TAX FORMULA FOR INDIVIDUALS

Income (broadly conceived)...	$xx,xxx
Less: Exclusions	(x,xxx)
Gross income...	$xx,xxx
Less: Deductions *for* adjusted gross income...................	(x,xxx)
Adjusted gross income..	$xx,xxx
Less: The greater of–	
Total itemized deductions	
or standard deduction...	(x,xxx)
Personal and dependency exemptions	(x,xxx)
Taxable income	$xx,xxx

BASIC STANDARD DEDUCTION AMOUNTS

	Standard Deduction Amount	
Filing Status	**1993**	**1994**
Single	$3,700	$3,800
Married, filing jointly	6,200	6,350
Surviving spouse	6,200	6,350
Head of household	5,450	5,600
Married, filing separately	3,100	3,175

AMOUNT OF EACH ADDITIONAL STANDARD DEDUCTION

Filing Status	**1993**	**1994**
Single	$900	$950
Married, filing jointly	700	750
Surviving spouse	700	750
Head of household	900	950
Married, filing separately	700	750

1995 ANNUAL EDITION

West's Federal Taxation:

Individual Income Taxes

1995 ANNUAL EDITION

West's Federal Taxation:

Individual Income Taxes

GENERAL EDITORS

William H. Hoffman, Jr., J.D., Ph.D., C.P.A.   James E. Smith, Ph.D., C.P.A.

Eugene Willis, Ph.D., C.P.A.

CONTRIBUTING AUTHORS

James H. Boyd,
Ph.D., C.P.A.
Arizona State University

D. Larry Crumbley,
Ph.D., C.P.A.
Texas A & M University

Steven C. Dilley,
J.D., Ph.D., C.P.A.
Michigan State University

Patrica C. Elliott,
D.B.A., C.P.A.
University of New Mexico

Mary Sue Gately,
Ph.D., C.P.A.
Texas Tech University

Jerome S. Horvitz,
J.D., LL.M. in Taxation
Suffolk University

William H. Hoffman, Jr.,
J.D., Ph.D., C.P.A.
University of Houston

David M. Maloney,
Ph.D., C.P.A.
University of Virginia

Marilyn Phelan,
J.D., Ph.D., C.P.A.
Texas Tech University

William A. Raabe,
Ph.D., C.P.A.
University of Wisconsin-Milwaukee

Boyd C. Randall,
J.D., Ph.D.
Brigham Young University

W. Eugene Seago,
J.D., Ph.D., C.P.A.
*Virginia Polytechnic Institute
and State University*

James E. Smith,
Ph.D., C.P.A.
College of William and Mary

Eugene Willis,
Ph.D., C.P.A.
University of Illinois at Urbana

West Publishing Company
Minneapolis/St. Paul • New York • Los Angeles • San Francisco

Copyediting:	Patricia A. Lewis
Composition:	Carlisle Communications, Ltd.
Text Design:	LightSource Images
Cover Design:	David Farr, *ImageSmythe*
Index:	Catalyst Communication Arts

West's Commitment to the Environment

In 1906, West Publishing Company began recycling materials left over from the production of books. This began a tradition of efficient and responsible use of resources. Today, up to 95 percent of our legal books and 70 percent of our college and school texts are printed on recycled, acid-free stock. West also recycles nearly 22 million pounds of scrap paper annually— the equivalent of 181,717 trees. Since the 1960s, West has devised ways to capture and recycle waste inks, solvents, oils, and vapors created in the printing process. We also recycle plastics of all kinds, wood, glass, corrugated cardboard, and batteries, and have eliminated the use of styrofoam book packaging. We at West are proud of the longevity and the scope of our commitment to the environment.

Production, Prepress, Printing and Binding by West Publishing Company.

MacInTax and *TurboTax* are registered trademarks of ChipSoft, Inc.

By **West Publishing Company**
  610 Opperman Drive
  P.O. Box 64526
  St. Paul, MN 55164–0526

Library of Congress Cataloging-in-Publication Data

Main entry under title:
  West's Federal Taxation.
  Includes index.
  1. Income tax—United States—Law
I. Hoffman, William H. III. Willis, Eugene

ISBN 0–314–02992–3, 0–314–03923–6
KF6369.W47   343'.73'052   77–20656

ISSN 0272–0329
1995 ANNUAL EDITION

PREFACE

This text is intended as a basis for a first course in Federal taxation for undergraduate or graduate accounting, business, and law students. With certain modifications in the coverage of the materials, the text may be used in a survey course on Federal taxation for undergraduate or graduate students. The materials may also be valuable as a tool for self-study, since they contain numerous clarifying examples adaptable to such an approach.

Tax policy considerations and historical developments are introduced in the text only to the extent that they shed light on the reason for a particular rule. The many simple and straightforward examples further clarify the materials by showing how a particular tax rule applies in an actual situation.

Since the original edition was issued in 1978, we have followed a policy of annually revising the text material to reflect statutory, judicial, and administrative changes in the Federal tax law and to correct any errors or other shortcomings. Not only do we encourage user input, we actively seek the advice of users as the basis for improving the text.

In the 1995 edition, the effects of the Revenue Reconciliation Act of 1993 (RRA of 1993) are integrated throughout the text and supplements. If any significant tax legislation is enacted in 1994, we will provide you with supplements on a timely basis.

Two sequence changes have been made in the 1995 edition. While we continue to recognize the importance of the coverage on passive activity losses and the at-risk limitations, we have moved this chapter from near the beginning of the materials on deductions (Part III) to the end (Chapter 11). We also recognize that studying the § 167 depreciation topic at the same time as the § 168 ACRS and MACRS cost recovery topics presents difficulties for students. Therefore, we have deleted the § 167 depreciation coverage from the chapter and have rewritten the text to reflect this deletion. For those professors who want their students to be exposed to § 167 depreciation, the material is now located in Appendix H.

Though the primary emphasis of the text is on the income taxation of individuals, Chapter 20 provides an overview of the Federal taxation of other forms of business organization (corporations and partnerships). This chapter could be of particular significance to students who do not plan to take a second course in Federal taxation. For others, Chapter 20 may serve as a lead-in to *West's Federal Taxation: Corporations, Partnerships, Estates, and Trusts.*

ENHANCED PEDAGOGICAL PLAN

In the 1995 edition, we have enhanced the pedagogy to assist the student in the learning process and to address the recommendations of the Accounting Education Change Commission (AECC).

- *Learning Objectives.* Each chapter begins with student learning objectives for the chapter. These behavioral objectives provide the students with guidance in learning the key concepts and principles.
- *Chapter Outline.* The learning objectives are followed by a topical outline of the material in the chapter. Page references appear in the outline to provide the student with ready access to each topic.
- *Chapter Introductions.* The introductions link the material in the current chapter to previous chapters and demonstrate its relevance. Frequently, the chapter introduction includes a "real world" illustration to help convey the relevance of the material.
- *Margin Notes.* Each of the learning objectives appears in the margin where the related material is introduced and helps to guide the student through the chapter.
- *Tax in the News.* Tax in the News items appear in each chapter as a boxed feature to enliven the text discussion. These items are drawn from today's business press and present current issues that are relevant to the chapter material.
- *Ethical Considerations.* Ethical Considerations features appear in each chapter presenting thought-provoking issues related to the chapter topics. In response to the recommendations of the AECC, they also demonstrate that many issues do not have a single correct answer. The questions raised in the Ethical Considerations were selected to provoke discussion and provide opportunities for debate (oral communication) based on the student's value system rather than to provide a defensible answer.
- *Key Terms.* Located before the Problem Materials in each chapter is a list of key terms to assist student learning. When the key term is introduced in the chapter, it appears in bold print. The list of key terms includes page references to the chapter coverage. In addition, each key term is defined in the Glossary (Appendix C).
- *Communication Assignments.* In recognition of the increasing emphasis in accounting and tax education on communication, identified items in the Problem Materials now include a written communication component. Selected Problems, Cumulative Problems, and Research Problems are identified as communication assignments with a "scroll" icon. These problems ask the student to prepare a tax client letter and a memorandum for the tax files. The discussion of the tax research process in Chapter 2 includes an illustration of these items.
- *Decision-Making Problems.* The Problem Materials include decision-making problems that are designed to enhance the student's analytical skills. These problems are identified with a "scales" icon.

SPECIAL FEATURES

A variety of other pedagogical devices are used to assist the student in the learning process. We recognize the importance of readability and continue to strive to make our text and supplements even more readable and understandable. The following features enhance the readability of the text:

- Including three levels of headings to aid in organization.
- Using bold print in the text to identify key terms the first time each term is used.
- Italicizing other key words to emphasize their importance to the student.
- Avoiding legal terminology except where it is beneficial.
- Using Concept Summaries to synthesize important concepts in chart or tabular form.

- Using Exhibits, Figures, and Tables to enhance presentations.
- Organizing the material in lists with bullets rather than presenting it in lengthy sentences.
- Using examples frequently to help the student understand the tax concept being discussed.
- Using a larger page size to provide a more open, accessible, and student-friendly textbook.

Once knowledge of the tax law has been acquired, it needs to be used. The tax minimization process, however, normally requires careful planning. Because we recognize the importance of planning procedures, most chapters include a separate section (called *Tax Planning Considerations*) illustrating the applications of these procedures to specific areas.

We believe that any basic course in Federal taxation should offer the reader the opportunity to learn and utilize the methodology of tax research. This knowledge is requisite in today's environment with its increased emphasis on the concept of "learning to learn." Chapter 2 and Appendix E are devoted to this methodology. Also, most chapters contain *Research Problems* that require the use of research tools. Solutions to these Research Problems can be found in the Instructor's Guide. The effectiveness of the text does not, however, depend on the coverage of tax research procedures. Consequently, the treatment of this subject may be omitted without impairing the continuity of the remaining textual materials.

Although it is not our purpose to approach taxation from the standpoint of preparing tax returns, some familiarity with forms is necessary. Because 1994 forms will not be available until later in the year, most tax return problems in this edition are written for tax year 1993. The 1993 problems may be solved manually, or many may be solved using the tax return preparation software (*TurboTax* or *MacInTax*) that may be purchased by students who use this text.

Appendix F contains two comprehensive tax return problems written for tax year 1993. Each of these problems lends itself for use as a term project because of the sophistication required for satisfactory completion. Solutions to the problems in Appendix F appear in the Instructor's Guide.

For the reader's convenience, Appendix B contains a full reproduction of most of the 1993 tax forms frequently encountered in actual practice.

Most tax textbooks are published in the spring, long before tax forms for the year of publication are available from the government. We believe that students should be exposed to the most current tax forms. As a result, we develop some new problems and provide adopters with reproducible copies of these problems, along with blank tax forms and solutions on the new forms. Shortly after the beginning of 1995, adopters will receive selected tax return problems solved on 1994 forms.

SUPPLEMENTS

Other products in our 1995 instructional package include the following:

- The *Instructor's Guide with Lecture Notes* contains lecture notes for each chapter and solutions to Research Problems and Comprehensive Tax Return problems found in the text. The lecture notes consist of a lecture outline that the professor can use as the basis for his or her classroom presentation. These lecture notes include not only material covered in the text, but also cases and other relevant material and teaching aids. The lecture notes are also available on disk in ASCII files.

- A *Solutions Manual* that has been carefully checked to ensure that it is error-free. The problems are arranged in accordance with the sequence of the material in the chapter. All problems are labeled by topical coverage in a matrix that also indicates which problems are new, modified, or unchanged in the new edition. The matrix also includes the problem number for the unchanged and modified problems in the prior edition. Approximately 20 percent of the problems in the 1995 edition are new or modified. The solutions are referenced to pages in the text.
- A *Test Bank* with questions and solutions referenced to pages in the text. The questions are arranged in accordance with the sequence of the material in the chapter. To assist the professor in selecting questions for an examination, all questions are labeled by topical coverage in a matrix that also indicates which questions are new, modified, or unchanged in the new edition. The matrix includes the question number for the unchanged and modified questions in the prior edition. Approximately 20 percent of the questions in the 1995 edition are new or modified.
- *Westest*, a microcomputer test generation program for IBM PCs and compatibles and the Macintosh family of computers.
- *West CD-ROM Federal Tax Library* (Compact Disk with Read-Only Memory) provides a complete tax research library on a desktop. The Federal Tax Library is a set of compact disks with a software package that reads the disks through a PC. Each disk has a remarkable storage capacity—roughly 1,000 times more than a single-sided floppy disk. A brief list of the library contents includes the complete IRS Code and Regulations, 1986 Tax Reform Act with Amendments and Legislative History, Federal Court Cases on Tax, Tax Court Cases, Revenue Rulings, and Revenue Procedures. The library is available to qualified adopters.
- A *Student Study Guide* prepared by Gerald E. Whittenburg, San Diego State University, includes a chapter review of key concepts and self-evaluation tests with solutions that are page referenced to the text.
- *Solutions Transparency Masters* for selected complex and cumulative problems, with a larger typeface for greater readability.
- *Astound Presentation Software* allows qualified adopters to create interactive lectures and manipulate graphs, charts, and figures during in-class lectures. The package contains approximately 25 transparency masters per chapter consisting of alternate figures, outlines, and key points.
- *Teaching Transparency Masters* include all screens from the Astound package reproduced as transparency masters for instructors who may wish to use traditional transparencies.
- A *Student Note-Taking Guide* includes selected screens from the Astound package consisting of chapter outlines and key points. This unique guide provides students with the core chapter information, so they can concentrate in class on learning key concepts instead of copying basic lecture outlines and transparencies. In addition, the charts and graphs in the Astound package have been printed and bound in a manner similar to accounting working papers. The pages include all the information from the Astound screens while still leaving room for student notes.
- *Teaching Transparency Acetates* contain charts and tables that can be used to enhance classroom lectures.
- *Instructor's Resource Notebook*—this three-ring binder can be used to house all or portions of the supplements and text that we will continue to offer in looseleaf form so you can reorganize the book and incorporate your supplemental materials to fit your course lectures.

- *WFT Individual Practice Sets*, 1994–95 edition, prepared by John B. Barrack, University of Georgia, is designed to cover all the common forms that a tax practitioner would use for the average client.
- Limited free use to qualified adopters of WESTLAW, a computer-assisted tax and legal research service that provides access to hundreds of valuable information sources.
- *West's Internal Revenue Code of 1986 and Treasury Regulations: Annotated and Selected 1995 Edition* by James E. Smith, College of William and Mary. This provides the opportunity for the student to be exposed to the Code and the Regulations in a single-volume book, which also contains useful annotations that help the student work with and understand the Code.
- *West's Federal Taxation Newsletter* is mailed to adopters twice a year. It focuses on new tax legislation and updated information.
- *WFT On-Line Electronic Bulletin Board* is the latest supplement from West that puts the most current information in your hands as soon as it is available. Qualified adopters can log onto the Bulletin Board from their home or office via a toll-free phone number and immediately gain access to the most recent taxation information available, including the Code and Regulations, case citations, new court rulings, and other newsworthy items. This information can then be transferred to a word-processing program for editing, printout, and classroom use while the information is still topical.

SOFTWARE

The trend toward increased use of the computer as an essential tool in tax practice has accelerated. To ensure that the West's Federal Taxation instructional package continues to set the pace in this important area, the following products are available to be used with the 1995 edition:

- *TurboTax* © Personal/1040 for DOS version 11.01 by Chipsoft, Inc., is a commercial tax preparation package. It teaches students how to prepare over 80 forms, schedules, and worksheets, and automatically performs all mathematical calculations and data transfers. *TurboTax* also assists students with tax planning and helps them prepare "anticipated" tax returns. The *TurboTax* package, available for student purchase, includes disks bound with a 200-page workbook containing exercises and problems. The software runs on IBM PCs and compatibles with 512K memory. *MacInTax®* and *TurboTax©ior Windows* are also available.
- *West's Federal Taxation: Tax Planning with Electronic Spreadsheets*, prepared by Samuel A. Hicks, Jr., Virginia Polytechnic Institute and State University, contains Lotus-based tax computation and planning templates for individual taxpayers and is available free to adopters.

These software products are powerful, easy to learn, and easy to use. We believe that tax education can be raised to a higher level through the use of computers and well-designed software. These software packages take the drudgery out of performing the complex computations required to solve difficult tax problems.

To enable students to take advantage of these new software products, the 1995 edition contains numerous tax return and tax planning problems. Problems that lend themselves to solutions using the software packages described above are identified by a computer symbol. The instructions for each of these problems indicate which software packages are appropriate for solving the problems.

ACKNOWLEDGMENTS

We are most appreciative of the many suggestions that we have received for revising the text, many of which have been incorporated in past editions and in the 1995 edition. In particular, we would like to thank all those users who responded to our questionnaire and those who have called or written with suggestions for improving the book, and those who did detailed reviews for this edition. They include Faye Bradwick, Indiana University of Pennsylvania; Gary W. Carter, University of Minnesota; Caroline K. Craig, Illinois State University; Joseph R. Danos, Southeastern Louisiana University; Christopher P. Hennessey, Babson College; Sherman R. Roser, St. Cloud State University; Marilyn Scheiner, Montgomery College; Joseph F. Schirger, University of Wisconsin at Oshkosh; Ralph B. Tower, Wake Forest University; James P. Trebby, Marquette University; and Mark A. Turner, Stephen F. Austin State University. We would also like to thank the people who have painstakingly worked through all the problems and test questions and generally acted as problem checkers to ensure the accuracy of the book and ancillary package. They are Tracey A. Anderson, Indiana University at South Bend; Caroline K. Craig, Illinois State University; Mark B. Persellin, St. Mary's University; Debra L. Sanders, Washington State University; Randall K. Serrett, University of Alaska at Fairbanks; Thomas Sternburg, University of Illinois at Urbana; and Raymond F. Wacker, Southern Illinois University at Carbondale.

Finally, this 1995 edition would not have been possible without the technical assistance of and manuscript review by Bonnie Hoffman, CPA, Freda Mulhall, CPA, and Nora Smith, M.Ed. We are indebted to them for their efforts.

William H. Hoffman, Jr.
James E. Smith
Eugene Willis

April 1, 1994

CONTENTS IN BRIEF

Preface   v

P A R T I   INTRODUCTION AND BASIC TAX MODEL

CHAPTER 1   An Introduction to Taxation and Understanding the Federal Tax Law   1–1

CHAPTER 2   Working with the Tax Law   2–1

CHAPTER 3   Tax Determination; Personal and Dependency Exemptions; An Overview of Property Transactions   3–1

P A R T II   GROSS INCOME

CHAPTER 4   Gross Income: Concepts and Inclusions   4–1

CHAPTER 5   Gross Income: Exclusions   5–1

P A R T III   DEDUCTIONS

CHAPTER 6   Deductions and Losses: In General   6–1

CHAPTER 7   Deductions and Losses: Certain Business Expenses and Losses   7–1

CHAPTER 8   Depreciation, Cost Recovery, Amortization, and Depletion   8–1

CHAPTER 9   Deductions: Employee Expenses   9–1

CHAPTER 10   Deductions and Losses: Certain Itemized Deductions   10–1

CHAPTER 11   Passive Activity Losses   11–1

P A R T IV   SPECIAL TAX COMPUTATION METHODS, PAYMENT PROCEDURES, AND TAX CREDITS

CHAPTER 12   Alternative Minimum Tax   12–1

CHAPTER 13   Tax Credits and Payment Procedures   13–1

PART V   PROPERTY TRANSACTIONS

CHAPTER 14   **Property Transactions: Determination of Gain or Loss and Basis Considerations   14–1**

CHAPTER 15   **Property Transactions: Nontaxable Exchanges   15–1**

CHAPTER 16   **Property Transactions: Capital Gains and Losses   16–1**

CHAPTER 17   **Property Transactions: Section 1231 and Recapture Provisions   17–1**

PART VI   ACCOUNTING PERIODS, ACCOUNTING METHODS, AND DEFERRED COMPENSATION

CHAPTER 18   **Accounting Periods and Methods   18–1**

CHAPTER 19   **Deferred Compensation   19–1**

PART VII   CORPORATIONS AND PARTNERSHIPS

CHAPTER 20   **Corporations and Partnerships   20–1**

Appendixes   A–1

Subject Index   I–1

CONTENTS

Preface   v

PART I   INTRODUCTION AND BASIC TAX MODEL

CHAPTER 1   **An Introduction to Taxation and Understanding the Federal Tax Law   1–1**

History of U.S. Taxation   1–2

Early Periods   1–2

Revenue Acts   1–3

Historical Trends   1–3

Criteria Used in the Selection of a Tax Structure   1–4

The Tax Structure   1–5

Tax Base   1–5

Tax Rates   1–5

Incidence of Taxation   1–5

Major Types of Taxes   1–6

Property Taxes   1–6

Tax in the News: Share of Property Taxes: Commercial versus Residential   1–7

Transaction Taxes   1–8

Ethical Considerations: Avoiding the Sales Tax   1–10

Death Taxes   1–11

Gift Taxes   1–12

Ethical Considerations: The Annual Exclusion for Gifts   1–13

Income Taxes   1–14

Tax in the News: America's Quarterback Is Taxed in Different Parts of America   1–16

Employment Taxes   1–16

Other U.S. Taxes   1–17

Value Added Taxes   1–18

Tax Administration   1–18

Internal Revenue Service   1–18

The Audit Process   1–19

Tax in the News: A Little Flushed   1–20

Statute of Limitations   1–21

Interest and Penalties   1–22

Tax Practice   1–23

Understanding the Federal Tax Law   1–24

Revenue Needs   1–24

Economic Considerations   1–24

Social Considerations   1–26

Equity Considerations   1–27

Political Considerations   1–30

Influence of the Internal Revenue Service   1–31

Influence of the Courts   1–33

Summary   1–34

Problem Materials   1–35

CHAPTER 2   **Working with the Tax Law   2–1**

Tax Sources   2–2

Statutory Sources of the Tax Law   2–2

Tax in the News: Crafting Tax Laws   2–4

Tax in the News: The Complexity of Tax Laws   2–7

Administrative Sources of the Tax Law   2–8

Judicial Sources of the Tax Law   2–12

Ethical Considerations: Choosing Cases for Appeal   2–16

Working with the Tax Law—Tax Research   2–22

Identifying the Problem   2–23

Refining the Problem   2–23

Locating the Appropriate Tax Law Sources   2–23

Assessing the Validity of the Tax Law Sources   2–25

Tax in the News: Internal Revenue Code: Interpretation Pitfalls   2–26

Arriving at the Solution or at Alternative Solutions   2–29

Communicating Tax Research   2–29

Working with the Tax Law—Tax Planning   2–32

Nontax Considerations   2–32

Tax Avoidance and Tax Evasion   2–32

Ethical Considerations: Tax Avoidance   2–33

Follow-up Procedures   2–33

Tax Planning—A Practical Application   2–33

Computer-Assisted Tax Research   2–34

Problem Materials   2–35

CHAPTER 3   Tax Determination; Personal and Dependency Exemptions; An Overview of Property Transactions   3–1

Tax Formula   3–3

Components of the Tax Formula   3–3

Application of the Tax Formula   3–8

Individuals Not Eligible for the Standard Deduction   3–9

Special Limitations for Individuals Who Can Be Claimed as Dependents   3–9

Personal and Dependency Exemptions   3–9

Personal Exemptions   3–10

Tax in the News: The Shrinking Personal and Dependency Exemption   3–10

Dependency Exemptions   3–11

Ethical Considerations: Claiming a Dependent   3–11

Tax Determination   3–15

Tax Table Method   3–15

Tax Rate Schedule Method   3–16

Computation of Net Taxes Payable or Refund Due   3–17

Unearned Income of Children under Age 14 Taxed at Parents' Rate   3–18

Filing Considerations   3–20

Filing Requirements   3–20

Filing Status   3–23

Ethical Considerations: The Marriage Penalty   3–24

Tax in the News: Taxing Wedded Bliss   3–25

Gains and Losses from Property Transactions—In General   3–26

**Gains and Losses from Property Transactions—
Capital Gains and Losses   3–27**

Definition of a Capital Asset   3–27

*Tax in the News: Losing a Good Loss or Effectively Using
the Alternative Tax   3–27*

Computation of Net Capital Gains and Losses   3–29

Capital Loss Limitation   3–28

Tax Planning Considerations   3–28

Taking Advantage of Tax Rate Differentials   3–29

Income of Minor Children   3–30

Dependency Exemptions   3–30

Problem Materials   3–32

PART II GROSS INCOME

CHAPTER 4   **Gross Income: Concepts and Inclusions   4–1**

Gross Income—What Is It?   4–3

Definition   4–3

Economic and Accounting Concepts   4–3

*Tax in the News: IRS Cracks Down on Sales of Frequent
Flier Miles   4–4*

Comparison of the Accounting and Tax Concepts of Income   4–5

Form of Receipt   4–6

Recovery of Capital Doctrine   4–6

Year of Inclusion   4–6

Taxable Year   4–6

Accounting Methods   4–7

Exceptions Applicable to Cash Basis Taxpayers   4–9

Exceptions Applicable to Accrual Basis Taxpayers   4–12

Income Sources   4–14

Personal Services   4–14

Income from Property   4–15

Income Received by an Agent   4–16

Income from Partnerships, S Corporations, Trusts, and Estates   4–16

Income in Community Property States   4–17

Items Specifically Included in Gross Income   **4–19**

Alimony and Separate Maintenance Payments   4–19

Ethical Considerations: Structuring a Divorce   4–22

Imputed Interest on Below-Market Loans   4–23

Income from Annuities   4–27

Prizes and Awards   4–30

Group Term Life Insurance   4–31

Tax in the News: Employers May Tailor Group Term Life Insurance   4–32

Unemployment Compensation   4–33

Social Security Benefits   4–33

Ethical Considerations: Taxing Social Security Benefits   4–34

Tax Planning Considerations   **4–35**

Nontaxable Economic Benefits   4–35

Tax Deferral   4–35

Shifting Income to Relatives   4–37

Accounting for Community Property   4–38

Alimony   4–38

Problem Materials   **4–39**

CHAPTER 5   **Gross Income: Exclusions**   **5–1**

Items Specifically Excluded from Gross Income   **5–2**

Statutory Authority   **5–2**

Gifts and Inheritances   **5–3**

Life Insurance Proceeds   **5–5**

General Rule   5–5

Exceptions to Exclusion Treatment   5–5

*Tax in the News: Tax-Exempt Life Insurance Benefits
for the Terminally Ill*   5–6

Employee Death Benefits   **5–7**

Gift versus Compensation   5–7

Scholarships   **5–8**

General Information   5–8

Timing Issues   5–9

Disguised Compensation   5–9

Qualified Tuition Reduction Plans   5–9

Ethical Considerations: Excluding Scholarships from Taxation   5–10

Compensation for Injuries and Sickness   5–10

Damages   5–10

Ethical Considerations: Excluding Punitive Damages from Taxation   5–12

Workers' Compensation   5–12

Accident and Health Insurance Benefits   5–12

Employer-Sponsored Accident and Health Plans   5–13

Medical Reimbursement Plans   5–14

Meals and Lodging   5–14

Furnished for the Convenience of the Employer   5–14

Other Housing Exclusions   5–16

Other Employee Fringe Benefits   5–17

Specific Benefits   5–17

Cafeteria Plans   5–17

Tax in the News: Turning Tuition Reimbursement On and Off   5–18

General Classes of Excluded Benefits   5–18

Taxable Fringe Benefits   5–24

Foreign Earned Income   5–24

Interest on Certain State and Local Government Obligations   5–26

Dividends   5–27

General Information   5–27

Stock Dividends   5–27

Educational Savings Bonds   5–28

Tax in the News: Adding Appeal to Savings Bonds   5–28

Tax Benefit Rule   5–29

Income from Discharge of Indebtedness   5–30

Tax Planning Considerations   5–31

Life Insurance   5–31

Employee Benefits   5–31

Investment Income   5–32

Problem Materials   5–33

PART III DEDUCTIONS

CHAPTER 6   Deductions and Losses: In General   6-1

Classification of Deductible Expenses   6-2
Deductions for Adjusted Gross Income   6-3
Itemized Deductions   6-4
Trade or Business Expenses and Production of Income Expenses   6-4
Business and Nonbusiness Losses   6-7
Reporting Procedures   6-7

Deductions and Losses—Timing of Expense Recognition   6-7
Importance of Taxpayer's Method of Accounting   6-7
Cash Method Requirements   6-8
Accrual Method Requirements   6-9

Disallowance Possibilities   6-10
Public Policy Limitation   6-10
Ethical Considerations: Obtaining Zoning Variances   6-11
Political Contributions and Lobbying Activities   6-13
Excessive Executive Compensation   6-14
Tax in the News: The Truly Rich Say Thank You   6-15
Investigation of a Business   6-15
Hobby Losses   6-16
Tax in the News: Pleasure versus Work   6-16
Ethical Considerations: When Is a Dairy Farm a Trade or Business?   6-17
Rental of Vacation Homes   6-19
Ethical Considerations: Renting for One More Day   6-20
Expenditures Incurred for Taxpayer's Benefit or Taxpayer's Obligation   6-23
Disallowance of Personal Expenditures   6-25
Disallowance of Deductions for Capital Expenditures   6-25
Transactions between Related Parties   6-26
Substantiation Requirements   6-28
Expenses and Interest Relating to Tax-Exempt Income   6-29

Tax Planning Considerations   6-30
Time Value of Tax Deductions   6-30
Unreasonable Compensation   6-30

Excessive Executive Compensation   6–32

Shifting Deductions   6–32

Hobby Losses   6–32

Capital Expenditures   6–33

Problem Materials   6–34

CHAPTER 7   **Deductions and Losses: Certain Business Expenses and Losses   7–1**

Bad Debts   7–3

Specific Charge-off Method   7–3

Business versus Nonbusiness Bad Debts   7–4

Loans between Related Parties   7–5

Ethical Considerations: Writing Off a Loan to a Friend   7–6

Loss of Deposits in Insolvent Financial Institutions   7–6

Worthless Securities   7–7

Tax in the News: Little of $100 Billion Loss Can Be Retrieved   7–8

Small Business Stock   7–8

Losses of Individuals   7–9

Events That Are Not Casualties   7–10

Theft Losses   7–10

Ethical Considerations: Deducting a Theft Loss   7–11

When to Deduct Casualty Losses   7–11

Tax in the News: Clinton Declares Parts of Three States Major Federal Disaster Areas   7–12

Measuring the Amount of Loss   7–12

Statutory Framework for Deducting Losses of Individuals   7–15

Personal Casualty Gains and Losses   7–16

Research and Experimental Expenditures   7–17

Expense Method   7–18

Deferral and Amortization Method   7–18

Net Operating Losses   7–19

Carryback and Carryover Periods   7–20

Computation of the Net Operating Loss   7–21

Ethical Considerations: Net Operating Losses   7–23

Recomputation of Tax Liability for Year to Which Net Operating Loss Is Carried   7–23

Calculation of the Remaining Net Operating Loss   7–24

Tax Planning Considerations   7–25

Documentation of Related-Taxpayer Loans, Casualty Losses, and Theft Losses   7–25

Small Business Stock   7–26

Casualty Losses   7–26

Net Operating Losses   7–26

Problem Materials   7–27

CHAPTER 8   **Depreciation, Cost Recovery, Amortization, and Depletion**   8–1

Tax in the News: Shorter Cost Recovery Schedules for Phone Companies   8–2

Overview   8–3

Accelerated Cost Recovery System (ACRS and MACRS)   8–4

General Considerations   8–4

Eligible Property under ACRS or MACRS   8–5

Personalty: Recovery Periods and Methods   8–5

Realty: Recovery Periods and Methods   8–10

Straight-Line Election under ACRS and MACRS   8–13

Election to Expense Assets   8–14

Business and Personal Use of Automobiles and Other Listed Property   8–16

Ethical Considerations: Substantiating Business Mileage   8–21

Alternative Depreciation System (ADS)   8–21

Amortization   8–22

Tax in the News: Supreme Court Expands Amortization Deductions   8–23

Ethical Considerations: Allocating Intangible Assets When a Business Is Sold   8–24

Depletion   8–24

Intangible Drilling and Development Costs (IDC)   8–25

Depletion Methods   8–25

Tax in the News: Supreme Court Decision Affects Depletion Tax Preference   8–27

Reporting Procedures   8–28

Tax Planning Considerations   8–29

Cost Recovery   8–29

Amortization   8–33

Depletion   8–34

Tables   8–34

Problem Materials   8–43

CHAPTER 9 **Deductions: Employee Expenses**   **9–1**

Employee versus Self-Employed   **9–2**
Tax in the News: Misclassified Workers   9–3

Employee Expenses—In General   **9–4**

Transportation Expenses   **9–4**
Qualified Expenditures   9–4
Computation of Automobile Expenses   9–6

Travel Expenses   **9–7**
Definition of Travel Expenses   9–7
Away-from-Home Requirement   9–7
Ethical Considerations: The Same Job But Different Deductions   9–8
Restrictions on Travel Expenses   9–8
Combined Business and Pleasure Travel   9–9

Moving Expenses   **9–11**
Distance Test   9–12
Time Test   9–12
Treatment of Moving Expenses   9–13

Education Expenses   **9–13**
General Requirements   9–13
Requirements Imposed by Law or by the Employer for Retention of Employment   9–14
Maintaining or Improving Existing Skills   9–14
Classification of Specific Items   9–15
Other Provisions Dealing with Education   9–15

Entertainment Expenses   **9–16**

Dollar Limitations   **9–16**
Tax in the News: Protests from the Restaurant Industry   9–17

Classification of Expenses   **9–17**

Restrictions upon Deductibility   **9–17**
Ethical Considerations: Reciprocal Entertaining   9–18
Ethical Considerations: Plan for the $25 Limitation   9–19

Other Employee Expenses   **9–20**
Office in the Home   9–20
Miscellaneous Employee Expenses   9–21
Contributions to Infividual Retirement Accounts   9–22

Classification of Employee Expenses   9–22

Accountable Plans   9–23

Nonaccountable Plans   9–24

Reporting Procedures   9–24

Limitations on Itemized Deductions   9–25

Miscellaneous Itemized Deductions Subject to the 2 Percent Floor   9–25

Miscellaneous Itemized Deductions Not Subject to the 2 Percent Floor   9–26

Tax Planning Considerations   9–26

Self-Employed Individuals   9–26

Shifting Deductions between Employer and Employee   9–27

Transportation and Travel Expenses   9–27

Moving Expenses   9–27

Education Expenses   9–28

Entertainment Expenses   9–28

Problem Materials   9–29

CHAPTER 10   **Deductions and Losses: Certain Itemized Deductions   10–1**

General Classification of Expenses   10–2

Medical Expenses   10–2

General Requirements   10–2

Medical Expenses Defined   10–3

Capital Expenditures for Medical Purposes   10–4

Transportation and Lodging Expenses for Medical Treatment   10–5

Amounts Paid for Medical Insurance Premiums   10–6

Medical Expenses Incurred for Spouse and Dependents   10–6

Year of Deduction   10–7

Reimbursements   10–7

Taxes   10–8

Deductibility as a Tax   10–8

Property Taxes, Assessments, and Apportionment of Taxes   10–9

State and Local Income Taxes   10–10

Interest   10–11

Allowed and Disallowed Items   10–11

Restrictions on Deductibility and Timing Considerations   10–15

Classification of Interest Expense   10–16

Charitable Contributions   **10–16**

Criteria for a Gift   10–16

Qualified Organizations   10–18

Time of Deduction   10–18

Tax in the News: The Rationale for the New Reporting Requirements   10–19

Record-keeping and Valuation Requirements   10–19

Limitations on Charitable Contribution Deduction   10–20

Miscellaneous Itemized Deductions   **10–24**

Ethical Considerations: Increasing Itemized Deductions through Bunching   10–25

Other Miscellaneous Deductions   **10–25**

Comprehensive Example of Schedule A   **10–25**

Overall Limitation on Certain Itemized Deductions   **10–27**

Effective Utilization of Itemized Deductions   10–28

Utilization of Medical Deductions   10–28

Protecting the Interest Deduction   10–29

Assuring the Charitable Contribution Deduction   10–30

Problem Materials   **10–32**

CHAPTER 11   **Passive Activity Losses**   **11–1**

The Tax Shelter Problem   **11–2**

At-Risk Limits   **11–3**

Passive Loss Limits   **11–4**

Taxpayers Subject to the Passive Loss Rules   11–4

Passive Activities Defined   11–6

Material Participation   11–7

Tax in the News: Economics or Politics?   11–11

Tax in the News: Economic Effects of a Tax Law Change   11–12

Ethical Considerations: Applying the Rules on Rental Real Estate   11–12

Rental Activities   11–13

Identification of Passive Activity   11–16

Classification of Income and Losses   11–18

Income Not Treated as Passive   11–19

Deductions Not Treated as Passive   11–20

Suspended Losses   11–20

Passive Credits   11–22

Real Estate Rental Activities   11–23

Dispositions of Passive Interests   11–25

Transition Rules for Passive Losses (1987–1990)   11–27

Tax Planning Considerations   11–28

Utilizing Passive Losses   11–28

Tax in the News: Taking Advantage of the Real Estate Professionals Exemption   11–29

Problem Materials   11–30

PART IV SPECIAL TAX COMPUTATION METHODS, PAYMENT PROCEDURES, AND TAX CREDITS

CHAPTER 12   **Alternative Minimum Tax   12–1**

Individual Alternative Minimum Tax   12–2

A New Concept: Alternative Tax Adjusted Gross Income   12–5

AMTI Limitations Based on Income   12–6

Ethical Considerations: The Cost of Complying with the ATAGI Requirements   12–7

AMT Adjustments   12–8

Tax in the News: The Appeal of Incentive Stock Options   12–13

AMT Preferences   12–18

Tax in the News: A Plan to Donate Stock and Still Benefit from Future Appreciation   12–20

Other Components of the AMT Formula   12–21

Illustration of the AMT Computation   12–22

AMT Credit   12–24

Corporate Alternative Minimum Tax   12–24

AMT Adjustments   12–25

Tax Preferences   12–27

Exemption   12–28

Other Aspects of the AMT   12–28

Tax Planning Considerations   12–28

Avoiding Preferences and Adjustments   12–28

Controlling the Timing of Preferences and Adjustments   12–29

Taking Advantage of the AMT/Regular Tax Rate Differential   12–29

Problem Materials   12–30

CHAPTER 13 **Tax Credits and Payment Procedures** **13–1**

Tax Policy Considerations **13–3**

Overview and Priority of Credits **13–4**

Refundable versus Nonrefundable Credits 13–4

General Business Credit 13–5

Treatment of Unused General Business Credits 13–6

Specific Business-Related Tax Credit Provisions **13–7**

Investment Tax Credit: Introduction 13–7

Regular Investment Tax Credit 13–7

Tax Credit for Rehabilitation Expenditures 13–8

Ethical Considerations: Using the Rehabilitation Expenditures Credit 13–9

Business Energy Credits 13–10

Jobs Credit 13–10

Research Activities Credit 13–11

Tax in the News: Research Activities Credit 13–15

Low-Income Housing Credit 13–15

Disabled Access Credit 13–16

Tax in the News: Consider Low-Income-Housing Investments 13–16

Other Tax Credits **13–17**

Earned Income Credit **13–17**

Tax Credit for Elderly or Disabled Taxpayers 13–19

Foreign Tax Credit 13–20

Credit for Child and Dependent Care Expenses 13–21

Ethical Considerations: Using the Credit for Child and Dependent Care Expenses 13–24

Payment Procedures **13–26**

Procedures Applicable to Employers 13–26

Tax in the News: Nannygate 13–28

Ethical Considerations: Withholding for Domestic Workers 13–34

Procedures Applicable to Self-Employed Persons 13–34

Tax Planning Considerations **13–39**

Foreign Tax Credit 13–39

Credit for Child and Dependent Care Expenses 13–39

Adjustments to Increase Withholding 13–41

Adjustments to Avoid Overwithholding   13–41

Problem Materials   13–42

▼ **PART V** PROPERTY TRANSACTIONS

CHAPTER 14 **Property Transactions: Determination of Gain or Loss and Basis Considerations**   14–1

Determination of Gain or Loss   14–3

Realized Gain or Loss   14–3

Recognized Gain or Loss   14–6

Nonrecognition of Gain or Loss   14–6

Recovery of Capital Doctrine   14–7

Basis Considerations   14–8

Determination of Cost Basis   14–8

Gift Basis   14–11

Property Acquired from a Decedent   14–14

Tax in the News: Carryover Basis versus Stepped-Up Basis   14–15

Ethical Considerations: Helping a Friend Increase Basis   14–16

Disallowed Losses   14–17

Ethical Considerations: Transactions between Spouses   14–18

Conversion of Property from Personal Use to Business or Income-Producing Use   14–19

Additional Complexities in Determining Realized Gain or Loss   14–21

Summary of Basis Adjustments   14–22

Tax Planning Considerations   14–24

Tax Consequences of Alice's Proposed Transaction   14–24

Cost Identification and Documentation Considerations   14–25

Selection of Property for Making Gifts   14–25

Selection of Property for Making Bequests   14–26

Disallowed Losses   14–26

Problem Materials   14–27

CHAPTER 15 **Property Transactions: Nontaxable Exchanges**   15–1

General Concept of a Nontaxable Exchange   15–2

Like-Kind Exchanges—§ 1031   15–3

Like-Kind Property   15–4

Tax in the News: My Land for Your Jail   15–5

Exchange Requirement   15–5

Boot   15–6

Basis and Holding Period of Property Received   15–7

Involuntary Conversions—§ 1033   15–9

General Scheme   15–9

Involuntary Conversion Defined   15–10

Ethical Considerations: Purchasing Property in Expectation of Condemnation   15–10

Computing the Amount Realized   15–10

Replacement Property   15–11

Time Limitation on Replacement   15–12

Ethical Considerations: Postponing Realized Gain from an Involuntary Conversion   15–13

Nonrecognition of Gain   15–14

Involuntary Conversion of a Personal Residence   15–15

Reporting Considerations   15–15

Sale of a Residence—§ 1034   15–15

Tax in the News: Presidentially Declared Disasters—The Back Door   15–16

Replacement Period   15–16

Principal Residence   15–18

Nonrecognition of Gain Requirements   15–19

Capital Improvements   15–20

Basis and Holding Period of the New Residence   15–20

Reporting Procedures   15–21

Sale of a Residence—§ 121   15–22

Exclusion Requirements   15–22

Ethical Considerations: A Couple's Approach to the § 121 Exclusion   15–23

Relationship to Other Provisions   15–23

Making and Revoking the Election   15–23

Computation Procedure   15–24

Other Nonrecognition Provisions   15–25

Exchange of Stock for Property—§ 1032   15–25

Certain Exchanges of Insurance Policies—§ 1035   15–25

Exchange of Stock for Stock of the Same Corporation—§ 1036   15–25

Certain Reacquisitions of Real Property—§ 1038   15–26

Transfers of Property between Spouses or Incident
to Divorce—§ 1041   15–26

Rollover of Publicly Traded Securities Gain into Specialized Small Business
Investment Companies—§ 1044   15–26

Tax Planning Considerations   15–27

Like-Kind Exchanges   15–27

Involuntary Conversions   15–27

Sale of a Personal Residence   15–28

Problem Materials   15–30

CHAPTER 16   Property Transactions: Capital Gains and Losses   16–1

General Considerations   16–2

Rationale for Separate Reporting of Capital Gains and Losses   16–2

General Scheme of Taxation   16–3

Capital Assets   16–3

Definition of a Capital Asset   16–3

Tax in the News: Garage Sales and Taxable Gains   16–4

Effect of Judicial Action   16–6

Statutory Expansions   16–6

*Ethical Considerations: Capital Gain Treatment for Real Estate
Developments*   16–8

Sale or Exchange   16–9

Worthless Securities   16–9

Special Rule—Retirement of Corporate Obligations   16–9

Options   16–10

Patents   16–12

Tax in the News: Who Owns the Invention?   16–13

Franchises, Trademarks, and Trade Names   16–13

Tax in the News: Franchises and the Early Retired   16–14

Lease Cancellation Payments   16–15

Holding Period   16–16

Review of Special Holding Period Rules   16–17

Special Rules for Short Sales   16–18

Tax Treatment of Capital Gains and Losses of Noncorporate Taxpayers   16–20

Treatment of Capital Gains   16–21

Ethical Considerations: Indexing Long-Term Capital Gains for Inflation   16–22

Treatment of Capital Losses   16–23

Reporting Procedures   16–24

Tax Treatment of Capital Gains and Losses of Corporate Taxpayers   16–25

Tax Planning Considerations   16–27

Importance of Capital Asset Status   16–27

Planning for Capital Asset Status   16–27

Ethical Considerations: Assuring Capital Asset Status   16–27

Effect of Capital Asset Status in Transactions Other Than Sales   16–28

Stock Sales   16–29

Maximizing Benefits   16–29

Year-End Planning   16–29

Problem Materials   16–30

CHAPTER 17   Property Transactions: Section 1231 and Recapture Provisions   17–1

Tax in the News: Fixed Assets for Sale   17–2

Section 1231 Assets   17–3

Relationship to Capital Assets   17–3

Justification for Favorable Tax Treatment   17–4

Property Included   17–5

Property Excluded   17–5

Special Rules for Certain § 1231 Assets   17–5

Ethical Considerations: Determining How Long an Asset Has Been Held   17–6

Tax in the News: Taking Deductions after the California Fires   17–8

General Procedure for § 1231 Computation   17–8

Section 1245 Recapture   17–12

Ethical Considerations: Does Applying the Recapture Rules Make a Difference?   17–12

Tax in the News: Recapturing the Amortization of Intangible Assets   17–13

Section 1245 Property   17–14

Observations on § 1245   17–15

Section 1250 Recapture   **17–15**

Computing Recapture on Nonresidential Real Property   17–16

Computing Recapture on Residential Rental Housing   17–18

Section 1250 Recapture Situations   17–18

Considerations Common to §§ 1245 and 1250   **17–19**

Exceptions   17–19

Other Applications   17–21

Special Recapture Provisions   **17–23**

Special Recapture for Corporations   17–23

Gain from Sale of Depreciable Property between Certain
Related Parties   17–23

Intangible Drilling Costs   17–23

Reporting Procedures   **17–23**

Tax Planning Considerations   **17–25**

Timing of § 1231 Gain   17–25

Timing of Recapture   17–29

Postponing and Shifting Recapture   17–29

Avoiding Recapture   17–29

Problem Materials   **17–30**

▼

PART VI ACCOUNTING PERIODS, ACCOUNTING METHODS, AND DEFERRED COMPENSATION

CHAPTER 18   Accounting Periods and Methods   18–1

Tax in the News: Acceleration of Income   18–2

Accounting Periods   **18–2**

In General   18–3

Making the Election   18–7

Changes in the Accounting Period   18–7

Taxable Periods of Less Than One Year   18–8

Mitigation of the Annual Accounting Period Concept   18–9

Accounting Methods   **18–10**

Permissible Methods   18–10

Cash Receipts and Disbursements Method—Cash Basis   18–11

Accrual Method   18–12

Tax in the News: Automobile Dealers Sandwiched between Two Tax Accounting Rules   18–15

Hybrid Method   18–15

Change of Method   18–15

Tax in the News: IRS Prohibits Changes from the Accrual to the Cash Method   18–16

Ethical Considerations: A Change in Accounting Method   18–17

Special Accounting Methods   18–19

Installment Method   18–19

Ethical Considerations: A Related-Party Installment Sale Has Unexpected Results   18–24

Disposition of Installment Obligations   18–25

Interest on Deferred Taxes   18–25

Electing Out of the Installment Method   18–26

Long-Term Contracts   18–26

Inventories   18–31

Determining Inventory Cost   18–32

Ethical Considerations: Protecting the LIFO Reserve   18–35

The LIFO Election   18–36

Tax Planning Considerations   18–37

Taxable Year   18–37

Cash Method of Accounting   18–37

Installment Method   18–37

LIFO   18–38

Problem Materials   18–38

CHAPTER 19   **Deferred Compensation   19–1**

Qualified Pension, Profit Sharing, and Stock Bonus Plans   19–3

Tax in the News: Dig It Out   19–3

Types of Plans   19–4

Ethical Considerations: Underfunded Pension Plans   19–5

Qualification Requirements   19–7

Tax Consequences to the Employee and Employer   19–12

Limitations on Contributions to and Benefits from Qualified Plans   19–16

Top-Heavy Plans   19–18

Cash or Deferred Arrangement Plans   19–19

Tax in the News: Choices in 401(k) Plans?   19–20

Retirement Plans for Self-Employed Individuals   19–20

Coverage Requirements   19–21

Contribution Limitations   19–21

Individual Retirement Accounts (IRAs)   19–22

General Rules   19–22

Penalty Taxes for Excess Contributions   19–25

Taxation of Benefits   19–25

Nonqualified Deferred Compensation Plans   19–27

Underlying Rationale for Tax Treatment   19–27

Tax Treatment to the Employer and Employee   19–28

Tax in the News: Golden Handcuffs   19–30

Ethical Considerations: Limiting Compensation for Executives But Not for Other Highly Paid Employees   19–31

Restricted Property Plans   19–31

General Provisions   19–31

Substantial Risk of Forfeiture   19–32

Special Election Available   19–32

Employer Deductions   19–33

Stock Options   19–34

In General   19–34

Incentive Stock Options   19–34

Nonqualified Stock Options   19–36

Tax Planning Considerations   19–37

Deferred Compensation   19–37

Qualified Plans   19–38

Self-Employed Retirement Plans   19–38

Individual Retirement Accounts   19–38

Comparison of § 401(k) Plan with IRA   19–39

Nonqualified Deferred Compensation (NQDC) Plans   19–40

Stock Options   19–40

Flexible Benefit Plans   19–41

Problem Materials   19–42

CHAPTER 20 Corporations and Partnerships   20–1

What Is a Corporation?   20–3

Compliance with State Law   20–3

Ethical Considerations: Filing Status: Corporation versus Individual   20–3

The Association Approach   20–4

Limited Liability Companies   20–4

Income Tax Considerations   20–5

General Tax Consequences of Different Forms
of Business Entities   20–5

Individuals and Corporations Compared—An Overview   20–5

Specific Provisions Compared   20–6

Deductions Available Only to Corporations   20–10

Tax in the News: There May Be No Free Parking   20–11

Determination of Comporate Tax Liability   20–13

Corporate Filing Requirements   20–14

Reconciliation of Corporate Taxable Income
and Accounting Income   20–14

Forming the Corporation   20–17

Capital Contributions   20–17

Transfers to Controlled Corporations   20–18

Operating the Corporation   20–19

Dividend Distributions   20–19

Stock Redemptions   20–22

Liquidating the Corporation   20–22

General Rule of § 331   20–22

Exception to the General Rule   20–23

Basis Determination—§§ 334 and 338   20–23

Effect of the Liquidation on the Corporation   20–23

Ethical Considerations: Necessity for Filing a Corporate Tax Return   20–24

The S Election   20–24

Justification for the Election   20–24

Tax in the News: Proposed S Corporation Legislation   20–26

Operational Rules   20–26

Partnerships   20–30

Nature of Partnership Taxation   20–30

Contents

Partnership Formation 20–30

Partnership Operation 20–32

Tax Planning Considerations **20–35**

Corporate versus Noncorporate Forms of Business Organization 20–35

Regular Corporation versus S Status 20–35

Use of an Entity to Reduce the Family Income Tax Burden 20–36

Problem Materials **20–37**

APPENDIXES

Tax Rate Schedules and Tables A–1

Tax Forms B–1

Glossary of Tax Terms C–1

Table of Code Sections Cited D–1

Table of Proposed Regulations and Regulations Cited D–9

Table of Revenue Proceedings and Revenue Rulings Cited D–13

Citator Example E–1

Comprehensive Tax Return Problems F–1

Table of Cases Cited G–1

Depreciation H–1

Subject Index I–1

INTRODUCTION AND BASIC TAX MODEL

Part I provides an introduction to taxation in the United States. Although the primary orientation of this text is income taxation, other types of taxes are also discussed briefly. The purposes of the Federal tax law are examined, and the legislative, administrative, and judicial sources of Federal tax law, including their application to the tax research process, are analyzed. Part I concludes with the introduction of the basic tax model for the individual taxpayer.

Chapter 1
An Introduction to Taxation and Understanding the Federal Tax Law

Chapter 2
Working with the Tax Law

Chapter 3
Tax Determination; Personal and Dependency Exemptions; An Overview of Property Transactions

AN INTRODUCTION TO TAXATION AND UNDERSTANDING THE FEDERAL TAX LAW

LEARNING OBJECTIVES

After completing Chapter 1, you should be able to:

1. Understand some of the history, including trends, of the Federal income tax.

2. Know some of the criteria for selecting a tax structure and understand the components of a tax structure.

3. Identify the different taxes imposed in the United States at the Federal, state, and local levels.

4. Understand the administration of the tax law including the audit process utilized by the IRS.

5. Appreciate some of the ethical guidelines involved in tax practice.

6. Recognize the economic, social, equity, and political considerations that justify various aspects of the tax law and the role played by the IRS and the courts in the evolution of the Federal tax system.

OUTLINE

History of U.S. Taxation, 1–2

Early Periods, 1–2

Revenue Acts, 1–3

Historical Trends, 1–3

Criteria Used in the Selection
of a Tax Structure, 1–4

The Tax Structure, 1–5

Tax Base, 1–5

Tax Rates, 1–5

Incidence of Taxation, 1–5

Major Types of Taxes, 1–6

Property Taxes, 1–6

Transaction Taxes, 1–8

Death Taxes, 1–11

Gift Taxes, 1–12

Income Taxes, 1–14

Employment Taxes, 1–16

Other U.S. Taxes, 1–17

Value Added Taxes, 1–18

Tax Administration, 1–18

Internal Revenue Service, 1–18

The Audit Process, 1–19

Statute of Limitations, 1–21

Interest and Penalties, 1–22

Tax Practice, 1–23

Understanding the Federal
Tax Law, 1–24

Revenue Needs, 1–24

Economic Considerations, 1–24

Social Considerations, 1–26

Equity Considerations, 1–27

Political Considerations, 1–30

Influence of the Internal Revenue
Service, 1–31

Influence of the Courts, 1–33

Summary, 1–34

The primary objective of this chapter is to provide an overview of the Federal tax system. Among the topics discussed are the following:

- A brief history of the Federal income tax.
- The different types of taxes imposed at the Federal, state, and local levels.
- Some highlights of tax law administration.
- Tax concepts that help explain the reasons for various tax provisions.
- The influence that the Internal Revenue Service (IRS) and the courts have had in the evolution of current tax law.

Why does a text devoted primarily to the Federal individual income tax discuss state and local taxes? A simple illustration shows the importance of non-Federal taxes.

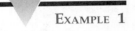

EXAMPLE 1

Rick is employed by Flamingo Corporation in San Antonio, Texas, at a salary of $54,000. Rick's employer offers him a chance to transfer to its New York City office at a salary of $60,000. Neither Texas nor San Antonio imposes an income tax, but New York State and New York City do. A quick computation indicates that the income taxes involved approximate $4,000. ▼

Although Rick must consider many nontax factors before he decides on a job change, he should also evaluate the tax climate. How do state and local taxes compare? In this case, what appears to be a $6,000 pay increase is only $2,000 when the income tax differential of $4,000 is taken into account.

HISTORY OF U.S. TAXATION

EARLY PERIODS

1 LEARNING OBJECTIVE
Understand some of the history, including trends, of the Federal income tax.

The concept of an income tax can hardly be regarded as a newcomer to the Western Hemisphere. An income tax was first enacted in 1634 by the English colonists in the Massachusetts Bay Colony, but the Federal government did not adopt this form of taxation until 1861. In fact, both the Federal Union and the

Confederate States of America used the income tax to raise funds to finance the Civil War. Although modest in its reach and characterized by broad exemptions and low rates, the income tax generated $376 million of revenue for the Federal government during the Civil War.

When the Civil War ended, the need for additional revenue disappeared, and the income tax was repealed. As was true before the war, the Federal government was able to finance its operations almost exclusively from customs duties (tariffs). It is interesting to note that the courts held that the Civil War income tax was not contrary to the Constitution.

When a new Federal income tax on individuals was enacted in 1894, its opponents were prepared to and did again challenge its constitutionality. The U.S. Constitution provided that " . . . No Capitation, or other direct, Tax shall be laid, unless in Proportion to the Census or Enumeration herein before directed to be taken." In *Pollock v. Farmers' Loan and Trust Co.,*[1] the U.S. Supreme Court found that the income tax was a direct tax that was unconstitutional because it was not apportioned among the states in proportion to their populations.

A Federal corporate income tax, enacted by Congress in 1909, fared better in the judicial system. The U.S. Supreme Court found this tax to be constitutional because it was treated as an excise tax.[2] In essence, it was a tax on the right to do business in the corporate form. As such, it was likened to a form of the franchise tax.[3] The corporate form of doing business had been developed in the late nineteenth century and was an unfamiliar concept to the framers of the U.S. Constitution. Since a corporation is an entity created under law, jurisdictions possess the right to tax its creation and operation. Using this rationale, many states still impose franchise taxes on corporations.

The ratification of the Sixteenth Amendment to the U.S. Constitution in 1913 sanctioned both the Federal individual and corporate income taxes and, as a consequence, neutralized the continuing effect of the *Pollock* decision.

REVENUE ACTS

Following ratification of the Sixteenth Amendment, Congress enacted the Revenue Act of 1913. Under this Act, a flat 1 percent tax was levied upon the income of corporations. Individuals paid a normal tax rate of 1 percent on taxable income after deducting a personal exemption of $3,000 for a single individual and $4,000 for a married taxpayer. Surtax rates of 1 to 6 percent were applied to high-income taxpayers.

Various revenue acts were passed between 1913 and 1939. In 1939, all of these revenue laws were codified into the Internal Revenue Code of 1939. In 1954, a similar codification of the revenue law took place. The current law is entitled the Internal Revenue Code of 1986, which largely carries over the provisions of the 1954 Code. To date, the Code has been amended several times since 1986. This matter is discussed further in Chapter 2 under Origin of the Internal Revenue Code.

HISTORICAL TRENDS

The income tax has proved to be a major source of revenue for the Federal government. Figure 1–1, which contains a breakdown of the major revenue

---

[1] 3 AFTR 2602, 15 S.Ct. 912 (USSC, 1895). See Chapter 2 for an explanation of the citations of judicial decisions.

[2] *Flint v. Stone Tracy Co.,* 3 AFTR 2834, 31 S.Ct. 342 (USSC, 1911).

[3] See the discussion of state franchise taxes later in the chapter.

▼ **FIGURE 1–1**
Federal Budget Receipts—1994

Individual income taxes	37%
Corporation income taxes	8
Social insurance taxes and contributions	31
Excise taxes	3
Borrowing	17
Other	4
	100%

sources,[4] demonstrates the importance of the income tax. *Estimated* income tax collections from individuals and corporations amount to 45 percent of the total receipts.

The need for revenues to finance the war effort during World War II converted the income tax into a *mass tax.* For example, in 1939, less than 6 percent of the U.S. population was subject to the Federal income tax. In 1945, over 74 percent of the population was subject to the Federal income tax.[5]

Certain changes in the income tax law are of particular significance in understanding the Federal income tax. In 1943, Congress passed the Current Tax Payment Act, which provided for the first pay-as-you-go tax system. A pay-as-you-go income tax system requires employers to withhold for taxes a specified portion of an employee's wages. Persons with income from other than wages must make periodic (e.g., quarterly) payments to the taxing authority (the Internal Revenue Service) for estimated taxes due for the year.

One trend that has caused considerable concern has been the increased complexity of the Federal income tax laws. Often, under the name of tax reform, Congress has added to this complexity by frequently changing the tax laws. Increasingly, this has forced many taxpayers to seek the assistance of tax professionals. At this time, therefore, substantial support exists for tax law simplification.

CRITERIA USED IN THE SELECTION
OF A TAX STRUCTURE

2   LEARNING OBJECTIVE
Know some of the criteria for selecting a tax structure and understand the components of a tax structure.

In the eighteenth century, Adam Smith identified the following *canons of taxation*, which are still considered when evaluating a particular tax structure:[6]

- *Equality.* Each taxpayer enjoys fair or equitable treatment by paying taxes in proportion to his or her income level. Ability to pay a tax is the measure of how equitably a tax is distributed among taxpayers.
- *Convenience.* Administrative simplicity has long been valued in formulating tax policy. If a tax is easily assessed and collected and its administrative costs are low, it should be favored. An advantage of the withholding (pay-as-you-go) system is its convenience for taxpayers.

[4] Budget of the United States Government for Fiscal Year 1994, Office of Management and Budget (Washington, D.C.: U.S. Government Printing Office, 1993).

[5] Richard Goode, *The Individual Income Tax* (Washington, D.C.: The Brookings Institution, 1964), pp. 2–4.
[6] *The Wealth of Nations,* Book V, Chapter II, Part II (New York: Dutton, 1910).

- *Certainty.* A tax structure is *good* if the taxpayer can readily predict when, where, and how a tax will be levied. Individuals and businesses need to know the likely tax consequences of a particular type of transaction.
- *Economy.* A *good* tax system involves only nominal collection costs by the government and minimal compliance costs on the part of the taxpayer. Although the government's cost of collecting Federal taxes amounts to less than one-half of 1 percent of the revenue collected, the complexity of our current tax structure imposes substantial taxpayer compliance costs.

By these canons, the Federal income tax is a contentious product. *Equality* is present as long as one accepts ability to pay as an ingredient of this component. *Convenience* exists due to a heavy reliance on pay-as-you-go procedures. *Certainty* probably generates the greatest controversy. In one sense, certainty is present since a mass of administrative and judicial guidelines exists to aid in interpreting the tax law. In another sense, however, certainty does not exist since many questions remain unanswered and frequent changes in the tax law by Congress lessen stability. *Economy* is present if only the collection procedure of the IRS is considered. Economy is not present, however, if one focuses instead on taxpayer compliance efforts.

THE TAX STRUCTURE

TAX BASE

A tax base is the amount to which the tax rate is applied. In the case of the Federal income tax, the tax base is *taxable income.* As noted later in the chapter (Figure 1–2), taxable income is gross income reduced by certain deductions (both business and personal).

TAX RATES

Tax rates are applied to the tax base to determine a taxpayer's liability. The tax rates may be proportional or progressive. A tax is *proportional* if the rate of tax remains constant for any given income level.

EXAMPLE 2

Bill has $10,000 of taxable income and pays a tax of $3,000, or 30%. Bob's taxable income is $50,000, and the tax on this amount is $15,000, or 30%. If this constant rate is applied throughout the rate structure, the tax is proportional. ▼

A tax is *progressive* if a higher rate of tax applies as the tax base increases. The Federal income tax, Federal gift and estate taxes, and most state income tax rate structures are progressive.

EXAMPLE 3

If Cora, a married individual filing jointly, has taxable income of $10,000, her tax for 1994 is $1,500 for an average tax rate of 15%. If, however, Cora's taxable income is $50,000, her tax will be $9,060 for an average tax rate of 18.12%. The tax is progressive since higher rates are applied to greater amounts of taxable income. ▼

INCIDENCE OF TAXATION

The degree to which various segments of society share the total tax burden is difficult to assess. Assumptions must be made concerning who absorbs the burden for paying the tax. For example, since dividend payments to shareholders are not deductible by a corporation and are generally taxable to shareholders, the same income is subject to a form of double taxation. Concern over double taxation is valid to the extent that corporations are *not* able to shift the corporate tax to the consumer through higher commodity prices. Many research studies have shown a high degree of shifting of the corporate income tax. When the corporate tax can be shifted, it becomes merely a consumption tax that is borne by the ultimate purchasers of goods.

The progressiveness of the U.S. Federal income tax rate structure for individuals has varied over the years. As late as 1986, for example, there were 15 rates, ranging from 0 to 50 percent. These later were reduced to two rates of 15 and 28 percent. Currently, there are five rates, ranging from 15 to 39.6 percent.

MAJOR TYPES OF TAXES

PROPERTY TAXES

3 **LEARNING OBJECTIVE**
Identify the different taxes imposed in the United States at the Federal, state, and local levels.

Normally referred to as **ad valorem taxes** because they are based on value, property taxes are a tax on wealth, or capital. In this regard, they have much in common with death taxes and gift taxes discussed later in the chapter. Although property taxes do not tax income, the income actually derived (or the potential for any income) may be relevant insofar as it affects the value of the property being taxed.

Property taxes fall into *two* categories: those imposed on realty and those imposed on personalty. Both have added importance since they usually generate a deduction for Federal income tax purposes (see Chapter 10).

Ad Valorem Taxes on Realty

Property taxes on realty are exclusively within the province of the states and their local political subdivisions (e.g., cities, counties, school districts). They represent a major source of revenue for *local* governments, but their importance at the *state* level has waned over the past few years.[7]

How realty is defined can have an important bearing on which assets are subject to tax. This is especially true in jurisdictions that do not impose ad valorem taxes on personalty. Primarily a question of state property law, **realty** generally includes real estate and any capital improvements that are classified as fixtures. Simply stated, a *fixture* is something so permanently attached to the real estate that its removal will cause irreparable damage. A built-in bookcase might well be a fixture, whereas a movable bookcase would not be a fixture. Certain items such as electrical wiring and plumbing cease to be personalty when installed in a building and become realty.

The following are some of the characteristics of ad valorem taxes on realty:

- Property owned by the Federal government is exempt from tax. Similar immunity usually is extended to property owned by state and local governments and by certain charitable organizations.
- Some states provide for lower valuations on property dedicated to agricultural use or other special uses (e.g., wildlife sanctuaries).

---

[7]Some states have imposed freezes on upward revaluations of residential housing.

- Some states partially exempt the homestead portion of property from taxation. Modern homestead laws normally protect some or all of a personal residence (including a farm or ranch) from the actions of creditors pursuing claims against the owner.
- Lower taxes may apply to a residence owned by an elderly taxpayer (e.g., age 65 and older).
- When non-income-producing property (e.g., a personal residence) is converted to income-producing property (e.g., a rental house), typically the appraised value increases.
- Some jurisdictions extend immunity from tax for a specified period of time (a *tax holiday*) to new or relocated businesses.

Unlike the ad valorem tax on personalty (see below), the tax on realty is difficult to avoid. Since real estate is impossible to hide, a high degree of taxpayer compliance is not surprising. The only avoidance possibility that is generally available is associated with the assessed value of the property. For this reason, the assessed value of the property—particularly, a value that is reassessed upward—may be subject to controversy and litigation.

Four methods are currently in use for assessing the value of real estate:

1. Actual purchase or construction price.
2. Contemporaneous sales prices or construction costs of comparable properties.
3. Cost of reproducing a building, less allowance for depreciation and obsolescence from the time of actual construction.
4. Capitalization of income from rental property.

Because all of these methods suffer faults and lead to inequities, a combination of two or more is not uncommon. For example, when real estate values and construction costs are rising, the use of actual purchase or construction price (method 1) places the purchaser of a new home at a definite disadvantage

---

TAX IN THE NEWS

SHARE OF PROPERTY TAXES: COMMERCIAL VERSUS RESIDENTIAL

The plunge in commercial real estate values means many homeowners are facing higher property taxes, cuts in public services, or both.

A projected 32 percent drop in commercial real estate values between 1989 and 1994 will leave many local governments with a declining property tax base, a new study said. The tax bill on an average commercial building will drop 25 percent during that period, while the tax bill for an average home will rise 40 percent, according to the study by the Urban Land Institute, a Washington real estate education and research organization.

By 1994, the erosion of commercial real estate values will leave homeowners shouldering 73 percent of the property tax load, up from 65 percent in 1989, the report said. Increasing homeowner tax burdens have turned property taxes into an extremely volatile political issue, with voters in a growing number of states capping rate increases.

SOURCE: Reprinted from Mitchell Pacelle, "Drop in Commercial Real-Estate Values Brings Tax Rise to Many Homeowners," *Wall Street Journal*, June 8, 1993. Reprinted by permission of the *Wall Street Journal*, © 1993 Dow Jones & Company, Inc. All rights reserved worldwide.

compared with an owner who acquired similar property years before. As another illustration, if the capitalization of income (method 4) deals with property subject to rent controls (e.g., Boston), the property may be undervalued.

The history of the ad valorem tax on realty has been marked by inconsistent application due to a lack of competent tax administration and definitive guidelines for assessment procedures. In recent years, however, some significant improvements have occurred. Some jurisdictions, for example, have computerized their reassessment procedures so they will have an immediate effect on all property located within the jurisdiction. Nevertheless, the property tax area continues to be controversial.

Ad Valorem Taxes on Personalty

Personalty can be defined as all assets that are not realty. It may be helpful to distinguish between the *classification* of an asset (realty or personalty) and the *use* to which it is placed. Both realty and personalty can be either business use or personal use property. Examples include a residence (realty that is personal use), an office building (realty that is business use), surgical instruments (personalty that is business use), and regular wearing apparel (personalty that is personal use).[8]

Personalty can also be classified as tangible property or intangible property. For ad valorem tax purposes, intangible personalty includes stocks, bonds, and various other securities (e.g., bank shares).

The following generalizations may be made concerning the ad valorem taxes on personalty:

- Particularly with personalty devoted to personal use (e.g., jewelry, household furnishings), taxpayer compliance ranges from poor to zero. Some jurisdictions do not even attempt to enforce the tax on these items. For automobiles devoted to personal use, many jurisdictions have converted from value as the tax base to arbitrary license fees based on the weight of the vehicle. Some jurisdictions also consider the vehicle's age (e.g., automobiles six years or older are not subject to the ad valorem tax because they are presumed to have little, if any, value).
- For personalty devoted to business use (e.g., inventories, trucks, machinery, equipment), taxpayer compliance and enforcement procedures are measurably better.
- Which jurisdiction possesses the authority to tax movable personalty (e.g., railroad rolling stock) always has been and continues to be a troublesome issue.
- Some jurisdictions impose an ad valorem tax on intangibles.

TRANSACTION TAXES

Transaction taxes, which characteristically are imposed at the manufacturer's, wholesaler's, or retailer's level, cover a wide range of transfers. Like many other types of taxes (e.g., income taxes, death taxes, and gift taxes), transaction taxes usually are not within the exclusive province of any level of taxing authority

---

[8] The distinction, important for ad valorem and for Federal income tax purposes, often becomes confused when personalty is referred to as "personal" property to distinguish it from "real" property. This designation does not give a complete picture of what is involved. The description "personal" residence, however, is clearer, since a residence can be identified as being realty. What is meant, in this case, is realty that is personal use property.

(Federal, state, local government). As the description implies, these levies place a tax on transfers of property and normally are determined by multiplying the value involved by a percentage rate.

Federal Excise Taxes

Long one of the mainstays of the Federal tax system, Federal **excise taxes** had declined in relative importance until recently. In late 1982, 1990, and 1993, Congress substantially increased the Federal excise taxes on such items as tobacco products, fuel and gasoline sales, telephone usage, and air travel passenger tickets. Other Federal excise taxes include the following:

- Manufacturers' excise taxes on trucks, trailers, tires, firearms, sporting equipment, coal, and the gas guzzler tax on automobiles.[9]
- Alcohol taxes.
- Luxury tax on automobiles. The tax is 10 percent of the retail price in excess of $32,000 (adjusted each year for inflation).
- Miscellaneous taxes (e.g., the tax on wagering).

The list of transactions covered, although seemingly impressive, has diminished over the years. At one time, for example, there was a Federal excise tax on admission to amusement facilities (e.g., theaters) and on the sale of such items as leather goods, jewelry, furs, and cosmetics.

When reviewing the list of both Federal and state excise taxes, one should recognize the possibility that the tax laws may be trying to influence social behavior. For example, the gas guzzler tax is intended as an incentive for the automobile companies to build cars that are fuel efficient. Since many consider alcohol and tobacco to be harmful to a person's health, why not increase their cost by imposing excise taxes and thereby discourage their use? Unfortunately, the evidence of the level of correlation between the imposition of an excise tax and consumer behavior is mixed.

State Excise Taxes

Many state and local excise taxes parallel the Federal version. Thus, all states tax the sale of gasoline, liquor, and tobacco products; however, the rates vary significantly. For gasoline products, for example, compare the 29 cents per gallon imposed by the state of Connecticut with the 9 cents per gallon levied by the state of Wyoming. For tobacco sales, contrast the 2.5 cents per pack of cigarettes in effect in Virginia with the 56 cents per pack applicable in New York. Given the latter situation, is it surprising that the smuggling of cigarettes for resale elsewhere is so widespread?

Other excise taxes found at some state and local levels include those on admission to amusement facilities; hotel occupancy and the rental of various other facilities; and the sale of playing cards, oleomargarine products, and prepared foods. Most states impose a transaction tax on the transfer of property that requires the recording of documents (e.g., real estate sales).[10] Some extend the tax to the transfer of stocks and other securities.

---

[9] The gas guzzler tax is imposed on the manufacturers of automobiles and progresses in amount as the mileage ratings per gallon of gas decrease.

[10] This type of tax has much in common with the stamp tax levied by Great Britain on the American colonies during the pre-revolutionary war period in U.S. history.

General Sales Taxes

The distinction between an excise tax and a general **sales tax** is easy to make. One is restricted to a particular transaction (e.g., the 18.4 cents per gallon Federal excise tax on the sale of gasoline), while the other covers a multitude of transactions (e.g., a 5 percent tax on *all* retail sales). In actual practice, however, the distinction is not always that clear. Some state statutes exempt certain transactions from the application of the general sales taxes (e.g., sales of food to be consumed off the premises, sales of certain medicines and drugs). Also, it is not uncommon to find that rates vary depending on the commodity involved. Many states, for example, allow preferential rates for the sale of agricultural equipment or apply different rates (either higher or lower than the general rate) to the sale of automobiles. With many of these special exceptions and classifications of rates, a general sales tax can take on the appearance of a collection of individual excise taxes.

A **use tax** is an ad valorem tax, usually at the same rate as the sales tax, on the use, consumption, or storage of tangible property. The purpose of a use tax is to prevent the avoidance of a sales tax. Every state that imposes a general sales tax levied on the consumer also has a use tax. Alaska, Delaware, Montana, New Hampshire, and Oregon have neither tax.

EXAMPLE 4   Susan resides in a jurisdiction that imposes a 5% general sales tax but lives near a state that has no sales or use tax at all. Susan purchases an automobile for $10,000 from a dealer located in the neighboring state. Has she saved $500 in sales taxes? The state use tax is designed to pick up the difference between the tax paid in another jurisdiction and what would have been paid in the state in which Susan resides. ▼

The use tax is difficult to enforce for many purchases and is therefore often avoided. In some cases, for example, it may be worthwhile to make purchases through an out-of-state mail-order business. In spite of shipping costs, the avoidance of the local sales tax that otherwise might be incurred could make the price of such products as computer components cheaper. Some states are taking steps to curtail this loss of revenue. For items such as automobiles (refer to Example 4), the use tax probably will be collected when the purchaser registers the item in his or her home state.

Local general sales taxes, over and above those levied by the state, are common. It is not unusual to find taxpayers living in the same state who pay different general sales taxes due to the location of their residence.

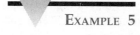

EXAMPLE 5   Pete and Sam both live in a state that has a general sales tax of 3%. Sam, however, resides in a city that imposes an additional general sales tax of 2%. Even though Pete and Sam live in the same state, one is subject to a rate of 3%, while the other pays a tax of 5%. ▼

ETHICAL CONSIDERATIONS

Avoiding the Sales Tax

You live in a jurisdiction that imposes a city and state sales tax of 8 percent. The sales tax is very broad and also applies to the performance of various services.

A severe storm damages the trees on your residential property. You consult Jerry Jones, a tree surgeon, who offers the following estimate for the cleanup work: $500 if paid by check or $450 if paid in cash. Jones says he will take care of the appropriate sales tax charge under either form of payment.

Jones does competent work, is bonded, and has no known history of impropriety. What are your options? You could simply pay him in cash, but it seems likely that Jones will not account for the sales tax charge if you select this option. Before paying him the cash, therefore, you could demand accountability by having Jones issue a receipt showing amounts for services rendered and sales tax charged. You have no responsibility to ensure that Jones actually pays the sales tax specified to the appropriate taxing authorities.

Severance Taxes

Severance taxes are an important source of revenue for many states. These transaction taxes are based on the notion that the state has an interest in its natural resources (e.g., oil, gas, iron ore, coal). Therefore, a tax is imposed when they are extracted.

DEATH TAXES

A **death tax** is a tax on the right to transfer property or to receive property upon the death of the owner. Consequently, a death tax falls into the category of an excise tax. If the death tax is imposed on the right to pass property at death, it is classified as an **estate tax.** If it taxes the right to receive property from a decedent, it is termed an **inheritance tax.** As is typical of other types of excise taxes, the value of the property transferred provides the base for determining the amount of the death tax.

The Federal government imposes only an estate tax. State governments, however, levy inheritance taxes, estate taxes, or both.

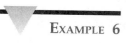

EXAMPLE 6

At the time of her death, Wilma lived in a state that imposes an inheritance tax but not an estate tax. Mary, one of Wilma's heirs, lives in the same state. Wilma's estate is subject to the Federal estate tax, and Mary is subject to the state inheritance tax. ▼

The Federal Estate Tax

The Revenue Act of 1916 incorporated the estate tax into the tax law. Never designed to generate a large amount of revenue, its original purpose was to prevent large concentrations of wealth from being kept within a family for many generations. Whether this objective has been accomplished is debatable. Like the income tax, estate taxes can be reduced through various planning procedures.

The gross estate includes property the decedent owned at the time of death. It also includes life insurance proceeds when paid to the estate or when paid to a beneficiary other than the estate if the deceased-insured had any ownership rights in the policy. Quite simply, the gross estate represents property interests subject to Federal estate taxation.[11] All property included in the gross estate is valued as of the date of death or, if the alternate valuation date is elected, six months later.[12]

Deductions from the gross estate in arriving at the taxable estate include funeral and administration expenses, certain taxes, debts of the decedent, casualty losses[13] incurred during the administration of the estate, transfers to charitable

---

[11] For further information on these matters, see *West's Federal Taxation: Corporations, Partnerships, Estates, and Trusts.*
[12] See the discussion of the alternate valuation date in Chapter 14.

[13] For a definition of casualty losses, see the Glossary of Tax Terms in Appendix C.

organizations, and, in some cases, the marital deduction. The marital deduction is available for amounts actually passing to a surviving spouse (a widow or widower).

Once the taxable estate has been determined and certain taxable gifts have been added to it, the estate tax can be computed. From the amount derived from the appropriate tax rate schedules, various credits should be subtracted to arrive at the tax, if any, that is due.[14] Although many other credits are also available, probably the most significant is the unified transfer tax credit. The main reason for this credit is to eliminate or reduce the estate tax liability for modest estates. For deaths after 1986, the amount of the credit is $192,800. Based on the estate tax rates, the credit covers a tax base of $600,000.

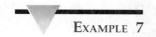

EXAMPLE 7

Ned made no taxable gifts before his death in 1994. If Ned's taxable estate amounts to $600,000 or less, no Federal estate tax is due because of the application of the unified transfer tax credit. Under the tax law, the estate tax on a taxable estate of $600,000 is $192,800. ▼

State Death Taxes

As noted earlier, states usually levy an inheritance tax, an estate tax, or both. The two forms of death taxes differ according to whether the tax is imposed on the heirs or on the estate.

Characteristically, an inheritance tax divides the heirs into classes based on their relationship to the decedent. The more closely related the heir, the lower the rates imposed and the greater the exemption allowed. Some states completely exempt from taxation amounts passing to a surviving spouse.

GIFT TAXES

Like a death tax, a **gift tax** is an excise tax levied on the right to transfer property. In this case, however, the tax is imposed on transfers made during the owner's life and not at death. Also, a gift tax applies only to transfers that are not supported by full and adequate consideration.

EXAMPLE 8

Carl sells property worth $20,000 to his daughter for $1,000. Although property worth $20,000 has been transferred, only $19,000 represents a gift, since this is the portion not supported by full and adequate consideration. ▼

The Federal Gift Tax

First enacted in 1932, the Federal gift tax was intended to complement the estate tax. In the absence of a tax applicable to lifetime transfers by gift, it would be possible to avoid the estate tax and escape taxation entirely.

Only taxable gifts are subject to the gift tax. For this purpose, a taxable gift is measured by the fair market value of the property on the date of transfer less the annual exclusion of $10,000 per donee and, in some cases, less the marital deduction, which allows tax-free transfers between spouses. Each donor is allowed an annual exclusion of $10,000 for each donee.[15]

---

[14] For tax purposes it is always crucial to appreciate the difference between a deduction and a credit. A *credit* is a dollar-for-dollar reduction of tax liability. A *deduction,* however, only benefits the taxpayer to the extent of his or her tax bracket. An estate in a 50% tax bracket, for example, would need $2 of deductions to prevent $1 of tax liability from developing. In contrast, $1 of credit neutralizes $1 of tax liability.

[15] The purpose of the annual exclusion is to avoid the need to report and pay a tax on *modest* gifts. Without the exclusion, the IRS could face a real problem of taxpayer noncompliance.

EXAMPLE 9

On December 31, 1993, Vera (a widow) gives $10,000 to each of her four married children, their spouses, and her eight grandchildren. On January 3, 1994, she repeats the same procedure. Due to the annual exclusion, Vera has not made a taxable gift, although she transferred $160,000 [$10,000 × 16 (number of donees)] in 1993 and $160,000 [$10,000 × 16 (number of donees)] in 1994 for a total of $320,000 ($160,000 + $160,000). ▼

ETHICAL
CONSIDERATIONS

The Annual Exclusion for Gifts

Arlene, a wealthy widow, would like to transfer $20,000 of cash to her son, Wilbur, in 1994 without exceeding the $10,000 per donee annual exclusion. To achieve this result, Arlene devises the following scheme: she gives $10,000 to Wilbur and $10,000 to her brother, George, who gives $10,000 to Wilbur.

A special election applicable to married persons allows one-half of the gift made by the donor-spouse to be treated as being made by the nondonor-spouse. This election to split the gifts of property made to third persons has the effect of increasing the number of annual exclusions available. Also, it allows the use of the nondonor-spouse's unified transfer tax credit and may lower the tax brackets that will apply.

For taxable gifts made after 1976, the gift tax rate schedule is the same as that applicable to the estate tax. The schedule is commonly referred to as the *unified transfer tax schedule.*

The Federal gift tax is *cumulative* in effect. What this means is that the tax base for current taxable gifts includes past taxable gifts. Although a credit is allowed for prior gift taxes, the result of adding past taxable gifts to current taxable gifts is to force the donor into a higher tax bracket.[16] Like the Federal estate tax rates, the Federal gift tax rates are progressive (see Example 3 earlier in this chapter).

The unified transfer tax credit is available for all taxable gifts made after 1976. As with the Federal estate tax, the amount of this credit is $192,800. There is, however, only one unified transfer tax credit, and it applies both to taxable gifts and to the Federal estate tax. In a manner of speaking, therefore, once the unified transfer tax credit has been exhausted for Federal gift tax purposes, it is no longer available to insulate a decedent from the Federal estate tax.

In summary, transfers by gift and transfers by death made after 1976 will be subject to the unified transfer tax. The same rates and credits apply. Further, taxable gifts made after 1976 will have to be added to the taxable estate in arriving at the tax base for applying the unified transfer tax at death.

State Gift Taxes

The states currently imposing a state gift tax are Connecticut, Delaware, Louisiana, New York, North Carolina, and Tennessee. Most of the laws provide for lifetime exemptions and annual exclusions. Like the Federal gift tax, the state taxes are

---

[16] For further information on the Federal gift tax, see *West's Federal Taxation: Corporations, Partnerships, Estates, and Trusts.*

cumulative in effect. But unlike the Federal version, the amount of tax depends on the relationship between the donor and the donee. Like state inheritance taxes, larger exemptions and lower rates apply when the donor and donee are closely related to each other.

INCOME TAXES

Income taxes are levied by the Federal government, most states, and some local governments. The trend in recent years has been to place greater reliance on this method of taxation. This trend is not consistent with what is happening in other countries, and in this sense, our system of taxation is somewhat different.

Income taxes generally are imposed on individuals, corporations, and certain fiduciaries (estates and trusts). Most jurisdictions attempt to assure the collection of income taxes by requiring certain pay-as-you-go procedures (e.g., withholding requirements for employees and estimated tax prepayments for other taxpayers).

On occasion, Congress has seen fit to impose additional taxes on income. Such impositions were justified either by economic considerations or by special circumstances resulting from wartime conditions. During World War II, the Korean conflict, and the Vietnam conflict, excess-profits taxes were imposed in addition to the regular Federal income tax. The taxes were aimed at the profiteering that occurs when the economy is geared to the production of war materials.

Another additional income tax is the surcharge approach. During the period from April 1, 1968, to July 1, 1970, for example, taxpayers were subject to a surcharge of 10 percent of the amount of their regular income tax liability. This led to the strange result that taxpayers had to pay, so to speak, an income tax on their income tax. Justifications for the special tax included the need to restrain what was regarded as an overactive economy, to curtail inflation, and to reduce the Federal deficit.

In light of current budget deficits, the surcharge approach has its advocates in Congress and therefore may be of more than historical interest. The advantage of the surcharge approach is that it represents a temporary solution to the problem. Thus, the tax can be imposed on a one-shot basis without compelling Congress to modify the regular income tax rates or base.

Federal Income Taxes

Chapters 3 through 19 deal with the application of the Federal income tax to individuals. The procedure for determining the Federal income tax applicable to individuals is summarized in Figure 1–2.

The application of the Federal corporate income tax does not require the computation of adjusted gross income (AGI) and does not provide for the standard deduction and personal and dependency exemptions. All allowable deductions of a corporation fall into the business-expense category. In effect, therefore, the taxable income of a corporation is the difference between gross income (net of exclusions) and deductions.

Chapter 20 summarizes the rules relating to corporations. For an in-depth treatment of the Federal income tax as it affects corporations, estates, and trusts, see *West's Federal Taxation: Corporations, Partnerships, Estates, and Trusts*, 1995 Edition, Chapters 2 through 9, 12, and 19.

State Income Taxes

All but the following states impose an income tax on individuals: Alaska, Florida, Nevada, South Dakota, Texas, Washington, and Wyoming.

▼ **FIGURE 1–2**

Formula for Federal Income Tax on Individuals

Income (broadly conceived)	$xx,xxx
Less: Exclusions (income that is not subject to tax)	(x,xxx)
Gross income (income that is subject to tax)	$xx,xxx
Less: Certain business deductions (usually referred to as deductions *for* adjusted gross income)	(x,xxx)
Adjusted gross income	$xx,xxx
Less: The greater of certain personal and employee deductions (usually referred to as *itemized deductions*) or The standard deduction (including any additional standard deduction) *and*	(x,xxx)
Less: Personal and dependency exemptions	(x,xxx)
Taxable income	$xx,xxx
Tax on taxable income (see Tax Rate Schedules in Appendix A)	$ x,xxx
Less: Tax credits (including Federal income tax withheld and other prepayments of Federal income taxes)	(xxx)
Tax due (or refund)	$ xxx

Some of the characteristics of state income taxes are summarized as follows:

- With few exceptions, all states require some form of withholding procedures.
- Most states use as the tax base the income determination made for Federal income tax purposes.
- A minority of states go even further and impose a flat rate upon AGI as computed for Federal income tax purposes. Several apply a rate to the Federal income tax liability. This is often referred to as the piggyback approach to state income taxation. Although the term *piggyback* does not lend itself to precise definition, in this context, it means making use, for state income tax purposes, of what was done for Federal income tax purposes.
- Because of the tie-in to the Federal return, the state may be notified of any changes made by the IRS upon audit of a Federal return.
- Most states allow a deduction for personal and dependency exemptions. Some states substitute a tax credit for a deduction.
- A diminishing minority of states allow a deduction for Federal income taxes.
- Most states allow their residents some form of tax credit for income taxes paid to other states.
- The due date for filing generally is the same as for the Federal income tax (the fifteenth day of the fourth month following the close of the tax year).

Nearly all states have an income tax applicable to corporations. It is difficult to determine those that do not because a state franchise tax sometimes is based in part on the income earned by the corporation.[17]

Local Income Taxes

Cities imposing an income tax include, but are not limited to, Baltimore, Cincinnati, Cleveland, Detroit, Kansas City (Mo.), Minneapolis, New York, Philadelphia, and St. Louis. The application of a city income tax is not limited to local residents.

---

[17] See the discussion of franchise taxes later in the chapter.

> ## TAX IN THE NEWS
>
> ### AMERICA'S QUARTERBACK IS TAXED IN DIFFERENT PARTS OF AMERICA
>
> One memorable afternoon last fall, Dallas Cowboy quarterback Troy Aikman eluded the 300-pound defensive linemen of the Philadelphia Eagles for most of a game at Veterans Stadium. But Mr. Aikman wasn't able to dodge an even more determined Philadelphian: the city tax collector.
>
> When he got home to Dallas, Mr. Aikman found in his mailbox an income tax bill. The City of Brotherly Love was asking him to ante up a pro rata share of his annual income for playing just that one game at the Vet.
>
> Unfair? Maybe so, but not uncommon. Strapped for cash in a spotty economic recovery and smarting from cutbacks in Federal funds, some states and cities with income taxes have decided to enforce tax laws on rich itinerants. It's easier than raising public hackles by increasing tax rates.
>
> "State officials will jump at any chance they see to get money without imposing higher taxes on current residents," says Steven Gold, of the Center for the Study of the States, in Albany, New York.
>
> The easiest targets are professional athletes, entertainers, and others who are just passing through but making big money while in town.
>
> SOURCE: Reprinted from Earl C. Gottschalk, Jr., "Some States and Cities with Income Taxes Go after Rich Visitors," *Wall Street Journal*, April 15, 1993, p. A1. Reprinted by permission of the *Wall Street Journal*, © 1993 Dow Jones & Company, Inc. All rights reserved worldwide.

EMPLOYMENT TAXES

Classification as an employee usually leads to the imposition of **employment taxes** and to the requirement that the employer withhold specified amounts for income taxes. The rules governing the withholding for income taxes are discussed in Chapter 13. The material that follows concentrates on the two major employment taxes: FICA (Federal Insurance Contributions Act—commonly referred to as the Social Security tax) and FUTA (Federal Unemployment Tax Act). Both taxes can be justified by social and public welfare considerations: FICA offers some measure of retirement security, and FUTA provides a modest source of income in the event of loss of employment.

Employment taxes come into play only if two conditions are satisfied. First, is the individual involved an *employee* (as opposed to *self-employed*)? The differences between an employee and a self-employed person are discussed in Chapter 9.[18] Second, if the individual involved is an employee, is he or she covered under FICA or FUTA or both? The coverage of both of these taxes is summarized in Exhibit 13–2 in Chapter 13.[19]

FICA Taxes

The **FICA tax** rates and wage base have steadily increased over the years. It is difficult to imagine that the initial rate in 1937 was only 1 percent of the first $3,000 of covered wages. Thus, the maximum tax due was only $30!

---

[18] See also Circular E, Employer's Tax Guide, issued by the IRS as Publication 15.

[19] Chapter 13 deals with the self-employment tax (the Social Security and Medicare taxes for self-employed persons).

Currently, the FICA tax has two components: Social Security tax (old age, survivors, and disability insurance) *and* Medicare tax (hospital insurance). The Social Security tax rate is 6.2 percent for 1993 and 1994, and the Medicare tax rate is 1.45 percent for these years. The base amount for Social Security is $57,600 for 1993 and $60,600 for 1994. The Revenue Reconciliation Act of 1993 removed the maximum base amount for the Medicare tax, formerly $135,000, for 1994 and thereafter. The employer must match the employee's portion.

A spouse employed by another spouse is subject to FICA. However, children under the age of 18 who are employed in a parent's trade or business are exempted.

FUTA Taxes

The purpose of the **FUTA tax** is to provide funds that the states can use to administer unemployment benefits. This leads to the somewhat unusual situation of one tax being handled by both Federal and state governments. The end result of such joint administration is to compel the employer to observe a double set of rules. Thus, state and Federal returns must be filed and payments made to both governmental units.

In 1994, FUTA applies at a rate of 6.2 percent on the first $7,000 of covered wages paid during the year to each employee. The Federal government allows a credit for FUTA paid (or allowed under a merit rating system) to the state. The credit cannot exceed 5.4 percent of the covered wages. Thus, the amount required to be paid to the IRS could be as low as 0.8 percent (6.2% − 5.4%).

States follow a policy of reducing the unemployment tax on employers who experience stable employment. Thus, an employer with little or no employee turnover might find that the state rate drops to as low as 0.1 percent or, in some states, even to zero. The reason for the merit rating credit is that the state has to pay fewer unemployment benefits when employment is steady.

FUTA differs from FICA in the sense that the incidence of taxation falls entirely upon the employer. A few states, however, levy a special tax on employees either to provide disability benefits or supplemental unemployment compensation, or both.

OTHER U.S. TAXES

To complete the overview of the U.S. tax system, some missing links need to be covered that do not fit into the classifications discussed elsewhere in this chapter.

Federal Customs Duties

One tax that has not yet been mentioned is the tariff on certain imported goods.[20] Generally referred to as customs duties or levies, this tax, together with selective excise taxes, provided most of the revenues needed by the Federal government during the nineteenth century. In view of present times, it is remarkable to note that tariffs and excise taxes alone paid off the national debt in 1835 and enabled the U.S. Treasury to pay a surplus of $28 million to the states.

In recent years, tariffs have served the nation more as an instrument for carrying out protectionist policies than as a means of generating revenue. Thus, a

---

[20] Less-developed countries that rely principally on one or more major commodities (e.g., oil, coffee) are prone to favor *export* duties as well.

particular U.S. industry might be saved from economic disaster, so the argument goes, by placing customs duties on the importation of foreign goods that can be sold at lower prices. Protectionists contend that the tariff therefore neutralizes the competitive edge held by the producer of the foreign goods.[21]

Protectionist policies seem more appropriate for less-developed countries whose industrial capacity has not yet matured. In a world where a developed country should have everything to gain by encouraging international free trade, such policies may be of dubious value. History shows that tariffs often lead to retaliatory action on the part of the nation or nations affected.

Miscellaneous State and Local Taxes

Most states impose a franchise tax on corporations. Basically, a **franchise tax** is levied on the right to do business in the state. The base used for the determination of the tax varies from state to state. Although corporate income considerations may come into play, this tax most often is based on the capitalization of the corporation (either with or without certain long-term indebtedness).

Closely akin to the franchise tax are **occupational taxes** applicable to various trades or businesses, such as a liquor store license, a taxicab permit, or a fee to practice a profession such as law, medicine, or accounting. Most of these are not significant revenue producers and fall more into the category of licenses than taxes. The revenue derived is used to defray the cost incurred by the jurisdiction in regulating the business or profession in the interest of the public good.

VALUE ADDED TAXES

At least in the Common Market countries of Western Europe, the **value added tax** (VAT) has gained acceptance as a major source of revenue. Although variously classified, a VAT resembles a national sales tax, since it taxes the increment in value as goods move through production and manufacturing stages to the marketplace. A VAT has its proponents in the United States as a partial solution to high Federal budget deficits and increases in employment taxes. Some have even suggested that a VAT could be utilized to furnish partial or total funding for a national health care program. Its incorporation as part of our tax system, however, is not likely in the immediate future.

Tax Administration

INTERNAL REVENUE SERVICE

4   LEARNING OBJECTIVE
Understand the administration of the tax law including the audit process utilized by the IRS.

The responsibility for administering the Federal tax laws rests with the Treasury Department. Administratively, the IRS is part of the Department of the Treasury and is responsible for enforcing the tax laws. The Commissioner of Internal Revenue is appointed by the President and is responsible for establishing policy and supervising the activities of the entire IRS organization.

The field organization of the IRS includes the following:

• Service Centers (10) that are primarily responsible for processing tax returns, including the selection of returns for audit. The Service Center

---

[21] The North American Free Trade Agreement (NAFTA), enacted in 1993, substantially reduced the tariffs on trade between Canada, Mexico, and the United States. However, NAFTA did not eliminate all tariffs on North American trade.

having proper jurisdiction is where taxpayers must file their Federal tax returns.

- District Directors (63) who are responsible for audits and for the collection of delinquent taxes. Each state has at least one District Director; several states (e.g., New York, California) have more.

THE AUDIT PROCESS

Selection of Returns for Audit

Due to budgetary limitations, only a small minority of returns are audited. For calendar year 1991, for example, only 1 percent of *all* individual income tax returns were examined.

The IRS utilizes mathematical formulas and statistical sampling techniques to select tax returns that are most likely to contain errors and to yield substantial amounts of additional tax revenues upon audit.

Though the IRS does not openly disclose all of its audit selection techniques, the following observations may be made concerning the probability of selection for audit:

- Certain groups of taxpayers are subject to audit much more frequently than others. These groups include individuals with gross income in excess of $50,000, self-employed individuals with substantial business income and deductions, and taxpayers with prior tax deficiencies. Also vulnerable are cash businesses (e.g., cafes and small service businesses) where the potential for tax avoidance is high.

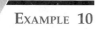

EXAMPLE 10

Jack owns and operates a liquor store on a cash-and-carry basis. Since all of Jack's sales are for cash, he might well be a prime candidate for an audit by the IRS. Cash transactions are easier to conceal than those made on credit. ▼

- If information returns (e.g., Form 1099, Form W–2) are not in substantial agreement with reported income, an audit can be anticipated.
- If an individual's itemized deductions are in excess of norms established for various income levels, the probability of an audit is increased.
- Filing of a refund claim by the taxpayer may prompt an audit of the return.
- Certain returns are selected on a random sampling basis under the Taxpayer Compliance Measurement Program (TCMP). The TCMP is used to develop, update, and improve the mathematical formulas and statistical sampling techniques used by the IRS.
- Information obtained from other sources (e.g., informants, news items) may lead to an audit. The tax law permits the IRS to pay rewards to persons who provide information that leads to the detection and punishment of those who violate the tax laws. The rewards may not exceed 10 percent of the taxes, fines, and penalties recovered as a result of such information.

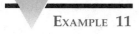

EXAMPLE 11

After 15 years of service, Rita is discharged by her employer, Dr. Smith. Shortly thereafter, the IRS receives an anonymous letter informing it that Dr. Smith keeps two separate sets of books, one of which substantially understates his cash receipts. ▼

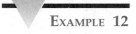

EXAMPLE 12

During a divorce proceeding, it is revealed that Leo, a public official, kept large amounts of cash in a shoe box at home. This information is widely disseminated by the news media and comes to the attention of the IRS. Needless to say, the IRS would be interested in knowing whether these funds originated from a taxable source and, if so, whether they were reported on Leo's income tax returns. ▼

Types of Audits

Once a return is selected for audit, the taxpayer is notified accordingly. If the issue involved is minor, the matter often can be resolved simply by correspondence (a **correspondence audit**) between the IRS and the taxpayer.

▼

EXAMPLE 13

During 1992, Janet received dividend income from Green Corporation. In early 1993, Green Corporation reported the payment on Form 1099–DIV (an information return for reporting dividend payments), the original being sent to the IRS and a copy to Janet. When preparing her income tax return for 1992, Janet apparently overlooked this particular Form 1099–DIV and failed to include the dividend on Schedule B, Interest and Dividend Income, of Form 1040. In 1994, the IRS sends a notice to Janet calling her attention to the omission and requesting a remittance for additional tax, interest, and penalty. Janet promptly mails a check to the IRS for the requested amount, and the matter is closed. ▼

Other examinations are generally classified as either office audits or field audits. An **office audit** usually is restricted in scope and is conducted in the facilities of the IRS. In contrast, a **field audit** involves an examination of numerous items reported on the return and is conducted on the premises of the taxpayer or the taxpayer's representative.

Upon the conclusion of the audit, the examining agent issues a Revenue Agent's Report (RAR) that summarizes the findings. The RAR will result in a refund (the tax was overpaid), a deficiency (the tax was underpaid), or a *no change* (the tax was correct) finding.

Settlement Procedures

If an audit results in an assessment of additional tax and no settlement is reached with the IRS agent, the taxpayer may attempt to negotiate a settlement with the IRS. If an appeal is desired, an appropriate request must be made to the Appeals Division of the IRS. In some cases, a taxpayer may be able to obtain a percentage settlement or a favorable settlement of one or more disputed issues. The Appeals

---

TAX IN THE NEWS

A LITTLE FLUSHED

Tax cheats beware! The IRS is prepared to follow you and your employees right into the bathroom. But only, says the IRS, for your own good.

This intrusion is part of an audit program in the Western Region that's cracking down on laundromats. The IRS doesn't trust cash businesses to keep accurate records, so the taxpersons are using water consumption to reconstruct laundromats' true income. But to be perfectly fair, they are careful to subtract the water used for toilet flushes, water fountains, wash basins and the like. Hence the necessity of measuring such flow.

In fact, the information from these audits will be incorporated into national guidelines for IRS employees checking on laundromats. Where water isn't metered, the auditors are devising ways to reconstruct income based on gas or electricity usage. Here they'll subtract what's used for heat and light.

SOURCE: Reprinted from "A Little Flushed" by Laura Saunders, *Forbes*, July 20, 1992, p. 19. Reprinted by permission of Forbes Magazine. © Forbes Inc., 1992.

Division is authorized to settle all disputes based on the *hazard of litigation* (the probability of favorable resolution of the disputed issue or issues if litigated).

If a satisfactory settlement is not reached within the administrative appeal process, the taxpayer may wish to litigate the case in the Tax Court, a Federal District Court, or the Court of Federal Claims. However, litigation is recommended only as a last resort because of the legal costs involved and the uncertainty of the final outcome. Tax litigation considerations are discussed more fully in Chapter 2.

STATUTE OF LIMITATIONS

A **statute of limitations** is a provision in the law that offers a party a defense against a suit brought by another party after the expiration of a specified period of time. The purpose of a statute of limitations is to preclude parties from prosecuting stale claims. The passage of time makes the defense of such claims difficult since witnesses may no longer be available or evidence may have been lost or destroyed. Found at the state and Federal levels, such statutes cover a multitude of suits, both civil and criminal.

For our purposes, the relevant statutes deal with the Federal income tax. The two categories involved cover both the period of limitations applicable to the assessment of additional tax deficiencies by the IRS and the period that deals with claims for refunds by taxpayers.

Assessment by the IRS

Under the general rule, the IRS may assess (impose) an additional tax liability against a taxpayer within *three years* of the filing of the income tax return. If the return is filed early, the three-year period begins to run from the due date of the return (usually April 15 for a calendar year individual taxpayer).

If a taxpayer omits an amount of gross income in excess of 25 percent of the gross income reported on the return, the statute of limitations is increased to six years.

▼

EXAMPLE 14

For 1989, Mark, a calendar year taxpayer, reported gross income of $400,000 on a timely filed income tax return. If Mark omitted more than $100,000 (25% × $400,000), the six-year statute of limitations would apply to the 1989 tax year. ▼

The six-year provision on assessments by the IRS applies only to the omission of income and does not cover other factors that might lead to an understatement of tax liability (e.g., overstatement of deductions and credits).

There is *no* statute of limitations on assessments of tax if *no return* is filed or if a *fraudulent* return is filed.

Limitations on Refunds

If a taxpayer believes that an overpayment of Federal income tax was made, a claim for refund should be filed with the IRS. A *claim for refund*, therefore, is a request to the IRS that it return to the taxpayer the excessive income taxes paid.[22]

---

[22]The forms to use in filing a claim for refund are discussed in Chapter 3.

A claim for refund generally must be filed within *three years* from the date the return was filed *or* within *two years* from the date the tax was paid, whichever is later. Income tax returns that are filed early are deemed to have been filed on the date the return was due.

INTEREST AND PENALTIES

Interest rates are determined quarterly by the IRS based on the existing Federal short-term rate. The rates for tax refunds (overpayments) are 1 percent below those applicable to assessments (underpayments). For the first quarter (January 1–March 31) of 1994, the rates were 6 percent for refunds and 7 percent for assessments.[23]

For assessments of additional taxes, the interest begins running on the unextended due date of the return.[24] With refunds, however, no interest is allowed if the overpayment is refunded to the taxpayer within 45 days of the date the return is filed. For this purpose, returns filed early are deemed to have been filed on the due date.

The tax law provides various penalties for lack of compliance by taxpayers. Some of these penalties are summarized as follows:

- For a *failure to file* a tax return by the due date (including extension—see Chapter 3), a penalty of 5 percent per month (up to a maximum of 25 percent) is imposed on the amount of tax shown as due on the return. Any fraction of a month counts as a full month.
- A penalty for a *failure to pay* the tax due (as shown on the return) is imposed in the amount of 0.5 percent per month (up to a maximum of 25 percent). Again, any fraction of a month counts as a full month. During any month in which both the failure to file penalty and the failure to pay penalty apply, the failure to file penalty is reduced by the amount of the failure to pay penalty.

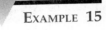

EXAMPLE 15

Adam files his tax return 18 days after the due date of the return. Along with the return, he remits a check for $1,000, which is the balance of the tax he owed. Disregarding the interest element, Adam's total penalties are as follows:

Failure to pay penalty (0.5% × $1,000)		$ 5
Plus:		
Failure to file penalty (5% × $1,000)	$50	
Less failure to pay penalty for the same period	(5)	
Failure to file penalty		45
Total penalties		$50

Note that the penalties for one full month are imposed even though Adam was delinquent by only 18 days. Unlike the method used to compute interest, any part of a month is treated as a whole month. ▼

- A *negligence* penalty of 20 percent is imposed if any of the underpayment was for intentional disregard of rules and regulations without intent to defraud. The penalty applies to just that portion attributable to the negligence.

---

[23]The rates applicable after March 31, 1994, were not available when this text went to press.

[24]Some additional taxes due for 1993 and generated by changes made by the Revenue Reconciliation Act of 1993 can be paid in installments *without* a charge for interest.

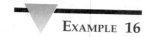

EXAMPLE 16

Cindy underpaid her taxes for 1993 in the amount of $20,000, of which $15,000 is attributable to negligence. Cindy's negligence penalty is $3,000 (20% × $15,000). ▼

- Various fraud penalties may be imposed. *Fraud* is a deliberate action on the part of the taxpayer evidenced by deceit, misrepresentation, concealment, etc. For possible fraud situations, refer to Examples 11 and 12. The burden of proving fraud is on the IRS. This is in contrast to the usual deficiency assessment made by the IRS, where the burden is on the taxpayer to show that he or she does not owe any additional tax.

TAX PRACTICE

The area of tax practice is largely unregulated. Virtually anyone can aid another in complying with the various tax laws. If a practitioner is a member of a profession, such as law or public accounting, he or she must abide by certain ethical standards. Furthermore, the Internal Revenue Code imposes penalties upon the preparers of Federal tax returns who violate proscribed acts and procedures.

Ethical Guidelines

5 LEARNING OBJECTIVE
Appreciate some of the ethical guidelines involved in tax practice.

The American Institute of CPAs has issued numerous guides for CPAs engaged in tax practice. Called "Statements on Responsibilities in Tax Practice," some of these are summarized below.

- Do not take questionable positions on a client's tax return in the hope that the return will not be selected for audit by the IRS. Any positions taken should be supported by a good-faith belief that they have a realistic chance of being sustained if challenged. The client should be fully advised of the risks involved and of the penalties that would result if the position taken is not successful.
- A practitioner can use a client's estimates if they are reasonable under the circumstances. If the tax law requires verification (e.g., receipts), the client should be so advised. In no event should an estimate be given the appearance of greater accuracy than is the case. For example, an estimate of $1,000 should not be deducted on a return as $999.
- Every effort should be made to answer questions appearing on tax returns. A question need not be answered if the information requested is not readily available, the answer is voluminous, or the question's meaning is uncertain. The failure to answer a question on a return cannot be justified on the grounds that the answer could prove disadvantageous to the taxpayer.
- Upon learning of an error on a past tax return, advise the client to correct it. Do not, however, inform the IRS of the error. If the error is material and the client refuses to correct it, consider withdrawing from the engagement. This will be necessary if the error has a carryover effect and prevents the current year's tax liability from being determined correctly.

Statutory Penalties Imposed on Tax Return Preparers

In addition to ethical constraints, a tax return preparer may be subject to certain statutorily sanctioned penalties, including the following:

- Various penalties involving procedural matters. Examples include failing to furnish the taxpayer with a copy of the return; endorsing a taxpayer's refund check; failing to sign the return as a preparer; failing to furnish one's identification number; and failing to keep copies of returns or maintain a client list.

- Understatement of a tax liability based on a position that lacks any realistic possibility of being sustained. If the position is not frivolous, the penalty can be avoided by disclosing it on the return.
- Any willful attempt to understate taxes. This usually results when a preparer disregards or makes no effort to obtain pertinent information from a client.

UNDERSTANDING THE FEDERAL TAX LAW

6   LEARNING OBJECTIVE
Recognize the economic, social, equity, and political considerations that justify various aspects of the tax law and the role played by the IRS and the courts in the evolution of the Federal tax system.

The Federal tax law is a mosaic of statutory provisions, administrative pronouncements, and court decisions. Anyone who has attempted to work with this body of knowledge would have to admit to its complexity. For the person who has to trudge through a mass of rules to find the solution to a tax problem, it may be of some consolation to know that the law's complexity can generally be explained. Whether sound or not, there is a reason for the formulation of every rule. Knowing these reasons, therefore, is a considerable step toward understanding the Federal tax law.

The Federal tax law has as its *major objective* the raising of revenue. But although the fiscal needs of the government are important, other considerations explain certain portions of the law. Economic, social, equity, and political factors also play a significant role. Added to these factors is the marked impact the IRS and the courts have had and will continue to have on the evolution of Federal tax law. These matters are treated in the remainder of the chapter, and, wherever appropriate, the discussion is referenced to subjects covered later in the text.

REVENUE NEEDS

The foundation of any tax system has to be the raising of revenue to cover the cost of government operations. Ideally, annual outlays should not exceed anticipated revenues, thereby leading to a balanced budget with no resulting deficit. Many states have achieved this objective by passing laws or constitutional amendments precluding deficit spending. Unfortunately, the Federal government has no such conclusive prohibition, and mounting annual deficits have become an increasing concern for many.

When finalizing the Tax Reform Act (TRA) of 1986, a deficit-conscious Congress was guided by the concept of **revenue neutrality.** The concept means that the changes made will neither increase nor decrease the net result reached under the prior rules. Revenue neutrality does not mean that any one taxpayer's tax liability will remain the same. Since the circumstances involved will differ, one taxpayer's increased tax liability could be another's tax savings. Although revenue-neutral tax reform does not reduce deficits, at least it does not aggravate the problem.

One can expect budget deficit considerations to play an ever-increasing role in shaping future tax policy. Recent tax legislation, the Revenue Reconciliation Act (RRA) of 1993, is intended to generate considerable revenue. Although it contains a few revenue loss provisions, these are more than made up by new taxes and increases in tax rates.

ECONOMIC CONSIDERATIONS

The use of the tax system in an effort to accomplish economic objectives has become increasingly popular in recent years. Generally, proponents of this goal use tax legislation to amend the Internal Revenue Code and promote measures designed to help control the economy or encourage certain activities and businesses.

Control of the Economy

Congress has used depreciation write-offs as a means of controlling the economy. Theoretically, shorter asset lives and accelerated methods should encourage additional investment in depreciable property acquired for business use. Conversely, longer asset lives and the required use of the straight-line method of depreciation dampen the tax incentive for capital outlays.

Compared with past law, TRA of 1986 generally cut back on faster write-offs for property acquired after 1986. Particularly hard hit was most depreciable real estate, where asset lives were extended from 19 years to as long as 31½ years and the straight-line method was made mandatory. In RRA of 1993, the recovery period for nonresidential real property was further extended to 39 years. This last change was in the interest of revenue neutrality to compensate for the liberalization of the passive activity loss rules (see Chapter 11).

A change in the tax rate structure has a more immediate impact on the economy. With lower tax rates, taxpayers are able to retain additional spendable funds. Although TRA of 1986 lowered tax rates for most taxpayers, it also reduced or eliminated many deductions and credits. Consequently, lower rates may not lead to lower tax liabilities. RRA of 1993 raised rates on higher-income individuals and corporations. Although this action was justified as a means of raising additional revenue, its impact on the economy is not yet clear.

Encouragement of Certain Activities

Without passing judgment on the wisdom of any such choices, it is quite clear that the tax law does encourage certain types of economic activity or segments of the economy. For example, the favorable treatment allowed research and development expenditures can be explained by the desire to foster technological progress. Under the tax law, such expenditures can be either deducted in the year incurred or capitalized and amortized over a period of 60 months or more. In terms of the timing of the tax savings, these options usually are preferable to capitalizing the cost with a write-off over the estimated useful life of the asset created. If the asset developed has an indefinite useful life, no write-off would be available without the two options allowed by the tax law.

Is it desirable to encourage the conservation of energy resources? Considering the world energy situation and our own reliance on foreign oil, the answer to this question has to be yes. The concern over energy usage was a prime consideration in the enactment of legislation to make various tax savings for energy conservation expenditures available to taxpayers.

Is preserving the environment a desirable objective? Ecological considerations explain why the tax law permits a 60-month amortization period for costs incurred in the installation of pollution control facilities.

Is it wise to stimulate U.S. exports of goods and services? Considering the pressing and continuing problem of a deficit in the U.S. balance of payments, the answer should be clear. Along this line, Congress has created Foreign Sales Corporations (FSCs), which are designed to encourage domestic exports of goods. The FSC provisions exempt a percentage of profits from export sales from the Federal income tax. Also in an international setting, Congress has deemed it advisable to establish incentives for U.S. citizens who accept employment overseas.

Such persons receive generous tax breaks through special treatment of their foreign-source income and certain housing costs.

Is saving desirable for the economy? Saving leads to capital formation and thereby makes funds available to finance home construction and industrial expansion. The tax law encourages saving by according preferential treatment to private retirement plans. Not only are contributions to Keogh (H.R. 10) plans and certain Individual Retirement Accounts (IRAs) deductible, but income from the contributions accumulates free of tax. As noted below, the encouragement of private-sector pension plans can also be justified under social considerations.

Encouragement of Certain Industries

No one can question the proposition that a sound agricultural base is necessary for a well-balanced national economy. Undoubtedly, this can explain why farmers are accorded special treatment under the Federal tax system. Among the benefits are the election to expense rather than capitalize certain soil and water conservation expenditures and fertilizers and the election to defer the recognition of gain on the receipt of crop insurance proceeds.

Encouragement of Small Business

At least in the United States, a consensus exists that what is good for small business is good for the economy as a whole. Whether valid or not, this assumption has led to a definite bias in the tax law favoring small business.

In the corporate tax area, several provisions can be explained by the desire to benefit small business. One provision permits the shareholders of a small business corporation to make a special election that generally will avoid the imposition of the corporate income tax.[25] Furthermore, such an election enables the corporation to pass through its operating losses to its shareholders.

SOCIAL CONSIDERATIONS

Some provisions of the Federal tax law, particularly those dealing with the income tax of individuals, can be explained by social considerations. Some notable examples and their rationales include the following:

- Certain benefits provided to employees through accident and health plans financed by employers are nontaxable to employees. Encouraging such plans is considered socially desirable since they provide medical benefits in the event of an employee's illness or injury.
- Most premiums paid by an employer for group term insurance covering the life of the employee are nontaxable to the employee. These arrangements can be justified on social grounds in that they provide funds for the family unit to help it adjust to the loss of wages caused by the employee's death.
- A contribution made by an employer to a qualified pension or profit sharing plan for an employee receives special treatment. The contribution and any income it generates will not be taxed to the employee until the funds are

---

[25] Known as the S election, it is discussed in Chapter 20.

distributed. Such an arrangement also benefits the employer by allowing a tax deduction when the contribution is made to the qualified plan. Private retirement plans are encouraged to supplement the subsistence income level the employee otherwise would have under the Social Security system.[26]

- A deduction is allowed for contributions to qualified charitable organizations.[27] The deduction attempts to shift some of the financial and administrative burden of socially desirable programs from the public (the government) to the private (the citizens) sector.

- A tax credit is allowed for amounts spent to furnish care for certain minor or disabled dependents to enable the taxpayer to seek or maintain gainful employment.[28] Who could deny the social desirability of encouraging taxpayers to provide care for their children while they work?

- A tax deduction is not allowed for certain expenditures deemed to be contrary to public policy. This disallowance extends to such items as fines, penalties, illegal kickbacks, bribes to government officials, and gambling losses in excess of gains. Social considerations dictate that the tax law should not encourage these activities by permitting a deduction.

Many other examples could be cited, but the conclusion would be unchanged. Social considerations do explain a significant part of the Federal tax law.

EQUITY CONSIDERATIONS

The concept of equity is relative. Reasonable persons can, and often do, disagree about what is fair or unfair. In the tax area, moreover, equity is most often tied to a particular taxpayer's personal situation. To illustrate, compare the tax positions of those who rent their personal residences with those who own their homes. Renters receive no Federal income tax benefit from the rent they pay. For homeowners, however, a large portion of the house payments they make may qualify for the Federal interest and property tax deductions. Although renters may have difficulty understanding this difference in tax treatment, the encouragement of home ownership can be justified on both economic and social grounds.

In the same vein, compare the tax treatment of a corporation with that of a partnership. Although the two businesses may be of equal size, similarly situated, and competitors in the production of goods or services, they are not treated comparably under the tax law. The corporation is subject to a separate Federal income tax; the partnership is not. Whether the differences in tax treatment can be justified logically in terms of equity is beside the point. The point is that the tax law can and does make a distinction between these business forms.

Equity, then, is not what appears fair or unfair to any one taxpayer or group of taxpayers. It is, instead, what the tax law recognizes. Some recognition of equity does exist, however, and explains part of the law. The concept of equity appears in tax provisions that alleviate the effect of multiple taxation and postpone the recognition of gain when the taxpayer lacks the ability or wherewithal to pay the tax. Equity considerations also mitigate the effect of the application of the annual accounting period concept and cope with the eroding results of inflation.

---

[26] The same rationale explains the availability of similar arrangements for self-employed persons (the H.R. 10, or Keogh, plan). See Chapter 19.

[27] The charitable contribution deduction is discussed in Chapter 10.
[28] See Chapter 13.

Alleviating the Effect of Multiple Taxation

The income earned by a taxpayer may be subject to taxes imposed by different taxing authorities. If, for example, the taxpayer is a resident of New York City, income might generate Federal, state of New York, and city of New York income taxes. To compensate for this apparent inequity, the Federal tax law allows a taxpayer to claim a deduction for state and local income taxes. The deduction does not, however, neutralize the effect of multiple taxation, since the benefit derived depends on the taxpayer's Federal income tax rate. Only a tax credit, rather than a deduction, would eliminate the effects of multiple taxation on the same income.

Equity considerations can explain the Federal tax treatment of certain income from foreign sources. Since double taxation results when the same income is subject to both foreign and U.S. income taxes, the tax law permits the taxpayer to choose between a credit and a deduction for the foreign taxes paid.

The Wherewithal to Pay Concept

The **wherewithal to pay** concept recognizes the inequity of taxing a transaction when the taxpayer lacks the means with which to pay the tax. It is particularly suited to situations in which the taxpayer's economic position has not changed significantly as a result of the transaction.

An illustration of the wherewithal to pay concept is the provision of the tax law dealing with the treatment of gain resulting from the sale of a personal residence. If the proceeds are rolled over (reinvested) in another personal residence within a specified time period, the gain will not be taxed (see Chapter 15).

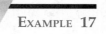

EXAMPLE 17

Ron sold his personal residence (cost of $60,000) for $100,000 and moved to another city. Shortly thereafter, he purchased a new personal residence for $100,000. ▼

In Example 17, Ron had a realized gain of $40,000 [$100,000 (selling price) − $60,000 (cost of residence)]. It would be inequitable to force Ron to pay a tax on this gain for two reasons. First, without disposing of the property acquired (the new residence), Ron would be hard-pressed to pay the tax. Second, his economic position has not changed significantly.

A warning is in order concerning the application of the wherewithal to pay concept. It applies only in situations specified by the tax law. Otherwise, the absence of cash and no apparent change in economic position will not prevent a transaction from being taxed.

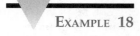

EXAMPLE 18

Assume the same facts as in Example 17 except that the sale and purchase involved rental houses and not personal residences. Now, the sale of the first rental house will result in a gain of $40,000 that will be subject to tax. The fact that Ron reinvested the $100,000 in another rental house is of no consequence. ▼

Reconciling the different results reached in Examples 17 and 18 may seem difficult. But simply stated, the tax law applies the wherewithal to pay concept to the rollover on the gain from the sale of a personal residence. It does not do so when a rental house is involved, as Example 18 illustrates.

Mitigating the Effect of the Annual Accounting Period Concept

For purposes of effective administration of the tax law, all taxpayers must report to and settle with the Federal government at periodic intervals. Otherwise, taxpayers would remain uncertain as to their tax liabilities, and the government would have difficulty judging revenues and budgeting expenditures. The period selected for final settlement of most tax liabilities, in any event an arbitrary determination, is one year. At the close of each year, therefore, a taxpayer's position becomes complete for that particular year. Referred to as the annual accounting period concept, its effect is to divide each taxpayer's life, for tax purposes, into equal annual intervals.

The finality of the annual accounting period concept could lead to dissimilar tax treatment for taxpayers who are, from a long-range standpoint, in the same economic position.

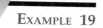

EXAMPLE 19   José and Alicia, both sole proprietors, have experienced the following results during the past four years:

Profit (or Loss)		
Year	José	Alicia
1991	$50,000	$150,000
1992	60,000	60,000
1993	70,000	70,000
1994	50,000	(50,000)

Although José and Alicia have the same profit of $230,000 over the period from 1991 to 1994, the finality of the annual accounting period concept places Alicia at a definite disadvantage for tax purposes. The net operating loss procedure offers Alicia some relief by allowing her to apply some or all of her 1994 loss to the earlier profitable years (in this case, 1991). Thus, with a net operating loss carryback, Alicia is in a position to obtain a refund for some of the taxes she paid on the $150,000 profit reported for 1991. ▼

The same reasoning used to support the deduction of net operating losses can explain the special treatment the tax law accords to excess capital losses and excess charitable contributions.[29] Carryback and carryover procedures help mitigate the effect of limiting a loss or a deduction to the accounting period in which it was realized. With such procedures, a taxpayer may be able to salvage a loss or a deduction that might otherwise be wasted.

The installment method of recognizing gain on the sale of property allows a taxpayer to spread tax consequences over the payout period.[30] The harsh effect of taxing all the gain in the year of sale is thereby avoided. The installment method can also be explained by the wherewithal to pay concept since recognition of gain is tied to the collection of the installment notes received from the sale of the property. Tax consequences, then, tend to correspond to the seller's ability to pay the tax.

Coping with Inflation

Because of the progressive nature of the income tax, a wage adjustment to compensate for inflation can increase the income tax bracket of the recipient.

---

[29] The tax treatment of these items is discussed in Chapters 7, 10, and 16.

[30] Under the installment method, each payment received by the seller represents both a recovery of capital (the nontaxable portion) and profit from the sale (the taxable portion). The tax rules governing the installment method are discussed in Chapter 18.

Known as *bracket creep*, its overall impact is an erosion of purchasing power. Congress recognized this problem and began to adjust various income tax components, such as tax brackets, standard deduction amounts, and personal and dependency exemptions, through an indexation procedure. Indexation is based upon the rise in the consumer price index over the prior year.

POLITICAL CONSIDERATIONS

A large segment of the Federal tax law is made up of statutory provisions. Since these statutes are enacted by Congress, is it any surprise that political considerations influence tax law? For purposes of discussion, the effect of political considerations on the tax law is divided into the following topics: special interest legislation, political expediency situations, and state and local government influences.

Special Interest Legislation

There is no doubt that certain provisions of the tax law can largely be explained by the political influence some pressure groups have had on Congress. Is there any other realistic reason that, for example, prepaid subscription and dues income are not taxed until earned while prepaid rents are taxed to the landlord in the year received?

A recent example of special interest legislation was a last minute amendment to TRA of 1986 made by former Senator Long (Louisiana) and Representative Pickle (Austin, Texas). Under the amendment, a charitable deduction was allowed for donations to certain institutions of higher education that enabled the donor to receive choice seating at athletic events. The definition of institutions of higher education was so limited, however, that only Louisiana State University and the University of Texas were qualified recipients. It was not until two years later that Congress modified the tax law to neutralize this apparent preferential treatment (see Chapter 10).

Special interest legislation is not necessarily to be condemned if it can be justified on economic, social, or some other utilitarian grounds. At any rate, it is an inevitable product of our political system.

Political Expediency Situations

Various tax reform proposals rise and fall in favor with the shifting moods of the American public. That Congress is sensitive to popular feeling is an accepted fact. Therefore, certain provisions of the tax law can be explained by the political climate at the time they were enacted.

Measures that deter more affluent taxpayers from obtaining so-called preferential tax treatment have always had popular appeal and, consequently, the support of Congress. Provisions such as the alternative minimum tax, the imputed interest rules, and the limitation on the deductibility of interest on investment indebtedness can be explained on this basis.[31]

Other changes explained at least partially by political expediency include the lowering of individual income tax rates, the increase in the personal and dependency exemptions, and the increase in the amount of the earned income credit. One of the expressed objectives of RRA of 1993 was to increase taxes levied on wealthy individuals by instituting new 36 and 39.6 percent rates on higher-income brackets.

---

[31] See Chapters 4, 10, and 12.

State and Local Government Influences

Political considerations have played a major role in the nontaxability of interest received on state and local obligations. In view of the furor that has been raised by state and local political figures every time any modification of this tax provision has been proposed, one might well regard it as next to sacred.

Somewhat less apparent has been the influence state law has had in shaping our present Federal tax law. Such was the case with community property systems. The nine states with community property systems are Louisiana, Texas, New Mexico, Arizona, California, Washington, Idaho, Nevada, and Wisconsin. The rest of the states are classified as common law jurisdictions. The difference between common law and community property systems centers around the property rights possessed by married persons. In a common law system, each spouse owns whatever he or she earns. Under a community property system, one-half of the earnings of each spouse is considered owned by the other spouse.

EXAMPLE 20

Al and Fran are husband and wife, and their only income is the $60,000 annual salary Al receives. If they live in New Jersey (a common law state), the $60,000 salary belongs to Al. If, however, they live in Arizona (a community property state), the $60,000 is divided equally, in terms of ownership, between Al and Fran. ▼

At one time, the tax position of the residents of community property states was so advantageous that many common law states actually adopted community property systems. Needless to say, the political pressure placed on Congress to correct the disparity in tax treatment was considerable. To a large extent this was accomplished in the Revenue Act of 1948, which extended many of the community property tax advantages to residents of common law jurisdictions.

The major advantage extended was the provision allowing married taxpayers to file joint returns and compute the tax liability as if the income had been earned one-half by each spouse. This result is automatic in a community property state, since half of the income earned by one spouse belongs to the other spouse. The income-splitting benefits of a joint return are now incorporated as part of the tax rates applicable to married taxpayers. See Chapter 3.

INFLUENCE OF THE INTERNAL REVENUE SERVICE

The influence of the IRS is apparent in many areas beyond its role in issuing the administrative pronouncements that make up a considerable portion of our tax law. In its capacity as the protector of the national revenue, the IRS has been instrumental in securing the passage of much legislation designed to curtail the most flagrant tax avoidance practices (to close tax loopholes). In its capacity as the administrator of the tax law, the IRS has sought and obtained legislation to make its job easier (to attain administrative feasibility).

The IRS as Protector of the Revenue

Innumerable examples can be given of provisions in the tax law that stem from the direct influence of the IRS. Usually, such provisions are intended to prevent a loophole from being used to avoid the tax consequences intended by Congress. Working within the letter of existing law, ingenious taxpayers and their advisers devise techniques that accomplish indirectly what cannot be accomplished directly. As a consequence, legislation is enacted to close the loopholes that taxpayers have located and exploited. Some tax law can be explained in this fashion and is discussed in the chapters to follow.

In addition, the IRS has secured from Congress legislation of a more general nature that enables it to make adjustments based on the substance, rather than the formal construction, of what a taxpayer has done. One such provision permits the IRS to make adjustments to a taxpayer's method of accounting when the method used by the taxpayer does not clearly reflect income.[32]

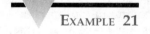
Example 21

Tina, a cash basis taxpayer, owns and operates a pharmacy. All drugs and other items acquired for resale (e.g., cosmetics) are charged to the purchases account and written off (expensed) for tax purposes in the year of acquisition. As this procedure does not clearly reflect income, it would be appropriate for the IRS to require that Tina establish and maintain an ending inventory account. ▼

Administrative Feasibility

Some of the tax law is justified on the grounds that it simplifies the task of the IRS in collecting the revenue and administering the law. With regard to collecting the revenue, the IRS long ago realized the importance of placing taxpayers on a pay-as-you-go basis. Elaborate withholding procedures apply to wages, while the tax on other types of income may be paid at periodic intervals throughout the year. The IRS has been instrumental in convincing the courts that accrual basis taxpayers should pay taxes on prepaid income in the year received and not when earned. The approach may be contrary to generally accepted accounting principles, but it is consistent with the wherewithal to pay concept.

Of considerable aid to the IRS in collecting revenue are the numerous provisions that impose interest and penalties on taxpayers for noncompliance with the tax law. Provisions such as the penalties for failure to pay a tax or to file a return that is due, the negligence penalty for intentional disregard of rules and regulations, and various penalties for civil and criminal fraud serve as deterrents to taxpayer noncompliance.

One of the keys to an effective administration of our tax system is the audit process conducted by the IRS. To carry out this function, the IRS is aided by provisions that reduce the chance of taxpayer error or manipulation and therefore simplify the audit effort that is necessary. An increase in the amount of the standard deduction, for example, reduces the number of individual taxpayers who will choose the alternative of itemizing their personal deductions.[33] With fewer deductions to check, the audit function is simplified.[34]

The audit function of the IRS has also been simplified by provisions of the tax law dealing with the burden of proof. Suppose, for example, the IRS audits a taxpayer and questions a particular deduction. Who has the burden of proving the propriety of the deduction? The so-called presumption of correctness that attaches in favor of any deficiency assessed by the IRS can be explained by the nature of our tax system. The Federal income tax is a self-assessed tax, which means that each taxpayer is responsible for rendering an accounting to the IRS of all of his or her transactions during the year. A failure to do so means that any doubts will be resolved in favor of the IRS. Only in the case of fraud (which could involve fines and penal sanctions) does the IRS carry the burden of proof.

---

[32] See Chapter 18.

[33] For a discussion of the standard deduction, see Chapter 3.

[34] The same justification was given by the IRS when it proposed to Congress the $100 limitation on personal casualty and theft losses. Imposition of the limitation eliminated many casualty and theft loss deductions and, as a consequence, saved the IRS considerable audit time. Later legislation, in addition to retaining the $100 feature, limits deductible losses to those in excess of 10% of a taxpayer's adjusted gross income. See Chapter 7.

INFLUENCE OF THE COURTS

In addition to interpreting statutory provisions and the administrative pronouncements issued by the IRS, the Federal courts have influenced tax law in two other respects.[35] First, the courts have formulated certain judicial concepts that serve as guides in the application of various tax provisions. Second, certain key decisions have led to changes in the Internal Revenue Code.

Judicial Concepts Relating to Tax

A leading tax concept developed by the courts deals with the interpretation of statutory tax provisions that operate to benefit taxpayers. The courts have established the rule that these relief provisions are to be narrowly construed against taxpayers if there is any doubt about their application.

EXAMPLE 22

When a taxpayer has a gain on the sale of a personal residence, the gain is not subject to Federal income tax if the proceeds from the sale are reinvested in another principal residence. The tax law specifies a period of time in which the reinvestment must take place. The courts have held that the nontaxability of gain is a relief provision to be narrowly construed. Thus, failure to meet the replacement period requirements, even if beyond the control of the taxpayer, will cause the gain to be taxed.[36] ▼

Important in this area is the *arm's length* concept. Particularly in dealings between related parties, transactions may be tested by looking to whether the taxpayers acted in an arm's length manner. The question to be asked is: Would unrelated parties have handled the transaction in the same way?

EXAMPLE 23

Rex, the sole shareholder of Silver Corporation, leases property to the corporation for a yearly rent of $6,000. To test whether the corporation should be allowed a rent deduction for this amount, the IRS and the courts will apply the arm's length concept. Would Silver Corporation have paid $6,000 a year in rent if it had leased the same property from an unrelated party (rather than from Rex)? Suppose it is determined that an unrelated third party would have paid an annual rent for the property of only $5,000. Under these circumstances, Silver Corporation will be allowed a deduction of only $5,000. The other $1,000 it paid for the use of the property represents a nondeductible dividend. Accordingly, Rex will be treated as having received rent income of $5,000 and dividend income of $1,000. ▼

Judicial Influence on Statutory Provisions

Some court decisions have been of such consequence that Congress has incorporated them into statutory tax law. For example, many years ago the courts found that stock dividends distributed to the shareholders of a corporation were not taxable as income. This result was largely accepted by Congress, and a provision in the tax statutes now covers the issue.

On occasion, however, Congress has reacted negatively to judicial interpretations of the tax law.

EXAMPLE 24

Nora leases unimproved real estate to Wade for 40 years. At a cost of $200,000, Wade erects a building on the land. The building is worth $100,000 when the lease terminates and Nora takes possession of the property. Does Nora have any income either when the improve-

[35] A great deal of case law is devoted to ascertaining congressional intent. The courts, in effect, ask: What did Congress have in mind when it enacted a particular tax provision?

[36] These rules are discussed further in Chapter 15.

ments are made or when the lease terminates? In a landmark decision, a court held that Nora must recognize income of $100,000 upon the termination of the lease. ▼

Congress felt that the result reached in Example 24 was inequitable in that it was not consistent with the wherewithal to pay concept. Consequently, the tax law was amended to provide that a landlord does not recognize any income either when the improvements are made (unless made in lieu of rent) or when the lease terminates.

SUMMARY

In addition to its necessary revenue-raising objective, the Federal tax law has developed in response to several other factors:

- *Economic considerations.* The emphasis here is on tax provisions that help regulate the economy and encourage certain activities and types of businesses.
- *Social considerations.* Some tax provisions are designed to encourage (or discourage) certain socially desirable (or undesirable) practices.
- *Equity considerations.* Of principal concern in this area are tax provisions that alleviate the effect of multiple taxation, recognize the wherewithal to pay concept, mitigate the effect of the annual accounting period concept, and recognize the eroding effect of inflation.
- *Political considerations.* Of significance in this regard are tax provisions that represent special interest legislation, reflect political expediency, and exhibit the effect of state and local law.
- *Influence of the IRS.* Many tax provisions are intended to aid the IRS in the collection of revenue and the administration of the tax law.
- *Influence of the courts.* Court decisions have established a body of judicial concepts relating to tax law and have, on occasion, led Congress to enact statutory provisions to either clarify or negate their effect.

These factors explain various tax provisions and thereby help in understanding why the tax law developed to its present state. The next step involves learning to work with the tax law, which is the subject of Chapter 2.

KEY TERMS*

Ad valorem tax, 1–6

Correspondence audit, 1–20

Death tax, 1–11

Employment taxes, 1–16

Estate tax, 1–11

Excise tax, 1–9

FICA tax, 1–16

Field audit, 1–20

Franchise tax, 1–18

FUTA tax, 1–17

Gift tax, 1–12

Inheritance tax, 1–11

Occupational tax, 1–18

Office audit, 1–20

Personalty, 1–8

Realty, 1–6

Revenue neutrality, 1–24

Sales tax, 1–10

Severance tax, 1–11

Statute of limitations, 1–21

Use tax, 1–10

Value added tax, 1–18

Wherewithal to pay, 1–28

*The page reference is the page on which the term is discussed in the text. See also the definition of the term in the Glossary (Appendix C).

PROBLEM
MATERIALS

DISCUSSION QUESTIONS

1. Irene, a middle management employee, is offered a pay increase by her employer. As a condition of the offer, Irene must move to another state. What tax considerations should Irene weigh before making a decision on whether to accept the offer?

2. A tax protester refuses to pay the Federal income tax on the grounds that the tax is unconstitutional. Any comment?

3. Before the ratification of the Sixteenth Amendment to the U.S. Constitution, the Federal income tax on corporations was held to be constitutional, whereas the Federal income tax on individuals was not. Why?

4. A tax law that was enacted in 1953 would be part of which Internal Revenue Code (i.e., 1939, 1954, or 1986)? Explain.

5. How does the pay-as-you-go procedure apply to wage earners? To persons who have income from other than wages?

6. Analyze the Federal income tax in light of Adam Smith's canons of taxation.

7. Is FICA a proportional or progressive tax? Explain.

8. What difference does it make whether a capital improvement to real estate is classified as a *fixture*?

9. Al is considering starting a new business that will require the construction of a manufacturing facility. Jefferson County, one of the geographic locations Al is considering, has proposed a tax holiday. What does this mean?

10. Ira inherits his mother's personal residence and converts it to rental property. The next year, the city and county raise the ad valorem taxes due on the property. Explain what the cause of the increase might be.

11. Lora lives in a city that has recently experienced a large increase in commercial office vacancies. She has noticed that the property tax on her personal residence has gone up. Could there be a causal connection? Explain.

12. Matt buys a new home for $150,000, its cost of construction plus the usual profit margin for the builder. The new home is located in a neighborhood largely developed 10 years ago when the homes sold for approximately $50,000 each. Assuming the homes of his neighbors are worth (in current values) in the vicinity of $150,000, could Matt be at a disadvantage with regard to the ad valorem tax on realty?

13. Recently, one of your friends successfully challenged a reappraisal of his personal residence by the county board of real estate tax assessors. He remarks to you that this should put him "in good shape for the next five years." What does he mean?

14. While out of town on business, Paul stays at a motel with an advertised room rate of $40 per night. When checking out, Paul is charged $44. What would be a plausible reason for the extra $4 Paul had to pay?

15. Agnes, a salesperson for a national firm, resides in New York. Every time Agnes travels to Virginia on business, she purchases at least a dozen cartons of cigarettes. Why?

16. Earl, a resident of Wyoming (which imposes a general sales tax), goes to Montana (which does not impose a general sales tax) to purchase his automobile. Will Earl successfully avoid the Wyoming sales tax? Explain.

17. When Alaska became a major oil producer, the state repealed its state income tax. Is there any correlation between these two events? Explain.

18. A death tax has been characterized as an excise tax. Do you agree? Why or why not?

19. Explain the difference between an inheritance tax and an estate tax.

20. What was the original objective of the Federal estate tax?

21. A decedent who leaves all of his property to his surviving spouse and to qualified charitable organizations will not be subject to a Federal estate tax. Explain.

22. The Federal gift tax is cumulative in nature. Explain.

23. How much property can Ida, a widow, give to her three married children, their spouses, and five grandchildren over a period of 12 years without making a taxable gift?

24. When married persons elect to split a gift, what tax advantages do they enjoy?

25. Reuben, a widower, plans on making taxable gifts of $600,000 and then passing $600,000 of his property by death. Because of the unified transfer tax credit, he believes that this approach will allow him to dispose of $1,200,000 without incurring the Federal gift tax and the Federal estate tax. Do you have any comment?

26. Contrast the major differences between the Federal income tax schemes applicable to individuals and to corporations.

27. When a state uses a "piggyback" approach for its state income tax, what is the state doing?

28. Chee lives in a state that imposes an income tax. His Federal income tax return for 1992 is audited in 1994, and, as a result of several adjustments made by the IRS, Chee has to pay additional Federal income tax. Several months later, Chee is notified that his 1992 state income tax return is to be audited. Are these two incidents a coincidence or does a reasonable explanation exist?

29. A person who does not live in Philadelphia will not pay this city's income tax. Comment on the validity of this statement.

30. Keith, a sole proprietor, owns and operates a grocery store. Keith's wife and his 17-year-old son work in the business and are paid wages. Will the wife and son be subject to FICA? Explain.

31. Dan, the owner and operator of a construction company that builds outdoor swimming pools, releases most of his construction personnel during the winter months. Should this hurt Dan's FUTA situation? Why or why not?

32. Compare FICA and FUTA in connection with each of the following:
    a. Incidence of taxation.
    b. Justification for taxation.
    c. Rates and base involved.

33. What is a value added tax (VAT) and how does it operate?

34. Norm, the owner and operator of a cash-and-carry military surplus retail outlet, has been audited many times by the IRS. When Norm mentions this fact to his next-door neighbor, an employee with Ford Motor Company, he is somewhat surprised to learn that the neighbor has never been audited by the IRS. Is there any explanation for this apparent disparity in treatment?

35. While Dr. Jones and her family are out of town on vacation, their home is burglarized. Among the items stolen and reported to the police are $35,000 in cash and gold coins worth $80,000. Shortly after the incident, Dr. Jones is audited by the IRS. Could there be any causal connection between the burglary and the audit? Explain.

36. Distinguish between a field audit and an office audit by the IRS.

37. As a result of an audit by the IRS of her Federal income tax return, Sophy receives an RAR. What does this mean?

38. For tax year 1986, Linda failed to file a Federal income tax return. In 1994, the IRS notifies Linda that it wants an accounting of her tax-related transactions for tax year 1986. Linda is not concerned about the request because three years have passed since the due date (April 15, 1987) of the return. Is Linda's defense based on the statute of limitations valid? Why or why not?

39. On a Federal income tax return filed five years ago, Michael inadvertently omitted a large amount of gross income.
    a. Michael seeks your advice as to whether the IRS is barred from assessing additional income tax in the event he is audited. What is your advice?
    b. Would your advice differ if you are the person who prepared the return in question? Explain.
    c. Suppose Michael asks you to prepare his current year's return. Would you do so? Explain.

40. Jill files her income tax return 45 days after the due date of the return without obtaining an extension from the IRS. Along with the return, she remits a check for $4,000, which is the balance of the tax she owes. Disregarding the interest element, what are Jill's penalties for failure to file and for failure to pay?

41. Ed overstated deductions on his Federal income tax return for 1993. Upon audit by the IRS, it is determined that the overstatement was partially the result of negligence. As a result, Ed owes additional income taxes of $10,000 ($8,000 attributable to the negligence). What is Ed's penalty?

42. In March 1994, Jim asks you to prepare his Federal income tax returns for tax years 1991, 1992, and 1993. In discussing this matter with him, you discover that he also has not filed for tax year 1990. When you mention this fact, Jim tells you that the statute of limitations precludes the IRS from taking any action as to this year.
    a. Is Jim correct about the application of the statute of limitations? Why?
    b. If Jim refuses to file for 1990, should you prepare returns for 1991 through 1993?

43. You are preparing Ellen's Federal income tax return for 1993. Although she has no records, she estimates that she has given cash of about $500 to various charities during the year. She suggests that it would "look better" if you listed $501 as charitable contributions. What should you do?

44. What is meant by revenue-neutral tax reform?

45. How does the tax law encourage research and development expenditures?

46. Discuss the probable justification for the following provisions of the tax law:
    a. The election permitted certain corporations to avoid the corporate income tax.
    b. A provision that excludes from gross income certain benefits furnished to employees through accident and health plans financed by employers.
    c. Nontaxable treatment for an employee for premiums paid by an employer for group term insurance covering the life of the employee.

47. The tax law encourages private retirement plans and contributions to charitable organizations. In terms of nonrevenue objectives, what is the common justification for this special tax treatment?

48. What purpose is served by allowing a deduction for home mortgage interest and property taxes?

49. Allowing a taxpayer a deduction for Federal income tax purposes for state income taxes paid eliminates the double taxation of the same income. Do you agree? Why or why not?

50. George sells a rental house for more than he paid for it. Shortly thereafter, George reinvests the proceeds in another rental house. Can George avoid the tax on any gain under the wherewithal to pay concept? Explain.

51. How does the tax law cope with the impact of inflation?

52. Forcing accrual basis taxpayers to recognize prepaid income when received (as opposed to when earned) accomplishes what objective?

53. On his income tax return for the year, Henry claims as a deduction certain charitable contributions that he did not make. When you question him about this, he responds:
    a. "How is the IRS going to prove that I did not make these contributions?"

    b. "Even if the IRS disallows the deductions, the worst that can happen is that I will owe the same amount of tax I would have paid anyway."

Comment on Henry's misconceptions about the tax law.

54. Edward leases real estate to Janet for a period of 20 years. Janet makes capital improvements to the property. When the lease expires, Edward reclaims the property, including the improvements made by Janet.
    a. Under current law, at what point does Edward recognize income as a result of Janet's improvements?
    b. Has the law in (a) always been the rule?
    c. What is the justification, if any, for the current rule?

2

WORKING WITH THE TAX LAW

LEARNING OBJECTIVES

After completing Chapter 2, you should be able to:

1. Distinguish between the statutory, administrative, and judicial sources of the tax law and understand the purpose of each source.

2. Locate and work with the appropriate tax law sources.

3. Understand the tax research process.

4. Communicate the results of the tax research process in a client letter and a tax file memorandum.

5. Apply tax research techniques and planning procedures and have an awareness of computer-assisted tax research.

OUTLINE

Tax Sources, 2–2

Statutory Sources of the Tax Law, 2–2

Administrative Sources of the Tax Law, 2–8

Judicial Sources of the Tax Law, 2–12

Working with the Tax Law—Tax Research, 2–22

Identifying the Problem, 2–23

Refining the Problem, 2–23

Locating the Appropriate Tax Law Sources, 2–23

Assessing the Validity of the Tax Law Sources, 2–25

Arriving at the Solution or at Alternative Solutions, 2–29

Communicating Tax Research, 2–29

Working with the Tax Law—Tax Planning, 2–32

Nontax Considerations, 2–32

Tax Avoidance and Tax Evasion, 2–32

Follow-up Procedures, 2–33

Tax Planning—A Practical Application, 2–33

Computer-Assisted Tax Research, 2–34

TAX SOURCES

1   LEARNING OBJECTIVE
Distinguish between the statutory, administrative, and judicial sources of the tax law and understand the purpose of each source.

Understanding taxation requires a mastery of the sources of the *rules of tax law.* These sources include not only legislative provisions in the form of the Internal Revenue Code, but also Congressional Committee Reports, Treasury Department Regulations, other Treasury Department pronouncements, and court decisions. Thus, the *primary sources* of tax information include pronouncements from all three branches of government: legislative, executive, and judicial.

In addition to being able to locate and interpret the sources of the tax law, a tax professional must understand the relative weight of authority within these sources. The tax law is of little significance, however, until it is applied to a set of facts and circumstances. This chapter, therefore, both introduces the statutory, administrative, and judicial sources of tax law and explains how the law is applied to individual and business transactions. It also explains how to apply research techniques and use planning procedures effectively.

A large part of tax research focuses on determining the intent of Congress. Although Congress often claims simplicity as one of its goals, a cursory examination of the tax law indicates that it has not been very successful in achieving this objective. Commenting on his 48-page tax return, James Michener, the author, said "it is unimaginable in that I graduated from one of America's better colleges, yet I am totally incapable of understanding tax returns."

Frequently, uncertainty in the tax law causes disputes between the Internal Revenue Service (IRS) and taxpayers. Due to these *gray areas* and the complexity of the tax law, a taxpayer may have more than one alternative for structuring a business transaction. In structuring business transactions and engaging in other tax planning activities, the tax adviser must be cognizant that the objective of tax planning is not necessarily to minimize the tax liability. Instead a taxpayer should maximize his or her after-tax return, which may include maximizing nontax as well as noneconomic benefits.

STATUTORY SOURCES OF THE TAX LAW

Origin of the Internal Revenue Code

Before 1939, the statutory provisions relating to Federal taxation were contained in the individual revenue acts enacted by Congress. Because dealing with many separate acts was inconvenient and confusing, in 1939 Congress codified all of the Federal tax laws. Known as the Internal Revenue Code of 1939, the codification arranged all Federal tax provisions in a logical sequence and placed them in a separate part of the Federal statutes. A further rearrangement took place in 1954 and resulted in the Internal Revenue Code of 1954, which continued in effect until 1986 when it was replaced by the Internal Revenue Code of 1986. Although Congress did not recodify the law in the Tax Reform Act (TRA) of 1986, the magnitude of the changes made by TRA of 1986 do provide some rationale for renaming the Federal tax law the Internal Revenue Code of 1986.

The following observations help clarify the codification procedure:

* With some exceptions, neither the 1939 nor the 1954 Code substantially changed the tax law existing on the date of its enactment. Much of the 1939 Code, for example, was incorporated into the 1954 Code; the major change was the reorganization and renumbering of the tax provisions.
* Although the 1986 Code resulted in substantial changes, only a minority of the statutory provisions were affected.[1]
* Statutory amendments to the tax law are integrated into the Code. For example, the Technical and Miscellaneous Revenue Act of 1988, the Revenue Reconciliation Act of 1989, the Revenue Reconciliation Act of 1990, and the Revenue Reconciliation Act of 1993 all became part of the Internal Revenue Code of 1986. Considering the tax legislation enacted in recent years, it appears that the tax law will continue to be amended frequently.

The Legislative Process

Federal tax legislation generally originates in the House of Representatives, where it is first considered by the House Ways and Means Committee. Tax bills originate in the Senate when they are attached as riders to other legislative proposals.[2] If acceptable to the House Ways and Means Committee, the proposed bill is referred to the entire House of Representatives for approval or disapproval. Approved bills are sent to the Senate, where they are considered by the Senate Finance Committee. The next step is referral from the Senate Finance Committee to the entire Senate. Assuming no disagreement between the House and Senate, passage by the Senate results in referral to the President for approval or veto. If the bill is approved or if the President's veto is overridden, the bill becomes law and part of the Internal Revenue Code of 1986.

When the Senate version of the bill differs from that passed by the House, the Joint Conference Committee, which includes members of both the House Ways and Means Committee and the Senate Finance Committee, is called upon to resolve the differences. Major tax bills frequently have differing versions. One reason bills are often changed in the Senate is that each individual senator has considerable latitude to make amendments when the Senate as a whole is voting

[1] This point is important in assessing judicial decisions interpreting provisions of the Internal Revenue Code of 1939 and the Internal Revenue Code of 1954. If the same provision was included in the Internal Revenue Code of 1986 and has not been subsequently amended, the decision has continuing validity.

[2] The Tax Equity and Fiscal Responsibility Act of 1982 originated in the Senate, and its constitutionality was unsuccessfully challenged in the courts. The Senate version of the Deficit Reduction Act of 1984 was attached as an amendment to the Federal Boat Safety Act.

TAX IN THE NEWS

CRAFTING TAX LAWS

They seem like an odd couple, the two committee chairmen who will be the central figures in the congressional conference that will write the final version of President Bill Clinton's budget package.

Senator Daniel Patrick Moynihan, the rookie chairman of the Finance Committee, has been a naval officer, a Harvard professor, an author, and a diplomat. Representative Dan Rostenkowski, the veteran chairman of the Ways and Means Committee, was an army private, a night-school dropout, a semipro baseball player, and a ward-heeler.

Mr. Moynihan, it is said on Capitol Hill, has written more books (16 at last count) than Mr. Rostenkowski has read. Mr. Rostenkowski, it is said, is so savvy he can pick the eccentric senator's pockets.

Their personalities are so different that one wonders whether the two lawmakers are up to their daunting challenge—to amalgamate the budget bills passed by the House and the Senate into one measure that can be approved by both houses in identical form and be signed by the President.

But the difference in their styles masks the fact that the senator from New York and congressman from Illinois are cut from the same bolt.

"Danny Rostenkowski and I are regulars, regular Democrats," Mr. Moynihan said. What he meant was that both are products of big-city political machines: Mr. Moynihan from Tammany Hall, Mr. Rostenkowski from Richard J. Daley's Chicago.

SOURCE: Excerpted from David E. Rosenbaum, "Crafting of the Budget Bill Unites a Democratic Odd Couple," *New York Times*, July 6, 1993, p. A1.

on a bill referred to it by the Senate Finance Committee.[3] In contrast, the entire House of Representatives either accepts or rejects what is proposed by the House Ways and Means Committee, and changes from the floor are rare. The deliberations of the Joint Conference Committee usually produce a compromise between the two versions, which is then voted on by both the House and the Senate. If both bodies accept the bill, it is referred to the President for approval or veto.

Referrals from the House Ways and Means Committee, the Senate Finance Committee, and the Joint Conference Committee are usually accompanied by Committee Reports. Because these Committee Reports often explain the provisions of the proposed legislation, they are a valuable source for ascertaining the *intent of Congress.* What Congress had in mind when it considered and enacted tax legislation is, of course, the key to interpreting such legislation by taxpayers, the IRS, and the courts. Since Regulations normally are not issued immediately after a statute is enacted, taxpayers often look to legislative history materials to determine congressional intent.

---

[3] During the passage of the Tax Reform Act of 1986, Senate leaders tried to make the bill *amendment proof* to avoid the normal amendment process.

The typical legislative process for dealing with tax bills is summarized as follows:

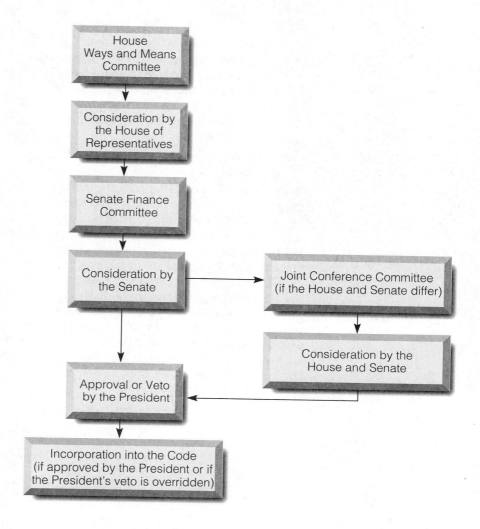

The role of the Joint Conference Committee indicates the importance of compromise in the legislative process. As an example of the practical effect of the compromise process, consider what happened to a new limitation on con- tributions by employees to their tax-sheltered annuities in the Tax Reform Act of 1986.

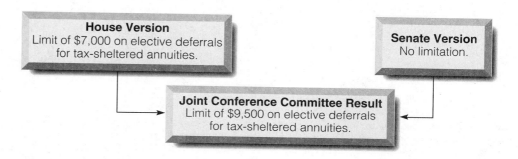

Arrangement of the Code

In working with the Code, it helps to understand the format. Note, for example, the following partial table of contents:

Subtitle A. Income Taxes
  Chapter 1. Normal Taxes and Surtaxes
    Subchapter A. Determination of Tax Liability
      Part I. Tax on Individuals
        Sections 1–5
      Part II. Tax on Corporations
        Sections 11–12

* * *

In referring to a provision of the Code, the *key* is usually the Section number. In citing Section 2(a) (dealing with the status of a surviving spouse), for example, it is unnecessary to include Subtitle A, Chapter 1, Subchapter A, Part I. Merely mentioning Section 2(a) will suffice, since the Section numbers run consecutively and do not begin again with each new Subtitle, Chapter, Subchapter, or Part. Not all Code Section numbers are used, however. Notice that Part I ends with Section 5 and Part II starts with Section 11 (at present there are no Sections 6, 7, 8, 9, and 10).[4]

Tax practitioners commonly refer to some specific areas of income taxation by their Subchapters. Some of the more common Subchapter designations include Subchapter C ("Corporate Distributions and Adjustments"), Subchapter K ("Partners and Partnerships"), and Subchapter S ("Tax Treatment of S Corporations and Their Shareholders"). In the last situation in particular, it is much more convenient to describe the subject of the applicable Code provisions (Sections 1361–1379) as S corporation status rather than as the "Tax Treatment of S Corporations and Their Shareholders."

Citing the Code

Code Sections often are broken down into subparts.[5] Section 2(a)(1)(A) serves as an example.

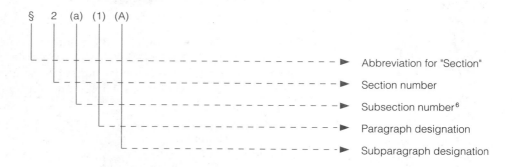

----

[4] When the 1954 Code was drafted, some Section numbers were intentionally omitted so that later changes could be incorporated into the Code without disrupting its organization. When Congress does not leave enough space, subsequent Code Sections are given A, B, C, etc., designations. A good example is the treatment of §§ 280A through 280H.

[5] Some Code Sections do not require subparts. See, for example, §§ 211 and 241.

[6] Some Code Sections omit the subsection designation and use the paragraph designation as the first subpart. See, for example, §§ 212(1) and 1221(1).

Broken down by content, § 2(a)(1)(A) becomes:

§ 2	Definitions and special rules (relating to the income tax imposed on individuals)
(a)	Definition of a surviving spouse
(1)	For purposes of § 1 (the determination of the applicable rate schedule), a surviving spouse must meet certain conditions.
(A)	One of the conditions necessary to qualify as a surviving spouse is that the taxpayer's spouse must have died during either of his or her two taxable years immediately preceding the present taxable year.

Throughout the remainder of the text, references to the Code Sections are in the form given above. The symbols "§" and "§§" are used in place of "Section" and "Sections." Unless otherwise stated, all Code references are to the Internal Revenue Code of 1986. The following table summarizes the format that will be used:

Complete Reference	Text Reference
Section 2(a)(1)(A) of the Internal Revenue Code of 1986	§ 2(a)(1)(A)
Sections 1 and 2 of the Internal Revenue Code of 1986	§§ 1 and 2
Section 2 of the Internal Revenue Code of 1954	§ 2 of the Internal Revenue Code of 1954
Section 12(d) of the Internal Revenue Code of 1939[7]	§ 12(d) of the Internal Revenue Code of 1939

---

[7] § 12(d) of the Internal Revenue Code of 1939 is the predecessor to § 2 of the Internal Revenue Code of 1954 and the Internal Revenue Code of 1986. Keep in mind that the 1954 Code superseded the 1939 Code and the 1986 Code has superseded the 1954 Code. Footnote 1 of this chapter explains why references to the 1939 or 1954 code are included.

Effect of Treaties

The United States signs certain tax treaties (sometimes called tax conventions) with foreign countries to render mutual assistance in tax enforcement and to avoid double taxation. The Technical and Miscellaneous Revenue Act of 1988 provided that neither a tax law nor a tax treaty takes general precedence. Thus, when there is a direct conflict, the most recent item will take precedence. A taxpayer must disclose on the tax return any position where a treaty overrides a tax law.[8] There is a $1,000 penalty per failure to disclose for individuals and a $10,000 per failure penalty for corporations.[9]

ADMINISTRATIVE SOURCES OF THE TAX LAW

The administrative sources of the Federal tax law can be grouped as follows: Treasury Department Regulations, Revenue Rulings and Revenue Procedures, and other administrative pronouncements (see Exhibit 2–1). All are issued by either the U.S. Treasury Department or one of its instrumentalities (e.g., the IRS or a District Director).

Treasury Department Regulations

Regulations are issued by the U.S. Treasury Department under authority granted by Congress.[10] Interpretive by nature, they provide taxpayers with considerable guidance on the meaning and application of the Code. Regulations may be issued in *proposed, temporary,* or *final* form. Regulations carry considerable weight and are an important factor to consider in complying with the tax law.

▼ **EXHIBIT 2–1**
Administrative Sources

Source	Location	Authority**
Regulations	*Federal Register**	Force and effect of law.
Proposed Regulations	*Federal Register** *Internal Revenue Bulletin* *Cumulative Bulletin*	Preview of final Regulations.
Temporary Regulations	*Federal Register** *Internal Revenue Bulletin* *Cumulative Bulletin*	May be cited as a precedent.
Revenue Rulings Revenue Procedures	*Internal Revenue Bulletin* *Cumulative Bulletin*	Do not have the force and effect of law.
General Counsel's Memoranda Actions on Decisions Technical Advice Memoranda	*Tax Analysts' Tax Notes*; RIA's *Internal Memoranda of the IRS*; CCH's *IRS Position Reporter*	May not be cited as a precedent.
Letter Rulings	Research Institute of America and Commerce Clearing House loose-leaf services	Applicable only to taxpayer addressed. No precedential force.

*Finalized, proposed, and temporary Regulations are published in soft-cover form by several publishers.
**Each of these sources may be substantial authority for purposes of the accuracy-related penalty in § 6662. A lower source has less weight than a higher source in this list. Notice 90–20, 1990–1 C.B. 328.

---

[8] § 7852(d).
[9] Reg. §§ 301.6114–1 and 301.6712–1.

[10] § 7805.

Since Regulations interpret the Code, they are arranged in the same sequence as the Code. A number is added at the beginning, however, to indicate the type of tax or administrative, procedural, or definitional matter to which they relate. For example, the prefix 1 designates the Regulations under the income tax law. Thus, the Regulations under Code § 2 are cited as Reg. § 1.2 with subparts added for further identification. The numbers of these subparts often do not correspond to the numbers of the Code subsections. The prefix 20 designates estate tax Regulations; 25 covers gift tax Regulations; 31 relates to employment taxes; and 301 refers to procedure and administration. This list is not all-inclusive.

New Regulations and changes to existing Regulations are usually issued in proposed form before they are finalized. The interval between the proposal of a Regulation and its finalization permits taxpayers and other interested parties to comment on the propriety of the proposal. **Proposed Regulations** under Code § 2, for example, are cited as Prop.Reg. § 1.2. The Tax Court indicates that proposed Regulations carry no more weight than a position advanced in a written brief prepared by a litigating party before the Tax Court. **Finalized Regulations** have the force and effect of law.[11]

Sometimes the Treasury Department issues **temporary Regulations** relating to elections and other matters where speed is important. These Regulations are issued without the comment period required for proposed Regulations. Temporary Regulations have the same authoritative value as final Regulations and may be cited as precedents. Temporary Regulations must now also be issued as proposed Regulations and automatically expire within three years after the date of issuance.[12] Obviously, temporary Regulations and the simultaneously issued proposed Regulations carry more weight than traditional proposed Regulations. An example of a temporary Regulation is Temp.Reg. § 1.1(i)–1T, which deals with the tax on unearned income of certain minor children (the kiddie tax). In the past, the Treasury Department has been slow to finalize temporary Regulations.

Proposed, temporary, and final Regulations are published in the *Federal Register* and are reproduced in major tax services. Final Regulations are issued as Treasury Decisions.

Regulations may also be classified as *legislative, interpretive,* or *procedural.* This classification scheme is discussed under Assessing the Validity of a Treasury Regulation later in the chapter.

Revenue Rulings and Revenue Procedures

Revenue Rulings are official pronouncements of the National Office of the IRS.[13] Like Regulations, they are designed to provide interpretation of the tax law. However, they do not carry the same legal force and effect as Regulations and usually deal with more restricted problems. In addition, Regulations are approved by the Secretary of the Treasury, whereas Revenue Rulings are not. Both Revenue Rulings and Revenue Procedures serve an important function by providing *guidance* to IRS personnel and taxpayers in routine tax matters.

Although letter rulings (discussed below) are not the same as Revenue Rulings, a Revenue Ruling often results from a specific taxpayer's request for a letter ruling. If the IRS believes that a taxpayer's request for a letter ruling deserves official publication because of its widespread impact, the holding will be converted into a Revenue Ruling and issued for the information and guidance of taxpayers, tax practitioners, and IRS personnel. Names, identifying descriptions,

---

[11] *F. W. Woolworth Co.,* 54 T.C. 1233 (1970); *Harris M. Miller,* 70 T.C. 448 (1978); and *James O. Tomerlin Trust,* 87 T.C. 876 (1986).

[12] § 7805(e).

[13] § 7805(a).

and money amounts are changed to disguise the identity of the taxpayer. In addition to resulting from taxpayer requests, Revenue Rulings arise from technical advice to District Offices of the IRS, court decisions, suggestions from tax practitioner groups, and various tax publications.

Revenue Procedures are issued in the same manner as Revenue Rulings, but deal with the internal management practices and procedures of the IRS. Familiarity with these procedures can increase taxpayer compliance and help the IRS administer the tax laws efficiently. A taxpayer's failure to follow a Revenue Procedure can result in unnecessary delay or cause the IRS to decline to act in a discretionary situation on behalf of the taxpayer.

Revenue Rulings and Revenue Procedures are published weekly by the U.S. Government in the *Internal Revenue Bulletin* (I.R.B.). Semiannually, the bulletins for a six-month period are gathered together, reorganized by Code Section classification, and published in a bound volume called the *Cumulative Bulletin* (C.B.).[14] The proper form for citing Revenue Rulings and Revenue Procedures depends on whether the item has been published in the *Cumulative Bulletin* or is only available in I.R.B. form. Consider, for example, the following transition:

Temporary
Citation

Rev.Rul. 92–62, I.R.B. No. 33, 5.
Explanation: Revenue Ruling Number 62, appearing on page 5 of the 33rd weekly issue of the *Internal Revenue Bulletin* for 1992.

Permanent
Citation

Rev.Rul. 92–62, 1992–2 C.B. 193.
Explanation: Revenue Ruling Number 62, appearing on page 193 of Volume 2 of the *Cumulative Bulletin* for 1992.

Since the second volume of the 1992 *Cumulative Bulletin* was not published until August of 1993, the I.R.B. citation had to be used until that time. After the publication of the *Cumulative Bulletin,* the C.B. citation is proper. The basic portion of both citations (Rev.Rul. 92–62) indicates that this document was the 62nd Revenue Ruling issued by the IRS during 1992.

Revenue Procedures are cited in the same manner, except that "Rev.Proc." is substituted for "Rev.Rul." Some recent Revenue Procedures had the following effects:

- Outlined the areas in which the IRS will not issue advance rulings.
- Provided relief for defined contribution plans with investments in life insurance companies in state delinquency proceedings.
- Announced new guidelines for public interest law firms.

Letter Rulings

Individual **(letter) rulings** are issued upon a taxpayer's request and describe how the IRS will treat a proposed transaction for tax purposes. They apply only to the taxpayer who asks for and obtains the ruling, but post-1984 letter rulings may be substantial authority for purposes of the accuracy-related penalty.[15] Though this procedure may sound like the only real way to carry out effective tax planning,

---

[14] Usually only two volumes of the *Cumulative Bulletin* are published each year. However, when Congress has enacted major tax legislation, other volumes may be published containing the congressional Committee Reports supporting the Revenue Act. See, for example, the two extra volumes for 1984 dealing with the Deficit Reduction Act of 1984. The 1984–3 *Cumulative Bulletin,* Volume 1, contains the text of the law itself; 1984–3, Volume 2, contains the Committee Reports. This makes a total of four volumes of the *Cumulative Bulletin* for 1984: 1984–1; 1984–2; 1984–3, Volume 1; 1984–3, Volume 2.

[15] Notice 90–20, 1990–1 C.B. 328. In this regard, letter rulings differ from Revenue Rulings, which are applicable to *all* taxpayers. Letter rulings may later lead to the issuance of a Revenue Ruling if the holding involved affects many taxpayers. In its Agents' Manual, the IRS indicates that letter rulings may be used as a guide with other research materials in formulating a District Office position on an issue. The IRS is required to charge a taxpayer a fee for letter rulings, determination letters, etc.

the IRS limits the issuance of individual rulings to restricted, preannounced areas of taxation. The main reason the IRS will not rule in certain areas is that they involve fact-oriented situations. Thus, it is not possible to obtain a ruling on many of the problems that are particularly troublesome for taxpayers.[16]

The law now requires the IRS to make individual rulings available for public inspection after identifying details are deleted.[17] Published digests of private letter rulings can be found in *Private Letter Rulings* (published by RIA), BNA *Daily Tax Reports,* and Tax Analysts & Advocates *Tax Notes. IRS Letter Rulings Reports* (published by Commerce Clearing House) contains both digests and full texts of all letter rulings. *Letter Ruling Review* (published by Tax Analysts) is a monthly publication that selects and discusses the more important of the over 300 letter rulings issued each month.

Letter rulings receive multidigit file numbers, which indicate the year and week of issuance as well as the number of the ruling during that week. Consider, for example, Ltt.Rul. 9327013 dealing with the low-income housing credit:

93	27	013
Year 1993	27th week of issuance	Number of the ruling issued during the 27th week

Other Administrative Pronouncements

Treasury Decisions (TDs) are issued by the Treasury Department to promulgate new Regulations, amend or otherwise change existing Regulations, or announce the position of the Government on selected court decisions. Like Revenue Rulings and Revenue Procedures, TDs are published in the *Internal Revenue Bulletin* and subsequently transferred to the *Cumulative Bulletin.*

The IRS publishes other administrative communications in the *Internal Revenue Bulletin* such as Announcements, Notices, LRs (proposed Regulations), and Prohibited Transaction Exemptions.

Like letter rulings, **determination letters** are issued at the request of taxpayers and provide guidance on the application of the tax law. They differ from letter rulings in that the issuing source is the District Director rather than the National Office of the IRS. Also, determination letters usually involve completed (as opposed to proposed) transactions. Determination letters are not published and are made known only to the party making the request.

The following examples illustrate the distinction between letter rulings and determination letters:

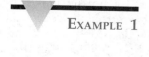

EXAMPLE 1   The shareholders of Red Corporation and Green Corporation want assurance that the consolidation of the corporations into Blue Corporation will be a nontaxable reorganization. The proper approach would be to request the National Office of the IRS to issue a letter ruling concerning the income tax effect of the proposed transaction. ▼

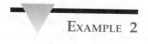

EXAMPLE 2   Chris operates a barber shop in which he employs eight barbers. To comply with the rules governing income tax and payroll tax withholdings, Chris wants to know whether the barbers working for him are employees or independent contractors. The proper procedure would be to request a determination letter on their status from the appropriate District Director. ▼

---

[16] Rev.Proc. 94–3, I.R.B. No. 1, 79 contains a list of areas in which the IRS will not issue advance rulings. From time to time, subse-quent Revenue Procedures are issued that modify or amplify Rev.Proc. 94–3.

[17] § 6110.

The National Office of the IRS releases **Technical Advice Memoranda** (TAMs) weekly. Although TAMs and letter rulings both give the IRS's determination of an issue, they differ in several respects. Letter rulings deal with proposed transactions and are issued to taxpayers at their request. In contrast, TAMs deal with completed transactions and are often requested in relation to exempt organizations and employee plans. Futhermore, TAMs arise from questions raised by IRS personnel during audits and are issued by the National Office of the IRS to its field personnel rather than to taxpayers. TAMs are not officially published and may not be cited or used as precedent.[18] They are assigned file numbers according to the same procedure used for letter rulings. For example, TAM 9327008 refers to the 8th TAM issued during the 27th week of 1993.

Several internal memoranda that constitute the working law of the IRS now must be released. These General Counsel Memoranda (GCMs) and Actions on Decisions (AODs) are not officially published, and the IRS indicates that they may not be cited as precedents by taxpayers.[19] However, these working documents do explain the IRS's position on various issues.

JUDICIAL SOURCES OF THE TAX LAW

The Judicial Process in General

After a taxpayer has exhausted some or all of the remedies available within the IRS (i.e., no satisfactory settlement has been reached at the agent or at the Appeals Division level), the dispute can be taken to the Federal courts. The dispute is first considered by a **court of original jurisdiction** (known as a trial court) with any appeal (either by the taxpayer or the IRS) taken to the appropriate appellate court. In most situations, the taxpayer has a choice of any of *four trial courts:* a **Federal District Court,** the **U.S. Court of Federal Claims,** the **U.S. Tax Court,** or the **Small Claims Division** of the U.S. Tax Court. The trial and appellate court scheme for Federal tax litigation is illustrated in Figure 2–1.

The broken line between the U.S. Tax Court and the Small Claims Division indicates that there is no appeal from the Small Claims Division. The jurisdiction of the Small Claims Division is limited to cases involving amounts of $10,000 or less. The proceedings of the Small Claims Division are informal (e.g., no necessity for the taxpayer to be represented by a lawyer or other tax adviser). Commissioners rather than Tax Court judges preside over these proceedings. The decisions of the Small Claims Division are not precedents for any other court decision and are not reviewable by any higher court. Proceedings can be faster and less expensive in the Small Claims Division.

American law, following English law, is frequently *made* by judicial decisions. Under the doctrine of *stare decisis,* each case (except in the Small Claims Division) has precedential value for future cases with the same controlling set of facts. Most Federal and state appellate court decisions and some decisions of trial courts are published. Almost 3.5 million judicial opinions have been published in the United States; over 30,000 cases are published each year.[20] Published court decisions are organized by jurisdiction (Federal or state) and level of court (trial or appellate).

A decision of a particular court is called its holding. Sometimes a decision includes dicta or incidental opinions beyond the current facts. Such passing remarks, illustrations, or analogies are not essential to the current holding.

[18] § 6110(j)(3). Post-1984 TAMs may be substantial authority for purposes of avoiding the accuracy-related penalty. Notice 90–20, 1990–1 C.B. 328.

[19] These are unofficially published by the publishers listed in Exhibit 2–1. Such internal memoranda for post-1984 may be substantial authority for purposes of the accuracy-related penalty. Notice 90–20, 1990–1 C.B. 328.

[20] Jacobstein and Mersky, *Fundamentals of Legal Research,* 5th ed. (Mineola, N.Y.: The Foundation Press, 1990).

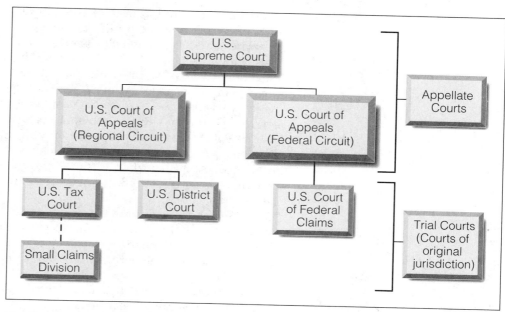

▼ **FIGURE 2–1**
Federal Judicial System

Although the holding has precedential value under *stare decisis*, dicta are not binding on a future court.

Trial Courts

The various trial courts (courts of original jurisdiction) differ in several respects:

- *Number of courts.* There is only one Court of Federal Claims and only one Tax Court, but there are many Federal District Courts. The taxpayer does not select the District Court that will hear the dispute but must sue in the one that has jurisdiction.
- *Number of judges.* Each District Court has only 1 judge, the Court of Federal Claims has 16 judges, and the Tax Court has 19 regular judges. The entire Tax Court, however, will review a case (the case is sent to court conference) only when more important or novel tax issues are involved. Most cases will be heard and decided by one of the 19 judges.
- *Location.* The Court of Federal Claims meets most often in Washington, D.C., whereas a District Court meets at a prescribed seat for the particular district. Each state has at least one District Court, and many of the more populous states have more than one. Therefore, the inconvenience and expense of traveling for the taxpayer and his or her counsel (present with many suits in the Court of Federal Claims) are largely eliminated. Although the Tax Court is officially based in Washington, D.C., the various judges travel to different parts of the country and hear cases at predetermined locations and dates. Although this procedure eases the distance problem for the taxpayer, it may mean a delay before the case comes to trial and is decided.
- *Jurisdiction of the Court of Federal Claims.* The Court of Federal Claims has jurisdiction over any claim against the United States that is based upon the Constitution, any Act of Congress, or any regulation of an executive department. Thus, the Court of Federal Claims hears nontax litigation as well as tax cases. This forum appears to be more favorable for issues having

an equitable or pro-business orientation (as opposed to purely technical issues) and for those requiring extensive discovery.[21]

- *Jurisdiction of the Tax Court and District Courts.* The Tax Court hears only tax cases and is the most popular forum. The District Courts hear nontax litigation as well as tax cases. Some Tax Court justices have been appointed from IRS or Treasury Department positions. For these reasons, some people suggest that the Tax Court has more expertise in tax matters.
- *Jury trial.* The only court in which a taxpayer can obtain a jury trial is a District Court. But since juries can only decide questions of fact and not questions of law, even taxpayers who choose the District Court route often do not request a jury trial. In that event, the judge will decide all issues. Note that a District Court decision is controlling only in the district in which the court has jurisdiction.
- *Payment of deficiency.* For the Court of Federal Claims or a District Court to have jurisdiction, the taxpayer must pay the tax deficiency assessed by the IRS and sue for a refund. A taxpayer who wins (assuming no successful appeal by the Government) recovers the tax paid plus appropriate interest. For the Tax Court, however, jurisdiction is usually obtained without first paying the assessed tax deficiency. In the event the taxpayer loses in the Tax Court (and does not appeal or an appeal is unsuccessful), the deficiency must be paid with appropriate interest. With the elimination of the deduction for personal (consumer) interest, the Tax Court route of delaying payment of the deficiency can become expensive. For example, to earn 11 percent after tax, a taxpayer with a 39.6 percent marginal tax rate would

CONCEPT SUMMARY 2–1

Federal Judicial System: Trial Courts

Issue	U.S. Tax Court	U.S. District Court	U.S. Court of Federal Claims
Number of judges per court	19*	1	16
Payment of deficiency before trial	No	Yes	Yes
Jury trial available	No	Yes	No
Types of disputes	Tax cases only	Most criminal and civil issues	Claims against the United States
Jurisdiction	Nationwide	Location of taxpayer	Nationwide
IRS acquiescence policy	Yes	No	No
Appeal route	U.S. Court of Appeals	U.S. Court of Appeals	U.S. Court of Appeals for the Federal Circuit

*There are also 14 special trial judges and 9 senior judges.

---

[21] T. D. Peyser, "The Case for Selecting the Claims Court to Litigate a Federal Tax Liability," *The Tax Executive* (Winter 1988): 149.

have to earn 18.2 percent. By paying the tax, a taxpayer limits underpayment interest and penalties on underpayment interest.

- *Termination of running of interest.* A taxpayer who selects the Tax Court may deposit a cash bond to stop the running of interest. The taxpayer must deposit both the amount of the tax and any accrued interest. If the taxpayer wins and the deposited amount is returned, the Government does not pay interest on the deposit.
- *Appeals.* Appeals from a District Court or a Tax Court decision are to the appropriate U.S. Court of Appeals. Appeals from the Court of Federal Claims go to the Court of Appeals for the Federal Circuit.
- *Bankruptcy.* When a taxpayer files a bankruptcy petition, the IRS, like other creditors, is prevented from taking action against the taxpayer. Sometimes a bankruptcy court may settle a tax claim.

Appellate Courts

The losing party can appeal a trial court decision to a **Circuit Court of Appeals.** The 11 geographical circuits, the circuit for the District of Columbia, and the Federal Circuit[22] appear in Figure 2–2. The appropriate circuit for an appeal depends upon where the litigation originated. For example, an appeal from New York goes to the Second Circuit.

▼ **FIGURE 2–2**
The Federal Courts of Appeals

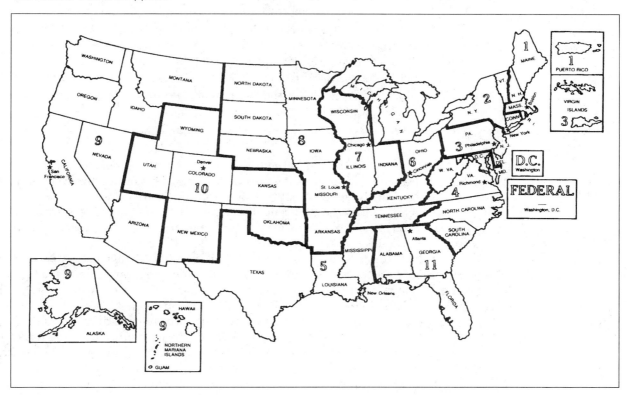

---

[22] The Court of Appeals for the Federal Circuit was created, effective October 1, 1982, by P.L. 97–164 (4/2/82) to hear decisions appealed from the Claims Court (now the Court of Federal Claims).

If the Government loses at the trial court level (District Court, Tax Court, or Court of Federal Claims), it need not (frequently does not) appeal. The fact that an appeal is not made, however, does not indicate that the IRS agrees with the result and will not litigate similar issues in the future. The IRS may decide not to appeal for a number of reasons. First, the current litigation load may be heavy, and as a consequence, the IRS may decide that available personnel should be assigned to other, more important cases. Second, the IRS may determine that this is not a good case to appeal. Perhaps the taxpayer is in a sympathetic position or the facts are particularly strong in his or her favor. In that event, the IRS may wait to test the legal issues involved with a taxpayer who has a much weaker case. Third, if the appeal is from a District Court or the Tax Court, the Court of Appeals of jurisdiction could have some bearing on whether the IRS chooses to go forward with an appeal. Based on past experience and precedent, the IRS may conclude that the chance for success on a particular issue might be more promising in another Court of Appeals. If so, the IRS will wait for a similar case to arise in a different jurisdiction.

ETHICAL
CONSIDERATIONS

Choosing Cases for Appeal

The U.S. Government loses a tax case against a prominent citizen in the U.S. District Court of Iowa. The taxpayer had set up three separate trusts for each of his three children (i.e., a total of nine trusts). The Government argued that under Reg. § 1.641(a)–0(c) these trusts should be consolidated and treated as three trusts to stop the taxpayer from mitigating the progressive tax structure (e.g., 39.6 percent top tax bracket).

The Government's attorneys decide that this conflict is not a good case to appeal. They feel that this taxpayer, a minister, is likely to win sympathy due to his profession and the facts are reasonably strong in his favor. Instead the Government appeals a similar multiple trust conflict in the U.S. District Court of Virginia. Here the taxpayer is a CPA who has established four separate trusts for her two children (i.e., a total of eight trusts). See *Estelle Morris Trusts*, 51 T.C. 20 (1968).

With the establishment of the Federal Circuit at the appellate level, a taxpayer has an alternative forum to the Court of Appeals of his or her home circuit for the appeal. Appeals from both the Tax Court and the District Court go to a taxpayer's home circuit. Now, when a particular circuit has issued an adverse decision, the taxpayer may wish to select the Court of Federal Claims route, since any appeal will be to the Federal Circuit.

District Courts, the Tax Court, and the Court of Federal Claims must abide by the **precedents** set by the Court of Appeals of jurisdiction. A particular Court of Appeals need not follow the decisions of another Court of Appeals. All courts, however, must follow the decisions of the **U.S. Supreme Court.**

Because the Tax Court is a national court (it hears and decides cases from all parts of the country), the observation made in the previous paragraph has caused problems. For many years, the Tax Court followed a policy of deciding cases based on what it thought the result should be, even though its decision might be appealed to a Court of Appeals that had previously decided a similar case differently. A number of years ago this policy was changed in the *Golsen*[23]

---

[23]*Jack E. Golsen*, 54 T.C. 742 (1970).

decision. Now the Tax Court will decide a case as it feels the law should be applied *only* if the Court of Appeals of appropriate jurisdiction has not yet passed on the issue or has previously decided a similar case in accord with the Tax Court's decision. If the Court of Appeals of appropriate jurisdiction has previously held otherwise, the Tax Court will conform under the *Golsen* rule even though it disagrees with the holding.

▼

EXAMPLE 3

Emily lives in Texas and sues in the Tax Court on Issue A. The Fifth Court of Appeals is the appellate court of appropriate jurisdiction. The Fifth Court of Appeals has already decided, in a case based on similar facts and involving a different taxpayer, that Issue A should be resolved against the Government. Although the Tax Court feels that the Fifth Court of Appeals is wrong, under its *Golsen* policy it will render judgment for Emily. Shortly thereafter, Rashad, a resident of New York, in a comparable case, sues in the Tax Court on Issue A. Assume that the Second Court of Appeals, the appellate court of appropriate jurisdiction, has never expressed itself on Issue A. Presuming the Tax Court has not reconsidered its position on Issue A, it will decide against Rashad. Thus, it is entirely possible for two taxpayers suing in the same court to end up with opposite results merely because they live in different parts of the country. ▼

Appeal to the U.S. Supreme Court is by **Writ of Certiorari.** If the Court accepts jurisdiction, it will grant the Writ (*Cert. Granted*). Most often, it will deny jurisdiction (*Cert. Denied*). For whatever reason or reasons, the Supreme Court rarely hears tax cases. The Court usually grants certiorari to resolve a conflict among the Courts of Appeals (e.g., two or more appellate courts have assumed opposing positions on a particular issue) or where the tax issue is extremely important. The granting of a Writ of Certiorari indicates that at least four members of the Supreme Court believe that the issue is of sufficient importance to be heard by the full Court.

The *role* of appellate courts is limited to a review of the record of trial compiled by the trial courts. Thus, the appellate process usually involves a determination of whether the trial court applied the proper law in arriving at its decision. Rarely will an appellate court disturb a lower court's fact-finding determination.

Both the Code and the Supreme Court indicate that Federal appellate courts are bound by findings of facts unless they are clearly erroneous.[24] This aspect of the appellate process is illustrated by a decision of the Court of Appeals for the District of Columbia involving whether a taxpayer was engaged in an activity for profit under § 183.[25] This appeals court specifically held that the "Tax Court's findings of facts are binding on Federal courts of appeals unless clearly erroneous." The Court applauded the Tax Court for the thoroughness of its factual inquiry but could "not place the stamp of approval upon its eventual legal outcome." In reversing and remanding the decision to the Tax Court, the appellate court said that "the language of § 183, its legislative history and the applicable Treasury regulation combine to demonstrate that the court's [Tax Court's] standard is erroneous as a matter of law." The appeals court held that this taxpayer's claims of deductibility were to be evaluated by proper legal standards.

An appeal can have any of a number of possible outcomes. The appellate court could approve (affirm) or disapprove (reverse) the lower court's finding, or it

---

[24] §§ 7482(a) and (c). *Comm. v. Duberstein*, 60–2 USTC ¶9515, 5 AFTR2d 1626, 80 S.Ct. 1190 (USSC, 1960). See Rule 52(a) of the Federal Rules of Civil Procedure.

[25] *Dreicer v. Comm.*, 81–2 USTC ¶9683, 48 AFTR2d 5884, 665 F.2d 1292 (CA–DC, 1981).

could send the case back for further consideration (remand). When many issues are involved, a mixed result is not unusual. Thus, the lower court could be affirmed (*aff'd*) on Issue A and reversed (*rev'd*) on Issue B, while Issue C is remanded (*rem'd*) for additional fact finding.

When more than one judge is involved in the decision-making process, disagreements are not uncommon. In addition to the majority view, one or more judges may concur (agree with the result reached but not with some or all of the reasoning) or dissent (disagree with the result). In any one case, of course, the majority view controls. But concurring and dissenting views can have an influence on other courts or, at some subsequent date when the composition of the court has changed, even on the same court.

Knowledge of several terms is important in understanding court decisions. The term *plaintiff* refers to the party requesting action in a court, and the *defendant* is the party against whom the suit is brought. Sometimes a court uses the terms *petitioner* and *respondent.* In general, "petitioner" is a synonym for "plaintiff," and "defendant" is a synonym for "respondent." At the trial court level, a taxpayer is normally the plaintiff (or petitioner), and the Government is the defendant (or respondent). If the taxpayer wins and the Government appeals as the new petitioner (or appellant), the taxpayer becomes the new respondent.

Judicial Citations—General

Having concluded a brief description of the judicial process, it is appropriate to consider the more practical problem of the relationship of case law to tax research. As previously noted, court decisions are an important source of tax law. The ability to cite and locate a case is, therefore, a must in working with the tax law. Judicial citations usually follow a standard pattern: case name, volume number, reporter series, page or paragraph number, and court (where necessary).

Judicial Citations—The U.S. Tax Court

A good starting point is with the Tax Court. The Court issues two types of decisions: Regular and Memorandum. The Chief Judge decides whether the opinion is issued as a Regular or Memorandum decision. The distinction between the two involves both substance and form. In terms of substance, *Memorandum* decisions deal with situations necessitating only the application of already established principles of law. *Regular* decisions involve novel issues not previously resolved by the Court. In actual practice, however, this distinction is not always preserved. Not infrequently, Memorandum decisions will be encountered that appear to warrant Regular status and vice versa. At any rate, do not conclude that Memorandum decisions possess no value as precedents. Both represent the position of the Tax Court and, as such, can be relied upon.

The Regular and Memorandum decisions issued by the Tax Court also differ in form. Memorandum decisions are officially published in mimeograph form only. Regular decisions are published by the U.S. Government in a series entitled *Tax Court of the United States Reports.* Each volume of these *Reports* covers a six-month period (January 1 through June 30 and July 1 through December 31) and is given a succeeding volume number. But, as was true of the *Cumulative Bulletin,* there is usually a time lag between the date a decision is rendered and the date it appears in bound form. A temporary citation might be necessary to aid the researcher in locating a recent Regular decision. Consider, for example, the temporary and permanent citations for *Rosemary S. Kovacs*, a decision filed on February 24, 1993:

Temporary Citation { *Rosemary S. Kovacs*, 100 T.C. ___ , No. 10 (1993).
Explanation: Page number left blank because not yet known.

Permanent Citation { *Rosemary S. Kovacs*, 100 T.C. 124 (1993).
Explanation: Page number now available.

Both citations tell us that the case will ultimately appear in Volume 100 of the *Tax Court of the United States Reports*. But until this volume is bound and made available to the general public, the page number must be left blank. Instead, the temporary citation identifies the case as being the 10th Regular decision issued by the Tax Court since Volume 99 ended. With this information, the decision can easily be located in either of the special Tax Court services published by Commerce Clearing House or Research Institute of America (formerly by Prentice-Hall). Once Volume 100 is released, the permanent citation can be substituted and the number of the case dropped.

Before 1943, the Tax Court was called the Board of Tax Appeals, and its decisions were published as the *United States Board of Tax Appeals Reports* (B.T.A.). These 47 volumes cover the period from 1924 to 1942. For example, the citation *Karl Pauli*, 11 B.T.A. 784 (1928) refers to the 11th volume of the *Board of Tax Appeals Reports*, page 784, issued in 1928.

One further distinction between Regular and Memorandum decisions of the Tax Court involves the IRS procedure of **acquiescence** ("A" or "Acq.") or **nonacquiescence** ("NA" or "Nonacq."). If the IRS loses in a Regular decision, it will usually indicate whether it agrees or disagrees with the result reached by the Court. This acquiescence or nonacquiescence will be published in the *Internal Revenue Bulletin* and the *Cumulative Bulletin*. The procedure is not followed for Memorandum decisions or for the decisions of other courts. The IRS can retroactively revoke an acquiescence. The IRS also sometimes announces that it will *or* will not follow a decision of another Federal court on similar facts. Such an announcement is not considered to be an acquiescence or nonacquiescence.

Most often the IRS issues nonacquiescences to Tax Court decisions that are not appealed. A nonacquiescence provides a warning to taxpayers that a similar case cannot be settled administratively. A taxpayer will incur fees and expenses appealing within the IRS even though the IRS may be unwilling to litigate a fact pattern similar to a nonacquiesce decision.[26]

Although Memorandum decisions are not published by the U.S. Government, they are published by Commerce Clearing House (CCH) and Research Institute of America (RIA [formerly by Prentice-Hall]). Consider, for example, the three different ways that *Jack D. Carr* can be cited:

Jack D. Carr, T.C. Memo. 1985–19
The 19th Memorandum decision issued by the Tax Court in 1985.

Jack D. Carr, 49 TCM 507
Page 507 of Vol. 49 of the CCH *Tax Court Memorandum Decisions.*

Jack D. Carr, RIA T.C.Mem.Dec. ¶85,019
Paragraph 85,019 of the RIA *T.C. Memorandum Decisions.*

---

[26] G. W. Carter, "Nonacquiescence: Winning by Losing," *Tax Notes* (September 19, 1988): 1301–1307.

Note that the third citation contains the same information as the first. Thus, ¶85,019 indicates the following information about the case: year 1985, 19th T.C. Memo. decision.[27] Although the RIA citation does not specifically include a volume number, the paragraph citation indicates that the decision can be found in the 1985 volume of the RIA Memorandum decision service.

Judicial Citations—The U.S. District Court, Court of Federal Claims, and Courts of Appeals

District Court, Court of Federal Claims, Court of Appeals, and Supreme Court decisions dealing with Federal tax matters are reported in both the CCH *U.S. Tax Cases* (USTC), and the RIA *American Federal Tax Reports* (AFTR) series. Federal District Court decisions, dealing with *both* tax and nontax issues, also are published by West Publishing Company in its *Federal Supplement Series.* The following examples illustrate three different ways of citing a District Court case:

Simons-Eastern Co. v. U.S., 73–1 USTC ¶9279 (D.Ct.Ga., 1972).

Explanation: Reported in the first volume of the *U.S. Tax Cases* (USTC) published by Commerce Clearing House for calendar year 1973 (73–1) and located at paragraph 9279 (¶9279).

Simons-Eastern Co. v. U.S., 31 AFTR2d 73–640 (D.Ct.Ga., 1972).

Explanation: Reported in the 31st volume of the second series of the *American Federal Tax Reports* (AFTR2d) published by RIA and beginning on page 640. The "73" preceding the page number indicates the year the case was published but is a designation used only in recent decisions.

Simons-Eastern Co. v. U.S., 354 F.Supp. 1003 (D.Ct.Ga., 1972).

Explanation: Reported in the 354th volume of the *Federal Supplement Series* (F.Supp.) published by West Publishing Company and beginning on page 1003.

In all of the preceding citations, note that the name of the case is the same (Simons-Eastern Co. being the taxpayer), as is the reference to the Federal District Court of Georgia (D.Ct.Ga.) and the year the decision was rendered (1972).[28]

Decisions of the Court of Federal Claims[29] and the Courts of Appeals are published in the USTCs, AFTRs, and a West Publishing Company reporter called the *Federal Second Series* (F.2d). Volume 999, published in 1993, is the last volume of the *Federal Second Series.* It is followed by the *Federal Third Series* (F.3d). Beginning with October 1982, the Court of Federal Claims decisions are published in another West Publishing Company reporter entitled the *Claims Court Reporter.* Beginning with Volume 27 on October 30, 1992, the name of the reporter changed to the *Federal Claims Reporter.* The following examples illustrate the different forms:

Finkbohner, Jr. v. U.S.,   (CA–11, 1986)

    86–1 USTC ¶9393 (CCH citation)
    57 AFTR2d 86–1400 (RIA citation)
    788 F.2d 723 (West citation)

Recchie v. U.S.,   (Cl.Ct., 1983)

    83–1 USTC ¶9312 (CCH citation)
    51 AFTR2d 83–1010 (RIA citation)
    1 Cl.Ct. 726 (West citation)

[27] In this text, the RIA citation for Memorandum decisions of the U.S. Tax Court is omitted. Thus, *Jack D. Carr* would be cited as 49 TCM 507, T.C. Memo. 1985–19.

[28] In this text, the case would be cited in the following form: *Simons-Eastern Co. v. U.S.,* 73–1 USTC ¶9279, 31 AFTR2d 73–640, 354 F.Supp. 1003 (D.Ct.Ga., 1972). Prentice-Hall Information Ser-

vices is now owned by Research Institute of America. Although new volumes will contain the RIA imprint, many of the older volumes will continue to have the P-H imprint.

[29] Before October 29, 1992, the Court of Federal Claims was called the Claims Court. Before October 1, 1982, the Court of Federal Claims was called the Court of Claims.

Note that *Finkbohner, Jr.* is a decision rendered by the Eleventh Court of Appeals in 1986 (CA–11, 1986), while *Recchie* was issued by the Court of Federal Claims in 1983 (Cl.Ct., 1983).

Judicial Citations—The U.S. Supreme Court

Like all other Federal tax decisions (except those rendered by the Tax Court), Supreme Court decisions are published by Commerce Clearing House in the USTCs and by RIA (formerly by Prentice-Hall) in the AFTRs. The U.S. Government Printing Office also publishes these decisions in the *United States Supreme Court Reports* (U.S.) as does West Publishing Company in its *Supreme Court Reporter* (S.Ct.) and the Lawyer's Co-operative Publishing Company in its *United States Reports, Lawyer's Edition* (L.Ed.). The following illustrates the different ways the same decision can be cited:

U.S. v. The Donruss Co.,   (USSC, 1969)

69–1 USTC ¶9167 (CCH citation)
23 AFTR2d 69–418 (RIA citation)
89 S.Ct. 501 (West citation)
393 U.S. 297 (U.S. Government Printing Office citation)
21 L.Ed.2d 495 (Lawyer's Co-operative Publishing Co. citation)

The parenthetical reference (USSC, 1969) identifies the decision as having been rendered by the U.S. Supreme Court in 1969. In this text, the citations of Supreme Court decisions will be limited to the CCH (USTC), RIA (AFTR), and West (S.Ct.) versions. For a summary, see Concept Summary 2–2.

CONCEPT SUMMARY 2–2

Judicial Sources

Court	Location	Authority
U.S. Supreme Court	S.Ct. Series (West) U.S. Series (U.S. Gov't.) L.Ed. (Lawyer's Co-op.) AFTR (RIA) USTC (CCH)	Highest authority
U.S. Courts of Appeal	Federal 2d (West) AFTR (RIA) USTC (CCH)	Next highest appellate court
Tax Court (Regular decisions)	U.S. Govt. Printing Office, RIA/CCH separate services	Highest trial court*
Tax Court (Memorandum decisions)	RIA T.C. Memo (RIA) TCM (CCH)	Less authority than regular T.C. decision
U.S. Court of Federal Claims**	Federal Claims Reporter (West) AFTR (RIA) USTC (CCH)	Similar authority as Tax Court
U.S. District Courts	F.Supp. Series (West) AFTR (RIA) USTC (CCH)	Lowest trial court
Small Claims Division of Tax Court	Not published	No precedent value

*Theoretically, the Tax Court, Court of Federal Claims, and District Courts are on the same level of authority. But some people believe that since the Tax Court hears and decides tax cases from all parts of the country (it is a national court), its decisions may be more authoritative than a Court of Federal Claims or District Court decision.
**Before October 29, 1992, the U.S. Claims Court.

WORKING WITH THE TAX LAW—TAX RESEARCH

Tax research is the method by which a tax practitioner or professor determines the best available solution to a situation that possesses tax consequences. In other words, it is the process of finding a competent and professional conclusion to a tax problem. The problem may originate from completed or proposed transactions. In the case of a completed transaction, the objective of the research is to determine the tax result of what has already taken place. For example, was the expenditure incurred by the taxpayer deductible or not deductible for tax purposes? When dealing with proposed transactions, the tax research process is directed toward the determination of possible tax consequences. To the extent that tax research leads to a choice of alternatives or otherwise influences the future actions of the taxpayer, it becomes the key to effective tax planning.

Tax research involves the following procedures:

- Identifying and refining the problem.
- Locating the appropriate tax law sources.
- Assessing the validity of the tax law sources.
- Arriving at the solution or at alternative solutions with due consideration given to nontax factors.
- Effectively communicating the solution to the taxpayer or the taxpayer's representative.
- Following up on the solution (where appropriate) in light of new developments.

These procedures are diagrammed in Figure 2–3. The broken lines reflect the steps of particular interest when tax research is directed toward proposed, rather than completed, transactions.

▼ **FIGURE 2–3**
Tax Research Process

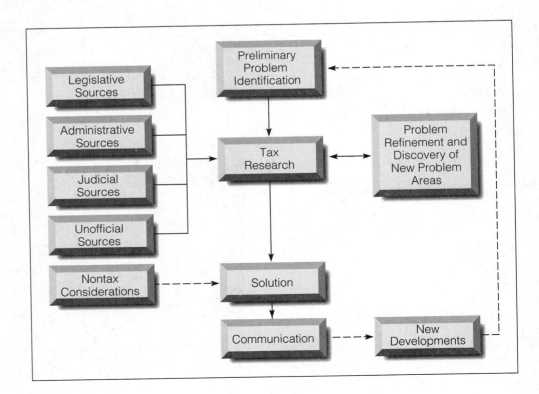

IDENTIFYING THE PROBLEM

Problem identification must start with a compilation of the relevant facts involved.[30] In this regard, *all* of the facts that may have a bearing on the problem must be gathered because any omission could modify the solution to be reached. To illustrate, consider what appears to be a very simple problem.

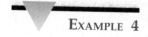

EXAMPLE 4

Early in December, Fred and Megan review their financial and tax situation with their son, Sam, and daughter-in-law, Dana. Fred and Megan are in the 28% tax bracket. Both Sam and Dana are age 21. Sam, a student at a nearby university, owns some publicly traded stock that he inherited from his grandmother. A current sale would result in approximately $7,000 of gross income. At this point, Fred and Megan provide about 55% of Sam and Dana's support. Although neither is now employed, Sam has earned $960 and Dana has earned $900. The problem: Should the stock be sold, and would the sale prohibit Fred and Megan from claiming Sam and Dana as dependents? ▼

REFINING THE PROBLEM

Initial reaction is that Fred and Megan in Example 4 could *not* claim Sam and Dana as dependents if the stock is sold, since Sam would then have earned more than the exemption amount under § 151(d).[31] However, Sam is a full-time student, and § 151(c)(1)(B) allows a son or daughter who is a full-time student and is under age 24 to earn more than the exemption amount without penalizing the parents with the loss of the dependency exemption. Thus, Sam could sell the stock without penalizing the parents with respect to the gross income test. However, the $7,000 income from the sale of the stock might lead to the failure of the greater than 50 percent support test, depending on how much Sam spends for his (or Dana's) support.

Assume, however, that further fact gathering reveals the following additional information:

- Sam does not really need to spend the proceeds from the sale of the stock.
- Sam receives a sizable portion of his own support from a scholarship.

With these new facts, additional research leads to § 152(d) and Reg. § 1.152–1(c), which indicate that a scholarship received by a student is not included for purposes of computing whether the parents furnished more than one-half of the child's support. Further, if Sam does not spend the proceeds from the sale of stock, the unexpended amount is not counted for purposes of the support test. Thus, it appears that the parents would not be denied the dependency exemptions for Sam and Dana.

LOCATING THE APPROPRIATE TAX LAW SOURCES

Once the problem is clearly defined, what is the next step? Although this is a matter of individual judgment, most tax research begins with the index volume of the tax service. If the problem is not complex, the researcher may bypass the tax service and turn directly to the Internal Revenue Code and Treasury Regulations.

---

[30] For an excellent discussion of the critical role of facts in carrying out tax research, see Ray M. Sommerfeld and G. Fred Streuling, *Tax Research Techniques*, Tax Study No. 5 (New York: The American Institute of Certified Public Accountants, 1981), Chapter 2.

[31] See the related discussion in Chapter 3.

For the beginner, the latter procedure saves time and will solve many of the more basic problems. If the researcher does not have a personal copy of the Code or Regulations, resorting to the appropriate volume(s) of a tax service will be necessary.[32] The major tax services available are as follows:

Standard Federal Tax Reporter, Commerce Clearing House.

United States Tax Reporter, Research Institute of America (entitled *Federal Taxes* prior to July 1992).

Federal Tax Coordinator 2d, Research Institute of America.

Tax Management Portfolios, Bureau of National Affairs.

Rabkin and Johnson, *Federal Income, Gift and Estate Taxation,* Matthew Bender, Inc.

Bender's Federal Tax Service, Matthew Bender, Inc.

Mertens Law of Federal Income Taxation, Callaghan and Co.

Working with the Tax Services

In this text, it is not feasible to teach the use of any particular tax service; this can be learned only by practice.[33] However, several important observations about the use of tax services cannot be overemphasized. First, never forget to check for current developments. The main text of any service is not revised frequently enough to permit reliance on that portion as the *latest* word on any subject. Where current developments can be found depends, of course, on which service is being used. The Commerce Clearing House service contains a special volume devoted to current matters. Both RIA's *U.S. Tax Reporter* and *Federal Tax Coordinator 2d* integrate the new developments into the body of the service throughout the year. Second, when dealing with a tax service synopsis of a Treasury Department pronouncement or a judicial decision, remember there is no substitute for the original source.

To illustrate, do not base a conclusion solely on a tax service's commentary on *Simons-Eastern Co. v. U.S.*[34] If the case is vital to the research, look it up. It is possible that the facts of the case are distinguishable from those involved in the problem being researched. This is not to say that the case synopsis contained in the tax service is wrong; it might just be misleading or incomplete.

Tax Periodicals

The various tax periodicals are another source of tax information. The best way to locate a journal article pertinent to a tax problem is through Commerce Clearing House's *Federal Tax Articles.* This three-volume service includes a subject index, a Code Section number index, and an author's index. The RIA (formerly P-H) tax service also has a topical "Index to Tax Articles" section that is organized using the RIA paragraph index system.

---

[32] Several of the major tax services publish paperback editions of the Code and Treasury Regulations that can be purchased at modest prices. These editions are usually revised twice each year. For an annotated and abridged version of the Code and Regulations that is published annually, see James E. Smith, *West's Internal Revenue Code of 1986 and Treasury Regulations: Annotated and Selected* (St. Paul, Minn.: West Publishing Company, 1994).

[33] The representatives of the various tax services are prepared to provide the users of their services with printed booklets and individual instruction on the use of the materials.

[34] Refer to Footnote 28.

The following are some of the more useful tax periodicals:

The Journal of Taxation
Warren, Gorham and Lamont
210 South Street
Boston, MA 02111

Tax Law Review
Warren, Gorham and Lamont
210 South Street
Boston, MA 02111

Trusts and Estates
Communication Channels, Inc.
6255 Barfield Road
Atlanta, GA 30328

Oil and Gas Tax Quarterly
Matthew Bender & Co.
235 East 45th Street
New York, NY 10017

The International Tax Journal
Panel Publishers
14 Plaza Road
Greenvale, NY 11548

TAXES—The Tax Magazine
Commerce Clearing House, Inc.
4025 West Peterson Avenue
Chicago, IL 60646

National Tax Journal
21 East State Street
Columbus, OH 43215

The Tax Adviser
1211 Avenue of the Americas
New York, NY 10036

The Practical Accountant
1 Penn Plaza
New York, NY 10119

Estate Planning
Warren, Gorham and Lamont
210 South Street
Boston, MA 02111

Taxation for Accountants
Warren, Gorham and Lamont
210 South Street
Boston, MA 02111

The Tax Executive
1300 North 17th Street
Arlington, VA 22209

Journal of Corporate Taxation
Warren, Gorham and Lamont
210 South Street
Boston, MA 02111

Journal of Taxation for Individuals
Warren, Gorham and Lamont
210 South Street
Boston, MA 02111

The Tax Lawyer
American Bar Association
1800 M Street, N.W.
Washington, DC 20036

Journal of the American Taxation Association
American Accounting Association
5717 Bessie Drive
Sarasota, FL 34233

Tax Notes
6830 Fairfax Drive
Arlington, VA 22213

ASSESSING THE VALIDITY OF THE TAX LAW SOURCES

Once a source has been located, the next step is to assess it in light of the problem at hand. Proper assessment involves careful interpretation of the tax law with consideration given to its relevance and validity. In connection with validity, an important step is to check for recent changes in the tax law.

Interpreting the Internal Revenue Code

The language of the Code can be extremely difficult to comprehend fully. For example, a subsection [§ 341(e)] relating to collapsible corporations contains *one* sentence of more than 450 words (twice as many as in the Gettysburg Address).

Within this same subsection is another sentence of 300 words. Research has shown that in one-third of the conflicts reaching the Tax Court, the Court could not discern the intent of Congress by simply reading the statute. Yet the overriding attitude of the Tax Court judges is that the statute comes first. Even when the statute is unworkable, the Court will not rewrite the law.[35]

Assessing the Validity of a Treasury Regulation

It is often stated that Treasury Regulations have the force and effect of law. This statement is certainly true for most Regulations, but some judicial decisions have held a Regulation or a portion thereof invalid. When a court holds a Regulation invalid, it usually does so on the ground that the Regulation is contrary to the intent of Congress when it enacted a particular Code Section. Most often the courts do not question the validity of Regulations because of the belief that "the first administrative interpretation of a provision as it appears in a new act often expresses the general understanding of the times or the actual understanding of those who played an important part when the statute was drafted."[36]

TAX IN THE NEWS

INTERNAL REVENUE CODE: INTERPRETATION PITFALLS

One author has noted 10 common pitfalls in interpreting the Code:

1. Determine the limitations and exceptions to a provision. Do not permit the language of the Code Section to carry greater or lesser weight than was intended.
2. Just because a Section fails to mention an item does not necessarily mean that the item is excluded.
3. Read definitional clauses carefully.
4. Do not overlook small words such as *and* and *or*. There is a world of difference between these two words.
5. Read the Code Section completely; do not jump to conclusions.
6. Watch out for cross-referenced and related provisions, since many Sections of the Code are interrelated.
7. At times Congress is not careful when reconciling new Code provisions with existing Sections. Conflicts among Sections, therefore, do arise.
8. Be alert for hidden definitions; terms in a particular Code Section may be defined in the same Section or in a separate Section.
9. Some answers may not be found in the Code; therefore, a researcher may have to consult the Regulations and/or judicial decisions.
10. Take careful note of measuring words such as *less than 50 percent*, *more than 50 percent*, and *at least 80 percent*.

SOURCE: Adapted by permission from Henry G. Wong, "Ten Common Pitfalls in Reading the Internal Revenue Code," *Practical Accountant*, July–August 1972, pp. 30–33. Reprinted with permission by Faulkner & Gray, Inc., 11 Penn Plaza, New York, NY 10001.

---

[35] T. L. Kirkpatrick and W. B. Pollard, "Reliance by the Tax Court on the Legislative Intent of Congress," *The Tax Executive* (Summer 1986): 358–359.

[36] *Augustus v. Comm.*, 41–1 USTC ¶9255, 26 AFTR 612, 118 F.2d 38 (CA–6, 1941).

Keep the following observations in mind when assessing the validity of a Regulation:

- IRS agents must give the Code and the Regulations issued thereunder equal weight when dealing with taxpayers and their representatives.
- Proposed Regulations provide a preview of future final Regulations, but they are not binding on the IRS or taxpayers.
- In a challenge, the burden of proof is on the taxpayer to show that the Regulation is wrong. However, a court may invalidate a Regulation that varies from the language of the statute and has no support in the Committee Reports.
- If the taxpayer loses the challenge, a 20 percent negligence penalty may be imposed.[37] This accuracy-related penalty applies to any failure to make a reasonable attempt to comply with the tax law and any disregard of rules and regulations.[38]
- Final Regulations tend to be legislative, interpretive, or procedural. **Procedural Regulations** neither establish tax laws nor attempt to explain tax laws. Procedural Regulations are *housekeeping-type instructions* indicating information that taxpayers should provide the IRS as well as information about the internal management and conduct of the IRS itself.
- Some **interpretive Regulations** merely reprint or rephrase what Congress stated in the Committee Reports that were issued when the tax legislation was enacted. Such Regulations are *hard* and *solid* and almost impossible to overturn because they clearly reflect the intent of Congress. An interpretive Regulation is given less deference than a legislative Regulation, however. The Supreme Court has told lower courts to analyze Treasury Regulations carefully before accepting the Treasury's interpretation.[39]
- In some Code Sections, Congress has given the *Secretary or his delegate* the authority to prescribe Regulations to carry out the details of administration or to otherwise complete the operating rules. Under such circumstances, it could almost be said that Congress is delegating its legislative powers to the Treasury Department. Regulations issued pursuant to this type of authority truly possess the force and effect of law and are often called **legislative Regulations** (e.g., consolidated return Regulations).
- Courts tend to apply a legislative reenactment doctrine. A particular Regulation is assumed to have received congressional approval if the Regulation was finalized many years earlier and Congress has not amended the Code Section pertaining to that Regulation.

Assessing the Validity of Other Administrative Sources of the Tax Law

Revenue Rulings issued by the IRS carry less weight than Treasury Department Regulations. Revenue Rulings are important, however, in that they reflect the position of the IRS on tax matters. In any dispute with the IRS on the interpretation of tax law, therefore, taxpayers should expect agents to follow the results reached in any applicable Revenue Rulings. A 1986 Tax Court decision, however, indicated that Revenue Rulings "typically do not constitute substantive authority for a position."[40] Most Revenue Rulings apply retroactively unless a specific statement indicates the extent to which a Ruling is to be applied without retroactive effect.[41]

---

[37] §§ 6662(a) and (b)(1).

[38] § 6662(c).

[39] *U.S. v. Vogel Fertilizer Co.*, 82–1 USTC ¶9134, 49 AFTR2d 82–491, 102 S.Ct. 821 (USSC, 1982); *National Muffler Dealers Assn., Inc.*, 79–1 USTC ¶9264, 43 AFTR2d 79–828, 99 S.Ct. 1304 (USSC, 1979).

[40] *Nelda C. Stark*, 86 T.C. 243 (1986). See also *Ann R. Neuhoff*, 75 T.C. 36 (1980). For a different opinion, however, see *Industrial Valley Bank & Trust Co.*, 66 T.C. 272 (1976).

[41] Rev.Proc. 87–1, 1987–1 C.B. 503.

Revenue Rulings further tell the taxpayer the IRS's reaction to certain court decisions. Recall that the IRS follows a practice of either acquiescing (agreeing) or nonacquiescing (not agreeing) with the *Regular* decisions of the Tax Court. This does not mean that a particular decision of the Tax Court is of no value if, for example, the IRS has nonacquiesced in the result. It does, however, indicate that the IRS will continue to litigate the issue involved.

Assessing the Validity of Judicial Sources of the Tax Law

The judicial process as it relates to the formulation of tax law has already been described. How much reliance can be placed on a particular decision depends upon the following variables:

- The level of the court. A decision rendered by a trial court (e.g., a Federal District Court) carries less weight than one issued by an appellate court (e.g., the Fifth Court of Appeals). Unless Congress changes the Code, decisions by the U.S. Supreme Court represent the last word on any tax issue.
- The legal residence of the taxpayer. If, for example, a taxpayer lives in Texas, a decision of the Fifth Court of Appeals means more than one rendered by the Second Court of Appeals. This result occurs because any appeal from a U.S. District Court or the Tax Court would be to the Fifth Court of Appeals and not to the Second Court of Appeals.[42]
- A Tax Court Regular decision carries more weight than a Memorandum decision since the Tax Court does not consider Memorandum decisions to be binding precedents.[43] Furthermore, a Tax Court *reviewed* decision carries even more weight. All of the Tax Court judges participate in a reviewed decision.
- A Circuit Court decision where certiorari has been requested and denied by the U.S. Supreme Court carries more weight than a Circuit Court decision that was not appealed. A Circuit Court decision heard *en banc* (all the judges participate) carries more weight than a normal Circuit Court case.
- Whether the decision represents the weight of authority on the issue. In other words, is it supported by the results reached by other courts?
- The outcome or status of the decision on appeal. For example, was the decision appealed and, if so, with what result?

In connection with the last two variables, the use of a citator is invaluable to tax research.[44] Citators and their use are discussed in Appendix E.

Assessing the Validity of Other Sources

Primary sources of tax law include the Constitution, legislative history materials, statutes, treaties, Treasury Regulations, IRS pronouncements, and judicial decisions. In general, the IRS considers only primary sources to constitute substantial authority. However, a researcher might wish to refer to *secondary materials* such as legal periodicals, treatises, legal opinions, General Counsel Memoranda, and written determinations. In general, secondary sources are not authority.

Until 1990, the IRS considered only primary sources to constitute substantial authority. In Notice 90–20,[45] the IRS expanded the list of substantial authority *for purposes of* the accuracy-related penalty in § 6662 to include a number of secondary

---

[42] Before October 1, 1982, an appeal from the then-named U.S. Court of Claims (the other trial court) was directly to the U.S. Supreme Court.

[43] *Severino R. Nico, Jr.,* 67 T.C. 647 (1977).

[44] The major citators are published by Commerce Clearing House, RIA, and Shepard's Citations, Inc.

[45] 1990–1 C.B. 328; see also Reg. § 1.6661–3(b)(2).

materials (e.g., letter rulings, General Counsel Memoranda, the Bluebook). As under former § 6661, "authority" does not include conclusions reached in treatises, legal periodicals, and opinions rendered by tax professionals.

A letter ruling or determination letter is substantial authority only to the taxpayer to whom it is issued, except as noted above with respect to the accuracy-related penalty.

Upon the completion of major tax legislation, the staff of the Joint Committee on Taxation (in consultation with the staffs of the House Ways and Means and Senate Finance Committees) often will prepare a General Explanation of the Act, commonly known as the Bluebook because of the color of its cover. The IRS will not accept this detailed explanation as having legal effect, except as noted above with respect to the accuracy-related penalty. The Bluebook does, however, provide valuable guidance to tax advisers and taxpayers until Regulations are issued, and some letter rulings and General Counsel Memoranda of the IRS cite its explanations.

ARRIVING AT THE SOLUTION OR AT ALTERNATIVE SOLUTIONS

Example 4 raised the question of whether a taxpayer would be denied dependency exemptions for a son and a daughter-in-law if the son sold some stock near the end of the year. A refinement of the problem supplies additional information:

- Sam was a full-time student during four calendar months of the year.
- Sam and Dana anticipate filing a joint return.

Additional research leads to Reg. § 1.151–3(b), which indicates that to qualify as a student, Sam must be a full-time student during each of *five* calendar months of the year at an educational institution. Thus, proceeds from Sam's sale of the stock would cause his parents to lose at least one dependency exemption because Sam's gross income would exceed the exemption amount. The parents still might be able to claim Dana as an exemption if the support test is met.

Section 151(c)(2) indicates that a supporting taxpayer is not permitted a dependency exemption for a married dependent if the married individual files a joint return. Initial reaction is that a joint return by Sam and Dana would be disastrous to the parents. However, more research uncovers two Revenue Rulings that provide an exception if neither the dependent nor the dependent's spouse is required to file a return but does so solely to claim a refund of tax withheld. The IRS asserts that each spouse must have gross income of less than the exemption amount.[46] Therefore, if Sam sells the stock and he and Dana file a joint return, the parents would lose the dependency exemption for both Sam and Dana. If the stock is not sold until January, both exemptions may still be available to the parents. However, under § 151(d)(2) a personal exemption is not available to a taxpayer who can be claimed as a dependent by another taxpayer (whether actually claimed or not). Thus, if the parents can claim Sam and Dana as dependents, Sam and Dana would lose their personal exemptions on their tax return.

4   **LEARNING OBJECTIVE**
Communicate the results of the tax research process in a client letter and a tax file memorandum.

COMMUNICATING TAX RESEARCH

Once satisfied that the problem has been researched adequately, the researcher may need to prepare a memo (and/or letter) setting forth the result. The form such a memo takes could depend on a number of considerations. For example, does an

---

[46] Rev.Rul. 54–567, 1954–2 C.B. 108; Rev.Rul. 65–34, 1965–1 C.B. 86.

employer or professor recommend a particular procedure or format for tax research memos? Is the memo to be given directly to the client or will it first go to the researcher's employer? Whatever form it takes, a good research memo should contain the following elements:

- A clear statement of the issue.
- In more complex situations, a short review of the fact pattern that raises the issue.
- A review of the tax law sources (e.g., Code, Regulations, Revenue Rulings, judicial authority).
- Any assumptions made in arriving at the solution.
- The solution recommended and the logic or reasoning supporting it.
- The references consulted in the research process.

In short, a good tax memo should tell the reader what was researched, the results of that research, and the justification for the recommendation made.[47]

Illustrations of the memorandum for the tax files and the client letter associated with Example 4 appear in Figures 2–4, 2–5, and 2–6.

▼ **FIGURE 2–4**
Client Letter

Hoffman, Smith, and Willis, CPAs
50 Kellogg Boulevard
St. Paul, Minnesota 55164

September 2, 1994

Mr. and Ms. Fred Taxpayer
111 Boulevard
Williamsburg, Virginia 23185

Dear Mr. and Ms. Taxpayer:

This letter is in response to your request for us to review your family's financial and tax situation. Our conclusions are based upon the facts as outlined in your August 15th letter. Any change in the facts may affect our conclusions.

You provide over 50% of the support for your son, Sam, and his wife, Dana. The scholarship Sam receives is not included in determining support. If the stock is not sold, you will qualify for a dependency exemption for both Sam and Dana.

However, if the stock is sold, a gain of approximately $7,000 will result. This amount will result in the gross income requirement being violated (i.e., potential dependent's gross income must not exceed $2,450) for Sam. Therefore, you will not qualify to receive a dependency exemption for Sam. In addition, if Sam sells the stock and he and Dana file a joint return, you also will not qualify for a dependency exemption for Dana.

From a tax planning perspective, Sam should not sell the stock in 1994. This will enable you to claim dependency exemptions for both Sam and Dana. If the stock is sold, Sam and Dana should not file a joint return. This will still enable you to qualify for a dependency exemption for Dana.

Should you need more information or need to clarify our conclusions, do not hesitate to contact me.

Sincerely yours,

John J. Jones, CPA
Partner

---

[47]See Chapter 6 of the publication cited in Footnote 30.

▼ **FIGURE 2-5**
Tax File Memorandum

August 19, 1994

TAX FILE MEMORANDUM

FROM: John J. Jones

SUBJECT: Fred and Megan Taxpayer
Engagement: Issues

Today I talked to Fred Taxpayer with respect to his August 15, 1994 letter requesting tax assistance. He wishes to know if his son, Sam, can sell stock worth $19,000 (basis = $12,000) without the parents losing the dependency exemptions for Sam and Sam's wife, Dana.

Fred Taxpayer is married to Megan, and Sam is a full-time student at a local university. Sam inherited the stock from his grandmother about five years ago. If he sells the stock, he will save the proceeds from the sale. Sam does not need to spend the proceeds if he sells the stock because he receives a $3,000 scholarship that he uses for his own support (i.e., to pay for tuition, books, and fees). Fred and Megan are in the 28% tax bracket and furnish approximately 55% of Sam and Dana's support.

ISSUE: If the stock is sold, would the sale prohibit Fred and Megan from claiming Sam and Dana as dependents? I told Fred that we would have an answer for him within two weeks.

▼ **FIGURE 2-6**
Tax File Memorandum

August 27, 1994

TAX FILE MEMORANDUM

FROM: John J. Jones

SUBJECT: Fred and Megan Taxpayer
Engagement: Conclusions

Section 152(a) provides that in order for a taxpayer to take a dependency exemption, the taxpayer must provide over 50% of the support of the potential dependent. Fred and Megan provide about 55% of the support of their son, Sam, and their daughter-in-law, Dana. If Sam should sell the stock in 1994, he would not need to spend the proceeds for support purposes (i.e., would save the proceeds). Thus, the stock sale would not affect his qualifying for the support test. In calculating the percentage of support provided by Fred and Megan, a $3,000 scholarship received by Sam is not counted in determining the amount of support Sam provides for himself [see Reg. § 1.152–1(c)].

Section 151(c)(1) provides that in order to qualify for a dependency exemption, the potential dependent's gross income must be less than the exemption amount (i.e., $2,450 in 1994). Without the stock sale, the gross income of both Sam ($960) and Dana ($900) will be below the exemption amount in 1994. The $3,000 Sam receives as a scholarship is excluded from his gross income under § 117(a) because he uses the entire amount to pay for his tuition, books, and fees at a local university.

The key issue then is whether the stock, which will generate $7,000 gain for Sam, will cause the gross income test to be violated. The gain will increase Sam's gross income to $7,960 ($7,000 + $960). However, § 151(c)(1)(B) permits a child's gross income to exceed the exemption amount if the child is a student under the age of 24. Under Reg. § 1.151–3(b), to qualify as a student, the person must be a full-time student during each of five calendar months. A telephone call to Megan provided the information that Sam was a student for only four months in 1994. Thus, since Sam is not eligible for the student exception, the sale of the stock by Sam in 1994 would result in Fred and Megan losing the dependency exemption for Sam.

The stock sale would also result in the loss of the dependency exemption for Dana if Sam and Dana file a joint return for 1994 [see § 151(c)(2)].

From a tax planning perspective, Sam should not sell the stock until 1995. This will enable Fred and Megan to claim dependency exemptions on their 1994 return for Sam and Dana. Note, however, that neither Sam nor Dana will be permitted to take a personal exemption deduction on their 1994 tax return since they are claimed as dependents on someone else's return [see § 151(d)(2)]. However, this will not produce any negative tax consequences since their tax liability will be zero if the stock is not sold in 1994.

WORKING WITH THE TAX LAW—TAX PLANNING

5 **LEARNING OBJECTIVE**
Apply tax research techniques
and planning procedures and
have an awareness of
computer-assisted tax research.

Tax research and tax planning are inseparable. The *primary* purpose of effective *tax planning* is to reduce the taxpayer's total tax bill. This does not mean that the course of action selected must produce the lowest possible tax under the circumstances. The minimization of tax liability must be considered in context with the legitimate business goals of the taxpayer.

A *secondary* objective of effective tax planning is to reduce or defer the tax in the current tax year. Specifically, this objective aims to accomplish one or more of the following: eradicating the tax entirely; eliminating the tax in the current year; deferring the receipt of income; converting ordinary income into capital gains; converting active to passive income; converting passive to active expense; proliferating taxpayers (i.e., forming partnerships and corporations or making lifetime gifts to family members); eluding double taxation; avoiding ordinary income; or creating, increasing, or accelerating deductions. However, this second objective should be approached with considerable reservation and moderation. For example, a tax election in one year may reduce taxes currently, but saddle future years with a disadvantageous tax position.

NONTAX CONSIDERATIONS

There is an honest danger that tax motivations may take on a significance that does not correspond to the true values involved. In other words, tax considerations may impair the exercise of sound business judgment by the taxpayer. Thus, the tax planning process can become a medium through which to accomplish ends that are socially and economically objectionable. All too often, planning seems to lean toward the opposing extremes of placing either too little or too much emphasis on tax considerations. The happy medium—a balance that recognizes the significance of taxes, but not beyond the point where planning detracts from the exercise of good business judgment—turns out to be the promised land that is seldom reached.

The remark is often made that a good rule is to refrain from pursuing any course of action that would not be followed were it not for certain tax considerations. This statement is not entirely correct, but it does illustrate the desirability of preventing business logic from being *sacrificed at the altar of tax planning.*

TAX AVOIDANCE AND TAX EVASION

A fine line exists between legal tax planning and illegal tax planning—tax avoidance versus tax evasion. **Tax avoidance** is merely tax minimization through legal techniques. In this sense, tax avoidance is the proper objective of all tax planning. Tax evasion, while also aimed at the elimination or reduction of taxes, connotes the use of subterfuge and fraud as a means to an end. Popular usage—probably because of the common goals involved—has so linked these two concepts that many individuals are no longer aware of the true distinctions between them. Consequently, some taxpayers have been deterred from properly taking advantage of planning possibilities. The now classic words of Judge Learned Hand in *Commissioner v. Newman* reflect the true values the taxpayer should have:

> Over and over again courts have said that there is nothing sinister in so arranging one's affairs as to keep taxes as low as possible. Everybody does so, rich or poor; and all do right, for nobody owes any public duty to pay more than the law demands: taxes

are enforced extractions, not voluntary contributions. To demand more in the name of morals is mere cant.[48]

ETHICAL CONSIDERATIONS

Tax Avoidance

In a speech class, a philosophy student argues that tax advisers are immoral because they help people cheat the government. Each time a tax adviser shows a taxpayer a tax planning idea that reduces the client's liability, all other taxpayers have to pay more taxes. Society would be better off if all tax advisers would work at improving our environment or living conditions in the inner cities.

As an accounting student, you argue that the primary purpose of tax planning is to reduce a taxpayer's overall liability. This advisory process can result in avoiding, deferring, or postponing the tax burden until the future. There is nothing illegal or immoral about tax avoidance. Taxpayers have every legal right to be concerned about tax avoidance and to arrange their affairs so as to pay no more taxes than the law demands. There is no difference between reducing a tax expense through the help of a tax adviser and reducing a cost of operating a business with the aid of a cost accountant.

FOLLOW-UP PROCEDURES

Because tax planning usually involves a proposed (as opposed to a completed) transaction, it is predicated upon the continuing validity of the advice based upon the tax research. A change in the tax law (either legislative, administrative, or judicial) could alter the original conclusion. Additional research may be necessary to test the solution in light of current developments (refer to the broken lines at the right in Figure 2–3).

TAX PLANNING—A PRACTICAL APPLICATION

Returning to the facts of Example 4, what could be done to protect the dependency exemptions for the parents? If Sam and Dana were to refrain from filing a joint return, both could be claimed by the parents. This result assumes that the stock is not sold.

An obvious tax planning tool is the installment method. Could the securities be sold using the installment method under § 453 so that most of the gain is deferred into the next year? Under the installment method, certain gains may be postponed and recognized as the cash proceeds are received. The problem is that the installment method is not available for stock traded on an established securities market.[49]

A little more research, however, indicates that Sam can sell the stock and postpone the recognition of gain until the following year by selling short an equal number of substantially identical shares and covering the short sale in the subsequent year with the shares originally held. Selling short means that Sam sells borrowed stock (substantially identical) and repays the lender with the stock held

---

[48]*Comm. v. Newman,* 47–1 USTC ¶9175, 35 AFTR 857, 159 F.2d 848 (CA–2, 1947).

[49]See Chapter 18 for a discussion of installment sales.

on the date of the short sale. This *short against the box* technique would allow Sam to protect his $7,000 profit and defer the closing of the sale until the following year.[50] Further, if the original shares have been held for the required long-term holding period before the date of the short sale, Sam would be able to obtain long-term capital gain treatment.[51] Thus, some research and planning would reap tax savings for this family. Note the critical role of obtaining the correct facts in attempting to resolve the proper strategy for the taxpayers.

Throughout this text, most chapters include observations on Tax Planning Considerations. Such observations are not all-inclusive but are intended to illustrate some of the ways in which the material covered can be effectively utilized to minimize taxes.

COMPUTER-ASSISTED TAX RESEARCH

The computer is being used more and more frequently in the day-to-day practice of tax professionals, students, and educators. Many software vendors offer tax return software programs for individual, corporate, partnership, and fiduciary returns. The use of computers, however, is not limited to batch-processed tax returns and computer timesharing for quantitative tax and problem-solving planning and calculations.

The microcomputer has become the revolutionary tool of the present—much as the electronic calculator did in the 1970s. Electronic spreadsheets are being used to replace the 14-column worksheet. The electronic spreadsheet approach can be used for retirement planning, 1040 projections, real estate projections, partnership allocations, consolidated tax return problems, compensation planning—wherever projections and calculations are needed. Many public accounting firms use internally prepared tax-related programs. Microcomputer software is available for estate planning calculations.

LEXIS, a computerized legal data bank from Mead Data Central, has been available since 1973 as a complement to the conventional research approach (available in many of the more than 100 graduate tax programs). WESTLAW, a competitive system from West Publishing Company, has been operational since 1975. Commerce Clearing House's legal data base is called ACCESS, and Research Institute of America's is called TAXRIA. With these data banks, one has immediate access to the current tax law, Regulations, proposed Regulations, letter rulings, Revenue Rulings, judicial decisions, daily tax services, code commentaries, and much more. Note, however, that WESTLAW, LEXIS, ACCESS, and TAXRIA are actually document retrieval systems that cannot interpret the law.

The latest development is the proliferation of Compact Disc–Read Only Memory (CD-ROM). By employing a key-word search technique, a person can browse through a tax service, IRS publications, and other tax information. Commerce Clearing House, Matthew Bender, Research Institute of America, and West Publishing Company offer CD-ROM products. For example, West provides a complete Federal tax library on only nine CDs. Although CD-ROM does not offer the on-line updating provided by WESTLAW, LEXIS, ACCESS, and TAXRIA, the CDs can be replaced periodically.

Computer-assisted tax research is useful in searching for facts because human indexing centers on legal theories rather than fact patterns. Computer searching also is useful in finding new court decisions not yet in the printed indexes.

---

[50]§§ 1233(a) and 1233(b)(2). See Chapter 16 for a discussion of short sales.

[51]Long-term capital gains may receive preferential tax rate treatment. In addition, if Sam had capital losses from other transactions, the capital gains and capital losses could be offset. See the discussion in Chapter 16.

Because computer searching probably does not find as many relevant cases as manual searching does, a combination of manual and computer searching can be quite effective.[52]

KEY TERMS

Acquiescence, 2–19

Circuit Court of Appeals, 2–15

Court of original jurisdiction, 2–12

Determination letters, 2–11

Federal District Court, 2–12

Finalized Regulation, 2–9

Interpretive Regulations, 2–27

Legislative Regulations 2–27

Letter rulings 2–10

Nonacquiescence, 2–19

Precedents, 2–16

Procedural Regulations, 2–27

Proposed Regulation, 2–9

Revenue Procedures 2–10

Revenue Rulings, 2–9

Small Claims Division, 2–12

Tax avoidance, 2–32

Tax research, 2–22

Technical Advice Memoranda (TAMs), 2–12

Temporary Regulation, 2–9

U.S. Court of Federal Claims, 2–12

U.S. Supreme Court, 2–16

U.S. Tax Court, 2–12

Writ of Certiorari, 2–17

PROBLEM MATERIALS

DISCUSSION QUESTIONS

1. Judicial decisions interpreting a provision of the Internal Revenue Code of 1939 or 1954 are no longer of any value in view of the enactment of the Internal Revenue Code of 1986. Assess the validity of this statement.

2. The Revenue Reconciliation Act of 1990 became part of the Internal Revenue Code of 1986. Explain this statement.

3. Where does tax legislation normally originate?

4. Why are Committee Reports of Congress important as a source of tax law?

5. Why are certain Code Section numbers missing from the Internal Revenue Code (e.g., §§ 6, 7, 8, 9, 10)?

6. If a treaty between the United States and a foreign country conflicts with a Section of the Internal Revenue Code and the taxpayer fails to disclose this position on the tax return, what is the penalty for failure to disclose?

7. Explain how Regulations are arranged. How would a proposed Regulation under § 66 be cited?

8. Distinguish between legislative, interpretive, and procedural Regulations.

---

[52] See p. 437 of the publication cited in Footnote 20; Thomas and Weinstein, *Computer-Assisted Legal and Tax Research* (Paramus, N.J.: Prentice-Hall, 1986); and Chapter 13 of W. A. Raabe, G. E. Whittenburg, and J. C. Bost, *West's Federal Tax Research*, 2d ed. (St. Paul, Minn.: West Publishing Co., 1990).

9. Distinguish between:
   a. Treasury Regulations and Revenue Rulings.
   b. Revenue Rulings and Revenue Procedures.
   c. Revenue Rulings and letter rulings.
   d. Letter rulings and determination letters.

10. Rank the following items from the highest authority to the lowest in the Federal tax law system:
    a. Interpretive Regulation.
    b. Legislative Regulation.
    c. Letter ruling.
    d. Revenue Procedure.
    e. Internal Revenue Code.
    f. Proposed Regulation.

11. Interpret each of the following citations:
    a. Rev.Rul. 65–235, 1965–2 C.B. 88.
    b. Rev.Proc. 87–56, 1987–2 C.B. 674.
    c. Ltt.Rul. 9046036.

12. You find a 1994 letter ruling in which the factual situation is identical to the approach you wish to take. Can you rely on this letter ruling?

13. Does the government publish letter rulings?

14. What is a Technical Advice Memorandum (TAM)?

15. a. What are Treasury Decisions (TDs)?
    b. What purpose do they serve?
    c. Where are they published?

16. What are the major differences between letter rulings and determination letters?

17. Summarize the trial and appellate court system for Federal tax litigation.

18. Which of the following statements would be considered advantages of the Small Claims Division of the Tax Court?
    a. Appeal to the Court of Appeals for the Federal Circuit is possible.
    b. A hearing of a deficiency of $11,200 is considered on a timely basis.
    c. Taxpayer can handle the litigation without using a lawyer or certified public accountant.
    d. Taxpayer can use other Small Claims Division decisions for precedential value.
    e. The actual hearing is held on an informal basis.
    f. Travel time will probably be reduced.

19. List an advantage and a disadvantage of using the U.S. Tax Court as the trial court for Federal tax litigation.

20. List an advantage and a disadvantage of using a U.S. District Court as the trial court for Federal tax litigation.

21. List an advantage and a disadvantage of using the U.S. Court of Federal Claims as the trial court for Federal tax litigation.

22. A taxpayer lives in Michigan. In a controversy with the IRS, the taxpayer loses at the trial court level. Describe the appeal procedure under the following different assumptions:
    a. The trial court was the Small Claims Division of the U.S. Tax Court.
    b. The trial court was the U.S. Tax Court.
    c. The trial court was a U.S. District Court.
    d. The trial court was the U.S. Court of Federal Claims.

23. Suppose the U.S. Government loses a tax case in the U.S. District Court of North Carolina but does not appeal the result. What does the failure to appeal signify?

24. Because the U.S. Tax Court is a national court, it always decides the same issue in a consistent manner. Assess the validity of this statement.

25. For the U.S. Tax Court, U.S. District Court, and the U.S. Court of Federal Claims, determine the following:
    a. Number of regular judges per court.
    b. Availability of a jury trial.
    c. Whether the deficiency must be paid before the trial.

26. In which of the following states could a taxpayer appeal the decision of a U.S. District Court to the Fifth Court of Appeals?
    a. Arkansas.
    b. Arizona.
    c. Alabama.
    d. Maine.
    e. None of the above.

27. Explain the fact-finding determination of a Federal Court of Appeals.

28. What is the Supreme Court's policy on hearing tax cases?

29. In assessing the validity of a prior court decision, discuss the significance of the following on the taxpayer's issue:
    a. The decision was rendered by the U.S. District Court of Wyoming. Taxpayer lives in Wyoming.
    b. The decision was rendered by the U.S. Court of Federal Claims. Taxpayer lives in Wyoming.
    c. The decision was rendered by the Second Court of Appeals. Taxpayer lives in California.
    d. The decision was rendered by the U.S. Supreme Court.
    e. The decision was rendered by the U.S. Tax Court. The IRS has acquiesced in the result.
    f. Same as (e) except that the IRS has issued a nonacquiescence as to the result.

30. Where can a researcher locate a 1989 U.S. District Court decision?

31. What is the difference between a Regular and a Memorandum decision of the U.S. Tax Court?

32. The IRS may acquiesce or nonacquiesce to what court decisions? Can an acquiescence be withdrawn retroactively?

33. Interpret each of the following citations:
    a. 54 T.C. 1514 (1970).
    b. 408 F.2d 1117 (CA–2, 1969).
    c. 69–1 USTC ¶9319 (CA–2, 1969).
    d. 23 AFTR2d 69–1090 (CA–2, 1969).
    e. 293 F.Supp. 1129 (D.Ct., Miss., 1967).
    f. 67–1 USTC ¶9253 (D.Ct., Miss., 1967).
    g. 19 AFTR2d 647 (D.Ct., Miss., 1967).
    h. 56 S.Ct. 289 (USSC, 1935).
    i. 36–1 USTC ¶9020 (USSC, 1935).
    j. 16 AFTR 1274 (USSC, 1935).
    k. 422 F.2d 1336 (Ct.Cls., 1970).

34. Explain the following abbreviations:

a.	CA–2	i.	USTC
b.	Cls.Ct.	j.	AFTR
c.	*aff'd.*	k.	F.2d
d.	*rev'd.*	l.	F.Supp.
e.	*rem'd.*	m.	USSC
f.	*Cert. Denied*	n.	S.Ct.
g.	*acq.*	o.	D.Ct.
h.	B.T.A.		

35. Give the Commerce Clearing House citation for the following courts:
    a. Small Claims Division of the Tax Court.
    b. Federal District Court.

c. U.S. Supreme Court.
d. U.S. Court of Federal Claims.
e. Tax Court Memorandum decision.

36. Where can you locate a published decision of the U.S. Court of Federal Claims?

37. Which of the following items can probably be found in the *Cumulative Bulletin*?
a. Revenue Ruling.
b. Small Claims Division of the U.S. Tax Court decision.
c. Letter ruling.
d. Revenue Procedure.
e. Proposed Regulation.
f. District Court decision.
g. Senate Finance Committee Report.
h. Acquiescences to Tax Court decisions.
i. Tax Court Memorandum decision.

38. In the tax research process, what does problem identification involve?

39. In tax law, what has the highest tax authority or reliability?

40. Since a Regulation has the force and effect of tax law, can a Regulation be overturned by a court?

41. Which court has the higher level of authority: the Tax Court or a U.S. District Court?

42. When might a researcher need to refer to a citator?

43. List the elements that a good tax research memo should include.

44. Defend the practice by which tax advisers such as CPAs use tax planning techniques to reduce the tax liability of their clients.

45. Which of the following would be considered differences between the Research Institute of America and Commerce Clearing House citators?
a. Distinguishes between the various issues in a particular court decision.
b. Lists all court decisions that cite the court decision being researched.
c. Allows a researcher to determine the validity of a Revenue Ruling.
d. Indicates whether a court decision is explained, criticized, followed, or overruled by a subsequent decision.
e. Pinpoints the exact page on which a decision is cited by another case.

46. You inherit a tax problem that was researched five months ago. You believe the answer is correct, but you are unfamiliar with the general area. How would you find some recent articles dealing with the subject area? How do you evaluate the reliability of the authority cited in the research report? How do you determine the latest developments pertaining to the research problem?

47. When might a researcher wish to consult one of the four computerized legal data banks?

PROBLEMS

48. Tom, an individual taxpayer, has just been audited by the IRS and, as a result, has been assessed a substantial deficiency (which has not yet been paid) in additional income taxes. In preparing his defense, Tom advances the following possibilities:
a. Although a resident of Kentucky, Tom plans to sue in a U.S. District Court in Oregon that appears to be more favorably inclined towards taxpayers.
b. If (a) is not possible, Tom plans to take his case to a Kentucky state court where an uncle is the presiding judge.
c. Since Tom has found a B.T.A. decision that seems to help his case, he plans to rely on it under alternative (a) or (b).

d. If he loses at the trial court level, Tom plans to appeal either to the U.S. Court of Federal Claims or to the U.S. Second Court of Appeals. The reason for this choice is the presence of relatives in both Washington, D.C., and New York. Staying with these relatives could save Tom lodging expense while his appeal is being heard by the court selected.

e. Whether or not Tom wins at the trial court or appeals court level, he feels certain of success on an appeal to the U.S. Supreme Court.

Evaluate Tom's notions concerning the judicial process as it applies to Federal income tax controversies.

49. Using the legend provided, identify the governmental unit that produces the following tax sources:

Legend

   T = U.S. Treasury Department
 NO = National Office of the IRS
 DD = District Director of the IRS
 NA = Not applicable

a. Proposed Regulations.
b. Revenue Procedures.
c. Letter rulings.
d. Determination letters.
e. Technical Advice Memoranda.
f. Treasury Decisions.
g. Revenue Rulings.

50. Using the legend provided, classify each of the following statements (more than one answer per statement may be appropriate):

Legend

 D = Applies to the U.S. District Court

 T = Applies to the U.S. Tax Court

 C = Applies to the U.S. Court of Federal Claims

 A = Applies to the U.S. Court of Appeals

 U = Applies to the U.S. Supreme Court

 N = Applies to none of the above

a. Decides only Federal tax matters.
b. Decisions are reported in the F.2d Series.
c. Decisions are reported in the USTCs.
d. Decisions are reported in the AFTRs.
e. Appeal is by Writ of Certiorari.
f. Court meets most often in Washington, D.C.
g. A jury trial is available.
h. Trial court.
i. Appellate court.
j. Appeal is to the Federal Circuit and bypasses the taxpayer's particular circuit court.
k. Has a Small Claims Division.
l. The only trial court where the taxpayer does not have to pay the tax assessed by the IRS first.

51. Using the legend provided, classify each of the following tax sources:

Legend

P = Primary tax source

S = Secondary tax source

B = Both

N = Neither

a. Sixteenth Amendment to the Constitution.
b. Tax treaty between the United States and France.
c. Revenue Rulings.
d. General Counsel Memoranda (1988).
e. Tax Court Memorandum decision.
f. *Yale Law Review* article.
g. Temporary Regulations (issued 1993).
h. District Court decision.
i. Small Claims Division of the U.S. Tax Court decision.
j. Senate Finance Committee report.

52. Using the legend provided, classify each of the following citations as to publisher:

Legend

RIA   = Research Institute of America

CCH = Commerce Clearing House

W   = West Publishing Company

U.S. = U.S. Government

O   = Others

a. 83–2 USTC ¶9600.
b. 52 AFTR2d 83–5954.
c. 49 T.C. 645 (1968).
d. 39 TCM 32 (1979).
e. 393 U.S. 297.
f. RIA T.C. Memo ¶80,582.
g. 89 S.Ct. 501.
h. 2 Cl.Ct. 601.
i. 159 F.2d 848.
j. 592 F.Supp. 18.
k. Rev.Rul. 76–332, 1976–2 C.B. 81.
l. 21 L.Ed.2d 495.

53. Using the legend provided, classify each of the following statements:

Legend

A = Tax avoidance

E = Tax evasion

N = Neither

a. Terry writes a $250 check as a charitable contribution on December 28, 1994, but does not mail the check to the charitable organization until January 10. She takes a deduction in 1994.

b. Robert decided not to report interest income from a bank because it was only $11.75.

c. Jim pays property taxes on his home in December 1994 rather than waiting until February 1995.

d. Jane switches her investments from taxable corporate bonds to tax-exempt municipal bonds.

e. Ted encourages his mother to save most of her Social Security benefits so that he will be able to claim her as a dependent.

RESEARCH PROBLEMS

Research Problem 1.   Locate the following Internal Revenue Code citations and give a brief description of them:
   a. § 63(a).
   b. § 195(a).
   c. § 7701(a)(2).

Research Problem 2.   Locate the following Regulation citations and give a brief description of them:
   a. Reg. § 1.151–3(a).
   b. Reg. § 1.1031(a)–3(g)(2).
   c. Reg. § 1.1502–75(c)(2)(i).

Research Problem 3.   What is the subject matter of Rev.Rul. 77–37, 1977–2 C.B. 568?

Research Problem 4.
   a. Using Volume 7 of *Bender's Federal Tax Service* in I:24.44 [2], define an Alaska Native Corporation.
   b. Using "S Corporation" Tax Management Portfolios (TMP) 60–7th, on page A–61, determine if royalties from a secret process are passive investment income.

Research Problem 5.
   a. Locate the Fall 1991 issue of *The Journal of the American Taxation Association*. On page 26, determine if the research and development credit is effective.
   b. Locate the September 1990 issue of *The Tax Adviser*, page 581, footnote 16. What types of companies does Rev.Rul. 85–135 refer to? Who is the employer of the authors?

Research Problem 6.   Determine the acquiescence/nonacquiescence position of the IRS with respect to the following:
   a. *Woods Investment Company*, 85 T.C. 274 (1985).
   b. *Henry W. Schwartz Corp.*, 60 T.C. 728 (1973).
   c. *Estate of Milton S. Lennard*, 61 T.C. 554 (1974).

Research Problem 7.   Locate the following tax services in your library and indicate the name of the publisher and whether the service is organized by topic or Code Section:
   a. *United States Tax Reporter.*
   b. *Standard Federal Tax Reporter.*
   c. *Federal Tax Coordinator 2d.*
   d. *Mertens Law of Federal Income Taxation.*
   e. *Tax Management Portfolios.*
   f. Rabkin & Johnson, *Federal Income, Gift & Estate Taxation.*
   g. *Bender's Federal Tax Service.*

Research Problem 8.   In the Tax Publications Matrix below, place an X if a court decision can be found in the publication. There may be more than one X in a row for a particular court.

Court	U.S. Govt. Printing Office	West Publishing Company				Research Institute of America			Commerce Clearing House	
		Federal Supp.	Federal 2d	Federal Claims Reporter	S.Ct.	BTA Memo	TC Memo	AFTR	TC Memo	USTC
U.S. Supreme Court										
Court of Appeals										
Court of Federal Claims										
District Court										
Tax Court (regular decisions)										
Tax Court (memo decisions)										
Board of Tax Appeal										
BTA Memo										

Research Problem 9.   Complete the following citations to the extent the research materials are available to you:
  a. Rev.Proc. 90– _____ , 1990–1 C.B. 427.
  b. *C. A. Daniel,* 53 TCM _____ .
  c. *Joyce Purcell,* 96 T.C. _____ (1986).
  d. *Sol Diamond,* 492 F.2d 286 (_____ , 1974).
  e. *Centel Communications Co., Inc.,* 90–2 USTC _____ (CA–7, 1990).
  f. Rev.Rul. 75–493, 1975– _____ C.B. 108.
  g. *U.S. v. Maclin P. Davis,* 397 U.S. _____ (USSC, 1970).

Research Problem 10.   Using the research materials available to you, answer the following questions:
  a. Has Prop.Reg. § 1.482–2 been finalized?
  b. What happened to *Golconda Mining Corp.,* 58 T.C. 736 (1972) on appeal?
  c. Does Rev.Rul. 69–185 still represent the position of the IRS on the issue involved?

Research Problem 11.   Determine the disposition of the following decisions:
  a. *Louis E. Roszkos,* 87 T.C. 1255 (1986).
  b. *John L. Jackson,* 86 T.C. 492 (1986).
  c. *Rollert Residuary Trust,* 80 T.C. 619 (1983).

Research Problem 12.   Determine the reliability of the following items:
  a. *Simpson v. U.S.,* 261 F.2d 497 (CA–7, 1958).
  b. Rev.Proc. 83–78, 1983–2 C.B. 595.
  c. *Estate of Grace E. Lang,* 64 T.C. 404 (1975).

Research Problem 13.   Did the IRS agree or disagree with the following court decisions?
  a. *Longue Vue Foundation,* 90 T.C. 150 (1988).
  b. *Charles Crowther,* 28 T.C. 1293 (1957).
  c. *Sidney Merians,* 60 T.C. 187 (1973).
  d. *Ray Durden,* 3 T.C. 1 (1944).

Research Problem 14.   Determine the reliability of the following decisions:
  a. *Maid of The Mist Corp. v. Comm.,* T.C.Memo. 1977–263, 36 TCM 1068 (1977).
  b. *Lazisky v. Comm.,* 72 T.C. 495 (1979).
  c. *Farm Service Cooperative v. Comm.,* 70 T.C. 145 (1978).
  d. *Tufts v. Comm.,* 81–2 USTC ¶9574 (CA–5, 1981), *rev'g* 70 T.C. 756 (1978).

Research Problem 15. Find the decision *Barbados #6 Ltd.*, 85 T.C. 900 (1985).
   a. Who was the presiding judge?
   b. Was the decision reviewed by the full court? If so, who dissented from the majority opinion?
   c. Who won?
   d. Was the decision entered under the Rule of 155?

Research Problem 16. During 1994, Frank lived with and supported a 20-year-old woman who was not his wife. He resides in a state that has a statute that makes it a misdemeanor for a man and woman who are not married to each other to live together. May Frank claim his *friend* as a dependent assuming he satisfies the normal tax rules for the deduction? Should Frank consider moving to another state?

Partial list of research aids:
§ 152(b)(5).
John T. Untermann, 38 T.C. 93 (1962).
S.Rept. 1983, 85th Cong., 2d Sess., reprinted in the 1958 Code Cong. & Adm. News 4791, 4804.

Research Problem 17. Locate *New York University's Forty-Third Annual Institute on Federal Taxation*.
   a. Turn to Chapter 35, page 35–35, Chart III, and determine the present cost of an employer's obligation to pay an employee $20,000 in 10 years. Assume a 12% employer rate of return.
   b. Turn to Chapter 56, page 56–19, and determine what IRA fees are deductible.

Tax Determination; Personal and Dependency Exemptions; An Overview of Property Transactions

LEARNING OBJECTIVES

After completing Chapter 3, you should be able to:

1. Understand and apply the components of the Federal income tax formula.

2. Apply the rules for arriving at personal and dependency exemptions.

3. Use the proper method for determining tax liability.

4. Recognize the filing requirements and the proper filing status.

5. Obtain an overview of property transactions.

6. Identify tax planning opportunities associated with the individual tax formula.

OUTLINE

Tax Formula, 3–3

Components of the Tax Formula, 3–3

Application of the Tax Formula, 3–8

Individuals Not Eligible for the Standard Deduction, 3–9

Special Limitations for Individuals Who Can Be Claimed as Dependents, 3–9

Personal and Dependency Exemptions, 3–10

Personal Exemptions, 3–10

Dependency Exemptions, 3–11

Tax Determination, 3–15

Tax Table Method, 3–15

Tax Rate Schedule Method, 3–16

Computation of Net Taxes Payable or Refund Due, 3–17

Unearned Income of Children under Age 14 Taxed at Parents' Rate, 3–18

Filing Considerations, 3–20

Filing Requirements, 3–20

Filing Status, 3–23

Gains and Losses from Property Transactions—In General, 3–26

Gains and Losses from Property Transactions—Capital Gains and Losses, 3–27

Definition of a Capital Asset, 3–27

Computation of Net Capital Gains and Losses, 3–28

Capital Loss Limitation, 3–28

Tax Planning Considerations, 3–29

Taking Advantage of Tax Rate Differentials, 3–29

Income of Minor Children, 3–30

Dependency Exemptions, 3–30

Individuals are subject to Federal income tax based on taxable income. This chapter explains how taxable income and the income tax of an individual taxpayer are determined.

To compute taxable income, it is necessary to understand the tax formula in Figure 3–1. Although the tax formula is rather simple, determining an individual's taxable income can be quite complex. The complexity stems from the numerous provisions that govern the determination of gross income and allowable deductions.

After computing taxable income, the appropriate rates must be applied. This requires a determination of the individual's filing status, since different rates apply for single taxpayers, married taxpayers, and heads of household. The basic tax rate structure is progressive, with rates ranging from 15 percent to 39.6 percent.[1] For comparison, the lowest rate structure ranged from 1 percent to 7 percent in 1913–1915, and the highest ranged from 23 percent to 94 percent during 1944–1945.

▼ **FIGURE 3–1**
Tax Formula

Income (broadly conceived)	$xx,xxx
Less: Exclusions	(x,xxx)
Gross income	$xx,xxx
Less: Deductions *for* adjusted gross income	(x,xxx)
Adjusted gross income	$xx,xxx
Less: The greater of— Total itemized deductions *or* the standard deduction	(x,xxx)
Personal and dependency exemptions	(x,xxx)
Taxable income	$xx,xxx

---

[1] The 1994 Tax Table was not available from the IRS at the date of publication of this text. The Tax Table for 1993 and the Tax Rate Schedules for 1993 and 1994 are reproduced in Appendix A. For quick reference, the 1993 and 1994 Tax Rate Schedules are also reproduced inside the front cover of this text.

Once the individual's tax has been computed, prepayments and credits are subtracted to determine whether the taxpayer owes additional tax or is entitled to a refund.

When property is sold or otherwise disposed of, a gain or loss may result, which could affect the determination of taxable income. Although property transactions are covered in detail in Chapters 14–17, an understanding of certain basic concepts helps in working with some of the materials to follow. The concluding portion of this chapter furnishes an overview of property transactions, including the distinction between realized and recognized gain or loss, the classification of such gain or loss (ordinary or capital), and treatment for income tax purposes.

TAX FORMULA

1 LEARNING OBJECTIVE
Understand and apply the components of the Federal income tax formula.

Most individuals compute taxable income using the tax formula shown in Figure 3–1. Special provisions govern the computation of taxable income and the tax liabilityfor certain minor children who have unearned income in excess of specified amounts. These provisions are discussed later in the chapter.

Before illustrating the application of the tax formula, a brief discussion of its components is necessary.

COMPONENTS OF THE TAX FORMULA

Income (Broadly Conceived)

Thisincludes all the taxpayer's income, both taxable and nontaxable. Although it is essentially equivalent to gross receipts, it does not include a return of capital or receipt of borrowed funds.

EXAMPLE 1

Dave needed money to purchase a house. He sold 5,000 shares of stock for $100,000. He had paid $40,000 for the stock. In addition, he borrowed $75,000 from a bank. Dave has taxable income of $60,000 from the sale of the stock ($100,000 selling price – $40,000 return of capital). He has no income from the $75,000 borrowed from the bank because he has an obligation to repay that amount. ▼

Exclusions

For various reasons, Congress has chosen to exclude certain types of income from the income tax base. The principal income exclusions are discussed in Chapter 5. A partial list of these exclusions is shown in Exhibit 3–1.

Gross Income

The Internal Revenue Code defines gross income broadly as "all income from whatever source derived."[2] It includes, but is not limited to, the items in the partial list in Exhibit 3-2 on page 3-5. It does not include unrealized gains. Gross income is discussed in Chapters 4 and 5.

---

[2] § 61(a).

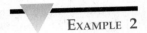

EXAMPLE 2

Beth received the following amounts during the year:

Salary	$30,000
Interest on savings account	900
Gift from her aunt	10,000
Prize won in state lottery	1,000
Alimony from ex-husband	12,000
Child support from ex-husband	6,000
Damages for injury in auto accident	25,000
Increase in the value of stock held for investment	5,000

Review Exhibits 3–1 and 3–2 to determine the amount Beth must include in the computation of taxable income and the amount she may exclude. Then check your answer in footnote 3.[3] ▼

Deductions for Adjusted Gross Income

Individual taxpayers have two categories of deductions: (1) deductions *for* adjusted gross income (deductions to arrive at adjusted gross income) and (2) deductions *from* adjusted gross income.

Deductions *for* adjusted gross income (AGI) include ordinary and necessary expenses incurred in a trade or business, one-half of self-employment tax paid, alimony paid, certain payments to an Individual Retirement Account, moving expenses (after 1993), forfeited interest penalty for premature withdrawal of time deposits, the capital loss deduction, and others.[4] The principal deductions *for* AGI are discussed in Chapters 6, 7, 8, 9, and 11.

Adjusted Gross Income (AGI)

AGI is an important subtotal that serves as the basis for computing percentage limitations on certain itemized deductions, such as medical expenses and charitable contributions. For example, medical expenses are deductible only to the extent they exceed 7.5 percent of AGI, and charitable contribution deductions may not exceed 50 percent of AGI. These limitations might be described as a 7.5 percent *floor* under the medical expense deduction and a 50 percent *ceiling* on the charitable contribution deduction.

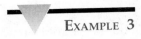

EXAMPLE 3

Keith earned a salary of $23,000 in the current tax year. He contributed $2,000 to his Individual Retirement Account (IRA) and sustained a $1,000 capital loss on the sale of Wren Corporation stock. His AGI is computed as follows:

Gross income		
Salary		$23,000
Less: Deductions *for* AGI		
IRA contribution	$2,000	
Capital loss	1,000	3,000
AGI		$20,000

▼

---

[3] Beth must include $43,900 in computing taxable income ($30,000 salary + $900 interest + $1,000 lottery prize + $12,000 alimony). She can exclude $41,000 ($10,000 gift from aunt + $6,000 child support + $25,000 damages). The unrealized gain on the stock held for investment is not included in gross income. Such gain will be included in gross income only when it is realized upon disposition of the stock.

[4] § 62.

▼ **EXHIBIT 3–1**
Partial List of Exclusions from
Gross Income

Accident insurance proceeds	Meals and lodging (if furnished for employer's convenience)
Annuities (to a limited extent)	Military allowances
Bequests	Minister's dwelling rental value allowance
Child support payments	Railroad retirement benefits (to a limited extent)
Cost-of-living allowance (for military)	Scholarship grants (to a limited extent)
Damages for personal injury or sickness	Social Security benefits (to a limited extent)
Death benefits (up to $5,000)	
Gifts received	Veterans' benefits
Group term life insurance, premium paid by employer (for coverage up to $50,000)	Welfare payments
Inheritances	Workers' compensation benefits
Life insurance paid on death	

▼ **EXHIBIT 3–2**
Partial List of Gross Income
Items

Alimony	Group term life insurance, premium paid by employer (for coverage over $50,000)
Annuities	
Awards	Hobby income
Back pay	Interest
Bargain purchase from employer	Jury duty fees
Bonuses	Living quarters, meals (unless furnished for employer's convenience)
Breach of contract damages	
Business income	Mileage allowance
Clergy fees	Military pay (unless combat pay)
Commissions	Notary fees
Compensation for services	Partnership income
Death benefits in excess of $5,000	Pensions
Debts forgiven	Prizes
Director's fees	Professional fees
Dividends	Punitive damages (in certain cases)
Embezzled funds	Rents
Employee awards (in certain cases)	Rewards
Employee benefits (except certain fringe benefits)	Royalties
	Salaries
Employee bonuses	Severance pay
Estate and trust income	Strike and lockout benefits
Farm income	Supplemental unemployment benefits
Fees	Tips and gratuities
Gains from illegal activities	Travel allowance (in certain cases)
Gains from sale of property	Wages
Gambling winnings	

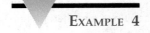

EXAMPLE 4

Assume the same facts as in Example 3, and that Keith also had medical expenses of $1,800. Medical expenses may be included in itemized deductions to the extent they exceed 7.5% of AGI. In computing his itemized deductions, Keith may include medical expenses of $300 [$1,800 medical expenses − $1,500 (7.5% × $20,000 AGI)]. ▼

Itemized Deductions

As a general rule, personal expenditures are disallowed as deductions in arriving at taxable income. However, Congress has chosen to allow specified personal expenses as **itemized deductions.** Such expenditures include medical expenses, certain taxes and interest, and charitable contributions.

In addition to these personal expenses, taxpayers are allowed itemized deductions for expenses related to (1) the production or collection of income and (2) the management of property held for the production of income.[5] These expenses, sometimes referred to as *nonbusiness expenses*, differ from trade or business expenses (discussed previously). Trade or business expenses, which are deductions *for* AGI, must be incurred in connection with a trade or business. Nonbusiness expenses, on the other hand, are expenses incurred in connection with an income-producing activity that does not qualify as a trade or business. Such expenses are itemized deductions.

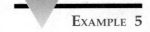

EXAMPLE 5

Leo is the owner and operator of a video game arcade. All allowable expenses he incurs in connection with the arcade business are deductions *for* AGI. In addition, Leo has an extensive portfolio of stocks and bonds. Leo's investment activity is not treated as a trade or business. All allowable expenses that Leo incurs in connection with these investments are itemized deductions. ▼

Itemized deductions include, but are not limited to, the expenses listed in Exhibit 3–3. See Chapter 10 for a detailed discussion of itemized deductions.

Standard Deduction

The **standard deduction** is a specified amount set by Congress, and the amount depends on the filing status of the taxpayer. The effect of the standard deduction is to exempt a taxpayer's income, up to the specified amount, from Federal income tax liability. In the past, Congress has attempted to set the tax-free amount represented by the standard deduction approximately equal to an estimated poverty level,[6] but it has not always been consistent in doing so.

The standard deduction is the sum of two components: the *basic* standard deduction and the *additional* standard deduction.[7] Table 3–1 lists the basic standard deduction allowed for taxpayers in each filing status. All taxpayers allowed a *full* standard deduction are entitled to the applicable amount listed in Table 3–1. The standard deduction amounts are subject to adjustment for inflation each year.

Certain taxpayers are not allowed to claim *any* standard deduction, and the standard deduction is *limited* for others. These provisions are discussed later in the chapter.

---

[5] § 212.

[6] S.Rep. No. 92–437, 92nd Cong., 1st Sess., 1971, p. 54. Another purpose of the standard deduction was discussed in Chapter 1 under Influence of the Internal Revenue Service—Administrative Feasibility. The size of the standard deduction has a direct bearing on the number of taxpayers who are in a position to itemize deductions. Reducing the number of taxpayers who itemize also reduces the audit effort required from the IRS.

[7] § 63(c)(1).

▼ **EXHIBIT 3–3**
Partial List of Itemized
Deductions

Medical expenses in excess of 7.5% of AGI

State and local income taxes

Real estate taxes

Personal property taxes

Interest on home mortgage

Investment interest (to a limited extent)

Charitable contributions (within specified percentage limitations)

Casualty and theft losses in excess of 10% of AGI

Miscellaneous expenses (to the extent such expenses exceed 2% of AGI)

   Union dues

   Professional dues and subscriptions

   Certain educational expenses

   Tax return preparation fee

   Investment counsel fees

   Unreimbursed employee business expenses (after 50% reduction for meals
     and entertainment)

▼ **TABLE 3–1**
Basic Standard Deduction
Amounts

Filing Status	Standard Deduction Amount	
	1993	1994
Single	$3,700	$3,800
Married, filing jointly	6,200	6,350
Surviving spouse	6,200	6,350
Head of household	5,450	5,600
Married, filing separately	3,100	3,175

A taxpayer who is age 65 or over *or* blind qualifies for an *additional standard deduction* of $750 or $950, depending on filing status (see amounts in Table 3–2). Two additional standard deductions are allowed for a taxpayer who is age 65 or over *and* blind. The additional standard deduction provisions also apply for a qualifying spouse who is age 65 or over or blind, but a taxpayer may not claim an additional standard deduction for a dependent.

To determine whether to itemize, the taxpayer compares the *total* standard deduction (the sum of the basic standard deduction and any additional standard deductions) to total itemized deductions. Taxpayers are allowed to deduct the *greater* of itemized deductions or the standard deduction. Taxpayers whose itemized deductions are less than the standard deduction compute their taxable income using the standard deduction rather than itemizing.

EXAMPLE 6

Sara, who is single, is 66 years old. She had total itemized deductions of $4,500 during 1994. Her total standard deduction is $4,750 ($3,800 basic standard deduction plus $950 additional standard deduction). Sara will compute her taxable income for 1994 using the standard deduction ($4,750), since it exceeds her itemized deductions ($4,500). ▼

▼ **TABLE 3–2**
Amount of Each Additional
Standard Deduction

Filing Status	1993	1994
Single	$900	$950
Married, filing jointly	700	750
Surviving spouse	700	750
Head of household	900	950
Married, filing separately	700	750

Exemptions

Exemptions are allowed for the taxpayer, for the taxpayer's spouse, and for each dependent of the taxpayer. The exemption amount is $2,350 in 1993 and $2,450 in 1994.

APPLICATION OF THE TAX FORMULA

The tax formula shown in Figure 3–1 is illustrated in Example 7.

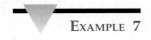

EXAMPLE 7

Grace, age 25, is single and has no dependents. She is a high school teacher and earned a $20,000 salary in 1994. Her other income consisted of a $1,000 prize won in a sweepstakes contest and $500 interest on municipal bonds received as a graduation gift in 1989. During 1994, she sustained a deductible capital loss of $1,000. Her itemized deductions are $3,900. Grace's taxable income for the year is computed as follows:

Income (broadly conceived)		
Salary		$20,000
Prize		1,000
Interest on municipal bonds		500
		$21,500
Less: Exclusion—		
Interest on municipal bonds		(500)
Gross income		$21,000
Less: Deduction *for* adjusted gross income—		
Capital loss		(1,000)
Adjusted gross income		$20,000
Less: The greater of—		
Total itemized deductions	$3,900	
or the standard deduction	$3,800	(3,900)
Personal and dependency exemptions		
(1 × $2,450)		(2,450)
Taxable income		$13,650

▼

The structure of the individual income tax return (Form 1040, 1040A, or 1040EZ) differs somewhat from the tax formula in Figure 3–1. On the tax return, gross income generally is the starting point in computing taxable income. With few exceptions, exclusions are not reported on the tax return.

INDIVIDUALS NOT ELIGIBLE FOR THE STANDARD DEDUCTION

The following individual taxpayers are ineligible to use the standard deduction and must therefore itemize:[8]

- A married individual filing a separate return where either spouse itemizes deductions.
- A nonresident alien.
- An individual filing a return for a period of less than 12 months because of a change in annual accounting period.

SPECIAL LIMITATIONS FOR INDIVIDUALS WHO CAN BE CLAIMED AS DEPENDENTS

Special rules apply to the standard deduction and personal exemption of an individual who can be claimed as a dependent on another person's tax return.

When filing his or her own tax return, a *dependent's* basic standard deduction is limited to the greater of $600 or the individual's earned income for the year.[9] However, if the individual's earned income exceeds the normal standard deduction, the standard deduction is limited to the appropriate standard deduction amount shown in Table 3–1. These limitations apply only to the basic standard deduction. A dependent who is 65 or over or blind or both is also allowed the additional standard deduction amount on his or her own return (refer to Table 3–2). These provisions are illustrated in Examples 8 through 11.

EXAMPLE 8

Susan, who is 17 years old and single, is claimed as a dependent on her parents' tax return. During 1994, she received $1,000 interest (unearned income) on a savings account. She also earned $400 from a part-time job. When Susan files her own tax return, her standard deduction is $600 (the greater of $600 or earned income of $400). ▼

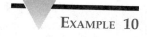

EXAMPLE 9

Assume the same facts as in Example 8, except that Susan is 67 years old and is claimed as a dependent on her son's tax return. In this case, when Susan files her own tax return, her standard deduction is $1,550 [$600 (the greater of $600 or earned income of $400) + $950 (the additional standard deduction allowed because Susan is 65 or over)]. ▼

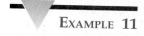

EXAMPLE 10

Peggy, who is 16 years old and single, earned $1,000 from a summer job and had no unearned income during 1994. She is claimed as a dependent on her parents' tax return. Her standard deduction for 1994 is $1,000 (the greater of $600 or earned income). ▼

EXAMPLE 11

Jack, who is a 20-year-old, single, full-time college student, is claimed as a dependent on his parents' tax return. He worked as a musician during the summer of 1994, earning $3,900. Jack's standard deduction is $3,800 (the greater of $600 or $3,900 earned income, but limited to the $3,800 standard deduction for a single taxpayer). ▼

A taxpayer who claims an individual as a dependent is allowed to claim an exemption for the dependent. The dependent cannot claim a personal exemption on his or her own return.

---

[8] § 63(c)(6).
[9] § 63(c)(5). The $600 amount is subject to adjustment for inflation each year. The amount was also $600 for 1993.

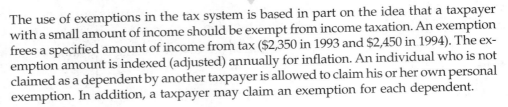

PERSONAL AND DEPENDENCY EXEMPTIONS

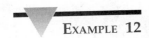

2   **LEARNING OBJECTIVE**
Apply the rules for arriving at
personal and dependency
exemptions.

The use of exemptions in the tax system is based in part on the idea that a taxpayer with a small amount of income should be exempt from income taxation. An exemption frees a specified amount of income from tax ($2,350 in 1993 and $2,450 in 1994). The exemption amount is indexed (adjusted) annually for inflation. An individual who is not claimed as a dependent by another taxpayer is allowed to claim his or her own personal exemption. In addition, a taxpayer may claim an exemption for each dependent.

EXAMPLE 12

Bonnie, who is single, supports her mother and father, who have no income of their own, and claims them as dependents on her tax return. Bonnie may claim a personal exemption for herself plus an exemption for each dependent. On her 1994 tax return, Bonnie may deduct $7,350 for exemptions ($2,450 per exemption × 3 exemptions). ▼

PERSONAL EXEMPTIONS

The Code provides a **personal exemption** for the taxpayer and an exemption for the spouse if a joint return is filed. However, when separate returns are filed, a married taxpayer cannot claim an exemption for his or her spouse unless the spouse has no gross income and is not claimed as the dependent of another taxpayer.

The determination of marital status generally is made at the end of the taxable year, except when a spouse dies during the year. Spouses who enter into a legal separation under a decree of divorce or separate maintenance before the end of the year are considered to be unmarried at the end of the taxable year. The following table illustrates the effect of death or divorce upon marital status:

	Marital Status for 1994
• Walt is the widower of Helen who died on January 3, 1994.	Walt and Helen are considered to be married for purposes of filing the 1994 return.
• Bill and Jane entered into a divorce decree that is effective on December 31, 1994.	Bill and Jane are considered to be unmarried for purposes of filing the 1994 return.

TAX IN THE NEWS

THE SHRINKING PERSONAL AND DEPENDENCY EXEMPTIONS

For the past decade, the amount of the personal and dependency exemptions has been indexed for the effect of inflation. As the result of this indexation, the amount has increased from $2,350 in 1993 to $2,450 in 1994.

Unfortunately, taxpayers today are not receiving as large an economic benefit from personal and dependency exemptions as they did several decades ago. This results from indexation not always having been part of the Internal Revenue Code and several changes in the amount over the years made by Congress.

Eugene Steuerle, a senior fellow at the Urban Institute in Washington, has calculated what the amount would be if it had been adjusted for both inflation and real growth in income since 1948. Rather than being $2,350 in 1993, the amount of a personal or dependency exemption would be $8,652.

SOURCE: Information from "Tax Report: A Special Summary and Forecast of Federal and State Tax Developments," *Wall Street Journal*, January 19, 1994, p. A1.

DEPENDENCY EXEMPTIONS

As indicated in Example 12, the Code allows a taxpayer to claim a dependency exemption for each eligible individual. A **dependency exemption** may be claimed for each individual for whom the following five tests are met:

- Support.
- Relationship or member of the household.
- Gross income.
- Joint return.
- Citizenship or residency.

Support Test

Over one-half of the support of the individual must be furnished by the taxpayer. Support includes food, shelter, clothing, medical and dental care, education, etc. However, a scholarship received by a student is not included for purposes of computing whether the taxpayer furnished more than half of the child's support.[10]

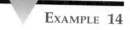

EXAMPLE 13 Hal contributed $2,500 (consisting of food, clothing, and medical care) toward the support of his son, Sam, who earned $1,500 from a part-time job and received a $2,000 scholarship to attend a local university. Assuming that the other dependency tests are met, Hal may claim Sam as a dependent since he has contributed more than half of Sam's support. The $2,000 scholarship is not included as support for purposes of this test. ▼

If the individual does not spend funds that have been received from any source, the unexpended amounts are not counted for purposes of the support test.

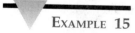

EXAMPLE 14 Emily contributed $3,000 to her father's support during the year. In addition, her father received $2,400 in Social Security benefits, $200 of interest, and wages of $600. Her father deposited the Social Security benefits, interest, and wages in his own savings account and did not use any of the funds for his support. Thus, the Social Security benefits, interest, and wages are not considered as support provided by Emily's father. Emily may claim her father as a dependent if the other tests are met. ▼

Capital expenditures for items such as furniture, appliances, and automobiles are included in total support if the item does, in fact, constitute support.[11]

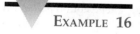

EXAMPLE 15 Norm purchased a television set costing $150 and gave it to his minor daughter. The television set was placed in the child's bedroom and was used exclusively by her. Norm should include the cost of the television set in determining the support of his daughter. ▼

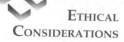

EXAMPLE 16 Mark paid $6,000 for an automobile that was titled and registered in his name. Mark's minor son is permitted to use the automobile equally with Mark. Since Mark did not give the automobile to his son, the $6,000 cost is not includible as a support item. However, out-of-pocket operating expenses incurred by Mark for the benefit of his son are includible as support. ▼

ETHICAL CONSIDERATIONS

Claiming a Dependent

Martha is a widow and lives with her only son, Roland, and his family. Martha's only income consists of $70,000 in interest from tax-exempt bonds. She invests all of the income in stocks in her name. The stocks do not pay dividends. Martha's will

---

[10] Reg. § 1.152–1(c).

[11] Rev.Rul. 57–344, 1957–2 C.B. 112; Rev.Rul. 58–419, 1958–2 C.B. 57.

provides that all of her property is to pass to Roland upon her death. Because of this expectation, Roland provides all of his mother's support. On his return, Roland claims a dependency exemption for his mother.

One exception to the support test involves a **multiple support agreement.** A multiple support agreement permits one of a group of taxpayers who furnish more than half of the support of an individual to claim a dependency exemption for that individual even if no one person provides more than 50 percent of the support.[12] Any person who contributed more than 10 percent of the support is entitled to claim the exemption if each person in the group who contributed more than 10 percent files a written consent. This provision frequently enables one of the children of aged dependent parents to claim an exemption when none of the children meets the 50 percent support test. Each person who is a party to the multiple support agreement must meet all other requirements (except the support requirement) for claiming the exemption. A person who does not meet the relationship or member-of-household requirement, for instance, cannot claim the dependency exemption under a multiple support agreement. It does not matter if he or she contributes more than 10 percent of the individual's support.

EXAMPLE 17   Wanda, who resides with her son, Adam, received $6,000 from various sources during 1994. This constituted her entire support for the year. She received support from the following:

	Amount	Percentage of Total
Adam, a son	$2,880	48
Bob, a son	600	10
Carol, a daughter	1,800	30
Diane, a friend	720	12
	$6,000	100

If Adam and Carol file a multiple support agreement, either may claim the dependency exemption for Wanda. Bob may not claim Wanda because he did not contribute more than 10% of her support. Bob's consent is not required in order for Adam and Carol to file a multiple support agreement. Diane does not meet the relationship or member-of-household test and cannot be a party to the agreement. The decision as to who claims Wanda rests with Adam and Carol. It is possible for Carol to claim Wanda, even though Adam furnished more of Wanda's support. ▼

Each person who qualifies under the more-than-10 percent rule (except for the person claiming the exemption) must complete Form 2120 (Multiple Support Declaration) waiving the exemption. The person claiming the exemption must attach all Forms 2120 to his or her own return. Form 2120 is reproduced in Appendix B.

A second exception to the 50 percent support requirement can occur for a child of parents who are divorced or separated under a decree of separate maintenance.

---

[12] § 152(c).

For decrees executed after 1984, the custodial parent is allowed to claim the exemption unless that parent agrees in writing not to claim a dependency exemption for the child.[13] Thus, claiming the exemption is dependent on whether or not a written agreement exists, *not* on meeting the support test.

EXAMPLE 18

Ira and Rita obtain a divorce decree in 1989. In 1994, their two children are in Rita's custody. Ira contributed over half of the support for each child. In the absence of a written agreement on the dependency exemptions, Rita (the custodial parent) is entitled to the exemptions in 1994. However, Ira may claim the exemptions if Rita agrees in writing. ▼

For the noncustodial parent to claim the exemption, the custodial parent must complete Form 8332 (Release of Claim to Exemption for Child of Divorced or Separated Parents). The release can apply to a single year, a number of specified years, or all future years. The noncustodial parent must attach a copy of Form 8332 to his or her return.

Relationship or Member-of-the-Household Test

To be claimed as a dependent, an individual must be either a relative of the taxpayer or a member of the taxpayer's household. The Code contains a detailed listing of the various blood and marriage relationships that qualify. Note, however, that the relationship test is met if the individual is a relative of either spouse. Once established by marriage, a relationship continues regardless of subsequent changes in marital status.

The following individuals may be claimed as dependents of the taxpayer if the other tests for dependency are met:[14]

- A son or daughter of the taxpayer or a descendant of either, such as a grandchild.
- A stepson or stepdaughter of the taxpayer.
- A brother, sister, stepbrother, or stepsister of the taxpayer.
- The father or mother of the taxpayer or an ancestor of either, such as a grandparent.
- A stepfather or stepmother of the taxpayer.
- A nephew or niece of the taxpayer.
- An uncle or aunt of the taxpayer.
- A son-in-law, daughter-in-law, father-in-law, mother-in-law, brother-in-law, or sister-in-law of the taxpayer.
- An individual who, for the entire taxable year of the taxpayer, has as his or her principal place of abode the home of the taxpayer and is a member of the taxpayer's household. This does not include an individual who, at any time during the taxable year, was the spouse of the taxpayer.

The following rules are also prescribed in the Code:[15]

- A legally adopted child is treated as a natural child.
- A foster child qualifies if the child's principal place of abode is the taxpayer's household.

---

[13] § 152(e).
[14] § 152(a). However, under § 152(b)(5), a taxpayer may not claim someone who is a member of his or her household as a dependent if their relationship is in violation of local law. For example, the dependency exemption was denied because the taxpayer's relation-

ship to the person claimed as a dependent constituted *cohabitation*, a crime under applicable state law. *Cassius L. Peacock, III*, 37 TCM 177, T.C.Memo. 1978–030.
[15] § 152(b)(2).

Gross Income Test

The dependent's gross income must be less than the exemption amount ($2,450 in 1994).[16] However, a parent may claim a dependency exemption for his or her child, even when the child's gross income exceeds $2,450, if the parent provided over half of the child's support and the child, at year-end, is under age 19 or is a full-time student under age 24. If the parent claims a dependency exemption, the dependent child may not claim a personal exemption on his or her own income tax return.

A child is defined as a son, stepson, daughter, stepdaughter, adopted son, or adopted daughter and may include a foster child.[17] For the child to qualify as a student for purposes of the dependency exemption, he or she must be a full-time student at an educational institution during some part of five calendar months of the year.[18] This exception to the gross income test for dependent children who are under age 19 or full-time students under age 24 permits a child or college student to earn money from part-time or summer jobs without penalizing the parent with the loss of the dependency exemption.

Joint Return Test

If a dependent is married, the supporting taxpayer (e.g., the parent of a married child) generally is not permitted a dependency exemption if the married individual files a joint return with his or her spouse.[19] The joint return rule does not apply, however, if the following conditions are met:

- The reason for filing is to claim a refund for tax withheld.
- No tax liability would exist for either spouse on separate returns.
- Neither spouse is required to file a return.

See Table 3–4 later in the chapter and the related discussion concerning income level requirements for filing a return.

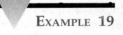

EXAMPLE 19

Paul provides over half of the support of his son Quinn. He also provides over half of the support of Vera, who is Quinn's wife. In 1994, Quinn had wages of $1,500, and Vera earned $1,800. Quinn and Vera file a joint return for the year. Neither Quinn nor Vera was required to file a return because each had income below the $2,450 level for married taxpayers filing separate returns. Paul is allowed to claim both as dependents. ▼

Citizenship or Residency Test

To be a dependent, the individual must be either a U.S. citizen, a U.S. resident, or a resident of Canada or Mexico for some part of the calendar year in which the taxpayer's tax year begins.

Phase-out of Exemptions

For tax years beginning after December 31, 1990, personal exemptions and exemptions for dependents are phased out as AGI exceeds specified threshold amounts. For 1994, the phase-out *begins* at the following threshold amounts:

Joint returns/Surviving spouse	$167,700
Head of household	139,750
Single	111,800
Married, filing separately	83,850

---

[16] § 151(c)(1).
[17] Reg. § 1.151–3(a).

[18] Reg. §§ 1.151–3(b) and (c).
[19] § 151(c)(2).

These threshold amounts are indexed for inflation each year.

Exemptions are phased out by 2 percent for each $2,500 (or fraction thereof) by which the taxpayer's AGI exceeds the threshold amounts. For a married taxpayer filing separately, the phase-out is 2 percent for each $1,250 or fraction thereof.

The allowable exemption amount can be determined with the following steps:

1. AGI – threshold amount = excess amount
2. Excess amount ÷ $2,500 = reduction factor [rounded up to the next whole increment (e.g., 18.1 = 19)] × 2 = phase-out percentage
3. Phase-out percentage (from step 2) × exemption amount = amount of exemptions phased out
4. Exemption amounts – phase-out amount = allowable exemption deduction

EXAMPLE 20 Frederico is married but files a separate return. His AGI is $103,850. He is entitled to one personal exemption.

1. $103,850 – $83,850 = $20,000 excess amount
2. [($20,000 ÷ $1,250) × 2] = 32% (phase-out percentage)
3. 32% × $2,450 = $784 amount of exemption phased out
4. $2,450 – $784 = $1,666 allowable exemption deduction ▼

Note that the exemption amount is completely phased out when the taxpayer's AGI exceeds the threshold amount by more than $122,500 ($61,250 for a married taxpayer filing a separate return), calculated as follows:

$122,501 ÷ $2,500 = 49.0004, rounded to 50 and multiplying by 2 = 100% (phase-out percentage).

EXAMPLE 21 Bill and Isabella file a joint return claiming two personal exemptions and one dependency exemption for their child. Their AGI equals $291,700.

$291,700 − $167,700 = $124,000 excess amount

Since the excess amount exceeds $122,500, the exemptions are completely phased out. ▼

TAX DETERMINATION

TAX TABLE METHOD

3 LEARNING OBJECTIVE
Use the proper method for determining tax liability.

Most taxpayers compute their tax using the **Tax Table.** Eligible taxpayers compute taxable income (as shown in Figure 3–1) and *must* determine their tax by reference to the Tax Table. The following taxpayers, however, may not use the Tax Table method:

- An individual who files a short period return (see Chapter 18).
- Individuals whose taxable income exceeds the maximum (ceiling) amount in the Tax Table. The 1993 Tax Table applies to taxable income below $100,000 for Form 1040.
- An estate or trust.

The 1994 Tax Table was not available at the date of publication of this text. Therefore, the 1993 Tax Table will be used to illustrate the tax computation using the Tax Table method.

EXAMPLE 22 Pedro, a single taxpayer, is eligible to use the Tax Table. For 1993, he had taxable income of $25,025. To determine Pedro's tax using the Tax Table (see Appendix A), find the $25,000 to $25,050 income line. The first column to the right of the taxable income column is for single taxpayers. Pedro's tax for 1993 is $4,134. ▼

TAX RATE SCHEDULE METHOD

The **Tax Rate Schedules** contain rates of 15, 28, 31, 36, and 39.6 percent. Separate schedules are provided for the following filing statuses: single, married filing jointly, married filing separately, and head of household. The rate schedules for 1993 and 1994 are reproduced inside the front cover of this text and also in Appendix A.

The rate schedules are adjusted for inflation each year. Comparison of the 1993 and 1994 schedules shows that the top amount to which the 15 percent bracket applies for single taxpayers rose from $22,100 in 1993 to $22,750 in 1994. Thus, inflation allowed $650 ($22,750 – $22,100) more taxable income to be subject to the lowest 15 percent rate.

The 1994 rate schedule for single taxpayers is reproduced in Table 3–3. This schedule is used to illustrate the tax computations in Examples 23, 24, and 25.

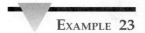

EXAMPLE 23

Pat had $18,000 of taxable income in 1994. His tax is $2,700 ($18,000 × 15%). ▼

Several terms are used to describe tax rates. The rates in the Tax Rate Schedules are often referred to as *statutory* (or nominal) rates. The *marginal* rate is the highest rate that is applied in the tax computation for a particular taxpayer. In Example 23, the statutory rate and the marginal rate are both 15 percent.

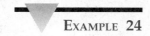

EXAMPLE 24

Chris is single and had taxable income of $41,450 in 1994. Her tax is $8,648.50 [$3,412.50 + 28%($41,450 – $22,750)]. ▼

The *average* rate is equal to the tax liability divided by taxable income. In Example 24, Chris had statutory rates of 15 percent and 28 percent, and a marginal rate of 28 percent. Chris's average rate was 20.9 percent ($8,648.50 tax liability ÷ $41,450 taxable income).

Note that $3,412.50, which is the starting point in the tax computation in Example 24, is 15 percent of the $22,750 taxable income in the first bracket. Income in excess of $22,750 is taxed at a 28 percent rate. This reflects the *progressive* (or graduated) rate structure on which the United States income tax system is based. A tax is progressive if a higher rate of tax applies as the tax base increases.

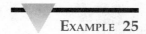

EXAMPLE 25

Carl had taxable income of $81,900 in 1994. His tax is $20,778.50 [$12,470.50 + 31%($81,900 – $55,100)]. Note that the effect of this computation is to tax part of Carl's

▼ **TABLE 3–3**
1994 Tax Rate Schedule for Single Taxpayers

If Taxable Income Is		The Tax Is:	Of the Amount Over
Over	But Not Over		
$ –0–	$ 22,750	15%	$ –0–
22,750	55,100	$ 3,412.50 + 28%	22,750
55,100	115,000	12,470.50 + 31%	55,100
115,000	250,000	31,039.50 + 36%	115,000
250,000		79,639.50 + 39.6%	250,000

income at 15%, part at 28%, and part at 31%. An alternative computational method provides a clearer illustration of the progressive rate structure:

Tax on $22,750 at 15%	$ 3,412.50
Tax on $55,100 − $22,750 at 28%	9,058.00
Tax on $81,900 − $55,100 at 31%	8,308.00
Total	$20,778.50

A special computation limits the tax rate on long-term capital gain to 28 percent of the gain. The alternative tax on long-term capital gain is discussed in detail in Chapter 16.

COMPUTATION OF NET TAXES PAYABLE OR REFUND DUE

The pay-as-you-go feature of the Federal income tax system requires payment of all or part of the taxpayer's income tax liability during the year. These payments take the form of Federal income tax withheld by employers or estimated tax paid by the taxpayer or both.[20] The payments are applied against the tax from the Tax Table or Tax Rate Schedules to determine whether the taxpayer will get a refund or pay additional tax.

Employers are required to withhold income tax on compensation paid to their employees and to pay this tax over to the government. The employer notifies the employee of the amount of income tax withheld on Form W–2 (Wage and Tax Statement). The employee should receive this form by January 31 after the year in which the income tax is withheld.

If taxpayers receive income that is not subject to withholding or income from which not enough tax is withheld, they must pay estimated tax. These individuals must file Form 1040–ES (Estimated Tax for Individuals) and pay in quarterly installments the income tax and self-employment tax estimated to be due (see Chapter 13 for a thorough discussion).

The income tax from the Tax Table or the Tax Rate Schedules is reduced first by the individual's tax credits. There is an important distinction between tax credits and tax deductions. Tax credits reduce the tax liability dollar-for-dollar. Tax deductions reduce taxable income on which the tax liability is based.

EXAMPLE 26

Gail is a taxpayer in the 28% tax bracket. As a result of incurring $1,000 in child care expenses (see Chapter 13 for details), she is entitled to a $200 child care credit ($1,000 child care expenses × 20% credit rate). She also contributed $1,000 to the American Cancer Society and included this amount in her itemized deductions. The child care credit results in a $200 reduction of Gail's tax liability for the year. The contribution to the American Cancer Society reduces taxable income by $1,000 and results in a $280 reduction in Gail's tax liability ($1,000 reduction in taxable income × 28% tax rate). ▼

Tax credits are discussed in Chapter 13. The following are several of the more common credits:

- Earned income credit.
- Credit for child and dependent care expenses.
- Credit for the elderly.
- Foreign tax credit.

---

[20] § 3402 for withholding; § 6202 for estimated payments.

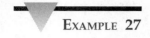
EXAMPLE 27

Kelly, age 30, is a head of household with two dependents. During 1994, Kelly had the following: taxable income, $30,000; income tax withheld, $3,950; estimated tax payments, $600; and credit for child care expenses, $200. Kelly's net tax payable is computed as follows:

Income tax (from 1994 Tax Rate Schedule, Appendix A)		$ 4,500
Less: Tax credits and prepayments—		
Credit for child care expenses	$ 200	
Income tax withheld	3,950	
Estimated tax payments	600	(4,750)
Net taxes payable or (refund due if negative)		$ (250)

UNEARNED INCOME OF CHILDREN UNDER AGE 14 TAXED AT PARENTS' RATE

Before the Tax Reform Act (TRA) of 1986, a dependent child could claim an exemption on his or her own return even if claimed as a dependent by the parents. This enabled a parent to shift investment income (such as interest and dividends) to a child by transferring ownership of the assets producing the income. The child would pay no tax on the income to the extent that it was sheltered by the child's exemption.

For pre-1987 years, an additional tax motivation existed for shifting income from parents to children. Although a child's unearned income in excess of the exemption amount was subject to tax, it was taxed at the child's rate, rather than the parents' rate.

To reduce the tax savings that result from shifting income from parents to children, the net **unearned income** (commonly called investment income) of certain minor children is taxed as if it were the parents' income.[21] Unearned income includes such income as taxable interest, dividends, capital gains, rents, royalties, pension and annuity income, and income (other than earned income) received as the beneficiary of a trust. This provision, commonly referred to as the *kiddie tax,* applies to any child for any taxable year if the child has not reached age 14 by the close of the taxable year, has at least one living parent, and has unearned income of more than $1,200. The *kiddie tax* provision does not apply to a child age 14 or older. However, the limitation on the use of the standard deduction and the unavailability of the personal exemption do apply to such a child as long as he or she is eligible to be claimed as a dependent by a parent.

The term *parent* is defined in the Senate Finance Committee Report as a parent or stepparent of the child. No statutory definition exists for the term.

Net Unearned Income

Net unearned income of a dependent child is computed as follows:

Unearned income
Less: $600
Less: The greater of
   • $600 of the standard deduction *or*
   • The amount of allowable itemized deductions directly connected with the production of the unearned income
Equals: Net unearned income

---

[21] § 1(g).

If net unearned income is zero (or negative), the child's tax is computed without using the parent's rate. If the amount of net unearned income (regardless of source) is positive, the net unearned income will be taxed at the parent's rate. The $600 amounts in the preceding formula are subject to adjustment for inflation each year (refer to footnote 9).

Tax Determination

If a child under age 14 has net unearned income, there are two options for computing the tax on the income. A separate return may be filed for the child, or the parents may elect to report the child's income on their own return. If a separate return is filed for the child, the tax on net unearned income (referred to as the *allocable parental tax*) is computed as though the income had been included on the parents' return. Form 8615 (reproduced in Appendix B) is used to compute the tax. The steps required in this computation are illustrated below.

EXAMPLE 28

Olaf and Olga have a child, Hans (age 10). In 1994, Hans received $2,600 of interest and dividend income and paid investment-related fees of $200. Olaf and Olga had $69,450 of taxable income, not including their child's investment income. Olaf and Olga do not make the parental election.

1. **Determine Hans's net unearned income**

Gross income	$ 2,600
Less: $600	(600)
Less: The greater of	
• $600 or	
• Investment expense	(600)
Equals: Net unearned income	$ 1,400

2. **Determine allocable parental tax**

Parents' taxable income	$ 69,450
Plus: Hans's net unearned income	1,400
Equals: Revised taxable income	$ 70,850
Tax on revised taxable income	$ 14,898
Less: Tax on parents' taxable income	(14,506)
Allocable parental tax	$ 392

3. **Determine Hans's nonparental source tax**

Hans's AGI	$ 2,600
Less: Standard deduction	(600)
Less: Personal exemption	(–0–)
Equals: Taxable income	$ 2,000
Less: Net unearned income	(1,400)
Nonparental source taxable income	$ 600
Equals: Tax ($600 × 15% rate)	$ 90

4. **Determine Hans's total tax liability**

Nonparental source tax (step 3)	$ 90
Allocable parental tax (step 2)	392
Total tax	$ 482

Election to Claim Certain Unearned Income on Parent's Return

If a child under age 14 meets all of the following requirements, the parent may elect to report the child's unearned income that exceeds $1,000 on the parent's own tax return:

- Gross income is from interest and dividends only.
- Gross income is more than $500 and less than $5,000.
- No estimated tax has been paid in the name and Social Security number of the child, and the child is not subject to backup withholding (see Chapter 13).

The child, then, is treated as having no gross income and is not required to file a tax return.

The parent(s) must also pay an additional tax equal to the smaller of $75 or 15 percent of the child's gross income over $500. If the child has any interest from certain private activity bonds, that amount is a tax preference to the parents for purposes of the parents' alternative minimum tax (see Chapter 12). Parents who have substantial itemized deductions based on AGI (see Chapter 10) may find that making the parental election also increases total taxes for the family unit. Taxes should be calculated both with the parental election and without it to determine the appropriate choice.

Other Provisions

If parents have more than one child subject to the tax on net unearned income, the tax for the children is computed as shown in Example 28 and then allocated to the children based on their relative amounts of income. For children of divorced parents, the taxable income of the custodial parent is used to determine the allocable parental tax. This parent is the one who may elect to report the child's unearned income. For married individuals filing separate returns, the individual with the greater taxable income is the applicable parent.

FILING CONSIDERATIONS

Under the category of filing considerations, the following questions need to be resolved:

- Is the taxpayer required to file an income tax return?
- If so, which form should be used?
- When and how should the return be filed?
- In computing the tax liability, which column of the Tax Table or which Tax Rate Schedule should be used?

The first three questions are discussed under Filing Requirements, and the last is treated under Filing Status.

4 LEARNING OBJECTIVE
Recognize the filing requirements and the proper filing status.

FILING REQUIREMENTS

General Rules

An individual must file a tax return if certain minimum amounts of gross income have been received. The general rule is that a tax return is required for every individual who has gross income that equals or exceeds the sum of the exemption amount plus the applicable standard deduction.[22] For example, a single taxpayer under age 65 must file a tax return in 1994 if gross income equals or exceeds $6,250 ($2,450 exemption plus $3,800 standard deduction). Table 3–4 lists the income levels[23] that require tax returns under the general rule and under certain special rules.

The additional standard deduction for being age 65 or older is considered in determining the gross income filing requirements. For example, note in Table 3–4 that the 1994 filing requirement for a single taxpayer age 65 or older is $7,200 ($3,800 basic standard deduction + $950 additional standard deduction + $2,450 exemption). However, the additional standard deduction for blindness is not taken into account. The 1994 filing requirement for a single taxpayer under age 65 and blind is $6,250 ($3,800 basic standard deduction + $2,450 exemption).

Filing Requirements for Dependents

Computation of the gross income filing requirement for an individual who can be claimed as a dependent on another person's tax return is subject to more complex rules. Such an individual must file a return if he or she has either of the following:

- Earned income only and gross income that is more than the total standard deduction (including any additional standard deduction) that the individual is allowed for the year.

▼ **TABLE 3–4**
Filing Levels

Filing Status	1993 Gross Income	1994 Gross Income
Single		
Under 65 and not blind	$ 6,050	$ 6,250
Under 65 and blind	6,050	6,250
65 or older	6,950	7,200
Married, filing joint return		
Both spouses under 65 and neither blind	$10,900	$11,250
Both spouses under 65 and one or both spouses blind	10,900	11,250
One spouse 65 or older	11,600	12,000
Both spouses 65 or older	12,300	12,750
Married, filing separate return		
All—whether 65 or older or blind	$ 2,350	$ 2,450
Head of household		
Under 65 and not blind	$ 7,800	$ 8,050
Under 65 and blind	7,800	8,050
65 or older	8,700	9,000
Qualifying widow(er)		
Under 65 and not blind	$ 8,550	$ 8,800
Under 65 and blind	8,550	8,800
65 or older	9,250	9,550

---

[22] The gross income amounts for determining whether a tax return must be filed are adjusted for inflation each year.

[23] § 6012(a)(1).

- Unearned income only and gross income of more than $600 plus any additional standard deduction that the individual is allowed for the year.
- Both earned and unearned income and gross income of more than the larger of earned income (but limited to the applicable basic standard deduction) or $600, plus any additional standard deduction that the individual is allowed for the year.

Thus, the filing requirement for a dependent who has no unearned income is the total of the *basic* standard deduction plus any *additional* standard deduction, which includes the additional deduction for blindness. For example, the 1994 filing requirement for a single dependent who is under 65 and not blind is $3,800, the amount of the basic standard deduction for 1994. The filing requirement for a single dependent under 65 and blind is $4,750 ($3,800 basic standard deduction + $950 additional standard deduction).

A self-employed individual with net earnings of $400 or more from a business or profession must file a tax return regardless of the amount of gross income.

Even though an individual has gross income below the filing level amounts and therefore does not owe any tax, he or she must file a return to obtain a tax refund of amounts withheld. A return is also necessary to obtain the benefits of the earned income credit allowed to taxpayers with little or no tax liability. Chapter 13 discusses the earned income credit.

Selecting the Proper Form

The 1994 tax forms had not been released at the date of publication of this text. The following comments apply to 1993 forms. It is possible that some provisions will change for the 1994 forms.

Individual taxpayers file a return on either Form 1040 (the long form), Form 1040A (the short form), or Form 1040EZ. Taxpayers who cannot use either Form 1040EZ or Form 1040A must use Form 1040. These forms are reproduced in Appendix B. Examine the forms to determine which form is appropriate for a particular taxpayer.

When and Where to File

Tax returns of individuals are due on or before the fifteenth day of the fourth month following the close of the tax year. For the calendar year taxpayer, the usual filing date is on or before April 15 of the following year.[24] When the due date falls on a Saturday, Sunday, or legal holiday, the last day for filing falls on the next business day. If the return is mailed to the proper address with sufficient postage and is postmarked on or before the due date, it is deemed timely filed.

If a taxpayer is unable to file the return by the specified due date, a four-month extension of time can be obtained by filing Form 4868 (Application for Automatic Extension of Time to File U.S. Individual Income Tax Return).[25] Further extensions may be granted by the IRS upon a showing of good cause by the taxpayer. For this purpose, Form 2688 (Application for Extension of Time to File U.S. Individual Income Tax Return) should be used. An extension of more than six months will not be granted if the taxpayer is in the United States.

Although obtaining an extension excuses a taxpayer from a penalty for failure to file, it does not insulate against the penalty for failure to pay.[26] If more tax is

---

[24] § 6072(a).
[25] Reg. § 1.6081–4.

[26] For an explanation of these penalties, refer to Chapter 1.

owed, the filing of Form 4868 should be accompanied by an additional remittance to cover the balance due.

The return should be sent or delivered to the Regional Service Center of the IRS for the area where the taxpayer lives.[27]

If an individual taxpayer needs to file an amended return (e.g., because of a failure to report income or to claim a deduction or tax credit), Form 1040X is filed. The form generally must be filed within three years of the filing date of the original return or within two years from the time the tax was paid, whichever is later.

FILING STATUS

The amount of tax will vary considerably depending on which Tax Rate Schedule is used. This is illustrated in the following example.

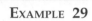

EXAMPLE 29 The following amounts of tax are computed using the 1994 Tax Rate Schedules for a taxpayer (or taxpayers in the case of a joint return) with $40,000 of taxable income (see Appendix A).

Filing Status	Amount of Tax
Single	$8,242.50
Married, filing joint return	6,260.00
Married, filing separate return	8,730.00
Head of household	7,235.00

Rates for Single Taxpayers

A taxpayer who is unmarried or separated from his or her spouse by a decree of divorce or separate maintenance and does not qualify for another filing status must use the rates for single taxpayers. Marital status is determined as of the last day of the tax year, except when a spouse dies during the year. In that case, marital status is determined as of the date of death. State law governs whether a taxpayer is considered married, divorced, or legally separated.

Under a special relief provision, however, married persons who live apart may be able to qualify as single. Married taxpayers who are considered single under the *abandoned spouse rules* are allowed to use the head of household rates. See the discussion of this filing status under Abandoned Spouse Rules later in the chapter.

Rates for Married Individuals

The joint return [Tax Rate Schedule Y, Code § 1(a)] was originally enacted in 1948 to establish equity between married taxpayers in common law states and those in community property states. Before the joint return rates were enacted, taxpayers in community property states were in an advantageous position relative to taxpayers in common law states because they could split their income. For instance, if one spouse earned $100,000 and the other spouse was not employed,

---

[27] The Regional Service Centers and the geographical area each covers can be found in *Your Federal Income Tax,* IRS Publication 17 for 1993.

each spouse could report $50,000 of income. Splitting the income in this manner caused the total income to be subject to lower marginal tax rates. Each spouse would start at the bottom of the rate structure.

Taxpayers in common law states did not have this income-splitting option, so their taxable income was subject to higher marginal rates. This inconsistency in treatment was remedied by the joint return provisions. The progressive rates in the joint return Tax Rate Schedule are constructed based on the assumption that income is earned equally by the two spouses.

If married individuals elect to file separate returns, each reports only his or her own income, exemptions, deductions, and credits, and each must use the Tax Rate Schedule applicable to married taxpayers filing separately. It is generally advantageous for married individuals to file a joint return, since the combined amount of tax is lower. However, special circumstances (e.g., significant medical expenses incurred by one spouse subject to the 7.5 percent limitation) may warrant the election to file separate returns. It may be necessary to compute the tax under both assumptions to determine the most advantageous filing status.

ETHICAL CONSIDERATIONS

The Marriage Penalty

When Congress enacted the rate structure available to those filing joint returns, it intended to favor married taxpayers. However, situations can exist where the parties would incur less tax if they were not married and filed separate returns. The additional tax that a joint return can cause, commonly called the **marriage penalty,** generally develops when *both* spouses have taxable income.

As an illustration, consider John and Betty. Both are employed and each earns taxable income of $55,000. If they *are not married* and file separate returns, each has a tax liability of $12,442.50, or a total of $24,885 ($12,442.50 × 2). If they are married, the filing of a joint return produces a tax of $26,405 on taxable income of $110,000 ($55,000 + $55,000). Thus, being married yields $1,520 ($26,405 – $24,885) more tax!

Should Congress tolerate a tax system that can impose a marriage penalty, making it cheaper for John and Betty to live together and avoid the altar?

The Code places some limitations on deductions, credits, etc., when married individuals file separately. If either spouse itemizes deductions, the other spouse must also itemize. Married taxpayers who file separately cannot take either of the following:

- The credit for child and dependent care expenses (in most instances).
- The earned income credit.

The joint return rates also apply for two years following the death of one spouse, if the surviving spouse maintains a household for a dependent child.[28] This is referred to as **surviving spouse** status.

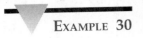

EXAMPLE 30

Fred dies in 1993 leaving Ethel with a dependent child. For the year of Fred's death (1993), Ethel files a joint return with Fred (presuming the consent of Fred's executor is obtained). For the next two years (1994 and 1995), Ethel, as a surviving spouse, may use the joint

---

[28]§ 2(a).

return rates. In subsequent years, Ethel may use the head-of-household rates if she continues to maintain a household as her home that is the domicile of the child. ▼

Rates for Heads of Household

Unmarried individuals who maintain a household for a dependent (or dependents) are entitled to use the **head-of-household** rates.[29] The tax liability using the head-of-household rates falls between the liability using the joint return Tax Rate Schedule and the liability using the Tax Rate Schedule for single taxpayers.

To qualify for head-of-household rates, a taxpayer must pay more than half the cost of maintaining a household as his or her home. The household must also be the principal home of a dependent relative as defined in § 152(a).[30] As a general rule, the dependent must live in the taxpayer's household for over half the year.

The general rule has two exceptions. One exception is that an unmarried child (child also means grandchild, stepchild, or adopted child) need not be a dependent in order for the taxpayer to qualify as a head of household. This exception also applies to a married child if the child is claimed by the noncustodial parent as a result of a written agreement between the custodial parent and the noncustodial parent (refer to Example 18).

EXAMPLE 31 Nancy maintains a household where she and Dan, her nondependent unmarried son, reside. Since Dan is not married, Nancy qualifies for the head-of-household rates. ▼

Another exception to the general rule is that head-of-household status may be claimed if the taxpayer maintains a separate home for his or her parent or parents if at least one parent qualifies as a dependent of the taxpayer.[31]

EXAMPLE 32 Rick, an unmarried individual, lives in New York City and maintains a household in Detroit for his dependent parents. Rick may use the head-of-household rates even though his parents do not reside in his New York home. ▼

TAX IN THE NEWS

TAXING WEDDED BLISS

How do you spell relief? This advertising slogan may have a new response: DIVORCE.

The penalty tax on marriage existed prior to the Revenue Reconciliation Act of 1993 (RRA of 1993). However, RRA of 1993 made it even worse for certain taxpayers. If the taxpayer and spouse each report taxable income of $250,000, the taxpayers can save $18,000 ($500,000 × 3.6%) by getting a divorce.

What produces this result? President Clinton wanted to impose a surtax of 3.6% on the income of millionaires. However, to raise the requisite amount of revenue from the surtax, it was necessary to define a "millionaire" in terms of taxable income of $250,000 and to ignore whether the amount was on a joint or a single taxpayer return.

SOURCE: Adapted from "Taxing Wedded Bliss," in Rob Norton, "Our Screwed-Up Tax Code," *Fortune,* September 6, 1993, p. 40. © 1993 Time Inc. All rights reserved.

---

[29] § 2(b).
[30] § 2(b)(1)(A)(i).

[31] § 2(b)(1)(B).

Abandoned Spouse Rules

When married persons file separate returns, several unfavorable tax consequences result. For example, the taxpayer must use the Tax Rate Schedule for married taxpayers filing separately. To mitigate such harsh treatment, Congress enacted provisions commonly referred to as the **abandoned spouse** rules. These rules allow a married taxpayer to file as a head of household if all of the following conditions are satisfied:

- The taxpayer does not file a joint return.
- The taxpayer paid more than one-half the cost of maintaining his or her home for the tax year.
- The taxpayer's spouse did not live in the home during the last six months of the tax year.
- The home was the principal residence of the taxpayer's child, stepchild, or adopted child for more than half the year.
- The taxpayer could claim the child, stepchild, or adopted child as a dependent.[32]

GAINS AND LOSSES FROM PROPERTY TRANSACTIONS—IN GENERAL

5   **LEARNING OBJECTIVE**
Obtain an overview of property transactions.

Gains and losses from property transactions are discussed in detail in Chapters 14 through 17. Because of their importance in the tax system, however, they are introduced briefly at this point.

When property is sold or otherwise disposed of, gain or loss may result. Such gain or loss has an effect on the income tax position of the party making the sale or other disposition when the *realized* gain or loss is *recognized* for tax purposes. Without realized gain or loss, generally, there can be no recognized gain or loss. The concept of realized gain or loss is expressed as follows:

$$\begin{array}{c} \text{Amount realized} \\ \text{from the sale} \end{array} - \begin{array}{c} \text{Adjusted basis of} \\ \text{the property} \end{array} = \begin{array}{c} \text{Realized gain} \\ \text{(or loss)} \end{array}$$

The amount realized is the selling price of the property less any costs of disposition (e.g., brokerage commissions) incurred by the seller. Simply stated, adjusted basis of the property is determined as follows:

Cost (or other original basis) at date of acquisition[33]

Add: Capital additions

Subtract: Depreciation (if appropriate) and other capital recoveries
              (see Chapter 8)

Equals: Adjusted basis at date of sale or other disposition

All realized gains are recognized (taxable) unless some specific part of the tax law provides otherwise (see Chapter 15 dealing with certain nontaxable exchanges). Realized losses may or may not be recognized (deductible) for tax purposes, depending on the circumstances involved. Generally, losses realized from the disposition of personal use property (property neither held for investment nor used in a trade or business) are not recognized.

---

[32] The dependency requirement does not apply, however, if the taxpayer could have claimed a dependency exemption except for the fact that the exemption was claimed by the noncustodial parent under a written agreement. Refer to Example 18 and the related discussion.

[33] Cost usually means purchase price plus expenses related to the acquisition of the property and incurred by the purchaser (e.g., brokerage commissions). For the basis of property acquired by gift or inheritance and other basis rules, see Chapter 14.

EXAMPLE 33

During the current year, Ted sells his sailboat (adjusted basis of $4,000) for $5,500. Ted also sells one of his personal automobiles (adjusted basis of $8,000) for $5,000. Ted's realized gain of $1,500 from the sale of the sailboat is recognized. On the other hand, the $3,000 realized loss on the sale of the automobile is not recognized and will not provide Ted with any deductible tax benefit. ▼

Once it has been determined that the disposition of property results in a recognized gain or loss, the next step is to classify the gain or loss as capital or ordinary. Although ordinary gain is fully taxable and ordinary loss is fully deductible, the same may not hold true for capital losses.

GAINS AND LOSSES FROM PROPERTY TRANSACTIONS—CAPITAL GAINS AND LOSSES

For tax years beginning after 1992, preferential tax treatment may apply to gains on capital assets that have been held for more than a year. The maximum rate on *net capital gain* (see Chapter 16 for details) is 28 percent. This provision could save 11.6 percent for taxpayers in the 39.6 percent bracket. Because of the potential tax savings on long-term capital gains, property transactions are important factors in effective tax planning.

DEFINITION OF A CAPITAL ASSET

Capital assets are defined in the Code as any property held by the taxpayer *other than* property listed in § 1221. The list in § 1221 includes inventory, accounts receivable, and depreciable property or real estate used in a business. Thus, the

---

TAX IN THE NEWS

LOSING A GOOD LOSS OR EFFECTIVELY USING THE ALTERNATIVE TAX

The highest tax rate for the individual taxpayer is 39.6%. The alternative rate on net capital gains is 28%. Therefore, the opportunity is provided to reduce the tax liability for high income taxpayers by having gains classified as long-term capital gains rather than as ordinary income or as short-term capital gains.

Another planning strategy is to offset capital losses against capital gains. Sometimes the conversion strategy (i.e., from ordinary income into capital gains) and the matching strategy (i.e., offsetting capital gains with capital losses) are not effectively used. This occurs when (1) short-term capital losses are used to offset long-term capital gains or (2) when a transaction which if delayed, and is not, would result in a short-term capital gain becoming a long-term capital gain.

By not recognizing the benefit of the 28% alternative tax rate, in the first case, the loss which has the potential for being deducted at a 39.6% (or 36% or 31%) rate offsets a gain which otherwise would be taxed at a 28% rate. In the second case, the gain is subject to a tax rate higher than 28% (i.e., 31%, 36%, or 39.6%) rather than being taxed at a 28% rate.

SOURCE: Information from Lynn Asinof, "Tricks to Avoid When Coming to Terms with the New Tax Law," *Wall Street Journal*, November 18, 1993, p. C1.

sale or exchange of assets in these categories usually results in ordinary income or loss treatment (see Chapter 17).

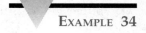

EXAMPLE 34

Kelly owns a pizza parlor. During the current year, he sells two automobiles. The first automobile, which had been used as a pizza delivery car for three years, was sold at a loss of $1,000. Because this automobile is an asset used in his business, Kelly has an ordinary loss deduction of $1,000, rather than a capital loss deduction. The second automobile, which Kelly had owned for two years, was his personal car. It was sold for a gain of $800. The personal car is a capital asset. Therefore, Kelly has a capital gain of $800. ▼

The principal capital assets held by an individual taxpayer include assets held for personal (rather than business) use, such as a personal residence or an automobile, and assets held for investment purposes (e.g., corporate securities and land).

COMPUTATION OF NET CAPITAL GAINS AND LOSSES

Capital gains and losses must be classified as short term (those on assets held for one year or less) and long term (those on assets held for more than one year). Short-term capital losses (STCL) are offset against short-term capital gains (STCG). The result is either net short-term capital gain (NSTCG) or net short-term capital loss (NSTCL).

Long-term capital losses (LTCL) are offset against long-term capital gains (LTCG), and the result is either net long-term capital gain (NLTCG) or net long-term capital loss (NLTCL).

Several combinations are possible after this first round of offsetting. For example, if the taxpayer has NSTCL and NLTCG, these amounts are offset. Likewise, if the taxpayer has NLTCL and NSTCG, a similar offsetting is required. In general, the offsetting continues as long as there is gain in any category and loss in any other category.

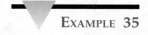

EXAMPLE 35

In the current year, Polly has the following capital gains and losses: STCL of $4,000, STCG of $3,000, LTCG of $6,000, and LTCL of $2,000. This results in NSTCL of $1,000 ($4,000 STCL – $3,000 STCG) and NLTCG of $4,000 ($6,000 LTCG – $2,000 LTCL). The $1,000 NSTCL is used to offset the $4,000 NLTCG, resulting in an excess of NLTCG over NSTCL of $3,000. ▼

CAPITAL LOSS LIMITATION

Capital losses are first offset against capital gains (as illustrated in Example 35). If, after this offsetting, an individual taxpayer has net capital losses, such losses are deductible as a deduction *for* AGI to a maximum of $3,000 per year. Any unused amounts are carried over for an indefinite period.

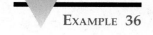

EXAMPLE 36

During the year, Tina has $1,000 of NLTCL and $2,000 of NSTCL. Tina's other income is $100,000. Her capital loss deduction for the year is $3,000, which consists of $2,000 NSTCL and $1,000 NLTCL. ▼

When a taxpayer has both short-term and long-term capital losses, and the losses together exceed $3,000, the short-term losses must be used first in applying the $3,000 limitation.

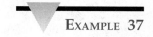

EXAMPLE 37

Matt has NSTCL of $2,500 and NLTCL of $5,000 for the year. His other income is $50,000. Matt uses the losses as follows:

NSTCL	$2,500
NLTCL	500
Maximum capital loss deduction	$3,000

The remaining NLTCL of $4,500 ($5,000 NLTCL – $500 used) may be carried forward for an indefinite period until used. See Chapter 16 for a detailed discussion of capital loss carryovers. ▼

Corporate Capital Losses

Corporate taxpayers may offset capital losses only against capital gains. Capital losses in excess of capital gains may not be used to reduce ordinary income of a corporation. A corporation's unused capital losses are subject to a carryback and carryover. Capital losses are initially carried back three years and then carried forward five years to offset capital gains that arise in those years. See Chapters 16 and 20 for a discussion of capital losses of corporate taxpayers.

TAX PLANNING CONSIDERATIONS

TAKING ADVANTAGE OF TAX RATE DIFFERENTIALS

It is natural for taxpayers to be concerned about the tax rates they are paying. How does a tax practitioner communicate information about rates to clients? There are several possibilities.

The marginal rate (refer to Examples 23 through 25) provides information that can help a taxpayer evaluate a particular course of action or structure a transaction in the most advantageous manner.

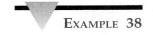

EXAMPLE 38

Ron, who is in the 28% marginal tax bracket for 1994, is considering the sale of corporate stock he has held as an investment for a $10,000 gain in December. If he sells the stock, his income tax increases by $2,800 ($10,000 gain × 28% marginal rate), and he has $7,200 of after-tax income ($10,000 – $2,800). ▼

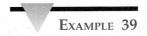

EXAMPLE 39

Assume the same facts as in Example 38 and that Ron plans to retire early in 1995. Upon retirement, Ron's only source of income will be nontaxable Social Security benefits and municipal bond interest. If Ron waits until 1995 to sell the stock, his tax on the gain is $1,500, and his after-tax income is $8,500 ($10,000 gain – $1,500 tax). By being aware of the effect of marginal tax rates, Ron can save $1,300 in tax. ▼

6   LEARNING OBJECTIVE
Identify tax planning opportunities associated with the individual tax formula.

The marginal rate analysis illustrated in Examples 38 and 39 for an income item can also help a taxpayer obtain the greatest tax benefit from a deductible expense. For example, a taxpayer who is in the 15 percent bracket this year and expects to be in the 31 percent bracket next year should, if possible, defer payment of deductible expenses until next year to maximize the tax benefit of the deduction.

A note of caution is in order with respect to shifting income and expenses between years. Congress has recognized the tax planning possibilities of such shifting and has enacted many provisions to limit a taxpayer's ability to do so. Some of these limitations on the shifting of income are discussed in Chapters 4, 5, and 18. Limitations that affect a taxpayer's ability to shift deductions are discussed in Chapters 6 through 11 and in Chapter 18.

A taxpayer's *effective rate* can be an informative measure of the effectiveness of tax planning. The effective rate is computed by dividing the taxpayer's tax liability by the total amount of income. A low effective rate can be considered an indication of effective tax planning.

One way of lowering the effective rate is to exclude income from the tax base. For example, a taxpayer might consider investing in tax-free municipal bonds rather than taxable corporate bonds. Although pre-tax income from corporate bonds is usually higher, after-tax income may be higher if the taxpayer invests in tax-free municipals.

Another way of lowering the effective rate is to make sure that the taxpayer's expenses and losses are deductible. For example, losses on investments in passive activities may not be deductible (see Chapter 11). Therefore, a taxpayer who plans to invest in an activity that will produce a loss in the early years should take steps to ensure that the business is treated as active rather than passive. Active losses are deductible while passive losses are not.

INCOME OF MINOR CHILDREN

Taxpayers can use several strategies to avoid or minimize the effect of the rules that tax the unearned income of certain minor children at the parents' rate. The kiddie tax rules do not apply once a child reaches age 14. Parents should consider giving a younger child assets that defer taxable income until the child reaches age 14. For example, U.S. government Series EE savings bonds can be used to defer income until the bonds are cashed in (see Chapter 4).

Growth stocks typically pay little in the way of dividends. However, the profit on an astute investment may more than offset the lack of dividends. The child can hold the stock until he or she reaches age 14. If the stock is sold then at a profit, the profit is taxed at the child's low rates.

Taxpayers in a position to do so can employ their children in their business and pay them a reasonable wage for the work they actually perform (e.g., light office help, such as filing). The child's earned income is sheltered by the standard deduction, and the parents' business is allowed a deduction for the wages. The kiddie tax rules have no effect on earned income, even if it is earned from the parents' business.

DEPENDENCY EXEMPTIONS

The Joint Return Test

A married person can be claimed as a dependent only if that individual does not file a joint return with his or her spouse. If a joint return has been filed, the damage may be undone if separate returns are substituted on a timely basis (on or before the due date of the return).

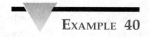

EXAMPLE 40

While preparing a client's 1993 income tax return on April 8, 1994, the tax practitioner discovered that the client's daughter filed a joint return with her husband in late January of 1994. Presuming the daughter otherwise qualifies as the client's dependent, the exemption is not lost if she and her husband file separate returns on or before April 15, 1994. ▼

An initial election to file a joint return must be considered carefully in any situation in which the taxpayers might later decide to amend their return and file separately. As indicated above, separate returns may be substituted for a joint return only if the amended returns are filed on or before the normal due date of the return. If the taxpayers in Example 40 attempt to file separate returns after April 15, 1994, the returns will not be accepted, and the joint return election is binding.[34]

Keep in mind that the filing of a joint return will not be fatal to the dependency exemption if the parties are filing solely to recover all income tax withholdings, neither is required to file a return, and no tax liability would exist on separate returns. The filing requirement for married persons filing separate returns applies. The application of these rules can be interesting when contrasting common law and community property jurisdictions.

---

[34] Reg. § 1.6013–1(a)(1).

EXAMPLE 41

In 1994, Abdel furnished 80% of the support of his son (Rashad) and daughter-in-law (Veneia). During the year, Veneia earned $2,500 from a part-time job. As a result, Veneia and Rashad filed a joint return to obtain a refund of all the income tax withheld. All parties reside in New York (a common law state). Presuming the joint return stands (refer to Example 40), Abdel cannot claim either Rashad or Veneia as his dependent. Although Veneia and Rashad filed a joint return to recover Veneia's withholdings, Veneia was required to file (she had gross income of $2,450 or more). ▼

EXAMPLE 42

Assume the same facts as in Example 41, except that all parties reside in Arizona (a community property state). Under these circumstances, Abdel may claim both Rashad and Veneia as dependents. Not only have they filed a joint return to recover all of Veneia's withholdings, but neither was required to file. Recall that in a community property state (unless otherwise altered by agreement between spouses, if permitted by state law), half of the wages of a spouse are attributable to the other spouse. Rashad and Veneia are treated as each having earned $1,250, which is less than the filing requirement for married persons filing separate returns. ▼

The Gross Income Test

The exception to the gross income test for a person under the age of 19 or a full-time student under the age of 24 applies only to a child of the taxpayer. The term *child* is limited to a son, stepson, daughter, stepdaughter, adopted son, or adopted daughter and may include a foster child.

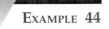

EXAMPLE 43

Assume the same facts as in Example 41, except that Rashad and Veneia (the son and daughter-in-law) do not file a joint return. Further assume that Veneia (the person who had gross income of $2,500) is a full-time student under age 24. Even though Abdel may claim Rashad as a dependent, Veneia does not qualify since she has gross income of $2,450 or more. The student exception to the gross income test does not apply because Veneia is not a *child* of Abdel. ▼

As was true with Example 42, the residence of the parties in a common law or a community property state can produce different results.

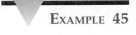

EXAMPLE 44

In 1994, Abdel furnishes 60% of the support of his son (Rashad) and daughter-in-law (Veneia), both over the age of 19. During the year, Veneia earns $5,000 from a part-time job, while Rashad is unemployed and not a full-time student. All parties reside in New Jersey (a common law state). Abdel may claim Rashad as a dependent, but Veneia does not qualify because of the gross income test. ▼

EXAMPLE 45

Assume the same facts as in Example 44, except that all parties reside in Washington (a community property state). Abdel may not claim either Rashad or Veneia as dependents because of the application of the gross income test. Each spouse is treated as having gross income of $2,500 (one-half of $5,000), which is not below the $2,450 filing level. ▼

The Support Test

Adequate records of expenditures for support should be maintained in the event a dependency exemption is questioned on audit by the IRS. The maintenance of adequate records is particularly important for exemptions arising from multiple support agreements.

Relationship to the Deduction for Medical Expenses

Generally, medical expenses are deductible only if they are paid on behalf of the taxpayer, his or her spouse, and their dependents. Since deductibility may rest on dependency status, planning is important in arranging multiple support agreements.

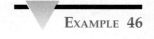

EXAMPLE 46

During the year, Zelda will be supported by her two sons (Vern and Vito) and her daughter (Maria). Each will furnish approximately one-third of the required support. If the parties decide that the dependency exemption should be claimed by the daughter under a multiple support agreement, any medical expenses incurred by Zelda should be paid by Maria. ▼

In planning a multiple support agreement, take into account which of the parties is most likely to exceed the 7.5 percent limitation (see Chapter 10). In Example 46, for instance, Maria might be a poor choice if she and her family do not expect to incur many medical and drug expenses of their own.

One exception permits the deduction of medical expenses paid on behalf of someone who is not a spouse or a dependent. If the person could be claimed as a dependent *except* for the gross income or joint return test, the medical expenses are, nevertheless, deductible. For additional discussion, see Chapter 10.

KEY TERMS

Abandoned spouse, 3–26	Marriage penalty, 3–24	Surviving spouse, 3–24
Dependency exemption, 3–11	Multiple support agreement, 3–12	Tax Rate Schedules, 3–16
Head of household, 3–25	Personal exemption, 3–10	Tax Table, 3–15
Itemized deductions, 3–6	Standard deduction, 3–6	Unearned income, 3–18

PROBLEM MATERIALS

DISCUSSION QUESTIONS

1. Rearrange the following components to show the formula for arriving at the amount of Federal taxable income:
   a. Deductions *for* AGI.
   b. The greater of the standard deduction or itemized deductions.
   c. Income (broadly conceived).
   d. Adjusted gross income.
   e. Exclusions.
   f. Personal and dependency exemptions.
   g. Gross income.

2. To obtain funds to buy a car, Demi borrows $6,000 from a bank. Her mother gives her the purchase balance of $7,000. What is Demi's gross income?

3. During the year, Leon had a salary of $32,000 and inherited $10,000 from his mother. He also won $3,000 in the state lottery. What is Leon's gross income?

4. During the year, Mildred's stock investment increased in value by $13,000. She also sold some stock for $4,500; the stock had cost $4,000. How do these facts affect Mildred's gross income?

5. What is the importance of determining adjusted gross income (AGI)?

6. For income tax purposes, what difference does it make whether an expense is *business* or *nonbusiness?*

X 7. Discuss the special limitations that apply to the personal exemption and standard deduction of an individual who can be claimed as a dependent of another taxpayer.

8. Discuss the marital status of the parties under the following circumstances:
   a. One spouse dies during the year.
   b. The spouses are divorced during the year.

9. Roy is a student at Lakeland Community College. He earned $6,500 during 1994. Under what circumstances will Roy's parents be allowed to claim him as a dependent?

10. If an individual who may qualify as a dependent does not spend funds that he or she has received (e.g., wages or Social Security benefits), are these unexpended amounts considered in applying the support test? Are they included in applying the gross income test?

11. Freda purchased a stereo system for her son Wes, age 16. The stereo was placed in Wes's room and used exclusively by him. Freda also purchased a new sports car, titled and registered in her own name, that was used 90% of the time by Wes. Should the cost of these items be considered as support in determining whether Freda may claim Wes as a dependent?

12. Carol provided 75% of the support of Debra, her niece. Debra was a full-time student during the year and earned $3,800 from a part-time job. Can Carol claim Debra as a dependent?

13. Cora's support is provided by her daughter (40%), her son (30%), and an unrelated friend (30%). Can Cora be claimed as a dependent by any of the individuals who contributed to her support? Explain.

X 14. When parents with children are divorced, who can claim the dependency exemptions? Do the parents have any flexibility in shifting the exemptions? Explain.

15. A taxpayer who is divorced continues to support his former mother-in-law. May he claim her as a dependent? Suppose she does not live with him. Does this make any difference?

16. Under what circumstances, if any, may a parent claim a married child as a dependent if the child files a joint return with his or her spouse?

17. Carlos is a U.S. citizen who lives and works in El Paso, Texas. He provides all of the support of his mother and two sisters who are Mexican citizens and residents.
   a. May Carlos claim his mother and sisters as dependents?
   b. Suppose the mother and sisters are citizens and residents of Honduras (not Mexico). Does this make a difference? Why or why not?

18. "Regardless of income, a person should be allowed to claim his or her personal and dependency exemptions." Do you agree with this statement? Why or why not?

19. Do taxpayers have a choice as to whether they can determine their income tax by using the tax *tables* or rate *schedules?*

X 20. What perceived abuse is the kiddie tax designed to correct?

21. A single individual age 65 or over and blind is required to file a Federal income tax return in 1994 if he or she has gross income of $7,200 or more (refer to Table 3–4).
   a. Explain how the $7,200 filing requirement was computed.
   b. In general, explain the effect of the additional standard deduction on the determination of gross income requirements for filing.

22. Jim and Jane are engaged to be married. Each has gross income of $40,000 for 1994. Assume that they plan to make use of the standard deduction and have no dependency exemptions or tax credits. If they marry before the end of 1994, what is the overall effect on the total Federal income taxes that they will pay?

23. Kim, age 67 and blind, earned $6,500 of interest and received Social Security benefits of $7,200 in 1994. Is Kim required to file a tax return?

24. Ali, age 67, is married to Leila, who is age 62 and blind. Ali and Leila file a joint return. How much gross income can they earn before they are required to file an income tax return for 1994?

25. Alicia, a high school student, earned $1,000 from a summer job during the current year. Alicia is aware that this amount is below the income level that will require her to file a return and therefore does not plan to file. Do you have any advice for Alicia?

26. What is the marriage penalty? When might it develop?

27. Ida's husband dies in 1994. Ida is planning to file as a surviving spouse for tax years 1994 through 1996. Comment regarding Ida's expectations.

28. What purpose is served by the abandoned spouse rules?

29. During the current year, Andre had a $5,000 long-term capital loss on the sale of common stock he had held as an investment. In addition, he had a $3,000 loss on the sale of his personal automobile, which he had owned for a year. How do these transactions affect Andre's taxable income?

30. Ten years ago, Ann purchased a personal residence for $140,000. In the current year, she sells the residence for $105,000. Ann's friend tells her she has a recognizable loss of $35,000 from the sale. Do you agree with the friend's comment? Elaborate.

31. List some assets that are not capital assets and some that are capital assets. Why is it important to determine whether an asset is an ordinary asset or a capital asset?

32. During the current year, Kate earned a salary of $40,000. She sold 20 shares of Robin Corporation common stock at a loss of $2,500 and sold her personal automobile at a gain of $1,500. Compute Kate's AGI.

33. If Cole has a salary of $41,000, net short-term capital gain of $1,000, and net long-term capital losses of $4,500, what is his AGI?

PROBLEMS

34. Compute the taxpayer's taxable income for 1994 in each of the following cases:
    a. Jack is married and files a joint return with his wife Alice. Jack and Alice have two dependent children. They have AGI of $50,000 and $8,300 of itemized deductions.
    b. Pete is an unmarried head of household with two dependents. He has AGI of $45,000 and itemized deductions of $5,200.
    c. Iris, age 22, is a full-time college student who is claimed as a dependent by her parents. She earns $3,900 from a part-time job and has interest income of $1,500.
    d. Matt, age 20, is a full-time college student who is claimed as a dependent by his parents. He earns $2,500 from a part-time job and has interest income of $4,100. His itemized deductions related to the investment income are $700.

Note: Problems 35 and 36 can be solved by referring to Figure 3–1, Exhibits 3–1 through 3–3, Tables 3–1 and 3–2, and the discussion under Deductions for Adjusted Gross Income in this chapter.

35. Compute taxable income for 1994 for Ned on the basis of the following information:

Filing status	Head of household
Salary	$45,000
Inheritance	20,000
Capital loss	2,500
Deductible contribution to IRA	2,000
Charitable contributions	7,000
Medical expenses	5,000
State and local income taxes	2,800
Interest on home mortgage	5,000
Number of dependents	2
Age	51

36. Compute taxable income for 1994 for Lori on the basis of the following information:

Filing status	Single
Salary	$57,000
Alimony received	10,000
Child support payments received	9,000
Gain from illegal activities	8,000
Deductible contribution to IRA	2,000
Moving expenses (deductible portion)	6,500
Theft loss (deductible portion)	5,100
State and local income taxes	900
Interest on home mortgage	3,900
Number of dependents	2
Age	34

37. Determine the amount of the standard deduction allowed for 1994 in each of the following situations:
    a. Lori, who is 17 years old and single, is claimed as a dependent on her parents' income tax return. During the year, she has interest income of $1,100 from a savings account and earns $1,200 from a job as a part-time sales clerk.
    b. Assume the same facts as in (a) except that Lori's income as a sales clerk is $500 (not $1,200).
    c. Assume the same facts as in (a) except that Lori's income as a sales clerk is $4,000 (not $1,200).

38. Determine the amount of the standard deduction allowed for 1994 in each of the following situations:
    a. Jesse, who is 69 years old and a widower, is claimed as a dependent on his daughter's income tax return. During the year, he earns $400 from a part-time job at a local supermarket.
    b. Assume the same facts as in (a) except the income is $800 (not $400).

X 39. Determine the correct number of personal and dependency exemptions in each of the following independent situations:
    a. Rick, age 66 and disabled, is a widower who maintains a home for his unmarried daughter who is 24 years old. The daughter earned $3,000 and attends college on a part-time basis. Rick provides more than 50% of her support.
    b. Wes, a bachelor age 45, provides more than 50% of the support of his father, age 70. Wes's father had gross income of $3,500 from a part-time job.
    c. Dan, age 45, is married and has two dependent foster children who live with him and are totally supported by Dan. One of the foster children, age 14, had $2,200 of gross income. Dan and his spouse file a joint return.
    d. Leo, age 67, is married and has a married daughter, age 22. His daughter attended college on a full-time basis and was supported by Leo. The daughter filed a joint return with her spouse. Leo filed a joint return with his spouse, age 62.

40. Compute the number of personal and dependency exemptions in the following independent situations:
    a. Mark, a single individual, provides 60% of the support of his mother, age 69. Mark's mother received dividend income of $1,000 and $1,500 in Social Security benefits.
    b. Adam, a married individual filing a joint return, provides 100% of the support of his son, age 21, who is a part-time student. Adam's son earned $2,500 during the year from part-time employment.
    c. Vern is divorced and provides $2,000 of child support for his child who is living with her mother, who provides support of $2,500. An agreement executed in 1986 between Vern and his former wife provides that the noncustodial parent is to receive the dependency exemption. Vern's former wife provides him with a completed Form 8332.

41. Carlos and Alicia, who are married and file a joint return, have four dependent children. They have AGI of $193,700. What is their allowable exemption deduction for 1994?

42. Ted and Sara are married and have no dependents. Ted has AGI of $92,300, and Sara has AGI of $67,000 in 1994.
    a. Compute the exemption deduction for Ted and Sara if they file a joint return.
    b. Compute the exemption deductions for Ted and Sara if they file separate returns.
    c. Explain why your answers to parts (a) and (b) differ.

43. Fred and Eve are married and file a joint return. Fred is 66 years of age, and Eve is 65. Fred's salary for 1994 was $33,000, and Eve earned $41,000. Eve won $10,000 in the state lottery and inherited $25,000 from her aunt. Fred incurred a $2,500 capital loss on stock he sold in December. Fred and Eve provided 90% of the support for Cora, their 23-year-old daughter, who is a full-time student. Fred and Eve also provided over half of the support of Jim, who is Cora's husband. Jim joined the army in March and earned $2,100. Cora and Jim filed a joint return. Fred and Eve also provide over half of the support of Eve's mother, Abbey, who lives in a nursing home. Abbey earned interest of $2,200 on a savings account and received Social Security benefits of $6,400. Fred and Eve had total itemized deductions of $7,800.
    a. Compute taxable income for Fred and Eve for 1994.
    b. Assume the same facts, except that Jim earned $6,100 in 1994. Compute taxable income for Fred and Eve for 1994.

44. Bob, age 13, is a full-time student supported by his parents who claim him on their tax return for 1994. Bob's parents present you with the following information and ask that you prepare Bob's 1994 Federal income tax return:

Wages from summer job	$2,100
Interest on savings account at First National Bank	950
Interest on City of Chicago bonds Bob received as a gift from his grandfather two years ago	750
Dividend from Owl Corporation	200

    a. What is Bob's taxable income for 1994?
    b. Bob's parents file a joint return for 1994 on which they report taxable income of $66,000. Compute Bob's 1994 tax liability.

45. Walter and Nancy provide 70% of the support of their daughter (age 21) and son-in-law (age 22). The son-in-law (John) is a full-time student at a local university, while the daughter (Irene) holds various part-time jobs from which she earns $4,500. Walter and Nancy engage you to prepare their tax return for 1994. During a meeting with them in late March of 1995, you learn that John and Irene have already filed a joint return in order to obtain a refund of Irene's income tax withholdings. What tax advice would you give based on the following assumptions:
    a. All parties live in Louisiana (a community property state).
    b. All parties live in New Jersey (a common law state).

46. Don is a wealthy executive who had taxable income of $200,000 in 1994. He is considering transferring title in a duplex he owns to his son Sam, age 16. Sam has no other income and is claimed as a dependent by Don. Net rent income from the duplex is $10,000 a year, which Sam will be encouraged to place in a savings account. Will the family save income taxes in 1994 if Don transfers title in the duplex to Sam? Explain.

47. Compute the 1994 tax liability for each of the following taxpayers:
    a. Norm and Nancy, both age 46, are married, have two dependent children, and file a joint return. Their combined salaries totaled $75,000. They had deductions *for* AGI of $6,000 and total itemized deductions of $8,100.
    b. Juan, age 45, is single and has no dependents. He had a salary of $62,000, deductions *for* AGI of $3,000, and total itemized deductions of $7,100.
    c. David and Susan, both age 65, are married, have no dependents, and file a joint return. Their combined salaries were $92,000. They had deductions *for* AGI of $2,000 and itemized deductions of $17,000.

48. Compute the 1994 tax liability for each of the following taxpayers:
    a. Ed, age 65, is single and has no dependents. He earned $94,260, had deductions *for* AGI of $4,000, and had itemized deductions of $3,700.
    b. George, who is single and has no dependents, has taxable income of $85,000.
    c. Pam, who is single and has no dependents, has taxable income of $95,000.
    d. Gus and Grace, both age 34, have one dependent child, Gail, age 10. Gus and Grace have taxable income of $96,000. Gail receives interest income of $3,000 during the year. Compute Gail's tax liability.

49. Peter, age 12, is claimed as a dependent on his parents' 1994 Federal income tax return, on which they reported taxable income of $95,000. During the summer, Peter earned $2,500 from a job as a model. His only other income consisted of $1,700 in interest on a savings account. Compute Peter's taxable income and tax liability.

50. Carmen, who is 12 years old, is claimed as a dependent on her parents' tax return. During 1994, she received $12,200 in dividends and interest and incurred itemized deductions of $800 related to the management of her portfolio assets. She also earned $2,000 wages from a part-time job. Compute the amount of income that is taxed at her parents' rate.

51. Ellen, who is 14 years old, is claimed as a dependent on her parents' tax return. During 1994, she received $9,000 in dividends and interest and incurred itemized deductions of $800 related to the management of her portfolio assets. She also earned $1,700 wages from a part-time job. Compute the amount of income that is taxed at her own rate.

52. Bruce and Wanda are young professionals who are employed in well-paying jobs. They have been dating each other for several years and are considering getting married in December 1994 or January 1995. For 1994, their respective AGIs are $65,000 and $68,000. They anticipate earning the same income in 1995. In both years, they will claim the standard deduction.
    a. What is Bruce and Wanda's income tax liability if they marry in 1994 and file a joint return?
    b. What is their income tax liability if they marry in 1994 and file separate returns?
    c. What is their income tax liability if they do not marry in 1994?
    d. Do you have any suggestions as to when Bruce and Wanda should get married?

    Compute the tax liability using the Tax Rate Schedules in Appendix A.

53. Which of the following individuals are required to file a tax return for 1994? Should any of these individuals file a return even if filing is not required? Why?
    a. Diego is married and files a joint return with his spouse, Juanita. Both Diego and Juanita are 47 years old. Their combined gross income was $9,000.
    b. Patsy is a dependent child under age 19 who received $1,000 in wages from a part-time job and $1,900 of dividend income.
    c. Dana is single and is 67 years old. His gross income from wages was $5,800.
    d. Jeff is a self-employed single individual with gross income of $4,400 from an unincorporated business. Business expenses amounted to $3,900.

54. Which of the following taxpayers must file a Federal income tax return for 1994?
    a. Bob, age 19, is a full-time college student. He is claimed as a dependent by his parents. He earned $3,900 wages during the year.
    b. Anita, age 12, is claimed as a dependent by her parents. She earned interest of $900 during the year.
    c. Earl, age 16, is claimed as a dependent by his parents. He earned wages of $2,700 and interest of $1,100 during the year.
    d. Karen, age 16 and blind, is claimed as a dependent by her parents. She earned wages of $2,600 and interest of $1,200 during the year.
    e. Pat, age 17, is claimed as a dependent by her parents. She earned interest of $300 during the year. In addition, she earned $550 during the summer operating her own business at the beach, where she painted caricatures of her customers.

55. Can Ron use Tax Rate Schedule Z (head of household) in 1994?
    a. Ron's wife died in 1993. Ron maintained a household for his two dependent children during 1994 and provided over one-half of the cost of the household.

b. Ron is unmarried and lives in an apartment. He supported his aged parents, who live in a separate home. Ron provides over one-half of the funds used to maintain his parents' home. Ron also claimed his parents as dependents since he provided more than one-half of their support during the year.

c. Ron is unmarried and maintains a household (over one-half of the cost) for his 18-year-old married daughter and her husband. His daughter filed a joint return with her husband solely for the purpose of obtaining a refund of income taxes that were withheld. Neither Ron's daughter nor her husband was required to file a return.

56. Indicate in each of the following situations which of the Tax Rate Schedules Vicki should use for calendar year 1994:

a. Vicki, the mother and sole support of her three minor children, was abandoned by her husband in late 1993.

b. Vicki is a widow whose husband died in 1993. Vicki furnishes all of the support of her household, which includes two dependent children.

c. Vicki furnishes all of the support of her parents, who live in their own home in a different city. Vicki's parents qualify as her dependents. Vicki is not married.

d. Vicki's household includes an unmarried stepchild, age 18, who has gross income of $6,000 during the year. Vicki furnishes all of the cost of maintaining the household. Vicki is not married.

57. Henry died on January 1, 1992. He was survived by his wife, Sue, and their 19-year-old son, Mike, who was a college sophomore. Mike was a full-time student in 1993 and earned $3,000 for the year. In 1994, Mike reduced his school load and became a part-time student. He earned $5,200 in 1994. Mike continues to live with his mother, who provides over half of his support. What is Sue's filing status in 1992, 1993, and 1994?

58. Tracy, age 66, is a widow. Her husband died in 1992. Tracy maintains a home in which she and her 28-year-old son reside. Her son Gary is a piano player at a local nightclub, where he earned $12,000 during 1994. Gary contributed $3,000 of his income toward household expenses and put the remainder in a savings account that he used to return to college full-time to pursue a master's degree in music starting in August 1994. Tracy contributed $12,000 toward household expenses. What is the most favorable filing status available to Tracy for 1994, and how many exemptions may she claim?

59. In the current year, Jill earned a salary of $50,000 and had a long-term loss of $6,000 on the sale of stock. She also had a $2,500 short-term gain on the sale of land held as an investment and a $2,000 gain on the sale of her personal automobile. She had owned the automobile for two years. Compute Jill's AGI.

60. Hazel, age 39, is single. She maintains a household that is the residence of her two children, Fran, age 8, and Sam, age 11. The children are claimed as dependents by their father, who provides $2,000 child support for each of them. During 1994, Hazel earned a salary of $100,000. Other items that affected her taxable income are as follows:

Total itemized deductions	$ 6,500
Capital gains	
Short-term	1,200
Long-term	3,500
Capital losses	
Short-term	(900)
Long-term	(7,600)
Interest income	2,100

Hazel provides all the support for her mother, Mabel, who lives in a nursing home. Mabel qualifies as Hazel's dependent.

a. Compute Hazel's AGI and taxable income for 1994.

b. What is Hazel's filing status for 1994?

61. Tina, age 61, earned a salary of $63,000 in 1994. She sold common stock that she had owned for 10 months at a loss of $1,500 and sold a fishing boat that she had bought in 1988 at a loss of $4,000. Tina also sold an antique desk for a gain of $10,000. She acquired the desk in 1953. Compute Tina's AGI for 1994.

62. Lee is a single, cash basis calendar year taxpayer. For the years 1993 and 1994, he expects AGI of $20,000 and the following itemized deductions:

Church pledge	$2,300
Interest on home mortgage	1,200
Property taxes	500

Discuss the tax consequences of the alternatives presented below. Assume for purposes of this problem that the interest and taxes are deductible in the year of payment.
a. In 1993, Lee pays his church pledge for 1993 and 1994 ($2,300 for each year).
b. Lee does nothing different.

63. Gina, a cash basis taxpayer, is single and has no dependents. She provides you with the following estimates for 1993 and 1994:

	1993	**1994**
Adjusted gross income	$56,000	$60,000
Charitable contributions	2,200	2,400
Interest on home mortgage	1,000	1,200
Property taxes	700	900

a. Can Gina decrease taxable income over the two-year period by prepaying her 1994 charitable contributions in 1993?
b. Advise Gina on when she should pay her charitable contributions. Compute the amount of Federal income tax she can save if she follows your recommendation.

64. Tom and Janet are married and have no dependents. Tom has AGI of $40,000, medical expenses of $5,400, and other itemized deductions of $2,800. Janet has AGI of $50,000, medical expenses of $1,400, and other itemized deductions of $2,800. Should Tom and Janet file a joint return or separate returns for 1994? Support your answer by computing tax liabilities.

65. Leon and Grace are married and have no dependents. For 1994, Leon has AGI of $49,300 and itemized deductions of $2,800. Grace has AGI of $51,900 and itemized deductions of $7,800.
a. Compute the tax liability for Leon and Grace if they file a joint return.
b. Compute the lowest combined tax liability for Leon and Grace if they file separate returns.

CUMULATIVE PROBLEMS

66. Vincent and Myrna Keller, both age 26, are married and have one daughter, Lana, who was born on December 28, 1993. Vincent's Social Security number is 266–77–2345, and Myrna's is 467–33–1289. They live at 403 Teal Street, Columbus, OH 43211.

Vincent is a claims adjuster for a large casualty insurance company, while Myrna is a full-time graduate student at Ohio State University. For 1993, Vincent earns $49,000 ($5,500 withheld for Federal income taxes). Myrna receives $3,500 as a gift from her father to help pay education expenses.

The Kellers have the following itemized deductions for 1993:

Charitable contributions	$ 500
State and local income taxes	2,000
Real estate taxes	1,800
Home mortgage interest	3,600

Part 1—Tax Computation

Complete a joint Federal income tax return for the Kellers for tax year 1993. Neither wishes to contribute to the Presidential Election Campaign Fund. If they have overpaid, they want the amount refunded. Use Form 1040 and Schedule A. Suggested software (if available): *TurboTax* or *MacInTax* for tax return or WFT tax planning software.

Part 2—Tax Planning

For tax year 1994, the Kellers will have the following changes in their tax position:

- Vincent has been awarded a 10% salary increase (effective January 1, 1994).

- Myrna expects to receive approximately the same amount of gifts from her father. Also, her uncle's estate will finally be settled, and she will receive an inheritance of about $40,000 worth of marketable securities.

- Myrna will receive $4,200 from a research assistantship she accepted from Ohio State University. (This amount does not qualify as a nontaxable scholarship.)

Write a letter to the Kellers concerning the tax ramifications of the changes that will take place in 1994. Advise them on any potential problems that could arise regarding the payment of sufficient taxes. You are the tax adviser for Myrna's parents and have been asked by them to write the letter.

67. Horace and Marcia Wall, 4030 Beachside Drive, Longboat Key, FL 33548, filed a joint Federal income tax return for 1992. Horace, age 64, is a manager for a Motel 6. His Social Security number is 344–99–7642. Marcia, who is 66, is a manager at Marie's Beauty Salon. Her Social Security number is 354–33–7890. The Walls come to you in early December 1993 seeking tax advice.

The Walls have received or will receive the following amounts during 1993:
a. Horace's salary, $50,000.
b. Marcia's salary, $44,000.
c. Interest on bonds issued by the City of Sarasota, $1,100.
d. Life insurance proceeds received on the death of Horace's mother, $90,000.
e. Value of property inherited from Horace's mother, $150,000.

In examining the Walls' records, you find the following items of possible tax consequence (all applicable to 1993):

f. They had itemized deductions as follows:

- Real estate taxes, $4,300.

- Home mortgage interest, $4,700.

- Charitable contributions (cash), $4,000.

g. Horace's employer withheld $7,400 of Federal income tax, and Marcia's employer withheld $6,300. In addition, they made estimated tax payments of $2,000.

The Walls' son Steven (S.S. no. 371–85–0033) lived with them during 1993 except for nine months during which he was away at college. Steven, age 23, is a law student and plans to graduate in 1995. During the summer, Steven earned $2,500 and used the money he earned to pay for his college expenses. His parents contributed $3,000 toward his support.

Part 1—Tax Computation

Compute the following amounts for the Walls if they file a joint return for 1993: gross income, adjusted gross income, taxable income, and net tax payable or refund due. Both wish to contribute $3 to the Presidential Election Campaign Fund. If you use tax forms for your computations, you will need Form 1040 and Schedule A. Suggested software (if available): *TurboTax* or *MacInTax* for tax return or WFT tax planning software.

Part 2—Tax Planning

Assume, instead the Walls are contemplating a divorce and would prefer not to file jointly. They have asked your firm to compute their tax liabilities if they file separately rather than jointly. If they file separately, they will split itemized deductions and estimated tax payments equally. Each spouse will report one-half of the bond interest since they owned the City of Sarasota bonds jointly (refer to item c). Marcia will claim an exemption for Steven (assume he qualifies as her dependent). Will the Walls have to pay more tax if they file separately?

a. Write a letter to the Walls explaining the result.
b. Prepare a memo for your firm's files.

Suggested software (if available): *TurboTax* or *MacInTax* for tax return or WFT tax planning software.

RESEARCH PROBLEMS

Research Problem 1.   Jerry, who is 13 years old, earned $1,200 from a paper route during 1994. In addition, he had two savings accounts. He earned interest of $1,200 on an account set up for him, in his name, by his grandparents. Jerry also earned $450 on a savings account he set up with earnings from his paper route over the last three years. How much of Jerry's interest income is treated as unearned income taxable at his parents' rate?

Research Problem 2.   In the state of Texas, a lawsuit was instituted charging that the state schools for the mentally retarded furnished inadequate, unsafe, and improper care, treatment, and education. As part of the settlement of this suit, the Texas Department of Mental Health offered to pay a fixed daily amount to third-party providers of these services. Under this arrangement, the taxpayers received $16,425 during the year for the care of their mentally retarded daughter. This amount covered a daily per diem for food and board, medical expenses, cost of special food, clothing, transportation, special laundry, home repairs, and other living expenses. The daughter lived with the taxpayers and during the year attended classes at a special school operated by the local school district.

Although the taxpayers did not pay for more than 50% of their daughter's support, they claimed her as a dependent for the year. The taxpayers contend that the amount they received from the state is a scholarship and, therefore, should not be taken into account in applying the support test. The IRS disagrees. What result?

Partial list of research aids:
§ 152(d).
Rev.Rul. 61–186, 1961–2 C.B. 30.
Rev.Rul. 64–221, 1964–2 C.B. 46.

Research Problem 3.   Jerry maintained a home in which he, his daughter (Fran), and his son-in-law (Ed) lived. Ed died in June 1991, and Fran continued to reside with Jerry for the rest of the year. Fran filed a joint return with Ed for 1991. Jerry filed his 1991 tax return as a head of household. The IRS claims that Jerry was not entitled to head-of-household status because Fran was considered married as of the end of 1991. Should Jerry accept the IRS position and file as a single taxpayer, or should he challenge them for the right to file as a head of household?

Partial list of research aids:
Hilliard v. U.S., 63–1 USTC ¶9126, 10 AFTR2d 6135, 310 F.2d 631 (CA–6, 1962).
§ 2(b).

II

GROSS INCOME

P art II presents the income component of the basic tax model. Included in this presentation are the determination of what is income and the statutory exclusions that are permitted in calculating gross income. Because the taxpayer's accounting method and accounting period affect when income is reported, an introductory discussion of these topics is also included.

Chapter 4

Gross Income: Concepts and Inclusions

Chapter 5

Gross Income: Exclusions

GROSS INCOME: CONCEPTS AND INCLUSIONS

LEARNING OBJECTIVES

After completing Chapter 4, you should be able to:

1. Explain the concepts of gross income and realization and distinguish between the economic, accounting, and tax concepts of gross income.

2. Describe the cash and accrual methods of accounting and the related effects of the choice of taxable year.

3. Identify who should pay the tax on a particular item of income in various situations.

4. Apply the Internal Revenue Code provisions on alimony, loans made at below-market interest rates, annuities, prizes and awards, group term life insurance, unemployment compensation, and Social Security benefits.

5. Identify tax planning strategies for minimizing gross income.

Gross Income—What Is It?, 4–3

Definition, 4–3

Economic and Accounting Concepts, 4–3

Comparison of the Accounting and Tax Concepts of Income, 4–5

Form of Receipt, 4–6

Recovery of Capital Doctrine, 4–6

Year of Inclusion, 4–6

Taxable Year, 4–6

Accounting Methods, 4–7

Exceptions Applicable to Cash Basis Taxpayers, 4–9

Exceptions Applicable to Accrual Basis Taxpayers, 4–12

Income Sources, 4–14

Personal Services, 4–14

Income from Property, 4–15

Income Received by an Agent, 4–16

Income from Partnerships, S Corporations, Trusts, and Estates, 4–16

Income in Community Property States, 4–17

Items Specifically Included in Gross Income, 4–19

Alimony and Separate Maintenance Payments, 4–19

Imputed Interest on Below-Market Loans, 4–23

Income from Annuities, 4–27

Prizes and Awards, 4–30

Group Term Life Insurance, 4–31

Unemployment Compensation, 4–33

Social Security Benefits, 4–33

Tax Planning Considerations, 4–35

Nontaxable Economic Benefits, 4–35

Tax Deferral, 4–35

Shifting Income to Relatives, 4–37

Accounting for Community Property, 4–38

Alimony, 4–38

Mr. Zarin lost over $2,500,000 of his own money gambling. The casino then allowed him to gamble on credit. After several months, his liability to the casino totaled more than $3,400,000. Following protracted negotiations, the casino agreed to settle its claim against Mr. Zarin for a mere $500,000. Although Mr. Zarin had paid for gambling losses of $3,000,000, the IRS had the audacity to ask him to pay tax on $2,900,000; that is, the amount the casino marked down his account.[1] Mr. Zarin undoubtedly found it difficult to understand how he could be deemed to have income in this situation.

Given an understanding of the income tax formula, though, it is not so apparent that Mr. Zarin did not have income from the "free" gambling he enjoyed. The starting point in the formula is the determination of gross income rather than "net income." Once gross income is determined, the next step is to determine the allowable deductions. In Mr. Zarin's way of thinking, these steps were collapsed.

This chapter is concerned with the first step in the computation of taxable income—the determination of gross income. Questions that are addressed include the following:

- What: What is income?
- When: In which tax period is the income recognized?
- Who: Who must include the item of income in gross income?

The Code provides an all-inclusive definition of gross income in § 61. Chapter 5 presents items of income that are specifically excluded from gross income (exclusions).

---

[1] *Zarin v. Comm.*, 90–2 USTC ¶50,530, 916 F.2d 110, 66 AFTR2d 90–5679, (CA–3, 1990).

GROSS INCOME—WHAT IS IT?

DEFINITION

1   **LEARNING OBJECTIVE**
Explain the concepts of gross income and realization and distinguish between the economic, accounting, and tax concepts of gross income.

Section 61(a) of the Internal Revenue Code defines the term **gross income** as follows:

> Except as otherwise provided in this subtitle, gross income means all income from whatever source derived.

This definition is derived from the language of the Sixteenth Amendment to the Constitution.

Supreme Court decisions have made it clear that all sources of income are subject to tax unless Congress specifically excludes the type of income received:

> The starting point in all cases dealing with the question of the scope of what is included in "gross income" begins with the basic premise that the purpose of Congress was to use the full measure of its taxing power.[2]

Although at this point we know that *income* is to be broadly construed, we still do not have a satisfactory definition of the term *income*. Congress left it to the judicial and administrative branches to thrash out the meaning of income. Early in the development of the income tax law, a choice was made between two competing models: economic income and accounting income.

ECONOMIC AND ACCOUNTING CONCEPTS

The term **income** is used in the Code but is not separately defined. Thus, early in the history of our tax laws, the courts were required to interpret "the commonly understood meaning of the term which must have been in the minds of the people when they adopted the Sixteenth Amendment to the Constitution."[3] In determining the definition of income, the Supreme Court rejected the economic concept of income.

Economists measure income (**economic income**) by first determining the fair market value of the individual's net assets at the beginning and end of the year (change in net worth). Then, to arrive at economic income, this change in net worth is added to the goods and services that person actually consumed during the period. Economic income also includes imputed values for such items as the rental value of an owner-occupied home and the value of food a taxpayer might grow for personal consumption.[4]

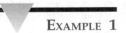
EXAMPLE 1

Helen's economic income is calculated as follows:

Fair market value of Helen's assets on December 31, 1994	$220,000	
Less liabilities on December 31, 1994	(40,000)	
Net worth on December 31, 1994		$180,000

---

[2] *James v. U.S.*, 61–1 USTC ¶9449, 7 AFTR2d 1361, 81 S.Ct. 1052 (USSC, 1961).

[3] *Merchants Loan and Trust Co. v. Smietanka*, 1 USTC ¶42, 3 AFTR 3102, 41 S.Ct. 386 (USSC, 1921).

[4] See Henry C. Simons, *Personal Income Taxation* (Chicago: University of Chicago Press, 1933), Ch. 2–3.

Fair market value of Helen's assets on January 1, 1994	$200,000	
Less liabilities on January 1, 1994	(80,000)	
Net worth on January 1, 1994		120,000
Increase in net worth		$ 60,000
Consumption		
Food, clothing, and other personal expenditures		25,000
Imputed rental value of Helen's home she owns and occupies		12,000
Economic income		$ 97,000

▼

The need to value assets annually would make compliance with the tax law burdensome and would cause numerous controversies between the taxpayer and the IRS over valuation. In addition, using market values to determine income for tax purposes could result in liquidity problems. That is, the taxpayer's assets may increase in value even though they are not readily convertible into the cash needed to pay the tax (e.g., commercial real estate). Thus, the IRS, Congress, and the courts have rejected the economic concept of income as impractical.

In contrast, the accounting concept of income is founded on the realization principle.[5] According to this principle, income (**accounting income**) is not recognized until it is realized. For realization to occur, (1) an exchange of goods or services must take place between the accounting entity and some independent,

---

TAX IN THE NEWS

IRS CRACKS DOWN ON SALES OF FREQUENT FLIER MILES

Employees often accumulate frequent flier miles for business trips paid for by their employer. The employees then use the frequent flier miles credits for vacations. Although the value of any credits received by employees while traveling for their employer seems to fit into the concept of gross income, the IRS to date has not attempted to value the credits. Reasons for not doing so include the difficulty of valuing the credits and in determining when the income should be recognized (e.g., when the credits are accumulated or when they are used to purchase a ticket).

Although frequent flier certificates are supposed to be nontransferable, a market for the certificates has developed. At least one office of the IRS has begun taxing employees who sell their frequent flier certificates. Many employees anxiously await IRS guidance on this issue.

SOURCE: Information from "Florida IRS Cracks Down on Sale of Air Flier Miles," *Wall Street Journal* (West Coast Edition), March 23, 1993, p. C20.

---

[5]See the American Accounting Association Committee Report on the "Realization Concept," *The Accounting Review* (April 1965): 312–322.

external group, and (2) in the exchange the accounting entity must receive assets that are capable of being objectively valued. Thus, the mere appreciation in the market value of assets before a sale or other disposition is not sufficient to warrant income recognition. In addition, the imputed savings that arise when an individual creates assets for his or her own use (e.g., feed grown for a farmer's own livestock) are not income because no exchange has occurred. The courts and the IRS have ruled, however, that embezzlement proceeds and buried treasures found satisfy the realization requirement and, therefore, must be recognized as income.[6]

The Supreme Court expressed an inclination toward the accounting concept of income when it adopted the realization requirement in *Eisner v. Macomber:*[7]

> Income may be defined as the gain derived from capital, from labor, or from both combined, provided it is understood to include profit gained through a sale or conversion of capital assets. . . . Here we have the essential matter: not a gain accruing to capital; not a *growth* or *increment* of value *in* investment; but a gain, a profit, something of exchangeable value, *proceeding from* the property, *severed from* the capital however invested or employed, and *coming in*, being "*derived*"—that is, *received* or *drawn by* the recipient for his separate use, benefit and disposal—*that* is, income derived from the property.

In summary, *income* represents an increase in wealth recognized for tax purposes only upon realization.

COMPARISON OF THE ACCOUNTING AND TAX CONCEPTS OF INCOME

Although income tax rules frequently parallel financial accounting measurement concepts, differences do exist. Of major significance, for example, is the fact that unearned (prepaid) income received by an accrual basis taxpayer often is taxed in the year of receipt. For financial accounting purposes, such prepayments are not treated as income until earned.[8] Because of this and other differences, many corporations report financial accounting income that is substantially different from the amounts reported for tax purposes (see Chapter 20, Reconciliation of Taxable Income and Accounting Income).

The Supreme Court provided an explanation for some of the variations between accounting and taxable income in a decision involving inventory and bad debt adjustments:[9]

> The primary goal of financial accounting is to provide useful information to management, shareholders, creditors, and others properly interested; the major responsibility of the accountant is to protect these parties from being misled. The primary goal of the income tax system, in contrast, is the equitable collection of revenue. . . . Consistently with its goals and responsibilities, financial accounting has as its foundation the principle of conservatism, with its corollary that 'possible errors in measurement [should] be in the direction of understatement rather than overstatement of net income and net assets.' In view of the Treasury's markedly different goals and responsibilities, understatement of income is not destined to be its guiding light.

---

[6] *Rutkin v. U.S.*, 52–1 USTC ¶9260, 41 AFTR2d 596, 72 S.Ct. 571 (USSC, 1952); Rev.Rul. 61, 1953–1 C.B. 17.
[7] 1 USTC ¶32, 3 AFTR 3020, 40 S.Ct. 189 (USSC, 1920).

[8] Similar differences exist in the deduction area.
[9] *Thor Power Tool Co. v. Comm.*, 79–1 USTC ¶9139, 43 AFTR2d 79–362, 99 S.Ct. 773 (USSC, 1979).

... Financial accounting, in short, is hospitable to estimates, probabilities, and reasonable certainties; the tax law, with its mandate to preserve the revenue, can give no quarter to uncertainty.

FORM OF RECEIPT

Gross income is not limited to cash received. "It includes income realized in any form, whether in money, property, or services. Income may be realized [and recognized], therefore, in the form of services, meals, accommodations, stock or other property, as well as in cash."[10]

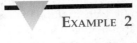

EXAMPLE 2   Ostrich Corporation allowed Bill, an employee, to use a company car for his vacation. Bill realized income equal to the rental value of the car for the time and mileage. ▼

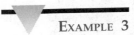

EXAMPLE 3   Terry owed $10,000 on a mortgage. The creditor accepted $8,000 in full satisfaction of the debt. Terry realized income of $2,000 from retiring the debt.[11] ▼

RECOVERY OF CAPITAL DOCTRINE

The Constitution grants Congress the power to tax income but does not define the term. Because the Constitution does not define income, it would seem that Congress could simply tax gross receipts. Although Congress does allow certain deductions, none are constitutionally required. However, the Supreme Court has held that there is no income subject to tax until the taxpayer has recovered the capital invested.[12] This concept is known as the **recovery of capital doctrine.**

In its simplest application, this doctrine means that sellers can reduce their gross receipts (selling price) by the adjusted basis of the property sold.[13] This net amount, in the language of the Code, is gross income.

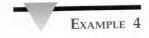

EXAMPLE 4   Dave sold common stock for $15,000. He had purchased the stock for $12,000. Dave's gross receipts are $15,000. This amount consists of a $12,000 recovery of capital and $3,000 of gross income. ▼

Collections on annuity contracts and installment payments received from sales of property must be allocated between recovery of capital and income. Annuities are discussed in this chapter, and installment sales are discussed in Chapter 18.

YEAR OF INCLUSION

2   LEARNING OBJECTIVE
Describe the cash and accrual methods of accounting and the related effects of the choice of taxable year.

TAXABLE YEAR

The annual accounting period or **taxable year** is a basic component of our tax system.[14] Generally, an entity must use the *calendar year* to report its income. However, a *fiscal year* (a period of 12 months ending on the last day of any month

---

[10] Reg. § 1.61–1(a).
[11] Reg. § 1.61–12. See *U.S. v. Kirby Lumber Co.,* 2 USTC ¶814, 10 AFTR 458, 52 S.Ct. 4 (USSC, 1931). Exceptions to this general rule are discussed in Chapter 5.

[12] *Doyle v. Mitchell Bros. Co.,* 1 USTC ¶17, 3 AFTR 2979, 38 S.Ct. 467 (USSC, 1916).
[13] For a definition of adjusted basis, see the Glossary of Tax Terms in Appendix C.
[14] See Accounting Periods in Chapter 18.

other than December) can be elected if the taxpayer maintains adequate books and records. This fiscal year option generally is not available to partnerships, S corporations, and personal service corporations, as discussed in Chapter 18.[15]

Determining the particular year in which the income will be taxed is important for determining when the tax must be paid. But the year each item of income is subject to tax can also affect the total tax liability over the entity's lifetime. This is true for the following reasons:

- With a progressive rate system, a taxpayer's marginal tax rate can change from year to year.
- Congress may change the tax rates.
- The relevant rates may change because of a change in the entity's status (e.g., a person may marry or a business may be incorporated).
- Several provisions in the Code are dependent on the taxpayer's gross income for the year (e.g., whether the person can be claimed as a dependent, as discussed in Chapter 3).

ACCOUNTING METHODS

The year an item of income is subject to tax often depends upon which acceptable **accounting method** the taxpayer regularly employs.[16] The three primary methods of accounting are (1) the cash receipts and disbursements method, (2) the accrual method, and (3) the hybrid method. Most individuals use the cash receipts and disbursements method of accounting, whereas most corporations use the accrual method. The Regulations require the accrual method for determining purchases and sales when inventory is an income-producing factor.[17] Some businesses employ a hybrid method that is a combination of the cash and accrual methods of accounting.

In addition to these overall accounting methods, a taxpayer may choose to spread the gain from the sale of property over the collection periods by using the installment method of income recognition. Contractors may either spread profits from contracts over the periods in which the work is done (the percentage of completion method) or defer all profit until the year in which the project is completed (the completed contract method, which can be used only in limited circumstances).[18]

The IRS has the power to prescribe the accounting method to be used by the taxpayer. Section 446(b) grants the IRS broad powers to determine if the accounting method used *clearly reflects income*:

> Exceptions—If no method of accounting has been regularly used by the taxpayer, or *if the method used does not clearly reflect income, the computation of taxable income shall be made under such method as, in the opinion of the Secretary . . . does clearly reflect income.*

A change in the method of accounting requires the consent of the IRS.[19]

Cash Receipts Method

Under the **cash receipts method,** property or services received are included in the taxpayer's gross income in the year of actual or constructive receipt by the

---

[15] §§ 441(a) and (d).
[16] See Accounting Methods in Chapter 18.
[17] Reg. § 1.446−1(c)(2)(i). Other circumstances in which the accrual method must be used are presented in Chapter 18.

[18] §§ 453(a) and (b), § 453A, and Reg. § 1.451−3. See Chapter 18 for limitations on the use of the installment method and the completed contract method.
[19] § 446(e). See Chapter 18.

taxpayer or agent, regardless of whether the income was earned in that year.[20] The income received need not be reduced to cash in the same year. All that is necessary for income recognition is that property or services received have a fair market value—a cash equivalent.[21] Thus, if a cash basis taxpayer receives a note in payment for services, he or she has income in the year of receipt equal to the fair market value of the note. However, a creditor's mere promise to pay (e.g., an account receivable), with no supporting note, is not usually considered to have a fair market value.[22] Thus, the cash basis taxpayer defers income recognition until the account receivable is collected.

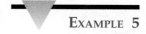

EXAMPLE 5

Dana, an accountant, reports her income by the cash method. In 1994, she performed an audit for Orange Corporation and billed the client for $5,000, which was collected in 1995. In 1994, Dana also performed an audit for Blue Corporation. Because of Blue's precarious financial position, Dana required Blue to issue an $8,000 secured negotiable note in payment of the fee. The note had a fair market value of $6,000. Dana collected $8,000 on the note in 1995. Dana's gross income for the two years is as follows:

	1994	1995
Fair market value of note received from Blue	$6,000	
Cash received		
From Orange on account receivable		$ 5,000
From Blue on note receivable		8,000
Less: Recovery of capital		(6,000)
Total gross income	$6,000	$ 7,000

Generally, a check received is considered a cash equivalent. Thus, a cash basis taxpayer must recognize the income when the check is received. This is true even though the taxpayer receives the check after banking hours.[23]

Accrual Method

Under the **accrual method,** an item is generally included in the gross income for the year in which it is earned, regardless of when the income is collected. The income is earned when (1) all the events have occurred that fix the right to receive such income and (2) the amount to be received can be determined with reasonable accuracy.[24]

Generally, the taxpayer's rights to the income accrue when title to property passes to the buyer or the services are performed for the customer or client.[25] If the rights to the income have accrued but are subject to a potential refund claim (e.g., under a product warranty), the income is reported in the year of sale and a deduction is allowed in subsequent years when actual claims accrue.[26]

Where the taxpayer's rights to the income are being contested (e.g., when a contractor fails to meet specifications), the year in which the income is subject to tax depends upon whether payment has been received. If payment has not been

---

[20] *Julia A. Strauss,* 2 B.T.A. 598 (1925). See the Glossary of Tax Terms in Appendix C for a discussion of the terms "cash equivalent doctrine" and "constructive receipt."

[21] Reg. §§ 1.446–1(a)(3) and (c)(1)(i).

[22] *Bedell v. Comm.,* 1 USTC ¶359, 7 AFTR 8469, 30 F.2d 622 (CA–2, 1929).

[23] *Charles F. Kahler,* 18 T.C. 31 (1952).

[24] Reg. § 1.451–1(a).

[25] *Lucas v. North Texas Lumber Co.,* 2 USTC ¶484, 8 AFTR 10276, 50 S.Ct. 184 (USSC, 1930).

[26] *Brown v. Helvering,* 4 USTC ¶1222, 13 AFTR 851, 54 S.Ct. 356 (USSC, 1933).

received, no income is recognized until the claim is settled. Only then is the right to the income established.[27] However, if the payment is received before the dispute is settled, the court-made **claim of right doctrine** requires the taxpayer to recognize the income in the year of receipt.[28]

EXAMPLE 6

A contractor completed a building in 1994 and presented a bill to the customer. The customer refused to pay the bill and claimed that the contractor had not met specifications. A settlement with the customer was not reached until 1995. No income would accrue to the contractor until 1995. If the customer paid for the work and then filed suit for damages, the contractor could not defer the income (the income would be taxable in 1994). ▼

The measure of accrual basis income is generally the amount the taxpayer has a right to receive. Unlike the cash basis, the fair market value of the customer's obligation is irrelevant in measuring accrual basis income.

EXAMPLE 7

Assume the same facts as in Example 5, except Dana is an accrual basis taxpayer. Dana must recognize $13,000 ($8,000 + $5,000) income in 1994, the year her rights to the income accrued. ▼

Hybrid Method

The **hybrid method** is a combination of the accrual method and the cash method. Generally, when the hybrid method is used, inventory is an income-producing factor. Therefore, the Regulations require that the accrual method be used for determining sales and cost of goods sold. In this circumstance, to simplify record keeping, the taxpayer accounts for inventory using the accrual method and uses the cash method for all other income and expense items (e.g., dividend and interest income). The hybrid method is primarily used by small businesses.

EXCEPTIONS APPLICABLE TO CASH BASIS TAXPAYERS

Constructive Receipt

Income that has not actually been received by the taxpayer is taxed as though it had been received—the income is **constructively received**—under the following conditions:

- The amount is made readily available to the taxpayer.
- The taxpayer's actual receipt is not subject to substantial limitations or restrictions.[29]

The rationale for the constructive receipt doctrine is that if the income is available, the taxpayer should not be allowed to postpone the income recognition. For instance, a taxpayer is not permitted to defer income for December services by refusing to accept payment until January. However, determining whether the income is *readily available* and whether *substantial limitations or restrictions exist* necessitates a factual inquiry that leads to a judgment call.[30] The following are some examples of the application of the constructive receipt doctrine.

---

[27] *Burnet v. Sanford and Brooks,* 2 USTC ¶636, 9 AFTR 603, 51 S.Ct. 150 (USSC, 1931).
[28] *North American Oil Consolidated Co. v. Burnet,* 3 USTC ¶943, 11 AFTR 16, 52 S.Ct. 613 (USSC, 1932).

[29] Reg. § 1.451–2(a).
[30] *Baxter v. Comm.,* 87–1 USTC ¶9315, 59 AFTR2d 87–1068, 816 F.2d 493 (CA–9, 1987).

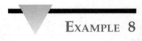

EXAMPLE 8

Ted is a member of a barter club. In 1994, Ted performed services for other club members and earned 1,000 points. Each point entitles him to $1 in goods and services sold by other members of the club; the points can be used at any time. In 1995, Ted exchanged his points for a new color TV. Ted must recognize $1,000 income in 1994 when the 1,000 points were credited to his account.[31] ▼

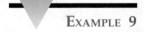

EXAMPLE 9

On December 31, an employer issued a bonus check to an employee but asked her to hold it for a few days until the company could make deposits to cover the check. The income was not constructively received on December 31 since the issuer did not have sufficient funds in its account to pay the debt.[32] ▼

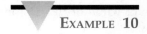

EXAMPLE 10

Rick owned interest coupons that matured on December 31. The coupons could be converted to cash at any bank at maturity. Thus, the income is constructively received on December 31.[33] ▼

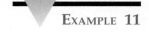

EXAMPLE 11

Dove Company mails dividend checks on December 31, 1994. The checks will not be received by shareholders until January. The shareholders do not realize income until 1995.[34] ▼

The constructive receipt doctrine does not reach income that the taxpayer is not yet entitled to receive even though he or she could have contracted to receive the income at an earlier date.

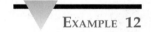

EXAMPLE 12

Sara offered to pay Ivan $100,000 for land in December 1994. Ivan refused but offered to sell the land to Sara on January 1, 1995, when Ivan would be in a lower tax bracket. If Sara accepts Ivan's offer, the gain is taxed to Ivan in 1995 when the sale is completed.[35] ▼

Income set apart or made available is not constructively received if its actual receipt is subject to *substantial restrictions*. The life insurance industry has used substantial restrictions as a cornerstone for designing life insurance contracts with favorable tax features. Ordinary life insurance policies provide (1) current protection—an amount payable in the event of death—and (2) a savings feature—a cash surrender value payable to the policyholder if he or she terminates the policy during his or her life. The annual increase in cash surrender value is not taxable because the policyholder must cancel the policy to actually receive the increase in value. Because the cancellation requirement is a substantial restriction, the policyholder does not constructively receive the annual increase in cash surrender value.[36] Employees often receive from their employers property subject to substantial restrictions. Generally, no income is recognized until the restrictions lapse.[37]

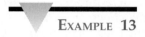

EXAMPLE 13

Carlos is a key employee of Red, Inc. The corporation gave stock with a value of $10,000 to Carlos. The stock could not be sold, however, for five years. Carlos will not be required to recognize income until the restrictions lapse at the end of five years. ▼

---

[31] Rev.Rul. 80–52, 1980–1 C.B. 100.
[32] *L. M. Fischer,* 14 T.C. 792 (1950).
[33] Reg. § 1.451–2(b).
[34] Reg. § 1.451–2(b).

[35] *Cowden v. Comm.,* 61–1 USTC ¶9382, 7 AFTR2d 1160, 289 F.2d 20 (CA–5, 1961).
[36] *Theodore H. Cohen,* 39 T.C. 1055 (1963).
[37] § 83(a). See also the discussion of Restricted Property Plans in Chapter 19.

Original Issue Discount

Lenders frequently make loans that require a payment at maturity of more than the amount of the original loan. The difference between the amount due at maturity and the amount of the original loan is actually interest but is referred to as **original issue discount.** Under the general rules of tax accounting, the cash basis lender would not report the original issue discount as interest income until the year the amount is collected, although an accrual basis borrower would deduct the interest as it is earned. However, the Code puts the lender and borrower on parity by requiring that the original issue discount be reported when it is earned, regardless of the taxpayer's accounting method.[38]

EXAMPLE 14

On July 1, 1994, Chee, a cash basis taxpayer, paid $82,645 for a 24-month certificate of deposit with a maturity value of $100,000. The effective interest rate on the certificate was 10%. Chee must report $4,132 interest income for 1994:

$$(.10 \times \$82,645)(1/2 \text{ year}) = \underline{\$4,132}$$ ▼

The original issue discount rules do not apply to U.S. savings bonds (discussed in the following paragraphs) or to obligations with a maturity date of one year or less from the date of issue.[39] See Chapter 16 for additional discussion of the tax treatment of original issue discount.

Series E and Series EE Bonds

Certain U.S. government savings bonds (Series E before 1980 and Series EE after 1979) are issued at a discount and are redeemable for fixed amounts that increase at stated intervals. No interest payments are actually made. The difference between the purchase price and the amount received on redemption is the bondholder's interest income from the investment.

The income from these savings bonds is generally deferred until the bonds are redeemed or mature. Furthermore, Series E bonds can be exchanged within one year of their maturity date for Series HH bonds, and the interest on the Series E bonds can be further deferred until maturity of the Series HH bonds.[40] Thus, U.S. savings bonds have attractive income deferral features not available with corporate bonds and certificates of deposit issued by financial institutions.

Of course, the deferral feature of government bonds issued at a discount is not an advantage if the investor has insufficient income to be subject to tax as the income accrues. In fact, the deferral may work to the investor's disadvantage if he or she has other income in the year the bonds mature or the bunching of the bond interest into one tax year creates a tax liability. Fortunately, U.S. government bonds have a provision for these investors. A cash basis taxpayer can elect to include in gross income the annual increment in redemption value.[41]

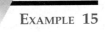

EXAMPLE 15

Kate purchases Series EE U.S. savings bonds for $500 (face value of $1,000) on January 2 of the current year. If the bonds are redeemed during the first six months, no interest is paid. At December 31, the redemption value is $519.60.

---

[38] §§ 1272(a)(3) and 1273(a).
[39] § 1272(a)(2).
[40] Treas. Dept. Circulars No. 1–80 and No. 2–80, 1980–1 C.B. 714, 715. Note that interest is paid at semiannual intervals on the Series

HH bonds and must be included in income as received. Refer to Chapter 5 for a discussion of the savings bond interest exclusion.
[41] § 454(a).

If Kate elects to report the interest income annually, she must report interest income of $19.60 for the current year. If she does not make the election, she will report no interest income for the current year. ▼

When a taxpayer elects to report the income from the bonds on an annual basis, the election applies to all such bonds the taxpayer owns at the time of the election and to all such securities acquired subsequent to the election. A change in the method of reporting the income from the bonds requires permission from the IRS.

Amounts Received under an Obligation to Repay

The receipt of funds with an obligation to repay that amount in the future is the essence of borrowing. Because the taxpayer's assets and liabilities increase by the same amount, no income is realized when the borrowed funds are received. Because amounts paid to the taxpayer by mistake and customer deposits are often classified as borrowed funds, receipt of the funds is not a taxable event.

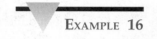

EXAMPLE 16

A landlord receives a damage deposit from a tenant. The landlord does not recognize income until the deposit is forfeited because the landlord has an obligation to repay the deposit if no damage occurs.[42] However, if the deposit is in fact a prepayment of rent, it is taxed in the year of receipt. ▼

EXCEPTIONS APPLICABLE TO ACCRUAL BASIS TAXPAYERS

Prepaid Income

For financial reporting purposes, advance payments received from customers are reflected as prepaid income and as a liability of the seller. However, for tax purposes, the prepaid income often is taxed in the year of receipt.

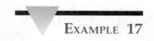

EXAMPLE 17

In December 1994, a tenant paid his January 1995 rent of $1,000. The accrual basis landlord must include the $1,000 in his 1994 income for tax purposes, although the unearned rent income is reported as a liability on the landlord's December 31, 1994, balance sheet. ▼

Taxpayers have repeatedly argued that deferral of income until it is actually earned properly matches revenues and expenses. Moreover, a proper matching of income with the expenses of earning the income is necessary to clearly reflect income, as required by the Code. The IRS responds that § 446(b) grants it broad powers to determine whether an accounting method clearly reflects income. The IRS further argues that generally accepted financial accounting principles should not dictate tax accounting for prepaid income because of the practical problems of collecting Federal revenues. Collection of the tax is simplest in the year the taxpayer receives the cash from the customer or client.

Over 40 years of litigation, the IRS has been only partially successful in the courts. In cases involving prepaid income from services to be performed at the demand of customers (e.g., dance lessons to be taken at any time in a 24-month period), the IRS's position has been upheld.[43] In such cases, the taxpayer's argument that deferral of the income was necessary to match the income with

---

[42] *John Mantell*, 17 T.C. 1143 (1952).
[43] *American Automobile Association v. U.S.*, 61–2 USTC ¶9517, 7 AFTR2d 1618, 81 S.Ct. 1727 (USSC, 1961); *Schlude v. Comm.*, 63–1 USTC ¶9284, 11 AFTR2d 751, 83 S.Ct. 601 (USSC, 1963).

expenses was not persuasive because the taxpayer did not know precisely when each customer would demand services and, thus, when the expenses would be incurred. However, taxpayers have had some success in the courts when the services were performed on a fixed schedule (e.g., a baseball team's season-ticket sales).[44] In some cases involving the sale of goods, taxpayers have successfully argued that the prepayments were mere deposits[45] or in the nature of loans.[46]

Against this background of mixed results in the courts, congressional intervention, and taxpayers' strong resentment of the IRS's position, in 1971 the IRS modified its prepaid income rules, as explained in the following paragraphs.

Deferral of Advance Payments for Goods

Generally, a taxpayer can elect to defer recognition of income from *advance payments for goods* if the method of accounting for the sale is the same for tax and financial reporting purposes.[47]

EXAMPLE 18   Brown Company will ship goods only after payment for the goods has been received. In December 1994, Brown received $10,000 for goods that were not shipped until January 1995. Brown can elect to report the income for tax purposes in 1995, assuming the company reports the income in 1995 for financial reporting purposes. ▼

Deferral of Advance Payments for Services

Revenue Procedure 71-21[48] permits an accrual basis taxpayer to defer recognition of income for *advance payments for services* to be performed by the end of the tax year following the year of receipt. No deferral is allowed if the taxpayer might be required to perform any services, under the agreement, after the tax year following the year of receipt of the advance payment.

EXAMPLE 19   Yellow Corporation, an accrual basis taxpayer, sells its services under 12-month, 18-month, and 24-month contracts. The corporation provides services to each customer every month. In April of 1994, Yellow Corporation sold the following customer contracts:

Length of Contract	Total Proceeds
12 months	$6,000
18 months	3,600
24 months	2,400

Fifteen hundred dollars of the $6,000 may be deferred ($3/12 \times \$6,000$), and $1,800 of the $3,600 may be deferred ($9/18 \times \$3,600$) because those amounts will not be earned until 1995. However, the entire $2,400 received on the 24-month contracts is taxable in the year of receipt (1994), since a part of the income will still be unearned by the end of the tax year following the year of receipt. ▼

---

[44] *Artnell Company v. Comm.*, 68-2 USTC ¶9593, 22 AFTR2d 5590, 400 F.2d 981 (CA-7, 1968). See also *Boise Cascade Corp. v. U.S.*, 76-1 USTC ¶9203, 37 AFTR2d 76-696, 530 F.2d 1367 (Ct. Cls., 1976).
[45] *Venstra & DeHavaan Coal Co.*, 11 T.C. 964 (1948).
[46] *Consolidated-Hammer Dry Plate & Film Co. v. Comm.*, 63-1 USTC ¶9494, 11 AFTR2d 1518, 317 F.2d 829 (CA-7, 1963); *Comm. v.*

Indianapolis Power & Light Co., 90-1 USTC ¶50,007, 65 AFTR2d 90-394, 110 S.Ct. 589 (USSC, 1990).
[47] Reg. § 1.451-5(b). See Reg. § 1.451-5(c) for exceptions to this deferral opportunity. The financial accounting conformity requirement is not applicable to contractors who use the completed contract method.
[48] 1971-2 C.B. 549.

Revenue Procedure 71–21 does *not apply* to prepaid rent or prepaid interest. These items are always taxed in the year of receipt. However, the term *rent* does not include payments for the use of space where the taxpayer also provides significant services (e.g., a hotel or motel). Amounts received under guarantee of warranty contracts are not eligible for deferral unless the goods are also sold without such contracts. The reason these amounts cannot be deferred is to prevent the seller of goods from simply carving a service charge out of the selling price for the goods and attempting to defer from income a service charge that may in reality be part of the price of the goods.

In summary, Revenue Procedure 71–21 will result in conformity of tax and financial accounting in a very limited number of prepaid income cases. It is not apparent why prepaid rents and interest may not be deferred, why revenues under some service contracts may be spread over two years, and why revenues under longer service contracts must be reported in one year. Although Revenue Procedure 71–21 has reduced the number of controversies involving prepaid income, a consistent policy has not yet evolved.

INCOME SOURCES

PERSONAL SERVICES

It is a well-established principle of taxation that income from personal services must be included in the gross income of the person who performs the services. This principle was first established in a Supreme Court decision, *Lucas v. Earl*.[49] Mr. Earl entered into a binding agreement with his wife under which Mrs. Earl was to receive one-half of Mr. Earl's salary. Justice Holmes used the celebrated **fruit and tree metaphor** to explain that the fruit (income) must be attributed to the tree from which it came (Mr. Earl's services). A mere **assignment of income** does not shift the liability for the tax.

However, services performed by an employee for the employer's customers are considered performed by the employer. Thus, the employer is taxed on the income from the services provided to the customer, and the employee is taxed on any compensation received from the employer.[50]

3 **LEARNING OBJECTIVE**
Identify who should pay the tax on a particular item of income in various situations.

EXAMPLE 20

Dr. Shontelle incorporated her medical practice and entered into a contract to work for the corporation for a salary. All patients contracted to receive their services from the corporation, and those services were provided through the corporation's employee, Dr. Shontelle. The corporation must include the patients' fees in its gross income. Dr. Shontelle must include her salary in her gross income. The corporation will be allowed a deduction for the reasonable salary paid to Dr. Shontelle (see the discussion of unreasonable compensation in Chapter 6). ▼

In the case of a child, the Code specifically provides that amounts earned from personal services must be included in the child's gross income. This result applies even though the income is paid to other persons (e.g., the parents).[51]

---

[49] 2 USTC ¶496, 8 AFTR 10287, 50 S.Ct. 241 (USSC, 1930).
[50] *Sargent v. Comm.*, 91–1 USTC ¶50,168, 67 AFTR2d 91–718, 929 F.2d 1252 (CA–8, 1991).

[51] § 73. For circumstances in which the child's unearned income is taxed at the parents' rate, see Unearned Income of Certain Minor Children Taxed at Parents' Rate in Chapter 3.

INCOME FROM PROPERTY

Income from property (interest, dividends, rent) must be included in the gross income of the *owner* of the property. If a father clips interest coupons from bonds shortly before the interest payment date and gives the coupons to his son, the interest will still be taxed to the father. A father who assigns rents from rental property to his daughter will be taxed on the rent since he retains ownership of the property.[52]

Often income-producing property is transferred after income from the property has accrued but before the income is recognized under the transferor's method of accounting. The IRS and the courts have developed rules to allocate the income between the transferor and the transferee.

Interest

According to the IRS, interest accrues daily. Therefore, the interest for the period that includes the date of the transfer is allocated between the transferor and transferee based on the number of days during the period that each owned the property.

EXAMPLE 21

Floyd, a cash basis taxpayer, gave his son, Seth, bonds with a face amount of $10,000 and an 8% stated annual interest rate. The gift was made on January 31, 1994, and the interest was paid on December 31, 1994. Floyd must recognize $68 in interest income (8% × $10,000 × $^{31}\!/_{365}$). Seth will recognize $732 in interest income ($800 − $68). ▼

When the transferor must recognize the income from the property depends upon the method of accounting and the manner in which the property was transferred. In the case of a gift of income-producing property, the donor must recognize his or her share of the accrued income at the time it would have been recognized had the donor continued to own the property.[53] However, if the transfer is a sale, the transferor must recognize the accrued income at the time of the sale. This results because the accrued interest will be included in the sales proceeds.

EXAMPLE 22

Assume the same facts as in Example 21, except the interest that was payable as of December 31 was not actually or constructively received by the bondholders until January 3, 1995. As a cash basis taxpayer, Floyd generally does not recognize interest income until it is received. If Floyd had continued to own the bonds, the interest would have been included in his 1995 gross income, the year it would have been received. Therefore, Floyd must include the $68 accrued income in his gross income as of January 3, 1995.

Further assume that Floyd sold identical bonds on the date of the gift. The bonds sold for $9,900, including accrued interest. On January 31, 1994, Floyd must recognize the accrued interest of $68 on the bonds sold. Thus, the selling price of the bonds is $9,832 ($9,900 − $68). ▼

Dividends

Unlike interest, dividends do not accrue on a daily basis because the declaration of a dividend is at the discretion of the corporation's board of directors. Generally,

---

[52] *Galt v. Comm.*, 54–2 USTC ¶9457, 46 AFTR 633, 216 F.2d 41 (CA–7, 1954); *Helvering v. Horst*, 40–2 USTC ¶9787, 24 AFTR 1058, 61 S.Ct. 144 (USSC, 1940).

[53] Rev.Rul. 72–312, 1972–1 C.B. 22.

dividends are taxed to the person who is entitled to receive them—the shareholder of record as of the corporation's record date.[54] Thus, if a taxpayer sells stock after a dividend has been declared but before the record date, the dividend generally will be taxed to the purchaser.

If a donor makes a gift of stock to someone (e.g., a family member) after the declaration date but before the record date, the Tax Court has held that the donor does not shift the dividend income to the donee. The *fruit* has sufficiently ripened as of the declaration date to tax the dividend income to the donor of the stock.[55] In a similar set of facts, the Fifth Court of Appeals concluded that the dividend income should be included in the gross income of the donee (the owner at the record date). In this case, the taxpayer gave stock to a qualified charity (a charitable contribution) after the declaration date and before the record date.[56]

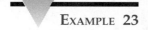

EXAMPLE 23

On June 20, the board of directors of Black Corporation declares a $10 per share dividend. The dividend is payable on June 30, to shareholders of record on June 25. As of June 20, Maria owned 200 shares of Black Corporation's stock. On June 21, Maria sold 100 of the shares to Norm for their fair market value and gave 100 of the shares to Sam (her son). Assume both Norm and Sam are shareholders of record as of June 25. Norm (the purchaser) will be taxed on $1,000 since he is entitled to receive the dividend. However, Maria (the donor) will be taxed on the $1,000 received by Sam (the donee) because the gift was made after the declaration date of the dividend. ▼

INCOME RECEIVED BY AN AGENT

Income received by the taxpayer's agent is considered to be received by the taxpayer. A cash basis principal must recognize the income at the time it is received by the agent.[57]

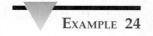

EXAMPLE 24

Jack, a cash basis taxpayer, delivered cattle to the auction barn in late December. The auctioneer, acting as the farmer's agent, sold the cattle and collected the proceeds in December. The auctioneer did not pay Jack until the following January. Jack must include the sales proceeds in his gross income for the year the auctioneer received the funds. ▼

INCOME FROM PARTNERSHIPS, S CORPORATIONS, TRUSTS, AND ESTATES

A *partnership* is not a separate taxable entity. Rather, the partnership merely files an information return (Form 1065), which serves to provide the data necessary for determining the character and amount of each partner's distributive share of the partnership's income and deductions. Each partner must then report his or her distributive share of the partnership's income and deductions for the partnership's tax year ending within or with his or her tax year. The income must be reported by each partner in the year it is earned, even if such amounts are not actually distributed to the partners. Because a partner pays tax on income as the partnership earns it, a distribution by the partnership to the partner is treated under the recovery of capital rules.[58]

---

[54] Reg. § 1.61–9(c). The record date is the cutoff for determining the shareholders who are entitled to receive the dividend.
[55] M. G. Anton, 34 T.C. 842 (1960).
[56] Caruth Corporation v. U.S., 89–1 USTC ¶9172, 63 AFTR2d 89–716, 865 F.2d 644 (CA–5, 1989).

[57] Rev.Rul. 79–379, 1979–2 C.B. 204.
[58] § 706(a) and Reg. § 1.706–1(a)(1). For further discussion, see Chapter 20.

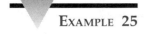

EXAMPLE 25

Tara owned a one-half interest in the capital and profits of T & S Company (a calendar year partnership). For tax year 1994, the partnership earned revenue of $150,000 and had operating expenses of $80,000. During the year, Tara withdrew from her capital account $2,500 per month (for a total of $30,000). For 1994, Tara must report $35,000 as her share of the partnership's profits [½ × ($150,000 − $80,000)] even though she received distributions of only $30,000. ▼

A *small business corporation* may elect to be taxed similarly to a partnership. Thus, the shareholders, rather than the corporation, pay the tax on the corporation's income.[59] The electing corporation is referred to as an *S corporation*. Generally, the shareholder reports his or her proportionate share of the corporation's income and deductions for the year, whether or not the corporation actually makes any distributions to the shareholder.

The *beneficiaries of estates and trusts* generally are taxed on the income earned by the estates or trusts that is actually distributed or required to be distributed to them.[60] Any income not taxed to the beneficiaries is taxable to the estate or trust.

INCOME IN COMMUNITY PROPERTY STATES

General Rules

State law in Louisiana, Texas, New Mexico, Arizona, California, Washington, Idaho, Nevada, and Wisconsin is based upon a community property system. All other states have a common law property system. The basic difference between common law and community property systems centers around the property rights of married persons. Questions about community property income most frequently arise when the husband and wife file separate returns.

Under a **community property** system, all property is deemed either to be separately owned by the spouse or to belong to the marital community. Property may be held separately by a spouse if it was acquired before marriage or received by gift or inheritance following marriage. Otherwise, any property is deemed to be community property. For Federal tax purposes, each spouse is taxed on one-half of the income from property belonging to the community.

The laws of Texas, Louisiana, Wisconsin, and Idaho distinguish between separate property and the income it produces. In these states, the income from separate property belongs to the community. Accordingly, for Federal income tax purposes, each spouse is taxed on one-half of the income. In the remaining community property states, separate property produces separate income that the owner-spouse must report on his or her Federal income tax return.

What appears to be income, however, may really represent a recovery of capital. A recovery of capital and gain realized on separate property retain their identity as separate property. Items such as nontaxable stock dividends, royalties from mineral interests, and gains and losses from the sale of property take on the same classification as the assets to which they relate.

EXAMPLE 26

Bob and Jane are husband and wife and reside in California. Among other transactions during the year, the following occurred:

- Nontaxable stock dividend received by Jane on stock that was given to her after her marriage by her mother.

---

[59] §§ 1361(a) and 1366. For further discussion, see Chapter 20.
[60] §§ 652(a) and 662(a). For further discussion of the taxation of income from partnerships, S corporations, trusts, and estates, see

West's Federal Taxation: Corporations, Partnerships, Estates, and Trusts, Chapters 10, 11, 12, and 19.

- Gain of $10,000 on the sale of unimproved land purchased by Bob before his marriage.
- Oil royalties of $15,000 from a lease Jane acquired after marriage with her separate funds.

Since the stock dividend was distributed on stock held by Jane as separate property, it also is her separate property. The same result occurs for the oil royalties Jane receives. All of the proceeds from the sale of unimproved land (including the gain of $10,000) are Bob's separate property. ▼

In all community property states, income from personal services (e.g., salaries, wages, income from a professional partnership) is generally treated as if one-half is earned by each spouse.

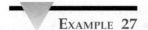

EXAMPLE 27

Fred and Wilma are married but file separate returns. Fred received $25,000 salary and $300 taxable interest on a savings account he established in his name. The deposits to the savings account were made from Fred's salary earned since the marriage. Wilma collected $2,000 taxable dividends on stock she inherited from her father. Wilma's gross income is computed as follows under three assumptions as to the state of residency of the couple:

	California	**Texas**	**Common Law States**
Dividends	$ 2,000	$ 1,000	$2,000
Salary	12,500	12,500	–0–
Interest	150	150	–0–
	$14,650	$13,650	$2,000

▼

Community Property Spouses Living Apart

The general rules for taxing the income from services performed by residents of community property states can create complications and even inequities for spouses who are living apart.

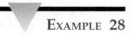

EXAMPLE 28

Cole and Debra were married but living apart for the first nine months of 1994 and were divorced as of October 1, 1994. In December 1994, Cole married Emily, who was married but living apart from Frank before their divorce in June 1994. Cole and Frank had no income from personal services in 1994.

Cole brought into his marriage to Emily a tax liability on one-half of Debra's earnings for the first nine months of the year. However, Emily left with Frank a tax liability on one-half of her earnings for the first six months of 1994. ▼

In circumstances such as those depicted in Example 28, the accrued tax liability could be factored into a property division being negotiated at a time when the parties do not need further complications. In other cases, an abandoned spouse could be saddled with a tax on income earned by a spouse whose whereabouts are unknown.

In 1980, Congress developed a simple solution to the many tax problems of community property spouses living apart. A spouse (or former spouse) will be taxed only on his or her actual earnings from personal services if the following conditions are met:[61]

- The individuals live apart for the entire year.
- They do not file a joint return with each other.
- No portion of the earned income is transferred between the individuals.

---

[61]§ 66.

EXAMPLE 29

Jim and Lori reside in a community property state, and both are gainfully employed. On July 1, 1994, they separated, and on June 30, 1995, they were divorced. Assuming their only source of income is wages, one-half of such income for each year is earned by June 30, and they did not file a joint return for 1994, each should report the following gross income:

	Jim's Separate Return	Lori's Separate Return
1994	One-half of Jim's wages	One-half of Jim's wages
	One-half of Lori's wages	One-half of Lori's wages
1995	All of Jim's wages	All of Lori's wages

The results would be the same if Jim or Lori married another person in 1995, except the newlyweds would probably file a joint return. ▼

The IRS may absolve from liability an *innocent spouse* who does not live apart for the entire year and files a separate return but omits his or her share of the community income received by the other spouse. To qualify for the innocent spouse relief, the taxpayer must not know or must have no reason to know of the omitted community income.

ITEMS SPECIFICALLY INCLUDED IN GROSS INCOME

4 LEARNING OBJECTIVE
Apply the Internal Revenue Code provisions on alimony, loans made at below-market interest rates, annuities, prizes and awards, group term life insurance, unemployment compensation, and Social Security benefits.

The general principles of gross income determination (discussed in the previous sections) as applied by the IRS and the courts have on occasion yielded results Congress found unacceptable. Consequently, Congress has provided more specific rules for determining the gross income from certain sources. Some of these special rules appear in §§ 71–90 of the Code.

ALIMONY AND SEPARATE MAINTENANCE PAYMENTS

When a married couple divorce or become legally separated, state law generally requires a division of the property accumulated during the marriage. In addition, one spouse may have a legal obligation to support the other spouse. The Code distinguishes between the support payments (alimony or separate maintenance) and the property division in terms of the tax consequences.

Alimony and separate maintenance payments are *deductible* by the party making the payments and are *includible* in the gross income of the party receiving the payments.[62] Thus, income is shifted from the income earner to the income beneficiary, who is better able to pay the tax on the amount received.

EXAMPLE 30

Pete and Tina were divorced, and Pete was required to pay Tina $15,000 of alimony each year. Pete earns $31,000 a year. The tax law presumes that because Tina received the $15,000, she is more able than Pete to pay the tax on that amount. Therefore, Tina must include the $15,000 in her gross income, and Pete is allowed to deduct $15,000 from his gross income. ▼

---

[62] §§ 71 and 215.

A transfer of property *other than cash* to a former spouse under a divorce decree or agreement is not a taxable event. The transferor is not entitled to a deduction and does not recognize gain or loss on the transfer. The transferee does not recognize income and has a cost basis equal to the transferor's basis.[63]

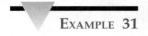

EXAMPLE 31

Paul transfers stock to Rosa as part of a 1994 divorce settlement. The cost of the stock to Paul is $12,000, and the stock's value at the time of the transfer is $15,000. Rosa later sells the stock for $16,000. Paul is not required to recognize gain from the transfer of the stock to Rosa, and Rosa has a realized and recognized gain of $4,000 ($16,000 − $12,000) when she sells the stock. ▼

In the case of cash payments, however, it is often difficult to distinguish payments under a support obligation (alimony) and payments for the other spouse's property (property settlement). In 1984, Congress developed objective rules to classify the payments.

Post-1984 Agreements and Decrees

Payments made under post-1984 agreements and decrees are *classified as alimony* only if the following conditions are satisfied:

1. The payments are in cash.
2. The agreement or decree does not specify that the payments are not alimony.
3. The payor and payee are not members of the same household at the time the payments are made.
4. There is no liability to make the payments for any period after the death of the payee.[64]

Requirement 1 simplifies the law by clearly distinguishing alimony from a property division; that is, if the payment is not in cash, it must be a property division. Requirement 2 allows the parties to determine by agreement whether or not the payments will be alimony. The prohibition on cohabitation—requirement 3—is aimed at assuring the alimony payments are associated with duplicative living expenses (maintaining two households).[65] Requirement 4 is an attempt to prevent alimony treatment from being applied to what is, in fact, a payment for property rather than a support obligation. That is, a seller's estate generally will receive payments for property due after the seller's death. Such payments after the death of the payee could not be for the payee's support.

Front-Loading

As a further safeguard against a property settlement being disguised as alimony, special rules apply to post-1986 agreements if payments in the first or second year exceed $15,000. If the change in the amount of the payments exceeds statutory limits, **alimony recapture** results to the extent of the excess alimony payments. In

---

[63] § 1041, added to the Code in 1984 to repeal the rule of *U.S. v. Davis*, 62–2 USTC ¶9509, 9 AFTR2d 1625, 82 S.Ct. 1190 (USSC, 1962). Under the Davis rule, which was applicable to pre-1985 divorces, a transfer incident to divorce was a taxable event.

[64] § 71(b)(1). This set of alimony rules can also apply to pre-1985 agreements and decrees if both parties agree in writing. The rules applicable to pre-1985 agreements and decrees are not discussed in this text.

[65] *Alexander Washington*, 77 T.C. 601 (1981) at 604.

the *third* year, the payor must include the excess alimony payments for the first and second years in gross income, and the payee is allowed a deduction for these excess alimony payments. The recaptured amount is computed as follows:[66]

$$R = D + E$$

$$D = B - (C + \$15{,}000)$$

$$E = A - \left(\frac{B - D + C}{2} + \$15{,}000\right)$$

R = amount recaptured in Year 3

D = recapture from Year 2

E = recapture from Year 1

A, B, C = payments in the first (A), second (B), and third (C) calendar years of the agreement or decree, where $D \geqslant 0$, $E \geqslant 0$

The recapture formula provides an objective technique for determining alimony recapture. Thus, at the time of the divorce, the taxpayers can ascertain the tax consequences. The general concept is that if the alimony payments decrease by over $15,000 between years in the first three years, there will be alimony recapture with respect to the decrease in excess of $15,000 each year. This rule is applied for the change between Year 2 and Year 3 (D in the above formula). However, rather than making the same calculation for Year 2 payments versus Year 1 payments, the Code requires that the *average* of the payments in Years 2 and 3 be compared with the Year 1 payments (E in the above formula). For this purpose, revised alimony for Year 2 (alimony deducted for Year 2 minus the alimony recapture for Year 2) is used.

EXAMPLE 32

Wes and Rita were divorced in 1994. Under the agreement, Rita was to receive $50,000 in 1994, $20,000 in 1995, and nothing thereafter. The payments were to cease upon Rita's death or remarriage. In 1996, Wes must include an additional $32,500 in gross income for alimony recapture, and Rita is allowed a deduction for the same amount.

$$D = \$20{,}000 - (\$0 + \$15{,}000) = \$5{,}000$$

$$E = \$50{,}000 - \left(\frac{\$20{,}000 - \$5{,}000 + \$0}{2} + \$15{,}000\right) = \$27{,}500$$

$$R = \$5{,}000 + \$27{,}500 = \$32{,}500$$

Note that for 1994 Wes deducts alimony of $50,000 and Rita includes $50,000 in her gross income. For 1995, the amount of the alimony deduction for Wes is $20,000 and Rita's gross income from the alimony is $20,000.

If $50,000 were paid in 1994 and nothing is paid for the following years, $35,000 would be recaptured in 1996.

$$D = \$0 - (\$0 + \$15{,}000) = -\$15{,}000, \text{ but D must be} \geqslant \$0$$

$$E = \$50{,}000 - \left(\frac{\$0 - \$0 + \$0}{2} + \$15{,}000\right) = \$35{,}000$$

$$R = \$0 + \$35{,}000 = \$35{,}000$$

---

[66]§ 71(f).

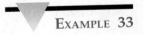

CONCEPT SUMMARY 4–1

Tax Treatment of Payments and Transfers Pursuant to Post-1984 Divorce Agreements and Decrees

	Payor	Recipient
Alimony	Deduction from gross income.	Included in gross income.
Alimony recapture	Included in gross income of the third year.	Deducted from gross income of the third year.
Child support	Not deductible.	Not includible in income.
Property settlement	No income or deduction.	No income or deduction; basis for the property is the same as the transferor's basis.

For 1985 and 1986 agreements and decrees, alimony recapture is required during the second and third years if payments decrease by more than $10,000. A special formula is applied to compute the recapture amounts.[67]

Post-1984 agreements and decrees are not subject to alimony recapture if the decrease in payments is due to the death of either spouse or the remarriage of the payee. Recapture is not applicable because these events typically terminate alimony under state laws. In addition, the recapture rules do not apply to payments where the amount is contingent (e.g., a percentage of income from certain property or a percentage of the payor spouse's compensation), the payments are to be made over a period of three years or longer (unless death, remarriage, or other contingency occurs), and the contingencies are beyond the payor's control.[68]

EXAMPLE 33 Under a 1994 divorce agreement, Ed was to receive an amount equal to one-half of Nina's income from certain rental properties for 1994–1997. Payments were to cease upon the death of Ed or Nina or upon the remarriage of Ed. Ed received $50,000 in 1994 and $50,000 in 1995; in 1996, however, the property was vacant, and Ed received nothing. Nina, who deducted alimony in 1994 and 1995, is not required to recapture any alimony in 1996 because the payments were contingent. ▼

ETHICAL CONSIDERATIONS

Structuring a Divorce

In many situations, the tax laws influence how transactions are structured. The tax laws can be especially influential in structuring divorce agreements. The law seems to say that as long as one party will report as income cash received from a former spouse, the paying party can claim a deduction, even though, in reality, the paying party is purchasing the other's share of the marital property. Thus, the paying party may obtain a deduction for purchasing a personal asset (e.g., a weekend home that was formerly jointly owned). The

---

[67] See § 421 of the Deficit Reduction Act of 1984 and § 1843(c)(2) of the Tax Reform Act of 1986.

[68] §§ 71(f)(5)(A) and (C).

alimony recapture provision limits the parties' ability to carry out such a transaction, but does not preclude it.

Assume that each former spouse is represented by competent tax and legal advisers and that one spouse is in a higher marginal tax bracket than the other. The divorcing couple can enter into an agreement that will increase each party's after-tax wealth at the government's expense.

One may question why the laws deliberately set forth rules that will cause a divorcing couple to engage in this arbitrage. One may also question whether a tax adviser should advise a client involved in divorce negotiations to exploit the tax laws in this manner.

Child Support

A taxpayer does not realize income from the receipt of child support payments made by his or her former spouse. This result occurs because the money is received subject to the duty to use the money for the child's benefit. The payor is not allowed to deduct the child support payments because the payments are made to satisfy the payor's legal obligation to support the child.

In many cases, it is difficult to determine whether an amount received is alimony or child support. Under pre-1985 decrees and agreements, according to the Supreme Court, if the decree or agreement does not specifically provide for child support, none of the payments will be treated as such.[69]

EXAMPLE 34

A pre-1985 divorce agreement provides that Matt is required to make periodic alimony payments of $500 per month to Grace. However, when Matt and Grace's child reaches age 21, marries, or dies (whichever occurs first), the payments will be reduced to $300 per month. Grace has custody of the child. Although it is reasonable to infer that $200 ($500 – $300) is for child support, the entire $500 is alimony because no payments are specified as child support. ▼

In 1984, Congress changed the results in Example 34 but only for post-1984 agreements and decrees. Under the revision, if the amount of the payments would be reduced upon the happening of a contingency related to a child (e.g., the child attains age 21 or dies), the amount of the future reduction in the payment will be deemed child support.[70]

EXAMPLE 35

The facts are the same as in Example 34, except that the agreement is a post-1984 agreement. Child support payments are $200 each month and alimony is $300 each month. ▼

IMPUTED INTEREST ON BELOW-MARKET LOANS

As discussed earlier in the chapter, generally no income is recognized unless it is realized. Realization generally occurs when the taxpayer performs services or sells goods and thus becomes entitled to a payment from the other party. It follows that no income is realized if the goods or services are provided at no charge. Under this

---

[69] *Comm. v. Lester,* 61–1 USTC 9463, 7 AFTR2d 1445, 81 S.Ct. 1343 (USSC, 1961).

[70] § 71(c)(2). Pre-1985 agreements can be amended so that the revision will apply [§ 422(e) of the Deficit Reduction Act of 1984].

interpretation of the realization requirement, before 1984, interest-free loans were used to shift income between taxpayers.

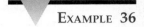

EXAMPLE 36

Veneia (daughter) is in the 20% tax bracket and has no investment income. Kareem (father) is in the 50% tax bracket and has $200,000 in a money market account earning 10% interest. Kareem would like Veneia to receive and pay tax on the income earned on the $200,000. Because Kareem would also like to have access to the $200,000 should he need the money, he does not want to make an outright gift of the money, nor does he want to commit the money to a trust.

Before 1984, Kareem could achieve his goals as follows. He could transfer the money market account to Veneia in exchange for her $200,000 non-interest-bearing note, payable on Kareem's demand. As a result, Veneia would receive the income, and the family's taxes would be decreased by $6,000.

Decrease in Kareem's tax—	
(.10 × $200,000).50 =	($10,000)
Increase in Veneia's tax—	
(.10 × $200,000).20 =	4,000
Decrease in the family's taxes	($ 6,000)

Under the 1984 amendments to the Code, Kareem in Example 36 is required to recognize **imputed interest** income.[71] Veneia is deemed to have incurred interest expense equal to Kareem's imputed interest income. Veneia's interest may be deductible on her return as investment interest if she itemizes deductions (see Chapter 10). To complete the fictitious series of transactions, Kareem is then deemed to have given Veneia the amount of the imputed interest she did not pay. The gift received by Veneia is not subject to income tax (see Chapter 5), although Kareem may be subject to the gift tax (unified transfer tax) on the amount deemed given to Veneia (refer to Chapter 1).

Imputed interest is calculated using the rate the Federal government pays on new borrowings and is compounded semiannually. This Federal rate is adjusted monthly and is published by the IRS.[72] Actually, there are three Federal rates: short-term (not over three years and including demand loans), mid-term (over three years but not over nine years), and long-term (over nine years).

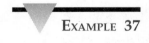

EXAMPLE 37

Assume the Federal rate applicable to the loan in Example 36 is 7% through June 30 and 8% from July 1 through December 31. Kareem made the loan on January 1, and the loan is still outstanding on December 31. Kareem must recognize interest income of $15,280, and Veneia has interest expense of $15,280. Kareem is deemed to have made a gift of $15,280 to Veneia.

Interest calculations	
January 1–June 30—	
.07($200,000) (½ year)	$ 7,000
July 1–December 31—	
.08($200,000 + $7,000) (½ year)	8,280
	$15,280

If interest is charged on the loan but is less than the Federal rate, the imputed interest is the difference between the amount that would have been charged at the Federal rate and the amount actually charged.

---

[71] § 7872(a)(1).

[72] §§ 7872(b)(2) and (f)(2).

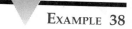

EXAMPLE 38

Assume the same facts as in Example 37, except that Kareem charged 6% interest, compounded annually.

Interest at the Federal rate	$ 15,280
Less interest charged (.06 × $200,000)	(12,000)
Imputed interest	$ 3,280

The imputed interest rules apply to the following *types* of below-market loans:[73]

1. Gift loans (made out of love, affection, or generosity, as in Example 36).
2. Compensation-related loans (employer loans to employees).
3. Corporation-shareholder loans (a corporation's loans to its shareholders).
4. Tax avoidance loans and other loans that significantly affect the borrower's or lender's Federal tax liability (discussed in the following paragraphs).

The effects of the first three types of loans on the borrower and lender are summarized in Concept Summary 4–2.

Tax Avoidance and Other Below-Market Loans

In addition to the three specific types of loans that are subject to the imputed interest rules, the Code includes a catchall provision for *tax avoidance loans* and other arrangements that have a significant effect on the tax liability of the borrower or lender. The Conference Report provides the following example of an arrangement that might be subject to the imputed interest rules.[74]

EXAMPLE 39

Annual dues for the Good Health Club are $400. In lieu of paying dues, a member can make a $4,000 deposit, refundable at the end of one year. The club can earn $400 interest on the deposit.

If interest were not imputed, an individual with $4,000 could, in effect, earn tax-exempt income on the deposit. That is, rather than invest the $4,000, earn $400 in interest, pay tax on the interest, and then pay $400 in dues, the individual could avoid tax on the interest by making the deposit. Thus, income and expenses are imputed as follows: interest income and nondeductible health club fees for the club member; income from fees and interest expense for the club. ▼

Many commercially motivated transactions could be swept into this other below-market loans category. However, the temporary Regulations have carved

CONCEPT SUMMARY 4–2

Effect of Certain Below-Market Loans on the Lender and Borrower

Type of Loan		Lender	Borrower
Gift	Step 1	Interest income	Interest expense
	Step 2	Gift made	Gift received
Compensation-related	Step 1	Interest income	Interest expense
	Step 2	Compensation expense	Compensation income
Corporation to shareholder	Step 1	Interest income	Interest expense
	Step 2	Dividend paid	Dividend income

---

[73] § 7872(c).

[74] H. Rep. No. 98–861, 98th Cong., 2d Sess., 1984, p. 1023.

out a frequently encountered exception for customer prepayments. If the prepayments are included in the recipient's income under the recipient's method of accounting, the payments are not considered loans and, thus, are not subject to the imputed interest rules.[75]

EXAMPLE 40

Landlord, a cash basis taxpayer, charges tenants a damage deposit equal to one month's rent on residential apartments. When the tenant enters into the lease, the landlord also collects rent for the last month of the lease.

The prepaid rent for the last month of the lease is taxed in the year received and thus is not considered a loan. The security deposit is not taxed when received and is therefore a candidate for imputed interest. However, no apparent tax benefit is derived by the landlord or the tenant, and thus the security deposit should not be subject to the imputed interest provisions. But if making the deposit would reduce the rent paid by the tenant, the tenant could derive a tax benefit, much the same as the club member in Example 39. ▼

Exceptions and Limitations

No interest is imputed on total outstanding *gift loans* of $10,000 or less between individuals, unless the loan proceeds are used to purchase income-producing property.[76] This exemption eliminates from these complex provisions immaterial amounts that do not result in apparent shifts of income. However, if the proceeds of such a loan are used to purchase income-producing property, the limitations discussed in the following paragraphs apply.

On loans of $100,000 or less between individuals, the imputed interest cannot exceed the borrower's net investment income for the year (gross income from all investments less the related expenses).[77] As discussed above, one of the purposes of the imputed interest rules is to prevent high-income taxpayers from shifting income to relatives in a lower marginal bracket. This shifting of investment income is considered to occur only to the extent the borrower has investment income. Thus, the income imputed to the lender is limited to the borrower's net investment income. As a further limitation, or exemption, if the borrower's net investment income for the year does not exceed $1,000, no interest is imputed on loans of $100,000 or less. However, these limitations for loans of $100,000 or less do not apply if a principal purpose of a loan is tax avoidance. According to the Senate Report, if a principal purpose of a loan is to shift income to a taxpayer in a lower tax bracket (as illustrated in Example 36), the purpose is a proscribed one. Therefore, in such a case interest is imputed, and the imputed interest is not limited to the borrower's net investment income.[78]

EXAMPLE 41

Vicki made interest-free gift loans as follows:

Borrower	Amount	Borrower's Net Investment Income	Purpose
Susan	$ 8,000	$ –0–	Education
Dan	9,000	500	Purchase of stock
Bonnie	25,000	–0–	Purchase of a business
Megan	90,000	15,000	Purchase of a residence
Olaf	120,000	–0–	Purchase of a residence

[75] Prop. Reg. § 1.7872–2(b)(1)(i).
[76] § 7872(c)(2).
[77] § 7872(d).

[78] *Deficit Reduction Tax Bill of 1984: Explanation of the Senate Finance Committee* (April 2, 1984), p. 484.

Assume that tax avoidance is not a principal purpose of any of the loans. The loan to Susan is not subject to the imputed interest rules because the $10,000 exception applies. The $10,000 exception does not apply to the loan to Dan because the proceeds were used to purchase income-producing assets. However, under the $100,000 exception, the imputed interest is limited to Dan's investment income ($500). Since the $1,000 exception also applies to this loan, no interest is imputed.

No interest is imputed on the loan to Bonnie because the $100,000 exception applies. Interest is imputed on the loan to Megan based on the lesser of (1) the borrower's $15,000 net investment income or (2) the interest as calculated by applying the Federal rate to the outstanding loan. None of the exceptions apply to the loan to Olaf because the loan was for more than $100,000.

Assume the relevant Federal rate is 10% and the loans were outstanding for the entire year. Vicki would recognize interest income, compounded semiannually, as follows:

Loan to Megan:

First 6 months (.10 × $90,000 × ½ year)	$ 4,500
Second 6 months (.10 × $94,500 × ½ year)	4,725
	$ 9,225

Loan to Olaf:

First 6 months (.10 × $120,000 × ½ year)	$ 6,000
Second 6 months (.10 × $126,000 × ½ year)	6,300
	$12,300
Total imputed interest ($9,225 + $12,300)	$21,525

▼

As with gift loans, there is a $10,000 exemption for *compensation-related loans* and *corporation-shareholder loans*. However, the $10,000 exception does not apply if tax avoidance is one of the principal purposes of a loan.[79] This vague tax avoidance standard makes practically all compensation-related and corporation-shareholder loans suspect. Nevertheless, the $10,000 exception should apply when an employee's borrowing was necessitated by personal needs (e.g., to meet unexpected expenses) rather than tax considerations.

INCOME FROM ANNUITIES

Annuity contracts generally require the purchaser (the annuitant) to pay a fixed amount for the right to receive a future stream of payments. Typically, the issuer of the contract is an insurance company and will pay the annuitant a cash value if the annuitant cancels the contract. The insurance company invests the amounts received from the annuitant, and the income earned serves to increase the cash value of the policy. No income is recognized at the time the cash value of the annuity increases because the taxpayer has not actually received any income. The income is not constructively received because, generally, the taxpayer must cancel the policy to receive the increase in value (the increase in value is subject to substantial restrictions).

EXAMPLE 42

Juanita, age 50, paid $30,000 for an annuity contract that is to pay her $500 per month beginning when she reaches age 65 and continuing until her death. If Juanita should cancel the policy after one year, she would receive $30,200. The $200 increase in value is not includible in Juanita's gross income as long as she does not actually receive the $200. ▼

---

[79] § 7872(c)(3).

CONCEPT SUMMARY 4–3

Exceptions to the Imputed Interest Rules For Below-Market Loans

Exception	Eligible Loans	Ineligible Loans and Limitations
De minimis—aggregate loans of $10,000 or less	Gift loans	Proceeds used to purchase income-producing assets.
	Employer-employee	Principal purpose is tax avoidance.
	Corporation-shareholder	Principal purpose is tax avoidance.
Aggregate loans of $100,000 or less	Between individuals	Principal purpose is tax avoidance. For all other loans, interest is imputed to the extent of the borrower's net investment income (NII), if the borrower's NII exceeds $1,000.

The tax accounting problem associated with receiving payments under an annuity contract is one of apportioning the amounts received between recovery of capital and income.

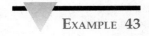

EXAMPLE 43

In 1994, Tom purchased for $15,000 an annuity intended as a source of retirement income. In 1996, when the cash value of the annuity was $17,000, Tom collected $1,000 on the contract. Is the $1,000 gross income, recovery of capital, or a combination of recovery of capital and income? ▼

The statutory solution to this problem depends upon whether the payments began before or after the annuity starting date and upon when the policy was acquired.

Collections before the Annuity Starting Date

Generally, an annuity contract specifies a date on which monthly or annual payments will begin—the annuity starting date. Often the contract will also allow the annuitant to collect a limited amount before the starting date. The amount collected may be characterized as either an actual withdrawal of the increase in cash value or a loan on the policy. In 1982, Congress changed the rules applicable to these withdrawals and loans.

Collections (including loans) equal to or less than the post–August 13, 1982, increases in cash value must be included in gross income. Amounts received in excess of post–August 13, 1982, increases in cash value are treated as a recovery of capital until the taxpayer's cost has been entirely recovered. Additional amounts are included in gross income.[80] The taxpayer may also be subject to a penalty on early distributions of 10 percent of the income recognized. The penalty generally applies if the amount is received before the taxpayer reaches age 59½ or is disabled.[81]

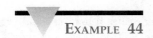

EXAMPLE 44

Juan, age 50, purchased an annuity policy for $30,000 in 1993. In 1995, when the cash value of the policy has increased to $33,000, Juan withdraws $4,000. Juan must recognize $3,000 of income ($33,000 cash value – $30,000 cost) and must pay a penalty of $300 ($3,000 × 10%).

---

[80] § 72(c)(3); Reg. § 1.72–9.   [81] § 72(q).

The remaining $1,000 is a recovery of capital and reduces Juan's basis in the annuity policy. ▼

The current rules were enacted because Congress perceived that the recovery of capital rule was being abused. Formerly, individuals could purchase annuity contracts that guaranteed an annual increase in cash value and withdraw the equivalent of interest on the contract but recognize no income. This is no longer possible. In addition, the individual must recognize income from borrowing on the contract (e.g., pledging the contract as security for a loan) as well as from an actual distribution.

Collections on and after the Annuity Starting Date

The annuitant can exclude from income (as a recovery of capital) the proportion of each payment that the investment in the contract bears to the expected return under the contract. The *exclusion amount* is calculated as follows:

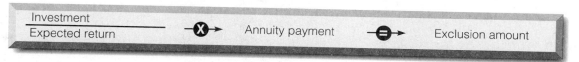

$$\frac{\text{Investment}}{\text{Expected return}} \ \otimes \ \text{Annuity payment} \ \ominus \ \text{Exclusion amount}$$

The *expected return* is the annual amount to be paid to the annuitant multiplied by the number of years the payments will be received. The payment period may be fixed (a *term certain*) or for the life of one or more individuals. When payments are for life, the taxpayer must use the annuity table published by the IRS to determine the expected return (see Table 4–1). This is an actuarial table that contains life expectancies.[82] The expected return is calculated by multiplying the appropriate multiple (life expectancy) by the annual payment.

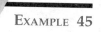

EXAMPLE 45

The taxpayer, age 54, purchased an annuity from an insurance company for $90,000. She was to receive $500 per month for life. Her life expectancy (from Table 4–1) is 29.5 years from the annuity starting date. Thus, her expected return is $500 × 12 × 29.5 = $177,000, and the exclusion amount is $3,051 [($90,000 investment/$177,000 expected return) × $6,000 annual payment]. The $3,051 is a nontaxable return of capital, and $2,949 is included in gross income. ▼

The exclusion ratio (investment ÷ expected return) applies until the annuitant has recovered his or her investment in the contract. Once the investment is recovered, the entire amount of subsequent payments is taxable. If the annuitant dies before recovering his or her investment, the unrecovered cost is deductible in the year the payments cease (usually the year of death).[83]

EXAMPLE 46

Assume the taxpayer in Example 45 received annuity payments for 30.5 years (366 months). For the last 12 months [366 – (12 × 29.5) = 12], the taxpayer would include $500 each month in gross income. If instead the taxpayer died after 36 months, she is eligible for a $80,847 deduction on her final tax return.

Cost of the contract	$90,000
Cost previously recovered $90,000/$177,000 × 36($500) =	(9,153)
Deduction	$80,847

▼

---

[82] The life expectancies in Table 4–1 apply for annuity investments made on or after July 1, 1986. See *Pension and Annuity Income,* IRS Publication 575 (Rev. Nov. 87), pp. 22–24 for the IRS table to use for investments made before July 1, 1986.

[83] § 72(b).

▼ **TABLE 4–1**
Ordinary Life Annuities:
One Life–Expected
Return Multiples

Age	Multiple	Age	Multiple	Age	Multiple
5	76.6	42	40.6	79	10.0
6	75.6	43	39.6	80	9.5
7	74.7	44	38.7	81	8.9
8	73.7	45	37.7	82	8.4
9	72.7	46	36.8	83	7.9
10	71.7	47	35.9	84	7.4
11	70.7	48	34.9	85	6.9
12	69.7	49	34.0	86	6.5
13	68.8	50	33.1	87	6.1
14	67.8	51	32.2	88	5.7
15	66.8	52	31.3	89	5.3
16	65.8	53	30.4	90	5.0
17	64.8	54	29.5	91	4.7
18	63.9	55	28.6	92	4.4
19	62.9	56	27.7	93	4.1
20	61.9	57	26.8	94	3.9
21	60.9	58	25.9	95	3.7
22	59.9	59	25.0	96	3.4
23	59.0	60	24.2	97	3.2
24	58.0	61	23.3	98	3.0
25	57.0	62	22.5	99	2.8
26	56.0	63	21.6	100	2.7
27	55.1	64	20.8	101	2.5
28	54.1	65	20.0	102	2.3
29	53.1	66	19.2	103	2.1
30	52.2	67	18.4	104	1.9
31	51.2	68	17.6	105	1.8
32	50.2	69	16.8	106	1.6
33	49.3	70	16.0	107	1.4
34	48.3	71	15.3	108	1.3
35	47.3	72	14.6	109	1.1
36	46.4	73	13.9	110	1.0
37	45.4	74	13.2	111	.9
38	44.4	75	12.5	112	.8
39	43.5	76	11.9	113	.7
40	42.5	77	11.2	114	.6
41	41.5	78	10.6	115	.5

PRIZES AND AWARDS

The fair market value of prizes and awards (other than scholarships exempted under § 117, to be discussed subsequently) must be included in income.[84] Therefore, TV giveaway prizes, door prizes, and awards from an employer to an employee in recognition of performance are fully taxable to the recipient.

[84] § 74.

An exception permits a prize or award to be excluded from gross income if all of the following requirements are satisfied:

- The prize or award is received in recognition of religious, charitable, scientific, educational, artistic, literary, or civic achievement.
- The recipient transfers the prize or award to a qualified governmental unit or nonprofit organization.
- The recipient was selected without any action on his or her part to enter the contest or proceeding.
- The recipient is not required to render substantial future services as a condition for receiving the prize or award.[85]

Because the transfer of the property to a qualified governmental unit or nonprofit organization ordinarily would be a charitable contribution (an itemized deduction as presented in Chapter 10), the exclusion produces beneficial tax consequences in the following situations:

- The taxpayer does not itemize deductions and thus would receive no tax benefit from the charitable contribution.
- The taxpayer's charitable contributions exceed the annual statutory ceiling on the deduction.
- Including the prize or award in gross income would reduce the amount of deductions the taxpayer otherwise would qualify for because of gross income limitations (e.g., the gross income test for a dependency exemption, the adjusted gross income limitation in calculating the medical expense deduction).

Another exception is provided for certain *employee achievement awards* in the form of tangible personal property (e.g., a gold watch). The awards must be made in recognition of length of service or safety achievement. Generally, the ceiling on the excludible amount is $400. However, if the award is a qualified plan award, the ceiling on the exclusion is $1,600.[86]

GROUP TERM LIFE INSURANCE

For many years, the IRS did not attempt to tax the value of life insurance protection provided to an employee by the employer. Some companies took undue advantage of the exclusion by providing large amounts of insurance protection for executives. Therefore, Congress enacted § 79, which created a limited exclusion for **group term life insurance.** Current law allows an exclusion for premiums on the first $50,000 of group term life insurance protection.

The benefits of this exclusion are available only to employees. Proprietors and partners are not considered employees. Moreover, the Regulations generally require broad-scale coverage of employees to satisfy the *group* requirement (e.g., shareholder-employees would not constitute a qualified group). The exclusion applies only to term insurance (protection for a period of time but with no cash surrender value) and not to ordinary life insurance (lifetime protection plus a cash surrender value that can be drawn upon before death).

As mentioned, the exclusion applies to the first $50,000 of group term life insurance protection. For each $1,000 coverage in excess of $50,000, the employee must include the amounts indicated in Table 4–2 in gross income.[87]

---

[85] § 74(b).
[86] §§ 74(c) and 274(j).

[87] Reg. § 1.79–3(d)(2) and Temp.Reg. § 1.79–3T.

▼ TABLE 4–2
Uniform Premiums for $1,000 of Group Term Life Insurance Protection

Attained Age on Last Day of Employee's Tax Year	Cost per $1,000 of Protection for One-Month Period
Under 30	8 cents
30–34	9 cents
35–39	11 cents
40–44	17 cents
45–49	29 cents
50–54	48 cents
55–59	75 cents
60–64	$1.17
65–69	$2.10
70 and over	$3.76

TAX IN THE NEWS

EMPLOYERS MAY TAILOR GROUP TERM LIFE INSURANCE

Many employees are willing to forgo group term life insurance coverage in excess of $50,000. The employees prefer the reduced coverage to having to pay taxes on the premiums associated with coverage in excess of $50,000. Employers have been reluctant to drop the coverage for these employees, however, because doing so could cause the plan to appear to discriminate in favor of higher paid employees and, thus, could jeopardize the exclusion from tax of the $50,000 coverage.

Recently, the employees' fears were allayed when the IRS ruled that such a plan would not violate the antidiscrimination requirements. A group term life insurance plan can permit employees to limit their coverage to $50,000 to avoid taxes. Employees who choose to limit their insurance coverage may not receive cash or any other benefit in lieu of the forgone coverage.

SOURCE: Adapted from "Employers Tailor Group Term Life Insurance to Trim Taxes on Employees," *Wall Street Journal*, June 9, 1993, p. A1. Reprinted by permission of the *Wall Street Journal*, © 1993 Dow Jones & Company, Inc. All rights reserved worldwide.

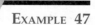

EXAMPLE 47

Finch Corporation has a group term life insurance policy with coverage equal to the employee's annual salary. Keith, age 52, is president of the corporation and receives an annual salary of $75,000. Keith must include $144 in gross income from the insurance protection for the year.

$$\frac{\$75,000 - \$50,000}{\$1,000} \times .48 \times 12 \text{ months} = \$144$$

▼

Generally, the amount that must be included in income, computed from Table 4–2, is much less than the price an individual would pay an insurance company for the same amount of protection. Thus, even the excess coverage provides some tax-favored income for employees when group term life insurance coverage in excess of $50,000 is desirable. However, if the plan discriminates in favor of certain key employees (e.g., officers), the key employees are not eligible for the exclusion.

In such a case, the key employees must include in gross income the greater of actual premiums paid by the employer or the amount calculated from the Uniform Premiums table in Table 4–2. The other employees are still eligible for the $50,000 exclusion and continue to use the Uniform Premiums table to compute the income from excess insurance protection.[88]

UNEMPLOYMENT COMPENSATION

In a series of rulings over a period of 40 years, the IRS exempted unemployment benefits from tax. These payments were considered social benefit programs for the promotion of the general welfare. After experiencing dissatisfaction with the IRS's treatment of unemployment compensation, Congress amended the Code to provide that the benefits are taxable.[89]

SOCIAL SECURITY BENEFITS

If a taxpayer's income exceeds a specified base amount, as much as 85 percent of Social Security retirement benefits must be included in gross income. The taxable amount of benefits is determined through the application of one of two formulas that utilize a unique measure of income—*modified adjusted gross income (MAGI)*.[90] MAGI is, generally, the taxpayer's adjusted gross income from all sources (other than Social Security) plus the foreign earned income exclusion and any tax-exempt interest income.

In the formulas, two sets of base amounts are established. The first set is as follows:

- $32,000 for married taxpayers who file a joint return.
- $0 for married taxpayers who do not live apart for the entire year but file separate returns.
- $25,000 for all other taxpayers.

The second set of base amounts is as follows:

- $44,000 for married taxpayers who file a joint return.
- $0 for married taxpayers who do not live apart for the entire year but file separate returns.
- $34,000 for all other taxpayers.

If MAGI plus one-half of Social Security benefits exceeds the first set of base amounts, but not the second set, the taxable amount of Social Security benefits is the *lesser* of the following:

- .50(Social Security benefits).
- .50[MAGI + .50(Social Security benefits) − base amount].

EXAMPLE 48 A married couple with adjusted gross income of $30,000, no tax-exempt interest, and $11,000 of Social Security benefits who file jointly must include $1,750 of the benefits in gross income. This works out as the lesser of the following:

1. .50($11,000) = $5,500.
2. .50[$30,000 + .50($11,000) − $32,000] = .50($3,500) = $1,750.

[88]§ 79(d).
[89]§ 85.
[90]§ 86.

If the couple's adjusted gross income were $15,000 and their Social Security benefits totaled $5,000, none of the benefits would be taxable, since .50[$15,000 + .50($5,000) − $32,000] is not a positive number. ▼

If MAGI plus one-half of Social Security benefits exceeds the second set of base amounts, the taxable amount of Social Security benefits is the *lesser* of the following:

- .85(Social Security benefits).
- Sum of:
  - .85[MAGI + .50(Social Security benefits) − base amount].
  - Lesser of:
    - Amount included through application of the first formula.
    - $4,500 ($6,000 for married filing jointly).

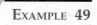

EXAMPLE 49

A married couple who file jointly have adjusted gross income of $72,000, no tax-exempt interest, and $12,000 of Social Security benefits. Their includible Social Security benefits would be $10,200.

Include the lesser of the following:

1. .85($12,000) = $10,200.
2. Sum of:
   a. .85[$72,000 + .50($12,000) − $44,000] = $28,900.
   b. Lesser of:
      - Amount calculated by the first formula, which is the lesser of:
        - .50($12,000) = $6,000.
        - .50[$72,000 + .50($12,000) − $32,000] = $23,000.
      - $6,000.

The sum equals $34,900 ($28,900 + $6,000). Since 85% of the Social Security benefits received is less than this amount, $10,200 is included in the couples' gross income. ▼

ETHICAL CONSIDERATIONS

Taxing Social Security Benefits

The taxation of Social Security benefits has gone through several phases. For many years, Social Security benefits were not subject to tax. Then in 1976, the Internal Revenue Code was amended to tax up to one-half of Social Security benefits received by individuals with gross income over a threshold amount (i.e., $25,000 or $32,000 depending on filing status). The apparent rationale for taxing 50 percent was that the employee had contributed half of the original payments and thus half of the benefits represented a recovery of capital.

As a result of the Revenue Reconciliation Act of 1993, taxpayers with adjusted gross income over the threshold amount (i.e., $34,000 or $44,000 depending on filing status) are required to include up to 85 percent of Social Security benefits in gross income. Under current law, as well as under pre-1993 law, if an individual dies before recovering his or her payments into the Social Security system, no loss can be claimed on the final return.

Now, two former U.S. senators (Paul Tsongas of Massachusetts and Warren Rudman of New Hampshire) are proposing that the receipt of Social Security benefits be based on the "wherewithal to pay" as part of a plan to eliminate the Federal deficit by the year 2000. Such a means-based approach would effectively result in a 100 percent inclusion for Social Security benefits combined with a 100 percent tax rate.

SOURCE: Information from David Wessel, "Ex-Senators Unveil a Plan to Cut Deficit," *Wall Street Journal*, September 21, 1993, p. A2; "A Deficit Solution: Former Senators Take Aim at Entitlement Spending," *Newport News (Virginia) Daily Press*, September 22, 1993, p. A6.

TAX PLANNING CONSIDERATIONS

5 **LEARNING OBJECTIVE**
Identify tax planning strategies for minimizing gross income.

The materials in this chapter have focused on the following questions:

- What is income?
- When is the income recognized?
- Who is the taxpayer?

Planning strategies suggested by these materials include the following:

- Maximize economic benefits that are not included in gross income.
- Defer the recognition of income.
- Shift income to taxpayers who are in a lower marginal tax bracket.

Some specific techniques for accomplishing these strategies are discussed in the following paragraphs.

NONTAXABLE ECONOMIC BENEFITS

Home ownership is the prime example of economic income from capital that is not subject to tax. If the taxpayer uses his or her capital to purchase investments, but pays rent on a personal residence, the taxpayer would pay the rent from after-tax income. However, if the taxpayer purchases a personal residence instead of the investments, the taxpayer would give up gross income from the forgone investments in exchange for the rent savings. The savings in rent enjoyed as a result of owning the home is not subject to tax. Thus, the homeowner will have substituted nontaxable for taxable income.

TAX DEFERRAL

General

Since deferred taxes are tantamount to interest-free loans from the government, the deferral of taxes is a worthy goal of the tax planner. However, the tax planner must also consider the tax rates for the years the income is shifted from and to. For example, a one-year deferral of income from a year in which the taxpayer's tax rate was 28 percent to a year in which the tax rate will be 39.6 percent would not be advisable if the taxpayer expects to earn less than a 11.6 percent after-tax return on the deferred tax dollars.

The taxpayer can often defer the recognition of income from appreciated property by postponing the event triggering realization (the final closing on a sale or exchange of property). If the taxpayer needs cash, obtaining a loan by using the appreciated property as collateral may be the least costly alternative. When the taxpayer anticipates reinvesting the proceeds, a sale may be inadvisable.

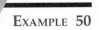

EXAMPLE 50

Ira owns 100 shares of Pigeon Company common stock with a cost of $20,000 and a fair market value of $50,000. Although the stock's value has increased substantially in the past three years, Ira thinks the growth days are over. If he sells the Pigeon stock, Ira will invest the proceeds from the sale in other common stock. Assuming Ira is in the 28% marginal tax bracket, he will have only $41,600 [$50,000 − .28($50,000 − $20,000)] to reinvest. The alternative investment must substantially outperform Pigeon in the future in order for the sale to be beneficial. ▼

Selection of Investments

Because no tax is due until a gain has been recognized, the law favors investments that yield appreciation rather than annual income.

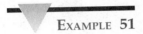

EXAMPLE 51

Vera can buy a corporate bond or an acre of land for $10,000. The bond pays $1,000 of interest (10%) each year, and Vera expects the land to increase in value 10% each year for the next 10 years. She is in the 40% (combined Federal and state) tax bracket. Assuming the bond would mature or the land would be sold in 10 years and Vera would reinvest the interest at a 10% before-tax return, she would accumulate the following amount at the end of 10 years.

		Bond	**Land**
Original investment		$10,000	$10,000
Annual income	$1,000		
Less tax	(400)		
	$ 600		
Compound amount reinvested for 10 years at 6% after-tax	× 13.18	7,908	
		$17,908	
Compound amount, 10 years at 10%			× 2.59
			$25,900
Less tax on sale: 40%($25,900 − $10,000)			(6,360)
			$19,540

Therefore, the value of the deferral that results from investing in the land rather than in the bond is $1,632 ($19,540 − $17,908). ▼

Series E and EE bonds can also be purchased for long-term deferrals of income. As discussed in the chapter, Series E bonds can be exchanged for new Series HH bonds to further postpone the tax. In situations where the taxpayer's goal is merely to shift income one year into the future, bank certificates of deposit are useful tools. If the maturity period is one year or less, all interest is reported in the year of maturity. Time certificates are especially useful for a taxpayer who realizes an unusually large gain from the sale of property in one year (and thus is in a high tax bracket) but expects his or her income to be less the following year.

Cash Basis

The timing of income from services can often be controlled through the use of the cash method of accounting. Although taxpayers are somewhat constrained by the constructive receipt doctrine (they cannot turn their backs on income), seldom will customers and clients offer to pay before they are asked. The usual lag between billings and collections (e.g., December's billings collected in January) will result in a continuous deferring of some income until the last year of operations. A salaried individual approaching retirement may contract with his or her employer before the services are rendered to receive a portion of compensation in the lower tax bracket retirement years.

Prepaid Income

For the accrual basis taxpayer who receives advance payments from customers, the transactions should be structured to avoid payment of tax on income before the time the income is actually earned. Revenue Procedure 71–21 provides the guidelines for deferring the tax on prepayments for services, and Reg. § 1.451–5 provides the guidelines for deferrals on sales of goods. In addition, both the cash and accrual basis taxpayer can sometimes defer income by stipulating that the payments are deposits rather than prepaid income. For example, a landlord should require an equivalent damage deposit rather than require prepayment of the last month's rent under the lease.

SHIFTING INCOME TO RELATIVES

The tax liability of a family can be minimized by shifting income from higher- to lower-bracket family members. This can be accomplished through gifts of income-producing property. Furthermore, in many cases, income can be shifted with no negative effect on the family's investment plans.

EXAMPLE 52

Adam, who is in the 28% tax bracket, would like to save for his children's education. All of the children are under 14 years of age. Adam could transfer income-producing properties to the children, and the children could each receive income of up to $600 each year (refer to Chapter 3) with no tax liability. The next $600 would be taxed at the child's tax rate. After a child has more than $1,200 income, there is no tax advantage to shifting more income to the child (because the income will be taxed at the parents' rate) until the child is 14 years old (when all income will be taxed according to the child's tax rate). ▼

The Uniform Gifts to Minors Act, a model law adopted by all states (but with some variations among the states), facilitates income shifting. Under the Act, a gift of intangibles (e.g., bank accounts, stocks, bonds, life insurance contracts) can be made to a minor but with an adult serving as custodian. Usually, a parent who makes the gift is also named as custodian. The state laws allow the custodian to sell or redeem and reinvest the principal and to accumulate or distribute the income, practically at the custodian's discretion provided there is no commingling of the child's income with the parent's property. Thus, the parent can give appreciated securities to the child, and the donor custodian can then sell the securities and reinvest the proceeds, thereby shifting both the gain and annual income to the child. Such planning is limited by the tax liability calculation provision for a child under the age of 14 (refer to Chapter 3).

U.S. government bonds (Series E and EE) can be purchased by the parent for his or her children. When this is done, the children generally should file a return and elect to report the income on the accrual basis.

EXAMPLE 53

Abby pays $7,500 for Series EE bonds in 1994 and immediately gives them to Wade (her son), who will enter college the year of original maturity of the bonds. The bonds have a maturity value of $10,000. Wade elects to report the annual increment in redemption value as income for each year the bonds are held. The first year the increase is $250, and Wade includes that amount in his gross income. If Wade has no other income, no tax will be due on the $250 bond interest, since such an amount will be more than offset by his available standard deduction. The following year, the increment is $260, and Wade includes this amount in income. Thus, over the life of the bonds, Wade will include $2,500 in income ($10,000 − $7,500), none of which will result in a tax liability, assuming he has no other income. However, if the election had not been made, Wade would be required to include $2,500 in income on the bonds in the year of original maturity, if they were redeemed as planned. This amount of income might result in a tax liability. ▼

In some cases, it may be advantageous for the child not to make the accrual election. For example, a child under age 14 with investment income of more than

$1,200 each year and parents in the 28, 31, 36, or 39.6 percent tax bracket would probably benefit from deferring the tax on the savings bond interest. The child would also benefit from the use of the usually lower tax rate (rather than subjecting the income to his or her parents' tax rate) if the bonds mature after the child is age 14 or older.

ACCOUNTING FOR COMMUNITY PROPERTY

The classification of income as community or separate property becomes important when either of two events occurs:

- Husband and wife, married taxpayers, file separate income tax returns for the year.
- Husband and wife obtain a divorce and therefore have to file separate returns for the year (refer to Chapter 3).

For planning purposes, it behooves married persons to keep track of the source of income (community or separate). To be in a position to do this effectively when income-producing assets are involved, it may be necessary to distinguish between separate and community property.[91]

ALIMONY

The person making the alimony payments favors a divorce settlement that includes a provision for deductible alimony payments. On the other hand, the recipient prefers that the payments do not qualify as alimony. If the payor is in a higher tax bracket than the recipient, both parties may benefit by increasing the payments and structuring them so that they qualify as alimony.

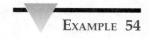
EXAMPLE 54

Carl and Polly are negotiating a divorce settlement. Carl has offered to pay Polly $10,000 each year for 10 years, but payments would cease upon Polly's death. Polly is willing to accept the offer, if the agreement will specify that the cash payments are not alimony. Carl is in the 36% tax bracket, and Polly's marginal rate is 15%.

If Carl and Polly agree that Carl will pay Polly $12,000 of alimony each year, both will have improved after-tax cash flows.

	Annual Cash Flows	
	Carl	**Polly**
Nonalimony payments	$(10,000)	$10,000
Alimony payments	$(12,000)	$12,000
Tax effects		
.36($12,000)	4,320	
.15($12,000)		(1,800)
After-tax cash flows	$ (7,680)	$10,200
Benefit of alimony option	$ 2,320	$ 200

Both parties benefit at the government's expense if the $12,000 alimony option is used. ▼

---

[91]Being able to distinguish between separate and community property is crucial to the determination of a property settlement incident to a divorce. It also is vital in the estate tax area (refer to Chapter 1) since the surviving wife's or husband's share of the community property is not included in the gross estate of the deceased spouse.

KEY TERMS

Accounting income, 4–4

Accounting method, 4–7

Accrual method, 4–8

Alimony and separate maintenance payments, 4–19

Alimony recapture, 4–20

Annuity, 4–27

Assignment of income, 4–14

Cash receipts method, 4–7

Claim of right doctrine, 4–9

Community property, 4–17

Constructive receipt, 4–9

Economic income, 4–3

Fruit and tree metaphor, 4–14

Gross income, 4–3

Group term life insurance, 4–31

Hybrid method, 4–9

Imputed interest, 4–24

Income, 4–3

Original issue discount, 4–11

Recovery of capital doctrine, 4–6

Taxable year, 4–6

PROBLEM MATERIALS

DISCUSSION QUESTIONS

1. The Internal Revenue Code contains a broad definition of gross income, but does not provide a listing of all possible types of income subject to tax. Would it improve the tax law if a complete listing of taxable sources of income were included in the Code?

2. Which of the following would be considered "income" for the current year by an economist but would not be gross income for tax purposes? Explain.
   a. Securities acquired two years ago for $10,000 had a value of $12,000 at the beginning of the current year and a value of $13,000 at the end of the year.
   b. An individual lives in the home he owns.
   c. A corporation obtained a loan from a bank.
   d. A shareholder paid a corporation $3,000 for property valued at $5,000.
   e. An individual owned property that was stolen. The cost of the property three years ago was $2,000, and an insurance company paid the owner $6,000 (the value of the property on the date of theft).
   f. An individual found a box of seventeenth-century Spanish coins while diving off the Virginia coast.
   g. An individual received a $200 rebate from the manufacturer upon the purchase of a new car.

3. According to economists, because our tax system does not impute income to homeowners for the rental value of their homes, the nonhomeowner who invests in securities (rather than a home) is taxed more heavily than the homeowner. This leads to overinvesting in homes. Why do you suppose the laws are not changed to tax homeowners on the rental value of their homes?

4. Evaluate the following alternative proposals for taxing the income from property:
   a. All assets would be valued at the end of the year, any increase in value that occurred during the year would be included in gross income, and any decrease in value would be deductible from gross income.
   b. No gain or loss would be recognized until the taxpayer sold or exchanged the property.
   c. Increases or decreases in the value of property traded on a national exchange (e.g., the New York Stock Exchange) would be reflected in gross income for the years the changes in value occurred. For all other assets, no gain or loss would be recognized until the property is sold or exchanged.

5. Able Utility Corporation's common stock pays $1 per share in dividends. However, the stock is highly unlikely to increase in value because Able is regulated by a public utility commission that will not allow the company to increase its charges to customers. In addition, market interest rates are not expected to decrease. Baker Technology Corporation does not pay any dividends, but the prospects for increases in the value of the stock are excellent because of the company's new products. How might the realization requirement of the income tax law affect an investor's decision between Able and Baker stock?

6. Leif had owned a tract of land for several years when the local government decided to build an airport near the property. The cost of the property to Leif was $50,000. The local government paid Leif $10,000 for invasion of his airspace. What is Leif's gross income from the receipt of the $10,000?

7. Why is the annual increase in the cash surrender value of a life insurance policy not subject to tax each year?

8. Sparrow, Inc., receives all of its income from repairing computers. The company reports its income by the cash method. On December 31, an employee went to a customer's office and repaired a computer. The customer gave Sparrow's employee a check for $300, but the employee did not remit the check to Sparrow until January of the following year. When is Sparrow required to recognize the income?

X 9. What is the major tax advantage of the cash method of accounting?

10. Lane is a self-employed consultant who reports his income by the cash method of accounting. In December 1994, Lane received a check for $5,000 from a client. Lane misplaced the check and did not find it until January 1995, when he deposited it in his bank account. Lane uses his deposit records to compute his income. Therefore, he included the $5,000 in his 1995 gross income.
a. In what year should Lane report the income?
b. Why does it matter whether Lane reports the income in 1994 or 1995, so long as he actually reports it?

11. Pat, an accrual basis taxpayer, performed services for a customer in 1994. Pat's total charge was $500, and the customer paid $200 when the work was begun. When Pat completed the services, the customer refused to pay the balance due of $300. In addition, at the end of 1994, the customer claimed the work did not meet contract specifications and filed a lawsuit against Pat for the return of the $200. The suit was settled in 1995 when the customer paid an additional $100. What is Pat's 1994 income from the contract?

12. In 1994, Nora, an accrual basis taxpayer, rendered services for a customer with a poor credit rating. Nora's charge for the service was $1,000. Nora sent a bill to the customer for $1,000 but reported only $500 of income. She justified reporting only $500 as follows: "I'm being generous reporting $500. I'll be lucky if I collect anything." How much should Nora include as gross income from the contract in 1994?

13. In January 1994, Carol, a cash basis taxpayer, purchased for $2,000 a five-year Series EE U.S. government bond with a maturity value of $3,000. She also purchased for $2,000 a three-year bank certificate of deposit with a maturity value of $2,500. Is Carol required to recognize any interest income in 1994?

14. Quinn (father) paid $200 for an automobile that needed repairs. He worked nights and weekends to restore the car. Several individuals offered to purchase the car for $2,800. Quinn gave the car and a list of potential buyers to Ron (son), whose college tuition was due in a few days. Ron sold the car for $2,800 and paid his tuition. Does Quinn have any taxable income from the transaction?

15. Olga, a cash basis taxpayer, sold a bond with accrued interest of $750, for $10,250. Olga's basis in the bond was $9,000. Compute Olga's income from this transaction.

16. Tom Sr. performed services for a client, but told the client to pay the fee to Tom Jr. Why is Tom Sr. required to pay the tax on the income even though Tom Jr. received the income?

17. Isabella transferred rental properties to a corporation. Isabella's objective was to minimize her liability for injuries that may occur on the property. The tenants continued to pay rents to Isabella. Who must include the rents in gross income?

18. Who pays the tax on (a) the income of an S corporation and on (b) the undistributed income of an estate?

19. Ted and Alice were residents of a community property state. In 1994, Ted left Alice for parts unknown. Ted and Alice were still married at year-end. How will Ted's absence complicate Alice's 1994 tax return?

20. What is the purpose of the front-loading rules related to alimony?

21. A post-1984 divorce agreement between Earl and Cora provides that Earl is to pay Cora $500 per month for 13 years. Earl and Cora have a child who is 8 years old. Termination of the monthly payments will coincide with the child's attaining age 21. Can the monthly payments qualify as alimony?

22. Hal and Nancy were divorced. They jointly owned a home in the mountains with a basis of $50,000 and a fair market value of $80,000. According to the terms of the divorce, Nancy gave Hal $40,000 for his one-half interest in the mountain home. Nancy later sold the house for $85,000. What is Nancy's gain from the sale?

23. In the case of a below-market loan between relatives, why is the lender required to recognize income although it is the borrower who appears to receive the economic benefit?

24. Mother loaned $80,000 to Son who used the money to buy a personal residence. Mother did not charge interest on the loan, although the market rate of interest was 8%. Son had investment income of $2,000. Do the imputed interest rules apply?

25. In the case of a corporation's loan to its controlling shareholder who is also an employee of the corporation, why would the corporation prefer that the loan be classified as an employer-employee loan rather than a corporation-shareholder loan?

26. Suppose the annuity tables used by the IRS were outdated and that people lived longer than the tables indicated. How would this affect Federal revenues?

27. Discuss the difference in tax treatment, if any, between a taxpayer who wins the Nobel Peace Prize and a taxpayer who is crowned Miss America.

28. Gail is a full-time employee of Purple Corporation. One of the fringe benefits the company offers its employees is group term life insurance protection equal to twice the employee's annual salary. Gail is 32 years old, and her annual salary is $45,000. What is Gail's gross income from the life insurance protection for the year?

29. When a taxpayer is receiving Social Security benefits, could a $1,000 increase in income from services cause the taxpayer's adjusted gross income to increase by more than $1,000?

30. Compare the taxation of amounts a retired worker receives from an annuity contract with the amounts she receives in Social Security benefits.

PROBLEMS

31. Determine the effects of the following on Anne's gross income for the year:
    a. Anne bought a used sofa for $25. After she took the sofa home, she discovered $15,000 in a secret compartment. Anne was unable to determine who placed the money in the sofa. Therefore, she put the money in her bank account.
    b. Anne also discovered oil on her property during the year, and the value of the land increased from $10,000 to $3,000,000.
    c. One year later, Anne found a diamond in the sofa she had purchased. Apparently, the diamond was in the sofa when Anne purchased it. The value of the diamond was $6,000, and Anne could not determine the former owner.

d. Anne's bank charges a $3 per month service charge. However, the fee is waived if the customer maintains an average balance for the month of at least $1,000. Anne's account exceeded the minimum deposit requirement, and as a result she was not required to pay any service charges for the year.

32. Compute the taxpayer's (1) economic income and (2) gross income for tax purposes from the following events:
    a. The taxpayer sold securities for $10,000. The securities cost $6,000 in 1990. The fair market value of the securities at the beginning of the year was $12,000.
    b. The taxpayer sold his business and received $15,000 under a covenant not to compete with the new owner.
    c. The taxpayer used her controlled corporation's automobile for her vacation. The rental value of the automobile for the vacation period was $800.
    d. The taxpayer raised vegetables in her garden. The fair market value of the vegetables was $900, and the cost of raising them was $100. She ate some of the vegetables and gave the remainder to neighbors.
    e. The local government changed the zoning ordinances so that some of the taxpayer's residential property was reclassified as commercial. Because of the change, the fair market value of the taxpayer's property increased by $10,000.
    f. During the year, the taxpayer borrowed $50,000 for two years at 9% interest. By the end of the year, interest rates had increased to 12%, and the lender accepted $49,000 in full satisfaction of the debt.

33. Kevin, a cash basis taxpayer, received the following from his employer during 1994:

    • Salary of $70,000.

    • Bonus of $10,000. In 1995, the company determined that the bonus had been incorrectly computed and required Kevin to repay $2,000.

    • Use of a company car for his vacation. Rental value for the period would have been $800. Kevin paid for the gas.

    • $4,000 advance for travel expenses. Kevin had spent only $2,500 at the end of the year.

    Determine the effects of these items on Kevin's gross income.

34. Determine the taxpayer's income for tax purposes in each of the following cases:
    a. In the current year, Seagull Corporation purchased $1,000,000 par value of its own bonds and paid the bondholders $980,000 plus $50,000 of accrued interest. The bonds had been issued 10 years ago at par and were to mature 25 years from the date of issue. Does the corporation recognize income from the purchase of the bonds?
    b. A shareholder of a corporation sold property to the corporation for $60,000 (the shareholder's cost). The value of the property on the date of sale was $50,000. Does the taxpayer have any gross income from the sale?
    c. Rex was a football coach at a state university. Because of his disappointing record, he was asked to resign and accept one-half of his pay for the remaining three years of his contract. Rex resigned, accepting $75,000.

35. Which of the following investments will yield the greater after-tax value assuming the taxpayer is in the 40% tax bracket (combined Federal and state) in all years and the investments will be liquidated at the end of five years?
    a. Land that will increase in value by 10% each year.
    b. A taxable bond yielding 10% before tax, and the interest can be reinvested at 10% before tax.
    c. Common stock that will increase in value at the rate of 5% (compounded) each year and pays dividends equal to 5% of the year-end value of the stock. The dividends can be reinvested at 10% before tax.
    d. A tax-exempt state government bond yielding 8%. The interest can be reinvested at a before-tax rate of 10%, and the bond matures in 10 years.

    Given: Compound amount of $1 at the end of five years:

Interest Rate	Factor
6%	1.33
8%	1.47
10%	1.61

Compound value of annuity payments at the end of five years:

Interest Rate	Factor
6%	5.64
8%	5.87
10%	6.11

X 36. Determine the taxpayer's income for tax purposes in each of the following cases:
   a. Zelda borrowed $30,000 from the First National Bank. She was required to deliver to the bank stocks with a value of $30,000 and a cost of $10,000. The stocks were to serve as collateral for the loan.
   b. Zelda owned a lot on Sycamore Street that measured 100 feet by 100 feet. The cost of the lot to her is $10,000. The city condemned a 10-foot strip of the land so that it could widen the street. Zelda received a $2,000 condemnation award.
   c. Zelda owned land zoned for residential use only. The land cost $5,000 and had a market value of $7,000. Zelda spent $500 and several hundred hours petitioning the county supervisors to change the zoning to A–1 commercial. The value of the property immediately increased to $20,000 when the county approved the zoning change.

37. Al is an attorney who conducts his practice as a sole proprietor. During the year, he received cash of $75,000 for legal services. At the beginning of the year, he had receivables from clients of $20,000. At the end of the year, his receivables totaled $35,000. During the year, he wrote off as uncollectible $10,000 in receivables from a client for services rendered during the previous year. Compute Al's gross income from the practice for the year:
   a. Using the cash basis of accounting.
   b. Using the accrual basis of accounting.

38. The taxpayer began operating a grocery store during the year. Her only books and records are based on cash receipts and disbursements, but she has asked you to compute her gross profit from the business for tax purposes.

Sales of merchandise	$260,000
Purchases of merchandise	190,000

You determine that as of the end of the year the taxpayer has accounts payable for merchandise of $9,000 and accounts receivable from customers totaling $1,500. The cost of merchandise on hand at the end of the year was $4,000. Compute the grocery store's accrual method gross profit for the year.

39. Dance, Inc., is a dance studio that sells dance lessons for cash, on open account, and for notes receivable. The company also collects interest on bonds held as an investment. The company's cash receipts for 1994 totaled $219,000:

Cash sales	$ 70,000
Collections on accounts receivable	120,000
Collections on notes receivable	20,000
Interest on bonds	9,000
	$219,000

The balances in accounts receivable, notes receivable, and accrued interest on bonds at the beginning and end of the year were as follows:

	1–1–94	12–31–94
Accounts receivable	$17,000	$20,000
Notes receivable	9,000	13,000
Accrued interest on bonds	2,500	4,000
	$28,500	$37,000

The fair market value of the notes is equal to 75% of their face amount. There were no bad debts for the year, and all notes were for services performed during the year. Compute the corporation's gross income:

a. Using the cash basis of accounting.

b. Using the accrual basis of accounting.

c. Using a hybrid method—accrual basis for lessons and cash basis for interest income.

40. Determine the effect of the following on the taxpayer's gross income for 1994:

a. Received his paycheck for $3,000 from his employer on December 31, 1994. He deposited the paycheck on January 2, 1995.

b. Received a bonus of $5,000 from his employer on January 10, 1995. The bonus was for the outstanding performance of his division during 1994.

c. Received a dividend check from IBM on November 28, 1994. He mailed the check back to IBM in December requesting that additional IBM stock be issued to him under IBM's dividend reinvestment plan.

41. Mohammed owns a life insurance policy. The cash surrender value of the policy increased $1,500 during the year. He purchased a certificate of deposit on June 30 of the current year for $44,500. The certificate matures in two years when its value will be $50,000 (interest rate of 6%). However, if Mohammed redeems the certificate before the end of the first year, he receives no interest. Mohammed also purchased a Series EE U.S. government savings bond for $7,460. The maturity value of the bond is $10,000 in six years (yield of 5%), and the redemption price of the bond increased by $400 during the year. Mohammed has owned no other savings bonds. What is Mohammed's current year gross income from the above items?

42. Pelican, Inc., an accrual basis taxpayer, sells and installs consumer appliances. Determine the effects of each of the following transactions on the company's 1994 gross income:

a. In December 1994, the company received a $1,200 advance payment from a customer. The payment was for an appliance that Pelican specially ordered from the manufacturer. The appliance had not arrived at the end of 1994.

b. At the end of 1994, the company installed an appliance and collected the full price of $750 for the item. However, the customer claimed the appliance was defective and asked the company for a refund. The company conceded that the appliance was defective, but claimed that the customer should collect from the manufacturer. The dispute had not been settled by the end of 1994. In early 1995, it was determined that Pelican did not install the appliance properly and the company was required to refund the full sales price.

c. At the end of 1994, a customer refused to pay for merchandise delivered in 1993. The customer claimed that the merchandise was defective. In 1994, the company replaced the merchandise at no charge to the customer.

d. The company sold an appliance for $1,200 (plus a market rate of interest) and received the customer's note for that amount. However, because of the customer's poor credit rating, the value of the note was only $700.

43. Freda is a cash basis taxpayer. Determine her 1994 gross income from the following transactions:

a. In 1992, Freda negotiated her 1993 salary. The employer offered to pay Freda $200,000 in 1993. Freda countered that she wanted $10,000 each month in 1993 and the remaining $80,000 in January 1994. Freda wanted the $80,000 income shifted to 1994 because she expected her 1994 tax rates to be lower. The employer agreed to Freda's terms.

b. In 1993, Freda was running short of cash and needed money for Christmas. Her employer loaned her $20,000 in November 1993. Freda signed a note for $20,000 plus 10% interest, the applicable Federal rate. In January 1994, the employer subtracted the $20,000 and $333 interest from the $80,000 due Freda and paid her $59,667.

c. On December 31, 1993, Zina offered to buy land from Freda for $30,000 (Freda's basis was $8,000). Freda refused to sell in 1993, but at that time, she contracted to sell the land to Zina in 1994 for $30,000.

44. The Heron Apartments requires its new tenants to pay the rent for the first and last months of the annual lease and a $400 damage deposit, all at the time the lease is signed. In December 1994, a tenant paid $800 for January 1995 rent, $800 for December 1995 rent, and $400 for the damage deposit. In January 1996, Heron refunded the tenant's damage deposit. What are the effects of these payments on Heron's taxable income for 1994, 1995, and 1996?

a. Assume Heron is a cash basis taxpayer.

b. Assume Heron is an accrual basis taxpayer.

45. Leo has asked you to review portions of his tax return. He provides you with the following information:

Gain on redemption of a 2-year 7% certificate of deposit

Proceeds received June 30, 1994	$10,000	
Purchase price July 1, 1992	(8,735)	
Gain		$1,265

Gain on redemption of a 6-month 6% certificate of deposit

Proceeds received March 31, 1994	$ 5,000	
Purchase price October 1, 1993	(4,855)	
Gain		145

Gain from 8% Series E savings bond

Proceeds received September 30, 1994	$ 2,500	
Purchase price June 30, 1981	(780)	
Gain		1,720
Distributions from a family partnership		1,500

Leo's share of the partnership's earnings were $1,400. Determine Leo's 1994 gross income from the above.

46. a. An automobile dealer has several new cars in inventory but often does not have the right combination of body style, color, and accessories. In some cases, the dealer makes an offer to sell a car at a certain price, accepts a deposit, and then orders the car from the manufacturer. When the car is received from the manufacturer, the sale is closed, and the dealer receives the balance of the sales price. At the end of the current year, the dealer has deposits totaling $8,200 for cars that have not been received from the manufacturer. When is the $8,200 subject to tax?

b. Grey Corporation, an exterminating company, is a calendar year taxpayer. It contracts to provide service to homeowners once a month under a one-year or a two-year contract. On April 1 of the current year, the company sold a customer a one-year contract for $60. How much of the $60 is taxable in the current year if the company is an accrual basis taxpayer? If the $60 is payment on a two-year contract, how much is taxed in the year the contract is sold?

c. Vera, an accrual basis taxpayer, owns an amusement park whose fiscal year ends September 30. To increase business during the fall and winter months, Vera sold passes that would allow the holder to ride free during the months of October through March. During the month of September, $6,000 was collected from the sale of passes for the upcoming fall and winter. When will the $6,000 be taxable to Vera?

d. The taxpayer is in the office equipment rental business and uses the accrual basis of accounting. In December, he collected $5,000 in rents for the following January. When is the $5,000 taxable?

47. a. Gus is a cash basis taxpayer. On September 1, 1994, Gus gave a corporate bond to his son, Hans. The bond had a face amount of $10,000 and paid $900 of interest each January 31. On December 1, 1994, Gus gave common stocks to his daughter, Dena. Dividends totaling $720 had been declared on the stocks on November 30, 1994, and were payable on January 15, 1995. Dena became the shareholder of record in time to collect the dividends. What is Gus's 1995 gross income from the bond and stocks?

    b. In 1994, Gus's mother was unable to pay her bills as they came due. Gus, his employer, and his mother's creditors entered into an arrangement whereby Gus's employer would withhold $500 per month from his salary and the employer would pay the $500 to the creditors. In 1994, $3,000 was withheld from Gus's salary and paid to the creditors. Is Gus required to pay tax on the $3,000?

    c. Gus is considering purchasing a zero coupon (no interest is paid until maturity) corporate bond for himself and for his minor son, Hans (age 4). The bonds have an issue price of $300 and pay $1,000 at the end of 10 years. Gus is in the 36% tax bracket, and Hans has no other taxable income. Would the zero coupon bond be an equally suitable investment for Gus and Hans?

48. Tracy, a cash basis taxpayer, is employed by Eagle Corporation, also a cash basis taxpayer. Tracy is a full-time employee of the corporation and receives a salary of $60,000 per year. He also receives a bonus equal to 10% of all collections from clients he serviced during the year. Determine the tax consequences of the following events to the corporation and to Tracy:

    a. On December 31, 1994, Tracy was visiting a customer. The customer gave Tracy a $3,000 check payable to the corporation for appraisal services Tracy performed during 1994. Tracy did not deliver the check to the corporation until January 1995.

    b. The facts are the same as in (a), except that the corporation is an accrual basis taxpayer and Tracy deposited the check on December 31, but the bank did not add the deposit to the corporation's account until January 1995.

    c. The facts are the same as in (a), except the customer told Tracy to hold the check until January when the customer could make a bank deposit that would cover the check.

49. Eve, Fran, and Gary each have a one-third interest in the capital and profits of the EFG Partnership. At the beginning of the year, each partner had a $50,000 balance in his or her capital account. The partnership's gross income for the year was $280,000, and its total expenses were $96,000. During the year, Eve contributed an additional $10,000 to the partnership and did not have any withdrawals from her capital account. Fran withdrew $30,000, and Gary withdrew $9,000. Compute each partner's taxable income from the partnership for the year.

50. Diego and Carmen lived together for part of the year but were divorced on December 31, 1994. Diego earned $30,000 salary from his employer during the year. Carmen's salary was $16,000. Carmen also received $8,000 in taxable dividends from stock held as separate property.

    a. If Diego and Carmen reside in Texas, how much income should each report on their separate tax returns for 1994?

    b. If amounts are withheld from their salaries, how are these amounts reported on Diego and Carmen's separate returns?

    c. If Diego and Carmen reside in a common law state, how much income should each report on their separate returns?

51. Hazel and Harry were married on June 30, 1994, and resided in Dallas, Texas. On December 31, 1994, they separated, and on March 31, 1995, they were divorced. On July 1, 1995, Harry moved to Grundy, Virginia, and remarried in December 1995. Hazel did not remarry. Hazel's and Harry's incomes for the relevant periods were as follows:

Salary	Harry	Hazel
January 1–June 30, 1994	$23,000	$15,000
July 1–December 31, 1994	24,000	16,000
January 1–March 31, 1995	25,000	18,000
April 1–December 31, 1995	40,000	20,000

In addition to the salaries listed, on January 31, 1995, Harry received $2,400 interest on savings certificates acquired on February 1, 1994. What is Hazel's gross income for 1994 and 1995 as computed on separate returns?

52. Liz and Doug were divorced on July 1 of the current year after 10 years of marriage. Their current year's income received before the divorce was as follows:

Doug's salary	$20,000
Liz's salary	25,000
Rent on apartments purchased by Liz 15 years ago	6,000
Dividends on stock Doug inherited from his mother 4 years ago	1,200
Interest on a savings account in Liz's name funded with her salary	600

Allocate the income to Liz and Doug assuming they live in:
a. California.
b. Texas.

53. Nell and Kirby are in the process of negotiating their divorce agreement. What would be the tax consequences to Nell and Kirby if the following, considered individually, become part of the agreement:
   a. Nell is to receive $1,000 per month until she dies or remarries. She also is to receive $500 per month for 12 years for her one-half interest in their personal residence. She paid for her one-half interest out of her earnings.
   b. Nell is to receive a principal sum of $100,000. Of this amount, $50,000 is to be paid in the year of the divorce, and $5,000 per year will be paid to her in each of the following 10 years or until her death.
   c. Nell is to receive stock in GM Corporation (value of $120,000 and basis of $75,000). The stock was jointly owned by Nell and Kirby. In exchange for the stock, Nell relinquished all of her rights to property accumulated during the marriage. She also is to receive $1,000 per month until her death or remarriage, but for a period of not longer than 10 years.
   d. Assume that Nell and Kirby are close to agreeing on the settlement described in (c). Nell has informed you that she plans to sell the stock soon after she receives it and move into her mother's residence. Nell has asked you for a memorandum explaining the tax consequences of accepting the settlement described in (c).

X 54. Under the terms of a post-1986 divorce agreement, Al is to receive payments from Karen as follows: $50,000 in Year 1, $40,000 in Year 2, and $20,000 each year for Years 3 through 10. Al is also to receive custody of their minor son. The payments will decrease by $5,000 per year if the son dies or when he attains age 21 and will cease upon Al's death.
   a. What will be Al's taxable alimony in Year 1?
   b. What will be the effect of the Years 2 and 3 payments on Al's taxable income?

55. Under the terms of their divorce agreement, Barry is to transfer common stock (cost of $25,000, market value of $60,000) to Sandra. Barry and Sandra have a 14-year-old child. Sandra will have custody of the child, and Barry is to pay $300 per month as child support. In addition, Sandra is to receive $1,000 per year for 10 years. However, the payments will be reduced to $750 per month when their child reaches age 21. In the first year under the agreement, Sandra receives the common stock and the correct cash payments for six months. How will the terms of the agreement affect Sandra's gross income?

56. Mary (mother) is in the 39.6% marginal tax bracket, and Joe (son) is in the 28% marginal tax bracket. Mary loaned Joe $30,000, which he used to buy a new automobile. Mary did not charge Joe interest on the loan. Joe has $1,200 investment income (and no investment expenses) for the year from securities he inherited from his grandfather.
   a. Assuming the relevant Federal rate is 6% and the loan is outstanding for the entire year, what are the effects of the above on Mary's and Joe's tax liability for the year?
   b. If Joe could obtain a 9% bank loan for the automobile and Mary could invest the $30,000 at 8% interest before tax, would the family's after-tax income be maximized through the bank loan or through the interfamily loan?

57. On June 30, 1994, Ridge borrowed $52,000 from his employer. On July 1, 1994, Ridge used the money as follows:

Interest-free loan to Ridge's controlled corporation (operated by Ridge on a part-time basis)	$21,000
Interest-free loan to Tab (Ridge's son)	11,000
National Bank of Grundy 9% certificate of deposit ($15,260 due at maturity, June 30, 1995)	14,000
National Bank of Grundy 10% certificate of deposit ($7,260 due at maturity, June 30, 1996)	6,000
	$52,000

Ridge's employer did not charge him interest. The applicable Federal rate was 12% throughout the relevant period. Tab had investment income of $800 for the year, and he used the loan proceeds to pay medical school tuition. There were no other outstanding loans between Ridge and Tab. What are the effects of the preceding transactions on Ridge's taxable income for 1994?

58. Indicate whether the imputed interest rules should apply in the following situations:
    a. Mitch is a cash basis attorney who charges his clients based on the number of hours it takes to do the job. The bill is due upon completion of the work. However, for clients who make an initial payment when the work begins, Mitch grants a discount on the final bill. The discount is equal to 10% interest on the deposit.
    b. Local Telephone Company requires that customers make a security deposit. The deposit is refunded after the customer has established a good record for paying the telephone bill. The company pays 6% interest on the deposits.
    c. Lynn asked Kelly for a $125,000 loan to purchase a new home. Kelly made the loan and did not charge interest. Kelly never intended to collect the loan, and at the end of the year Kelly told Lynn that the debt was forgiven.

59. Vito is the sole shareholder of Vito, Inc. He is also employed by the corporation. On June 30, 1994, Vito borrowed $8,000 from Vito, Inc., and on July 1, 1995, he borrowed an additional $3,000. Both loans were due on demand. No interest was charged on the loans, and the Federal rate was 10% for all relevant dates. Vito used the money to purchase stock, and he had no investment income. Determine the tax consequences to Vito and Vito, Inc. in each of the following situations:
    a. The loans are considered employer-employee loans.
    b. The loans are considered corporation-shareholder loans.

60. Otis purchased an annuity from an insurance company for $15,000 on January 1, 1994. The annuity was to pay him $1,500 per year for life. At the time he purchased the contract, his life expectancy was 15 years.
    a. Determine Otis's gross income from the annuity in the first year.
    b. Assume Otis lives 20 years after purchasing the contract. What would be his gross income in the nineteenth year?
    c. Assume Otis died in 1997, after collecting a total of $6,000. What will be the effect of the annuity on his 1997 gross income?

61. In 1994, Ahmad purchased an annuity for $50,000. He was 59 at the time he purchased the contract. Payments were to begin when Ahmad attained age 62. In 1994, when the cash surrender value had increased to $51,000, Ahmad exercised a right to receive $1,500 and accept reduced payments after age 62. In 1996, when he had a life expectancy of 22.5 years, Ahmad received his first annual $3,000 payment under the contract.
    a. What is Ahmad's income from the contract in 1994?
    b. Compute Ahmad's taxable collections under the annuity contract in 1996.

62. For each of the following, determine the amount that should be included in gross income:
    a. Joe was selected as the most valuable player in the Super Bowl. In recognition of this, he was awarded a sports car worth $60,000 and $50,000 in cash.
    b. Wanda won the Mrs. America beauty contest. She received various prizes valued at $75,000.

c. George was awarded the Nobel Peace Prize. He took the $345,000 check he received and donated it to State University, his alma mater.

63. The LMN Partnership has a group term life insurance plan. Each partner has $100,000 protection, and each employee has protection equal to twice his or her annual salary. Employee Alice (age 44) had $90,000 insurance under the plan, and partner Kay (age 46) had $100,000 coverage. The cost of Alice's coverage for the year was $180, and the cost of Kay's protection was $380.

   a. Assuming the plan is nondiscriminatory, how much must Alice and Kay include in gross income from the insurance?

   b. Assuming the plan is discriminatory, how much must Kay include in her gross income from the insurance?

64. Herbert was employed for the first six months of the year and earned $60,000 in salary. During the next six months, he collected $7,800 of unemployment compensation, borrowed $6,000 (using his personal residence as collateral), and withdrew $1,000 from his savings account (including $60 interest). His luck was not all bad, for in December he won $800 in the lottery on a $5 ticket. Calculate Herbert's gross income.

65. Linda and Don are married and file a joint return. In 1994, they received $9,000 in Social Security benefits and $28,000 taxable pension benefits, interest, and dividends.

   a. Compute the couple's adjusted gross income on a joint return.

   b. If Linda works part-time and earns $30,000, how much would Linda and Don's adjusted gross income increase?

   c. Don would like to know whether they should sell for $100,000 a corporate bond (at no gain or loss) that pays 8% in interest each year and use the proceeds to buy a $100,000 nontaxable State of Virginia bond that will pay $6,000 in interest each year.

66. Melissa and James are married and file a joint return. They receive $8,000 a year in Social Security benefits, $25,000 pension benefits (all taxable), and $10,000 a year in taxable interest and dividends. Melissa is considering doing some consulting and would earn a fee of $5,000. Assuming that Melissa and James have $12,000 in itemized deductions and personal and dependency exemptions, how much will their taxable income increase if Melissa receives the $5,000 fee?

67. Donna does not think she has an income tax problem but would like to discuss her situation with you just to make sure she will not get hit with an unexpected tax liability. Base your suggestions on the following relevant financial information:

   a. Donna's share of the SAT Partnership income is $70,000, but none of the income can be distributed because the partnership needs the cash for operations.

   b. Donna's Social Security benefits totaled $8,400, but Donna loaned the cash received to her nephew.

   c. Donna assigned to a creditor the right to collect $1,200 interest on some bonds she owned.

   d. Donna and her husband lived together in California until September, when they separated. Donna has heard rumors that her husband had substantial gambling winnings since they separated.

CUMULATIVE PROBLEMS

68. Dan and Freida Butler, husband and wife, file a joint return. The Butlers live at 625 Oak Street, Corbin, KY 27521. Dan's Social Security number is 482–61–1231, and Freida's is 162–79–1245.

   During 1994, Dan and Freida furnished over half of the total support of each of the following individuals:

   a. Gina, their daughter, age 22, who was married on December 21, 1993, has no income of her own, and for 1994 files a joint return with her husband, who earned $8,500 during 1994.

   b. Sam, their son, age 17, who had gross income of $2,900 and who dropped out of high school in February 1994.

   c. Ben Brow, Freida's brother, age 27, who is a full-time college student with gross income of $2,900.

Dan, a radio announcer for WJJJ, earned a salary of $36,000 in 1994. Freida was employed part-time as a real estate salesperson by Corbin Realty and was paid commissions of $18,000 in 1994. Freida sold a house on December 30, 1994, and will be paid a commission of $1,500 (not included in the $18,000) on the January 10, 1995, closing date.

Dan and Freida collected $15,000 on a certificate of deposit that matured on September 30, 1994. The certificate was purchased on October 1, 1992, for $12,397, and the yield to maturity was 10%.

Dan and Freida had itemized deductions as follows:

State income tax withheld	$1,900
Real estate taxes paid	900
Interest on home mortgage (paid to Corbin Savings and Loan)	5,600
Cash contributions to the Boy Scouts	420

Their employers withheld Federal income tax of $7,400 (Dan $4,400, Freida $3,000), and the Butlers paid estimated tax of $800.

Part 1—Tax Computation
Compute Dan and Freida's 1994 Federal income tax payable (or refund due). Suggested software (if available): *TurboTax* or *MacInTax* for tax return or WFT tax planning software.

Part 2—Tax Planning
Dan plans to reduce his work schedule and work only halftime for WJJJ in 1995. He has been writing songs for several years and wants to devote more time to developing a career as a songwriter. Because of the uncertainty in the music business, however, he would like you to make all computations assuming he will have no income from songwriting in 1995. To make up for the loss of income, Freida plans to increase the amount of time she spends selling real estate. She estimates she will be able to earn $33,000 in 1995. Assume all other income and expense items will be approximately the same as they were in 1994. Will the Butlers have more or less disposable income (after Federal income tax) in 1995? Write a letter to the Butlers that contains your advice and prepare a memo for the tax files. Suggested software (if available): WFT tax planning software.

69. Sam T. Seymour would like to forget 1993 (and almost did as a result of his drinking problem). Although he received a salary of $74,000 and $600 of interest income, a divorce nearly brought him to financial ruin. The divorce was final on February 28, 1993. Under the agreement, Sam was required to do the following:

- Pay his minor daughter Pam's private school tuition of $10,800.

- Pay his ex-wife, Patricia Ann Seymour, a $40,000 lump-sum payment on March 1, 1993, and $2,000 each month thereafter through February 1999. The payments are to cease upon Patricia's death.

- Transfer to Patricia stock acquired in 1986 for $40,000 that now has a market value of $82,000.

Patricia retained custody of Pam but spent only $4,000 for Pam's support in 1993. The divorce agreement was silent as to whether Sam could claim Pam as a dependent and as to whether the cash payments to Patricia would constitute alimony.

Sam paid the tuition and made the $40,000 lump-sum payment but, because he was dismissed from his job in August 1993, was able to make only seven of the monthly payments to Patricia.

On November 1, 1993, when the applicable Federal rate was 6%, Sam was compelled to borrow $35,000 from his mother (Mollie Seymour). He gave her a non-interest-bearing second mortgage on his residence. There were no other loans outstanding between Sam and his mother.

Other information relevant to Sam's 1993 return is as follows:

a. Sam's disabled brother, Fred Seymour, lived with Sam from April through December 1993. Fred's only income was $3,600 of Social Security disability payments, and Sam contributed $4,000 toward Fred's support. No one else contributed to Fred's support. Fred's Social Security number is 245–99–4444.

b. Sam's only deductible items were home mortgage interest, $2,080; state income tax, $2,180; county property taxes, $3,000; charitable contributions, $200.

c. Sam's employer withheld $13,127 of Federal income tax.

d. Sam is 47 years old, his Social Security number is 215–71–1041, and he lives at 170 Ford Street, Gretna, TN 37929.

e. Patricia Ann Seymour's Social Security number is 712–15–9701.

Compute Sam's 1993 Federal income tax payable (or refund due). If you use tax forms for your computations, you will need Form 1040 and Schedule A. Suggested software (if available): *TurboTax* or *MacInTax* for tax return or WFT tax planning software.

RESEARCH PROBLEMS

Research Problem 1.   Edith gave common stock to her daughter, Joyce. The cost of the stock was $20,000, and its fair market value was $150,000. The uniform transfer tax on the gift was $30,000. Edith was liable for the transfer tax, but the gift was made on the condition that Joyce would pay the gift tax (i.e., a "net gift"). Joyce paid the $30,000 in accordance with the agreement.

The IRS agent contends that Edith must treat the transactions as part sale and part gift. That is, 20% of the stock ($30,000/$150,000 = .20) was sold, and the balance was given to Joyce. According to the agent, Edith must recognize taxable gain of $26,000 [$30,000 − (.20)($20,000)]. Edith is having difficulty understanding why she would be required to recognize any income since she made a gift of property and did not receive anything. Write a letter to the taxpayer that contains your advice and prepare a memo for the tax files.

Research Problem 2.   Sam purchased a newly issued convertible bond for $10,000 in 1991. The bond was issued by Hammer, Inc., and was convertible into 1,000 shares of the company's common stock. In 1994, Sam asked your opinion about the tax consequences of exercising his conversion rights. The value of the 1,000 shares of Hammer common stock is $13,000. Advise Sam whether he must recognize gain if he converts the bond into common stock.

Research Problem 3.   Alicia is a commissioned agent for a large insurance company. During the year, she purchased a policy on her life and the lives of her children and received a commission. Alicia treated the commission on these policies as a reduction in cost rather than as income. However, during an audit the revenue agent indicates that Alicia must include the commission in her gross income. Alicia seeks your assistance in resolving the matter with the agent.

Partial list of research aids:
Ostheimer v. U.S., 59–1 USTC ¶9300, 3 AFTR2d 886, 264 F.2d 789 (CA–3, 1959).
Rev.Rul. 55–273, 1955–1 C.B. 221.

Research Problem 4.   The Great Electric Company requires new customers to make a $100 deposit to secure future payments for electricity. After the customer has established a good payment record (usually within two years), the company refunds the deposit to the customer. If the services are terminated before refund, the deposit is usually applied against the final bill. The IRS agent insists that the company must include the deposits in gross income for the year the deposits are received. Can you find authority for excluding the deposits from income?

5

GROSS INCOME: EXCLUSIONS

LEARNING OBJECTIVES

After completing Chapter 5, you should be able to:

1. Understand that statutory authority is required to exclude an item from gross income.

2. Identify the circumstances under which various items are excludible from gross income.

3. Determine the extent to which receipts can be excluded under the tax benefit rule.

4. Describe the circumstances under which income must be reported from the discharge of indebtedness.

5. Identify tax planning strategies for obtaining the maximum benefit from allowable exclusions.

Items Specifically Excluded from Gross Income, 5–2

Statutory Authority, 5–2

Gifts and Inheritances, 5–3

Life Insurance Proceeds, 5–5

General Rule, 5–5

Exceptions to Exclusion Treatment, 5–5

Employee Death Benefits, 5–7

Gift versus Compensation, 5–7

Scholarships, 5–8

General Information, 5–8

Timing Issues, 5–9

Disguised Compensation, 5–9

Qualified Tuition Reduction Plans, 5–9

Compensation for Injuries and Sickness, 5–10

Damages, 5–10

Workers' Compensation, 5–12

Accident and Health Insurance Benefits, 5–12

Employer-Sponsored Accident and Health Plans, 5–13

Medical Reimbursement Plans, 5–14

Meals and Lodging, 5–14

Furnished for the Convenience of the Employer, 5–14

Other Housing Exclusions, 5–16

Other Employee Fringe Benefits, 5–17

Specific Benefits, 5–17

Cafeteria Plans, 5–17

General Classes of Excluded Benefits, 5–18

Taxable Fringe Benefits, 5–24

Foreign Earned Income, 5–24

Interest on Certain State and Local Government Obligations, 5–26

Dividends, 5–27

General Information, 5–27

Stock Dividends, 5–27

Educational Savings Bonds, 5–28

Tax Benefit Rule, 5–29

Income from Discharge of Indebtedness, 5–30

Tax Planning Considerations, 5–31

Life Insurance, 5–31

Employee Benefits, 5–31

Investment Income, 5–32

ITEMS SPECIFICALLY EXCLUDED FROM GROSS INCOME

Chapter 4 discussed the concepts and judicial doctrines that affect the determination of gross income. If an income item is within the all-inclusive definition of gross income, the item can be excluded only if the taxpayer can locate specific authority for doing so. Chapter 5 focuses on the exclusions Congress has authorized.

Tax advisers spend countless hours trying to develop techniques to achieve tax-exempt status for income. Employee benefits planning is greatly influenced by the availability of certain types of exclusions. Taxes play an important role in employee benefits, as well as in other situations, because attaining an exclusion is another means of enhancing after-tax income. For example, for a person whose combined Federal and state marginal tax rate is 40 percent, $1.00 of tax-exempt income is equivalent to $1.66 in income subject to taxation. The tax adviser's ideal is to attach the right labels or provide the right wording to render income nontaxable without affecting the economics of the transaction.

STATUTORY AUTHORITY

1 LEARNING OBJECTIVE
Understand that statutory authority is required to exclude an item from gross income.

Sections 101 through 150 provide the authority for excluding specific items from gross income. In addition, other exclusions are scattered throughout the Code. Each exclusion has its own legislative history and reason for enactment. Certain exclusions are intended as a form of indirect welfare payments. Other exclusions prevent double taxation of income or provide incentives for socially desirable activities (e.g., nontaxable interest on certain U.S. government bonds where the owner uses the funds for educational expenses).

In some cases, Congress has enacted exclusions to rectify the effects of judicial decisions. For example, the Supreme Court held that the fair market value of improvements (not made in lieu of rent) made by a tenant to the landlord's property should be included in the landlord's gross income upon termination of the lease.[1] The landlord was required to include the value of the improvements in gross income even though the property had not been sold or otherwise disposed of. Congress provided relief in this situation by enacting § 109, which defers taxing the value of the improvements until the property is sold.[2]

Gifts and Inheritances

2   **Learning Objective**
Identify the circumstances under which various items are excludible.

Beginning with the Income Tax Act of 1913 and continuing to the present, Congress has allowed the recipient of a gift to exclude the value of the property from gross income. The exclusion applies to gifts made during the life of the donor (*inter vivos* gifts) and transfers that take effect upon the death of the donor (bequests and inheritances).[3] However, as discussed in Chapter 4, the recipient of a gift of income-producing property is subject to tax on the income subsequently earned from the property. Also, as discussed in Chapter 1, the donor or the decedent's estate may be subject to gift or estate taxes on the transfer.

In numerous cases, gifts are made in a business setting. For example, a salesperson gives a purchasing agent free samples; an employee receives cash from his or her employer on retirement; a corporation makes payments to employees who were victims of a natural disaster; a corporation makes a cash payment to a deceased employee's spouse. In these and similar instances, it is frequently unclear whether the payment was a gift or whether it represents compensation for past, present, or future services.

The courts have defined a **gift** as "a voluntary transfer of property by one to another without adequate [valuable] consideration or compensation therefrom."[4] If the payment is intended to be for services rendered, it is not a gift, even though the payment is made without legal or moral obligation and the payor receives no economic benefit from the transfer. To qualify as a gift, the payment must be made "out of affection, respect, admiration, charity or like impulses."[5] Thus, the cases on this issue have been decided on the basis of the donor's intent.

In a landmark case, *Comm. v. Duberstein*,[6] the taxpayer (Duberstein) received a Cadillac from a business acquaintance. Duberstein had supplied the businessman with the names of potential customers with no expectation of compensation. The Supreme Court concluded:

> . . . despite the characterization of the transfer of the Cadillac by the parties [as a gift] and the absence of any obligation, even of a moral nature, to make it, it was at the bottom a recompense for Duberstein's past service, or an inducement for him to be of further service in the future.

---

[1] *Helvering v. Bruun,* 40–1 USTC ¶9337, 24 AFTR 652, 60 S.Ct. 631 (USSC, 1940).

[2] If the tenant made the improvements in lieu of rent, the value of the improvements is not eligible for exclusion.

[3] § 102.

[4] *Estate of D. R. Daly,* 3 B.T.A. 1042 (1926).

[5] *Robertson v. U.S.,* 52–1 USTC ¶9343, 41 AFTR 1053, 72 S.Ct. 994 (USSC, 1952).

[6] 60–2 USTC ¶9515, 5 AFTR2d 1626, 80 S.Ct. 1190 (USSC, 1960).

Summary of Principal Exclusions from Gross Income

1. Donative items
   Gifts, bequests, inheritances, and employee death benefits [§§ 102 and 101(b)]
   Life insurance proceeds paid by reason of death (§ 101)
   Scholarships (§ 117)
2. Personal and welfare items
   Injury or sickness payments (§ 104)
   Public assistance payments (Rev.Rul. 71–425, 1971–2 C.B. 76)
   Amounts received under insurance contracts for certain living expenses (§ 123)
   Reimbursement for the costs of caring for a foster child (§ 131)
3. Wage and salary supplements
   a. Fringe benefits
      Accident and health benefits (§§ 105 and 106)
      Lodging and meals furnished for the convenience of the employer (§ 119)
      Rental value of parsonages (§ 107)
      Employee achievement awards [§ 74(c)]
      Employer contributions to employee group term life insurance (§ 79)
      Cafeteria plans (§ 125)
      Educational assistance payments (§ 127)*
      Child or dependent care (§ 129)
      Services provided to employees at no additional cost to the employer (§ 132)
      Employee discounts (§ 132)
      Working condition and *de minimis* fringes (§ 132)
      Athletic facilities provided to employees (§ 132)
      Qualified transportation fringe (§ 132)
      Qualified moving expense reimbursement (§ 132)
      Tuition reductions granted to employees of educational institutions (§ 117)
   b. Military benefits
      Combat pay (§ 112)
      Housing, uniforms, and other benefits (§ 134)
   c. Foreign earned income (§ 911)
4. Investor items
   Interest on state and local government obligations (§ 103)
   Improvements by tenant to landlord's property (§ 109)
5. Benefits for the elderly
   Social Security benefits (except in the case of certain higher-income taxpayers) (§ 86)
   Gain from the sale of personal residence by elderly taxpayers (§ 121)
6. Other benefits
   Income from discharge of indebtedness (§ 108)
   Recovery of a prior year's deduction that yielded no tax benefit (§ 111)
   Educational savings bonds (§ 135)

*Exclusion treatment applies for tax years beginning before January 1, 1995.

Duberstein was therefore required to include the fair market value of the automobile in gross income.

In the case of cash or other property *received by an employee* from his or her employer, Congress has eliminated any ambiguity. Transfers from an employer to an employee cannot be excluded as a gift unless the transfer fits into a statutory exclusion provision other than the one for gifts.[7]

LIFE INSURANCE PROCEEDS

GENERAL RULE

Life insurance proceeds paid to the beneficiary because of the death of the insured are exempt from income tax.[8]

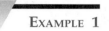

EXAMPLE 1

Mark purchased an insurance policy on his life and named his wife Linda as the beneficiary. Mark paid $24,000 in premiums. When he died, Linda collected the insurance proceeds of $50,000. The $50,000 is exempt from Federal income tax. ▼

Congress chose to exempt life insurance proceeds for the following reasons:

* For family members, life insurance proceeds serve much the same purpose as a nontaxable inheritance.
* In a business context (as well as in a family situation), life insurance proceeds replace an economic loss suffered by the beneficiary.

EXAMPLE 2

Gold Corporation purchased a life insurance policy to cover its key employee. If the proceeds were taxable, the corporation would require more insurance coverage to pay the tax as well as to cover the economic loss of the employee. ▼

Thus, in general, Congress concluded that making life insurance proceeds exempt from income tax was a good policy.

EXCEPTIONS TO EXCLUSION TREATMENT

The income tax exclusion applies only when the insurance proceeds are received because of the death of the insured. If the owner cancels the policy and receives the cash surrender value, he or she must recognize gain to the extent of the excess of the amount received over the cost of the policy (a loss is not deductible).[9]

Another exception to exclusion treatment applies if the policy is transferred after it is issued by the insurance company. If the policy is *transferred for valuable consideration,* the insurance proceeds are includible in the gross income of the transferee to the extent the proceeds received exceed the amount paid for the policy by the transferee plus any subsequent premiums paid.

---

[7] § 102(c).
[8] § 101(a).
[9] *Landfield Finance Co. v. U.S.,* 69–2 USTC ¶9680, 24 AFTR2d 69–5744, 418 F.2d 172 (CA–7, 1969).

TAX IN THE NEWS

TAX-EXEMPT LIFE INSURANCE BENEFITS FOR THE TERMINALLY ILL

In December 1992, the IRS issued proposed Regulations that would allow a terminally ill person to cash in his or her life insurance contract without recognizing gain. In the past, the taxpayer has been required to recognize gain equal to the difference between the proceeds from the policy and the total premiums paid. The proposed exclusion would allow the terminally ill to receive the economic benefits of owning the policy when the benefits are most needed and at little cost to the Federal government. A person would be deemed terminally ill if the attending physician indicated that the taxpayer was not expected to live for an additional 12 months.

SOURCE: Information from Robert Pear, "Benefits Proposed for the Terminally Ill," *New York Times,* December 16, 1992, p. A29.

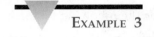

EXAMPLE 3

Adam pays premiums of $500 for an insurance policy in the face amount of $1,000 upon the life of Beth and subsequently transfers the policy to Carol for $600. Carol receives the proceeds of $1,000 on the death of Beth. The amount that Carol can exclude from gross income is limited to $600 plus any premiums she paid subsequent to the transfer. ▼

The Code, however, provides exceptions to the rule illustrated in the preceding example. The four exceptions that permit exclusion treatment include transfers to the following:

1. A partner of the insured.
2. A partnership in which the insured is a partner.
3. A corporation in which the insured is an officer or shareholder.
4. A transferee whose basis in the policy is determined by reference to the transferor's basis.

The first three exceptions facilitate the use of insurance contracts to fund buy-sell agreements.

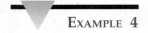

EXAMPLE 4

Rick and Sam are equal partners who have an agreement that allows either partner to purchase the interest of a deceased partner for $50,000. Neither partner has sufficient cash to actually buy the other partner's interest, but each has a life insurance policy on his own life in the amount of $50,000. Rick and Sam could exchange their policies (usually at little or no taxable gain), and upon the death of either partner, the surviving partner could collect tax-free insurance proceeds. The proceeds could then be used to purchase the decedent's interest in the partnership. ▼

The fourth exception applies to policies that were transferred pursuant to a tax-free exchange or were received by gift.[10]

Investment earnings arising from the reinvestment of life insurance proceeds are generally subject to income tax. Often the beneficiary will elect to collect the

---

[10] See the discussion of gifts in Chapter 14 and tax-free exchanges in Chapters 15 and 20.

insurance proceeds in installments. The annuity rules (discussed in Chapter 4) are used to apportion the installment payment between the principal element (excludible) and the interest element (includible).[11]

EMPLOYEE DEATH BENEFITS

GIFT VERSUS COMPENSATION

Frequently, an employer makes payments (**death benefits**) to a deceased employee's surviving spouse, children, or other beneficiaries. If the decedent had a nonforfeitable right to the payments (e.g., the decedent's accrued salaries), the amounts are generally taxable to the recipient just the same as if the employee had lived and collected the payments. But where the employer makes voluntary payments, the gift issue arises. Generally, the IRS considers such payments to be compensation for prior services rendered by the deceased employee.[12] However, some courts have held that payments to an employee's surviving spouse or other beneficiaries are gifts if the following are true:[13]

- The payments were made to the surviving spouse and children rather than to the employee's estate.
- The employer derived no benefit from the payments.
- The surviving spouse and children performed no services for the employer.
- The decedent had been fully compensated for services rendered.
- Payments were made pursuant to a board of directors' resolution that followed a general company policy of providing payments for families of deceased employees (but not exclusively for families of shareholder-employees).

When all of the above conditions are true, the payment is presumed to have been made *as an act of affection or charity.* When one or more of these conditions is not true, the surviving spouse and children may still be deemed the recipients of a gift if the payment is made in light of the survivors' financial needs.[14]

Automatic $5,000 Exclusion

Section 101(b) attempts to eliminate or reduce controversy in this area by providing an *automatic exclusion* of the first $5,000 paid by the employer to the employee's beneficiaries by reason of the death of the employee. The maximum total exclusion on behalf of a deceased employee is $5,000 regardless of the number of employers paying the benefit. The $5,000 exclusion must be apportioned among the beneficiaries on the basis of each beneficiary's percentage of the total death benefits received. When the employer's payments exceed $5,000, the beneficiaries may still be able to exclude the entire amount received as a gift if they are able to show gratuitous intent on the part of the employer. Note that this exclusion does not apply to the decedent's accrued salary.

---

[11] Reg. §§ 1.72–7(c)(1) and 1.101–7T.
[12] Rev.Rul. 62–102, 1962–2 C.B. 37.
[13] *Estate of Sydney J. Carter v. Comm.,* 72–1 USTC ¶9129, 29 AFTR2d 332, 453 F.2d 61 (CA–2, 1972), and the cases cited there.

[14] *Simpson v. U.S.,* 58–2 USTC ¶9923, 2 AFTR2d 6036, 261 F.2d 497 (CA–7, 1958), *cert. denied,* 79 S.Ct. 724 (USSC, 1958).

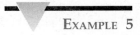

EXAMPLE 5

When Antonio died, his employer paid his accrued salary of $3,000 to Josefina, Antonio's widow. The employer's board of directors also authorized payments to Josefina ($4,000), Antonio's daughter ($2,000), and Antonio's son ($2,000) "in recognition of Antonio's many years of service to the company."

The $3,000 accrued salary is compensation for past services and was owed to Antonio at the time of his death. Therefore, the $3,000 is includible in gross income. The additional payments to the widow and children were not owed to Antonio. Because the payments were made in recognition of Antonio's past service, under the *Duberstein* decision, the payments are not gifts. However, the employee death benefit exclusion enables the widow and children to exclude the following amounts:

$$\text{Widow} \quad \frac{\$4,000}{\$8,000} \times \$5,000 = \$2,500$$

$$\text{Daughter} \quad \frac{\$2,000}{\$8,000} \times \$5,000 = 1,250$$

$$\text{Son} \quad \frac{\$2,000}{\$8,000} \times \$5,000 = \underline{1,250}$$

$$\underline{\underline{\$5,000}}$$

Besides avoiding the gift issue in many cases, the employee death benefit exclusion is intended to allow a substitute for tax-exempt life insurance proceeds.

SCHOLARSHIPS

GENERAL INFORMATION

Payments or benefits received by a student at an educational institution may be (1) compensation for services, (2) a gift, or (3) a scholarship. If the payments or benefits are received as compensation for services (past or present), the fact that the recipient is a student generally does not render the amounts received nontaxable.[15]

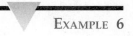

EXAMPLE 6

State University waives tuition for all graduate teaching assistants. The tuition waived is intended as compensation for services and is therefore included in the graduate assistant's gross income. ▼

As discussed earlier, gifts are not includible in gross income.

The **scholarship** rules are intended to provide exclusion treatment for education-related benefits that cannot qualify as gifts but are not compensation for services. According to the Regulations, "a scholarship is an amount paid or allowed to, or for the benefit of, an individual to aid such individual in the pursuit of study or research."[16] The recipient must be a candidate for a degree (either undergraduate or graduate) at an educational institution.[17]

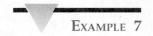

EXAMPLE 7

Terry enters a contest sponsored by a local newspaper. Each contestant is required to submit an essay on local environmental issues. The prize is one year's tuition at State University.

[15] Reg. § 1.117–2(a). See *C. P. Bhalla*, 35 T.C. 13 (1960), for a discussion of the distinction between a scholarship and compensation. See also *Bingler v. Johnson*, 69–1 USTC ¶9348, 23 AFTR2d 1212, 89 S.Ct. 1439 (USSC, 1969). For potential exclusion treatment, see the subsequent discussion of qualified tuition reductions.

[16] Prop.Reg. § 1.117–6(a)(3)(i).

[17] § 117(a).

Terry wins the contest. The newspaper has a legal obligation to Terry (as contest winner). Thus, the benefits are not a gift. However, since the tuition payment aids Terry in pursuing her studies, the payment is a scholarship. ▼

A scholarship recipient may exclude from gross income the amount used for tuition and related expenses (fees, books, supplies, and equipment required for courses), provided the conditions of the grant do not require that the funds be used for other purposes.[18] Amounts received for room and board are *not* excludible and are treated as earned income for purposes of calculating the standard deduction for a taxpayer who is another taxpayer's dependent.[19]

EXAMPLE 8

Kelly received a scholarship of $9,500 from State University to be used to pursue a bachelor's degree. She spent $4,000 on tuition, $3,000 on books and supplies, and $2,500 for room and board. Kelly may exclude $7,000 ($4,000 + $3,000) from gross income. The $2,500 spent for room and board is includible in Kelly's gross income.

The scholarship was Kelly's only source of income. Her parents provided more than 50% of Kelly's support and claimed her as a dependent. Kelly's standard deduction will equal her $2,500 gross income. Thus, she has no taxable income. ▼

TIMING ISSUES

Frequently, the scholarship recipient is a cash basis taxpayer who receives the money in one tax year but pays the educational expenses in a subsequent year. The amount eligible for exclusion may not be known at the time the money is received. In that case, the transaction is held *open* until the educational expenses are paid.[20]

EXAMPLE 9

In August 1994, Sanjay received $10,000 as a scholarship for the academic year 1994–1995. Sanjay's expenditures for tuition, books, and supplies were as follows:

August–December 1994	$3,000
January–May 1995	4,500
	$7,500

Sanjay's gross income for 1995 includes $2,500 ($10,000 − $7,500) that is not excludible as a scholarship. None of the scholarship is included in his gross income in 1994. ▼

DISGUISED COMPENSATION

Some employers make scholarships available solely to the children of key employees. The tax objective of these plans is to provide a nontaxable fringe benefit to the executives by making the payment to the child in the form of an excludible scholarship. However, the IRS has ruled that the payments are generally includible in the gross income of the parent-employee.[21]

QUALIFIED TUITION REDUCTION PLANS

Employees (including retired and disabled former employees) of nonprofit educational institutions are allowed to exclude a tuition waiver from gross income, if the

[18] § 117(b).
[19] Prop.Reg. § 1.117–6(h).
[20] Prop.Reg. § 1.117–6(b)(2).

[21] Rev.Rul. 75–448, 1975–2 C.B. 55. *Richard T. Armantrout,* 67 T.C. 996 (1977).

waiver is pursuant to a **qualified tuition reduction plan**.[22] The plan may not discriminate in favor of highly compensated employees. The exclusion applies to the employee, the employee's spouse, and the employee's dependent children. The exclusion also extends to tuition reductions granted by any nonprofit educational institution to employees of any other nonprofit educational institution (reciprocal agreements).

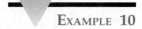

EXAMPLE 10 ABC University allows the dependent children of XYZ University employees to attend ABC University with no tuition charge. XYZ University grants reciprocal benefits to the children of ABC University employees. The dependent children can also attend tuition-free the university where their parents are employed. Employees who take advantage of these benefits are not required to recognize gross income. ▼

Generally, the exclusion is limited to *undergraduate* tuition waivers. However, in the case of teaching or research assistants, graduate tuition waivers may also qualify for exclusion treatment. According to the proposed Regulations, the exclusion is limited to the value of the benefit in excess of the employee's reasonable compensation.[23] Thus, a tuition reduction that is a substitute for cash compensation cannot be excluded.

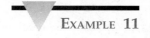

EXAMPLE 11 Susan is a graduate research assistant. She receives a $5,000 salary for 500 hours of service over a nine-month period. This pay, $10 per hour, is reasonable compensation for Susan's services. In addition, Susan receives a waiver of $6,000 for tuition. Susan may exclude the tuition waiver from gross income. ▼

ETHICAL CONSIDERATIONS

Excluding Scholarships from Taxation

Although scholarships are frequently much like gifts, they are also frequently much like compensation for services. University personnel spend countless hours attempting to assure that the amounts paid to good students and good athletes are not subject to tax. On the other hand, these same university personnel may also spend time trying to assure that the payments to the students are valid cost components of a research project funded by a grant.

Is it fair not to tax the gifted student who receives a scholarship when the less capable student, who works part-time, must pay his or her tuition with after-tax dollars?

COMPENSATION FOR INJURIES AND SICKNESS

DAMAGES

A person who suffers harm caused by another is often entitled to **compensatory damages.** The tax consequences of the receipt of damages depend on the type of harm the taxpayer has experienced. The taxpayer may seek recovery for (1) a loss of income, (2) expenses incurred, (3) property destroyed, or (4) personal injury.

---

[22] § 117(d).   [23] Prop.Reg. § 1.117–6(d).

Generally, reimbursement for a loss of income is taxed the same as the income replaced. The recovery of an expense is not income, unless the expense was deducted. Damages that are a recovery of the taxpayer's previously deducted expenses are generally taxable under the tax benefit rule, discussed later in this chapter.

A payment for damaged or destroyed property is treated as an amount received in a sale or exchange of the property. Thus, the taxpayer has a realized gain if the damage payments received exceed the property's basis. Damages for personal injuries receive special treatment under the Code.

Personal Injury

The legal theory of personal injury damages is that the amount received is intended "to make the plaintiff [the injured party] whole as before the injury."[24] It follows that if the damage payments received were subject to tax, the after-tax amount received would be less than the actual damages incurred and the injured party would not be "whole as before the injury."

Congress has specifically excluded from gross income the amount of any damage payments received (whether by suit or agreement) on account of personal injuries or sickness. The courts have applied the exclusion to any personal wrong committed against the taxpayer (e.g., breach of promise to marry, invasion of privacy, libel, slander, assault, battery). The exclusion also applies to compensation for loss of income (ordinarily taxable, as previously discussed) and recovery of expenses (except medical expenses deducted by the taxpayer) resulting from the personal injury.[25] According to the Supreme Court, however, the damages are taxable if under the Federal or state law establishing the taxpayer's right of recovery, the recovery is limited to the loss of income.[26]

In libel and slander cases, a single event can cause both a personal injury and damage to a business reputation. Damage to a business reputation is measured on the basis of estimated loss of income. Taxpayers argue that the amount received for loss of income in these cases is no different from the payments in other personal injury cases and thus should be excluded. According to the IRS, however, the business reputation damages are separate from the personal injury and are taxable.[27]

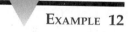

EXAMPLE 12

Tom, a television announcer, was dissatisfied with the manner in which Ron, an attorney, was defending the television station in a libel case. Tom stated on the air that Ron was botching the case. Ron sued Tom for slander, claiming damages for loss of income from clients and potential clients who heard Tom's statement. Ron's claim is for damages to his business reputation, and the amounts received are taxable.

Ron collected on the suit against Tom and was on his way to a party to celebrate his victory when a negligent driver, Norm, drove his truck into Ron's automobile, injuring Ron. Ron filed suit for the personal injuries and claimed as damages the loss of income for the period he was unable to work as a result of the injury. All amounts Ron received from Norm, including the reimbursement for lost income, are nontaxable because the claims are based on a personal injury. ▼

[24] *C. A. Hawkins,* 6 B.T.A. 1023 (1928).
[25] § 104(a)(2) and Rev.Rul. 85–97, 1985–2 C.B. 50.
[26] *U.S. v. Burke,* 92–1 USTC ¶50,254, 69 AFTR2d 92–1293, 112 S.Ct. 1867 (USSC, 1992).

[27] Rev.Rul. 85–143, 1985–2 C.B. 55, in which the IRS announced it would not follow the Ninth Court of Appeals decision in *Roemer v. Comm.,* 83–2 USTC ¶9600, 52 AFTR2d 83–5954, 716 F.2d 693 (CA–9, 1983). See also *Wade E. Church,* 80 T.C. 1104 (1983).

Punitive Damages

In addition to seeking compensatory damages, the injured party may seek **punitive damages,** which are often awarded to punish the defendant for gross negligence or the intentional infliction of harm. While some courts have held that punitive damages are taxable under the broad concept of gross income, other courts have permitted exclusion treatment.[28] The Revenue Reconciliation Act of 1989 clarified congressional intent on this issue by providing that punitive damages are includible in gross income *unless* the claim arises out of physical injury or physical sickness.[29] Thus, punitive damages received for loss of personal reputation are taxable, although the compensatory damages are excludible. Punitive damages arising out of a physical injury claim are excludible.

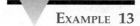

EXAMPLE 13

Assume Ron in Example 12 also received punitive damages in each suit. The punitive damages Ron received from Norm may be excluded from gross income because the damages arose out of the physical injury claim. Ron's punitive damages received from Tom are taxable because the damages did not arise from a physical injury or sickness claim. ▼

ETHICAL CONSIDERATIONS

Excluding Punitive Damages from Taxation

Punitive damages received because of a personal physical injury are excluded from tax while all other punitive damages received are taxable. If the damages are awarded as punishment to the wrongdoer, rather than compensation to the injured, why should any punitive damages be excluded from gross income? Because the punitive damages are awarded *in addition to the actual damages* the recipient suffered, the recipient is just as capable of paying tax as someone who receives income for services rendered.

Generally, a defendant will not settle a case that requires a payment for punitive damages. Thus, the exclusion of punitive damages is an additional incentive for the plaintiff to use the court system rather than settling the case in a more efficient manner.

WORKERS' COMPENSATION

State workers' compensation laws require the employer to pay fixed amounts for specific job-related injuries. The state laws were enacted so that the employee will not have to go through the ordeal of a lawsuit (and possibly not collect damages because of some defense available to the employer) to recover the damages. Although the payments are intended, in part, to compensate for a loss of future income, Congress has specifically exempted workers' compensation benefits from inclusion in gross income.[30]

ACCIDENT AND HEALTH INSURANCE BENEFITS

The income tax treatment of accident and health insurance benefits depends on whether the policy providing the benefits was purchased by the taxpayer or the

---

[28] Rev.Rul. 84–108, 1984–2 C.B. 32; *Glenshaw Glass v. Comm.,* 55–1 USTC ¶9308, 47 AFTR 162, 75 S.Ct. 473 (USSC, 1955); *Roemer v. Comm.,* 83–2 USTC ¶9600, 52 AFTR2d 83–5954, 716 F.2d 693 (CA–9, 1983).

[29] § 104(a).

[30] § 104(a)(1).

CONCEPT SUMMARY 5–2

Taxation of Damages

Type of Claim	Taxation of Award or Settlement
Breach of contract (generally loss of income)	Taxable.
Property damages	Recovery of cost, gain to the extent of the excess over basis, or loss to the extent of basis over the amount realized.
Personal injury	
Physical	All amounts (compensatory and punitive) are excluded unless previously deducted (e.g., medical expenses).
Nonphysical, general	Compensatory damages are excluded (unless previously deducted), and punitive damages are taxable.
Nonphysical, only compensation is loss of income	Taxable.

taxpayer's employer. Benefits collected under an accident and health insurance policy *purchased by the taxpayer* are excludible. In this case, benefits collected under the taxpayer's insurance policy are excluded even though the payments are a substitute for income.[31]

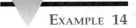

EXAMPLE 14   Bonnie purchased a medical and disability insurance policy. The insurance company paid Bonnie $200 per week to replace wages she lost while in the hospital. Although the payments serve as a substitute for income, the amounts received are tax-exempt benefits collected under Bonnie's insurance policy. ▼

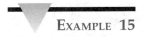

EXAMPLE 15   Joe's injury results in a partial paralysis of his left foot. He receives $5,000 from his accident insurance company for the injury under a policy he had purchased. The $5,000 accident insurance proceeds are tax-exempt. ▼

A different set of rules applies if the accident and health insurance protection was *purchased by the individual's employer*, as discussed in the following section.

EMPLOYER-SPONSORED ACCIDENT AND HEALTH PLANS

Congress encourages employers to provide employees, retired former employees, and their dependents with **accident and health benefits** and disability insurance plans. The *premiums* are deductible by the employer and excluded from the employee's income.[32] Although § 105(a) provides the general rule that the employee has includible income when he or she collects the insurance *benefits*, two exceptions are provided.

Section 105(b) generally excludes payments received for medical care of the employee, spouse, and dependents. However, if the payments are for expenses

---

[31] § 104(a)(3).

[32] § 106, Reg. § 1.106–1, and Rev.Rul. 82–196, 1982–1 C.B. 106.

that do not meet the Code's definition of medical care,[33] the amount received must be included in gross income. In addition, the taxpayer must include in gross income any amounts received for medical expenses that were deducted by the taxpayer on a prior return.

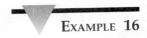

EXAMPLE 16

In 1994, Tab's employer-sponsored health insurance plan paid $4,000 for hair transplants that did not meet the Code's definition of medical care. Tab must include the $4,000 in his gross income for 1994. ▼

Section 105(c) excludes payments for the permanent loss or the loss of the use of a member or function of the body or the permanent disfigurement of the employee, spouse, or a dependent. Payments that are a substitute for salary (e.g., related to the period of time absent) are includible.

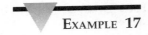

EXAMPLE 17

Jill lost an eye in an automobile accident unrelated to her work. As a result of the accident, Jill incurred $2,000 of medical expenses, which she deducted on her return. She collected $10,000 from an accident insurance policy carried by her employer. The benefits were paid according to a schedule of amounts that varied with the part of the body injured (e.g., $10,000 for loss of an eye, $20,000 for loss of a hand). Because the payment was for loss of a *member or function of the body,* § 105(c) applies and the $10,000 is excluded from income. Jill was absent from work for a week as a result of the accident. Her employer provided her with insurance for the loss of income due to illness or injury. Jill collected $500, which is includible in gross income. ▼

MEDICAL REIMBURSEMENT PLANS

In lieu of providing the employee with insurance coverage for hospital and medical expenses, the employer may agree to reimburse the employee for these expenses. The amounts received through the insurance coverage (insured plan benefits) are excluded from income under § 105 (as previously discussed). Unfortunately in terms of cost considerations, the insurance companies that issue this type of policy usually require a broad coverage of employees. An alternative is to have a plan that is not funded with insurance (a self-insured arrangement). The benefits received under a self-insured plan can be excluded from the employee's income, if the plan does not discriminate in favor of highly compensated employees.[34]

MEALS AND LODGING

FURNISHED FOR THE CONVENIENCE OF THE EMPLOYER

As discussed in Chapter 4, income can take any form, including meals and lodging. However, § 119 excludes from income the value of meals and lodging provided to the employee and the employee's spouse and dependents under the following conditions:[35]

- The meals and/or lodging are *furnished* by the employer, on the employer's *business premises,* for the *convenience of the employer.*

---

[33] See the discussion of medical care in Chapter 10.
[34] § 105(h).

[35] § 119(a). The meals and lodging are also excluded from FICA and FUTA tax. *Rowan Companies, Inc. v. U.S.,* 81–1 USTC ¶9479, 48 AFTR2d 81–5115, 101 S.Ct. 2288 (USSC, 1981).

- In the case of lodging, the *employee* is *required* to accept the lodging as a condition of employment.

The courts have construed both of these requirements strictly.

The following two questions have been raised with regard to the *furnished by the employer* requirement:

- Who is considered an *employee*?
- What is meant by *furnished*?

The IRS and some courts have reasoned that because a partner is not an employee, the exclusion does not apply to a partner. However, the Tax Court and the Fifth Court of Appeals have ruled in favor of the taxpayer on this issue.[36]

The Supreme Court held that a cash meal allowance was ineligible for the exclusion because the employer did not actually furnish the meals.[37] Similarly, one court denied the exclusion where the employer paid for the food and supplied the cooking facilities but the employee prepared the meal.[38]

The *on the employer's business premises* requirement, applicable to both meals and lodging, has resulted in much litigation. The Regulations define business premises as simply "the place of employment of the employee."[39] Thus, the Sixth Court of Appeals held that a residence, owned by the employer and occupied by an employee, two blocks from the motel that the employee managed was not part of the business premises.[40] However, the Tax Court considered an employer-owned house across the street from the hotel that was managed by the taxpayer to be on the business premises of the employer.[41] Perhaps these two cases can be reconciled by comparing the distance from the lodging facilities to the place where the employer's business was conducted. The closer the lodging to the business operations, the more likely the convenience of the employer is served.

The *convenience of the employer* test is intended to focus on the employer's motivation for furnishing the meals and lodging rather than on the benefits received by the employee. If the employer furnishes the meals and lodging primarily to enable the employee to perform his or her duties properly, it does not matter that the employee considers these benefits to be a part of his or her compensation.

The Regulations give the following examples in which the tests for excluding meals are satisfied:[42]

- A waitress is required to eat her meals on the premises during the busy lunch and breakfast hours.
- A bank furnishes a teller meals on the premises to limit the time the employee is away from his or her booth during the busy hours.
- A worker is employed at a construction site in a remote part of Alaska. The employer must furnish meals and lodging due to the inaccessibility of other facilities.

The *employee required* test applies only to lodging. If the employee's use of the housing would serve the convenience of the employer, but the employee is not required to use the housing, the exclusion is not available.

---

[36] Rev.Rul. 80, 1953–1 C.B. 62; *Comm. v. Doak*, 56–2 USTC ¶9708, 49 AFTR 1491, 234 F.2d 704 (CA–4, 1956); *Comm. v. Moran*, 56–2 USTC ¶9879, 50 AFTR 64, 236 F.2d 595 (CA–8, 1956); *Robinson v. U.S.*, 60–1 USTC ¶9152, 5 AFTR2d 315, 273 F.2d 503 (CA–3, 1959); *Briggs v. U.S.*, 56–2 USTC ¶10020, 50 AFTR 667, 238 F.2d 53 (CA–10, 1956), but see *G. A. Papineau*, 16 T.C. 130 (1951); *Armstrong v. Phinney*, 68–1 USTC ¶9355, 21 AFTR2d 1260, 394 F.2d 661 (CA–5, 1968).

[37] *Comm. v. Kowalski*, 77–2 USTC ¶9748, 40 AFTR2d 6128, 98 S.Ct. 315 (USSC, 1977).

[38] *Tougher v. Comm.*, 71–1 USTC ¶9398, 27 AFTR2d 1301, 441 F.2d 1148 (CA–9, 1971).

[39] Reg. § 1.119–1(c)(1).

[40] *Comm. v. Anderson*, 67–1 USTC ¶9136, 19 AFTR2d 318, 371 F.2d 59 (CA–6, 1966).

[41] *J. B. Lindeman*, 60 T.C. 609 (1973).

[42] Reg. § 1.119–1(f).

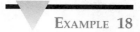

EXAMPLE 18

VEP, a utilities company, has all of its service personnel on 24-hour call for emergencies. The company encourages its employees to live near the plant so that the employees can respond quickly to emergency calls. Company-owned housing is available rent-free. Only 10 of the employees live in the company housing because it is not suitable for families.

Although the company-provided housing serves the convenience of the employer, it is not required. Therefore, the employees who live in the company housing cannot exclude its value from gross income. ▼

In addition, if the employee has the *option* of cash or lodging, the *required* test is not satisfied.

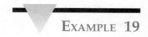

EXAMPLE 19

Khalid is the manager of a large apartment complex. The employer gives Khalid the option of rent-free housing (value of $6,000 per year) or an additional $5,000 per year. Khalid selects the housing option. Therefore, he must include $6,000 in gross income. ▼

OTHER HOUSING EXCLUSIONS

Employees of Educational Institutions

An employee of an educational institution may be able to exclude the value of campus housing provided by the employer. Generally, the employee does not recognize income if he or she pays annual rents equal to or greater than 5 percent of the appraised value of the facility. If the rent payments are less than 5 percent of the value of the facility, the deficiency must be included in gross income.[43]

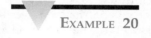

EXAMPLE 20

Swan University provides on-campus housing for its full-time faculty during the first three years of employment. The housing is not provided for the convenience of the employer. Professor Edith pays $3,000 annual rent for the use of a residence with an appraised value of $100,000 and an annual rental value of $12,000. Edith must recognize $2,000 gross income [.05($100,000) – $3,000 = $2,000] for the value of the housing provided to her. ▼

Ministers of the Gospel

Ministers of the gospel can exclude (1) the rental value of a home furnished as compensation or (2) a rental allowance paid to them as compensation, to the extent the allowance is used to rent or provide a home.[44] The housing or housing allowance must be provided as compensation for the conduct of religious worship, the administration and maintenance of religious organizations, or the performance of teaching and administrative duties at theological seminaries.

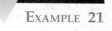

EXAMPLE 21

Pastor Bill is allowed to live rent-free in a house owned by the congregation. The annual rental value of the house is $6,000 and is provided as part of the pastor's compensation for ministerial services. Assistant Pastor Olga is paid a $4,500 cash housing allowance. She uses the $4,500 to pay rent and utilities on a home she and her family occupy. Neither Pastor Bill nor Assistant Pastor Olga is required to recognize gross income associated with the housing or housing allowance. ▼

[43]§ 119(d).   [44]§ 107 and Reg. § 1.107–1.

Military Personnel

Military personnel are allowed housing exclusions under various circumstances. Authority for these exclusions generally is found in Federal laws that are not part of the Internal Revenue Code.[45]

OTHER EMPLOYEE FRINGE BENEFITS

SPECIFIC BENEFITS

In recent years, Congress has enacted exclusions to encourage employers to (1) finance and make available child care facilities, (2) provide athletic facilities for employees, and (3) finance certain employees' education. These provisions are summarized as follows:

- The employee does not have to include in gross income the value of child and dependent care services paid for by the employer and incurred to enable the employee to work. The exclusion cannot exceed $5,000 per year ($2,500 if married and filing separately). For a married couple, the annual exclusion cannot exceed the earned income of the spouse who has the lesser amount of earned income. For an unmarried taxpayer, the exclusion cannot exceed the taxpayer's earned income.[46]
- The value of the use of a gymnasium or other athletic facilities by employees, their spouses, and their dependent children may be excluded from an employee's gross income. The facilities must be on the employer's premises, and substantially all of the use of the facilities must be by employees and their family members.[47]
- Qualified employer-provided educational assistance (tuition, fees, books, and supplies) at the undergraduate and graduate levels is excludible from gross income. The exclusion is subject to an annual employee statutory ceiling of $5,250.[48]

CAFETERIA PLANS

Generally, if an employee is offered a choice between cash and some other form of compensation, the employee is deemed to have constructively received the cash even when the noncash option is elected. Thus, the employee has gross income regardless of the option chosen.

An exception to this constructive receipt treatment is provided under the **cafeteria plan** rules. Under such a plan, the employee is permitted to choose between cash and nontaxable benefits (e.g., group term life insurance, health and accident protection, and child care). If the employee chooses the otherwise nontaxable benefits, the cafeteria plan rules enable the benefits to remain nontaxable.[49] Cafeteria

[45] H. Rep. No. 99–841, 99th Cong., 2d Sess., p. 548 (1986). See also § 134.
[46] § 129. The exclusion applies to the same types of expenses that, if they were paid by the employee (and not reimbursed by the employer), would be eligible for the Credit for Child and Dependent Care Expense discussed in Chapter 13.

[47] § 132(j)(4).
[48] § 127. Exclusion treatment applies for tax years beginning before January 1, 1995.
[49] § 125.

plans provide tremendous flexibility in tailoring the employee pay package to fit individual needs. Some employees (usually the younger group) prefer cash, while others (usually the older group) will opt for the fringe benefit program.

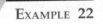

EXAMPLE 22　　Hawk Corporation offers its employees (on a nondiscriminatory basis) a choice of any one or all of the following benefits:

	Cost
Group term life insurance	$ 200
Hospitalization insurance for family members	2,400
Child care payments	1,800
	$4,400

If a benefit is not selected, the employee receives cash equal to the cost of the benefit. Kay, an employee, has a spouse who works for another employer that provides hospitalization insurance but no child care payments. Kay elects to receive the group term life insurance, the child care payments, and $2,400 of cash. Only the $2,400 must be included in Kay's gross income. ▼

GENERAL CLASSES OF EXCLUDED BENEFITS

An employer can confer numerous forms and types of economic benefits on employees. Under the all-inclusive concept of income, the benefits are taxable unless one of the provisions previously discussed specifically excludes the item from gross income. The amount of the income is the fair market value of the benefit. This reasoning can lead to results that Congress considers unacceptable, as illustrated in the following example.

EXAMPLE 23　　Vern is employed in New York as a ticket clerk for Trans National Airlines. He has a sick mother in Miami, Florida, but has no money for plane tickets. Trans National has daily

flights from New York to Miami that often leave with empty seats. The cost of a ticket is $400, and Vern is in the 28% tax bracket. If Trans National allows Vern to fly without charge to Miami, under the general gross income rules, Vern has income equal to the value of a ticket. Therefore, Vern must pay $112 tax (.28 × $400) on a trip to Miami. Because Vern does not have $112, he cannot visit his mother, and the airplane flies with another empty seat. ▼

If Trans National in Example 23 will allow employees to use resources that would otherwise be wasted, why should the tax laws interfere with the employee's decision to take advantage of the available benefit? Thus, to avoid the undesirable results that occur in Example 23 and in similar situations as well as to create uniform rules for fringe benefits, Congress established six broad classes of nontaxable employee benefits:[50]

- No-additional-cost services.
- Qualified employee discounts.
- Working condition fringes.
- *De minimis* fringes.
- Qualified transportation fringe.
- Qualified moving expense reimbursement.

No-Additional-Cost Services

Example 23 illustrates the **no-additional-cost service** type of fringe benefit. The services will be nontaxable if all of the following conditions are satisfied:

- The employee receives services, as opposed to property.
- The employer does not incur substantial additional cost, including forgone revenue, in providing the services to the employee.
- The services are offered to customers in the ordinary course of the business in which the employee works.[51]

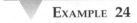

EXAMPLE 24

Assume that Vern in Example 23 can fly without charge only if the airline cannot fill the seats with paying customers. That is, Vern must fly on standby. Although the airplane may burn slightly more fuel because Vern is on the airplane and Vern may receive the same meal as paying customers, the additional costs would not be substantial. Thus, the trip could qualify as a no-additional-cost service.

On the other hand, assume that Vern is given a reserved seat on a flight that is frequently full. The employer would be forgoing revenue to allow Vern to fly. This forgone revenue would be a substantial additional cost, and thus the benefit would be taxable. ▼

Note that if Vern were employed in a hotel owned by Trans National, the receipt of the airline ticket would be taxable because Vern did not work in that line of business. However, the Code allows the exclusion for reciprocal benefits offered by employers in the same line of business.

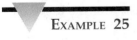

EXAMPLE 25

Grace is employed as a desk clerk for Plush Hotels, Inc. The company and Chain Hotels, Inc., have an agreement that allows any of their employees to stay without charge in either company's resort hotels during the off-season. Grace would not be required to recognize income from taking advantage of the plan by staying in a Chain Hotel. ▼

The no-additional-cost exclusion extends to the employee's spouse and dependent children and to retired and disabled former employees. In the Regulations, the IRS has conceded that partners who perform services for the partnership

---

[50] See, generally, § 132.   [51] Reg. § 1.132–2.

are employees for purposes of the exclusion.[52] (As discussed earlier in the chapter, the IRS's position is that partners are not employees for purposes of the § 119 meals and lodging exclusion.) However, the exclusion is not allowed to highly compensated employees unless the benefit is available on a nondiscriminatory basis.

Qualified Employee Discounts

When the employer sells goods or services (other than no-additional-cost benefits just discussed) to the employee for a price that is less than the price charged regular customers, the employee realizes income equal to the discount. However, the discount, referred to as a **qualified employee discount,** can be excluded from the gross income of the employee, subject to the following conditions and limitations:

- The exclusion is not available for real property (e.g., a house) or for personal property of the type commonly held for investment (e.g., common stocks).
- The property or services must be from the same line of business in which the employee works.
- In the case of *property,* the exclusion is limited to the *gross profit component* of the price to customers.
- In the case of *services,* the exclusion is limited to 20 percent of the customer price.[53]

EXAMPLE 26

Silver Corporation, which operates a department store, sells a television set to a store employee for $300. The regular customer price is $500, and the gross profit rate is 25%. The corporation also sells the employee a service contract for $120. The regular customer price for the contract is $150. The employee must recognize $75 income.

Customer price for property	$ 500
Less: Gross profit (25%)	(125)
	$ 375
Employee price	(300)
Income	$ 75
Customer price for service	$ 150
Less: 20 percent	(30)
	$ 120
Employee price	(120)
Income	$ –0–

▼

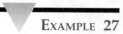

EXAMPLE 27

Assume the same facts as in Example 26, except the employee is a clerk in a hotel operated by Silver Corporation. Because the line of business requirement is not met, the employee must recognize $200 income ($500 – $300) from the purchase of the television and $30 income ($150 – $120) from the service contract. ▼

As in the case of no-additional-cost benefits, the exclusion applies to employees (including service partners), employees' spouses and dependent children, and retired and disabled former employees. However, the exclusion does not apply to highly compensated individuals unless the discount is available on a nondiscriminatory basis.

---

[52] Reg. § 1.132–1(b).   [53] § 132(c).

Working Condition Fringes

Generally, an employee is not required to include in gross income the cost of property or services provided by the employer if the employee could deduct the cost of those items if he or she had actually paid for them.[54] These benefits are called **working condition fringes.**

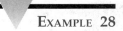

EXAMPLE 28   Mitch is a certified public accountant employed by an accounting firm. The employer pays Mitch's annual dues to professional organizations. Mitch is not required to include the payment of the dues in gross income because if he had paid the dues, he would have been allowed to deduct the amount as an employee business expense (as discussed in Chapter 9). ▼

In many cases, this exclusion merely avoids reporting income and an offsetting deduction. However, in two specific situations, the working condition fringe benefit rules allow an exclusion where the expense would not be deductible if paid by the employee:

- Automobile salespeople are allowed to exclude the value of certain personal use of company demonstrators (e.g., commuting to and from work).[55]
- The employee business expense would be eliminated by the 2 percent floor on miscellaneous deductions under § 67 (see Chapter 10).

Unlike the other fringe benefits discussed previously, working condition fringes can be made available on a discriminatory basis and still qualify for the exclusion.

De Minimis Fringes

As the term suggests, *de minimis* **fringe** benefits are so small that accounting for them is impractical. The House Report contains the following examples of *de minimis* fringes:

- The typing of a personal letter by a company secretary, occasional personal use of a company copying machine, occasional company cocktail parties or picnics for employees, occasional supper money or taxi fare for employees because of overtime work, and certain holiday gifts of property with a low fair market value are excluded.
- Subsidized eating facilities (e.g., an employees' cafeteria) operated by the employer are excluded if located on or near the employer's business premises, if revenue equals or exceeds direct operating costs, and if nondiscrimination requirements are met.

When taxpayers venture beyond the specific examples contained in the House Report and the Regulations, there is obviously much room for disagreement as to what is *de minimis*. However, note that except in the case of subsidized eating facilities, the *de minimis* fringe benefits can be granted in a manner that favors highly compensated employees.

Qualified Transportation Fringe

The Energy Policy Act of 1992 created a new category of nontaxable employee benefits called the **qualified transportation fringe.** The intent was to encourage the use of mass transit for commuting to and from work. The qualified transpor-

---

[54] § 132(d).   [55] § 132(j)(3).

tation fringe encompasses the following transportation benefits provided by the employer to the employee:[56]

1. Transportation in a commuter highway vehicle between the employee's residence and the place of employment.
2. A transit pass.
3. Qualified parking.

Statutory dollar limits are placed on the amount of the exclusion. Categories (1) and (2) above are combined for purposes of applying the limit. In this case, the limit on the exclusion is $60 per month. Category (3) has a separate limit. For qualified parking, the limit on the exclusion is $155 per month. Both of these dollar limits are to be indexed annually for inflation.

A *commuter highway vehicle* is any highway vehicle with a seating capacity of at least 6 adults (excluding the driver). In addition, at least 80 percent of the vehicle's use must be for transporting employees between their residences and place of employment.

Qualified parking includes the following:

• Parking provided to an employee on or near the employer's business premises.
• Parking provided to an employee on or near a location from which the employee commutes to work via mass transit, in a commuter highway vehicle, or in a carpool.

Qualified transportation fringes may be provided directly by the employer or may be in the form of cash reimbursements.

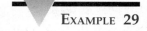

EXAMPLE 29

Gray Corporation's offices are located in the center of a large city. The company pays for parking spaces to be used by the company officers. Steve, a vice president, receives $250 of such benefits each month. The parking space rental qualifies as a qualified transportation fringe. Of the $250 benefit received each month by Steve, $155 is excludible from gross income. The balance of $95 is included in his gross income. The same result would occur if Steve paid for the parking and was reimbursed by his employer. ▼

Qualified Moving Expense Reimbursement

The Revenue Reconciliation Act of 1993 provides that qualified moving expenses that are reimbursed or paid by the employer are excludible from gross income. A qualified moving expense is one that would be deductible under § 217. See the discussion of moving expenses in Chapter 9.

Nondiscrimination Provisions

For no-additional-cost services and qualified employee discounts, if the plan is discriminatory in favor of highly compensated employees, these key employees are denied exclusion treatment. However, the non-highly compensated employees who receive benefits from the plan can still enjoy exclusion treatment for the no-additional-cost services and qualified employee discounts.[57]

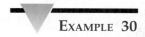

EXAMPLE 30

Dove Company's officers are allowed to purchase goods from the company at a 25% discount. Other employees are allowed only a 15% discount. The company's gross profit margin on these goods is 30%.

---

[56] § 132(f).   [57] § 132(j)(1).

CONCEPT SUMMARY 5–3

General Classes of Excluded Benefits

Benefit	Description and Examples	Coverage Allowed	Effect of Discrimination
1. No-additional-cost services	The employee takes advantage of the employer's excess capacity (e.g., free passes for airline employees).	Current, retired, and disabled employees; their spouses and dependent children; spouses of deceased employees. Partners are treated as employees.	No exclusion for highly compensated employees.
2. Qualified discounts on goods	The employee is allowed to purchase the employer's merchandise at a price that is not less than the employer's cost.	Same as 1. above.	Same as 1. above.
3. Qualified discounts on services	The employee is allowed a discount (maximum of 20%) on services the employer offers to customers.	Same as 1. above.	Same as 1. above.
4. Working condition fringes	Expenses paid by the employer that would be deductible if paid by the employee (e.g., a mechanic's tools). Also, includes auto salesperson's use of a car held for sale.	Current employees, partners, directors, and independent contractors.	No effect.
5. *De minimis* items	Expenses so immaterial that accounting for them is not warranted (e.g., occasional supper money, personal use of the copy machine).	*Any recipient* of a fringe benefit.	No effect.
6. Qualified transportation fringe	Transportation benefits provided by the employer to employees including commuting in a commuter highway vehicle, a transit pass, and qualified parking.	Current employees.	No effect.
7. Qualified moving expense reimbursement	Qualified moving expenses that are paid or reimbursed by the employer. A qualified moving expense is one that would be deductible under § 217.	Current employees.	No effect.

Peggy, an officer in the company, purchased goods from the company for $750 when the price charged to customers was $1,000. Peggy must include $250 in gross income because the plan is discriminatory.

Leo, an employee of the company who is not an officer, purchased goods for $850 when the customer price was $1,000. Leo is not required to recognize income because he received a qualified employee discount. ▼

De minimis (except in the case of subsidized eating facilities) and working condition fringe benefits can be provided on a discriminatory basis. The *de minimis* benefits are not subject to tax because the accounting problems that would be created are out of proportion to the amount of additional tax that would result. A nondiscrimination test would simply add to the compliance problems. In the case of working condition fringes, the types of services required vary with the job. Therefore, a nondiscrimination test probably could not be satisfied, although usually there is no deliberate plan to benefit a chosen few.

TAXABLE FRINGE BENEFITS

If the fringe benefits cannot qualify for any of the specific exclusions or do not fit into any of the general classes of excluded benefits, the taxpayer must recognize gross income equal to the fair market value of the benefits. Obviously, problems are frequently encountered in determining values. The IRS has issued extensive Regulations addressing the valuation of personal use of an employer's automobiles and meals provided at an employer-operated eating facility.[58]

If a fringe benefit plan discriminates in favor of highly compensated employees, generally those employees are not allowed to exclude the benefits they receive that other employees do not enjoy. However, the highly compensated employees, as well as the other employees, are generally allowed to exclude the nondiscriminatory benefits.[59]

EXAMPLE 31

MED Company has a medical reimbursement plan that reimburses officers for 100% of their medical expenses, but reimburses all other employees for only 80% of their medical expenses. Cliff, the president of the company, was reimbursed $1,000 during the year for medical expenses. Cliff must include $200 in gross income [(1 − .80) × $1,000 = $200]. Mike, an employee who is not an officer, received $800 (80% of his actual medical expenses) under the medical reimbursement plan. None of the $800 is includible in his gross income. ▼

FOREIGN EARNED INCOME

A U.S. citizen is generally subject to U.S. tax on his or her income regardless of the income's geographic origin. The income may also be subject to tax in the foreign country, and thus the taxpayer must carry a double tax burden. Out of a sense of fairness and to encourage U.S. citizens to work abroad (so that exports might be increased), Congress has provided alternative forms of relief from taxes on foreign earned income. The taxpayer can elect *either* (1) to include the foreign income in his or her taxable income and then claim a credit for foreign taxes paid or (2) to

---

[58] Reg. § 1.61–2 T(j). Generally, the income from the personal use of the employer's automobile is based on the lease value of the automobile (what it would have cost the employee to lease the

automobile). Meals are valued at 150% of the employer's direct costs (e.g., food and labor) of preparing the meals.

[59] §§ 79(d), 105(h), 127(b)(2), and 132(j)(1). See the discussion of the term "highly compensated employee" in Chapter 19.

exclude the foreign earnings from his or her U.S. gross income (the **foreign earned income exclusion**).[60] The foreign tax credit option is discussed in Chapter 13, but as is apparent from the following discussion, most taxpayers will choose the exclusion.

Foreign earned income consists of the earnings from the individual's personal services rendered in a foreign country (other than as an employee of the U.S. government). To qualify for the exclusion, the taxpayer must be either of the following:

• A bona fide resident of the foreign country (or countries).
• Present in a foreign country (or countries) for at least 330 days during any 12 consecutive months.[61]

EXAMPLE 32

Sandra's trips to and from a foreign country in connection with her work were as follows:

Arrived in Foreign Country	Arrived in United States
March 10, 1993	February 1, 1994
March 7, 1994	June 1, 1994

During the 12 consecutive months ending on March 10, 1994, Sandra was present in the foreign country for at least 330 days (365 days less 28 days in February and 7 days in March 1994). Therefore, all income earned in the foreign country through March 10, 1994, is eligible for the exclusion. The income earned from March 11, 1994, through May 31, 1994, is also eligible for the exclusion because Sandra was present in the foreign country for 330 days during the 12 consecutive months ending on May 31, 1994. ▼

The exclusion is *limited* to $70,000 per year. For married persons, both of whom have foreign earned income, the exclusion is computed separately for each spouse. Community property rules do not apply (the community property spouse is not deemed to have earned one-half of the other spouse's foreign earned income). A taxpayer who is present in the country for less than the entire year must compute the maximum exclusion on a daily basis ($70,000 divided by the number of days in the entire year and multiplied by the number of days present in the foreign country during the year).

EXAMPLE 33

Keith qualifies for the foreign earned income exclusion. He was present in France for all of 1994 except for 7 days in December, when he was in the United States. Keith's salary for 1994 is $90,000. If Keith had been in France for all of the 365 days in 1994, he would have been able to exclude $70,000. However, since he was not present in the foreign country for 7 days, his exclusion is limited to $68,658 as follows:

$$\$70,000 \times \frac{358 \text{ days in foreign country}}{365 \text{ days in the year}} = \$68,658$$

▼

In addition to the exclusion for foreign earnings, the *reasonable housing costs* incurred by the taxpayer and the taxpayer's family in a foreign country in excess of a base amount may be excluded from gross income. The base amount is 16 percent of the U.S. government pay scale for a GS–14 (Step 1) employee, which varies from year to year.[62]

---

[60] § 911(a).
[61] § 911(d). For the definition of resident, see Reg. § 1.871–2(b). Under the Regulations, a taxpayer is not a resident if he or she is there for a definite period (e.g., until completion of a construction contract).
[62] § 911(c).

As previously mentioned, the taxpayer may elect to include the foreign earned income in gross income and claim a credit (an offset against U.S. tax) for the foreign tax paid. The credit alternative may be advantageous if the individual's foreign earned income far exceeds the excludible amount so that the foreign taxes paid exceed the U.S. tax on the amount excluded. However, once an election is made, it applies to all subsequent years unless affirmatively revoked. A revocation is effective for the year of the change and the four subsequent years.

INTEREST ON CERTAIN STATE AND LOCAL GOVERNMENT OBLIGATIONS

At the time the Sixteenth Amendment was ratified by the states, there was some question as to whether the Federal government possessed the constitutional authority to tax interest on state and local government obligations. Taxing such interest was thought to violate the doctrine of intergovernmental immunity in that the tax would impair the state and local governments' ability to finance their operations.[63] Thus, interest on state and local government obligations was specifically exempted from Federal income taxation.[64] However, the Supreme Court recently concluded that there is no constitutional prohibition against levying a nondiscriminatory Federal income tax on state and local government obligations.[65] Nevertheless, currently the statutory exclusion still exists.

Obviously, the exclusion of the interest reduces the cost of borrowing for state and local governments. A taxpayer in the 36 percent tax bracket requires only a 5.12 percent yield on a tax-exempt bond to obtain the same after-tax income as a taxable bond paying 8 percent interest [5.12% ÷ (1 − .36) = 8%].

The lower cost for the state and local governments is more than offset by the revenue loss of the Federal government. Also, tax-exempt interest is considered to be a substantial loophole for the very wealthy. For these reasons, bills have been introduced in Congress calling for Federal government subsidies to state and local governments that voluntarily choose to issue taxable bonds. Under the proposals, the tax-exempt status of existing bonds would not be eliminated.

The current exempt status applies solely to state and local government bonds. Thus, income received from the accrual of interest on a condemnation award or an overpayment of state income tax is fully taxable.[66] Nor does the exemption apply to gains on the sale of tax-exempt securities.

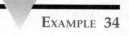

EXAMPLE 34

Megan purchases State of Virginia bonds for $10,000 on July 1, 1993. The bonds pay $400 interest each June 30th and December 31st. On March 31, 1994, Megan sells the bonds for $10,500 plus $200 accrued interest. Megan must recognize a $500 gain ($10,500 − $10,000), but the $200 accrued interest is exempt from taxation. ▼

State and local governments have developed sophisticated financial schemes to attract new industry. For example, local municipalities have issued bonds to finance the construction of plants to be leased to private enterprise. Because the

[63] *Pollock v. Farmer's Loan & Trust Co.*, 3 AFTR 2602, 15 S.Ct. 912 (USSC, 1895).
[64] § 103(a).
[65] *South Carolina v. Baker III*, 88–1 USTC ¶9284, 61 AFTR2d 88–995, 108 S.Ct. 1355 (USSC, 1988).

[66] *Kieselbach v. Comm.*, 43–1 USTC ¶9220, 30 AFTR 370, 63 S.Ct. 303 (USSC, 1943); *U.S. Trust Co. of New York v. Anderson*, 3 USTC ¶1125, 12 AFTR 836, 65 F.2d 575 (CA–2, 1933).

financing could be arranged with low-interest municipal obligations, the plants could be leased at a lower cost than the private business could otherwise obtain. However, Congress has placed limitations on the use of tax-exempt securities to finance private business.[67]

DIVIDENDS

GENERAL INFORMATION

A *dividend* is a payment to a shareholder with respect to his or her stock. Dividends to shareholders are taxable only to the extent the payments are made from *either* the corporation's *current earnings and profits* (in many cases the same as net income per books) or its *accumulated earnings and profits* (in many cases the same as retained earnings per books).[68] Distributions that exceed earnings and profits are treated as a nontaxable recovery of capital and reduce the shareholder's basis in the stock. Once the shareholder's basis is reduced to zero, any subsequent distributions are taxed as capital gains (see Chapter 14).[69]

Some payments are frequently referred to as dividends but are not considered dividends for tax purposes:

- Dividends received on deposits with savings and loan associations, credit unions, and banks are actually interest (a contractual rate paid for the use of money).
- Patronage dividends paid by cooperatives (e.g., for farmers) are rebates made to the users and are considered reductions in the cost of items purchased from the association. The rebates are usually made after year-end (after the cooperative has determined whether it has met its expenses) and are apportioned among members on the basis of their purchases.
- Mutual insurance companies pay dividends on unmatured life insurance policies that are considered rebates of premiums.
- Shareholders in a mutual investment fund are allowed to report as capital gains their proportionate share of the fund's gains realized and distributed. The capital gain and ordinary income portions are reported on the Form 1099 that the fund supplies its shareholders each year.

STOCK DIVIDENDS

When a corporation issues a simple stock dividend (e.g., common stock issued to common shareholders), the shareholder has merely received additional shares that represent the same total investment. Thus, the shareholder does not realize income.[70] However, if the shareholder has the *option* of receiving either cash or stock in the corporation, the individual realizes gross income whether he or she receives stock or cash.[71] A taxpayer who elects to receive the stock could be deemed to be in constructive receipt of the cash he or she has rejected.[72] However, the amount of the income in this case is the value of the stock received, rather than the cash the shareholder has rejected. See Chapter 14 for a detailed discussion of stock dividends.

---

[67] See § 103(b).

[68] § 316(a).

[69] § 301(c). See Chapter 4, *West's Federal Taxation: Corporations, Partnerships, Estates, and Trusts,* for a detailed discussion of corporate distributions.

[70] *Eisner v. Macomber,* 1 USTC ¶32, 3 AFTR 3020, 40 S.Ct. 189 (USSC, 1920); § 305(a).

[71] § 305(b).

[72] Refer to the discussion of constructive receipt in Chapter 4.

EDUCATIONAL SAVINGS BONDS

The cost of a college education has risen dramatically during the past 10 years, increasing at a rate almost twice the change in the general price level. The U.S. Department of Education estimates that by the year 2007, the cost of attending a publicly supported university for four years will exceed $60,000. For a private university, the cost is expected to exceed $200,000.[73] Consequently, Congress has attempted to assist low- to middle-income parents in saving for their children's college education.

The assistance is in the form of an interest income exclusion on **educational savings bonds.**[74] The interest on Series EE U.S. government savings bonds may be excluded from gross income if the bond proceeds are used to pay qualified higher education expenses. The exclusion applies only if both of the following requirements are satisfied:

- The savings bonds are issued after December 31, 1989.
- The savings bonds are issued to an individual who is at least 24 years old at the time of issuance.

The exclusion is not available for a married couple who file separate returns.

The redemption proceeds must be used to pay qualified higher education expenses. *Qualified higher education expenses* consist of tuition and fees paid to an eligible educational institution for the taxpayer, spouse, or dependent. In calculating qualified higher education expenses, the tuition and fees paid are reduced by excludible scholarships and veterans' benefits received. If the redemption proceeds (both principal and interest) exceed the qualified higher education expenses, only a pro rata portion of the interest will qualify for exclusion treatment.

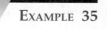

EXAMPLE 35

Tracy's redemption proceeds from qualified savings bonds during the taxable year were $6,000 (principal of $4,000 and interest of $2,000). Tracy's qualified higher education expenses were $5,000. Since the redemption proceeds exceed the qualified higher education expenses, only $1,667 ($5,000/$6,000 × $2,000) of the interest is excludible. ▼

TAX IN THE NEWS

ADDING APPEAL TO SAVINGS BONDS

In 1992, a proposal introduced in Congress would have exempted any interest on U.S. government savings bonds from tax, if the bond proceeds were spent on higher education, regardless of the taxpayer's adjusted gross income. This proposal met staunch opposition when the state and local governments realized that exempt Federal bonds would directly compete with state and local bonds for investment dollars.

SOURCE: Information from Alison Leigh Cowan, "Market Place: Adding Appeal to Savings Bonds," *New York Times,* October 6, 1992, p. D8.

---

[73] See generally, Knight and Knight, "New Ways to Manage Soaring Tuition Costs," *Journal of Accountancy* (March 1989): 207.

[74] § 135.

The exclusion is limited by the application of the wherewithal to pay concept. That is, once the modified adjusted gross income exceeds a threshold amount, the phase-out of the exclusion begins. *Modified adjusted gross income (MAGI)* is adjusted gross income prior to the § 911 foreign earned income exclusion and the educational savings bond exclusion. The threshold amounts are adjusted for inflation each year. For 1994, the phase-out begins at $46,900 ($70,350 on a joint return).[75] The phase-out is completed when MAGI exceeds the threshold amount by more than $15,000 ($30,000 on a joint return). The otherwise excludible interest is reduced by the amount calculated as follows:

$$\frac{\text{MAGI} - \$46,900}{\$15,000} \times \frac{\text{Excludible interest}}{\text{before phase-out}} = \frac{\text{Reduction in}}{\text{excludible interest}}$$

On a joint return, $70,350 is substituted for $46,900 (in 1994), and $30,000 is substituted for $15,000.

EXAMPLE 36

Assume the same facts as in Example 35, except that Tracy's MAGI for 1994 is $50,000. The phase-out will result in Tracy's interest exclusion being reduced by $345 [($50,000 – $46,900)/ $15,000 × $1,667]. Therefore, Tracy's exclusion is $1,322 ($1,667 – $345). ▼

Tax Benefit Rule

3 **LEARNING OBJECTIVE**
Determine the extent to which receipts can be excluded under the tax benefit rule.

Generally, if a taxpayer obtains a deduction for an item in one year and in a later year recovers all or a portion of the prior deduction, the recovery is included in gross income in the year received.[76]

EXAMPLE 37

A taxpayer deducted as a loss a $1,000 receivable from a customer when it appeared the amount would never be collected. The following year, the customer paid $800 on the receivable. The taxpayer must report the $800 as income in the year it is received. ▼

However, the § 111 **tax benefit rule** provides that no income is recognized upon the recovery of a deduction, or the portion of a deduction, that did not yield a tax benefit in the year it was taken. If the taxpayer in Example 37 had no tax liability in the year of the deduction (e.g., itemized deductions and personal exemptions exceeded adjusted gross income), the recovery would be partially or totally excluded from income in the year of the recovery.[77]

EXAMPLE 38

Before deducting a $1,000 loss from an uncollectible business receivable, Ali had taxable income of $200, computed as follows:

Adjusted gross income	$ 13,300
Itemized deductions and personal exemptions	(13,100)
Taxable income	$ 200

The business bad debt deduction yields only a $200 tax benefit. That is, taxable income is reduced by only $200 (to zero) as a result of the bad debt deduction. Therefore, if the customer makes a payment on the previously deducted receivable in a subsequent year, only the first $200 will be a recovery of a prior deduction and thus will be taxable. Any additional amount collected will be nontaxable because only $200 of the loss yielded a reduction in taxable income. ▼

---

[75] The indexed amounts for 1993 are $45,500 and $68,250.
[76] § 111(a).

[77] Itemized deductions are discussed in Chapter 10.

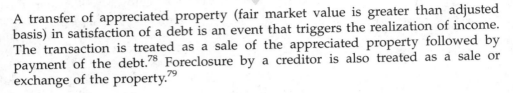

INCOME FROM DISCHARGE OF INDEBTEDNESS

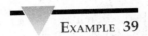

4 ▼ **LEARNING OBJECTIVE**
Describe the circumstances
under which income must be
reported from the discharge of
indebtedness.

A transfer of appreciated property (fair market value is greater than adjusted basis) in satisfaction of a debt is an event that triggers the realization of income. The transaction is treated as a sale of the appreciated property followed by payment of the debt.[78] Foreclosure by a creditor is also treated as a sale or exchange of the property.[79]

▼ **EXAMPLE 39**

Juan owed the State Bank $100,000 on an unsecured note. Juan satisfied the note by transferring to the bank common stock with a basis of $60,000 and a fair market value of $100,000. Juan must recognize $40,000 gain on the transfer. Juan also owed the bank $50,000 on a note secured by land. When Juan's basis in the land was $20,000 and the land's fair market value was $50,000, the bank foreclosed on the loan and took title to the land. Juan must recognize a $30,000 gain on the foreclosure. ▼

In some cases, a creditor will not exercise his or her right of foreclosure and will even forgive a portion of the debt to assure the vitality of the debtor. In such cases, the debtor realizes income from discharge of indebtedness.

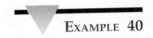

▼ **EXAMPLE 40**

Brown Corporation is unable to meet the mortgage payments on its factory building. Both the corporation and the mortgage holder are aware of the depressed market for industrial property in the area. Foreclosure would only result in the creditor's obtaining unsalable property. To improve Brown Corporation's financial position and thus improve Brown's chances of obtaining the additional credit from other lenders necessary for survival, the creditor agrees to forgive all amounts past due and to reduce the principal amount of the mortgage. ▼

Generally, the income realized by the debtor from the forgiveness of a debt is taxable.[80] A similar debt discharge (produced by a different creditor motivation) associated with personal use property is illustrated in Example 41.

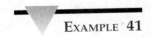

▼ **EXAMPLE 41**

In 1989, Joyce borrowed $60,000 from National Bank to purchase her personal residence. Joyce agreed to make monthly principal and interest payments for 15 years. The interest rate on the note was 7%. In 1994, when the balance on the note had been reduced through monthly payments to $48,000, the bank offered to accept $45,000 in full settlement of the note. The bank made the offer because interest rates had increased to 11%. Joyce accepted the bank's offer. As a result, Joyce must recognize $3,000 ($48,000 − $45,000) income.[81] ▼

The following discharge of indebtedness situations are subject to special treatment:[82]

1. Creditors' gifts.
2. Discharges under Federal bankruptcy law.
3. Discharges that occur when the debtor is insolvent.
4. Discharge of the farm debt of a solvent taxpayer.

---

[78] Reg. § 1.1001–2(a).
[79] Estate of Delman v. Comm., 73 T.C. 15 (1979).
[80] U.S. v. Kirby Lumber Co., 2 USTC ¶814, 10 AFTR 458, 52 S.Ct. 4 (USSC, 1931), codified in § 61(a)(12).

[81] Rev.Rul. 82–202, 1982–1 C.B. 35.
[82] §§ 108 and 1017.

5. Discharge of **qualified real property business indebtedness.**
6. A seller's cancellation of the buyer's indebtedness.
7. A shareholder's cancellation of the corporation's indebtedness.
8. Forgiveness of loans to students.

If the creditor reduces the debt as an act of *love, affection or generosity*, the debtor has simply received a nontaxable gift (situation 1). Rarely will a gift be found to have occurred in a business context. A businessperson may settle a debt for less than the amount due, but as a matter of business expediency (e.g., high collection costs or disputes as to contract terms) rather than generosity.[83]

In situations 2, 3, 4, and 5, the Code allows the debtor to reduce his or her basis in the assets by the realized gain from the discharge.[84] Thus, the realized gain is merely deferred until the assets are sold (or depreciated). Similarly, in situation 6 (a price reduction), the debtor reduces the basis in the specific assets financed by the seller.[85]

A shareholder's cancellation of the corporation's indebtedness to him or her (situation 7) usually is considered a contribution of capital to the corporation. Thus, the corporation's paid-in capital is increased, and its liabilities are decreased by the same amount.[86]

Many states make loans to students on the condition that the loan will be forgiven if the student practices a profession in the state upon completing his or her studies. The amount of the loan that is forgiven (situation 8) is excluded from gross income.[87]

TAX PLANNING CONSIDERATIONS

The present law excludes certain types of economic gains from taxation. Therefore, taxpayers may find tax planning techniques helpful in obtaining the maximum benefits from the exclusion of such gains. Following are some of the tax planning opportunities made available by the exclusions described in this chapter.

5 **LEARNING OBJECTIVE**
Identify tax planning strategies for obtaining the maximum benefit from allowable exclusions.

LIFE INSURANCE

Life insurance offers several favorable tax attributes. As discussed in Chapter 4, the annual increase in the cash surrender value of the policy is not taxable (because no income has been actually or constructively received). By borrowing on the policy's cash surrender value, the owner can actually receive the policy's increase in value in cash but without recognizing income.

EMPLOYEE BENEFITS

Generally, employees view accident and health insurance, as well as life insurance, as necessities. Employees can obtain group coverage at much lower rates than individuals would have to pay for the same protection. Premiums paid by the employer can be excluded from the employees' gross income. Because of the exclusion, employees will have a greater after-tax and after-insurance income if the employer pays a lower salary but also pays the insurance premiums.

---

[83] *Comm. v. Jacobson,* 49–1 USTC ¶9133, 37 AFTR 516, 69 S.Ct. 358 (USSC, 1949).
[84] §§ 108(a), (c), (e), and (g). Note that § 108(b) provides that other tax attributes (e.g., net operating loss) will be reduced by the

realized gain from the debt discharge prior to the basis adjustment unless the taxpayer elects to apply the basis adjustment first.
[85] § 108(e)(5).
[86] § 108(e)(6).
[87] § 108(f).

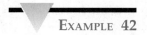

EXAMPLE 42

Pat receives a salary of $30,000. The company has group insurance benefits, but Pat was required to pay his own premiums as follows:

Hospitalization and medical insurance	$1,400
Term life insurance ($30,000 coverage)	200
Disability insurance	400
	$2,000

To simplify the analysis, assume Pat's tax rate on income is 28%. After paying taxes of $8,400 (.28 × $30,000) and $2,000 for insurance, Pat has $19,600 ($30,000 − $8,400 − $2,000) for his other living needs.

If Pat's employer reduced Pat's salary by $2,000 (to $28,000) but paid his insurance premiums, Pat's tax liability would be only $7,840 ($28,000 × .28). Thus, Pat would have $20,160 ($28,000 − $7,840) to meet his other living needs. The change in the compensation plan would save $560 ($20,160 − $19,600). ▼

Similarly, employees must often incur expenses for child care and parking. The employee can have more income for other uses if the employer pays these costs for the employee but reduces the employee's salary by the cost of the benefits.

The use of cafeteria plans has increased dramatically in recent years. These plans allow employees to tailor their benefits to meet their individual situations. Thus, where both spouses in a married couple are working, duplications of benefits can be avoided and other needed benefits can often be added. If less than all of the employee's allowance is spent, the employee can receive cash.

The meals and lodging exclusion enables employees to receive from their employer what they ordinarily must purchase with after-tax dollars. Although the requirements that the employee live and take his or her meals on the employer's premises limit the tax planning opportunities, in certain situations, the exclusion is an important factor in the employee's compensation (e.g., hotels, motels, restaurants, farms, and ranches).

The employees' discount provision is especially important for manufacturers and wholesalers. Employees of manufacturers can avoid tax on the manufacturer's, wholesaler's, and retailer's markups. The wholesaler's employees can avoid tax on an amount equal to the wholesale and retail markups.

It should be recognized that the exclusion of benefits is generally available only to employees. Proprietors and partners must pay tax on the same benefits their employees receive tax-free. By incorporating and becoming an employee of the corporation, the former proprietor or partner can also receive these tax-exempt benefits. Thus, the availability of employee benefits is a consideration in the decision to incorporate.

INVESTMENT INCOME

Tax-exempt state and local government bonds are almost irresistible investments for many high-income taxpayers. To realize the maximum benefit from the exemption, the investor can purchase zero coupon bonds. Like Series EE U.S. government savings bonds, these investments pay interest only at maturity. The advantage of the zero coupon feature is that the investor can earn tax-exempt interest on the accumulated principal and interest. If the investor purchases a bond that pays the interest each year, the interest received may be such a small amount that an additional tax-exempt investment cannot be made. In addition, reinvesting the interest may entail transaction costs (broker's fees). The zero coupon feature avoids these problems.

Series EE U.S. government savings bonds can earn tax-exempt interest if the bond proceeds are used for qualified higher education expenses. Many taxpayers can foresee these expenditures being made for their children's educations. In deciding whether to invest in the bonds, however, the investor must take into account the income limitations for excluding the interest from gross income.

KEY TERMS

Accident and health benefits, 5–13

Cafeteria plan, 5–17

Compensatory damages, 5–10

De minimis fringes, 5–21

Death benefits, 5–7

Educational savings bonds, 5–28

Foreign earned income exclusion, 5–25

Gift, 5–3

Life insurance proceeds, 5–5

No-additional-cost service, 5–19

Punitive damages, 5–12

Qualified employee discount, 5–20

Qualified real property business indebtedness, 5–31

Qualified transportation fringe, 5–21

Qualified tuition reduction plan, 5–10

Scholarship, 5–8

Tax benefit rule, 5–29

Working condition fringes, 5–21

PROBLEM MATERIALS

DISCUSSION QUESTIONS

1. Tim owned land that was leased to a corporation under a 20-year lease with no renewal options. In 1980, when 15 years were remaining on the lease, the tenant constructed a building on the property. The value of the building was $100,000, and its estimated useful life was 35 years. In 1994, the lease expired, the tenant moved, and Tim began using the building. The building's value when the lease expired was $75,000.
   a. Did Tim realize income in 1980 or in 1994?
   b. When is Tim required to recognize income from the value attributable to the building?

2. Bob gave Finch Company common stock to his son, Earl, before any dividends had been declared. Bob gave his mother the right to collect dividends on 100 shares of Finch Company common stock, but otherwise retained all incidents of ownership of the stock. Later in the year of the gifts, Finch Company paid $1 per share dividends. What are the tax consequences of these transactions upon Bob, Earl, and Bob's mother?

3. Violet Company gave $500 to each household in the community that had suffered a flood loss. The purpose of the payments was to help the flood victims. If some of the recipients are employees of Violet Company, can the employees exclude the payments from gross income?

4. Matt's truck was stalled on the side of the road. Abby stopped to help and called Al, who agreed to repair the truck for $75. Matt paid Al $75 and Abby $25. The payment to Al was made because of a contractual obligation and therefore is not a gift. The payment to Abby was not made because of a contractual obligation. Does this mean that the payment Abby received is a gift?

5. What are the two principal tax benefits of buying life insurance that has a cash surrender value?

6. Black Corporation purchased a $1,000,000 insurance policy on the life of the company's president. The company paid $100,000 of premiums, the president died, and the company collected the face amount of the policy. How much must Black Corporation include in gross income?

7. Grace died while employed by Seagull Company. Seagull paid Grace's husband $2,000 in sales commissions that Grace had earned and $3,000 under the company's policy of making payments to the spouse of a deceased employee. Is any of the $5,000 that Grace's husband received subject to income tax?

8. Yellow Company provides its employees with $10,000 group term life insurance. Red Company does not provide insurance but generally gives the family of a deceased employee $10,000. Compare the tax consequences of the insured and uninsured plans.

9. James received an academic scholarship to State University. Under the scholarship agreement, he received tuition ($1,500), books ($400), and room and board ($5,000). What is James's gross income from the scholarship?

10. José is a graduate assistant at State University. He receives $7,000 a year in salary. In addition, tuition of $4,000 is waived. The tuition waiver is available to all full- and part-time employees. The fair market value of José's services is $11,000. How much is José required to include in his gross income?

11. Ted and Olaf were traveling together in a defectively manufactured automobile. As a result of the defects, the automobile ran off the road and crashed into a tree. Ted and Olaf each broke an arm in the accident. Ted was a baseball pitcher and was unable to pitch for one year as a result of the accident. He received a $400,000 damage award in a suit against the automobile manufacturer. Olaf was a 65-year-old retiree and received $25,000 as an award for damages. The difference in the damage awards was largely due to Ted's greater loss of earnings. Is Ted taxed on any of the $400,000 received?

12. Sara was injured in an automobile accident by a person who was intoxicated at the time of the accident. She settled with the defendant's insurance company and received $15,000 for the medical expenses associated with a whiplash, $6,000 for lost wages, and $5,000 of punitive damages. How much of the settlement is Sara required to include in gross income?

13. Wes purchases an accident and health insurance plan that was advertised in the Sunday newspaper. The annual premiums are $400. During the year, Wes received payments of $1,200 under the plan.
    a. How much of the $1,200 must Wes include in his gross income?
    b. Would the tax consequences differ if the $1,200 represented amounts paid by the insurance company to replace lost wages while Wes was hospitalized?

14. What nontaxable fringe benefits are available to employees that are not available to partners and proprietors?

15. How does one determine if the meals and lodging supplied by the employer are to serve a valid business purpose? Is the tax treatment of meals and lodging affected if the employer advertises that the meals and lodging provided are one of the employees' fringe benefits?

16. Paula is employed by a telemarketing firm that pays a fixed amount for unlimited long-distance telephone calls. Employees are allowed to use the toll-free line for 5 minutes each month at no charge to the employee. The normal charge for the calls Paula made during the year was $75. How much is Paula required to include in gross income?

17. Eagle Life Insurance Company pays its employees $.25 per mile for driving their personal automobiles to and from work. The company reimburses each employee who rides the bus $45 a month for the cost of a pass. Tom collected $60 for his automobile mileage, and Ted received $45 as reimbursement for the cost of a bus pass.
    a. What are the effects of the above on Tom and Ted's gross income?

    b. Assume that Tom and Ted are in the 28% marginal tax bracket, and the actual before-tax cost for Tom to drive to and from work is $.25 per mile. What are Tom and Ted's after-tax costs of commuting to and from work?

18. Jane works at a bakery and is allowed to take home bread that could not be sold during the day. The bakery gives the day-old bread to the employees because it has no other use for the goods. Is Jane required to recognize income as a result of receiving the bread?

19. Gary is employed by Pelican, Inc., an automobile manufacturing company. Pelican sells Gary a new automobile at company cost of $12,000. The price charged a dealer would have been $14,000, and the retail price of the automobile is $17,000. What is Gary's gross income from the purchase of the automobile?

20. Flamingo Company provides officers with a 30% discount on merchandise, but provides other employees with only a 10% discount. The company's gross profit rate on the goods is 40%. If Zack, an officer in the company, is allowed to buy goods for $70 when the regular price is $100, how much is Zack required to include in gross income?

21. Rashad is a U.S. citizen who worked in a foreign country for the period July 1, 1994, through May 31, 1995. Is Rashad entitled to any foreign earned income exclusion for 1994?

22. Falcon Corporation is opening a branch in Kazonbi, an African country that does not levy an income tax on citizens of foreign countries. Carl, a U.S. citizen, is considering two offers from his employer, Falcon Corporation. He can work for 6 months in Kazonbi and 6 months in the United States and receive a salary of $4,000 per month, or he can work in Kazonbi for 12 months at the same monthly salary. Carl would like to spend as much time in the United States as possible and prefers the first alternative. However, he asks your advice as to how income taxes might affect his decision.

23. When is interest received from a state or local government subject to tax?

24. Donna and George are married, file a joint return, and are in the 36% marginal tax bracket. They would like to save for their child's education. What would be the advantage of buying State of Virginia bonds as compared to buying Series EE U.S. government bonds?

25. Chee owns 100 shares of stock in Sparrow Corporation. The corporation declares a dividend that gives Chee the option of receiving 10 additional shares of Sparrow stock or $200 cash. Chee elects to receive 10 additional shares of stock. What are the tax consequences to Chee?

26. In 1994, Mary received a $2,000 sales commission. However, in 1995, her employer discovered that Mary should have received only a $1,500 commission in 1994. Therefore, the employer withheld $500 from Mary's 1995 commission. Mary's standard deduction and personal exemption for 1994 exceeded her gross income. What effect would the tax benefit rule have on Mary's gross income for 1995?

27. In 1994, Fred paid $2,400 in life insurance premiums. The premiums are not deductible on his return. The policy is with a "mutual company," which means that the company rebates premiums if it has profits for the year. The rebates are termed dividends. In 1995, Fred received a $200 dividend attributable to premiums paid in 1994. Fred also received a $700 factory rebate on a personal automobile he purchased during the year. How should Fred report these items on his return?

28. How does the tax treatment of a corporation's income generated by the retirement of bonds for less than book value (issue price plus amortized discount or less amortized premium) differ from the income derived from a shareholder's forgiveness of the corporation's indebtedness?

29. In 1988, Moustafa purchased real estate for $500,000. To finance the transaction, Moustafa borrowed $200,000 from the bank, invested $80,000 of his money, and gave

the seller a note for $220,000. In 1994, when the balance on the note to the bank was $200,000, Moustafa negotiated a reduction in principal to $150,000. In addition, the seller reduced the balance due on his note from $210,000 to $150,000. What are the tax consequences of the debt adjustments to Moustafa?

30. What special tax benefits are available to students and their parents?

PROBLEMS

31. Determine whether the following may be excluded from gross income as gifts, bequests, scholarships, prizes, or life insurance proceeds:
    a. Uncle told Nephew, "Come live with me and take care of me in my old age and you can have all my property after my death." Nephew complied with Uncle's request. Uncle's will made Nephew sole beneficiary of the estate.
    b. Uncle told Nephew, "If you study hard and make the dean's list this year, I will pay your tuition for the following year." Nephew made the dean's list, and Uncle paid the tuition.
    c. Uncle told Nephew, "If you make the dean's list this year, I will pay you $500." Nephew made the dean's list, and Uncle paid the $500.
    d. Diane cashed in her life insurance contract and collected $10,000. She had paid premiums totaling $7,000.
    e. Fred received $500 from his employer to pay the medical expenses of Fred's child. The payment was not part of a medical reimbursement plan, and the employer made the payment out of compassion.

32. Determine the taxable life insurance proceeds in the following cases:
    a. Manuel purchased a sports franchise and player contracts from Steve. As part of the transaction, Manuel purchased a life insurance contract on a key player from Steve for $50,000. One month later, the player was killed in an automobile accident, and Manuel collected $500,000 on the life insurance contract.
    b. Kareem and Vito formed a partnership and agreed that upon the death of either partner, the surviving partner would purchase the decedent's partnership interest. Kareem purchased a life insurance policy on Vito's life and paid $5,000 in premiums. Upon Vito's death, Kareem collected $100,000 on the life insurance policy and used the proceeds to purchase Vito's interest in the partnership.
    c. Same as (b), except the partnership was incorporated and Kareem and Vito owned all the stock. Upon incorporation, Kareem and Vito transferred their life insurance policies to the corporation in exchange for stock. When Vito died, the corporation redeemed (purchased) Vito's stock, using the $100,000 life insurance proceeds.

33. The Egret Company, which is in the 40% (combined Federal and state) marginal tax bracket, estimated that if its current president should die, the company would incur $200,000 in costs to find a suitable replacement. In addition, profits on various projects the president is responsible for would likely decrease by $300,000. How much insurance should the company carry on the life of its president to compensate for the after-tax loss that would result from the president's death, assuming the $200,000 costs of finding a president are deductible and the lost profits would have been taxable?

34. Determine whether the taxpayer has gross income in each of the following situations:
    a. Jim is a waiter in a restaurant. The rule of thumb is that a customer should leave the waiter a tip equal to 15% of the customer's bill for food and beverages. Jim collected $6,000 in tips during the year.
    b. Tara works at a grocery store, bagging groceries and carrying them to the customers' automobiles. Her employer posts a sign saying that the employees are paid by the hour and the customer is not expected to tip them. Tara received $1,800 in tips from customers.
    c. Sheila worked at a hotel. Her home was damaged by a fire. Sheila's employer allowed her to stay at the hotel for no charge until she could return to her home. The normal charge for the room Sheila occupied during this period was $500, and the hotel had several vacant rooms.

35. Donald died at age 35. He was married and had four minor children. Donald's employer, Lark Painting Company, made payments to his wife as follows:

Donald's accrued salary at date of death	$4,000
Family death benefits under long-standing company policy ($2,000 is paid to the spouse and $1,500 is paid to each child of a deceased employee)	2,000
A payment authorized by the board of directors to help his wife pay debts accumulated by Donald	7,000

In addition, Donald's wife was the beneficiary of her husband's life insurance policy of $50,000. Lark Painting Company had paid for the policy. Donald had excluded all of the premiums paid by the employer from gross income as group term life insurance. His wife left the insurance proceeds with the insurance company and elected to receive an annuity of $4,000 each year for life. Her life expectancy is 40 years. She collected one $4,000 payment at the end of the current year. A joint return was filed in the year of Donald's death. Which of the above amounts must be included in gross income?

36. Alejandro was awarded an academic scholarship to State University. He received $5,000 in August and $6,000 in December 1994. Alejandro had enough personal savings to pay all expenses as they came due. Alejandro's expenditures for the relevant period were as follows:

Tuition, August 1994	$2,900
Tuition, December 1994	3,200
Room and board	
August–December 1994	3,000
January–May 1995	2,400
Books and educational supplies	
August–December 1994	800
January–May 1995	950

Determine the effect on Alejandro's gross income for 1994 and 1995.

37. Walt made the all-state football team during his junior and senior years in high school. He accepted an athletic scholarship from State University. The scholarship provided the following:

Tuition and fees	$4,000
Room and board	2,500
Books and supplies	500

Determine the effect of the scholarship on Walt's gross income.

38. Determine the taxpayer's taxable damages in each of the following cases:
    a. Orange Corporation collected $500,000 for damages to its business reputation.
    b. Don collected $100,000 in lost wages caused by age discrimination by his employer. Under the relevant law, a successful plaintiff can recover only lost wages.
    c. Kirby was injured in an automobile accident and collected $10,000 for loss of the use of his left arm, $15,000 for pain and suffering, $9,000 in lost wages, $5,000 for medical expenses, and $10,000 of punitive damages. None of the medical expenses had been deducted because Kirby's insurance policy paid the hospital and doctor.
    d. Nell received $10,000 of damages for invasion of her privacy by a photographer and $5,000 of punitive damages.

39. Tom was accused of shoplifting. He sued the store and collected $1,000 for actual damages to his personal reputation and $10,000 in punitive damages for the outrageous behavior by the store's security guard. Tom's wife, Jane, slipped on a banana peel in the same store and collected $5,000 in medical expenses she incurred (the expenses were not deducted on their return) and $1,500 in lost wages (wages she would have earned

if she had not been injured). Must any of these amounts be included in Tom and Jane's income reported on a joint return?

40. Rex, age 45, is an officer of Blue Company, which provided him with the following nondiscriminatory fringe benefits in 1994:
    a. Hospitalization insurance for Rex and his dependents. The cost of coverage for Rex was $450, and the additional cost for Rex's dependents was $400.
    b. Reimbursement of $700 from an uninsured medical reimbursement plan available to all employees.
    c. Group term life insurance protection of $120,000. (Each employee received coverage equal to twice his or her annual salary.)
    d. Salary continuation payments of $2,600 while Rex was hospitalized for an illness.

    While Rex was ill, he collected $1,600 on a salary continuation insurance policy he had purchased. Determine the amounts Rex must include in gross income.

41. Ramon served as the manager of an orphanage in 1994. In this connection, he had the following transactions:
    a. He received no salary from his job but was given room and board (valued at $9,600) on the premises. No other person was employed by the orphanage, which is a tax-exempt organization.
    b. The orphanage paid $500 in tuition for a night course Ramon took at a local university. The course was in the field of philosophy and dealt with the meaning of life. The payment was authorized by the orphanage's trustees in a written resolution.
    c. The orphanage paid $900 of the premiums on Ramon's life insurance policy and all of his medical expenses of $1,800. Again, the payment was made pursuant to a resolution approved by the trustees.

    Determine the effect of these transactions on Ramon's gross income.

42. The UVW Union and HON Corporation are negotiating contract terms. Assume the union members are in the 28% marginal tax bracket and all benefits would be provided on a nondiscriminatory basis. Write a letter to the UVW Union members explaining the tax consequences of the options discussed below.
    a. The company would impose a $100 deductible on medical insurance benefits. Most employees incur more than $100 each year in medical expenses.
    b. Employees would get an additional paid holiday with the same annual income (the same pay but less work).
    c. An employee who did not need health insurance (because the employee's spouse works and receives family coverage) would be allowed to receive the cash value of the coverage.

43. Determine the taxpayer's gross income for each of the following:
    a. Alice is the manager of a plant. The company owns a house one mile from the plant (rental value of $6,000) that Alice is allowed to occupy.
    b. Pam works for an insurance company that allows employees to eat in the cafeteria for $.50 a meal. Generally, the cost to the insurance company of producing a meal is $5.00, and a comparable meal could be purchased for $4.00. Pam ate 150 meals in the cafeteria during the year.
    c. Wade is a Methodist minister and receives a housing allowance of $600 per month from his church. Wade is buying his home and uses the $600 to make house payments ($450) and to pay utilities ($150).
    d. Floyd is a college professor and lives in campus housing. He is not charged rent. The value of the house is $100,000, and the annual rental value is $7,200.

44. Does the taxpayer recognize gross income in the following situations?
    a. Ann is a registered nurse working in a community hospital. She is not required to take her lunch on the hospital premises, but she can eat in the cafeteria at no charge. The hospital adopted this policy to encourage employees to stay on the premises and be available in case of emergencies. During the year, Ann ate most of her meals on the premises. The total value of those meals was $750.

b. Ira is the manager of a hotel. His employer will allow him to live in one of the rooms rent-free or to receive a $600 per month cash allowance for rent. Ira elected to live in the hotel.

c. Seth is a forest ranger and lives in his employer's cabin in the forest. He is required to live there, and because there are no restaurants nearby, the employer supplies Seth with groceries that he cooks and eats on the premises.

d. Rocky is a partner in the BAR Ranch (a partnership). He is the full-time manager of the ranch. BAR has a business purpose for Rocky's living on the ranch.

45. Thrush Corporation provides a health insurance plan for all of its employees. The plan pays for all medical care after the first $500 incurred for the year. Under the company's cafeteria plan, which is available to all employees, an employee can receive either (1) insurance that will pay his or her regular salary while he or she is away from work due to illness and reimbursement for the first $500 of medical expenses or (2) $1,200 cash. Sam elected to receive the additional insurance and reimbursement of medical expenses.

a. What is Sam's gross income from the above assuming the only benefits he collected were $400 in reimbursement for medical expenses?

b. What is Sam's gross income from the above assuming that he collected $400 on the medical reimbursement plan and $4,000 under the wage continuation insurance?

46. Ed is employed by FUN Bowling Lanes, Inc. Determine Ed's gross income in each of the following situations:

a. Ed's children are allowed to use the lanes without charge. Each child can also bring a friend without charge. This benefit is available to all employees. During the year, the children bowled 100 games, and the usual charge was $1.50 per game. Friends of Ed's children bowled 90 games.

b. The company has a lunch counter. Ed is allowed to take home the leftover donuts each night. The company's cost was $450, and the value of the donuts Ed took home was $100.

c. The company pays Ed's subscription to *Bowling Lanes Management*, a monthly journal.

47. Snowbird Corporation would like you to review its employee fringe benefits program with regard to the effects of the plan on the company's president (Polly), who is also the majority shareholder:

a. All employees receive free tickets to State University football games. Polly is seldom able to attend the games and usually gives her tickets to her nephew. The cost of Polly's tickets for the year was $75.

b. The company pays all parking fees for its officers but not for other employees. The company paid $1,200 for Polly's parking for the year.

c. Employees are allowed to use the copy machine for personal purposes as long as the privilege is not abused. Polly is president of a trade association and made extensive use of the copy machine to prepare mailings to members of the association. The cost of the copies was $900.

d. The company is in the household moving business. Employees are allowed to ship goods without charge whenever there is excess space on a truck. Polly purchased a dining room suite for her daughter. Company trucks delivered the furniture to the daughter. Normal freight charges would have been $600.

e. The company has a storage facility for household goods. Officers are allowed a 20% discount on charges for storing their goods. All other employees are allowed a 10% discount. Polly's discounts for the year totaled $400.

48. Eli works for a company that operates a cruise ship. All employees are allowed to take a one-week cruise each year at no cost to the employee. The employee is provided with a room, meals, and general recreation on the ship. Determine the tax consequences of Eli accepting a trip under the following assumptions:

a. Eli must travel on a standby basis; that is, Eli can travel only if the ship is not completely booked. The room Eli occupies has maid service, and the sheets and towels are changed each day.

b. Eli takes his meals with the other customers who pay a fixed amount for the cruise that includes meals and lodging.

c. The recreation consists of the use of the pool, dancing, and bingo games.

d. All guests must pay for their drinks and snacks between meals, but Eli and the other employees are given a 20% discount.

e. Employees at Eli's level and above are provided with free parking at the pier. Parking for the week would cost $70. This group comprises about 25% of all employees of the company.

49. Pedro is a U.S. citizen and a production manager for Parrot Company. On May 1, 1993, Pedro was temporarily assigned to the Monterrey, Mexico, plant. On August 6, 1993, he returned to the United States for medical treatment. On September 1, 1993, he returned to his duties in Monterrey. Except for a two-week period in the United States (December 16–31, 1993), he worked in Monterrey until December 1, 1994, when he was transferred to Boston, Massachusetts. Pedro's salary was $4,000 per month in 1993 and $5,000 per month in 1994. His housing expense did not exceed the base amount. Compute Pedro's foreign earned income exclusion in 1993 and 1994.

50. Determine Hazel's gross income from the following receipts for the year:

Gain on sale of Augusta County bonds	$ 600
Interest on U.S. government savings bonds	900
Interest on state income tax refund	150
Interest on Augusta County bonds	900
Patronage dividend from Potato Growers Cooperative	1,700

The patronage dividend was received in March of the current year for amounts paid and deducted in the previous year as expenses of Hazel's profitable cash basis farming business.

51. Determine Jack's taxable income from the following items:

a. Jack owns 100 shares of Roadrunner Company common stock. The company has a dividend reinvestment plan. Under the plan, Jack can receive an $18 cash dividend or an additional share of stock with a fair market of $18. Jack elected to take the stock.

b. Jack owns 100 shares of Bat Corporation. The company declared a dividend, and Jack was to receive an additional share of the company's common stock with a fair market value of $18. Jack did not have the option to receive cash. However, a management group announced a plan to repurchase all available shares for $18 each. The offer was part of a takeover defense.

c. Jack also collected $125 on a corporate debenture. The corporation had been in bankruptcy for several years. Jack had correctly deducted the cost of the bond in a prior year because the bankruptcy judge had informed the bondholders they would not receive anything in the final liquidation. Later the company collected on an unanticipated claim and had the funds to make partial payment on the bonds.

52. Lynn recently inherited $25,000. She is considering using the money to finance a college education for her 5-year-old child. Lynn does not expect her gross income to ever exceed $40,000 a year. She is very concerned with the safety of the principal and has decided to invest the $25,000 in Series EE U.S. government savings bonds. The bonds earn 5% interest each year. At the end of 13 years, when Lynn's child is 18 and ready to go to college, the bonds will be worth $44,375. This would pay a substantial portion of the cost of a 4-year college education at that time. Write a letter to Lynn advising her as to whether the Series EE bonds will be an appropriate investment for financing her child's college education, including whether the bonds should be purchased in Lynn's name or in the child's name (with Lynn as custodian).

53. How does the tax benefit rule apply in the following cases?

a. In 1993, Wilma paid Vera $5,000 for locating a potential client. The deal fell through, and in 1994, Vera refunded the $5,000 to Wilma.

b. In 1993, Wilma paid an attorney $300 for services in connection with a title search. Because the attorney was negligent, Wilma incurred some additional costs in acquiring the land. In 1994, the attorney refunded his $300 fee to Wilma.

c. In 1994, Wilma received a $90 dividend with respect to 1994 premiums on her life insurance policy.

d. In 1994, a cash basis farmer received a $400 patronage dividend with respect to 1993 purchases of cattle feed.

54. Fran, who is in the 36% tax bracket, recently collected $100,000 on a life insurance policy she carried on her father. She currently owes $120,000 on her personal residence and $120,000 on business property. National Bank holds the mortgage on both pieces of property and has agreed to accept $100,000 in complete satisfaction of either mortgage. The interest rate on the mortgages is 8%, and both mortgages are payable over 10 years. Fran can also purchase Montgomery County school bonds yielding 8%. What would be the tax consequences of each of the following alternatives, assuming Fran currently deducts the mortgage interest on her tax return?

a. Retire the mortgage on the residence.

b. Retire the mortgage on the business property.

c. Purchase tax-exempt bonds but not pay off either mortgage.

Which alternative should Fran select?

55. Robin Company is experiencing financial troubles and is considering negotiating the following with its creditors. Determine the tax consequences to Robin of the following plan:

a. The Motor Finance Company will cancel $1,500 in accrued interest. Robin had deducted the interest in the prior year. Motor Finance Company will also reduce the principal on the note by $1,000. The note financed the purchase of equipment from a local dealer.

b. The Trust Land Company, which sold Robin land and buildings, will reduce the mortgage on the building by $15,000.

c. Ridge, the sole shareholder in the corporation, will cancel a $50,000 receivable from the corporation in exchange for additional stock.

CUMULATIVE PROBLEMS

56. Oliver W. Hand was divorced from Sandra D. Hand on May 12, 1993. On September 6, 1994, Oliver married Beulah Crane. Oliver and Beulah will file a joint return for 1994. Oliver's Social Security number is 262–60–3814. Beulah's number is 259–68–4184, and she will adopt "Hand" as her married name. The Hands live at 210 Mason Drive, Atlanta, GA 30304. Sandra's Social Security number is 219–74–1361.

Oliver is 49 and is employed by Atom, Inc., as an electrical engineer. His salary for 1994 was $55,000. Beulah is 30 and earned $35,000 as a marriage counselor in 1994. She was employed by Family Counselors, Inc.

The divorce agreement required Oliver to make 132 monthly payments to Sandra. The payments are $1,200 per month for 84 months, at which time the payments decrease to $1,000 per month. Oliver and Sandra have a 14-year-old daughter, Daisy Hand. If Daisy should die before she attains age 21, Oliver's remaining payments to Sandra would be reduced to $1,000 per month. Sandra was granted custody of Daisy and can document that she provided $2,000 of support for Daisy. Oliver made 12 payments in 1994.

Oliver's employer provided him with group term life insurance coverage in the amount of $90,000 in 1994.

Beulah's employer provided Beulah with free parking in a parking garage adjacent to the office building where Beulah works. The monthly charge to the general public is $50.

Oliver received dividends of $40 on Z Corporation stock he owned before marriage, and Beulah received dividends of $50 on her separately owned M Corporation stock. They received dividends of $400 on jointly owned B Corporation stock, which they acquired after marriage. Oliver and Beulah live in a common law state.

Combined itemized deductions for Oliver and Beulah in 1994 were as follows:

State income taxes withheld		
Oliver	$2,900	
Beulah	800	$3,700
Real estate taxes on residence		1,500
Home mortgage interest (paid to Atlanta Federal Savings and Loan)		4,020
Cash contributions to church		900

In 1994, Beulah received a refund of 1993 state income taxes of $600. She had deducted state income taxes withheld as an itemized deduction on her 1993 return. Oliver received a $400 refund on his 1993 state income taxes. He had used the standard deduction in 1993.

Additional information:

- Oliver's employer withheld Federal income tax of $7,650 and $4,208 of FICA (Social Security) tax. Beulah's employer withheld $2,900 of Federal income tax and $2,678 of FICA tax.

Part 1—Tax Computation
Compute the Hands' net tax payable (or refund due) for 1994. Suggested software (if available): *TurboTax* or *MacInTax* for tax return or WFT tax planning software.

Part 2—Tax Planning
Assume the Hands came to you in early December of 1994 seeking tax planning advice for 1994 and 1995. They provide you with the following information:

a. All the facts previously presented will be essentially the same in 1995 except for the items described in (b), (c), (d), and (e).
b. Oliver inherited $100,000 from his mother on December 1. He will use part of his inheritance to pay off the mortgage on the Hands' residence on January 3, 1995. Consequently, there will be no mortgage interest expense in 1995.
c. Oliver expects a 6% salary increase in 1995, and Beulah expects a 10% increase.
d. The Hands have pledged to contribute $2,400 to their church in 1995 (as opposed to $900 contributed in 1994). However, they could use Oliver's inherited funds to pay the pledge before the end of 1994 if you advise them to do so to achieve an overall tax savings.
e. The Hands acquired 100 shares of ABC Corporation stock on July 5, 1994, at a total cost of $2,000. The value of the stock has increased rapidly, and it is now worth $5,000. The Hands plan to sell the stock and ask whether they should sell it in 1994 or wait until 1995.

Advise the Hands as to the appropriate tax planning strategy for 1994 and 1995. Support your recommendations by computing their tax liabilities for 1994 and 1995 considering the various available alternatives. Suggested software (if available): WFT tax planning software.

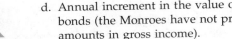

57. Archie S. Monroe (Social Security number 363–33–1411) is 35 years old and is married to Annie B. Monroe (Social Security number 259–68–4284). The Monroes live at 215 Adams Dr., Thor, VA 24317. They file a joint return and have two dependent children (Barry and Betty). In 1994, Archie and Annie had the following transactions:

a. Salary received by Archie from Allen Steel Company (Archie is vice president). $69,000
b. Interest received on jointly owned State of Nebraska bonds. 8,000
c. Group term life insurance premiums paid by Archie's employer (coverage of $60,000). 220
d. Annual increment in the value of Series EE government savings bonds (the Monroes have not previously included the accrued amounts in gross income). 300

e. Taxable dividends received from Allen Steel Company, a U.S. corporation (the stock was jointly owned). Of the $6,300 in dividends, $1,000 was mailed on December 31, 1994, and received by Archie and Annie on January 4, 1995.   6,300

f. Alimony payments to Archie's former wife (Rosa T. Monroe, Social Security number 800–60–2580) under a divorce decree.   7,000

g. Itemized deductions:

State income tax	1,950
Real estate tax on residence	1,300
Interest on personal residence (paid to Thor Federal Savings)	3,200
Cash contribution to church	700

h. Federal income tax withheld.   9,634

Part 1—Tax Computation
Compute the Monroes' net tax payable (or refund due) for 1994. Suggested software (if available): *TurboTax* or *MacInTax* for tax return or *WFT* tax planning software.

Part 2—Tax Planning
The Monroes plan to sell 200 shares of AXE stock they purchased on July 12, 1982, at a cost of $18,000. The stock is worth $10,000 in December 1994, and the Monroes' broker predicts a continued decline in value. Annie plans to resume her career as a model in 1995, and her earnings will move the Monroes into the 31% bracket. How much Federal income tax will the Monroes save for 1994 if they sell the stock in 1994? Should they sell the stock in 1994 or 1995? Write a letter to the Monroes that contains your advice and prepare a memo for the tax files. Suggested software (if available): *WFT* tax planning software.

RESEARCH PROBLEMS

Research Problem 1. David is the minister at the First Baptist Church. As part of his compensation, David receives an $800 per month housing allowance. David is purchasing his residence, and he uses the $800 each month to make mortgage and property tax payments. The mortgage interest and property taxes are deducted (as itemized deductions) on David's tax return. The examining IRS agent thinks David would be enjoying a double benefit if the housing allowance is excluded and the itemized deductions are allowed. In addition, the agent contends that the housing allowance exclusion should apply only where the church provides the residence or the minister uses the funds to pay rent. Therefore, the agent maintains that David should include in gross income the $800 received each month. David has asked your assistance in this matter. Write a letter to David that contains your advice and prepare a memo for the tax files.

Research Problem 2. Dan was recently hired as manager of Fertile Farm, Inc. Dan is required to live in the employer's house on the farm. Dan and the employer are trying to decide how to arrange terms with the electric company. The employer would like the utility account to be in Dan's name, but with the employer reimbursing Dan $200 each month. The $200 should be adequate to cover all charges. The employer requests this arrangement because the previous manager established the account in the company's name and left town without paying the bill. Dan has asked your tax advice on the matter.

Partial list of research aids:
Rev.Rul. 68–579, 1968–2 C.B. 61.

Research Problem 3. Ted is considering giving his daughter securities with a value of $100,000. Ted's basis in the securities is $10,000. If Ted makes the gift, he will owe $25,000 of uniform transfer tax on the transaction. However, the daughter has agreed to pay the transfer tax. Ted would like to know if any income tax consequences will result from his daughter paying the transfer tax.

Research Problem 4. Snipe Company is closing one of its plants. The company's management is very concerned about employee morale at other plants. To minimize the damage to employee relations, the company has decided to pay the costs of "outplacement services" for the employees of the plant to be closed. The services include the use of a consultant in writing resumés, identifying potential employers, and writing to those employers. The company has asked your advice as to whether the employees would be required to include the costs of the services in their gross incomes.

P·A·R·T

III

DEDUCTIONS

Part III presents the deduction component of the basic tax model. Deductions are classified as business versus nonbusiness, "for" versus "from," employee versus employer, active versus passive, and reimbursed versus unreimbursed. The effect of each of these classifications is analyzed. The presentation includes not only the deductions that are permitted, but also limitations and disallowances associated with deductions. Because deductions can exceed gross income, the treatment of losses is also included.

Chapter 6

Deductions and Losses: In General

Chapter 7

Deductions and Losses: Certain Business Expenses and Losses

Chapter 8

Depreciation, Cost Recovery, Amortization, and Depletion

Chapter 9

Deductions: Employee Expenses

Chapter 10

Deductions and Losses: Certain Itemized Deductions

Chapter 11

Passive Activity Losses

6

DEDUCTIONS AND LOSSES: IN GENERAL

LEARNING OBJECTIVES

After completing Chapter 6, you should be able to:

1. Differentiate between deductions *for* and *from* adjusted gross income and understand the relevance of the differentiation.

2. Describe the cash and accrual methods of accounting.

3. Apply the Internal Revenue Code deduction disallowance provisions associated with the following: public policy limitations, political activities, excessive executive compensation, investigation of business opportunities, hobby losses, vacation home rentals, payment of others' expenses, personal expenditures, capital expenditures, related-party transactions, and expenses related to tax-exempt income.

4. Identify tax planning opportunities for maximizing deductions and minimizing the disallowance of deductions.

Classification of Deductible
Expenses, 6–2

Deductions for Adjusted Gross
Income, 6–3

Itemized Deductions, 6–4

Trade or Business Expenses and
Production of Income Expenses,
6–4

Business and Nonbusiness Losses,
6–7

Reporting Procedures, 6–7

Deductions and Losses—Timing of
Expense Recognition, 6–7

Importance of Taxpayer's Method
of Accounting, 6–7

Cash Method Requirements, 6–8

Accrual Method Requirements,
6–9

Disallowance Possibilities, 6–10

Public Policy Limitation, 6–10

Political Contributions and Lobbying
Activities, 6–13

Excessive Executive
Compensation, 6–14

Investigation of a Business, 6–15

Hobby Losses, 6–16

Rental of Vacation Homes, 6–19

Expenditures Incurred for
Taxpayer's Benefit or Taxpayer's
Obligation, 6–23

Disallowance of Personal
Expenditures, 6–25

Disallowance of Deductions for
Capital Expenditures, 6–25

Transactions between Related
Parties, 6–26

Substantiation Requirements, 6–28

Expenses and Interest Relating to
Tax-Exempt Income, 6–29

Tax Planning Considerations, 6–30

Time Value of Tax Deductions, 6–30

Unreasonable Compensation, 6–30

Excessive Executive
Compensation, 6–32

Shifting Deductions, 6–32

Hobby Losses, 6–32

Capital Expenditures, 6–33

CLASSIFICATION OF DEDUCTIBLE EXPENSES

1 LEARNING OBJECTIVE
Differentiate between
deductions *for* and *from* AGI
and understand the relevance
of the differentiation.

The tax law has an all-inclusive definition of income; that is, income from whatever source derived is includible in gross income. Income cannot be excluded unless there is a specific statement to that effect in the Internal Revenue Code.

Similarly, deductions are disallowed unless a specific provision in the tax law permits them. The inclusive definition of income and the exclusive definition of deductions may not seem fair to taxpayers, but it is the structure of the tax law.

The courts have held that whether and to what extent deductions are allowed depends on legislative grace.[1] In other words, any exclusions from income and all deductions are gifts from Congress!

It is important to classify deductible expenses as **deductions for adjusted gross income** (AGI) or **deductions from adjusted gross income.** Deductions *for* AGI can be claimed whether or not the taxpayer itemizes. Deductions *from* AGI result in a tax benefit only if they exceed the taxpayer's standard deduction. If itemized deductions (*from* AGI) are less than the standard deduction, they provide no tax benefit.

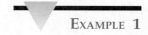
EXAMPLE 1

Steve is a self-employed CPA. Ralph is one of Steve's employees. During the year, Steve and Ralph incur the following expenses:

	Steve	Ralph
Dues in American Institute of CPAs and Virginia Society of CPAs	$ 400	$ 300
Subscriptions to professional journals	500	200
Registration fees for tax conferences	800	800
	$1,700	$1,300

---

[1] *New Colonial Ice Co. v. Helvering,* 4 USTC ¶1292, 13 AFTR 1180, 54 S.Ct. 788 (USSC, 1934).

Steve does not reimburse any of his employees for dues, subscriptions, or educational programs.

Steve's expenses are classified as a deduction *for* AGI. Therefore, he can deduct the $1,700 on his Federal income tax return. Ralph's expenses are classified as deductions *from* AGI. Ralph will be able to benefit from the $1,300 of expenses on his Federal income tax return only if he itemizes deductions. If he takes the standard deduction instead, the $1,300 of expenses will have no effect on the calculation of his taxable income. Even if Ralph does itemize deductions, he must reduce the $1,300 of expenses, which are classified as miscellaneous itemized deductions, by 2% of his AGI. As this example illustrates, whether a deduction is classified as *for* AGI or *from* AGI can affect the benefit the taxpayer receives from the deduction. ▼

Deductions *for* AGI are also important in determining the *amount* of itemized deductions because many itemized deductions are limited to amounts in excess of specified percentages of AGI. Examples of itemized deductions that are limited by AGI are medical expenses and personal casualty losses. Itemized deductions that are deductible only to the extent that they exceed a specified percentage of AGI are increased when AGI is decreased. Likewise, when AGI is increased, these itemized deductions are decreased.

EXAMPLE 2 Tina earns a salary of $20,000 and has no other income. She itemizes deductions during the current year. Medical expenses for the year are $1,800. Since medical expenses are deductible only to the extent they exceed 7.5% of AGI, Tina's medical expense deduction is $300 [$1,800 − (7.5% × $20,000)]. If Tina had a $2,000 deduction *for* AGI, her medical expense deduction would be $450 [$1,800 − (7.5% × $18,000)], or $150 more. If the $2,000 deduction was *from* AGI, her medical expense deduction would remain $300 since AGI is unchanged. ▼

DEDUCTIONS FOR ADJUSTED GROSS INCOME

To understand how deductions of individual taxpayers are classified, it is necessary to examine the role of § 62. The purpose of § 62 is to classify various deductions as deductions *for* AGI. It does not provide the statutory authority for taking the deduction. For example, § 212 allows individuals to deduct expenses attributable to income-producing property. Section 212 expenses that are attributable to rents or royalties are classified as deductions *for* AGI. Likewise, a deduction for trade or business expenses is allowed by § 162. These expenses are classified as deductions *for* AGI.

If a deduction is not listed in § 62, it is an itemized deduction, *not* a deduction *for* AGI. Following is a *partial* list of the items classified as deductions *for* AGI by § 62:

- Expenses attributable to a trade or business carried on by the taxpayer. A trade or business does not include the performance of services by the taxpayer as an employee.
- Expenses incurred by a taxpayer in connection with the performance of services as an employee if the expenses are reimbursed and other conditions are satisfied.
- Deductions that result from losses on the sale or exchange of property by the taxpayer.
- Deductions attributable to property held for the production of rents and royalties.
- The deduction for payment of alimony.
- Certain contributions to pension, profit sharing, and annuity plans of self-employed individuals.

- The deduction for certain retirement savings allowed by § 219 (e.g., IRAs).
- The penalty imposed on premature withdrawal of funds from time savings accounts or deposits.
- The deduction for moving expenses.

These items are covered in detail in various chapters in the text.

ITEMIZED DEDUCTIONS

The Code defines **itemized deductions** as the deductions allowed other than "the deductions allowable in arriving at adjusted gross income."[2] Thus, if a deduction is not properly classified as a deduction *for* AGI, then it is classified as an itemized deduction.

Section 212 allows deductions for ordinary and necessary expenses paid or incurred for the following:

- The production or collection of income.
- The management, conservation, or maintenance of property held for the production of income.
- Expenses paid in connection with the determination, collection, or refund of any tax.

Section 212 expenses related to rent and royalty income are deductions *for* AGI.[3] Expenses paid in connection with the determination, collection, or refund of taxes related to the income of sole proprietorships, rents and royalties, or farming operations are deductions *for* AGI. All other § 212 expenses are itemized deductions (deductions *from* AGI). For example, investment-related expenses (e.g., safe deposit box rentals) are deductible as itemized deductions attributable to the production of investment income.[4]

Taxpayers are allowed to deduct certain expenses that are primarily personal in nature. These expenses, which generally are not related to the production of income, are deductions *from* AGI (itemized deductions). Some of the more frequently encountered deductions in this category include the following:

- Contributions to qualified charitable organizations (not to exceed a specified percentage of AGI).
- Medical expenses (in excess of 7.5 percent of AGI).
- State and local taxes (e.g., real estate taxes and state and local income taxes).
- Personal casualty losses (in excess of an aggregate floor of 10 percent of AGI and a $100 floor per casualty).
- Certain personal interest (e.g., mortgage interest on a personal residence).

Itemized deductions are discussed in detail in Chapter 10.

TRADE OR BUSINESS EXPENSES AND PRODUCTION OF INCOME EXPENSES

Section 162(a) permits a deduction for all ordinary and necessary expenses paid or incurred in carrying on a trade or business. These include reasonable salaries paid for services, expenses for the use of business property, and one-half of self-employment taxes paid (see Chapter 13). Such expenses are deducted *for* AGI.

---

[2] § 63(d).
[3] § 62(a)(4).

[4] Reg. § 1.212–1(g).

It is sometimes difficult to determine whether an expenditure is deductible as a trade or business expense. The term "trade or business" is not defined in the Code or Regulations, and the courts have not provided a satisfactory definition. It is usually necessary to ask one or more of the following questions to determine whether an item qualifies as a trade or business expense:

- Was the use of the particular item related to a business activity? For example, if funds are borrowed for use in a business, the interest is deductible as a business expense.
- Was the expenditure incurred with the intent to realize a profit or to produce income? For example, expenses in excess of the income from raising horses are not deductible if the activity is classified as a personal hobby rather than a trade or business.
- Were the taxpayer's operation and management activities extensive enough to indicate the carrying on of a trade or business?

Section 162 *excludes* the following items from classification as trade or business expenses:

- Charitable contributions or gifts.
- Illegal bribes and kickbacks and certain treble damage payments.
- Fines and penalties.

A bribe paid to a domestic official is not deductible if it is illegal under the laws of the United States. Foreign bribes are deductible unless they are unlawful under the Foreign Corrupt Practices Act of 1977.[5]

Ordinary and Necessary Requirement

The terms **ordinary and necessary** are found in both §§ 162 and 212. To be deductible, any trade or business expense must be "ordinary and necessary." In addition, compensation for services must be "reasonable" in amount.

Many expenses that are necessary are *not* ordinary. Neither "ordinary" nor "necessary" is defined in the Code or Regulations. The courts have held that an expense is *necessary* if a prudent businessperson would incur the same expense and the expense is expected to be appropriate and helpful in the taxpayer's business.[6]

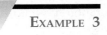

EXAMPLE 3

Pat purchased a manufacturing concern that had just been adjudged bankrupt. Because the business had a poor financial rating, Pat satisfied some of the obligations to employees and outside salespeople incurred by the former owners. Pat had no legal obligation to pay these debts, but felt this was the only way to keep salespeople and employees. The Second Court of Appeals found that the payments were necessary in that they were both appropriate and helpful.[7] However, the Court held that the payments were *not* ordinary but were in the nature of capital expenditures to build a reputation. Therefore, no deduction was allowed. ▼

An expense is *ordinary* if it is normal, usual, or customary in the type of business conducted by the taxpayer and is not capital in nature.[8] However, an expense need not be recurring to be deductible as ordinary.

---

[5] § 162(c)(1).

[6] *Welch v. Helvering*, 3 USTC ¶1164, 12 AFTR 1456, 54 S.Ct. 8 (USSC, 1933).

[7] *Dunn and McCarthy, Inc. v. Comm.*, 43–2 USTC ¶9688, 31 AFTR 1043, 139 F.2d 242 (CA–2, 1943).

[8] *Deputy v. DuPont*, 40–1 USTC ¶9161, 23 AFTR 808, 60 S.Ct. 363 (USSC, 1940).

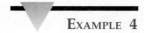
EXAMPLE 4

Albert engaged in a mail-order business. The post office judged that his advertisements were false and misleading. Under a fraud order, the post office stamped "fraudulent" on all letters addressed to Albert's business and returned them to the senders. Albert spent $30,000 on legal fees in an unsuccessful attempt to force the post office to stop. The legal fees (though not recurring) were ordinary business expenses because they were normal, usual, or customary in the circumstances.[9] ▼

For § 212 deductions, the law requires that expenses bear a reasonable and proximate relationship to (1) the production or collection of income or to (2) the management, conservation, or maintenance of property held for the production of income.[10]

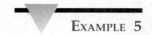
EXAMPLE 5

Wendla owns a small portfolio of investments, including 10 shares of Hawk, Inc., common stock worth $1,000. She incurred $350 in travel expenses to attend the annual shareholders' meeting at which she voted her 10 shares against the current management group. No deduction is permitted because a 10-share investment is insignificant in value in relation to the travel expenses incurred.[11] ▼

Reasonableness Requirement

The Code refers to **reasonableness** solely with respect to salaries and other compensation for services.[12] But the courts have held that for any business expense to be ordinary and necessary, it must also be reasonable in amount.[13]

What constitutes reasonableness is a question of fact. If an expense is unreasonable, the excess amount is not allowed as a deduction. The question of reasonableness generally arises with respect to closely held corporations where there is no separation of ownership and management.

Transactions between the shareholders and the closely held company may result in the disallowance of deductions for excessive salaries and rent expense paid by the corporation to the shareholders. The courts will view an unusually large salary in light of all relevant circumstances and may find that the salary is reasonable despite its size.[14] If excessive payments for salaries and rents are closely related to the percentage of stock owned by the recipients, the payments are generally treated as dividends.[15] Since dividends are not deductible by the corporation, the disallowance results in an increase in the corporate taxable income. Deductions for reasonable salaries will not be disallowed *solely* because the corporation has paid insubstantial portions of its earnings as dividends to its shareholders.

EXAMPLE 6

Sparrow Corporation, a closely held corporation, is owned equally by Lupe, Carlos, and Ramon. The company has been highly profitable for several years and has not paid dividends. Lupe, Carlos, and Ramon are key officers of the company, and each receives a salary of $200,000. Salaries for similar positions in comparable companies average only $100,000. Amounts paid the owners in excess of $100,000 may be deemed unreasonable, and, if so, a total of $300,000 in salary deductions is disallowed. The disallowed amounts are treated as dividends rather than salary income to Lupe, Carlos, and Ramon because the payments are proportional to stock ownership. Salaries are deductible by the corporation, but dividends are not. ▼

---

[9] *Comm. v. Heininger,* 44–1 USTC ¶9109, 31 AFTR 783, 64 S.Ct. 249 (USSC, 1943).
[10] Reg. § 1.212–1(d).
[11] *J. Raymond Dyer,* 36 T.C. 456 (1961).
[12] § 162(a)(1).

[13] *Comm. v. Lincoln Electric Co.,* 49–2 USTC ¶9388, 38 AFTR 411, 176 F.2d 815 (CA–6, 1949).
[14] *Kennedy, Jr. v. Comm.,* 82–1 USTC ¶9186, 49 AFTR2d 82–628, 671 F.2d 167 (CA–6, 1982), *rev'g* 72 T.C. 793 (1979).
[15] Reg. § 1.162–8.

BUSINESS AND NONBUSINESS LOSSES

Section 165 provides for a deduction for losses not compensated for by insurance. As a general rule, deductible losses of individual taxpayers are limited to those incurred in a trade or business or in a transaction entered into for profit. Individuals are also allowed to deduct losses that are the result of a casualty. Casualty losses include, but are not limited to, fire, storm, shipwreck, and theft. See Chapter 7 for a further discussion of this topic. Deductible personal casualty losses are reduced by $100 per casualty, and the aggregate of all personal casualty losses is reduced by 10 percent of AGI. A personal casualty loss is an itemized deduction. See Concept Summary 6–2 on p. 6–34 for the classification of expenses.

REPORTING PROCEDURES

All deductions *for* and *from* AGI wind up on pages 1 and 2 of Form 1040. All deductions *for* AGI are reported on page 1. The last line on page 1 is adjusted gross income.

The first item on page 2 is also adjusted gross income. Itemized deductions are entered next, followed by the deduction for personal and dependency exemptions. The result is taxable income.

Most of the deductions *for* AGI on page 1 originate on supporting schedules. Examples include business expenses (Schedule C) and rent, royalty, partnership, and fiduciary deductions (Schedule E). Other deductions *for* AGI, such as IRAs, Keogh retirement plans, and alimony, are entered directly on page 1 of Form 1040.

All itemized deductions on page 2 are carried over from Schedule A. Some Schedule A deductions originate on other forms. Examples include home mortgage interest, investment interest, noncash charitable contributions in excess of $500, casualty losses, and unreimbursed employee expenses.

Form 1040 becomes a summary of the detailed information entered on the other schedules and forms. See Figure 6–1.

DEDUCTIONS AND LOSSES—TIMING OF EXPENSE RECOGNITION

IMPORTANCE OF TAXPAYER'S METHOD OF ACCOUNTING

2   LEARNING OBJECTIVE
Describe the cash and accrual methods of accounting.

A taxpayer's **accounting method** is a major factor in determining taxable income. The method used determines when an item is includible in income and when an item is deductible on the tax return. Usually, the taxpayer's regular method of record keeping is used for income tax purposes.[16] The taxing authorities do not require uniformity among all taxpayers. They do require that the method used clearly reflect income and that items be handled consistently.[17] The most common methods of accounting are the **cash method** and the **accrual method.**

Throughout the portions of the Code dealing with deductions, the phrase "paid or incurred" is used. *Paid* refers to the cash basis taxpayer who gets a deduction only in the year of payment. *Incurred* concerns the accrual basis taxpayer who obtains the deduction in the year in which the liability for the expense becomes certain (refer to Chapter 4).

---

[16] § 446(a).   [17] §§ 446(b) and (e); Reg. § 1.446–1(a)(2).

▼ **FIGURE 6–1**
Format of Form 1040

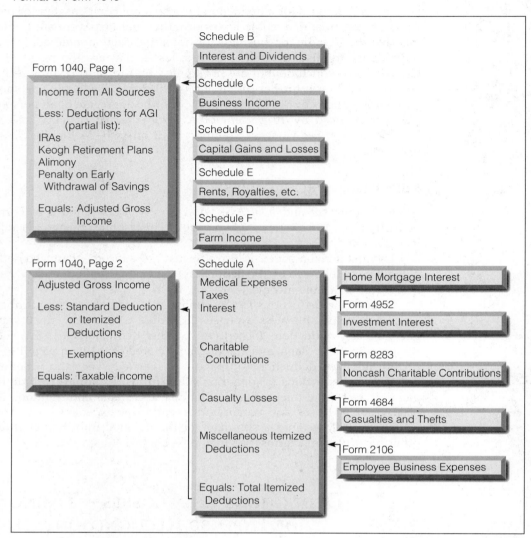

CASH METHOD REQUIREMENTS

The expenses of cash basis taxpayers are deductible only when they are actually paid with cash or other property. Promising to pay or issuing a note does not satisfy the actually paid requirement.[18] However, the payment can be made with borrowed funds. At the time taxpayers charge expenses on their bank credit cards, they are allowed to claim the deduction. They are deemed to have simultaneously borrowed money from the credit card issuer and constructively paid the expenses.[19]

Although the cash basis taxpayer must have actually or constructively paid the expense, payment does not assure a current deduction. Cash basis and accrual basis taxpayers cannot take a current deduction for capital expenditures except

[18] *Page v. Rhode Island Trust Co., Exr.,* 37–1 USTC ¶9138, 19 AFTR 105, 88 F.2d 192 (CA–1, 1937).

[19] Rev.Rul. 78–39, 1978–1 C.B. 73. See also Rev.Rul. 80–335, 1980–2 C.B. 170, which applies to pay-by-phone arrangements.

through amortization, depletion, or depreciation over the life (actual or statutory) of the asset. The Regulations set forth the general rule that an expenditure that creates an asset having a useful life that extends substantially beyond the end of the tax year must be capitalized.[20]

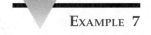
EXAMPLE 7

John, a cash basis taxpayer, rents property from Carl. On July 1, 1994, John paid $2,400 rent for the 24 months ending June 30, 1996. The prepaid rent extends 18 months after the close of the tax year—substantially beyond the year of payment. Therefore, John must capitalize the prepaid rent and amortize the expense on a monthly basis. His deduction for 1994 is $600. ▼

The Tax Court and the IRS took the position that an asset that will expire or be consumed by the end of the tax year following the year of payment must be prorated. The Ninth Court of Appeals held that such expenditures are currently deductible, however, and the Supreme Court apparently concurs.[21]

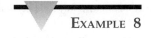
EXAMPLE 8

Assume the same facts as in Example 7 except that John was required to pay only 12 months rent in 1994. He paid $1,200 on July 1, 1994. The entire $1,200 would be deductible in 1994. ▼

The payment must be required, not a voluntary prepayment, to obtain the current deduction under the one-year rule.[22] The taxpayer must also demonstrate that allowing the current deduction will not result in a material distortion of income. Generally, the deduction will be allowed if the item is recurring or was made for a business purpose rather than to manipulate income.[23]

As Chapter 18 explains, not all taxpayers are allowed to use the cash method.[24]

ACCRUAL METHOD REQUIREMENTS

The period in which an accrual basis taxpayer can deduct an expense is determined by applying the *economic performance test*.[25] This test is met only when the service, property, or use of property giving rise to the liability is actually performed for, provided to, or used by the taxpayer.[26]

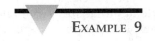
EXAMPLE 9

On December 15, 1994, a rusted water main broke and flooded the business premises of Chris, an accrual basis, calendar year taxpayer. An outside firm surveyed the damage and estimated the cleanup fee at $6,000. Chris signed a contract (paying 20% down) on December 20, 1994. Because of the holidays, the cleanup crew did not start work until January 2, 1995. Chris cannot deduct the $1,200 until 1995, when the services are performed. ▼

An exception to the economic performance requirements allows certain *recurring items* to be deducted if the following conditions are met:

• The item is recurring in nature and is treated consistently by the taxpayer.
• Either the accrued item is not material, or accruing it results in better matching of income and expenses.

[20] Reg. § 1.461–1(a).
[21] *Zaninovich v. Comm.*, 80–1 USTC ¶9342, 45 AFTR2d 80–1442, 616 F.2d 429 (CA–9, 1980), *rev'g* 69 T.C. 605 (1978). Cited by the Supreme Court in *Hillsboro National Bank v. Comm.*, 83–1 USTC ¶9229, 51 AFTR2d 83–874, 103 S.Ct. 1134 (USSC, 1983).
[22] *Bonaire Development Co. v. Comm.*, 82–2 USTC ¶9428, 50 AFTR2d 82–5167, 679 F.2d 159 (CA–9, 1982).

[23] *Keller v. Comm.*, 84–1 USTC ¶9194, 53 AFTR2d 84–663, 725 F.2d 1173 (CA–8, 1984), *aff'g* 79 T.C. 7 (1982).
[24] § 448.
[25] § 461(h)(1).
[26] §§ 461(h)(2)(A) and (B).

- The all-events test is met. This test is met when all the events have occurred that determine the fact of the liability and the amount of the liability can be determined with reasonable accuracy.[27]
- Economic performance occurs within a reasonable period (but not later than 8½ months after the close of the taxable year).[28]

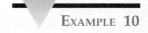

EXAMPLE 10

Rick, an accrual basis, calendar year taxpayer, entered into a monthly maintenance contract during the year. He makes a monthly accrual at the end of every month for this service and pays the fee sometime between the first and fifteenth of the following month when services are performed. The amount involved is immaterial, and all the other tests are met. The December 1994 accrual is deductible even though the service is performed on January 12, 1995. ▼

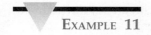

EXAMPLE 11

Rita, an accrual basis, calendar year taxpayer, shipped merchandise sold on December 30, 1994, via Greyhound Van Lines on January 2, 1995, and paid the freight charges at that time. Since Rita reported the sale of the merchandise in 1994, the shipping charge should also be deductible in 1994. This procedure results in a better matching of income and expenses. ▼

Reserves for estimated expenses (frequently employed for financial accounting purposes) generally are not allowed for tax purposes because the economic performance test cannot be satisfied.

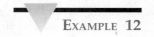

EXAMPLE 12

Blackbird Airlines is required by Federal law to test its engines after 3,000 flying hours. Aircraft cannot return to flight until the tests have been conducted. An unrelated aircraft maintenance company does all of the company's tests for $1,500 per engine. For financial reporting purposes, the company accrues an expense based upon $.50 per hour of flight and credits an allowance account. The actual amounts paid for maintenance are offset against the allowance account. For tax purposes, the economic performance test is not satisfied until the work has been done. Therefore, the reserve method cannot be used for tax purposes. ▼

DISALLOWANCE POSSIBILITIES

3   **LEARNING OBJECTIVE**
Apply the Internal Revenue Code deduction disallowance provisions associated with the following: public policy limitations, political activities, excessive executive compensation, investigation of business opportunities, hobby losses, vacation home rentals, payment of others' expenses, personal expenditures, capital expenditures, related-party transactions, and expenses related to tax-exempt income.

The tax law provides for the disallowance of certain types of expenses. Without specific restrictions in the tax law, taxpayers might attempt to deduct certain items that in reality are personal expenditures. For example, specific tax rules are provided to determine whether an expenditure is for trade or business purposes or related to a personal hobby.

Certain disallowance provisions are a codification or extension of prior court decisions. After the courts denied deductions for payments considered to be in violation of public policy, the tax law was changed to provide specific authority for the disallowance of these deductions. Discussions of specific disallowance provisions in the tax law follow.

PUBLIC POLICY LIMITATION

Justification for Denying Deductions

The courts developed the principle that a payment that is in violation of public policy is not a necessary expense and is not deductible.[29] Although a bribe or fine, may be appropriate, helpful, and even contribute to the profitability of an activity,

---

[27] Reg. § 1.461–1(a)(2).
[28] § 461(h)(3)(A).

[29] *Tank Truck Rentals, Inc. v. Comm.*, 58–1 USTC ¶9366, 1 AFTR2d 1154, 78 S.Ct. 507 (USSC, 1958).

the courts held that to allow such expenses would frustrate clearly defined public policy. A deduction would dilute the effect of the penalty since the government would be indirectly subsidizing a taxpayer's wrongdoing.

Accordingly, the IRS was free to restrict deductions if, in its view, the expenses were contrary to public policy. But since the law did not explain which actions violated public policy, taxpayers often had to go to court to determine whether or not their expense fell into this category.

Furthermore, the public policy doctrine could be arbitrarily applied in cases where no clear definition had emerged. To solve these problems, Congress enacted legislation that attempts to limit the use of the doctrine. Under the legislation, deductions are disallowed for certain specific types of expenditures that are considered contrary to public policy:

- Bribes and kickbacks (in the case of foreign bribes and kickbacks, only if the payments violate the U.S. Foreign Corrupt Practices Act of 1977).
- Fines and penalties paid to a government for violation of law.

EXAMPLE 13   Brown Corporation, a moving company, consistently loads its trucks with weights in excess of the limits allowed by state law. The additional revenue more than offsets the fines levied. The fines are for a violation of public policy and are not deductible. ▼

- Two-thirds of the treble damage payments made to claimants resulting from violation of the antitrust law.[30]

No deduction is permitted for a kickback that is illegal under state law if the state law is generally enforced. The kickback must also subject the payer to a criminal penalty or the loss of license or privilege to engage in a trade or business.

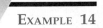

EXAMPLE 14   During the year Keith, an insurance salesman, paid $5,000 to Karen, a real estate broker. The payment represented 20% of the commissions Keith earned from customers referred by Karen. Under state law, the splitting of commissions by an insurance salesperson is an act of misconduct that could warrant a revocation of the salesperson's license. Keith's $5,000 payments to Karen are not deductible provided the state law is generally enforced. ▼

ETHICAL CONSIDERATIONS

Obtaining Zoning Variances

Tex is a real estate developer. He has a contract with a major retailer to handle its land acquisitions in the southeastern part of the state. One of Tex's major responsibilities is to secure the requisite zoning to enable the retailer to build and operate its retail outlets. Typically, obtaining proper zoning is more of a procedural activity than a strategic activity.

Tex has identified a site he would like to acquire for the retailer in a small historic city surrounded by two counties with substantially greater populations. Tex and the retailer have agreed that it is imperative that the site be in the city rather than in one of the counties. The city has very restrictive zoning for commercial properties, and the retailer will have to obtain several zoning variances.

---

[30]§§ 162(c), (f), and (g).

Tex's normal strategy in such a situation is to hire the leading law firm in the community to represent him in dealing with the property owner, the city planning commission, and the city council. In this instance, however, the senior partner in the major law firm is also the city mayor, so Tex adopts the following strategy. He hires another law firm as his representative on this acquisition, but so as not to antagonize the mayor and potentially adversely affect the city council's approval of the zoning variances, he pays a $10,000 retainer to the mayor's law firm to serve as his legal representative on any real estate acquisitions during the next 12-month period in the two adjoining counties. Tex deducts the $10,000 payment as an ordinary and necessary business expense. He is successful in securing the zoning variances and acquires the site for the retailer. During the following 12-month period, Tex does not need to use the services of the mayor's law firm.

Legal Expenses Incurred in Defense of Civil or Criminal Penalties

To deduct legal expenses, the taxpayer must be able to show that the origin and character of the claim are directly related to a trade or business, an income-producing activity, or the determination, collection, or refund of a tax. Personal legal expenses are not deductible. Thus, legal fees incurred in connection with a criminal defense are deductible only if the crime is associated with the taxpayer's trade or business or income-producing activity.[31]

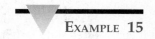

EXAMPLE 15

Debra, a financial officer of Blue Corporation, incurred legal expenses in connection with her defense in a criminal indictment for evasion of Blue's income taxes. Debra may deduct her legal expenses because she is deemed to be in the trade or business of being an executive. The legal action impairs her ability to conduct this business activity.[32] ▼

Deductible legal expenses associated with the following are deductible *for* AGI:

- Ordinary and necessary expenses incurred in connection with a trade or business.
- Ordinary and necessary expenses incurred in conjunction with rental or royalty property held for the production of income.

All other deductible legal expenses are deductible *from* AGI. For example, legal expenses generally are deductible *from* AGI if they are for fees for tax advice relative to the preparation of an individual's income tax return. Contrast this with the deduction *for* classification of legal fees for tax advice relative to the preparation of the portion of the tax return for a sole proprietor's trade or business (Schedule C) or an individual's rental or royalty income (Schedule E).

Expenses Relating to an Illegal Business

The usual expenses of operating an illegal business (e.g., a numbers racket) are deductible.[33] However, § 162 disallows a deduction for fines, bribes to public officials, illegal kickbacks, and other illegal payments.

---

[31] *Comm. v. Tellier,* 66–1 USTC ¶9319, 17 AFTR2d 633, 86 S.Ct. 1118 (USSC, 1966).

[32] Rev.Rul. 68–662, 1968–2 C.B. 69.

[33] *Comm. v. Sullivan,* 58–1 USTC ¶9368, 1 AFTR2d 1158, 78 S.Ct. 512 (USSC, 1958).

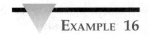

EXAMPLE 16

Sam owns and operates an illegal gambling establishment. In connection with this activity, he had the following expenses during the year:

Rent	$ 60,000
Payoffs to the police	40,000
Depreciation on equipment	100,000
Wages	140,000
Interest	30,000
Criminal fines	50,000
Illegal kickbacks	10,000
Total	$430,000

All of the usual expenses (rent, depreciation, wages, and interest) are deductible; payoffs, fines, and kickbacks are not deductible. Of the $430,000 spent, $330,000 is deductible and $100,000 is not. ▼

An exception applies to expenses incurred in illegal trafficking in drugs.[34] *Drug dealers* are not allowed a deduction for ordinary and necessary business expenses incurred in their business. In arriving at gross income from the business, however, dealers may reduce total sales by the cost of goods sold.[35] In this regard, no distinction is made between legal and illegal businesses in calculating gross income. Treating cost of goods sold as a negative income item rather than as a deduction item produces the unseemly result that a drug dealer's taxable income is reduced by cost of goods sold.

POLITICAL CONTRIBUTIONS AND LOBBYING ACTIVITIES

Political Contributions

Generally, no business deduction is permitted for direct or indirect payments for political purposes.[36] Historically, the government has been reluctant to accord favorable tax treatment to business expenditures for political purposes. Allowing deductions might encourage abuses and enable businesses to have undue influence upon the political process.

Lobbying Expenditures

Prior to the effect of the Revenue Reconciliation Act of 1993 (RRA of 1993), a deduction was allowed for certain expenses incurred to influence legislation (appearances before or statements filed with legislative bodies or individual legislators). For the expense to qualify as a deductible lobbying expenditure, the proposed legislation had to be of direct interest to the taxpayer. A direct interest existed if the legislation would, or could reasonably be expected to, affect the trade

---

[34] § 280E.
[35] Reg. § 1.61–3(a). Gross income is defined as sales minus cost of goods sold. Thus, while § 280E prohibits any deductions for drug dealers, it does not modify the normal definition of gross income.

[36] § 276.

or business of the taxpayer. No deduction was allowed for expenses incurred to influence the public on legislative matters or for any political campaign.

RRA of 1993 generally repeals this lobbying deduction.[37] Any lobbying expenses incurred in attempting to influence state or Federal legislation or the actions of certain high-ranking public officials (e.g., the President, Vice-President, cabinet-level officials, and the two most senior officials in each agency of the executive branch) are no longer deductible. The disallowance also applies to a pro rata portion of the membership dues of trade associations and other groups that are used for lobbying activities.

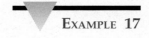

EXAMPLE 17

Egret Company pays a $10,000 annual membership fee to the Free Trade Group, a trade association for plumbing wholesalers. The trade association estimates that 70% of its dues are allocated to lobbying activities. Thus, Egret Company's deduction is limited to $3,000 ($10,000 × 30%). ▼

There are three exceptions to this repeal of the lobbying expenses deduction. An exception is provided for influencing local legislation (e.g., city and county governments). Second, the disallowance provision does not apply to activities devoted solely to monitoring legislation. Third, a *de minimis* exception is provided for annual in-house expenditures not exceeding $2,000 (lobbying expenses other than those paid to professional lobbyists or any portion of dues used by associations for lobbying).

EXCESSIVE EXECUTIVE COMPENSATION

Prior to the effect of RRA of 1993, there was no statutory dollar limit on the deduction for executive compensation. The only limitation was the reasonableness requirement (discussed earlier in this chapter) for shareholder-employees of closely held corporations.

RRA of 1993 includes the so-called millionaires provision, which applies to publicly held corporations.[38] The provision does not limit the amount of compensation that can be paid to an employee. Instead, it limits the amount the employer can deduct for the compensation of a covered executive to $1 million annually. Covered employees include the chief executive officer and the four other most highly compensated officers.

Employee compensation *excludes* the following:

- Commissions based on individual performance.
- Certain performance-based compensation based on company performance according to a formula approved by a board of directors compensation committee (comprised solely of two or more outside directors) and by shareholder vote. The performance attainment must be certified by this compensation committee.
- Payments to tax-qualified retirement plans.
- Payments that are excludible from the employees' gross income (e.g., certain fringe benefits).

[37] § 162(e).
[38] A publicly held corporation, for this provision, is a corporation that has at least one class of stock registered under the Securities Act of 1934.

TAX IN THE NEWS

THE TRULY RICH SAY THANK YOU

When the Revenue Reconciliation Act of 1993 was being debated, there was concern that the $1 million limit on compensation deductions would apply to all employees rather than only to the top five executives of publicly held corporations.

Barbra Streisand, a certified FOB, is supposedly going to receive $20 million for two days' work at the MGM Grand Casino in Las Vegas on December 31, 1993, and January 1, 1994. Chris Webber, the number 1 pick in the NBA draft, has reached agreement on a $74.4 million 15-year contract with the Golden State Warriors. One wonders if these payments would have been as lucrative if the payer could deduct only $1 million each year. Perhaps, however, placing the compensation deduction limit on executives only is sound tax policy. Maybe we need to treat potentially greedy executives differently than others. Scrutiny may be needed for them whereas no special scrutiny is needed for someone who makes more than a million dollars serenading lounge lizards, dunking basketballs, or hitting baseballs.

Thomas Sowell has raised the issue to a higher level by asking whether the government has the expertise to decide for private businesses what salaries they should pay. Charles Elson has concluded that the President has missed the point completely in apparently concluding that executive salaries above $1 million are somehow inherently suspect. To him, the relevant issue is overcompensation, not high compensation. Some executives are worth every cent they earn while others are not. The overcompensation of some executives is the result of a failure in the bargaining process between the corporate board and the executives over salary.

SOURCE: Information from Charles M. Elson, "Manager's Journal: A Board-Based Solution to Overpaid CEOs," *Wall Street Journal*, September 27, 1993, p. A22; "The FOB Loophole," *Wall Street Journal*, October 14, 1993, p. A16; Dick Marlowe, "Business Trends: Executive Salaries Show No Sign of Slowing Down," *Newport News (Virginia) Daily Press*, October 14, 1993, p. C6; "Briefs: Webber Agrees to 15-Year Deal," *Newport News (Virginia) Daily Press*, October 18, 1993, p. D2; Thomas Sowell, "Clinton Policymakers Don't Know, But They Don't Care," *Jacksonville, Florida, Times-Union*, October 23, 1993, p. A16; "Streisand to Take the Stage New Year's at MGM Grand," *Wall Street Journal*, November 3, 1993, p. B8.

INVESTIGATION OF A BUSINESS

Investigation expenses are expenses paid or incurred to determine the feasibility of entering a new business or expanding an existing business. They include such costs as travel, engineering and architectural surveys, marketing reports, and various legal and accounting services. How such expenses are treated for tax purposes depends on a number of variables, including the following:

- The current business, if any, of the taxpayer.
- The nature of the business being investigated.
- The extent to which the investigation has proceeded.
- Whether or not the acquisition actually takes place.

If the taxpayer is in a business the *same as or similar to* that being investigated, all expenses in this connection are deductible in the year paid or incurred. The tax result is the same whether or not the taxpayer acquires the business being investigated.[39]

---

[39] *York v. Comm.*, 58–2 USTC ¶9952, 2 AFTR2d 6178, 261 F.2d 421 (CA–4, 1958).

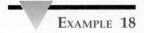

EXAMPLE 18

Terry, an accrual basis sole proprietor, owns and operates three motels in Georgia. In 1994, Terry incurs expenses of $8,500 in investigating the possibility of acquiring several additional motels located in South Carolina. The $8,500 is deductible in 1994 whether or not Terry acquires the motels in South Carolina. ▼

When the taxpayer is *not* in a business that is the same as or similar to the one being investigated, the tax result depends on whether the new business is acquired. If the business is not acquired, all investigation expenses generally are nondeductible.[40]

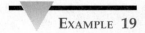

EXAMPLE 19

Lynn, a retired merchant, incurs expenses in traveling from Rochester, New York, to California to investigate the feasibility of acquiring several auto care centers. If no acquisition takes place, none of the expenses are deductible. ▼

If a taxpayer is in a different business than the one being investigated and actually acquires the new business, the expenses must be capitalized. At the election of the taxpayer, the expenses may be amortized over a period of 60 months or more.[41]

HOBBY LOSSES

Business or investment expenses are deductible only if the taxpayer can show that the activity was entered into for the purpose of making a profit. Certain activities may have either profit-seeking or personal attributes, depending upon individual circumstances. An example is raising horses and operating a farm used as a

---

TAX IN THE NEWS

PLEASURE VERSUS WORK

One of the factors normally considered in distinguishing between a hobby and a trade or business is the enjoyment of the taxpayer. Another factor considered is the amount of time and effort the taxpayer devotes to the activity.

Woody Rowland, a former IRS attorney who now is in private practice, tells of a case he was litigating before the Tax Court for the government. The taxpayer, a woman, raised breeding horses. The activity consistently reported losses. According to Rowland, "her losses were so great for so many years that it was hard to believe she was in it as a business." Rowland thought he had the case won until the taxpayer testified ". . . what it was like to stay up all night with the mares when they were foaling and how much time and effort the horses required." Although the taxpayer very much enjoyed what she was doing, both Rowland and the Tax Court judge knew at that moment that the activity was a trade or business.

SOURCE: Information and quotation from "Taxes . . . ," *Money*, September 1993, p. 122.

---

[40] Rev.Rul. 57–418, 1957–2 C.B. 143; *Morton Frank,* 20 T.C. 511   [41] § 195.
(1953); and *Dwight A. Ward,* 20 T.C. 332 (1953).

weekend residence. While personal losses are not deductible, losses attributable to profit-seeking activities may be deducted and used to offset a taxpayer's other income. For this reason, the tax law limits the deductibility of **hobby losses.**

General Rules

If an individual can show that an activity has been conducted with the intent to earn a profit, losses from the activity are fully deductible. The hobby loss rules apply only if the activity is not engaged in for profit. Hobby expenses are deductible only to the extent of hobby income.[42]

The Regulations stipulate that the following nine factors should be considered in determining whether an activity is profit-seeking or a hobby:[43]

- Whether the activity is conducted in a businesslike manner.
- The expertise of the taxpayers or their advisers.
- The time and effort expended.
- The expectation that the assets of the activity will appreciate in value.
- The previous success of the taxpayer in the conduct of similar activities.
- The history of income or losses from the activity.
- The relationship of profits earned to losses incurred.
- The financial status of the taxpayer (e.g., if the taxpayer does not have substantial amounts of other income, this may indicate that the activity is engaged in for profit).
- Elements of personal pleasure or recreation in the activity.

ETHICAL CONSIDERATIONS

When Is a Dairy Farm a Trade or Business?

Wes has been an orthopedic surgeon in New Orleans for 25 years. With the increase in tax rates in 1993, he would like to devote less time to his medical practice, spend more time with his family, and pay less in income taxes. His net income from his medical practice has been about $500,000 per year for the past five years.

Wes grew up on a dairy farm in southeastern Louisiana. He has many fond memories of his childhood and believes this would be an excellent environment for his 12-year-old daughter and 10-year-old son.

Wes purchases a dairy farm across Lake Pontchartrain from New Orleans. He hires two full-time employees to handle the milking operations and other part-time employees as needed for other farm functions. In addition, Wes and all his family members participate in performing various activities on the farm.

Wes commutes to New Orleans four days each week for his orthopedic surgeon practice. Because he is devoting less time to his medical practice, his net income from the practice decreases to $350,000. Wes has a loss of $75,000 for the dairy farm that he attributes to depressed milk prices and his inexperience at running the farm. He considers both the medical practice and the dairy farm to be trades or businesses. Therefore on his Federal income tax return, the $75,000 net loss is offset against the $350,000 net income. Assume that the net income and net loss from the medical practice and the dairy farm, respectively, remain approximately the same for the next four years.

---

[42] § 183(b)(2).

[43] Reg. §§ 1.183–2(b)(1) through (9).

Presumptive Rule of § 183

The Code provides a rebuttable presumption that an activity is profit-seeking if the activity shows a profit in at least three of any five prior consecutive years.[44] If the activity involves horses, a profit in at least two of seven consecutive years meets the presumptive rule. If these profitability tests are met, the activity is presumed to be a trade or business rather than a personal hobby. In this situation, the IRS bears the burden of proving that the activity is personal rather than trade or business related.

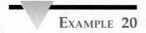

EXAMPLE 20

Camille, an executive for a large corporation, is paid a salary of $200,000. Her husband is a collector of antiques. Several years ago, he opened an antique shop in a local shopping center and spends most of his time buying and selling antiques. He occasionally earns a small profit from this activity but more frequently incurs substantial losses. If the losses are business related, they are fully deductible against Camille's salary income on a joint return. In resolving this issue, consider the following:

- Initially determine whether the antique activity has met the three-out-of-five years profit test.
- If the presumption is not met, the activity may nevertheless qualify as a business if the taxpayer can show that the intent is to engage in a profit-seeking activity. It is not necessary to show actual profits.
- Attempt to fit the operation within the nine criteria prescribed in the Regulations and listed above. These criteria are the factors considered in trying to rebut the § 183 presumption. ▼

If an activity is deemed to be a hobby, the expenses are deductible only to the extent of the income from the hobby. These expenses must be deducted in the following order:

- Amounts deductible under other Code sections without regard to the nature of the activity, such as property taxes.
- Amounts deductible under other Code sections if the activity had been engaged in for profit, but only if those amounts do not affect adjusted basis. Examples include maintenance, utilities, and supplies.
- Amounts deductible under other Code sections if the activity had been engaged in for profit, which affect adjusted basis.[45] Examples include depreciation, amortization, and depletion.

These deductions are deductible *from* AGI as itemized deductions to the extent they exceed 2 percent of AGI.[46]

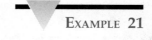

EXAMPLE 21

Jim, the vice president of an oil company, has AGI of $80,000. He decides to pursue painting in his spare time. He uses a home studio, comprising 10% of the home's square footage. During the current year, Jim incurs the following expenses:

Frames	$ 350
Art supplies	300
Fees paid to models	1,000
Home studio expenses:	
Total property taxes	900
Total home mortgage interest	10,000
Depreciation on 10% of home	500
Total home maintenance and utilities	3,600

---

[44] § 183(d).
[45] Reg. § 1.183–1(b)(1).

[46] Reg. § 1.67–1T(a)(1)(iv) and Rev. Rul. 75–14, 1975–1 C.B. 90.

During the year, Jim sold paintings for a total of $3,200. If the activity is held to be a hobby, Jim is allowed deductions as follows:

Gross income		$ 3,200
Deduct: Taxes and interest (10% of $10,900)		(1,090)
Remainder		$ 2,110
Deduct: Frames	$ 350	
Art supplies	300	
Models' fees	1,000	
Maintenance and utilities (10%)	360	(2,010)
Remainder		$ 100
Depreciation ($500, but limited to $100)		(100)
Net income		$ –0–

Jim includes the $3,200 of income in AGI, making his AGI $83,200. The taxes and interest are itemized deductions, deductible in full. The remaining $2,110 of expenses are reduced by 2% of his AGI ($1,664) so the net deduction is $446. Since the property taxes and home mortgage interest are deductible anyway, the net effect is a $2,754 ($3,200 less $446) increase in taxable income. ▼

EXAMPLE 22

If Jim's activity in Example 21 is held to be a business, he could deduct expenses totaling $2,510 ($2,010 plus $500 of depreciation) *for* AGI, in addition to the $1,090 of taxes and interest. All these expenses would be trade or business expenses deductible *for* AGI. His reduction in AGI would be as follows:

Gross income		$ 3,200
Less: Taxes and interest	$1,090	
Other business expenses	2,010	
Depreciation	500	(3,600)
Reduction in AGI		$ (400)

▼

RENTAL OF VACATION HOMES

Restrictions on the deductions allowed for part-year rentals of personal **vacation homes** were written into the law to prevent taxpayers from deducting essentially personal expenses as rental losses. Many taxpayers who owned vacation homes had formerly treated the homes as rental property and generated rental losses as deductions *for* AGI. For example, a summer cabin would be rented for 2 months per year, used for vacationing for 1 month, and left vacant the rest of the year. The taxpayer would then deduct 11 months' depreciation, maintenance, etc., as rental expenses, resulting in a rental loss. Section 280A eliminates this treatment by allowing deductions on residences used primarily for personal purposes only to the extent of the income generated. Only a break-even situation is allowed; no losses can be deducted.

There are three possible tax treatments for residences used for both personal and rental purposes. The treatment depends upon the relative time the residence is used for personal purposes versus rental use.

Primarily Personal Use

If the residence is rented for *less than 15 days* per year, it is treated as a personal residence. The rent income is excluded from gross income, and mortgage interest and real estate taxes are allowed as itemized deductions, as with any personal residence.[47] No other expenses (e.g., depreciation, utilities, maintenance) are deductible.

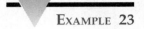

EXAMPLE 23

Dixie owns a vacation cottage on the lake. During the current year, she rented it for $1,600 for two weeks, lived in it two months, and left it vacant the remainder of the year. The year's expenses amounted to $6,000 interest expense, $500 property taxes, $1,500 utilities and maintenance, and $2,400 depreciation. Since the property was not rented for at least 15 days, the income is excluded, the interest and property tax expenses are itemized deductions, and the remaining expenses are nondeductible personal expenses. ▼

ETHICAL
CONSIDERATIONS

Renting for One More Day

June is a widow who lives in Williamsburg, Virginia. For the past five years (since the death of her husband), she has rented her home for one week to a professional golfer who is participating in the A–B Golf Classic. The rent income is $1,500. During this week, June visits her sister in Charlotte. A neighbor who is a CPA advises June that she does not need to report the $1,500 on her Federal income tax return because she did not rent her house for more than two weeks during the year.

In 1994, June has the opportunity to rent the house for $2,800 for an additional week in December to the golfer and his family who would like to spend Christmas in Williamsburg. She checks with her CPA neighbor to verify she will not have to include the rent income in her gross income. June agrees to rent her house and to visit her sister through New Year's Day.

The golfer and his family arrived on December 20 and were scheduled to depart on December 27. On December 26, the golfer's wife calls June at her sister's, explains that their two-year-old child is ill, and asks if they can rent for an additional day until the child feels better. June says yes, of course, but indicates she will not accept any rent for the additional day.

When June returns home on January 2, 1995, she finds the check on her kitchen counter is for $3,200 rather than for $2,800. The check is enclosed in a Christmas card from the golfer and his family.

On her 1994 Federal income tax return, June does not report any rent income or deduct any rental expenses. According to her records, she rented her house for exactly two weeks.

Primarily Rental Use

If the residence is not used for personal purposes for more than the greater of (1) 14 days or (2) 10 percent of the total days rented, the residence is treated as rental property.[48] The expenses must be allocated between personal and rental days if there are any personal use days during the year. The deduction of the expenses allocated to rental days can exceed rent income and result in a rental loss. The loss may be deductible under the passive loss rules (discussed in Chapter 11).

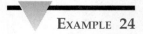

EXAMPLE 24

Assume Dixie in Example 23 rented the cottage for 120 days. The cottage is primarily rental use if she did not use it for personal purposes for more than 14 days. ▼

---

[47] § 280A(g).

[48] § 280A(d) and Prop.Reg. § 1.280A–3(c).

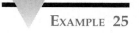
EXAMPLE 25

Assume Dixie in Example 23 rented the cottage for 200 days. She could use it for personal use for no more than 20 days (10% of the rental days) for it to be primarily rental use. ▼

EXAMPLE 26

Assume that Dixie in Example 23 used the cottage for 12 days and rented it for 48 days for $4,800. Since she did not use the cottage for more than 14 days, the cottage is treated as rental property. The expenses must be allocated between personal and rental days.

	Percentage of Use	
	Rental 80%	Personal 20%
Income	$4,800	$ –0–
Expenses		
Interest ($6,000)	($4,800)	($1,200)
Property taxes ($500)	(400)	(100)
Utilities and maintenance ($1,500)	(1,200)	(300)
Depreciation ($2,400)	(1,920)	(480)
Total expenses	($8,320)	($2,080)
Rental loss	($3,520)	$ –0–

Dixie deducts the $3,520 rental loss *for* AGI (assuming she meets the passive loss rules, discussed in Chapter 11). She also has itemized interest of $1,200 and taxes of $100 associated with the personal use. The portion of utilities and maintenance and depreciation attributable to personal use is not deductible. ▼

Personal/Rental Use

If the residence is rented for 15 or more days *and* is used for personal purposes for more than the greater of (1) 14 days or (2) 10 percent of the total days rented, it is treated as a personal/rental use residence. Expenses are allowed only to the extent of income.

EXAMPLE 27

Assume that Dixie in Example 23 rented the property for 30 days and lived in it for 30 days. The residence is classified as personal/rental use property since she used it more than 14 days and rented it for more than 14 days. The expenses must be allocated between rental use and personal use, and the rental expenses are allowed only to the extent of rent income. ▼

If a residence is classified as personal/rental use property, the expenses that are deductible anyway (e.g., real estate taxes) must be deducted first. If a positive net income results, otherwise nondeductible expenses that do not affect adjusted basis (e.g., maintenance, utilities, insurance) are allowed next. Finally, depreciation is allowed if any positive balance remains.

Expenses must be allocated between personal and rental days before the limits are applied. The courts have held that real estate taxes and mortgage interest, which accrue ratably over the year, are allocated on the basis of 365 days.[49] The

---

[49] *Bolton v. Comm.,* 82–2 USTC ¶9699, 51 AFTR2d 83–305, 694 F.2d 556 (CA–9, 1982).

IRS, however, disagrees and allocates real estate taxes and mortgage interest on the basis of total days of use.[50] Other expenses (utilities, maintenance, depreciation, etc.) are allocated on the basis of total days used.

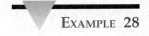

EXAMPLE 28

Sue rents her vacation home for 60 days and lives in the home for 30 days. The limitations on personal/rental use residences apply. Sue's gross rent income is $10,000. For the entire year (not a leap year), the real estate taxes are $2,190; her mortgage interest expense is $10,220; utilities and maintenance expense equals $2,400; and depreciation is $9,000. Using the IRS approach, these amounts are deductible in this specific order:

Gross income	$10,000
Deduct: Taxes and interest (60/90 × $12,410)	(8,273)
Remainder to apply to rental operating expenses and depreciation	$ 1,727
Deduct: Utilities and maintenance (60/90 × $2,400)	(1,600)
Balance	$ 127
Deduct: Depreciation (60/90 × $9,000 = $6,000 but limited to above balance)	(127)
Net rent income	$ –0–

The nonrental use portion of taxes and interest ($4,137 in this case) is deductible if the taxpayer elects to itemize (see Chapter 10). The personal use portion of utilities, maintenance, and depreciation is not deductible in any case. Also note that the basis of the property is not reduced by the $5,873 depreciation not allowed ($6,000 – $127) because of the above limitation. (See Chapter 14 for a discussion of the reduction in basis for depreciation allowed or allowable.) ▼

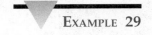

EXAMPLE 29

Using the court's approach in allocating property taxes and interest, Sue, in Example 28, would have this result:

Gross income	$10,000
Deduct: Taxes and interest (60/365 × $12,410)	(2,040)
Remainder to apply to rental operating expenses and depreciation	$ 7,960
Deduct: Utilities and maintenance (60/90 × $2,400)	(1,600)
Balance	$ 6,360
Deduct: Depreciation (60/90 × $9,000, but limited to $6,360)	(6,000)
Net rent income	$ 360

Sue can deduct $10,370 ($12,410 paid – $2,040 deducted as expense in computing rent income) of personal use interest and taxes as itemized deductions. ▼

Note the contrasting results in Examples 28 and 29. The IRS's approach (Example 28) results in no rental gain or loss and an itemized deduction for real estate taxes and mortgage interest of $4,137. In Example 29, Sue has net rent income of $360 and $10,370 of itemized deductions. The court's approach decreases her taxable income by $10,010 ($10,370 itemized deductions less $360 net rent income). The IRS's approach reduces her taxable income by only $4,137.

---

[50] Prop.Reg. § 1.280A–3(d)(4).

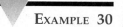

EXAMPLE 30

Assume that Sue in Example 28 had not lived in the home at all during the year. The house is rental property. The rental loss is calculated as follows:

Gross income	$10,000
Expenses	
Taxes and interest	($12,410)
Utilities and maintenance	(2,400)
Depreciation	(9,000)
Total expenses	($23,810)
Rental loss	($13,810)

Whether any of the rental loss would be deductible depends upon whether Sue actively participated in the rental activity and met the other requirements for passive losses (discussed in Chapter 10). ▼

Conversion to Rental Property

A related issue is whether or not a taxpayer's *primary residence* is subject to the preceding rules if it is converted to rental property. If the rules apply, a taxpayer who converts his or her personal residence to rental property during the tax year, without any tax avoidance motive, could have the allowable deductions limited to the rent income. This would occur if the personal use exceeded the greater of 14 days or 10 percent of rental days test (a likely situation). The Code provides that during a *qualified rental period,* any personal use days are not counted as personal use days in terms of classifying the use of the residence as *personal/rental use* rather than as *primarily rental use.*[51] In effect, the deduction for expenses of the property incurred during a qualified rental period is not subject to the personal use test of the vacation home rules. A qualified rental period is a consecutive period of 12 or more months. The period begins or ends in the taxable year in which the residence is rented or held for rental at a fair price. The residence must not be rented to a related party. If the property is sold before the 12-month period expires, the qualified rental period is the actual time rented.

EXAMPLE 31

Rhonda converts her residence to rental property on May 1 and rents it for the remainder of 1994 for $5,600 and for all of 1995 for $8,400. The house would be classified as personal/rental use property (personal use days during 1994 are greater than both 14 days and 10% of rental days) except that this is a qualified rental period. Therefore, Rhonda's deduction for rental expenses is not limited to the gross income of $5,600 in 1994. ▼

See Concept Summary 6–1 for a summary of the vacation home rules.

EXPENDITURES INCURRED FOR TAXPAYER'S BENEFIT OR TAXPAYER'S OBLIGATION

An expense must be incurred for the taxpayer's benefit or arise from the taxpayer's obligation. An individual cannot claim a tax deduction for the payment of the expenses of another individual.

---

[51] § 280A(d).

CONCEPT SUMMARY 6–1

Vacation/Rental Home

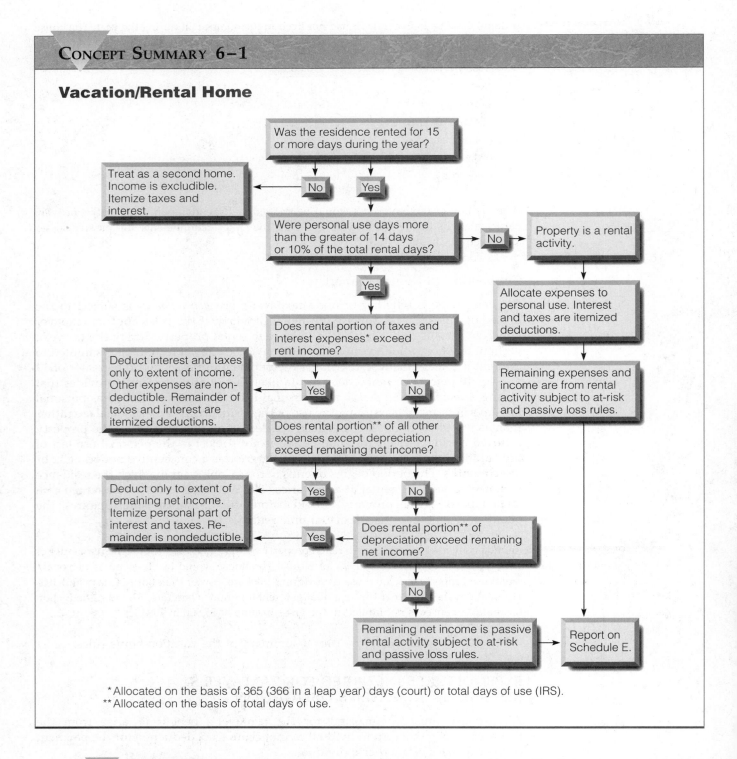

*Allocated on the basis of 365 (366 in a leap year) days (court) or total days of use (IRS).
**Allocated on the basis of total days of use.

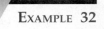

EXAMPLE 32

During the current year, Fred pays the interest on his son, Vern's, home mortgage. Neither Fred nor Vern can take a deduction for the interest paid. Fred is not entitled to a deduction because the mortgage is not his obligation. Vern cannot claim a deduction because he did not pay the interest. The tax result would have been more favorable had Fred made a cash gift to Vern and let him pay the interest. The interest then could have been deducted by the son, and Fred might not have been liable for any gift taxes depending upon the amount involved. A deduction would have been created with no cash difference to the family. ▼

One exception to this rule is the payment of medical expenses for a dependent. Such expenses are deductible by the payer.[52]

DISALLOWANCE OF PERSONAL EXPENDITURES

Section 262 states that "except as otherwise expressly provided in this chapter, no deduction shall be allowed for personal, living, or family expenses." To justify a deduction, an individual must be able to identify a particular Section of the Code that sanctions the deduction (e.g., charitable contributions, medical expenses). Sometimes the character of a particular expenditure is not easily determined.

EXAMPLE 33 During the current year, Howard pays $1,500 in legal fees and court costs to obtain a divorce from his wife, Vera. Involved in the divorce action is a property settlement that concerns the disposition of income-producing property owned by Howard. In a similar situation, the Tax Court held that the taxpayer could not deduct any such costs.[53] "Although fees primarily related to property division concerning his income-producing property, they weren't ordinary and necessary expenses paid for conservation or maintenance of property held for production of income. Legal fees incurred in defending against claims that arise from a taxpayer's marital relationship aren't deductible expenses regardless of possible consequences on taxpayer's income-producing property." ▼

The IRS has clarified the issue of the deduction of legal fees incurred in connection with a divorce.[54] To be deductible, an expense must relate solely to tax advice in a divorce proceeding. For example, legal fees attributable to the determination of dependency exemptions of children are deductible if the fees are distinguishable from the general legal fees incurred in obtaining a divorce. Other examples are the costs of creating a trust to make periodic alimony payments and the determination of the tax consequences of a property settlement. Therefore, it is advisable to request an itemization of attorney's fees to substantiate a deduction for the tax-related amounts.

DISALLOWANCE OF DEDUCTIONS FOR CAPITAL EXPENDITURES

The Code specifically disallows a deduction for "any amount paid out for new buildings or for permanent improvements or betterments made to increase the value of any property or estate."[55] The Regulations further define capital expenditures to include those expenditures that add to the value or prolong the life of property or adapt the property to a new or different use.[56] Incidental repairs and maintenance of the property are not capital expenditures and can be deducted as ordinary and necessary business expenses. Repairing a roof is a deductible expense, but replacing a roof is a capital expenditure subject to depreciation

---

[52] § 213(a).
[53] *Harry H. Goldberg*, 29 TCM 74, T.C.Memo. 1970–27.
[54] Rev.Rul. 72–545, 1972–2 C.B. 179.

[55] § 263(a)(1).
[56] Reg. § 1.263(a)–1(b).

deductions over its useful life. The tune-up of a delivery truck is an expense; a complete overhaul probably is a capital expenditure.

Capitalization versus Expense

When an expenditure is capitalized rather than expensed, the deduction is at best deferred and at worst lost forever. Although an immediate tax benefit for a large cash expenditure is lost, the cost may be deductible in increments over a longer period of time.

If the expenditure is for a tangible asset that has an ascertainable life, it is capitalized and may be deducted as depreciation (or cost recovery) over the life of the asset (for depreciation) or over a statutory period (for cost recovery under either ACRS or MACRS).[57] Land is not subject to depreciation (or cost recovery) since it does not have an ascertainable life.

EXAMPLE 34

Stan purchased a prime piece of land located in an apartment-zoned area. Stan paid $500,000 for the property, which had an old but usable apartment building on it. He immediately had the building demolished at a cost of $100,000. The $500,000 purchase price and the $100,000 demolition costs must be capitalized, and the basis of the land is $600,000. Since land is a nondepreciable asset, no deduction is allowed. More favorable tax treatment might result if Stan rented the apartments in the old building for a period of time to attempt to establish that there was no intent to demolish the building. If Stan's attempt is successful, it might be possible to allocate a substantial portion of the original purchase price of the property to the building (a depreciable asset). When the building is later demolished, any remaining adjusted basis can be deducted as an ordinary (§ 1231) loss. (See Chapter 17 for a discussion of the treatment of § 1231 assets.) ▼

If the expenditure is for an intangible asset (e.g., copyright, patent, covenant not to compete, goodwill), the capitalized expenditure can be amortized. Prior to the effect of RRA of 1993, only intangible assets with ascertainable lives (e.g., copyright, patent, covenant not to compete) could be amortized. Intangible assets with indeterminate lives (e.g., goodwill) could not be amortized. The amortization period generally was the life of the asset, and the amortization method was the straight-line method.

RRA of 1993 provides that intangibles acquired after August 10, 1993, are to be amortized over a 15-year period using the straight-line method.[58] This statutory change can produce both positive and negative results. On the positive side, goodwill is now subject to amortization. On the negative side, intangibles with an actual life shorter than 15 years must be amortized over the longer 15-year statutory period (e.g., a covenant not to compete with a 10-year life).

TRANSACTIONS BETWEEN RELATED PARTIES

The Code places restrictions on the recognition of gains and losses from **related-party transactions.** Without these restrictions, relationships created by birth, marriage, and business would provide endless possibilities for engaging in financial transactions that produce tax savings with no real economic substance or change. For example, to create an artificial loss, a wife could sell investment property to her husband at a loss and deduct the loss on their joint return. Her

---

[57] See Chapter 8 for the discussion of depreciation and cost recovery.   [58] § 197.

husband could then hold the asset indefinitely, and the family would sustain no real economic loss. A complex set of laws has been designed to eliminate such possibilities.

Losses

The Code provides for the disallowance of any "losses from sales or exchanges of property . . . directly or indirectly" between related parties.[59] When the property is subsequently sold to a nonrelated party, any gain recognized is reduced by the loss previously disallowed. Any disallowed loss not used by the related-party buyer to offset his or her recognized gain on a subsequent sale or exchange to an unrelated party is permanently lost.

EXAMPLE 35 Freida sells common stock with a basis of $1,000 to her son, Bill, for $800. Bill sells the stock several years later for $1,100. Freida's $200 loss is disallowed upon the sale to Bill, and only $100 of gain ($1,100 selling price – $800 basis – $200 disallowed loss) is taxable to him upon the subsequent sale. ▼

EXAMPLE 36 George sells common stock with a basis of $1,050 to his son, Ray, for $800. Ray sells the stock eight months later to an unrelated party for $900. Ray's gain of $100 ($900 selling price – $800 basis) is not recognized because of George's previously disallowed loss of $250. Note that the offset may result in only partial tax benefit upon the subsequent sale (as in this case). If the property had not been transferred to Ray, George could have recognized a $150 loss upon the subsequent sale to the unrelated party ($1,050 basis – $900 selling price). ▼

EXAMPLE 37 Pete sells common stock with a basis of $1,000 to an unrelated third party for $800. Pete's son repurchased the same stock in the market on the same day for $800. The $200 loss is not allowed because the transaction is an indirect sale between related parties.[60] ▼

Unpaid Expenses and Interest

The law prevents related taxpayers from engaging in tax avoidance schemes where one related taxpayer uses the accrual method of accounting and the other uses the cash basis. An accrual basis, closely held corporation, for example, could borrow funds from a cash basis individual shareholder. At the end of the year, the corporation would accrue and deduct the interest, but the cash basis lender would not recognize interest income since no interest had been paid. Section 267 specifically defers the deduction of the accruing taxpayer until the recipient taxpayer must include it in income; that is, when it is actually paid to the cash basis taxpayer. This *matching* provision applies to interest as well as other expenses, such as salaries and bonuses.

Relationships and Constructive Ownership

Section 267 operates to disallow losses and defer deductions only between related parties. Losses or deductions generated by similar transactions with an unrelated party are allowed. *Related parties* include the following:

---

[59] § 267(a)(1).
[60] *McWilliams v. Comm.*, 47–1 USTC ¶9289, 35 AFTR 1184, 67 S.Ct. 1477 (USSC, 1947).

- Brothers and sisters (whether whole, half, or adopted), spouse, ancestors (parents, grandparents), and lineal descendants (children, grandchildren) of the taxpayer.
- A corporation owned more than 50 percent (directly or indirectly) by the taxpayer.
- Two corporations that are members of a controlled group.
- A series of other complex relationships between trusts, corporations, and individual taxpayers.

Constructive ownership provisions are applied to determine whether the taxpayers are related. Under these provisions, stock owned by certain relatives or related entities is *deemed* to be owned by the taxpayer for purposes of applying the loss and expense deduction disallowance provisions. A taxpayer is deemed to own not only his or her stock but the stock owned by his or her lineal descendants, ancestors, brothers and sisters or half-brothers and half-sisters, and spouse. The taxpayer is also deemed to own his or her proportionate share of stock owned by any partnership, corporation, estate, or trust of which he or she is a member. An individual is deemed to own any stock owned, directly or indirectly, by his or her partner. However, constructive ownership by an individual of the partnership's and the other partner's shares does not extend to the individual's spouse or other relatives (no double attribution).

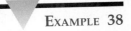

EXAMPLE 38

The stock of Sparrow Corporation is owned 20% by Ted, 30% by Ted's father, 30% by Ted's mother, and 20% by Ted's sister. On July 1 of the current year, Ted loaned $10,000 to Sparrow Corporation at 8% annual interest, principal and interest payable on demand. For tax purposes, Sparrow uses the accrual basis, and Ted uses the cash basis. Both are on a calendar year. Since Ted is deemed to own the 80% owned by his parents and sister, he constructively owns 100% of Sparrow Corporation. If the corporation accrues the interest within the taxable year, no deduction can be taken until payment is made to Ted. ▼

SUBSTANTIATION REQUIREMENTS

The tax law is built on a voluntary system. Taxpayers file their tax returns, report income and take deductions to which they are entitled, and pay their taxes through withholding or estimated tax payments during the year. The taxpayer has the burden of proof for substantiating expenses deducted on the returns and must retain adequate records. Upon audit, the IRS will disallow any undocumented or unsubstantiated deductions. These requirements have resulted in numerous conflicts between taxpayers and the IRS.

Some events throughout the year should be documented as they occur. For example, it is generally advisable to receive a pledge payment statement from one's church, in addition to a canceled check (if available) for proper documentation of a charitable contribution.[61] In addition, for charitable contributions made after December 31, RRA of 1993 requires that the donor obtain a receipt from the donee for contributions of $250 or more. Other types of deductible expenditures may require receipts or some other type of support.

Specific and *more stringent* rules for deducting travel, entertainment, and gift expenses are discussed in Chapter 9. Certain mixed-use (both personal and business use) and listed property are also subject to the adequate records requirement (discussed in Chapter 8).

---

[61] Rev.Proc. 92–71, 1992-2 C.B. 437, addresses circumstances where checks are not returned by a financial institution or where electronic transfers are made.

EXPENSES AND INTEREST RELATING TO TAX-EXEMPT INCOME

Certain income, such as interest on municipal bonds, is tax-exempt.[62] The law also allows the taxpayer to deduct expenses incurred for the production of income.[63] Deduction disallowance provisions, however, make it impossible to make money at the expense of the government by excluding interest income and deducting interest expense.[64]

EXAMPLE 39

Sandy, a taxpayer in the 36% bracket, purchased $100,000 of 6% municipal bonds. At the same time, she used the bonds as collateral on a bank loan of $100,000 at 8% interest. A positive cash flow would result from the tax benefit as follows:

Cash paid out on loan	($8,000)
Cash received from bonds	6,000
Tax savings from deducting interest expense (36% of $8,000 interest expense)	2,880
Net positive cash flow	$ 880

To eliminate the possibility illustrated in Example 39, the Code specifically disallows as a deduction the expenses of producing tax-exempt income. Interest on any indebtedness incurred or continued to purchase or carry tax-exempt obligations also is disallowed.

Judicial Interpretations

It is often difficult to show a direct relationship between borrowings and investment in tax-exempt securities. Suppose, for example, that a taxpayer borrows money, adds it to existing funds, buys inventory and stocks, then later sells the inventory and buys municipal bonds. A series of transactions such as these can completely obscure any connection between the loan and the tax-exempt investment. One solution would be to disallow interest on any debt to the extent that the taxpayer holds any tax-exempt securities. This approach would preclude individuals from deducting part of their home mortgage interest if they owned any municipal bonds. The law was not intended to go to such extremes. As a result, judicial interpretations have tried to be reasonable in disallowing interest deductions.

In one case, a company used municipal bonds as collateral on short-term loans to meet seasonal liquidity needs.[65] The Court disallowed the interest deduction on the grounds that the company could predict its seasonal liquidity needs. The company could anticipate the need to borrow the money to continue to carry the tax-exempt securities. The same company *was* allowed an interest deduction on a building mortgage, even though tax-exempt securities it owned could have been sold to pay off the mortgage. The Court reasoned that short-term liquidity needs would have been impaired if the tax-exempt securities were sold. Furthermore, the Court ruled that carrying the tax-exempt securities bore no relationship to the long-term financing of a construction project.

---

[62] § 103.
[63] § 212.
[64] § 265.

[65] *The Wisconsin Cheeseman, Inc. v. U.S.*, 68–1 USTC ¶9145, 21 AFTR2d 383, 388 F.2d 420 (CA–7, 1968).

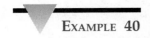

EXAMPLE 40

In January of the current year, Gayle borrowed $100,000 at 8% interest. She used the loan proceeds to purchase 5,000 shares of stock in White Corporation. In July, she sold the stock for $120,000 and reinvested the proceeds in City of Denver bonds, the income from which is tax-exempt. Assuming the $100,000 loan remained outstanding throughout the entire year, the interest attributable to the period in which the bonds were held cannot be deducted. ▼

TAX PLANNING CONSIDERATIONS

4 ▼ **LEARNING OBJECTIVE**
Identify tax planning opportunities for maximizing deductions and minimizing the disallowance of deductions.

TIME VALUE OF TAX DEDUCTIONS

Cash basis taxpayers often have the ability to make early payments for their expenses at the end of the tax year. This permits the payments to be deducted currently instead of in the following tax year. In view of the time value of money, a tax deduction this year may be worth more than the same deduction next year. Before employing this strategy, the taxpayer must consider next year's expected income and tax rates and whether a cash-flow problem may develop from early payments. Thus, the time value of money as well as tax rate changes must be considered when an expense can be paid and deducted in either of two years.

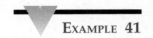

EXAMPLE 41

Jena pledged $5,000 to her church's special building fund. She can make the contribution in December 1994 or January 1995. Jena is in the 36% tax bracket in 1994, and in the 31% bracket in 1995. She itemizes in both years. Assume Jena's discount rate is 8%. If she takes the deduction in 1994, she saves $365 ($1,800 – $1,435), due to the decrease in the tax rates and the time value of money.

	1994	**1995**
Contribution	$5,000	$5,000
Tax bracket	.36	.31
Tax savings	$1,800	$1,550
Discounted @ 8%	1.0	.926
Savings in present value	$1,800	$1,435

▼

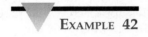

EXAMPLE 42

Assume the same facts as in Example 41, except that Jena is in the 31% bracket in both 1994 and 1995. By taking the deduction in 1994, Jena saves $115 ($1,550 – $1,435), due to the time value of money.

	1994	**1995**
Contribution	$5,000	$5,000
Tax bracket	.31	.31
Tax savings	$1,550	$1,550
Discounted @ 8%	1.0	.926
Savings in present value	$1,550	$1,435

▼

UNREASONABLE COMPENSATION

In substantiating the reasonableness of a shareholder-employee's compensation, an internal comparison test is sometimes useful. If it can be shown that nonshareholder-employees and shareholder-employees in comparable positions receive comparable compensation, it is indicative that compensation is not unreasonable.

CONCEPT SUMMARY 6–2

Classification of Expenses

Expense Item	Deductible For AGI	Deductible From AGI	Not Deductible	Applicable Code §
Investment expenses				
Rent and royalty	X			§ 62(a)(4)
All other investments		X[4]		§ 212
Employee expenses				
Commuting expenses			X	§ 262
Travel and transportation[1]		X[4,5]		§ 162(a)(2)
Reimbursed expenses[1]	X			§ 62(a)(2)(A)
Moving expenses	X			§ 62(a)(15)
Entertainment[1]		X[4,5]		§ 162(a)
All other employee expenses[1]		X[4,5]		§ 162(a)
Certain expenses of performing artists	X			§ 62(a)(2)(B)
Trade or business expenses	X			§§ 162 and 62(a)(1)
Casualty losses				
Business	X			§ 165(c)(1)
Personal		X[6]		§ 165(c)(3)
Tax determination				
Collection or refund expenses	X[8]	X[4]		§§ 212 and 62(a)(1) or (4)
Bad debts	X			§§ 166 and 62(a)(1) or (3)
Medical expenses		X[7]		§ 213
Charitable contributions		X		§ 170
Taxes				
Trade or business	X			§§ 162 and 62(a)(1)
Personal taxes				
Real property		X		§ 164(a)(1)
Personal property		X		§ 164(a)(2)
State and local income		X		§ 164(a)(3)
Investigation of a business[2]	X			§§ 162 and 62(a)(1)
Interest				
Business	X			§§ 162 and 62(a)(1)
Personal		X[3]	X[9]	§ 163(a), (d), & (h)
All other personal expenses			X	§ 262

1. Deduction *for* AGI if reimbursed, an adequate accounting is made, and employee is required to repay excess reimbursements.
2. Provided certain criteria are met.
3. Subject to the excess investment interest and the qualified residence interest provisions.
4. Subject (in the aggregate) to a 2%-of-AGI floor imposed by § 67.
5. Only 50% of meals and entertainment are deductible.
6. Subject to a 10%-of-AGI floor and a $100 floor.
7. Subject to a 7.5%-of-AGI floor.
8. Only the portion relating to business, rental, or royalty income or losses.
9. Other personal interest is disallowed.

Another possibility is to demonstrate that the shareholder-employee has been underpaid in prior years. For example, the shareholder-employee may have agreed to take a less-than-adequate salary during the unprofitable formative years of the business. He or she would expect the "postponed" compensation to be paid in later, more profitable years. The agreement should be documented, if possible, in the corporate minutes.

Keep in mind that in testing for reasonableness, the *total* pay package must be considered. Look at all fringe benefits or perquisites, such as contributions by the corporation to a qualified pension plan. Even though those amounts are not immediately available to the covered shareholder-employee, they must be taken into account.

EXCESSIVE EXECUTIVE COMPENSATION

With the new $1 million limit on the deduction of compensation of covered employees, many corporations and their executives must engage in additional tax planning. Previously, concerns over the deductibility of compensation related primarily to closely held corporations. The new limit applies specifically to publicly held corporations. In many instances, it will now be necessary for these corporations to restructure the compensation packages of their top executives in order to deduct payments in excess of $1 million. Opportunities include compensation payable on a commission basis, certain other performance-based compensation, payments to qualified retirement plans, and payments that are excludible fringe benefits.

SHIFTING DEDUCTIONS

Taxpayers should manage their obligations to avoid the loss of a deduction. Deductions can be shifted among family members, depending upon who makes the payment. For example, a father buys a condo for his daughter and puts the title in both names. The taxpayer who makes the payment gets the deduction for the property taxes. If the condo is owned by the daughter only and her father makes the payment, neither is entitled to a deduction.

HOBBY LOSSES

To demonstrate that an activity has been entered into for the purpose of making a profit, a taxpayer should treat the activity as a business. The business should engage in advertising, use business letterhead stationery, and maintain a business phone.

If a taxpayer's activity earns a profit in three out of five consecutive years, the presumption is that the activity is engaged in for profit. It may be possible for a cash basis taxpayer to meet these requirements by timing the payment of expenses or the receipt of revenues. The payment of certain expenses incurred before the end of the year might be made in the following year. The billing of year-end sales might be delayed so that collections are received in the following year.

Keep in mind that the three-out-of-five-years rule under § 183 is not absolute. All it does is shift the presumption. If a profit is not made in three out of five years, the losses may still be allowed if the taxpayer can show that they are due to the nature of the business. For example, success in artistic or literary endeavors can take a long time. Also, due to the present state of the economy, even full-time farmers and ranchers are often unable to show a profit. How can one expect a part-time farmer or rancher to do so?

Merely satisfying the three-out-of-five-years rule does not guarantee that a taxpayer is automatically home free. If the three years of profits are insignificant relative to the losses of other years, or if the profits are not from the ordinary operation of the business, the taxpayer is vulnerable. The IRS may still be able to establish that the taxpayer is not engaged in an activity for profit.

EXAMPLE 43

Ashley had the following gains and losses in an artistic endeavor:

1990	($ 50,000)
1991	(65,000)
1992	400
1993	200
1994	125

Under these circumstances, the IRS might try to overcome the presumption. ▼

If Ashley in Example 43 could show conformity with the factors enumerated in the Regulations[66] or could show evidence of business hardships (e.g., injury, death, or illness), the government cannot override the presumption.[67]

CAPITAL EXPENDITURES

The Revenue Reconciliation Act of 1993 (RRA of 1993) has modified the planning strategy associated with goodwill and covenants not to compete. Prior to RRA of 1993, on the sale of a sole proprietorship where the sales price exceeded the fair market value of the tangible assets and stated intangible assets, a natural tax conflict typically existed between the seller and the buyer. The seller's preference was for the excess amount to be allocated to goodwill. Goodwill is a capital asset whereas a covenant not to compete produces ordinary income treatment (see Chapter 16). The buyer's preference was for the excess amount to be allocated to a covenant not to compete because it could be amortized over the covenant life whereas goodwill was not eligible for amortization.

RRA of 1993 provides that both a covenant and goodwill are to be amortized over a statutory 15-year period. Therefore, the tax results for the buyer are the same. The seller's motive was not affected by RRA of 1993. Therefore, the seller and buyer, in negotiating the sales price, should factor in the tax benefit to the seller of having the excess amount labeled goodwill rather than a covenant not to compete. Of course, if the noncompetition aspects of a covenant are important to the buyer, part of the excess amount can be assigned to a covenant.

---

[66] Reg. §§ 1.183–2(b)(1) through (9).
[67] *Faulconer, Sr. v. Comm.*, 84–2 USTC ¶9955, 55 AFTR2d 85–302, 748 F.2d 890 (CA–4, 1984), *rev'g* 45 TCM 1084, T.C.Memo. 1983–165.

KEY TERMS

Accounting method, 6–7

Accrual method, 6–7

Cash method, 6–7

Constructive ownership, 6–28

Deductions *for* adjusted gross income, 6–2

Deductions *from* adjusted gross income, 6–2

Hobby losses, 6–17

Itemized deductions, 6–4

Ordinary and necessary, 6–5

Reasonableness, 6–6

Related-party transactions, 6–26

Vacation home, 6–19

PROBLEM MATERIALS

DISCUSSION QUESTIONS

1. "All income must be reported and all deductions are allowed unless specifically disallowed in the Code." Discuss.

2. Tyson, who had AGI of $30,000, had deductions of $5,000. Would it matter to Tyson whether they were *for* or *from* AGI? Why or why not?

3. If a taxpayer is audited and $1,000 of income is added to his AGI, will his tax increase (ignoring penalties and interest) be equal to $1,000 multiplied by his marginal tax bracket? Discuss.

4. Are the following items deductible *for* AGI, deductible *from* AGI, or nondeductible personal items?
   a. Unreimbursed travel expenses of an employee.
   b. Alimony payments.
   c. Charitable contributions.
   d. Medical expenses.
   e. Rentals for safe deposit box in which stocks and bonds are kept.
   f. Repairs made on a personal residence.
   g. Expenses related to tax-exempt municipal bonds.
   h. Reimbursed travel expenses of an employee.
   i. Moving expenses.

5. Are the following expenditures deductible *for* AGI, deductible *from* AGI, nondeductible personal items, or capital expenditures?
   a. Repairs made to a rental property.
   b. State income taxes.
   c. Investment advice subscriptions.
   d. Child support payments.
   e. New roof on rental property.
   f. New roof on personal residence.
   g. Mortgage interest on personal residence.

6. Larry and Susan each invest $10,000 in separate investment activities. They each incur deductible expenses of $800 associated with their respective investments. Explain why Larry's expenses are properly classified as deductions *from* AGI (itemized deductions) and Susan's expenses are appropriately classified as deductions *for* AGI.

7. Define and contrast the "ordinary" and "necessary" tests for business expenses.

8. When Jason died, he left equal shares of stock to his four children, although he made it clear that he wanted Jill and John to run the company. This was quite all right with the other two children, who were to receive $100,000 each per year from the company and were free to pursue their own interests. Jill and John each received reasonable salaries of $250,000 and $210,000, respectively. They paid the other two children salaries of $100,000 each. What were they trying to accomplish from a tax standpoint? Will it work? If not, what are the tax consequences to the corporation and to the other two children?

9. Don uses the second story of a building for his residence and the first story for his business. The uninsured building is destroyed by a fire. Are the tax consequences the same for the residence part of the building and the business part?

10. Describe the cash method and the accrual method of accounting with respect to deductions.

11. Landry, a cash basis taxpayer, decides to reduce his taxable income for 1994 by buying $10,000 worth of supplies on December 28, 1994. The supplies will be used up in 1995.
   a. Can Landry deduct this expenditure in 1994?
   b. Would your answer differ if Landry bought the supplies because a supplier was going out of business and had given him a significant discount on the supplies?

12. What is the "actually paid" requirement for the deduction of an expense by a cash basis taxpayer? Does actual payment ensure a deduction?

13. What is the significance of the economic performance test?

14. Why can't the reserve method be used for tax purposes?

15. Linda operates a drug-running operation. Which of the following expenses she incurs are deductible?
   a. Bribes paid to border guards.
   b. Salaries to employees.
   c. Price paid for drugs purchased for resale.
   d. Kickbacks to police.
   e. Rent on an office.

16. Kelly is an executive in Gray Corporation. He used insider information to buy Gray stock just before public announcement of the discovery of huge oil reserves on company-owned property. He was caught and incurred legal expenses and treble damage payments. Can Kelly deduct either expense?

17. Gordon anticipates that being positively perceived by the individual who is elected mayor will be beneficial for his business. Therefore, he contributes to the campaigns of both the Democratic and the Republican candidates. The Republican candidate is elected mayor. Can Gordon deduct any of the political contributions he made?

18. What is the significance of one's present occupation in the deductibility of expenses incurred in investigating another business?

19. What factors should be considered in determining whether an activity is profit-seeking or a hobby? Discuss.

20. What is meant by the statement that § 183 is a "presumptive rule"?

21. Discuss the tax treatment of the rental of a vacation home if it is:
   a. Rented 10 days during the year.
   b. Rented 130 days during the year; used personally for 12 days.
   c. Rented for 250 days; used personally for 40 days.

22. Contrast the differing results obtained in a personal/rental situation by allocating property taxes and interest on the IRS's basis and the court's basis. Which method would the taxpayer prefer?

23. Hank was transferred from Phoenix to North Dakota on March 1 of the current year. He immediately put his home in Phoenix up for rent. The home was rented May 1 to November 30 and was vacant during the month of December. It was rented again on January 1 for six months. What expenses, if any, can Hank deduct on his return? Which deductions are *for* AGI and which ones are *from* AGI?

24. Explain which, if any, legal fees incurred obtaining a divorce are deductible. Are they deductible *for* or *from* AGI?

25. Igor repaired the roof on his factory at a cost of $1,500 in the current year. During the same year, Raisa replaced the roof on her small rental house for $1,500. Both taxpayers are on the cash basis. Are their expenditures treated the same on their tax returns? Why or why not?

26. Discuss the reasons for the disallowance of losses between related parties. Would it make any difference if a parent sold stock to an unrelated third party and the child repurchased the same number of shares of the stock in the market the same day?

27. Tara sold 100 shares of Eagle Company stock to Frank, her brother, for $8,000. She had originally paid $7,100 for the stock. Frank later sold the stock for $6,000 on the open market. What are the tax consequences to Tara and Frank?

28. Would your answer to Question 27 differ if Tara had sold the stock to Frank for $6,500?

29. Helen owns 20% of Black Corporation; 20% of Black's stock is owned by Sara, Helen's mother; 15% is owned by Richard, Helen's brother; the remaining 45% is owned by unrelated parties. Helen is on the cash basis, and Black Corporation is on the accrual basis. On December 31, 1994, Black accrued Helen's salary of $5,000 and paid it on April 4, 1995. Both are on a calendar year. What is the tax effect to Helen and Black?

30. Why are taxpayers required to substantiate their expenditures in order to obtain a deduction on their returns?

PROBLEMS

31. Ted filed his 1993 tax return, claiming two exemptions and itemizing his deductions as follows:

AGI (salary)			$20,000
Less: Itemized deductions:			
Medical expenses	$ 1,800		
Less: 7.5% of AGI	(1,500)	$ 300	
Charitable contributions		1,900	
Interest		5,300	
Taxes		900	
Miscellaneous	$ 600		
Less: 2% of AGI	(400)	200	
Total itemized deductions			(8,600)
			$11,400
Less: 2 exemptions			(4,700)
Taxable income			$ 6,700

In 1994, Ted realized that he had forgotten to deduct his $2,000 IRA contribution for 1993. On an amended return, what is his new AGI? Taxable income?

32. Sandra and Roy each own 50% of the stock of Wren Corporation. The net income of the corporation for 1994, before shareholder-employee salaries, is $800,000. In prior years, Sandra received a salary of $150,000, and Roy received a salary of $100,000, both of

which are comparable to the salaries paid for similar positions in comparable companies. Sandra and Roy decide to pay themselves the following salaries for 1994:

Sandra	$500,000
Roy	300,000

a. What are Sandra and Roy trying to achieve with the increased salaries?

b. If the additional salaries are allowed, what are the tax consequences to Sandra, Roy, and Wren Corporation?

c. If the additional salaries are disallowed, what are the tax consequences to Sandra, Roy, and Wren Corporation?

33. Peggy, who is single, has a sole proprietorship and keeps her books on the cash basis. Following is a summary of her receipts, disbursements, and other items related to her business account for 1994:

Receipts	
Sales	$28,000
Dividend received from AT&T	300
Interest on savings account	450
Long-term capital gain on sale of stock	1,200
Disbursements	
Rent on buildings used 75% for business and 25% for living quarters	6,000
Salary paid to part-time secretary	3,000
Taxes	
Gross receipts tax on sales	840
State income taxes	750
Charitable contributions	1,400
Insurance on business property (policy runs from October 1, 1994, to September 30, 1995)	1,200
Depreciation on business equipment	1,000
Business supplies	980

Calculate Peggy's AGI for 1994.

34. Duck, Inc., an accrual basis corporation, sponsored a rock concert on December 29, 1994. Gross receipts were $300,000. The following expenses were incurred and paid as indicated:

Expense		**Payment Date**
Rental of coliseum	$ 25,000	December 21, 1994
Cost of goods sold:		
Food	30,000	December 30, 1994
Souvenirs	60,000	December 30, 1994
Performers	100,000	January 5, 1995
Cleaning of coliseum	10,000	February 1, 1995

Since the coliseum was not scheduled to be used again until January 15, the company with which Duck had contracted did not actually perform the cleanup until January 8–10, 1995.

Calculate Duck's net income from the concert for tax purposes for 1994.

35. Andrew, a cash basis taxpayer, had the following income and expenses in his local trucking business:

Service fees collected	$322,000
Expenses	
Salaries paid to drivers	185,000
Repairs and maintenance on trucks	15,000
Supplies	8,000
Fuel purchased	63,000
Fines for overloading trucks	4,200
Depreciation on trucks	30,600
Purchase price of two new trucks (paid $40,000 down and signed an installment note for the balance)	120,000
Interest paid on truck installment note	4,000
Protection money paid to local gang so trucks would not be vandalized	12,000

What is Andrew's net income from this business for tax purposes?

36. David runs an illegal numbers racket. His gross income was $500,000. He incurred the following expenses:

Illegal kickbacks	$20,000
Salaries	80,000
Rent	24,000
Utilities and telephone	9,000
Bribes to police	25,000
Interest	6,000
Depreciation on equipment	12,000

   a. What is his net income from this business that is includible in taxable income?
   b. If the business was an illegal drug operation, would your answer differ?

37. Tim traveled to a neighboring state to investigate the purchase of two restaurants. His expenses included travel, legal, accounting, and miscellaneous expenses. The total was $12,000. He incurred the expenses in March and April 1994.
   a. What can Tim deduct in 1994 if he was in the restaurant business and did not acquire the two restaurants?
   b. What can Tim deduct in 1994 if he was in the restaurant business and acquired the two restaurants and began operating them on July 1, 1994?
   c. What can Tim deduct in 1994 if he did not acquire the two restaurants and was not in the restaurant business?
   d. What can he deduct in 1994 if he acquired the two restaurants but was not in the restaurant business when he acquired them? Operations began on July 1, 1994.

38. Matt is a promoter, real estate developer, and investor. Because he has inherited wealth, he can afford to be somewhat of a wheeler-dealer. He is single, age 41. During 1994, Matt incurred expenses in traveling to the state capitol to testify against proposed legislation for a green belt around the city because it interfered with some of his development plans. The expenses amounted to $900. He also spent $300 traveling to various locations to speak to civic groups against the proposed legislation.

Matt also incurred $1,600 of expense investigating the purchase of a computer franchising operation. He did not purchase the operation because he felt that his lack of expertise in that type of business was too big an obstacle to overcome.

Matt's other income and expenses for the year were as follows:

Income	
Interest	$ 80,000
Dividends	160,000
Short-term capital loss	(50,000)
Long-term capital gains	175,000
Fees for promotion and development	24,000
Expenses	
Office expenses	17,000
Expenses incurred on land held for resale	6,000
Tax advice on stock investments	5,000
All other itemized deductions	34,000

Assume Matt's self-employment tax is $862. Calculate Matt's AGI for 1994.

39. Larry made a fortune in the stock market and retired at age 42. He bought a charming home in Vermont and incurred the following expenses in turning it into a country inn:

Repairs and maintenance	$14,000
Utilities	4,800
Depreciation	50,000
Interest on house mortgage	18,000
Property taxes	5,000
Supplies and food	20,000
All other expenses	10,000

a. Assuming that Larry's endeavor was deemed a hobby and he had income of $30,000, what would he have to include in income? What could he deduct, assuming an AGI of $200,000 (not counting the $30,000 from the inn)?

b. Assuming that Larry's endeavor was a bona fide business, how would your answer change?

40. Samantha is an executive with an AGI of $100,000 before consideration of income or loss from her miniature horse business. Her income comes from winning horse shows, stud fees, and sales of yearlings. Her home is on 20 acres, 18 of which she uses to pasture the horses and upon which she has erected stables, paddocks, fences, tack houses, and so forth.

Samantha uses an office in her home that is 10% of the square footage of the house. She uses the office exclusively for keeping records of breeding lines, histories, and show and veterinary records. Her records show the following income and expenses for the current year:

Income from fees, prizes, and sales	$22,000
Expenses	
Entry fees	1,000
Feed and veterinary bills	4,000
Supplies	900
Publications and dues	500
Travel to horse shows (no meals)	2,300
Salaries and wages of employees	8,000
Depreciation on horse equipment	3,000
Depreciation on horse farm improvements	7,000
Depreciation on 10% of home	1,000
Total home mortgage interest	24,000
Total property taxes on home	2,200
Total property taxes on horse farm improvements	800

The mortgage interest is only on her home. The horse farm improvements are not mortgaged.

How must Samantha treat the income and expenses of the operation if the miniature horse activity is held to be a hobby?

41. How would your answer in Problem 40 differ if the horse operation was held to be a business?

42. Louis makes macramé animals in his spare time. He sold $3,000 worth of animals during the year and incurred expenses as follows:

Supplies	$1,800
Depreciation on business property	1,100
Advertising	300

How are these items treated if the endeavor is a hobby? A business?

43. In 1994, Anna rented her vacation home for 60 days, used it personally for 20 days, and left it vacant for 285 days. She had the following income and expenses:

Rent income	$ 6,000
Expenses	
Real estate taxes	2,000
Interest on mortgage	9,000
Repairs	1,000
Roof replacement	12,000
Depreciation	8,000

Compute Anna's net rent income or loss and the amounts she can itemize on her tax return, using the court's approach in allocating property taxes and interest.

44. How would your answer in Problem 43 differ using the IRS's method of allocating property taxes and interest?

45. How would your answer in Problem 43 differ if Anna had rented the house for 90 days and had used it personally for 12 days?

46. Chee, single, age 40, had the following income and expenses in 1994:

Income	
Salary	$ 43,000
Rental of vacation home (rented 60 days, used personally 60 days, vacant 245 days)	4,000
Municipal bond interest	2,000
Dividend from General Motors	400
Expenses	
Interest	
On home mortgage	8,400
On vacation home	4,758
On loan used to buy municipal bonds	3,100
Taxes	
Property tax on home	2,200
Property tax on vacation home	1,098
State income tax	3,300
Charitable contributions	1,100
Tax return preparation fee	300
Utilities and maintenance on vacation home	2,600
Depreciation on rental 50% of vacation home	3,500

Calculate Chee's taxable income for 1994 before personal exemptions.

47. During 1994, Robert pays the following amounts associated with his own residence and that of his daughter, Anne:

- Property taxes:
  On home owned by Robert $3,000
  On home owned by Anne 1,500

  - Mortgage interest:
  Associated with Robert's home 8,000
  Associated with Anne's home 4,500

  - Repairs to:
  Robert's home 1,200
  Anne's home 700

  - Utilities:
  Robert's home 2,700
  Anne's home 1,600

  - Replacement of roof:
  Robert's home 4,000

  a. Which of these expenses can Robert deduct?
  b. Which of these expenses can Anne deduct?
  c. Are the deductions *for* AGI or *from* AGI (itemized)?

48. Lee incurred the following expenses in the current tax year. Indicate, in the spaces provided, whether each expenditure is deductible *for* AGI, *from* AGI, or not deductible.

Expense Item	Deductible For AGI	Deductible From AGI	Not Deductible
a. Lee's personal medical expenses			
b. Lee's dependent daughter's medical expenses			
c. Real estate taxes on rental property			
d. Real estate taxes on Lee's personal residence			
e. Real estate taxes on daughter's personal residence			
f. Lee's state income taxes			
g. Interest on rental property mortgage			
h. Interest on Lee's personal residence mortgage			
i. Interest on daughter's personal residence mortgage			
j. Interest on business loans			
k. Charitable contributions			
l. Depreciation on rental property			
m. Utilities & maintenance on:			
(1) Rental property			
(2) Lee's home			
(3) Daughter's home			
n. Depreciation on auto used in Lee's business			
o. Depreciation on Lee's personal auto			
p. Depreciation on daughter's personal auto			

49. Janet sold stock (basis of $40,000) to her brother, Fred, for $32,000.
    a. What are the tax consequences to Janet?
    b. What are the tax consequences to Fred if he later sells the stock for $42,000? For $28,000? For $36,000?

50. The Robin Corporation is owned as follows:

Irene	20%
Paul, Irene's husband	20%
Sylvia, Irene's mother	15%
Ron, Irene's father	25%
Quinn, an unrelated party	20%

Robin is on the accrual basis, and Irene and Paul are on the cash basis. Irene and Paul each loaned the Robin Corporation $10,000 out of their separate funds. On December 31, 1994, Robin accrued interest at 7% on both loans. The interest was paid on February 4, 1995. What is the tax treatment of this interest expense/income to Irene, Paul, and Robin?

51. What is Kim's constructive ownership of Wren Corporation, given the following information?

Shares owned by Kim	900
Shares owned by Sam, Kim's uncle	600
Shares owned by Barbara, Kim's partner	30
Shares owned by Green, a partnership owned by Kim and Barbara equally	300
Shares owned by Vera, Kim's granddaughter	570
Shares owned by unrelated parties	600

52. Chris has a brokerage account and buys on the margin, which resulted in an interest expense during the year of $8,000. Income generated through the brokerage account was as follows:

Municipal interest	$30,000
Taxable dividends, interest, and capital gains	70,000

How much investment interest can Chris deduct?

53. Jay's sole proprietorship has the following assets

	Basis	Fair Market Value
Cash	$ 10,000	$ 10,000
Accounts receivable	18,000	18,000
Inventory	25,000	30,000
Patent	22,000	40,000
Land	50,000	75,000
	$125,000	$173,000

The building in which Jay's business is located is leased. The lease expires at the end of the year.

Jay is age 70 and would like to retire. He expects to be in the 36% tax bracket. Jay is negotiating the sale of the business with Lois, a key employee. They have agreed on the

fair market value of the assets, as indicated above, and agree the total purchase price should be about $200,000.
a. Advise Jay regarding how the sale should be structured.
b. Advise Lois regarding how the purchase should be structured.
c. What might they do to achieve an acceptable compromise?

CUMULATIVE PROBLEMS

54. John and Mary Jane Sanders are married, filing jointly. Their address is 204 Shoe Lane, Blacksburg, VA 24061. They are expecting their first two children (twins) in early 1995. John's salary in 1994 was $60,000, from which $11,000 of Federal income tax and $3,500 of state income tax were withheld. Mary Jane made $35,000 and had $4,000 of Federal income tax and $2,000 of state income tax withheld.

Mary Jane's father lived with them until his death in October. His only source of income was Social Security benefits of $4,800. Of this amount, he deposited $2,800 in a savings account. The remainder of his support, including funeral expenses of $5,000, was provided by John and Mary Jane.

They had $600 of savings account interest and $900 of dividends during the year.

They made charitable contributions of $2,000 during the year and paid an additional $200 in state income taxes in 1994 upon filing their 1993 state income tax return. Their deductible home mortgage interest was $8,200, and their property taxes came to $2,100. They had no other deductible expenses.

Part 1—Tax Computation
Calculate their tax (or refund) due for 1994. Suggested software (if available): WFT tax planning software.

Part 2—Tax Planning
Assume that they come to you for advice in December 1994. John has learned that he will receive a $25,000 bonus. He wants to know if he should take it in December 1994 or in January 1995. Mary Jane will quit work on December 31 to stay home with the twins. Their itemized deductions will decrease by $2,000 because Mary Jane will not have state income taxes withheld. Write a letter to John and Mary Jane that contains your advice and prepare a memo for the tax files. Suggested software (if available): WFT tax planning software.

55. Linda Maples, age 49, is single and lives at 321 Poplar Road, Springfield, IL 60740. Her Social Security number is 648–23–9981. Linda's husband died in 1992, and she has dependent twins, Joshua and Samantha, age 10. Joshua's Social Security number is 648–92–3471, and Samantha's is 648–92–3472.

Linda is an accountant and earned $65,000 in 1993. Her employer withheld $9,600 in Federal income tax, $1,300 in state income tax, and the correct amount of FICA tax.

Linda received $100,000 from her late husband's life insurance policy in March and promptly invested in mutual funds. On December 10, 1993, she sold 100 shares of Unco stock for $7,000. She had purchased the stock on March 18, 1993, for $8,000. She had the following interest and dividends in 1993:

First National Bank savings account	$ 800
Total dividends from United Mutual Fund	5,000
Capital gains portion from United Mutual Fund	2,000

An examination of her records reveals the following:

- Linda made charitable contributions of $3,000 and gave used clothing worth $200 to the Salvation Army.

- Her deceased husband's employer gave her and the two children $5,000 each.

- Linda received a $300 state income tax refund in 1993. She and her husband had itemized on their joint return in 1992 and deducted the full amount.

- Linda paid unreimbursed medical expenses of $5,800 for herself and her children.

- Her deductible mortgage interest was $9,000, home property taxes were $900, and she had deductible personal property taxes of $150.

- She does not wish to contribute $3 to the Presidential Election Campaign Fund.

Calculate Linda's net tax payable or refund due for 1993. If you use tax forms, you will need Form 1040 and Schedules A, B, and D. Suggested software (if available): *TurboTax* or *MacInTax* for tax return solutions or WFT tax planning software.

RESEARCH PROBLEMS

Research Problem 1.   Noel is an employee of the U.S. Immigration Service and is stationed at Dorval International Airport in Montreal. Noel received a Living Quarters Allowance (LQA) of $10,000. An LQA is a stipend provided to qualifying Federal employees stationed abroad who are not otherwise provided with housing and is excludible from gross income under § 912(1)(C).

Noel and Janet, his spouse, purchased a house in Montreal and lived in it during the tax year. They deducted mortgage interest of $9,000 and property taxes of $2,000. A revenue agent disallowed a portion of these deductions under § 265 (Expenses and Interest Relating to Tax-Exempt Income). The disallowed amount was the portion that was allocable to the tax-exempt LQA. Advise Noel on the appropriate treatment of the disallowed property taxes and mortgage interest.

Research Problem 2.   Gray Chemical Company manufactured pesticides that were toxic. Over the course of several years, the toxic waste contaminated the air and water around the company's plant. Several employees suffered toxic poisoning, and the Environmental Protection Agency cited the company for violations. In court, the judge found Gray guilty and imposed fines of $15 million. The company voluntarily set up a charitable fund for the purpose of bettering the environment and funded it with $8 million. The company incurred legal expenses in setting up the foundation and defending itself in court. The court reduced the fine from $15 million to $7 million.

Gray Chemical Company deducted the $8 million paid to the foundation and the legal expenses incurred. The IRS disallowed both deductions on the grounds that the payment was, in fact, a fine and in violation of public policy.

Gray has contacted you regarding the deductibility of the $7 million fine, the $8 million payment to the foundation, and the legal fees. Write a letter to Gray that contains your advice and prepare a memo for the tax files.

Partial list of research aids:
§ 162(a) and (f).
Reg. § 1.162–21(b).

Research Problem 3.   Darlene is a graduate student working on her Ph.D. in microbiology. She attended the university under the G.I. bill, which pays her tuition and books in full. The G.I. benefits are not taxable. She was appointed to a research team, and the university paid her a monthly stipend of $450 for the year. She was required to register and pay tuition for the semesters she was on the research team. Her tuition was still paid by the V.A. Can she deduct the tuition as a business expense?

Partial list of research aids:
§ 265.
Rev.Rul. 83–3, 1983–1 C.B. 72.

Research Problem 4.   Stan is a self-employed lawyer. One of his hobbies is songwriting. He had one song published in 1991. Over the next three years, Stan spent a considerable amount of time writing songs and meeting with producers. He has not shown a profit. He maintains a separate room in his house for the sole purpose of writing music, and he deducted a pro rata share of the utility bills and other home expenses. He incurred other expenses amounting to $4,000. Will his expenses for this endeavor be disallowed as a hobby loss?

DEDUCTIONS AND LOSSES: CERTAIN BUSINESS EXPENSES AND LOSSES

LEARNING OBJECTIVES

After completing Chapter 7, you should be able to:

1. Determine the amount, classification, and timing of the bad debt deduction.

2. Understand the tax treatment of worthless securities including §1244 stock.

3. Distinguish between deductible and nondeductible losses of individuals.

4. Identify a casualty and determine the classification, amount, and timing of casualty and theft losses.

5. Recognize and apply the alternative tax treatments for research and experimental expenditures.

6. Determine the amount of the net operating loss and recognize the impact of the carryback and carryover provisions.

7. Identify tax planning opportunities in deducting certain business expenses, business losses, and personal losses.

OUTLINE

Bad Debts, 7–3

Specific Charge-Off Method, 7–3

Business versus Nonbusiness Bad Debts, 7–4

Loans between Related Parties, 7–5

Loss of Deposits in Insolvent Financial Institutions, 7–6

Worthless Securities, 7–7

Small Business Stock, 7–8

Losses of Individuals, 7–9

Events That Are Not Casualties, 7–10

Theft Losses, 7–10

When to Deduct Casualty Losses, 7–11

Measuring the Amount of Loss, 7–12

Statutory Framework for Deducting Losses of Individuals, 7–15

Personal Casualty Gains and Losses, 7–16

Research and Experimental Expenditures, 7–17

Expense Method, 7–18

Deferral and Amortization Method, 7–18

Net Operating Losses, 7–19

Carryback and Carryover Periods, 7–20

Computation of the Net Operating Loss, 7–21

Recomputation of Tax Liability for Year to Which Net Operating Loss Is Carried, 7–23

Calculation of the Remaining Net Operating Loss, 7–24

Tax Planning Considerations, 7–25

Documentation of Related-Taxpayer Loans, Casualty Losses, and Theft Losses, 7–25

Small Business Stock, 7–26

Casualty Losses, 7–26

Net Operating Losses, 7–26

Working with the tax formula for individuals requires the proper classification of items that are deductible *for* adjusted gross income (AGI) and items that are deductions *from* AGI (itemized deductions). Business expenses and losses, discussed in this chapter, are reductions of gross income to arrive at the taxpayer's AGI. Expenses and losses incurred in connection with a transaction entered into for profit and attributable to rents and royalties are deducted for AGI. All other expenses and losses incurred in connection with a transaction entered into for profit are deducted *from* AGI.

The situation of Robert P. Groetzinger provides an interesting insight into the importance of the proper classification for the individual taxpayer. In January 1978, Groetzinger terminated his employment with a private company and devoted virtually all of his working time to pari-mutuel wagering on dog races. He had no other profession or employment, and his only sources of income, apart from his gambling winnings, were interest, dividends, and sales from investments. During the tax year in question, he went to the track six days a week and devoted 60 to 80 hours per week in preparing and making wagers to his own account.

The tax question that this case presents is whether Groetzinger's gambling activities constitute a trade or business. If the gambling is a trade or business, his gambling losses are deductions *for* AGI. If the gambling activity is not a trade or business, the losses are itemized deductions, and Groetzinger's taxes increase by $2,142.[1]

Deductible losses on personal use property are deducted as an itemized deduction. Itemized deductions are deductions *from* AGI. While the general coverage of itemized deductions is in Chapter 10, casualty and theft losses on personal use property are discussed in this chapter.

In determining the amount and timing of the deduction for bad debts, proper classification is again important. A business bad debt is classified as a deduction *for* AGI, and a nonbusiness bad debt is classified as a short-term capital loss.

---

[1]*Groetzinger v. Comm.,* 85–1 USTC ¶9622, 56 AFTR2d 85–5683, 771 F.2d 269 (CA–7, 1985).

Other topics discussed in Chapter 7 are research and experimental expenditures and the net operating loss deduction.

BAD DEBTS

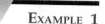

1 LEARNING OBJECTIVE
Determine the amount, classification, and timing of the bad debt deduction.

If a taxpayer sells goods or provides services on credit and the account receivable subsequently becomes worthless, a **bad debt** deduction is permitted only if income arising from the creation of the account receivable was previously included in income.[2] No deduction is allowed, for example, for a bad debt arising from the sale of a product or service when the taxpayer is on the cash basis because no income is reported until the cash has been collected. Permitting a bad debt deduction for a cash basis taxpayer would amount to a double deduction because the expenses of the product or service rendered are deducted when payments are made to suppliers and to employees, or at the time of the sale.

A bad debt can also result from the nonrepayment of a loan made by the taxpayer or from purchased debt instruments.

EXAMPLE 1

Tracy, an individual engaged in the practice of accounting, performed accounting services for Pat for which she charged $8,000. Pat never paid the bill, and his whereabouts are unknown.

If Tracy is an accrual basis taxpayer, the $8,000 is included in income when the services are performed. When it is determined that Pat's account will not be collected, the $8,000 is expensed as a bad debt.

If Tracy is a cash basis taxpayer, the $8,000 is not included in income until payment is received. When it is determined that Pat's account will not be collected, the $8,000 is not deducted as a bad debt expense since it was never recognized as income. ▼

SPECIFIC CHARGE-OFF METHOD

For tax years beginning after 1986, taxpayers (other than certain financial institutions) may use only the **specific charge-off method** in accounting for bad debts. Certain financial institutions are allowed to use the **reserve method** for computing deductions for bad debts.

A taxpayer using the specific charge-off method may claim a deduction when a specific business debt becomes either partially or wholly worthless or when a specific nonbusiness debt becomes wholly worthless.[3] For the business debt, the taxpayer must satisfy the IRS that the debt is partially worthless and must demonstrate the amount of worthlessness.

If a business debt previously deducted as partially worthless becomes totally worthless in a future year, only the remainder not previously deducted can be deducted in the future year.

In the case of total worthlessness, a deduction is allowed for the entire amount in the year the debt becomes worthless. The amount of the deduction depends on the taxpayer's basis in the bad debt. If the debt arose from the sale of services or products and the face amount was previously included in income, that amount is deductible. If the taxpayer purchased the debt, the deduction is equal to the amount the taxpayer paid for the debt instrument.

---

[2] Reg. § 1.166–1(e).

[3] § 166(a) and Reg. § 1.166.

One of the more difficult tasks is determining if and when a bad debt is worthless. The loss is deductible only in the year of partial or total worthlessness for business debts and only in the year of total worthlessness for nonbusiness debts. Legal proceedings need not be initiated against the debtor when the surrounding facts indicate that such action will not result in collection.

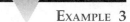

EXAMPLE 2

In 1992, Jill loaned $1,000 to Kay, who agreed to repay the loan in two years. In 1994, Kay disappeared after the note became delinquent. If a reasonable investigation by Jill indicates that she cannot find Kay or that a suit against Kay would not result in collection, Jill can deduct the $1,000 in 1994. ▼

Bankruptcy is generally an indication of at least partial worthlessness of a debt. Bankruptcy may create worthlessness before the settlement date. If this is the case, the deduction must be taken in the year of worthlessness, not in the later year upon settlement.

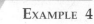

EXAMPLE 3

In Example 2, assume Kay filed for personal bankruptcy in 1993 and that the debt is a business debt. At that time, Jill learned that unsecured creditors (including Jill) were ultimately expected to receive 20¢ on the dollar. In 1994, settlement is made and Jill receives only $150. She should deduct $800 ($1,000 loan − $200 expected settlement) in 1993 and $50 in 1994 ($200 balance − $150 proceeds). Jill is not permitted to wait until 1994 to deduct the entire $850. ▼

If a receivable has been written off as uncollectible during the current tax year and is subsequently collected during the current tax year, the write-off entry is reversed. If a receivable has been written off as uncollectible, the collection of the receivable in a later tax year may result in income being recognized. Income will result if the deduction yielded a tax benefit in the year it was taken. See Examples 37 and 38 in Chapter 5.

BUSINESS VERSUS NONBUSINESS BAD DEBTS

A **nonbusiness bad debt** is a debt unrelated to the taxpayer's trade or business either when it was created or when it became worthless. The nature of a debt depends on whether the lender was engaged in the business of lending money or whether there is a proximate relationship between the creation of the debt and the lender's trade or business. The use to which the borrowed funds are put by the debtor is of no consequence. Loans to relatives or friends are the most common type of nonbusiness bad debt.

EXAMPLE 4

José loaned his friend, Esther, $1,500. Esther used the money to start a business, which subsequently failed. Even though proceeds of the loan were used in a business, the loan is a nonbusiness bad debt because the business was Esther's, not José's. ▼

The distinction between a business bad debt and a nonbusiness bad debt is important. A **business bad debt** is deductible as an ordinary loss in the year incurred, whereas a nonbusiness bad debt is always treated as a short-term capital loss. Thus, regardless of the age of a nonbusiness bad debt, the deduction may be of limited benefit due to the capital loss limitations on deductibility in any one year. The maximum amount of a net short-term capital loss that an individual can deduct against ordinary income in any one year is $3,000 (see Chapter 16 for a detailed discussion). Although no deduction is allowed when a nonbusiness bad debt is partially worthless, the taxpayer is entitled to deduct the net amount of the loss upon final settlement.

The following example is an illustration of business bad debts adapted from the Regulations.[4]

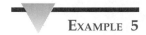

EXAMPLE 5

In 1993, Leif sold his business but retained a claim (note or account receivable) against Bob. The claim became worthless in 1994. Leif's loss is treated as a business bad debt because the debt was created in the conduct of his former trade or business. Leif is accorded business bad debt treatment even though he was holding the note as an investor and was no longer in a trade or business when the claim became worthless. ▼

The nonbusiness bad debt provisions are *not* applicable to corporations. It is assumed that any loans made by a corporation are related to its trade or business. Therefore, any bad debts of a corporation are business bad debts.

LOANS BETWEEN RELATED PARTIES

Loans between related parties (especially family members) raise the issue of whether the transaction was a *bona fide* loan or a gift. The Regulations state that a bona fide debt arises from a debtor-creditor relationship based on a valid and enforceable obligation to pay a fixed or determinable sum of money. Thus, individual circumstances must be examined to determine whether advances between related parties are gifts or loans. Some considerations are these:

- Was a note properly executed?
- Was there a reasonable rate of interest?
- Was collateral provided?
- What collection efforts were made?
- What was the intent of the parties?

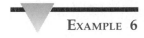

EXAMPLE 6

Lana loans $2,000 to her widowed mother for an operation. Lana's mother owns no property and is not employed, and her only income consists of Social Security benefits. No note is issued for the loan, no provision for interest is made, and no repayment date is

---

CONCEPT SUMMARY 7–1

Specific Charge-Off Method

Expense deduction and account write-off	The expense arises and the write-off takes place when a specific business account becomes either partially or wholly worthless or when a specific nonbusiness account becomes wholly worthless.
Recovery of accounts previously written off	If the account recovered was written off during the current taxable year, the write-off entry is reversed. If the account recovered was written off during a previous taxable year, income is created subject to the tax benefit rule.

---

[4]Reg. § 1.166–5(d).

mentioned. In the current year, Lana's mother dies leaving no estate. Assuming the loan is not repaid, Lana cannot take a deduction for a nonbusiness bad debt because the facts indicate that no debtor-creditor relationship existed. ▼

ETHICAL CONSIDERATIONS

Writing Off a Loan to a Friend

Loans to family members and friends raise concerns with respect to whether a deductible bad debt exists. The fact that the debtor is a family member or friend does not preclude a deduction for a bad debt. However, evidence must show that the debt is bona fide and that it is in fact worthless.

Frank, an engineer, loans $5,000 to Chris, a friend from high school who is a musician. Chris uses the money to cut a record. The loan, which is evidenced by a formal written instrument, has a maturity date of three years and an 8 percent interest rate.

The record is unsuccessful, and at the maturity date, Chris does not repay the loan. Frank writes Chris twice requesting repayment. Frank hears from another friend that Chris is now divorced and has a drinking problem.

Frank decides to give up trying to collect the loan. Since Frank's combined Federal and state tax rate is 44 percent, he decides he can live without $2,800 ($5,000 × 56%). He deducts the $5,000 as a nonbusiness bad debt on his Federal and state tax returns.

LOSS OF DEPOSITS IN INSOLVENT FINANCIAL INSTITUTIONS

Qualified individuals can *elect* to deduct losses on deposits in qualified financial institutions as personal casualty losses in the year in which the amount of the loss can be reasonably estimated. If the election is made to treat a loss on a deposit as a personal casualty loss, no bad debt deduction for the loss will be allowed.[5] As a personal casualty loss, the loss is subject to the $100 per event floor and the 10 percent of AGI aggregate floor. Both floors limiting casualty losses are explained later in the chapter. The amount of loss to be recognized under the election is the difference between (1) the taxpayer's basis in the deposit and (2) a reasonable estimate of the amount to be received.

A *qualified individual* is any individual other than:

- An owner of 1 percent or more of the value of the stock of the institution in which the loss was sustained.
- An officer of the institution.
- Certain relatives and other persons who are tax-related to such owners and officers.

A *qualified financial institution* is a commercial bank, thrift institution, insured credit union, or any similar institution chartered and supervised under Federal or state law. A *deposit*, for purposes of this provision, is any deposit, withdrawal certificate, or withdrawable or repurchasable share of or in a qualified financial institution. The term *insolvent* generally denotes a situation where the liabilities exceed the fair market value of the assets.

If the individual does not elect to deduct the loss as a casualty loss, it will be treated as a nonbusiness bad debt and, hence, as a short-term capital loss. As a short-term capital loss, it will be subject to the capital loss limitation rules (see the discussion in Chapter 16).

[5] § 165(l).

Concept Summary 7–2

Bad Debt Deductions

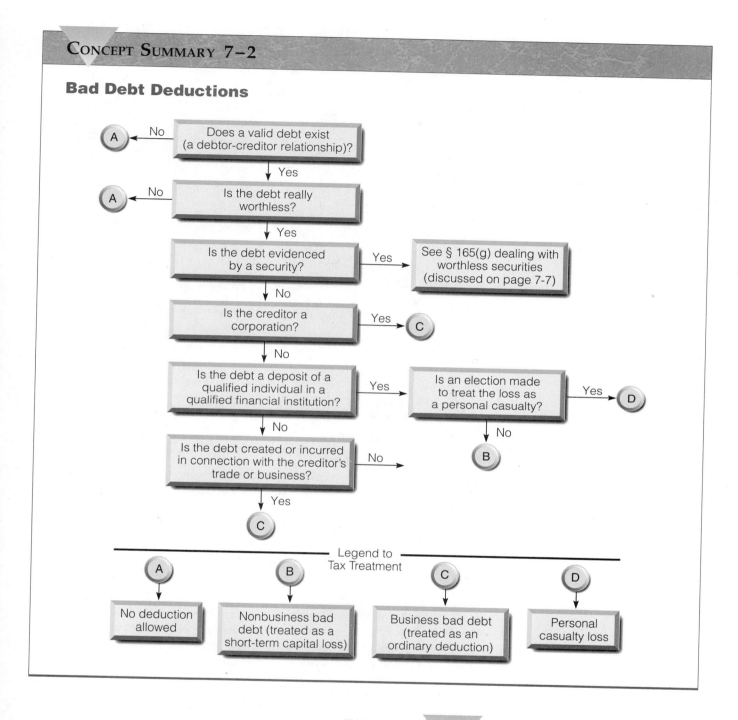

2   **LEARNING OBJECTIVE**
Understand the tax treatment of worthless securities including § 1244 stock.

WORTHLESS SECURITIES

A loss is allowed under § 165 for securities that become *completely* worthless during the year (**worthless securities**).[6] Such securities are shares of stock, bonds, notes, or other evidence of indebtedness issued by a corporation or government.

---

[6] § 165(g).

TAX IN THE NEWS

LITTLE OF $100 BILLION LOSS CAN BE RETRIEVED

During the 1980s, the savings and loan industry was a playpen for white-collar criminals. Losses from the debacle are estimated at roughly $100 billion, and while reckless lending in an overheated real estate market accounted for much of that, fraud by savings and loan officers and directors added billions of dollars to the bill for taxpayers.

In fact, fraud contributed to the collapse of 35 percent of the more than 650 savings institutions under the control of the Resolution Trust Corporation, the agency created to clean up the industry's mess.

How much of the money can be recovered by financial investigators?

Most experts estimate that only 5 percent to 10 percent of the losses can be traced and retrieved. Some former savings executives have stashed away millions, but most of the money has been squandered and spent, the experts say.

SOURCE: Excerpted from Steve Lohr, "Little of $100 Billion Loss Can Be Retrieved," *New York Times*, February 20, 1992, p. D7. © 1992 by The New York Times Company. Reprinted by permission.

The losses generated are treated as capital losses deemed to have occurred on the *last day* of the taxable year. By treating the loss as having occurred on the last day of the taxable year, a loss that would otherwise have been classified as short term (if the date of worthlessness was used) may be classified as a long-term capital loss. Capital losses may be of limited benefit due to the $3,000 capital loss limitation.

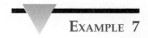

EXAMPLE 7 Ali, a calendar year taxpayer, owns stock in Owl Corporation (a publicly held company). The stock was acquired as an investment on November 30, 1993, at a cost of $5,000. On April 1, 1994, the stock became worthless. Since the stock is deemed to have become worthless as of December 31 of 1994, Ali has a capital loss from an asset held for 13 months (a long-term capital loss). ▼

SMALL BUSINESS STOCK

The general rule is that shareholders receive capital gain or loss treatment upon the sale or exchange of stock. However, it is possible to receive an ordinary loss deduction if the loss is sustained on **small business stock—§ 1244 stock.** This loss could arise from a sale of the stock or from the stock becoming worthless. Only *individuals*[7] who acquired the stock *from* the corporation are eligible to receive ordinary loss treatment under § 1244. The ordinary loss treatment is limited to $50,000 ($100,000 for married individuals filing jointly) per year. Losses on § 1244 stock in excess of the statutory limits receive capital loss treatment.

The corporation must meet certain requirements for the loss on § 1244 stock to be treated as an *ordinary*—rather than a capital—loss. The major requirement is that the total amount of money and other property received by the corporation for stock as a contribution to capital (or paid-in surplus) does not exceed $1,000,000.

---

[7] The term "individuals" for this purpose includes a partnership but not a trust or an estate.

The $1,000,000 test is made at the time the stock is issued. Section 1244 stock can be common or preferred stock. Section 1244 applies only to losses. If § 1244 stock is sold at a gain, the Section has no application, and the gain will be capital gain.

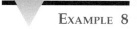

EXAMPLE 8

On July 1, 1992, Iris, a single individual, purchased 100 shares of Eagle Corporation common stock for $100,000. The Eagle stock qualified as § 1244 stock. On June 20, 1994, Iris sold all of the Eagle stock for $20,000. Because the Eagle stock is § 1244 stock, Iris would have $50,000 of ordinary loss and $30,000 of long-term capital loss. ▼

LOSSES OF INDIVIDUALS

3   **LEARNING OBJECTIVE**
Distinguish between deductible and nondeductible losses of individuals.

An individual may deduct the following losses under § 165(c):

- Losses incurred in a trade or business.
- Losses incurred in a transaction entered into for profit.
- Losses caused by fire, storm, shipwreck, or other casualty or by theft.

An individual taxpayer may deduct losses to property used in the taxpayer's trade or business or losses to property used in a transaction entered into for profit. Examples include a loss on property used in a proprietorship, a loss on property held for rent, or a loss on stolen bearer bonds. Note that an individual's losses on property used in a trade or business or on transactions entered into for profit are not limited to losses caused by fire, storm, shipwreck, or other casualty or by theft.

A taxpayer suffering losses from damage to nonbusiness property can deduct only those losses attributable to fire, storm, shipwreck, or other casualty or theft. Although the meaning of the terms *fire, storm, shipwreck,* and *theft* is relatively free from dispute, the term *other casualty* needs further clarification. It means casualties analogous to fire, storm, or shipwreck. The term also includes accidental loss of property provided the loss qualifies under the same rules as any other casualty. These rules are that the loss must result from an event that is (1) identifiable; (2) damaging to property; and (3) sudden, unexpected, and unusual in nature.

A *sudden event* is one that is swift and precipitous and not gradual or progressive. An *unexpected event* is an event that is ordinarily unanticipated and occurs without the intent of the individual who suffers the loss. An *unusual event* is one that is extraordinary and nonrecurring and does not commonly occur during the activity in which the taxpayer was engaged when the destruction occurred.[8] Examples include hurricanes, tornadoes, floods, storms, shipwrecks, fires, auto accidents, mine cave-ins, sonic booms, and vandalism. Weather that causes damages (drought, for example) must be unusual and severe for the particular region. Damage must be to the taxpayer's property to qualify as a **casualty loss.**

A taxpayer can take a deduction for a casualty loss from an automobile accident only if the damage was not caused by the taxpayer's willful act or willful negligence.

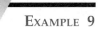

EXAMPLE 9

Ted parks his car on a hill and fails to set the brake properly and to curb the wheels. As a result of Ted's negligence, the car rolls down the hill and is damaged. The repairs to Ted's car should qualify for casualty loss treatment since Ted's act of negligence appears to be simple rather than willful. ▼

---

[8] Rev.Rul. 72–592, 1972–2 C.B. 101.

EVENTS THAT ARE NOT CASUALTIES

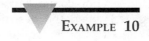

4 **LEARNING OBJECTIVE**
Identify a casualty and determine the classification, amount, and timing of casualty and theft losses.

Not all acts of God are treated as casualty losses for income tax purposes. Because a casualty must be sudden, unexpected, and unusual, progressive deterioration (such as erosion due to wind or rain) is not a casualty because it does not meet the suddenness test.

Examples of nonsudden events that generally do not qualify as casualties include disease and insect damages. When the damage was caused by termites over a period of several years, some courts have disallowed a casualty loss deduction.[9] On the other hand, some courts have held that termite damage over periods of up to 15 months after infestation constituted a sudden event and was, therefore, deductible as a casualty loss.[10] Despite the existence of some judicial support for the deductibility of termite damage as a casualty loss, the current position of the IRS is that termite damage is not deductible.[11]

Other examples of events that are not casualties are losses resulting from a decline in value rather than an actual loss of the property. No loss was allowed where the taxpayer's home declined in value as a result of a landslide that destroyed neighboring homes but did no actual damage to the taxpayer's home.[12] Similarly, a taxpayer was allowed a loss for the actual flood damage to his property but not for the decline in market value due to the property's being flood-prone.[13]

THEFT LOSSES

Theft includes, but is not necessarily limited to, larceny, embezzlement, and robbery.[14] Theft does not include misplaced items.[15]

Theft losses are computed like other casualty losses (discussed in the following section), but the *timing* for recognition of the loss differs. A theft loss is deducted in the year of discovery, not the year of the theft (unless, of course, the discovery occurs in the same year as the theft). If, in the year of the discovery, a claim exists (e.g., against an insurance company) and there is a reasonable expectation of recovering the adjusted basis of the asset from the insurance company, no deduction is permitted.[16] If, in the year of settlement, the recovery is less than the asset's adjusted basis, a partial deduction may be available. If the recovery is greater than the asset's adjusted basis, gain may be recognized.

EXAMPLE 10

Keith's new sailboat, which he uses for personal purposes, was stolen from the storage marina in December 1992. He discovered the loss on June 3, 1993, and filed a claim with his insurance company that was settled on January 30, 1994. Assuming there is a reasonable expectation of full recovery, no deduction is allowed in 1993. A partial deduction may be available in 1994 if the actual insurance proceeds are less than the lower of the fair market value or the adjusted basis of the asset. (Loss measurement rules are discussed later in this chapter.) ▼

---

[9] Fay v. Helvering, 41–2 USTC ¶9494, 27 AFTR 432, 120 F.2d 253 (CA–2, 1941); *U.S. v. Rogers,* 41–1 USTC ¶9442, 27 AFTR 423, 120 F.2d 244 (CA–9, 1941).

[10] *Rosenberg v. Comm.,* 52–2 USTC ¶9377, 42 AFTR 303, 198 F.2d 46 (CA–8, 1952); *Shopmaker v. U.S.,* 54–1 USTC ¶9195, 45 AFTR 758, 119 F.Supp. 705 (D.Ct.Mo., 1953).

[11] Rev.Rul. 63–232, 1963–2 C.B. 97.

[12] H. Pulvers v. Comm., 69–1 USTC ¶9222, 23 AFTR2d 69–678, 407 F.2d 838 (CA–9, 1969).

[13] *S. L. Solomon,* 39 TCM 1282, T.C.Memo. 1980–87.

[14] Reg. § 1.165–8(d).

[15] *Mary Francis Allen,* 16 T.C. 163 (1951).

[16] Reg. §§ 1.165–1(d)(2) and 1.165–8(a)(2).

ETHICAL
CONSIDERATIONS

Deducting a Theft Loss

Theft losses of personal use assets are itemized deductions in the year of discovery. The taxpayer must show that the property was actually stolen. Losses due to mislaying or losing property cannot be deducted. If there is no positive proof that a theft occurred, all of the details and evidence should be presented. If the reasonable inferences point to a theft, the Tax Court has allowed a deduction. If the inferences point to a mysterious (unexplained) disappearance, however, the deduction will be disallowed.

A taxpayer went shopping in a major city, riding the subway to and from the city. During the day, he purchased items using money from his wallet. When he arrived home, his wallet was missing. He is considering claiming a theft loss deduction for the wallet and the money it contained.

WHEN TO DEDUCT CASUALTY LOSSES

General Rule

Generally, a casualty loss is deducted in the year the loss occurs. However, no casualty loss is permitted if a reimbursement claim with a *reasonable prospect of full recovery* exists.[17] If the taxpayer has a partial claim, only part of the loss can be claimed in the year of the casualty, and the remainder is deducted in the year the claim is settled.

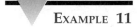

EXAMPLE 11

Chee's new sailboat was completely destroyed by fire in 1994. Its cost and fair market value were $10,000. Chee's only claim against the insurance company was on a $7,000 policy that was not settled by year-end. The following year, 1995, Chee settled with the insurance company for $6,000. Chee is entitled to a $3,000 deduction in 1994 and a $1,000 deduction in 1995. If Chee held the sailboat for personal use, the $3,000 deduction in 1994 would be reduced first by $100 and then by 10% of Chee's 1994 AGI. The $1,000 deduction in 1995 would be reduced by 10% of Chee's 1995 AGI (see the following discussion on the $100 and 10% floors). ▼

If a taxpayer receives reimbursement for a casualty loss sustained and deducted in a previous year, an amended return is not filed for that year. Instead, the taxpayer must include the reimbursement in gross income on the return for the year in which it is received to the extent that the previous deduction resulted in a tax benefit.

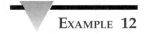

EXAMPLE 12

Fran had a deductible casualty loss of $5,000 on her 1993 tax return. Fran's taxable income for 1993 was $60,000. In June 1994, Fran was reimbursed $3,000 for the prior year's casualty loss. Fran would include the entire $3,000 in gross income for 1994 because the deduction in 1993 produced a tax benefit. ▼

Disaster Area Losses

An exception to the general rule for the time of deduction is allowed for **disaster area losses,** which are casualties sustained in an area designated as a disaster area

---

[17] Reg. § 1.165–1(d)(2)(i).

> ### TAX IN THE NEWS
>
> ### CLINTON DECLARES PARTS OF THREE STATES MAJOR FEDERAL DISASTER AREAS
>
> President Clinton yesterday declared parts of waterlogged Illinois, Iowa, and Missouri major disaster areas as the Mississippi and Missouri rivers breached more levees and flooded out thousands more bottom-land residents.
>
> Clinton's declaration, similar to earlier declarations upstream, makes available immediately federal assistance for grants, low-interest loans and temporary housing.
>
> The sun was shining in many affected areas yesterday, but more drenching rain, lightning, and tornadoes were predicted last night as a stubborn Bermuda high-pressure area remained firmly planted over the Atlantic Ocean, blocking an increasingly unwelcome storm system from leaving the upper Midwest. Eight inches of rain was recorded at Kansas City on Friday night and yesterday morning, adding to the flow in the Missouri River.
>
> Several severe thunderstorms, some with wind gusts to 55 mph, drenched an already saturated east central and southeast Iowa last night, and in northeast Iowa similar storms included hail as well. About 3,500 people were ordered evacuated in West Des Moines. Two tornadoes were sighted near Platteville, Wisconsin, 20 miles northeast of Dubuque, Iowa, and travel was difficult because so many roads have been closed—including two interstate highways leading into Des Moines—because of high water the Iowa Department of Public Safety said there was no place to detour drivers.
>
> SOURCE: Excerpted from Don Phillips, "Clinton Declares Parts of 3 States Major Federal Disaster Areas," *Washington Post*, July 11, 1993, p. A3. © 1993, Washington Post Writers Group. Reprinted with permission.

by the President of the United States.[18] In such cases, the taxpayer may *elect* to treat the loss as having occurred in the taxable year immediately preceding the taxable year in which the disaster actually occurred. The rationale for this exception is to provide immediate relief to disaster victims in the form of accelerated tax benefits.

If the due date, plus extensions, for the prior year's return has not passed, a taxpayer makes the election to claim the disaster area loss on the prior year's tax return. If the disaster occurs after the prior year's return has been filed, it is necessary to file either an amended return or a refund claim. In any case, the taxpayer must show clearly that such an election is being made.

Disaster loss treatment also applies in the case of a personal residence that has been rendered unsafe for use as a residence because of a disaster. This provision applies when, within 120 days after the President designates the area as a disaster area, the state or local government where the residence is located orders the taxpayer to demolish or relocate the residence.[19]

MEASURING THE AMOUNT OF LOSS

Amount of Loss

The rules for determining the amount of a loss depend in part on whether business use, income-producing use, or personal use property was involved.

---

[18] § 165(h).   [19] § 165(k).

Another factor that must be considered is whether the property was partially or completely destroyed.

If business property or property held for the production of income (e.g., rental property) is *completely destroyed,* the loss is equal to the adjusted basis of the property at the time of destruction.

EXAMPLE 13

Vicki's automobile, which was used only for business purposes, was destroyed by fire. Vicki had unintentionally allowed her insurance coverage to expire. The fair market value of the automobile was $9,000 at the time of the fire, and its adjusted basis was $10,000. Vicki is allowed a loss deduction of $10,000 (the basis of the automobile). The $10,000 loss is a deduction *for* AGI. ▼

A different measurement rule applies for *partial destruction* of business property and income-producing property and for *partial* or *complete destruction* of personal use property. In these situations, the loss is the *lesser* of the following:

1. The adjusted basis of the property.
2. The difference between the fair market value of the property before the event and the fair market value immediately after the event.

EXAMPLE 14

Kelly's uninsured automobile, which was used only for business purposes, was damaged in a wreck. At the date of the wreck, the fair market value of the automobile was $12,000, and its adjusted basis was $9,000. After the wreck, the automobile was appraised at $4,000. Kelly's loss deduction is $8,000 (the lesser of the adjusted basis or the decrease in fair market value). The $8,000 loss is a deduction *for* AGI. ▼

The deduction for the loss of property that is part business and part personal must be computed separately for the business portion and the personal portion.

Any insurance recovery reduces the loss for business, production of income, and personal use losses. In fact, a taxpayer may realize a gain if the insurance proceeds exceed the amount of the loss. Chapter 17 discusses the treatment of net gains and losses on business property and income-producing property.

A taxpayer will not be permitted to deduct a casualty loss for damage to insured personal use property unless he or she files a *timely insurance claim* with respect to the damage to the property. This rule applies to the extent that any insurance policy provides for full or partial reimbursement for the loss.[20]

Generally, an appraisal before and after the casualty is needed to measure the amount of the loss. However, the *cost of repairs* to the damaged property is acceptable as a method of establishing the loss in value provided the following criteria are met:

- The repairs are necessary to restore the property to its condition immediately before the casualty.
- The amount spent for such repairs is not excessive.
- The repairs do not extend beyond the damage suffered.
- The value of the property after the repairs does not, as a result of the repairs, exceed the value of the property immediately before the casualty.[21]

Reduction for $100 and 10 Percent of AGI Floors

The amount of the loss for personal use property must be further reduced by a $100 *per event* floor and a 10 percent of AGI *aggregate* floor.[22] The $100 floor applies

---

[20] § 165(h)(4)(E).
[21] Reg. § 1.165–7(a)(2)(ii).

[22] § 165(c)(3).

separately to each casualty and applies to the entire loss from each casualty (e.g., if a storm damages both a taxpayer's residence and automobile, only $100 is subtracted from the total amount of the loss). The losses are then added together, and the total is reduced by 10 percent of the taxpayer's AGI. The resulting loss is the taxpayer's itemized deduction for casualty and theft losses.

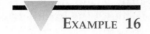

EXAMPLE 15

Rocky, who had AGI of $30,000, was involved in a motorcycle accident. His motorcycle, which was used only for personal use and had a fair market value of $12,000 and an adjusted basis of $9,000, was completely destroyed. He received $5,000 from his insurance company. Rocky's casualty loss deduction is $900 [$9,000 basis − $5,000 insurance − $100 floor − $3,000 (.10 × $30,000 AGI)]. The $900 casualty loss is an itemized deduction (*from* AGI). ▼

When a nonbusiness casualty loss is spread between two taxable years because of the *reasonable prospect of recovery* doctrine, the loss in the second year is not reduced by the $100 floor. This result occurs because this floor is imposed per event and has already reduced the amount of the loss in the first year. However, the loss in the second year is still subject to the 10 percent floor based on the taxpayer's second-year AGI (refer to Example 11).

Taxpayers who suffer qualified disaster area losses can elect to deduct the losses in the year preceding the year of occurrence. The disaster loss is treated as having occurred in the preceding taxable year. Hence, the 10 percent of AGI floor is determined by using the AGI of the year for which the deduction is claimed.[23]

Multiple Losses

The rules for computing loss deductions where multiple losses have occurred are explained in Examples 16 and 17.

EXAMPLE 16

During the year, Tim had the following casualty losses:

Asset	Adjusted Basis	Fair Market Value of Asset		Insurance Recovery
		Before the Casualty	After the Casualty	
A	$900	$600	$-0-	$400
B	300	800	250	100

Assets A and B were used in Tim's business at the time of the casualty. The following losses are allowed:

Asset A: $500. The complete destruction of a business asset results in a deduction of the adjusted basis of the property (reduced by any insurance recovery) regardless of the asset's fair market value.

Asset B: $200. The partial destruction of a business (or personal use) asset results in a deduction equal to the lesser of the adjusted basis ($300) or the decline in value ($550), reduced by any insurance recovery ($100).

Both Asset A and Asset B losses are deductions *for* AGI. The $100 floor and the 10% of AGI floor do not apply because the assets are business assets. ▼

---

[23] § 165(i).

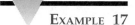

EXAMPLE 17

During the year, Emily had AGI of $20,000 and the following casualty losses:

| Asset | Adjusted Basis | Fair Market Value of Asset | | Insurance Recovery |
		Before the Casualty	After the Casualty	
A	$ 900	$ 600	$ –0–	$200
B	2,500	4,000	1,000	–0–
C	800	400	100	250

Assets A, B, and C were held for personal use, and the losses to these three assets are from three different casualties. The loss for each asset is computed as follows:

Asset A: $300. The lesser of the adjusted basis of $900 or the $600 decline in value, reduced by the insurance recovery of $200, minus the $100 floor.

Asset B: $2,400. The lesser of the adjusted basis of $2,500 or the $3,000 decline in value, minus the $100 floor.

Asset C: $0. The lesser of the adjusted basis of $800 or the $300 decline in value, reduced by the insurance recovery of $250, minus the $100 floor.

Emily's itemized casualty loss deduction for the year is $700:

Asset A loss	$ 300
Asset B loss	2,400
Asset C loss	–0–
Total loss	$ 2,700
Less: 10% of AGI (10% × $20,000)	(2,000)
Itemized casualty loss deduction	$ 700

STATUTORY FRAMEWORK FOR DEDUCTING LOSSES OF INDIVIDUALS

Casualty and theft losses incurred by an individual in connection with a trade or business are deductible *for* AGI.[24] These losses are not subject to the $100 per event and the 10 percent of AGI limitations.

Casualty and theft losses incurred by an individual in a transaction entered into for profit are not subject to the $100 per event and the 10 percent of AGI limitations. If these losses are attributable to rents or royalties, the deduction is *for* AGI.[25] However, if these losses are not connected with property held for the production of rents and royalties, they are deductions *from* AGI. More specifically, these losses are classified as other miscellaneous itemized deductions. An example of this type of loss would be the theft of a security. The aggregate of certain miscellaneous itemized deductions is subject to a 2 percent of AGI floor (explained in Chapter 9).

Casualty and theft losses attributable to personal use property are subject to the $100 per event and the 10 percent of AGI limitations. These losses are itemized deductions, but they are not subject to the 2 percent of AGI floor.[26]

---

[24] § 62(a)(1).
[25] § 62(a)(4).

[26] § 67(b)(3).

PERSONAL CASUALTY GAINS AND LOSSES

If a taxpayer has personal casualty and theft gains as well as losses, a special set of rules applies for determining the tax consequences. A **personal casualty gain** is the recognized gain from a casualty or theft of personal use property. A **personal casualty loss** for this purpose is a casualty or theft loss of personal use property after the application of the $100 floor. A taxpayer who has both gains and losses for the taxable year must first net (offset) the personal casualty gains and personal casualty losses. If the gains exceed the losses, the gains and losses will be treated as gains and losses from the sale of capital assets. The capital gains and losses will be short term or long term, depending on the period the taxpayer held each of the assets. In the netting process, personal casualty and theft gains and losses are not netted with the gains and losses on business and income-producing property.

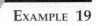

EXAMPLE 18

During the year, Cliff had the following personal casualty gains and losses (after deducting the $100 floor):

Asset	Holding Period	Gain or (Loss)
A	Three months	($ 300)
B	Three years	(2,400)
C	Two years	3,200

Cliff would compute the tax consequences as follows:

Personal casualty gain	$ 3,200
Personal casualty loss ($300 + $2,400)	(2,700)
Net personal casualty gain	$ 500

Cliff would treat all of the gains and losses as capital gains and losses and would have the following:

Short-term capital loss (Asset A)	$ 300
Long-term capital loss (Asset B)	2,400
Long-term capital gain (Asset C)	3,200

If personal casualty losses exceed personal casualty gains, all gains and losses are treated as ordinary items. The gains—and the losses to the extent of gains—will be treated as ordinary income and ordinary loss in computing AGI. Losses in excess of gains are deducted as itemized deductions to the extent the losses exceed 10 percent of AGI.[27]

EXAMPLE 19

During the year, Hazel had AGI of $20,000 and the following personal casualty gain and loss (after deducting the $100 floor):

Asset	Holding Period	Gain or (Loss)
A	Three years	($2,700)
B	Four months	200

[27] § 165(h).

CONCEPT SUMMARY 7–3

Casualty Gains and Losses

	Business Use or Income-Producing Property	Personal Use Property
Event creating the loss	Any event.	Casualty or theft loss.
Amount	The lesser of the decline in fair market value or the adjusted basis, but always the adjusted basis if the property is totally destroyed.	The lesser of the decline in fair market value or the adjusted basis.
Insurance	Insurance proceeds received reduce the amount of the loss.	Insurance proceeds received (or for which there is an unfiled claim) reduce the amount of the loss.
$100 floor	Not applicable.	Applicable per event.
Gains and losses	Gains and losses are netted (see detailed discussion in Chapter 17).	Personal casualty and theft gains and losses are netted.
Gains exceeding losses		The gains and losses are treated as gains and losses from the sale of capital assets.
Losses exceeding gains		The gains—and the losses to the extent of gains—are treated as ordinary items in computing AGI. The losses in excess of gains, to the extent they exceed 10% of AGI, are itemized deductions.

Hazel would compute the tax consequences as follows:

Personal casualty loss	($2,700)
Personal casualty gain	200
Net personal casualty loss	($2,500)

Hazel would treat the gain and the loss as ordinary items. The $200 gain and $200 of the loss would be included in computing AGI. Hazel's itemized deduction for casualty losses would be computed as follows:

Casualty loss in excess of gain ($2,700 − $200)	$ 2,500
Less: 10% of AGI (10% × $20,000)	(2,000)
Itemized deduction	$ 500

RESEARCH AND EXPERIMENTAL EXPENDITURES

5 **LEARNING OBJECTIVE**
Recognize and apply the alternative tax treatments for research and experimental expenditures.

Section 174 covers the treatment of research and experimental expenditures. The Regulations define **research and experimental expenditures** as follows:

. . . all such costs incident to the development of an experimental or pilot model, a plant process, a product, a formula, an invention, or similar property, and the improvement of already existing property of the type mentioned. The term does not include expenditures such as those for the ordinary testing or inspection of materials or products for quality control or those for efficiency surveys, management studies, consumer surveys, advertising, or promotions.[28]

Expenses in connection with the acquisition or improvement of land or depreciable property are not research and experimental expenditures. Rather, they increase the basis of the land or depreciable property. However, depreciation on a building used for research may be a research and experimental expense. Only the depreciation that is a research and experimental expense (not the cost of the asset) is subject to the three alternatives discussed below.

The law permits the following *three alternatives* for the handling of research and experimental expenditures:

- Expensed in the year paid or incurred.
- Deferred and amortized.
- Capitalized.

If the costs are capitalized, a deduction is not available until the research project is abandoned or is deemed worthless. Since many products resulting from research projects do not have a definite and limited useful life, a taxpayer should ordinarily elect to write off the expenditures immediately or to defer and amortize them. It is generally preferable to elect an immediate write-off of the research expenditures because of the time value of the tax deduction.

The law also provides for a research activities credit. The credit amounts to 20 percent of certain research and experimental expenditures.[29] (The credit is discussed more fully in Chapter 13.)

EXPENSE METHOD

A taxpayer can elect to expense all of the research and experimental expenditures incurred in the current year and all subsequent years. The consent of the IRS is not required if the method is adopted for the first taxable year in which such expenditures were paid or incurred. Once the election is made, the taxpayer must continue to expense all qualifying expenditures unless a request for a change is made to, and approved by, the IRS. In certain instances, a taxpayer may incur research and experimental expenditures before actually engaging in any trade or business activity. In such instances, the Supreme Court has applied a liberal standard of deductibility and permitted a deduction in the year of incurrence.[30]

DEFERRAL AND AMORTIZATION METHOD

Alternatively, research and experimental expenditures may be deferred and amortized if the taxpayer makes an election.[31] Under the election, research and experimental expenditures are amortized ratably over a period of not less than 60 months. A deduction is allowed beginning with the month in which the taxpayer first realizes benefits from the experimental expenditure. The election is binding, and a change requires permission from the IRS.

---

[28] Reg. § 1.174–2(a)(1).
[29] § 41. See the information in Chapter 13 on the termination date for the research activities credit.

[30] *Snow v. Comm.,* 74–1 USTC ¶9432, 33 AFTR2d 74–1251, 94 S.Ct. 1876 (USSC, 1974).
[31] § 174(b)(2).

EXAMPLE 20

Gold Corporation decided to develop a new line of adhesives. The project was begun in 1994. Gold incurred the following expenses in 1994 in connection with the project:

Salaries	$25,000
Materials	8,000
Depreciation on machinery	6,500

Gold incurred the following expenses in 1995 in connection with the project:

Salaries	$18,000
Materials	2,000
Depreciation on machinery	5,700

The benefits from the project will be realized starting in March 1996. If Gold Corporation elects a 60-month deferral and amortization period, there will be no deduction prior to March 1996, the month benefits from the project begin to be realized. The deduction for 1996 would be $10,867, computed as follows:

Salaries ($25,000 + $18,000)	$43,000
Materials ($8,000 + $2,000)	10,000
Depreciation ($6,500 + $5,700)	12,200
Total	$65,200
$65,200 × (10 months/60 months) =	$10,867

The option to treat research and experimental expenditures as deferred expense is usually employed when a company does not have sufficient income to offset the research and experimental expenses. Rather than create net operating loss carryovers that might not be utilized because of the 15-year limitation on such carryovers, the deferral and amortization method may be used. The deferral of research and experimental expenditures should also be considered if the taxpayer expects higher tax rates in the future.

NET OPERATING LOSSES

6   **LEARNING OBJECTIVE**
Determine the amount of the net operating loss and recognize the impact of the carryback and carryover provisions.

The requirement that every taxpayer file an annual income tax return (whether on a calendar year or a fiscal year) may result in certain inequities for taxpayers who experience cyclical patterns of income or expense. Inequities result from the application of a progressive rate structure to taxable income determined on an annual basis. A **net operating loss (NOL)** in a particular tax year would produce no tax benefit if the Code did not provide for the carryback and carryforward of such losses to profitable years.

EXAMPLE 21

Juanita has a business that realizes the following taxable income or loss over a five-year period: Year 1, $50,000; Year 2, ($30,000); Year 3, $100,000; Year 4, ($200,000); and Year 5, $380,000. She is married and files a joint return. Hubert, on the other hand, has a taxable income pattern of $60,000 every year. He, too, is married and files a joint return. Note that both Juanita and Hubert have total taxable income of $300,000 over the five-year period.

Assume there is no provision for carryback or carryover of NOLs. Juanita and Hubert would have the following five-year tax bills:

Year	Juanita's Tax	Hubert's Tax
1	$ 9,060	$11,860
2	–0–	11,860
3	23,305	11,860
4	–0–	11,860
5	126,785	11,860
	$159,150	$59,300

The computation of tax is made without regard to any NOL benefit. Rates applicable to 1994 are used to compute the tax.

Even though Juanita and Hubert realized the same total taxable income ($300,000) over the five-year period, Juanita had to pay taxes of $159,150, while Hubert paid taxes of only $59,300. ▼

To provide partial relief from this inequitable tax treatment, a deduction is allowed for NOLs.[32] This provision permits NOLs for any one year to be offset against taxable income of other years. The NOL provision is intended as a form of relief for business income and losses. Thus, only losses from the operation of a trade or business (or profession), casualty and theft losses, or losses from the confiscation of a business by a foreign government can create an NOL. In other words, a salaried individual with itemized deductions and personal exemptions in excess of gross income is not permitted to deduct the excess amounts as an NOL. On the other hand, a personal casualty loss is treated as a business loss and can therefore create (or increase) an NOL for an individual.

CARRYBACK AND CARRYOVER PERIODS

General Rules

An NOL must be applied initially to the three taxable years preceding the year of the loss (unless an election is made not to carry the loss back at all). It is carried first to the third prior year, then to the second prior year, then to the immediately preceding tax year (or until used up). If the loss is not fully used in the carryback period, it must be carried forward to the first year after the loss year, and then forward to the second, third, etc., year after the loss year. The carryover period is 15 years. A loss sustained in 1994 is used in this order: 1991, 1992, 1993, 1995 through 2009.

If the loss is being carried to a preceding year, an amended return is filed on Form 1040X, or a quick refund claim is filed on Form 1045. In any case, a refund of taxes previously paid is requested. When the loss is carried forward, the current return shows an NOL deduction for the prior year's loss.

Sequence of Use of NOLs

Where there are NOLs in two or more years, the rule is always to use the earliest year's loss first until it is completely absorbed. The later years' losses can then be

[32] § 172.

used until they also are absorbed or lost. Thus, one year's return could show NOL carryovers from two or more years. Each loss is computed and applied separately.

Election to Forgo Carryback

A taxpayer can *irrevocably elect* not to carry back an NOL to any of the three prior years. In that case, the loss is available as a carryover for 15 years. A taxpayer would make the election if it is to his or her tax advantage. For example, a taxpayer might be in a low marginal tax bracket in the carryback years but expect to be in a high marginal tax bracket in future years. Therefore, it would be to the taxpayer's advantage to use the NOL to offset income in years when the tax rate is high rather than use it when the tax rate is relatively low.

COMPUTATION OF THE NET OPERATING LOSS

Since the NOL provisions apply solely to business-related losses, certain adjustments must be made so that the loss more closely resembles the taxpayer's *economic* loss. The required adjustments for corporate taxpayers are usually insignificant because a corporation's tax loss is generally similar to its economic loss. However, in computing taxable income, individual taxpayers are allowed deductions for such items as personal and dependency exemptions and itemized deductions that do not reflect actual business-related economic losses.

To arrive at the NOL (economic loss) for an individual, taxable income must be adjusted by adding back the following items:[33]

1. No deduction is allowed for personal and dependency exemptions. These amounts do not reflect economic, or business, outlays and hence must be added back.
2. The NOL carryover or carryback from another year is not allowed in the computation of the current year's NOL.
3. Capital losses and nonbusiness deductions are limited in determining the current year's NOL. These limits are as follows:
   a. The excess of nonbusiness capital losses over nonbusiness capital gains must be added back.
   b. The excess of nonbusiness deductions over the sum of nonbusiness income and *net* nonbusiness capital gains must be added back. *Net nonbusiness capital gains* are the excess of nonbusiness capital gains over nonbusiness capital losses. *Nonbusiness income* includes such passive items as dividends and interest. It does not include such items as salaries, rents, and gains and losses on the sale or exchange of business assets. *Nonbusiness deductions* are total itemized deductions less personal casualty and theft losses.

      A taxpayer who does not itemize deductions computes the excess of nonbusiness deductions over nonbusiness income by substituting his or her standard deduction for total itemized deductions.
   c. The excess of business capital losses over the sum of business capital gains and the excess of nonbusiness income and net nonbusiness capital gains over nonbusiness deductions must be added back.
   d. The add-back for net nonbusiness capital losses and excess business capital losses does not include net capital losses not included in the current year computation of taxable income because of the capital loss limitation provisions (discussed in Chapter 16).

[33] § 172(d); Reg. § 1.172–3(a).

The capital loss and nonbusiness deduction limits are illustrated in Examples 22 through 25.

EXAMPLE 22

For 1994, taxpayer and spouse have $6,000 of nonbusiness capital losses and $4,000 of nonbusiness capital gains. They must add back $2,000 ($6,000 − $4,000) in determining the excess of nonbusiness capital losses over nonbusiness capital gains. ▼

EXAMPLE 23

For 1994, taxpayer and spouse have $2,000 of nonbusiness capital gains, $1,000 of nonbusiness capital losses, $2,000 of interest income, and no itemized deductions. They must add back $3,350 {$6,350 standard deduction − [$2,000 interest income + $1,000 ($2,000 − $1,000) net nonbusiness capital gains]}. Note that, in this example, there is no excess of nonbusiness capital losses over nonbusiness capital gains. ▼

EXAMPLE 24

For 1994, taxpayer and spouse have $2,000 of nonbusiness capital gains, $1,000 of nonbusiness capital losses, $9,000 of interest income, $9,500 of itemized deductions (none of which are personal casualty and theft losses), $4,000 of business capital losses, and $1,000 of business capital gains. They must add back $2,500 {$4,000 business capital losses − [$1,000 business capital gains + ($9,000 nonbusiness income + $1,000 net nonbusiness capital gains − $9,500 nonbusiness deductions)]}. Note that, in this example, there is no excess of nonbusiness capital losses over nonbusiness capital gains, nor is there an excess of nonbusiness deductions over the sum of nonbusiness income and net nonbusiness capital gains. ▼

EXAMPLE 25

For 1994, taxpayer and spouse have $2,000 of nonbusiness capital gains, $3,000 of nonbusiness capital losses, $8,000 of interest income, $9,000 of itemized deductions (none of which are personal casualty and theft losses), $8,000 of business capital losses, and $4,000 of business capital gains. They must add back $1,000 ($9,000 − $8,000), the excess of nonbusiness deductions over nonbusiness income, and $3,000, the excess of combined capital losses. Because of the capital loss limitations, only $3,000 of the loss would have been used in computing taxable income for the year. ▼

Example 26 illustrates the computation of an NOL.

EXAMPLE 26

James opened a retail store in 1993 and experienced an NOL of $185 for that year. James had no taxable income for 1990, 1991, or 1992. James is married, has no dependents, and files a joint return. For 1994, James and his wife had the following taxable income:

Gross income from the business	$ 67,000	
Less: Business expenses	(71,000)	($ 4,000)
Salary from a part-time job		875
Interest on savings account		525
Nonbusiness long-term capital gain		1,000
NOL carryover from 1993		(185)
Net loss on rental property		(100)
Adjusted gross income		($ 1,885)
Less: Itemized deductions		
Interest expense	$ 3,000	
Taxes	4,300	
Casualty loss	2,000	
Total itemized deductions		(9,300)
Exemptions (2 × $2,450)		(4,900)
Taxable income		($16,085)

James's NOL is computed as follows:

Taxable income				($16,085)
Add:				
Net operating loss from 1993			$ 185	
Personal exemptions (2)			4,900	
Excess of nonbusiness deductions over nonbusiness income				
Total itemized deductions		$ 9,300		
Less: Casualty loss		(2,000)		
		$ 7,300		
Less: Interest	$ 525			
Less: Long-term capital gain	1,000	(1,525)	5,775	10,860
Net operating loss				($ 5,225)

The NOL can be thought of as follows:

Business loss	($ 4,000)
Rental loss	(100)
Casualty loss	(2,000)
Salary income	875
Net operating loss	($ 5,225)

▼

ETHICAL CONSIDERATIONS

Net Operating Losses

Adam is aware that the net operating loss carryback and carryover provisions enable him to carry back current period losses for 3 years and to carry the losses forward for 15 years. He also is aware of the time value of money concept. In addition, he recognizes that certain adjustments must be made in converting negative taxable income into an NOL.

Adam discusses with you, his accountant, the projections for his new business for the next five years, which show losses in the first two years, profits in the subsequent three years, and a cumulative profit of $90,000 for the five-year period. Adam indicates that if he delays certain transactions (by modifying the contract dates) from Years 1 and 2 into Years 3 and 4, he can convert the losses for the first two years into small profits with the cumulative projected profits for the five years remaining at $90,000. He raises the issues with you of the benefit and appropriateness of doing so.

RECOMPUTATION OF TAX LIABILITY FOR YEAR TO WHICH NET OPERATING LOSS IS CARRIED

When an NOL is carried back to a nonloss year, the taxable income and income tax for the carryback year must be recomputed by including the NOL as a deduction *for* AGI. Several deductions (such as medical expenses and charitable contributions) are based on the amount of AGI. When an NOL is carried back, all such deductions *except* the charitable contributions deduction must be recomputed on the basis of the new AGI after the NOL has been applied. The deduction for charitable contributions is determined without regard to any NOL carryback but with regard to any other modification affecting AGI. Furthermore, any tax credits limited by or based upon the tax must be recomputed, based on the recomputed tax.

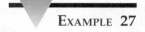

EXAMPLE 27

Peggy sustained an NOL of $11,000 in 1995. Because Peggy had no taxable income in 1992 or 1993, the loss is carried back to 1994. For 1994, the joint income tax return of Peggy and her husband was as follows:

Salary income		$10,000
Dividends		4,000
Net long-term capital gain		1,400
Adjusted gross income		$15,400
Itemized deductions		
Charitable contributions	$2,700	
Interest	4,800	
Taxes	1,420	(8,920)
Exemptions (2 × $2,450)		(4,900)
Taxable income		$ 1,580
Tax (married filing jointly)		$ 237

Peggy's new tax liability for the carryback year is computed as follows:

Adjusted gross income		$ 15,400
Less: Net operating loss		(11,000)
Recomputed adjusted gross income		$ 4,400
Itemized deductions		
Charitable contributions	$2,700	
Interest	4,800	
Taxes	1,420	(8,920)
Exemptions (2 × $2,450)		(4,900)
Recomputed taxable income		$ (9,420)
Tax		$ –0–
Tax originally paid and refund claim		$ 237

CALCULATION OF THE REMAINING NET OPERATING LOSS

After computing the amount of the refund claim for the initial carryback year, it is then necessary to determine the extent to which any NOL remains to carry over to future years. The amount of this carryover loss is the excess of the NOL over the taxable income of the year to which the loss is being applied. However, the taxable income of the year to which the loss is being applied must be determined with the following *modifications:*

- No deduction is allowed for excess capital losses over capital gains.
- No deduction is allowed for the NOL that is being carried back. However, deductions are allowed for NOLs occurring before the loss year.
- Any deductions claimed that are based on or limited by AGI must be determined after making the preceding adjustments. However, charitable contributions do not take into account any NOL carryback.
- No deduction is allowed for personal and dependency exemptions.

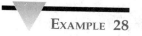

EXAMPLE 28

Referring to the facts in Example 27, the NOL carryover from 1994 available for future years would be ($4,520), computed as follows:

Salary income		$10,000
Dividends		4,000
Net long-term capital gain		1,400
Adjusted gross income		$15,400
Itemized deductions		
Charitable contributions	$2,700	
Interest	4,800	
Taxes	1,420	(8,920)
Exemptions (not allowed)		–0–
Modified taxable income		$ 6,480
Net operating loss		($11,000)
Modified taxable income		6,480
Net operating loss to carry forward		($ 4,520)

Since the ending figure is negative, it represents the NOL remaining to carry over to 1996 or later years.

TAX PLANNING CONSIDERATIONS

DOCUMENTATION OF RELATED-TAXPAYER LOANS, CASUALTY LOSSES, AND THEFT LOSSES

7   **LEARNING OBJECTIVE**
Identify tax planning opportunities in deducting certain business expenses, business losses, and personal losses.

Since non-bona fide loans between related taxpayers may be treated as gifts, adequate documentation is needed to substantiate a bad debt deduction if the loan subsequently becomes worthless. Documentation should include proper execution of the note (legal form) and the establishment of a bona fide purpose for the loan. In addition, it is desirable to stipulate a reasonable rate of interest and a fixed maturity date.

Since a theft loss is not permitted for misplaced items, a loss should be documented by a police report and evidence of the value of the property (e.g., appraisals, pictures of the property, newspaper clippings). Similar documentation

---

CONCEPT SUMMARY 7–4

Computation of Net Operating Loss

Taxable income shown on the return
Add back:

1. Personal and dependency exemptions.
2. Net operating loss carryover or carryback from another year.
3. The excess of nonbusiness capital losses over nonbusiness capital gains.
4. The excess of nonbusiness deductions over the sum of nonbusiness income plus *net* nonbusiness capital gains.
5. The excess of business capital losses over the sum of business capital gains plus the excess of nonbusiness income and *net* nonbusiness capital gains over nonbusiness deductions. The add-back from the total of items 3 and 5 will not exceed $3,000 because of the capital loss limitation rules.

Equals the net operating loss

of the value of property should be provided to support a casualty loss deduction because the amount of loss is measured by the decline in fair market value of the property.

Casualty loss deductions must be reported on Form 4684 (see Appendix B).

SMALL BUSINESS STOCK

Because § 1244 limits the amount of loss classified as ordinary loss on a yearly basis, a taxpayer might maximize the benefits of § 1244 by selling the stock in more than one taxable year. The result could be that the losses in any one taxable year would not exceed the § 1244 limits on ordinary loss.

EXAMPLE 29

Mitch, a single individual, purchased small business stock in 1992 for $150,000 (150 shares at $1,000 per share). On December 20, 1994, the stock is worth $60,000 (150 shares at $400 per share). Mitch wants to sell the stock at this time. Mitch earns a salary of $80,000 a year, has no other capital transactions, and does not expect any in the future. If Mitch sells all of the small business stock in 1994, his recognized loss will be $90,000 ($60,000 – $150,000). The loss will be characterized as a $50,000 ordinary loss and a $40,000 long-term capital loss. In computing taxable income for 1994, Mitch could deduct the $50,000 ordinary loss but could deduct only $3,000 of the capital loss. The remainder of the capital loss could be carried over and used in future years subject to the $3,000 limitation if Mitch has no capital gains. If Mitch sells 82 shares in 1994, he will recognize an ordinary loss of $49,200 [82 × ($1,000 – $400)]. If Mitch then sells the remainder of the shares in 1995, he will recognize an ordinary loss of $40,800 [68 × ($1,000 – $400)]. Mitch could deduct the $49,200 ordinary loss in computing 1994 taxable income and the $40,800 ordinary loss in computing 1995 taxable income. ▼

CASUALTY LOSSES

A special election is available for taxpayers who sustain casualty losses in an area designated by the President as a disaster area. This election affects only the timing, not the calculation, of the deduction. The deduction can be taken in the year before the year in which the loss occurred. Thus, an individual can take the deduction on the 1993 return for a loss occurring between January 1 and December 31, 1994. The benefit, of course, is a faster refund (or reduction in tax). It will also be advantageous to carry the loss back if the taxpayer's tax rate in the carryback year is higher than the tax rate in the year of the loss.

To find out if an event qualifies as a disaster area loss, one can look in any of the major tax services, the Weekly Compilation of Presidential Documents, or the *Internal Revenue Bulletin.*

NET OPERATING LOSSES

In certain instances, it may be advisable for a taxpayer to elect not to carry back an NOL. For an individual, the benefits from the loss carryback could be scaled down or lost due to the economic adjustments that must be made to taxable income for the year to which the loss is carried. For example, a taxpayer should attempt to minimize the number of taxable years to which an NOL is carried. The more years to which the NOL is applied, the more benefits are lost from adjustments for items such as personal and dependency exemptions.

The election not to carry back the loss might also be advantageous if there is a disparity in marginal tax rates applicable to different tax years.

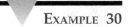

EXAMPLE 30 Abby sustained an NOL of $10,000 in Year 4. Her marginal tax bracket in Year 1 was 15%. In Year 5, however, she expects her bracket to be 39.6% due to a large profit she will make on a business deal. If Abby carries her loss back, her refund will be $1,500 (15% × $10,000). If she elects not to carry it back to Year 1 but chooses, instead, to carry it forward, her savings will be $3,960 (39.6% × $10,000). Even considering the time value of an immediate tax refund, Abby appears to be better off using the carryover approach. ▼

KEY TERMS

Bad debt, 7–3	Personal casualty gain, 7–16	Small business stock, 7–8
Business bad debt, 7–4	Personal casualty loss, 7–16	Specific charge-off method, 7–3
Casualty loss, 7–9	Research and experimental expenditures, 7–17	Theft loss, 7–10
Disaster area losses, 7–11		Worthless securities, 7–7
Net operating loss (NOL), 7–19	Reserve method, 7–3	
Nonbusiness bad debt, 7–4	Section 1244 stock, 7–8	

PROBLEM MATERIALS

DISCUSSION QUESTIONS

1. Explain why a bad debt deduction is not allowed for a bad debt arising from the sale of inventory by a cash basis taxpayer.

2. Discuss whether legal proceedings must be brought against a debtor in order to show that a debt is worthless.

3. Bill made a loan to a friend three years ago to help the friend purchase an automobile. Bill's friend has notified him that the car has been sold and the most he will be able to repay is 50% of the loan. Discuss the possibility of Bill taking a bad debt deduction for half of the loan.

4. Discuss the difference between business and nonbusiness bad debts. How is the distinction determined? How is each treated on the return?

5. What factors are to be considered in determining whether a bad debt arising from a loan between related parties is, in fact, a bad debt?

6. Discuss a taxpayer's options for the tax treatment of a loss incurred on a deposit in a qualified financial institution. Also note the consequences of each option.

7. Explain the tax consequences of selling § 1244 stock at a gain.

8. Discuss the ordinary loss limitations on the sale of § 1244 stock and the advantages of such a characterization.

9. Jim, an individual, discovers that his personal residence has been extensively damaged by termites. Discuss whether he may take a deduction for the damage to his home.

10. Discuss the provision for determining the year in which a theft loss is deductible.

11. What is a disaster area loss? Why might a taxpayer benefit from making the disaster area loss election?

12. Discuss the tax consequences of property being partially destroyed in determining the amount of a casualty loss assuming no insurance proceeds are received.

✗ 13. How is a personal casualty loss computed? A business casualty loss? What effect do insurance proceeds have on both types of losses?

14. Discuss the tax consequences of not making an insurance claim when insured personal use property is subject to a casualty or theft loss.

15. Mark's 10-year-old automobile was extensively damaged in a collision in which he was not at fault. The original cost of the automobile was $10,000, and the cost of repairing it was $5,000. Discuss any problems with using the $5,000 as the measurement of the loss.

16. Discuss the reduction of personal casualty losses by the $100 and 10% of AGI floors.

17. When casualty losses exceed casualty gains, only the amount of the casualty loss in excess of casualty gains is subject to the 10% of AGI floor. Discuss the significance of netting losses against gains in this manner rather than having the entire casualty loss subject to the 10% of AGI floor.

18. If a taxpayer is required to spread a personal casualty loss between two years under the reasonable prospect of recovery doctrine, how will the $100 per event floor and the 10% of AGI limitation be treated?

19. Bonnie sustained a loss on a duplex damaged by fire. She owns the duplex and lives in one unit. She rents out the other unit to a tenant. Discuss the tax treatment of the loss on Bonnie's individual tax return.

20. Discuss the computation of a personal casualty loss.

21. Why do most taxpayers elect to write off research and experimental expenditures rather than capitalize and amortize such amounts? Are there some situations in which the capitalization and amortization approach would be preferable?

22. If a business does not elect to expense or amortize research expenditures, what is the possibility of writing off such expenditures?

23. Why can the sale of small business stock (§ 1244 stock) at a loss create or increase an NOL?

✗ 24. Discuss the periods to which NOLs may be carried. Can the taxpayer elect not to carry an NOL back to any one year? What possible benefit might result from not carrying a loss back to a particular year?

25. Why are such items as nonbusiness deductions and personal and dependency exemptions not allowed in computing the NOL?

26. If an individual has no nonbusiness capital transactions for the year, discuss the treatment of the excess of nonbusiness income over nonbusiness deductions with respect to the NOL.

27. Discuss the calculation of the NOL remaining after a carryback to a particular tax year.

PROBLEMS

28. John is the sole proprietor of Crow Loan Company. On May 1, 1993, Crow loaned Sara $10,000. In 1994, Sara filed for bankruptcy. At that time, it was revealed that Sara's creditors could expect to receive 60 cents on the dollar. In March 1995, final settlement was made and Crow received $4,000. How much loss can Crow deduct and in which year?

29. In 1992, Jack loaned his mother $10,000. In 1994, his mother told him that she would try and pay him $1,000. In 1995, Jack's mother filed for bankruptcy and told Jack that she would be unable to pay him anything. Determine Jack's possible deductions with respect to the loan.

30. In 1993, Wilma deposited $20,000 with a commercial bank. On July 1, 1994, Wilma was notified that the bank was insolvent, and subsequently she received only 30% of the

deposit. Wilma also has a salary of $5,000, long-term capital gain of $12,000, and itemized deductions (other than casualty and theft) of $7,000. Determine Wilma's possible deductions with respect to the deposit.

31. Seth, a married taxpayer filing a joint return, had the following items for 1994:

    • Salary of $150,000.

    • Gain of $30,000 on the sale of stock Seth acquired three years ago.

    • Loss of $120,000 on the sale of § 1244 stock Seth acquired two years ago.

    • Stock acquired on December 15, 1993, for $5,000 became worthless on March 28, 1994.

    Determine Seth's AGI for 1994.

32. John and Joyce, married and filing a joint return, have the following items for the current year:

    • Worthless stock of $7,000. The stock was acquired on November 1 of the prior year and became worthless on March 15 of the current year.

    • Gain of $3,000 on the sale of § 1244 stock acquired two years earlier.

    • Loss of $75,000 on the sale of § 1244 stock acquired three months earlier.

    • Salary of $90,000.

    Determine John and Joyce's AGI for the current year.

33. When Helen returned from a vacation in Hawaii on November 8, 1994, she discovered that a burglar had stolen her silver, stereo, and color television. In the process of removing these items, the burglar damaged some furniture that originally cost $1,400. Helen's silver cost $3,640 and was valued at $6,500; the stereo system cost $8,400 and was valued at $6,200; the television cost $840 and was worth $560. Helen filed a claim with her insurance company and was reimbursed in the following amounts on December 20, 1994.

Silver	$2,800
Stereo	5,600
Television	490

    The insurance company disputed the reimbursement claimed by Helen for the damaged furniture, but she protested and was finally paid $280 on January 30, 1995. The repairs to the furniture totaled $448. Helen's AGI for 1994 was $20,000, and it was $500 for 1995. How much can Helen claim as a casualty and theft loss? In which year?

34. Eduardo owned 50 acres of land in Florida that he farmed. A hurricane hit the area and destroyed a farm building and some farm equipment and damaged a barn. Applicable information is as follows:

Item	Adjusted Basis	FMV Before	FMV After	Insurance Proceeds
Building	$50,000	$65,000	$ –0–	$30,000
Equipment	35,000	29,000	–0–	27,000
Barn	80,000	90,000	70,000	5,000

    a. How much is Eduardo's loss?
    b. Assuming the loss occurred on August 24, 1995, and that the President designated the area as a disaster area, what options are available to Eduardo with respect to the timing of the loss deduction?

35. On January 7 of the current year, Wade dropped off to sleep while driving home from a business trip. Luckily, he was only slightly injured in the resulting accident, but his car was completely destroyed.

   Wade had purchased the car new two years ago and had driven it 64,000 miles at the time of the accident. Of these miles, 28,000 were business miles; the remaining miles were personal miles. The car cost $7,200 new. Wade has taken $1,985 of depreciation for the business use of the car. He carried zero deductible collision insurance on the car. Wade made no claim on his insurance policy because he was afraid that if he did his insurance premiums would increase.

   After Wade's release from the hospital the day after the accident, he could not find his wallet (cost $65, fair replacement value $30) or its contents, which included $350 in cash and $500 in traveler's checks. The traveler's checks were replaced by the issuing company. He also was unable to locate the stone from his diamond ring. The stone cost his wife $2,500 when purchased nine years ago and was worth $6,400 at the time of the loss.

   a. Determine the amount of Wade's deductible loss *for* AGI.
   b. Determine the amount of the loss deductible *from* AGI, assuming AGI for the year is $25,000.

36. On September 17 of the current year, Kathy was involved in an accident with her business automobile. The automobile had a fair market value of $2,000 before the accident, and it was worthless after the accident. Kathy had a basis of $3,000 in the car at the time of the accident. The car was covered by an insurance policy that insured the car for 60% of fair market value. Because Kathy was afraid that the policy would be canceled, she made no claim against the insurance policy for damages to the car. Kathy earned a salary of $60,000 for the current year. Determine the amount of Kathy's deductible loss.

37. Green Corporation, a manufacturing company, decided to develop a new line of fireworks. Because of the danger involved, Green purchased an isolated parcel of land for $300,000 and constructed a building for $400,000. The building was to be used for research and experimentation in creating the new fireworks. The project was begun in 1994. Green had the following expenses in 1994 in connection with the project:

Salaries	$80,000
Utilities	10,000
Materials	20,000
Insurance	30,000
Cost of market survey to determine profit potential for new fireworks line	15,000
Depreciation on the building	10,000

Green had the following expenses in 1995 in connection with the project:

Salaries	$90,000
Utilities	15,000
Materials	25,000
Insurance	24,000
Depreciation on the building	13,000

The benefits from the project will be realized starting in June 1996.

   a. If Green Corporation elects to expense research and experimental expenditures, determine the amount of the deduction for 1994, 1995, and 1996.
   b. If Green Corporation elects a 60-month deferral and amortization period, determine the amount of the deduction for 1994, 1995, and 1996.

38. Rex and Rosa, who file a joint return, had the following items for their 1994 tax return:

    - Rex's salary—$40,000.

    - Rosa's salary—$42,000.

    - Dividends from domestic corporations—$12,000.

    - During the year, a fire completely destroyed an apartment building owned by Rex and Rosa. The building was worth $400,000 at the time of the fire, and Rex and Rosa had a basis for the building of $375,000. The building was insured for 60% of its fair market value.

    - Other itemized deductions—$10,000.

    a. What is Rex and Rosa's taxable income for 1994?
    b. What is Rex and Rosa's NOL for 1994?

39. Carol, a single taxpayer, had the following items of income and expense during 1994:

Gross receipts from business	$120,000
Business expenses	150,000
Carol's salary	10,000
Interest from Blue Company bonds	12,000
Itemized deductions	8,000

    a. Determine the amount of Carol's 1994 taxable income.
    b. Determine the amount of Carol's 1994 NOL.

40. Gus, who is married and files a joint return, owns a grocery store. In 1994, his gross sales were $286,000 and operating expenses were $310,000. Other items on his 1994 return were as follows:

Nonbusiness capital gains (short-term)	$10,000
Nonbusiness capital losses (long-term)	9,000
Itemized deductions	10,000
Ordinary nonbusiness income	4,000
Salary from part-time job	10,000

    During the years 1991 and 1992, Gus had no taxable income. In 1993, Gus had taxable income of $24,400 computed as follows:

Net business income		$60,000
Interest income		2,000
Adjusted gross income		$62,000
Less: Itemized deductions		
Charitable contributions of $40,000, limited to 50% of AGI	$31,000	
Medical expenses of $6,550, limited to the amount in excess of 7.5% of AGI ($6,550 – $4,650)	1,900	
Total itemized deductions		(32,900)
Exemptions (2 × 2,350)		(4,700)
Taxable income		$24,400

    a. What is Gus's 1994 NOL?
    b. Determine Gus's recomputed taxable income for 1993.

41. During 1994, Rick and his wife Sara had the following items of income and expense to report:

• Gross receipts from business	$400,000
• Business expenses	525,000
• Interest income from bank savings accounts	8,000
• Sara's salary	50,000
• Long-term capital gain on stock held as an investment	4,000
• Itemized deductions	15,000

a. Assuming Rick and Sara file a joint return, what is their taxable income for 1994?
b. What is the amount of Rick and Sara's NOL for 1994?

42. Assume that in addition to the information in Problem 41, Rick had no taxable income for the years 1991 and 1992 and $7,000 of taxable income for 1993 computed as follows:

Salary		$ 25,000
Capital loss		(1,000)
Adjusted gross income		$ 24,000
Less: Itemized deductions		
Charitable contributions of $20,000, limited to 50% of AGI	$12,000	
Medical expenses of $2,100, limited to the amount in excess of 7.5% of AGI ($2,100 – $1,800)	300	
Total itemized deductions		(12,300)
Exemptions (2 × $2,350)		(4,700)
Taxable income		$ 7,000

Determine the amount of Rick and Sara's 1994 NOL to be carried forward to 1995.

43. Fran is single and had the following income and deductions for 1994:

Business receipts	$ 90,000
Business expenses	130,000
Dividends from domestic corporations	20,000
Interest received from bank savings account	6,000
Itemized deductions	10,000
1993 NOL carried to 1994	25,000

a. What is Fran's taxable income for 1994?
b. What is Fran's NOL for 1994?

44. Soong, single and age 32, had the following items for the tax year 1994:

• Salary of $40,000.

• Interest income from U.S. government bonds of $2,000.

• Dividends from a foreign corporation of $500.

• Sale of small business § 1244 stock on October 20, 1994, for $10,000. The stock had been acquired two years earlier for $65,000.

• Business bad debt of $3,000.

• Nonbusiness bad debt of $5,000.

• Sale of small business § 1244 stock on November 12, 1994, for $4,000. The stock had been acquired on June 5, 1994, for $800.

- Sale of common stock on December 4, 1994, for $40,000. The stock was acquired four years ago for $18,000.

- Total itemized deductions of $8,000.

Determine Soong's NOL for 1994.

45. Nell, single and age 38, had the following income and expense items in 1994:

Nonbusiness bad debt	$ 6,000
Business bad debt	2,000
Nonbusiness long-term capital gain	4,000
Nonbusiness short-term capital loss	3,000
Salary	40,000
Interest income	1,000

Determine Nell's AGI for 1994.

46. Assume that in addition to the information in Problem 45, Nell had the following items in 1994:

Personal casualty gain on an asset held for four months	$10,000
Personal casualty loss on an asset held for two years	1,000

Determine Nell's AGI for 1994.

47. Assume that in addition to the information in Problems 45 and 46, Nell had the following items in 1994:

Personal casualty loss on an asset held for five years	$50,000
Interest expense on home mortgage	3,000

Determine Nell's taxable income and NOL for 1994.

CUMULATIVE PROBLEMS

48. Ned Wilson, age 60, single, and retired, has no dependents. Ned lives at 231 Wander Lane, Salt Lake City, UT 84201. Ned's Social Security number is 985–12–3774. During 1994, Ned had the following income and expense items:

a. On January 27, 1993, Ned deposited $8,000 in a savings account at the ABC Financial Company. The savings account bore interest at 15%, compounded semiannually. Ned received a $600 interest payment on July 27, 1993, but received no interest payments thereafter. The finance company filed for bankruptcy on January 12, 1994. Ned received a $710 check in final settlement of his account from the bankruptcy trustee on December 20, 1994.

b. On January 1, 1994, a fire severely damaged a two-story building owned by Ned, who occupied the second story of the building as a residence and had recently opened a hardware store on the ground level. The following information is available with respect to the incident:

	Adjusted Basis	Fair Market Value	
		Before	After
Building	$64,000	$130,000	$50,000
Inventory	35,000	55,000	None
Store equipment	3,000	1,800	None
Home furnishings	12,600	6,000	800
Personal auto	8,900	7,800	7,600

Ned's fire insurance policy paid the following amounts for damages covered by the policy:

Building	$50,000	(policy maximum)
Inventory	33,000	
Store equipment	None	
Home furnishings	1,000	(policy maximum)
Personal auto	None	

Assume all of the destroyed property was acquired on December 15, 1993.

c. On March 1, 1989, Ned loaned a neighboring businessman $15,000. The debtor died of a heart attack on June 21, 1994. Ned had no security and was unable to collect anything from the man's estate.

d. Ned received $112,000 of interest income from Salt Lake City Bank.

e. On March 3, 1994, Ned sold a piece of real estate he had been holding for speculation for $90,000. Ned had bought the land July 18, 1979, for $52,800.

f. Ned made a charitable contribution of $13,000.

g. Ned made four quarterly estimated tax payments of $7,000 each.

Part 1—Tax Computation
Compute Ned's 1994 Federal income tax payable (or refund due), assuming he deducts the lost deposit as a bad debt. Suggested software (if available): *TurboTax* or *MacInTax* for tax return or WFT tax planning software.

Part 2—Tax Planning
Determine whether Ned should elect to treat the deposit in ABC Financial Company as a casualty loss rather than as a bad debt. Suggested software (if available): *TurboTax* or *MacInTax* for tax return or WFT tax planning software.

49. Jane Smith, age 40, is single and has no dependents. She is employed as a legal secretary by Legal Services, Inc. She owns and operates Typing Services located near the campus of San Jose State University at 1986 Campus Drive. She is a cash basis taxpayer. Jane lives at 2020 Oakcrest Road, San Jose, CA 95134. Jane's Social Security number is 123–89–6666. Jane indicates that she wishes to designate $3 to the Presidential Election Campaign Fund. During 1993, Jane had the following income and expense items:

a. $40,000 salary from Legal Services, Inc.

b. $15,000 gross receipts from her typing services business.

c. $300 cash dividend from Buffalo Mining Company, a Canadian corporation.

d. $1,000 Christmas bonus from Legal Services, Inc.

e. $10,000 life insurance proceeds on the death of her sister.

f. $5,000 check given to her by her wealthy aunt.

g. $100 won in a bingo game.

h. Expenses connected with the typing service:

Office rent	$5,000
Supplies	2,400
Utilities and telephone	3,680
Wages to part-time typists	4,000
Payroll taxes	600
Equipment rentals	3,000

i. $8,000 interest expense on a home mortgage (paid to San Jose Savings and Loan).

j. $5,000 fair market value of silverware stolen from her home by a burglar on October 12, 1993. Jane had paid $4,000 for the silverware on July 1, 1984. She was reimbursed $1,500 by her insurance company.

k. Jane had loaned $2,100 to a friend, Joan Jensen, on June 3, 1990. Joan declared bankruptcy on August 14, 1993, and was unable to repay the loan.

l. Legal Services, Inc., withheld Federal income tax of $5,000 and the required amount of FICA tax.

Part 1—Tax Computation

Compute Jane Smith's 1993 Federal income tax payable (or refund due). If you use tax forms for your computations, you will need Forms 1040 and 4684 and Schedules A, C, and D. Suggested software (if available): *TurboTax* or *MacInTax* for tax return or WFT tax planning software.

Part 2—Tax Planning

In 1994, Jane plans to continue her job with Legal Services, Inc. Therefore, items a, d, and l will recur in 1994. Jane plans to continue her typing services business (refer to item b) and expects gross receipts of $20,000. She projects that all business expenses (refer to item h) will increase by 10%, except for office rent, which, under the terms of her lease, will remain the same as in 1993. Items e, f, g, j, and k will not recur in 1994. Items c and i will be approximately the same as in 1993.

Jane would like you to compute the minimum amount of estimated tax she will have to pay for 1994 so that she will not have to pay any additional tax upon filing her 1994 Federal income tax return. Write a letter to Jane that contains your advice and prepare a memo for the tax files. Suggested software (if available): *TurboTax* or *MacInTax* for tax return or WFT tax planning software.

RESEARCH PROBLEMS

Research Problem 1. While Ralph Jones was in the process of obtaining a divorce, his wife, without Ralph's knowledge, had the furniture removed from his apartment. Discuss whether Ralph would be entitled to a tax deduction for the loss of the furniture.

Partial list of research aids:
Landis G. Brown, 30 TCM 257, T.C.Memo. 1971–60.
Jerry L. Goode, 42 TCM 1209, T.C.Memo. 1981–548.

Research Problem 2. John Morgan made deductible alimony payments of $60,000 for the year. The payments were deductible for AGI under §§ 62(a)(10) and 215. Because of the large deduction, John has a negative taxable income for the year. Discuss the possibility of John having an NOL for the year as a result of the alimony payments.

Research Problem 3. George Johnson, a resident of St. Paul, Minnesota, parked his car on a lake while he was watching an iceboat race. During the race, the ice beneath his car unexpectedly gave way, and the car sank to the bottom of the lake. Write a letter to George advising him as to whether he can claim a casualty loss for the damage to the car. Also prepare a memo for the tax files.

Research Problem 4. John Smith had $250,000 of personal savings on deposit in the Equity Savings and Loan Association. During the current year, an employee embezzled large sums of money from Equity. As a result, Equity was declared insolvent. At the present, it appears as though John will recover none of his deposit. Discuss the possibility of John taking the $250,000 loss as a theft loss on his tax return.

DEPRECIATION, COST RECOVERY, AMORTIZATION, AND DEPLETION

LEARNING OBJECTIVES

After completing Chapter 8, you should be able to:

1. Understand the rationale for the cost consumption concept and identify the relevant time periods for depreciation, ACRS, and MACRS.

2. Determine the amount of cost recovery under ACRS and MACRS including the effects of the §179 expensing election and the limitations on listed property.

3. Identify intangible assets that are eligible for amortization and calculate the amount of the deduction.

4. Determine the amount of depletion expense including being able to apply the alternative tax treatments for intangible drilling and development costs.

5. Perform the reporting procedures for cost recovery.

6. Identify tax planning opportunities for cost recovery, amortization, and depletion.

OUTLINE

Overview, 8–3

Accelerated Cost Recovery System (ACRS and MACRS), 8–4

General Considerations, 8–4

Eligible Property under ACRS or MACRS, 8–5

Personalty: Recovery Periods and Methods, 8–5

Realty: Recovery Periods and Methods, 8–10

Straight-Line Election under ACRS and MACRS, 8–13

Election to Expense Assets, 8–14

Business and Personal Use of Automobiles and Other Listed Property, 8–16

Alternative Depreciation System (ADS), 8–21

Amortization, 8–22

Depletion, 8–24

Intangible Drilling and Development Costs, 8–25

Depletion Methods, 8–25

Reporting Procedures, 8–28

Tax Planning Considerations, 8–29

Cost Recovery, 8–29

Amortization, 8–33

Depletion, 8–34

Tables, 8–34

1   LEARNING OBJECTIVE
Understand the rationale for the cost consumption concept and identify the relevant time periods for depreciation, ACRS, and MACRS.

The Internal Revenue Code provides for a deduction for the consumption of the cost of an asset through depreciation, cost recovery, amortization, or depletion. These deductions are applications of the recovery of capital doctrine (discussed in Chapter 4).

A distinction is made between tangible and intangible property. Tangible property is any property with physical substance (e.g., equipment, buildings), while intangible property lacks such substance (e.g., goodwill, patents).

The **depreciation** rules were completely overhauled by the Economic Recovery Tax Act of 1981 (ERTA). Hence, *most* property placed in service after December 31, 1980, is subject to the accelerated **cost recovery** system (ACRS). However, property placed in service before January 1, 1981, that is still in use, as well as *certain* property placed in service after December 31, 1980, is subject to the pre-ERTA depreciation rules. The Tax Reform Act (TRA) of 1986 completely revised the ACRS rules for property placed in service after December 31, 1986 (MACRS). Therefore, a knowledge of all of the depreciation and cost recovery rules may be needed as Example 1 illustrates.

TAX IN THE NEWS

SHORTER COST RECOVERY SCHEDULES FOR PHONE COMPANIES

Federal regulators are considering ways to modify broadcast and telecommunications rules that could boost the economy and eventually help change the competitive landscape.

Among the ideas being discussed among Federal Communications Commission members and their staffs are accelerating depreciation rates for phone companies and easing ownership limits on radio and television stations.

One of the commission members, Sherrie Marshall, would like to see revisions to depreciation schedules for the phone companies. "This should spur investment in our telephone networks," a move that could lead to greater use of optical fiber and advanced switching technologies.

SOURCE: Adapted from Mary Lu Carnevale, "FCC is Considering Changes in Rules That Could Stimulate Economic Growth," *Wall Street Journal*, February 6, 1992, p. A16. Reprinted by permission of the *Wall Street Journal*, © 1993 Dow Jones & Company, Inc. All rights reserved worldwide.

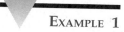

EXAMPLE 1

The Brown Company owns machinery purchased in 1980. The machinery has a 15-year useful life. The business also owns equipment purchased in 1986 that has a 10-year cost recovery life. In 1990, the business purchased a computer. To compute the depreciation and cost recovery for 1994, Brown will use the pre-ERTA depreciation rules for the equipment, the pre-TRA of 1986 cost recovery rules (ACRS) for the equipment, and the post-TRA of 1986 cost recovery rules (MACRS) for the computer. ▼

This chapter initially focuses on the ACRS and MACRS rules.[1] The chapter then concludes with a discussion of the amortization of intangible property and the depletion of natural resources.

ACRS was one of many provisions in ERTA that were intended to stimulate the economy. The following features of ACRS result in accelerated write-offs:

- Cost recovery periods are shorter than the estimated useful lives required under the pre-1981 depreciation system.
- The use of salvage value, required under the § 167 depreciation system, is eliminated under ACRS.
- For many assets, the methods for computing ACRS deductions are more generous than the allowable methods for computing depreciation.

For assets placed in service after 1986, ACRS is replaced with MACRS. The basic effect of MACRS is to somewhat dampen the economic stimulus effect of ACRS. MACRS cost recovery periods are generally longer than ACRS cost recovery periods. In addition, the cost recovery methods available under MACRS are, in most cases, not as generous as the methods available under ACRS.

OVERVIEW

Taxpayers may write off the cost of certain assets that are used in a trade or business or held for the production of income. A write-off may take the form of depreciation (or cost recovery), depletion, or amortization. Tangible assets, other than natural resources, are *depreciated*. Natural resources, such as oil, gas, coal, and timber, are *depleted*. Intangible assets, such as copyrights and patents, are *amortized*. Generally, no write-off is allowed for an asset that does not have a determinable useful life.

CONCEPT SUMMARY 8–1

Depreciation and Cost Recovery: Relevant Time Periods

System	Date Property Is Placed in Service
§ 167 depreciation	Before January 1, 1981, and *certain* property placed in service after December 31, 1980.
Original accelerated cost recovery system (ACRS)	After December 31, 1980, and before January 1, 1987.
Modified accelerated cost recovery system (MACRS)	After December 31, 1986.

---

[1] § 168. Pre-ERTA depreciation rules are covered in Appendix H.

ACRS and MACRS provide separate cost recovery tables for realty (real property) and personalty (personal property). Realty generally includes land and buildings permanently affixed to the land. Write-offs are not available for land because it does not have a determinable useful life. Cost recovery allowances for real property, other than land, are based on recovery lives specified in the law. For most types of realty, cost recovery allowances are specified in tables provided by the IRS.

Personalty is defined as any asset that is not realty.[2] Personalty includes furniture, machinery, equipment, and many other types of assets. Do not confuse personalty (or personal property) with *personal use* property. Personal use property is any property (realty or personalty) that is held for personal use rather than for use in a trade or business or an income-producing activity. Write-offs are not allowed for personal use assets.

In summary, both realty and personalty can be either business use/income-producing property or personal use property. Examples include a residence (realty that is personal use), an office building (realty that is business use), a dump truck (personalty that is business use), and regular wearing apparel (personalty that is personal use). It is imperative that this distinction between the *classification* of an asset (realty or personalty) and the *use* to which the asset is put (business or personal) be understood.

ACCELERATED COST RECOVERY SYSTEM (ACRS AND MACRS)

GENERAL CONSIDERATIONS

2   LEARNING OBJECTIVE
Determine the amount of cost recovery under ACRS and MACRS including the effects of the § 179 expensing election and the limitations on listed property.

Under the **accelerated cost recovery system (ACRS),** the cost of an asset is recovered over a predetermined period that is generally shorter than the useful life of the asset or the period the asset is used to produce income. The ACRS system was designed to encourage investment, improve productivity, and simplify the law and its administration. However, the pre-ACRS depreciation rules will continue to apply in the following situations:

- Property placed in service after 1980 whose life is not based on years (e.g., units-of-production method).
- The remaining depreciation on property placed in service by the taxpayer before 1981.
- Personal property acquired after 1980 if the property was owned or used during 1980 by the taxpayer or a related person (antichurning rule).[3]
- Property that is amortized (e.g., leasehold improvements).

The basis of cost recovery property must be reduced by the cost recovery allowed and by not less than the allowable amount. The *allowed* cost recovery is the cost recovery actually taken, whereas the *allowable* cost recovery is the amount that could have been taken under the applicable cost recovery method. If the taxpayer does not claim any cost recovery on property during a particular year, the basis of the property must still be reduced by the amount of cost recovery that should have been deducted (the allowable cost recovery).

---

[2] Refer to Chapter 1 for a further discussion.
[3] § 168(f). The antichurning rules may also require the use of pre-TRA of 1986 ACRS rules on property placed in service after December 31, 1986 (property that otherwise would be subject to MACRS).

The basis for cost recovery generally is the adjusted cost basis used to determine gain if property is sold or otherwise disposed of. However, if personal use assets are converted to business or income-producing use, the basis for cost recovery and for loss is the *lower* of the adjusted basis or the fair market value at the time the property was converted. As a result of this lower-of-basis rule, losses that occurred while the property was personal use property will not be recognized for tax purposes through the cost recovery of the property.

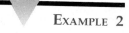

EXAMPLE 2

Hans acquires a personal residence for $120,000. Four years later, when the fair market value is only $100,000, he converts the property to rental use. The basis for cost recovery is $100,000, since the fair market value is less than the adjusted basis. The $20,000 decline in value is deemed to be personal (since it occurred while the property was held for personal use) and therefore nondeductible. ▼

ELIGIBLE PROPERTY UNDER ACRS OR MACRS

Assets used in a trade or business or for the production of income are eligible for cost recovery if they are subject to wear and tear, decay or decline from natural causes, or obsolescence. Assets that do not decline in value on a predictable basis or that do not have a determinable useful life (e.g., land, stock, antiques) are not eligible for cost recovery.

PERSONALTY: RECOVERY PERIODS AND METHODS

Classification of Property: ACRS

ACRS provides that the cost of eligible personalty (and certain realty) is recovered over 3, 5, 10, or 15 years. Property is classified by recovery period as follows:

3 years . . . . Autos, light-duty trucks, R & D equipment, racehorses over 2 years old and other horses over 12 years old, and personalty with an ADR* midpoint life of 4 years or less.[4]

5 years . . . . Most other equipment except long-lived public utility property. Also includes single-purpose agricultural structures and petroleum storage facilities, which are designated as § 1245 property under the law.

10 years . . . . Public utility property with an ADR midpoint life greater than 18 but not greater than 25 years, burners and boilers using coal as a primary fuel if used in a public utility power plant and if replacing or converting oil- or gas-fired burners or boilers, railroad tank cars, mobile homes, and realty with an ADR midpoint life of 12.5 years or less (e.g., theme park structures).

15 years . . . . Public utility property with an ADR midpoint life exceeding 25 years (except certain burners and boilers using coal as a primary fuel).

*ADR refers to the Asset Depreciation Range system.

Taxpayers who own 10-year or 15-year ACRS property continue to compute cost recovery allowances under the ACRS rules. However, all cost has already been recovered on any 3-year or 5-year ACRS property.

---

[4] Rev.Proc. 83–35, 1983–1 C.B. 745 is the source for the ADR midpoint lives.

Taxpayers had the choice of using (1) the straight-line method over the regular or optional (see below) recovery period or (2) a prescribed accelerated method over the regular recovery period. These two methods are both part of the ACRS system, but a convenient name is not provided for either method. Hereafter, the straight-line method will be referred to as the *optional* (or *elective*) *straight-line method*. The method using percentages prescribed in the Code will be referred to as the *statutory percentage method*.

The rates to be used in computing the deduction under the statutory percentage method are shown in Table 8–1 (all tables are located at the end of the chapter prior to the Problem Materials) and are based on the 150 percent declining-balance method, using the half-year convention[5] and an assumption of zero salvage value. The rates in the cost recovery tables at the end of the chapter reflect the relevant methods, conventions, and assumptions.

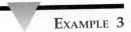

EXAMPLE 3   Green Utilities acquired 15-year public utility property in 1985 at a cost of $100,000. The property was placed in service on September 1, 1985. Green's cost recovery allowance for 1994 is determined from Table 8–1. The cost recovery percentage for 1994 (recovery year 10) is 6%, and the cost recovery allowance is $6,000 ($100,000 cost × 6%). ▼

Note that in 1985, Green got a half-year's cost recovery deduction (since the **half-year convention** is reflected in the percentages in Table 8–1) although it held the property only four months.

In the year that personal property is disposed of, no cost recovery is allowed.

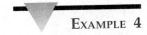

EXAMPLE 4   Assume the same facts as in the previous example and that the property is sold in May 1995. Green is not allowed a cost recovery deduction for the property in 1995. ▼

Reduction of Basis for Investment Tax Credit

For personalty placed in service after 1982 and before January 1, 1986, taxpayers were required to reduce the basis of the property for the ACRS write-off by one-half the amount of the investment tax credit taken on the property.[6] The investment tax credit was not allowed on realty (see Chapter 13 for details).

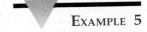

EXAMPLE 5   Transrail Company acquired a railroad tank car on September 4, 1985 for $100,000. The tank car was 10-year ACRS property, and Transrail claimed a $10,000 investment tax credit ($100,000 × 10% investment tax credit rate). The basis of the tank car was reduced by $5,000 (one-half of the $10,000 investment tax credit). Therefore, the basis for cost recovery was $95,000. The cost recovery allowance for 1994 is $8,550 ($95,000 cost recovery basis × 9% rate for recovery year 10). ▼

As an alternative to reducing the basis of the property, a taxpayer could elect to take a *reduced* investment tax credit. Under this election, the investment tax credit was 8 percent (rather than 10 percent) for recovery property other than three-year property and 4 percent (instead of 6 percent) for three-year property. In Example 5, if the reduced investment tax credit election were made, Transrail's cost recovery basis would be $100,000 rather than $95,000.

---

[5] The half-year convention assumes all property is placed in service at mid-year and thus provides for a half-year's cost recovery.

[6] § 48(q).

TRA of 1986 generally repealed the investment tax credit for property placed in service after December 31, 1985. Therefore, the reduction of basis for the investment tax credit does not apply to such property.

Classification of Property: MACRS

The general effect of TRA of 1986 was to lengthen asset lives. The **modified accelerated cost recovery system (MACRS)** provides that the cost recovery basis of eligible personalty (and certain realty) is recovered over 3, 5, 7, 10, 15, or 20 years. Property is classified by recovery period under MACRS as follows:[7]

3-year 200% class..... ADR midpoints of 4 years and less.[8] Excludes automobiles and light trucks. Includes racehorses more than 2 years old and other horses more than 12 years old.

5-year 200% class..... ADR midpoints of more than 4 years and less than 10 years, adding automobiles, light trucks, qualified technological equipment, renewable energy and biomass properties that are small power production facilities, research and experimentation property, semiconductor manufacturing equipment, and computer-based central office switching equipment.

7-year 200% class..... ADR midpoints of 10 years and more and less than 16 years, adding single-purpose agricultural or horticultural structures and property with no ADR midpoint not classified elsewhere. Includes railroad track and office furniture, fixtures, and equipment.

10-year 200% class..... ADR midpoints of 16 years and more and less than 20 years.

15-year 150% class..... ADR midpoints of 20 years and more and less than 25 years, including sewage treatment plants, and telephone distribution plants and comparable equipment used for the two-way exchange of voice and data communications.

20-year 150% class..... ADR midpoints of 25 years and more, other than real property with an ADR midpoint of 27.5 years and more, and including sewer pipes.

Accelerated depreciation is allowed for these six MACRS classes of property. Two hundred percent declining-balance is used for the 3-, 5-, 7-, and 10-year classes, with a switchover to straight-line depreciation when it yields a larger amount. One hundred and fifty percent declining-balance is allowed for the 15- and 20-year classes, with an appropriate straight-line switchover.[9]

Taxpayers may *elect* the straight-line method to compute cost recovery allowances for each of these classes of property. Certain property is not eligible for accelerated cost recovery and must be depreciated under an alternative depreciation system (ADS). Both the straight-line election and ADS are discussed later in the chapter.

The original ACRS system gave the taxpayer a half-year of cost recovery for the tax year an asset was placed in service but allowed the taxpayer to recover the balance of the cost recovery basis over the years remaining in the property's recovery period. No cost recovery deduction was permitted for the year of disposition or retirement of the property. Thus, conceptually, the taxpayer was

[7] § 168(e).

[8] Rev.Proc. 87–56, 1987–2 C.B. 674 is the source for the ADR midpoint lives.

[9] § 168(b).

considered to have placed property in service at the beginning of the recovery period but was allowed only a half-year's worth of cost recovery for the year it was placed in service.

By contrast, MACRS views property as placed in service in the middle of the first year.[10] Thus, for example, the statutory recovery period for three-year property begins in the middle of the year an asset is placed in service and ends three years later. In practical terms, this means that taxpayers must wait an extra year to recover the cost of depreciable assets. That is, the actual write-off periods are 4, 6, 8, 11, 16, and 21 years. MACRS also allows for a half-year of cost recovery in the year of disposition or retirement.

The procedure for computing the cost recovery allowance under MACRS is the same as under the original ACRS method. The cost recovery basis is multiplied by the percentages that reflect the applicable cost recovery method and the applicable convention. The percentages are shown in Table 8–2.

EXAMPLE 6   Kareem acquires a five-year class asset on April 10, 1994, for $30,000. Kareem's cost recovery deduction for 1994 is $6,000 [$30,000 × .20 (Table 8–2)]. ▼

EXAMPLE 7   Assume the same facts as in Example 6, and that Kareem disposes of the asset on March 5, 1996. Kareem's cost recovery deduction for 1996 is $2,880 [$30,000 × ½ × .192 (Table 8–2)]. ▼

Mid-Quarter Convention

Under the original ACRS rules for personal property, the half-year convention was used no matter when property was acquired during the year. Thus, if a substantial dollar amount of assets was acquired late in the tax year, the half-year convention still applied. The law now contains a provision to curtail the benefits of such a tax strategy. If more than 40 percent of the value of property other than eligible real estate (see Realty: Recovery Periods and Methods: MACRS for a discussion of eligible real estate) is placed in service during the last quarter of the year, a **mid-quarter convention** applies.[11] Property acquisitions are then grouped by the quarter they were acquired for cost recovery purposes. Acquisitions during the first quarter are allowed 10.5 months of cost recovery; the second quarter, 7.5 months; the third quarter, 4.5 months; and the fourth quarter, 1.5 months. The percentages are shown in Table 8–3.

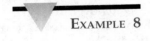

EXAMPLE 8   Silver Corporation acquires the following five-year class property in 1994:

Property Acquisition Dates	Cost
February 15	$ 200,000
July 10	400,000
December 5	600,000
Total	$1,200,000

If Silver Corporation uses the statutory percentage method, the cost recovery allowances for the first two years are computed as indicated below. Since more than 40% ($600,000/$1,200,000 = 50%) of the acquisitions are in the last quarter, the mid-quarter convention applies.

---

[10]§ 168(d)(4)(A).   [11]§ 168(d)(3).

1994

February 15	[$200,000 × .35 (Table 8–3)]	$ 70,000
July 10	($400,000 × .15)	60,000
December 5	($600,000 × .05)	30,000
Total		$160,000

1995

February 15	[$200,000 × .26 (Table 8–3)]	$ 52,000
July 10	($400,000 × .34)	136,000
December 5	($600,000 × .38)	228,000
Total		$416,000

CONCEPT SUMMARY 8–2

Cost Recovery Periods: MACRS

Class of Property	Examples
3-year	Tractor units for use over-the-road.
	Any horse that is not a racehorse and is more than 12 years old at the time it is placed in service.
	Any racehorse that is more than 2 years old at the time it is placed in service.
	Breeding hogs.
	Special tools used in the manufacturing of motor vehicles such as dies, fixtures, molds, and patterns.
5-year	Automobiles and taxis.
	Light and heavy general-purpose trucks.
	Buses.
	Trailers and trailer-mounted containers.
	Typewriters, calculators, and copiers.
	Computers and peripheral equipment.
	Breeding and dairy cattle.
7-year	Office furniture, fixtures, and equipment.
	Breeding and work horses.
	Agricultural machinery and equipment.
	Single-purpose agricultural or horticultural structures.
	Railroad track.
10-year	Vessels, barges, tugs, and similar water transportation equipment.
	Assets used for petroleum refining, manufacture of grain and grain mill products, manufacture of sugar and sugar products, and manufacture of vegetable oils and vegetable oil products.
15-year	Land improvements.
	Assets used for industrial steam and electric generation and/or distribution systems.
	Assets used in the manufacture of cement.
	Assets used in pipeline transportation.
	Electric utility nuclear production plant.
	Municipal wastewater treatment plant.
20-year	Farm buildings except single-purpose agricultural and horticultural structures.
	Gas utility distribution facilities.
	Water utilities.
	Municipal sewer.

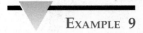

EXAMPLE 9

Assume the same facts as in Example 8, except that Silver Corporation sells the $400,000 asset on November 30 of 1995. The cost recovery allowance for 1995 is computed as follows:

February 15	[$200,000 × .26 (Table 8–3)]	$ 52,000
July 10	[$400,000 × .34 × (3.5/4)]	119,000
December 5	($600,000 × .38)	228,000
Total		$399,000

REALTY: RECOVERY PERIODS AND METHODS

ACRS

Under the original ACRS rules, realty was assigned a 15-year recovery period. Real property other than low-income housing is depreciated using the 175 percent declining-balance method, with a switchover to straight-line depreciation when it yields a larger amount. Low-income housing is depreciated using the 200 percent declining-balance method, with an appropriate straight-line switchover. In either case, zero salvage value is assumed. Statutory percentages for real property are shown in Table 8–4, which contains rates for low-income housing as well as for other 15-year real estate. As explained later in the chapter, taxpayers were allowed to elect the straight-line method for real property.

The half-year convention does not apply to 15-year real property. As a result, Table 8–4 is structured differently from Tables 8–1 and 8–2. The cost recovery deduction for 15-year real property is based on the month the asset is placed in service rather than on the half-year convention.

EXAMPLE 10

Alicia purchased a warehouse for $100,000 on January 1, 1984. The cost recovery allowance for the years 1984 through 1994, using the statutory percentage method, is as follows (see Table 8–4 for percentages):

1984—$12,000 (12% × $100,000)

1985—$10,000 (10% × $100,000)

1986—$ 9,000 (9% × $100,000)

1987—$ 8,000 (8% × $100,000)

1988—$ 7,000 (7% × $100,000)

1989—$ 6,000 (6% × $100,000)

1990—$ 6,000 (6% × $100,000)

1991—$ 6,000 (6% × $100,000)

1992—$ 6,000 (6% × $100,000)

1993—$ 5,000 (5% × $100,000)

1994—$ 5,000 (5% × $100,000)

EXAMPLE 11

Assume the same facts as in Example 10, except the property is low-income housing. Cost recovery deductions using the statutory percentage method for 1984 through 1994 are as follows (see Table 8–4 for percentages):

1984—$13,000 (13% × $100,000)

1985—$12,000 (12% × $100,000)

1986—$10,000 (10% × $100,000)

1987—$ 9,000 (9% × $100,000)

1988—$ 8,000 (8% × $100,000)

1989—$ 7,000 (7% × $100,000)

```
1990—$ 6,000   (6% × $100,000)
1991—$ 5,000   (5% × $100,000)
1992—$ 5,000   (5% × $100,000)
1993—$ 5,000   (5% × $100,000)
1994—$ 4,000   (4% × $100,000)
```

The Deficit Reduction Act of 1984 changed the recovery period for real property to 18 years. This applies generally to property placed in service after March 15, 1984. However, the 15-year recovery period was retained for low-income housing as well as for other real property placed in service before March 16, 1984.

Eighteen-year real property placed in service after June 22, 1984, is subject to a **mid-month convention**.[12] This means that real property placed in service at any time during a particular month is treated as if it were placed in service in the middle of the month. This allows for one-half month's cost recovery for the month the property is placed in service. If the property is disposed of before the end of the recovery period, one-half month's cost recovery is permitted for the month of disposition regardless of the specific date of disposition. Statutory percentages for 18-year real property with a mid-month convention are shown in Table 8–5.

EXAMPLE 12   Rex purchased a building for $300,000 and placed it in service on August 21, 1984. The first year's cost recovery using the statutory percentage method is $12,000 (4% × $300,000). (See Table 8–5 for percentages.) ▼

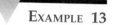

EXAMPLE 13   Assume the same facts as in Example 12 and that Rex disposes of the building on May 3, 1994. The cost recovery in the year of disposition is $5,625 ($300,000 × 5% × 4.5/12). ▼

Public Law 99–121 extended the minimum recovery period for real property (except low-income housing) from 18 years to 19 years. This applies to property placed in service after May 8, 1985, and before January 1, 1987. Statutory percentages for 19-year real property are shown in Table 8–6. Because the percentages are determined using a mid-month convention, the computation of cost recovery is mechanically the same as for 18-year property with the mid-month convention.

MACRS

Under MACRS, the cost recovery period for residential rental real estate is 27.5 years, and the straight-line method is used for computing the cost recovery allowance. **Residential rental real estate** includes property where 80 percent or more of the gross rental revenues are from nontransient dwelling units (e.g., an apartment building). Hotels, motels, and similar establishments are not residential rental property. Low-income housing is classified as residential rental real estate. Nonresidential real estate has a recovery period of 31.5 years (39 years for such property placed in service after May 12, 1993) and is also depreciated using the straight-line method.[13]

---

[12] A transitional rule, which provides for a full-month convention, is effective for property placed in service after March 15, 1984, and

before June 23, 1984. The cost recovery tables for property placed in service during this period are not included in this chapter.

[13] §§ 168(b), (c), and (e).

Some items of real property are not treated as real estate for purposes of MACRS. For example, single-purpose agricultural structures are in the 7-year MACRS class. Land improvements are in the 15-year MACRS class.

All eligible real estate is depreciated using the mid-month convention. Regardless of when during the month the property is placed in service, it is deemed to have been placed in service at the middle of the month. In the year of disposition, a mid-month convention is also used.

Cost recovery is computed by multiplying the applicable rate (Table 8–7) by the cost recovery basis.

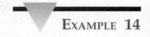
EXAMPLE 14

Ann acquired a building on April 1, 1993, for $800,000. If the building is classified as residential rental real estate, the cost recovery allowance for 1994 is $29,088 (.03636 × $800,000). If the building is classified as nonresidential real estate, the 1994 cost recovery allowance is $25,400 (.03175 × $800,000). (See Table 8–7 for percentages.) ▼

As part of the deficit reduction legislation of the Clinton administration (Revenue Reconciliation Act of 1993), nonresidential real estate placed in service after May 12, 1993, is subject to a 39-year recovery period. Property placed in service before 1994 that, as of May 12, 1993, was subject to a binding contract to construct or purchase may still be treated as 31.5-year property under the prior rules.

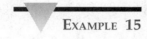
EXAMPLE 15

Assume the same facts as in Example 14, except Ann acquired the nonresidential building on November 19, 1994. The 1994 cost recovery allowance is $2,568 (.00321 × $800,000). (See Table 8-7 for percentages.) ▼

CONCEPT SUMMARY 8–3

Statutory Percentage Method under ACRS and MACRS

	Personal Property	ACRS Real Property		
		15-Year	18-Year	19-Year
Convention	Half-year	Full-month	Mid-month	Mid-month
Cost recovery deduction in the year of disposition	None	Full-month for month of disposition	Half-month for month of disposition	Half-month for month of disposition

	MACRS	
	Personal Property	Real Property*
Convention	Half-year or mid-quarter	Mid-month
Cost recovery deduction in the year of disposition	Half-year for year of disposition or half-quarter for quarter of disposition	Half-month for month of disposition

*Straight-line method must be used.

STRAIGHT-LINE ELECTION UNDER ACRS AND MACRS
ACRS

Under ACRS, taxpayers could *elect* to write off an asset using the straight-line method rather than the statutory percentage method. The straight-line recovery period could be the same as the prescribed recovery period under the statutory percentage method, or a longer period. The allowable straight-line recovery periods for each class of property are summarized as follows:

3-year property	3, 5, or 12 years
5-year property	5, 12, or 25 years
10-year property	10, 25, or 35 years
15-year property	15, 35, or 45 years
18-year real property and low-income housing (placed in service after March 15, 1984)	18, 35, or 45 years
19-year real property and low-income housing (placed in service after May 8, 1985)	19, 35, or 45 years

If the straight-line option was elected for personal property, the half-year convention applies in computing the cost recovery deduction. The effect of electing the straight-line method for personal property is to extend the statutory recovery period by one year (e.g., three to four and five to six years). There is no cost recovery deduction in the year of the disposition of the property.

EXAMPLE 16

On May 6, 1985, Owl Utilities paid $20,000 for coal-fired boilers to replace gas-fired boilers (10-year property). Owl elected to compute the cost recovery allowance using the optional straight-line method and the regular cost recovery period. Owl's cost recovery allowance for 1985 was $1,000 ($20,000 basis × 10% straight-line rate × ½ year). The cost recovery allowance is $2,000 for 1994 ($20,000 basis × 10% straight-line rate) and $1,000 for 1995 ($20,000 basis × 10% straight-line rate × ½ year). These cost recovery allowances reflect the half-year convention for the first and last years of the cost recovery period. ▼

For each class of personal property, the straight-line election applied to *all* assets in a *particular class* that were placed in service during the year for which the election was made. The election applies for the entire recovery period of these assets. The election is not binding for personal property of the same class placed in service in another taxable year.

Under the straight-line option for 15-year *real* property, the first year's cost recovery deduction and the cost recovery deduction for the year of disposition are computed on the basis of the number of months the property was in service during the year.

EXAMPLE 17

Kate acquired a store building on October 1, 1983, at a cost of $150,000. She elected the straight-line method using a recovery period of 15 years. Kate's cost recovery deduction for 1983 was $2,500 [($150,000 ÷ 15) × 3/12]. ▼

EXAMPLE 18

Assume the same facts as in Example 17 and that Kate disposes of the asset on September 30, 1994. Kate's cost recovery deduction for 1994 is $7,500 [($150,000 ÷ 15) × 9/12]. ▼

Under the straight-line option for 18-year or 19-year real property, the cost recovery allowances in the year the property is placed in service and in the year of disposition are computed in the same manner (except for the use of different rates) as under the statutory percentage method. Note that 18-year and 19-year real property use a mid-month convention, whereas 15-year real property uses a full-month convention. Table 8–8 contains the applicable percentages to be used under the straight-line option for 19-year real property. (The tables that contain the percentages for 18-year real property using the straight-line method over 18, 35, and 45 years and 19-year real property using the straight-line method over 35 and 45 years are not reproduced in this text.)

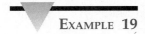

EXAMPLE 19

Ned acquired 19-year real property on October 1, 1986, at a cost of $150,000. He elected the straight-line method of cost recovery. Ned's cost recovery deduction for 1986 was $1,650 [$150,000 × 1.1% (Table 8–8)]. ▼

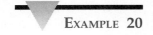

EXAMPLE 20

Assume the same facts as in Example 19 and that Ned disposes of the asset on September 20, 1994. Ned's cost recovery deduction for 1994 is $5,631 [($150,000 × 5.3% × 8.5/12) (Table 8–8)]. ▼

The straight-line election for 15-year, 18-year, or 19-year real property may be made on a *property-by-property* basis within the same year.

MACRS

Although MACRS requires straight-line depreciation for all eligible real estate as previously discussed, the taxpayer may *elect* to use the straight-line method for personal property.[14] The property is depreciated using the class life (recovery period) of the asset with a half-year convention or a mid-quarter convention, whichever is applicable. The election is available on a class-by-class and year-by-year basis. The percentages for the straight-line election with a half-year convention appear in Table 8–9.

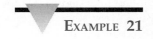

EXAMPLE 21

Terry acquires a 10-year class asset on August 4, 1994, for $100,000. He elects the straight-line method of cost recovery. Terry's cost recovery deduction for 1994 is $5,000 ($100,000 × .050). His cost recovery deduction for 1995 is $10,000 ($100,000 × .100). (See Table 8–9 for percentages.) ▼

ELECTION TO EXPENSE ASSETS

Section 179 (Election to Expense Certain Depreciable Business Assets) permits the taxpayer to elect to write off up to $17,500[15] of the acquisition cost of *tangible personal property* used in a trade or business. Amounts that are expensed under § 179 may not be capitalized and depreciated. The **§ 179 expensing** election is an annual election and applies to the acquisition cost of property placed in service that year. The immediate expense election is not available for real property or for property used for the production of income.[16]

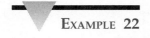

EXAMPLE 22

Kelly acquires machinery (five-year class) on February 1, 1994, at a cost of $40,000 and elects to expense $17,500 under § 179. Kelly's statutory percentage cost recovery deduction for 1994 is $4,500 [($40,000 cost – $17,500 expensed) × .200]. (See Table 8–2 for percentage.) Kelly's total deduction for 1994 is $22,000 ($17,500 + $4,500). ▼

---

[14] § 168(b)(5).

[15] This amount was $10,000 for property placed in service in tax years beginning before January 1, 1993.

[16] §§ 179(b) and (d). The amount shown is per taxpayer, per year. On a joint return, the statutory amounts apply to the couple. If the taxpayers are married and file separate returns, each spouse is eligible for 50% of the statutory amount.

CONCEPT SUMMARY 8–4

Straight-Line Election under ACRS and MACRS

ACRS

	Personal Property	Real Property		
		15-Year	18-Year	19-Year
Convention	Half-year	Full-month	Mid-month	Mid-month
Cost recovery deduction in the year of disposition	None	Full-month for month of disposition	Half-month for month of disposition	Half-month for month of disposition
Elective or mandatory	Elective	Elective	Elective	Elective
Breadth of election	Class by class	Property by property	Property by property	Property by property

MACRS

	Personal Property	Real Property
Convention	Half-year or mid-quarter	Mid-month
Cost recovery deduction in the year of disposition	Half-year for year of dispositon or half-quarter for quarter of disposition	Half-month for month of disposition
Elective or mandatory	Elective	Mandatory
Breadth of election	Class by class	

Annual Limitations

Two additional limitations apply to the amount deductible under § 179. First, the ceiling amount on the deduction is reduced dollar-for-dollar when property (other than eligible real estate) placed in service during the taxable year exceeds $200,000. Second, the amount expensed under § 179 cannot exceed the aggregate amount of taxable income derived from the conduct of any trade or business by the taxpayer. Taxable income of a trade or business is computed without regard to the amount expensed under § 179. Any § 179 expensed amount in excess of taxable income is carried forward to future taxable years and added to other amounts eligible for expensing (and is subject to the ceiling rules for the carryforward years).

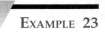

EXAMPLE 23

Jill owns a computer service and operates it as a sole proprietorship. In 1994, she will net $11,000 before considering any § 179 deduction. If Jill spends $204,000 on new equipment, her § 179 expense deduction is computed as follows:

§ 179 deduction before adjustment	$17,500
Less: Dollar limitation reduction ($204,000 – $200,000)	(4,000)
Remaining § 179 deduction	$13,500
Business income limitation	$11,000
§ 179 deduction allowed	$11,000
§ 179 deduction carryforward ($13,500 – $11,000)	$ 2,500

Effect on Basis

The basis of the property for cost recovery purposes is reduced by the § 179 amount after it is adjusted for property placed in service in excess of $200,000. This adjusted amount does not reflect any business income limitation.

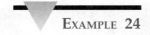

EXAMPLE 24

Assume the same facts as in Example 23 and that the new equipment is five-year class property. Jill's statutory percentage cost recovery deduction for 1994 is $38,100 [($204,000 – $13,500) × .200]. (See Table 8–2 for percentage.) ▼

Conversion to Personal Use

Conversion of the expensed property to personal use at any time results in recapture income (see Chapter 17). A property is converted to personal use if it is not used predominantly in a trade or business. Regulations provide for the mechanics of the recapture.[17]

BUSINESS AND PERSONAL USE OF AUTOMOBILES AND OTHER LISTED PROPERTY

Limits exist on ACRS and MACRS deductions with respect to business and personal use of automobiles and other listed property.[18] If the listed property is *predominantly used* for business, the taxpayer is allowed to use the statutory percentage method to recover the cost. In cases where the property is *not predominantly used* for business, the cost is recovered using a straight-line recovery.

Listed property includes the following:

- Any passenger automobile.
- Any other property used as a means of transportation.
- Any property of a type generally used for purposes of entertainment, recreation, or amusement.
- Any computer or peripheral equipment, with the exception of equipment used exclusively at a regular business establishment, including a qualifying home office.
- Any cellular telephone or other similar telecommunications equipment.
- Any other property specified in the Regulations.[19]

Automobiles and Other Listed Property Used Predominantly in Business

For listed property to be considered as predominantly used in business, the percentage of use for business must exceed 50 percent.[20] The use of listed property for production of income does not qualify as business use for purposes of the more-than-50 percent test. However, if the more-than-50 percent test is met, both production of income and business use percentages are used to compute the cost recovery deduction.

EXAMPLE 25

On September 1, 1994, Shontelle places in service listed five-year recovery property. The property cost $10,000. If Shontelle uses the property 40% for business and 25% for the production of income, the property will not be considered as predominantly used for business. The cost would be recovered using straight-line cost recovery. If, however, Shontelle uses the property 60% for business and 25% for the production of income, the property will be considered as used predominantly for business. Therefore, she may use the statutory percentage method. Shontelle's cost recovery allowance for the year would be $1,700 ($10,000 × .200 × 85%). ▼

---

[17] Reg. § 1.179–1(e).
[18] § 280F.

[19] § 280F(d)(4).
[20] § 280F(b)(4).

The method for determining the percentage of business usage for listed property is specified in the Regulations. The Regulations provide that for automobiles a mileage-based percentage is to be used. Other listed property is to use the most appropriate unit of time (e.g., hours) the property is actually used (rather than available for use).[21]

The law places special limitations on the cost recovery deduction for passenger automobiles. These statutory dollar limits were imposed on passenger automobiles because of the belief that the tax system was being used to underwrite automobiles whose cost and luxury far exceeded what was needed for their business use.

A *passenger automobile* is any four-wheeled vehicle manufactured for use on public streets, roads, and highways with an unloaded gross vehicle weight rating of 6,000 pounds or less.[22] This definition specifically excludes vehicles used directly in the business of transporting people or property for compensation such as taxicabs, ambulances, hearses, and trucks and vans as prescribed by the Regulations.

The following limits apply to the cost recovery deductions for passenger automobiles:[23]

Year	Recovery Limitation
1	$2,860
2	4,600
3	2,750
Succeeding years until the cost is recovered	1,675

These limits are imposed before any percentage reduction for personal use. In addition, the limitation in the first year includes any amount the taxpayer elects to expense under § 179.[24] If the passenger automobile is used partly for personal use, the personal use percentage is ignored for the purpose of determining the unrecovered cost available for deduction in later years.

EXAMPLE 26

On July 1, 1994, Dan places in service an automobile that cost $15,000. The car is always used 80% for business and 20% for personal use. The cost recovery for the automobile would be as follows:

1994—$2,288   [$15,000 × 20% (limited to $2,860) × 80%]
1995—$3,680   [$15,000 × 32% (limited to $4,600) × 80%]
1996—$2,200   [$15,000 × 19.2% (limited to $2,750) × 80%]
1997—$1,340   [$15,000 × 11.52% (limited to $1,675) × 80%]
1998—$1,340   [$15,000 × 11.52% (limited to $1,675) × 80%]
1999—$1,152   [$1,440 unrecovered cost ($15,000 – $13,560*) (limited to $1,675) × 80%]

*($2,860 + $4,600 + $2,750 + $1,675 + $1,675). Although the statutory percentage method appears to restrict the deduction to $691 [$15,000 × 5.76% (limited to $1,675) × 80%], the unrecovered cost of $1,440 (limited to $1,675) multiplied by the business usage percentage is deductible. At the start of 1997 (year 4), there is an automatic switch to the straight-line cost recovery method. Under this method, the unrecovered cost up to the maximum allowable limit ($1,675) is deductible in the last year of the recovery period (1999 or year 6). Because the limit may restrict the deduction (it does not in this example), any remaining unrecovered cost is deductible in the next or succeeding year(s), subject to the maximum allowable yearly limit ($1,675), multiplied by the business usage percentage.

[21] Reg. § 1.280F–6T(e).
[22] § 280F(d)(5).

[23] § 280F(a)(2). The 1993 amounts are used because the indexed amounts for 1994 were not available at the time of this writing.
[24] § 280F(d)(1).

The total cost recovery for the years 1994–1999 is $12,000 (80% business usage × $15,000). ▼

The cost recovery limitations are maximum amounts. If the regular calculation produces a lesser amount of cost recovery, the lesser amount is used.

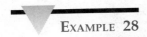

EXAMPLE 27 On April 2, 1994, Gail places in service an automobile that cost $10,000. The car is always used 70% for business and 30% for personal use. The cost recovery allowance for 1994 is $1,400 ($10,000 × 20% × 70%), which is less than $2,002 ($2,860 × 70%). ▼

Note that the cost recovery limitations apply *only* to passenger automobiles and not to other listed property.

Automobiles and Other Listed Property Not Used Predominantly in Business

The cost of listed property that does not pass the more-than-50 percent business usage test in the year the property is placed in service must be recovered using the straight-line method.[25] The straight-line method to be used is that required under the alternative depreciation system (explained later in the chapter). This system requires a straight-line recovery period of five years for automobiles. However, even though the straight-line method is used, the cost recovery allowance for passenger automobiles cannot exceed the dollar limitations.

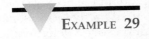

EXAMPLE 28 On July 27, 1994, Fred places in service an automobile that cost $20,000. The auto is used 40% for business and 60% for personal use. The cost recovery allowance for 1994 is $800 [$20,000 × 10% (Table 8–11) × 40%]. ▼

EXAMPLE 29 Assume the same facts as in Example 28, except that the auto cost $50,000. The cost recovery allowance for 1994 is $1,144 [$50,000 × 10% (Table 8–11) = $5,000 (limited to $2,860) × 40%]. ▼

If the listed property fails the more-than-50 percent business usage test, the straight-line method must be used for the remainder of the property's life. This applies even if at some later date the business usage of the property increases to more than 50 percent. However, even though the straight-line method must continue to be used, the amount of cost recovery will reflect the increase in business usage.

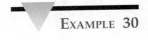

EXAMPLE 30 Assume the same facts as in Example 28, except that in 1995, Fred uses the auto 70% for business and 30% for personal use. Fred's cost recovery allowance for 1995 is $2,800 [$20,000 × 20% (Table 8–11) × 70%]. ▼

Change from Predominantly Business Use

If the business use percentage of listed property falls to 50 percent or lower after the year the property is placed in service, the property is subject to *cost recovery recapture*. The amount required to be recaptured and included in the taxpayer's return as ordinary income is the excess depreciation.

Excess depreciation is the excess of the cost recovery deduction taken in prior years using the statutory percentage method over the amount that would have been allowed if the straight-line method had been used since the property was placed in service.[26]

---

[25]§ 280F(b)(2).

[26]§ 280F(b)(3).

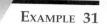

EXAMPLE 31

Seth purchased a car on January 22, 1994, at a cost of $20,000. Business usage was 80% in 1994, 70% in 1995, 40% in 1996, and 60% in 1997. Statutory percentage cost recovery deductions in 1994 and 1995 are $2,288 (80% × $2,860) and $3,220 (70% × $4,600), respectively. Seth's excess depreciation to be recaptured as ordinary income in 1996 is $1,108, calculated as follows:

1994	
Statutory percentage allowance	$ 2,288
Straight-line ($20,000 × 10% × 80%)	(1,600)
Excess	$ 688

1995	
Statutory percentage allowance	$ 3,220
Straight-line ($20,000 × 20% × 70%)	(2,800)
1995 excess	$ 420
1994 excess	688
Total excess	$ 1,108

▼

After the business usage of the listed property drops below the more-than-50 percent level, the straight-line method must be used for the remaining life of the property.

EXAMPLE 32

Assume the same facts as in Example 31. Seth's cost recovery allowance for the years 1996 and 1997 would be $1,100 and $1,005, computed as follows:

1996—$1,100	[($20,000 × 20%) limited to $2,750 × 40%]
1997—$1,005	[($20,000 × 20%) limited to $1,675 × 60%]

▼

Leased Automobiles

A taxpayer who leases a passenger automobile must report an *inclusion amount* in gross income. The inclusion amount is computed from an IRS table for each taxable year for which the taxpayer leases the automobile. The purpose of this provision is to prevent taxpayers from circumventing the cost recovery dollar limitations by leasing, instead of purchasing, an automobile.

The dollar amount of the inclusion is based on the fair market value of the automobile and is prorated for the number of days the auto is used during the taxable year. The prorated dollar amount is then multiplied by the business and income-producing usage percentage to determine the amount to be included in gross income.[27] The taxpayer deducts the lease payments, multiplied by the business and income-producing usage percentage. The net effect is that the annual deduction for the lease payment is reduced by the inclusion amount.

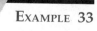

EXAMPLE 33

On April 1, 1994, Jim leases and places in service a passenger automobile worth $40,000. The lease is to be for a period of five years. During the taxable years 1994 and 1995, Jim uses the automobile 70% for business and 30% for personal use. Assuming the dollar amounts

---

[27] Reg. § 1.280F–7T(a).

from the IRS table for 1994 and 1995 are $143 and $314, Jim must include $75 in gross income for 1994 and $220 for 1995, computed as follows:

| 1994 | $143 × (275/365) × 70% = $75 |
| 1995 | $314 × (365/365) × 70% = $220 |

In addition, Jim can deduct 70% of the lease payments each year because this is the business use percentage. ▼

Substantiation Requirements

Listed property is now subject to the substantiation requirements of § 274. This means that the taxpayer must prove the business usage as to the amount of expense or use, the time and place of use, the business purpose for the use, and the business relationship to the taxpayer of persons using the property. Substantiation requires adequate records or sufficient evidence corroborating the taxpayer's statement. However, these substantiation requirements do not apply to

CONCEPT SUMMARY 8–5

Listed Property Cost Recovery

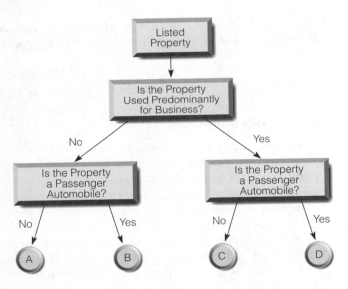

Legend to Tax Treatment

A　Straight-line cost recovery reduced by the personal use percentage.

B　Straight-line cost recovery subject to the recovery limitations ($2,860, $4,600, $2,750, $1,675) and reduced by the personal use percentage.

C　Statutory percentage cost recovery reduced by the personal use percentage.

D　Statutory percentage cost recovery subject to the recovery limitations ($2,860, $4,600, $2,750, $1,675) and reduced by the personal use percentage.

vehicles that, by reason of their nature, are not likely to be used more than a *de minimis* amount for personal purposes.[28]

Substantiating Business Mileage

J ake, a physician, uses his car to go from his office to the hospital to see patients. He makes this trip at least once daily and quite often two or three times a day. In addition, he uses the car for commuting to his office from home and for other personal use.

Last year, as instructed by his CPA, Jake maintained a mileage log that he kept in the glove compartment of his car. He recorded his business mileage at the end of each day.

This year Jake maintained the mileage log for the month of January and compared it with his log for last year. This year's mileage was within 10 miles of last year's. Concluding that maintaining the log was a waste of his time, Jake recorded no entries for the rest of 1994.

At his annual meeting with his CPA to discuss his 1994 tax return, Jake said that his business mileage and personal use mileage were "the same as last year."

ALTERNATIVE DEPRECIATION SYSTEM (ADS)

The **alternative depreciation system (ADS)** must be used for the following:[29]

- To calculate the portion of depreciation treated as an alternative minimum tax (AMT) adjustment for purposes of the corporate and individual AMT (see Chapters 12 and 20).
- To compute depreciation allowances for property for which any of the following is true:
  - Used predominantly outside the United States.
  - Leased or otherwise used by a tax-exempt entity.
  - Financed with the proceeds of tax-exempt bonds.
  - Imported from foreign countries that maintain discriminatory trade practices or otherwise engage in discriminatory acts.
- To compute depreciation allowances for earnings and profits purposes (see Chapter 20).

In general, ADS depreciation is computed using straight-line recovery without regard to salvage value. However, for purposes of the AMT, depreciation of personal property is computed using the 150 percent declining-balance method with an appropriate switch to the straight-line method.

The taxpayer must use the half-year or the mid-quarter convention, whichever is applicable, for all property other than eligible real estate. The mid-month convention is used for eligible real estate. The applicable ADS rates are found in Tables 8–10, 8–11, and 8–12.

The recovery periods under ADS are as follows:[30]

- The ADR midpoint life for property that does not fall into any of the following listed categories.
- Five years for qualified technological equipment, automobiles, and light-duty trucks.

---

[28] §§ 274(d) and (i).
[29] § 168(g).

[30] The class life for certain properties described in § 168(e)(3) are specially determined under § 168(g)(3)(B).

• Twelve years for personal property with no class life.
• Forty years for all residential rental property and all nonresidential real property.

Taxpayers may *elect* to use the 150 percent declining-balance method to compute the regular tax rather than the 200 percent declining-balance method that is available for personal property. Hence, if the election is made, there will be no difference between the cost recovery for computing the regular tax and the AMT. However, taxpayers who make this election must use the ADS recovery periods in computing the cost recovery for the regular tax, and the ADS recovery periods generally are longer than the regular recovery periods under MACRS.

The following are examples of the classification of property by class life for the ADS recovery periods:[31]

3-year	Special tools used in the manufacture of motor vehicles, breeding hogs.
5-year	Automobiles, light general-purpose trucks.
7-year	Breeding and dairy cattle.
9.5-year	Computer-based telephone central office switching equipment.
10-year	Office furniture, fixtures, and equipment, railroad track.
12-year	Racehorses more than 2 years old at the time they are placed in service.

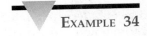

EXAMPLE 34

On March 1, 1994, Abby purchases computer-based telephone central office switching equipment for $80,000. If Abby uses statutory percentage cost recovery (assuming no § 179 election), the cost recovery allowance for 1994 is $16,000 [$80,000 × 20% (Table 8–2, 5-year class property)]. If Abby elects to use ADS 150% declining-balance cost recovery (assuming no § 179 election), the cost recovery allowance for 1994 is $6,312 [$80,000 × 7.89% (Table 8–10, 9.5-year class property)]. ▼

In lieu of depreciation under the regular MACRS method, taxpayers may *elect* straight-line under ADS for property that qualifies for the regular MACRS method. The election is available on a class-by-class and year-by-year basis for property other than eligible real estate. The election for eligible real estate is on a property-by-property basis. One reason for making this election is to avoid a difference between deductible depreciation and earnings and profits depreciation.

EXAMPLE 35

Polly acquires an apartment building on March 17, 1994, for $700,000. She takes the maximum cost recovery allowance for determining taxable income. Polly's cost recovery allowance for computing 1994 taxable income is $20,153 [$700,000 × .02879 (Table 8–7)]. However, Polly's cost recovery for computing her earnings and profits is only $13,853 [$700,000 × .01979 (Table 8–12)]. ▼

3 **LEARNING OBJECTIVE**
Identify intangible assets that are eligible for amortization and calculate the amount of the deduction.

AMORTIZATION

Prior to the Revenue Reconciliation Act of 1993 (RRA of 1993), the tax treatment of intangible assets had become a source of much controversy between taxpayers and the IRS. Disputes arose as to whether a covenant not to compete (an amortizable

---

[31] Rev.Proc. 87–56, 1987–2 C.B. 674 is the source for the recovery periods.

SUPREME COURT EXPANDS AMORTIZATION DEDUCTIONS

The Supreme Court has protected business from what could have been a multibillion-dollar tax hit in a case involving the treatment of intangible assets such as newspaper-subscriber lists.

The 5–4 high court ruling will benefit companies in a wide range of industries, including publishing, financial services, and insurance. The Court said that if companies can determine the dollar value and useful life of lists of readers, clients, or policy holders, they may seek Federal tax deductions based on the amortization of those intangible assets.

The majority rejected the long-established position of the IRS that such customer information generally can't be the basis for amortization deductions. It's difficult to project the extent of the government's revenue losses, but they could run into billions of dollars a year.

The issue of intangible-asset amortization frequently arises in the context of takeovers. This decision probably will make it easier for Congress to pass proposed pro-business legislation that would set specific amortization rules for intangible assets acquired in takeovers. That's because after taking account of the likely reduction in projected government revenues resulting from the Court ruling, the bill itself would be less likely to add further to the Federal deficit. Lawmakers and President Clinton might have wanted to avoid legislation that would enlarge the deficit amid the broader controversy over taxes and spending.

SOURCE: Adapted from Paul M. Barrett, "Business Wins Case over IRS in Top Court," *Wall Street Journal,* April 21, 1993, p. A3. Reprinted by permission of the *Wall Street Journal,* © 1993 Dow Jones & Company, Inc. All rights reserved worldwide.

asset) was separate and distinct from goodwill and going-concern value (a nonamortizable asset) or merely a transfer of goodwill.

Under RRA of 1993, taxpayers can claim an **amortization** deduction on intangible assets called "amortizable § 197 intangibles." The amount of the deduction is determined by amortizing the adjusted basis of such intangibles ratably over a 15-year period beginning in the month in which the intangible is acquired.[32]

An *amortizable § 197 intangible* is any § 197 intangible acquired after August 10, 1993, and held in connection with the conduct of a trade or business or for the production of income. Section 197 intangibles include goodwill and going-concern value, franchises (except sports franchises), trademarks, and trade names. Covenants not to compete, copyrights, and patents are also included if they are acquired in connection with the acquisition of a business. Generally, self-created intangibles are not § 197 intangibles. The 15-year amortization period applies regardless of the actual useful life of an amortizable § 197 intangible. No other depreciation or amortization deduction is permitted with respect to any amortizable § 197 intangible except those permitted under the 15-year amortization rules.

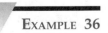

EXAMPLE 36

On June 1, 1994, Sally purchased and began operating the Falcon Cafe. Ninety thousand dollars of the purchase price is correctly allocated to goodwill. The deduction for amortization for 1994 is $3,500 [($90,000/15) × (7/12)]. ▼

---

[32]§ 197(a).

Allocating Intangible Assets When a Business Is Sold

Marge and Stan are negotiating Stan's purchase of Marge's business. Both are in the 36 percent tax bracket. They have agreed that the tangible assets of the business are worth $100,000. Marge's adjusted basis for these assets is $70,000. The only other asset of the business is the going-concern value. Marge believes that this asset is worth about $50,000. Stan believes that it is worth somewhat less, probably about $40,000.

Marge and Stan are handling their own negotiations since they do not believe in wasting money on attorneys or CPAs when such professional services are not required. Stan knows from an MBA class he took five years ago that goodwill is not deductible, but that a covenant not to compete can be deducted over the covenant period. Stan believes that Marge, who is age 67 and in poor health, is going to retire. In order to maximize the tax benefits to himself, Stan increases his offer from $140,000 to $145,000 (i.e., "we'll split the difference") if Marge will agree to sign a five-year covenant with $45,000 of the $145,000 purchase price allocated to the covenant. Marge, who believes that the tax consequences of the sale ($145,000 amount realized – $70,000 adjusted basis = $75,000 recognized gain) will be the same regardless of whether the $45,000 is for goodwill or for a covenant, accepts the offer.

▼ DEPLETION ▼

4   LEARNING OBJECTIVE
Determine the amount of depletion expense including being able to apply the alternative tax treatments for intangible drilling and development costs.

Natural resources (e.g., oil, gas, coal, gravel, timber) are subject to **depletion,** which is simply a form of depreciation applicable to natural resources. Land generally cannot be depleted.

The owner of an interest in the natural resource is entitled to deduct depletion. An owner is one who has an economic interest in the property.[33] An economic interest requires the acquisition of an interest in the resource in place and the receipt of income from the extraction or severance of that resource. Like depreciation, depletion is a deduction *for* adjusted gross income.

Although all natural resources are subject to depletion, oil and gas wells are used as an example in the following paragraphs to illustrate the related costs and issues.

In developing an oil or gas well, the producer must make four types of expenditures.

- Natural resource costs.
- Intangible drilling and development costs.
- Tangible asset costs.
- Operating costs.

Natural resources are physically limited, and the costs to acquire them (e.g., oil under the ground) are, therefore, recovered through depletion. Costs incurred in making the property ready for drilling such as the cost of labor in clearing the property, erecting derricks, and drilling the hole are **intangible drilling and development costs (IDC).** These costs generally have no salvage value and are a

---

[33] Reg. § 1.611–1(b).

lost cost if the well is dry. Costs for tangible assets such as tools, pipes, and engines are capital in nature. These costs must be capitalized and recovered through depreciation (cost recovery). Costs incurred after the well is producing are operating costs. These costs would include expenditures for such items as labor, fuel, and supplies. Operating costs are deductible when incurred (on the accrual basis) or when paid (on the cash basis).

The expenditures for depreciable assets and operating costs pose no unusual problems for producers of natural resources. The tax treatment of depletable costs and intangible drilling and development costs is quite a different matter.

INTANGIBLE DRILLING AND DEVELOPMENT COSTS

Intangible drilling and development costs (IDC) can be handled in one of two ways at the option of the taxpayer. They can be *either* charged off as an expense in the year in which they are incurred *or* capitalized and written off through depletion. The taxpayer makes the election in the first year such expenditures are incurred either by taking a deduction on the return or by adding them to the depletable basis. No formal statement of intent is required. Once made, the election is binding on both the taxpayer and the IRS for all such expenditures in the future. If the taxpayer fails to make the election to expense IDC on the original timely filed return the first year such expenditures are incurred, an automatic election to capitalize them has been made and is irrevocable.

As a general rule, it is more advantageous to expense IDC. The obvious benefit of an immediate write-off (as opposed to a deferred write-off through depletion) is not the only advantage. Since a taxpayer can use percentage depletion, which is calculated without reference to basis (see Example 40), the IDC may be completely lost as a deduction if they are capitalized.

DEPLETION METHODS

There are two methods of calculating depletion: cost and percentage. Cost depletion can be used on any wasting asset (and is the only method allowed for timber). Percentage depletion is subject to a number of limitations, particularly for oil and gas deposits. Depletion should be calculated both ways, and generally the method that results in the *larger* deduction is used. The choice between cost and percentage depletion is an annual election.

Cost Depletion

Cost depletion is determined by using the adjusted basis of the asset.[34] The basis is divided by the estimated recoverable units of the asset (e.g., barrels, tons) to arrive at the depletion per unit. The depletion per unit then is multiplied by the number of units sold (*not* the units produced) during the year to arrive at the cost depletion allowed. Cost depletion, therefore, resembles the units-of-production method of calculating depreciation.

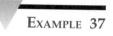

EXAMPLE 37

On January 1, 1994, Pablo purchased the rights to a mineral interest for $1,000,000. At that time, the remaining recoverable units in the mineral interest were estimated to be 200,000. The depletion per unit is $5 [$1,000,000 (adjusted basis) ÷ 200,000 (estimated recoverable units)]. If during the year 60,000 units were mined and 25,000 were sold, the cost depletion would be $125,000 [$5 (depletion per unit) × 25,000 (units sold)]. ▼

---

[34] § 612.

If the taxpayer later discovers that the original estimate was incorrect, the depletion per unit for future calculations must be redetermined based on the revised estimate.[35]

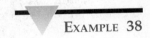

EXAMPLE 38

Assume the same facts as in Example 37. In 1995, Pablo realizes that an incorrect estimate was made. The remaining recoverable units now are determined to be 400,000. Based on this new information, the revised depletion per unit is $2.1875 [$875,000 (adjusted basis) ÷ 400,000 (estimated recoverable units)]. Note that the adjusted basis is the original cost ($1,000,000) reduced by the depletion claimed in 1994 ($125,000). If 30,000 units are sold in 1995, the depletion for the year would be $65,625 [$2.1875 (depletion per unit) × 30,000 (units sold)]. ▼

Percentage Depletion

Percentage depletion (also referred to as statutory depletion) is a specified percentage provided for in the Code. The percentage varies according to the type of mineral interest involved. A sample of these percentages is shown in Exhibit 8–1. The rate is applied to the gross income from the property, but in no event may percentage depletion exceed 50 percent of the taxable income from the property before the allowance for depletion.[36]

▼ **EXHIBIT 8–1**
Sample of Percentage Depletion Rates

22% Depletion	
Cobalt	Sulfur
Lead	Tin
Nickel	Uranium
Platinum	Zinc
15% Depletion	
Copper	Oil and gas
Gold	Oil shale
Iron	Silver
14% Depletion	
Borax	Magnesium carbonates
Calcium carbonates	Marble
Granite	Potash
Limestone	Slate
10% Depletion	
Coal	Perlite
Lignite	Sodium chloride
5% Depletion	
Gravel	Pumice
Peat	Sand

[35]§ 611(a).
[36]§ 613(a). Special rules apply for certain oil and gas wells under § 613A (e.g., the 50% ceiling is replaced with a 100% ceiling, and the percentage depletion may not exceed 65% of the taxpayer's taxable income from all sources before the allowance for depletion).

EXAMPLE 39

Assuming gross income of $100,000, a depletion rate of 22%, and other expenses relating to the property of $60,000, the depletion allowance is determined as follows:

Gross income	$100,000
Less: Other expenses	(60,000)
Taxable income before depletion	$ 40,000
Depletion allowance [the lesser of $22,000 (22% × $100,000) or $20,000 (50% × $40,000)]	(20,000)
Taxable income after depletion	$ 20,000

The adjusted basis of the property is reduced by $20,000, the depletion allowed. If the other expenses had been only $55,000, the full $22,000 could have been deducted, and the adjusted basis would have been reduced by $22,000. ▼

Note that percentage depletion is based on a percentage of the gross income from the property and makes no reference to cost. Thus, when percentage depletion is used, it is possible to deduct more than the original cost of the property. If percentage depletion is used, however, the adjusted basis of the property (for computing cost depletion) must be reduced by the amount of percentage depletion taken until the adjusted basis reaches zero.

Effect of Intangible Drilling Costs on Depletion

The treatment of IDC has an effect on the depletion deduction in two ways. If the costs are capitalized, the basis for cost depletion is increased. As a consequence, the cost depletion is increased. If IDC are expensed, they reduce the taxable income from the property. This reduction may result in application of the provision that limits depletion to 50 percent (100 percent for certain oil and gas wells) of taxable income before deducting depletion.

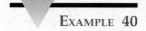

EXAMPLE 40

Iris purchased the rights to an oil interest for $1,000,000. The recoverable barrels were estimated to be 200,000. During the year, 50,000 barrels were sold for $2,000,000. Regular expenses amounted to $800,000, and IDC were $650,000. If the IDC are capitalized, the depletion per unit is $8.25 ($1,000,000 + $650,000 ÷ 200,000 barrels), and the following taxable income results:

Gross income	$2,000,000
Less: Expenses	(800,000)
Taxable income before depletion	$1,200,000
Cost depletion ($8.25 × 50,000) = $412,500	
Percentage depletion (15% × $2,000,000) = $300,000	
Greater of cost or percentage depletion	(412,500)
Taxable income	$ 787,500

If the IDC are expensed, the taxable income is $250,000, calculated as follows:

Gross income	$ 2,000,000
Less: Expenses, including IDC	(1,450,000)
Taxable income before depletion	$ 550,000
Cost depletion [($1,000,000 ÷ 200,000 barrels) × 50,000 barrels] = $250,000	
Percentage depletion (15% of $2,000,000 = $300,000, limited to 100% of $550,000 taxable income before depletion) = $300,000	
Greater of cost or percentage depletion	(300,000)
Taxable income	$ 250,000

For further restrictions on the use or availability of the percentage depletion method, see § 613.

REPORTING PROCEDURES

5　LEARNING OBJECTIVE
Perform the reporting procedures for cost recovery.

Sole proprietors engaged in a business should file a Schedule C, Profit or Loss from Business, to accompany Form 1040. Schedule C for 1993 is presented because the 1994 form was not yet available.

The top part of page 1 requests certain key information about the taxpayer (e.g., name, address, Social Security number) and the business methods involved (e.g., accounting method and inventory method used). Part I provides for the reporting of items of income. If the business requires the use of inventories and the computation of cost of goods sold (see Chapter 18 for when this is necessary), Part III must be completed and the cost of goods sold amount transferred to line 4 of Part I.

Part II allows for the reporting of deductions. Some of the deductions discussed in Chapters 7 and 8 and their location on the form are bad debts (line 9), depletion (line 12), and depreciation (line 13). Other expenses (line 27) include those items not already covered (see lines 8–26). An example would be research and experimental expenditures.

If depreciation is claimed, it should be supported by completing Form 4562. Form 4562 for 1993 is presented because the 1994 form was not yet available. The amount listed on line 20 of Form 4562 is then transferred to line 13 of Part II of Schedule C.

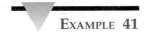 **EXAMPLE 41**

Thomas Andrews, Social Security number 123–45–6789, was employed as an accountant until July 1992, when he opened his own practice. His address is 279 Mountain View, Ogden, UT 84201. Andrews keeps his books on the accrual basis and had the following revenue and business expenses in 1993:

   a. Revenue from accounting practice, $80,000.
   b. Bad debts, $2,000.
   c. Automobile expenses, $3,000.
   d. Insurance, $800.
   e. Office supplies, $4,000.
   f. Rent, $12,000.
   g. Furniture and fixtures acquired on July 15, 1992, for $8,000. Andrews used the statutory percentage cost recovery method.
   h. Business automobile acquired on May 20, 1992, for $10,000. Andrews used the statutory percentage cost recovery method. The automobile, which was driven 12,000 miles during 1993, was used only for business purposes.
   i. Microcomputer acquired on May 7, 1993, for $21,500. Andrews elects § 179 and uses the statutory percentage cost recovery method.

Andrews would report the above information on Schedule C and Form 4562 as illustrated on the following pages. ▼

COST RECOVERY

 TAX PLANNING CONSIDERATIONS

Cost recovery schedules should be reviewed annually for possible retirements, abandonments, and obsolescence.

 EXAMPLE 42

An examination of the cost recovery schedule of Eagle Company reveals the following:

   • Asset A was abandoned when it was discovered that the cost of repairs would be in excess of the cost of replacement. Asset A had an adjusted basis of $3,000.
   • Asset J became obsolete this year, at which point, its adjusted basis was $8,000.

Assets A and J should be written off for an additional expense of $11,000 ($3,000 + $8,000). ▼

 6 LEARNING OBJECTIVE
Identify tax planning opportunities for cost recovery, amortization, and depletion.

Because of the deductions for cost recovery, interest, and ad valorem property taxes, investments in real estate can be highly attractive. In figuring the economics of such investments, one should be sure to take into account any tax savings that result.

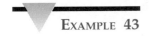 **EXAMPLE 43**

In early January 1993, Vern purchased residential rental property for $170,000 (of which $20,000 was allocated to the land and $150,000 to the building). Vern made a down payment of $25,000 and assumed the seller's mortgage for the balance. Under the mortgage agreement, monthly payments of $1,000 are required and are applied toward interest, taxes, insurance, and principal. Since the property was already occupied, Vern continued to receive rent of $1,200 per month from the tenant. Vern actively participates in this activity and hence comes under the special rule for a rental real estate activity with respect to the limitation on passive activity losses (refer to Chapter 11). Vern is in the 31% tax bracket.

Form **4562**	**Depreciation and Amortization**	OMB No. 1545-0172
Department of the Treasury Internal Revenue Service	**(Including Information on Listed Property)** ▶ See separate instructions. ▶ Attach this form to your return.	**19**93 Attachment Sequence No. **67**

Name(s) shown on return	Identifying number
Thomas Andrews	123-45-6789

Business or activity to which this form relates Accounting Services

Part I Election To Expense Certain Tangible Property (Section 179) (Note: *If you have any "Listed Property," complete Part V before you complete Part I.*)

1	Maximum dollar limitation (If an enterprise zone business, see instructions.)	1	$17,500
2	Total cost of section 179 property placed in service during the tax year (see instructions) . .	2	$21,500
3	Threshold cost of section 179 property before reduction in limitation	3	$200,000
4	Reduction in limitation. Subtract line 3 from line 2, but do not enter less than -0-	4	
5	Dollar limitation for tax year. Subtract line 4 from line 1, but do not enter less than -0-. (If married filing separately, see instructions.)	5	$17,500

(a) Description of property	(b) Cost	(c) Elected cost	
6 5-Year Class Prop.-Microcomputer	$21,500	$17,500	

7	Listed property. Enter amount from line 26.	7	
8	Total elected cost of section 179 property. Add amounts in column (c), lines 6 and 7 . . .	8	17,500
9	Tentative deduction. Enter the smaller of line 5 or line 8	9	17,500
10	Carryover of disallowed deduction from 1992 (see instructions).	10	
11	Taxable income limitation. Enter the smaller of taxable income or line 5 (see instructions) . .	11	17,500
12	Section 179 expense deduction. Add lines 9 and 10, but do not enter more than line 11 . .	12	17,500
13	Carryover of disallowed deduction to 1994. Add lines 9 and 10, less line 12 ▶	13	

Note: *Do not use Part II or Part III below for listed property (automobiles, certain other vehicles, cellular telephones, certain computers, or property used for entertainment, recreation, or amusement). Instead, use Part V for listed property.*

Part II MACRS Depreciation For Assets Placed in Service ONLY During Your 1993 Tax Year (Do Not Include Listed Property)

(a) Classification of property	(b) Month and year placed in service	(c) Basis for depreciation (business/investment use only—see instructions)	(d) Recovery period	(e) Convention	(f) Method	(g) Depreciation deduction
14 General Depreciation System (GDS) (see instructions):						
a 3-year property						
b 5-year property		4,000	5-YR	HY	200DB	800
c 7-year property						
d 10-year property						
e 15-year property						
f 20-year property						
g Residential rental property			27.5 yrs.	MM	S/L	
			27.5 yrs.	MM	S/L	
h Nonresidential real property				MM	S/L	
				MM	S/L	
15 Alternative Depreciation System (ADS) (see instructions):						
a Class life					S/L	
b 12-year			12 yrs.		S/L	
c 40-year			40 yrs.	MM	S/L	

Part III Other Depreciation (Do Not Include Listed Property)

16	GDS and ADS deductions for assets placed in service in tax years beginning before 1993 (see instructions)	16	1,959
17	Property subject to section 168(f)(1) election (see instructions)	17	
18	ACRS and other depreciation (see instructions)	18	

Part IV Summary

19	Listed property. Enter amount from line 25.	19	3,200
20	**Total.** Add deductions on line 12, lines 14 and 15 in column (g), and lines 16 through 19. Enter here and on the appropriate lines of your return. (Partnerships and S corporations—see instructions)	20	23,459
21	For assets shown above and placed in service during the current year, enter the portion of the basis attributable to section 263A costs (see instructions)	21	

For Paperwork Reduction Act Notice, see page 1 of the separate instructions.   Cat. No. 12906N   Form **4562** (1993)

Form 4562 (1993) Page **2**

Part V	Listed Property—Automobiles, Certain Other Vehicles, Cellular Telephones, Certain Computers, and Property Used for Entertainment, Recreation, or Amusement

*For any vehicle for which you are using the standard mileage rate or deducting lease expense, complete **only** 22a, 22b, columns (a) through (c) of Section A, all of Section B, and Section C if applicable.*

Section A—Depreciation and Other Information (Caution: *See instructions for limitations for automobiles.*)

22a Do you have evidence to support the business/investment use claimed? ☒ Yes ☐ No   **22b** If "Yes," is the evidence written? ☒ Yes ☐ No

(a) Type of property (list vehicles first)	(b) Date placed in service	(c) Business/ investment use percentage	(d) Cost or other basis	(e) Basis for depreciation (business/investment use only)	(f) Recovery period	(g) Method/ Convention	(h) Depreciation deduction	(i) Elected section 179 cost
23 Property used more than 50% in a qualified business use (see instructions):								
Automobile	5/20/92	100 %	10,000	10,000	5-YR	200DB-HY	3,200	
		%						
		%						
24 Property used 50% or less in a qualified business use (see instructions):								
		%				S/L –		
		%				S/L –		
		%				S/L –		

25 Add amounts in column (h). Enter the total here and on line 19, page 1 . . . . . | **25** | 3,200

26 Add amounts in column (i). Enter the total here and on line 7, page 1 . . . . | **26** |

Section B—Information Regarding Use of Vehicles—*If you deduct expenses for vehicles:*
- *Always complete this section for vehicles used by a sole proprietor, partner, or other "more than 5% owner," or related person.*
- *If you provided vehicles to your employees, first answer the questions in Section C to see if you meet an exception to completing this section for those vehicles.*

		(a) Vehicle 1		(b) Vehicle 2		(c) Vehicle 3		(d) Vehicle 4		(e) Vehicle 5		(f) Vehicle 6	
27	Total business/investment miles driven during the year (DO NOT include commuting miles)	12,000											
28	Total commuting miles driven during the year	–0–											
29	Total other personal (noncommuting) miles driven	–0–											
30	Total miles driven during the year. Add lines 27 through 29	12,000											
		Yes	No	Yes	No	Yes	No	Yes	No	Yes	No	Yes	No
31	Was the vehicle available for personal use during off-duty hours?		X										
32	Was the vehicle used primarily by a more than 5% owner or related person?	X											
33	Is another vehicle available for personal use?	X											

Section C—Questions for Employers Who Provide Vehicles for Use by Their Employees

Answer these questions to determine if you meet an exception to completing Section B. **Note:** *Section B must always be completed for vehicles used by sole proprietors, partners, or other more than 5% owners or related persons.*

		Yes	No
34	Do you maintain a written policy statement that prohibits all personal use of vehicles, including commuting, by your employees?		
35	Do you maintain a written policy statement that prohibits personal use of vehicles, except commuting, by your employees? (See instructions for vehicles used by corporate officers, directors, or 1% or more owners.)		
36	Do you treat all use of vehicles by employees as personal use?		
37	Do you provide more than five vehicles to your employees and retain the information received from your employees concerning the use of the vehicles?		
38	Do you meet the requirements concerning qualified automobile demonstration use (see instructions)? . . .		

Note: *If your answer to 34, 35, 36, 37, or 38 is "Yes," you need not complete Section B for the covered vehicles.*

Part VI	Amortization

(a) Description of costs	(b) Date amortization begins	(c) Amortizable amount	(d) Code section	(e) Amortization period or percentage	(f) Amortization for this year
39 Amortization of costs that begins during your 1993 tax year:					

40 Amortization of costs that began before 1993 . . . . | **40** |

41 **Total.** Enter here and on "Other Deductions" or "Other Expenses" line of your return . . . | **41** |

SCHEDULE C (Form 1040) Department of the Treasury Internal Revenue Service	**Profit or Loss From Business** (Sole Proprietorship) ▶ Partnerships, joint ventures, etc., must file Form 1065. ▶ Attach to Form 1040 or Form 1041. ▶ See Instructions for Schedule C (Form 1040).	OMB No. 1545-0074 19**93** Attachment Sequence No. **09**

Name of proprietor Thomas Andrews	Social security number (SSN) 123 : 45 : 6789

A	Principal business or profession, including product or service (see page C-1) Accounting Services	**B** Enter principal business code (see page C-6) ▶ 7 6 5 8

C Business name. If no separate business name, leave blank.   Andrews Accounting Services   **D** Employer ID number (EIN), if any

E Business address (including suite or room no.) ▶ 279 Mountain View
City, town or post office, state, and ZIP code   Ogden, UT 84201

F Accounting method: (1) ☐ Cash   (2) ☒ Accrual   (3) ☐ Other (specify) ▶ ....

G	Method(s) used to value closing inventory:	(1) ☐ Cost	(2) ☐ Lower of cost or market	(3) ☐ Other (attach explanation)	(4) ☒ Does not apply (if checked, skip line H)	Yes	No

H Was there any change in determining quantities, costs, or valuations between opening and closing inventory? If "Yes," attach explanation . . . . | | X

I Did you "materially participate" in the operation of this business during 1993? If "No," see page C-2 for limit on losses. . . . | ▶ ☐

J If you started or acquired this business during 1993, check here . . . . ▶ ☐

Part I   Income

1	Gross receipts or sales. **Caution:** If this income was reported to you on Form W-2 and the "Statutory employee" box on that form was checked, see page C-2 and check here . . . . ▶ ☐	**1**	80,000
2	Returns and allowances	**2**	
3	Subtract line 2 from line 1	**3**	80,000
4	Cost of goods sold (from line 40 on page 2)	**4**	
5	**Gross profit.** Subtract line 4 from line 3	**5**	80,000
6	Other income, including Federal and state gasoline or fuel tax credit or refund (see page C-2) . . ▶	**6**	
7	**Gross income.** Add lines 5 and 6 . . . . ▶	**7**	80,000

Part II   Expenses. Caution: Do not enter expenses for business use of your home on lines 8–27. Instead, see line 30.

8	Advertising	**8**		19 Pension and profit-sharing plans	**19**	
9	Bad debts from sales or services (see page C-3) . .	**9**	2,000	20 Rent or lease (see page C-4):		
				a Vehicles, machinery, and equipment .	**20a**	
10	Car and truck expenses (see page C-3)	**10**	3,000	b Other business property . .	**20b**	12,000
11	Commissions and fees. . .	**11**		21 Repairs and maintenance . .	**21**	
12	Depletion.	**12**		22 Supplies (not included in Part III) .	**22**	
13	Depreciation and section 179 expense deduction (not included in Part III) (see page C-3) . .	**13**	23,459	23 Taxes and licenses	**23**	
				24 Travel, meals, and entertainment:		
14	Employee benefit programs (other than on line 19) . .	**14**		a Travel	**24a**	
15	Insurance (other than health) .	**15**	800	b Meals and entertainment .		
16	Interest:			c Enter 20% of line 24b subject to limitations (see page C-4) .		
a	Mortgage (paid to banks, etc.) .	**16a**		d Subtract line 24c from line 24b .	**24d**	
b	Other	**16b**		25 Utilities	**25**	
17	Legal and professional services	**17**		26 Wages (less jobs credit) . .	**26**	
18	Office expense	**18**	4,000	27 Other expenses (from line 46 on page 2)	**27**	

28	**Total expenses** before expenses for business use of home. Add lines 8 through 27 in columns. . ▶	**28**	45,259
29	Tentative profit (loss). Subtract line 28 from line 7	**29**	34,741
30	Expenses for business use of your home. Attach **Form 8829**	**30**	
31	**Net profit or (loss).** Subtract line 30 from line 29. • If a profit, enter on **Form 1040, line 12,** and ALSO on **Schedule SE, line 2** (statutory employees, see page C-5). Fiduciaries, enter on Form 1041, line 3. • If a loss, you MUST go on to line 32.	**31**	34,741
32	If you have a loss, check the box that describes your investment in this activity (see page C-5). • If you checked 32a, enter the loss on **Form 1040, line 12,** and ALSO on **Schedule SE, line 2** (statutory employees, see page C-5). Fiduciaries, enter on Form 1041, line 3. • If you checked 32b, you MUST attach **Form 6198.**	32a ☐ All investment is at risk. 32b ☐ Some investment is not at risk.

For Paperwork Reduction Act Notice, see Form 1040 instructions.   Cat. No. 11334P   Schedule C (Form 1040) 1993

During 1994, Vern's expenses were as follows:

Interest	$10,000
Taxes	800
Insurance	1,000
Repairs and maintenance	2,200
Depreciation ($150,000 × .03636)	5,454
Total	$19,454

The deductible loss from the rental property is computed as follows:

Rent income ($1,200 × 12 months)	$ 14,400
Less expenses (see above)	(19,454)
Net loss	$ (5,054)

But what is Vern's overall position for the year when the tax benefit of the loss is taken into account? Considering just the cash intake and outlay, it is summarized as follows:

Intake—		
Rent income	$14,400	
Tax savings [31% (income tax bracket) × $5,054 (loss from the property)]	1,567	$ 15,967
Outlay—		
Mortgage payments ($1,000 × 12 months)	$12,000	
Repairs and maintenance	2,200	(14,200)
Net cash benefit		$ 1,767

It should be noted, however, that should Vern cease being an active participant in the rental activity, the passive activity loss rules would apply, and Vern could lose the current period benefit of the loss.

AMORTIZATION

When a business is purchased, goodwill and covenants not to compete are both subject to a statutory amortization period of 15 years. Therefore, the purchaser does not derive any tax benefits when part of the purchase price is assigned to a covenant rather than to goodwill.

Thus, from the purchaser's perspective, bargaining for a covenant should be based on legal rather than tax reasons. Note, however, that from the seller's perspective, goodwill is a capital asset and the covenant is an ordinary income asset.

Since the amortization period for both goodwill and a covenant is 15 years, the purchaser may want to attempt to minimize these amounts if the purchase price can be assigned to assets with shorter lives (e.g., inventory, receivables, and personalty). Conversely, the purchaser may want to attempt to maximize these amounts if otherwise part of the purchase price will be assigned to assets with longer recovery periods (e.g., realty) or to assets not eligible for cost recovery (e.g., land).

DEPLETION

Since the election to use the cost or percentage depletion method is an annual election, a taxpayer can use cost depletion (if higher) until the basis is exhausted and then switch to percentage depletion in the following years.

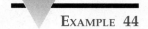
EXAMPLE 44

Assume the following facts for Melissa:

Remaining depletable basis	$ 11,000
Gross income (10,000 units)	100,000
Expenses (other than depletion)	30,000

Since cost depletion is limited to the basis of $11,000 and if the percentage depletion is $22,000 (assume a 22% rate), Melissa would choose the latter. Her basis is then reduced to zero. In future years, however, she can continue to take percentage depletion since percentage depletion is taken without reference to the remaining basis. ▼

The election to expense intangible drilling and development costs is a one-time election. Once the election is made to either expense or capitalize the intangible drilling and development costs, it is binding on all future expenditures. The permanent nature of the election makes it extremely important for the taxpayer to determine which treatment will provide the greatest tax advantage. (Refer to Example 40 for an illustration of the effect of using the two different alternatives for a given set of facts.)

TABLES

Summary of Tables

Table 8–1   Original ACRS statutory percentage table for personalty.
Applicable depreciation method: 150 percent declining-balance switching to straight-line.
Applicable recovery periods: 3, 5, 10, 15 years.
Applicable convention: half-year.

Table 8–2   Modified ACRS statutory percentage table for personalty.
Applicable depreciation methods: 200 or 150 percent declining-balance switching to straight-line.
Applicable recovery periods: 3, 5, 7, 10, 15, 20 years.
Applicable convention: half-year.

Table 8–3   Modified ACRS statutory percentage table for personalty.
Applicable depreciation method: 200 percent declining-balance switching to straight-line.
Applicable recovery periods: 3, 5, 7 years.
Applicable convention: mid-quarter.

Table 8–4   Original ACRS statutory percentage table for realty.
Applicable depreciation methods: 200 or 175 percent declining-balance switching to straight-line.
Applicable recovery period: 15 years.
Applicable convention: full-month.

Table 8–5   Original ACRS statutory percentage table for realty.
Applicable depreciation method: 175 percent declining-balance switching to straight-line.
Applicable recovery period: 18 years.
Applicable convention: mid-month.

Table 8–6   Original ACRS statutory percentage table for realty.
Applicable depreciation method: 175 percent declining-balance switching to straight-line.
Applicable recovery period: 19 years.
Applicable convention: mid-month.

Table 8–7   Modified ACRS straight-line table for realty.
Applicable depreciation method: straight-line.
Applicable recovery periods: 27.5, 31.5, 39 years.
Applicable convention: mid-month.

Table 8–8   Original ACRS optional straight-line table for realty.
Applicable depreciation method: straight-line.
Applicable recovery period: 19 years.
Applicable convention: mid-month.

Table 8–9   Modified ACRS optional straight-line table for personalty.
Applicable depreciation method: straight-line.
Applicable recovery periods: 3, 5, 7, 10, 15, 20 years.
Applicable convention: half-year.

Table 8–10   Alternative minimum tax declining-balance table for personalty.
Applicable depreciation method: 150 percent declining-balance switching to
straight-line.
Applicable recovery periods: 3, 5, 9.5, 10 years.
Applicable convention: half-year.

Table 8–11   Alternative depreciation system straight-line table for personalty.
Applicable depreciation method: straight-line.
Applicable recovery periods: 5, 9.5, 12 years.
Applicable convention: half-year.

Table 8–12   Alternative depreciation system straight-line table for realty.
Applicable depreciation method: straight-line.
Applicable recovery period: 40 years.
Applicable convention: mid-month.

▼ TABLE 8–1
ACRS Statutory Percentages for Property Other Than 15-Year Real Property, 18-Year Real Property, or 19-Year Real Property Assuming Half-Year Convention

For Property Placed in Service after December 31, 1980, and before January 1, 1987

Recovery Year	The Applicable Percentage for the Class of Property Is:			
	3-Year	5-Year	10-Year	15-Year Public Utility
1	25	15	8	5
2	38	22	14	10
3	37	21	12	9
4		21	10	8
5		21	10	7
6			10	6
7			9	6
8			9	6
9			9	6
10			9	6
11				6
12				6
13				6
14				6
15				6

▼ **TABLE 8–2**
MACRS Accelerated Depreciation for Personal Property Assuming Half-Year Convention

For Property Placed in Service after December 31, 1986

Recovery Year	3-Year (200% DB)	5-Year (200% DB)	7-Year (200% DB)	10-Year (200% DB)	15-Year (150% DB)	20-Year (150% DB)
1	33.33	20.00	14.29	10.00	5.00	3.750
2	44.45	32.00	24.49	18.00	9.50	7.219
3	14.81*	19.20	17.49	14.40	8.55	6.677
4	7.41	11.52*	12.49	11.52	7.70	6.177
5		11.52	8.93*	9.22	6.93	5.713
6		5.76	8.92	7.37	6.23	5.285
7			8.93	6.55*	5.90*	4.888
8			4.46	6.55	5.90	4.522
9				6.56	5.91	4.462*
10				6.55	5.90	4.461
11				3.28	5.91	4.462
12					5.90	4.461
13					5.91	4.462
14					5.90	4.461
15					5.91	4.462
16					2.95	4.461
17						4.462
18						4.461
19						4.462
20						4.461
21						2.231

*Switchover to straight-line depreciation.

▼ **TABLE 8–3**
MACRS Accelerated Depreciation for Personal Property Assuming Mid-Quarter Convention

For Property Placed in Service after December 31, 1986 (Partial Table*)

3-Year

Recovery Year	First Quarter	Second Quarter	Third Quarter	Fourth Quarter
1	58.33	41.67	25.00	8.33
2	27.78	38.89	50.00	61.11

5-Year

Recovery Year	First Quarter	Second Quarter	Third Quarter	Fourth Quarter
1	35.00	25.00	15.00	5.00
2	26.00	30.00	34.00	38.00

7-Year

Recovery Year	First Quarter	Second Quarter	Third Quarter	Fourth Quarter
1	25.00	17.85	10.71	3.57
2	21.43	23.47	25.51	27.55

*The figures in this table are taken from the official tables that appear in Rev.Proc. 87–57, 1987–2 C.B. 687. Because of their length, the complete tables are not presented.

▼ **TABLE 8–4**
ACRS Statutory Percentages for
15-Year Real Property

For Property Placed in Service after December 31, 1980, and before January 1, 1987: 15-Year Real Property— Low-Income Housing

And the Month in the First Recovery Year the Property Is Placed in Service Is:

If the Recovery Year Is:	1	2	3	4	5	6	7	8	9	10	11	12
	The Applicable Percentage Is (Use the Column for the Month in the First Year the Property Is Placed in Service):											
1	13	12	11	10	9	8	7	6	4	3	2	1
2	12	12	12	12	12	12	12	13	13	13	13	13
3	10	10	10	10	11	11	11	11	11	11	11	11
4	9	9	9	9	9	9	9	9	10	10	10	10
5	8	8	8	8	8	8	8	8	8	8	8	9
6	7	7	7	7	7	7	7	7	7	7	7	7
7	6	6	6	6	6	6	6	6	6	6	6	6
8	5	5	5	5	5	5	5	5	5	5	6	6
9	5	5	5	5	5	5	5	5	5	5	6	6
10	5	5	5	5	5	5	5	5	5	5	5	5
11	4	5	5	5	5	5	5	5	5	5	5	5
12	4	4	4	5	4	5	5	5	5	5	5	5
13	4	4	4	4	4	4	5	4	5	5	5	5
14	4	4	4	4	4	4	4	4	4	5	4	4
15	4	4	4	4	4	4	4	4	4	4	4	4
16	—	—	1	1	2	2	2	3	3	3	4	4

For Property Placed in Service after December 31, 1980, and before March 16, 1984: 15-Year Real Property— Other Than Low-Income Housing

	1	2	3	4	5	6	7	8	9	10	11	12
1	12	11	10	9	8	7	6	5	4	3	2	1
2	10	10	11	11	11	11	11	11	11	11	11	12
3	9	9	9	9	10	10	10	10	10	10	10	10
4	8	8	8	8	8	8	9	9	9	9	9	9
5	7	7	7	7	7	7	8	8	8	8	8	8
6	6	6	6	6	7	7	7	7	7	7	7	7
7	6	6	6	6	6	6	6	6	6	6	6	6
8	6	6	6	6	6	6	5	6	6	6	6	6
9	6	6	6	6	5	6	5	5	5	6	6	6
10	5	6	5	6	5	5	5	5	5	5	6	6
11	5	5	5	5	5	5	5	5	5	5	6	5
12	5	5	5	5	5	5	5	5	5	5	5	5
13	5	5	5	5	5	5	5	5	5	5	5	5
14	5	5	5	5	5	5	5	5	5	5	5	5
15	5	5	5	5	5	5	5	5	5	5	5	5
16	—	—	1	1	2	2	3	3	4	4	4	5

▼ **TABLE 8–5**
ACRS Cost Recovery Table
for 18-Year Real Property

For Property Placed in Service after June 22, 1984, and before May 9, 1985: 18-Year Real Property (18-Year 175% Declining Balance) (Assuming Mid-Month Convention)

If The Recovery Year Is:	And the Month in the First Recovery Year the Property Is Placed in Service Is:											
	1	2	3	4	5	6	7	8	9	10	11	12
	The Applicable Percentage Is (Use the Column for the Month in the First Year the Property Is Placed in Service):											
1	9	9	8	7	6	5	4	4	3	2	1	0.4
2	9	9	9	9	9	9	9	9	9	10	10	10.0
3	8	8	8	8	8	8	8	8	9	9	9	9.0
4	7	7	7	7	7	8	8	8	8	8	8	8.0
5	7	7	7	7	7	7	7	7	7	7	7	7.0
6	6	6	6	6	6	6	6	6	6	6	6	6.0
7	5	5	5	5	6	6	6	6	6	6	6	6.0
8	5	5	5	5	5	5	5	5	5	5	5	5.0
9	5	5	5	5	5	5	5	5	5	5	5	5.0
10	5	5	5	5	5	5	5	5	5	5	5	5.0
11	5	5	5	5	5	5	5	5	5	5	5	5.0
12	5	5	5	5	5	5	5	5	5	5	5	5.0
13	4	4	4	5	4	4	5	4	4	4	5	5.0
14	4	4	4	4	4	4	4	4	4	4	4	4.0
15	4	4	4	4	4	4	4	4	4	4	4	4.0
16	4	4	4	4	4	4	4	4	4	4	4	4.0
17	4	4	4	4	4	4	4	4	4	4	4	4.0
18	4	3	4	4	4	4	4	4	4	4	4	4.0
19		1	1	1	2	2	2	3	3	3	3	3.6

▼ **TABLE 8–6**
ACRS Cost Recovery Table
for 19-Year Real Property

For Property Placed in Service after May 8, 1985, and before January 1, 1987
19-Year Real Property (19-Year 175% Declining Balance)
(Assuming Mid-Month Convention)

If the Recovery Year Is:	And the Month in the First Recovery Year the Property Is Placed in Service Is:											
	1	2	3	4	5	6	7	8	9	10	11	12
	The Applicable Percentage Is (Use the Column for the Month in the First Year the Property Is Placed in Service):											
1	8.8	8.1	7.3	6.5	5.8	5.0	4.2	3.5	2.7	1.9	1.1	0.4
2	8.4	8.5	8.5	8.6	8.7	8.8	8.8	8.9	9.0	9.0	9.1	9.2
3	7.6	7.7	7.7	7.8	7.9	7.9	8.0	8.1	8.1	8.2	8.3	8.3
4	6.9	7.0	7.0	7.1	7.1	7.2	7.3	7.3	7.4	7.4	7.5	7.6
5	6.3	6.3	6.4	6.4	6.5	6.5	6.6	6.6	6.7	6.8	6.8	6.9
6	5.7	5.7	5.8	5.9	5.9	5.9	6.0	6.0	6.1	6.1	6.2	6.2
7	5.2	5.2	5.3	5.3	5.3	5.4	5.4	5.5	5.5	5.6	5.6	5.6
8	4.7	4.7	4.8	4.8	4.8	4.9	4.9	5.0	5.0	5.1	5.1	5.1
9	4.2	4.3	4.3	4.4	4.4	4.5	4.5	4.5	4.5	4.6	4.6	4.7
10	4.2	4.2	4.2	4.2	4.2	4.2	4.2	4.2	4.2	4.2	4.2	4.2
11	4.2	4.2	4.2	4.2	4.2	4.2	4.2	4.2	4.2	4.2	4.2	4.2
12	4.2	4.2	4.2	4.2	4.2	4.2	4.2	4.2	4.2	4.2	4.2	4.2
13	4.2	4.2	4.2	4.2	4.2	4.2	4.2	4.2	4.2	4.2	4.2	4.2
14	4.2	4.2	4.2	4.2	4.2	4.2	4.2	4.2	4.2	4.2	4.2	4.2
15	4.2	4.2	4.2	4.2	4.2	4.2	4.2	4.2	4.2	4.2	4.2	4.2
16	4.2	4.2	4.2	4.2	4.2	4.2	4.2	4.2	4.2	4.2	4.2	4.2
17	4.2	4.2	4.2	4.2	4.2	4.2	4.2	4.2	4.2	4.2	4.2	4.2
18	4.2	4.2	4.2	4.2	4.2	4.2	4.2	4.2	4.2	4.2	4.2	4.2
19	4.2	4.2	4.2	4.2	4.2	4.2	4.2	4.2	4.2	4.2	4.2	4.2
20	0.2	0.5	0.9	1.2	1.6	1.9	2.3	2.6	3.0	3.3	3.7	4.0

▼ **TABLE 8–7**
MACRS Straight-Line
Depreciation for Real Property
Assuming Mid-Month
Convention*

For Property Placed in Service after December 31, 1986: 27.5-Year Residential Real Property

| Recovery Year(s) | The Applicable Percentage Is (Use the Column for the Month in the First Year the Property Is Placed in Service): | | | | | | | | | | | |
	1	2	3	4	5	6	7	8	9	10	11	12
1	3.485	3.182	2.879	2.576	2.273	1.970	1.667	1.364	1.061	0.758	0.455	0.152
2–18	3.636	3.636	3.636	3.636	3.636	3.636	3.636	3.636	3.636	3.636	3.636	3.636
19–27	3.637	3.637	3.637	3.637	3.637	3.637	3.637	3.637	3.637	3.637	3.637	3.637
28	1.970	2.273	2.576	2.879	3.182	3.485	3.636	3.636	3.636	3.636	3.636	3.636
29	0.000	0.000	0.000	0.000	0.000	0.000	0.152	0.455	0.758	1.061	1.364	1.667

For Property Placed in Service after December 31, 1986 and before May 13, 1993: 31.5-Year Nonresidential Real Property

| Recovery Year(s) | The Applicable Percentage Is (Use the Column for the Month in the First Year the Property Is Placed in Service): | | | | | | | | | | | |
	1	2	3	4	5	6	7	8	9	10	11	12
1	3.042	2.778	2.513	2.249	1.984	1.720	1.455	1.190	0.926	0.661	0.397	0.132
2–19	3.175	3.175	3.175	3.175	3.175	3.175	3.175	3.175	3.175	3.175	3.175	3.175
20–31	3.174	3.174	3.174	3.174	3.174	3.174	3.174	3.174	3.174	3.174	3.174	3.174
32	1.720	1.984	2.249	2.513	2.778	3.042	3.175	3.175	3.175	3.175	3.175	3.175
33	0.000	0.000	0.000	0.000	0.000	0.000	0.132	0.397	0.661	0.926	1.190	1.455

For Property Placed in Service after May 12, 1993: 39-Year Nonresidential Real Property

| Recovery Year(s) | The Applicable Percentage Is (Use the Column for the Month in the First Year the Property Is Placed in Service): | | | | | | | | | | | |
	1	2	3	4	5	6	7	8	9	10	11	12
1	2.461	2.247	2.033	1.819	1.605	1.391	1.177	0.963	0.749	0.535	0.321	0.107
2–39	2.564	2.564	2.564	2.564	2.564	2.564	2.564	2.564	2.564	2.564	2.564	2.564
40	0.107	0.321	0.535	0.749	0.963	1.177	1.391	1.605	1.819	2.033	2.247	2.461

*The official tables contain a separate row for each year. For ease of presentation, certain years are grouped in these tables. In some instances, this will produce a difference of .001 for the last digit when compared with the official tables.

▼ **TABLE 8–8**
ACRS Cost Recovery Table for
19-Year Real Property:
Optional Straight-Line

For Property Placed in Service after May 8, 1985, and before January 1, 1987: 19-Year Real Property for Which an Optional 19-Year Straight-Line Method Is Elected (Assuming Mid-Month Convention)

If the Recovery Year Is:	And the Month in the First Recovery Year the Property Is Placed in Service Is:											
	1	2	3	4	5	6	7	8	9	10	11	12
	The Applicable Percentage Is (Use the Column for the Month in the First Year the Property Is Placed in Service):											
1	5.0	4.6	4.2	3.7	3.3	2.9	2.4	2.0	1.5	1.1	.7	.2
2	5.3	5.3	5.3	5.3	5.3	5.3	5.3	5.3	5.3	5.3	5.3	5.3
3	5.3	5.3	5.3	5.3	5.3	5.3	5.3	5.3	5.3	5.3	5.3	5.3
4	5.3	5.3	5.3	5.3	5.3	5.3	5.3	5.3	5.3	5.3	5.3	5.3
5	5.3	5.3	5.3	5.3	5.3	5.3	5.3	5.3	5.3	5.3	5.3	5.3
6	5.3	5.3	5.3	5.3	5.3	5.3	5.3	5.3	5.3	5.3	5.3	5.3
7	5.3	5.3	5.3	5.3	5.3	5.3	5.3	5.3	5.3	5.3	5.3	5.3
8	5.3	5.3	5.3	5.3	5.3	5.3	5.3	5.3	5.3	5.3	5.3	5.3
9	5.3	5.3	5.3	5.3	5.3	5.3	5.3	5.3	5.3	5.3	5.3	5.3
10	5.3	5.3	5.3	5.3	5.3	5.3	5.3	5.3	5.3	5.3	5.3	5.3
11	5.3	5.3	5.3	5.3	5.3	5.3	5.3	5.3	5.3	5.3	5.3	5.3
12	5.3	5.3	5.3	5.3	5.3	5.3	5.3	5.3	5.3	5.3	5.3	5.3
13	5.3	5.3	5.3	5.3	5.3	5.3	5.3	5.3	5.3	5.3	5.3	5.3
14	5.2	5.2	5.2	5.2	5.2	5.2	5.2	5.2	5.2	5.2	5.2	5.2
15	5.2	5.2	5.2	5.2	5.2	5.2	5.2	5.2	5.2	5.2	5.2	5.2
16	5.2	5.2	5.2	5.2	5.2	5.2	5.2	5.2	5.2	5.2	5.2	5.2
17	5.2	5.2	5.2	5.2	5.2	5.2	5.2	5.2	5.2	5.2	5.2	5.2
18	5.2	5.2	5.2	5.2	5.2	5.2	5.2	5.2	5.2	5.2	5.2	5.2
19	5.2	5.2	5.2	5.2	5.2	5.2	5.2	5.2	5.2	5.2	5.2	5.2
20	.2	.6	1.0	1.5	1.9	2.3	2.8	3.2	3.7	4.1	4.5	5.0

▼ **TABLE 8–9**
MACRS Straight-Line
Depreciation for Personal
Property Assuming Half-Year
Convention*

For Property Placed in Service after December 31, 1986

ACRS Class	% First Recovery Year	Other Recovery Years Years	%	Last Recovery Year Year	%
3-year	16.67	2–3	33.33	4	16.67
5-year	10.00	2–5	20.00	6	10.00
7-year	7.14	2–7	14.29	8	7.14
10-year	5.00	2–10	10.00	11	5.00
15-year	3.33	2–15	6.67	16	3.33
20-year	2.50	2–20	5.00	21	2.50

*The official table contains a separate row for each year. For ease of presentation, certain years are grouped in this table. In some instances, this will produce a difference of .01 for the last digit when compared with the official table.

▼ **TABLE 8–10**
Alternative Minimum Tax: 150%
Declining-Balance Assuming
Half-Year Convention

For Property Placed in Service after December 31, 1986 (Partial Table*)

Recovery Year	3-Year 150%	5-Year 150%	9.5-Year 150%	10-Year 150%
1	25.00	15.00	7.89	7.50
2	37.50	25.50	14.54	13.88
3	25.00**	17.85	12.25	11.79
4	12.50	16.66**	10.31	10.02
5		16.66	9.17**	8.74**
6		8.33	9.17	8.74
7			9.17	8.74
8			9.17	8.74
9			9.17	8.74
10			9.16	8.74
11				4.37

*The figures in this table are taken from the official table that appears in Rev.Proc. 87–57, 1987–2 C.B. 687. Because of its length, the complete table is not presented.
**Switchover to straight-line depreciation.

▼ **TABLE 8–11**
ADS Straight-Line for Personal
Property Assuming Half-Year
Convention

For Property Placed in Service after December 31, 1986 (Partial Table*)

Recovery Year	5-Year Class	9.5-Year Class	12-Year Class
1	10.00	5.26	4.17
2	20.00	10.53	8.33
3	20.00	10.53	8.33
4	20.00	10.53	8.33
5	20.00	10.52	8.33
6	10.00	10.53	8.33
7		10.52	8.34
8		10.53	8.33
9		10.52	8.34
10		10.53	8.33
11			8.34
12			8.33
13			4.17

*The figures in this table are taken from the official table that appears in Rev.Proc. 87–57, 1987–2 C.B. 687. Because of its length, the complete table is not presented. The tables for the mid-quarter convention also appear in Rev.Proc. 87–57.

▼ **TABLE 8–12**
ADS Straight-Line for Real
Property Assuming Mid-Month
Convention

For Property Placed in Service after December 31, 1986

Recovery Year	Month Placed in Service											
	1	2	3	4	5	6	7	8	9	10	11	12
1	2.396	2.188	1.979	1.771	1.563	1.354	1.146	0.938	0.729	0.521	0.313	0.104
2–40	2.500	2.500	2.500	2.500	2.500	2.500	2.500	2.500	2.500	2.500	2.500	2.500
41	0.104	0.312	0.521	0.729	0.937	1.146	1.354	1.562	1.771	1.979	2.187	2.396

KEY TERMS

Accelerated cost recovery system (ACRS), 8–4

Alternative depreciation system (ADS), 8–21

Amortization, 8–23

Cost depletion, 8–25

Cost recovery, 8–2

Depletion, 8–24

Depreciation, 8–2

Half-year convention, 8–6

Intangible drilling and development costs (IDC), 8–24

Listed property, 8–16

Mid-month convention, 8–11

Mid-quarter convention, 8–8

Modified accelerated cost recovery system (MACRS), 8–7

Percentage depletion, 8–26

Residential rental real estate, 8-11

Section 179 expensing, 8–14

PROBLEM MATERIALS

DISCUSSION QUESTIONS

1. Distinguish between cost recovery, amortization, and depletion.

2. Discuss whether personal property (personalty) is subject to cost recovery.

3. Distinguish between allowed and allowable cost recovery.

4. If a personal use asset is converted to business use, why is it necessary to compute cost recovery on the lower of fair market value or adjusted basis at the date of conversion?

5. Discuss whether a parking lot that is used in a business is subject to cost recovery.

6. Discuss the half-year convention as it is used in the MACRS rules.

7. Discuss when the mid-quarter convention must be used.

8. Discuss the mid-month convention as it is used in the MACRS rules.

9. Discuss how the determination is made as to whether a building is residential rental real estate.

10. What is the cost recovery period for nonresidential realty placed in service in 1994?

11. Discuss the applicable conventions if a taxpayer elects to use straight-line cost recovery for property placed in service after December 31, 1986.

12. If a taxpayer makes a straight-line election under MACRS, discuss the possibility of taking a cost recovery deduction, for personal and real property, in the year of disposition.

13. Discuss whether an election to use straight-line cost recovery under MACRS can be applied on an asset-by-asset basis.

X 14. Discuss the limitation on the § 179 amount that can be expensed and its impact on the basis of the property.

15. Discuss what factors are used in determining whether the more-than-50% business use test has been satisfied.

16. If a taxpayer does not pass the more-than-50% business use test on an automobile, discuss whether the statutory dollar limitations on cost recovery are applicable.

17. Discuss the tax consequences that result when a passenger automobile, which failed the more-than-50% business usage test during the first two years, satisfies the test for the third year.

18. Discuss whether § 179 should be elected for a passenger automobile.

19. Explain the reason for the inclusion amount with respect to leased passenger automobiles.

20. Explain how an inclusion amount is determined with respect to leased passenger automobiles.

21. Discuss the extent to which the 150% declining-balance method can be used under the alternative depreciation system.

22. Explain the amortization period of a § 197 intangible if the actual useful life is less than 15 years.

23. What is the amortization period for self-created goodwill?

24. Discuss the options for handling intangible drilling and development costs.

25. Briefly discuss the differences between cost depletion and percentage depletion.

PROBLEMS

26. On January 1, 1990, Black Company acquired an asset (three-year property) for $10,000 for use in its business. In the years 1990 and 1991, Black took $3,333 and $4,445 of cost recovery. The allowable cost recovery for the years 1992 and 1993 was $1,481 and $741, but Black did not take the deductions. In those years, Black had net operating losses, and the company wanted to "save" the deductions for later years. On January 1, 1994, the asset was sold for $2,000. Calculate the gain or loss on the sale of the asset in 1994.

X 27. Eve acquired a personal residence in 1990 for $70,000. In January 1994, when the fair market value was $80,000, she converted the residence to rental property.
   a. Calculate the amount of cost recovery that can be taken in 1994.
   b. What would your answer be if the property were worth only $50,000 in 1994?

28. Lori acquired a 10-year class asset on March 1, 1986, for $20,000. She did not elect immediate expensing under § 179. On October 5, 1994, Lori sells the asset.
   a. Determine Lori's cost recovery for 1986.
   b. Determine Lori's cost recovery for 1994.

29. Walt acquires a seven-year class asset on February 17, 1994, for $40,000. He does not elect immediate expensing under § 179. On January 2, 1999, Walt sells the asset.
   a. Determine Walt's cost recovery for 1994.
   b. Determine Walt's cost recovery for 1999.

30. Pedro acquires a 10-year class asset on April 4, 1994, for $150,000. Pedro does not elect immediate expensing under § 179, but does elect the straight-line method. On June 2, 2000, Pedro sells the asset.
   a. Determine Pedro's cost recovery for 1994.
   b. Determine Pedro's cost recovery for 2000.

31. Debra acquired a building for $300,000 (exclusive of land) on January 1, 1984. Calculate the cost recovery using the statutory percentage method for 1984 and 1994 if:
    a. The real property is low-income housing.
    b. The real property is a factory building.

32. On December 2, 1984, Wade purchased and placed in service a warehouse. The warehouse cost $800,000. Wade used the statutory percentage cost recovery method. On July 7, 1994, Wade sold the warehouse.
    a. Determine Wade's cost recovery for 1984.
    b. Determine Wade's cost recovery for 1994.

33. On March 10, 1994, James purchased and placed in service a warehouse. The warehouse cost $1,000,000. If James uses the statutory percentage cost recovery method, determine his cost recovery for 1994.

34. Tina, who is single, acquired a new copier (five-year class property) on March 2, 1994, for $28,000. What is the maximum amount that Tina can deduct in 1994 assuming the following:
    a. The taxable income derived from Tina's trade or business (without regard to the amount expensed under § 179) is $100,000.
    b. The taxable income derived from Tina's trade or business (without regard to the amount expensed under § 179) is $5,000.

35. Jack owns a small business that he operates as a sole proprietor. In 1994, Jack will net $9,000 of business income before consideration of any § 179 deduction. Jack spends $208,000 on new equipment in 1994. If Jack also has $3,000 of § 179 deduction carryforwards from 1993, determine his § 179 expense deduction for 1994 and the amount of any carryforward.

36. Olga is the proprietor of a small business. In 1994, her business income, before consideration of any § 179 deduction, is $5,000. Olga spends $203,000 on new equipment and furniture for 1994. If Olga elects to take the § 179 deduction on a desk that cost $20,000 (included in the $203,000), determine her total cost recovery for 1994 with respect to the desk.

37. On March 10, 1994, Yoon purchased three-year class property for $20,000. On December 15, 1994, Yoon purchased five-year class property for $50,000.
    a. Calculate Yoon's cost recovery for 1994, assuming he does not make the § 179 election or use straight-line cost recovery.
    b. Calculate Yoon's cost recovery for 1994, assuming he does elect to use § 179 and does not elect to use straight-line cost recovery.
    c. Assuming Yoon's marginal tax rate is 36%, determine his tax benefit from electing § 179.

38. Pat acquires a warehouse on November 1, 1993, at a cost of $4,500,000. On January 30, 2005, Pat sells the warehouse. Calculate Pat's cost recovery for 1993. For 2005.

39. On July 1, 1994, Wilma places in service a computer (five-year class property). The computer cost $20,000. Wilma used the computer 65% for business. The remainder of the time, she used the computer for personal purposes. If Wilma does not elect § 179, determine her cost recovery deduction for the computer for 1994.

40. On February 16, 1994, Ron purchased and placed into service a new car. The purchase price was $18,000. Ron drove the car 12,000 miles during the remainder of the year, 9,000 miles for business and 3,000 miles for personal use. Ron used the statutory percentage method of cost recovery. Calculate the total deduction Ron may take for 1994 with respect to the car.

41. On June 5, 1994, Leo purchased and placed in service a $19,000 car. The business use percentage for the car is always 100%. Compute Leo's cost recovery deduction in 2000.

42. On June 14, 1994, Helen purchased and placed in service a new car. The purchase price was $16,000. The car was used 75% for business and 25% for personal use in both 1994

and 1995. In 1996, the car was used 40% for business and 60% for personal use. Compute the cost recovery deduction for the car in 1996 and the cost recovery recapture.

43. In 1994, Paul purchased a computer (five-year property) for $120,000. The computer was used 60% for business, 20% for income production, and 20% for personal use. In 1995, the usage changed to 40% for business, 30% for income production, and 30% for personal use. Compute the cost recovery deduction for 1995 and any cost recovery recapture. Assume Paul did not make a § 179 election on the computer in 1994.

44. Midway through 1994, Abdel leases and places in service a passenger automobile. The lease will run for five years, and the payments are $430 per month. During 1994, Abdel uses the car 70% for business use and 30% for personal use. Assuming the inclusion dollar amount from the IRS table is $64, determine the tax consequences to Abdel from the lease for the year 1994.

45. Use the information given in Problem 44, but assume the inclusion dollar amount is $139. Abdel uses the car 60% for business use and 40% for personal use in 1995. Determine Abdel's tax consequences from the lease in 1995.

46. Dennis Harding is considering acquiring an automobile that he will use 100% for business. The purchase price of the automobile would be $30,500. If Dennis leased the car for five years, the lease payments would be $350 per month. Dennis will acquire the car on January 1, 1994. The inclusion dollar amounts from the IRS table for the next five years are $92, $201, $299, $358, and $412. Dennis desires to know the effect on his adjusted gross income of purchasing versus leasing the car for the next five years. Write a letter to Dennis and present your calculations. Also prepare a memo for the tax files.

47. On March 5, 1994, Nell purchased computer-based telephone equipment for $40,000. The assets are seven-year class property and have an ADS midpoint of 9.5 years. Determine Nell's cost recovery deduction for computing 1994 taxable income using the straight-line method under the alternative depreciation system and assuming she does not make a § 179 election.

48. In 1994, Muhammad purchased a light-duty truck for $12,000. The truck is used 100% for business. Muhammad did not make a § 179 election with respect to the truck. If Muhammad uses the statutory percentage method, determine his cost recovery deduction for 1994 for computing taxable income and for computing his alternative minimum tax.

49. In June 1994, Cardinal, Inc., purchased and placed in service railroad track costing $600,000.
   a. Calculate Cardinal's cost recovery deduction for 1994 for computing taxable income, assuming Cardinal does not make the § 179 election or use straight-line cost recovery.
   b. Calculate Cardinal's cost recovery deduction for 1994 for computing taxable income, assuming Cardinal does not make the § 179 election but does elect to use ADS 150% declining-balance cost recovery.

50. On August 1, 1994, Jake acquired a dental practice from Bob for $250,000. The purchase price was allocated $200,000 to the tangible assets of the practice and $50,000 to the goodwill. Determine Jake's deduction for the amortization of the goodwill for 1994.

51. Wes acquired a mineral interest during the year for $5,000,000. A geological survey estimated that 250,000 tons of the mineral remained in the deposit. During the year, 80,000 tons were mined, and 45,000 tons were sold for $6,000,000. Other expenses amounted to $4,000,000. Assuming the mineral depletion rate is 22%, calculate Wes's lowest taxable income.

52. Chris purchased an oil interest for $2,000,000. Recoverable barrels were estimated to be 500,000. During the year, 120,000 barrels were sold for $3,840,000, regular expenses (including cost recovery) were $1,240,000, and IDC were $1,000,000. Calculate Chris's taxable income under the expensing and capitalization methods of handling IDC.

CUMULATIVE PROBLEMS

53. John Smith, age 31, is single and has no dependents. At the beginning of 1994, John started his own excavation business and named it Earth Movers. John lives at 1045 Center Street, Lindon, UT, and his business is located at 381 State Street, Lindon, UT. The zip code for both addresses is 84059. John's Social Security number is 321–09–6456, and the business identification number is 98–1234567. John is a cash basis taxpayer. During 1994, John had the following items in connection with his business:

Fees for services	$255,000
Building rental expense	30,000
Office furniture and equipment rental expense	5,000
Office supplies	1,500
Utilities	2,000
Salary for secretary	25,000
Salary for equipment operators	70,000
Payroll taxes	9,000
Fuel and oil for the equipment	20,000
Purchase of three front-end loaders on January 15, 1994, for $175,000. John made the election under § 179.	175,000
Purchase of a new dump truck on January 18, 1994	30,000

During 1994, John had the following additional items:

Interest income from First National Bank	$9,000
Dividends from Exxon	1,500
Quarterly estimated tax payments	11,500

On October 8, 1994, John inherited IBM stock from his Aunt Mildred. John had been her favorite nephew. According to the data provided by the executor of Aunt Mildred's estate, the stock had been valued for estate tax purposes at $70,000. On October 9, 1994, John sold the stock for its fair market value of $75,000 and used the proceeds to buy an Acura NSX. John uses the car 100% for his personal use.

Assuming John does not itemize his deductions, compute his Federal income tax payable (or refund due). Suggested software (if available): *TurboTax* or *MacInTax* for tax return or WFT tax planning software.

54. Bob Brown, age 30, is single and has no dependents. He was employed as a barber until May 1993 by Hair Cuts, Inc. In June 1993, Bob opened his own styling salon, the Style Shop, located at 465 Willow Drive, St. Paul, MN 55455. Bob is a cash basis taxpayer. He lives at 1021 Snelling Avenue, St. Paul, MN 55455. His Social Security number is 321–56–7102. Bob does not wish to designate $3 to the Presidential Election Campaign Fund. During 1993, Bob had the following income and expense items:
   a. $20,800 salary from Hair Cuts, Inc.
   b. $2,400 Federal income tax withheld by Hair Cuts, Inc.
   c. $600 cash dividend from General Motors.
   d. $7,000 gross receipts from his own hair styling business.
   e. Expenses connected with Bob's hair styling business:

   • $100 laundry and cleaning

   • $4,400 rent

   • $700 supplies

   • $600 utilities and telephone

   f. Bob purchased and installed a fancy barber chair on June 3, 1993. The chair cost $6,400. Bob did not make the § 179 election.

g. Bob purchased and installed furniture and fixtures on June 5, 1993. These items cost $7,000. Bob did not make the § 179 election.

h. Bob had no itemized deductions.

Compute Bob Brown's 1993 Federal income tax payable (or refund due). If you use tax forms for your computations, you will need Forms 1040 and 4562 and Schedules B and C. Suggested software (if available): *TurboTax* or *MacInTax* for tax return or WFT tax planning software.

RESEARCH PROBLEMS

Research Problem 1.   Harry, who is one of your clients, is considering building a golf course in the resort area of Sun River, Oregon. Because the land is unimproved, all of the sand traps, greens, fairways, and tees will need to be constructed. Write a letter to Harry that contains your advice on whether any deductions can be taken for the landscaping improvements. Also prepare a memo for the tax files.

Research Problem 2.   Doug operates a restaurant in a small town. In May of the current year, Doug had a new septic tank installed for the restaurant. The town plans to construct a sewage system in five years. At that time, Doug will be required to be connected to the town system, and his septic tank will be obsolete. Doug believes that depreciation should represent wear, tear, and obsolescence, and, hence, he believes he should use a five-year life for the depreciation of the septic tank. Discuss the proper period and method for depreciating the septic tank.

Partial list of research aids:
J. O. Miller, 56 TCM 1242, T.C.Memo. 1989–66.
Rev.Proc. 87–56, 1987–2 C.B. 674.

Research Problem 3.   Sandra purchased the following personal property during 1994:

Date	Asset	Cost
June 1	Machine A	$20,000
July 10	Machine B	10,000
November 15	Machine C	25,000

Sandra elects to take the § 179 expense on Machine C. Discuss what convention Sandra must use to determine her cost recovery deduction for 1994.

Research Problem 4.   Gabriella is a professor of violin at the University of Minnesota. She is also a concert violinist. Gabriella purchased her violin for $80,000. Discuss whether Gabriella's violin is of a character subject to cost recovery using MACRS with the violin being classified as five-year property.

9

DEDUCTIONS: EMPLOYEE EXPENSES

LEARNING OBJECTIVES

After completing Chapter 9, you should be able to:

1. Distinguish between employee and self-employed status.

2. Recognize deductible transportation expenses.

3. Know how travel expenses are treated.

4. Understand the moving expense deduction.

5. Differentiate between deductible and nondeductible education expenses.

6. Understand how entertainment expenses are treated.

7. Recognize other employee expenses.

8. Appreciate the difference between accountable and non-accountable employee plans.

9. Know how to apply the limitations on miscellaneous itemized deductions.

10. Develop tax planning ideas related to employee business expenses.

OUTLINE

Employee versus Self-Employed, 9–2

Employee Expenses—In General, 9–4

Transportation Expenses, 9–4

Qualified Expenditures, 9–4

Computation of Automobile Expenses, 9–6

Travel Expenses, 9–7

Definition of Travel Expenses, 9–7

Away-from-Home Requirement, 9–7

Restrictions on Travel Expenses, 9–8

Combined Business and Pleasure Travel, 9–9

Moving Expenses, 9–11

Distance Test, 9–12

Time Test, 9–12

Treatment of Moving Expenses, 9–13

Education Expenses, 9–13

General Requirements, 9–13

Requirements Imposed by Law or by the Employer for Retention of Employment, 9–14

Maintaining or Improving Existing Skills, 9–14

Classification of Specific Items, 9–15

Other Provisions Dealing with Education, 9–15

Entertainment Expenses, 9–16

Dollar Limitations, 9–16

Classification of Expenses, 9–17

Restrictions upon Deductibility, 9–17

Other Employee Expenses, 9–20

Office in the Home, 9–20

Miscellaneous Employee Expenses, 9–21

Contributions to Individual Retirement Accounts, 9–22

Classification of Employee Expenses, 9–22

Accountable Plans, 9–23

Nonaccountable Plans, 9–24

Reporting Procedures, 9–24

Limitations on Itemized Deductions, 9–25

Miscellaneous Itemized Deductions Subject to the 2 Percent Floor, 9–25

Miscellaneous Itemized Deductions Not Subject to the 2 Percent Floor, 9–26

Tax Planning Considerations, 9–26

Self-Employed Individuals, 9–26

Shifting Deductions between Employer and Employee, 9–27

Transportation and Travel Expenses, 9–27

Moving Expenses, 9–27

Education Expenses, 9–28

Entertainment Expenses, 9–28

Unreimbursed Employee Business Expenses, 9–28

Considering the large number of taxpayers affected, the tax treatment of job-related expenses is unusually complex. To resolve this matter in a systematic fashion, a number of key questions must be asked:

- Is the taxpayer an *employee* or *self-employed?*
- If an employee, what expenses *qualify* as deductions?
- How are the expenses that qualify *classified* for tax purposes?
- To the extent the expenses are classified as deductions *from* AGI, are they subject to any *limitation?*

Once these questions have been posed and answered, the chapter considers various planning procedures available to maximize the deductibility of employee expenses.

EMPLOYEE VERSUS SELF-EMPLOYED

1 LEARNING OBJECTIVE
Distinguish between employee and self-employed status.

The determination of employment status is already controversial and can be expected to become an even greater problem in the future. Businesses are increasingly relying on the services of self-employed persons (i.e., **independent contractors**) for numerous reasons. Unlike employees, self-employed persons do not have to be included in various fringe benefit programs (e.g., group term life insurance) and retirement plans. Since they are not covered by FICA and FUTA (see Chapter 1), these payroll costs are avoided. Also, there is fear that any new national health care system will place added financial burdens on employers.

The IRS is very much aware of the tendency of businesses to wrongly classify workers. In terms of tax consequences, employment status also makes a great deal of difference to the persons who perform the services. Expenses of self-employed taxpayers, to the extent allowable, are classified as deductions *for* AGI and are reported on Schedule C (Profit or Loss From Business) of Form 1040.[1] With the exception of reimbursement under an accountable plan (see later in the chapter), expenses of employees are deductions *from* AGI. They are reported on Form 2106 (Employee Business Expenses) and Schedule A (Itemized Deductions) of Form 1040.[2]

But when does an employer-employee relationship exist? Such a relationship exists when the employer has the right to specify the end result and the ways and means by which that result is to be attained.[3] An employee is subject to the will and control of the employer with respect not only to what shall be done but also to how it shall be done. If the individual is subject to the direction or control of another only to the extent of the end result but not as to the means of accomplishment, an employer-employee relationship does not exist. An example is the preparation of a taxpayer's return by an independent CPA.

Certain factors may indicate an employer-employee relationship. They include (1) the right to discharge without legal liability the person performing the service, (2) the furnishing of tools or a place to work, and (3) payment based on time spent rather than the task performed. Each case is tested on its own merits, and the right to control the means and methods of accomplishment is the definitive test. Generally, physicians, lawyers, dentists, contractors, subcontractors, and others who offer services to the public are not classified as employees.

EXAMPLE 1

Arnold is a lawyer whose major client accounts for 60% of his billings. He does the routine legal work and income tax returns at the client's request. He is paid a monthly retainer in addition to amounts charged for extra work. Arnold is a self-employed individual. Even though most of his income comes from one client, he still has the right to determine how the end result of his work is attained. ▼

---

[1] §§ 62(a)(1) and 162(a). See Appendix B for a reproduction of Schedule C.

[2] See Appendix B for a reproduction of Form 2106 and Schedule A.
[3] Reg. § 31.3401(c)–(1)(b).

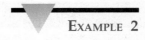

EXAMPLE 2   Ellen is a lawyer hired by Arnold to assist him in the performance of services for the client mentioned in Example 1. Ellen is under Arnold's supervision; he reviews her work and pays her an hourly fee. Ellen is an employee of Arnold. ▼

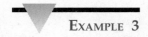

EXAMPLE 3   Frank is a licensed practical nurse who works as a private-duty nurse. He is under the supervision of the patient's doctor and is paid by the patient. Frank is not an employee of either the patient (who pays him) or the doctor (who supervises him). The ways and means of attaining the end result (care of the patient) are under his control. ▼

Employees in a special category are also allowed to file Schedule C to report income and deduct expenses *for* AGI. These employees are called statutory employees because they are not common law employees under the rules explained above. The wages or commissions paid to statutory employees are not subject to Federal income tax withholding but are subject to Social Security tax.

EMPLOYEE EXPENSES—IN GENERAL

Once the employment relationship has been established, employee expenses fall into one of the following categories:

- Transportation.
- Travel.
- Moving.
- Education.
- Entertainment.
- Other.

These expenses are discussed below in the order presented.

Keep in mind, however, that these expenses are not necessarily limited to employees. A deduction for business transportation, for example, is equally available to taxpayers who are self-employed.

TRANSPORTATION EXPENSES

QUALIFIED EXPENDITURES

2   LEARNING OBJECTIVE
Recognize deductible transportation expenses.

An employee may deduct unreimbursed employment-related transportation expenses as an itemized deduction *from* AGI. **Transportation expenses** include only the cost of transporting the employee from one place to another when the employee is not away from home *in travel status*. Such costs include taxi fares, automobile expenses, tolls, and parking.

Commuting Expenses

Commuting between home and one's place of employment is a personal, nondeductible expense. The fact that one employee drives 30 miles to work and another employee walks six blocks is of no significance.[4]

---

[4] *Tauferner v. U.S.,* 69–1 USTC ¶9241, 23 AFTR2d 69–1025, 407 F.2d 243 (CA–10, 1969).

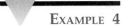

EXAMPLE 4

Geraldo is employed by Sparrow Corporation. He drives 22 miles each way to work. One day Geraldo drove to a customer's office from his place of work. The drive was a 14-mile round trip to the customer's office. Geraldo can take a deduction for 14 miles of business transportation. The remaining 44 miles are a nondeductible commuting expense. ▼

The rule that disallows a deduction for commuting expenses has several exceptions. An employee who uses an automobile to transport heavy tools to work and who otherwise would not drive to work will be allowed a deduction, but only for the additional costs incurred to transport the work implements. Additional costs are those exceeding the cost of commuting by the same mode of transportation without the tools. For example, the rental of a trailer for transporting tools is deductible, but the expenses of operating the automobile are not deductible.[5] The Supreme Court has held that a deduction is permitted only when the taxpayer can show that the automobile would not have been used without the necessity to transport tools or equipment.[6]

Another exception is provided for an employee who has a second job. The expenses of getting from one job to another are deductible. If the employee goes home between jobs, the deduction is based on the distance between jobs.

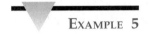

EXAMPLE 5

In the current year, Cynthia holds two jobs, a full-time job with Blue Corporation and a part-time job with Wren Corporation. During the 250 days that she works (adjusted for weekends, vacation, and holidays), Cynthia customarily leaves home at 7:30 A.M. and drives 30 miles to the Blue Corporation plant, where she works until 5:00 P.M. After dinner at a nearby cafe, Cynthia drives 20 miles to Wren Corporation and works from 7:00 to 11:00 P.M. The distance from the second job to Cynthia's home is 40 miles. Her deduction is based on 20 miles (the distance between jobs). ▼

If the taxpayer is required to incur a transportation expense to travel between work stations, that expense is deductible.

EXAMPLE 6

Thomas, a general contractor, drove from his home to his office, then drove to three building sites to perform his required inspections, and finally drove home. The costs of driving to his office and driving home from the last inspection site are nondeductible commuting expenses. The other transportation costs are deductible. ▼

Likewise, the commuting costs from home to a temporary work station and from the temporary work station to home are deductible.[7]

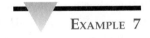

EXAMPLE 7

Vivian works for a firm in downtown Denver and commutes to work. She occasionally works in a customer's office. On one such occasion, Vivian drove directly to the customer's office, a round-trip distance from her home of 40 miles. She did not go into her office, which is a 52-mile round-trip. Her mileage is deductible. ▼

Also deductible is the reasonable travel cost between the general working area and a temporary work station outside that area. What constitutes the general working area depends on the facts and circumstances of each situation. Furthermore, if an employee customarily works on several temporary assignments in a localized area, that localized area becomes the regular place of employment.

---

[5] Rev.Rul. 75–380, 1975–2 C.B. 59.
[6] *Fausner v. Comm.*, 73–2 USTC ¶9515, 32 AFTR2d 73–5202, 93 S.Ct. 2820 (USSC, 1973).

[7] Rev.Rul. 90–23, 1990–1 C.B. 28.

Transportation from home to these locations becomes a personal, nondeductible commuting expense.

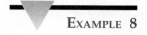

EXAMPLE 8

Sam, a building inspector in Minneapolis, regularly inspects buildings for building code violations for his employer, a general contractor. During one busy season, the St. Paul inspector became ill, and Sam was required to inspect several buildings in St. Paul. The expenses for transportation for the trips to St. Paul are deductible. ▼

COMPUTATION OF AUTOMOBILE EXPENSES

A taxpayer has two choices in computing automobile expenses. The actual operating cost, which includes depreciation, gas, oil, repairs, licenses, and insurance, may be used. Records must be kept that detail the automobile's personal and business use. Only the percentage allocable to business transportation and travel is allowed as a deduction. Complex rules for the computation of depreciation (discussed in Chapter 8) apply if the actual expense method is used.

Use of the **automatic mileage method** is the second alternative. For 1994 the deduction is based on 29 cents per mile for all business miles.[8] Parking fees and tolls are allowed in addition to expenses computed using the automatic mileage method.

Generally, a taxpayer may elect either method for any particular year. However, the following restrictions apply:

- The vehicle must be owned by the taxpayer.
- If two or more vehicles are in use (for business purposes) at the *same* time (not alternately), a taxpayer may not use the automatic mileage method.
- A basis adjustment is required if the taxpayer changes from the automatic mileage method to the actual operating cost method. Depreciation is considered allowed for the business miles in accordance with the following schedule for the most recent five years:

Year	Rate per Mile
1994	12 cents
1993	11.5 cents
1992	11.5 cents
1991	11 cents
1990	11 cents

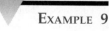

EXAMPLE 9

Tim purchased his automobile in 1991 for $9,000. It is used 90% for business purposes. Tim drove the automobile for 10,000 business miles in 1993; 8,500 miles in 1992; and 6,000 miles in 1991. At the beginning of 1994, the basis of the business portion is $5,312.

Cost ($9,000 × 90%)	$ 8,100
Less depreciation:	
1993 (10,000 miles × 11.5 cents)	(1,150)
1992 (8,500 miles × 11.5 cents)	(978)
1991 (6,000 × 11 cents)	(660)
Adjusted business basis 1/1/94	$ 5,312

▼

---

[8] Rev.Proc. 93–51, I.R.B. No. 42, 30. The rate was 28 cents a mile for 1992 and 1993.

- Use of the standard mileage rate in the first year the auto is placed in service is considered an election to exclude the auto from the MACRS method of depreciation (discussed in Chapter 8).
- A taxpayer may not switch to the automatic mileage method if the MACRS statutory percentage method or the election to expense under § 179 has been used.

TRAVEL EXPENSES

DEFINITION OF TRAVEL EXPENSES

3 LEARNING OBJECTIVE
Know how travel expenses are treated.

An itemized deduction is allowed for unreimbursed travel expenses related to a taxpayer's employment. **Travel expenses** are more broadly defined in the Code than are transportation expenses. Travel expenses include transportation expenses and meals and lodging while away from home in the pursuit of a trade or business. Meals cannot be lavish or extravagant under the circumstances. Transportation expenses (as previously discussed) are deductible even though the taxpayer is not away from home. A deduction for travel expenses is available only if the taxpayer is away from his or her tax home. Travel expenses also include reasonable laundry and incidental expenses.

AWAY-FROM-HOME REQUIREMENT

The crucial test for the deductibility of travel expenses is whether or not the employee is away from home overnight. "Overnight" need not be a 24-hour period, but it must be a period substantially longer than an ordinary day's work and must require rest, sleep, or a relief-from-work period.[9] A one-day business trip is not travel, and meals and lodging for such a trip are not deductible.

Temporary Assignments

The employee must be away from home for a temporary period. If the taxpayer-employee is reassigned to a new post for an indefinite period of time, that new post becomes his or her tax home. *Temporary* indicates that the assignment's termination is expected within a reasonably short period of time. The position of the IRS is that the tax home is the business location, post, or station of the taxpayer. Thus, travel expenses are not deductible if a taxpayer is reassigned for an indefinite period and does not move his or her place of residence to the new location.

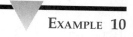 EXAMPLE 10

Malcolm's employer opened a branch office in San Diego. Malcolm was assigned to the new office for three months to train a new manager and to assist in setting up the new office. He tried commuting from his home in Los Angeles for a week and decided that he could not continue driving several hours a day. He rented an apartment in San Diego, where he lived during the week. He spent weekends with his wife and children at their home in Los Angeles. Malcolm's rent, meals, laundry, incidentals, and automobile expenses in San Diego are deductible. To the extent that Malcolm's transportation expense related to his weekend trips home exceeds what his cost of meals and lodging would have been, the excess is personal and nondeductible. ▼

[9] *U.S. v. Correll,* 68–1 USTC ¶9101, 20 AFTR2d 5845, 88 S.Ct. 445 (USSC, 1967); Rev.Rul. 75–168, 1975–1 C.B. 58.

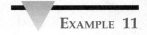

EXAMPLE 11

Assume that Malcolm in Example 10 was transferred to the new location to become the new manager permanently. His wife and children continued to live in Los Angeles until the end of the school year. Malcolm is no longer "away from home" because the assignment is not temporary. His travel expenses are not deductible. ▼

To curtail controversy in this area, the Code specifies that a taxpayer "*shall not* be treated as *temporarily* away from home during any period of employment if such period exceeds 1 year."[10]

Determining the Tax Home

Under ordinary circumstances, there is no problem in determining the location of a taxpayer's tax home. The tax home is the area in which the taxpayer derives his or her principal source of income or is based on the amount of time spent in each area when the taxpayer has more than one place of employment.

It is possible for a taxpayer never to be away from his or her tax home. In other words, the tax home follows the taxpayer.[11] Thus, all meals and lodging remain personal and are not deductible.

ETHICAL CONSIDERATIONS

The Same Job But Different Deductions

Two unrelated taxpayers, Bill and Bob, are employed as long-haul truck drivers. Bill is single, stores his clothes and other belongings at his parents' home, and stops there for periodic visits. Most of the time, Bill is on the road, sleeping in his truck and in motels. Bob is married and owns his own home where his wife and children live. Bob spends Christmas with his family and usually goes home to vote. He spends about as much time on the road as Bill does.

For tax purposes, the deductibility of Bill's and Bob's travel expenses may differ. Bill cannot deduct his meals and lodging while on the road whereas Bob may be able to do so.

RESTRICTIONS ON TRAVEL EXPENSES

The possibility always exists that taxpayers will attempt to treat vacation or pleasure travel as deductible business travel. To prevent such practices, the law contains restrictions on certain travel expenses.

Conventions

For travel expenses to be deductible, the convention must be directly related to the taxpayer's trade or business.[12]

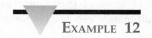

EXAMPLE 12

Dr. Hill, a pathologist who works for a hospital in Ohio, travels to Las Vegas to attend a two-day session on recent developments in estate planning. No deduction is allowed for Dr. Hill's travel expenses. ▼

---

[10] § 162(a). Added by the Comprehensive National Energy Policy Act of 1992.

[11] *Moses Mitnick*, 13 T.C. 1 (1949).

[12] § 274(h)(1).

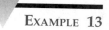

EXAMPLE 13   Assume the same facts as in Example 12 except that the convention deals entirely with recent developments in forensic medicine. Under these circumstances, a travel deduction is allowed. ▼

If the proceedings of the convention are videotaped, the taxpayer must attend convention sessions to view the videotaped materials along with other participants. This requirement does not disallow deductions for costs (other than travel, meals, and entertainment) of renting or using videotaped materials related to business.

EXAMPLE 14   A CPA is unable to attend a convention at which current developments in taxation are discussed. She pays $200 for videotapes of the lectures that she views at home later. The $200 is an itemized deduction if the CPA is an employee. If she is self-employed, the $200 is a deduction *for* AGI. ▼

RRA of 1993 recently amended the Code to place stringent restrictions on the deductibility of travel expenses of the taxpayer's spouse or dependent.[13] Generally, the accompaniment by the spouse or dependent must serve a bona fide business purpose, and the expenses must be otherwise deductible.

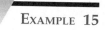

EXAMPLE 15   Assume the same facts as in Example 13 with the additional fact that Dr. Hill is accompanied by Mrs. Hill. Mrs. Hill is not employed, but possesses secretarial skills and takes notes during the proceedings. No deduction is allowed for Mrs. Hill's travel expenses.

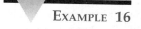

EXAMPLE 16   Modify the facts in Example 15 to make Mrs. Hill a nurse trained in pathology, who is employed by Dr. Hill as his assistant. Now, Mrs. Hill's travel expenses will qualify for deduction. ▼

Education

Travel as a form of education is not deductible.[14] If, however, the education qualifies as a deduction, the travel involved is allowed.

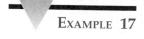

EXAMPLE 17   Greta, a German teacher, travels to Germany to maintain general familiarity with the language and culture. No travel expense deduction is allowed. ▼

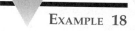

EXAMPLE 18   Jean-Claude, a scholar of French literature, travels to Paris to do specific library research that cannot be done elsewhere and to take courses that are offered only at the Sorbonne. The travel costs are deductible, assuming that the other requirements for deducting education expenses (discussed later in the chapter) are met. ▼

COMBINED BUSINESS AND PLEASURE TRAVEL

To be deductible, travel expenses need not be incurred in the performance of specific job functions. Travel expenses incurred in attending a professional convention are deductible by an employee if attendance is connected with services as an employee. For example, an employee of a law firm could deduct travel expenses incurred in attending a meeting of the American Bar Association.

Domestic Travel

Travel deductions have been used in the past by persons who claimed a tax deduction for what was essentially a personal vacation. As a result, several

---

[13] § 274(m)(3).   [14] § 274(m)(2).

provisions have been enacted to govern deductions associated with combined business and pleasure trips. If the business/pleasure trip is from one point in the United States to another point in the United States, the transportation expenses are deductible only if the trip is *primarily for business*.[15] If the trip is primarily for pleasure, no transportation expenses can be taken as a deduction. Meals, lodging, and other expenses must be allocated between business and personal days.

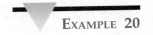

EXAMPLE 19

In 1994, Hana traveled from Seattle to New York primarily for business. She spent five days conducting business and three days sightseeing and attending shows. Her plane and taxi fare amounted to $560. Her meals amounted to $100 per day, and lodging and incidental expenses were $150 per day. She can deduct the transportation charges of $560, since the trip was primarily for business (five days of business versus three days of sightseeing). Meals are limited to five days and will be subject to the 50% cutback (discussed later in the chapter) for a total of $250 [5 days × ($100 × 50%)], and other expenses are limited to $750 (5 days × $150). All the travel expenses are miscellaneous itemized deductions. ▼

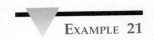

EXAMPLE 20

Assume Hana goes to New York for a two-week vacation. While there, she spends several hours renewing acquaintances with people in her company's New York office. Her transportation expenses are not deductible. ▼

Foreign Travel

When the trip is *outside the United States,* special rules apply.[16] Transportation expenses must be allocated between business and personal unless (1) the taxpayer is away from home for seven days or less *or* (2) less than 25 percent of the time was for personal purposes. No allocation is required if the taxpayer has no substantial control over arrangements for the trip or the desire for a vacation is not a major factor in taking the trip. If the trip is primarily for pleasure, no transportation charges are deductible. Days devoted to travel are considered as business days. Weekends, legal holidays, and intervening days are considered business days, provided that both preceding and succeeding days were business days.

EXAMPLE 21

In 1994, Robert took a trip from New York to Japan primarily for business purposes. He was away from home from June 10 through June 19. He spent three days vacationing and seven days conducting business (including two travel days). His air fare was $2,500, his meals amounted to $100 per day, and lodging and incidental expenses were $160 per day. Since Robert was away from home for more than seven days and more than 25% of his time was devoted to personal purposes, only 70% (7 days business/10 days total) of the transportation is deductible. His deductions are as follows:

Transportation (70% × $2,500)		$1,750
Lodging ($160 × 7)		1,120
Meals ($100 × 7)	$ 700	
Less: 50% cutback (discussed later)	(350)	350
Total		$3,220

If Robert had been gone the same period of time but had spent only two days (rather than three) vacationing, no allocation of transportation is required. Since the pleasure portion of the trip is less than 25% of the total, all of the air fare qualifies for the travel deduction. ▼

---

[15] Reg. § 1.162–2(b)(1).

[16] § 274(c) and Reg. § 1.274–4.

Certain restrictions are imposed on the deductibility of expenses paid or incurred to attend conventions located outside the North American area. The expenses will be disallowed unless it is established that the meeting is directly related to a trade or business of the taxpayer. Disallowance will also occur unless the taxpayer shows that it is as reasonable for the meeting to be held in a foreign location as within the North American area.

The foreign convention rules will not operate to bar a deduction to an employer if the expense is compensatory in nature. For example, a trip to Rome won by a top salesperson is included in the gross income of the employee and is fully deductible by the employer.

MOVING EXPENSES

4 LEARNING OBJECTIVE
Understand the moving expense deduction.

RRA of 1993 significantly changed the tax treatment of moving expenses. In large part, the changes reduced the amount and types of expenditures that are deductible. The changes are not retroactive and apply only to expenses incurred after 1993. The text discussion that follows is based on the new law. For transitional use, however, Concept Summary 9–1 shows the tax rules applicable to pre-1994 situations.

CONCEPT SUMMARY 9–1

Comparison of Pre-1994 and Post-1993 Moving Expense Rules

	Pre-1994	Post-1993
Distance test	35 miles	50 miles
Classification	*dfrom* AGI	*dfor* AGI
Direct expenses:		
Cost of moving household and personal effects	Allowed	Allowed
Transportation of household	Allowed	Allowed
Lodging during move	Allowed	Allowed
Meals during move	20% cutback	Not allowed
Ceiling limit	None	None
Indirect expenses:		
1. Househunting trips[a]	1 + 2 = $1,500 limit	
2. Temporary living[b]	1 + 2 + 3 = $3,000 limit	Not allowed
3. Certain residential buying and selling expenses and lease expenses[c]		

a. Expenses of traveling to new place of employment to look for a home after employment is obtained.
b. Meals and lodging expenses while living in temporary quarters in the general area of the new job (30-day limit).
c. Includes commissions, escrow fees, legal expenses, points paid for financing, transfer taxes, and advertising. Also includes cost of getting into or out of a lease.

Moving expenses are deductible for moves in connection with the commencement of work at a new principal place of work.[17] Both employees and self-employed individuals can deduct these expenses. To be eligible for a moving expense deduction, a taxpayer must meet two basic tests: distance and time.

DISTANCE TEST

To meet the distance test, the taxpayer's new job location must be at least 50 miles farther from the taxpayer's old residence than the old residence was from the former place of employment. In this regard, the location of the new residence is not relevant. This eliminates a moving deduction for taxpayers who purchase a new home in the same general area without changing their place of employment. Those who accept a new job in the same general area as the old job location are also eliminated.

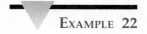

EXAMPLE 22

Harry is permanently transferred to a new job location. The distance from Harry's former home to his new job (80 miles) exceeds the distance from his former home to his old job (30 miles) by at least 50 miles. Harry has met the distance test for a moving expense deduction. (See the following diagram.)

If Harry was not employed before the move, his new job must be at least 50 miles from his former residence. In this instance, the distance test would be met if Harry had not been previously employed. ▼

TIME TEST

To meet the time test, an employee must be employed on a full-time basis at the new location for 39 weeks in the 12-month period following the move. If the taxpayer is a self-employed individual, he or she must work in the new location for 78 weeks during the next two years. The first 39 weeks must be in the first 12 months. The taxpayer can work either as a self-employed individual or as an employee. The time test is suspended if the taxpayer dies, becomes disabled, or is discharged or transferred by the new employer through no fault of the employee.

A taxpayer might not be able to meet the 39-week test by the due date of the tax return for the year of the move. For this reason, two alternatives are allowed. The taxpayer can take the deduction in the year the expenses were incurred, even though the 39-week test has not been met. If the taxpayer later fails to meet the test, either (1) the income of the following year must be increased by an amount equal to the deduction previously claimed for moving expenses, or (2) an amended return must be filed for the year of the move. The second alternative is to wait until the test is met and then file an amended tax return for the year of the move.

---

[17] § 217(a).

TREATMENT OF MOVING EXPENSES

What Is Included

"Qualified" moving expenses include *reasonable* expenses of:

- Moving household goods and personal effects.
- Traveling from the former residence to the new place of residence.

For this purpose, *traveling* includes lodging, but not meals, for the taxpayer and members of the household.[18]

EXAMPLE 23

Jill is transferred by her employer from the Atlanta office to the San Francisco office. In this connection, she spends the following amounts:

Cost of moving furniture	$2,800
Transportation	700
Meals	200
Lodging	300

Jill's total qualified moving expense is $3,800 ($2,800 + $700 + $300). ▼

The moving expense deduction is allowed regardless of whether the employee is transferred by the existing employer or is employed by a new employer. It is allowed if the employee moves to a new area and obtains employment or switches from self-employed status to employee status (and vice versa). The moving expense deduction is also allowed if an individual is unemployed before obtaining employment in a new area.

How Treated

Qualified moving expenses that are paid (or reimbursed) by the employer are not reported as part of the gross income of the employee.[19] Moving expenses that are paid (or reimbursed) by the employer and are not qualified moving expenses are included in the employee's gross income and are not deductible. Qualified moving expenses that are not reimbursed and those of self-employed taxpayers are deductions *for* AGI.[20]

Form 3903 is used to report the details of the moving expense deduction if the employee is not reimbursed or a self-employed person is involved.

EDUCATION EXPENSES

GENERAL REQUIREMENTS

5 LEARNING OBJECTIVE
Differentiate between deductible and nondeductible education expenses.

An employee may deduct expenses incurred for education (**education expenses**) as ordinary and necessary business expenses provided the expenses were incurred for either of two reasons:

1. To maintain or improve existing skills required in the present job.
2. To meet the express requirements of the employer or the requirements imposed by law to retain his or her employment status.

---

[18] § 217(b).
[19] §§ 132(a)(6) and (g).
[20] § 62(a)(15).

Education expenses are not deductible if the education is for either of the following purposes:

1. To meet the minimum educational standards for qualification in the taxpayer's existing job.
2. To qualify the taxpayer for a new trade or business.[21]

Fees incurred for professional qualification exams (the bar exam, for example) and fees for review courses (such as a CPA review course) are not deductible.[22] A deduction may be allowed for nonaccounting courses that also maintain and improve an accountant's existing skills in a present job.[23] If the education incidentally results in a promotion or raise, the deduction still can be taken as long as the education maintained and improved existing skills and did not qualify a person for a new trade or business. A change in duties is not always fatal to the deduction if the new duties involve the same general work. For example, the IRS has ruled that a practicing dentist's education expenses incurred to become an orthodontist are deductible.[24]

REQUIREMENTS IMPOSED BY LAW OR BY THE EMPLOYER FOR RETENTION OF EMPLOYMENT

Teachers are permitted to deduct education expenses if additional courses are required by the employer or are imposed by law. Many states require a minimum of a bachelor's degree and a specified number of additional courses to retain a teaching job. In addition, some public school systems have imposed a master's degree requirement and require teachers to make satisfactory progress toward a master's degree in order to keep their positions. If the required education is the minimum degree required for the job, no deduction is allowed.

A taxpayer classified as an Accountant I who went back to school to obtain a bachelor's degree was not allowed to deduct the expenses. Although some courses tended to maintain and improve his existing skills in his entry-level position, the degree was the minimum requirement for his job.[25]

Expenses incurred for education required by law for various professions will also qualify for deduction.

EXAMPLE 24

In order to satisfy the State Board of Public Accountancy rules for maintaining her CPA license, Nancy takes an auditing course sponsored by a local college. The cost of the education will be deductible. ▼

MAINTAINING OR IMPROVING EXISTING SKILLS

The "maintaining or improving existing skills" requirement in the Code has been difficult for both taxpayers and the courts to interpret. For example, a business executive may be permitted to deduct the costs of obtaining an M.B.A. on the grounds that the advanced management education is undertaken to maintain and improve existing management skills. The executive would be eligible to deduct

---

[21] Reg. §§ 1.162–5(b)(2) and (3).
[22] Reg. § 1.212–1(f) and Rev.Rul. 69–292, 1969–1 C.B. 84.
[23] *Howard Sherman Cooper,* 38 TCM 955, T.C.Memo. 1979–241.

[24] Rev.Rul. 74–78, 1974–1 C.B. 44.
[25] Reg. § 1.162–5(b)(2)(iii) Example (2); *Collin J. Davidson,* 43 TCM 743, T.C.Memo. 1982–119.

the costs of specialized, nondegree management courses that were taken for continuing education or to maintain or improve existing skills. If the business executive incurred the expenses to obtain a law degree, they would not be deductible because the education constitutes training for a new trade or business. The Regulations deny a self-employed accountant a deduction for expenses relating to law school.[26]

CLASSIFICATION OF SPECIFIC ITEMS

Education expenses include books, tuition, typing, and transportation (e.g., from the office to night school) and travel (e.g., meals and lodging while away from home at summer school).

EXAMPLE 25

Bill, who holds a bachelor of education degree, is a secondary education teacher in the Los Angeles school system. The school board recently changed its minimum education requirement for new teachers by prescribing five years of college training instead of four. Under a grandfather clause, teachers who have only four years of college will continue to qualify if they show satisfactory progress toward a graduate degree. Bill enrolls at the University of California and takes three graduate courses. His unreimbursed expenses for this purpose are as follows:

Books and tuition	$2,600
Lodging while in travel status (June–August)	1,150
Meals while in travel status	800
Laundry while in travel status	220
Transportation	600

Bill has an itemized deduction as follows:

Books and tuition	$2,600
Lodging	1,150
Meals less 50% cutback (see below)	400
Laundry	220
Transportation	600
	$4,970

OTHER PROVISIONS DEALING WITH EDUCATION

The focus of this chapter is on the deduction aspects of certain items. For education, however, two important provisions involve the income aspects. One deals with the exclusion of certain scholarships from gross income.[27] The other deals with the exclusion from gross income of employer amounts provided under certain educational assistance programs.[28] Both of these provisions are discussed in Chapter 5.

---

[26] Reg. § 1.162–5(b)(3)(ii) Example (1).
[27] § 117.

[28] § 127.

ENTERTAINMENT EXPENSES

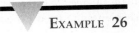

6   LEARNING OBJECTIVE
Understand how entertainment expenses are treated.

Many taxpayers attempt to deduct personal entertainment expenses as business expenses. For this reason, the tax law restricts the deductibility of entertainment expenses. The Code contains strict record-keeping requirements and provides restrictive tests for the deduction of certain types of **entertainment expenses.**

DOLLAR LIMITATIONS

Under RRA of 1993, only 50 percent of meal and entertainment expenses are allowed as a deduction.[29] The limitation applies in the context of both employment and self-employment status. The 50 percent cutback is effective for tax years beginning after 1993 (previously the cutback was 20 percent). Although the cutback can apply to either the employer or the employee, it will not apply twice. The cutback applies to the one who really pays (economically) for the meals or entertainment.

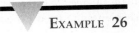

EXAMPLE 26

Jane, an employee of Pelican Corporation, entertains one of her clients. If Pelican Corporation does not reimburse Jane, she is subject to the cutback adjustment. If, however, Pelican Corporation reimburses Jane (or pays for the entertainment directly), Pelican will suffer the cutback. ▼

What Is Covered

Transportation expenses are not affected by this provision—only meals and entertainment. The cutback also applies to taxes and tips relating to meals and entertainment. Cover charges, parking fees at an entertainment location, and room rental fees for a meal or cocktail party are also subject to the 50 percent rule.

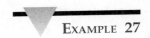

EXAMPLE 27

Joe pays a $30 cab fare to meet his client for dinner. The meal costs $120, and Joe leaves a $20 tip. His deduction is $100 [($120 + $20) × 50% + $30 cab fare]. ▼

What Is Not Covered

The cutback rule has a number of exceptions. One exception covers the case where the full value of the meals or entertainment is included in the compensation of the employee (or independent contractor).[30]

EXAMPLE 28

Myrtle wins an all-expense-paid trip to Europe for selling the most insurance for her company during the year. Her employer treats this trip as additional compensation to Myrtle. The cutback adjustment does not apply to the employer. ▼

Another exception applies to meals and entertainment in a subsidized eating facility or where the *de minimis* fringe benefit rule is met (see Chapter 5).[31]

EXAMPLE 29

General Hospital has an employee cafeteria on the premises for its doctors, nurses, and other employees. The cafeteria operates at cost. The cutback rule does not apply to General Hospital. ▼

---

[29] § 274(n).
[30] §§ 274(e)(2) and (9).

[31] § 274(n)(2).

EXAMPLE 30

Canary Corporation gives a ham, a fruitcake, and a bottle of wine to each employee at year-end. Since the *de minimis* fringe benefit exclusion applies to business gifts of packaged foods and beverages, their *full* cost is deductible by Canary. ▼

A somewhat similar exception applies to employer-paid recreational activities for employees (e.g., the annual Christmas party or spring picnic).[32]

CLASSIFICATION OF EXPENSES

Entertainment expenses are categorized as follows: those *directly related* to business and those *associated with* business.[33] Directly related expenses are related to an actual business meeting or discussion. These expenses can be contrasted with entertainment expenses that are incurred to promote goodwill, such as maintaining existing customer relations. To obtain a deduction for directly related entertainment, it is not necessary to show that actual benefit resulted from the expenditure as long as there was a reasonable expectation of benefit. To qualify as directly related, the expense should be incurred in a clear business setting. If there is little possibility of engaging in the active conduct of a trade or business due to the nature of the social facility, it may be difficult to qualify the expenditure as directly related to business.

Expenses associated with, rather than directly related to, business entertainment must serve a specific business purpose, such as obtaining new business or continuing existing business. These expenditures qualify only if the expenses directly precede or follow a bona fide business discussion. Entertainment occurring on the same day as the business discussion meets the test.

RESTRICTIONS UPON DEDUCTIBILITY

Business Meals

Any business meal is deductible only if the following are true:[34]

- The meal is directly related to or associated with the active conduct of a trade or business.

---

[32] § 274(e)(4).
[33] § 274(a)(1)(A).

[34] § 274(k).

- The expense is not lavish or extravagant under the circumstances.
- The taxpayer (or an employee) is present at the meal.

A business meal with a business associate or customer is not deductible unless business is discussed before, during, or after the meal. This requirement is not intended to disallow the deduction for a meal consumed while away from home on business.

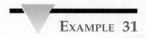

EXAMPLE 31

Lacy travels to San Francisco for a business convention. She pays for dinner with three colleagues and is not reimbursed by her employer. They do not discuss business. She can deduct 50% of the cost of her meal. However, she cannot deduct the cost of her colleagues' meals. ▼

The *clear business purpose* test requires that meals be directly related to or associated with the active conduct of a business. A meal is not deductible if it serves no business purpose.

ETHICAL CONSIDERATIONS

Reciprocal Entertaining

Walter (an attorney), Susan (an insurance broker), Richard (a realtor), and Nancy (a banker) are all good friends and do business with each other. Richard's accountant suggests that each might derive a substantial tax benefit if they went to lunch together as often as possible and rotated the tab. Richard discusses the suggestion with his friends, and they agree to follow it.

The taxpayer or an employee must be present at the business meal for the meal to be deductible.[35] An independent contractor who renders significant services to the taxpayer is treated as an employee.

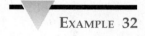

EXAMPLE 32

Lance, a party to a contract negotiation, buys dinner for other parties to the negotiation but does not attend the dinner. No deduction is allowed. ▼

Club Dues

RRA of 1993 denies *any* deduction for club dues.[36] Prior to 1994, some deduction for such dues was allowed if the taxpayer could show that the facility was used more than 50 percent of the time for business (i.e., the "primary use" test). Even though the dues may no longer be deductible, however, actual entertainment at the club may qualify.

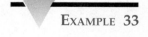

EXAMPLE 33

During 1994, Vincent spent $1,400 on business lunches at the Lakeside Country Club. The annual membership fee was $6,000, and Vincent used the facility 60% of the time for business. Presuming the lunches meet the business meal test, Vincent may claim $700 (50% × $1,400) as a deduction. None of the club dues are deductible. ▼

[35] § 274(k)(1)(B).

[36] §§ 274(a)(3).

Ticket Purchases for Entertainment

A deduction for the cost of a ticket for an entertainment activity is limited to the face value of the ticket.[37] This limitation is applied before the 50 percent rule. The face value of a ticket includes any tax. Under this rule, the excess payment to a scalper for a ticket is not deductible. Similarly, the fee to a ticket agency for the purchase of a ticket is not deductible.

Expenditures for the rental or use of a luxury skybox at a sports arena in excess of the face value of regular tickets are disallowed as deductions. If a luxury skybox is used for entertainment that is directly related to or associated with business, the deduction is limited to the face value of nonluxury box seats. All seats in the luxury skybox are counted, even when some seats are unoccupied.

The taxpayer may also deduct stated charges for food and beverages under the general rules for business entertainment. The deduction for skybox seats, food, and beverages is limited to 50 percent of cost.

EXAMPLE 34

In the current year, Condor Co. pays $6,000 to rent a 10-seat skybox at City Stadium for three football games. Nonluxury box seats at each event range in cost from $25 to $35 a seat. In March, a Condor Co. representative and five clients use the skybox for the first game. The entertainment follows a bona fide business discussion, and Condor Co. spends $86 for food and beverages during the game. The deduction for the first sports event is as follows:

Food and beverages	$ 86
Deduction for seats ($35 × 10 seats)	350
Total entertainment expense	$436
50% limitation	×.50
Deduction	$218

Business Gifts

Business gifts are deductible to the extent of $25 per donee per year.[38] An exception is made for gifts costing $4 or less (e.g., pens with the employee's or company's name on them) or promotional materials. Such items are not treated as business gifts subject to the $25 limitation. In addition, incidental costs such as engraving of jewelry and nominal charges for gift-wrapping, mailing, and delivery are not included in the cost of the gift in applying the limitation. Gifts to superiors and employers are not deductible.

Records must be maintained to substantiate business gifts.

ETHICAL CONSIDERATIONS

Plan for the $25 Limitation

Roger has a key client (Clara) to whom he usually sends a holiday gift. Roger has discovered that Clara is particularly fond of a brand of wine that retails for approximately $50. On December 31, 1994, Roger gives Clara a $25 gift certificate to Richard's Wine Emporium. Roger repeats the procedure on January 1, 1995. The

---

[37] § 274(l).

[38] § 274(b)(1).

transactions are properly substantiated and Roger claims a business gift deduction of $25 for tax years 1994 and 1995.

OTHER EMPLOYEE EXPENSES

OFFICE IN THE HOME

7   LEARNING OBJECTIVE
Recognize other employee expenses.

Employees and self-employed individuals are not allowed a deduction for **office in the home expenses** unless a portion of the residence is used exclusively on a regular basis as either:

- The principal place of business for any trade or business of the taxpayer.
- A place of business used by clients, patients, or customers.

Employees must meet an additional test: The use must be for the convenience of the employer rather than merely being "appropriate and helpful."[39]

The precise meaning of "principal place of business" was recently resolved by the U.S. Supreme Court. In a divided opinion, the Court established a two-pronged test.[40] First, determine the relative importance of the activities performed at each business location (i.e., inside and outside the personal residence). Second, compare the time spent at each business location.

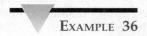

EXAMPLE 35

Dr. Smith is a self-employed anesthesiologist. During the year, he spends 30 to 35 hours per week administering anesthesia and postoperative care to patients in three hospitals, none of which provides him with an office. He also spends two to three hours per day in a room in his home that he uses exclusively as an office. He does not meet patients there, but he performs a variety of tasks related to his medical practice (e.g., contacting surgeons, bookkeeping, reading medical journals). None of Dr. Smith's expenses of the office in the home are deductible because the hospital procedures (i.e., administering to patients) are more important than those done at home. Also, more business time is spent outside the home than inside. ▼

EXAMPLE 36

Lori is a salesperson. Her only office is a room in her home that she uses regularly and exclusively to set up appointments, store product samples, and write up orders and other reports for the companies whose products she sells. Lori makes most of her sales to customers by telephone or mail from her home office. She spends an average of 30 hours a week working at home and 12 hours a week visiting prospective customers to deliver products and occasionally take orders. Under these circumstances, Lori qualifies for the office in the home deduction. Visiting customers is less important to the business than the activities conducted in Lori's office.[41] ▼

The exclusive use requirement means that a specific part of the home must be used solely for business purposes. A deduction, if permitted, will require an allocation of total expenses of operating the home between business and personal use based on floor space or number of rooms.

---

[39] § 280A(c)(1).
[40] *Comm. v. Soliman*, 93–1 USTC ¶50,014, 71 AFTR2d 93–463, 113 S.Ct. 701 (USSC, 1993) *rev'g.* 91–1 USTC ¶50,291, 67 AFTR2d 91–1112, 935 F.2d 52 (CA–4, 1991) and 94 T.C. 20 (1990).

[41] Notice 93–12, I.R.B. No. 8, 46.

Even if the taxpayer meets the above requirements, the allowable home office expenses cannot exceed the gross income from the business less all other business expenses attributable to the activity. Furthermore, the home office expenses that would be allowable as itemized deductions anyway (e.g., mortgage interest and real estate taxes) must be deducted first. All home office expenses of an employee are miscellaneous itemized deductions, except those (such as interest) that qualify as other personal itemized deductions. Home office expenses of a self-employed individual are trade or business expenses and are deductible *for* AGI.

Any disallowed home office expenses can be carried forward and used in future years subject to the same limitations.

EXAMPLE 37

Rick is a certified public accountant employed by a regional CPA firm as a tax manager. He operates a separate business in which he refinishes furniture in his home. For this business, he uses two rooms in the basement of his home exclusively and regularly. The floor space of the two rooms constitutes 10% of the floor space of his residence. Gross income from the business totals $8,000. Expenses of the business (other than home office expenses) are $6,500. Rick incurs the following home office expenses:

Real property taxes on residence	$4,000
Interest expense on residence	7,500
Operating expenses of residence	2,000
Depreciation on residence (based on 10% business use)	250

Rick's deductions are determined as follows:

Business income		$ 8,000
Less: Other business expenses		(6,500)
		$ 1,500
Less: Allocable taxes ($4,000 × 10%)	$400	
Allocable interest ($7,500 × 10%)	750	(1,150)
		$ 350
Allocable operating expenses of the residence ($2,000 × 10%)		(200)
		$ 150
Allocable depreciation ($250, limited to remaining income)		(150)
		$ –0–

Rick has a carryover of $100 (the unused excess depreciation). Because he is self-employed, the allocable taxes and interest ($1,150), the other deductible office expenses ($200 + $150), and $6,500 of other business expenses are deductible *for* AGI. ▼

Form 8829 (Expenses for Business Use of Your Home) is available from the IRS for computation of the office in the home deduction.

The home office limitation cannot be circumvented by leasing part of one's home to an employer, using it as a home office, and deducting the expenses as a rental expense under § 212.

MISCELLANEOUS EMPLOYEE EXPENSES

Deductible miscellaneous employee expenses include special clothing and its upkeep, union dues, and professional expenses. Also deductible are professional dues, professional meetings, and employment agency fees for seeking employment in the same trade or business, whether or not a new job is secured.

To be deductible, special clothing must be both specifically required as a condition of employment and not generally adaptable for regular wear. For example, a police officer's uniform is not suitable for off-duty activities. An exception is clothing used to the extent that it takes the place of regular clothing (e.g., military uniforms).

EXAMPLE 38

Captain Roberts is on active duty in the U.S. Marines. The cost of his regular uniforms is not deductible since such clothing is suitable for regular wear. Military regulations, however, generally preclude marines from wearing battle fatigues when they are off the military base. The cost of the fatigues, to the extent it exceeds any clothing allowance, would qualify as a deduction. ▼

The current position of the IRS is that expenses incurred in seeking employment are deductible if the taxpayer is seeking employment in the same trade or business. The deduction is allowed whether or not the attempts to secure employment are successful. An unemployed taxpayer can take a deduction providing there has been no substantial lack of continuity between the last job and the search for a new one. No deduction is allowed for persons seeking their first job or seeking employment in a new trade or business.

The basic cost of one telephone in the home is not deductible, even if used for business. Any long-distance or toll charges relating to business are deductible.

CONTRIBUTIONS TO INDIVIDUAL RETIREMENT ACCOUNTS

An important and popular deduction *for* AGI is the amount contributed to an Individual Retirement Account (IRA). This amount may be as great as $2,000 per year for an individual (or $2,250 for spousal IRAs). IRAs are covered in detail in Chapter 19.

CLASSIFICATION OF EMPLOYEE EXPENSES

8 LEARNING OBJECTIVE
Appreciate the difference between accountable and nonaccountable employee plans.

The classification of employee expenses depends on whether they are reimbursed by the employer under an accountable plan. If so, then they are not reported by the employee at all. In effect, therefore, this result is equivalent to treating the expenses as deductions *for* AGI.[42] If the expenses are reimbursed under a nonaccountable plan or are not reimbursed at all, then they are classified as deductions *from* AGI and can only be claimed if the employee-taxpayer itemizes. An exception is made for moving expenses and the employment-related expenses of a qualified performing artist.[43] Here, deduction *for* AGI classification is allowed.

For classification purposes, therefore, the difference between accountable and nonaccountable plans is significant.

---

[42] § 62(a)(2).
[43] As defined in § 62(b).

ACCOUNTABLE PLANS

In General

An **accountable plan** requires the employee to satisfy these two requirements:

- Adequately account for (substantiate) the expenses. An employee renders an *adequate accounting* by submitting a record, with receipts and other substantiation, to the employer.[44]
- Return any excess reimbursement or allowance. An "excess reimbursement or allowance" is any amount that the employee does not adequately account for as an ordinary and necessary business expense.

Substantiation

The law provides that no deduction will be allowed for any travel, entertainment, business gift, or listed property (automobiles, computers) expenditure unless properly substantiated by adequate records. The records should contain the following information:[45]

- The amount of the expense.
- The time and place of travel or entertainment (or date of gift).
- The business purpose of the expense.
- The business relationship of the taxpayer to the person entertained (or receiving the gift).

This means the taxpayer must maintain an account book or diary in which the above information is recorded at the time of the expenditure. Documentary evidence, such as itemized receipts, is required to support any expenditure for lodging while traveling away from home and for any other expenditure of $25 or more. If a taxpayer fails to keep adequate records, each expense must be established by a written or oral statement of the exact details of the expense and by other corroborating evidence.[46]

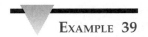

EXAMPLE 39

Bertha has travel expenses substantiated only by canceled checks. The checks establish the date, place, and amount of the expenditure. Because neither the business relationship nor the business purpose is established, the deduction will be disallowed.[47] ▼

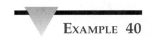

EXAMPLE 40

Dwight has travel and entertainment expenses substantiated by a diary showing the time, place, and amount of the expenditure. His oral testimony provides the business relationship and business purpose; however, since he has no receipts, any expenditures of $25 or more will be disallowed.[48] ▼

Deemed Substantiation

In lieu of reimbursing actual expenses for travel away from home, many employers reduce their paperwork by adopting a policy of reimbursing employees with a *per diem* allowance, a flat dollar amount per day of business travel. Of the substantiation requirements listed above, the *amount* of the expense is proved, or

---

[44] Reg. § 1.162–17(b)(4).
[45] § 274(d).
[46] Reg. § 1.274–5T(c)(3).

[47] *William T. Whitaker,* 56 TCM 47, T.C.Memo. 1988–418.
[48] *W. David Tyler,* 43 TCM 927, T.C.Memo. 1982–160.

deemed substantiated, by using such a per diem allowance or reimbursement procedure. The amount of expenses that is deemed substantiated is equal to the lesser of the per diem allowance or the amount of the Federal per diem rate.

The regular Federal per diem rate is the highest amount that the Federal government will pay to its employees for lodging and meals[49] while in travel status away from home in a particular area. The rates are different for different locations.

To avoid the need to keep a current list of the per diem rate in effect for each city or locale, a simplified method, called the *high-low method,* can be used. The high-low method specifies a limited number of high travel cost locations where the per diem is considered to be the same for all cities on the list. All other cities are considered to have the same, but lower, Federal per diem rate in effect.[50]

The use of the standard Federal per diem for meals constitutes an adequate accounting. Employees and self-employed persons can use the standard meal allowance instead of deducting the actual cost of daily meals, even if not reimbursed. There is no standard lodging allowance, however. An employee who receives a reimbursement of not more than the Federal standard mileage rate for automobile business miles substantiated will be treated as rendering an adequate accounting.

Only the amount of the expense is considered substantiated under the deemed substantiated method. The other substantiation requirements must be provided: place, date, business purpose of the expense, and the business relationship of the parties involved.

NONACCOUNTABLE PLANS

A **nonaccountable plan** is one in which an adequate accounting or return of excess amounts, or both, is not required. All reimbursements of expenses are reported in full as wages on the employee's Form W–2. Any allowable expenses are deductible in the same manner as are unreimbursed expenses.

Unreimbursed Employee Expenses

Unreimbursed employee expenses are treated in a straightforward manner. Meals and entertainment expenses are subject to the 50 percent limit. Total unreimbursed employee business expenses are usually reported as miscellaneous itemized deductions subject to the 2 percent-of-AGI floor (see below). If the employee could have received, but did not seek, reimbursement for whatever reason, none of the employment-related expenses are deductible.

Failure to Comply with Accountable Plan Requirements

An employer may have an accountable plan and require employees to return excess reimbursements or allowances, but an employee may fail to follow the rules of the plan. In that case, the expenses and reimbursements are subject to nonaccountable plan treatment.

REPORTING PROCEDURES

The reporting requirements range from no reporting at all (accountable plans when all requirements are met) to the use of some or all of three forms: Form W–2 (Wage

---

[49] The meals per diem also covers incidental expenses, including laundry and cleaning of clothing and tips for waiters. Taxi fares and telephone calls are not included.

[50] Each current edition of *Your Federal Income Tax* (IRS Publication 17) contains the list and amounts for that year.

and Tax Statement), Form 2106 (Employee Expenses), and Schedule A (Itemized Deductions) for nonaccountable plans and unreimbursed employee expenses.

Reimbursed employee expenses that are adequately accounted for under an accountable plan are deductible *for* AGI on Form 2106. Allowed excess expenses, expenses reimbursed under a nonaccountable plan, and unreimbursed expenses are deductible *from* AGI on Schedule A, subject to the 2 percent-of-AGI floor.

When a reimbursement under an accountable plan is paid in separate amounts relating to designated expenses such as meals or entertainment, no problem arises. The reimbursements and expenses are reported as such on the appropriate forms. If the reimbursement is made in a single amount, an allocation must be made to determine the appropriate portion of the reimbursement that applies to meals and entertainment and to other employee expenses.

EXAMPLE 41

Elizabeth, who is employed by Green Company, had AGI of $42,000. During the year, she incurred $2,000 of transportation and lodging expense and $1,000 of meals and entertainment expense, all fully substantiated. Elizabeth received $1,800 reimbursement under an accountable plan. The reimbursement rate that applies to meals and entertainment is 33.33% ($1,000 meals and entertainment expense/$3,000 total expenses). Thus, $600 ($1,800 × 33.33%) of the reimbursement applies to meals and entertainment, and $1,200 ($1,800 – $600) applies to transportation and lodging. Elizabeth's itemized deduction will consist of the $800 ($2,000 total – $1,200 reimbursement) of unreimbursed transportation and lodging expenses and $400 ($1,000 – $600) of unreimbursed meal and entertainment expenses as follows:

Transportation and lodging	$ 800
Meals and entertainment ($400 × 50%)	200
Total (reported on Form 2106)	$1,000
Less: 2% of $42,000 AGI (see limitation discussed below)	(840)
Deduction (reported on Schedule A)	$ 160

In summary, Elizabeth must report $3,000 of expenses and the $1,800 reimbursement on Form 2106 and $160 as a miscellaneous itemized deduction on Schedule A. ▼

LIMITATIONS ON ITEMIZED DEDUCTIONS

9   LEARNING OBJECTIVE
Know how to apply the limitations on miscellaneous itemized deductions.

Many itemized deductions, such as medical expenses and charitable contributions, are subject to limitations expressed as a percentage of AGI. These limitations may be expressed as floors or ceilings. These limitations are discussed in Chapter 10.

MISCELLANEOUS ITEMIZED DEDUCTIONS SUBJECT TO THE 2 PERCENT FLOOR

Certain miscellaneous itemized deductions, including most *unreimbursed employee business expenses*, must be aggregated and then reduced by 2 percent of AGI.[51] Expenses subject to the 2 percent floor include the following:

- All § 212 expenses, except expenses of producing rent and royalty income (refer to Chapter 6).

---
[51] § 67.

- All unreimbursed employee expenses (after 50 percent reduction, if applicable) except moving.
- Professional dues and subscriptions.
- Union dues and work uniforms.
- Employment-related education expenses.
- Malpractice insurance premiums.
- Expenses of job hunting (including employment agency fees and resumé-writing expenses).
- Home office expenses of an employee or outside salesperson.
- Legal, accounting, and tax return preparation fees.
- Hobby expenses (up to hobby income).
- Investment expenses, including investment counsel fees, subscriptions, and safe deposit box rental.
- Custodial fees relating to income-producing property or an IRA or a Keogh plan.
- Any fees paid to collect interest or dividends.
- Appraisal fees establishing a casualty loss or charitable contribution.

MISCELLANEOUS ITEMIZED DEDUCTIONS NOT SUBJECT TO THE 2 PERCENT FLOOR

Certain miscellaneous itemized deductions, including the following, are not subject to the 2 percent floor:

- Impairment-related work expenses of handicapped individuals.
- Gambling losses to the extent of gambling winnings.
- Certain terminated annuity payments.

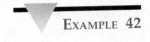

EXAMPLE 42

Ted, who has AGI of $20,000, has the following miscellaneous itemized deductions:

Gambling losses (to extent of gains)	$ 1,200
Tax return preparation fees	300
Unreimbursed employee transportation	200
Professional dues and subscriptions	260
Safe deposit box rental	30

Ted's itemized deductions are as follows:

Deduction not subject to 2% floor (gambling losses)		$1,200
Deductions subject to 2% floor ($300 + $200 + $260 + $30)	$ 790	
Less 2% of AGI	(400)	390
Total miscellaneous itemized deductions		$1,590

If Ted's AGI were $40,000, the floor would be $800 (2% of $40,000), and he could not deduct any expenses subject to the 2% floor. ▼

TAX PLANNING CONSIDERATIONS

SELF-EMPLOYED INDIVIDUALS

Some taxpayers have the flexibility to be classified as either employees or self-employed individuals. Examples include real estate agents and direct sellers. These taxpayers should carefully consider all factors and not automatically assume that self-employed status is preferable.

10   **LEARNING OBJECTIVE**
Develop tax planning ideas related to employee business expenses.

It is advantageous to deduct one's business expenses *for* AGI and avoid the 2 percent floor. However, a self-employed individual may have higher expenses, such as local gross receipts taxes, license fees, franchise fees, personal property taxes, and occupation taxes. The record-keeping and filing requirements can be quite burdensome.

One of the most expensive considerations is the Social Security tax versus the self-employment tax. For an employee in 1994, for example, the Social Security tax applies at a rate of 6.2 percent on a base amount of wages of $60,600, and the Medicare tax applies at a rate of 1.45 percent with no limit on the base amount. For self-employed persons, the rate, but not the base amount, for each tax doubles. Even though a deduction *for* AGI is allowed for one-half of the self-employment tax paid, an employee and a self-employed individual are not in the same tax position on equal amounts of earnings. The self-employment tax is explained in Chapter 13. For the applicability of these taxes to employees, see Chapter 1.

After analyzing all these factors, a taxpayer may decide that employee status is preferable to self-employed status.

SHIFTING DEDUCTIONS BETWEEN EMPLOYER AND EMPLOYEE

An employee can avoid the 2 percent floor for employee business expenses. Typically, an employee incurs travel and entertainment expenses in the course of employment. The employer gets the deduction if it reimburses the employee, and the employee gets the deduction *for* AGI. An adequate accounting must be made, and excess reimbursements cannot be kept.

TRANSPORTATION AND TRAVEL EXPENSES

Adequate detailed records should be kept of all transportation and travel expenses. Since the regular mileage allowance is 29 cents per mile, a new, expensive automobile used primarily for business may generate a higher expense based on actual cost. The election to expense part of the cost of the automobile under § 179, MACRS depreciation, insurance, repairs and maintenance, automobile club dues, and other related costs may result in automobile expenses greater than the automatic mileage allowance.

If a taxpayer wishes to sightsee or vacation on a business trip, it would be beneficial to schedule business on both a Friday and a Monday to turn the weekend into business days for allocation purposes. It is especially crucial to schedule appropriate business days when foreign travel is involved.

MOVING EXPENSES

Persons who retire and move to a new location incur personal nondeductible moving expenses. If the retired person accepts a full-time job in the new location before moving, the moving expenses become deductible.

EXAMPLE 43

At the time of his retirement from the national office of a major accounting firm, Gordon had an annual salary of $220,000. He moves from New York City to Seattle to retire. In order to qualify for the moving expense deduction, Gordon accepts a full-time teaching position at a Seattle junior college at an annual salary of $15,000. If Gordon satisfies the 39-week test, his moving expenses will be deductible. The disparity between the two salaries (previous and current) is of no consequence. ▼

EDUCATION EXPENSES

Education expenses are treated as nondeductible personal items unless the individual is employed or is engaged in a trade or business. A temporary leave of absence for further education is one way to reasonably assure that the taxpayer is still qualified, even if a full-time student. An individual was permitted to deduct education expenses even though he resigned from his job, returned to school full-time for two years, and accepted another job in the same field upon graduation. The Court held that the student had merely suspended active participation in his field.[52]

If the time out of the field is too long, educational expense deductions will be disallowed. For example, a teacher who left the field for four years to raise her child and curtailed her employment searches and writing activities was denied a deduction. She was not actively engaged in the trade or business of being an educator.[53]

To secure the deduction, an individual should arrange his or her work situation to preserve employee or business status.

ENTERTAINMENT EXPENSES

Proper documentation of expenditures is essential because of the strict recordkeeping requirements and the restrictive tests that must be met. For example, credit card receipts and canceled checks as the sole source of documentation may be inadequate to substantiate the business purpose and business relationship.[54] Taxpayers should maintain detailed records of amounts, time, place, business purpose, and business relationships. A credit card receipt details the place, date, and amount of the expense. A notation made on the receipt of the names of the person(s) attending, the business relationship, and the topic of discussion should constitute proper documentation.

Associated with or goodwill entertainment is not deductible unless a business discussion is conducted immediately before or after the entertainment. Furthermore, a business purpose must exist for the entertainment. Taxpayers should arrange for a business discussion before or after such entertainment. They must provide documentation of the business purpose, such as obtaining new business from a prospective customer.

Unreimbursed meals and entertainment are subject to the 50 percent rule in addition to the 2 percent floor. Consequently, the procedure of negotiating a salary reduction, as discussed below under Unreimbursed Employee Business Expenses, is even more valuable to the taxpayer.

UNREIMBURSED EMPLOYEE BUSINESS EXPENSES

The 2 percent floor for unreimbursed employee business expenses offers a tax planning opportunity for married couples. If one spouse has high miscellaneous expenses subject to the floor, it may be beneficial for the couple to file separate returns. If they file jointly, the 2 percent floor will be based on the incomes of both. Filing separately will lower the reduction to 2 percent of only one spouse's income.

Other provisions of the law should be considered, however. For example, filing separately could cost a couple losses of up to $25,000 from self-managed rental units under the passive activity loss rules (discussed in Chapter 11).

---

[52] *Stephen G. Sherman,* 36 TCM 1191, T.C.Memo. 1977–301.
[53] *Brian C. Mulherin,* 42 TCM 834, T.C.Memo. 1981–454; *George A. Baist,* 56 TCM 778, T.C.Memo. 1988–554.

[54] *Kenneth W. Guenther,* 54 TCM 382, T.C.Memo. 1987–440.

Another possibility is to negotiate a salary reduction with one's employer in exchange for the 100 percent reimbursement of employee expenses. The employee would be better off because the 2 percent floor would not apply. The employer would be better off because certain expense reimbursements are not subject to Social Security and other payroll taxes.

KEY TERMS

Accountable plan,
9–23

Automatic mileage
method,   9–6

Education expenses,
9–13

Entertainment
expenses,   9–16

Independent
contractor,   9–2

Moving expenses,
9–12

Nonaccountable plan,
9–24

Office in the home
expenses,   9–20

Transportation
expenses,   9–4

Travel expenses,
9–7

PROBLEM MATERIALS

DISCUSSION QUESTIONS

X   1. What difference does it make if an individual's expenses are classified as employment-related expenses or as expenses from self-employment?

X   2. Discuss the factors that may indicate an employer-employee relationship.

3. Why might a business prefer to classify a worker as an independent contractor (i.e., self-employed) rather than as an employee?

4. Under what circumstances will heavy tools used in a taxpayer's trade or business justify some deduction for commuting expenses?

5. Chris has two jobs. He drives 40 miles to his first job. The distance from the first job to the second is 32 miles. During the year, he worked 200 days at both jobs. On 150 days, he drove from his first job to the second job. On the remaining 50 days, he drove home (40 miles) and then to the second job (42 miles). How much can he deduct?

X   6. What are the two methods the taxpayer can choose in computing a deduction for automobile expenses?

7. Irene decides to claim the automatic mileage method for the business use of her car. She believes that this method will avoid a reduction in the car's basis through depreciation. Is Irene correct? Why or why not?

8. How will the following affect the decision of whether to use the automatic mileage method in deducting the business use of an auto?
a. The cost of the automobile.
b. The miles per gallon obtained.

9. Distinguish between transportation expenses and travel expenses.

10. Under the "away-from-home" requirement, what is the significance of the "overnight" concept? What does "overnight" require?

11. Jim works in St. Louis. On Tuesday morning he flies to San Francisco for a business meeting. After the meeting, Jim has lunch by himself and then flies back to St. Louis that same evening. Is the cost of Jim's lunch deductible? Why or why not?

12. Is it possible for a person never to be away from his or her tax home? Explain.

13. Can a taxpayer be away from home on a temporary assignment that lasts 13 months? Explain.

14. Dr. Fuerst, a practicing orthodontist in Buffalo, travels to New York City to attend a two-day convention on experimental orthodontia procedures. Mr. Fuerst accompanies his wife since he prepares their tax return and knows how to properly prepare the required substantiation for the trip. Comment on the deductibility of the trip.

15. If any pleasure is involved, then the travel deduction is not allowed. Comment on the validity of this statement.

16. Josephine took a combined business and pleasure trip to Europe. She traveled to London from New York on Friday, vacationed on Saturday and Sunday, conducted business on Monday, got snowed in at the airport on Tuesday, traveled to Paris on Wednesday, relaxed on Thursday (a legal holiday), conducted business on Friday, went sightseeing on Saturday and Sunday, picked up business samples and papers on Monday, and flew back to New York on Tuesday. What portion of her air fare can she deduct?

17. RRA of 1993 significantly modified the rules governing the moving expense deduction. Were such changes pro- or anti-taxpayer? Illustrate.

18. What are the distance requirements for moving expenses?

19. For the moving expense deduction, what is the time test for employees? Self-employed persons?

20. Under what circumstances, if any, may the time test for the moving expense deduction be suspended?

21. Under current rules, what expenses qualify for the moving expense deduction?

22. What difference does it make if a taxpayer is improving existing skills or acquiring new ones for the purpose of the education deduction? On what general tax principle is the justification for this rule based?

23. What expenses can qualify for the education deduction?

24. Janet wins the salesperson of the year award as an employee of the Peacock Buick dealership. The award consists of a five-day expenses-paid trip to LaCosta, California. For this award, is Janet subject to the 50% cutback adjustment? Is Peacock Buick subject to the cutback adjustment?

25. Discuss the difference between entertainment that is *directly related to* business and entertainment that is *associated with* business.

26. Discuss the requirements for the deductibility of business meals.

27. Crow Corporation has an annual Fourth of July outing for all of its employees. Will the cost of the outing be subject to the 50% cutback? Why or why not?

28. What limits are imposed on the deduction of expenses for tickets purchased for business entertainment? How are such expenses treated on an employee's return if they are reimbursed? Not reimbursed?

29. To what extent may a taxpayer take a deduction for business gifts to a business associate? To an employee? To a superior?

30. How are deductible home office expenses treated for tax purposes? Is the deduction *for* or *from* AGI?

31. Lieutenant Hebert is on active duty with the U.S. Navy. To what extent, if any, is the cost of her uniforms deductible?

32. Cynthia, a CPA, is currently employed by a public accounting firm. On a part-time basis, she earns a law degree. After attending a bar review course, she takes and passes the state bar exam. Currently, she is incurring costs in seeking employment with a law firm. Comment on the deductibility to Cynthia of each of the following expenditures:

a. The cost of attending law school.
b. The cost of the bar review course.
c. The cost of seeking employment with a law firm.

33. How does the tax treatment of meals and entertainment differ from the treatment of other employee business expenses? Does the treatment differ if the expenses are reimbursed?

34. What constitutes an adequate accounting to an employer?

35. What tax return reporting procedures must be followed by an employee under the following circumstances?
    a. Expenses and reimbursements are equal under an accountable plan.
    b. Reimbursements at the appropriate Federal per diem rate exceed expenses, and an adequate accounting is made to the employer.
    c. Expenses exceed reimbursements under a nonaccountable plan.

36. Can an employee who receives a reimbursement of 15 cents per mile for job-related automobile expenses deduct any excess expense amounts on his or her tax return?

37. Jeff Johnson has spent his life in Boston. This year he plans to retire from a national brokerage house and relocate to Albuquerque, New Mexico. He consults you as a tax adviser and wants information regarding the deductibility of his moving expenses. Write a letter to Jeff giving him advice on this matter.

PROBLEMS

38. Georgia purchased a new automobile for $16,000 in 1991. She used it 80% for business purposes, driving 12,000 business miles in 1991, 10,000 business miles in 1992, 8,000 business miles in 1993, and 5,000 business miles in 1994.

    Georgia used the automatic mileage method for all years. What is the adjusted basis of the business portion of her automobile on January 1, 1995?

39. Louis took a business trip from Chicago to Seattle. He spent two days in travel, conducted business for eight days, and visited friends for five days. He incurred the following expenses:

Air fare	$ 900
Lodging	2,100
Meals	1,500
Entertainment of clients	500

    Louis received no reimbursements. What amount can he deduct?

40. Nadine took a business trip of 10 days. Seven days were spent on business (including travel time) and 3 days were personal. Her unreimbursed expenses were as follows:

Air fare	$3,000
Lodging (per day)	400
Meals (per day)	200
Entertainment of clients	600

    a. How much can Nadine deduct if the trip is within the United States?
    b. How much can she deduct if the trip is outside the United States?

41. Samuel traveled from New York to Helsinki primarily on business for his employer. He spent 16 days (including travel) on business and 4 days sightseeing. His expenses were as follows:

Air fare	$3,600
Meals	2,250
Lodging	2,850
Incidental expenses	300

Samuel was not reimbursed. How are these expenses reported assuming an AGI of $100,000?

42. Hal, an investment counselor, attended a conference on the impact of the new tax law on investment choices. His unreimbursed expenses were as follows:

Air fare	$250
Lodging	500
Meals	300
Tuition and fees	400

a. How much can Hal deduct on his return? Are the expenses *for* or *from* AGI?
b. Would your answer differ if Hal were a self-employed physician?

43. David, a professor of French history, went to France during the year to research documents available only in France. His time on the trip was spent entirely on business. No vacation days were involved, and David kept adequate records. David received no reimbursements for the following carefully documented expenses:

Air fare and other transportation	$1,600
Hotels	1,200
Meals	900

a. What can David deduct in 1994 if he has AGI of $30,000 and no other miscellaneous itemized deductions? Are the deductions *for* or *from* AGI?
b. Would your answer differ if David had gone to France to soak up the culture and brush up on his French?

✗ 44. Dorothy is an employee of Cardinal Corporation, a commercial property broker involved in the leasing of office space. She takes a client to dinner and incurs the following expenses:

Taxi (to and from restaurant)	$ 35
Cover charge	40
Meal cost	140
Tip	28

Assume the event is adequately substantiated.
a. If Dorothy is not reimbursed, how much can she claim as a deduction?
b. If Dorothy is reimbursed (under an adequate accounting), how much can Cardinal Corporation claim?

45. During 1994, Kevin, the assistant manager of a truck leasing firm, made gifts that cost the following amounts:

To Darlene (Kevin's secretary) for Christmas ($2 was for gift wrapping)	$27
To George (Kevin's boss) on his birthday	25
To Susan (a key client) for Christmas	30
To John (a key client) for Christmas	20

Presuming Kevin has adequate substantiation and is not reimbursed, how much can he deduct?

✗ 46. Camille is a professor who consults on the side. She uses one-fifth of her home exclusively for her consulting business, and clients regularly meet her there. Camille is single and under 65. Her AGI (before considering consulting income) is $40,000. Other relevant data follow:

Income from consulting business	$4,000
Consulting expenses other than home office	1,400
Total costs relating to home	
Interest and taxes	8,000
Utilities	1,400
Maintenance and repairs	900
Depreciation (business part only)	1,200

Calculate Camille's AGI for 1994.

47. Paige incurred the following expenses related to her employment as a chief executive officer:

Lodging while away from home	$2,800
Meals while away from home	1,200
Entertainment while away from home	2,000
Dues, subscriptions, and books	1,000
Transportation expenses	4,000

Her AGI was $100,000, and she received $6,600 under her employer's accountable plan. What are Paige's deductions *for* and *from* AGI?

48. Kenneth received $4,400 in reimbursements under an accountable plan after he had made an adequate accounting to his employer. His expenses were as follows:

Transportation expenses	$3,200
Meals	1,400
Lodging and incidentals	2,300
Dues, phone, and subscriptions	100
Entertainment	1,000

How much can Kenneth deduct *for* and *from* AGI? Assume he had AGI of $50,000 and no other miscellaneous itemized deductions.

X 49. Patrick, an executive with Gray Corporation, incurred the following employee business expenses:

Lodging	$2,000
Meals	1,600
Transportation	2,400
Entertainment	1,500
Phone	500

Patrick received $5,600 under an accountable plan to cover the above expenses. He made an adequate accounting. In addition to incurring the above expenses, Patrick incurred expenses in attending a seminar on communications for executives. He paid $500 for transportation, $100 for meals, and $300 for fees and books. He was not reimbursed.

Patrick's salary was $50,000. His only other income was interest of $800. He is 47 and single.

Calculate Patrick's AGI and itemized employee expenses.

50. Thelma, who is age 42 and single, earned a salary of $60,000. She had other income consisting of interest of $2,000, dividends of $1,600, and long-term capital gains of $4,000.

Thelma incurred the following expenses during the year:

Transportation	$2,300
Meals	1,600
Dues and subscriptions	800
Entertainment of clients	300
Total	$5,000

Thelma received reimbursements of $3,000 under an accountable plan. Calculate her AGI and itemized employee business expenses.

CUMULATIVE PROBLEMS

51. Julie Stern is 34 and single with a dependent mother who lives with her. Julie's Social Security number is 436–22–1234. Her address is 1000 Glenside, Pullman, WA 99164. Julie's salary is $49,000, from which the proper amounts were withheld for Federal income tax, Social Security tax, and Medicare tax. The state where Julie lives does not impose an income tax.

Examination of Julie's 1994 records reveals the following:

Other receipts:	
Dividends from Texaco stock	$ 600
Interest from savings account	1,300
Interest on municipal bond	200
State lottery winnings	250
Itemized deductions:	
Interest expense on home mortgage	4,500
Property taxes on residence	1,800
Charitable contributions	600

During the year, Julie drove her automobile 13,000 miles (2,000 commuting, 2,000 personal, and 9,000 business). She uses the automatic mileage method. Her employee expenses (none of which are reimbursed) are:

Business meals and entertainment	$4,100
Business gifts (all $25 or less)	400
Professional dues and publications	600
Tuition and materials for special course to maintain existing skills	1,200

Compute Julie's Federal taxable income for 1994. Suggested software (if available): *TurboTax* or *MacInTax* for tax return or WFT tax planning software.

52. George M. and Martha J. Jordan have no dependents and are both under age 65. George is a statutory employee of Consolidated Jobbers (business code is 2634), and his Social Security number is 582–99–4444. Martha is an executive with General Corporation, and her Social Security number is 241–88–6642. The Jordans live at 321 Oak Street, Lincoln, NV 89553. They both want to contribute to the Presidential Election Campaign Fund.

In 1993, George earned $49,000 in commissions. His employer withholds FICA but not Federal income taxes. George paid $10,000 in estimated taxes. Martha earned $62,000, from which $9,000 was withheld for Federal income taxes. Neither George nor Martha received any expense reimbursements.

George uses his two-year-old car (purchased on January 3, 1991) on sales calls and keeps a log of all miles driven. In 1993, he drove 36,000 miles, 24,554 of them for business. He made several out-of-state sales trips, incurring transportation costs of $1,600, meals of $800, and lodging costs of $750. He also spent $1,400 during the year taking customers to lunch.

Martha incurred the following expenses related to her work: taxi fares of $125, business lunches of $615, and a yearly commuter train ticket of $800. During the year, Martha received $1,200 in interest from the employees' credit union, $100,000 life insurance proceeds upon the death of her mother in December, and $500 in dividends from General Motors. She contributed $2,000 to her Individual Retirement Account. Neither George nor Martha is covered by an employee retirement plan. Martha gave a gift valued at $500 to the president of her firm upon his promotion to that position.

The Jordans had additional expenditures as follows:

Charitable contributions (cash)	$1,200
Medical and dental expenses	1,400
Real property taxes	1,200
Home mortgage interest	9,381
Tax return preparation fee	150

Part 1—Tax Computation
Compute the Jordans' Federal income tax payable or refund due, assuming they file a joint income tax return for 1993. If they have a refund due, they want the amount refunded. You will need Form 1040, Form 2106, and Schedules A, B, and C. Suggested software (if available): *TurboTax* or *MacInTax* for tax return or WFT tax planning software if tax return solutions are not desired.

Part 2—Tax Planning
Martha and George ask your help in deciding what to do with the $100,000 Martha inherited in 1993. They are considering three conservative investment alternatives:

• Invest in 8% long-term U.S. bonds.

• Invest in 7% Series EE bonds and elect to defer the interest earned.

• Invest in 6% municipal bonds.

a. Calculate the best alternative for next year. Assume that Martha and George will have the same income and deductions in 1994, except for the income from the investment they choose.
b. What other factors should the Jordans take into account?
c. Write a memo to the Jordans, explaining their alternatives.

Suggested software (if available): *TurboTax* or *MacInTax* for tax return or WFT tax planning software.

RESEARCH PROBLEMS

Research Problem 1.   Green Corporation is in the business of supplying customers with temporary personnel who work at customers' offices, receive their assignments by telephone, and rarely go into Green Corporation's offices. Several times during the year, Green rented a yacht for recreational cruises for its employees. No temporary employees were expressly excluded from taking the cruises. Very few of the temporary employees even learned of the cruises, however, because notices were posted in Green's offices on a "first-come, first-served" basis. The IRS disallowed Green's deduction for the cruises under § 274(e)(4), claiming that temporary employees were, in fact, excluded from the cruises. Is the IRS correct?

Research Problem 2.   Alan, a heart specialist, left his job in Texas to accept a position in a California medical center. In addition to seeing patients, he was required to work on the hospital's heart transplant project under the supervision of Dr. Hume. Dr. Hume was an impossible boss, who had already had two other doctors removed from the team. Dr. Hume had Alan terminated from the project after 35 weeks of employment. Will Alan be able to deduct his moving expenses?

Partial list of research aids:
§ 217(c)(2).

Research Problem 3.   Rick Beam has been an independent sales representative for various textile manufacturers for many years. His products consist of soft goods, such as tablecloths, curtains, and drapes. Rick's customers are clothing store chains, department stores, and smaller specialty stores. The employees of these companies who are responsible for purchasing merchandise are known as buyers. These companies generally prohibit their buyers from accepting gifts from manufacturers' sales representatives.

Each year Rick gives cash gifts (never more than $25) to most of the buyers who are his customers. Generally, he cashes a large check in November and gives the money personally to the buyers around Christmas. Rick says, "This is one of the ways that I maintain my relationship with my buyers." He maintains adequate substantiation of all the gifts.

Rick's deductions for these gifts have been disallowed by the IRS, based on Code § 162(c)(2). Rick is confused and comes to you, a CPA, for advice.
a. Write a letter to Rick concerning his tax position on this issue.
b. Prepare a memo for your files supporting the advice you have given.

Research Problem 4.   Jesse maintains a home office that he uses exclusively for business. He is an employee of the Ace Company, which provides him with an office, and has a consulting business on the side.

He used his home office 80% of the time in his consulting business and 20% of the time in connection with his job with Ace. Can he deduct his home office expenses?

Partial list of research aids:
§ 280A(c)(1).

Deductions and Losses: Certain Itemized Deductions

LEARNING OBJECTIVES

After completing Chapter 10, you should be able to:

1. Distinguish between deductible and nondeductible personal expenses.

2. Define and compute the medical expense deduction.

3. Contrast deductible taxes and nondeductible fees, and handle the Federal tax treatment of state and local income taxes.

4. Distinguish between deductible and nondeductible interest and apply the appropriate limitations to deductible interest.

5. Understand charitable contributions and their related measurement problems and percentage limitations.

6. List the business and personal expenditures that are deductible as miscellaneous itemized or as other itemized deductions.

7. Recognize the limitation applicable to high-income taxpayers.

8. Identify the tax planning procedures that can maximize the benefit of itemized deductions.

▼ OUTLINE

General Classification of Expenses, 10–2

Medical Expenses, 10–2

General Requirements, 10–2

Medical Expenses Defined, 10–3

Capital Expenditures for Medical Purposes, 10–4

Transportation and Lodging Expenses for Medical Treatment, 10–5

Amounts Paid for Medical Insurance Premiums, 10–6

Medical Expenses Incurred for Spouse and Dependents, 10–6

Year of Deduction, 10–7

Reimbursements, 10–7

Taxes, 10–8

Deductibility as a Tax, 10–8

Property Taxes, Assessments, and Apportionment of Taxes, 10–9

State and Local Income Taxes, 10–10

Interest, 10–11

Allowed and Disallowed Items, 10–11

Restrictions on Deductibility and Timing Considerations, 10–15

Classification of Interest Expense, 10–16

Charitable Contributions, 10–16

Criteria for a Gift, 10–16

Qualified Organizations, 10–18

Time of Deduction, 10–18

Record-Keeping and Valuation Requirements, 10–19

Limitations on Charitable Contribution Deduction, 10–20

Miscellaneous Itemized Deductions, 10–24

Other Miscellaneous Deductions, 10–25

Comprehensive Example of Schedule A, 10–25

Overall Limitation on Certain Itemized Deductions, 10–27

Tax Planning Considerations, 10–28

Effective Utilization of Itemized Deductions, 10–28

Utilization of Medical Deductions, 10–28

Protecting the Interest Deduction, 10–29

Assuring the Charitable Contribution Deduction, 10–30

▼ General Classification of Expenses

1 ▼ Learning Objective
Distinguish between deductible and nondeductible personal expenses.

As a general rule, personal expenditures are disallowed by § 262 of the Code. However, Congress has chosen to allow certain personal expenditures to be deducted as itemized deductions. Personal expenditures that are deductible as itemized deductions include medical expenses, certain taxes, mortgage interest, investment interest, and charitable contributions. These expenditures and other personal expenditures that are allowed as itemized deductions are covered in this chapter. Any personal expenditures not specifically allowed as itemized deductions by the tax law are nondeductible.

Allowable itemized deductions are deductible *from* AGI in arriving at taxable income if the taxpayer elects to itemize. The election to itemize is appropriate when total itemized deductions exceed the standard deduction based on the taxpayer's filing status (refer to Chapter 3).[1]

▼ Medical Expenses

GENERAL REQUIREMENTS

2 ▼ Learning Objective
Define medical expenses and compute the medical expense deduction.

Medical expenses paid for the care of the taxpayer, spouse, and dependents are allowed as an itemized deduction to the extent the expenses are not reimbursed. The **medical expense** deduction is limited to the amount by which such expenses *exceed* 7.5 percent of the taxpayer's AGI.

---

[1]The total standard deduction is the sum of the basic standard deduction and the additional standard deduction (refer to Chapter 3).

Chapter 3 also describes the situations in which a taxpayer is not eligible for the standard deduction.

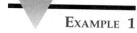

EXAMPLE 1 During 1994, Iris had medical expenses of $4,800, of which $1,000 was reimbursed by her insurance company. If her AGI for the year is $40,000, the itemized deduction for medical expenses is limited to $800 [$4,800 − $1,000 = $3,800 − (7.5% × $40,000)]. ▼

MEDICAL EXPENSES DEFINED

The term *medical care* includes expenditures incurred for the "diagnosis, cure, mitigation, treatment, or prevention of disease, or for the purpose of affecting any structure or function of the body."[2] A *partial* list of deductible and nondeductible medical items appears in Exhibit 10–1.

A medical expense does not have to relate to a particular ailment to be deductible. Since the definition of medical care is broad enough to cover preventive measures, the cost of periodic physical and dental exams qualifies even for a taxpayer in good health.

Amounts paid for unnecessary *cosmetic surgery* are not deductible medical expenses. However, if cosmetic surgery is deemed necessary, it is deductible as a medical expense. Cosmetic surgery is necessary when it ameliorates (1) a deformity arising from a congenital abnormality, (2) a personal injury, or (3) a disfiguring disease.

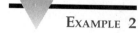

EXAMPLE 2 Art, a calendar year taxpayer, paid $11,000 to a plastic surgeon for a face lift. Art, age 75, merely wanted to improve his appearance. The $11,000 does not qualify as a medical expense since the surgery was unnecessary. ▼

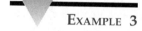

EXAMPLE 3 As a result of a serious automobile accident, Marge's face is disfigured. The cost of restorative cosmetic surgery is deductible as a medical expense. ▼

The deductibility of *nursing home expenses* depends on the medical condition of the patient and the nature of the services rendered.[3] If an individual enters a home for the aged for personal or family considerations and not because he or she requires medical or nursing attention, deductions are allowed only for the costs

▼ **EXHIBIT 10–1**
Illustration of Deductible and Nondeductible Medical Expenses

Deductible	Nondeductible
Medical (including dental, mental, and hospital) care	Funeral, burial, or cremation expenses
Prescription drugs	Nonprescription drugs (except insulin)
Special equipment	Bottled water
Wheelchairs	Toiletries, cosmetics
Crutches	Diaper service, maternity clothes
Artificial limbs	Programs for the *general* improvement of health
Eyeglasses (including contact lenses)	Weight reduction
Hearing aids	Health spas
Transportation for medical care	Stop-smoking clinics
Medical and hospital insurance premiums	Social activities (e.g., dancing and swimming lessons)
	Unnecessary cosmetic surgery

[2] § 213(d)(1)(A).

[3] Reg. § 1.213–1(e)(1)(v).

attributable to the medical and nursing care. However, if obtaining medical care is the primary purpose for entering the facility, the expenses are deductible in their entirety.

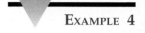

EXAMPLE 4

Norman has a chronic heart ailment. His family decided to place Norman in a nursing home equipped to provide medical and nursing care facilities. Total nursing home expenses amount to $15,000 per year. Of this amount, $4,500 is directly attributable to medical and nursing care. Since Norman is in need of significant medical and nursing care and is placed in the facility primarily for this purpose, all $15,000 of the nursing home costs are deductible (subject to the 7.5% floor). ▼

Tuition expenses of a dependent at a special school may be deductible as a medical expense. The cost of medical care can include the expenses of a special school for a mentally or physically handicapped individual. The deduction is allowed if a principal reason for sending the individual to the school is the school's special resources for alleviating the infirmities. In this case, the cost of meals and lodging, in addition to the tuition, is a proper medical expense deduction.[4]

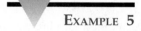

EXAMPLE 5

Jason's daughter Marcia attended public school through the seventh grade. Because Marcia was a poor student, she was examined by a psychiatrist who diagnosed an organic problem that created a learning disability. Upon the recommendation of the psychiatrist, Marcia is enrolled in a private school so that she can receive individual attention. The school has no special program for students with learning disabilities and does not provide special medical treatment. The expense related to Marcia's attendance is not deductible as a medical expense. The cost of any psychiatric care, however, qualifies as a medical expense. ▼

Example 5 shows that the recommendation of a physician does not automatically make the expenditure deductible.

CAPITAL EXPENDITURES FOR MEDICAL PURPOSES

Some examples of *capital expenditures* for medical purposes are swimming pools if the taxpayer does not have access to a neighborhood pool and air conditioners if they do not become permanent improvements (e.g., window units).[5] Other examples include dust elimination systems,[6] elevators,[7] and a room built to house an iron lung. These expenditures are medical in nature if they are incurred as a medical necessity upon the advice of a physician, the facility is used primarily by the patient alone, and the expense is reasonable.

Capital expenditures normally are adjustments to basis and are not deductible. However, both a capital expenditure for a permanent improvement and expenditures made for the operation or maintenance of the improvement may qualify as medical expenses. If a capital expenditure qualifies as a medical expense, the allowable cost is deductible in the year incurred. The tax law makes no provision for depreciating medical expenses as it does for other capital expenditures.

A capital improvement that ordinarily would not have a medical purpose qualifies as a medical expense if it is directly related to prescribed medical care and

[4] *Donald R. Pfeifer*, 37 TCM 816, T.C.Memo. 1978–189. Also see Rev.Rul. 78–340, 1978–2 C.B. 124.
[5] Rev.Rul. 55–261, 1955–1 C.B. 307, modified by Rev.Rul. 68–212, 1968–1 C.B. 91.
[6] *F. S. Delp*, 30 T.C. 1230 (1958).
[7] *Riach v. Frank*, 62–1 USTC ¶9419, 9 AFTR2d 1263, 302 F.2d 374 (CA–9, 1962).

is deductible to the extent that the expenditure *exceeds* the increase in value of the related property. Appraisal costs related to capital improvements are also deductible, but not as medical expenses. These costs are expenses incurred in the determination of the taxpayer's tax liability.[8]

EXAMPLE 6   Fred's physician advises him to install an elevator in his residence so that his wife, who is afflicted with heart disease, will not be required to climb the stairs. The cost of installing the elevator is $3,000, and the increase in the value of the residence is determined to be only $1,700. Therefore, $1,300 ($3,000 − $1,700) is deductible as a medical expense. Additional utility costs to operate the elevator and maintenance costs are deductible as medical expenses as long as the medical reason for the capital expenditure continues to exist. ▼

The full cost of certain home-related capital expenditures incurred to enable a physically handicapped individual to live independently and productively qualifies as a medical expense. These expenditures are subject to the 7.5 percent floor only, and the increase in the home's value is deemed to be zero. Qualifying costs include expenditures for constructing entrance and exit ramps to the residence, widening hallways and doorways to accommodate wheelchairs, installing support bars and railings in bathrooms and other rooms, and adjusting electrical outlets and fixtures.[9]

TRANSPORTATION AND LODGING EXPENSES FOR MEDICAL TREATMENT

Payments for transportation to and from a point of treatment for medical care are deductible as medical expenses (subject to the 7.5 percent floor). Transportation expenses for medical care include bus, taxi, train, or plane fare, charges for ambulance service, and out-of-pocket expenses for the use of an automobile. A mileage allowance of nine cents per mile[10] may be used instead of actual out-of-pocket automobile expenses. Whether the taxpayer chooses to claim out-of-pocket automobile expenses or the nine cents per mile automatic mileage option, related parking fees and tolls can also be deducted. The cost of meals while en route to obtain medical care is not deductible.

A deduction is also allowed for the transportation expenses of a parent who must accompany a child who is receiving medical care or for a nurse or other person giving medical assistance to a person who is traveling to get medical care and cannot travel alone.

A deduction is allowed for lodging while away from home for medical expenses if the following requirements are met:[11]

- The lodging is primarily for and essential to medical care.
- Medical care is provided by a doctor in a licensed hospital or a similar medical facility (e.g., a clinic).
- The lodging is not lavish or extravagant under the circumstances.
- There is no significant element of personal pleasure, recreation, or vacation in the travel away from home.

The deduction for lodging expenses included as medical expenses cannot exceed $50 *per* night for *each* person. The deduction is allowed not only for the patient but

---

[8] § 212(3).
[9] For a complete list of the items that qualify, see Rev.Rul. 87–106, 1987–2 C.B. 67.

[10] Rev.Proc. 93–51, I.R.B. No. 42, 30.
[11] § 213(d)(2).

also for a person who must travel with the patient (e.g., a parent traveling with a child who is receiving medical care).

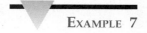

EXAMPLE 7

Herman, a resident of Winchester, Kentucky, is advised by his family physician that Martha, Herman's dependent and disabled mother, needs specialized treatment for her heart condition. Consequently, Herman and Martha fly to Cleveland, Ohio, where Martha receives the therapy at a heart clinic on an out-patient basis. Expenses in connection with the trip are as follows:

Round trip airfare ($250 each)	$500
Lodging in Cleveland for two nights ($60 each per night)	240

Herman's medical expense deduction for transportation is $500, and his medical expense deduction for lodging is $200 ($50 per night per person). Because Martha is disabled, it is assumed that his accompanying her is justified. ▼

No deduction is allowed for the cost of meals unless they are part of the medical care and are furnished at a medical facility. When allowable, such meals are not subject to the 50 percent limit.

AMOUNTS PAID FOR MEDICAL INSURANCE PREMIUMS

Medical insurance premiums are included with other medical expenses subject to the 7.5 percent floor. Premiums paid by the taxpayer under a group plan or an individual plan are included as medical expenses. If an employer pays all or part of the taxpayer's medical insurance premiums, the amount paid by the employer is not included in gross income by the employee. Likewise, the premium is not included in the employee's medical expenses.

If a taxpayer is *self-employed,* up to 25 percent of insurance premiums paid for medical coverage is deductible as a *business* expense. Any excess can be treated as a *medical* expense. The deduction is not allowed to any taxpayer who is eligible to participate in a subsidized health plan maintained by any employer of the taxpayer or of the taxpayer's spouse.

MEDICAL EXPENSES INCURRED FOR SPOUSE AND DEPENDENTS

In computing the medical expense deduction, a taxpayer may include medical expenses for a spouse and for a person who was a dependent at the time the expenses were paid or incurred. In determining dependency status for medical expense deduction purposes, neither the gross income nor the joint return tests (see Chapter 3) apply.

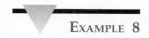

EXAMPLE 8

Ernie (age 22) is married and a full-time student at a university. During 1994, Ernie incurred medical expenses that were paid by Matilda (Ernie's mother). She provided more than half of Ernie's support for the year. Even if Ernie files a joint return with his wife, Matilda may claim the medical expenses she paid for him. Matilda would combine Ernie's expenses with her own in applying the 7.5% floor. ▼

For divorced persons with children, a special rule applies to the noncustodial parent. The noncustodial parent may claim any medical expenses he or she pays even though the custodial parent claims the children as dependents. This rule applies if the dependency exemptions could have been shifted to the noncustodial parent by the custodial parent's waiver (refer to Chapter 3).

▼

EXAMPLE 9

Irv and Joan are divorced in 1993, and Joan is awarded custody of their child, Keith. During 1994, Irv makes the following payments to Joan: $3,600 for child support and $2,500 for Keith's medical bills. Together, Irv and Joan provide more than half of Keith's support. Even though Joan claims Keith as a dependent, Irv can combine the medical expenses that he pays for Keith with his own. ▼

YEAR OF DEDUCTION

Regardless of a taxpayer's method of accounting, medical expenses are deductible only in the year *paid.* In effect, this places all individual taxpayers on a cash basis as far as the medical expense deduction is concerned. One exception, however, is allowed for deceased taxpayers. If the medical expenses are paid within one year from the day following the day of death, they can be treated as being paid at the time they were *incurred.*[12] Thus, such expenses may be reported on the final income tax return of the decedent or on earlier returns if incurred before the year of death.

No current deduction is allowed for payment of medical care to be rendered in the future unless the taxpayer is under an obligation to make the payment.[13] Whether an obligation to make the payment exists depends upon the policy of the physician or the institution furnishing the medical care.

▼

EXAMPLE 10

Upon the recommendation of his regular dentist, in late December 1994 Gary consults Dr. Smith, a prosthodontist, who specializes in crown and bridge work. Dr. Smith tells Gary that he can do the restorative work for $12,000. To cover his lab bill, however, Dr. Smith requires that 40% of this amount be prepaid. Accordingly, Gary pays $4,800 in December 1994. The balance of $7,200 is paid when the work is completed in July 1995. Under these circumstances, the qualifying medical expenses are $4,800 for 1994 and $7,200 in 1995. The result would be the same even if Gary prepaid the full $12,000 in 1994. ▼

REIMBURSEMENTS

If medical expenses are reimbursed in the same year as paid, no problem arises. The reimbursement merely reduces the amount that would otherwise qualify for the medical expense deduction. But what happens if the reimbursement is received in a later year than the expenditure? Unlike casualty losses where reasonable prospect of recovery must be considered (refer to Chapter 7), the expected reimbursement is disregarded in measuring the amount of the deduction. Instead, the reimbursement is accounted for separately in the year in which it occurs.

Under the *tax benefit rule,* a taxpayer who receives an insurance reimbursement for medical expenses deducted in a previous year might have to include the reimbursement in gross income in the year of receipt. However, taxpayers are not required to report more than the amount previously deducted as medical expenses. Thus, a taxpayer who did not itemize deductions in the year the expenses were paid did not receive a tax benefit and is not required to include a reimbursement in gross income.

The tax benefit rule does apply to reimbursements if the taxpayer itemized deductions in the previous year. In this case, the taxpayer may be required to report some or all of the medical expense reimbursement in income in the year the reimbursement is received. Under the tax benefit rule, the taxpayer must include

---

[12] § 213(c).

[13] *Robert S. Basset,* 26 T.C. 619 (1956).

the reimbursement in income up to the amount of the deductions that decreased income tax in the earlier year.

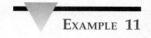

EXAMPLE 11

Homer has AGI of $20,000 for 1993. He was injured in a car accident and paid $1,300 for hospital expenses and $700 for doctor bills. Homer also incurred medical expenses of $600 for his dependent child. In 1994, Homer was reimbursed $650 by his insurance company for the medical expenses attributable to the car accident. His deduction for medical expenses in 1993 is computed as follows:

Hospitalization	$ 1,300
Bills for doctor's services	700
Medical expenses for dependent	600
Total	$ 2,600
Less: 7.5% of $20,000	(1,500)
Medical expense deduction (assuming Homer itemizes his deductions)	$ 1,100

Assume that Homer would have elected to itemize his deductions even if he had no medical expenses in 1993. If the reimbursement for medical care had occurred in 1993, the medical expense deduction would have been only $450 [$2,600 (total medical expenses) – $650 (reimbursement) – $1,500 (floor)], and Homer would have paid more income tax.

Since the reimbursement was made in a subsequent year, Homer would include $650 in gross income for 1994. If Homer had not itemized in 1993, he would not include the $650 reimbursement in 1994 gross income because he would have received no tax benefit in 1993. ▼

TAXES

3 **LEARNING OBJECTIVE**
Contrast deductible taxes and nondeductible fees, licenses, etc.

Section 164 permits the deduction of certain state and local taxes paid or accrued by a taxpayer. The deduction was created to relieve the burden of multiple taxes upon the same source of revenue.

DEDUCTIBILITY AS A TAX

A distinction must be made between a tax and a fee, since fees are not deductible unless incurred as an ordinary and necessary business expense or as an expense in the production of income.

The IRS has defined a tax as follows:

> A tax is an enforced contribution exacted pursuant to legislative authority in the exercise of taxing power, and imposed and collected for the purpose of raising revenue to be used for public or governmental purposes, and not as payment for some special privilege granted or service rendered. Taxes are, therefore, distinguished from various other contributions and charges imposed for particular purposes under particular powers or functions of the government. In view of such distinctions, the question whether a particular contribution or charge is to be regarded as a tax depends upon its real nature.[14]

---

[14] Rev.Rul. 57–345, 1957–2 C.B. 132, and Rev.Rul. 70–622, 1970–2 C.B. 41.

Accordingly, fees for dog licenses, automobile inspection, automobile titles and registration, hunting and fishing licenses, bridge and highway tolls, drivers' licenses, parking meter deposits, postage, etc., are not deductible. These items, however, could be deductible if incurred as a business expense or for the production of income. Deductible and nondeductible taxes are summarized in Exhibit 10–2.[15]

PROPERTY TAXES, ASSESSMENTS, AND APPORTIONMENT OF TAXES

Property Taxes

State, local, and foreign taxes on real property are generally deductible only by the person upon whom the tax is imposed. Deductible personal property taxes must be *ad valorem* (assessed in relation to the value of the property). Therefore, a motor vehicle tax based on weight, model, year, and horsepower is not an ad valorem tax. However, a tax based on value and other criteria may qualify in part.

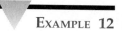

EXAMPLE 12

A state imposes a motor vehicle registration tax on 4% of the value of the vehicle plus 40 cents per hundredweight. Belle, a resident of the state, owns a car having a value of $4,000 and weighing 3,000 pounds. Belle pays an annual registration fee of $172. Of this amount, $160 (4% of $4,000) is deductible as a personal property tax. The remaining $12, based on the weight of the car, is not deductible. ▼

Assessments for Local Benefits

As a general rule, real property taxes do not include taxes assessed for local benefits since such assessments tend to increase the value of the property (e.g., special assessments for streets, sidewalks, curbing, and other similar improvements). A taxpayer cannot deduct the cost of a new sidewalk (relative to a personal residence), even though the construction was required by the city and the sidewalk may have provided an incidental benefit to the public welfare.[16] Such assessments are added to the adjusted basis of the taxpayer's property.

▼ **EXHIBIT 10–2**
Deductible and Nondeductible Taxes

Deductible	Nondeductible
State, local, and foreign real property taxes	Federal income taxes
	FICA taxes imposed on employees
State and local personal property taxes	Employer FICA taxes paid on domestic household workers
State, local, and foreign income taxes	Estate, inheritance, and gift taxes
	General sales taxes
The environmental tax	Federal, state, and local excise taxes (e.g., gasoline, tobacco, spirits)
	Foreign income taxes if the taxpayer chooses the foreign tax credit option
	Taxes on real property to the extent such taxes are to be apportioned and treated as imposed on another taxpayer

---

[15] Most deductible taxes are listed in § 164, while the nondeductible items are included in § 275.

[16] *Erie H. Rose*, 31 TCM 142, T.C.Memo. 1972–39; Reg. § 1.164–4(a).

Apportionment of Real Property Taxes between Seller and Purchaser

Real estate taxes for the entire year are apportioned between the buyer and seller on the basis of the number of days the property was held by each during the real property tax year. This apportionment is required whether the tax is paid by the buyer or the seller or is prorated according to the purchase agreement. It is the apportionment that determines who is entitled to deduct the real estate taxes in the year of sale. In making the apportionment, the assessment date and the lien date are disregarded. The date of sale counts as a day the property is owned by the buyer.

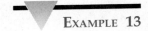
EXAMPLE 13

A county's real property tax year runs from April 1 to March 31. Susan, the owner on April 1, 1994, of real property located in the county, sells the real property to Bob on June 30, 1994. Bob owns the real property from June 30, 1994, through March 31, 1995. The tax for the real property tax year April 1, 1994, through March 31, 1995, is $730. The portion of the real property tax treated as imposed upon Susan, the seller, is $180 (90/365 × $730, April 1 through June 29, 1994), and $550 (275/365 × $730, June 30, 1994 through March 31, 1995) of the tax is treated as imposed upon Bob, the purchaser. ▼

If the actual real estate taxes are not prorated between the buyer and seller as part of the purchase agreement, adjustments are required. The adjustments are necessary to determine the amount realized by the seller and the adjusted basis of the property to the buyer. If the buyer pays the entire amount of the tax, he or she has, in effect, paid the seller's portion of the real estate tax and has therefore paid more for the property than the actual purchase price. Thus, the amount of real estate tax that is apportioned to the seller (for Federal income tax purposes) and paid by the buyer is added to the buyer's adjusted basis. The seller must increase the amount realized on the sale by the same amount.

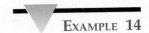
EXAMPLE 14

Seth sells real estate on October 3, 1994, for $50,000. The buyer, Wilma, pays the real estate taxes of $1,095 for the calendar year, which is the real estate property tax year. Of the real estate taxes, $825 (for 275 days) is apportioned to and is deductible by the seller, Seth, and $270 (for 90 days) of the taxes is deductible by Wilma. The buyer has, in effect, paid Seth's real estate taxes of $825 and has therefore paid $50,825 for the property. Wilma's basis is increased to $50,825, and the amount realized by Seth from the sale is increased to $50,825. ▼

The opposite result occurs if the seller (rather than the buyer) pays the real estate taxes. In this case, the seller reduces the amount realized from the sale by the amount that has been apportioned to the buyer. The buyer is required to reduce his or her adjusted basis by a corresponding amount.

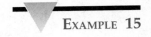
EXAMPLE 15

Ruth sells real estate to Butch for $50,000 on October 3, 1994. While Ruth held the property, she paid the real estate taxes of $1,095 for the calendar year, which is the real estate property tax year. Although Ruth paid the entire $1,095 of real estate taxes, $270 of that amount is apportioned to Butch and is therefore deductible by him. The effect is that the buyer, Butch, has paid only $49,730 for the property. The amount realized by Ruth, the seller, is reduced by $270, and Butch reduces his basis in the property to $49,730. ▼

STATE AND LOCAL INCOME TAXES

4 LEARNING OBJECTIVE
Be able to handle the Federal tax treatment of state and local income taxes.

The position of the IRS is that state and local income taxes imposed upon an individual are deductible only as itemized deductions, even if the taxpayer's sole source of income is from a business, rents, or royalties.

Cash basis taxpayers are entitled to deduct state income taxes withheld by the employer in the year the taxes are withheld. In addition, estimated state income tax payments are deductible in the year the payment is made by cash basis taxpayers even if the payments relate to a prior or subsequent year.[17] If the taxpayer overpays state income taxes because of excessive withholdings or estimated tax payments, the refund received is included in gross income of the following year to the extent that the deduction reduced the tax liability in the prior year.

EXAMPLE 16

Leona, a cash basis, unmarried taxpayer, had $800 of state income tax withheld during 1994. Additionally in 1994, Leona paid $100 that was due when she filed her 1993 state income tax return and made estimated payments of $300 on her 1994 state income tax. When Leona files her 1994 Federal income tax return in April 1995, she elects to itemize deductions, which amount to $5,500, including the $1,200 of state income tax payments and withholdings, all of which reduce her tax liability.

As a result of overpaying her 1994 state income tax, Leona receives a refund of $200 early in 1995. She will include this amount in her 1995 gross income in computing her Federal income tax. It does not matter whether Leona received a check from the state for $200 or applied the $200 toward her 1995 state income tax. ▼

INTEREST

5 LEARNING OBJECTIVE
Distinguish between deductible and nondeductible interest and apply the appropriate limitations to deductible interest.

A deduction for interest has been allowed since the income tax law was enacted in 1913. Despite its long history of congressional acceptance, the interest deduction has been one of the most controversial areas in the tax law. The controversy centered around the propriety of allowing the deduction of interest charges for the purchase of consumer goods and services and interest on borrowings used to acquire investments (investment interest). TRA of 1986 effectively put an end to this controversy by eliminating the deduction for personal interest. **Investment interest** and **qualified residence** (mortgage) **interest** continue to be deductible, subject to limits discussed below.

ALLOWED AND DISALLOWED ITEMS

The Supreme Court has defined *interest* as compensation for the use or forbearance of money.[18] The general rule permits a deduction for interest paid or accrued within the taxable year on indebtedness.[19]

Investment Interest

Taxpayers frequently borrow funds that they use to acquire investment assets. When the interest expense is large relative to the income from the investments, substantial tax benefits could result. Congress has therefore limited the deductibility of interest on funds borrowed for the purpose of purchasing or continuing to hold investment property. Investment interest expense is *now* limited to net investment income for the year.[20]

---

[17] Rev.Rul. 71–190, 1971–1 C.B. 70. See also Rev.Rul. 82–208, 1982–2 C.B. 58, where a deduction is not allowed when the taxpayer cannot, in good faith, reasonably determine that there is additional state income tax liability.

[18] *Old Colony Railroad Co. v. Comm.*, 3 USTC ¶880, 10 AFTR 786, 52 S.Ct. 211 (USSC, 1932).
[19] § 163(a).
[20] § 163(d).

Investment income is gross income from interest, dividends, annuities, and royalties not derived in the ordinary course of a trade or business. Income from a passive activity and income from a real estate activity in which the taxpayer actively participates are not included in investment income.

Net capital gain attributable to the disposition of property producing the types of income just enumerated or from property held for investment purposes is *not* included in investment income.

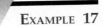

EXAMPLE 17

Terry incurred $13,000 of interest expense related to her investments in 1994. Her investment income included $4,000 of interest, $2,000 of dividends, and a $5,000 net capital gain on the sale of securities. Her investment income for purposes of computing the investment income limitation is $6,000 ($4,000 interest + $2,000 dividends). ▼

Taxpayers may *elect* to include the capital gains as investment income, but only if they agree to reduce capital gains qualifying for the alternative tax computation for net capital gain (see Chapter 16) by an equivalent amount.

Net investment income is the excess of investment income over investment expenses. Investment expenses are those deductible expenses directly connected with the production of investment income. Investment expenses *do not* include interest expense. When investment expenses fall into the category of miscellaneous itemized deductions that are subject to the 2 percent-of-AGI floor, some may not enter into the calculation of net investment income because of the floor.

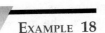

EXAMPLE 18

Gina has AGI of $80,000, which includes dividends and interest income of $18,000. Besides investment interest expense, she paid $3,000 of city ad valorem property tax on stocks and bonds and had the following miscellaneous itemized expenses:

Safe deposit box rental (to hold investment securities)	$ 120
Investment counsel fee	1,200
Unreimbursed business travel	850
Uniforms	600

Before Gina can determine her investment expenses for purposes of calculating net investment income, those miscellaneous expenses that are not investment expenses are disallowed before any investment expenses are disallowed under the 2%-of-AGI floor. This is accomplished by selecting the *lesser* of the following:

1. The amount of investment expenses included in the total of miscellaneous itemized deductions subject to the 2%-of-AGI floor.
2. The amount of miscellaneous expenses deductible after the 2%-of-AGI rule is applied.

The amount under item 1 is $1,320 [$120 (safe deposit box rental) + $1,200 (investment counsel fee)]. The item 2 amount is $1,170 [$2,770 (total of miscellaneous expenses) − $1,600 (2% of $80,000 AGI)].

Then, Gina's investment expenses are calculated as follows:

Deductible miscellaneous deductions investment expense (the lesser of item 1 or item 2)	$1,170
Plus: Ad valorem tax on investment property	3,000
Total investment expenses	$4,170

Gina's net investment income is $13,830 ($18,000 investment income − $4,170 investment expenses). ▼

After net investment income is determined, deductible investment interest expense can be calculated.

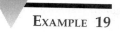

EXAMPLE 19 For 1994, Adam is a single person employed by a law firm. His investment activities for the year are as follows:

Net investment income	$30,000
Investment interest expense	44,000

Adam's investment interest deduction for 1994 is $30,000. ▼

The amount of investment interest disallowed is carried over to future years. In Example 19, therefore, the amount that is carried over to 1995 is $14,000 ($44,000 investment interest expense – $30,000 allowed). No limit is placed on the carryover period. The investment interest expense deduction is determined by completing Form 4952 (see Appendix B).

Qualified Residence Interest

Qualified residence interest is interest paid or accrued during the taxable year on indebtedness (subject to limitations) *secured* by any property that is a qualified residence of the taxpayer. Qualified residence interest falls into two categories: (1) interest on acquisition indebtedness and (2) interest on home equity loans. Before discussing each of these categories, however, the term qualified residence must be defined.

A *qualified residence* includes the taxpayer's principal residence and one other residence of the taxpayer or spouse. The *principal residence* is one that meets the requirement for nonrecognition of gain upon sale under § 1034 (see Chapter 15). The *one other residence,* or second residence, refers to one that is used as a residence if not rented or, if rented, meets the requirements for a personal residence under the rental of vacation home rules (refer to Chapter 6). A taxpayer who has more than one second residence can make the selection each year of which one is the qualified second residence. A residence includes, in addition to a house in the ordinary sense, cooperative apartments, condominiums, and mobile homes and boats that have living quarters (sleeping accommodations and toilet and cooking facilities).

Although in most cases interest paid on a home mortgage would be fully deductible, there are limitations.[21] Interest paid or accrued during the tax year on aggregate *acquisition indebtedness* of $1,000,000 or less ($500,000 for married persons filing separate returns) is deductible as qualified residence interest. **Acquisition indebtedness** refers to amounts incurred in acquiring, constructing, or substantially improving a qualified residence of the taxpayer.

Qualified residence interest also includes interest on **home equity loans.** These loans utilize the personal residence of the taxpayer as security. Because the funds from home equity loans can be used for personal purposes (e.g., auto purchases, medical expenses), what would otherwise have been nondeductible consumer interest becomes deductible qualified residence interest.

However, interest is deductible only on the portion of a home equity loan that does not exceed the *lesser of*:

- The fair market value of the residence, reduced by the acquisition indebtedness, *or*
- $100,000 ($50,000 for married persons filing separate returns).

---

[21] § 163(h)(3).

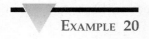

EXAMPLE 20   Larry owns a personal residence with a fair market value of $150,000 and an outstanding first mortgage of $120,000. Therefore, his equity in his home is $30,000 ($150,000 − $120,000). Larry issues a lien on the residence and in return borrows $15,000 to purchase a new family automobile. All interest on the $135,000 of debt is treated as qualified residence interest. ▼

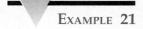

EXAMPLE 21   Leon and Pearl, married taxpayers, took out a mortgage on their home for $200,000 in 1983. In March 1994, when the home had a fair market value of $400,000 and they owed $195,000 on the mortgage, Leon and Pearl took out a home equity loan for $120,000. They used the funds to purchase a boat to be used for recreational purposes. For 1994 on a joint return, Leon and Pearl can deduct all of the interest on the first mortgage since it is acquisition indebtedness. Of the $120,000 home equity loan, only the interest on the first $100,000 is deductible. The interest on the remaining $20,000 is not deductible because it exceeds the statutory ceiling of $100,000. ▼

Interest Paid for Services

Mortgage loan companies commonly charge a fee for finding, placing, or processing a mortgage loan. Such fees are often called **points** and are expressed as a percentage of the loan amount. In periods of tight money, a borrower may have to pay points to obtain the necessary financing. To qualify as deductible interest, the points must be considered compensation to a lender solely for the use or forbearance of money. The points cannot be a form of service charge or payment for specific services if they are to qualify as deductible interest.[22]

Points must be capitalized and are amortized and deductible ratably over the life of the loan. A special exception permits the purchaser of a personal residence to deduct qualifying points in the year of payment.[23] The exception also covers points paid to obtain funds for home improvements.

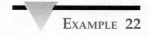

EXAMPLE 22   During 1994, Thelma purchased a new residence for $130,000 and paid points of $2,600 to obtain mortgage financing. At Thelma's election, the $2,600 can be claimed as an interest deduction for tax year 1994. ▼

Points paid to refinance an existing home mortgage cannot be immediately expensed but must be capitalized and amortized as interest expense over the life of the new loan.[24]

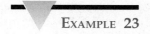

EXAMPLE 23   Sandra purchased her residence four years ago, obtaining a 30-year mortgage at an annual interest rate of 12%. In 1994, Sandra refinances the mortgage in order to reduce the interest rate to 9%. To obtain the refinancing, she had to pay points of $2,600. The $2,600 paid comes under the usual rule applicable to points. The $2,600 must be capitalized and amortized over the life of the mortgage. ▼

Points paid by the *seller* are not deductible because the debt on which they are paid is not the debt of the seller. Points paid by the seller are treated as a reduction of the selling price of the property.

Prepayment Penalty

When a mortgage or loan is paid off in full in a lump sum before its term (early), the lending institution may require an additional payment of a certain percentage

---

[22] Rev.Rul. 67–297, 1967–2 C.B. 87.
[23] § 461(g)(2).

[24] Rev.Rul. 87–22, 1987–1 C.B. 146.

applied to the unpaid amount at the time of prepayment. This is known as a prepayment penalty and is considered to be interest (e.g., personal, qualified residence, investment) in the year paid. The general rules for deductibility of interest also apply to prepayment penalties.

Interest Paid to Related Parties

Nothing prevents the deduction of interest paid to a related party as long as the payment actually took place and the interest meets the requirements for deductibility. Recall from Chapter 6 that a special rule for related taxpayers applies when the debtor uses the accrual basis and the related creditor is on the cash basis. If this rule is applicable, interest that has been accrued but not paid at the end of the debtor's tax year is not deductible until payment is made and the income is reportable by the cash basis recipient.

Tax-Exempt Securities

The tax law provides that no deduction is allowed for interest on debt incurred to purchase or carry tax-exempt securities.[25] A major problem for the courts has been to determine what is meant by the words *to purchase or carry.* Refer to Chapter 6 for a detailed discussion of these issues.

RESTRICTIONS ON DEDUCTIBILITY AND TIMING CONSIDERATIONS

Taxpayer's Obligation

Allowed interest is deductible if the related debt represents a bona fide obligation for which the taxpayer is liable.[26] Thus, a taxpayer may not deduct interest paid on behalf of another individual. For interest to be deductible, both the debtor and creditor must intend for the loan to be repaid. Intent of the parties can be especially crucial between related parties such as a shareholder and a closely held corporation. A shareholder may not deduct interest paid by the corporation on his or her behalf.[27] Likewise, a husband may not deduct interest paid on his wife's property if he files a separate return, except in the case of qualified residence interest. If both husband and wife consent in writing, either the husband or the wife may deduct the allowed interest on the principal residence and one other residence.

Time of Deduction

Generally, interest must be paid to secure a deduction unless the taxpayer uses the accrual method of accounting. Under the accrual method, interest is deductible ratably over the life of the loan.

EXAMPLE 24

On November 1, 1994, Ramon borrows $1,000 to purchase appliances for a rental house. The loan is payable in 90 days at 12% interest. On the due date in January 1995, Ramon pays the $1,000 note and interest amounting to $30. Ramon can deduct the accrued portion (2/3 × $30 = $20) of the interest in 1994 only if he is an accrual basis taxpayer. Otherwise, the entire amount of interest ($30) is deductible in 1995. ▼

---

[25] § 265(a)(2).
[26] *Arcade Realty Co.,* 35 T.C. 256 (1960).

[27] *Continental Trust Co.,* 7 B.T.A. 539 (1927).

Prepaid Interest

Accrual method reporting is imposed on cash basis taxpayers for interest pre payments that extend beyond the end of the taxable year.[28] Such payments must be allocated to the tax years to which the interest payments relate. These provisions are intended to prevent cash basis taxpayers from *manufacturing* tax deductions before the end of the year by prepaying interest.

CLASSIFICATION OF INTEREST EXPENSE

Whether interest is deductible *for* AGI or as an itemized deduction *(from)* depends on whether the indebtedness has a business, investment, or personal purpose. If the indebtedness is incurred in relation to a business (other than performing services as an employee) or for the production of rent or royalty income, the interest is deductible *for* AGI. However, if the indebtedness is incurred for personal use, such as qualified residence interest, any deduction allowed is reported on Schedule A of Form 1040 if the taxpayer elects to itemize. If the taxpayer is an employee who incurs debt in relation to his or her employment, the interest is considered to be personal, or consumer, interest. Business expenses appear on Schedule C of Form 1040, and expenses related to rents or royalties are reported on Schedule E.

    If a taxpayer deposits money in a certificate of deposit (CD) that has a term of one year or less and the interest cannot be withdrawn without penalty, the full amount of the interest must still be included in income, even though part of the interest is forfeited due to an early withdrawal. However, the taxpayer will be allowed a deduction *for* AGI as to the forfeited amount.

CHARITABLE CONTRIBUTIONS

6   **LEARNING OBJECTIVE**
Understand charitable contributions and their related measurement problems and percentage limitations.

Section 170 permits individuals and corporations to deduct contributions made to qualified domestic organizations. Contributions to qualified charitable organizations serve certain social welfare needs and therefore relieve the government of the cost of providing these needed services to the community.

    The **charitable contribution** provisions are among the most complex in the tax law. To determine the amount deductible as a charitable contribution, several important questions must be answered:

- What constitutes a charitable contribution?
- Was the contribution made to a qualified organization?
- When is the contribution deductible?
- What record-keeping and reporting requirements apply to charitable contributions?
- How is the value of donated property determined?
- What special rules apply to contributions of property that has increased in value?
- What percentage limitations apply to the charitable contribution deduction?

These questions are addressed in the sections that follow.

CRITERIA FOR A GIFT

Section 170(c) defines a *charitable contribution* as a gift made to a qualified organization. The major elements needed to qualify a contribution as a gift are a

---

[28] § 461(g)(1).

donative intent, the absence of consideration, and acceptance by the donee. Consequently, the taxpayer has the burden of establishing that the transfer was made from motives of *disinterested generosity* as established by the courts.[29] This test is quite subjective and has led to problems of interpretation (refer to the discussion of gifts in Chapter 5).

Benefit Received Rule

When a donor derives a tangible benefit from a contribution, he or she cannot deduct the value of the benefit.

EXAMPLE 25

Ralph purchases a ticket at $100 for a special performance of the local symphony (a qualified charity). If the price of a ticket to a symphony concert is normally $35, Ralph is allowed only $65 as a charitable contribution. ▼

An exception to this benefit rule provides for the deduction of an automatic percentage of the amount paid for the right to purchase athletic tickets from colleges and universities.[30] Under this exception, 80 percent of the amount paid to or for the benefit of the institution qualifies as a charitable contribution deduction.

EXAMPLE 26

Janet donates $500 to State University's athletic department. The payment guarantees that Janet will have preferred seating on the 50-yard line. Subsequently, Janet buys four $35 game tickets. Under the exception to the benefit rule, she is allowed a $400 (80% of $500) charitable contribution deduction for the taxable year.

If, however, Janet's $500 donation includes four $35 tickets, that portion [$140 ($35 × 4)] and the remaining portion of $360 ($500 – $140) are treated as separate amounts. Thus, Janet is allowed a charitable contribution deduction of $288 (80% of $360). ▼

Contribution of Services

No deduction is allowed for a contribution of one's services to a qualified charitable organization. However, unreimbursed expenses related to the services rendered may be deductible. For example, the cost of a uniform (without general utility) that is required to be worn while performing services may be deductible, as are certain out-of-pocket transportation costs incurred for the benefit of the charity. In lieu of these out-of-pocket costs for an automobile, a standard mileage rate of 12 cents per mile is allowed.[31] Deductions are permitted for transportation, reasonable expenses for lodging, and the cost of meals while away from home incurred in performing the donated services. The travel may not involve a significant element of personal pleasure, recreation, or vacation.[32]

EXAMPLE 27

Grace, a delegate representing her church in Miami, Florida, travels to a two-day national meeting in Denver, Colorado, in February. After the meeting, Grace spends two weeks at a nearby ski resort. Under these circumstances, none of the transportation, meals, or lodging is deductible since the travel involved a significant element of personal pleasure, recreation, or vacation. ▼

---

[29] *Comm. v. Duberstein,* 60–2 USTC ¶9515, 5 AFTR2d 1626, 80 S.Ct. 1190 (USSC, 1960).
[30] § 170(l).

[31] § 170(i).
[32] § 170(j).

Nondeductible Items

In addition to the benefit received rule and the restrictions placed on contribution of services, the following items may *not* be deducted as charitable contributions:

- Dues, fees, or bills paid to country clubs, lodges, fraternal orders, or similar groups.
- Cost of raffle, bingo, or lottery tickets.
- Cost of tuition.
- Value of blood given to a blood bank.
- Donations to homeowners associations.
- Gifts to individuals.
- Rental value of property used by a qualified charity.

QUALIFIED ORGANIZATIONS

To be deductible, a contribution must be made to one of the following organizations:[33]

- A state or possession of the United States or any subdivisions thereof.
- A corporation, trust, or community chest, fund, or foundation that is situated in the United States and is organized and operated exclusively for religious, charitable, scientific, literary, or educational purposes or for the prevention of cruelty to children or animals.
- A veterans' organization.
- A fraternal organization operating under the lodge system.
- A cemetery company.

The IRS publishes a list of organizations that have applied for and received tax-exempt status under § 501 of the Code.[34] This publication is updated frequently and may be helpful in determining if a gift has been made to a qualifying charitable organization.

Because gifts made to needy individuals are not deductible, a deduction will not be permitted if a gift is received by a donee in an individual capacity rather than as a representative of a qualifying organization.

TIME OF DEDUCTION

A charitable contribution generally is deducted in the year the payment is made. This rule applies to both cash and accrual basis individuals. A contribution is ordinarily deemed to have been made on the delivery of the property to the donee. For example, if a gift of securities (properly endorsed) is made to a qualified charitable organization, the gift is considered complete on the day of delivery or mailing. However, if the donor delivers the certificate to his or her bank or broker or to the issuing corporation, the gift is considered complete on the date the stock is transferred on the books of the corporation.

A contribution made by check is considered delivered on the date of mailing. Thus, a check mailed on December 31, 1994, is deductible on the taxpayer's 1994 tax return. If the contribution is charged on a bank credit card, the date the charge is made determines the year of deduction.

---

[33] § 170(c).

[34] Although this *Cumulative List of Organizations*, IRS Publication 78 (available by purchase from the Superintendent of Documents, U.S. Government Printing Office, Washington, DC 20402), may be helpful, qualified organizations are not required to be listed. Not all organizations that qualify are listed in this publication (e.g., American Red Cross, University of Cleveland).

THE RATIONALE FOR THE NEW REPORTING REQUIREMENTS

Sometimes tax laws do not seem to make sense. However, each provision usually has a logical explanation. The new law requires that taxpayers obtain a written acknowledgment from the charity for any gift of more than $250. A canceled check is no longer sufficient proof that a deductible contribution was made. In addition, if the taxpayer receives any goods or services as a result of making the contribution, the acknowledgment must place a value on the goods or services. Any contribution deductions that are not documented as required by law are subject to disallowance. These requirements place a greater reporting burden on both the taxpayer and the charity. Why did Congress feel it was necessary to enact these new reporting requirements? A recent news item gave examples of the types of situations in which taxpayers were suspected of overstating their contribution deductions:

- A taxpayer writes a check to a church to pay for day care, counseling, or other services provided by the church and deducts the amount as a charitable contribution.
- A taxpayer writes a tuition check to a private school and deducts the amount as a charitable contribution.
- Parents attend a fund-raising auction for their child's school and bid $300 for a weekend at a cabin in the mountains donated by another parent. The *value* of the lodging must be determined and subtracted from the amount paid to arrive at the deductible amount.

One may question whether enough is at stake to justify imposing these burdensome new reporting rules on taxpayers and charities. However, revenue estimates, which are required for each provision in a tax bill, predict that the new reporting requirements will raise $469 million in additional tax revenues over a five-year period.

SOURCE: Information from Albert B. Crenshaw, "Changing the Ground Rules on Charity," *Washington Post*, November 14, 1993, pp. H1, H3.

RECORD-KEEPING AND VALUATION REQUIREMENTS

Record-Keeping Requirements

No deduction is allowed for contributions of $250 or more unless the taxpayer obtains *contemporaneous written substantiation* of the contribution from the charitable organization. The substantiation must specify the amount of cash and a description (but not value) of any property other than cash contributed. To qualify as contemporaneous, the substantiation must be obtained before the earlier of (1) the due date (including extensions) of the return for the year the contribution is claimed or (2) the date such return is filed. This requirement applies to contributions made on or after January 1, 1994.[35]

---

[35]§ 170 (f)(8). This substantiation requirement does not apply if the donee organization files a return that includes the required information.

Additional information is required if the value of the donated property is over $500 but not over $5,000. Also, the taxpayer must file Section A of Form 8283 (Noncash Charitable Contributions) for such contributions.

For noncash contributions with a claimed value in excess of $5,000 ($10,000 in the case of nonpublicly traded stock), the taxpayer must obtain a qualified appraisal and must file Section B of Form 8283. This schedule must show a summary of the appraisal and must be attached to the taxpayer's return. Failure to comply with these reporting rules may result in disallowance of the charitable contribution deduction. Additionally, significant overvaluation exposes the taxpayer to rather stringent penalties.

Valuation Requirements

Property donated to a charity is generally valued at fair market value at the time the gift is made. The Code and Regulations give very little guidance on the measurement of the fair market value except to say, "The fair market value is the price at which the property would change hands between a willing buyer and a willing seller, neither being under any compulsion to buy or sell and both having reasonable knowledge of relevant facts."

Generally, charitable organizations do not attest to the fair market value of the donated property. Nevertheless, the taxpayer must maintain reliable written evidence of the following information concerning the donation:

- The fair market value of the property and how that value was determined.
- The amount of the reduction in the value of the property (if required) for certain appreciated property and how that reduction was determined.
- Terms of any agreement with the charitable organization dealing with the use of the property and potential sale or other disposition of the property by the organization.
- A signed copy of the appraisal if the value of the property was determined by appraisal. Only for a contribution of art with an aggregate value of $20,000 or more must the appraisal be attached to the taxpayer's return.

LIMITATIONS ON CHARITABLE CONTRIBUTION DEDUCTION

In General

The potential charitable contribution deduction is the total of all donations, both money and property, that qualify for the deduction. After this determination is made, the actual amount of the charitable contribution deduction that is allowed for individuals for the tax year is limited as follows:

- If the qualifying contributions for the year total 20 percent or less of AGI, they are fully deductible.
- If the qualifying contributions are more than 20 percent of AGI, the deductible amount may be limited to either 20 percent, 30 percent, or 50 percent of AGI, depending on the type of property given and the type of organization to which the donation is made.
- In any case, the maximum charitable contribution deduction may not exceed 50 percent of AGI for the tax year.

To understand the complex rules for computing the amount of a charitable contribution, it is necessary to understand the distinction between capital gain property and ordinary income property. In addition, it is necessary to understand when the 50 percent, 30 percent, and 20 percent limitations apply. If a taxpayer's contributions for the year exceed the applicable percentage limitations, the excess contributions may be carried forward and deducted during a five-year carryover period. These topics are discussed in the sections that follow.

Ordinary Income Property

Ordinary income property is any property that, if sold, will result in the recognition of ordinary income. The term includes inventory for sale in the taxpayer's trade or business, a work of art created by the donor, and a manuscript prepared by the donor. It also includes, for purposes of the charitable contribution calculation, a capital asset held by the donor for less than the required holding period for long-term capital gain treatment. To the extent that disposition of property results in the recognition of ordinary income due to the recapture of depreciation, it is ordinary income property.[36]

If ordinary income property is contributed, the deduction is equal to the fair market value of the property less the amount of ordinary income that would have been reported if the property were sold. In most instances, the deduction is limited to the adjusted basis of the property to the donor.

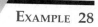

EXAMPLE 28

Tim owned stock in White Corporation that he donated to a university on May 1, 1994. Tim had purchased the stock for $2,500 on March 3, 1994, and the stock had a value of $3,600 when he made the donation. Since he had not held the property long enough to meet the long-term capital gain requirement, Tim would have recognized a short-term capital gain of $1,100 if he had sold the property. Since short-term capital gain property is treated as ordinary income property for charitable contribution purposes, Tim's charitable contribution deduction is limited to the property's adjusted basis of $2,500 ($3,600 – $1,100 = $2,500). ▼

In Example 28, suppose the stock had a fair market value of $2,300 (rather than $3,600) when it was donated to charity. Because the fair market value now is less than the adjusted basis, the charitable contribution deduction is $2,300.

Capital Gain Property

Capital gain property is any property that would have resulted in the recognition of long-term capital gain or § 1231 gain if the property had been sold by the donor. As a general rule, the deduction for a contribution of capital gain property is equal to the fair market value of the property.

Two major exceptions preclude the deductibility of the appreciation on long-term capital gain property. One exception concerns certain private foundations. Private foundations are organizations that traditionally do not receive their funding from the general public (e.g., the Ford Foundation). Generally, foundations fall into two categories: operating and nonoperating. A private *operating* foundation is one that spends substantially all of its income in the active conduct of the charitable undertaking for which it was established.[37] Other private foundations are *nonoperating* foundations. However, if a private nonoperating foundation distributes the contributions it receives according to special rules within two and one-half months following the year of the contribution, the organization is treated the same as public charities and private operating foundations. Often, only the private foundation knows its status (operating or nonoperating) for sure, and the status can change from year to year.

---

[36]For a more complete discussion of the difference between ordinary income and capital gain property, see Chapter 16.

[37]§ 4942.

If capital gain property is contributed to a private nonoperating foundation, the taxpayer must reduce the contribution by the long-term capital gain that would have been recognized if the property had been sold at its fair market value. The effect of this provision is to limit the deduction to the property's adjusted basis.

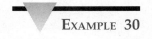

EXAMPLE 29

Walter purchases stock for $800 on January 1, 1975, and donates it to a private nonoperating foundation on June 21, 1994, when it is worth $2,000. Walter's charitable contribution is $800 ($2,000 – $1,200), the stock's basis. ▼

If, in Example 29, Walter had donated the stock to either a public charity or a private operating foundation, his charitable contribution would be $2,000, the fair market value of the stock.

A second exception applying to capital gain property relates to *tangible personalty.*[38] If tangible personalty is contributed to a public charity such as a museum, church, or university, the charitable deduction may have to be reduced. The amount of the reduction is the long-term capital gain that would have been recognized if the property had been sold for its fair market value. The reduction is required *if* the property is put to an unrelated use. The term *unrelated use* means a use that is unrelated to the exempt purpose or function of the charitable organization.

A taxpayer in this instance must establish that the property is not in fact being put to an unrelated use by the donee. The taxpayer must also establish that at the time of the contribution it was reasonable to anticipate that the property would not be put to an unrelated use. For a contribution of personalty to a museum, if the work of art is the kind of art normally retained by the museum, it is reasonable for a donor to anticipate that the work of art will not be put to an unrelated use. This is the case even if the object is later sold or exchanged by the museum.[39]

EXAMPLE 30

Myrtle contributes a Picasso painting, for which she paid $20,000, to a local museum. It had a value of $30,000 at the time of the donation. The museum displayed the painting for two years and subsequently sold it for $50,000. The charitable contribution is $30,000. It is not reduced by the unrealized appreciation since the painting was put to a related use even though it was later sold by the museum. ▼

Fifty Percent Ceiling

Contributions made to public charities may not exceed 50 percent of an individual's AGI for the year. Excess contributions may be carried over to the next five years. The 50 percent ceiling on contributions applies to the following types of public charities:

- A church or a convention or association of churches.
- An educational organization that maintains a regular faculty and curriculum.
- A hospital or medical school.
- An organization supported by the government that holds property or investments for the benefit of a college or university.

---

[38] Tangible personalty is all property that is not realty (land and buildings) and does not include intangible property such as stock or securities.

[39] Reg. § 1.170A–4(b)(3)(ii)(b).

- A Federal, state, or local governmental unit.
- An organization normally receiving a substantial part of its support from the public or a governmental unit.

In the remaining discussion of charitable contributions, public charities and private foundations (both operating and nonoperating) that qualify for the 50 percent ceiling will be referred to as *50 percent organizations*.

The 50 percent ceiling also applies to contributions to the following organizations:

- All private operating foundations.
- Certain private nonoperating foundations that distribute the contributions they receive to public charities and private operating foundations within two and one-half months following the year they receive the contribution.
- Certain private nonoperating foundations in which the contributions are pooled in a common fund and the income and principal sum are paid to public charities.

Thirty Percent Ceiling

A 30 percent ceiling applies to contributions of cash and ordinary income property to private nonoperating foundations that are not 50 percent organizations. The 30 percent ceiling also applies to contributions of appreciated capital gain property to 50 percent organizations unless the taxpayer makes a special election (see below).

In the event the contributions for any one tax year involve both 50 percent and 30 percent property, the allowable deduction comes first from the 50 percent property.

EXAMPLE 31

During 1994, Lisa made the following donations to her church: cash of $2,000 and unimproved land worth $30,000. Lisa had purchased the land four years ago for $22,000 and held it as an investment. Therefore, it is long-term capital gain property. Lisa's AGI for 1994 is $50,000. Disregarding percentage limitations, Lisa's potential deduction for 1994 is $32,000 [$2,000 (cash) + $30,000 (fair market value of land)].

In applying the percentage limitations, however, the *current* deduction for the land is limited to $15,000 [30% (limitation applicable to long-term capital gain property) × $50,000 (AGI)]. Thus, the total deduction for 1994 is $17,000 ($2,000 cash + $15,000 land). Note that the total deduction does not exceed $25,000, which is 50% of Lisa's AGI. ▼

Under a special election, a taxpayer may choose to forgo a deduction of the appreciation on capital gain property. Referred to as the *reduced deduction election*, this enables the taxpayer to move from the 30 percent limitation to the 50 percent limitation.

EXAMPLE 32

Assume the same facts as in Example 31, except that Lisa makes the reduced deduction election. Now the deduction for 1994 becomes $24,000 [$2,000 (cash) + $22,000 (basis in land)] because both donations fall under the 50% limitation. Thus, by making the election, Lisa has increased her charitable contribution deduction for 1994 by $7,000 [$24,000 − $17,000 (Example 31)]. ▼

Although the reduced deduction election appears attractive, it should be considered carefully. The election sacrifices a deduction for the appreciation on long-term capital gain property that might eventually be allowed. Note that in Example 31, the potential deduction was $32,000, yet in Example 32 only $24,000 is allowed. The reason the potential deduction is decreased by $8,000 ($32,000 − $24,000) is that no carryover is allowed for the amount sacrificed by the election.

Twenty Percent Ceiling

A 20 percent ceiling applies to contributions of appreciated long-term capital gain property to private nonoperating foundations that are not 50 percent organizations.

Contribution Carryovers

Contributions that exceed the percentage limitations for the current year can be carried over for five years. In the carryover process, such contributions do not lose their identity for limitation purposes. Thus, if the contribution originally involved 30 percent property, the carryover will continue to be classified as 30 percent property in the carryover year.

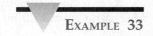

EXAMPLE 33

Assume the same facts as in Example 31. Because only $15,000 of the $30,000 value of the land was deducted in 1994, the balance of $15,000 may be carried over to 1995. But the carryover will still be treated as long-term capital gain property and is subject to the 30%-of-AGI limitation. ▼

In applying the percentage limitations, current charitable contributions must be claimed first before any carryovers can be considered. If carryovers involve more than one year, they are utilized in a first-in, first-out order.

MISCELLANEOUS ITEMIZED DEDUCTIONS

7   LEARNING OBJECTIVE
List the business and personal expenditures that are deductible either as miscellaneous itemized deductions or as other itemized deductions.

According to § 262, no deduction is allowed for personal, living, or family expenses. However, a taxpayer may incur a number of expenditures related to employment. If an employee or outside salesperson incurs unreimbursed business expenses or expenses that are reimbursed under a nonaccountable plan, including travel and transportation, the expenses are deductible as **miscellaneous itemized deductions.**[40] Certain other expenses also fall into the special category of miscellaneous itemized deductions. Some are deductible only if, in total, they exceed 2 percent of the taxpayer's AGI. These miscellaneous itemized deductions include (but are not limited to) the following:

- Professional dues to membership organizations.
- Uniforms or other clothing that cannot be used for normal wear.
- Fees incurred for the preparation of one's tax return or fees incurred for tax litigation before the IRS or the courts.
- Job-hunting costs.
- Fee paid for a safe deposit box used to store papers and documents relating to taxable income-producing investments.
- Investment expenses that are deductible under § 212 as discussed in Chapter 6.
- Appraisal fees to determine the amount of a casualty loss or the fair market value of donated property.
- Hobby losses up to the amount of hobby income (see Chapter 6).

Certain employee business expenses that are reimbursed are not itemized deductions, but are deducted *for* AGI. Employee business expenses are discussed in depth in Chapter 9.

---

[40] Actors and performing artists who meet certain requirements are not subject to this rule.

ETHICAL
CONSIDERATIONS

Increasing Itemized Deductions through Bunching

ABig Six accounting firm recommends that its clients "bunch" their miscellaneous itemized deductions subject to the 2 percent floor in order to increase itemized deductions. The strategy is implemented over a three-year period. To help clients achieve this bunching, the firm does not bill for tax services performed in year 1. In year 2, the firm bills the client for the year 1 services and for the services performed in year 2. Also in year 2, the client is billed in advance for tax services to be provided in year 3. Thus, tax preparation fees for three years are "bunched" in the middle year. The firm recommends that clients handle other expenses that are subject to the 2 percent floor in the same way, if possible. Comment on this firm's policy.

OTHER MISCELLANEOUS DEDUCTIONS

Certain expenses and losses do not fall into any category of itemized deductions already discussed but are nonetheless deductible.

- Casualty and theft losses, discussed in Chapter 7.
- Gambling losses up to the amount of gambling winnings.
- Impairment-related work expenses of a handicapped person.
- The unrecovered investment in an annuity contract when the annuity ceases by reason of death, discussed in Chapter 4.

The amount of each expense that is allowable as a deduction may be limited by the rules within a particular category (casualty and theft losses, gambling losses).

The category of casualty and theft losses is a separate line item on Schedule A (Form 1040). The remaining expenses and losses are deductible as "Other Miscellaneous Deductions."

COMPREHENSIVE EXAMPLE OF SCHEDULE A

Harry and Jean Brown, married filing jointly, had the following transactions for the current year:

• Medicines that required a prescription	$ 430
• Doctor and dentist bills paid and not reimbursed	2,120
• Medical insurance premium payments	1,200
• Contact lenses	175
• Transportation for medical purposes (425 miles × 9 cents/mile + $4.75 parking)	43
• State income tax withheld	620
• Real estate taxes	1,580
• Interest paid on qualified residence mortgage	2,840
• Charitable contributions in cash	860

- Transportation in performing charitable services
  (860 miles × 12 cents/mile + $15.80 parking and tolls)   119
- Unreimbursed employee expenses (from a Form 2106)   870
- Tax return preparation   150
- Professional expenses (dues and publications)   135
- Safe deposit box (used for keeping investment documents
  and tax records)   35

The Browns' AGI is $40,000. The completed Schedule A for 1993 reports itemized deductions totaling $7,377.

SCHEDULES A&B (Form 1040) Department of the Treasury Internal Revenue Service	Schedule A—Itemized Deductions (Schedule B is on back) ▶ Attach to Form 1040. ▶ See Instructions for Schedules A and B (Form 1040).	OMB No. 1545-0074 1993 Attachment Sequence No. 07

Name(s) shown on Form 1040   Harry and Jean Brown

Your social security number   371 : 30 : 3987

Medical and Dental Expenses		Caution: Do not include expenses reimbursed or paid by others.				
	1	Medical and dental expenses (see page A-1)	1	3,968		
	2	Enter amount from Form 1040, line 32. **2** 40,000				
	3	Multiply line 2 above by 7.5% (.075)	3	3,000		
	4	Subtract line 3 from line 1. If zero or less, enter -0- ▶	4			968
Taxes You Paid (See page A-1.)	5	State and local income taxes	5	620		
	6	Real estate taxes (see page A-2)	6	1,580		
	7	Other taxes. List—include personal property taxes ▶	7			
	8	Add lines 5 through 7 ▶	8			2,200
Interest You Paid (See page A-2.) Note: Personal interest is not deductible.	9a	Home mortgage interest and points reported to you on Form 1098	9a	2,840		
	b	Home mortgage interest not reported to you on Form 1098. If paid to the person from whom you bought the home, see page A-3 and show that person's name, identifying no., and address ▶				
			9b			
	10	Points not reported to you on Form 1098. See page A-3 for special rules	10			
	11	Investment interest. If required, attach Form 4952. (See page A-3.)	11			
	12	Add lines 9a through 11 ▶	12			2,840
Gifts to Charity (See page A-3.)		Caution: If you made a charitable contribution and received a benefit in return, see page A-3.				
	13	Contributions by cash or check	13	979		
	14	Other than by cash or check. If over $500, you **MUST** attach Form 8283	14			
	15	Carryover from prior year	15			
	16	Add lines 13 through 15 ▶	16			979
Casualty and Theft Losses	17	Casualty or theft loss(es). Attach Form 4684. (See page A-4.) ▶	17			
Moving Expenses	18	Moving expenses. Attach Form 3903 or 3903-F. (See page A-4.) ▶	18			
Job Expenses and Most Other Miscellaneous Deductions (See page A-5 for expenses to deduct here.)	19	Unreimbursed employee expenses—job travel, union dues, job education, etc. If required, you **MUST** attach Form 2106. (See page A-4.) ▶	19	870		
	20	Other expenses—investment, tax preparation, safe deposit box, etc. List type and amount ▶ Tax Preparation 150, profession expenses 135, safe deposit 35	20	320		
	21	Add lines 19 and 20	21	1,190		
	22	Enter amount from Form 1040, line 32. **22** 40,000				
	23	Multiply line 22 above by 2% (.02)	23	800		
	24	Subtract line 23 from line 21. If zero or less, enter -0- ▶	24			390
Other Miscellaneous Deductions	25	Other—from list on page A-5. List type and amount ▶	25			
Total Itemized Deductions	26	Is the amount on Form 1040, line 32, more than $108,450 (more than $54,225 if married filing separately)? • **NO.** Your deduction is not limited. Add lines 4, 8, 12, 16, 17, 18, 24, and 25 and enter the total here. Also enter on Form 1040, line 34, the **larger** of this amount or your standard deduction. • **YES.** Your deduction may be limited. See page A-5 for the amount to enter.	26			7,377

For Paperwork Reduction Act Notice, see Form 1040 instructions.   Cat. No. 11330X   Schedule A (Form 1040) 1993

OVERALL LIMITATION ON CERTAIN ITEMIZED DEDUCTIONS

8 ▼ **LEARNING OBJECTIVE**
Recognize the limitation on certain itemized deductions applicable to high-income taxpayers.

Itemized deductions are subject to a reduction if AGI exceeds specified threshold amounts. The threshold amount for 1994 is $111,800 ($55,900 for married persons filing a separate return). These threshold amounts are adjusted annually for inflation.[41] The cutback adjustment is reflected on line 26 of Schedule A of Form 1040. For computation purposes, the instructions for Form 1040 contain an "Itemized Deductions Worksheet." The worksheet is retained by the taxpayer for his or her records and is not filed with the tax return.

The cutback applies to all itemized deductions *except* the following:

- Medical expenses.
- Investment interest.
- Casualty and theft losses.
- Wagering losses to the extent of wagering gains.

The cutback adjustment is 3 percent of the excess of AGI over the threshold amount. In no case, however, may the cutback be more than 80 percent of the covered itemized deductions.

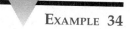

EXAMPLE 34

Hal and Mary are married, calendar year taxpayers and file a joint return. For 1994, they have AGI of $261,800. Their itemized deductions for the year amount to $20,000 and are entirely attributable to qualified residence interest, property taxes on their residence, charitable contributions, and state income taxes. The excess over the threshold amount is $150,000 [$261,800 (AGI) – $111,800 (threshold amount for 1994)]. Thus, the cutback adjustment under the 3% rule is $4,500 (3% of $150,000). As a result, only $15,500 [$20,000 (covered itemized deductions) – $4,500 (cutback adjustment)] of itemized deductions is allowed. The 80% limitation does not come into play because it would permit a larger cutback adjustment of $16,000 (80% × $20,000). ▼

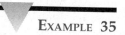

EXAMPLE 35

Assume the same facts as in the preceding example, except that Hal and Mary have the following itemized deductions: medical expenses of $32,000 and state income taxes of $5,000. Of the medical expenses, only $12,365 [$32,000 – (7.5% × $261,800)] can be claimed. Note, however, that the cutback adjustment does not apply to medical expenses. For the state income taxes, the cutback rules yield the following results:

- Under the 3% rule—

3% × $150,000 (excess amount) = $4,500

- Under the 80% rule—

80% × $5,000 (covered itemized deductions) = $4,000

Thus, the 80% rule must be used since it provides a smaller cutback ($4,000 versus $4,500). Therefore, the total allowable itemized deductions are $13,365 [$12,365 (medical expenses) + $1,000 (state income taxes less cutback)]. ▼

The cutback adjustment is applied after taking into account other Code provisions that reduce the allowable deduction (e.g., the 2 percent-of-AGI floor that applies to miscellaneous itemized deductions).

---

[41] § 68. The threshold amount for 1993 was $108,450 ($54,225 for married persons filing a separate return).

TAX PLANNING
CONSIDERATIONS

9 — LEARNING OBJECTIVE
Identify the tax planning
procedures that can maximize
the benefit of itemized
deductions.

EFFECTIVE UTILIZATION OF ITEMIZED DEDUCTIONS

Since an individual may use the standard deduction in one year and itemize deductions in another year, it is frequently possible to obtain maximum benefit by shifting itemized deductions from one year to another. For example, if a taxpayer's itemized deductions and the standard deduction are approximately the same for each year of a two-year period, the taxpayer should use the standard deduction in one year and shift itemized deductions (to the extent permitted by law) to the other year. The individual could, for example, prepay a church pledge for a particular year or avoid paying end-of-the-year medical expenses to shift the deduction to the following year.

UTILIZATION OF MEDICAL DEDUCTIONS

When a taxpayer anticipates that medical expenses will approximate the percentage floor, much might be done to generate a deductible excess. Any of the following procedures can help build a deduction by the end of the year:

- Incur the obligation for needed dental work or have needed work carried out.[42] Orthodontic treatment, for example, may have been recommended for a member of the taxpayer's family.
- Have elective remedial surgery that may have been postponed from prior years (e.g., tonsillectomies, vasectomies, correction of hernias, hysterectomies).
- Incur the obligation for capital improvements to the taxpayer's personal residence recommended by a physician (e.g., an air filtration system to alleviate a respiratory disorder).

As an aid to taxpayers who may experience temporary cash-flow problems at the end of the year, the use of bank credit cards is deemed to be payment for purposes of timing the deductibility of charitable and medical expenses.

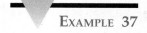

EXAMPLE 36

On December 13, 1994, Marge (a calendar year taxpayer) purchases two pairs of prescription contact lenses and one pair of prescribed orthopedic shoes for a total of $305. These purchases are separately charged to Marge's credit card. On January 6, 1995, Marge receives her statement containing these charges and makes payment shortly thereafter. The purchases are deductible as medical expenses in the year charged (1994) and not in the year the account is settled (1995). ▼

Recognizing which expenditures qualify for the medical deduction also may be crucial to exceeding the percentage limitations.

EXAMPLE 37

Mortimer employs Lana (an unrelated party) to care for his incapacitated and dependent mother. Lana is not a trained nurse but spends approximately one-half of the time performing nursing duties (e.g., administering injections and providing physical therapy) and the rest of the time doing household chores. An allocable portion of Lana's wages that Mortimer pays (including the employer's portion of FICA taxes) qualifies as a medical expense. ▼

---

[42] Prepayment of medical expenses does not generate a current deduction unless the taxpayer is under an obligation to make the payment.

To assure a deduction for the entire cost of nursing home care for an aged dependent, it is helpful if the transfer of the individual to the home is for medical reasons and is recommended by a doctor. In addition, the nursing home facilities should be adequate to provide the necessary medical and nursing care. To assure a deduction for all of the nursing home expenses, it is necessary to show that the individual was placed in the home for required medical care rather than for personal or family considerations.

Proper documentation is required to substantiate medical expenses. The taxpayer should keep all receipts for credit card or other charge purchases of medical services and deductible drugs as well as all cash register receipts. In addition, medical transportation mileage should be recorded.

If a taxpayer or a dependent of the taxpayer must be institutionalized in order to receive adequate medical care, it may be good tax planning to make a lump-sum payment that will cover medical treatment for future periods. It is advisable to negotiate a contract with the institution so that the expense is fixed and the payment is not a mere deposit.

PROTECTING THE INTEREST DEDUCTION

Although the deductibility of prepaid interest by a cash basis taxpayer has been severely restricted, a notable exception allows a deduction for points paid to obtain financing for the purchase or improvement of a principal residence in the year of payment. However, such points must actually be paid by the taxpayer obtaining the loan and must represent a charge for the use of money. It has been held that points paid from the mortgage proceeds do not satisfy the payment requirement.[43] Also, the portion of the points attributable to service charges does not represent deductible interest.[44] Taxpayers financing home purchases or improvements usually should direct their planning toward avoiding these two hurdles to immediate deductibility.

In rare instances, a taxpayer may find it desirable to forgo the immediate expensing of points in the year paid. Instead, it could prove beneficial to capitalize the points and write them off as interest expense over the life of the mortgage.

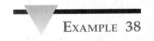

EXAMPLE 38

Geraldine purchases a home on December 15, 1994, for $95,000 with $30,000 cash and a 15-year mortgage of $65,000 financed by the Greater Metropolis National Bank. Geraldine pays two points in addition to interest allocated to the period from December 15 until December 31, 1994, at an annual rate of 10%. Since Geraldine does not have enough itemized deductions to exceed the standard deduction for 1994, she should elect to capitalize the interest expense by amortizing the points over 15 years. In this instance, Geraldine would deduct $86.67 for 1995, as part of her qualified residence interest expense [$1,300 (two points) divided by 15 years], if she elects to itemize that year. ▼

Because personal (consumer) interest is not deductible, taxpayers should consider making use of home equity loans. Recall that these loans utilize the personal residence of the taxpayer as security. Since the tracing rules do not apply to home equity loans, the funds from these loans can be used for personal purposes (e.g., auto loans, education). By making use of home equity loans, therefore, what would have been nondeductible consumer interest becomes deductible qualified residence interest.

[43] *Alan A. Rubnitz,* 67 T.C. 621 (1977).   [44] *Donald L. Wilkerson,* 70 T.C. 240 (1978).

ASSURING THE CHARITABLE CONTRIBUTION DEDUCTION

For a charitable contribution deduction to be available, the recipient must be a qualified charitable organization. Sometimes the mechanics of how the contribution is carried out can determine whether or not a deduction results.

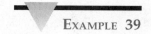

EXAMPLE 39

Fumiko wants to donate $5,000 to her church's mission in Kobe, Japan. In this regard, she considers three alternatives:

1. Send the money directly to the mission.
2. Give the money to her church with the understanding that it is to be passed on to the mission.
3. Give the money directly to the missionary in charge of the mission who is currently in the United States on a fund-raising trip.

If Fumiko wants to obtain a deduction for the contribution, she should choose alternative 2. A direct donation to the mission (alternative 1) is not deductible because the mission is a foreign charity. A direct gift to the missionary (alternative 3) does not comply since an individual cannot be a qualified charity for income tax purposes.[45] ▼

When making noncash donations, the type of property chosen can have decided implications in determining the amount, if any, of the deduction.

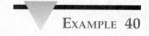

EXAMPLE 40

Samantha wants to give $60,000 in value to her church in some form other than cash. In this connection, she considers four alternatives:

1. Stock held for two years as an investment with a basis of $100,000 and a fair market value of $60,000.
2. Stock held for five years as an investment with a basis of $10,000 and a fair market value of $60,000.
3. The rent-free use for a year of a building that normally leases for $5,000 a month.
4. A valuable stamp collection held as an investment and owned for 10 years with a basis of $10,000 and a fair market value of $60,000. The church plans to sell the collection if and when it is donated.

Alternative 1 is ill-advised as the subject of the gift. Even though Samantha would obtain a deduction of $60,000, she would forgo the potential loss of $40,000 that would be recognized if the property were sold.[46] Alternative 2 makes good sense since the deduction still is $60,000 and none of the $50,000 of appreciation that has occurred must be recognized as income. Alternative 3 yields no deduction at all and is not a wise choice. Alternative 4 involves tangible personalty that the recipient does not plan to use. As a result, the amount of the deduction is limited to $10,000, the stamp collection's basis.[47] ▼

For property transfers (particularly real estate), the ceiling limitations on the amount of the deduction allowed in any one year (50 percent, 30 percent, or 20 percent of AGI, as the case may be) could be a factor to take into account. With proper planning, donations can be controlled to stay within the limitations and therefore avoid the need for a carryover of unused charitable contributions.

---

[45] *Thomas E. Lesslie*, 36 TCM 495, T.C.Memo. 1977–111.
[46] *LaVar M. Withers*, 69 T.C. 900 (1978).

[47] No reduction of appreciation is necessary in alternative 2 since stock is intangible property and not tangible personalty.

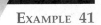

EXAMPLE 41

Andrew wants to donate a tract of unimproved land held as an investment to the University of Maryland (a qualified charitable organization). The land has been held for six years and has a current fair market value of $300,000 and a basis to Andrew of $50,000. Andrew's AGI for the current year is estimated to be $200,000, and he expects much the same for the next few years. In the current year, he deeds (transfers) an undivided one-fifth interest in the real estate to the university. ▼

What has Andrew in Example 41 accomplished for income tax purposes? In the current year, he will be allowed a charitable contribution deduction of $60,000 (⅕ × $300,000), which will be within the applicable limitation of AGI (30% × $200,000). Presuming no other charitable contributions for the year, Andrew has avoided the possibility of a carryover. In future years, Andrew can arrange donations of undivided interests in the real estate to stay within the bounds of the percentage limitations. The only difficulty with this approach is the need to revalue the real estate each year before the donation, since the amount of the deduction is based on the fair market value of the interest contributed at the time of the contribution.

It may be wise to avoid a carryover of unused charitable contributions, if possible, because that approach may be dangerous in several respects. First, the carryover period is limited to five years. Depending on the taxpayer's projected AGI rather than actual AGI, some of the amount carried over may expire without tax benefit after the five-year period has ended. Second, unused charitable contribution carryovers do not survive the death of the party making the donation and as a consequence are lost.

EXAMPLE 42

Tiffany dies in October 1994. In completing her final income tax return for 1994, Tiffany's executor determines the following information: AGI of $104,000 and a donation by Tiffany to her church of stock worth $60,000. Tiffany had purchased the stock two years ago for $50,000 and held it as an investment. Tiffany's executor makes the reduced deduction election and, as a consequence, claims a charitable contribution deduction of $50,000. With the election, the potential charitable contribution deduction of $50,000 ($60,000 – $10,000) is less than the 50% ceiling of $52,000 ($104,000 × 50%). If the executor had not made the election, the potential charitable contribution deduction of $60,000 would have been reduced by the 30% ceiling to $31,200 ($104,000 × 30%). No carryover of the $28,800 ($60,000 – $31,200) would have been available. ▼

KEY TERMS

Acquisition indebtedness, 10–13

Capital gain property, 10–21

Charitable contribution, 10–16

Home equity loans, 10–13

Investment income, 10–12

Investment interest, 10–11

Medical expense, 10–2

Miscellaneous itemized deductions, 10–24

Net investment income, 10–12

Ordinary income property, 10–21

Points, 10–14

Qualified residence interest, 10–11

<table>
<tr><td>

PROBLEM
MATERIALS

</td></tr>
</table>

DISCUSSION QUESTIONS

1. Dan, a self-employed individual taxpayer, prepared his own income tax return for the past year and asked you to check it over for accuracy. Your review indicates that Dan failed to claim certain business entertainment expenses.
   a. Will the correction of this omission affect the amount of medical expenses Dan can deduct? Explain.
   b. Would it matter if Dan were employed rather than self-employed?

2. Ninfa is in perfect health. During the current year, however, she pays $450 for an annual physical exam and $80 for a dental checkup. Do these expenses qualify for the medical deduction? Why or why not?

3. Under what circumstances, if any, will the cost of cosmetic surgery qualify as a deductible medical expense?

4. What are the criteria for determining whether the cost of a nursing home can qualify as a medical expense?

5. Hugo has a history of heart disease. Upon the advice of his doctor, he installs an elevator in his residence so he does not have to climb stairs. Is this a valid medical expense? If it is, how much of the expense is deductible?

6. Abby, who lives in California, discovers that she has a rare disease that can be treated only at the Mayo Clinic in Rochester, Minnesota. She travels to Rochester for treatment and incurs costs for airfare and for meals and lodging while being treated as an outpatient. Discuss the deductibility of these costs and any limits that will apply to the deduction.

7. Steve, who has a back problem that requires regular exercise, tells the other members of his golf foursome that his doctor has recommended that he go to Florida and play golf for the winter. He happily takes his doctor's advice and incurs expenses for transportation, meals, lodging, and greens fees while in Florida. Discuss the deductibility of these costs and any limits that will apply to the deduction.

8. If Ida's medical expense deduction was $500 in 1994 and the amount reduced her tax liability, how would a $300 insurance reimbursement be treated if received in 1995? Received in 1994? What if Ida had not itemized deductions in 1994 and received the $300 reimbursement in 1995?

9. Juan had medical expenses of $3,800 and AGI of $60,000 in 1994. He has other itemized deductions of $4,100 for the year. Can you suggest any tax planning ideas that might enable Juan to increase his itemized deductions for the year?

10. Susan and Anna, who are sisters, both itemize deductions. Susan, who lives in Arizona, can deduct part of the cost of licensing her automobile. Anna, who lives in Illinois, cannot deduct any part of her automobile license fees. Explain.

11. The city of Galveston, Texas, assessed beachfront property owners for the construction of jetties to protect shorelines from the destructive effects of the ocean. Is this assessment deductible?

12. A seller of property pays real estate taxes apportioned to the buyer. What are the income tax consequences to each party?

13. Bertha paid $2,600 in state income taxes in 1993. She received a state income tax refund of $500 in 1994 and was not required to report the refund as income for Federal income tax purposes. Earl, who paid state income tax of $3,300 in 1993, received a $700 state income tax refund in 1994. He did not report the $700 as income for Federal income tax purposes and received a notice from the IRS several months later informing him that he was required to report the amount as income. Explain why Earl's state income tax refund was treated differently than Bertha's refund.

14. Why has Congress imposed limitations on the deductibility of interest when funds are borrowed for the purpose of purchasing or continuing to hold investment property?

15. Ed borrows $20,000 and purchases an automobile. Jack borrows $20,000 to purchase a diamond engagement ring for his fiancée. Ed qualifies for an interest deduction on the amount he borrowed, but Jack does not. Can you offer any explanation for the difference?

16. As to the deductibility of "points," comment on the following:
   a. Those paid by the seller.
   b. Those paid to finance the purchase of a rental house.
   c. Those relating to the rendering of personal services.
   d. When capitalization and amortization might be advisable.
   e. Points paid from the mortgage proceeds.

17. Ellen borrows $50,000 from her parents for a down payment on a condominium. She paid interest of $4,200 in 1992, $0 in 1993, and $11,000 in 1994. The IRS disallows the deduction. Can you offer any explanation for the disallowance?

18. Walter was credited with interest of $3,000 on a one-year certificate of deposit. Because he withdrew the deposit before the maturity date, the bank assessed a $140 penalty. How should Walter report this information on his tax return?

19. An accountant normally charges $100 an hour when preparing financial statements for clients. If the accountant performs accounting services for a church without charge, can she deduct the value of the donated services on her tax return?

20. John would like to attend the annual convention of his church, which is to be held in another state. Advise John on some of the tax implications that would result if he makes the trip.

21. Zane donated property that cost $1,000 and was worth $3,000 to a charity. Under what circumstances will Zane be allowed to deduct $3,000 for this charitable contribution? Under what circumstances will he be limited to a $1,000 deduction?

22. What is capital gain property? What tax treatment is required if capital gain property is contributed to a private nonoperating foundation? To a public charity? What difference does it make if the contribution is tangible personalty and it is put to a use unrelated to the donee's business?

23. During 1994, Shirley donated five dresses to the Salvation Army. She had purchased the dresses three years ago at a cost of $1,200 and worn them as personal attire. Because the dresses are long-term capital assets, Shirley plans to deduct $1,200 on her 1994 income tax return. Comment on Shirley's understanding of the tax law governing charitable contributions.

24. In the year of her death, Sharon made significant charitable contributions of long-term capital gain property. In fact, the amount of the contributions exceeds 30% of her AGI. What might be a possible alternative for the executor of Sharon's estate who prepares her final income tax return?

25. In 1993, Vern had an excess charitable contribution that he could not deduct because of the percentage limitations. In 1994, Vern made further charitable contributions. In applying the percentage limitations for 1994, how are these transactions handled?

26. Regarding the cutback adjustment for certain itemized deductions, comment on the following:
   a. The threshold amount.
   b. Itemized deductions not covered.
   c. The 3% and 80% rules.

PROBLEMS

27. Bill and Nancy are married and together have AGI of $60,000. They have no dependents and filed a joint return in 1994. Each pays $900 for hospitalization insurance. During the year, they paid the following amounts for medical care: $6,200 in doctor and dentist

bills and hospital expenses and $800 for prescribed medicine and drugs. They received an insurance reimbursement for hospitalization in December 1994 for $1,200. Determine the deduction allowable for medical expenses paid in 1994.

28. Dave is divorced and claims his father (Jesse) and his son (Sammy) as dependents. During the current year, he pays the following expenses:

Tuition (including room and board) to send Sammy to Prospect Military Academy	$11,000
To Dr. Brown (a child psychiatrist) for consultations with Sammy	1,600
Room and board at Happy Farms Assisted Living Home on behalf of Jesse	22,000
Doctor and hospital charges to correct Jesse's hernia	3,100

Upon Dr. Brown's recommendation, Sammy was sent to Prospect Military Academy to alleviate a truancy problem. The academy provides no medical care but does impose strict discipline. Jesse moved to Happy Farms because he felt living with Dave was too dull. Disregarding percentage limitations, how much qualifies as a medical expense on Dave's tax return for:
   a. Sammy?
   b. Jesse?

29. Upon the advice of his physician, George, a heart patient, installs an elevator in his personal residence at a cost of $8,000. The elevator has a cost recovery period of five years. A neighbor who is in the real estate business charges George $60 for an appraisal that places the value of the residence at $60,000 before the improvement and $62,000 after. The value increases because George lives in a region where many older people retire and therefore would find the elevator an attractive feature in a home. As a result of the operation of the elevator, George noticed an increase of $75 in his utility bills for the current year. Disregarding percentage limitations, which of the above expenditures qualify as a medical expense deduction?

30. Julia had medical expenses of $9,000 and AGI of $100,000 in 1994. She had other itemized deductions of $8,200 for the year. Julia expects that her insurance company will reimburse her for all of her medical expenses in January 1995. What is the maximum amount Julia can deduct as itemized deductions for 1994? If she deducts the maximum allowable amount in 1994, will this affect her taxable income in 1995? What factors should Julia consider in deciding whether to deduct the medical expenses in 1994?

31. During 1994, Agnew paid the following medical expenses:

On behalf of Sylvester (Agnew's son by a former marriage)	$8,000
On behalf of Roger (Agnew's uncle)	6,100
Hospital bill for an operation performed on Agnew in 1993	5,200

Of the $8,000 spent on Sylvester, $7,000 was for orthodontia services to be performed in 1995. The dentist required this amount as a deposit for the braces to be applied to Sylvester's teeth. Agnew could claim Sylvester as a dependent, but Sylvester's mother refuses to sign the custodial parent's waiver. Roger could be claimed as Agnew's dependent except for the gross income test. For these items, what amount qualifies as Agnew's medical expenses for 1994?

32. Fran is employed as a real estate broker. For calendar year 1994, Fran has $50,000 in wages from her job and pays $3,800 in medical insurance premiums. During the year, she paid the following other medical expenses:

Doctor and hospital bills for Herb and Georgia (Fran's parents)	$6,000
Doctor and dentist bills for Fran	3,200
Prescribed medicines for Fran	800
Nonprescribed insulin for Fran	350

Herb and Georgia would qualify as Fran's dependents except that they file a joint return. Fran's medical insurance policy does not cover them. Fran filed a claim for $2,100 for her own expenses with her insurance company in December 1994. She received the $2,100 reimbursement in January 1995. Discuss the tax treatment of these various expenses.

33. In Clay County, the real property tax year is the calendar year. The real property tax becomes a personal liability of the owner of real property on January 1 in the current real property tax year, 1994. The tax is payable on July 1, 1994. On May 1, 1994, Joe sells his house to Celia for $280,000. On July 1, 1994, Celia pays the entire real estate tax of $4,015 for the year ending December 31, 1994.
    a. How much of the property taxes may Joe deduct?
    b. How much of the property taxes may Celia deduct?

34. Assume the same facts as in Problem 33.
    a. What is Celia's basis for the residence?
    b. How much did Joe realize from the sale of the residence?

35. Roland uses the cash method of accounting and lives in a state that imposes an income tax (including withholding from wages). On April 14, 1994, he files his state return for 1993, paying an additional $500 in state income taxes. During 1994, his withholdings for state income tax purposes amount to $3,700. On April 13, 1995, he files his state return for 1994 claiming a refund of $900. Roland receives the refund on August 3, 1995.
    a. If Roland itemizes deductions, how much may he claim as a deduction for state income taxes on his Federal return for calendar year 1994 (filed in April 1995)?
    b. How will the refund of $900 received in 1995 be treated for Federal income tax purposes?

36. In 1994, Myrna has $8,000 of investment income and the following miscellaneous deductions:

Unreimbursed employee business expenses (meals included at 50%)	$1,400
Tax return preparation fee	440
Investment expenses	500

For purposes of the investment interest expense limitation, what is the total of Myrna's net investment income in each of the following independent situations:
    a. AGI of $20,000.
    b. AGI of $60,000.
    c. AGI of $110,000.

37. Clark is married and files a joint tax return for 1994. Clark has investment interest expense of $95,000 for a loan made to him in 1994 to purchase a parcel of unimproved land. His income from investments (dividends and interest) totaled $15,000. After reducing his miscellaneous deductions by the applicable 2% floor, the deductible portion amounted to $2,500. In addition to $1,100 of investment expenses included in miscellaneous deductions, Clark paid $3,000 of real estate taxes on the unimproved land. Clark also has $3,000 as a net long-term capital gain from the sale of another parcel of unimproved land. Calculate Clark's investment interest deduction for 1994.

X 38. Veronica borrowed $200,000 to acquire a parcel of land to be held for investment purposes. During 1994, she paid interest of $20,000 on the loan. She had AGI of $50,000 for the year. Other items related to Veronica's investments include the following:

Investment income	$10,200
Long-term gain on sale of stock	4,000
Investment counsel fees	1,500

Veronica is unmarried and elected to itemize her deductions. She had no miscellaneous deductions other than the investment counsel fees. Determine Veronica's investment interest deduction for 1994.

39. In 1994, Earl borrows $150,000 to purchase an airplane (to be used for pleasure purposes) by placing a lien on his personal residence. At this time, the first mortgage on the residence has a balance of $260,000, and the residence has a fair market value of $390,000. How should Earl determine his interest deduction?

40. Ted and his wife Alice own a personal residence in the city. For many years, they have owned a beach house 50 miles away. They do not rent out the beach house because they spend every weekend there. Last year, they purchased a condominium in Boulder, Colorado, for their son to live in while he attends college. During 1994, they paid the following mortgage interest (each mortgage is secured by the respective property): $7,800 on their personal residence, $5,500 on the beach house, and $9,000 on the condominium. How much can Ted and Alice deduct for the year as qualified residence interest?

41. Ron and Tom are equal owners in Robin Corporation. On July 1, 1994, each loans the corporation $30,000 at annual interest of 10%. Ron and Tom are brothers. Both shareholders are on the cash method of accounting, while Robin Corporation is on the accrual method. All parties use the calendar year for tax purposes. On June 30, 1995, Robin repays the loans of $60,000 together with the specified interest of $6,000.
    a. How much of the interest can Robin Corporation deduct in 1994? In 1995?
    b. When is the interest taxed to Ron and Tom?

42. In 1994 Peter pays $800 to become a charter member of State University's Athletic Council. The membership ensures that Peter will receive choice seating at all of State's home football games. Also in 1994, Peter pays $150 (the regular retail price) for season tickets for himself and his wife. For these items, how much qualifies as a charitable contribution?

43. Diego's child attends a parochial school operated by the church the family attends. Diego made a donation of $300 to the church in lieu of the normal registration fee of $100 for children of nonmembers. In addition, the regular tuition of $75 per week is paid to the school. Based on this information, what is Diego's charitable contribution?

44. Determine the amount of the charitable deduction allowed in each of the following situations:
    a. Donation of Wren Corporation stock (a publicly traded corporation) to taxpayer's church. The stock cost the taxpayer $2,000 four months ago and has a fair market value of $3,000 on the date of the donation.
    b. Donation of a painting to the Salvation Army. The painting cost the taxpayer $2,000 five years ago and has a fair market value of $3,500 on the date of the donation.
    c. The local branch of the American Red Cross uses a building rent-free for half of the current year. The building normally rents for $500 a month.
    d. Donation by a cash basis farmer to a church of a quantity of grain worth $900. The farmer raised the grain in the preceding year at a cost of $650, all of which was deducted for income tax purposes.

45. During 1994, Al made the following contributions to his church:

Cash	$40,000
Stock in Thrush Corporation (a publicly traded corporation)	60,000

The stock in Thrush Corporation was acquired as an investment three years ago at a cost of $20,000. Al's AGI for 1994 is $140,000.
    a. What is Al's charitable contribution deduction for 1994?
    b. How are excess amounts, if any, treated?

46. Mae died in 1994. Before she died, Mae made a gift of stock in Eagle Corporation (a publicly traded corporation) to her church. The stock was worth $35,000 and had been acquired as an investment two years ago at a cost of $30,000. In the year of her death, Mae had AGI of $60,000. In completing her final income tax return, how should Mae's executor handle the charitable contribution?

47. On December 30, 1994, Roberta purchased four tickets to a charity ball sponsored by the city of San Diego for the benefit of underprivileged children. Each ticket cost $200 and

had a fair market value of $35. On the same day as the purchase, Roberta gave the tickets to the minister of her church for personal use by his family. At the time of the gift of the tickets, Roberta pledged $4,000 to the building fund of her church. The pledge was satisfied by check dated December 31, 1994, but not mailed until January 3, 1995.

a. Presuming Roberta is a cash basis and calendar year taxpayer, how much can she deduct as a charitable contribution for 1994?

b. Would the amount of the deduction be any different if Roberta is an accrual basis taxpayer? Explain.

48. Classify each of the following independent expenditures as nondeductible (ND) items, business (dfor) deductions, or itemized (dfrom) deductions. (Note: In many cases, it may be necessary to refer to the materials in earlier chapters of the text.)

a. Interest allowed on home mortgage accrued by a cash basis taxpayer.

b. State income taxes paid by a sole proprietor of a business.

c. Subscription to the *Wall Street Journal* paid by a vice president of a bank and not reimbursed by her employer.

d. Automobile mileage for attendance at weekly church services.

e. Street-paving assessment paid to the county by a homeowner.

f. Speeding ticket paid by the owner-operator of a taxicab.

g. Interest and taxes paid by the owner of residential rental property.

h. Business entertainment expenses (properly substantiated) paid by a self-employed taxpayer.

i. State and Federal excise taxes on tobacco paid by a self-employed taxpayer who gave his clients cigars as Christmas presents. The business gifts were properly substantiated and under $25 each.

j. State and Federal excise taxes on cigarettes purchased by a heavy smoker for personal consumption.

k. Federal excise taxes (18.4 cents per gallon) on the purchase of gasoline for use in the taxpayer's personal automobile.

l. Theft loss of personal jewelry worth $300 but which originally cost $75.

m. Maternity clothing purchased by a taxpayer who is pregnant.

n. Medical expenses paid by an employer on behalf of an employee.

o. Qualified residence interest paid by a taxpayer on a loan obtained to build an artist studio in his personal residence. Assume that taxpayer's art activities are classified as a hobby.

p. Assume the same facts as in (o) except that the art activities are classified as a trade or business.

49. Some miscellaneous deductions are subject to the 2%-of-AGI floor while other deductions are not. In this connection, comment on the tax treatment of the following:

a. Job hunting costs.

b. Appraisal fees to determine the amount of a casualty loss.

c. Gambling losses up to the amount of gambling winnings.

d. Hobby loss up to the amount of hobby income.

e. Job uniforms not suited for normal wear.

f. Casualty and theft losses.

g. Medical expenses.

50. For calendar year 1994, Clyde and Trisha file a joint return reflecting AGI of $150,000. Their itemized deductions are as follows:

Medical expenses	$11,000
Casualty loss (not covered by insurance)	18,000
Interest on home mortgage	17,000
Property taxes on home	12,000
Charitable contributions	15,000
State income tax	9,000

After all necessary adjustments are made, what is the amount of itemized deductions Clyde and Trisha may claim?

51. Kareem and Veneia are married and file a joint return. For 1994, they have AGI of $305,520. Their itemized deductions for the year total $39,000 and consist of the following:

Medical expenses	$32,000
Interest on home mortgage	3,000
State income tax	4,000

After all necessary adjustments are made, what is the amount of itemized deductions Kareem and Veneia may claim?

52. Ben and Laura are married and file a joint return. For 1994, they have AGI of $358,450, which included net investment income of $41,000 before deducting investment interest. Compute Ben and Laura's allowable itemized deductions for 1994 based on the following information:

Investment interest	$11,000
Casualty loss (after applicable limitations)	8,000
Qualified residence interest	5,400
Property taxes	4,700
Charitable contributions	2,900
State income taxes	5,300

53. Assume the same facts as in Problem 52, except that Ben and Laura have AGI of $708,450.

CUMULATIVE PROBLEMS

54. Alice and Bruce Byrd are married taxpayers, ages 47 and 45, who file a joint return. Their Social Security numbers are 034–48–4382 and 016–50–9556, respectively. They live at 473 Revere Avenue, Ames, MA 01850. Alice is a receptionist for a dental clinic and earns an annual salary of $28,000. Bruce is the manager of several fast-food outlets owned and operated by Plymouth Corporation. His annual salary is $41,000.

The Byrds have two children, Cynthia (age 23 and S.S. no. 017–44–9126) and John (age 22 and S.S. no. 017–27–4148), who live with them. Both are full-time students at a nearby college. Bruce's mother, Myrtle Byrd (age 74 and S.S. no. 016–15–8266), also lives with them. Her sole source of income is a Social Security benefit, which she deposits in a savings account.

During 1993, a particularly harsh storm struck the Ames area. As a result, the Byrds suffered severe flood damage to the basement and foundation of their personal residence, which was purchased in 1985 at a cost of $80,000. Based on an appraisal, the fair market value of the house was $110,000 before the storm and $100,000 after. The Byrds' homeowner's insurance policy does not cover damage due to flooding. The cost of the appraisal was $300.

During 1993, the Byrds furnished one-third of the total support of Alice's widower father, Sam Harper (age 70 and S.S. no. 034–82–8583). Sam lives alone and receives the rest of his support from Alice's sister and brother (one-third each). They have signed a multiple support agreement allowing Alice to claim the father as a dependent for 1993.

The Byrds had the following expenses relating to their personal residence during 1993:

Property taxes	$2,100
Interest on home mortgage	6,200
Repairs to roof	1,300
Utilities	2,500
Fire and theft insurance	900

Medical expenses for 1993 include:

Medical insurance premiums	$2,800
Doctor bill incurred in 1992 and not paid until 1993	1,400
Operation for Sam Harper	3,600

The operation for Sam Harper represents the one-third Alice contributed toward her father's support.

Other relevant information follows:

- During 1993, Myrtle gave Alice and Bruce a tract of undeveloped land (basis of $30,000 and fair market value of $40,000), which she had inherited from her husband (Bruce's father).

- Alice and Bruce had $2,956 withheld from their salaries for state income taxes. When they filed their 1992 state return in 1993, they paid additional tax of $210.

- During 1993, Alice and Bruce attended a dinner dance sponsored by the Ames Police Disability Association (a qualified charitable organization). The Byrds paid $80 for the tickets. Cost of comparable entertainment would normally be $50. The Byrds contributed $1,200 to their church and gave used clothing (cost of $500 and fair market value of $100) to the Salvation Army. All donations are supported by receipts.

- In 1993, the Byrds received interest income of $750 from a savings account they maintained.

- Alice's employer requires that all nurses wear uniforms to work. During 1993, Alice spent $240 on new uniforms and $82 on laundry charges. Bruce paid $84 for an annual subscription to the *Journal of Franchise Management*. Neither Alice's nor Bruce's employers reimburse for employee expenses.

- Alice and Bruce had $5,532 ($2,586 for Alice and $2,946 for Bruce) of Federal income tax withheld in 1993 and paid no estimated Federal income tax. Neither Alice nor Bruce wishes to designate $3 to the Presidential Election Campaign Fund.

Compute net tax payable or refund due for Alice and Bruce Byrd for 1994. If they have overpaid, the amount is to be refunded. If you use tax forms for your computations, you will need Form 1040, Schedule A, and Form 4684. Suggested software (if available): *TurboTax* or *MacInTax* for tax return or WFT tax planning software.

55. Sam Worthing, age 45, is married and has two dependent children. In 1994, he incurred the following:

Salary received from his employer, Geophysics, Inc.		$95,000
Cost of art supplies. Sam took up painting as a hobby and plans to sell the paintings to friends and art galleries but had no willing purchasers during 1994.		1,000
Contribution of shares of Xerox stock to his church (fair market value of $3,000, cost of $800, and acquired in 1976).		6,000
Sam's wife, Irene, had a diamond ring that was stolen in April 1994. A police report was filed, but her ring was not recovered. It is not covered by insurance. The ring had recently been appraised at $9,500, which was also its original cost.		9,500
Travel (meals included at 50%) and auto expenses incurred in connection with Sam's employment (none of which was reimbursed).		3,500
Sam and his family moved from Nashville to Boston during the year and incurred the following unreimbursed expenses:		
Moving van	$2,500	
Transportation expenses (meals included at 50%)	2,000	4,500

Sam incurred and paid the following personal expenses:

Medical and dental bills for the family	3,500
State and local income and property taxes	4,800

Determine the Worthings' AGI and taxable income for 1994, assuming that a joint return is filed and that there are no other items of income or expense. Suggested software (if available): *TurboTax* or *MacInTax* for tax return or WFT tax planning software.

RESEARCH PROBLEMS

Research Problem 1. Jane suffers from a degenerative spinal disorder. Her physician recommended the installation of a swimming pool at her residence for her use to prevent the onset of permanent paralysis. Jane's residence had a market value of approximately $500,000 before the swimming pool was installed. The swimming pool was built, and an appraiser estimated that the value of Jane's home increased by $98,000 because of the addition.

The pool cost $194,000, and Jane claimed a medical deduction on her tax return of $96,000. Upon audit of the return, the IRS determined that an adequate pool should have cost $70,000 and would increase the property value by only $31,000. Thus, the IRS claims that Jane should be entitled to a deduction of only $39,000.

a. Is there any ceiling limitation on the amount deductible as a medical expense?
b. Can capital expenditures be deducted as medical expenses?
c. What is the significance of a "minimum adequate facility"? Should aesthetic or architectural qualities be considered in this determination?

Research Problem 2.   Several years ago, Lester, a cash basis taxpayer, obtained a mortgage from State Bank to purchase a personal residence. In December 1994, $9,500 of interest was due on the mortgage, but Lester had only $75 in his checking account. On December 31, 1994, Lester borrowed $9,500 from State Bank, evidenced by a note, and the proceeds were deposited in his checking account. On the same day, Lester issued a check in the identical amount of $9,500 to State Bank for the interest expense due. Is this interest expense deductible for the tax year 1994?

Partial list of research aids:
§ 163(h)(3).
William M. Roberts, 53 TCM 787, T.C.Memo. 1987–235.

Research Problem 3.   Julio and his wife purchased a new residence. Because they were unable to obtain conventional mortgage financing, they borrowed the purchase price at City National Bank. Under the terms of the loan, they agreed to pay interest and make very modest repayments of the principal for three years. At the end of three years, the full amount of the loan would "balloon" and become due. During the three-year term of the loan, the taxpayers made the interest payments and only some of the repayments of principal.

By the end of the three-year loan, Julio and his wife managed to obtain long-term (30-year) mortgage financing with State Savings and Loan. Thus, the outstanding amounts due City National were rolled over into the new mortgage with State Savings and Loan.

As a cost of securing the refinancing, the couple had to pay points. These were paid from their own funds and not from the mortgage proceeds. Julio and his wife concede that they did not possess the economic means to meet the balloon payment requirement under the City National Bank loan agreement.

Determine the income tax treatment of the points paid to State Savings and Loan.

Partial list of research aids:
§ 461(g)(2).

Research Problem 4.   Falcon Corporation is the owner and operator of a large daily metropolitan newspaper. For at least 80 years, Falcon has collected and maintained a "clippings library." The library is a collection of past news items from Falcon's and other newspapers. The 7,800,000 items are well-preserved, cataloged, and cross-listed under various categories. Falcon estimates that it has spent in excess of $10 million compiling and organizing the library. However, since this amount was deducted as incurred, the income tax basis of the library is zero. The fair market value of the library is $3 million.

Falcon Corporation contributes the clippings library to the state historical society (a qualified organization) and claims a charitable contribution deduction of $3 million. Upon audit, the IRS disallows the entire amount of the deduction because the basis of the property is zero. Who is correct?

Partial list of research aids:
§§ 170(e)(1)(A) and 1221(3).

Research Problem 5.   The city of Sacramento wished to establish a scenic corridor along portions of Interstate 5, but did not have the funds to purchase all of the land involved and to make the necessary improvements (e.g., terracing and other landscaping). Likewise, the city was fearful of any personal liability that might result from the operation of the scenic corridor. If, however, state funding could be obtained to cover the improvements and liability costs, the project would be carried out. State funding was a possible but not a probable likelihood.

In 1992, all but one of the property owners affected by the project donated the necessary land to the city. The city purchased the land of the one owner who refused to make a donation. The city agreed to return the land to the donors in the event the project was not carried out. By 1994, it became certain that state funding would not be forthcoming. Therefore, the city returned the land to the donors, except for the parcel it had purchased.

William Baird, one of the donors, claimed a charitable deduction for the fair market value of the land transferred in 1992. Upon audit of William's 1992 income tax return, the IRS disallowed the deduction and assessed the penalty for overvaluation. Is the IRS correct?

a. Write a letter to William that contains your tax advice.
b. Prepare a memo for your firm's tax files.

Partial list of research aids:
§ 6659 [now § 6662(b)(3)].
Reg. § 1.170A–1(e).
Ronald W. McCrary, 92 T.C. 827 (1989).

11

PASSIVE ACTIVITY LOSSES

LEARNING OBJECTIVES

After completing Chapter 11, you should be able to:

1. Discuss tax shelters and the reasons for at-risk and passive loss limitations.

2. Explain the at-risk limitation.

3. Identify taxpayers who are subject to the passive loss limits.

4. Understand the rationale for the passive loss limitations.

5. Describe how the passive loss rules limit deductions for losses.

6. Discuss the definition of passive activities.

7. Analyze and apply the tests for material participation.

8. Consider special rules related to rental activities.

9. Apply the rules for identifying passive activities.

10. Discuss the real estate rental exception.

11. Determine the proper tax treatment upon the disposition of a passive activity.

12. Suggest tax planning strategies to minimize the effect of the passive loss limitations.

OUTLINE

The Tax Shelter Problem, 11–2

At-Risk Limits, 11–3

Passive Loss Limits, 11–4

Taxpayers Subject to the Passive Loss Rules, 11–4

Passive Activities Defined, 11–6

Material Participation, 11–7

Rental Activities, 11–13

Identification of Passive Activity, 11–16

Classification of Income and Losses, 11–18

Income Not Treated as Passive, 11–19

Deductions Not Treated as Passive, 11–20

Suspended Losses, 11–20

Passive Credits, 11–22

Real Estate Rental Activities, 11–23

Dispositions of Passive Interests, 11–25

Transition Rules for Passive Losses (1987–1990), 11–27

Tax Planning Considerations, 11–28

Utilizing Passive Losses, 11–28

THE TAX SHELTER PROBLEM

1 LEARNING OBJECTIVE
Discuss tax shelters and the reasons for at-risk and passive loss limitations.

Before Congress enacted legislation to reduce or eliminate their effectiveness, **tax shelters** were popular investments for tax avoidance purposes. The typical tax shelter relied heavily on nonrecourse financing[1] and generated large losses in the early years of the activity. Investors would offset these tax shelter losses against other types of income. At the very least, the tax shelter deductions deferred income taxes for the investor until the activity was sold. In the best of situations, additional tax savings were realized because sale of the activity produced capital gain, which was taxed at much lower rates than ordinary income. The following example illustrates what was possible *before* Congress enacted legislation to curb tax shelter abuses.

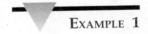
EXAMPLE 1

Bob, who earned a salary of $100,000, invested $20,000 for a 10% interest in a tax shelter. Through the use of $800,000 of nonrecourse financing, the partnership acquired assets worth $1 million. Depreciation, interest, and other deductions related to the activity resulted in a loss of $400,000, of which Bob's share was $40,000. Bob was allowed to deduct the $40,000 loss, even though he had invested and stood to lose only $20,000. ▼

A review of Example 1 shows that the taxpayer took a *two-for-one* write-off ($40,000 deduction, $20,000 investment). In the heyday of tax shelters, promoters often promised *multiple* write-offs for the investor.

The first major provision aimed at the tax shelter strategy was the **at-risk limitation** enacted in 1976. The objective of the at-risk rule is to limit a taxpayer's tax shelter deductions to the amount at risk, that is, the amount the taxpayer stands to lose if the investment turns out to be a financial disaster. Under the current at-risk rules, Bob in Example 1 would not be allowed to deduct more than $20,000.[2] The remaining $20,000 would be suspended under the at-risk rules and would be deductible in the future if his at-risk amount increased.

The second major attack on tax shelters came in the Tax Reform Act of 1986. The passive loss limits in that legislation have nearly made the term *tax shelter* obsolete. Now such investments are generally referred to as passive investments, or *passive activities*, rather than tax shelters.

---

[1] Nonrecourse debt is an obligation for which the endorser is not personally liable. An example of nonrecourse debt is a liability on real estate acquired by a partnership without the partnership or any of the partners assuming any liability for the mortgage. The acquired property generally is pledged as collateral for the loan.

[2] If the investment is in a *passive activity*, the deduction is limited further under the passive loss rules.

The passive loss rules require the taxpayer to segregate income and losses into three categories: active, passive, and portfolio. In general, the passive loss limits disallow the deduction of passive losses against active or portfolio income, even if the taxpayer is at risk for the amount of the loss. Refer again to Example 1. Under current law, the at-risk rules and passive loss limits work together to disallow the entire $40,000 loss in the year it is incurred. However, the *suspended* passive loss may be carried forward and deducted in the future if the taxpayer has passive income or disposes of the activity.

AT-RISK LIMITS

2 **LEARNING OBJECTIVE**
Explain the at-risk limitation.

The at-risk provisions limit the deductibility of losses from business and income-producing activities. These provisions, which apply to individuals and closely held corporations, are designed to prevent a taxpayer from deducting losses in excess of the actual economic investment in an activity.

Under the at-risk rules, a taxpayer's deductible losses from an activity for any taxable year are limited to the amount the taxpayer has at risk at the end of the taxable year (the amount the taxpayer could actually lose in the activity). The initial amount considered at risk is generally the sum of the following:[3]

- The amount of cash and the adjusted basis of property contributed to the activity.
- Amounts borrowed for use in the activity for which the taxpayer is personally liable or has pledged as security property not used in the activity.

This amount generally is increased each year by the taxpayer's share of income and is decreased by the taxpayer's share of losses and withdrawals from the activity. Partners are jointly and severally liable for recourse debts of the partnership. Therefore, a partner's at-risk amount is increased when the partnership increases its debt, and is decreased when the partnership reduces its debt.

A taxpayer generally is not considered at risk with respect to borrowed amounts if either of the following is true:

- The taxpayer is not personally liable for repayment of the debt (nonrecourse loans).
- The lender has an interest (other than as a creditor) in the activity.

Although taxpayers are generally not considered at risk for nonrecourse loans, there is an important exception. This exception provides that, in the case of an activity involving the holding of real property, a taxpayer is considered at risk for his or her share of any qualified nonrecourse financing that is secured by real property used in the activity.

Any losses disallowed for any given taxable year by the at-risk rules may be deducted in the first succeeding year in which the rules do not prevent the deduction. However, if the losses are incurred in a passive activity, they are subject to the passive loss limitations.

EXAMPLE 2

In 1994, Sue invests $40,000 in an oil partnership that, by the use of nonrecourse loans, spends $60,000 on intangible drilling costs applicable to her interest. Sue's interest in the partnership is subject to the at-risk limits but is not subject to the passive loss limits. Since

---

[3] § 465(b)(1).

Sue has only $40,000 of capital at risk, she cannot deduct more than $40,000 against her other income and must reduce her at-risk amount to zero ($40,000 at-risk amount – $40,000 loss deducted). The nondeductible loss of $20,000 ($60,000 loss – $40,000 allowed) can be carried over to 1995. ▼

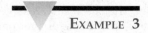

EXAMPLE 3

In 1995, Sue has taxable income from the oil partnership of $15,000 and invests an additional $5,000 in the venture. Her at-risk amount is now $20,000 ($0 beginning balance + $15,000 taxable income + $5,000 additional investment). This enables Sue to deduct the carried-over loss, and again requires her to reduce her at-risk amount to zero ($20,000 at-risk amount – $20,000 carried-over loss). ▼

Recapture of previously allowed losses is required to the extent the at-risk amount is reduced below zero.[4] This rule applies if the amount at risk is reduced below zero by distributions to the taxpayer, by changes in the status of indebtedness from recourse to nonrecourse, or by the commencement of a guarantee or other similar arrangement that affects the taxpayer's risk of loss.

PASSIVE LOSS LIMITS

TAXPAYERS SUBJECT TO THE PASSIVE LOSS RULES

3   LEARNING OBJECTIVE
Identify taxpayers who are subject to the passive loss limits.

The **passive loss** rules apply to individuals, estates, trusts, closely held C corporations, and personal service corporations.[5] Passive income or loss from investments in S corporations or partnerships (see Chapter 20) flows through to the owners, and the passive loss rules are applied at the owner level.

Before enactment of the passive loss limits, taxpayers were able to defer or avoid taxes by investing in tax shelters that produced losses. These losses were used to offset income from other sources.

EXAMPLE 4

Karen, a physician, earned $150,000 from her practice in 1985 (before the passive loss rules were enacted). She also received $10,000 in dividends and interest on various portfolio investments. During the year, she acquired a 20% interest in a tax shelter that produced a $300,000 loss not subject to the at-risk limits. In 1985, Karen would have been allowed to deduct her $60,000 share of the tax shelter loss, resulting in AGI of $100,000 ($150,000 salary + $10,000 dividends and interest – $60,000 tax shelter loss). ▼

4   LEARNING OBJECTIVE
Understand the rationale for the passive loss limitations.

Why would a taxpayer ever intentionally invest in an activity that would produce losses? There is a logical answer. Under the most favorable tax shelter scenario, the investor would take loss deductions for several years, then the tax shelter would be sold at a gain. Upon the sale of the tax shelter, the taxpayer would, in effect, report income to the extent of the previously deducted losses plus an additional gain due to appreciation of the investment. Deduction of the losses had the effect of deferring taxes. In addition, all or part of the gain would have been subject to the much lower capital gain rates that existed before the Tax Reform Act of 1986.

5   LEARNING OBJECTIVE
Describe how the passive loss rules limit deductions for losses.

As a general rule, under current law taxpayers who are subject to the passive loss limitations cannot offset passive losses against active income or portfolio income.

---

[4] § 465(e).   [5] § 469(a).

EXAMPLE 5 Assume the same facts as in Example 4, except that the year is 1994 and that Karen does not materially participate in the operations of the activity. Her $60,000 share of the loss is a *passive loss* and is not deductible in 1994. It is treated as a *suspended loss,* which is carried over to the future. If Karen has passive income from this investment, or from other passive investments, in the future, she can offset the suspended loss against that passive income. If she does not have passive income to offset the suspended loss in the future, she will be allowed to offset the loss against other types of income when she eventually disposes of the passive activity. Karen's AGI in 1994 is $160,000 ($150,000 salary + $10,000 portfolio income), compared to $100,000 based on the same set of facts for tax year 1985. ▼

Personal Service Corporations

Application of the passive loss limitation to **personal service corporations** is intended to prevent taxpayers from sheltering personal service income by creating personal service corporations and acquiring passive activities at the corporate level.

EXAMPLE 6 Five attorneys, who earn a total of $1 million a year in their individual practices, form a personal service corporation. Shortly after its formation, the corporation invests in a passive activity that produces a $200,000 loss during the year. Because the passive loss rules apply to personal service corporations, the corporation may not deduct the $200,000 loss. ▼

Determination of whether a corporation is a *personal service corporation* is based on rather broad definitions. A personal service corporation is a corporation that meets *both* of the following conditions:

- The principal activity is the performance of personal services.
- Such services are substantially performed by owner-employees.

Personal service corporations include those in the fields of health, law, engineering, architecture, accounting, actuarial science, performing arts, and consulting.[6] A corporation is treated as a personal service corporation if more than 10 percent of the stock (by value) is held by owner-employees.[7] A shareholder is treated as an owner-employee if he or she is an employee or shareholder on *any day* during the testing period.[8] For these purposes, shareholder status and employee status do not even have to occur on the same day.

Closely Held Corporations

Application of the passive loss rules to closely held (non-personal service) corporations also is intended to prevent individuals from incorporating to avoid the passive loss limitation. A corporation is classified as a **closely held corporation** if, at any time during the taxable year, more than 50 percent of the value of its outstanding stock is owned, directly or indirectly, by or for not more than five individuals. Closely held corporations (other than personal service corporations) may offset passive losses against *active* income, but not against portfolio income.

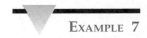

EXAMPLE 7 Silver Corporation, a closely held C corporation, has $500,000 of passive losses from a rental activity, $400,000 of active income, and $100,000 of portfolio income. The corporation may offset $400,000 of the $500,000 passive loss against the $400,000 of active business

---

[6] § 448(d).
[7] § 469(j)(2).

[8] § 269A(b)(2).

income, but may not offset the remainder against the $100,000 of portfolio income. Thus, $100,000 of the passive loss is suspended ($500,000 passive loss – $400,000 offset against active income). ▼

Application of the passive loss limitation to closely held corporations prevents taxpayers from transferring their portfolio investments to such corporations in order to offset passive losses against portfolio income.

PASSIVE ACTIVITIES DEFINED

6   **LEARNING OBJECTIVE**
Discuss the definition of passive activities.

Code § 469 specifies that the following types of activities are to be treated as passive:

- Any trade or business or income-producing activity in which the taxpayer does not materially participate.
- All rental activities, except real property trades or businesses in which the taxpayer materially participates.

As originally enacted, § 469 required that a taxpayer participate on a *regular, continuous,* and *substantial* basis in order to be a material participant. In many situations, however, it was difficult or impossible to determine whether the taxpayer had met these vague **material participation** standards. Temporary Regulations under § 469,[9] issued in February 1988, help taxpayers cope with these material participation issues.

The Temporary Regulations provide seven tests that can be applied to determine whether a taxpayer is a material participant in an activity. One of these tests specifies that a taxpayer who participates more than 500 hours a year in a nonrental trade or business activity is a material participant.

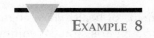
EXAMPLE 8

Juan spends 40 hours a week, 50 weeks a year, operating a restaurant that he owns. He also owns a men's clothing store in another state that is operated by an employee. Because Juan participates for more than 500 hours during the year, the restaurant is treated as an active business. However, because he does not participate in the operations of the clothing store, it is a passive activity. ▼

The seven tests for material participation provided by the Temporary Regulations, including the test reflected in Example 8, are discussed in detail under Material Participation later in the chapter.

Although the Code specifies that *rental activities* are to be treated as passive, identifying passive rental activities can be complicated. The general rule is that an activity is a rental activity if customers are charged rental fees for the use of tangible property (real or personal).

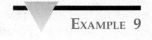
EXAMPLE 9

Sara owns an apartment building and spends an average of 60 hours a week in its operation. The rental activity does not qualify under any of the six exceptions provided by the Temporary Regulations. Consequently, it is treated as a rental activity and is automatically classified as a passive activity, even though Sara spends more than 500 hours a year in its operation. ▼

Application of the passive loss limits to rental activities is complicated by the fact that some activities that involve rentals of real or personal property are not

[9] The Temporary Regulations are also Proposed Regulations. Temporary Regulations have the same effect as final Regulations. Refer to Chapter 2 for a discussion of the different categories of Regulations.

treated as rental activities for purposes of the passive loss provisions. The Temporary Regulations contain six exceptions that allow rental activities to escape *automatic* passive activity classification. The following example illustrates one of the exceptions.

▼ **EXAMPLE 10**

Dan owns a videotape rental business. Because the average period of customer use is seven days or less, Dan's videotape business is not treated as a rental activity. ▼

The fact that Dan's videotape business in Example 10 is not treated as a rental activity does not necessarily mean that it is classified as a nonpassive activity. Instead, the videotape business is treated as a trade or business activity subject to the material participation standards. If Dan is a material participant, the business is treated as active. If he is not a material participant, it is treated as a passive activity.

The six rental exceptions provided in the Temporary Regulations, including the exception illustrated in Example 10, are discussed in detail under Rental Activities later in the chapter.

MATERIAL PARTICIPATION

7 **LEARNING OBJECTIVE**
Analyze and apply the tests for material participation.

If an individual taxpayer materially participates in a nonrental trade or business activity, any loss from that activity is treated as an active loss that can be offset against active income. If a taxpayer does not materially participate, however, the loss is treated as a passive loss, which can only be offset against passive income. Therefore, controlling whether a particular activity is treated as active or passive is an important part of the tax strategy of a taxpayer who owns an interest in one or more businesses. Consider the following examples.

▼ **EXAMPLE 11**

Nora, a corporate executive, earns a salary of $200,000 per year. In addition, she owns a separate business in which she participates. The business produces a loss of $100,000 in 1994. If Nora materially participates in the business, the $100,000 loss is an active loss that may be offset against her active income from her corporate employer. If she does not materially participate, the loss is passive and is suspended. Nora may use the suspended loss in the future only if she has passive income or disposes of the activity. ▼

▼ **EXAMPLE 12**

Kay, an attorney, earns $250,000 a year in her law practice. She owns interests in two activities, A and B, in which she participates in 1994. Activity A, in which she does *not* materially participate, produces a loss of $50,000. Kay has not yet met the material participation standard for Activity B, which produces income of $80,000. However, she can meet the material participation standard if she spends an additional 50 hours in Activity B during the year. Should Kay attempt to meet the material participation standard for Activity B? If she continues working in Activity B and becomes a material participant, the $80,000 income from the activity is *active,* and the $50,000 passive loss from Activity A must be suspended. A more favorable tax strategy is for Kay to *not meet* the material participation standard for Activity B, thus making the income from that activity passive. This enables her to offset the $50,000 passive loss from Activity A against the passive income from Activity B. ▼

It is possible to devise numerous scenarios in which the taxpayer could control the tax outcome by increasing or decreasing his or her participation in different activities. Examples 11 and 12 demonstrate some of the possibilities. The conclusion reached in most analyses of this type is that taxpayers will benefit by having profitable activities classified as passive, so that any passive losses can be used to offset passive income. If the activity produces a loss, however, the taxpayer will benefit if it is classified as active so the loss is not subject to the passive loss limitations.

As discussed above, a nonrental trade or business in which a taxpayer owns an interest must be treated as a passive activity unless the taxpayer materially participates. The Staff of the Joint Committee on Taxation explained the importance of the material participation standard as follows:[10]

> Congress believed that there were several reasons why it was appropriate to examine the materiality of a taxpayer's participation in an activity in determining the extent to which such taxpayer should be permitted to use tax benefits from the activity. A taxpayer who materially participated in an activity was viewed as more likely than a passive investor to approach the activity with a significant nontax economic profit motive, and to form a sound judgment as to whether the activity had genuine economic significance and value. A material participation standard identified an important distinction between different types of taxpayer activities. It was thought that, in general, the more passive investor seeks a return on capital invested, including returns in the form of reductions in the taxes owed on unrelated income, rather than an ongoing source of livelihood. A material participation standard reduced the importance, for such investors, of the tax-reduction features of an investment, and thus increased the importance of the economic features in an investor's decision about where to invest his funds.

The Temporary Regulations provide seven tests for determining whether a taxpayer is a material participant. These tests are discussed below.

Tests Based on Current Participation

Material participation is achieved by meeting any one of seven tests provided in the Regulations. The first four tests are quantitative tests that require measurement, in hours, of the taxpayer's participation in the activity during the year.

1. *Does the individual participate in the activity for more than 500 hours during the year?*

The purpose of the 500-hour requirement is to restrict deductions from the types of trade or business activities Congress intended to treat as passive activities. The 500-hour standard for material participation was adopted for the following reasons:[11]

- Few investors in traditional tax shelters devote more than 500 hours a year to such an investment.
- The IRS believes that income from an activity in which the taxpayer participates for more than 500 hours a year should not be treated as passive.

2. *Does the individual's participation in the activity for the taxable year constitute substantially all of the participation in the activity of all individuals (including nonowner employees) for the year?*

EXAMPLE 13

Ned, a physician, operates a separate business in which he participates for 80 hours during the year. He is the only participant and has no employees in the separate business. Ned meets the material participation standards of Test 2. If he had employees, it would be difficult to apply Test 2, because the Temporary Regulations do not define the term *substantially all.* ▼

---

[10] *General Explanation of the Tax Reform Act of 1986 ("Blue Book"),* prepared by The Staff of the Joint Committee on Taxation, May 4, 1987, H.R. 3838, 99th Cong., p. 212.

[11] T.D. 8175, 1988–1 C.B. 191.

3. *Does the individual participate in the activity for more than 100 hours during the year, and is the individual's participation in the activity for the year not less than the participation of any other individual (including nonowner employees) for the year?*

EXAMPLE 14

Judy, a college professor, owns a separate business in which she participates 110 hours during the year. She has an employee who works 90 hours during the year. Judy meets the material participation standard under Test 3, but probably does not meet it under Test 2 because her participation is only 55% of the total participation. It is unlikely that 55% would meet the *substantially all* requirement of Test 2. ▼

Tests 2 and 3 are included because the IRS recognizes that the operation of some activities does not require more than 500 hours of participation during the year.

4. *Is the activity a significant participation activity for the taxable year, and does the individual's aggregate participation in all significant participation activities during the year exceed 500 hours?*

A **significant participation activity** is one in which the individual's participation exceeds 100 hours during the year. This test treats taxpayers whose aggregate participation in several significant participation activities exceeds 500 hours as material participants. Test 4 thus accords the same treatment to an individual who devotes an aggregate of more than 500 hours to several significant participation activities as to an individual who devotes more than 500 hours to a single activity.

EXAMPLE 15

Mike owns five different businesses. He participated in each activity during the year as follows:

Activity	Hours of Participation
A	110
B	140
C	120
D	150
E	100

Activities A, B, C, and D are significant participation activities, and Mike's aggregate participation in those activities is 520 hours. Therefore, Activities A, B, C, and D are not treated as passive activities. Activity E is not a significant participation activity (not more than 100 hours), so it is not included in applying the 500-hour test. Activity E is treated as a passive activity, unless Mike meets one of the other material participation tests for that activity. ▼

EXAMPLE 16

Assume the same facts as in the previous example, except that Activity A does not exist. All of the activities are now treated as passive. Activity E is not counted in applying the more than 500-hour test, so Mike's aggregate participation in significant participation activities is 410 hours (140 in Activity B + 120 in Activity C + 150 in Activity D). He could meet the significant participation test for Activity E by participating for one more hour in the activity. This would cause Activities B, C, D, and E to be treated as nonpassive activities. Before deciding whether to participate for at least one more hour in Activity E, Mike should assess how the participation would affect his overall tax liability. ▼

Tests Based on Prior Participation

Tests 5 and 6 are based on material participation in prior years. Under these tests, a taxpayer who is no longer a participant in an activity can continue to be *classified* as a material participant. The IRS takes the position that material participation in a trade or business for a long period of time is likely to indicate that the activity represents the individual's principal livelihood, rather than a passive investment. Consequently, withdrawal from the activity, or reduction of participation to the point where it is not material, does not change the classification of the activity from active to passive.

> 5. *Did the individual materially participate in the activity for any 5 taxable years (whether consecutive or not) during the 10 taxable years that immediately precede the taxable year?*

Test 1 (the 500-hour test) is the only test that can be used in determining whether a taxpayer was a material participant in an activity for any taxable year beginning before 1987. Tests 2 through 7 are irrelevant for this purpose.[12]

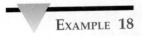

EXAMPLE 17   Dawn, who owns a 50% interest in a restaurant, was a material participant in the operations of the restaurant from 1988 through 1992. She retired at the end of 1992 and is no longer involved in the restaurant except as an investor. Dawn will be treated as a material participant in the restaurant in 1993. Even if she does not become involved in the restaurant as a material participant again, she will continue to be treated as a material participant in 1994, 1995, 1996, and 1997. In 1998 and later years, Dawn's share of income or loss from the restaurant will be classified as passive. ▼

> 6. *Is the activity a personal service activity, and did the individual materially participate in the activity for any three preceding taxable years (whether consecutive or not)?*

As indicated above, the material participation standards differ for personal service activities and other businesses. An individual who was a material participant in a personal service activity for *any three years* prior to the taxable year continues to be treated as a material participant after withdrawal from the activity.

EXAMPLE 18   Evan, a CPA, retires from the EFG Partnership after working full-time in the partnership for 30 years. As a retired partner, he will continue to receive a share of the profits of the firm for the next 10 years, even though he will not participate in the firm's operations. Evan also owns an interest in a passive activity that produces a loss for the year. He continues to be treated as a material participant in the EFG Partnership, and his income from the partnership is active income. He is not allowed to offset the loss from his passive investment against the income from the EFG Partnership. ▼

Facts and Circumstances Test

Test 7 is a facts and circumstances test to determine whether the taxpayer has materially participated.

> 7. *Based on all the facts and circumstances, did the individual participate in the activity on a regular, continuous, and substantial basis during the year?*

---

[12] Temp. and Prop.Reg. § 1.469–5T(j).

The Temporary Regulations do not define what constitutes regular, continuous, and substantial participation except to say that the taxpayer's activities will *not* be considered material participation under Test 7 in the following three circumstances:[13]

- The taxpayer satisfies the participation standards (whether or not a *material participant*) of any Code section other than § 469.
- The taxpayer manages the activity, unless

  - no other person receives compensation for management services, and
  - no individual spends more hours during the tax year managing the activity than does the taxpayer.

- The taxpayer participates in the activity for 100 hours or less during the tax year.

A part of the Temporary Regulations has been reserved for further development of this test. Presumably, additional guidelines will be issued in the future. For the time being, taxpayers should rely on Tests 1 through 6 in determining whether the material participation standards have been met.

Material Participation in a Real Property Trade or Business

After 1993, losses from real estate rental activities are *not* treated as passive losses for certain real estate professionals. To qualify for nonpassive treatment, a taxpayer must satisfy both the following requirements:

- More than half of the personal services that the taxpayer performs in trades or businesses are performed in real property trades or businesses in which the taxpayer materially participates.
- The taxpayer performs more than 750 hours of services in these real property trades or businesses as a material participant.

Taxpayers who do not satisfy the above requirements must continue to treat losses from real estate rental activities as passive losses.

TAX IN THE NEWS

ECONOMICS OR POLITICS?

Allowing real estate professionals to deduct passive losses from real estate activities is a very significant relief provision. It is interesting to speculate why passive losses of real estate professionals, which were disallowed by the Tax Reform Act of 1986, will be deductible for years after 1993. One would hope that Congress did an economic analysis and found that disallowing passive loss deductions had an adverse effect on the real estate industry that could be corrected by the new provision. However, an alternative explanation is more likely. Common Cause reports that real estate political action committees (PACs) gave nearly $17 million to current members of Congress from 1987 through 1992.

SOURCE: Information from Laura Saunders, "With Shelter for Some . . . ," *Forbes*, July 5, 1993, p. 44.

---

[13] Temp. and Prop.Reg. § 1.469–5T(b)(2).

TAX IN THE NEWS

ECONOMIC EFFECTS OF A TAX LAW CHANGE

It is a well-accepted notion that tax law changes can have widespread economic effects. The Mortgage Bankers Association of America estimates that removal of the passive loss limitation from real estate will cause a 3 to 5 percent rise in the market resale values of commercial property in the United States.

SOURCE: Information from Kenneth R. Harney, "The Ground Floor: Dr. Clinton's Prescription for Property," *Barron's*, March 1, 1993, p. 59.

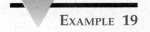

EXAMPLE 19

During 1994, Della performed personal service activities as follows: 900 hours as a personal financial planner, 550 hours in a real estate development and leasing business, and 600 hours in real estate rental activities. Any loss Della incurred in either real estate activity will *not* be subject to the passive loss rules, since more than 50% of her personal services were devoted to real property trades or businesses, and her material participation in those real estate activities exceeded 750 hours. Thus, any loss from the real estate rental activity could offset active and portfolio sources of income. ▼

On a joint return, the requirements for nonpassive treatment of losses must be met by one spouse or the other. That is, the spouses cannot combine their services in order to meet the requirements. Services performed by an employee are not treated as being related to a real estate trade or business unless the employee performing the services has at least a 5 percent ownership interest in the employer. Additionally, a closely held regular corporation may also qualify for the passive loss relief if more than 50 percent of its gross receipts for the year are derived from real property trades or businesses in which it materially participates.

ETHICAL CONSIDERATIONS

Applying the Rules on Rental Real Estate

Ted, a management consultant, owns rental real estate that produces a profit of $60,000 in 1994. He earned $120,000 in his consulting business and had a $40,000 loss on a passive activity (not real estate). Ted worked for 800 hours in the real estate business during the year, but characterizes the $60,000 profit as passive income so he can utilize the $40,000 passive loss. He claims that he is doing nothing wrong because the law is designed only to protect the passive loss deduction of real estate professionals and is not applicable to profits. Ted asks you to prepare his return. What actions will you take?

Participation Defined

Participation generally includes any work done by an individual in an activity that he or she owns. Participation does not include work if it is of a type not customarily done by owners *and* if one of its principal purposes is to avoid the disallowance of passive losses or credits. Also, work done in an individual's capacity as an investor (e.g., reviewing financial reports in a nonmanagerial capacity) is not counted in applying the material participation tests. Participation by an owner's spouse counts as participation by the owner.[14]

▼ **EXAMPLE 20**

Tom, who is a partner in a CPA firm, owns a computer store that has operated at a loss during the year. In order to offset this loss against the income from his CPA practice, Tom would like to avoid having the computer business classified as a passive activity. Through December 15, he has worked 400 hours in the business in management and selling activities. During the last two weeks of December, he works 80 hours in management and selling activities and 30 hours doing janitorial chores. Also during the last two weeks in December, Tom's wife participates 40 hours as a salesperson. She has worked as a salesperson in the computer store in prior years, but has not done so during the current year. If any of Tom's work is of a type not customarily done by owners *and* if one of its principal purposes is to avoid the disallowance of passive losses or credits, it is not counted in applying the material participation tests. It is likely that Tom's 480 hours of participation in management and selling activities will count as participation, but the 30 hours spent doing janitorial chores will not. However, the 40 hours of participation by his wife will count, and Tom will qualify as a material participant under the more-than-500-hour rule (480 + 40 = 520). ▼

Limited Partners

A *limited* partner is one whose liability to third-party creditors of the partnership is limited to the amount the partner has invested in the partnership. A partnership must have at least one *general* partner, who is fully liable in an individual capacity for the debts of the partnership to third parties. Generally, a *limited partner* is not considered a material participant unless he or she qualifies under Test 1, 5, or 6 in the above list. However, a *general partner* may qualify as a material participant by meeting any of the seven tests. If an unlimited, or general, partner also owns a limited interest in the same limited partnership, all interests are treated as a general interest.[15]

RENTAL ACTIVITIES

8 **LEARNING OBJECTIVE**
Consider special rules related to rental activities.

As discussed previously, § 469 specifies that all rental activities are to be treated as passive activities.[16] A **rental activity** is defined as any activity where payments are received principally for the use of tangible property.[17] However, Temporary Regulations provide that in certain circumstances activities involving rentals of real and personal property are *not* to be treated as rental activities.[18]

Activities covered by any of the following six exceptions in the Temporary Regulations are not *automatically* treated as passive activities. Instead, the activities are subject to the material participation tests.

1. *The average period of customer use for the property is seven days or less.*

Under this exception, activities involving the short-term use of tangible property such as automobiles, videocassettes, tuxedos, tools, and other such property are not treated as rental activities. The provision also applies to short-term rentals of hotel or motel rooms.

This exception is based on the presumption that a person who rents property for seven days or less is generally required to provide *significant services* to the

---

[14] Temp. and Prop.Reg. § 1.469–5T(f)(3).
[15] Temp. and Prop.Reg. § 1.469–5T(e)(3)(ii).
[16] § 469(c)(2).

[17] § 469(j)(8).
[18] Temp. and Prop.Reg. § 1.469–1T(e)(3)(ii).

customer. Providing such services supports a conclusion that the person is engaged in a service business rather than a rental business.

   2. *The average period of customer use for the property is 30 days or less, and the owner of the property provides significant personal services.*

For longer-term rentals, the presumption that significant services are provided is not automatic, as it is in the case of the seven-day exception. Instead, the taxpayer must be able to *prove* that significant personal services are rendered in connection with the activity. Therefore, an understanding of what constitutes significant personal services is necessary in order to apply the rule.

Significant personal services include only services provided by *individuals*. This provision excludes such items as telephone and cable television services. Four additional categories of *excluded services* are not considered significant personal services:[19]

- Services necessary to permit the lawful use of the property.
- Services performed in connection with the construction of improvements to property.
- Services performed in connection with the performance of repairs that extend the property's useful life for a period substantially longer than the average period for which the property is used by customers.
- Services similar to those commonly provided in connection with long-term rentals of high-grade commercial or residential real property (including cleaning and maintenance of common areas, routine repairs, trash collection, elevator service, and security at entrances or perimeters).

   3. *The owner of the property provides extraordinary personal services. The average period of customer use is of no consequence in applying this test.*

Extraordinary personal services are services provided by individuals where the customers' use of the property is incidental to their receipt of the services. For example, a patient's use of a hospital bed is incidental to his or her use of medical services. Another example is the use of a boarding school's dormitory, which is incidental to the scholastic services received.

   4. *The rental of the property is treated as incidental to a nonrental activity of the taxpayer.*

Rentals of real property incidental to a nonrental activity are not considered a passive activity. The Temporary Regulations provide that the following rentals are not passive activities:[20]

- *Property held primarily for investment.* This occurs where the principal purpose for holding the property is the expectation of gain from the appreciation of the property and the gross rent income is less than 2 percent of the lesser of (1) the unadjusted basis or (2) the fair market value of the property.

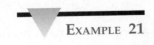

EXAMPLE 21

Anna invests in vacant land for the purpose of realizing a profit on its appreciation. She leases the land during the period it is held. The unadjusted basis is $250,000, and the fair market value is $350,000. The lease payments are $4,000 per year. Because gross rent income is less than 2% of $250,000, the activity is not a rental activity. ▼

[19] Temp. and Prop.Reg. § 1.469–1T(e)(3)(iv).

[20] Temp. and Prop.Regs. §§ 1.469–1T(e)(3)(vi)(B) through (E).

- *Property used in a trade or business.* This occurs where the property is owned by a taxpayer who is an owner of the trade or business using the rental property. The property must also have been used in the trade or business during the year or during at least two of the five preceding taxable years. The 2 percent test above also applies in this situation.

EXAMPLE 22

A farmer owns land with an unadjusted basis of $250,000 and a fair market value of $350,000. He used it for farming purposes in 1992 and 1993. In 1994, he leased the land to another farmer for $4,000. The activity is not a rental activity. ▼

- *Property held for sale to customers.* If property is held for sale to customers and rented during the year, the rental of the property is not a rental activity. If, for instance, an automobile dealer rents automobiles held for sale to customers to persons who are having their own cars repaired, the activity is not a rental activity.

EXAMPLE 23

A taxpayer acquires land upon which to construct a shopping center. Before beginning construction, she rents it to a business for use as a parking lot. Since she did not acquire the land as an investment, nor use it in her trade or business, nor hold it for sale to customers, the rental is a rental activity. ▼

- *Lodging rented for the convenience of an employer.* If an employer provides lodging for an employee incidental to the employee's performance of services in the employer's trade or business, no rental activity exists.

EXAMPLE 24

Joe has a farming business. He rents houses on his property to migrant workers during the harvest season. Joe does not have a rental activity. ▼

- A partner who rents property to a partnership that is used in the partnership's trade or business does not have a rental activity.

EXAMPLE 25

Betty, the owner of a business, transfers the business assets to a partnership, retaining the land and building as her separate property. She then rents the property to the partnership. Betty does not have a rental activity. ▼

These rules were written to prevent taxpayers from converting active or portfolio income into a passive activity for the purpose of offsetting other passive losses.

5. *The taxpayer customarily makes the property available during defined business hours for nonexclusive use by various customers.*

EXAMPLE 26

Pat is the owner-operator of a public golf course. Some customers pay daily greens fees each time they use the course, while others purchase weekly, monthly, or annual passes. The golf course is open every day from sunrise to sunset, except on certain holidays and on days when the course is closed due to weather conditions. Pat is not engaged in a rental activity, regardless of the average period customers use the course. ▼

6. *The property is provided for use in an activity conducted by a partnership, S corporation, or joint venture in which the taxpayer owns an interest.*

EXAMPLE 27

Kim, a partner in the ABC Partnership, contributes the use of a building to the partnership. The partnership has net income of $30,000 during the year, of which Kim's share is $10,000. Unless the partnership is engaged in a rental activity, none of Kim's income from the partnership is income from a rental activity. ▼

IDENTIFICATION OF PASSIVE ACTIVITY

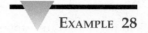

9 LEARNING OBJECTIVE
Apply the rules for identifying passive activities.

Identifying what constitutes an activity is a necessary first step in applying the passive loss limitations. Taxpayers who are involved in complex business operations need to be able to determine whether a given segment of their overall business operations constitutes a separate activity or is to be treated as part of a single activity. Proper treatment is necessary in order to determine whether income or loss from an activity is active or passive.

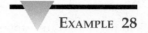

EXAMPLE 28

Ben owns a business with two separate departments. Department A generates net income of $120,000, and Department B generates a net loss of $95,000. Ben participates for 700 hours in the operations of Department A and for 100 hours in Department B. If Ben is allowed to treat both departments as a single activity, he is a material participant in the activity because his participation (700 + 100) exceeds 500 hours. Therefore, Ben can offset the $95,000 loss from Department B against the $120,000 income from Department A. ▼

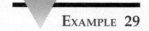

EXAMPLE 29

Assume the same facts as in the previous example. If Ben is required to treat each department as a separate activity, he is a material participant in Department A (700 hours), and the $120,000 profit is active income. However, he is not a material participant in Department B (100 hours), and the $95,000 loss is a passive loss. Ben cannot offset the $95,000 passive loss from Department B against the $120,000 of active income from Department A. ▼

Upon disposition of a passive activity, a taxpayer is allowed to offset suspended losses from the activity against other types of income. Therefore, identifying what constitutes an activity is of crucial importance.

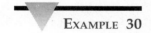

EXAMPLE 30

Linda owns a business with two departments. She participates for 200 hours in Department A, which had a net loss of $125,000 in the current year. Linda participates for 250 hours in Department B, which had a $70,000 net loss. She disposes of Department B during the year. She is allowed to treat the two departments as separate activities. Linda can offset the passive loss from Department B against other types of income in the following order: gain from disposition of the passive activity, other passive income, and nonpassive income. She has a suspended loss of $125,000 from Department A. ▼

The IRS has issued Proposed Regulations that set forth rules for grouping a taxpayer's trade or business activities and rental activities for purposes of applying the passive loss limitations.[21] These Proposed Regulations, which apply to tax years ending after May 10, 1992, provide a *facts and circumstances test* to determine whether a taxpayer's activities constitute an appropriate economic unit. Taxpayers may use *any reasonable method* in applying the facts and circumstances test.

In general, one or more trade or business or rental activities of a taxpayer will be treated as a single activity if the activities constitute an *appropriate economic unit.* The following five factors are given the greatest weight in determining whether activities constitute an appropriate economic unit. It is not necessary to meet all of these conditions in order to treat multiple activities as a single activity.[22]

- Similarities and differences in types of business conducted in the various trade or business or rental activities.
- The extent of common control over the various activities.
- The extent of common ownership of the activities.

---

[21] Prop.Reg. § 1.469–4.   [22] Prop.Reg. § 1.469–4(c)(2).

• The geographical location of the different units.
• Interdependencies among the activities.

The following examples, adapted from the Proposed Regulations, illustrate the application of the general rules for grouping activities.[23]

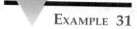

EXAMPLE 31

George owns a men's clothing store and a video game parlor in Chicago. He also owns a men's clothing store and a video game parlor in Milwaukee. Reasonable methods of applying the facts and circumstances test may result in any of the following groupings:

• All four activities may be grouped into a single activity.
• The clothing stores may be grouped into an activity, and the video parlors may be grouped into a separate activity.
• The Chicago activities may be grouped into an activity, and the Milwaukee activities may be grouped into a separate activity.
• Each of the four activities may be treated as a separate activity.   ▼

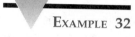

EXAMPLE 32

Sharon, an individual, is a partner in a business that sells snack items to drugstores. She also is a partner in a partnership that owns and operates a warehouse. Both partnerships, which are under common control, are located in the same industrial park. The predominant part of the warehouse business is warehousing items for the snack business, and it is the only warehousing business in which Sharon is involved. Sharon should treat the snack business and the warehousing business as a single activity. ▼

Taxpayers should carefully consider all tax factors in deciding how to group their activities. Once activities have been grouped, they cannot be regrouped unless the original grouping was clearly inappropriate or there has been a material change in facts and circumstances. If a regrouping is necessary for either of these reasons, the taxpayer is required to disclose to the IRS all information relevant to the regrouping.

Grouping Rental Activities

Two rules deal specifically with the grouping of rental activities. These provisions are designed to prevent taxpayers from grouping rental activities with other businesses in a way that would result in a tax advantage.

First, a rental activity may be grouped with a trade or business activity only if one activity is insubstantial in relation to the other. That is, the rental activity must be insubstantial in relation to the trade or business activity, or the trade or business activity must be insubstantial in relation to the rental activity. The Proposed Regulations provide no guidelines as to the meaning of insubstantial.[24]

Second, taxpayers generally may not treat an activity involving the rental of real property and an activity involving the rental of personal property as a single activity.

Regrouping of Activities

Although the Proposed Regulations allow taxpayers great latitude in grouping activities, they grant the IRS the right to regroup activities when both of the following conditions exist:[25]

---

[23] Prop.Reg. § 1.469–4(c)(3).
[24] Prop.Reg. § 1.469–4(d).

[25] Prop.Reg. § 1.469–4(h).

- The taxpayer's grouping fails to reflect one or more appropriate economic units.
- One of the primary purposes of the taxpayer's grouping is to avoid the passive loss limitations.

The following example, adapted from the Proposed Regulations, illustrates a situation where the IRS would exercise its prerogative to regroup a taxpayer's activities.

EXAMPLE 33

Baker, Edwards, Andrews, Clark, and Henson are physicians who operate their own separate practices. Each of the physicians owns interests in activities that generate passive losses, so they devise a plan to set up an entity that will generate passive income. They form the BEACH Partnership to acquire and operate X-ray equipment, and each receives a limited partnership interest. They select an unrelated person to operate the X-ray business as a general partner, and none of the limited partners participates in the activity. Substantially all of the services provided by BEACH are provided to the physicians who own limited partnership interests, and fees are set at a level that assures a profit for BEACH. Each physician treats his medical practice and his interest in the partnership as separate activities and offsets losses from passive investments against income from the partnership. The IRS would interpret the physicians' separate groupings as attempts to avoid the passive loss limitations and would regroup each medical practice and the services performed by the partnership as an appropriate economic unit. ▼

CLASSIFICATION OF INCOME AND LOSSES

The passive loss rules require classification of income and losses into three categories: active, passive, and portfolio. **Active income** includes, but is not limited to, the following:

- Wages, salary, commissions, bonuses, and other payments for services rendered by the taxpayer.
- Profit from a trade or business in which the taxpayer is a material participant.
- Gain on the sale or other disposition of assets used in an active trade or business.
- Income from intangible property if the taxpayer's personal efforts significantly contributed to the creation of the property.
- Income from a qualified low-income housing project that is not subject to the passive loss limitations under transitional rules.

Portfolio income includes, but is not limited to, the following:

- Interest, dividends, annuities, and royalties not derived in the ordinary course of a trade or business.
- Gain or loss from the disposition of property that produces portfolio income or is held for investment purposes.

Code § 469 provides that income or loss from the following activities is treated as *passive:*

- Any trade or business or income-producing activity in which the taxpayer does not materially participate.
- Any rental activity, whether the taxpayer materially participates or not.

Although the Code defines rental activities as passive activities, an exception allows losses from certain real estate rental activities to be offset against nonpassive (active or portfolio) income. The exception is discussed under Real Estate Rental Activities later in the chapter.

INCOME NOT TREATED AS PASSIVE

Certain items of income and expense are not taken into account in computing passive activity losses.[26] Some of these income items are discussed in this section. Others are beyond the scope of this text. Deductions that are not treated as passive are covered in the following section.

Portfolio income of an activity is not included in computing the passive income or loss from the activity. This provision negates any tax benefit taxpayers would otherwise achieve by transferring assets that produce portfolio income to an activity that produces a passive loss. Thus, it is possible that an activity might produce a passive loss *and* portfolio income in the same year.

EXAMPLE 34

Lou owns an activity that produces a passive loss of $15,000 during the year. He transfers to the activity corporate stock that produces portfolio income of $15,000. The passive loss cannot be offset against the portfolio income. Lou must report a passive loss of $15,000 and portfolio income of $15,000 from the activity. ▼

Portfolio income includes interest, annuities, royalties, dividends, and other items. However, such income is included in the passive loss computation if it is *derived* in the ordinary course of business.[27] For example, interest earned on loans made in the ordinary course of a trade or business of lending money is not treated as portfolio income. In addition, interest on accounts receivable arising from the performance of services or the sale of property is not treated as portfolio income if the business customarily offers credit to customers.

Gains on dispositions of portfolio assets are also treated as portfolio income. The rules for determining whether other gain is to be treated as portfolio income are very complex and are beyond the scope of this text. Refer to the Temporary and Proposed Regulations for additional information.[28]

Compensation paid to or on behalf of an individual for services performed or to be performed is not treated as passive activity gross income.[29]

EXAMPLE 35

Mara owns 50% of the stock of Greene, Inc., an S corporation that owns rental real estate. Greene pays Mara a $10,000 salary for services she performs for the corporation in connection with managing the rental real estate. The corporation has a $30,000 passive loss on the property during the year. Mara must report compensation income of $10,000 and a passive loss of $15,000 ($30,000 × 50%). ▼

The following are some of the other income items that are specifically excluded from the passive loss computation:[30]

- Gross income of an individual from intangible property (such as a patent, copyright, or literary, musical, or artistic composition) if the taxpayer's personal efforts significantly contributed to the creation of the property.
- Gross income attributable to a refund of any state, local, or foreign income, war profits, or excess profits tax.
- Gross income of an individual for a covenant not to compete.

[26] Temp. and Prop.Reg. § 1.469–2T(a)(2).
[27] Temp. and Prop.Reg. § 1.469–2T(c)(3).
[28] Temp. and Prop.Reg. § 1.469–2T(c)(2).
[29] Temp. and Prop.Reg. § 1.469–2T(c)(4).
[30] Temp. and Prop.Reg. § 1.469–2T(c)(7).

DEDUCTIONS NOT TREATED AS PASSIVE

The general rule is that a deduction is treated as a passive activity deduction if and only if the deduction arises in connection with the conduct of an activity that is a passive activity. The Temporary Regulations list several items that are not treated as passive activity deductions:[31]

- Any deduction for an expense that is clearly and directly allocable to portfolio income.
- Any deduction for a loss from the disposition of property of a type that produces portfolio income.
- Any deduction related to a dividend if the dividend is not included in passive activity gross income.
- Any deduction for qualified residence interest or interest that is capitalized under a capitalization provision.
- Any miscellaneous itemized deduction that is disallowed by operation of the 2 percent floor.

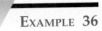

EXAMPLE 36

Chris, who owns a sole proprietorship that is a passive activity, calculated a loss for the activity as follows:

Operating income	$ 50,000
Dividends on stock held for investment	15,000
Total income	$ 65,000
– Expenses:	
Operating expenses (wages, rent, supplies, etc.)	(60,000)
Investment interest	(8,000)
– Loss on sale of stock held for investment	(5,000)
= Net loss	$ (8,000)

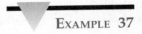

EXAMPLE 37

In computing Chris's passive loss, the net loss of $8,000 in Example 36 must be modified because the computation included gross income and deductions that are not to be considered in computing a passive loss. The passive loss is computed as follows:

Operating income	$ 50,000
– Operating expenses (wages, rent, supplies, etc.)	(60,000)
= Passive loss	$(10,000)

A comparison of Examples 36 and 37 shows that the portfolio income is not included in computing the passive loss, and that no deduction is taken for the investment interest or the loss on the portfolio investment.

SUSPENDED LOSSES

The determination of whether a loss is suspended under the passive loss rule is made after application of the at-risk rules, as well as other provisions relating to the measurement of taxable income. A loss that is not allowed for the year because the taxpayer is not at risk with respect to it is suspended under the at-risk provision and not under the passive loss rule.

---

[31] Temp. and Prop.Reg. § 1.469–2T(d).

A taxpayer's basis is reduced by deductions (e.g., depreciation) even if the deductions are not currently usable because of the passive loss rule.

EXAMPLE 38

Jack's adjusted basis in a passive activity is $10,000 at the beginning of 1992. His loss from the activity in 1992 is $4,000. Since Jack had no passive activity income, the $4,000 cannot be deducted. At year-end, Jack has an adjusted basis of $6,000 in the activity and a suspended loss of $4,000. ▼

EXAMPLE 39

Jack in Example 38 had a loss of $9,000 in the activity in 1993. Since the $9,000 exceeds his at-risk amount ($6,000) by $3,000, that $3,000 loss is disallowed by the at-risk rules. If Jack has no passive activity income, the remaining $6,000 is suspended under the passive activity rules. At year-end, he has a $3,000 loss suspended under the at-risk rules, $10,000 of suspended passive losses, and an adjusted basis in the activity of zero. ▼

EXAMPLE 40

Jack in Example 39 realized a $1,000 gain in 1994. Because the $1,000 increases his at-risk amount, $1,000 of the $3,000 unused loss can be reclassified as a passive loss. If he has no other passive income, the $1,000 income is offset against $1,000 of suspended passive losses. At the end of 1994, Jack has no taxable passive income, $2,000 ($3,000 − $1,000) of unused losses under the at-risk rules, $10,000 of (reclassified) suspended passive losses ($10,000 + $1,000 of reclassified unused at-risk losses − $1,000 of passive losses offset against passive gains), and an adjusted basis in the activity of zero. ▼

EXAMPLE 41

In 1995, Jack had no gain or loss from the activity in Example 40. He contributed $5,000 more to the passive activity. Because the $5,000 increases his at-risk amount, the $2,000 of losses suspended under the at-risk rules is reclassified as a passive loss. Jack gets no passive loss deduction in 1995. At year-end, he has no suspended losses under the at-risk rules, $12,000 of suspended passive losses ($10,000 + $2,000 of reclassified suspended at-risk losses), and an adjusted basis of $3,000 ($5,000 additional investment − $2,000 of reclassified losses). ▼

Carryovers of Suspended Losses

To determine the suspended loss for an activity, passive activity losses must be allocated among all activities in which the taxpayer has an interest. The allocation to the activity is made by multiplying the disallowed passive activity loss from all activities by a fraction. The numerator of the fraction is the loss from the activity, and the denominator is the sum of the losses for the taxable year from all activities having losses.

EXAMPLE 42

Ted has investments in three passive activities (acquired in 1993) with the following income and losses for that year:

Activity A	$(30,000)
Activity B	(20,000)
Activity C	25,000
Net passive loss	$(25,000)
Allocated to:	
A ($25,000 × $30,000/$50,000)	$ 15,000
B ($25,000 × $20,000/$50,000)	10,000
Total suspended losses	$(25,000)

▼

Suspended losses are carried over indefinitely and are offset in the future against any passive income from the activities to which they relate.[32]

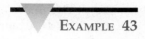

Assume the same facts as in Example 42 and that Activity A produces $15,000 of income in 1994. The disallowed loss of $15,000 from 1992 for Activity A is offset against the income from Activity A. ▼

Upon the taxable disposition of a passive activity, the suspended passive losses from that activity can be offset against the taxpayer's active and portfolio income. See Dispositions of Passive Interests later in the chapter.

PASSIVE CREDITS

Credits arising from passive activities are limited much like passive losses. They can be utilized only against regular tax attributable to passive income,[33] which is calculated by comparing the tax on all income (including passive income) with the tax on income excluding passive income.

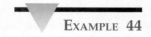

EXAMPLE 44   A taxpayer owes $50,000 of tax, disregarding net passive income, and $80,000 of tax, considering both net passive and other taxable income (disregarding the credits in both cases). The amount of tax attributable to the passive income is $30,000.

Tax due (before credits) including net passive income	$ 80,000
Less: Tax due (before credits) without including net passive income	(50,000)
Tax attributable to passive income	$ 30,000

▼

The taxpayer in the preceding example can claim a maximum of $30,000 of passive activity credits; the excess credits are carried over. These passive activity credits (such as the jobs credit, low-income housing credit, research activities credit, and rehabilitation credit) can be used against the *regular* tax attributable to passive income only. If a taxpayer has a net loss from passive activities during a given year, no credits can be used. Likewise, if a taxpayer has net passive income but the alternative minimum tax applies to that year, no passive activity credits can be used. (The alternative minimum tax is discussed in Chapter 12.) In addition, the unused passive losses are carried over.

Carryovers of Passive Credits

Tax credits attributable to passive activities can be carried forward indefinitely much like suspended passive losses. Unlike passive losses, however, passive credits can be lost forever when the activity is disposed of in a taxable transaction.

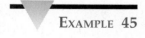

EXAMPLE 45   Alicia sells a passive activity for a gain of $10,000. The activity had suspended losses of $40,000 and suspended credits of $15,000. The $10,000 gain is offset by $10,000 of the suspended losses, and the remaining $30,000 of suspended losses is deductible against Alicia's active and portfolio income. The suspended credits are lost forever because the sale of the activity did not generate any tax. This is true even if Alicia has positive taxable income or is subject to the alternative minimum tax. ▼

---

[32] § 469(b).   [33] § 469(d)(2).

EXAMPLE 46

If Alicia in Example 45 had realized a $100,000 gain on the sale of the passive activity, the $15,000 of suspended credits could have been used to the extent of regular tax attributable to the net passive income.

Gain on sale	$100,000
Less: Suspended losses	40,000
Net gain	$ 60,000

If the tax attributable to the net gain of $60,000 is $15,000 or more, the entire $15,000 of suspended credits can be used. If the tax attributable to the gain is less than $15,000, the excess of the suspended credit over the tax attributable to the gain is lost forever. ▼

When a taxpayer has adequate regular tax liability from passive activities to trigger the use of suspended credits, the credits lose their character as passive credits. They are reclassified as regular tax credits and made subject to the same limits as other credits (discussed in Chapter 13).

REAL ESTATE RENTAL ACTIVITIES

10 **LEARNING OBJECTIVE**
Discuss the real estate rental exception.

The passive loss limits contain three exceptions related to real estate activities. These exceptions allow all or part of real estate rental losses to be offset against active or portfolio income, even though the activity is a passive activity.

The first exception allows real estate rental losses of certain real estate professionals to be treated as nonpassive (refer to the discussion preceding Example 19). The second exception provides favorable treatment for investors in low-income housing. Under a transition rule, losses from certain investments in low-income housing are not treated as passive losses for a period of up to seven years from the date of the original investment.

The third exception is more significant in that it is not restricted to low-income housing. This exception allows individuals to deduct up to $25,000 of losses on real estate rental activities against active and portfolio income.[34] The annual $25,000 deduction is reduced by 50 percent of the taxpayer's AGI in excess of $100,000. Thus, the entire deduction is phased out at $150,000. If married individuals file separately, the $25,000 deduction is reduced to zero unless they lived apart for the entire year. If they lived apart for the entire year, the loss amount is $12,500 each, and the phase-out begins at $50,000. AGI for purposes of the phase-out is calculated without regard to IRA deductions, Social Security benefits, and net losses from passive activities.

To qualify for the $25,000 exception, a taxpayer must meet the following requirements:[35]

- Actively participate in the real estate rental activity.
- Own 10 percent or more (in value) of all interests in the activity during the entire taxable year (or shorter period during which the taxpayer held an interest in the activity).

The difference between *active participation* and *material participation* is that the former can be satisfied without regular, continuous, and substantial involvement in operations as long as the taxpayer participates in the making of management decisions in a significant and bona fide sense. In this context, relevant management decisions include such decisions as approving new tenants, deciding on rental terms, and approving capital or repair expenditures.

---

[34] § 469(i).   [35] § 469(i)(6).

The $25,000 allowance is available after all active participation rental losses and gains are netted and applied to other passive income. If a taxpayer has a real estate rental loss in excess of the amount that can be deducted under the real estate rental exception, that excess is treated as a passive loss.

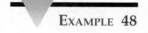

EXAMPLE 47

Diane, who has $90,000 of AGI before considering rental activities, has $85,000 of losses from a real estate rental activity in which she actively participates. She also actively participates in another real estate rental activity from which she has $25,000 of income. She has other passive income of $36,000. The net rental loss of $60,000 is offset by the $36,000 of passive income, leaving $24,000 that can be deducted against other income. ▼

The $25,000 offset allowance is an aggregate of both deductions and credits in deduction equivalents. The deduction equivalent of a passive activity credit is the amount of deductions that reduces the tax liability for the taxable year by an amount equal to the credit.[36] The deduction equivalent is the deduction necessary to reduce one's tax liability by an amount equal to the credit. A taxpayer with $5,000 of credits and a tax bracket of 28 percent would have a deduction equivalent of $17,857 ($5,000 divided by 28 percent).

If the total deduction and deduction equivalent exceed $25,000, the taxpayer must allocate on a pro rata basis, first among the losses (including real estate rental activity losses suspended in prior years) and then to credits in the following order: (1) credits other than rehabilitation credits, (2) rehabilitation credits, and (3) low-income housing credits.

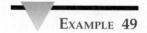

EXAMPLE 48

Kevin is an active participant in a real estate rental activity that produces $8,000 of income, $26,000 of deductions, and $1,500 of credits. Kevin, who is in the 28% tax bracket, may deduct the net passive loss of $18,000 ($8,000 – $26,000). After deducting the loss, he has an available deduction equivalent of $7,000 ($25,000 – $18,000 passive loss). Therefore, the maximum amount of credits that he may claim is $1,960 ($7,000 × 28%). Since the actual credits are less than this amount, Kevin may claim the entire $1,500 credit. ▼

EXAMPLE 49

Kelly, who is in the 28% tax bracket, is an active participant in three separate real estate rental activities. She has $20,000 of losses from Activity A, $10,000 of losses from Activity B, and $4,200 of passive credits from Activity C. Kelly's deduction equivalent from the credits is $15,000 ($4,200 ÷ .28). Total passive deductions and deduction equivalents are $45,000 ($20,000 + $10,000 + $15,000) and therefore exceed the maximum allowable amount of $25,000. Kelly must allocate pro rata first from among losses and then from among credits. Deductions from Activity A are limited to $16,667 {$25,000 × [$20,000 ÷ ($20,000 + $10,000)]}, and deductions from Activity B are limited to $8,333 {$25,000 × [$10,000 ÷ ($20,000 + $10,000)]}.

Since the amount of passive deductions exceeds the $25,000 maximum, the deduction balance of $5,000 and passive credit of $4,200 must be carried forward. Kelly's suspended losses and credits by activity are as follows:

	Total	Activity A	B	C
Allocated losses	$30,000	$ 20,000	$10,000	$ –0–
Allocated credits	4,200	–0–	–0–	4,200
Utilized losses	25,000	(16,667)	(8,333)	–0–
Suspended losses	5,000	3,333	1,667	–0–
Suspended credits	4,200	–0–	–0–	4,200

▼

[36] § 469(j)(5).

DISPOSITIONS OF PASSIVE INTERESTS

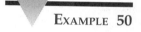

11 LEARNING OBJECTIVE
Determine the proper tax
treatment upon the disposition
of a passive activity.

When a taxpayer disposes of his or her entire interest in a passive activity, the actual economic gain or loss on the investment finally can be determined. As a result, under the passive loss rules, upon a fully taxable disposition, any overall loss from the activity realized by the taxpayer is recognized and allowed against any income. Special rules apply to dispositions of certain property that disallow their classification as passive income. Included in these rules are dispositions of partnership interests and S corporation stock, partial interests in property, property used in more than one activity, and substantially appreciated property formerly used in a nonpassive activity.[37]

Since the purpose of the disposition rule is to allow the taxpayer's real economic losses to be deducted, credits (which are not related to the measurement of such loss) are not allowable specially by reason of a disposition. Credits are allowed only when there is sufficient tax on passive income to absorb them.

A fully taxable disposition generally includes a sale of the property to a third party at arm's length and thus, presumably, for a price equal to the property's fair market value. Gain recognized upon a transfer of an interest in a passive activity generally is treated as passive and is first offset by the suspended losses from that activity.

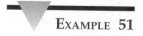

EXAMPLE 50

Kim sold an apartment building with an adjusted basis of $100,000 for $180,000. In addition, Kim has suspended losses of $60,000 associated with that specific apartment building. The total gain, $80,000, and the taxable gain, $20,000, are calculated as follows:

Net sales price	$ 180,000
Less: Adjusted basis	(100,000)
Total gain	$ 80,000
Less: Suspended losses	(60,000)
Taxable gain (passive)	$ 20,000

If current and suspended losses of the passive activity exceed the gain realized or if the sale results in a realized loss, the sum of

- any loss from the activity for the tax year (including losses suspended in the activity disposed of), plus
- any loss realized on the disposition

in excess of

- net income or gain for the tax year from all passive activities (without regard to the activity disposed of)

is treated as a loss that is not from a passive activity.

EXAMPLE 51

Dean sold an apartment building with an adjusted basis of $100,000 for $150,000. In addition, he has current and suspended losses of $60,000 associated with that specific apartment building and has no other passive activities. The total gain, $50,000, and the deductible loss, $10,000, are calculated as follows:

Net sales price	$ 150,000
Less: Adjusted basis	(100,000)
Total gain	$ 50,000
Less: Suspended losses	(60,000)
Deductible loss	$ (10,000)

---

[37] Temp. and Prop.Regs. §§ 1.469–2T(c)(2)(i) through (iii).

The $10,000 deductible loss is offset against Dean's ordinary income and portfolio income. ▼

Disposition of a Passive Activity at Death

A transfer of a taxpayer's interest in an activity by reason of the taxpayer's death results in suspended losses being allowed (to the decedent) to the extent they exceed the amount, if any, of the step-up in basis allowed.[38] Suspended losses are lost to the extent of the amount of the basis increase. The losses allowed generally are reported on the final return of the deceased taxpayer.

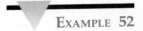

EXAMPLE 52   A taxpayer dies with passive activity property having an adjusted basis of $40,000, suspended losses of $10,000, and a fair market value at the date of the decedent's death of $75,000. The increase (i.e., step-up) in basis (see Chapter 14) is $35,000 (fair market value at date of death in excess of adjusted basis). None of the $10,000 suspended loss is deductible by either the decedent or the beneficiary. The suspended losses ($10,000) did not exceed the step-up in basis ($35,000). ▼

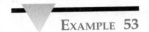

EXAMPLE 53   A taxpayer dies with passive activity property having an adjusted basis of $40,000, suspended losses of $10,000, and a fair market value at the date of the decedent's death of $47,000. Since the step-up in basis under § 1014 would be only $7,000 ($47,000 − $40,000), the suspended losses allowed are limited to $3,000 ($10,000 suspended loss at time of death − $7,000 increase in basis). The $3,000 loss available to the decedent is reported on the decedent's final income tax return. ▼

Disposition of a Passive Activity by Gift

In a disposition of a taxpayer's interest in a passive activity by gift, the suspended losses are added to the basis of the property.[39]

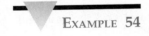

EXAMPLE 54   A taxpayer makes a gift of passive activity property having an adjusted basis of $40,000, suspended losses of $10,000, and a fair market value at the date of the gift of $100,000. The taxpayer cannot deduct the suspended losses in the year of the disposition. The suspended losses transfer with the property and are added to the adjusted basis of the property. ▼

Installment Sale of a Passive Activity

An installment sale of a taxpayer's entire interest in a passive activity triggers the recognition of the suspended losses.[40] The losses are allowed in each year of the installment obligation in the ratio that the gain recognized in each year bears to the total gain on the sale.

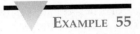

EXAMPLE 55   Stan sold his entire interest in a passive activity for $100,000. His adjusted basis in the property was $60,000. If he uses the installment method, his gross profit ratio is 40% ($40,000/$100,000). If Stan received a $20,000 down payment, he would recognize a gain of $8,000 (40% of $20,000). If the activity had a suspended loss of $25,000, Stan would deduct $5,000 [($8,000 ÷ $40,000) × $25,000] of the suspended loss in the first year. ▼

Passive Activity Changes to Active

If a formerly passive activity becomes an active one, suspended losses are allowed to the extent of income from the now active business.[41] If any of the suspended

---

[38] § 469(g)(2).
[39] § 469(j)(6).

[40] § 469(g)(3).
[41] § 469(f).

loss remains, it continues to be treated as a loss from a passive activity. The excess suspended loss can be deducted from passive income or carried over to the next tax year and deducted to the extent of income from the now active business in the succeeding year(s). The activity must continue to be the same activity.

Nontaxable Exchange of a Passive Activity

In a nontaxable exchange of a passive investment, the taxpayer keeps the suspended losses, which generally become deductible when the acquired property is sold. If the activity of the old and new property are the same, suspended losses can be used.

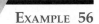

EXAMPLE 56

A taxpayer exchanged a duplex for a limited partnership interest in a § 721 nonrecognition transaction (see Chapter 20 for details). The suspended losses from the duplex are not deductible until the limited partnership interest is sold. Two separate activities exist: a real estate rental activity and a limited partnership activity. If the taxpayer had continued to own the duplex and the duplex had future taxable income, the suspended losses would have become deductible before the time of disposition. ▼

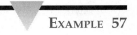

EXAMPLE 57

In a § 1031 nontaxable exchange (see Chapter 15 for details), a taxpayer exchanged a duplex for an apartment building. The suspended losses from the duplex are deductible against future taxable income of the apartment building. The same activity exists. ▼

TRANSITION RULES FOR PASSIVE LOSSES (1987–1990)

The passive loss rules disallow 100 percent of losses on passive activities acquired after October 22, 1986. However, under transition rules the disallowance provisions for losses on passive activities acquired before October 23, 1986, were phased in over five years. If a taxpayer had a loss on a passive activity acquired before October 23, 1986 (the date TRA of 1986 was enacted), a percentage of the loss was deductible under the transition rules. Congress enacted the phase-in schedule to provide some relief to taxpayers who had committed their investment funds to passive activities prior to enactment of the passive loss limitations. The following table shows the percentages that applied during the five-year phase-in period.

Taxable Years Beginning in	Losses and Credits Allowed	Losses and Credits Disallowed
1987	65%	35%
1988	40%	60%
1989	20%	80%
1990	10%	90%
1991	0%	100%

Although the transition percentages do not allow the deduction of passive losses after 1990, it is necessary to understand how they affected taxpayers during the transition period. Losses suspended under the transition rules can be deducted in future years when the taxpayer has passive income, or upon a taxable disposition of the activity that produced the loss. Thus, the transition rules will continue to affect the computation of passive gains and losses as long as a taxpayer continues to own any pre-October 23, 1986 activity with suspended losses incurred during the transition period.

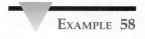

EXAMPLE 58

Erin acquired a passive activity in 1984. In 1990, she realized a loss of $10,000 on this activity. Under the transition rules, $1,000 (10% of $10,000) was deductible in 1990. The $9,000 disallowed loss is a suspended loss that can be carried forward and deducted against passive income in later years. If Erin has no passive income in later years, the suspended loss can be deducted when she disposes of the passive activity in a fully taxable transaction (see Example 50). If she had acquired the passive activity after October 22, 1986, no deduction would have been allowed in 1990, and the entire $10,000 would have been suspended. ▼

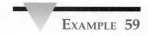

EXAMPLE 59

Assume that Erin in Example 58 had another loss of $20,000 on the pre-enactment passive activity in 1992. Pre-enactment passive activity losses were not deductible in 1992. The entire $20,000 loss would be suspended. ▼

If a taxpayer had both pre-enactment and post-enactment activities prior to 1991, the transition percentage was applied to the lesser of (1) the pre-enactment passive activity loss or (2) the net passive loss from pre-enactment and post-enactment activities.

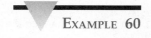

EXAMPLE 60

Steve has two passive activity investments. Investment A was purchased in 1985, and Investment B was purchased in 1987. In 1990, Investment A generated a $10,000 loss, and Investment B generated an $8,000 gain. Steve's net passive loss was $2,000 ($10,000 loss – $8,000 gain). The allowable deduction was $200 (10% of $2,000). The remaining $1,800 would have been suspended and carried over. ▼

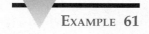

EXAMPLE 61

In Example 60, if Investment A had generated income of $10,000 and Investment B had generated an $8,000 loss, the net passive gain of $2,000 would have been included in income. ▼

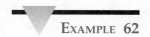

EXAMPLE 62

In Example 60, assume Investment A (the pre-enactment activity) had generated a loss of $10,000 and Investment B had generated a loss of $8,000. The net passive loss was $18,000. Only $1,000 (10% of $10,000) could have been deducted in 1990. The remaining $17,000 ($8,000 post-enactment loss plus 90% of the $10,000 pre-enactment loss) would have been suspended and carried over to the future. ▼

UTILIZING PASSIVE LOSSES

TAX PLANNING
CONSIDERATIONS

12 LEARNING OBJECTIVE
Suggest tax planning strategies to minimize the effect of the passive loss limitations.

Taxpayers who have passive activity losses (PALs) should adopt a strategy of generating passive activity income that can be sheltered by existing passive losses. One approach is to buy an interest in any passive activity that is generating income (referred to as passive income generators, or PIGs). Then the PAL can be offset against income from the PIG. From a tax perspective, it would be foolish to buy a loss-generating passive activity (PAL) unless one has other passive income (PIG) to shelter or the activity is rental real estate that can qualify for the $25,000 exception.

A taxpayer with existing passive losses might consider buying rental property. If a large down payment is made and the straight-line method of MACRS (discussed in Chapter 8) is elected, a positive net income could be realized. The income would be sheltered by other passive losses, depreciation expense would be spread out evenly and preserved for future years, and depreciation recapture (discussed in Chapter 17) is avoided upon the sale of the property. Future gain realized upon the sale of the rental property could be sheltered by existing suspended passive losses.

TAX IN THE NEWS

TAKING ADVANTAGE OF THE REAL ESTATE PROFESSIONALS EXCEPTION

It is interesting to follow the development of tax law. Careful observation discloses a pattern where Congress passes a provision that is unfavorable to taxpayers, tax advisers find a loophole in favor of the taxpayer, then Congress closes the loophole. Indeed, a particular provision may be subject to several such rounds. One tax planner suggests the following strategy to take advantage of the new provisions allowing deductions for passive losses of qualifying real estate professionals:

- One spouse earns a high salary that places a couple in the top Federal and state tax brackets. The other spouse is not employed.
- Neither spouse works in the real property business. However, the couple identifies rental real estate that currently produces a loss, but has solid prospects for long-term capital gains, which will be taxed at a favorable capital gains rate upon disposition.
- To qualify for the real estate professionals exception to the passive loss limitations, the unemployed spouse takes a training course to become a real estate agent. This spouse works part-time (751) hours as a real estate agent. Thus, the passive loss from the rental property can be offset against income earned by the other spouse.

Experienced observers of tax law development expect that Congress will eventually take action to close this potential loophole.

SOURCE: Information from Kenneth R. Harney, "The Ground Floor: Tax Bill Winners? Don't Be So Sure," *Barron's*, August 16, 1993, p. 48.

Taxpayers with passive losses should consider all other trades or businesses in which they have an interest. If they show that they do not materially participate in the activity, the activity becomes a passive activity. Any income generated could be sheltered by existing passive losses and suspended losses. Family partnerships in which certain members do not materially participate would qualify. The silent partner in any general partnership engaged in a trade or business would also qualify.

KEY TERMS

Active income, 11–18

At-risk limitation, 11–2

Closely held corporation, 11–5

Extraordinary personal services, 11–14

Material participation, 11–6

Passive loss, 11–4

Personal service corporation, 11–5

Portfolio income, 11–18

Rental activity, 11–13

Significant participation activity, 11–9

Tax shelters, 11–2

PROBLEM MATERIALS

DISCUSSION QUESTIONS

1. Congress has passed two major provisions to inhibit taxpayers' ability to use tax shelters to reduce or defer Federal income tax. Explain.

2. Alice invested $50,000 for a 25% interest in a partnership in which she is not a material participant. The partnership borrowed $100,000 from a bank and used the proceeds to acquire a building. What is Alice's at-risk amount if the $100,000 was borrowed on a recourse loan?

3. Eric invested $40,000 for a 20% interest in a partnership in which he is not a material participant. The partnership borrowed $200,000 from a bank and used the proceeds to acquire machinery. What is Eric's at-risk amount if the $200,000 was borrowed on a nonrecourse loan?

4. List some events that increase and decrease an investor's at-risk amount, and discuss some strategies that a taxpayer can employ to increase the at-risk amount in order to claim a higher deduction for losses.

5. What constitutes a taxpayer's initial at-risk amount, and what causes increases and decreases in the amount at risk?

6. Roy invested $10,000 in a cattle-feeding operation that used nonrecourse notes to purchase $100,000 in feed, which was fed to the cattle and expensed. His share of the expense was $18,000. How much can Roy deduct?

7. Gray Corporation has $100,000 of active income and a $55,000 passive loss for the year. Under what circumstances is the corporation prohibited from deducting the loss? Under what circumstances is the corporation allowed to deduct the loss?

8. Hi-Tech Consulting, Inc., is a corporation owned by four engineers, all of whom work full-time for the corporation. The corporation has eight other full-time employees, all on the clerical staff. Hi-Tech provides consulting services to inventors. The corporation has invested in a passive activity that produced a $60,000 loss in 1994. Can Hi-Tech deduct the loss in 1994? Explain.

9. Jane owns an interest in a dress shop in which she works 450 hours during the year. She has three full-time employees in the dress shop. Jane also owns an apartment building in which she participates 1,200 hours during the year. She has no employees for the apartment activity. Is either activity a passive activity? Explain.

10. Discuss whether the passive loss rules apply to the following: individuals, closely held regular corporations, S corporations, partnerships, and personal service corporations.

11. How is passive activity defined in the Code, and what aspects of the definition have been clarified by the Temporary Regulations?

12. What is the significance of the term *material participation*? Why is the extent of a taxpayer's participation in an activity important in determining whether a loss from the activity is deductible or nondeductible?

13. Manuel owns an interest in an activity that produces a $100,000 loss during the year. Would he generally prefer to have the activity classified as active or passive? Discuss.

14. Kim owns an interest in an activity that produces $100,000 of income during the year. Would Kim generally prefer to have the activity classified as active or passive? Discuss.

15. Laura owns an apartment building and a videotape rental business. She participates for more than 500 hours in the operations of each activity. Are the businesses active or passive?

16. Why did the IRS adopt the more-than-500-hour standard for material participation?

17. Keith, a physician, operates a separate business that he acquired in 1985. He participated for 90 hours in the business during the current year, and the business incurred a loss of $20,000. Under what circumstances will the loss be deductible as an ordinary loss?

18. Jan, an attorney, operates a separate business that she acquired in 1985. She has one part-time employee in the business. Jan participated for 130 hours in the business during the current year, and the business incurred a loss of $20,000. Under what circumstances will the loss be deductible as an ordinary loss?

19. Zelda, a professor, operates three separate businesses, all acquired in 1985. She participates for less than 500 hours in each business. Each business incurs a loss during the year. Are there any circumstances under which Zelda may treat the losses as active?

20. In 1993, Paul retired as a partner in a CPA firm he founded 30 years ago. He continues to share in the profits, although he no longer participates in the activities of the firm. Paul also owns an interest in a passive activity that he acquired in 1984. The passive activity produced a loss of $50,000 in 1994. Can Paul offset the passive loss against his income from the CPA firm?

21. Hilda incurred a loss of $60,000 on a real estate rental activity in 1994. Under what circumstances can Hilda treat the entire loss as nonpassive?

22. Under what circumstances can a closely held corporation treat rental real estate losses as nonpassive?

23. Can an employer treat services performed by an employee as being related to a real estate trade or business?

24. What are *extraordinary personal services*, and what is their importance in determining whether a rental activity is treated as a passive activity?

25. Discuss which types of services are treated as significant personal services. Which types are not treated as significant personal services?

26. The Proposed Regulations set forth a *facts and circumstances test* for determining what constitutes an activity. Describe this test and comment on the significance of the term *appropriate economic unit*.

27. What factors are given the greatest weight in determining whether activities constitute an appropriate economic unit?

28. The Proposed Regulations prohibit grouping rental activities in certain circumstances. Discuss these rules.

29. Under what circumstances may the IRS regroup activities in a different way than the taxpayer has grouped them? Give an example of a situation to which the regrouping rule would be applied.

30. Discuss the following issues in connection with the calculation of passive losses:
    a. What constitutes a passive activity?
    b. What types of income are not treated as passive income?
    c. What types of deductions are not treated as passive deductions?

31. What is a suspended loss? Why is it important to allocate suspended losses in cases where a taxpayer has interests in more than one passive activity?

32. Upon a taxable disposition of a passive activity, the taxpayer can utilize any suspended losses and credits related to that activity. True or false? Explain.

33. Matt owns a small apartment building that sustained a loss during the year. Under what circumstances can Matt deduct a loss from the rental activity, and what limitations apply?

34. In connection with passive activities, what is a *deduction equivalent?* How is a deduction equivalent computed?

35. What is the difference between material participation and active participation under the passive loss rules?

36. Upon the taxable disposition of a passive activity, what happens to the suspended losses? The suspended credits?

37. Felicia owns a passive activity that she acquired in 1985. She incurred losses on the activity in 1987 through 1990. This is the only passive activity she has ever owned. How

will these passive losses affect Felicia's taxable income when she disposes of the activity?

38. In 1990, Jay incurred a $100,000 loss on a passive activity that he acquired in 1985 and a $40,000 loss on a passive activity he acquired in 1988. How much was Jay allowed to deduct in 1990?

39. In 1990, April incurred a $100,000 loss on a passive activity that she acquired in 1985 and had $40,000 of income on a passive activity she acquired in 1988. How much was April allowed to deduct in 1990?

PROBLEMS

40. Kelly, who earned a salary of $200,000, invested $40,000 for a 20% working interest in an oil and gas limited partnership (not a passive activity) in 1993. Through the use of $800,000 of nonrecourse financing, the partnership acquired assets worth $1 million. Depreciation, interest, and other deductions related to the activity resulted in a loss of $150,000, of which Kelly's share was $30,000. Kelly's share of loss from the partnership was $15,000 in 1994. How much of the loss from the partnership can Kelly deduct?

41. In 1993, Fred invested $50,000 in a limited partnership that has a working interest in an oil well (not a passive activity). In 1993, his share of the partnership loss was $35,000. In 1994, his share of the partnership loss was $25,000. How much can Fred deduct in 1993 and 1994?

42. Brown Corporation, a personal service corporation, earned active income of $500,000 in 1994. The corporation received $60,000 in dividends during the year. In addition, Brown incurred a loss of $80,000 from an investment in a passive activity acquired in 1990. What is Brown's income for 1994 after considering the passive investment?

43. Green Corporation, a closely held, non-personal service corporation, earned active income of $50,000 in 1994. Green received $60,000 in dividends during the year. In addition, Green incurred a loss of $80,000 from an investment in a passive activity acquired in 1993. What is Green's net income for 1994 after considering the passive investment?

44. Bob, an attorney, earned $200,000 from his law practice in 1994. He received $45,000 in dividends and interest during the year. In addition, he incurred a loss of $50,000 from an investment in a passive activity acquired in 1990. What is Bob's net income for 1994 after considering the passive investment?

45. Tina acquired passive Activity A in January 1985 and Activity B in September 1986. Until 1993, Activity A was profitable. Activity A produced a loss of $100,000 in 1993, and a loss of $50,000 in 1994. Tina has passive income of $10,000 from Activity B in 1993 and $20,000 in 1994. After offsetting passive income, how much of the net losses may she deduct?

46. In 1985, Kay acquired an interest in a partnership in which she is not a material participant. The partnership was profitable until 1993. Kay's basis in her partnership interest at the beginning of 1993 was $40,000. In 1993, Kay's share of the partnership loss was $35,000. In 1994, her share of the partnership income was $15,000. How much can Kay deduct in 1993 and 1994?

47. Lee acquired a 20% interest in the ABC Partnership for $60,000 in 1985. The partnership was profitable until 1994, and Lee's basis in the partnership interest was $120,000 at the end of 1993. ABC incurred a loss of $400,000 in 1994 and reported income of $200,000 in 1995. Assuming Lee is not a material participant in ABC, how much of his loss from ABC Partnership is deductible in 1994 and 1995, respectively?

48. Hazel has two investments in nonrental passive activities. Activity A, which was acquired in 1985, was profitable until 1993. Activity B was acquired in 1993. Hazel's share of the loss from Activity A was $10,000 in 1993, and her share of the loss from Activity B was $6,000. What was the total of Hazel's suspended losses from these activities as of the end of 1993?

49. Joe acquired an activity in 1990. The loss from the activity was $50,000 in 1994. He had AGI of $140,000 before considering the loss from the activity. The activity is an apartment building, and Joe is an active participant. What is his AGI after the loss is considered?

50. Beth acquired an activity in 1990. The loss from the activity was $50,000 in 1994. She had AGI of $140,000 before considering the loss from the activity. The activity is an apartment building, and Beth is not an active participant. What is her AGI after considering the activity?

51. Ray acquired an activity in 1990. The loss from the activity was $50,000 in 1994. He had AGI of $140,000 before considering the loss from the activity. The activity is a bakery, and Ray is not a material participant. What is his AGI after considering this activity?

52. Ann acquired an activity in 1990. The loss from the activity was $50,000 in 1994. She had AGI of $140,000 before considering the loss from the activity. The activity is a service station, and Ann is a material participant. What is her AGI after considering this activity?

53. Ken has a $40,000 loss from an investment in a partnership in which he does not participate. He paid $30,000 for his interest in the partnership. How much of the loss is disallowed by the at-risk rules? How much is disallowed by the passive loss rules?

54. In 1994, Sue invested $20,000 for an interest in a partnership in which she is a material participant. Her share of the partnership's loss for the year was $25,000. Discuss the tax treatment of Sue's share of the loss, and compute her at-risk amount.

55. Assume the same facts as in Problem 54 and that Sue's share of the partnership's income in 1995 is $15,000. What will be the net effect on her taxable income for 1995?

56. Soong, a physician, earned $200,000 from his practice in 1994. He also received $18,000 in dividends and interest on various portfolio investments. During the year, he paid $45,000 to acquire a 20% interest in a partnership that produced a $300,000 loss.
    a. Compute Soong's AGI assuming he does not participate in the operations of the partnership.
    b. Compute Soong's AGI assuming he is a material participant in the operations of the partnership.

57. White, Inc., earned $400,000 from operations in 1994. White also received $36,000 in dividends and interest on various portfolio investments. During the year, White paid $150,000 to acquire a 20% interest in a passive activity that produced a $200,000 loss.
    a. How will this affect White's taxable income, assuming the corporation is a personal service corporation?
    b. How will this affect White's taxable income, assuming the corporation is a closely held, non-personal service corporation?

58. Ahmad owns four activities. He participated for 120 hours in Activity A, 150 hours in Activity B, 140 hours in Activity C, and 100 hours in Activity D. Which of the following statements is correct?
    a. Activities A, B, C, and D are all significant participation activities.
    b. Activities A, B, and C are significant participation activities.
    c. Ahmad is a material participant with respect to Activities A, B, and C.
    d. Ahmad is a material participant with respect to Activities A, B, C, and D.
    e. None of the above.

59. Dena owns interests in five businesses and has full-time employees in each business. She participates for 100 hours in Activity A, 120 hours in Activity B, 130 hours in Activity C, 140 hours in Activity D, and 125 hours in Activity E. Which of the following statements is correct?
    a. All five of Dena's activities are significant participation activities.
    b. Dena is a material participant with respect to all five activities.
    c. Dena is not a material participant in any of the activities.
    d. Dena is a material participant with respect to Activities B, C, D, and E.
    . None of the above.

60. Maria, who owns a 50% interest in a restaurant, has been a material participant in the restaurant activity for the last 20 years. She retired from the restaurant at the end of 1993 and will not participate in the restaurant activity in the future. However, she continues to be a material participant in a retail store in which she is a 50% partner. The restaurant operations resulted in a loss for 1994, and Maria's share of the loss is $80,000. Her share of the income from the retail store is $150,000. She does not own interests in any other activities. Which of the following statements is correct?

   a. Maria cannot deduct the $80,000 loss from the restaurant because she is not a material participant.

   b. Maria can offset the $80,000 loss against the $150,000 of income from the retail store.

   c. Maria will not be able to deduct any losses from the restaurant until 1999.

   d. None of the above.

61. During 1994, Donald worked 1,200 hours as a computer consultant, 600 hours in a real estate development business, and 500 hours in real estate rental activities. He earned $60,000 as a computer consultant, but lost $18,000 in the development business and $26,000 in the real estate rental business. How should Donald treat the losses on his 1994 Federal income tax return?

62. During 1994, Maria Castro worked 1,200 hours as a computer consultant, 320 hours in a real estate development business, and 400 hours in real estate rental activities. Jorge, her husband, worked 250 hours in the real estate development business and 180 hours in the real estate rental business. Maria earned $60,000 as a computer consultant, but the Castros lost $18,000 in the development business and $26,000 in the real estate rental business. How should they treat the losses on their joint 1994 Federal income tax return?

63. Greg, a syndicated radio talk show host from Cincinnati, earns a $400,000 salary in 1994. He works approximately 30 hours per week in this job, which leaves him time to participate in several businesses he acquired in 1994. He owns a movie theater and a drugstore in Cincinnati. He also owns a movie theater and a drugstore in Indianapolis and a drugstore in Louisville. A preliminary analysis on December 1, 1994, shows projected profits and losses for the various businesses as follows:

	Profit (Loss)
Cincinnati movie theater (95 hours participation)	$ 56,000
Cincinnati drugstore (140 hours participation)	(89,000)
Indianapolis movie theater (90 hours participation)	34,000
Indianapolis drugstore (170 hours participation)	(41,000)
Louisville drugstore (180 hours participation)	(15,000)

Greg has full-time employees in each of the five businesses listed above. Consider all possible groupings for Greg's activities. Write a letter to him suggesting the grouping method and other strategies that will provide the greatest tax advantage. Greg does not know much about the tax law, so you should provide a concise, nontechnical explanation.

64. Leanne has investments in four passive activity partnerships purchased in 1984. In 1993, the income and losses were as follows:

Activity	Income (Loss)
A	$ 60,000
B	(60,000)
C	(30,000)
D	(10,000)

In 1994, she sold her interest in Activity D for a $20,000 gain. Activity D, which had been profitable until 1993, had a $3,000 loss in 1994. How will the sale of Activity D affect Leanne's taxable income in 1994?

65. Hal and Wanda are married with no dependents and live together in Ohio, which is not a community property state. Since Wanda has large medical expenses, they seek your advice about filing separately to save taxes. Their income and expenses for 1994 are as follows:

Hal's salary	$ 60,000
Wanda's salary	20,000
Dividends and interest (joint)	1,500
Rental loss from actively managed units (joint)	(22,000)
Wanda's medical expenses	5,800
All other itemized deductions:*	
Hal	8,000
Wanda	2,000

*None subject to limitations.

Determine whether Hal and Wanda should file jointly or separately for 1994.

66. Ida, who has AGI of $80,000 before considering rental activities, is active in three separate real estate rental activities and is in the 28% tax bracket. She had $12,000 of losses from Activity A, $18,000 of losses from Activity B, and income of $10,000 from Activity C. She also had $2,100 of tax credits from Activity A. Calculate her deductions and credits allowed and the suspended losses and credits.

67. Chris, who owns a sole proprietorship that is a passive activity, calculated a loss for the activity as follows:

Operating income	$ 75,000
Dividends on stock held for investment	22,500
Total income	$ 97,500
Less expenses:	
Operating expenses (wages, rent, supplies, etc.)	(90,000)
Investment interest	(12,000)
Less: Loss on sale of stock held for investment	(7,500)
Net loss	$(12,000)

Compute Chris's passive loss from the activity based on the above information.

68. Ella has $105,000 of losses from a real estate rental activity in which she actively participates. She has other rental income of $25,000 and other passive income of $32,000. How much rental loss can Ella deduct against active and portfolio income (ignoring at-risk rules)? Does she have any suspended losses to carry over?

69. Faye died owning an interest in a passive activity property with an adjusted basis of $80,000, suspended losses of $8,000, and a fair market value of $85,000. What can be deducted on her final income tax return?

70. In 1993, Nina gave her son a passive activity with an adjusted basis of $100,000. Fair market value of the activity was $180,000, and the activity had suspended losses of $25,000. In 1994, her son realized income from the passive activity of $12,000. What is the effect on Nina and her son in 1993 and 1994?

71. Ray, who owns a sole proprietorship that is a passive activity, calculated a loss for the activity as follows:

Operating income	$ 70,000
Dividends on stock held for investment	25,000
Total income	$ 95,000
Less expenses:	
Operating expenses (wages, rent, supplies, etc.)	(90,000)
Investment interest	(6,000)
Less: Loss on sale of stock held for investment	(4,000)
Net loss	$ (5,000)

Compute Ray's passive loss for the year.

72. Sam invested $150,000 in a passive activity in 1982. On January 1, 1993, his adjusted basis in the activity was $30,000. His shares of the losses in the activity were as follows:

Year	Gain (Loss)
1993	$(40,000)
1994	(30,000)
1995	50,000

How much can Sam deduct in 1993 and 1994? What is his taxable income from the activity in 1995? Keep in mind the at-risk rules as well as the passive loss rules.

73. Tonya sold a passive activity in 1994 for $150,000. Her adjusted basis was $50,000. She used the installment method of reporting the gain. The activity had suspended losses of $12,000. Tonya received $60,000 in the year of sale. What is her gain? How much of the suspended losses can she deduct?

74. If Tonya in Problem 73 had no suspended losses, was in the 28% tax bracket, and had $10,000 of tax credits attributable to the activity, how much of the credits could she use in 1994?

RESEARCH PROBLEMS

Research Problem 1.   Leon Lane is a married individual who files a separate return for the taxable year. He is employed full-time as an attorney. Leon, who also owns an interest in a minor league baseball team, does no work in connection with the activity during the year. He anticipates that the activity will result in a loss for the taxable year. Leon pays his wife to work as an office receptionist in connection with the activity for an average of 20 hours a week during the year. Write a letter to Leon and explain whether he will be allowed to deduct his share of the loss from the activity.

Research Problem 2.   George owns interests in three business activities, X, Y, and Z. George does not materially participate in any of the activities considered separately, but he does participate for 110 hours in Activity X, 160 hours in Activity Y, and 125 hours in Activity Z. George does not own interests in any other businesses. His net passive income (loss) for the taxable year from Activities X, Y, and Z is as follows:

	X	Y	Z
Gross income	$ 600	$ 700	$ 900
Deductions	(200)	(1,000)	(300)
Net income (loss)	$ 400	$ (300)	$ 600

How much of the gross income from the three activities is treated as income that is not from a passive activity?

Research Problem 3.   Marcia owns six grocery stores and a warehouse that receives and stores goods and delivers the goods to the different grocery stores as needed. How many separate activities does Marcia have? How are the income and expenses of the warehouse treated?

SPECIAL TAX COMPUTATION METHODS, PAYMENT PROCEDURES, AND TAX CREDITS

Part IV presents several topics that relate to the theme of tax liability determination. The taxpayer must calculate the tax liability in accordance with the basic tax formula and also in accordance with the tax formula for the alternative minimum tax (AMT). The basic tax formula was presented in Part I, and the AMT formula is covered in Part IV. Tax credits reduce the amount of the calculated tax liability. The specific procedures for the timing of the payment of the tax liability are also discussed.

Chapter 12
Alternative Minimum Tax

Chapter 13
Tax Credits and Payment Procedures

12

ALTERNATIVE MINIMUM TAX

LEARNING OBJECTIVES

After completing Chapter 12, you should be able to:

1. Explain the rationale for the individual alternative minimum tax.

2. Apply the formula for computing alternative minimum taxable income.

3. Discuss the role of adjustments in the computation of the alternative minimum tax and explain the adjustments required.

4. Differentiate tax preferences from alternative minimum tax adjustments and discuss specific tax preferences.

5. Apply the formula for computing the alternative minimum tax.

6. Describe the role of the alternative minimum tax credit in the alternative minimum tax structure.

7. Understand the basic features of the corporate alternative minimum tax.

Individual Alternative Minimum Tax, 12–2

A New Concept: Alternative Tax Adjusted Gross Income, 12–5

AMTI Limitations Based on Income, 12–6

AMT Adjustments, 12–8

AMT Preferences, 12–18

Other Components of the AMT Formula, 12–21

Illustration of the AMT Computation, 12–22

AMT Credit, 12–24

Corporate Alternative Minimum Tax, 12–24

AMT Adjustments, 12–25

Tax Preferences, 12–27

Exemption, 12–28

Other Aspects of the AMT, 12–28

Tax Planning Considerations, **12–28**

Avoiding Preferences and Adjustments, 12–28

Controlling the Timing of Preferences and Adjustments, 12–29

Taking Advantage of the AMT/Regular Tax Rate Differential, 12–29

1 LEARNING OBJECTIVE
Explain the rationale for the individual alternative minimum tax.

The tax law contains many incentives that are intended to influence the economic and social behavior of taxpayers (refer to Chapter 1). Some taxpayers have been able to take advantage of enough of these incentives to avoid or minimize any liability for Federal income tax. Although these taxpayers were reducing taxes legally, Congress became concerned about the inequity that results when taxpayers with substantial economic incomes can avoid paying any income tax. The **alternative minimum tax (AMT)** was enacted as a backup to the income tax. The rationale for the AMT was expressed as follows:

> [T]he minimum tax should serve one overriding objective: to ensure that no taxpayer with substantial economic income can avoid significant tax liability by using exclusions, deductions, and credits. Although these provisions may provide incentives for worthy goals, they become counterproductive when taxpayers are allowed to use them to avoid virtually all tax liability. The ability of high-income taxpayers to pay little or no tax undermines respect for the entire tax system and, thus, for the incentive provisions themselves. In addition, even aside from public perceptions . . . it is inherently unfair for high-income taxpayers to pay little or no tax due to their ability to utilize tax preferences.[1]

The individual AMT is discussed in the first part of this chapter. The corporate AMT is similar to the individual AMT, but differs in several important ways. Details of the corporate AMT are presented in the last part of the chapter.

INDIVIDUAL ALTERNATIVE MINIMUM TAX

2 LEARNING OBJECTIVE
Apply the formula for computing alternative minimum taxable income.

The AMT is separate from, but parallel to, the income tax system. Most income and expense items are treated the same way for both income tax and AMT purposes. For example, a taxpayer's salary is included in computing taxable income and is also included in alternative minimum taxable income (AMTI). Alimony paid is allowed as a deduction *for* AGI for both income tax and AMT

---

[1] *General Explanation of the Tax Reform Act of 1986 ("Blue Book"),* prepared by The Staff of the Joint Committee on Taxation, May 4, 1987, H.R. 3838, 99th Cong., pp. 432–433.

purposes. Certain itemized deductions, such as gambling losses, are allowed for both income tax and AMT purposes.

On the other hand, some income and expense items are treated differently for income tax and AMT purposes. For example, interest income on bonds issued by state, county, or local governments is *excluded* in computing taxable income. However, interest on such bonds is *included* in computing AMTI if the bonds are private activity bonds issued after August 7, 1986. The deduction for personal and dependency exemptions is *allowed* for income tax purposes, but is *disallowed* for AMT purposes.

In other cases, certain items are considered in both the income tax and AMT computations, but the amounts are different. For example, the completed contract method can be used to report income from some long-term contracts for income tax purposes, but the percentage of completion method is required for AMT purposes. Thus, the amount of income included in taxable income will differ from the amount included in AMTI. Depreciation is allowed as a deduction for both income tax and AMT purposes, but the *amount* of the income tax deduction will be different from the amount of the AMT deduction.

The parallel but separate nature of the AMT means that AMTI will differ from taxable income. It would be possible to compute AMTI by direct application of the AMT provisions, using the following formula:

> Gross income computed by applying the AMT rules
>
> **Minus:** Deductions computed by applying the AMT rules
>
> **Equals:** AMTI before tax preferences
>
> **Plus:** Tax preferences
>
> **Equals:** Alternative minimum taxable income

While the direct approach for computing AMTI appears quite logical, the tax forms provide a very different approach. The tax form approach for computing AMTI uses taxable income as the starting point, as shown in Figure 12–1.

The purpose of the AMT formula is to *reconcile* taxable income to AMTI. This reconciliation is similar to a bank reconciliation, which reconciles a checkbook balance to a bank balance by considering differences between the depositor's records and the bank's records. The reconciliation of taxable income to AMTI is accomplished by entering reconciling items to account for differences between income tax provisions and AMT provisions. These reconciling items are referred to as **AMT adjustments** or **tax preferences.** *Adjustments* can be either positive or negative, as shown in the formula in Figure 12–1. Tax preferences are always positive.

▼ **FIGURE 12–1**
Alternative Minimum Taxable Income (AMTI) Formula

> Taxable income
>
> **Plus:** Positive AMT adjustments
>
> **Minus:** Negative AMT adjustments
>
> **Equals:** Taxable income after AMT adjustments
>
> **Plus:** Tax preferences
>
> **Equals:** Alternative minimum taxable income

Adjustments

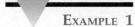

3   LEARNING OBJECTIVE
Discuss the role of adjustments in the computation of the alternative minimum tax and explain the adjustments required.

The concept of AMT adjustments was introduced in the Tax Reform Act of 1986. Most adjustments relate to *timing differences* that arise because of *separate* income tax and AMT treatments. Adjustments that are caused by timing differences will eventually *reverse;* that is, positive adjustments will be offset by negative adjustments in the future, and vice versa.

For example, **circulation expenditures** can give rise to a timing difference that requires an AMT adjustment. For income tax purposes, circulation expenditures can be deducted in the year incurred. For AMT purposes, however, circulation expenditures must be deducted over a three-year period. This difference in treatment will be used to illustrate the role of adjustments in the formula for computing AMTI.

EXAMPLE 1

Bob had taxable income of $100,000 in 1993. In computing taxable income, he deducted $30,000 of circulation expenditures incurred in 1993. Bob's allowable deduction for AMT purposes was only $10,000. Therefore, an AMT adjustment was required in 1993 as follows:

Taxable income		$100,000
+AMT adjustment:		
Circulation expenditures deducted for income tax purposes	$ 30,000	
–Circulation expenditures allowed for AMT purposes	(10,000)	
Positive adjustment		20,000
=AMTI before tax preferences		$120,000
+Tax preferences		–0–
AMTI		$120,000

Analysis of this computation shows that the allowable AMT deduction is $20,000 less than the allowable income tax deduction. Therefore, AMTI will be $20,000 greater than taxable income. This is accomplished by entering a positive AMT adjustment of $20,000. ▼

EXAMPLE 2

Assume that Bob from Example 1 has taxable income of $95,000 in 1994. He is allowed to deduct $10,000 of circulation expenditures for AMT purposes, but is not allowed a deduction for income tax purposes because all $30,000 was deducted in 1993. Therefore, a *negative* AMT adjustment is required.

Taxable income		$ 95,000
–AMT adjustment:		
Circulation expenditures allowed for income tax purposes	$ –0–	
Circulation expenditures deducted for AMT purposes	(10,000)	
Negative adjustment		(10,000)
=AMTI before tax preferences		$ 85,000
+Tax preferences		–0–
AMTI		$ 85,000

Analysis of this computation shows that the allowable AMT deduction is $10,000 more than the allowable income tax deduction. Therefore, AMTI will be $10,000 less than taxable income. This is accomplished by entering a negative AMT adjustment of $10,000. ▼

As noted previously, timing differences eventually reverse. Therefore, total positive adjustments will be offset by total negative adjustments with respect to a particular item.

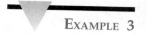

EXAMPLE 3   Refer to Examples 1 and 2. The difference in income tax and AMT treatments of circulation expenditures will result in AMT adjustments over a three-year period.

Year	Income Tax Deduction	AMT Deduction	AMT Adjustment
1993	$30,000	$10,000	+$20,000
1994	–0–	10,000	–10,000
1995	–0–	10,000	–10,000
Total	$30,000	$30,000	$ –0–

As column 3 illustrates, positive and negative AMT adjustments with respect to a particular item will eventually net to zero. ▼

The adjustments for circulation expenditures and other items are discussed in detail under AMT Adjustments.

Preferences

4   LEARNING OBJECTIVE
Differentiate tax preferences from alternative minimum tax adjustments and discuss specific tax preferences.

Some deductions allowed to taxpayers for regular income tax purposes provide extraordinary tax savings. Congress has chosen to single out these items, which are referred to as tax preferences. The AMT is designed to take back all or part of the tax benefits derived through the use of preferences in the computation of taxable income for regular income tax purposes. This is why taxable income, which is the starting point in computing AMTI, is increased by tax preference items. The effect of adding these preference items is to disallow for *AMT purposes* those preferences that were allowed in the regular income tax computation. Tax preferences include the following items, which are discussed in detail under AMT Preferences:

- Percentage depletion in excess of the property's adjusted basis.
- Excess intangible drilling costs reduced by 65 percent of the net income from oil, gas, and geothermal properties.
- Interest on certain private activity bonds.
- Excess of accelerated over straight-line depreciation on real property placed in service before 1987.
- Excess of accelerated over straight-line depreciation on *leased* personal property placed in service before 1987.
- Excess of amortization allowance over depreciation on pre-1987 certified pollution control facilities.

A NEW CONCEPT: ALTERNATIVE TAX ADJUSTED GROSS INCOME

Form 6251 (Alternative Minimum Tax—Individuals) for 1993 reflects a new concept—**alternative tax adjusted gross income (ATAGI).** The concept of ATAGI was created in a Technical Advice Memorandum.[2] A TAM is an IRS interpretation of a technical tax issue, usually issued in response to a question raised by IRS personnel.

---
[2] TAM 9320003, February 1, 1993.

In the case addressed, the taxpayers had reported a *loss* for income tax purposes, but reported a *positive* AMTI. As a result of the income tax loss, the percentage limitations prevented the taxpayers from taking a charitable contribution deduction. However, they filed an *amended* return and took a charitable contribution deduction for AMT purposes by applying the percentage limitation to the positive ATAGI, which resulted in a refund of AMT that had been paid with the original return. In TAM 9320003, the IRS held in favor of the taxpayers and concluded that ATAGI is to be used as the base for applying percentage limitations when the limitations are applicable for computing AMTI.

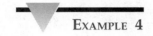

EXAMPLE 4

Erika's AGI is $20,000, and her ATAGI is $90,000. She contributed $50,000 to a public charity. Erika's charitable contribution deduction for income tax purposes is $10,000 ($20,000 AGI × 50% limit). Her deduction for AMT purposes is $45,000 ($90,000 ATAGI × 50% limit). She will have a negative AMT adjustment of $35,000 ($10,000 income tax deduction − $45,000 AMT deduction). ▼

Implementation of the concept of ATAGI provides an interesting insight into the development of tax law. ATAGI is not mentioned in the Code or the Regulations, nor did it evolve from case law. Furthermore, § 6110(j)(3) of the Internal Revenue Code states specifically that a TAM may not be cited as *precedent* for a position. However, the IRS's position is now reflected on Form 6251 and must be followed by *all* taxpayers on their 1993 returns. In effect, the "law" was developed by the IRS and the form writers, not by Congress.

The concept of ATAGI is not well developed at the date of this writing. The formula for computing ATAGI is set forth in a worksheet that accompanies Form 6251 for 1993. This ATAGI computation, with some items rearranged and/or expanded for clarity, is shown in Figure 12–2.

The complexity of the formula for computing ATAGI has aroused criticism. On November 12, 1993, the American Institute of Certified Public Accountants sent a letter to the Commissioner of the IRS decrying the dramatic increase in complexity caused by the ATAGI computation.[3] The letter asserts that *circular* computations are required to determine ATAGI, that the Form 6251 instructions do not provide the necessary guidance for making the computations, and that advanced algebraic equations are needed to solve the computations correctly. The letter suggests that the IRS should make the computation of ATAGI voluntary or totally eliminate it as a step toward simplification. Therefore, coverage of the ATAGI computation will be limited in this text until it is further developed by the IRS.

AMTI LIMITATIONS BASED ON INCOME

TAM 9320003 also requires that certain items that are limited by income for income tax purposes be refigured using a different limitation for AMT purposes. Recall that the deduction for percentage depletion cannot exceed 50 percent of the taxable income from the property before the allowance for depletion (refer to Chapter 8). The taxpayers in TAM 9320003 did not take an income tax deduction for percentage depletion on their original return because they had no taxable income. However, they amended their return and claimed an AMT deduction for percentage depletion based on a positive AMTI. The IRS held that the taxpayers' action was appropriate.

---

[3] Letter to Margaret Milner Richardson, Commissioner of Internal Revenue, from Harvey L. Coustan, Chairman, Tax Executive Committee of the American Institute of Certified Public Accountants.

▼ **FIGURE 12–2**
Formula for Computation
of ATAGI

Adjusted gross income		xx,xxx
Minus: Refund of taxes deducted on a previous income tax return		(xxx)
Plus: Portion of AMT adjustment for investment interest that is allocable to Schedule E of Form 1040		x,xxx
Plus (minus if negative) the following preferences and adjustments:		
Post-1986 depreciation	x,xxx	
Adjusted gain or loss	x,xxx	
Incentive stock options	x,xxx	
Passive activities	x,xxx	
Proceeds from estates and trusts	x,xxx	
Tax-exempt interest from private activity bonds issued after August 7, 1986	x,xxx	x,xxx
Plus (minus if negative) other adjustments:		
Circulation expenditures	x,xxx	
Depletion	x,xxx	
Depreciation (pre-1987)	x,xxx	
Installment sales	x,xxx	
Intangible drilling costs	x,xxx	
Long-term contracts	x,xxx	
Loss limitations	x,xxx	
Mining costs	x,xxx	
Pollution control facilities	x,xxx	
Research and experimental expenditures	x,xxx	
Tax shelter farm activities	x,xxx	
Related adjustments	x,xxx	x,xxx
Plus: Income tax net operating loss deduction		x,xxx
Minus: Alternative tax net operating loss deduction		(xxx)
Equals: Alternative tax adjusted gross income (ATAGI)		x,xxx

This interpretation regarding percentage depletion extends to any item limited by income (e.g., earned income, AGI, modified AGI, or taxable income from a business). The instructions to Form 6251 for 1993 list several items that must be recalculated for AMT purposes because they are limited in some way by income. The list includes the § 179 expense deduction, the self-employed health insurance deduction, taxable Social Security benefits, and personal casualty losses.

**ETHICAL
CONSIDERATIONS**

The Cost of Complying with the ATAGI Requirements

Based on preliminary computations, you have concluded that Ira, one of your major clients, will be subject to the AMT in 1993. You inform him that numerous additional calculations will be required to comply with the ATAGI requirements, but they probably will make very little difference in the amount of tax he will owe. You also explain that there is considerable uncertainty as to the proper methods for performing these calculations and that your additional fee for doing them will be $1,500. Ira asks you if his return is likely to be audited, and you tell him that an audit is unlikely. He then says that he will not pay the additional fee and asks you to go ahead and file his return. You must decide whether to file the return without doing the ATAGI calculations, do the calculations and not charge Ira an additional fee, or terminate the professional engagement.

AMT ADJUSTMENTS

Circulation Expenditures

For income tax purposes, circulation expenditures, other than those the taxpayer elects to charge to a capital account, may be expensed in the year incurred.[4] These expenditures include expenses incurred to establish, maintain, or increase the circulation of a newspaper, magazine, or other periodical.

Circulation expenditures are not deductible in the year incurred for AMT purposes. In computing AMTI, these expenditures must be capitalized and amortized ratably over the three-year period beginning with the year in which the expenditures were made.[5]

The AMT adjustment for circulation expenditures is the amount expensed for income tax purposes minus the amount that can be amortized for AMT purposes. The adjustment can be either positive or negative (refer to Examples 1, 2, and 3). A taxpayer can avoid the AMT adjustments for circulation expenditures by electing to write off the expenditures over a three-year period for regular income tax purposes.[6]

Direction of Adjustments

It is necessary to determine not only the amount of an adjustment, but also whether the adjustment is positive or negative. Careful study of Example 3 reveals the following pattern with regard to *deductions*:

- If the deduction allowed for income tax purposes exceeds the deduction allowed for AMT purposes, the difference is a positive adjustment.
- If the deduction allowed for AMT purposes exceeds the deduction allowed for income tax purposes, the difference is a negative adjustment.

Conversely, the direction of an adjustment attributable to an *income* item can be determined as follows:

- If the income reported for income tax purposes exceeds the income reported for AMT purposes, the difference is a negative adjustment.
- If the income reported for AMT purposes exceeds the income reported for income tax purposes, the difference is a positive adjustment.

Depreciation of Post-1986 Real Property

For real property placed in service after 1986, AMT depreciation is computed under the alternative depreciation system (ADS), which uses the straight-line

---

[4] § 173(a).
[5] § 56(b)(2)(A)(i).

[6] § 59(e)(2)(A).

method over a 40-year life. The depreciation lives for regular tax purposes are 27.5 years for residential rental property and 39 years for all other real property.[7] The difference between AMT depreciation and regular tax depreciation is treated as an adjustment in computing the AMT. The differences will be positive during the regular tax life of the asset because the cost is written off over a shorter period for regular tax purposes. For example, during the 27.5-year income tax life of residential real property, the regular tax depreciation will exceed the AMT depreciation because AMT depreciation is computed over a 40-year period.

Table 8–7 is used to compute regular income tax depreciation on real property placed in service after 1986. For AMT purposes, depreciation on real property placed in service after 1986 is computed under the ADS (refer to Table 8–12).

EXAMPLE 5

In January 1994, Sara placed in service a residential building that cost $100,000. Depreciation for 1994 for income tax purposes is $3,485 ($100,000 cost × 3.485% from Table 8–7). For AMT purposes, depreciation is $2,396 ($100,000 cost × 2.396% from Table 8–12). In computing AMTI for 1994, Sara has a positive adjustment of $1,089 ($3,485 income tax depreciation – $2,396 AMT depreciation). ▼

After real property has been held for the entire depreciation period for income tax purposes, the asset will be fully depreciated. However, the depreciation period under the ADS is 41 years due to application of the half-year convention, so depreciation will continue for AMT purposes. This causes negative adjustments after the property has been fully depreciated for income tax purposes.

EXAMPLE 6

Assume the same facts as in the previous example, and compute the AMT adjustment for 2022 (the twenty-ninth year of the asset's life). Income tax depreciation is zero (refer to Table 8–7). AMT depreciation is $2,500 ($100,000 cost × 2.500% from Table 8–12). Therefore, Sara has a negative AMT adjustment of $2,500 ($0 income tax depreciation – $2,500 AMT depreciation). ▼

After real property is fully depreciated for both income tax and AMT purposes, the positive and negative adjustments that have been made for AMT purposes will net to zero.

Depreciation of Post-1986 Personal Property

For most personal property placed in service after 1986, the modified ACRS (MACRS) deduction for regular income tax purposes is based on the 200 percent declining-balance method with a switch to straight-line when that method produces a larger depreciation deduction for the asset. Refer to Table 8–2 for computing income tax depreciation.

For AMT purposes, the taxpayer must use the ADS. This method is based on the 150 percent declining-balance method with a similar switch to straight-line for all personal property. Refer to Table 8–10 for percentages to be used in computing AMT depreciation.

All personal property placed in service after 1986 may be taken into consideration in computing one net adjustment. Using this netting process, the AMT adjustment for a tax year is the difference between the total MACRS depreciation

---

[7]The 39-year life generally applies to nonresidential real property placed in service on or after May 13, 1993.

for all personal property computed for regular tax purposes and the total ADS depreciation computed for AMT purposes. When the total of MACRS deductions exceeds the total of ADS deductions, the amount of the adjustment is positive. When the total of ADS deductions exceeds the total of MACRS deductions, the adjustment for AMTI is negative.

The MACRS deduction for personal property is larger than the ADS deduction in the early years of an asset's life. However, the ADS deduction is larger in the later years. This is so because ADS lives (based on class life) are longer than MACRS lives (based on recovery period).[8] Over the ADS life of the asset, the same amount of depreciation is deducted for both regular tax and AMT purposes. In the same manner as other timing adjustments, the AMT adjustments for depreciation will net to zero over the ADS life of the asset.

The taxpayer may elect to use the ADS for regular income tax purposes. If this election is made, no AMT adjustment is required because the depreciation deduction is the same for regular tax and for the AMT.

Pollution Control Facilities

For regular tax purposes, the cost of certified pollution control facilities may be amortized over a period of 60 months. For AMT purposes, the cost of these facilities placed in service after 1986 must be depreciated under the ADS over the appropriate class life, determined as explained above for depreciation of post-1986 property. The required adjustment for AMTI is equal to the difference between the amortization deduction allowed for regular tax purposes and the depreciation deduction computed under the ADS. The adjustment may be positive or negative.

Expenditures Requiring 10-Year Write-off for AMT Purposes

Certain expenditures that may be deducted in the year incurred for income tax purposes must be written off over a 10-year period for AMT purposes. These rules apply to (1) mining exploration and development costs and (2) research and experimental expenditures.

In computing taxable income, taxpayers are allowed to deduct certain mining exploration and development expenditures. The deduction is allowed for expenditures paid or incurred during the taxable year for exploration[9] (ascertaining the existence, location, extent, or quality of a deposit or mineral) and for development of a mine or other natural deposit, other than an oil or gas well. Mining development expenditures are expenses paid or incurred after the existence of ores and minerals in commercially marketable quantities has been disclosed.

For AMT purposes, however, mining exploration and development costs must be capitalized and amortized ratably over a 10-year period.[10] The AMT adjustment for mining exploration and development costs that are expensed is equal to the amount expensed minus the allowable expense if the costs had been capitalized and amortized ratably over a 10-year period. This provision does not apply to costs relating to an oil or gas well.

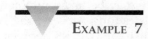

EXAMPLE 7

In 1994, Eve incurs $150,000 of mining exploration expenditures and deducts this amount for income tax purposes. For AMT purposes, these mining exploration expenditures must be amortized over a 10-year period. Eve must make a positive adjustment for AMTI of

[8]Class lives and recovery periods are established for all assets in Rev.Proc. 87–56, 1987–2 C.B. 674.

[9]§ 617(a).
[10]§ 56(a)(2).

$135,000 ($150,000 allowed for income tax – $15,000 for AMT) for 1994, the first year. In each of the next nine years for AMT purposes, Eve is required to make a negative adjustment of $15,000 ($0 allowed for regular tax – $15,000 for AMT). ▼

To avoid the AMT adjustments for mining exploration and development costs, a taxpayer may elect to write off the expenditures over a 10-year period for income tax purposes.[11]

Similar rules apply to computation of the adjustment for research and experimental expenditures.

Passive Activity Losses

Losses on passive activities are not deductible in computing either the income tax or the AMT. This does not, however, eliminate the possibility of adjustments attributable to passive activities.

The rules for computing taxable income differ from the rules for computing AMTI. It follows, then, that the rules for computing a loss for income tax purposes differ from the AMT rules for computing a loss. Therefore, any *passive loss* computed for income tax purposes may differ from the passive loss computed for AMT purposes.[12]

EXAMPLE 8

Soong acquired two passive activities in 1994. He received net passive income of $10,000 from Activity A and had no AMT adjustments or preferences in connection with the activity. Activity B had gross income of $27,000 and operating expenses (not affected by AMT adjustments or preferences) of $19,000. Soong claimed MACRS depreciation of $20,000 for Activity B; depreciation under the ADS would have been $15,000. In addition, Soong deducted $10,000 of percentage depletion in excess of basis. The following comparison illustrates the differences in the computation of the passive loss for income tax and AMT purposes for Activity B.

	Income Tax	AMT
Gross income	$27,000	$27,000
Deductions:		
Operating expenses	$19,000	$19,000
Depreciation	20,000	15,000
Depletion	10,000	–0–
Total deductions	$49,000	$34,000
Passive loss	$22,000	$ 7,000

Because the adjustment for depreciation ($5,000) applies and the preference for depletion ($10,000) is not taken into account in computing AMTI, the regular tax passive activity loss of $22,000 for Activity B is reduced by these amounts, resulting in a passive activity loss for AMT purposes of $7,000. ▼

For income tax purposes, Soong would offset the $10,000 of net passive income from Activity A with $10,000 of the passive loss from Activity B. For AMT purposes, he would offset the $10,000 of net passive income from Activity A with

---

[11] §§ 59(e)(2)(D) and (E).

[12] See Chapter 11.

the $7,000 passive activity loss allowed from Activity B, resulting in passive activity income of $3,000. Thus, in computing AMTI, Soong makes a positive passive loss adjustment of $3,000 [$10,000 (passive activity loss allowed for regular tax) – $7,000 (passive activity loss allowed for the AMT)]. To avoid duplication, the AMT adjustment for depreciation and the preference for depletion are *not* reported separately. They are accounted for in determining the AMT passive loss adjustment.

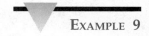

EXAMPLE 9

Assume the same facts as in the previous example. For regular tax purposes, Soong has a suspended passive loss of $12,000 [$22,000 (amount of loss) – $10,000 (used in 1994)]. This suspended passive loss can offset passive income in the future or can offset active or portfolio income when Soong disposes of the loss activity (refer to Chapter 11). For AMT purposes, Soong's suspended passive loss is $0 [$7,000 (amount of loss) – $7,000 (amount used in 1994)]. ▼

Use of Completed Contract Method of Accounting

For any long-term contract entered into after March 1, 1986, taxpayers are required to use the percentage of completion method for AMT purposes. However, in limited circumstances, taxpayers can use the completed contract method for income tax purposes.[13] Thus, a taxpayer recognizes a different amount of income for regular tax purposes than for AMT purposes. The resulting AMT adjustment is equal to the difference between income reported under the percentage of completion method and the amount reported using the completed contract method. The adjustment can be either positive or negative, depending on the amount of income recognized under the different methods.

A taxpayer can avoid an AMT adjustment on long-term contracts by using the percentage of completion method for regular income tax purposes rather than the completed contract method.

Incentive Stock Options

Incentive stock options (ISOs) are granted by employers to help attract new personnel and retain those already employed. At the time an ISO is granted, the employer corporation sets an option price for the corporate stock. If the value of the stock increases during the option period, the employee can obtain stock at a favorable price by exercising the option. Employees are generally restricted as to when they can dispose of stock acquired under an ISO (e.g., a certain length of employment may be required). Therefore, the stock may not be freely transferable until some specified period has passed. See Chapter 19 for details regarding ISOs.

The exercise of an ISO does not increase regular taxable income.[14] However, for AMT purposes, the excess of the fair market value of the stock over the exercise price is treated as an adjustment in the first taxable year in which the rights in the stock are freely transferable or are not subject to a substantial risk of forfeiture.

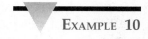

EXAMPLE 10

In 1992, Manuel exercised an ISO that had been granted by his employer, Gold Corporation. Manuel acquired 1,000 shares of Gold stock for the option price of $20 per share. The stock

---

[13] See Chapter 18 for a detailed discussion of the completed contract and percentage of completion methods of accounting.

[14] § 421(a).

TAX IN THE NEWS

THE APPEAL OF INCENTIVE STOCK OPTIONS

The higher tax rates for 1993 have increased the popularity of incentive stock options. The *Wall Street Journal* reported that Michael J. Blumenfield, chairman of Sport Supply Group, Inc., elected to take stock options in lieu of his salary for 1993. If his company's stock increases in value, the tax savings can be significant. There are two primary tax reasons for the popularity of ISOs:

The taxpayer does not have to report income upon *exercise* of the options. Income tax will be *deferred* until the stock is sold at a gain.

If required holding period rules are satisfied, the taxpayer will report long-term capital gain on sale of the stock acquired under the ISO. This could save the taxpayer as much as 11.6 percent in tax (39.6 percent top marginal rate – 28 percent rate applicable to long-term capital gain).

The alternative minimum tax is a potential threat to the use of ISOs as a tax-saving vehicle. The spread between the fair market value of the stock and the exercise price is an AMT adjustment in the first taxable year in which the rights in the stock are freely transferable or not subject to a substantial risk of forfeiture.

SOURCE: Information from Scott McCartney, "Stock Options Can Be a Valuable Tax-Cutting Tool," *Wall Street Journal*, November 24, 1993, p. C1, C17.

---

became freely transferable in 1994. The fair market value of the stock at the date of exercise was $50 per share. For AMT purposes, Manuel has a positive gain or loss adjustment (see below) of $30,000 ($50,000 fair market value – $20,000 option price) for 1994. The transaction does not affect regular taxable income in 1992 or 1994. ▼

No adjustment is required if the taxpayer exercises the option and disposes of the stock in the same year. Nor is there an adjustment if the amount realized on the disposition is less than the value of the option at the time it was exercised.

The income tax basis of stock acquired through exercise of ISOs is different from the AMT basis. The income tax basis of the stock is equal to its cost, whereas the AMT basis is equal to the fair market value on the date the options are exercised. Consequently, the gain or loss upon disposition of the stock is different for income tax purposes and AMT purposes.

▼
EXAMPLE 11

Assume the same facts as in the previous example and that Manuel sells the stock for $60,000 in 1996. His gain for income tax purposes is $40,000 ($60,000 amount realized – $20,000 income tax basis). For AMT purposes, the gain is $10,000 ($60,000 amount realized – $50,000 AMT basis). Therefore, Manuel has a $30,000 negative adjustment in computing AMT in 1996 ($40,000 income tax gain – $10,000 AMT gain). Note that the $30,000 negative adjustment upon disposition in 1996 offsets the $30,000 positive adjustment upon exercise of the ISO in 1994. ▼

Adjusted Gain or Loss

When property is sold during the year or a casualty occurs to business or income-producing property, gain or loss reported for regular income tax may be different than gain or loss determined for the AMT. This difference occurs because the adjusted basis of the property for AMT purposes must reflect any current and prior AMT adjustments for the following:

- Depreciation.
- Circulation expenditures.
- Research and experimental expenditures.
- Mining exploration and development costs.
- Amortization of certified pollution control facilities.

A negative gain or loss adjustment is required if

- the gain for AMT purposes is less than the gain for income tax purposes;
- the loss for AMT purposes is more than the loss for income tax purposes; or
- a loss is computed for AMT purposes and a gain is computed for income tax purposes.

Otherwise, the AMT gain or loss adjustment is positive.

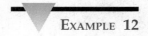

EXAMPLE 12

In January 1994, Kate paid $100,000 for a duplex acquired for rental purposes. Income tax depreciation in 1994 was $3,485 ($100,000 cost × 3.485% from Table 8–7). AMT depreciation was $2,396 ($100,000 cost × 2.396% from Table 8–12). For AMT purposes, Kate made a positive adjustment of $1,089 ($3,485 income tax depreciation – $2,396 AMT depreciation). ▼

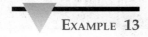

EXAMPLE 13

Kate sold the duplex on December 20, 1995, for $105,000. Income tax depreciation for 1995 is $3,485 [($100,000 cost × 3.636% from Table 8–7) × 11.5/12]. AMT depreciation for 1995 is $2,396 [($100,000 cost × 2.500% from Table 8–12) × 11.5/12]. Kate's AMT adjustment for 1995 was $1,089 ($3,485 income tax depreciation – $2,396 AMT depreciation). ▼

Because depreciation on the duplex differs for income tax and AMT purposes, the adjusted basis is different for income tax and AMT purposes. Consequently, the gain or loss on disposition of the duplex is different for income tax and AMT purposes.

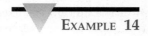

EXAMPLE 14

The adjusted basis of Kate's duplex for income tax purposes is $93,030 ($100,000 cost – $3,485 depreciation for 1994 – $3,485 depreciation for 1995). For AMT purposes, the adjusted basis is $95,208 ($100,000 cost – $2,396 depreciation for 1994 – $2,396 depreciation for 1995). The income tax gain is $11,970 ($105,000 amount realized – $93,030 income tax basis). The AMT gain is $9,792 ($105,000 amount realized – $95,208 AMT basis). Because the income tax and AMT gain on the sale of the duplex differ, Kate must make a negative AMT adjustment of $2,178 ($11,970 income tax gain – $9,792 AMT gain). Note that this negative adjustment offsets the $2,178 total of the two positive adjustments for depreciation ($1,089 in 1994 + $1,089 in 1995). ▼

Alternative Tax Net Operating Loss Deduction

In computing taxable income, taxpayers are allowed to deduct net operating loss (NOL) carryovers and carrybacks (refer to Chapter 7). The income tax NOL must be modified, however, in computing AMTI. The starting point in computing the alternative tax NOL deduction (ATNOLD) is the regular NOL computed for income tax purposes. The ATNOLD, however, is determined by applying AMT adjustments and ignoring tax preferences. Thus, preferences that have been deducted in computing the income tax NOL are added back, thereby reducing or eliminating the ATNOLD.

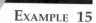

EXAMPLE 15

In 1994, Adam incurred an NOL of $100,000. Adam had no AMT adjustments, but his deductions included tax preferences of $18,000. His ATNOLD carryover to 1995 is $82,000 ($100,000 regular tax NOL – $18,000 tax preferences deducted in computing the NOL). ▼

In Example 15, if the adjustment was not made to the income tax NOL, the $18,000 in tax preference items deducted in 1994 would have the effect of reducing AMTI in the year the 1994 NOL is utilized. This would weaken the entire concept of the AMT.

A taxpayer who has an ATNOLD that is carried back or over to another year must use the ATNOLD against AMTI in the carryback or carryover year even if the regular tax, rather than the AMT, applies.

EXAMPLE 16

Matt's ATNOLD for 1995 (carried over from 1994) is $10,000. AMTI before considering the ATNOLD is $25,000. If Matt's regular income tax exceeds the AMT, the AMT does not apply. Nevertheless, Matt's ATNOLD of $10,000 is "used up" in 1995 and is not available for carryover to a later year. ▼

For income tax purposes, the NOL can be carried back 3 years and forward 15 years. However, the taxpayer may elect to forgo the 3-year carryback. These rules generally apply to the ATNOLD as well, except that the election to forgo the 3-year carryback is not available for the ATNOLD unless the taxpayer elected it for the income tax NOL.

Itemized Deductions

Taxes (state, local, foreign income, and property taxes) and miscellaneous itemized deductions that are subject to the 2 percent of AGI floor are not allowed in computing AMT. A positive AMT adjustment in the total amount of the income tax deduction for each is required. Moreover, if the taxpayer's gross income includes the recovery of any tax deducted as an itemized deduction for income tax purposes, a negative AMT adjustment in the amount of the recovery is allowed for AMTI purposes. For example, state, local, and foreign income taxes can be deducted for income tax purposes, but cannot be deducted in computing AMTI. Because of this, any refund of such taxes from a prior year is not included in AMTI. Therefore, the taxpayer must make a negative adjustment if an income tax refund has been included in computing regular taxable income. Under the tax benefit rule, a tax refund is included in taxable income to the extent that the taxpayer obtained a tax benefit by deducting the tax in a prior year.

Itemized deductions that are allowed for AMT purposes include the following:

- Casualty losses.
- Gambling losses.
- Charitable contributions.
- Medical expenses in excess of 10 percent of AGI.
- Estate tax on income in respect of a decedent.
- Qualified interest.

The 3 percent floor that applies to income tax itemized deductions of certain high-income taxpayers (refer to Chapter 10) does not apply in computing AMT. The effect of the 3 percent floor is to disallow a portion of the taxpayer's itemized deductions for income tax purposes. Because this floor does not apply for AMT purposes, taxable income, which is the starting point for computing AMTI, must be reduced by the amount of the disallowed deductions. Although this reduction has the same effect on AMTI as a negative adjustment, it is not shown on Form 6251 as such. Instead, it is shown on a separate line as a subtraction from taxable income.

Medical Expenses. The rules for determining the AMT deductions for medical expenses are sufficiently complex to require further explanation. For income tax purposes, medical expenses are deductible to the extent they exceed 7.5 percent of AGI. However, for AMT purposes, medical expenses are deductible only to the extent they exceed 10 percent of ATAGI.

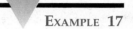

EXAMPLE 17

Joann incurred medical expenses of $16,000 in 1994. She had AGI of $100,000 and ATAGI of $120,000 for the year. Her AMT adjustment for medical expenses is computed as follows:

	Income Tax	AMT
Medical expenses incurred	$16,000	$16,000
Less reduction:		
$100,000 AGI × 7.5%	7,500	
$120,000 ATAGI × 10%		12,000
Medical expense deduction	$ 8,500	$ 4,000

Joann's AMT adjustment for medical expenses is $4,500 ($8,500 income tax deduction – $4,000 AMT deduction). ▼

Interest in General. The AMT itemized deduction allowed for interest expense includes only qualified housing interest and investment interest to the extent of net investment income that is included in the determination of AMTI.

In computing regular taxable income, taxpayers who itemize can deduct the following types of interest (refer to Chapter 10):

• Qualified residence interest.
• Investment interest, subject to the investment interest limitations (discussed under Investment Interest below).

Housing Interest. Under current income tax rules, taxpayers who itemize can deduct qualified *residence* interest on up to two residences. The deduction is limited to interest on acquisition indebtedness up to $1 million and home equity indebtedness up to $100,000. Acquisition indebtedness is debt that is incurred in acquiring, constructing, or substantially improving a qualified residence of the taxpayer and is secured by the residence. Home equity indebtedness is indebtedness secured by a qualified residence of the taxpayer, but does not include acquisition indebtedness.

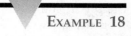

EXAMPLE 18

Gail, who used the proceeds of a mortgage to acquire a personal residence, paid mortgage interest of $112,000 in 1994. Of this amount, $14,000 is attributable to acquisition indebtedness in excess of $1 million. For income tax purposes, Gail may deduct mortgage interest of $98,000 ($112,000 total – $14,000 disallowed). ▼

The mortgage interest deduction for AMT purposes is limited to *qualified housing interest,* rather than *qualified residence interest.* Qualified housing interest includes only interest incurred to acquire, construct, or substantially improve the taxpayer's principal residence. It also includes interest on one other dwelling used for personal purposes. When additional mortgage interest is incurred (e.g., through a home equity loan), interest paid is deductible as qualified housing interest for AMT purposes only if:

- The proceeds are used to acquire or substantially improve a qualified residence.
- Interest on the prior loan was qualified housing interest.
- The amount of the loan was not increased.

A positive AMT adjustment is required in the amount of the difference between qualified *residence* interest allowed as an itemized deduction for regular tax purposes and qualified *housing* interest allowed in the determination of AMTI.

Investment Interest. Investment interest is deductible for income tax purposes and for AMT purposes to the extent of qualified net investment income.

▼
EXAMPLE 19 For the year, Jill had net investment income of $16,000 before deducting investment interest. She incurred investment interest expense of $30,000 during the year. Her investment interest deduction is $16,000. ▼

Even though investment interest is deductible for both income tax and AMT purposes, an adjustment is required if the amount of investment interest deductible for income tax purposes differs from the amount deductible for AMT purposes. For example, an adjustment will arise if proceeds from a home equity loan are used to purchase investments. Interest on a home equity loan is deductible as qualified residence interest for income tax purposes, but is not deductible for AMT purposes unless the proceeds are used to acquire or substantially improve a qualified residence. For AMT purposes, however, interest on a home equity loan is deductible as investment interest expense if proceeds from the loan are used for investment purposes.

To determine the AMT adjustment for interest expense, it is necessary to compute the investment interest deduction for both income tax and AMT purposes. This computation is illustrated in the following example.

▼
EXAMPLE 20 Tom had $20,000 interest income from corporate bonds and $5,000 dividends from preferred stock. He reported the following amounts of investment income for income tax and AMT purposes:

	Income Tax	**AMT**
Corporate bond interest	$20,000	$20,000
Preferred stock dividends	5,000	5,000
Net investment income	$25,000	$25,000

Tom incurred investment interest expense of $10,000 related to the corporate bonds. He also incurred $4,000 interest on a home equity loan and used the proceeds of the loan to purchase preferred stock. For income tax purposes, this $4,000 is deductible as mortgage interest. His *investment* interest expense for income tax and AMT purposes is computed below:

	Income Tax	AMT
To carry corporate bonds	$10,000	$10,000
On home equity loan to carry preferred stock	–0–	4,000
Total investment interest expense	$10,000	$14,000

Investment interest expense is deductible to the extent of net investment income. Because the amount deductible for income tax purposes ($10,000) differs from the amount deductible for AMT purposes ($14,000), an AMT adjustment is required. The adjustment is computed as follows:

AMT deduction for investment interest expense	$14,000
Income tax deduction for investment interest expense	10,000
Negative AMT adjustment	$ 4,000

▼

Other Adjustments

The standard deduction is not allowed as a deduction in computing AMTI. Although it would be rare for a person who does not itemize to be subject to the AMT, it is possible. In such a case, the taxpayer would be required to enter a positive adjustment for the standard deduction in computing the AMT.

The exemption amount deducted for income tax purposes is not allowed in computing AMT. Therefore, taxpayers must enter a positive AMT adjustment for the exemption amount claimed in computing the income tax. A separate exemption (discussed below) is allowed for AMT purposes. To allow both the income tax exemption amount and the AMT exemption amount would result in extra benefits for taxpayers.

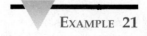

EXAMPLE 21

Eli, who is single, has no dependents and does not itemize deductions. He earned a salary of $106,250 in 1994. Based on this information, Eli's taxable income for 1994 is $100,000 ($106,250 – $3,800 standard deduction – $2,450 exemption). ▼

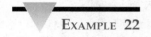

EXAMPLE 22

Assume the same facts as in Example 21. In addition, assume Eli's tax preferences for the year totaled $150,000. Eli's AMTI is $256,250 ($100,000 taxable income + $3,800 adjustment for standard deduction + $2,450 adjustment for exemption + $150,000 tax preferences). ▼

AMT PREFERENCES

Percentage Depletion

Congress originally enacted the percentage depletion rules to provide taxpayers with incentives to invest in the development of specified natural resources. Percentage depletion is computed by multiplying a rate specified in the Code times the gross income from the property (refer to Chapter 8). The percentage rate is based on the type of mineral involved. The basis of the property is reduced by the amount of percentage depletion taken until the basis reaches zero. However, once the basis of the property reaches zero, taxpayers are allowed to continue taking percentage depletion deductions. Thus, over the life of the property, depletion deductions may greatly exceed the cost of the property.

The percentage depletion preference is equal to the excess of the regular tax deduction for percentage depletion over the adjusted basis of the property at the end of the taxable year. Basis is determined without regard to the depletion deduction for the taxable year. This preference item is figured separately for each piece of property for which the taxpayer is claiming depletion.

EXAMPLE 23

Kim owns a mineral property that qualifies for a 22% depletion rate. The basis of the property at the beginning of the year was $10,000. Gross income from the property for the year was $100,000. For regular tax purposes, Kim's percentage depletion deduction (assume it is not limited by taxable income from the property) is $22,000. For AMT purposes, Kim has a tax preference of $12,000 ($22,000 − $10,000). ▼

Intangible Drilling Costs

In computing the income tax, taxpayers are allowed to deduct certain intangible drilling and development costs in the year incurred, although such costs are normally capital in nature. The deduction is allowed for costs incurred in connection with oil and gas wells and geothermal wells.

For AMT purposes, excess **intangible drilling costs (IDC)** for the year are treated as a preference. The preference for excess IDC is computed as follows:

IDC expensed in the year incurred

Minus: Deduction if IDC were capitalized and amortized over 10 years

Equals: Excess of IDC expense over amortization

Minus: 65% of net oil and gas income

Equals: Tax preference item

EXAMPLE 24

Ben, who incurred IDC of $50,000 during the year, elected to expense that amount. His net oil and gas income for the year was $60,000. Ben's tax preference for IDC is $6,000 [($50,000 IDC − $5,000 amortization) − (65% × $60,000 income)]. ▼

Interest on Private Activity Bonds

Income from private activity bonds is not included in taxable income, and expenses related to carrying such bonds are not deductible for income tax purposes. However, interest on private activity bonds is included as a preference in computing AMTI. Therefore, expenses incurred in carrying the bonds are offset against the interest income in computing AMTI.

Depreciation

For real property and leased personal property placed in service before 1987, there is an AMT preference for the excess of accelerated depreciation over straight-line depreciation. However, examination of the cost recovery tables for pre-1987 real property (refer to Chapter 8) reveals that from the eighth year on, accelerated depreciation will not exceed straight-line depreciation. Consequently, after 1992 taxpayers will no longer have preferences attributable to pre-1987 real property.

Accelerated depreciation on pre-1987 leased personal property was computed using specified ACRS percentages (refer to Table 8–1, Chapter 8). AMT depreciation was based on the straight-line method, which was computed using the half-year convention, no salvage value, and a longer recovery period.[15] As a result, in the early years of the life of the asset, the cost recovery allowance used in computing income tax was greater than the straight-line depreciation deduction allowed in computing AMT. The excess depreciation was treated as a tax preference item.

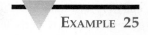

EXAMPLE 25

Paul acquired personal property on January 1, 1986, at a cost of $30,000. The property, which was placed in service as leased personal property on January 1, was 10-year ACRS property. Paul's 1986 depreciation deduction for regular tax purposes was $2,400 ($30,000 cost × 8% rate from Table 8–1). For AMT purposes, the asset was depreciated over the AMT life of 15 years using the straight-line method with the half-year convention. Thus, AMT depreciation for 1986 was $1,000 [($30,000 ÷ 15) × ½ year convention]. Paul's tax preference for 1986 was $1,400 ($2,400 − $1,000). ACRS depreciation for 1994 is $2,700 ($30,000 × 9% ACRS rate), and straight-line depreciation is $2,000 ($30,000 ÷ 15). ▼

The preference item for excess depreciation on leased personal property is figured separately for each piece of property. No preference is reported in the year the taxpayer disposes of the property.

Amortization of Certified Pollution Control Facilities

Under § 169 of the Code, for income tax purposes, taxpayers may elect to amortize the cost of certified pollution control facilities over a period of 60 months. For

---

TAX IN THE NEWS

A PLAN TO DONATE STOCK AND STILL BENEFIT FROM FUTURE APPRECIATION

For several years prior to 1993, taxpayers were required to report an AMT preference equal to the excess of fair market value over the adjusted basis of appreciated long-term capital gain property contributed to a charity. The preference was repealed for contributions of tangible personal property made after June 30, 1992, and contributions of other property made after December 31, 1992. This makes it more attractive to give appreciated assets to charity.

Consider the following scenario: Taxpayer holds stock with a basis of $10,000 and a fair market value of $50,000. Taxpayer needs a large income tax deduction for 1993, which will result if Taxpayer gives the stock to charity. However, Taxpayer thinks the stock is a good investment and would like to hold it for future appreciation.

The *Wall Street Journal* reported a plan to address Taxpayer's problem. Under this plan, Taxpayer would donate the existing stock to charity and immediately replace it with an equal number of shares of the same company's stock. Discuss the merits of this plan.

SOURCE: Information from "Tax Report: A Special Summary and Forecast of Federal and State Tax Developments," *Wall Street Journal*, December 22, 1993, p. A1.

---

[15] The specified lives for AMT purposes are 5 years for 3-year property, 8 years for 5-year property, 15 years for 10-year property, and 22 years for 15-year property.

pre-1987 facilities, excess amortization is a tax preference item. Excess amortization equals the amortization deducted by the taxpayer minus the amount that would have been deducted if the asset had been depreciated over its longer useful life or cost recovery period.

OTHER COMPONENTS OF THE AMT FORMULA

Alternative minimum taxable income is a somewhat confusing term. For income tax purposes, once taxable income has been computed, it is possible to compute the income tax. But even after AMTI has been computed, the AMT cannot be computed until the *AMT base* has been determined. To arrive at the AMT base, the AMT exemption must be deducted. This procedure is shown in the AMT formula in Figure 12–3.

Exemption Amount

The initial exemption amount is $45,000 for married taxpayers filing joint returns, $33,750 for single taxpayers, and $22,500 for married taxpayers filing separate returns. However, the exemption is phased out at a rate of 25 cents on the dollar when AMTI exceeds the levels listed below:

- $112,500 for single taxpayers.
- $150,000 for married taxpayers filing jointly.
- $75,000 for married taxpayers filing separately.

The following example explains the calculation of the phase-out of the AMT exemption.

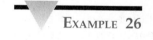

EXAMPLE 26   Grace, who is single, has AMTI of $192,500 for the year. Her $33,750 initial exemption amount is reduced by $20,000 [($192,500 – $112,500) × 25% phase-out rate]. Grace's AMT exemption is $13,750 ($33,750 exemption – $20,000 reduction). ▼

▼ **FIGURE 12–3**
Alternative Minimum Tax
Formula

> Regular taxable income
>
> **Plus or minus:** Adjustments
>
> **Equals:** Taxable income after AMT adjustments
>
> **Plus:** Tax preferences
>
> **Equals:** Alternative minimum taxable income
>
> **Minus:** Exemption
>
> **Equals:** Alternative minimum tax base
>
> **Times:** 26% or 28% rate
>
> **Equals:** Tentative minimum tax before foreign tax credit
>
> **Minus:** Alternative minimum tax foreign tax credit
>
> **Equals:** Tentative minimum tax
>
> **Minus:** Regular tax liability*
>
> **Equals:** Alternative minimum tax (if amount is positive)
>
> *This is the regular tax liability for the year reduced by any allowable foreign tax credit. It does not include any tax on lump-sum distributions from pension plans, any investment tax credit recapture, or any low-income credit recapture. See § 55(c).

The following table shows the beginning and end of the AMT exemption phase-out range for each filing status.

Status	Exemption	Phase-out Begins at	Phase-out Ends at
Married, joint	$45,000	$150,000	$330,000
Single or head of household	33,750	112,500	247,500
Married, separate	22,500	75,000	165,000

AMT Rate Schedule

A graduated, two-tier AMT rate schedule applies to noncorporate taxpayers for tax years beginning after 1992. A 26 percent rate applies to the first $175,000 of the AMT base ($87,500 for married, filing separately), and a 28 percent rate applies to the AMT base in excess of $175,000 ($87,500 for married, filing separately).

Regular Tax Liability

The AMT is equal to the tentative minimum tax minus the *regular tax liability*. In most cases, the regular tax liability is equal to the amount of tax from the Tax Table or Tax Rate Schedules decreased by any foreign tax credit allowable for income tax purposes. Because only the foreign tax credit is allowed as a reduction of the tentative minimum tax, taxpayers who pay AMT lose the benefit of all other nonrefundable credits.

In an AMT year, the taxpayer's total tax liability is equal to the tentative minimum tax (refer to Figure 12–3). The tentative minimum tax consists of two components: the regular tax liability and the AMT. The disallowance of credits does not affect a taxpayer's total liability in an AMT year. However, it does decrease the amount of the AMT and, as a consequence, reduces the minimum tax credit available to be carried forward. Thus, for AMT purposes, the government denies all the credits (except the foreign tax credit) that apply in computing the income tax liability. Furthermore, the foreign tax credit cannot offset more than 90 percent of the tentative minimum tax.

It is also possible that taxpayers who have adjustments and preferences but *do not pay* AMT will lose the benefit of some or all of their nonrefundable credits. This result occurs because a taxpayer may claim nonrefundable credits only to the extent that his or her regular tax liability exceeds the tentative minimum tax.

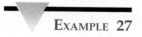

EXAMPLE 27

Vern has total nonrefundable credits of $10,000, regular tax liability of $33,000, and tentative minimum tax of $25,000. He can claim only $8,000 of the nonrefundable credits in the current year. The disallowed $2,000 credit is lost unless a carryover provision applies.

5 **LEARNING OBJECTIVE**
Apply the formula for computing the alternative minimum tax.

ILLUSTRATION OF THE AMT COMPUTATION

The computation of the AMT is illustrated in the following example.

EXAMPLE 28

Hans, who is single, had taxable income for 1994 as follows:

Salary		$ 92,000
Interest		8,000
Adjusted gross income		$100,000
Less itemized deductions:		
Medical expenses ($17,500 – 7.5% of $100,000 AGI)[a]	$10,000	
State income taxes	4,000	
Interest[b]		
Home mortgage (for qualified housing)	20,000*	
Investment interest	3,300*	
Contributions (cash)	5,000*	
Casualty losses ($14,000 – 10% of $100,000 AGI)	4,000*	(46,300)
		$ 53,700
Less exemption		(2,450)
Taxable income		$ 51,250

[a]Assume ATAGI is $100,000, the same amount as AGI. Total medical expenses were $17,500, reduced by 7.5% of AGI, resulting in an itemized deduction of $10,000. However, for AMT purposes, the reduction is 10%, which leaves an AMT itemized deduction of $7,500 ($17,500 – 10% of $100,000 AGI). Therefore, an adjustment of $2,500 ($10,000 – $7,500) is required for medical expenses disallowed for AMT purposes.

[b]In this illustration, all interest is deductible in computing AMTI. Qualified housing interest is deductible. Investment interest ($3,300) is deductible to the extent of net investment income included in the minimum tax base. For this purpose, the $8,000 of interest income is treated as net investment income.

Deductions marked by an asterisk are allowed as *alternative tax itemized deductions,* and AMT adjustments are required for the other itemized deductions. Thus, adjustments are required for state income taxes and for medical expenses to the extent the medical expenses deductible for income tax purposes are not deductible in computing AMT (see note a above). In addition to the items that affected taxable income, Hans had $35,000 interest on private activity bonds (an exclusion preference). AMTI is computed as follows:

Taxable income		$ 51,250
Plus:	Adjustments	
	State income taxes	4,000
	Medical expenses (see note a above)	2,500
	Personal exemption	2,450
Plus:	Tax preference (interest on private activity bonds)	35,000
Equals:	AMTI	$ 95,200
Minus:	AMT exemption	30,000
Equals:	Minimum tax base	$ 65,200
Times:	AMT rate	×26%
		$ 16,952
Minus:	Regular tax on taxable income	(11,393)
Equals:	AMT	$ 5,559

AMT CREDIT

As discussed previously, timing differences give rise to adjustments to the minimum tax base. In later years, the timing differences reverse, as was illustrated in several of the preceding examples. To provide equity for the taxpayer when timing differences reverse, the regular tax liability may be reduced by a tax credit for prior years' minimum tax liability attributable to timing differences. The **alternative minimum tax credit** may be carried over indefinitely. Therefore, there is no need to keep track of when the minimum tax credit arose.

▼ **Example 29**

Assume the same facts as in Example 3. Also assume that in 1993, Bob paid AMT as a result of the $20,000 positive adjustment arising from the circulation expenditures. In 1994, $10,000 of the timing difference reverses, resulting in regular taxable income that is $10,000 greater than AMTI. Because Bob has already paid AMT as a result of the write-off of circulation expenditures, he is allowed an AMT credit in 1994. ▼

The AMT credit is applicable only for the AMT that results from timing differences. It is not available in connection with **exclusions,** which include the following:

- The standard deduction.
- Personal exemptions.
- Medical expenses, to the extent deductible for income tax purposes but not deductible in computing AMT.
- Other itemized deductions not allowable for AMT purposes, including miscellaneous itemized deductions, taxes, and interest expense.
- Excess percentage depletion.
- Tax-exempt interest on specified private activity bonds.

▼ **Example 30**

Don, who is single, has zero taxable income for 1994. He also has positive timing adjustments of $300,000 and exclusions of $100,000. His AMTI is $400,000 because his AMT exemption is phased out completely due to the level of AMTI. Don's tentative AMT is $108,500 [($175,000 × 26% AMT rate) + ($225,000 × 28% rate)]. ▼

To determine the amount of AMT credit to carry over, the AMT must be recomputed reflecting only the exclusions and the AMT exemption amount.

▼ **Example 31**

Assume the same facts as in the previous example. If there had been no positive timing adjustments for the year, Don's tentative AMT would have been $17,225 [($100,000 exclusions − $33,750 exemption) × 26% AMT rate]. Don may carry over an AMT credit of $91,275 ($108,500 AMT − $17,225 related to exclusions). ▼

CORPORATE ALTERNATIVE MINIMUM TAX

The AMT applicable to corporations is similar to that applicable to noncorporate taxpayers. However, there are several important differences:

- The corporate AMT rate is 20 percent versus a top rate of 28 percent for noncorporate taxpayers.
- The AMT exemption for corporations is $40,000 reduced by 25 percent of the amount by which AMTI exceeds $150,000.
- Tax preferences applicable to noncorporate taxpayers are also applicable to corporate taxpayers, but some adjustments differ (see below).

▼ FIGURE 12–4
AMT Formula for Corporations

Taxable income
Plus: Income tax NOL deduction
Plus or minus: AMT adjustments
Plus: Tax preferences
Equals: AMTI before ATNOLD
Minus: ATNOLD (limited to 90% of AMTI before ATNOLD)
Equals: AMTI
Minus: Exemption
Equals: AMT base
Times: 20% rate
Equals: AMT before AMT foreign tax credit
Minus: AMT foreign tax credit (limited to 90% of AMT before AMT foreign tax credit)
Equals: Tentative minimum tax
Minus: Regular tax liability before credits minus regular foreign tax credit
Equals: AMT if positive

Although there are computational differences, the corporate AMT and the noncorporate AMT have the identical objective: to force taxpayers who are more profitable than their taxable income reflects to pay additional tax. The formula for determining the corporate AMT appears in Figure 12–4.

AMT ADJUSTMENTS

Adjustments Applicable to Individuals and Corporations

The following adjustments that were discussed in connection with the individual AMT also apply to the corporate AMT:

- Excess of ACRS over ADS depreciation on real and personal property placed in service after 1986.
- Mining and exploration expenditures (AMT requires amortization over 10 years versus immediate expensing allowed for income tax purposes).
- Income on long-term contracts (AMT requires percentage of completion method; completed contract method is allowed in limited circumstances for income tax purposes).
- Pollution control facilities placed in service after 1986 (AMT requires ADS depreciation over the asset's ADR life; 60-month amortization is allowed for income tax purposes).
- Dispositions of assets (if gain or loss for AMT purposes differs from gain or loss for income tax purposes).
- Allowable ATNOLD (which cannot exceed 90 percent of AMTI before deduction for ATNOLD).

Adjustments Applicable Only to Corporations

Three AMT adjustments are applicable only to corporations:

- The Merchant Marine capital construction fund adjustment.
- The adjustment for special deductions allowed to Blue Cross/Blue Shield organizations.
- The adjusted current earnings (ACE) adjustment.

The first two adjustments apply to specific types of corporations and are not discussed in the chapter. On the other hand, the **ACE adjustment** generally applies to all corporations[16] and is expected to have a significant impact on both tax and financial accounting.

ACE Adjustment.   Corporations are subject to an AMT adjustment equal to 75 percent of the excess of ACE over AMTI before the ACE adjustment. Historically, the government has not required conformity between tax accounting and financial accounting. For many years, the only *direct* conformity requirement was that a corporation that used the LIFO method for tax accounting also had to use LIFO for financial accounting.[17] Through the ACE adjustment, Congress is *indirectly* imposing a conformity requirement on corporations. While a corporation may still choose to use different methods for tax and financial accounting purposes, it may no longer be able to do so without incurring AMT as a result of the ACE adjustment. Thus, a corporation may incur AMT not only because of specifically targeted adjustments and preferences, but also as a result of any methods that cause ACE to exceed AMTI before the ACE adjustment.

The ACE adjustment can be either a positive or a negative amount. AMTI is increased by 75 percent of the excess of ACE over unadjusted AMTI. Or AMTI is reduced by 75 percent of the excess of unadjusted AMTI over ACE. The negative adjustment is limited to the aggregate of the positive adjustments under ACE for prior years, reduced by the previously claimed negative adjustments. See Concept Summary 12–1. Thus, the ordering of the timing differences is crucial because any lost negative adjustment is permanent. Unadjusted AMTI is AMTI without the ACE adjustment or the ATNOLD.[18]

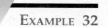

EXAMPLE 32

A calendar year corporation has the following data:

	1993	1994	1995
Pre-adjusted AMTI	$3,000	$3,000	$3,100
Adjusted current earnings	4,000	3,000	2,000

In 1993, because ACE exceeds unadjusted AMTI by $1,000, $750 (75% × $1,000) is included as a positive adjustment to AMTI. No adjustment is necessary for 1994. As unadjusted AMTI exceeds ACE by $1,100 in 1995, there is a potential negative adjustment to AMTI of $825. Since the total increases to AMTI for prior years equal $750 and there are no negative adjustments, only $750 of the potential negative adjustment reduces AMTI for 1995. Further, $75 of the negative amount is lost forever. Prior book income adjustments are ignored for limitation purposes. ▼

ACE should not be confused with current earnings and profits. Although many items are treated in the same manner, certain variations exist. For example, Federal income taxes, deductible in computing earnings and profits, are not deductible in determining ACE.

---

[16] The ACE adjustment does not apply to S corporations, regulated investment companies, real estate investment trusts, or REMICs. § 56(g)(6).

[17] § 472(c).
[18] §§ 56(g)(1) and (2).

CONCEPT SUMMARY 12–1

Determining the ACE Adjustment*

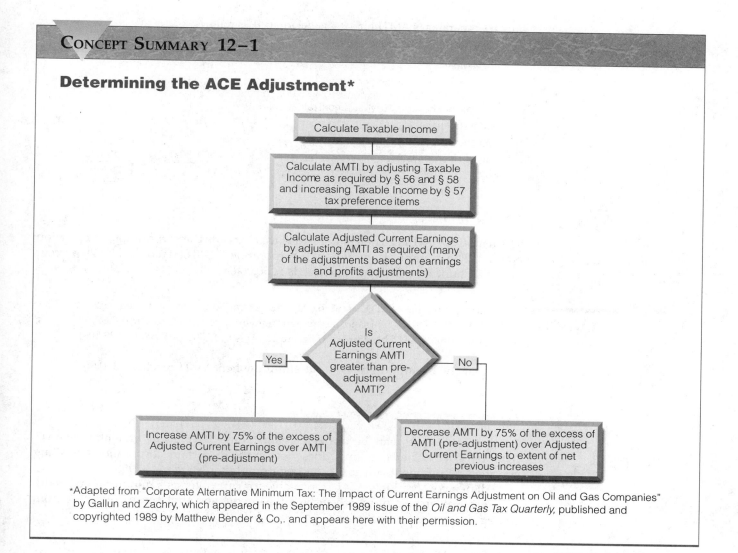

*Adapted from "Corporate Alternative Minimum Tax: The Impact of Current Earnings Adjustment on Oil and Gas Companies" by Gallun and Zachry, which appeared in the September 1989 issue of the *Oil and Gas Tax Quarterly*, published and copyrighted 1989 by Matthew Bender & Co,. and appears here with their permission.

The starting point for computing ACE is AMTI, which is defined as regular taxable income after AMT adjustments (other than the ATNOLD and ACE adjustments) and tax preferences. The resulting figure is adjusted for several items in order to arrive at ACE.

TAX PREFERENCES

AMTI includes designated tax preference items. In some cases, this has the effect of subjecting nontaxable income to the AMT. Tax preference items that apply to individuals also apply to corporations.

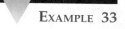

EXAMPLE 33

The following information applies to Brown Corporation (a calendar year taxpayer) for 1994:

Taxable income	$200,000
Mining exploration costs	50,000
Percentage depletion claimed (the property has a zero adjusted basis)	70,000
Interest on City of Elmira (Michigan) private activity bonds	30,000

Brown Corporation's AMTI for 1994 is determined as follows:

Taxable income		$200,000
Adjustments:		
Excess mining exploration costs [$50,000 (amount expensed) – $5,000 (amount allowed over a 10-year amortization period)]		45,000
Tax preferences:		
Excess depletion	$70,000	
Interest on private activity bonds	30,000	100,000
AMTI		$345,000

EXEMPTION

The tentative AMT is 20 percent of AMTI that exceeds the corporation's exemption amount. The exemption amount for a corporation is $40,000 reduced by 25 percent of the amount by which AMTI exceeds $150,000.

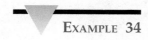

EXAMPLE 34

Blue Corporation has AMTI of $180,000. The exemption amount is reduced by $7,500 [25% × ($180,000 – $150,000)], and the amount remaining is $32,500 ($40,000 – $7,500). Thus, Blue Corporation's AMT base (refer to Figure 12–4) is $147,500 ($180,000 – $32,500). ▼

Note that the exemption phases out entirely when AMTI reaches $310,000.

OTHER ASPECTS OF THE AMT

Foreign tax credits can be applied against only 90 percent of tentative AMT liability. The 90 percent limit does not apply to certain corporations meeting specified requirements for tax years beginning after March 31, 1990.

All of a corporation's AMT is available for carryover as a minimum tax credit. This is so regardless of whether the adjustments and preferences originate from timing differences or exclusions.

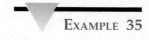

EXAMPLE 35

In Example 33, the AMTI exceeds $310,000, so no exemption is allowed. The tentative minimum tax is $69,000 (20% of $345,000). The regular tax liability is $61,250, and the AMT liability is $7,750 ($69,000 – $61,250). The amount of the minimum tax credit carryover is $7,750, which is all of the current year's AMT. ▼

TAX PLANNING
CONSIDERATIONS

AVOIDING PREFERENCES AND ADJUSTMENTS

Several strategies and elections are available to help taxpayers avoid having preferences and adjustments.

- A taxpayer who is in danger of incurring AMT liability should not invest in tax-exempt private activity bonds unless doing so makes good investment sense. Any AMT triggered by interest on private activity bonds reduces the yield on an investment in the bonds. Other tax-exempt bonds or taxable corporate bonds might yield a better after-tax return.
- A taxpayer may elect to expense certain costs in the year incurred or to capitalize and amortize the costs over some specified period. The decision should be based on the present discounted value of after-tax cash flows

under the available alternatives. Costs subject to elective treatment include circulation expenditures, mining exploration and development costs, and research and experimental expenditures.

CONTROLLING THE TIMING OF PREFERENCES AND ADJUSTMENTS

The AMT exemption often keeps items of tax preference from being subject to the AMT. To use the AMT exemption effectively, taxpayers should avoid bunching preferences and positive adjustments in any one year. To avoid this bunching, taxpayers should attempt to control the timing of such items when possible.

TAKING ADVANTAGE OF THE AMT/REGULAR TAX RATE DIFFERENTIAL

A taxpayer who cannot avoid triggering the AMT in a given year can usually save taxes by taking advantage of the rate differential between the AMT and the regular tax.

EXAMPLE 36

Peter, who expects to be in the 31% tax bracket in 1995, is subject to the AMT in 1994. He is considering the sale of a parcel of land at a gain of $100,000. If he sells the land in 1995, he will have to pay tax of $28,000 ($100,000 gain × 28% alternative capital gains rate). However, if he sells the land in 1994, he will pay tax of $26,000 ($100,000 gain × 26% AMT rate). Thus, accelerating the sale into 1994 will save Peter $2,000 in tax. ▼

EXAMPLE 37

Cora, who expects to be in the 39.6% tax bracket in 1995, is subject to the AMT in 1994. She is going to contribute $10,000 in cash to her alma mater, State University. If Cora makes the contribution in 1995, she will save tax of $3,960 ($10,000 contribution × 39.6% regular tax rate). However, if she makes the contribution in 1994, she will save tax of $2,600 ($10,000 contribution × 26% AMT rate). Thus, deferring the contribution until 1995 will save Cora $1,360 in tax. ▼

This deferral/acceleration strategy should be considered for any income or expenses where the taxpayer can control the timing. This strategy applies to corporations as well as to individuals.

KEY TERMS

ACE adjustment, 12–26

Alternative minimum tax (AMT),   12–2

Alternative minimum tax credit,   12–24

Alternative tax adjusted gross income (ATAGI), 12–5

AMT adjustments, 12–3

Circulation expenditures,   12–4

Exclusions,   12–24

Incentive stock options (ISOs), 12–12

Intangible drilling costs (IDC),   12–19

Tax preferences, 12–3

PROBLEM
MATERIALS

DISCUSSION QUESTIONS

1. Two elements in the AMT formula are tax preferences and AMT adjustments. Explain how these elements differ.

2. Discuss the ATAGI computation and give an example of how it could result in an AMT adjustment.

3. Adjustments considered in computing the AMT can be either positive or negative. Give an example of an AMT adjustment, including amounts. Explain the rationale behind the concept of positive and negative adjustments.

4. Why is it necessary for individual taxpayers to compute taxable income on Form 1040 *before* computing AMTI on Form 6251?

5. Bob incurred $36,000 of circulation expenditures in 1993 and expensed that amount. Compute Bob's AMT adjustments for 1993, 1994, and 1995 and indicate whether the adjustments are positive or negative.

6. During the year, Fran earned $18,000 interest on private activity bonds and incurred interest expense of $7,000 in connection with the bonds. How will this affect Fran's taxable income? AMT?

7. Tom, who owns and operates a sole proprietorship, acquired machinery and placed it in service in February 1994. If Tom has to pay AMT in 1994, he will be required to make an AMT adjustment for depreciation on the machinery. True or false? Explain.

8. How can an individual taxpayer avoid having an AMT adjustment for research and experimental expenditures?

9. Passive losses are not deductible in computing either taxable income or AMTI. Therefore, no adjustment for passive losses is required for AMT purposes. True or false? Explain.

10. Certain taxpayers have the option of using either the percentage of completion method or the completed contract method for reporting profit on long-term contracts. What impact could the AMT have on this decision?

11. Megan, a corporate executive, plans to exercise an incentive stock option granted by her employer to purchase 100 shares of the corporation's stock for an option price of $20 per share. The stock is currently selling for $65 per share. Explain the possible consequences of this action on Megan's regular tax and AMT.

12. Ramon acquired stock under an incentive stock option plan in 1991. All conditions of employment were satisfied in 1993, and the stock became freely transferable. Ramon sold the stock in 1994. Discuss the possible effects on taxable income and AMTI in each of the three years (1991, 1993, 1994).

13. Could computation of the AMT ever require an adjustment for the standard deduction? Explain.

14. Abby, who had AGI of $100,000 and ATAGI of $130,000, incurred medical expenses of $17,000 during the year. Compute her medical expense deductions for income tax and AMT purposes. How much is Abby's AMT adjustment, and is it positive or negative?

15. The following itemized deductions are allowed for income tax purposes: medical expenses, state and local income taxes, real estate taxes, personal property taxes, home mortgage interest, investment interest, charitable contributions of cash, charitable contributions of long-term capital gain property, casualty losses, moving expenses, unreimbursed employee business expenses, and gambling losses. Which of these itemized deductions can result in an AMT adjustment?

16. In computing the alternative tax itemized deduction for interest, it is possible that some interest allowed as an itemized deduction for income tax purposes will not be allowed. Explain.

17. What is the purpose of the AMT credit? Briefly describe how the credit is computed.

✗ 18. Discuss tax planning strategies for minimizing the AMT.

19. Lee, an equipment dealer who will be subject to the AMT in 1994, has an opportunity to make a large sale of equipment in December 1994 or January 1995. Discuss tax planning strategies Lee should consider in connection with the sale.

20. Discuss the similarities and differences between the individual AMT and the corporate AMT.

21. Some observers believe the ACE adjustment will cause corporations to change some of the methods they use for financial accounting and tax accounting purposes. Comment.

22. Is it ever advisable for a taxpayer to accelerate income into an AMT year? Explain and give an example of how this acceleration might be accomplished.

23. Is it ever advisable for a taxpayer to defer deductions from an AMT year into a non-AMT year where the regular income tax applies? Explain and give an example of how such a deferral might be accomplished.

PROBLEMS

24. Keri's AGI is $40,000, and her ATAGI is $100,000. She contributed $55,000 to a public charity. What is Keri's charitable contribution deduction for income tax purposes? For AMT purposes?

25. Lance is a landlord who owns two apartment buildings. He acquired Longwood Acres on February 21, 1986, for $300,000, with $60,000 of the cost allocated to the land. He acquired Colony Square on April 5, 1990, for $800,000, and $200,000 of the cost was allocated to land. Neither apartment complex is low-income housing. Lance elected to write off the cost of each building as fast as possible. What is the effect of depreciation (cost recovery) on Lance's AMTI for 1994?

26. Jim owns and operates Jimco, a sole proprietorship. On January 3, Jimco acquired a warehouse for $200,000 and allocated $40,000 of the cost to land. Jim claimed depreciation at the MACRS rate of 3.042%. The alternative depreciation system (ADS) rate for the first recovery year is 2.396%. Compute Jim's AMT adjustment for depreciation with respect to the warehouse, and indicate whether the adjustment is positive or negative.

27. In January 1994, Helen acquired and placed in service a residential building costing $320,000 and allocated $40,000 of the cost to land. For regular tax purposes, she depreciated the building over a 27.5-year period. Compute Helen's AMT adjustment for depreciation with respect to the building, and indicate whether the adjustment is positive or negative.

28. Vera sold an apartment building in October 1993 for $210,000. She had acquired the building in April 1990 for $200,000 and had deducted MACRS depreciation of $25,453 ($5,152 in 1990, $7,272 in 1991, $7,272 in 1992, and $5,757 in 1993). What adjustments were required in computing Vera's AMTI in each year (1990, 1991, 1992, and 1993)?

29. In 1994, Gary incurred $150,000 of mining and exploration expenditures. He elects to deduct the expenditures as quickly as the tax law allows for income tax purposes.
    a. How will Gary's treatment of mining and exploration expenditures affect his income tax and AMT computations for 1994?
    b. How can Gary avoid having AMT adjustments related to the mining and exploration expenditures?
    c. What factors should Gary consider in deciding whether to deduct the expenditures in the year incurred?

30. Freda acquired a passive activity in 1994. Gross income from operations of the activity was $150,000. Operating expenses, not including depreciation, were $135,000. Income tax depreciation of $37,500 was computed under MACRS (post-1986 ACRS). AMT depreciation, computed under ADS, was $24,000. Compute Freda's passive loss for income tax purposes and for AMT purposes.

31. In 1992, Diego exercised an incentive stock option, acquiring 1,000 shares of stock at an option price of $65 per share. The fair market value of the stock at the date of exercise was $92 per share. In 1994, the rights in the stock become freely transferable and are not subject to a substantial risk of forfeiture. How do these transactions affect Diego's AMTI in 1992 and 1994?

32. Otis is a vice president of Greene Corporation. He acquired 1,000 shares of Greene stock in 1992 under the corporation's incentive stock option plan for an option price of $43 per share. At the date of exercise, the fair market value of the stock was $65 per share. The stock became freely transferable in 1993, and Otis sold the 1,000 shares for $69 per share in 1994. How do these transactions affect Otis's AMTI in 1992, 1993, and 1994?

33. In 1991, Lori exercised an incentive stock option that had been granted by her employer, Black Corporation. Lori acquired 100 shares of Black stock for the option price of $175 per share. The rights in the stock become freely transferable and not subject to a substantial risk of forfeiture in 1993. The fair market value of the stock at the date of exercise was $210 per share. Lori sells the stock for $320 per share in 1994. What is the amount of her AMT adjustment in 1994?

34. Vito owns and operates a news agency (as a sole proprietorship). During 1993, he incurred expenses of $60,000 to increase circulation of newspapers and magazines that his agency distributes. For income tax purposes, he elected to expense the $60,000 in 1993. In addition, he incurred $30,000 in circulation expenditures in 1994 and again elected expense treatment. What AMT adjustments will be required in 1993 and 1994 as a result of the circulation expenditures?

35. Ken, who is single and has no dependents, had AGI of $100,000 and ATAGI of $110,000 in 1994. Ken's potential itemized deductions were as follows:

Medical expenses (before percentage limitation)	$15,000
State income taxes	3,000
Real estate taxes	7,000
Mortgage (qualified housing and residence) interest	9,000
Cash contributions to various charities	4,000
Unreimbursed employee expenses (before percentage limitation)	4,300

What is the amount of Ken's AMT adjustment for itemized deductions for 1994?

36. During the current year, Yoon earned $10,000 in dividends on corporate stock and incurred $13,000 of investment interest expense related to his stock holdings. Yoon also earned $5,000 interest on private activity bonds during the year and incurred interest expense of $3,500 in connection with the bonds. How much investment interest expense can Yoon deduct for income tax and AMT purposes for the year?

37. Tom, who is single, owns a personal residence in the city. He also owns a cabin near a ski resort in the mountains. He uses the cabin as a vacation home. In February 1993, he borrowed $60,000 on a home equity loan and used the proceeds to pay off credit card obligations and other debt. During 1994, he paid the following amounts of interest:

On his personal residence	$12,000
On the cabin	4,800
On the home equity loan	5,000
On credit card obligations	1,200

What amount, if any, must Tom recognize as an AMT adjustment in 1994?

38. Walter and Edith Benton, who are married with two dependents, had AGI of $110,000 in 1994. Their AGI included net investment income of $10,000 and gambling income of

$2,500. They incurred the following expenses during the year, all of which resulted in itemized deductions for income tax purposes:

Medical expenses (before 7.5%-of-AGI floor)	$9,500
State income taxes	2,800
Personal property tax	900
Real estate tax	9,100
Interest on personal residence	8,600
Interest on home equity loan (proceeds were used to buy a new fishing boat)	1,800
Investment interest expense	2,600
Charitable contribution (cash)	4,200
Unreimbursed employee expenses (before 2%-of-AGI floor)	3,800

What is the amount of the Bentons' AMT adjustment for itemized deductions in 1994, and is it positive or negative?

39. Assume the same facts as in the preceding problem and that the Bentons also earned interest of $5,000 on private activity bonds. They borrowed the money to buy these bonds and paid interest of $3,900 on the loan.

40. Bill, who is single with no dependents, had AGI of $100,000 and ATAGI of $120,000 in 1994. His AGI included net investment income of $14,000 and gambling income of $1,100. Bill incurred the following expenses during the year, all of which resulted in itemized deductions for income tax purposes:

Medical expenses (before 7.5%-of-AGI floor)	$11,000
State income taxes	3,200
Personal property tax	1,000
Real estate tax	8,400
Interest on personal residence	12,200
Interest on vacation home (never rented to others)	3,800
Interest on home equity loan (proceeds were used to buy a new automobile)	2,700
Investment interest expense	3,300
Charitable contribution	5,000
Casualty loss (after $100 floor, before 10%-of-AGI floor)	13,000
Unreimbursed employee expenses (before 2%-of-AGI floor)	2,400
Gambling losses	900

What is the amount of Bill's AMT adjustment for itemized deductions in 1994, and is it positive or negative?

41. Peggy, who is single and has no dependents, had taxable income of $102,000 and tax preferences of $72,500 in 1994. She did not itemize deductions for income tax purposes. Compute Peggy's AMT exemption for 1994.

42. Carl, who is single, has no dependents and does not itemize deductions. He had taxable income of $79,900 in 1994. His tax preferences totaled $90,000. What is Carl's AMTI for 1994?

43. Tara, who is single, has no dependents and does not itemize. She has the following items relative to her tax return for 1994:

Bargain element from the exercise of an incentive stock option (no restrictions apply to the stock)	$ 45,000
Accelerated depreciation on equipment acquired before 1987 (straight-line depreciation would have yielded $26,000)	41,000
Percentage depletion in excess of property's adjusted basis	50,000
Taxable income for regular tax purposes	121,000

a. Determine Tara's AMT adjustments and preferences for 1994.

b. Calculate the AMT (if any) for 1994.

44. Beth, who is single, has the following items for 1994:

Income

Salary	$105,000
Interest from bank	12,000
Interest on corporate bonds	7,000
Dividends	6,000
Short-term capital gain	8,000

Expenses

Unreimbursed employee business expenses (no meals or entertainment)	4,000
Total medical expenses	24,000
State income taxes	6,500
Real property taxes	6,800
Home mortgage (qualified housing) interest	7,200

Casualty loss on vacation home

Decline in value	20,000
Adjusted basis	70,000
Insurance proceeds	12,000
Tax preferences	116,000

Compute Beth's tax liability for 1994 before credits or prepayments.

45. Anna incurred an income tax net operating loss of $40,000 in 1994. She had positive AMT adjustments of $8,700 resulting from itemized deductions not allowed for AMT purposes. Her business deductions included tax preferences of $9,200. What is Anna's ATNOLD carryover to 1995?

46. The following itemized deductions were reported on Eve's Schedule A for 1994. On the basis of this information and the additional information in the notes below, determine the effect of Eve's itemized deductions on AMTI.

Medical expenses (before 7.5% floor)	$12,000
State income taxes	4,600
Real estate taxes	2,400
Mortgage (qualified housing) interest	5,400
Investment interest	2,100
Charitable contributions	8,600
Unreimbursed employee expenses (before 2% floor)	2,800
Gambling losses	1,500

Additional information:

a. Eve's AGI for 1994 was $100,000, and her ATAGI was $90,000.

b. Eve reported $800 of interest income and $1,500 of dividends for the year.

c. Eve earned $1,300 interest on private activity bonds.

47. Lynn is single and has no dependents. Based on the financial information presented below, compute Lynn's AMT for 1994.

Income:

Salary	$33,000
Taxable interest on corporate bonds	1,800
Dividend income	1,900
Business income	64,000

Expenditures:

Medical expenses	$12,000
State income taxes	6,000
Real estate taxes	8,500
Mortgage (qualified housing) interest	9,200
Investment interest	5,500
Cash contributions to various charities	2,900

Additional information:

a. The $64,000 business income is from Acme Office Supplies Company, a sole proprietorship Lynn owns and operates. Acme claimed MACRS depreciation of $3,175 on real property used in the business. ADS depreciation on the property would have been $2,500.

b. Lynn received interest of $27,000 on City of Columbus private activity bonds.

48. Hal and Wilma filed a joint return in 1994. Details are shown below. They have no dependents. Based on the items listed below and other relevant financial information presented in the subsequent notes, compute Hal and Wilma's AMT for the year.

Income:

Hal's salary	$60,000
Dividend income (jointly owned stock)	5,500
Wilma's business income	70,000

Expenditures:

State income taxes	$ 1,500
Real estate taxes	4,800
Mortgage interest	8,600
Investment interest	7,000
Charitable contributions	28,000

Additional information:

a. Wilma's business income was derived from a news agency (sole proprietorship) she owns and operates. During 1994, Wilma incurred expenses of $30,000 to increase circulation of newspapers and magazines her agency distributes. She elected to expense these items for income tax purposes.

b. Hal and Wilma earned $12,000 interest on State of New York bonds they acquired in 1988. These bonds are classified as private activity bonds.

49. Emily owns a coal mine that had a basis of $12,000 at the beginning of the year. The property qualifies for a 15% depletion rate. Gross income from the property was $140,000, and net income before the percentage depletion deduction was $60,000. What is Emily's tax preference for excess depletion?

50. Rita incurred and expensed intangible drilling costs (IDC) of $70,000 during 1994. Her net oil and gas income was $60,000. What is the amount of Rita's tax preference item for IDC?

51. Pat, who is single and has no dependents, had a salary of $90,000 in 1994. She had interest and dividend income of $6,000, gambling income of $4,000, and $40,000 interest income from private activity bonds. Pat presents the following additional information:

Medical expenses	$12,000
State income taxes	4,100
Real estate taxes	2,800
Mortgage interest on residence	3,100
Investment interest expense	1,800
Gambling losses	5,100

Compute Pat's tentative minimum tax for 1994 (rounded to the nearest dollar).

52. Jack, who is single with no dependents and does not itemize, provides you with the following information for 1994:

Short-term capital loss	$ 5,000
Long-term capital gain	25,000
Municipal bond interest received on private activity bonds acquired in 1989	9,000
Dividends from General Motors	1,500
Excess of FMV over cost of incentive stock options (the rights became freely transferable and not subject to a substantial risk of forfeiture in 1994)	35,000

What is the total amount of Jack's tax preference items and AMT adjustments for 1994?

53. Bonnie, who is single, had taxable income of $0 in 1994. She has positive timing adjustments of $200,000 and exclusion items of $100,000 for the year. What is the amount of Bonnie's AMT credit for carryover to 1995?

54. Rosa, who is single, had taxable income of $100,000 for 1994. She had positive AMT adjustments of $50,000, negative AMT adjustments of $15,000, and tax preference items of $57,500.
   a. Compute her AMTI.
   b. Compute Rosa's tentative minimum tax.

55. White Corporation, a calendar year taxpayer, has AMTI of $300,000 for 1994. What is White's tentative minimum tax for 1994?

56. Browne Corporation, a calendar year taxpayer, has AMTI (before the ACE adjustment) of $600,000 for 1994. Browne's ACE is $1,500,000. What is Browne's tentative minimum tax for 1994?

57. In each of the following independent situations, determine the tentative AMT:

	AMTI (Before the Exemption Amount)
Quincy Corporation	$150,000
Redland Corporation	160,000
Tanzen Corporation	320,000

58. Gray Corporation (a calendar year corporation) reports the following information for the years listed below:

	1993	1994	1995
Unadjusted AMTI	$3,000	$2,000	$5,000
Adjusted current earnings	4,000	3,000	2,000

Compute the ACE adjustment for each year.

59. For 1994, Brown Corporation (a calendar year taxpayer) had the following transactions:

Taxable income	$100,000
Depreciation for regular tax purposes on realty in excess of ADS (placed in service in 1988)	150,000
Excess amortization of certified pollution control facilities	10,000
Tax-exempt interest on municipal bonds (funds were used for nongovernmental purposes)	30,000
Percentage depletion in excess of the property's basis	60,000

   a. Determine Brown Corporation's AMTI for 1994.
   b. Determine the AMT base (refer to Figure 12–4).
   c. Determine the tentative minimum tax.
   d. What is the amount of the AMT?

CUMULATIVE PROBLEMS

60. Ned, who is single and age 46, has no dependents. In 1994, he earned a salary of $65,000 as vice president of ABC Manufacturing Corporation. Over the years, he has invested wisely and owns several thousand shares of stock and an apartment complex.

   In January 1994, Ned sold 500 shares of stock for a gain of $12,000. He had owned the stock for 11 months. Ned received dividends of $800 on the stock he retained.

   On May 20, 1991, Ned exercised his rights under ABC's incentive stock option plan. For an option price of $26,000, he acquired stock worth $53,000. The stock became freely transferable in 1994.

   On September 15, Ned contributed 100 shares of JKL Corporation stock to the American Red Cross. The basis of the stock was $32 per share, and its fair market value was $70 per share.

   Gross rent income from the apartment complex, which was acquired in 1982, was $150,000. Deductible expenses for the complex were $180,000. Ned actively participates in the management of the complex.

   Ned received $24,000 interest on private activity bonds in 1994. His itemized deductions were as follows: state and local income taxes, $4,100; property taxes on residence, $3,900; mortgage interest on home (qualified housing), $16,500.

   Compute Ned's lowest legal tax liability, before prepayments or credits, for 1994.

61. Ron, age 38, is single and has no dependents. He is independently wealthy as a result of having inherited sizable holdings in real estate and corporate stocks and bonds. Ron is a minister at First Methodist Church, but he accepts no salary from the church. However, he does reside in the church's parsonage free of charge. The rental value of the parsonage is $400 a month. The church also provides him a cash grocery allowance of $100 a week. Examination of Ron's financial records provides the following information for 1994:

   a. On January 16, 1994, Ron sold 2,000 shares of stock for a gain of $10,000. The stock was acquired four months ago.
   b. He received $85,000 of interest on private activity bonds in 1994.
   c. He received gross rent income of $145,000 from an apartment complex he owns and manages.
   d. Expenses related to the apartment complex, which he acquired in 1983, were $230,000.
   e. Ron's dividend and interest income (on a savings account) totaled $26,000.
   f. Ron had the following itemized deductions *from* AGI:

   • $3,000 fair market value of stock contributed to Methodist church (basis of stock was $1,000).

   • $3,000 interest on consumer purchases.

- $1,600 state and local taxes.

- $7,000 medical expenses (before 7.5% floor).

Compute Ron's tax, including AMT if applicable, before prepayments or credits, for 1994.

62. Robert M. and Jane R. Armstrong live at 1802 College Avenue, Carmel, IN 46302. They are married and file a joint return for 1993. The Armstrongs have two dependent children, Ellen J. and Sean M., who are 10-year-old twins. Ellen's Social Security number is 333–42–3368, and Sean's is 333–42–3369.

Robert (224–36–9987) is a factory foreman, and Jane (443–56–3421) is a computer systems analyst. The Armstrongs' W–2 forms for 1993 reflect the following information:

	Robert	**Jane**
Salary (Indiana Foundry, Inc.)	$45,000	
Salary (Carmel Computer Associates)		$70,000
Federal income tax withheld	6,600	13,600
Social Security wages	45,000	55,500
Social Security withheld	2,790	3,441
Medicare wages	45,000	70,000
Medicare tax withheld	653	1,015
State wages	45,000	70,000
State income tax withheld	1,350	2,100

In addition to their salaries, the Armstrongs had the following income items in 1993:

Interest income (Carmel Sanitation District Bonds)	$15,000
Interest income (Carmel National Bank)	800
Dividend income (Able Computer Corporation)	2,200
Gambling income	2,000

Jane inherited $200,000 from her grandfather in January and invested the money in the Carmel Sanitation District Bonds, which are private activity bonds.

The Armstrongs incurred the following expenses during 1993:

Medical expenses (doctor and hospital bills)	$15,000
Real property tax on personal residence	2,600
Mortgage interest on personal residence (reported on Form 1098)	3,600
Investment interest expense	1,200
Contributions	10,300
Gambling losses	1,500

On March 1, Robert and Jane contributed Ace stock to the Carmel Salvation Army, a public charity. They had acquired the stock on February 9, 1979, for $1,500. The stock was listed on the New York Stock Exchange at a value of $10,300 on the date of the contribution.

Use Forms 1040, 4952, 6251, and 8283 and Schedules A and B to compute the AMT for Robert and Jane Armstrong for 1993. Suggested software (if available): *TurboTax* or *MacInTax*. Write a letter to the Armstrongs indicating whether they have a refund or balance due for 1993, and suggest possible tax planning strategies for 1994.

RESEARCH PROBLEMS

Research Problem 1.   Tony is a full-time gambler whose only source of income is money that he wins from his gambling activities. The IRS contends that Tony's gambling losses should be treated as itemized deductions for purposes of computing the AMT. Tony argues that the gambling losses should be treated as trade or business expenses. Who is correct, Tony or the IRS?

Research Problem 2. Carol owns two warehouses that were placed in service before 1987. Accelerated depreciation for 1990 on Warehouse A was $12,000, and straight-line depreciation would have been $8,000. On Warehouse B, accelerated depreciation was $6,000, and straight-line depreciation would have been $7,500. What was the amount of Carol's tax preference for excess depreciation in 1990?

TAX CREDITS AND PAYMENT PROCEDURES

LEARNING OBJECTIVES

After completing Chapter 13, you should be able to:

1. Understand the use of tax credits as a tool of Federal tax policy.

2. Distinguish between refundable and nonrefundable credits and understand the order in which they can be used by taxpayers.

3. Describe various business-related tax credits.

4. Describe several other tax credits that are available primarily to individual taxpayers.

5. Understand the tax withholding and payment procedures applicable to employers and self-employed persons.

6. Identify tax planning opportunities related to tax credits and payment procedures.

OUTLINE

Tax Policy Considerations, 13–3

Overview and Priority of Credits, 13–4

Refundable versus Nonrefundable Credits, 13–4

General Business Credit, 13–5

Treatment of Unused General Business Credits, 13–6

Specific Business-Related Tax Credit Provisions, 13–7

Investment Tax Credit: Introduction, 13–7

Regular Investment Tax Credit, 13–7

Tax Credit for Rehabilitation Expenditures, 13–8

Business Energy Credits, 13–10

Jobs Credit, 13–10

Research Activities Credit, 13–11

Low-Income Housing Credit, 13–15

Disabled Access Credit, 13–16

Other Tax Credits, 13–17

Earned Income Credit, 13–17

Tax Credit for Elderly or Disabled Taxpayers, 13–19

Foreign Tax Credit, 13–20

Credit for Child and Dependent Care Expenses, 13–21

Payment Procedures, 13–26

Procedures Applicable to Employers, 13–26

Procedures Applicable to Self-Employed Persons, 13–34

Tax Planning Considerations, 13–39

Foreign Tax Credit, 13–39

Credit for Child and Dependent Care Expenses, 13–39

Adjustments to Increase Withholding, 13–41

Adjustments to Avoid Overwithholding, 13–41

As explained in Chapter 1, Federal tax law often serves other purposes besides merely raising revenue for the government. Evidence of equity, social, and economic considerations, among others, is found throughout the tax law. These considerations also bear heavily in the area of **tax credits.** Consider the following examples:

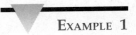
EXAMPLE 1

Paul and Peggy, husband and wife, are both employed outside the home. Their combined salaries are $50,000. However, after paying for child care expenses of $2,000 on behalf of their daughter, Polly, the net economic benefit from both spouses working is $48,000. The child care expenses are, in a sense, business related in that they would not have been incurred if both spouses did not work outside the home. If no tax benefits are associated with the child care expenditures, $50,000 is subject to tax.

Another couple, Alicia and Diego, also have a child, John. Diego stays at home to care for John (the value of those services is $2,000) while Alicia earns a $48,000 salary. Because the value of Diego's services rendered is not subject to tax, only Alicia's earnings of $48,000 are subject to tax. ▼

The credit for child and dependent care expenses is allowed to mitigate the inequity felt by working taxpayers who must pay for child care services in order to work outside the home.

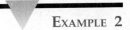
EXAMPLE 2

Olaf is a retired taxpayer who received $8,000 of Social Security benefits as his only source of income in 1994. His Social Security benefits are excluded from gross income. Therefore, Olaf's income tax is $0. In 1994, Olga, a single taxpayer 66 years of age, has $8,000 of income from a pension plan funded by her former employer. Assuming Olga has no itemized deductions or deductions *for* AGI, her income tax for 1994 (before credits) is $120. ▼

The tax credit for elderly or disabled taxpayers was enacted to mitigate this inequity.

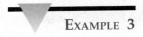
EXAMPLE 3

Jane is a single parent who depends on the government's "safety net" for survival—she receives Aid for Dependent Children in the amount of $10,000 per year. However, she very much wishes to work. Jane has located a job that will pay $10,500 per year and has found an individual to care for her child at no cost. But, with the $803.25 ($10,500 × 7.65%) payroll deduction for Social Security and Medicare taxes, the economic benefit from working is less than remaining reliant on the government ($9,696.75 as compared to $10,000). ▼

To help offset the effect of Social Security and Medicare taxes on wages of the working poor and to provide an incentive to work, the earned income credit is used to increase the after-tax earnings of qualified individuals. In addition, the earned income credit helps offset the regressive nature of certain taxes, such as the Social Security and Medicare taxes, which impose a relatively larger burden on low-income taxpayers than on more affluent taxpayers.

These three tax credits and many of the other important tax credits available to individuals and other types of taxpayers are a major focus of this chapter. The chapter begins by discussing important tax policy considerations relevant to tax credits. Tax credits are categorized as being either refundable or nonrefundable. The distinction between refundable and nonrefundable credits is important because it may affect the taxpayer's ability to enjoy a tax benefit from a particular credit.

Next an overview of the priority of tax credits is presented. The credit portion of the chapter continues with a discussion of the credits available to businesses and to individual taxpayers and the ways in which credits enter into the calculation of the tax liability.

The Federal tax system has long been based on the pay-as-you-go concept. That is, taxpayers or their employers are required to make regular deposits with the Federal government during the year as payment toward the tax liability that will be determined at the end of the tax year. These deposits are in effect refundable credits. In addition to presenting the procedures used in calculating these payments and the special problems self-employed persons encounter in estimating their payments, the penalties on underpayment are discussed.

TAX POLICY CONSIDERATIONS

1 LEARNING OBJECTIVE
Understand the use of tax credits as a tool of Federal tax policy.

Congress has generally used tax credits to achieve social or economic objectives or to provide equity for different types of taxpayers. For example, the investment tax credit, which was a part of our tax law for over 20 years beginning in the early 1960s, was expected to encourage economic growth, improve the competitive position of American industry at home and abroad, and help alleviate the nation's balance of payments problem.[1] The credit was repealed in the mid-1980s because Congress considered it too costly. President Clinton, however, believed such a credit would be a valuable way of stimulating our economy and proposed its reenactment in 1993. Although the President succeeded in winning congressional approval for most of his proposals, the investment tax credit was not reenacted. Nevertheless, the notion of the investment tax credit continues to surface from time to time, leading some to suggest that the credit is "down, but not out."

A tax credit should not be confused with an income tax deduction. Certain expenditures of individuals (e.g., business expenses) are permitted as deductions from gross income in arriving at adjusted gross income (AGI). Additionally, individuals are allowed to deduct certain nonbusiness and investment-related expenses *from* AGI. Whereas the tax benefit received from a tax deduction depends on the tax rate, a tax credit is not affected by the tax rate of the taxpayer.

---

[1] Remarks of the Secretary of the Treasury, quoted in S.Rept. 1881, 87th Cong., 2nd Sess., reported in 1962–3 C.B. 707.

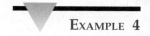

EXAMPLE 4

Assume Congress wishes to encourage a certain type of expenditure. One way to accomplish this objective is to allow a tax credit of 25% for such expenditures. Another way is to allow an itemized deduction for the expenditures. Assume Abby's tax rate is 15%, while Bill's tax rate is 39.6%. In addition, assume that Carmen does not incur enough qualifying expenditures to itemize deductions. The following tax benefits are available to each taxpayer for a $1,000 expenditure:

	Abby	**Bill**	**Carmen**
Tax benefit if a 25% credit is allowed	$250	$250	$250
Tax benefit if an itemized deduction is allowed	150	396	–0–

As these results indicate, tax credits provide benefits on a more equitable basis than do tax deductions. Equally apparent in this case is that the deduction approach benefits only taxpayers who itemize deductions, while the credit approach benefits all taxpayers who make the specified expenditure. ▼

For many years, Congress has used the tax credit provisions of the Code liberally in implementing tax policy. Although budget constraints and economic considerations often have dictated the repeal of some credits, other credits, such as those applicable to expenses incurred for child and dependent care and expenses related to making businesses more accessible to disabled individuals, have been kept to respond to important social policy considerations. Other credits, such as the one applicable to taxes paid on income generated in foreign countries, have been retained based on economic considerations. Finally, as the myriad of tax proposals that are always before Congress make clear, the use of tax credits as a tax policy tool continues to evolve as economic and political circumstances change.

OVERVIEW AND PRIORITY OF CREDITS

REFUNDABLE VERSUS NONREFUNDABLE CREDITS

2 LEARNING OBJECTIVE
Distinguish between refundable and nonrefundable credits and understand the order in which they can be used by taxpayers.

As illustrated in Exhibit 13–1, certain credits are refundable while others are nonrefundable. **Refundable credits** are paid to the taxpayer even if the amount of the credit (or credits) exceeds the taxpayer's tax liability.

EXAMPLE 5

Ted, who is single, had taxable income of $21,000 in 1994. His income tax from the 1994 Tax Rate Schedule is $3,150. During 1994, Ted's employer withheld income tax of $3,500. Ted is entitled to a refund of $350 because the credit for tax withheld on wages is a refundable credit. ▼

Nonrefundable credits are not paid if they exceed the taxpayer's tax liability.

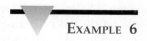

EXAMPLE 6

Tina is single, age 67, and retired. Her taxable income for 1994 is $1,320, and the tax on this amount is $198. Tina's tax credit for the elderly is $225. This credit can be used to reduce her net tax liability to zero, but it will not result in a refund, even though the credit ($225) exceeds Tina's tax liability ($198). This result occurs because the tax credit for the elderly is a nonrefundable credit. ▼

Some nonrefundable credits, such as the foreign tax credit, are subject to carryover provisions if they exceed the amount allowable as a credit in a given year. Other nonrefundable credits, such as the tax credit for the elderly (refer to Example 6), are not subject to carryover provisions and are lost if they exceed the

▼ **EXHIBIT 13–1**
Partial Listing of Refundable and
Nonrefundable Credits

Refundable Credits

Taxes withheld on wages

Earned income credit

Nonrefundable Credits

Credit for child and dependent care expenses

Credit for the elderly and disabled

Foreign tax credit

General business credit, which is the sum of the following:

- Investment tax credit, which includes:
  - Regular investment tax credit
  - Tax credit for rehabilitation expenditures
  - Business energy credit
- Jobs credit
- Research activities credit
- Low-income housing credit
- Disabled access credit

---

limitations. Because some credits are subject to carryover provisions while others are not, the order in which credits are offset against the tax liability is important. The Code provides that nonrefundable credits are to be offset against a taxpayer's income tax liability in the order shown in Exhibit 13–1.

GENERAL BUSINESS CREDIT

As shown in Exhibit 13–1, the **general business credit** is comprised of a number of other credits, each of which is computed separately under its own set of rules. The general business credit combines these credits into one amount to limit the amount of business credits that can be used to offset a taxpayer's income tax liability. The idea behind combining the credits is to prevent a taxpayer from completely avoiding his or her income tax liability in any one year by offsetting it with business credits that would otherwise be available.

Two special rules apply to the general business credit. First, any unused credit must be carried back 3 years, then forward 15 years. Second, for any tax year, the general business credit is limited to the taxpayer's *net income tax* reduced by the greater of:[2]

- The *tentative minimum tax.*
- 25 percent of *net regular tax liability* that exceeds $25,000.[3]

In order to understand the general business credit limitation, several terms need defining:

- *Net income tax* is the sum of the regular tax liability and the alternative minimum tax reduced by certain nonrefundable tax credits.
- *Tentative minimum tax* for this purpose is reduced by the foreign tax credit allowed.

---

[2] § 38(c).

[3] This amount is $12,500 for married taxpayers filing separately unless one of the spouses is not entitled to the general business credit.

- *Regular tax liability* is determined from the appropriate tax table or tax rate schedule, based on taxable income. However, the regular tax liability does not include certain taxes (e.g., alternative minimum tax).
- *Net regular tax liability* is the regular tax liability reduced by certain nonrefundable credits (e.g., credit for child and dependent care expenses, foreign tax credit).

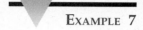

EXAMPLE 7

Floyd's general business credit for 1994 is $70,000. His net income tax is $150,000, tentative minimum tax is $130,000, and net regular tax liability is $150,000. He has no other tax credits. Floyd's general business credit allowed for the tax year is computed as follows:

Net income tax	$ 150,000
Less: The greater of	
• $130,000 (tentative minimum tax)	
• $31,250 [25% × ($150,000 – $25,000)]	(130,000)
Amount of general business credit allowed for tax year	$ 20,000

Floyd then has $50,000 ($70,000 – $20,000) of unused general business credits that may be carried back or forward as discussed below. ▼

TREATMENT OF UNUSED GENERAL BUSINESS CREDITS

Unused general business credits are initially carried back three years (to the earliest year in the sequence first) and are applied to reduce tax during these years. Thus, the taxpayer may receive a tax refund as a result of the carryback. Any remaining unused credits are then carried forward 15 years.[4]

A FIFO method is applied to the carryovers, carrybacks, and utilization of credits earned during a particular year. The oldest credits are used first in determining the amount of the general business credit. The FIFO method minimizes the potential for loss of a general business credit benefit due to the expiration of credit carryovers, since the earliest years are used before the current credit for the taxable year.

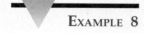

EXAMPLE 8

This example illustrates the use of general business credit carryovers.

General business credit carryovers		
1991	$ 4,000	
1992	6,000	
1993	2,000	
Total carryovers	$12,000	
1994 general business credit		$40,000
Total credit allowed in 1994 (based on tax liability)	$50,000	
Less: Utilization of carryovers		
1991	(4,000)	
1992	(6,000)	
1993	(2,000)	
Remaining credit allowed	$38,000	
Applied against		
1994 general business credit		(38,000)
1994 unused amount carried forward to 1995		$ 2,000

▼

---

[4]§ 39(a)(1).

SPECIFIC BUSINESS-RELATED TAX CREDIT PROVISIONS

3 ▼ **LEARNING OBJECTIVE**
Describe various business-related tax credits.

Each component of the general business credit is determined separately under its own set of rules. The components are explained here in the order listed in Exhibit 13–1.

INVESTMENT TAX CREDIT: INTRODUCTION

Since its original enactment in 1962, the **investment tax credit (ITC)** has been suspended, reinstated, repealed, and reenacted in response to varying economic conditions and political pressures. These changes in the tax laws have created a nightmare for tax practitioners. This phenomenon continued with the TRA of 1986, which repealed the *regular* investment tax credit for most property placed in service after 1985. However, other components of the ITC (*rehabilitation expenditures credit* and *business energy credit*) are still allowed in certain situations. In addition, practitioners will have to deal with carryover provisions related to the ITC for many years in the future. Because of these factors, an awareness of the pre-1986 ITC is necessary. Each of the ITC components is discussed below.

REGULAR INVESTMENT TAX CREDIT

Qualifying Property

Prior to its repeal by TRA of 1986, the ITC was allowed for most business tangible personal property (e.g., automobiles, machinery, furniture) and was not allowed for most real property (e.g., land, buildings). In addition, up until 1991, qualifying property also included certain property placed in service after 1985 that satisfied several restrictive requirements.

Computation of Qualified Investment and Amount of the Credit

Because of the carryover provisions applicable to the ITC, it is necessary to understand how the credit was computed. The ITC was based on the aggregate amount, without limit, of qualifying new property and limited amounts of used property that were placed in service during a given year.

The credit was based on the property's recovery period under ACRS (refer to Chapter 8 for details). To avoid a reduction of the asset's basis, the taxpayer could have elected a reduced ITC rate. Rates for the full credit and the reduced credit were as follows:

Recovery Period (in years)	Full Credit Rate	Reduced Credit Rate
3	6%	4%
5, 10, or 15	10%	8%

EXAMPLE 9

If Susan had placed into service five-year property costing $100,000 that qualified for the ITC, her allowable credit would have been $10,000 ($100,000 × 10%), assuming she chose to use the full credit rate. If she chose the reduced credit rate, the ITC would have been $8,000 ($100,000 × 8%). ▼

Reduction of Investment Tax Credit

In general, for ITC carryovers from pre-1986 years, a 35 percent reduction of the ITC is required. This applies to the regular ITC, regardless of when the property was placed in service.

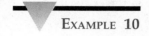

EXAMPLE 10

In an earlier year, Gary placed property into service that qualified for the ITC. The property, five-year recovery property, cost $10,000 and generated a tentative ITC of $1,000 ($10,000 × 10%). However, Gary was not able to actually use the ITC generated in his tax computation until 1994. The $1,000 ITC carried forward to 1994 produces a credit of $650 [$1,000 – $350 (reduction amount)]. ▼

TAX CREDIT FOR REHABILITATION EXPENDITURES

Taxpayers are allowed a tax credit for expenditures incurred to rehabilitate industrial and commercial buildings and certified historic structures. The **rehabilitation expenditures credit,** which is an extension of the regular ITC, is intended to discourage businesses from moving from older, economically distressed areas (e.g., inner city) to newer locations and to encourage the preservation of historic structures.

Congress has changed the credit rates and the structures to which the credit applies from time to time to ensure that the credit accomplishes its intended purpose. The current operating features of this credit follow:[5]

Rate of the Credit for Rehabilitation Expenses	Nature of the Property
10%	Nonresidential buildings, other than certified historic structures, originally placed in service before 1936
20%	Residential and nonresidential certified historic structures

When taking the credit, the basis of a rehabilitated building must be reduced by the full rehabilitation credit allowed.[6]

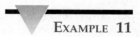

EXAMPLE 11

Juan spent $60,000 to rehabilitate a building (adjusted basis of $40,000) that had originally been placed in service in 1932. He is allowed a credit of $6,000 (10% × $60,000) for rehabilitation expenditures. Juan then increases the basis of the building by $54,000 [$60,000 (rehabilitation expenditures) – $6,000 (credit allowed)]. If the building were a historic structure, the credit allowed would be $12,000 (20% × $60,000), and the building's depreciable basis would increase by $48,000 [$60,000 (rehabilitation expenditures) – $12,000 (credit allowed)]. ▼

To qualify for the credit, buildings must be substantially rehabilitated. A building has been *substantially rehabilitated* if qualified rehabilitation expenditures exceed the greater of (1) the adjusted basis of the property before the rehabilitation or (2) $5,000. Qualified rehabilitation expenditures do not include the cost of

---

[5]§ 47.   [6]§ 50(c).

▼ **TABLE 13–1**
Recapture Calculation for
Rehabilitation Expenditures
Credit

If the Property Is Held for	The Recapture Percentage Is
Less than 1 year	100
One year or more but less than 2 years	80
Two years or more but less than 3 years	60
Three years or more but less than 4 years	40
Four years or more but less than 5 years	20
Five years or more	0

acquiring a building, the cost of facilities related to a building (such as a parking lot), and the cost of enlarging an existing building. Stringent rules apply concerning the retention of internal and external walls.

Recapture of Tax Credit for Rehabilitation Expenditures

The rehabilitation credit taken must be recaptured if the rehabilitated property is disposed of prematurely or if it ceases to be qualifying property. The **rehabilitation expenditures credit recapture** is based on a holding period requirement of five years and is added to the taxpayer's regular tax liability in the recapture year. In addition, the recapture amount is *added* to the adjusted basis of the rehabilitation expenditures for purposes of determining the amount of gain or loss realized on the property's disposition.

The portion of the credit recaptured is a specified percentage of the credit that was taken by the taxpayer. This percentage is based on the period the property was held by the taxpayer, as shown in Table 13–1.

EXAMPLE 12

On March 15, 1991, Rashad placed in service $30,000 of rehabilitation expenditures on a building qualifying for the 10% credit. A credit of $3,000 ($30,000 × 10%) was allowed, and the basis of the building was increased by $27,000 ($30,000 − $3,000). The building was sold on December 15, 1994. Rashad must recapture a portion of the rehabilitation credit based on the schedule in Table 13–1. Because he held the rehabilitated property for more than three years but less than four, 40% of the credit, or $1,200, must be added to his 1994 tax liability. Also, the adjusted basis of the rehabilitation expenditures is increased by the $1,200 recaptured amount. ▼

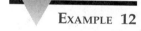

ETHICAL
CONSIDERATIONS

Using the Rehabilitation Expenditures Credit

The tax credit for rehabilitation expenditures is available to help offset the costs related to substantially rehabilitating certain buildings. The credit is calculated on the rehabilitation expenditures incurred and not on the acquisition cost of the building itself.

You are a developer who buys, sells, and does construction work on real estate in the inner city of your metropolitan area. A potential customer approaches you about acquiring one of your buildings that easily could qualify for the 20 percent rehabilitation credit on historic structures. The stated sales price of the structure is $100,000, and the rehabilitation expenditures, if the job is done correctly, would be about $150,000.

Your business has been slow recently due to the sluggish real estate market in your area, and the potential customer makes the following proposal: if you reduce the sales price of the building to $75,000, he will pay you $175,000 to perform the rehabilitation work. Although the buyer's total expenditures would be the same, he would benefit from this approach by obtaining a larger tax credit ($25,000 increased rehabilitation costs × 20% = $5,000).

It has been a long time since you have sold any of your real estate.

BUSINESS ENERGY CREDITS

Since 1978, a **business energy credit** has been allowed to encourage the conservation of natural resources and the development of alternative energy sources (to oil and natural gas). Many of these credits have now expired. The most important business energy credits that remain are the 10 percent credits for solar energy property and geothermal property.

JOBS CREDIT

The **jobs credit** (also referred to as the targeted jobs credit) was enacted to encourage employers to hire individuals from one or more of the following target groups traditionally subject to high rates of unemployment:[7]

- Vocational rehabilitation referrals.
- Economically disadvantaged youths (age 18 to 22).
- Economically disadvantaged Vietnam-era veterans.
- Recipients of certain Social Security supplemental security income benefits.
- General assistance recipients.
- Youths (age 16 to 19) participating in cooperative education programs.
- Economically disadvantaged ex-convicts.
- Eligible work incentive employees.
- Qualified summer youth employees (age 16 and 17).

The credit is available for wages paid to employees in their first year of service if they begin working for their employer before 1995.

Computation of the Regular Jobs Credit

The regular jobs credit is equal to 40 percent of the first $6,000 of wages (per eligible employee) for the *first 12 months* of employment. Thus, the credit is not available for any wages paid to an employee after his or her first year of employment. However, if the employee's first year of employment overlaps two of the employer's tax years, the employer may take the credit over two tax years. If the jobs credit is elected, the employer's tax deduction for wages is reduced by the amount of the credit. For an employer to qualify for the credit, an unemployed individual must be certified by a local jobs service office of a state employment security agency. The jobs credit is not available for wages paid to certain related parties.

Wages will be taken into account in computing the regular jobs credit only if paid to an individual who is employed for at least 90 days or has completed 120 hours of work. The equivalent thresholds for qualified summer youth employees (discussed below) are 14 days or 20 hours.

[7]§ 51.

EXAMPLE **13**

In January 1994, Green Company hires four handicapped individuals (certified to be eligible employees for the jobs credit). Each of these employees is paid wages of $7,000 during the year. Green Company's jobs credit is $9,600 [($6,000 × 40%) × 4 employees]. If the tax credit is taken, Green must reduce its deduction for wages paid by $9,600. No credit is available for wages paid to these employees after their first year of employment. ▼

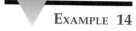

EXAMPLE **14**

On June 1, 1994, Maria, a calendar year taxpayer, hired a member of a targeted group and obtained the required certification. During the last seven months of 1994, this employee is paid $3,500. Maria is allowed a jobs credit of $1,400 ($3,500 × 40%). The employee continues to work for Maria in 1995 and is paid $7,000 through May 31. Because up to $6,000 of first-year wages are eligible for the credit, Maria is also allowed a 40% credit on $2,500 [$6,000 – $3,500 (wages paid in 1994)] of wages paid in 1995, or $1,000 ($2,500 × 40%). None of this employee's wages paid after May 31, the end of the first year of employment, are eligible for the jobs credit. Likewise, no credit is allowed for wages paid to persons newly hired after December 31, 1994. ▼

Computation of the Jobs Credit for Qualified Summer Youth Employees

The credit for qualified summer youth employees is allowed on wages for services during any 90-day period between May 1 and September 15 if the employee is hired before 1995. A qualified summer youth employee generally must be age 16 or 17 on the hiring date. The maximum wages eligible for the credit are $3,000 per summer youth employee. Thus, the maximum credit per employee for 1994 is $1,200 ($3,000 × 40%). If the employee continues employment after the 90-day period as a member of another targeted group, the amount of wages subject to the regular jobs credit must be reduced by the wages paid to the employee as a qualified summer youth employee.

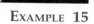

EXAMPLE **15**

Blue Corporation employs Tim as a qualified summer youth employee beginning May 1, 1994. After 90 days, Tim continues his employment as a member of a second targeted group. Tim was paid $2,000 as a qualified summer youth employee. As a member of the second targeted group, Tim is paid another $5,000 during the year. Of the $7,000 total paid to Tim, only $6,000 qualifies for the jobs credit. This amount consists of the $2,000 wages paid under the qualified summer youth employee program plus $4,000 ($6,000 – $2,000) paid to Tim as a member of the other targeted group. Blue Corporation's jobs credit will be 40% of $6,000 ($2,000 + $4,000), or $2,400. ▼

RESEARCH ACTIVITIES CREDIT

To encourage research and experimentation, usually described as research and development (R & D), a credit is allowed for certain qualifying expenditures paid or incurred through June 30, 1995. The **research activities credit** is the *sum* of two components: an incremental research activities credit and a basic research credit.[8]

Incremental Research Activities Credit

The incremental research activities credit applies at a 20 percent rate to the *excess* of qualified research expenses for the current taxable year (the credit year) over the base amount. These components of the credit are explained below.

In general, *research expenditures* qualify if the research relates to discovering information technological in nature that is intended for use in the development of

[8]§ 41.

a new or improved business component of the taxpayer. Such expenses qualify fully if the research is performed in-house (by the taxpayer or employees). If the research is conducted by persons outside the taxpayer's business (under contract), only 65 percent of the amount paid qualifies for the credit.[9]

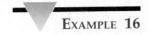

EXAMPLE 16

Sungho incurs the following research expenditures for the tax year.

In-house wages, supplies, computer time	$50,000
Paid to XYZ Scientific Foundation for research	30,000

Sungho's qualified research expenditures are $69,500 [$50,000 + ($30,000 × 65%)]. ▼

Beyond the general guidelines described above, the Code does not give specific examples of qualifying research. However, the credit is *not* allowed for research that falls into certain categories, including the following:[10]

- Research conducted after the beginning of commercial production of the business component.
- Surveys and studies such as market research, testing, and routine data collection.
- Research conducted *outside* the United States.
- Research in the social sciences, arts, or humanities.

The *base amount* for the credit year is determined by multiplying the taxpayer's fixed base percentage by the average gross receipts for the four preceding taxable years. The fixed base percentage depends on whether the taxpayer is an existing firm or a start-up company. For purposes of the incremental research activities credit, an *existing firm* is one that both incurred qualified research expenditures *and* had gross receipts during each of at least three years from 1984 to 1988. A *start-up company* is one that did not have both of the above during each of at least three years in the same 1984–1988 period.

For existing firms, the fixed base percentage is the ratio of total qualified research expenses for the 1984–1988 period to total gross receipts for this same period. Gross receipts are net of sales returns and allowances. The fixed base percentage cannot exceed a maximum ratio of .16, or 16 percent. A start-up company is *assigned* a fixed base percentage ratio of .03, or 3 percent, for each of its first five tax years after 1993. For subsequent years, the base percentage is calculated based on the taxpayer's actual experience.

To calculate the incremental research activities credit available for 1994, the following template may be used. Essentially, the steps lead to the multiplication of the excess or incremental research expenditures incurred by the tax credit rate.

1. Calculate the fixed base percentage for the period 1984–1988 (aggregate research expenses ÷ aggregate gross receipts).   _____

2. Calculate the average gross receipts for the four preceding years.   _____

3. Multiply the line 2 amount by the lesser of the line 1 amount or 16%.   _____

4. Subtract from the qualified research expenditures for the current year the line 3 amount or, if greater, 50% of the current year's qualified research expenditures. This is the excess research expenditures incurred.   _____

5. Multiply the line 4 amount by 20%. This is the incremental research activities credit.   _____

---

[9] § 41(b)(3)(A).   [10] § 41(d).

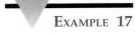

EXAMPLE 17

Jack, a calendar year taxpayer, has both gross receipts (net of sales returns and allowances) and qualified research expenses as follows:

	Gross Receipts	Qualified Research Expenses
1984	$150,000	$25,000
1985	300,000	45,000
1986	400,000	30,000
1987	350,000	35,000
1988	450,000	50,000
1989	425,000	60,000
1990	450,000	65,000
1991	450,000	50,000
1992	500,000	55,000
1993	650,000	73,000
1994	700,000	80,000

Using the template above, calculate Jack's incremental research activities credit.

1. Calculate the fixed base percentage for the period 1984–1988 (aggregate research expenses ÷ aggregate gross receipts). ($185,000 ÷ $1,650,000) ___11.21%___

2. Calculate the average gross receipts for the four preceding years. [($450,000 + $450,000 + $500,000 + $650,000) ÷ 4] $512,500

3. Multiply the line 2 amount by the lesser of the line 1 amount or 16%. ($512,500 × 11.21%) $ 57,451

4. Subtract from the qualified research expenditures for the current year the line 3 amount or, if greater, 50% of the current year's qualified research expenditures. This is the excess research expenditures incurred. ($80,000 − $57,451) $ 22,549

5. Multiply the line 4 amount by 20%. This is the incremental research activities credit. $ 4,510 ▼

As indicated in the template, a special rule limits the credit available for taxpayers who have incurred small amounts of research and experimentation costs during the base period. The rule provides that in no event shall the base amount be less than 50 percent of qualified research expenses for the credit year.

EXAMPLE 18

Assume the same facts as in Example 17, except that qualified research and experimentation expenses in 1994 were $200,000. Incremental research and experimentation expenditures eligible for the credit are $100,000, and the tax credit is computed as follows:

1. Calculate the fixed base percentage for the period 1984–1988 (aggregate research expenses ÷ aggregate gross receipts). ($185,000 ÷ $1,650,000) ___11.21%___

2. Calculate the average gross receipts for the four preceding years. [($450,000 + $450,000 + $500,000 + $650,000) ÷ 4] $512,500

3. Multiply the line 2 amount by the lesser of the line 1 amount or 16%. ($512,500 × 11.21%) $ 57,451

4. Subtract from the qualified research expenditures for the current year the line 3 amount or, if greater, 50% of the current year's qualified research expenditures. This is the excess research expenditures incurred. ($200,000 − $100,000) $100,000

5. Multiply the line 4 amount by 20%. This is the incremental research activities credit. $ 20,000 ▼

Qualified research and experimentation expenditures are not only eligible for the 20 percent credit, but can also be *expensed* in the year incurred.[11] In this regard, a taxpayer has two choices:[12]

- Use the full credit and reduce the expense deduction for research expenses by 100 percent of the credit.
- Retain the full expense deduction and reduce the credit by the product of 50 percent of the credit times the maximum corporate tax rate.

As an alternative to the expense deduction, the taxpayer may *capitalize* the research expenses and *amortize* them over 60 months or more. In this case, the amount capitalized and subject to amortization is reduced by the full amount of the credit *only* if the credit exceeds the amount allowable as a deduction.

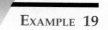

EXAMPLE 19

Assume the same facts as in Example 18, which shows that the potential incremental research activities credit is $20,000. The expense that the taxpayer can deduct currently and the credit are as follows:

	Credit Amount	Deduction Amount
• Full credit and reduced deduction		
$20,000 – $0	$20,000	
$200,000 – $20,000		$180,000
• Reduced credit and full deduction		
$20,000 – [(.50 × $20,000) × .35]	16,500	
$200,000 – $0		200,000
• Full credit and capitalize and elect to amortize costs over 60 months		
$20,000 – $0	20,000	
$200,000/60 × 12		40,000

Basic Research Credit

Corporations (but not S corporations or personal service corporations) are allowed an additional 20 percent credit for basic research payments through June 30, 1995, in *excess* of a base amount. This credit is not available to individual taxpayers. *Basic research payments* are defined as amounts paid in cash to a qualified basic research organization.

Basic research is defined generally as any original investigation for the advancement of scientific knowledge not having a specific commercial objective. The definition excludes basic research conducted outside the United States and basic research in the social sciences, arts, or humanities. This reflects the intent of Congress to encourage high-tech research in the United States.

The calculation of this additional credit for basic research expenditures is complex and is based on expenditures in excess of a specially defined base amount.[13] The portion of the basic research expenditures that does not exceed the base amount is not eligible for the basic research credit, but the amount does become a component of the regular credit for incremental research activities.

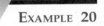

EXAMPLE 20

Orange Corporation, a qualifying corporation, pays $75,000 to a university for basic research. Assume that Orange's base amount is $50,000. The basic research activities credit allowed is $5,000 [($75,000 − $50,000) × 20%]. The $50,000 of current year basic research expenditures that are not eligible for the credit because they do not exceed the base amount are treated as contract research expenses for purposes of the regular incremental research activities credit. ▼

LOW-INCOME HOUSING CREDIT

To encourage building owners to make affordable housing available for low-income individuals, Congress has made a credit available to owners of qualified low-income housing projects.[14]

More than any other, the **low-income housing credit** is influenced by nontax factors. For example, certification of the property by the appropriate state or local agency authorized to provide low-income housing credits is required. These credits are issued based on a nationwide allocation.

The amount of credit is based on the qualified basis of the property. The qualified basis depends on the number of units rented to low-income tenants. Tenants are low-income tenants if their income does not exceed a specified percentage of the area median gross income. The amount of credit is determined by multiplying the qualified basis by the applicable percentage and is allowed over a 10-year period if the property continues to meet the required conditions.

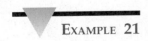

EXAMPLE 21

Sarah spends $100,000 to build a qualified low-income housing project completed January 1, 1994. The entire project is rented to low-income families. The credit rate for property placed in service during January 1994 is 8.36%.[15] Sarah may claim a credit of $8,360

---

[14] § 42.
[15] Rev.Rul. 94–1, I.R.B. No. 1, 6. The rate is subject to adjustment every month by the IRS.

($100,000 × 8.36%) in 1994 and in each of the following nine years. Generally, first-year credits are prorated based on the date the project is placed in service. A full year's credit is taken in each of the next nine years, and any remaining first-year credit is claimed in the eleventh year. ▼

Recapture of a portion of the credit may be required if the number of units set aside for low-income tenants falls below a minimum threshold, if the taxpayer disposes of the property or the interest in it, or if the taxpayer's amount at risk decreases.

DISABLED ACCESS CREDIT

The **disabled access credit** is designed to encourage small businesses to make their businesses more accessible to disabled individuals. The credit is available for any eligible access expenditures paid or incurred by an eligible small business. The credit is calculated at the rate of 50 percent of the eligible expenditures that exceed $250 but do not exceed $10,250. Thus, the maximum amount for the credit is $5,000 ($10,000 × 50%).[16]

An *eligible small business* is one that during the previous year either had gross receipts of $1 million or less or had no more than 30 full-time employees. An eligible business can include a sole proprietorship, partnership, regular corporation, or S corporation. However, in the case of a partnership or S corporation, the limitation on the eligible expenditures is determined at both the entity and the owner level.

Eligible access expenditures are generally any reasonable and necessary amounts that are paid or incurred to make certain changes to facilities. These changes must

---

TAX IN THE NEWS

CONSIDER LOW-INCOME-HOUSING INVESTMENTS

Both Clinton and Congress favor giving juicy tax credits to investors in complex new low-income-housing limited partnerships. With the top Federal tax rate now 39.6 percent, the timing couldn't be better. "As rates rise, investors look for shelter—and low-income housing is one of the last shelters left," says Michael Marsh, a tax manager at Grant Thornton in Kansas City, Missouri. "Unfortunately," he adds, "the tax credits may entice investors who don't understand the risks."

Attractive as the credits sound, there are substantial risks. Chief among them: If a project fails to meet strict Federal rules each year, investors retroactively lose up to a third of the credits they've taken to date. If a deal goes bankrupt, both principal and credits are lost. Moreover, low-income deals are sometimes hyped, with financial planners spinning tales of big gains and rarely mentioning their commissions of as much as 10 percent. Best advice: Don't invest unless you or a trusted adviser can evaluate a plan sponsor's prospectus and record.

SOURCE: Adapted from "Your Taxes," *Money,* January 1993, pp. 80, 82, by special permission; © 1993, Time Inc. All rights reserved.

---

[16] § 44.

involve the removal of architectural, communication, physical, or transportation barriers that would otherwise make a business inaccessible to disabled and handicapped individuals. Examples of qualifying projects include installing ramps, widening doorways, and adding raised markings on elevator control buttons. However, eligible expenditures do *not* include amounts that are paid or incurred in connection with any facility that has been placed into service after the enactment (November 5, 1990) of the provision.

To the extent a disabled access credit is available, no deduction or credit is allowed under any other provision of the tax law. The adjusted basis for depreciation is reduced by the amount of the credit.

EXAMPLE 22

In 1994, Red, Inc., an eligible business, made $11,000 of capital improvements to business realty that had been placed in service in June 1990. The expenditures were intended to make Red's business more accessible to the disabled and were considered eligible expenditures for purposes of the disabled access credit. The amount of the credit is $5,000 [($10,250 – $250) × 50%]. Although $11,000 of eligible expenditures were incurred, only the excess of $10,250 over $250 qualifies for the credit. Further, the depreciable basis of the capital improvement is $6,000 because the basis must be reduced by the amount of the credit [$11,000 (cost) – $5,000 (amount of the credit)]. ▼

OTHER TAX CREDITS

EARNED INCOME CREDIT

4   LEARNING OBJECTIVE
Describe several other tax credits that are available primarily to individual taxpayers.

The **earned income credit,** which has been a part of the law for many years, consistently has been justified as a means of providing tax equity to the working poor. President Clinton successfully pushed for the credit's liberalization in the 1993 tax legislation to help offset regressive taxes that are a part of our tax system, such as the gasoline and Social Security taxes. In addition, the credit has been designed to encourage economically disadvantaged individuals to become contributing members of the workforce.[17] Not only did the Revenue Reconciliation Act of 1993 (RRA of 1993) result in a more generous earned income credit than in previous years, but the current version is also easier to compute.

In 1994, the earned income credit is determined by multiplying a maximum amount of earned income by the appropriate credit percentage. See Table 13–2. Generally, earned income includes employee compensation and net earnings from self-employment but excludes items such as interest, dividends, pension benefits, and alimony. If a taxpayer has children, the credit percentage used in the calculation depends on the number of qualifying children. Thus, in 1994, the maximum basic earned income credit for a taxpayer with one qualifying child is $2,038 ($7,750 × 26.3%) and $2,527 ($8,425 × 30.0%) for a taxpayer with two or more qualifying children. However, the maximum basic earned income credit is phased out completely if the taxpayer's earned income or AGI exceeds certain thresholds as shown in Table 13–2. To the extent that the greater of earned income or AGI exceeds $11,000 in 1994, the difference, multiplied by the appropriate phase-out percentage, is subtracted from the maximum basic earned income credit.

---

[17]§ 32.

▼ **TABLE 13–2**
Earned Income Credit and
Phase-out Percentages

Tax Year	Number of Qualifying Children	Maximum Earned Income	Credit Percentage	Phase-out Begins	Phase-out Percentage	Phase-out Ends
1994	One child	$7,750	26.3	$11,000	15.98	$23,760
	Two or more children	8,425	30.0	11,000	17.68	25,300
1995	One child	6,170	34.0	11,310	15.98	24,440
	Two or more children	8,660	36.0	11,310	20.22	26,728

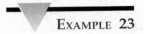

EXAMPLE 23　In 1994, Grace, who otherwise qualifies for the earned income credit, receives wages of $14,000 and has no other income. She has one qualifying child. Grace's earned income credit is $2,038 ($7,750 × 26.3%) reduced by $479 [($14,000 – $11,000) × 15.98%]. Thus, Grace's earned income credit is $1,559. If Grace has two or more qualifying children, the calculation would produce a credit of $2,527 ($8,425 × 30.0%) reduced by $530 [($14,000 – $11,000) × 17.68%]. Thus, Grace's earned income credit would be $1,997. ▼

Earned Income Credit Table

It is not necessary to compute the credit as was done in Example 23. As part of the tax simplification process, the IRS issues an Earned Income Credit Table for the determination of the appropriate amount of the earned income credit. This table and a worksheet are included in the instructions to both Form 1040 and Form 1040A.

Eligibility Requirements

Eligibility for the credit may depend not only on the taxpayer meeting the earned income and AGI thresholds, but whether he or she has a qualifying child. A *qualifying child* must meet the following tests:

- *Relationship test.* The individual must be a son, daughter, descendant of the taxpayer's son or daughter, stepson, stepdaughter, or an eligible foster child of the taxpayer. A legally adopted child of the taxpayer is considered the same as a child by blood.
- *Residency test.* The qualifying child must share the taxpayer's principal place of abode, which must be located within the United States, for more than one-half of the tax year of the taxpayer. Temporary absences (e.g., due to illness or education) are disregarded for purposes of this test. For foster children, however, the child must share the taxpayer's home for the entire year.
- *Age test.* The child must not have reached the age of 19 (24 in the case of a full-time student) as of the end of the tax year. In addition, a child who is permanently and totally disabled at any time during the year is considered to meet the age test.

RRA of 1993 liberalized the earned income credit by making it available to workers without children for the first time. However, this opportunity is available only to taxpayers aged 25 through 64 who cannot be claimed as a dependent on another taxpayer's return. The credit is calculated on a maximum earned income of $4,000 times 7.65 percent and reduced by 7.65 percent of earned income over $5,000. This credit is phased out completely at $9,000.

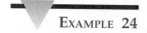

EXAMPLE 24

Walt, who is single, 28 years of age, and is not claimed as a dependent on anyone else's return, earns $6,500 during 1994. Even though he does not have any qualifying children, he qualifies for the earned income credit. His credit is $306 ($4,000 × 7.65%) reduced by $115 [($6,500 − $5,000) × 7.65%]. Thus, Walt's earned income credit is $191. If, instead, Walt's earned income is $4,900, his earned income credit would be $306. In this situation, there is no phase-out of the maximum credit because his earned income is not in excess of $5,000. ▼

Advance Payment

The earned income credit is a form of negative income tax (a refundable credit for taxpayers who do not have a tax liability). An eligible individual may elect to receive advance payments of the earned income credit from his or her employer (rather than receiving the credit from the IRS upon filing the tax return). The IRS is required to notify taxpayers who have qualifying children of this option if they have received tax refunds in previous years because of the credit. The amount that can be received in advance is limited to 60 percent of the credit that is available to a taxpayer with only one qualifying child. If this election is made, the taxpayer must file a certificate of eligibility (Form W−5) with his or her employer and *must* file a tax return for the year the income is earned.

TAX CREDIT FOR ELDERLY OR DISABLED TAXPAYERS

The credit for the elderly was originally enacted in 1954 as the retirement income credit to provide tax relief for those who were not receiving substantial benefits from tax-free Social Security payments.[18]

Currently, the **tax credit for the elderly or disabled** applies to the following:

- Taxpayers age 65 or older.
- Taxpayers under age 65 who are retired with a permanent and total disability and who have disability income from a public or private employer on account of the disability.

The *maximum* allowable credit is $1,125 (15% × $7,500 of qualifying income), but the credit will be less for a taxpayer who receives Social Security benefits or has AGI exceeding specified amounts. Under these circumstances, the base used in the credit computation is reduced. Many taxpayers receive Social Security benefits or have AGI high enough to reduce the base for the credit to zero.

The eligibility requirements and the tax computation are somewhat complicated. Consequently, an individual may elect to have the IRS compute his or her tax and the amount of the tax credit.

The credit generally is based on an initial amount (referred to as the *base amount*) and the filing status of the taxpayer in accordance with Table 13–3. To qualify for the credit, married taxpayers who live together must file a joint return. For taxpayers under age 65 who are retired on permanent and total disability, the base amounts could be less than those shown in Table 13–3 because these amounts are limited to taxable disability income.

---

[18] § 22. This credit is not subject to indexation.

▼ **TABLE 13–3**
Base Amounts for Tax Credit for
Elderly or Disabled

Status	Base Amount
Single, head of household, or surviving spouse	$5,000
Married, joint return, only one spouse qualified	5,000
Married, joint return, both spouses qualified	7,500
Married, separate returns, spouses live apart the entire year	3,750 each

This initial base amount is *reduced* by (1) Social Security, Railroad Retirement, and certain excluded pension benefits and (2) one-half of the taxpayer's AGI in excess of a threshold amount that is a function of the taxpayer's filing status. The credit may be calculated using the procedure presented in the following template:

Base amount ($3,750, $5,000, or $7,500—see
   Table 13–3)   _____

Less: Qualifying nontaxable benefits: _____

    One-half of excess of AGI over:
        $7,500 for single, head of household, or
           surviving spouse taxpayers
        $10,000 for married taxpayers
        $5,000 for married taxpayers filing
           separately   _____

Total reductions   _____

Balance subject to credit   ══════════

Multiply balance subject to credit by 15%—this is
   the tax credit allowed   ══════════

EXAMPLE **25**

Paul and his wife Peggy are both over age 65 and received Social Security benefits of $2,400 in 1994. On a joint return, they reported AGI of $14,000.

Base amount ($3,750, $5,000, or $7,500—see Table 13–3)		$ 7,500
Less: Qualifying nontaxable benefits:	$2,400	
One-half of excess of AGI over:		
$7,500 for single, head of household, or surviving spouse taxpayers		
$10,000 for married taxpayers		
$5,000 for married taxpayers filing separately	2,000	
Total reductions		(4,400)
Balance subject to credit		$ 3,100
Multiply balance subject to credit by 15%—this is the tax credit allowed		$ 465

▼

The credit for the elderly is reduced by any alternative minimum tax. Schedule R of Form 1040 is used to calculate and report the credit.

FOREIGN TAX CREDIT

Both individual taxpayers and corporations may claim a tax credit for foreign income tax paid on income earned and subject to tax in another country or a U.S. possession.[19] As an alternative, a taxpayer may claim a deduction instead of a

---

[19] Section 27 provides for the credit, but the qualifications and calculation procedure for the credit are contained in §§ 901–908.

credit.[20] In most instances, the **foreign tax credit (FTC)** is advantageous since it is a direct offset against the tax liability.

The purpose of the FTC is to mitigate double taxation since income earned in a foreign country is subject to both U.S. and foreign taxes. However, the ceiling limitation formula may result in some form of double taxation or taxation at rates in excess of U.S. rates when the foreign tax rates are higher than the U.S. rates. This is a distinct possibility because U.S. tax rates are lower than those of many foreign countries.

Other special tax treatments applicable to taxpayers working outside the United States include the foreign earned income exclusion (refer to Chapter 5) and limitations on deducting expenses of employees working outside the United States (refer to Chapter 9). Recall from the earlier discussion that a taxpayer may not take advantage of *both* the FTC and the foreign earned income exclusion.

Computation

Taxpayers are required to compute the FTC based upon an overall limitation.[21] The FTC allowed is the *lesser* of the foreign taxes imposed or the *overall limitation* determined according to the following formula:

$$\frac{\text{Foreign-source taxable income}}{\text{Worldwide taxable income}} \times \text{U.S. tax before FTC}$$

For individual taxpayers, worldwide taxable income in the overall limitation formula is determined *before* personal and dependency exemptions are deducted.

EXAMPLE 26

In 1994, Carlos, a calendar year taxpayer, has $10,000 of income from Country Y, which imposes a 15% tax, and $20,000 from Country Z, which imposes a 50% tax. He has taxable income of $60,200 from within the United States, is married filing a joint return, and claims two dependency exemptions. Thus, although Carlos's taxable income for purposes of determining U.S. tax is $90,200, taxable income amounts used in the limitation formula are not reduced by personal and dependency exemptions. Thus, for this purpose, taxable income is $100,000 [$90,200 + (4 × $2,450)]. Assume that Carlos's U.S. tax before the credit is $20,316. Overall limitation:

$$\frac{\text{Foreign-source taxable income}}{\text{Worldwide taxable income}} = \frac{\$30,000}{\$100,000} \times \$20,316 = \$6,095$$

In this case, $6,095 is allowed as the FTC because this amount is less than the $11,500 of foreign taxes imposed [$1,500 (Country Y) + $10,000 (Country Z)]. ▼

Thus, the overall limitation may result in some of the foreign income being subjected to double taxation. Unused FTCs [e.g., the $5,405 ($11,500 − $6,095) from Example 26] can be carried back two years and forward five years.

Only foreign income taxes, war profits taxes, and excess profits taxes (or taxes paid in lieu of such taxes) qualify for the credit. In determining whether or not a tax is an income tax, U.S. criteria are applied. Thus, value added taxes (VAT), severance taxes, property taxes, and sales taxes do not qualify because they are not regarded as taxes on income. Such taxes may be deductible, however.

CREDIT FOR CHILD AND DEPENDENT CARE EXPENSES

A credit is allowed to taxpayers who incur employment-related expenses for child or dependent care.[22] The **credit for child and dependent care expenses** is a

[20] § 164.
[21] § 904.

[22] § 21.

specified percentage of expenses incurred to enable the taxpayer to work or to seek employment. Expenses on which the credit for child and dependent care expenses is based are subject to limitations.

Eligibility

To be eligible for the credit, an individual must maintain a household for either of the following:

- A dependent under age 13.
- A dependent or spouse who is physically or mentally incapacitated.

Generally, married taxpayers must file a joint return to obtain the credit. The credit may also be claimed by the custodial parent for a nondependent child under age 13 if the noncustodial parent is allowed to claim the child as a dependent under a pre-1985 divorce agreement or under a waiver in the case of a post-1984 agreement.

Eligible Employment-Related Expenses

Eligible expenses include amounts paid for household services and care of a qualifying individual that are incurred to enable the taxpayer to be employed. Child and dependent care expenses include expenses incurred in the home, such as payments for a housekeeper. Out-of-the-home expenses incurred for the care of a dependent under the age of 13 also qualify for the credit. In addition, out-of-the-home expenses incurred for an older dependent or spouse who is physically or mentally incapacitated qualify for the credit if that person regularly spends at least eight hours each day in the taxpayer's household. This makes the credit available to taxpayers who keep handicapped older children and elderly relatives in the home instead of institutionalizing them. Out-of-the-home expenses incurred for services provided by a dependent care center will qualify only if the center complies with all applicable laws and regulations of a state or unit of local government.

Child care payments to a relative are eligible for the credit unless the relative is a dependent of the taxpayer or the taxpayer's spouse or is a child (under age 19) of the taxpayer.

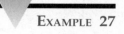

EXAMPLE 27   Wilma is an employed mother of an eight-year-old child. She pays her mother, Rita, $1,500 per year to care for the child after school. Wilma does not claim Rita as a dependent. Wilma pays her daughter Eleanor, age 17, $900 for the child's care during the summer. Of these amounts, only the $1,500 paid to Rita qualifies as employment-related child care expenses. ▼

Earned Income Ceiling

The total for qualifying employment-related expenses is limited to an individual's earned income. For married taxpayers, this limitation applies to the spouse with the *lesser* amount of earned income. Special rules are provided for taxpayers with nonworking spouses who are disabled or are full-time students. If a nonworking spouse is physically or mentally disabled or is a full-time student, he or she is *deemed* to have earned income. The deemed amount is $200 per month if there is one qualifying individual in the household or $400 per month if there are two or more qualifying individuals in the household. In the case of a student-spouse, the student's income is *deemed* to be earned only for the months that the student is enrolled on a full-time basis at an educational institution.

Calculation of the Credit

In general, the credit is equal to a percentage of *unreimbursed* employment-related expenses up to $2,400 for one qualifying individual and $4,800 for two or more individuals. The credit rate varies between 20 percent and 30 percent, depending on the taxpayer's AGI. The following chart shows the applicable percentage for taxpayers as AGI increases:

Adjusted Gross Income		
Over	**But Not Over**	**Applicable Rate of Credit**
$ 0	$10,000	30%
10,000	12,000	29%
12,000	14,000	28%
14,000	16,000	27%
16,000	18,000	26%
18,000	20,000	25%
20,000	22,000	24%
22,000	24,000	23%
24,000	26,000	22%
26,000	28,000	21%
28,000	No limit	20%

EXAMPLE 28

Nancy, who has two children under age 13, worked full-time while her spouse, Ron, was attending college for 10 months during the year. Nancy earned $21,000 and incurred $5,000 of child care expenses. Ron is *deemed* to be fully employed and to have earned $400 for each of the 10 months (or a total of $4,000). Since Nancy and Ron have AGI of $21,000, they are allowed a credit rate of 24%. Nancy and Ron are limited to $4,000 in qualified child care expenses (the lesser of $4,800 or $4,000). They are entitled to a tax credit of $960 (24% × $4,000) for the year. ▼

Dependent Care Assistance Program

Recall from Chapter 5 that a taxpayer is allowed an exclusion from gross income for a limited amount reimbursed for child or dependent care expenses. However, the taxpayer is not allowed both an exclusion from income and a child and dependent care credit on the same amount. The $2,400 and $4,800 ceilings for allowable child and dependent care expenses are reduced dollar for dollar by the amount of reimbursement.[23]

EXAMPLE 29

Assume the same facts as in Example 28, except that of the $5,000 paid for child care, Nancy was reimbursed $2,500 by her employer under a qualified dependent care assistance program. Under the employer's plan, the reimbursement reduces Nancy's taxable wages. Thus, Nancy and Ron have AGI of $18,500 ($21,000 − $2,500). The maximum amount of child care expenses for two or more dependents of $4,800 is reduced by the $2,500 reimbursement, resulting in a tax credit of $575 [25% × ($4,800 − $2,500)]. ▼

Reporting Requirements

The credit is claimed by completing and filing Form 2441, Credit for Child and Dependent Care Expenses (see Appendix B).

---

[23]§ 21(c).

ETHICAL CONSIDERATIONS

Using the Credit for Child and Dependent Care Expenses

Your friends, Bob and Carol, have hired a child care provider to come into their home for three hours a day to care for their child while they both are at work. The child care provider, Delores, charges $1,800 for her services for the year. Bob and Carol learn that up to $2,400 of qualifying expenditures will generate a credit for child and dependent care expenses and that qualifying expenditures can include payments for housecleaning services. As a result, they ask Delores whether she would be interested in working several hours more per week, after Bob returns from work, for the sole purpose of cleaning the house. Delores seems interested. For Bob and Carol, the net cost of the additional services would be $480 [$600 – ($600 × 20%)] due to the availability of the tax credit.

You learn of Bob and Carol's opportunity, but think it is unfair. If you hired Delores to perform similar housecleaning services, your net cost would be $600 and not $480 because you do not qualify for the credit. You are not sure that Bob and Carol should "take advantage" of the system in this way. How do you suppose Bob and Carol will feel, or should feel, about this "abuse" if you approach them?

CONCEPT SUMMARY 13–1

Tax Credits

Credit	Computation	Comments
Tax withheld on wages (§ 31)	Amount is reported to employee on W–2 form.	Refundable credit.
Earned income (§ 32)	Amount is determined by reference to Earned Income Credit Table published by IRS. Computations of underlying amounts in Earned Income Credit Table are illustrated in Example 23.	Refundable credit. A form of negative income tax to assist low-income taxpayers. Earned income and AGI must be less than certain threshold amounts. Generally, one or more qualifying children must reside with the taxpayer.
Child and dependent care (§ 21)	Rate ranges from 20% to 30% depending on AGI. Maximum base for credit is $2,400 for one qualifying individual, $4,800 for two or more.	Nonrefundable personal credit. No carryback or carryforward. Benefits taxpayers who incur employment-related child or dependent care expenses in order to work or seek employment. Eligible dependents include children under age 13 or dependent (any age) or spouse who is physically or mentally incapacitated.
Elderly or disabled (§ 22)	15% of sum of base amount minus reductions for (a) Social Security and other nontaxable benefits and (b) excess AGI. Base amount is fixed by law (e.g., $5,000 for a single taxpayer).	Nonrefundable personal credit. No carryback or carryforward. Provides relief for taxpayers not receiving substantial tax-free retirement benefits.

Credit	Computation	Comments
Foreign tax (§ 27)	Foreign income/total worldwide taxable income × U.S. tax = overall limitation. Lesser of foreign taxes imposed or overall limitation.	Nonrefundable credit. Unused credits may be carried back two years and forward five years. Purpose is to prevent double taxation of foreign income.

General business (§ 38)	May not exceed net income tax minus the greater of tentative minimum tax or 25% of net regular tax liability that exceeds $25,000.	Nonrefundable credit.
		  Components include investment tax credit, jobs credit, research activities credit, low-income housing credit, and disabled access credit.
		  Unused credit may be carried back 3 years and forward 15 years. FIFO method applies to carryovers, carrybacks, and credits earned during current year.

Investment (§ 46)	Qualifying investment times regular percentage, energy percentage, or rehabilitation percentage, depending on type of property.
	  Part of general business credit and subject to its limitations.
		Nonrefundable credit.
		  Part of general business credit and therefore subject to same carryback, carryover, and FIFO rules.
		  Regular credit repealed.
		  Energy percentage is 10%.
		  Regular rehabilitation rate is 10%; rate for certified historic structures is 20%.

Jobs (§ 51)	Regular credit is 40% of first $6,000 of wages paid to each eligible employee. Qualified summer youth employee (QSYE) credit is 40% of first $3,000 of wages paid to QSYE.
	  Eligible employees must begin work before 1995.
		Nonrefundable credit.
		  Part of general business credit and therefore subject to same carryback, carryover, and FIFO rules.
		  Purpose is to encourage employment of specified groups. QSYE generally must be age 16 or 17 on hiring date.

Research activities (§ 41)	Incremental credit is 20% of excess of computation year expenditures minus the base amount.
	  Basic research credit is allowed to certain corporations for 20% of cash payments to qualified organizations that exceed a specially calculated base amount.
		Nonrefundable credit.
		  Part of general business credit and therefore subject to same carryback, carryover, and FIFO rules.
		  Purpose is to encourage high-tech research in the United States.

Low-income housing (§ 42)	Appropriate rate times eligible basis (portion of project attributable to low-income units).	Nonrefundable credit.
		  Part of general business credit and therefore subject to same carryback, carryover, and FIFO rules
		  Credit is available each year for 10 years.
		  Recapture may apply.

Disabled access (§ 44)	Credit is 50% of eligible access expenditures that exceed $250, but do not exceed $10,250. Maximum credit is $5,000.	Nonrefundable credit.
		  Part of general business credit and therefore subject to same carryback, carryover, and FIFO rules.
		  Available only to eligible small businesses.

PAYMENT PROCEDURES

5 ▼ **LEARNING OBJECTIVE**
Understand the tax withholding and payment procedures applicable to employers and self-employed persons.

The tax law contains elaborate rules that require the prepayment of various Federal taxes. Consistent with the pay-as-you-go approach to the collection of taxes, these rules carry penalties for lack of compliance.[24] Prepayment procedures fall into two major categories: those applicable to employers and those applicable to self-employed persons. For employers, both payroll taxes (FICA and FUTA) and income taxes may be involved. With self-employed taxpayers, the focus is on the income tax and the self-employment tax.

PROCEDURES APPLICABLE TO EMPLOYERS

Employment taxes include FICA (Federal Insurance Contributions Act) and FUTA (Federal Unemployment Tax Act). The employer usually is responsible for withholding the employee's share of FICA (commonly referred to as Social Security tax) and appropriate amounts for income taxes. In addition, the employer must match the FICA portion withheld and fully absorb the cost of FUTA. The sum of the employment taxes and the income tax withholdings must be paid to the IRS at specified intervals.

The key to employer compliance in this area involves the resolution of the following points:

- Ascertaining which employees and wages are covered by employment taxes and are subject to withholding for income taxes.
- Arriving at the amount to be paid and/or withheld.
- Reporting and paying employment taxes and income taxes withheld to the IRS on a timely basis through the use of proper forms.

Coverage Requirements

Circular E (Employer's Tax Guide), Publication 15, issued by the IRS contains a complete list of which employees and which wages require withholdings for income taxes and employment taxes. A portion of this list appears in Exhibit 13–2. In working with Exhibit 13–2, consider the following observations:

- The designation "Exempt" in the income tax withholding column does not mean that the amount paid is nontaxable to the employee. It merely relieves the employer from having to withhold.

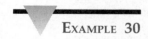

EXAMPLE 30

Lee works for Yellow Corporation and has the type of job where tips are not common but do occur. If Lee's total tips amount to less than $20 per month, Yellow Corporation need not withhold Federal income taxes on the tips. Nevertheless, Lee must include the tips in his gross income. ▼

- In some cases, income tax withholding is not required but is voluntary. This is designated "Exempt (withhold if both employer and employee voluntarily agree)."

---

[24]See, for example, § 3403 (employer liable for any taxes withheld and not paid over to the IRS), § 6656 (up to 15% penalty on amounts withheld and not paid over), and § 6654 (penalty for failure by an individual to pay estimated income taxes).

▼ **EXHIBIT 13–2**
Withholding Classifications

Special Classes of Employment and Special Types of Payment	Treatment under Different Employment Taxes		
	Income Tax Withholding	Social Security and Medicare	Federal Unemployment
Dismissal or severance pay.	Withhold	Taxable	Taxable
Family employees:			
a. Son or daughter employed by parent (or by partnership consisting only of parents).	Withhold	Exempt until age 18	Exempt until age 21
b. Spouse employed by spouse.	Withhold	Taxable if in course of spouse's business.	Exempt
c. Parent employed by a son or daughter.	Withhold	Taxable if in course of the son's or daughter's business. For household work in private home of employer, see Section 13 on page 12 of Circular E.	Exempt
Household workers (domestic service in private homes; farmers, see Circular A).	Exempt (withhold if both employer and employee voluntarily agree).	Taxable if paid $50 or more in cash in quarter.	Taxable if employer paid cash wages of $1,000 or more in any calendar quarter in the current or preceding year.
Interns working in hospitals.	Withhold	Taxable	Exempt
Meals and lodging including those furnished at a bargain charge to the employee.	a. Meals—subject to withholding and taxable unless furnished for employer's convenience and on the employer's premises. b. Lodging—subject to withholding and taxable unless furnished on employer's premises, for the employer's convenience, and as a condition of employment.		
Ministers of churches performing duties as such.	Exempt (withhold if both employer and employee voluntarily agree).	Exempt	Exempt
Moving expenses, reimbursement for.	Exempt if it is reasonable to believe expenses are deductible by the employee; otherwise taxable.		
Newspaper carrier under age 18.	Exempt (withhold if both employer and employee voluntarily agree).	Exempt	Exempt
Tips, if less than $20 in a month.	Exempt	Exempt	Exempt
Workers' compensation.	Exempt	Exempt	Exempt

EXAMPLE 31

Pat is employed as a gardener by a wealthy family. In the past, he has encountered difficulty in managing his finances so as to be in a position to pay the income tax due every April 15. To ease the cash-flow problem that develops in April, Pat asks his employer to withhold income taxes from his wages. ▼

• The Social Security and Medicare (FICA) column refers to the employer's share. The same is true of the Federal Unemployment (FUTA) column since the employee does not contribute to this tax.

TAX IN THE NEWS

NANNYGATE

Each year in the United States vast amounts of income are not reported to the Internal Revenue Service. Estimates indicate unreported payments for child care alone total $11 billion annually. It is widely acknowledged much of the labor in this so-called underground economy is provided by undocumented aliens. Although this issue usually gets little publicity, it became almost a national obsession earlier this year when it was found Zoë Baird, a nominee for U.S. attorney general, had illegally hired a Peruvian couple to perform household and baby-sitting duties. To make matters worse, she paid their Social Security taxes only after she learned she was being considered for a cabinet post. One possible reason for Ms. Baird's problems is that two complex and little-publicized aspects of the law—payroll taxes and immigration—were involved.

SOURCE: Excerpted from Larry Tunnell, Raymond A. Zimmerman, and Cindy Seipel, "Nannygate: An Overview of Payroll Tax Rules and Immigration Laws," *Journal of Accountancy,* July 1993, p. 36.

Amount of FICA Taxes

The FICA tax is comprised of two components: Social Security tax (old age, survivors, and disability insurance) *and* Medicare tax (hospital insurance). The tax rates and wage base under FICA have increased both frequently and substantially over the years. There appears to be every reason to predict that the rates and/or base amount will continue to rise in the future. As Table 13–4 shows, the top base amount has differed for the Medicare portion and for the Social Security portion. Also note that Table 13–4 represents the employee's share of the tax. The employer must match the employee's portion.

Withholdings from employees must continue until the maximum base amount is reached. In 1994, for example, FICA withholding ceases for the Social Security portion (6.2 percent) once the employee has earned wages subject to FICA in the amount of $60,600. For the Medicare portion (1.45 percent), however, the employer is required to withhold on all wages without limit. This contrasts with prior years when a maximum base existed for the Medicare portion also.

▼ **TABLE 13–4**
FICA Rates and Base

| | Social Security Tax | | | | Medicare Tax | | | | |
	Percent	×	Base Amount	+	Percent	×	Base Amount	=	Maximum Tax
1990	6.20%	×	$51,300	+	1.45%	×	$ 51,300	=	$3,924.45
1991	6.20%	×	53,400	+	1.45%	×	125,000	=	5,123.30
1992	6.20%	×	55,500	+	1.45%	×	130,200	=	5,328.90
1993	6.20%	×	57,600	+	1.45%	×	135,000	=	5,528.70
1994	6.20%	×	60,600	+	1.45%	×	Unlimited	=	Unlimited
1995 on	6.20%	×	*	+	1.45%	×	Unlimited	=	Unlimited

*Not yet determined by Congress.

▼
EXAMPLE 32

In 1994, Keshia earned a salary of $140,000 from her employer. Therefore, FICA taxes withheld from her salary are $3,757 ($60,600 × 6.2%) plus $2,030 ($140,000 × 1.45%) for a total of $5,787. In addition to paying the amount withheld from Keshia's salary to the government, her employer will also have to pay $5,787. ▼

In at least two situations, it is possible for an employee to have paid excess FICA taxes.

▼
EXAMPLE 33

During 1994, Kevin changed employers in the middle of the year and earned $40,000 (all of which was subject to FICA) from each job. As a result, each employer withheld $3,060 [(6.2% × $40,000) + (1.45% × $40,000)] for a total of $6,120. Although each employer acted properly, Kevin's total FICA tax liability for the year is only $4,917 [(6.2% × $60,600) + (1.45% × $80,000)]. Thus, Kevin has overpaid his share of FICA taxes by $1,203 [$6,120 (amount paid) − $4,917 (amount of correct liability)]. He should claim this amount as a tax credit when filing his income tax return for 1994. The tax credit will reduce any income tax Kevin might owe or, possibly, generate a tax refund. ▼

▼
EXAMPLE 34

During 1994, Lori earned $60,000 from her regular job and $20,000 from a part-time job (all of which was subject to FICA). As a result, one employer withheld $4,590 [(6.2% × $60,000) + (1.45% × $60,000)] while the other employer withheld $1,530 [(6.2% × $20,000) + (1.45% × $20,000)] for a total of $6,120. Lori's total FICA tax liability for the year is only $4,917 [(6.2% × $60,600) + (1.45% × $80,000)]. Thus, Lori has overpaid her share of FICA taxes by $1,203 [$6,120 (amount paid) − $4,917 (amount of correct liability)]. She should claim this amount as a tax credit when filing her income tax return for 1994. ▼

In Examples 33 and 34, the employee was subject to overwithholding. In both cases, however, the employee was able to obtain a credit for the excess withheld. The same result does not materialize for the portion paid by the employer. Since this amount is not refundable, in some situations employers may pay more FICA taxes than the covered employees.

The mere fact that a husband and wife are both employed does not, by itself, result in overwithholding of FICA taxes.

▼
EXAMPLE 35

During 1994, Jim and Betty (husband and wife) are both employed, and each earns wages subject to FICA of $40,000. Accordingly, each has $3,060 FICA withheld [(6.2% × $40,000) + (1.45% × $40,000)] for a total of $6,120. Since neither spouse paid FICA tax on wages in excess of $60,600 (Social Security tax) [see Table 13–4], there is no overwithholding. ▼

A spouse employed by another spouse is subject to FICA. However, children under the age of 18 who are employed in a parent's trade or business are exempted.

Amount of Income Tax Withholding

Arriving at the amount to be withheld for income tax purposes is not so simple. It involves three basic steps:[25]

- Have the employee complete Form W–4, Employee's Withholding Allowance Certificate.

---

[25] The withholding provisions are contained in §§ 3401 and 3402. These Sections will not be referenced specifically in the discussion that follows.

- Determine the employee's payroll period.
- Compute the amount to be withheld, usually using either the wage-bracket tables or the percentage method.

Form W–4 reflects the employee's marital status and **withholding allowances.** Generally, it need not be filed with the IRS and is retained by the employer as part of the payroll records.

The employer need not verify the number of exemptions claimed. Any misinformation in the form will be attributed to the employee. However, if the employer has reason to believe that the employee made a false statement, the IRS District Director should be notified. In the meantime, the Form W–4 should be honored. Employees are subject to both civil and criminal penalties for filing false withholding statements.

On Form W–4 an employee may claim *withholding allowances* for the following: personal exemptions for self and spouse (unless either is claimed as a dependent of another person) and dependency exemptions. One *special withholding allowance* may be claimed if the employee is single and has only one job, if the employee is married and has only one job and the spouse is not employed, or if wages from a second job or a spouse's wages (or both) are $1,000 or less. An additional allowance is available if the employee expects to file using the head of household status or if the employee expects to claim a credit for child and dependent care expenses on qualifying expenditures of at least $1,500. An employee who plans to itemize deductions or claim adjustments to income (e.g., alimony, deductible IRA contributions) should use the worksheet provided on Form W–4 to determine the correct number of additional allowances.

To avoid having too little tax withheld, some employees may find it necessary to reduce their withholding allowances. This might be the case for an employee who has more than one job or who has other sources of income that are not subject to adequate withholding. Likewise, a married employee who has a working spouse or more than one job might wish to claim fewer allowances.

If both spouses of a married couple are employed, they may allocate their total allowances between themselves as they see fit. The same allocation procedure is required if a taxpayer has more than one job. In no event should the same allowance be claimed more than once at the same time. It is permissible to declare *fewer* allowances than the taxpayer is entitled to in order to increase the amount of withholding. Doing so, however, does not affect the number of exemptions allowable on the employee's income tax return. An employee is also permitted to have the employer withhold a certain dollar amount in addition to the required amount. This additional dollar amount can be arbitrary or calculated in accordance with a worksheet and tables on Form W–4.

▼
EXAMPLE 36

Carl, who earns $15,000, is married to Carol, who earns $25,000. They have three dependent children and will claim the standard deduction. Together they should be entitled to five allowances [2 (for personal exemptions) + 3 (for dependency exemptions)]. The special withholding allowance is not available since both spouses earn more than $1,000. If Carl were the spouse first employed and his Form W–4 reflects five allowances, Carol's Form W–4 should report none. They could, however, reallocate their allowances between them as long as the total claimed does not exceed five. ▼

The period of service for which an employee is paid is known as the *payroll period.* Daily, weekly, biweekly, semimonthly, and monthly periods are the most common arrangements. If an employee has no regular payroll period, he or she is considered to be paid on a daily basis.

Once the allowances are known (as reflected on Form W–4) and the payroll period determined, the amount to be withheld for Federal income taxes can be

▼ TABLE 13–5
Withholding Table

MARRIED Persons—MONTHLY Payroll Period
(For Wages Paid in 1993)

If the wages are–		And the number of withholding allowances claimed is—										
At least	But less than	0	1	2	3	4	5	6	7	8	9	10
		The amount of income tax to be withheld is—										
$0	$520	$0	$0	$0	$0	$0	$0	$0	$0	$0	$0	$0
520	540	2	0	0	0	0	0	0	0	0	0	0
540	560	5	0	0	0	0	0	0	0	0	0	0
560	580	8	0	0	0	0	0	0	0	0	0	0
580	600	11	0	0	0	0	0	0	0	0	0	0
600	640	16	0	0	0	0	0	0	0	0	0	0
640	680	22	0	0	0	0	0	0	0	0	0	0
680	720	28	0	0	0	0	0	0	0	0	0	0
720	760	34	4	0	0	0	0	0	0	0	0	0
760	800	40	10	0	0	0	0	0	0	0	0	0
800	840	46	16	0	0	0	0	0	0	0	0	0
840	880	52	22	0	0	0	0	0	0	0	0	0
880	920	58	28	0	0	0	0	0	0	0	0	0
920	960	64	34	5	0	0	0	0	0	0	0	0
960	1,000	70	40	11	0	0	0	0	0	0	0	0
1,000	1,040	76	46	17	0	0	0	0	0	0	0	0
1,040	1,080	82	52	23	0	0	0	0	0	0	0	0
1,080	1,120	88	58	29	0	0	0	0	0	0	0	0
1,120	1,160	94	64	35	5	0	0	0	0	0	0	0
1,160	1,200	100	70	41	11	0	0	0	0	0	0	0
1,200	1,240	106	76	47	17	0	0	0	0	0	0	0
1,240	1,280	112	82	53	23	0	0	0	0	0	0	0
1,280	1,320	118	88	59	29	0	0	0	0	0	0	0
1,320	1,360	124	94	65	35	6	0	0	0	0	0	0
1,360	1,400	130	100	71	41	12	0	0	0	0	0	0
1,400	1,440	136	106	77	47	18	0	0	0	0	0	0
1,440	1,480	142	112	83	53	24	0	0	0	0	0	0
1,480	1,520	148	118	89	59	30	1	0	0	0	0	0
1,520	1,560	154	124	95	65	36	7	0	0	0	0	0
1,560	1,600	160	130	101	71	42	13	0	0	0	0	0
1,600	1,640	166	136	107	77	48	19	0	0	0	0	0
1,640	1,680	172	142	113	83	54	25	0	0	0	0	0
1,680	1,720	178	148	119	89	60	31	1	0	0	0	0
1,720	1,760	184	154	125	95	66	37	7	0	0	0	0
1,760	1,800	190	160	131	101	72	43	13	0	0	0	0
1,800	1,840	196	166	137	107	78	49	19	0	0	0	0
1,840	1,880	202	172	143	113	84	55	25	0	0	0	0
1,880	1,920	208	178	149	119	90	61	31	2	0	0	0
1,920	1,960	214	184	155	125	96	67	37	8	0	0	0
1,960	2,000	220	190	161	131	102	73	43	14	0	0	0
2,000	2,040	226	196	167	137	108	79	49	20	0	0	0
2,040	2,080	232	202	173	143	114	85	55	26	0	0	0
2,080	2,120	238	208	179	149	120	91	61	32	3	0	0
2,120	2,160	244	214	185	155	126	97	67	38	9	0	0
2,160	2,200	250	220	191	161	132	103	73	44	15	0	0
2,200	2,240	256	226	197	167	138	109	79	50	21	0	0
2,240	2,280	262	232	203	173	144	115	85	56	27	0	0
2,280	2,320	268	238	209	179	150	121	91	62	33	3	0
2,320	2,360	274	244	215	185	156	127	97	68	39	9	0
2,360	2,400	280	250	221	191	162	133	103	74	45	15	0
2,400	2,440	286	256	227	197	168	139	109	80	51	21	0
2,440	2,480	292	262	233	203	174	145	115	86	57	27	0
2,480	2,520	298	268	239	209	180	151	121	92	63	33	4
2,520	2,560	304	274	245	215	186	157	127	98	69	39	10
2,560	2,600	310	280	251	221	192	163	133	104	75	45	16
2,600	2,640	316	286	257	227	198	169	139	110	81	51	22
2,640	2,680	322	292	263	233	204	175	145	116	87	57	28
2,680	2,720	328	298	269	239	210	181	151	122	93	63	34
2,720	2,760	334	304	275	245	216	187	157	128	99	69	40
2,760	2,800	340	310	281	251	222	193	163	134	105	75	46
2,800	2,840	346	316	287	257	228	199	169	140	111	81	52
2,840	2,880	352	322	293	263	234	205	175	146	117	87	58
2,880	2,920	358	328	299	269	240	211	181	152	123	93	64
2,920	2,960	364	334	305	275	246	217	187	158	129	99	70
2,960	3,000	370	340	311	281	252	223	193	164	135	105	76
3,000	3,040	376	346	317	287	258	229	199	170	141	111	82
3,040	3,080	382	352	323	293	264	235	205	176	147	117	88
3,080	3,120	388	358	329	299	270	241	211	182	153	123	94
3,120	3,160	394	364	335	305	276	247	217	188	159	129	100
3,160	3,200	400	370	341	311	282	253	223	194	165	135	106

computed. The computation usually is made by using the wage-bracket tables or the percentage method.

Wage-bracket tables are available for daily, weekly, biweekly, semimonthly, and monthly payroll periods for single (including heads of household) and married taxpayers. An extract of the tables dealing with married persons on a monthly payroll period is reproduced in Table 13–5.

The data in Table 13–5 are for the period after December 31, 1993. Example 37 illustrates the use of withholding tables.

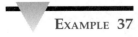

EXAMPLE 37

Tom is married and has three dependent children and no additional allowances for itemized deductions, adjustments to income, or child care credit. In his job with Pink Corporation, he earns $2,770 in May 1994. Assuming Tom's wife is not employed and all available allowances are claimed on Form W–4, Pink should withhold $154 a month from his wages. This amount is taken from the six allowances column in the $2,760–$2,800 wage bracket. The six allowances result from personal exemptions (two) plus the special withholding allowance (one) plus dependency exemptions (three). ▼

Although the wage-bracket table requires few, if any, calculations, the percentage method is equally acceptable. Its use may be necessary for payroll periods where no wage-bracket tables are available (quarterly, semiannual, and annual payroll periods) and where wages paid exceed the amount allowed for use of the wage-bracket tables. The percentage method is particularly useful when payroll computations are computerized. This method, however, requires the use of a conversion chart based on one withholding allowance. That is, the amount of one allowance is equal to the exemption amount divided by the number of payroll periods in a year. For example, the amount of one allowance for a taxpayer who is paid weekly is $47.12 ($2,450/52 payroll periods).

Payroll Period	Amount of One Allowance
Daily	$ 9.42
Weekly	47.12
Biweekly	94.23
Semimonthly	102.08
Monthly	204.17
Quarterly	612.50
Semiannual	1,225.00
Annual	2,450.00

To use the percentage method, proceed as follows:

Step 1. Multiply the amount of one allowance (as specified in the conversion chart) by the employee's total allowances (taken from Form W–4).
Step 2. Subtract the product reached in step 1 from the employee's wages. The remainder is called "amount of wages."
Step 3. Using the result derived in step 2, compute the income tax withholding under the proper percentage-method table.

The table used in applying the percentage method for those with monthly payroll periods is reproduced in Table 13–6.

An illustration of the percentage method follows.

▼ TABLE 13–6
Table for Percentage Method of Withholding[26]

TABLE 4—MONTHLY Payroll Period

(a) SINGLE person (including head of household)—				(b) MARRIED person—			
If the amount of wages (after subtracting withholding allowances) is:		The amount of income tax to withhold is:		If the amount of wages (after subtracting withholding allowances) is:		The amount of income tax to withhold is:	
Not over $210		$0		Not over $517		$0	
Over—	But not over—		of excess over—	Over—	But not over—		of excess over—
$210	—$1,954 . .	15%	—$210	$517	—$3,396 . . .	15%	—$517
$1,954	—$4,081 . .	$261.60 plus 28%	—$1,954	$3,396	—$6,771 . . .	$431.85 plus 28%	—$3,396
$4,081	. . . .	$857.16 plus 31%	—$4,081	$6,771		$1,376.85 plus 31%	—$6,771

[26] This table is for wages paid after December 1993.

EXAMPLE 38

Assume the same facts as in Example 37, except that Tom's income tax withholding is determined using the percentage method.

Step 1. $204.17 (amount of one allowance for a monthly payroll period) × 6 (total allowances) = $1,225.02.

Step 2. $2,770 (monthly salary) – $1,225.02 (step 1) = $1,544.98 (amount of wages).

Step 3. Referring to Table 13–6: 15% × $1,015.98 (excess of step 2 amount over $529) = $152. ▼

Note that the wage-bracket tables yield an amount for income tax withholding of $154 (refer to Example 37) while the percentage method results in $152 (refer to Example 38). The difference occurs because the wage-bracket table amounts are derived by computing the withholding on the median wage within each bracket.

Reporting and Payment Procedures

Proper handling of employment taxes and income tax withholdings requires considerable compliance effort on the part of the employer. Among the Federal forms that have to be filed are the following:

Form Designation	Title
SS–4	Application for Employer Identification Number
W–2	Wage and Tax Statement
W–3	Transmittal of Income and Tax Statements
940 or 940 EZ	Employer's Annual Federal Unemployment Tax Return
941	Employer's Quarterly Federal Tax Return

Form SS–4 is the starting point since it provides the employer with an identification number that must be used on all of the other forms filed with the IRS and the Social Security Administration. The number issued consists of nine digits and is hyphenated between the second and third digits (e.g., 72–1987316).

Form W–2 furnishes essential information to employees concerning wages paid, FICA, and income tax withholdings. Copies of Form W–2 are distributed to several parties for various purposes: to enable the employee to complete his or her income tax return, to inform the Social Security Administration of the amount of FICA wages earned by the employee, and to serve as a permanent record for the employer and employee of the payroll information contained on the form. Form W–2 must be furnished to an employee not later than January 31 of the following year. If an employee leaves a place of employment before the end of the year, Form W–2 can be given to him or her at any time after employment ends prior to the following January 31. However, if the terminated employee asks for Form W–2, it must be given to him or her within 30 days after the request or the final wage payment, whichever is later.

Form W–3 must accompany the copies of Forms W–2 filed by the employer with the Social Security Administration. Its basic purpose is to summarize and reconcile the amounts withheld for FICA and income taxes from *all* employees.

Form 940 (or Form 940 EZ) constitutes the employer's annual accounting for FUTA purposes. It must be filed on or before January 31 of the following year and must be accompanied by the payment of any undeposited FUTA due the Federal government.

Regardless of whether or not deposits[27] are required, most employers must settle their employment taxes every quarter. To do this, Form 941 must be filed on or before the last day of the month following the end of each calendar quarter.

Withholding on Other Amounts

Withholding is required for pension payments unless the taxpayer affirmatively *elects* to have *no* tax withheld. Part of the reason for this provision is to ease the burden on retirees of filing and paying quarterly estimated tax payments. In addition, on certain supplemental wages such as bonuses and commissions, the law permits withholdings to be made based on a flat 28 percent rate.

Backup Withholding

Some types of payments made to individuals by banks or businesses are subject to backup withholding under certain conditions. Backup withholding is designed to ensure that income tax is collected on interest and other payments reported on a Form 1099. If backup withholding applies, the payer must withhold 31 percent of the amount paid. Backup withholding applies when the taxpayer does not give the business or bank his or her identification number in the required manner and in other situations.[28]

ETHICAL CONSIDERATIONS

Withholding for Domestic Workers

Although most businesses have little difficulty implementing the withholding requirements, many individuals are ignorant of or confused about the rules relating to workers they hire on a personal basis, especially part-time employees.

Recently, your neighbor has hired a domestic worker, Simon, to clean his house twice a month. Since your house also needs cleaning, you inquire about Simon's qualifications, fees, hours, and so forth. You learn that his fee depends on whether he is paid by check or in cash. He charges $60 per visit if he is paid by check and $50 if he is paid in cash. Further, he does not mention employer withholding for income or FICA taxes. In fact, based on his fee structure, you have the distinct impression that Simon prefers that his employers not pay withholding or FICA taxes or file a Form W–2 with the government at the end of the year.

Your neighbor reports that Simon does a very good job, and you would like to establish an employment relationship with him as soon as possible. How do you proceed in terms of deciding on the method of payment and your withholding and reporting duties?

PROCEDURES APPLICABLE TO SELF-EMPLOYED PERSONS

Although the following discussion largely centers on self-employed taxpayers, some of the procedures may be applicable to employed persons. In many cases, for example, employed persons may be required to pay estimated tax if they have

---

[27] Deposit requirements are specified in each current issue of Circular E, *Employer's Tax Guide,* IRS Publication 15. Under current rules, most employers must make deposits on a monthly or semiweekly basis.

[28] § 3406(a).

income other than wages that is not subject to withholding. An employee may conduct a second trade or business in a self-employment capacity. Depending on the circumstances, the second job may require the payment of a self-employment tax. In addition, taxpayers whose income consists primarily of rentals, dividends, or interest (this list is not all-inclusive) may be required to pay estimated tax.

Estimated Tax for Individuals

Estimated tax is the amount of tax (including alternative minimum tax and self-employment tax) an individual expects to owe for the year after subtracting tax credits and income tax withheld. Any individual who has estimated tax for the year of $500 or more *and* whose withholding does not equal or exceed the required annual payment (discussed below) must make quarterly payments.[29] Otherwise, a penalty may be assessed. No quarterly payments are required (no penalty will apply on an underpayment) if the taxpayer's estimated tax is under $500. No penalty will apply if the taxpayer had no tax liability for the preceding tax year *and* the preceding tax year was a taxable year of 12 months *and* the taxpayer was a citizen or resident for the entire preceding tax year. In this regard, having no tax liability is not the same as having no additional tax to pay.

The required annual payment must first be computed. This is the *smaller* of the following amounts:

- Ninety percent of the tax shown on the current year's return.
- One hundred percent of the tax shown on the preceding year's return (the return must cover the full 12 months of the preceding year). In certain circumstances, however, this option is not available.

In general, one-fourth of this required annual payment is due on April 15, June 15, and September 15 of the tax year and January 15 of the following year.

An equal part of withholding is deemed paid on each due date. Thus, the quarterly installment of the required annual payment reduced by the applicable withholding is the estimated tax to be paid. Payments are to be accompanied by the payment voucher for the appropriate date from Form 1040–ES.

Married taxpayers may make joint estimated tax payments even though a joint income tax return is not subsequently filed. In such event, the estimated tax payments may be applied against the separate return liability of the spouses as they see fit. If a husband and wife cannot agree on a division of the estimated tax payments, the Regulations provide that the payments are to be allocated in proportion to the tax liability on the separate returns.

Penalty on Underpayments

A nondeductible penalty is imposed on the amount of underpayment of estimated tax. The rate for this penalty is the same as the rate for underpayments of tax and is adjusted quarterly to reflect changes in the average prime rate.

An *underpayment* occurs when any installment (the sum of estimated tax paid and income tax withheld) is less than 25 percent of the required annual payment. The penalty is applied to the amount of the underpayment for the period of the underpayment.[30]

---

[29] § 6654(c)(1).

[30] § 6654(b)(2).

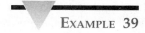

EXAMPLE 39

Marta made the following payments of estimated tax for 1994 and had no income tax withheld:

April 15, 1994	$1,400
June 15, 1994	2,300
September 15, 1994	1,500
January 17, 1995	1,800

Marta's actual tax for 1994 is $8,000, and her tax in 1993 was $10,000. Therefore, each installment should have been at least $1,800 [($8,000 × 90%) × 25%]. Of the payment on June 15, $400 will be credited to the unpaid balance of the first quarterly installment due on April 15,[31] thereby effectively stopping the underpayment penalty for the first quarterly period. Of the remaining $1,900 payment on June 15, $100 is credited to the September 15 payment, resulting in this third quarterly payment being $200 short. Then $200 of the January 17 payment is credited to the September 15 shortfall, ending the period of underpayment for that portion due. The January 17, 1995, installment is now underpaid by $200, and a penalty will apply from January 17, 1995, to April 15, 1995 (unless paid sooner). Marta's underpayments for the periods of underpayment are as follows:

1st installment due:	$400 from April 15–June 15
2nd installment due:	Paid in full
3rd installment due:	$200 from September 15, 1994–January 17, 1995
4th installment due:	$200 from January 17–April 15, 1995

If a possible underpayment of estimated tax is indicated, Form 2210 should be filed to compute the penalty due or to justify that no penalty applies.

Self-Employment Tax

The tax on self-employment income is levied to provide Social Security and Medicare benefits (old age, survivors, and disability insurance and hospital insurance) for self-employed individuals. Individuals with net earnings of $400 or more from self-employment are subject to the **self-employment tax.**[32] For 1994, the self-employment tax is 15.3 percent on self-employment income up to $60,600 and 2.9 percent on self-employment income in excess of $60,600. In other words, for 1994 the self-employment tax is 12.4 percent of self-employment earnings up to $60,600 (for the Social Security portion) *plus* 2.9 percent of the total amount of self-employment earnings (for the Medicare portion). See Table 13–7.

▼ **TABLE 13–7**
Self-Employment Tax: Social Security and Medicare Portions

Year		Tax Rate	Ceiling Amount
1993	Social Security portion	12.4%	$ 57,600
	Medicare portion	2.9%	135,000
	Aggregate rate	15.3%	
1994	Social Security portion	12.4%	$ 60,600
	Medicare portion	2.9%	Unlimited
	Aggregate rate	15.3%	

---

[31] Payments are credited to unpaid installments in the order in which the installments are required to be paid. § 6654(b)(3).

[32] § 6017.

▼ FIGURE 13–1
1994 Self-Employment
Tax Worksheet

1. Net earnings from self-employment. _____
2. Multiply line 1 by 92.35%. _____
3. If the amount on line 2 is $60,600 or less, multiply the line 2 amount by 15.3%. This is the self-employment tax. _____
4. If the amount on line 2 is more than $60,600, multiply the excess of line 2 over $60,600 by 2.9% and add $9,271.80. This is the self-employment tax. _____

Currently, self-employed taxpayers are allowed a deduction from net earnings from self-employment, at one-half of the self-employment rate, for purposes of determining self-employment tax[33] *and* an income tax deduction for one-half the amount of self-employment tax paid.[34]

Determining the amount of self-employment tax to be paid for 1994 involves completing the steps in Figure 13–1. The result of step 3 or 4 is the amount of self-employment tax to be paid. For *income tax purposes*, the amount to be reported is net earnings from self-employment before the deduction for one-half of the self-employment tax. Then the taxpayer is allowed a deduction *for* AGI of one-half of the self-employment tax.

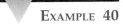

EXAMPLE 40

Using the format in Figure 13–1, the self-employment tax is determined for two taxpayers with net earnings from self-employment for 1994 as follows: Ned, $55,000 and Terry, $80,000.

Ned's Self-Employment Tax Worksheet

1. Net earnings from self-employment.	$55,000.00
2. Multiply line 1 by 92.35%.	$50,792.50
3. If the amount on line 2 is $60,600 or less, multiply the line 2 amount by 15.3%. This is the self-employment tax.	$ 7,771.25
4. If the amount on line 2 is more than $60,600, multiply the excess over $60,600 by 2.9% and add $9,271.80. This is the self-employment tax.	

Terry's Self-Employment Tax Worksheet

1. Net earnings from self-employment.	$80,000.00
2. Multiply line 1 by 92.35%.	$73,880.00
3. If the amount on line 2 is $60,600 or less, multiply the line 2 amount by 15.3%. This is the self-employment tax.	_____
4. If the amount on line 2 is more than $60,600, multiply the excess over $60,600 by 2.9% and add $9,271.80. This is the self-employment tax.	$ 9,656.92

For income tax purposes, Ned has net earnings from self-employment of $55,000 and a deduction *for* AGI of $3,885.63 (one-half of $7,771.25). Terry has net earnings from self-employment of $80,000 and a deduction *for* AGI of $4,828.46 (one-half of $9,656.92). Both taxpayers benefit from the deduction for one-half of the self-employment tax paid.

---

[33] § 1402(a)(12).

[34] § 164(f).

For 1993, the self-employment tax computations are similar to those for 1994. The only differences are that the tax bases were lower for 1993 than they are for 1994 and that the calculation for the Medicare portion in 1993 was limited to earnings of up to $135,000 (see Table 13–7 and Figure 13–2). ▼

If an individual also receives wages subject to FICA tax in 1994, the ceiling amount of the Social Security portion on which the self-employment tax is computed is reduced. Thus, self-employment tax may be reduced if a self-employed individual also receives FICA wages in excess of the ceiling amount.

EXAMPLE 41

In 1994, Kelly had $42,000 of net earnings from the conduct of a bookkeeping service (trade or business activity). She also received wages as an employee amounting to $25,000 during the year. The amount of Kelly's self-employment income subject to the Social Security portion (12.4%) is $35,600, producing a tax of $4,414.40 ($35,600 × 12.4%). All of Kelly's net self-employment earnings are subject to the Medicare portion of the self-employment tax of 2.9%. Therefore, the self-employment tax on this portion is $1,124.82 ($38,787 × 2.9%).

	Social Security Portion
Ceiling amount	$60,600
Less: FICA wages	25,000
Net ceiling	$35,600
Net self-employment income ($42,000 × 92.35%)	$38,787
Lesser of net ceiling or net self-employment income	$35,600

▼

Net earnings from self-employment include gross income from a trade or business less allowable trade or business deductions, the distributive share of any partnership income or loss derived from a trade or business activity, and net income from the rendering of personal services as an independent contractor. Gain or loss from the disposition of property (including involuntary conversions) is excluded from the computation of self-employment income unless the property involved is inventory.

Director's fees, which are paid to a nonemployee, are also considered self-employment income because a director is considered to be engaged in a trade or business activity. However, director's fees received on a deferred basis are not

▼ FIGURE 13–2
1993 Self-Employment
Tax Worksheet

1. Net earnings from self-employment. _____

2. Multiply line 1 by 92.35%. _____

3. If the amount on line 2 is $57,600 or less, multiply the line 2 amount by 15.3%. This is the self-employment tax. _____

4. If the amount on line 2 is more than $57,600 but less than $135,000, multiply the excess of line 2 over $57,600 by 2.9% and add $8,812.80. This is the self-employment tax. _____

5. If the amount on line 2 is $135,000 or more, enter $11,057.40. This is the self-employment tax. _____

subject to the self-employment tax until the fees are paid or constructively received and thus are subject to the income tax.

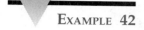

EXAMPLE 42

Tara, a former treasurer, is retired from Emerald Company but is retained as a corporate director. She performs these duties in 1994 under a deferred arrangement whereby she will be paid $12,000 in 1996, at which time she will be 70 years old. In 1994, the year earned, none of the director's fees will be subject to self-employment tax. For income tax purposes and for self-employment tax purposes, the $12,000 of director's fees will be subject to tax in 1996, the year received. ▼

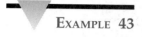

EXAMPLE 43

Assume the same facts as in Example 42, except that Tara is not retired. In addition to the director's fees, she is paid a salary of $150,000 in her capacity as treasurer of the company. Because her salary exceeds the Social Security portion wage base ($60,600) for FICA tax purposes, the director's fees are not subject to the Social Security portion of the self-employment tax if they were paid in 1994. If not paid until 1996, the director's fees will be subject to both portions of the self-employment tax in 1996 unless Tara's salary in 1996 exceeds the Social Security wage base. Thus, she will need to consider both the income tax deferral consequences and the self-employment tax consequences for the year the director's fees are to be paid. ▼

An employee who performs services on a part-time basis as an independent contractor or an employee who is engaged in a separate trade or business activity may be subject to the self-employment tax.

TAX PLANNING CONSIDERATIONS

FOREIGN TAX CREDIT

A U.S. citizen or resident working abroad (commonly referred to as an *expatriate*) may elect to take either a foreign tax credit or the foreign earned income exclusion. In cases where the income tax of a foreign country is higher than the U.S. income tax, the credit choice usually is preferable. If the reverse is true, electing the foreign earned income exclusion probably reduces the overall tax burden.

6 **LEARNING OBJECTIVE**
Identify tax planning opportunities related to tax credits and payment procedures.

Unfortunately, the choice between the credit and the earned income exclusion is not without some limitations. The election of the foreign earned income exclusion, once made, can be revoked for a later year. However, once revoked, the earned income exclusion will not be available for a period of five years unless the IRS consents to an earlier date. This will create a dilemma for expatriates whose job assignments over several years shift between low- and high-bracket countries.

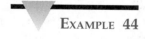

EXAMPLE 44

In 1993, Ira, a calendar year taxpayer, is sent by his employer to Saudi Arabia (a low-tax country). For 1993, therefore, Ira elects the foreign earned income exclusion. In 1994, Ira's employer transfers him to France (a high-tax country). Accordingly, he revokes the foreign earned income exclusion election for 1994 and chooses instead to use the foreign tax credit. If Ira is transferred back to Saudi Arabia (or any other low-tax country) within five years, he no longer may utilize the foreign earned income exclusion. ▼

CREDIT FOR CHILD AND DEPENDENT CARE EXPENSES

A taxpayer may incur employment-related expenses that also qualify as medical expenses (e.g., a nurse is hired to provide in-the-home care for an ill and incapacitated dependent parent). Such expenses may be either deducted as medical expenses (subject to the 7.5 percent limitation) or utilized in determining the credit for child and dependent care expenses. If the dependent care credit is chosen and the employment-related expenses exceed the limitation ($2,400, $4,800, or earned income, as the case may be), the excess may be considered a medical expense. If, however, the taxpayer chooses to deduct qualified employment-related expenses as medical expenses, any portion that is not deductible because of the 7.5 percent limitation may not be used in computing the credit for child and dependent care expenses.

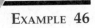

EXAMPLE 45

Alicia, a single taxpayer, has the following tax position for tax year 1994.

Adjusted gross income		$30,000
Potential itemized deductions *from* AGI—		
Other than medical expenses	$2,500	
Medical expenses	6,000	$ 8,500

All of Alicia's medical expenses were incurred to provide nursing care for her disabled father while she was working. The father lives with Alicia and qualifies as her dependent. ▼

What should Alicia do in this situation? One approach would be to use $2,400 of the nursing care expenses to obtain the maximum dependent care credit allowed of $480 (20% × $2,400). The balance of these expenses should be claimed as medical expenses. After a reduction of 7.5 percent of AGI, this would produce a medical expense deduction of $1,350 [$3,600 (remaining medical expenses) − (7.5% × $30,000)].

Another approach would be to claim the full $6,000 as a medical expense and forgo the dependent care credit. After the 7.5 percent adjustment of $2,250 (7.5% × $30,000), a deduction of $3,750 remains.

The choice, then, is between a credit of $480 plus a deduction of $1,350 or a credit of $0 plus a deduction of $3,750. Which is better, of course, depends on the relative tax savings involved.

One of the traditional goals of *family tax planning* is to minimize the total tax burden within the family unit. With proper planning and implementation, the child and dependent care expenses credit can be used to help achieve this goal. For example, payments to certain relatives for the care of qualifying dependents and children qualify for the credit if the care provider is *not* a dependent of the taxpayer or the taxpayer's spouse or is *not* a child (under age 19) of the taxpayer. Thus, if the care provider is in a lower tax bracket than the taxpayer, the following benefits result:

- Income is shifted to a lower-bracket family member.
- The taxpayer qualifies for the credit for child and dependent care expenses.

In addition, the goal of minimizing the family income tax liability can be enhanced in some other situations, but only if the credit's limitations are recognized and avoided. For example, tax savings may still be enjoyed even if the qualifying expenditures incurred by a cash basis taxpayer have already reached the annual ceiling ($2,400 or $4,800). To the extent that any additional payments can be shifted into future tax years, the benefit from the credit may be preserved on these excess expenditures.

EXAMPLE 46

Andre, a calendar year and cash basis taxpayer, has spent $2,400 by December 1 on qualifying child care expenditures for his dependent 11-year-old son. The $200 that is due the care provider for child care services rendered in December does not generate a tax credit benefit if the amount is paid in the current year because the $2,400 ceiling has been reached. However, if the payment can be delayed until the next year, the total credit over the two-year period for which Andre is eligible may be increased. ▼

A similar shifting of expenditures to a subsequent year may be wise if the potential credit otherwise generated would exceed the tax liability available to absorb the credit.

ADJUSTMENTS TO INCREASE WITHHOLDING

The penalty for underpayment of estimated tax by individuals is computed for each quarter of the tax year. A taxpayer can play *catch-up* to a certain extent. Each quarterly payment is credited to the unpaid portion of any previous required installment. Thus, the penalty stops on that portion of the underpayment for the previous quarter. Since income tax withheld is assumed to have been paid evenly throughout the year and is allocated equally among the four installments in computing any penalty, a taxpayer who would otherwise be subject to a penalty for underpayment should increase withholdings late in the year. This can be done by changing the number of allowances claimed on Form W–4 or by special arrangement with the employer to increase the amount withheld.

A similar way to avoid (or reduce) a penalty for underpayment is to have the employer continue Social Security withholding beyond the base amount.

EXAMPLE 47

Rose, a calendar year taxpayer, earns $72,000 from her job. In late August 1994, she realizes that she will be subject to a penalty for underpayment of estimated tax due to income from outside sources. Consequently, she instructs her employer to continue FICA withholdings for the rest of 1994. If this is done, an extra $11,400 [$72,000 (annual salary) – $60,600 (base amount of the Social Security portion for 1994)] will be subject to the 6.2% Social Security portion of the FICA tax [7.65% (total FICA rate) – 1.45% (Medicare portion of the FICA rate)]. Thus, Rose generates an additional $707 (6.2% × $11,400) that will be deemed withheld ratably during 1994. ▼

ADJUSTMENTS TO AVOID OVERWITHHOLDING

Publication 505, Tax Withholding and Estimated Tax, contains worksheets that taxpayers may use to take advantage of special provisions for avoiding overwithholding. Extra exemptions for withholding purposes are allowed if the taxpayer has unusually large itemized deductions, deductions *for* AGI, or tax credits. Net losses from Schedules C, D, E, and F may be considered in computing the number of extra withholding exemptions. Net operating loss carryovers may also be considered in the computation. A taxpayer who is entitled to extra withholding exemptions for any of these reasons should file a new Form W–4, Employee's Withholding Allowance Certificate, with his or her employer.

KEY TERMS

Business energy credit, 13–10	Earned income credit, 13–17	General business credit, 13–5
Credit for child and dependent care expenses, 13–21	Employment taxes, 13–26	Investment tax credit (ITC), 13–7
Disabled access credit, 13–16	Estimated tax, 13–35	Jobs credit, 13–10
	Foreign tax credit (FTC), 13–21	Low-income housing credit, 13–15

Nonrefundable credit, 13–4	Rehabilitation expenditures credit recapture, 13–9	Tax credits, 13–2
Refundable credit, 13–4	Research activities credit, 13–11	Tax credit for the elderly or disabled, 13–19
Rehabilitation expenditures credit, 13–8	Self-employment tax, 13–36	Withholding allowance, 13–30

PROBLEM
MATERIALS

DISCUSSION QUESTIONS

1. Would an individual taxpayer receive greater benefit from deducting an expenditure or from taking a credit equal to 25% of the expenditure?

2. What is a refundable credit? Give examples. What is a nonrefundable credit? Give examples.

3. Discuss the order in which credits are offset against the tax liability. Why is the order in which credits are utilized important?

4. Discuss the treatment of unused general business credits.

5. The regular investment tax credit was repealed generally for property placed in service after December 31, 1985. Is there any way a taxpayer can benefit currently from unused ITC related to investment credit property placed in service on or before that date? Explain.

6. Vic is considering the purchase and renovation of an old building. He has heard about the tax credit for rehabilitation expenditures but does not know the specific rules applicable to the credit. He has asked you to explain the most important details to him. What will you tell Vic?

7. If property on which the tax credit for rehabilitation expenditures was claimed is prematurely disposed of or ceases to be qualified property, how is the tax liability affected in the year of the disposition or disqualification?

8. Discuss the general requirements for obtaining benefit from the regular jobs credit.

9. In 1994, TUV Corporation hired Chris, who is certified as a member of a targeted group for purposes of the jobs credit. Chris was paid $11,000 during the year. How much is TUV Corporation's deduction for wages paid to Chris during 1994?

10. What credit provisions in the tax law were enacted to encourage technological development in the United States?

11. Explain the alternatives a taxpayer has in claiming the deduction and credit for research and experimentation expenditures incurred.

12. Explain the purpose of the disabled access credit and describe the general characteristics of its computation.

13. During 1994, Rust Corporation made some structural changes to its facility to provide easier access for disabled persons. These changes cost $12,000 and were qualifying expenditures for purposes of the disabled access credit. Determine the amount of the disabled access credit and the depreciable basis for these capital improvements.

14. Briefly discuss the requirements that must be satisfied for a taxpayer to qualify for the earned income credit.

15. What three tests must be met for a child to be considered a qualifying child for purposes of the earned income credit? Describe.

16. Individuals who receive substantial Social Security benefits are usually not eligible for the tax credit for the elderly or disabled because these benefits effectively eliminate the base upon which the credit is computed. Explain.

17. What purpose is served by the overall limitation to the foreign tax credit?

18. Do all foreign taxes qualify for the U.S. foreign tax credit? Explain.

19. In general, when would an individual taxpayer find it more beneficial to take advantage of the foreign earned income exclusion rather than the foreign tax credit in computing his or her income tax liability?

20. Pete is not concerned with the credit for child and dependent care expenses because his AGI is considerably in excess of $20,000. Is Pete under a misconception regarding the tax law? Explain.

21. Gary and Gail are married and have a dependent child eight years of age. Gary earned $15,000 during 1994. Gail, a full-time student for the entire year, was not employed. Gary and Gail believe they are not entitled to the credit for child and dependent care expenses because Gail was not employed. Is this correct? Explain your answer.

22. Polly and her spouse, Leo, file a joint return and expect to report AGI of $95,000 in 1994. Polly's employer offers a child and dependent care reimbursement plan that allows up to $2,500 of qualifying expenses to be reimbursed in exchange for a $2,500 reduction in the employee's salary. Because Polly and Leo have one minor child requiring child care that costs $2,500 each year, she is wondering if she should sign up for the program instead of taking advantage of the credit for child and dependent care expenses. Analyze the effect of the two alternatives. How would your answer differ if Polly and Leo's AGI was $10,000 instead of $95,000?

23. Discuss the rationale underlying the enactment of the following tax credits:
    a. Tax credit for rehabilitation expenditures.
    b. Low-income housing credit.
    c. Disabled access credit.
    d. Earned income credit.
    e. Foreign tax credit.
    f. Credit for child and dependent care expenses.

24. Elaborate rules exist that require employers to prepay various types of Federal taxes. Summarize the major issues that an employer must resolve if it is to comply with the requirements.

25. At a social function you attended in early July of 1994, you overhear a guest, the CEO of a corporation, remark, "Thank goodness this is the end of FICA for a while!" Interpret this remark.

26. Keith, a sole proprietor, owns and operates a grocery store. Keith's wife and his 17-year-old son work in the business and are paid wages. Will the wife and son be subject to FICA? Explain.

27. Although Vicki is entitled to four allowances, she claimed just one on her Form W–4.
    a. Why would Vicki claim fewer allowances than she is entitled to?
    b. Is this procedure permissible?
    c. Will this affect the number of exemptions Vicki can claim on her Federal income tax return?

28. If the employer is not required to withhold income taxes on an item of income paid to an employee, does this mean that the item is nontaxable? Explain.

29. Describe the exposure (i.e., wage base and tax rate) that a self-employed individual has to the self-employment tax for 1994.

30. You read that self-employed taxpayers get a double deduction for one-half of the self-employment tax, not only as a deduction in computing the self-employment tax but also as a deduction *for* AGI. Is this true? Explain.

PROBLEMS

31. Dan has a tentative general business credit of $110,000 for 1994. His net regular tax liability before the general business credit is $125,000; tentative minimum tax is $100,000. Compute Dan's allowable general business credit for 1994.

32. Tan Corporation has the following general business credit carryovers:

1990	$ 5,000
1991	15,000
1992	5,000
1993	20,000
Total carryovers	$45,000

    If the general business credit generated by activities during 1994 equals $45,000 and the total credit allowed during the current year is $80,000 (based on tax liability), what amounts of the current general business credit and carryovers are utilized against the 1994 income tax liability? What is the amount of unused credit carried forward to 1995?

33. In 1985, Gus placed $100,000 of five-year assets and $60,000 of three-year assets into service in his business. All of the assets were new at the time and met the definition of qualified property for purposes of the regular investment tax credit. Because of limited tax exposure since 1985, Gus has been unable to utilize the credit until the current year. Assuming that the full credit rates were used to compute the ITC, determine the amount of regular ITC that would be available as a carryover to the current tax year.

34. On August 1, 1991, Earl acquired and placed in service a pre-1936 office building. The cost was $250,000, of which $50,000 applied to the land. In order to keep tenants, Earl spent $250,000 renovating the building in 1994. The expenses were of the type that qualify for the rehabilitation credit. These improvements were placed in service on May 1.
    a. Compute Earl's rehabilitation tax credit for 1994.
    b. Determine cost recovery for the year.
    c. What is Earl's basis in the property at the end of 1994?

35. Diane Lawson acquires a qualifying historic structure for $250,000 (excluding the cost of land) in 1994 with full intentions of substantially rehabilitating the building. Write a letter to Diane and a memo to the tax files explaining the computation that determines the rehabilitation tax credit available to her and the impact on the depreciable basis, assuming either $200,000 or $400,000 is incurred for the rehabilitation project.

36. Redbird Company hired six handicapped individuals (qualifying Redbird for the jobs credit) in March 1994. Three of these individuals received wages of $7,000 each during 1994 while the other three received wages of $5,000 each.
    a. Calculate the amount of the jobs credit for 1994.
    b. Assume Redbird paid total wages of $120,000 to its employees during the year. How much of this amount is deductible in 1994 if the jobs credit is elected?

37. Leon, the sole owner of Wren Corporation, is in need of one additional factory worker. Due to the high rate of unemployment in the community, many people apply for the opening. As Leon reviews the applications, two individuals stand out: George, whose employment would give rise to a jobs credit for Wren Corporation, and Jason, whose employment would not give rise to the jobs credit. If George were hired, a reasonable salary would be $15,000 while Jason would have to be paid $16,000. Training costs incurred by Wren would probably be $1,400 higher if George were hired, while Jason's relative efficiencies on the job as compared to George would probably approach $1,000.
    a. Assuming that Wren is in the 34% tax bracket, from a quantitative point of view, would it be better to hire George or Jason?
    b. Would your answer change if you were to consider intangible aspects (e.g., such as goodwill from the community) of the hiring decision?

38. Matt, a calendar year taxpayer, furnishes the following information. Gross receipts are net of returns and allowances.

	Gross Receipts	Qualified Research Expenses
1994	$180,000	$30,000
1993	170,000	50,000
1992	160,000	35,000
1991	120,000	45,000
1990	120,000	50,000
1989	125,000	30,000
1988	120,000	45,000
1987	135,000	40,000
1986	110,000	20,000
1985	95,000	–0–
1984	80,000	30,000

a. Using the template in the text, determine Matt's incremental research activities credit for 1994.
b. Matt is in the 28% tax bracket. Determine which approach to the research expenditures and the research activities credit (other than capitalization and subsequent amortization) would provide the greatest tax benefit in the current year.

39. Assume the same facts as in the previous problem, except that Matt incurs $60,000 of qualified research expenditures in 1994. Using the template in the text, compute the incremental research activities credit for 1994.

40. Rose Corporation is an eligible small business for purposes of the disabled access credit. During the year, Rose Corporation makes the following expenditures on a structure originally placed in service in 1984:

Removal of architectural barriers	$4,250
Acquired equipment for disabled persons	3,000
	$7,250

In addition, $3,500 was expended on a building placed in service in the current year, to ensure easy accessibility by disabled individuals. Calculate the amount of the disabled access credit available to Rose Corporation.

41. Which of the following individuals qualify for the earned income credit for 1994?
a. Kristy is single, 23 years of age, and has no children. She earns $5,000.
b. Kareem is single, 32 years of age, and has no children. He earns $5,000.
c. Carlos maintains a household for a dependent 13-year-old daughter and qualifies for the head of household filing status. Carlos's income consists of a $30,000 salary.
d. Floyd and Grace are married, file a joint return, and have two children. Their combined income consists of salary of $14,000 and interest income of $50.

42. Irene, who qualifies for the earned income credit, has three qualifying children who live with her. Irene earns a salary of $13,500 during 1994. Calculate Irene's earned income credit for the year.

43. Vern, a widower, lives in an apartment with his three minor children (ages 3, 4, and 5) whom he supports. Vern earned $17,100 during 1994. He contributed $1,000 to an IRA and uses the standard deduction. Calculate the amount, if any, of Vern's earned income credit.

44. Joe, age 67, and Emily, age 66, are married retirees who received the following income and retirement benefits during 1994:

Fully taxable pension from Joe's former employer	$ 5,000
Dividends and interest	8,000
Social Security benefits	1,750
	$14,750

Assume Joe and Emily file a joint return, have no deductions *for* AGI, and do not itemize. Are they eligible for the tax credit for the elderly or disabled? If so, calculate the amount of the credit using the template shown in the chapter, assuming their actual tax liability (before credits) is $150.

45. Kim, a U.S. citizen and resident, owns and operates a novelty goods business. During 1994, Kim has taxable income of $100,000, made up as follows: $50,000 from foreign sources and $50,000 from U.S. sources. In calculating taxable income, the standard deduction is used. The income from foreign sources is subject to foreign income taxes of $26,000. For 1994, Kim files a joint return claiming his three children as dependents. Assuming Kim chooses to claim the foreign taxes as an income tax credit, what is his income tax liability for 1994?

46. Egret Corporation, a U.S. corporation, is a manufacturing concern that sells most of its products in the United States. It does, however, do some business in Europe through various branches. During 1994, Egret had taxable income of $500,000, of which $350,000 was U.S.-sourced and $150,000 was foreign-sourced. Foreign income taxes paid are $45,000. Egret's U.S. income tax liability before any foreign tax credit is $170,000. What is Egret's U.S. income tax net of the allowable foreign tax credit?

47. Purple Corporation is an international wholesaler headquartered in the United States. Of its worldwide taxable income of $3 billion, $1.25 billion was foreign-sourced. Before any credits, the U.S. income tax liability is $1.05 billion. If income taxes paid to foreign countries totaled $600 million, what is Purple's U.S. income tax liability after benefiting from the foreign tax credit?

48. Pat and Jeri are husband and wife, and both are gainfully employed. They have three children under the age of 13. During 1994, Pat earned $60,000, while Jeri earned $4,900. In order for them to work, they paid $5,800 to various unrelated parties to care for their children. Assuming Pat and Jeri file a joint return, what, if any, is their credit for child and dependent care expenses for 1994?

49. Jim and Jill are husband and wife and have two dependent children under the age of 13. They both are gainfully employed and during 1994 earned salaries as follows: $12,000 (Jim) and $3,000 (Jill). To care for their children while they work, they pay Megan (Jim's mother) $3,600. Megan does not qualify as a dependent of Jim and Jill. Assuming Jim and Jill file a joint return, what, if any, is their credit for child and dependent care expenses?

50. Kevin and Jane are husband and wife and have one dependent child, age 9. Kevin is a full-time student for all of 1994, while Jane earns $18,000 as a nurse's aid. In order to provide care for their child while Kevin attends classes and Jane works, they pay Sara (Jane's 17-year-old sister) $2,300. Sara is not the dependent of Kevin and Jane. Assuming Kevin and Jane file a joint return, what, if any, is their credit for child and dependent care expenses?

51. During 1994, Greg Cruz worked for Maple Corporation and Gray Company. He earned $60,000 at Maple Corporation where he was a full-time employee. Greg also worked part-time for Gray Company for wages of $30,000.
   a. Did Greg experience an overwithholding of FICA taxes? Write a letter to Greg and a memo for the tax files in which you explain your conclusion.
   b. Did Maple Corporation and Gray Company overpay the employer's portion of FICA? Explain.

52. In each of the following independent situations, determine the maximum withholding allowances permitted Eli (an employee) on Form W–4:
   a. Eli is single with no dependents.

b. Eli is married to a nonemployed spouse, and they have no dependents.

c. Eli is married to Vera, an employed spouse, and they have three dependent children. On the Form W–4 that she filed with the employer, Vera claimed zero allowances.

d. Assume the same facts as in (c), except that Eli and Vera fully support Eli's mother, who lives with them. The mother (age 70 and blind) qualifies as their dependent. (Refer to Chapter 3.)

e. Eli is single with no dependents but works for two employers, one on a full-time basis and the other on a part-time basis. The Form W–4 filed with the first employer (the full-time job) reflects two withholding exemptions. The wages from each job exceed $1,000.

f. Assume the same facts as in (e), except that Eli is married to a nonemployed spouse.

53. Norm is married to a nonemployed spouse and has four dependents. He is employed by Beige Corporation and is paid a monthly salary of $2,620 ($31,440 per year). Using these facts, determine the amount to be withheld by Beige Corporation for Federal income tax purposes under the wage-bracket tables and under the percentage method for 1994.

54. During 1994, Helen, the owner of a store, had the following income and expenses:

Gross profit on sales	$63,000
Income from part-time job (subject to FICA)	24,000
Business expenses (related to store)	15,000
Fire loss on store building	1,200
Dividend income	200
Long-term capital gain on the sale of a stock investment	2,000

Compute Helen's self-employment tax using the format illustrated in the text.

55. In 1994, Fran has self-employed earnings of $150,000. Compute Fran's self-employment tax liability and the allowable income tax deduction for the self-employment tax paid using the format illustrated in the text.

CUMULATIVE PROBLEMS

56. Hal and Wanda Atkins, ages 38 and 36, are married and file a joint return. Their Social Security numbers are 123–32–1232 and 456–65–4321, respectively. Hal and Wanda's household includes Sam, their 10-year-old son, and Fred, who is Hal's 76-year-old father. Sam's Social Security number is 789–87–6543, and Fred's Social Security number is 123–87–1232. Fred is very ill and has been confined to bed for most of the year. He has no income of his own and is fully supported by Hal and Wanda. Hal and Wanda had the following income and expenses during 1994:

Hal's wages	$18,000
Wanda's salary	24,000
Interest from First National Bank	450
Unemployment compensation received by Hal, who was laid off for five months during the year	4,500
Dividends received on January 3, 1995; the corporation mailed the check on December 31, 1994	250
Amounts paid to Nora, Hal's niece, for household help and caring for Sam and Fred while Hal and Wanda were working	5,500
Unreimbursed travel expenses (including meals of $600) incurred by Wanda in connection with her job	1,650
Total itemized deductions (not including any potential deductions mentioned elsewhere in the problem)	4,700
Federal income taxes withheld by their employers	3,700

Compute net tax payable or refund due for Hal and Wanda for 1994. Suggested software (if available): *TurboTax* or *MacInTax* for tax return or WFT tax planning software.

57. James R. Jordan lives at 2322 Branch Road, Mesa, AZ 85202. He is a tax accountant with Mesa Manufacturing Company. He also writes computer software programs for tax practitioners and has a part-time tax practice. James, age 35, is single and has no dependents. His Social Security number is 111–35–2222. He wants to contribute $3 to the Presidential Election Campaign Fund.

   During 1993, James earned a salary of $45,680 from his employer. He received interest of $890 from Home Federal Savings and Loan and $435 from Home State Bank. He received dividends of $620 from Acme Corporation, $470 from Jason Corporation, and $360 from General Corporation.

   James received a $1,600 income tax refund from the state of Arizona on May 12, 1993. On his 1992 Federal income tax return, he reported total itemized deductions of $6,700, which included $2,000 of state income tax withheld by his employer.

   Fees earned from his part-time tax practice in 1993 totaled $4,200. He paid $500 to have the tax returns processed by a computerized tax return service.

   On February 1, 1993, James bought 500 shares of Acme Corporation common stock for $17.60 a share. On July 16, James sold the stock for $15 a share.

   James bought a used pickup truck for $3,000 on June 5, 1993. He purchased the truck from his brother-in-law, who was unemployed and was in need of cash. On November 2, 1993, he sold the truck to a friend for $3,400.

   On January 2, 1983, James acquired 100 shares of Jason Corporation common stock for $30 a share. He sold the stock on December 19, 1993, for $75 a share.

   During 1993, James received royalties of $15,000 on a software program he had written. James incurred the following expenditures in connection with his software writing activities:

Cost of microcomputer (100% business use)	$8,000
Cost of printer (100% business use)	2,000
Supplies	650
Fee paid to computer consultant	3,500

   James elected to expense the maximum portion of the cost of the microcomputer and printer allowed under the provisions of § 179. This equipment was placed in service on January 15, 1993.

   Although his employer suggested that James attend a convention on current developments in corporate taxation, James was not reimbursed for the travel expenses of $1,360 he incurred in attending the convention. The $1,360 included $200 for the cost of meals.

   During 1993, James paid $300 for prescription medicines and $2,875 in doctor bills, hospital bills, and medical insurance premiums. His employer withheld state income tax of $1,954. James paid real property taxes of $1,766 on his home. Interest on his home mortgage was $3,845, and interest to credit card companies was $320. James contributed $20 each week to his church and $10 each week to the United Way. Professional dues and subscriptions totaled $350.

   James's employer withheld Federal income taxes of $9,500 during 1993. James paid estimated taxes of $1,600. What is the amount of James's net tax payable or refund due for 1993? If James has a tax refund due, he wants to have it credited toward his 1994 income tax. If you use tax forms for your solution, you will need Forms 1040, 2106, and 4562 and Schedules A, B, C, D, and SE. Suggested software (if available): *TurboTax* or *MacInTax* for tax return or WFT tax planning software.

RESEARCH PROBLEMS

Research Problem 1. Matthew Mark, who is the pastor of your church, asks your advice concerning a tax issue that was briefly discussed on the evening television news. According to the news story, the fair rental value of a home provided to a minister is excluded in calculating income tax. This exclusion is clearly provided by § 107. However, Mark did not understand whether the fair rental value of the home should be included in the base for computing the self-employment tax. Mark admitted that he had never included the rental value in computing his self-employment tax and said that "such taxation just wouldn't be right because the home is clearly excluded from income tax." How do you respond to your pastor?

Partial list of research aids:
§§ 107(1) and 1402(a)(8).

Research Problem 2.   Karen has been participating in a carpool arrangement from her home to her work with others in her office for a number of years. Carpooling has worked out well from her perspective because the physical and financial burdens of driving to and from work are reduced by being shared equally among several people. However, her family situation has changed recently, and she is now required to delay her departure for work until her 8-year-old child's school bus arrives each morning. Although she looked for help with this problem, she was unable to find anyone to care for her child during the early morning hours. Unfortunately, the others in the carpool were not willing to leave for work any later than they previously had. Therefore, the only recourse for Karen was to give up her carpool and to begin driving to and from work by herself. Karen figures that the cost of individually driving to and from work for the year was $1,000, while the cost of the carpool arrangement was $200. Because the incremental $800 costs relate to and are necessary for the care of her dependent child, she feels that they should be considered qualifying expenditures for purposes of the credit for child and dependent care expenses. Karen approaches you and asks your advice. Write a letter to Karen that contains your advice and prepare a memo for the tax files.

Research Problem 3.   Isabella, a lover of early twentieth-century American history and architecture, discovers a 1920s house in a downtown district of Atlanta during a recent visit. She decides not only to purchase and renovate this particular home, but also to move the structure to her hometown of Little Rock, Arkansas, so her community can enjoy its architectural features. Also, being aware of the availability of the tax credit for rehabilitation expenditures incurred on old structures, she wants to maximize her use of the provision once the renovation work begins in Arkansas. Comment on whether the renovation expenditures incurred will qualify for the tax credit for rehabilitation expenditures.

Research Problem 4.   Black Corporation is in the business of creating, manufacturing, and distributing board games based on science fiction themes. The research underlying the creation of the games is extensive and is absolutely necessary to make the games as intriguing and alluring as possible. In the current year alone, Black Corporation has spent over $100,000 on research activities where employees assigned to the project consulted libraries, government documents, museums, and various other sources. The controller at Black Corporation is under the impression the research expenditures incurred qualify for the research activities credit under § 41. What is your reaction to his impression?

V

PROPERTY TRANSACTIONS

Part V presents the tax treatment of sales, exchanges, and other dispositions of property. Included are the determination of the realized gain or loss, recognized gain or loss, and the classification of the recognized gain or loss as capital or ordinary. The topic of basis is evaluated both in terms of its effect on the calculation of the gain or loss and in terms of the determination of the basis of any contemporaneous or related subsequent acquisitions of property.

Chapter 14

Property Transactions: Determination of Gain or Loss
and Basis Considerations

Chapter 15

Property Transactions: Nontaxable Exchanges

Chapter 16

Property Transactions: Capital Gains or Losses

Chapter 17

Property Transactions: Section 1231 and Recapture Provisions

14

PROPERTY TRANSACTIONS: DETERMINATION OF GAIN OR LOSS AND BASIS CONSIDERATIONS

LEARNING OBJECTIVES

After completing Chapter 14, you should be able to:

1. Understand the computation of realized gain or loss on property dispositions.

2. Distinguish between realized and recognized gain or loss.

3. Apply the recovery of capital doctrine.

4. Explain how basis is determined for various methods of asset acquisition.

5. Describe various loss disallowance provisions.

6. Identify tax planning opportunities related to selected property transactions.

OUTLINE

Determination of Gain or Loss, 14–3

Realized Gain or Loss, 14–3

Recognized Gain or Loss, 14–6

Nonrecognition of Gain or Loss, 14–6

Recovery of Capital Doctrine, 14–7

Basis Considerations, 14–8

Determination of Cost Basis, 14–8

Gift Basis, 14–11

Property Acquired from a Decedent, 14–14

Disallowed Losses, 14–17

Conversion of Property from Personal Use to Business or Income-Producing Use, 14–19

Additional Complexities in Determining Realized Gain or Loss, 14–21

Summary of Basis Adjustments, 14–22

Tax Planning Considerations, 14–24

Tax Consequences of Alice's Proposed Transaction, 14–24

Cost Identification and Documentation Considerations, 14–25

Selection of Property for Making Gifts, 14–25

Selection of Property for Making Bequests, 14–26

Disallowed Losses, 14–26

This chapter and the following three chapters are concerned with the income tax consequences of property transactions (the sale or other disposition of property). The following questions are considered with respect to the sale or other disposition of property:

- Is there a realized gain or loss?
- If so, is the gain or loss recognized?
- If the gain or loss is recognized, is it ordinary or capital?
- What is the basis of any replacement property that is acquired?

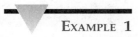

EXAMPLE 1

Alice owns a house that she received from her mother seven months ago. Her mother's cost for the house was $75,000. Alice is considering selling the house to her favorite nephew, Dan, for $75,000. Alice anticipates she will have no gain or loss on the transaction. She comes to you for advice.

As Alice's tax adviser, you need answers to the following questions:

- You are aware that Alice's mother died around the time Alice indicates she received the house from her mother. Did Alice receive the house by gift prior to her mother's death? If so, what was the mother's adjusted basis? If instead Alice inherited the house from her mother, what was the fair market value of the house on the date of her mother's death?
- Was the house Alice's principal residence during the period she owned it and was it her principal residence prior to receiving it from her mother?
- How long did Alice's mother own the house?
- What is the fair market value of the house?
- Does Alice intend for the transaction with Dan to be a sale or part sale and part gift?
- What does Alice intend to do with the sale proceeds?

Once you have the answers to these questions, you can advise Alice on the tax consequences of the proposed transaction. ▼

Chapters 14 and 15 discuss the determination of realized and recognized gain or loss and the basis of property. Chapters 16 and 17 cover the classification of the recognized gain or loss as ordinary or capital.

DETERMINATION OF GAIN OR LOSS

REALIZED GAIN OR LOSS

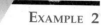

LEARNING OBJECTIVE
Understand the computation of realized gain or loss on property dispositions.

Realized gain or loss is measured by the difference between the amount realized from the sale or other disposition of property and the property's adjusted basis on the date of disposition. If the amount realized exceeds the property's adjusted basis, the result is a **realized gain.** Conversely, if the property's adjusted basis exceeds the amount realized, the result is a **realized loss.**[1]

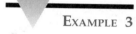

EXAMPLE 2

Tab sells Swan Corporation stock with an adjusted basis of $3,000 for $5,000. Tab's realized gain is $2,000. If Tab had sold the stock for $2,000, he would have had a $1,000 realized loss. ▼

Sale or Other Disposition

The term *sale or other disposition* is defined broadly in the tax law and includes virtually any disposition of property. Thus, transactions such as trade-ins, casualties, condemnations, thefts, and bond retirements are treated as dispositions of property. The most common disposition of property is through a sale or exchange. The key factor in determining whether a disposition has taken place usually is whether an identifiable event has occurred[2] as opposed to a mere fluctuation in the value of the property.[3]

EXAMPLE 3

Lori owns Tan Corporation stock that cost $3,000. The stock has appreciated in value by $2,000 since Lori purchased it. Lori has no realized gain since mere fluctuation in value is not a disposition or identifiable event for tax purposes. Nor would Lori have a realized loss had the stock declined in value by $2,000. ▼

Amount Realized

The **amount realized** from a sale or other disposition of property is the sum of any money received plus the fair market value of other property received. The amount realized also includes any real property taxes treated as imposed on the seller that are actually paid by the buyer.[4] The reason for including these taxes in the amount realized is that by paying the taxes, the purchaser is, in effect, paying an additional amount to the seller of the property.

The amount realized also includes any liability on the property disposed of, such as a mortgage debt, if the buyer assumes the mortgage or the property is sold subject to the mortgage.[5] The amount of the liability is included in the amount

---

[1] § 1001(a) and Reg. § 1.1001–1(a).
[2] Reg. § 1.1001–1(c)(1).
[3] *Lynch v. Turrish,* 1 USTC ¶18, 3 AFTR 2986, 38 S.Ct. 537 (USSC, 1918).

[4] § 1001(b) and Reg. § 1.1001–1(b). Refer to Chapter 10 for a discussion of this subject.
[5] *Crane v. Comm.,* 47–1 USTC ¶9217, 35 AFTR 776, 67 S.Ct. 1047 (USSC, 1947). Although a legal distinction exists between the direct assumption of a mortgage and taking property subject to a mortgage, the tax consequences in calculating the amount realized are the same.

realized even if the debt is nonrecourse and the amount of the debt is greater than the fair market value of the mortgaged property.[6]

EXAMPLE 4   Barry sells property on which there is a mortgage of $20,000 to Cole for $50,000 cash. Barry's amount realized from the sale is $70,000 if Cole assumes the mortgage or takes the property subject to the mortgage. ▼

The **fair market value** of property received in a sale or other disposition has been defined by the courts as the price at which property will change hands between a willing seller and a willing buyer when neither is compelled to sell or buy.[7] Fair market value is determined by considering the relevant factors in each case.[8] An expert appraiser is often required to evaluate these factors in arriving at fair market value. When the fair market value of the property received cannot be determined, the value of the property surrendered may be used.[9]

In calculating the amount realized, selling expenses such as advertising, commissions, and legal fees relating to the disposition are deducted. The amount realized is the net amount received directly or indirectly by the taxpayer from the disposition of property in the form of cash or anything else of value.

Adjusted Basis

The **adjusted basis** of property disposed of is the property's original basis adjusted to the date of disposition.[10] Original basis is the cost or other basis of the property on the date the property is acquired by the taxpayer. *Capital additions* increase and *recoveries of capital* decrease the original basis so that on the date of disposition the adjusted basis reflects the unrecovered cost or other basis of the property.[11] Adjusted basis is determined as follows:

> Cost (or other adjusted basis) on date of acquisition
> + Capital additions
> – Capital recoveries
> = Adjusted basis on date of disposition

Capital Additions

Capital additions include the cost of capital improvements and betterments made to the property by the taxpayer. These expenditures are distinguishable from expenditures for the ordinary repair and maintenance of the property that are neither capitalized nor added to the original basis (refer to Chapter 6). The latter expenditures are deductible in the current taxable year if they are related to business or income-producing property. Amounts representing real property taxes treated as imposed on the seller but paid or assumed by the buyer are part of the cost of the property.[12] Any liability on property that is assumed by the buyer is also included in the buyer's original basis of the property. The same rule applies

[6] *Comm. v. Tufts,* 83–1 USTC ¶9328, 51 AFTR2d 83–1132, 103 S.Ct. 1826 (USSC, 1983).

[7] *Comm. v. Marshman,* 60–2 USTC ¶9484, 5 AFTR2d 1528, 279 F.2d 27 (CA–6, 1960).

[8] *O'Malley v. Ames,* 52–1 USTC ¶9361, 42 AFTR 19, 197 F.2d 256 (CA–8, 1952).

[9] *U.S. v. Davis,* 62–2 USTC ¶9509, 9 AFTR2d 1625, 82 S.Ct. 1190 (USSC, 1962).

[10] § 1011(a) and Reg. § 1.1011–1.

[11] § 1016(a) and Reg. § 1.1016–1.

[12] Reg. §§ 1.1001–1(b)(2) and 1.1012–1(b). Refer to Chapter 10 for a discussion of this subject.

if property is acquired subject to a liability. Amortization of the discount on bonds increases the adjusted basis of the bonds.[13]

Capital Recoveries

The following are examples of capital recoveries:

1. *Depreciation and cost recovery allowances.* The original basis of depreciable property is reduced by the annual depreciation charges (or cost recovery allowances) while the property is held by the taxpayer. The amount of depreciation that is subtracted from the original basis is the greater of the *allowed* or *allowable* depreciation on an annual basis.[14] In most circumstances, the allowed and allowable depreciation amounts are the same (refer to Chapter 8).
2. *Casualties and thefts.* A casualty or theft may result in the reduction of the adjusted basis of property.[15] The adjusted basis is reduced by the amount of the deductible loss. In addition, the adjusted basis is reduced by the amount of insurance proceeds received. However, the receipt of insurance proceeds may result in a recognized gain rather than a deductible loss. The gain increases the adjusted basis of the property.[16]

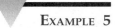

EXAMPLE 5   An insured truck used in a trade or business is destroyed in an accident. The adjusted basis is $8,000, and the fair market value is $6,500. Insurance proceeds of $6,500 are received. The amount of the casualty loss is $1,500 ($6,500 insurance proceeds − $8,000 adjusted basis). The adjusted basis is reduced by the $1,500 casualty loss and the $6,500 of insurance proceeds received. ▼

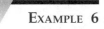

EXAMPLE 6   An insured truck used in a trade or business is destroyed in an accident. The adjusted basis is $6,500, and the fair market value is $8,000. Insurance proceeds of $8,000 are received. The amount of the casualty gain is $1,500 ($8,000 insurance proceeds − $6,500 adjusted basis). The adjusted basis is increased by the $1,500 casualty gain and is reduced by the $8,000 of insurance proceeds received ($6,500 basis before casualty + $1,500 casualty gain − $8,000 insurance proceeds = $0 basis). ▼

3. *Certain corporate distributions.* A corporate distribution to a shareholder that is not taxable is treated as a return of capital, and it reduces the basis of the shareholder's stock in the corporation.[17] For example, if a corporation makes a cash distribution to its shareholders and has no earnings and profits, the distributions are treated as a return of capital. Once the basis of the stock is reduced to zero, the amount of any subsequent distributions is a capital gain if the stock is a capital asset. These rules are illustrated in Example 21 of Chapter 20.
4. *Amortizable bond premium.* The basis in a bond purchased at a premium is reduced by the amortizable portion of the bond premium.[18] Investors in taxable bonds may *elect* to amortize the bond premium, but the premium

---

[13] §§ 1232(a)(2)(A) and 1232A(a) and (c)(5). See Chapter 16 for a discussion of bond discount and the related amortization.
[14] § 1016(a)(2) and Reg. § 1.1016–3(a)(1)(i).
[15] Refer to Chapter 7 for the discussion of casualties and thefts.
[16] Reg. § 1.1016–6(a).

[17] § 1016(a)(4) and Reg. § 1.1016–5(a).
[18] § 1016(a)(5) and Reg. § 1.1016–5(b). The accounting treatment of bond premium amortization is the same as for tax purposes. The amortization results in a decrease in the bond investment account.

on tax-exempt bonds *must be* amortized.[19] The amount of the amortized premium on taxable bonds is permitted as an interest deduction. Therefore, the election produces the opportunity for an annual interest deduction to offset ordinary income in exchange for a larger capital gain or smaller capital loss on the disposition of the bond. No such interest deduction is permitted for tax-exempt bonds.

The amortization deduction is allowed for taxable bonds because the premium is viewed as a cost of earning the taxable interest from the bonds. The reason the basis of taxable bonds is reduced is that the amortization deduction is a recovery of the cost or basis of the bonds. The basis of tax-exempt bonds is reduced even though the amortization is not allowed as a deduction. No amortization deduction is permitted on tax-exempt bonds since the interest income is exempt from tax and the amortization of the bond premium merely represents an adjustment of the effective amount of such income.

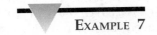

EXAMPLE 7

Antonio purchases Eagle Corporation taxable bonds with a face value of $100,000 for $110,000, thus paying a premium of $10,000. The annual interest rate is 7%, and the bonds mature 10 years from the date of purchase. The annual interest income is $7,000 (7% × $100,000). If Antonio elects to amortize the bond premium, the $10,000 premium is deducted over the 10-year period. Antonio's basis for the bonds is reduced each year by the amount of the amortization deduction. Note that if the bonds were tax-exempt, amortization of the bond premium and the basis adjustment would be mandatory. However, no deduction would be allowed for the amortization. ▼

RECOGNIZED GAIN OR LOSS

2 **LEARNING OBJECTIVE**
Distinguish between realized and recognized gain or loss.

Recognized gain is the amount of the realized gain included in the taxpayer's gross income.[20] A **recognized loss,** on the other hand, is the amount of a realized loss that is deductible for tax purposes.[21] As a general rule, the entire amount of a realized gain or loss is recognized.[22]

Concept Summary 14–1 summarizes the realized gain or loss and recognized gain or loss concepts.

NONRECOGNITION OF GAIN OR LOSS

In certain cases, a realized gain or loss is not recognized upon the sale or other disposition of property. One of the exceptions to the recognition of gain or loss involves nontaxable exchanges, which are covered in Chapter 15. Additional exceptions include losses realized upon the sale, exchange, or condemnation of personal use assets (as opposed to business or income-producing property) and gains realized upon the sale of a residence by taxpayers 55 years of age or older (see Chapter 15). In addition, realized losses from the sale or exchange of business or income-producing property between certain related parties are not recognized.[23]

Sale, Exchange, or Condemnation of Personal Use Assets

A realized loss from the sale, exchange, or condemnation of personal use assets (e.g., a personal residence or an automobile not used at all for business or

---

[19] § 171(c).
[20] § 61(a)(3) and Reg. § 1.61–6(a).
[21] § 165(a) and Reg. § 1.165–1(a).

[22] § 1001(c) and Reg. § 1.1002–1(a).
[23] § 267(a)(1).

income-producing purposes) is not recognized for tax purposes. An exception exists for casualty or theft losses from personal use assets (see Chapter 7). In contrast, any gain realized from the sale or other disposition of personal use assets is, generally, fully taxable. The following examples illustrate the tax consequences of the sale of personal use assets.

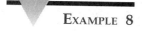

EXAMPLE 8   Freda sells an automobile, which is held exclusively for personal use, for $6,000. The adjusted basis of the automobile is $5,000. Freda has a realized and recognized gain of $1,000. ▼

EXAMPLE 9   Freda sells the automobile in Example 8 for $4,000. She has a realized loss of $1,000, but the loss is not recognized. ▼

RECOVERY OF CAPITAL DOCTRINE

Doctrine Defined

3   **LEARNING OBJECTIVE**
Apply the recovery of capital doctrine.

The **recovery of capital doctrine** is very significant and pervades all the tax rules relating to property transactions. The doctrine derives its roots from the very essence of the income tax—a tax on income. Therefore, as a general rule, a taxpayer is entitled to recover the cost or other original basis of property acquired and is not taxed on that amount.

The cost or other original basis of depreciable property is recovered through annual depreciation deductions. The basis is reduced as the cost is recovered over the period the property is held. Therefore, when property is sold or otherwise disposed of, it is the adjusted basis (unrecovered cost or other basis) that is compared to the amount realized from the disposition to determine realized gain or loss.

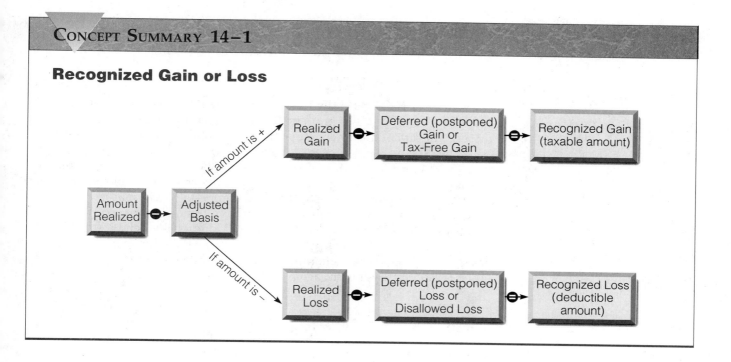

CONCEPT SUMMARY 14–1

Recognized Gain or Loss

Relationship of the Recovery of Capital Doctrine to the Concepts of Realization and Recognition

If a sale or other disposition results in a realized gain, the taxpayer has recovered more than the adjusted basis of the property. Conversely, if a sale or other disposition results in a realized loss, the taxpayer has recovered less than the adjusted basis.

The general rules for the relationship between the recovery of capital doctrine and the realized and recognized gain and loss concepts are summarized as follows:

Rule 1. A realized gain that is *never recognized* results in the *permanent recovery* of more than the taxpayer's cost or other basis for tax purposes. For example, all or a portion of the realized gain on the sale of a personal residence by taxpayers 55 years of age or older can be excluded from gross income under § 121.

Rule 2. A realized gain on which *recognition is postponed* results in the *temporary recovery* of more than the taxpayer's cost or other basis for tax purposes. For example, an exchange of like-kind property under § 1031, an involuntary conversion under § 1033, and a replacement of a personal residence under § 1034 are all eligible for postponement treatment.

Rule 3. A realized loss that is *never recognized* results in the *permanent recovery* of less than the taxpayer's cost or other basis for tax purposes. For example, a loss on the sale of an automobile held for personal use is not deductible.

Rule 4. A realized loss on which *recognition is postponed* results in the *temporary recovery* of less than the taxpayer's cost or other basis for tax purposes. For example, the realized loss on the exchange of like-kind property under § 1031 is postponed.

These rules are illustrated in discussions to follow in this and the next chapter.

BASIS CONSIDERATIONS

DETERMINATION OF COST BASIS

4   **LEARNING OBJECTIVE**
Explain how basis is determined for various methods of asset acquisition.

The basis of property is generally the property's cost. Cost is the amount paid for the property in cash or other property.[24] This general rule follows logically from the recovery of capital doctrine; that is, the cost or other basis of property is to be recovered tax-free by the taxpayer.

A *bargain purchase* of property is an exception to the general rule for determining basis. A bargain purchase may result when an employer transfers property to an employee at less than the property's fair market value (as compensation for services) or when a corporation transfers property to a shareholder at less than the property's fair market value (a dividend). The basis of property acquired in a bargain purchase is the property's fair market value.[25] If the basis of the property were not increased by the bargain amount, the taxpayer would be taxed on this amount again at disposition.

---

[24]§ 1012 and Reg. § 1.1012–1(a).

[25]Reg. §§ 1.61–2(d)(2)(i) and 1.301–1(j).

<table><tr><td>**EXAMPLE 10**</td><td>Wade buys a machine from his employer for $10,000 on December 30, 1994. The fair market value of the machine is $15,000. Wade must include the $5,000 difference between cost and the fair market value of the machine in gross income for the taxable year 1994. The bargain element represents additional compensation to Wade. His basis for the machine is $15,000, the machine's fair market value. ▼</td></tr></table>

Identification Problems

Cost identification problems are frequently encountered in securities transactions. For example, the Regulations require that the taxpayer adequately identify the particular stock that has been sold.[26] A problem arises when the taxpayer has purchased separate lots of stock on different dates or at different prices and cannot adequately identify the lot from which a particular sale takes place. In this case, the stock is presumed to come from the first lot or lots purchased (a FIFO presumption).[27] When securities are left in the custody of a broker, it may be necessary to provide specific instructions and receive written confirmation as to which securities are being sold.

<table><tr><td>**EXAMPLE 11**</td><td>Polly purchases 100 shares of Olive Corporation stock on July 1, 1992, for $5,000 ($50 a share) and another 100 shares of Olive stock on July 1, 1993, for $6,000 ($60 a share). She sells 50 shares of the stock on January 2, 1994. The cost of the stock sold, assuming Polly cannot adequately identify the shares, is $50 a share, or $2,500. This is the cost Polly will compare to the amount realized in determining the gain or loss from the sale. ▼</td></tr></table>

Allocation Problems

When a taxpayer acquires *multiple assets in a lump-sum purchase,* the total cost must be allocated among the individual assets.[28] Allocation is necessary because some of the assets acquired may be depreciable (e.g., buildings) and others not (e.g., land). In addition, only a portion of the assets acquired may be sold, or some of the assets may be capital or § 1231 assets that receive special tax treatment upon subsequent sale or other disposition. The lump-sum cost is allocated on the basis of the fair market values of the individual assets acquired.

<table><tr><td>**EXAMPLE 12**</td><td>Harry purchases a building and land for $800,000. Because of the depressed nature of the industry in which the seller was operating, Harry was able to negotiate a very favorable purchase price. Appraisals of the individual assets indicate that the fair market value of the building is $600,000 and that of the land is $400,000. Harry's basis for the building is $480,000 ($600,000/$1,000,000 × $800,000), and his basis for the land is $320,000 ($400,000/$1,000,000 × $800,000). ▼</td></tr></table>

If a business is purchased and **goodwill** is involved, a special allocation rule applies. Initially, the purchase price is assigned to the assets, excluding goodwill, to the extent of their total fair market value. This assigned amount is allocated among the assets on the basis of the fair market value of the individual assets acquired. Goodwill is then assigned the residual amount of the purchase price. The resultant allocation is applicable to both the buyer and the seller.[29]

---

[26] Reg. § 1.1012–1(c)(1).
[27] *Kluger Associates, Inc.,* 69 T.C. 925 (1978).
[28] Reg. § 1.61–6(a).
[29] § 1060.

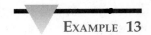

EXAMPLE 13

Rocky sells his business to Paul. They agree that the values of the individual assets are as follows:

Inventory	$ 50,000
Building	500,000
Land	200,000
Goodwill	150,000

After negotiations, Rocky and Paul agree on a sales price of $1 million. Applying the residual method with respect to goodwill results in the following allocation of the $1 million purchase price:

Inventory	$ 50,000
Building	500,000
Land	200,000
Goodwill	250,000

The residual method requires that all of the excess of the purchase price over the fair market value of the assets ($1,000,000 − $900,000 = $100,000) be allocated to goodwill. Without this requirement, the purchaser could allocate the excess pro rata to all of the assets, including goodwill, based on their respective fair market values. This would have resulted in only $166,667 [$150,000 + ($150,000 ÷ $900,000 × $100,000)] being assigned to goodwill. ▼

In the case of *nontaxable stock dividends,* the allocation depends upon whether the dividend is a common stock dividend on common stock or a preferred stock dividend on common stock. If the dividend is common on common, the cost of the original common shares is allocated to the total shares owned after the dividend.[30]

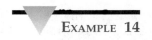

EXAMPLE 14

Susan owns 100 shares of Sparrow Corporation common stock for which she paid $1,100. She receives a 10% common stock dividend, giving her a new total of 110 shares. Before the stock dividend, Susan's basis was $11 per share ($1,100 ÷ 100 shares). The basis of each share after the stock dividend is $10 ($1,100 ÷ 110 shares). ▼

If the dividend is preferred stock on common, the cost of the original common shares is allocated between the common and preferred shares on the basis of their relative fair market values on the date of distribution.[31]

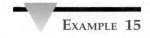

EXAMPLE 15

Fran owns 100 shares of Cardinal Corporation common stock for which she paid $1,000. She receives a stock dividend of 50 shares of preferred stock on her common stock. The fair market values on the date of distribution of the preferred stock dividend are $30 a share for common stock and $40 a share for preferred stock. Thus, the total fair market value is $3,000 ($30 × 100) for common stock and $2,000 ($40 × 50) for preferred stock. The basis of Fran's common stock after the dividend is $600, or $6 a share ($3,000/$5,000 × $1,000), and the basis of the preferred stock is $400, or $8 a share ($2,000/$5,000 × $1,000). ▼

In the case of *nontaxable stock rights,* the basis of the rights is zero unless the taxpayer elects or is required to allocate a portion of the cost of the stock to the rights. If the fair market value of the rights is 15 percent or more of the fair market value of the stock, the taxpayer is required to allocate. If the value of the rights is less than 15 percent of the fair market value of the stock, the taxpayer may elect to

---

[30] §§ 305(a) and 307(a). The holding period of the new shares includes the holding period of the old shares. § 1223(5) and Reg.

§ 1.1223–1(e). See Chapter 16 for a discussion of the importance of the holding period.
[31] Reg. § 1.307–1(a).

allocate.[32] The result is that either the rights will have no basis or the cost of the stock on which the rights are received will be allocated between the stock and rights on the basis of their relative fair market values.

▼
EXAMPLE 16

Donald receives nontaxable stock rights with a fair market value of $1,000. The fair market value of the stock on which the rights were received is $8,000 (cost $10,000). Donald does not elect to allocate. The basis of the rights is zero. If he exercises the rights, the basis of the new stock will be the exercise (subscription) price. ▼

▼
EXAMPLE 17

Assume the same facts as in Example 16, except the fair market value of the rights is $3,000. Donald must allocate because the value of the rights is 15% or more of the value of the stock ($3,000/$8,000 = 37.5%). The basis of the rights is $2,727 ($3,000/$11,000 × $10,000), and the basis of the stock is $7,273 ($8,000/$11,000 × $10,000). If Donald exercises the rights, the basis of the new stock will be the exercise (subscription) price plus the basis of the rights. If he sells the rights, he will recognize gain or loss. This allocation rule applies only when the rights are exercised or sold. Therefore, if the rights are allowed to lapse (expire), they have no basis, and the basis of the original stock is the stock's cost, $10,000. ▼

The holding period of nontaxable stock rights includes the holding period of the stock on which the rights were distributed. However, if the rights are exercised, the holding period of the newly acquired stock begins with the date the rights are exercised.[33] The significance of the holding period for capital assets is discussed in Chapter 16.

GIFT BASIS

When a taxpayer receives property as a **gift,** there is no cost to the recipient. Thus, under the cost basis provision, the donee's basis would be zero. However, this would violate the statutory intent that gifts are not subject to the income tax. With a zero basis, a sale by the donee would result in all of the amount realized being treated as realized gain. Therefore, a basis is assigned to the property received depending on the following:[34]

- The date of the gift.
- The basis of the property to the donor.
- The amount of the gift tax paid.
- The fair market value of the property.

Gift Basis Rules if No Gift Tax Is Paid

Property received by gift can be referred to as *dual basis* property; that is, the basis for gain and the basis for loss might not be the same amount. The present basis rules for gifts of property are as follows:

- If the donee subsequently disposes of gift property in a transaction that results in a gain, the basis to the donee is the same as the donor's adjusted basis.[35] The donee's basis in this case is referred to as the *gain basis*. Therefore, a *realized gain* results if the amount realized from the disposition exceeds the donee's gain basis.

---

[32] § 307(b).
[33] § 1223(5) and Reg. §§ 1.1223–1(e) and (f).
[34] § 102(a).

[35] § 1015(a) and Reg. § 1.1015–1(a)(1). See Reg. § 1.1015–1(a)(3) for cases in which the facts necessary to determine the donor's adjusted basis are unknown. Refer to Example 24 for the effect of depreciation deductions by the donee.

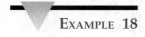
EXAMPLE 18

Melissa purchased stock in 1993 for $10,000. She gave the stock to her son, Joe, in 1994, when the fair market value was $15,000. Assume no gift tax is paid on the transfer and Joe subsequently sells the property for $15,000. Joe's basis is $10,000, and he has a realized gain of $5,000. ▼

- If the donee subsequently disposes of gift property in a transaction that results in a loss, the basis to the donee is the *lower* of the donor's adjusted basis or fair market value on the date of the gift. The donee's basis in this case is referred to as the *loss basis.* Therefore, a *realized loss results* if the amount realized from the disposition is less than the donee's loss basis.

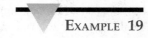
EXAMPLE 19

Burt purchased stock in 1993 for $10,000. He gave the stock to his son, Cliff, in 1994, when the fair market value was $7,000. Assume no gift tax is paid on the transfer. Cliff later sells the stock for $6,000. Cliff's basis is $7,000 (fair market value is less than donor's adjusted basis of $10,000), and the loss from the sale is $1,000 ($6,000 amount realized − $7,000 basis). ▼

The amount of the loss basis will differ from the amount of the gain basis only if at the date of the gift the adjusted basis of the property exceeds the property's fair market value. Note that the loss basis rule prevents the donee from receiving a tax benefit from the decline in value while the donor held the property. Therefore, in Example 19, Cliff has a loss of only $1,000 rather than a loss of $4,000. The $3,000 difference represents the decline in value while Burt held the property. Ironically, however, the gain basis rule may eventually result in the donee's being subject to income tax on the appreciation that occurred while the donor held the property, as illustrated in Example 18.

If the amount realized from sale or other disposition is *between* the basis for loss and the basis for gain, no gain or loss is realized.

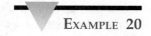
EXAMPLE 20

Assume the same facts as in Example 19, except that Cliff sold the stock for $8,000. The application of the gain basis rule produces a loss of $2,000 ($8,000 − $10,000). The application of the loss basis rule produces a gain of $1,000 ($8,000 − $7,000). Therefore, Cliff recognizes neither a gain nor a loss because the amount realized is between the gain basis and the loss basis. ▼

Adjustment for Gift Tax

If gift taxes are paid by the donor, the donee's gain basis may exceed the adjusted basis of the property to the donor. This occurs only if the fair market value of the property at the date of the gift is greater than the donor's adjusted basis (the property has appreciated in value). The portion of the gift tax paid that is related to the appreciation is added to the donor's basis in calculating the donee's gain basis for the property. In this circumstance, the following formula is used for calculating the donee's gain basis:[36]

---

[36] § 1015(d)(6).

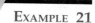

EXAMPLE 21

Bonnie made a gift of stock to Peggy in 1994, when the fair market value of the stock was $40,000. Bonnie had purchased the stock in 1981 for $10,000. Because the unrealized appreciation is $30,000 ($40,000 fair market value − $10,000 adjusted basis) and the fair market value is $40,000, three-fourths ($30,000/$40,000) of the gift tax paid is added to the basis of the property. If Bonnie paid gift tax of $4,000, Peggy's basis in the property is $13,000 [$10,000 + $3,000 (¾ of the $4,000 gift tax)]. ▼

EXAMPLE 22

Don made a gift of stock to Matt in 1994, when the fair market value of the stock was $40,000. Gift tax of $4,000 was paid by Don, who had purchased the stock in 1981 for $45,000. Because there is no unrealized appreciation at the date of the gift, none of the gift tax paid is added to Don's basis in calculating Matt's gain basis. Therefore, Matt's gain basis is $45,000. ▼

For *gifts made before 1977*, the full amount of the gift tax paid is added to the donor's basis. However, the ceiling on this total is the fair market value of the property at the date of the gift. Thus, in Example 21, if the gift had been made before 1977, the basis of the property would be $14,000 ($10,000 + $4,000). In Example 22, the gain basis would still be $45,000 ($45,000 + $0).

Holding Period

The **holding period** for property acquired by gift begins on the date the donor acquired the property if the gain basis rule applies.[37] The holding period starts on the date of the gift if the loss basis rule applies.[38] The significance of the holding period for capital assets is discussed in Chapter 16.

The following example summarizes the basis and holding period rules for gift property:

EXAMPLE 23

Jill acquires 100 shares of Wren Corporation stock on December 30, 1981, for $40,000. On January 3, 1994, when the stock has a fair market value of $38,000, Jill gives it to Dennis and pays gift tax of $4,000. There is no increase in basis for a portion of the gift tax paid because the property has not appreciated in value at the time of the gift. Therefore, Dennis's gain basis is $40,000. Dennis's basis for determining loss is $38,000 (fair market value) because the fair market value on the date of the gift is less than the donor's adjusted basis.

- If Dennis sells the stock for $45,000, he has a recognized gain of $5,000. The holding period for determining whether the capital gain is short term or long term begins on December 30, 1981, the date Jill acquired the property.
- If Dennis sells the stock for $36,000, he has a recognized loss of $2,000. The holding period for determining whether the capital loss is short term or long term begins on January 3, 1994, the date of the gift.
- If Dennis sells the property for $39,000, there is no gain or loss since the amount realized is less than the gain basis of $40,000 and more than the loss basis of $38,000. ▼

Basis for Depreciation

The basis for depreciation on depreciable gift property is the donee's gain basis.[39] This rule is applicable even if the donee later sells the property at a loss and uses the loss basis rule in calculating the amount of the realized loss.

---

[37] § 1223(2) and Reg. § 1.1223−1(b).
[38] Rev.Rul. 59−86, 1959−1 C.B. 209.

[39] § 1011 and Reg. §§ 1.1011−1 and 1.167(g)−1.

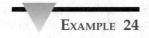

EXAMPLE 24

Vito gave a machine to Tina in 1994, when the adjusted basis was $32,000 (cost of $40,000 – accumulated depreciation of $8,000) and the fair market value was $26,000. No gift tax was paid. Tina's gain basis at the date of the gift is $32,000, and her loss basis is $26,000. During 1994, Tina deducts depreciation (cost recovery) of $10,240 ($32,000 × 32%). Therefore, at the end of 1994, Tina's gain basis and loss basis are calculated as follows:

	Gain Basis	**Loss Basis**
Donor's basis or fair market value	$ 32,000	$ 26,000
Depreciation	(10,240)	(10,240)
	$ 21,760	$ 15,760

▼

PROPERTY ACQUIRED FROM A DECEDENT

General Rules

The basis of property acquired from a decedent is generally the property's fair market value at the date of death (referred to as the *primary valuation amount*).[40] The property's basis is the fair market value six months after the date of death if the executor or administrator of the estate *elects* the alternate valuation date for estate tax purposes. This amount is referred to as the *alternate valuation amount*.

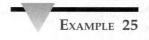

EXAMPLE 25

Linda and various other family members inherited property from Linda's father, who died in 1994. At the date of death, her father's adjusted basis for the property Linda inherited was $35,000. The property's fair market value at date of death was $50,000. The alternate valuation date was not elected. Linda's basis for income tax purposes is $50,000. This is commonly referred to as a *stepped-up basis.* ▼

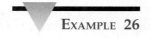

EXAMPLE 26

Assume the same facts as in Example 25, except the property's fair market value at date of death was $20,000. Linda's basis for income tax purposes is $20,000. This is commonly referred to as a *stepped-down basis.* ▼

If an estate tax return does not have to be filed because the estate is below the threshold amount for being subject to the estate tax, the alternate valuation date and amount are not available. Even if an estate tax return is filed and the executor elects the alternate valuation date, the six months after death date is available only for property that the executor has not distributed before this date. Any property distributed or otherwise disposed of by the executor during this six-month period will have an adjusted basis to the beneficiary equal to the fair market value on the date of distribution or other disposition.[41]

The alternate valuation date can be *elected only* if the election results in both the value of the gross estate and the estate tax liability being reduced below the amounts they would have been if the primary valuation date had been used. This provision prevents the alternate valuation election from being used to increase the basis of the property to the beneficiary for income tax purposes without simultaneously increasing the estate tax liability (because of estate tax deductions or credits).[42]

---

[40] § 1014(a).
[41] § 2032(a)(1) and Rev.Rul. 56–60, 1956–1 C.B. 443.

[42] § 2032(c).

▼
EXAMPLE 27

Nancy inherited all the property of her father, who died in 1994. Her father's adjusted basis for the property at date of death was $35,000. The property's fair market value was $750,000 at date of death and $760,000 six months after death. The alternate valuation date cannot be elected because the value of the gross estate has increased during the six-month period. Nancy's basis for income tax purposes is $750,000. ▼

▼
EXAMPLE 28

Assume the same facts as in Example 27, except the property's fair market value six months after death was $745,000. If the executor elects the alternate valuation date, Nancy's basis for income tax purposes is $745,000. ▼

▼
EXAMPLE 29

Assume the same facts as in the previous example, except the property is distributed four months after the date of the decedent's death. At the distribution date, the property's fair market value is $747,500. Since the executor elected the alternate valuation date, Nancy's basis for income tax purposes is $747,500. ▼

For inherited property, both unrealized appreciation and decline in value are taken into consideration in determining the basis of the property for income tax purposes. Contrast this with the carryover basis rules for property received by gift.

Deathbed Gifts

The Code contains a provision designed to eliminate a tax avoidance technique referred to as *deathbed gifts.* If the time period between the date of the gift of appreciated property and the date of the donee's death is not longer than one year, the usual basis rule (stepped-up basis) for inherited property may not apply. The adjusted basis of such property inherited by the donor or his or her spouse from the donee shall be the same as the decedent's adjusted basis for the property

---

TAX IN THE NEWS

CARRYOVER BASIS VERSUS STEPPED-UP BASIS

According to the old saying, "what goes around comes around." A good example is the proposal to replace the stepped-up basis (i.e., fair market value) for inherited property with a carryover basis.

The Tax Reform Act of 1976 amended the Code to provide that a beneficiary's basis for inherited property would be a carryover basis. The provision had a future effective date. Prior to that date, Senator Harry F. Byrd, Jr., of Virginia (now retired) was successful in attaching a rider to the Crude Oil Windfall Profit Tax Act of 1980, which repealed the carryover basis provision.

Several proposals to resurrect carryover basis for inherited property surfaced during the debates over the Revenue Reconciliation Act of 1993. Those who support carryover basis point out that it would make the basis rules for gifts during life and transfers at death symmetrical and would generate additional revenue. Opponents counter that the inherited property may be subject to the Federal estate tax and that determining the decedent's basis for the property may be difficult in many instances.

The proposals for carryover basis were not included in the Revenue Reconciliation Act of 1993. But the question still remains: Is carryover basis an issue whose time has come?

rather than the fair market value at the date of death or the alternate valuation date.[43]

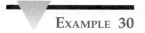

EXAMPLE 30

Ned gives stock to his uncle, Vern, in 1994. Ned's basis for the stock is $1,000, and the fair market value is $9,000. No gift tax is paid. Eight months later, Ned inherits the stock from Vern. At the date of Vern's death, the fair market value of the stock is $12,000. Ned's adjusted basis for the stock is $1,000. ▼

ETHICAL CONSIDERATIONS

Helping a Friend Increase Basis

Holly owns stock with an adjusted basis of $2,500 and a fair market value of $9,500. Holly expects the stock to continue to appreciate. Alice, Holly's best friend, has recently been operated on for cancer. Alice's physicians have told her that her life expectancy is between six months and one and a half years.

One day at lunch, the two friends were discussing their tax situations (both feel they pay too much), when Alice mentioned that she had read a newspaper article about a tax planning opportunity that might be suitable for Holly. Holly would make a gift of the appreciated stock to Alice. In her will, Alice would bequeath the stock to Holly. Since Alice is confident that she will live longer than a year, the basis of the stock to Holly would be the fair market value on the date of Alice's death. Alice would "feel good" because she had helped Holly "beat the tax system."

Survivor's Share of Property

Both the decedent's share and the survivor's share of *community property* have a basis equal to fair market value on the date of the decedent's death.[44] This result applies to the decedent's share of the community property because the property flows to the surviving spouse from the estate (fair market value basis for inherited property). Likewise, the surviving spouse's share of the community property is deemed to be acquired by bequest, devise, or inheritance from the decedent. Therefore, it will also have a basis equal to fair market value.

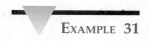

EXAMPLE 31

Floyd and Vera reside in a community property state. They own community property (200 shares of Crow stock) that was acquired in 1974 for $100,000. Assume that Floyd dies in 1994, when the securities are valued at $300,000. One-half of the Crow stock is included in Floyd's estate. If Vera inherits Floyd's share of the community property, the basis for determining gain or loss is:

$300,000 [$150,000 (Vera's share of one-half of the community property) + $150,000 (½ × $300,000, the value of Crow stock at the date of Floyd's death)] for the 200 shares of Crow stock. ▼

In a *common law* state, only one-half of jointly held property of spouses (tenants by the entirety or joint tenants with rights of survivorship) is includible in

---

[43] § 1014(e).

[44] § 1014(b)(6). See the listing of community property states in Chapter 4.

the estate.[45] In such a case, no adjustment of the basis is permitted for the excluded property interest (the surviving spouse's share).

EXAMPLE 32

Assume the same facts as in the previous example, except that the property is jointly held by Floyd and Vera who reside in a common law state. Also assume that Floyd purchased the property and made a gift of one-half of the property when the stock was acquired, with no gift tax being paid. Only one-half of the Crow stock is included in Floyd's estate. Vera's basis for determining gain or loss in the excluded half is not adjusted upward for the increase in value to date of death. Therefore, Vera's basis is $200,000 ($50,000 + $150,000). ▼

Holding Period of Property Acquired from a Decedent

The holding period of property acquired from a decedent is *deemed to be long term* (held for the required long-term holding period). This provision applies regardless of whether the property is disposed of at a gain or a loss.[46]

DISALLOWED LOSSES

Related Taxpayers

5 LEARNING OBJECTIVE
Describe various loss disallowance provisions.

Section 267 provides that realized losses from sales or exchanges of property, directly or indirectly, between certain related parties are not recognized. This loss disallowance provision applies to several types of **related-party transactions.** The most common involve (1) members of a family and (2) transactions between an individual and a corporation in which the individual owns, directly or indirectly, more than 50 percent in value of the corporation's outstanding stock. Section 707 provides a similar loss disallowance provision if the related parties are a partner and a partnership in which the partner owns, directly or indirectly, more than 50 percent of the capital interests or profits interests in the partnership. The rules governing the relationships covered by § 267 were discussed in Chapter 6. See Chapter 15 for the discussion of the special rules under § 1041 for property transfers between spouses or incident to divorce.

If income-producing or business property is transferred to a related taxpayer and a loss is disallowed, the basis of the property to the recipient is the property's cost to the transferee. However, if a subsequent sale or other disposition of the property results in a realized gain, the amount of gain is reduced by the loss that was previously disallowed.[47] This *right of offset* is not applicable if the original sale involved the sale of a personal use asset (e.g., the sale of a personal residence between related taxpayers). Likewise, this right of offset is available only to the original transferee (the related-party buyer).

EXAMPLE 33

Pedro sells business property with an adjusted basis of $50,000 to his daughter, Josefina, for its fair market value of $40,000.

- Pedro's realized loss of $10,000 is not recognized.
- How much gain will Josefina recognize if she sells the property for $52,000? Josefina recognizes a $2,000 gain. Her realized gain is $12,000 ($52,000 less her basis of $40,000), but she can offset Pedro's $10,000 loss against the gain.
- How much gain will Josefina recognize if she sells the property for $48,000? Josefina recognizes no gain or loss. Her realized gain is $8,000 ($48,000 less her basis of

---

[45] § 2040(a).
[46] § 1223(11).

[47] § 267(d) and Reg. § 1.267(d)–1(a).

$40,000), but she can offset $8,000 of Pedro's $10,000 loss against the gain. Note that Pedro's loss can only offset Josefina's gain. It cannot create a loss for Josefina.

- How much loss will Josefina recognize if she sells the property for $38,000? Josefina recognizes a $2,000 loss, the same as her realized loss ($38,000 less $40,000 basis). Pedro's loss does not increase Josefina's loss. His loss can be offset only against a gain. Since Josefina has no realized gain, Pedro's loss cannot be used and is never recognized. This example assumes that the property is business or income producing to Josefina. If not, her $2,000 loss is personal and is not recognized. ▼

The loss disallowance rules are designed to achieve two objectives. First, the rules prevent a taxpayer from directly transferring an unrealized loss to a related taxpayer in a higher tax bracket who could receive a greater tax benefit from the recognition of the loss. Second, the rules eliminate a substantial administrative burden on the Internal Revenue Service as to the appropriateness of the selling price (fair market value or not). The loss disallowance rules are applicable even where the selling price is equal to fair market value and can be validated (e.g., listed stocks).

The holding period of the buyer for the property is not affected by the holding period of the seller. That is, the buyer's *holding period* includes only the period of time he or she has held the property.[48]

ETHICAL CONSIDERATIONS

Transactions between Spouses

Ted and Lisa, both age 53, have been married for 10 years. At the time of their marriage, they both had substantial assets, so they signed a premarital agreement, establishing that their assets would not be commingled and that each would retain separate title to his or her respective assets.

As a result of their marriage, Ted and Lisa's Federal tax liability has been larger than it would have been if they were single (i.e., the marriage penalty). Ted and Lisa each own a 50 percent interest in some undeveloped land. Ted believes that they will be successful in having the land rezoned from residential to commercial. The rezoning could result in as much as a fourfold increase in the fair market value of the land. Based on her conversations with two members of the Planning Commission, Lisa has serious doubts that the rezoning request will be approved.

Ted has offered to buy Lisa's interest in the land for $300,000. Lisa's adjusted basis is $500,000. The land has declined in value since Ted and Lisa purchased it in accordance with a general decline in residential real estate values in the area.

Lisa's CPA informs her that her realized loss of $200,000 on the sale would be disallowed under § 267 as a transaction between related parties. He also informs her that if the land appreciates as a result of the rezoning, Ted, but not Lisa, could use her disallowed loss from the sale to Ted to reduce his recognized gain on a subsequent sale of the land.

From Lisa's perspective, this is the last straw. Their marriage is producing too many negative tax consequences. She proposes to Ted that they get a divorce "for tax purposes" and continue to live together as man and wife. Only Lisa, Ted, and their attorney will be aware that they are no longer married.

---

[48] §§ 267(d) and 1223(2) and Reg. § 1.267(d)–1(c)(3).

Wash Sales

Section 1091 stipulates that in certain cases, a realized loss on the sale or exchange of stock or securities is not recognized. Specifically, if a taxpayer sells or exchanges stock or securities and within 30 days before *or* after the date of the sale or exchange acquires substantially identical stock or securities, any loss realized from the sale or exchange is not recognized because the transaction is a **wash sale.**[49] The term *acquire* means acquire by purchase or in a taxable exchange and includes an option to purchase substantially identical securities. *Substantially identical* means the same in all important particulars. Corporate bonds and preferred stock are normally not considered substantially identical to the corporation's common stock. However, if the bonds and preferred stock are convertible into common stock, they may be considered substantially identical under certain circumstances.[50] Attempts to avoid the application of the wash sales rules by having a related taxpayer repurchase the securities have been unsuccessful.[51] The wash sales provisions do *not* apply to gains.

Recognition of the loss is disallowed because the taxpayer is considered to be in substantially the same economic position after the sale and repurchase as before the sale and repurchase. This disallowance rule does not apply to taxpayers engaged in the business of buying and selling securities.[52] Investors, however, are not allowed to create losses through wash sales to offset income for tax purposes.

Realized loss that is not recognized is added to the *basis* of the substantially identical stock or securities whose acquisition resulted in the nonrecognition of loss.[53] In other words, the basis of the replacement stock or securities is increased by the amount of the unrecognized loss. If the loss were not added to the basis of the newly acquired stock or securities, the taxpayer would never recover the entire basis of the old stock or securities.

The basis of the new stock or securities includes the unrecovered portion of the basis of the formerly held stock or securities. Therefore, the *holding period* of the new stock or securities begins on the date of acquisition of the old stock or securities.[54]

EXAMPLE 34

Bhaskar owns 100 shares of Green Corporation stock (adjusted basis of $20,000), 50 shares of which he sells for $8,000. Ten days later, he purchases 50 shares of the same stock for $7,000. Bhaskar's realized loss of $2,000 ($8,000 amount realized − $10,000 adjusted basis of 50 shares) is not recognized because it resulted from a wash sale. Bhaskar's basis in the newly acquired stock is $9,000 ($7,000 purchase price + $2,000 unrecognized loss from the wash sale). ▼

The taxpayer may acquire less than the number of shares sold in a wash sale. In this case, the loss from the sale is prorated between recognized and unrecognized loss on the basis of the ratio of the number of shares acquired to the number of shares sold.[55]

CONVERSION OF PROPERTY FROM PERSONAL USE TO BUSINESS OR INCOME-PRODUCING USE

As discussed previously, losses from the sale of personal use assets are not recognized for tax purposes, but losses from the sale of business and income-

---

[49] § 1091(a) and Reg. §§ 1.1091–1(a) and (f).
[50] Rev.Rul. 56–406, 1956–2 C.B. 523.
[51] *McWilliams v. Comm.*, 47–1 USTC ¶9289, 35 AFTR 1184, 67 S.Ct. 1477 (USSC, 1947).

[52] Reg. § 1.1091–1(a).
[53] § 1091(d) and Reg. § 1.1091–2(a).
[54] § 1223(4) and Reg. § 1.1223–1(d).
[55] § 1091(b) and Reg. § 1.1091–1(c).

producing assets are deductible. Can a taxpayer convert a personal use asset that has declined in value to business (or income-producing) use and then sell the asset to recognize a business (or income-producing) loss? The tax law prevents this by specifying that the *original basis for loss* on personal use assets converted to business or income-producing use is the *lower* of the property's adjusted basis or fair market value on the date of conversion.[56] The *gain basis* for converted property is the property's adjusted basis on the date of conversion. The tax law is not concerned with gains on converted property because gains are recognized regardless of whether property is business, income producing, or personal use.

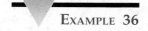

EXAMPLE 35

Diane's personal residence has an adjusted basis of $75,000 and a fair market value of $60,000. Diane converts the personal residence to rental property. Her basis for loss is $60,000 (lower of $75,000 adjusted basis and fair market value of $60,000). The $15,000 decline in value is a personal loss and can never be recognized for tax purposes. Diane's basis for gain is $75,000. ▼

The basis for loss is also the *basis for depreciating* the converted property.[57] This is an exception to the general rule that provides that the basis for depreciation is the gain basis (e.g., property received by gift). This exception prevents the taxpayer from recovering a personal loss indirectly through depreciation of the higher original basis. After the property is converted, both its basis for loss and its basis for gain are adjusted for depreciation deductions from the date of conversion to the date of disposition. These rules apply only if a conversion from personal to business or income-producing use has actually occurred.

EXAMPLE 36

At a time when his personal residence (adjusted basis of $40,000) is worth $50,000, Keith converts one-half of it to rental use. The property is not MACRS recovery property. At this point, the estimated useful life of the residence is 20 years and there is no estimated salvage value. After renting the converted portion for five years, Keith sells the property for $44,000. All amounts relate only to the building; the land has been accounted for separately. Keith has a $2,000 realized gain from the sale of the personal use portion of the residence and a $7,000 realized gain from the sale of the rental portion. These gains are computed as follows:

	Personal Use	Rental
Original basis for gain and loss—adjusted basis on date of conversion (fair market value is greater than the adjusted basis)	$20,000	$20,000
Depreciation—five years	None	5,000
Adjusted basis—date of sale	$20,000	$15,000
Amount realized	22,000	22,000
Realized gain	$ 2,000	$ 7,000

▼

As discussed in Chapter 15, Keith may be able to defer recognition of part or all of the $2,000 gain from the sale of the personal use portion of the residence under § 1034. The $7,000 gain from the rental portion is recognized.

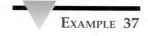

EXAMPLE 37

Assume the same facts as in the previous example, except that the fair market value on the date of conversion is $30,000 and the sales proceeds are $16,000. Keith has a $12,000 realized

---

[56] Reg. § 1.165–9(b)(2).

[57] Reg. § 1.167(g)–1.

loss from the sale of the personal use portion of the residence and a $3,250 realized loss from the sale of the rental portion. These losses are computed as follows:

	Personal Use	Rental
Original basis for loss—fair market value on date of conversion (fair market value is less than the adjusted basis)	*	$15,000
Depreciation—five years	None	3,750
Adjusted basis—date of sale	$20,000	$11,250
Amount realized	8,000	8,000
Realized loss	$12,000	$ 3,250

*Not applicable.

The $12,000 loss from the sale of the personal use portion of the residence is not recognized. The $3,250 loss from the rental portion is recognized. ▼

ADDITIONAL COMPLEXITIES IN DETERMINING REALIZED GAIN OR LOSS

Amount Realized

The calculation of the amount realized may appear to be one of the least complex areas associated with property transactions. However, because numerous positive and negative adjustments may be required, the calculation of this amount can be complex and confusing. In addition, the determination of the fair market value of the items received by the taxpayer can be difficult. The following example provides insight into various items that can have an impact on the amount realized.

EXAMPLE 38   Ridge sells an office building and the associated land on October 1, 1994. Under the terms of the sales contract, Ridge is to receive $600,000 in cash. The purchaser is to assume Ridge's mortgage of $300,000 on the property. To enable the purchaser to obtain adequate financing to pay the $600,000, Ridge is to pay the $15,000 in points charged by the lender. The broker's commission on the sale is $45,000. The purchaser agrees to pay the $12,000 in property taxes for the entire year. The amount realized by Ridge is calculated as follows:

Selling price		
Cash	$600,000	
Mortgage assumed by purchaser	300,000	
Seller's property taxes paid by purchaser ($12,000 × $\frac{9}{12}$)	9,000	$909,000
Less		
Broker's commission	$ 45,000	
Points paid by seller	15,000	(60,000)
Amount realized		$849,000

▼

Adjusted Basis

Three types of items tend to complicate the determination of adjusted basis. First, the applicable tax provisions for calculating the adjusted basis are dependent on how the property was acquired (e.g., purchase, taxable exchange, nontaxable exchange, gift, inheritance). Second, if the asset is subject to depreciation, cost recovery, amortization, or depletion, adjustments must be made to the basis during the time period the asset is held by the taxpayer. Upon disposition of the asset, the taxpayer's records for both of these items may be deficient. For example, the donee does not know the amount of the donor's basis or the amount of gift tax paid by the donor, or the taxpayer does not know how much depreciation he or she has deducted. Third, the complex positive and negative adjustments encountered in calculating the amount realized are also involved in calculating the adjusted basis.

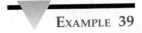

EXAMPLE 39

Jane purchased a personal residence in 1989. The purchase price and the related closing costs were as follows:

Purchase price	$125,000
Recording costs	140
Title fees and title insurance	815
Survey costs	115
Attorney's fees	750
Appraisal fee	60

Other relevant tax information for the house during the time Jane owned it follows:

- Constructed a swimming pool for medical reasons. The cost was $10,000, of which $3,000 was deducted as a medical expense.
- Added a solar heating system. The cost was $15,000.
- Deducted home office expenses of $6,000. Of this amount, $3,200 was for depreciation.
- None of the closing costs were deducted as moving expenses.

The adjusted basis for the house is calculated as follows:

Purchase price	$125,000
Recording costs	140
Title fees and title insurance	815
Survey costs	115
Attorney's fees	750
Appraisal fee	60
Swimming pool ($10,000 – $3,000)	7,000
Solar heating system	15,000
	$148,880
Less: Depreciation deducted on home office	(3,200)
Adjusted basis	$145,680

SUMMARY OF BASIS ADJUSTMENTS

Some of the more common items that either increase or decrease the basis of an asset appear in Concept Summary 14–2.

In discussing the topic of basis, a number of specific techniques for determining basis have been presented. Although the various techniques are responsive to and mandated by transactions occurring in the marketplace, they do possess enough common characteristics to be categorized as follows:

- The basis of the asset may be determined by reference to the asset's cost.
- The basis of the asset may be determined by reference to the basis of another asset.

CONCEPT SUMMARY 14-2

Adjustments to Basis

Item	Effect	Refer to Chapter	Explanation
Amortization of bond discount.	Increase	16	Amortization is mandatory for certain taxable bonds and elective for tax-exempt bonds.
Amortization of bond premium.	Decrease	14	Amortization is mandatory for tax-exempt bonds and elective for taxable bonds.
Amortization of covenant not to compete.	Decrease	16	Covenant must be for a definite and limited time period. The amortization period is a statutory period of 15 years.
Amortization of intangibles.	Decrease	8	Even goodwill is now subject to amortization.
Assessment for local benefits.	Increase	10	To the extent not deductible as taxes (e.g., assessment for streets and sidewalks that increase the value of the property versus one for maintenance or repair or for meeting interest charges).
Bad debts.	Decrease	7	Only the specific charge-off method is permitted.
Capital additions.	Increase	14	Certain items, at the taxpayer's election, can be capitalized or deducted (e.g., selected medical expenses).
Casualty.	Decrease	7	For a casualty loss, the amount of the adjustment is the summation of the deductible loss and the insurance proceeds received. For a casualty gain, the amount of the adjustment is the insurance proceeds received reduced by the recognized gain.
Condemnation.	Decrease	15	See casualty explanation.
Cost recovery.	Decrease	8	§ 168 is applicable to tangible assets placed in service after 1980 whose useful life is expressed in terms of years.
Depletion.	Decrease	8	Use the greater of cost or percentage depletion. Percentage depletion can still be deducted when the basis is zero.
Depreciation.	Decrease	8	§ 167 is applicable to tangible assets placed in service before 1981 and to tangible assets not depreciated in terms of years.
Easement.	Decrease		If the taxpayer does not retain any use of the land, all of the basis is allocable to the easement transaction. However, if only part of the land is affected by the easement, only part of the basis is allocable to the easement transaction.
Improvements by lessee to lessor's property.	Increase	5	Adjustment occurs only if the lessor is required to include the fair market value of the improvements in gross income under § 109.
Imputed interest.	Decrease	18	Amount deducted is not part of the cost of the asset.
Inventory: lower of cost or market.	Decrease	18	Not available if the LIFO method is used.
Limited expensing under § 179.	Decrease	8	Occurs only if the taxpayer elects § 179 treatment.

Item	Effect	Refer to Chapter	Explanation
Medical capital expenditure permitted as a medical expense.	Decrease	10	Adjustment is the amount of the deduction (the effect on basis is to increase it by the amount of the capital expenditure net of the deduction).
Real estate taxes; apportionment between the buyer and seller.	Increase or decrease	10	To the extent the buyer pays the seller's pro rata share, the buyer's basis is increased. To the extent the seller pays the buyer's pro rata share, the buyer's basis is decreased.
Rebate from manufacturer.	Decrease		Since the rebate is treated as an adjustment to the purchase price, it is not included in the buyer's gross income.
Stock dividend.	Decrease	5	Adjustment occurs only if the stock dividend is nontaxable. While the basis per share decreases, the total stock basis does not change.
Stock rights.	Decrease	14	Adjustment occurs only for nontaxable stock rights and only if the fair market value of the rights is at least 15% of the fair market value of the stock or, if less than 15%, the taxpayer elects to allocate the basis between the stock and the rights.
Theft.	Decrease	7	See casualty explanation.

- The basis of the asset may be determined by reference to the asset's fair market value.
- The basis of the asset may be determined by reference to the basis of the asset to another taxpayer.

TAX PLANNING CONSIDERATIONS

6   LEARNING OBJECTIVE
Identify tax planning opportunities related to selected property transactions.

TAX CONSEQUENCES OF ALICE'S PROPOSED TRANSACTION

In Example 1 earlier in the chapter, Alice's tax adviser asked a number of questions in order to advise her on a proposed transaction. Alice provided the following answers:

- Alice inherited the house from her mother. The fair market value of the house at the date of her mother's death, based on the estate tax return, was $200,000. Based on an appraisal, the house is worth $230,000. Alice's mother lived in the house for 48 years. According to the mother's attorney, her adjusted basis for the house was $75,000.
- As a child, Alice lived in the house for 10 years. She has not lived there during the 35 years she has been married.
- The house has been vacant during the seven months that Alice has owned it. She has been trying to decide whether she should sell it for its fair market value or sell it to her nephew for $75,000. Alice has suggested a $75,000 price for the sale to Dan because she believes this is the amount at which she will have no gain or loss.
- Alice intends to invest the $75,000 in stock.

You advise Alice that her adjusted basis for the house is the $200,000 fair market value on the date of her mother's death. If Alice sells the house for $230,000 (assuming no selling expenses), she would have a recognized gain of $30,000 ($230,000 amount realized − $200,000 adjusted basis). The house is a capital asset, and her holding period is long term since she inherited the house. Thus, the gain would be classified as a long-term capital gain. If, instead, Alice sells the house to her nephew for $75,000, she will have a part sale and part gift. The realized gain on the sale of $9,783 is recognized.

Amount realized	$75,000
Adjusted basis	(65,217)*
Realized gain	$ 9,783
Recognized gain	$ 9,783

*[($75,000/$230,000) × $200,000] = $65,217.

The gain is classified as a long-term capital gain. Alice is then deemed to have made a gift to Dan of $155,000 ($230,000 − $75,000).

With this information, Alice can make an informed selection between the two options.

COST IDENTIFICATION AND DOCUMENTATION CONSIDERATIONS

When multiple assets are acquired in a single transaction, the contract price must be allocated for several reasons. First, some of the assets may be depreciable while others are not. From the different viewpoints of the buyer and the seller, this may produce a tax conflict that needs to be resolved. That is, the seller prefers a high allocation for nondepreciable assets, whereas the purchaser prefers a high allocation for depreciable assets (see Chapters 16 and 17). Second, the seller needs to know the amount realized on the sale of the capital assets and the ordinary income assets so that the recognized gains and losses can be classified as capital or ordinary. For example, an allocation to goodwill or to a covenant not to compete (see Chapters 8, 16, and 17) produces different tax consequences to the seller. Third, the buyer needs the adjusted basis of each asset to calculate the realized gain or loss on a subsequent sale or other disposition of each asset.

SELECTION OF PROPERTY FOR MAKING GIFTS

A donor can achieve several tax advantages by making gifts of appreciated property. Income tax on the unrealized gain that would have occurred had the donor sold the property is avoided by the donor. A portion of this amount can be permanently avoided because the donee's adjusted basis is increased by part or all of any gift tax paid by the donor. Even without this increase in basis, the income tax liability on the sale of the property by the donee can be less than the income tax liability that would have resulted from the donor's sale of the property, if the donee is in a lower tax bracket than the donor. In addition, any subsequent appreciation during the time the property is held by the lower tax bracket donee results in a tax savings on the sale or other disposition of the property. Such gifts of appreciated property can be an effective tool in family tax planning.

Taxpayers should generally not make gifts of depreciated property (property that, if sold, would produce a realized loss) because the donor does not receive an income tax deduction for the unrealized loss element. In addition, the donee receives no benefit from this unrealized loss upon the subsequent sale of the property because of the loss basis rule. The loss basis rule provides that the donee's basis is the lower of the donor's basis or fair market value at the date of the gift. If the donor anticipates that the donee will sell the property upon receiving it, the donor should sell the property and take the loss deduction, assuming the loss is deductible. The donor can then give the proceeds from the sale to the donee.

SELECTION OF PROPERTY FOR MAKING BEQUESTS

A decedent's will should generally make bequests of appreciated property. Doing so enables both the decedent and the heir to avoid income tax on the unrealized gain because the recipient takes the fair market value as his or her basis.

Taxpayers generally should not make bequests of depreciated property (property that, if sold, would produce a realized loss) because the decedent does not receive an income tax deduction for the unrealized loss element. In addition, the heir will receive no benefit from this unrealized loss upon the subsequent sale of the property.

EXAMPLE 40

On the date of her death, Marta owned land held for investment purposes. The land had an adjusted basis of $600,000 and a fair market value of $100,000. If Marta had sold the property before her death, the recognized loss would have been $500,000. If Ramon inherits the property and sells it for $60,000, the recognized loss will be $40,000 (the decline in value since Marta's death). In addition, regardless of the period of time Ramon holds the property, the holding period is long term (see Chapter 16). ▼

From an income tax perspective, it is preferable to transfer appreciated property as a bequest rather than as a gift. This results because inherited property receives a step-up in basis, whereas property received by gift has a carryover basis to the donee. However, in making this decision, the estate tax consequences of the bequest should also be weighed against the gift tax consequences of the gift.

DISALLOWED LOSSES

Section 267 Disallowed Losses

Taxpayers should be aware of the desirability of avoiding transactions that activate the loss disallowance provisions for related parties. This is so even in light of the provision that permits the related-party buyer to offset his or her realized gain by the related-party seller's disallowed loss. Even with this offset, several inequities exist. First, the tax benefit associated with the disallowed loss ultimately is realized by the wrong party (the related-party buyer rather than the related-party seller). Second, the tax benefit of this offset to the related-party buyer does not occur until the buyer disposes of the property. Therefore, the longer the time period between the purchase and disposition of the property by the related-party buyer, the less the economic benefit. Third, if the property does not appreciate to at least its adjusted basis to the related-party seller during the time period the related-party buyer holds it, part or all of the disallowed loss is permanently lost. Fourth, since the right of offset is available only to the original transferee (the related-party buyer), all of the disallowed loss is permanently lost if the original transferee subsequently transfers the property by gift or bequest.

EXAMPLE 41

Tim sells property with an adjusted basis of $35,000 to Wes, his brother, for $25,000, the fair market value of the property. The $10,000 realized loss to Tim is disallowed by § 267. If Wes subsequently sells the property to an unrelated party for $37,000, he has a recognized gain of $2,000 (realized gain of $12,000 reduced by disallowed loss of $10,000). Therefore, from the perspective of the family unit, the original $10,000 realized loss ultimately is recognized. However, if Wes sells the property for $29,000, he has a recognized gain of $0 (realized gain of $4,000 reduced by disallowed loss of $4,000 necessary to offset the realized gain). From the perspective of the family unit, $6,000 of the realized loss of $10,000 is permanently wasted ($10,000 realized loss − $4,000 offset permitted). ▼

Wash Sales

The wash sales provisions can be avoided if the security is replaced within the statutory time period with a similar rather than a substantially identical security. For example, the sale of Bethlehem Steel common stock and a purchase of Inland Steel common stock is not treated as a wash sale. Such a procedure can enable the taxpayer to use an unrealized capital loss to offset a recognized capital gain. The taxpayer can sell the security before the end of the taxable year, offset the recognized capital loss against the capital gain, and invest the sales proceeds in a similar security.

Because the wash sales provisions do not apply to gains, it may be desirable to engage in a wash sale before the end of the taxable year. This recognized capital gain may be used to offset capital losses or capital loss carryovers from prior years. Since the basis of the replacement stock or securities will be the purchase price, the taxpayer in effect has exchanged a capital gain for an increased basis for the stock or securities.

KEY TERMS

Adjusted basis, 14–4	Goodwill, 14–9	Recognized loss, 14–6
Amount realized, 14–3	Holding period, 14–13	Recovery of capital doctrine, 14–7
Fair market value, 14–4	Realized gain, 14–3	Related-party transaction, 14–17
Gift, 14–11	Realized loss, 14–3	
	Recognized gain, 14–6	Wash sale, 14–19

PROBLEM MATERIALS

DISCUSSION QUESTIONS

1. Upon the sale or other disposition of property, what four questions should be considered for income tax purposes?

✗ 2. In addition to sales and exchanges, what are some other transactions that are treated as dispositions of property?

3. Ivan invests in land and Grace invests in taxable bonds. The land appreciates by $5,000 each year, and the bonds earn interest of $5,000 each year. After holding the land and bonds for five years, Ivan and Grace sell them. There is a $25,000 realized gain on the sale of the land and no realized gain or loss on the sale of the bonds. Are the tax consequences to Ivan and Grace the same for each of the five years? Explain.

4. Carol and Dave each purchase 100 shares of stock of Burgundy, Inc., a publicly owned corporation, in July for $10,000 each. Carol sells her stock on December 31 for $14,000. Since Burgundy's stock is listed on a national exchange, Dave is able to ascertain that

his shares are worth $14,000 on December 31. Does the tax law treat the appreciation in value of the stock differently for Carol and Dave? Explain.

5. If a taxpayer sells property for cash, the amount realized consists of the net proceeds from the sale. For each of the following, indicate the effect on the amount realized:
   a. The property is sold on credit.
   b. A mortgage on the property is assumed by the buyer.
   c. The purchaser pays real property taxes that are treated as imposed on the seller.

6. If the buyer pays real property taxes that are treated as imposed on the seller, what are the effects on the seller's amount realized and the buyer's adjusted basis for the property? If the seller pays real property taxes that are treated as imposed on the buyer, what are the effects on the seller's amount realized and the buyer's adjusted basis for the property?

7. Tom is negotiating to buy some land. Under the first option, Tom will give Sandra $70,000 and assume her mortgage on the land for $30,000. Under the second option, Tom will give Sandra $100,000, and she will immediately pay off the mortgage. Tom would like for his basis for the land to be as high as possible. Given this objective, which option should Tom select?

8. Edith purchases land from Gail. Edith gives Gail $40,000 in cash and agrees to pay Gail an additional $80,000 one year later plus interest at 8%.
   a. What is Edith's adjusted basis for the land at the date purchased?
   b. What is Edith's adjusted basis for the land one year later?

9. The taxpayer owns land and a building with an adjusted basis of $50,000 and a fair market value of $250,000. The property is subject to a mortgage of $400,000. Since the taxpayer is in arrears on the mortgage payments, the creditor is willing to accept the property in return for canceling the amount of the mortgage.
   a. How can the adjusted basis of the property be less than the amount of the mortgage?
   b. If the creditor's offer is accepted, what are the effects on the amount realized, the adjusted basis, and the realized gain or loss?
   c. Does it matter in (b) if the mortgage is recourse or nonrecourse?

10. Distinguish between the terms *allowed depreciation* and *allowable depreciation*. What effects do allowed depreciation and allowable depreciation have on adjusted basis?

11. Chris and Jeff each own an automobile that each uses exclusively in his respective trade or business. The adjusted basis of each automobile is $17,000, and the fair market value is $11,000. Both automobiles are destroyed in accidents. Chris's automobile is insured, and he receives insurance proceeds of $11,000. Jeff's automobile is uninsured. Explain how the adjusted basis for each automobile is reduced to zero, even though one is insured and the other is uninsured.

12. Abby owns stock in Orange Corporation and Blue Corporation. She receives a $1,000 distribution from both corporations. The instructions from Orange state that the $1,000 is a dividend. The instructions from Blue state that the $1,000 is not a dividend. What could cause the instructions to differ as to the tax consequences?

13. A taxpayer who acquires a taxable bond at a discount is required to amortize the discount, whereas a taxpayer who acquires a tax-exempt bond at a discount may elect to amortize the discount. What effect does the amortization have on the adjusted basis for the bonds? Why is the amortization mandatory for the taxable bond but elective for the tax-exempt bond?

14. A taxpayer who acquires a taxable bond at a premium may elect to amortize the premium, whereas a taxpayer who acquires a tax-exempt bond at a premium must amortize the premium. Why would a taxpayer make the amortization election for taxable bonds? What effect does the mandatory amortization of tax-exempt bonds have on taxable income?

15. Kara owns two assets that she is considering selling. One has appreciated in value by $3,000, and the other has declined in value by $3,000. Both assets are held for personal

use. Kara believes that she should sell both assets in the same taxable year so that the loss of $3,000 can offset the gain of $3,000. Advise Kara regarding the tax consequences.

16. Explain the relationship between the recovery of capital doctrine and (a) realized gain and (b) recognized gain or loss.

17. Lee owns a life insurance policy that will pay $100,000 to Rita, his spouse, on his death. At the date of Lee's death, he had paid total premiums on the policy of $65,000. In accordance with § 101(a)(1), Rita excludes the $100,000 of insurance proceeds. Discuss the relationship, if any, between the § 101 exclusion and the recovery of capital doctrine.

18. How is the basis of the property determined in a bargain purchase, and why is this method used?

19. How is cost allocated for lump-sum purchases?

20. Discuss the differences in tax treatment for allocating basis to nontaxable stock dividends when the form of the dividend is a common stock dividend on common stock versus a preferred stock dividend on common stock.

21. Discuss the differences in tax treatment when stock rights are allocated a cost basis and when stock rights have no cost basis. When does each of these situations occur?

22. Why must gifts of property be given a basis to the donee?

23. Why does the Code contain both a gain basis rule and a loss basis rule for gift property? Under what circumstances will these rules produce different basis amounts?

24. Under what circumstances is it possible to recognize no gain or loss on the sale of an asset previously received as a gift?

25. Discuss the differences in tax treatment between property sold before death and inherited property. Why is this important?

26. Gary makes a gift of an appreciated building to Carmen. She dies three months later, and Gary inherits the building from her. During the period that Carmen held the building, she deducted depreciation and made a capital expenditure. What effect might these items have on Gary's basis for the inherited building?

27. Immediately before his death in 1994, Kirby sells securities (adjusted basis of $100,000) for their fair market value of $20,000. The sale was not to a related party. The securities were community property, and Kirby is survived by his wife, Zina, who inherits all of his property.
    a. Did Kirby act wisely? Why or why not?
    b. Suppose the figures are reversed (sale for $100,000 of property with an adjusted basis of $20,000). Would the sale be wise? Why or why not?

28. What is the holding period for property received by gift? What is the holding period for inherited property?

29. What are related-party transactions, and why are they important?

30. What is a wash sale? Why isn't a realized loss recognized on a wash sale? How is the recovery of capital doctrine maintained?

PROBLEMS

31. Anne sold her home for $290,000 in 1994. Selling expenses were $17,000. She had purchased it in 1988 for $190,000. During the period of ownership, Anne had:

    • Deducted $57,500 office-in-home expenses, which included $17,500 in depreciation. (Refer to Chapter 9.)

    • Deducted a casualty loss of residential trees destroyed by a hurricane. The total loss was $17,000 (after the $100 floor and the 10%-of-AGI floor), and Anne's insurance company reimbursed Anne for $12,500. (Refer to Chapter 7.)

- Paid street paving assessment of $6,000 and added sidewalks for $10,000.

- Installed an elevator for medical reasons. The total cost was $20,000, and Anne deducted $11,000 as medical expenses. (Refer to Chapter 10.)

- Paid legal expenses of $3,000 in connection with the move to the home in 1988. Anne deducted these expenses as moving expenses. (Refer to Chapter 9.)

- Received $7,500 from a utility company for an easement to install underground utility lines across the property.

What is Anne's realized gain?

32. Kareem bought a rental house at the beginning of 1989 for $80,000, of which $10,000 is allocated to the land and $70,000 to the building. Early in 1991, he had a tennis court built in the backyard at a cost of $5,000. Kareem has deducted $32,200 for depreciation on the house and $1,300 for depreciation on the court. At the beginning of 1994, he sells the house and tennis court for $125,000 cash.
   a. What is Kareem's realized gain or loss?
   b. If an original mortgage of $20,000 is still outstanding and the buyer assumes the mortgage in addition to the cash payment, what is Kareem's realized gain or loss?
   c. If the buyer takes the property subject to the mortgage, what is Kareem's realized gain or loss?

33. Norm is negotiating the sale of a tract of his land to Pat. Use the following classification scheme to classify each of the items contained in the proposed sales contract:

Legend

DARN = Decreases amount realized by Norm
IARN = Increases amount realized by Norm
DABN = Decreases adjusted basis to Norm
IABN = Increases adjusted basis to Norm
DABP = Decreases adjusted basis to Pat
IABP = Increases adjusted basis to Pat

   a. Norm is to receive cash of $50,000.
   b. Norm is to receive Pat's note payable for $25,000, payable in three years.
   c. Pat assumes Norm's mortgage of $5,000 on the land.
   d. Pat agrees to pay the realtor's sales commission of $8,000.
   e. Pat agrees to pay the property taxes on the land for the entire year. If each party paid his or her respective share, Norm's share would be $1,000, and Pat's share would be $3,000.
   f. Pat pays legal fees of $500.
   g. Norm pays legal fees of $750.

34. Nell owns a personal use automobile that has an adjusted basis of $8,000. The fair market value of the automobile is $4,500.
   a. Calculate the realized and recognized loss if Nell sells the automobile for $4,500.
   b. Calculate the realized and recognized loss if Nell exchanges the automobile for another automobile worth $4,500.
   c. Calculate the realized and recognized loss if the automobile is stolen and Nell receives insurance proceeds of $4,500.

35. Mitch's automobile, which is used exclusively in his business, is stolen. The adjusted basis is $22,000, and the fair market value is $23,000. Mitch's AGI is $45,000.
   a. If Mitch receives insurance proceeds of $22,500, what effect do the theft and the receipt of the insurance proceeds have on the adjusted basis of the automobile?
   b. If the automobile is not insured, what effect do the theft and the absence of insurance have on the adjusted basis of the automobile?

36. Lynn owns 60% and Debra owns 40% of the stock of Pelican Corporation. Lynn's adjusted basis is $60,000, and Debra's adjusted basis is $40,000. Pelican has no earnings and profits. Pelican makes cash distributions of $90,000 to Lynn and $60,000 to Debra.
    a. What effect do the cash distributions have on each shareholder's adjusted basis for the stock?
    b. What effect do the cash distributions have on each shareholder's gross income?

37. Chee paid $215,000 for bonds with a face value of $200,000 at the beginning of 1990. The bonds mature in 10 years and pay 9% interest per year.
    a. If Chee sells the bonds for $225,000 at the beginning of 1994, is there a realized gain or loss? If so, how much?
    b. If Chee trades the bonds at the beginning of 1995 for stock worth $230,000, is there a realized gain or loss? If so, how much?

38. Which of the following would definitely result in a recognized gain or loss?
    a. Kay sells her lakeside cabin, which has an adjusted basis of $10,000, for $15,000.
    b. Adam sells his personal residence, which has an adjusted basis of $15,000, for $10,000.
    c. Carl's personal residence is on the site of a proposed airport and is condemned by the city. Carl receives $55,000 for the house, which has an adjusted basis of $65,000.
    d. Olga's land is worth $40,000 at the end of the year. Olga had purchased the land six months earlier for $25,000.
    e. Jack gives stock to his niece. Jack's adjusted basis is $8,000, and the fair market value is $5,000.

39. Hubert's personal residence is condemned as part of an urban renewal project. His adjusted basis for the residence is $160,000. He receives condemnation proceeds of $150,000 and invests the proceeds in stock.
    a. Calculate Hubert's realized and recognized gain or loss.
    b. If the condemnation proceeds are $180,000, what are Hubert's realized and recognized gain or loss?
    c. What are Hubert's realized and recognized gain or loss in (a) if the house was rental property?

40. Walt is a real estate agent for Governor's Farms, a residential real estate development. Because of his outstanding sales performance, Walt is permitted to buy a lot that normally would sell for $125,000 for $100,000. Walt is the only real estate agent for Governor's Farms who is permitted to do so.
    a. Does Walt have gross income from the transaction?
    b. What is Walt's adjusted basis for the land?

41. Karen makes the following purchases and sales of stock:

Transaction	Date	No. of Shares	Company	Price per Share
Purchase	1–1–92	300	MDG	$ 75
Purchase	6–1–92	150	GRU	300
Purchase	11–1–92	60	MDG	70
Sale	12–3–92	180	MDG	70
Purchase	3–1–93	120	GRU	375
Sale	8–1–93	90	GRU	330
Sale	1–1–94	150	MDG	90
Sale	2–1–94	75	GRU	500

Assuming that Karen is unable to identify the particular lots that are sold with the original purchase, what is the realized gain or loss on each type of stock as of:
    a. 7–1–92.
    b. 12–31–92.

c. 12–31–93.

d. 7–1–94.

42. Frank purchases 100 shares of Bluebird Corporation stock on June 3, 1994, for $100,000. On August 25, 1994, Frank purchases an additional 50 shares of Bluebird stock for $40,000. According to market quotations, Bluebird stock is selling for $850 per share on December 31, 1994. Frank sells 60 shares of Bluebird stock on March 1, 1995, for $54,000.

a. What is the adjusted basis of Frank's Bluebird stock on December 31, 1994?

b. What is Frank's recognized gain or loss from the sale of Bluebird stock on March 1, 1995, assuming the shares sold are from the shares purchased on June 3, 1994?

c. What is Frank's recognized gain or loss from the sale of Bluebird stock on March 1, 1995, assuming Frank cannot adequately identify the shares sold?

43. Paula purchases the assets of a sole proprietorship from Seth. The adjusted basis of each of the assets on Seth's books and the fair market value of each asset as agreed to by Paula and Seth are as follows:

Asset	Seth's Adjusted Basis	FMV
Accounts receivable	$ –0–	$ 10,000
Notes receivable	15,000	20,000
Machinery and equipment	85,000	100,000
Building	100,000	300,000
Land	200,000	350,000

The purchase price is $900,000. Determine Paula's basis for each of the assets of the sole proprietorship.

44. Shontelle owns 1,000 shares of Gray Corporation stock with a basis of $15,000 and a fair market value of $20,000. She receives nontaxable stock rights to purchase additional shares. The rights have a fair market value of $2,000.

a. What is the basis of the stock and the basis of the stock rights?

b. What is the recognized gain or loss if the stock rights are sold for $2,000?

c. What is the recognized gain or loss if the stock rights are allowed to lapse?

45. Rick received various gifts over the years. He has decided to dispose of the following assets that he received as gifts:

a. In 1945, he received land worth $20,000. The donor's adjusted basis was $32,000. Rick sells the land for $87,000 in 1994.

b. In 1950, he received stock in Gold Company. The donor's adjusted basis was $1,000. The fair market value on the date of the gift was $3,000. Rick sells the stock for $3,500 in 1994.

c. In 1961, he received land worth $12,000. The donor's adjusted basis was $25,000. Rick sells the land for $9,000 in 1994.

d. In 1990, he received stock worth $30,000. The donor's adjusted basis was $40,000. Rick sells the stock in 1994 for $37,000.

What is the realized gain or loss from each of the preceding transactions? Assume in each of the gift transactions that no gift tax was paid.

46. Beth received a car from Sam as a gift. Sam paid $7,000 for the car. He had used it for business purposes and had deducted $2,000 for depreciation up to the time he gave the car to Beth. The fair market value of the car is $3,500.

a. Assuming Beth uses the car for business purposes, what is her basis for depreciation?

b. If the estimated useful life is two years (from the date of the gift), what is her depreciation deduction for each year? Use the straight-line method.

c. If Beth sells the car for $800 one year after receiving it, what is her gain or loss?

d. If Beth sells the car for $4,000 one year after receiving it, what is her gain or loss?

47. Ron receives a gift of property (after 1976) that has a fair market value of $100,000 on the date of gift. The donor's adjusted basis for the property was $40,000. Assume the donor paid gift tax of $15,000 on the gift.
   a. What is Ron's basis for gain and loss and for depreciation?
   b. If Ron had received the gift of property before 1977, what would his basis be for gain and loss and for depreciation?

48. Liz receives a gift of income-producing property that has an adjusted basis of $70,000 on the date of the gift. The fair market value of the property on the date of the gift is $50,000. The donor paid gift tax of $4,000. Liz later sells the property for $54,000. Determine her recognized gain or loss.

49. Ira is planning to make a charitable contribution of stock worth $20,000 to the Boy Scouts. The stock Ira is considering contributing has an adjusted basis of $15,000. A friend has suggested that Ira sell the stock and contribute the $20,000 in proceeds rather than contribute the stock.
   a. Should Ira follow the friend's advice? Why?
   b. Assume the fair market value is only $13,000. In this case, should Ira follow the friend's advice? Why?
   c. Rather than make a charitable contribution to the Boy Scouts, Ira is going to make a gift to Nancy, his niece. Advise Ira regarding (a) and (b).

50. Dena inherits property from Mary, her mother. Mary's adjusted basis for the property is $100,000, and the fair market value is $725,000. Six months after Mary's death, the fair market value is $740,000. Dena is the sole beneficiary of Mary's estate.
   a. Can the executor of Mary's estate elect the alternate valuation date?
   b. What is Dena's basis for the property?

51. Earl's estate includes the following assets available for distribution to Robert, one of Earl's beneficiaries:

Asset	Earl's Adjusted Basis	FMV at Date of Death	FMV at Alternate Valuation Date
Cash	$10,000	$ 10,000	$ 10,000
Stock	40,000	125,000	60,000
Apartment building	60,000	300,000	325,000
Land	75,000	100,000	110,000

The fair market value of the stock six months after Earl's death was $60,000. However, believing that the stock would continue to decline in value, the executor of the estate distributed the stock to Robert one month after Earl's death. Robert immediately sold the stock for $85,000.
   a. Determine Robert's basis for the assets if the primary valuation date and amount apply.
   b. Determine Robert's basis for the assets if the executor elects the alternate valuation date and amount.

52. Dan bought a hotel for $720,000 in January 1991. In January 1994, he died and left the hotel to Ed. Dan had deducted $42,000 of cost recovery on the hotel before his death. The fair market value in January 1994 was $780,000.
   a. What is the basis of the property to Ed?
   b. If the land is worth $240,000, what is Ed's basis for cost recovery?

53. Emily makes a gift of 100 shares of appreciated stock to her uncle, George, on January 5, 1994. The basis of the stock is $3,150, and the fair market value is $5,250. George dies on October 8, 1994. During the period that George held the stock, he received a 5% nontaxable stock dividend. Under the provisions of George's will, Emily inherits 100

shares of the stock. The value of the stock for Federal estate tax purposes is $55 per share.
  a. What is the basis of the inherited stock to Emily?
  b. What is the basis of the inherited stock to Emily if she had given the stock to George on January 5, 1993?

54. Larry and Grace live in Louisiana, a community property state. They own land (community property) that has an adjusted basis to them of $100,000. At the date of Grace's death, the fair market value of the land is $140,000. Six months after Grace's death, the land is worth $150,000. What is Larry's basis for the land?

55. Joyce owns undeveloped real estate with an adjusted basis of $80,000. She sells the real estate to her sister, Iris, for its fair market value of $65,000.
  a. Calculate Joyce's realized and recognized gain or loss.
  b. If Iris later sells the real estate for $72,000, calculate her realized and recognized gain or loss.
  c. Assume instead that Joyce sold the real estate to Iris for its fair market value of $90,000. Calculate Joyce's realized and recognized gain or loss.

56. Ted owns a 60% capital and profits interest in TS Partnership, which sells property to Ted for $65,000. The partnership's adjusted basis for the property is $90,000.
  a. Calculate the realized and recognized loss to the partnership.
  b. Calculate the basis of the property to Ted.
  c. If Ted subsequently sells the property for $87,000, calculate his realized and recognized gain or loss.
  d. If Ted gives the property to his daughter, Donna, who subsequently sells it for $87,000, calculate Donna's realized and recognized gain or loss. Assume no gift tax is paid on the gift and the fair market value on the date of the gift is $80,000.
  e. Determine the tax consequences in (a) through (d) if Ted is a shareholder and TS is a corporation.

57. Doug owns three pieces of land in western Virginia. Parcel A has an adjusted basis of $75,000; parcel B, $125,000; and parcel C, $175,000. Doug sells parcel A to his father-in-law for $50,000, parcel B to his partner for $120,000, and parcel C to his mother for $150,000.
  a. What is the recognized gain (loss) from the sale of each of the parcels of land?
  b. If Doug's father-in-law sells his land for $90,000, what is his recognized gain (loss)?
  c. If Doug's partner sells his land for $130,000, what is his recognized gain (loss)?
  d. If Doug's mother sells her land for $165,000, what is her recognized gain (loss)?

58. On September 15, 1994, Veneia decides to revise her stock holdings as follows:

Date	Company	No. of Shares	Trans- action	Price	Cost
9–10–94	Delta	100	Buy	$25/share	
9–15–94	Kodak	120	Sell	20/share	$25/share
9–15–94	Ford	70	Sell	25/share	20/share
9–15–94	IBM	95	Sell	5/share	10/share
9–15–94	Xerox	220	Sell	8/share	5/share
9–15–94	Delta	100	Sell	20/share	30/share
10– 4–94	Ford	100	Buy	20/share	
10– 8–94	ABC	120	Buy	7/share	
10–14–94	American	50	Buy	4/share	
10–25–94	Kodak	95	Buy	30/share	

  a. What is the recognized gain or loss for each of the stocks sold on September 15?
  b. Explain why the gain or loss is or is not recognized on each sale.

59. Kristy owns 100 shares of stock in Magenta Corporation. Her adjusted basis for the stock is $5,000. On December 21, Kristy sells the stock in the marketplace for $12,000. She purchases 100 shares of Magenta stock in the marketplace on January 5 of the following year for $12,000.
    a. What is Kristy trying to achieve from a tax perspective?
    b. Will she succeed?
    c. Using the same data, except that Kristy's adjusted basis for the stock is $15,000, respond to (a) and (b).

60. James retires from a public accounting firm to enter private practice. He had bought a home two years earlier for $40,000. Upon opening his business, he converts one-fourth of his home into an office. The fair market value of the home on the date of conversion (January 1, 1988) is $75,000. The adjusted basis is $56,000 (ignore land). James lives and works in the home for six years (after converting it to business use) and sells it at the end of the sixth year. He deducted $6,148 of cost recovery using the statutory percentage method.
    a. How much gain or loss is recognized if James sells the property for $44,000?
    b. If he sells the property for $70,000?

61. Surendra's personal residence originally cost $150,000 (ignore land). After living in the house for five years, he converts it to rental property. At the date of conversion, the fair market value of the house is $130,000.
    a. Calculate Surendra's basis for loss for the rental property.
    b. Calculate Surendra's basis for depreciation for the rental property.
    c. Calculate Surendra's basis for gain for the rental property.

62. Hun, age 93, has accumulated substantial assets during his life. Among his many assets are the following, which he is considering giving to Koji, his grandson.

Assets	Adjusted Basis	Fair Market Value
Red Corporation stock	$ 50,000	$700,000
Silver Corporation stock	70,000	71,000
Emerald Corporation stock	200,000	50,000

Hun has been in ill health for the past five years. His physician has informed him that he probably will not live for more than six months. Advise Hun which of the stocks should be transferred as gifts and which as bequests.

CUMULATIVE PROBLEMS

63. Ada Johnson, age 28, is single and has no dependents. Her Social Security number is 444–11–3333, and she resides at 210 Avenue G, Kentwood, LA 70444. Her salary in 1994 was $52,000. She incurred unreimbursed expenses of $1,800 for travel and $500 for entertainment in connection with her job as an assistant personnel director. In addition, she had the following items of possible tax consequence in 1994:
    a. Itemized deductions (not including any potential deductions mentioned previously), $12,000.
    b. Proceeds from the October 8, 1994, sale of land inherited from her father on June 15, 1994 (fair market value on June 15 was $35,000; her father's adjusted basis was $15,000), $55,000.
    c. Proceeds from the November 1, 1994, sale of 50 shares of Pigeon Corporation stock received as a gift from her father on October 5, 1976, when the fair market value of the stock was $6,000 (her father's adjusted basis in the stock was $5,500, and he paid gift tax of $800 on the transfer), $9,500.
    d. Proceeds from the November 5, 1994, sale of her personal automobile, for which she had paid $4,500 in 1986, $3,100.

e. Proceeds from the December 3, 1994, sale of 10 shares of Swan Corporation stock to her brother (she had paid $85 per share for the stock on February 7, 1994), $600.

f. Dividends received from a domestic corporation, $480.

Part 1—Tax Computation

Ada's employer withheld Federal income tax of $14,880. Compute Ada's net tax payable or refund due for 1994. Suggested software (if available): *TurboTax* or *MacInTax* or WFT tax planning software.

Part 2—Tax Planning

As of the beginning of 1995, Ada is promoted to the position of personnel director. The promotion will result in a salary increase. Her new position will result in an estimated increase in her expenses for travel from $1,800 to $4,000 and in her expenses for entertainment from $500 to $4,000. Her employer has offered her the following options.

a. Salary increase of $20,000.

b. Salary increase of $12,000 and reimbursement for all travel and entertainment expenses not in excess of $8,000.

Ada estimates that her itemized deductions (excluding any potential deductions for travel and entertainment) will remain at $12,000. She anticipates that no dividends will be received and no proceeds from asset sales will be received.

Calculate Ada's tax liability for 1995 under both option (a) and option (b). Write a letter to Ada that contains your advice and prepare a memo for the tax files. Suggested software (if available): WFT tax planning software.

64. Kenneth Cloud, age 67, is married and files a joint return with his wife, Sarah, age 65. Kenneth and Sarah are both retired. In 1993, they received Social Security benefits of $9,000. Kenneth's Social Security number is 366–55–1111, and Sarah's is 555–66–2222. They reside at 405 College Drive, Hammond, LA 70408.

Kenneth, who retired on January 1, 1993, receives benefits from a qualified pension plan of $600 a month for life. His total contributions to the plan were $62,000. Kenneth's life expectancy at the annuity starting date on January 1, 1993, was 18.4 years.

Sarah, who retired on December 31, 1992, started receiving benefits of $800 a month on January 1, 1993. Her life expectancy was 20 years from the annuity starting date, and her investment in the qualified pension plan was $57,600.

Sarah enjoyed playing the slot machines at the casino in New Orleans. Her net winnings for the year were $1,000. When Kenneth visited his brother in Richmond, Virginia, he bought a lottery ticket for $1 and won $20,000.

On September 27, 1993, Kenneth and Sarah received a 10% stock dividend on 50 shares of stock they owned. They had paid $11 a share for the stock on March 5, 1976. On December 16, 1993, they sold the 5 shares received as a stock dividend for $30 a share.

On January 10, 1993, Sarah sold the car she had used in commuting to and from work. She paid $5,000 for the car in 1984 and sold it for $3,500.

Kenneth and Sarah received a gift of 100 shares of stock from their son Thomas on July 14, 1978. Thomas's basis in the stock was $30 a share, and the fair market value at the date of gift was $20 a share. No gift tax was paid. Kenneth and Sarah sold the stock on October 8, 1993, for $15 a share.

Sarah's mother died on May 1, 1993. Sarah inherited her mother's personal residence, which had a fair market value of $112,000 on May 1. Her mother's adjusted basis was $80,000. At the end of 1993, Sarah was still listing the house with a realtor. The realtor estimated the house was worth $120,000 at December 31, 1993.

Kenneth and Sarah paid estimated Federal income tax of $3,100 and had itemized deductions of $6,800. If they have overpaid their Federal income tax, they want the amount refunded. Both Kenneth and Sarah wish to have $3 go to the Presidential Election Campaign Fund.

Compute their net tax payable or refund due for 1993. If you use tax forms for your computations, you will need Form 1040 and Schedules A, D, and R. Suggested software (if available): *TurboTax* or *MacInTax* or WFT tax planning software.

RESEARCH PROBLEMS

Research Problem 1.   On January 1, 1994, Bart, a major shareholder in Copper Corporation, purchases land from the company for $300,000. The fair market value of the land is $1,200,000, and the adjusted basis in the hands of the corporation is $400,000.
a. What are the possible tax consequences to Bart?
b. What is the basis of the land to Bart?
c. What is the tax consequence to Copper Corporation?

Research Problem 2.   Terry owns real estate with an adjusted basis of $600,000 and a fair market value of $1,100,000. The amount of the nonrecourse mortgage on the property is $2,500,000. Because of substantial past and projected future losses associated with the real estate development (occupancy rate of only 37% after three years), Terry deeds the property to the creditor.
a. What are the tax consequences to Terry?
b. Assume the data are the same, except the fair market value of the property is $2,525,000. Therefore, when Terry deeds the property to the creditor, she also receives $25,000 from the creditor. What are the tax consequences to Terry?

Partial list of research aids:
Rev.Rul. 76–111, 1976–1 C.B. 214.
Crane v. Comm., 47 USTC ¶9217, 35 AFTR 776, 67 S.Ct. 1047 (USSC, 1947).

Research Problem 3.   Olaf gives stock worth $400,000 to Hazel. Olaf's adjusted basis in the stock is $50,000. The gift taxes due are $118,400. As a condition for receiving the gift of stock, Hazel agrees to pay the gift tax. The stock is transferred to Hazel on February 5, 1994.
a. What are the income tax consequences to Olaf?
b. What are the income tax consequences to Olaf if the gift was made on February 5, 1981?

Research Problem 4.   Wilma owns land that has an adjusted basis of $75,000 and a fair market value of $200,000. She has owned the land for five years. The land is subject to a mortgage of $100,000. Wilma, an alumna of State University, donates the land to State University. The university assumes Wilma's mortgage on the land. What are the tax consequences to Wilma?

Partial list of research aids:
Leo G. Ebben, 45 TCM 1283, T.C.Memo. 1983–200.

C·H·A·P·T·E·R

15

PROPERTY TRANSACTIONS: NONTAXABLE EXCHANGES

LEARNING OBJECTIVES

After completing Chapter 15, you should be able to:

1. Understand the rationale for nonrecognition (postponement) of gain or loss in certain property transactions.

2. Apply the nonrecognition provisions and basis determination rules for like-kind exchanges.

3. Explain the nonrecognition provisions available on the involuntary conversion of property.

4. Describe the provisions for postponing recognition of gain on the sale and replacement of a personal residence.

5. Discuss the provisions for permanent exclusion of gain on the sale of a personal residence by taxpayers age 55 and older.

6. Identify tax planning opportunities related to the nonrecognition provisions discussed in the chapter.

General Concept of a Nontaxable Exchange, 15–2

Like-Kind Exchanges— § 1031, 15–3

Like-Kind Property, 15–4

Exchange Requirement, 15–5

Boot, 15–6

Basis and Holding Period of Property Received, 15–7

Involuntary Conversions— § 1033, 15–9

General Scheme, 15–9

Involuntary Conversion Defined, 15–10

Computing the Amount Realized, 15–10

Replacement Property, 15–11

Time Limitation on Replacement, 15–12

Nonrecognition of Gain, 15–14

Involuntary Conversion of a Personal Residence, 15–15

Reporting Considerations, 15–15

Sale of a Residence— § 1034, 15–15

Replacement Period, 15–16

Principal Residence, 15–18

Nonrecognition of Gain Requirements, 15–19

Capital Improvements, 15–20

Basis and Holding Period of the New Residence, 15–20

Reporting Procedures, 15–21

Sale of a Residence—§ 121, 15–22

Exclusion Requirements, 15–22

Relationship to Other Provisions, 15–23

Making and Revoking the Election, 15–23

Computation Procedure, 15–24

Other Nonrecognition Provisions, 15–25

Exchange of Stock for Property—§ 1032, 15–25

Certain Exchanges of Insurance Policies—§ 1035, 15–25

Exchange of Stock for Stock of the Same Corporation—§ 1036, 15–25

Certain Reacquisitions of Real Property—§ 1038, 15–26

Transfers of Property between Spouses or Incident to Divorce—§ 1041, 15–26

Rollover of Publicly Traded Securities Gain into Specialized Small Business Investment Companies—§ 1044, 15–26

Tax Planning Considerations, 15–27

Like-Kind Exchanges, 15–27

Involuntary Conversions, 15–27

Sale of a Personal Residence, 15–28

GENERAL CONCEPT OF A NONTAXABLE EXCHANGE

1 LEARNING OBJECTIVE
Understand the rationale for nonrecognition (postponement) of gain or loss in certain property transactions.

A taxpayer who is going to replace a productive asset (e.g., machinery) used in a trade or business may structure the transactions as a sale of the old asset and the purchase of a new asset. Using this approach, any realized gain or loss on the asset sale is recognized. The basis of the new asset is its cost. Conversely, the taxpayer may be able to trade the old asset for the new asset. This exchange of assets may qualify for nontaxable exchange treatment.

The tax law recognizes that nontaxable exchanges result in a change in the *form* but not in the *substance* of the taxpayer's relative economic position. The replacement property received in the exchange is viewed as substantially a continuation of the old investment.[1] Additional justification for nontaxable exchange treatment is that this type of transaction does not provide the taxpayer with the wherewithal to pay the tax on any realized gain. The nonrecognition provisions do not apply to realized losses from the sale or exchange of personal use assets. Such losses are not recognized because they are personal in nature and not because of any nonrecognition provision.

In a **nontaxable exchange,** realized gains or losses are not recognized. However, the nonrecognition is usually temporary. The recognition of gain or loss is *postponed* (deferred) until the property received in the nontaxable exchange is subsequently disposed of in a taxable transaction. This is accomplished by assigning a carryover basis to the replacement property.

---
[1] Reg. § 1.1002–1(c).

EXAMPLE 1

Debra exchanges property with an adjusted basis of $10,000 and a fair market value of $12,000 for property with a fair market value of $12,000. The transaction qualifies for nontaxable exchange treatment. Debra has a realized gain of $2,000 ($12,000 amount realized – $10,000 adjusted basis). Her recognized gain is $0. Her basis in the replacement property is a carryover basis of $10,000. Assume the replacement property is nondepreciable. If Debra subsequently sells the replacement property for $12,000, her realized and recognized gain will be the $2,000 gain that was postponed (deferred) in the nontaxable transaction. If the replacement property is depreciable, the carryover basis of $10,000 is used in calculating depreciation. ▼

In some nontaxable exchanges, only part of the property involved in the transaction qualifies for nonrecognition treatment. If the taxpayer receives cash or other nonqualifying property, part or all of the realized gain from the exchange is recognized. In these instances, gain is recognized because the taxpayer has changed or improved his or her relative economic position and has the wherewithal to pay income tax to the extent of cash or other property received.

It is important to distinguish between a nontaxable disposition, as the term is used in the statute, and a tax-free transaction. First, a direct exchange is not required in all circumstances (e.g., replacement of involuntarily converted property or sale and replacement of a personal residence). Second, as previously mentioned, the term *nontaxable* refers to postponement of recognition via a carryover basis. In a *tax-free* transaction, the nonrecognition is permanent (e.g., see the discussion later in the chapter of the § 121 election by a taxpayer age 55 or over to exclude gain on the sale of a residence). Therefore, the basis of any property acquired does not depend on the basis of the property disposed of by the taxpayer.

LIKE-KIND EXCHANGES—§ 1031

2   **LEARNING OBJECTIVE**
Apply the nonrecognition provisions and basis determination rules for like-kind exchanges.

Section 1031 provides for nontaxable exchange treatment if the following requirements are satisfied:[2]

- The form of the transaction is an exchange.
- Both the property transferred and the property received are held either for productive use in a trade or business or for investment.
- The property is like-kind property.

Like-kind exchanges include business for business, business for investment, investment for business, or investment for investment property. Property held for personal use, inventory, and partnership interests (both limited and general) do not qualify under the like-kind exchange provisions. Securities, even though held for investment, do not qualify for like-kind exchange treatment.

The nonrecognition provision for like-kind exchanges is *mandatory* rather than elective. A taxpayer who wants to recognize a realized gain or loss will have to structure the transaction in a form that does not satisfy the statutory requirements for a like-kind exchange. This topic is discussed further under Tax Planning Considerations.

---

[2]§ 1031(a) and Reg. § 1.1031(a)–1(a).

LIKE-KIND PROPERTY

"The words 'like-kind' refer to the nature or character of the property and not to its grade or quality. One kind or class of property may not . . . be exchanged for property of a different kind or class."[3]

Although the term *like-kind* is intended to be interpreted very broadly, three categories of exchanges are not included. First, livestock of different sexes do not qualify as like-kind property. Second, real estate can be exchanged only for other real estate, and personalty can be exchanged only for other personalty. For example, the exchange of a machine (personalty) for an office building (realty) is not a like-kind exchange. *Real estate* (or **realty**) includes principally rental buildings, office and store buildings, manufacturing plants, warehouses, and land. It is immaterial whether real estate is improved or unimproved. Thus, unimproved land can be exchanged for an apartment house. **Personalty** includes principally machines, equipment, trucks, automobiles, furniture, and fixtures. Third, real property located in the United States exchanged for foreign real property (and vice versa) does not qualify as like-kind property.

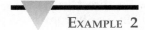

EXAMPLE 2

Wade made the following exchanges during the taxable year:

a. Inventory for a machine used in business.
b. Land held for investment for a building used in business.
c. Stock held for investment for equipment used in business.
d. A business truck for a business truck.
e. An automobile used for personal transportation for an automobile used in business.
f. Livestock for livestock of a different sex.
g. Land held for investment in New York for land held for investment in London.

Exchanges (b), investment real property for business real property, and (d), business personalty for business personalty, qualify as exchanges of like-kind property. Exchanges (a), inventory; (c), stock; (e), personal use automobile (not held for business or investment purposes); (f), livestock of different sexes; and (g), U.S. and foreign real estate do not qualify. ▼

A special provision applies if the taxpayers involved in the exchange are *related parties* under § 267(b). To qualify for like-kind exchange treatment, the taxpayer and the related party must not dispose of the like-kind property received in the exchange within the two-year period following the date of the exchange. If such an early disposition does occur, the postponed gain is recognized as of the date of the early disposition. Dispositions due to death, involuntary conversions, and certain non-tax avoidance transactions are not treated as early dispositions.

Regulations dealing with § 1031 like-kind exchange treatment were finalized in April 1991.[4] These Regulations provide that if the exchange transaction involves multiple assets of a business (e.g., a television station for another television station), the determination of whether the assets qualify as like-kind property will not be made at the business level. Instead, the underlying assets must be evaluated.

The Regulations also provide for greater specificity in determining whether depreciable tangible personal property is of a like kind or class. Such property held for productive use in a business is of a like class only if the exchanged property is within the same *general business asset class* (as specified by the IRS in

---

[3] Reg. § 1.1031(a)–1(b).

[4] Reg. §§ 1.1031(a)–2 and (j)–1.

TAX IN THE NEWS

My Land for Your Jail

The Colonial Williamsburg Foundation (CW) has offered to swap 30 acres of undeveloped woodland for the Williamsburg Jail and Courthouse. A few years ago CW built a replica of the eighteenth-century Public Hospital (i.e., insane asylum). Now it is attempting to acquire the adjacent twentieth-century jail and courthouse in a § 1031 trade.

Why does CW want to own a twentieth-century jail and courthouse? It doesn't. CW wants the land for eventual expansion of its DeWitt Wallace Decorative Arts Gallery, which is located behind the Public Hospital. In addition, CW wants to preserve green space in Williamsburg, which would be threatened if a new courthouse and jail are built on land adjacent to the current courthouse and jail in Bicentennial Park.

Although the foundation is tax-exempt, the undeveloped 30 acres are owned by CW's for-profit subsidiary Williamsburg Developments, Inc. Therefore, to avoid recognizing the realized gain on the exchange, the subsidiary needs to avail itself of the § 1031 like-kind exchange provisions. Fortunately, the undeveloped land and the courthouse and jail are like-kind property.

SOURCE: Information from Bentley Boyd, "CW Presses for Moving Courthouse," *Newport News (Virginia) Daily Press*, September 15, 1993, pp. C1, C2; Bentley Boyd, "CW Boosts Proposal for Courthouse," *Newport News (Virginia) Daily Press*, September 29, 1993, pp. B1, B2.

Rev.Proc. 87–57 or as subsequently modified) or the same *product class* (as specified by the Department of Commerce). Property included in a general business asset class is evaluated under this system rather than under the product class system.

The following are examples of general business asset classes:

- Office furniture, fixtures, and equipment.
- Information systems (computers and peripheral equipment).
- Airplanes.
- Automobiles and taxis.
- Buses.
- Light general-purpose trucks.
- Heavy general-purpose trucks.

The new Regulations have made it more difficult for depreciable tangible personal property to qualify for § 1031 like-kind exchange treatment. For example, the exchange of office equipment for a computer does not qualify as an exchange of like-kind property. Even though both assets are depreciable tangible personal property, they are not like-kind property because they are in different general business asset classes.

EXCHANGE REQUIREMENT

The transaction must actually involve a direct exchange of property to qualify as a like-kind exchange. The sale of old property and the purchase of new property, even though like-kind, is generally not an exchange. However, if the two transactions are mutually dependent, the IRS may treat them as a like-kind exchange. For example, if the taxpayer sells an old business machine to a dealer and purchases a new one from the same dealer, like-kind exchange treatment could result.[5]

The taxpayer may want to avoid nontaxable exchange treatment. Recognition of gain gives the taxpayer a higher basis for depreciation (see Example 31). To the extent that such gains would, if recognized, either receive favorable capital gain treatment or be passive activity income that could offset passive activity losses, it may be preferable to avoid the nonrecognition provisions through an indirect exchange transaction. For example, a taxpayer may sell property to one individual and subsequently purchase similar property from another individual. The taxpayer may also want to avoid nontaxable exchange treatment so that a realized loss can be recognized.

BOOT

If the taxpayer in a like-kind exchange gives or receives some property that is not like-kind property, recognition may occur. Property that is not like-kind property, including cash, is referred to as **boot.** Although the term *boot* does not appear in the Code, tax practitioners commonly use it rather than saying "property that is not like-kind property."

The *receipt* of boot will trigger recognition of gain if there is realized gain. The amount of the recognized gain is the *lesser* of the boot received or the realized gain (realized gain serves as the ceiling on recognition).

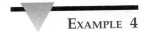

EXAMPLE 3 Emily and Fran exchange machinery, and the exchange qualifies as like-kind under § 1031. Since Emily's machinery (adjusted basis of $20,000) is worth $24,000 and Fran's machine has a fair market value of $19,000, Fran also gives Emily cash of $5,000. Emily's recognized gain is $4,000, the lesser of the realized gain ($24,000 amount realized − $20,000 adjusted basis = $4,000) or the fair market value of the boot received ($5,000). ▼

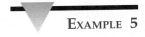

EXAMPLE 4 Assume the same facts as in the previous example, except that Fran's machine is worth $21,000 (not $19,000). Under these circumstances, Fran gives Emily cash of $3,000 to make up the difference. Emily's recognized gain is $3,000, the lesser of the realized gain ($24,000 amount realized − $20,000 adjusted basis = $4,000) or the fair market value of the boot received ($3,000). ▼

The receipt of boot does not result in recognition if there is realized loss.

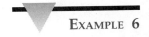

EXAMPLE 5 Assume the same facts as in Example 3, except the adjusted basis of Emily's machine is $30,000. Emily's realized loss is $6,000 ($24,000 amount realized − $30,000 adjusted basis = $6,000 realized loss). The receipt of the boot of $5,000 does not trigger recognition. Therefore, the recognized loss is $0. ▼

The *giving* of boot usually does not trigger recognition. If the boot given is cash, any realized gain or loss is not recognized.

EXAMPLE 6 Fred and Gary exchange equipment in a like-kind exchange. Fred receives equipment with a fair market value of $25,000 and Fred transfers equipment worth $21,000 (adjusted basis of $15,000) and cash of $4,000. Fred's realized gain is $6,000 ($25,000 amount realized − $15,000 adjusted basis − $4,000 cash). However, none of the realized gain is recognized. ▼

---

[5] Rev.Rul. 61–119, 1961–1 C.B. 395.

If, however, the boot given is appreciated or depreciated property, gain or loss is recognized to the extent of the differential between the adjusted basis and the fair market value of the boot. For this purpose, *appreciated or depreciated property* is defined as property whose adjusted basis is not equal to the fair market value.

EXAMPLE 7

Assume the same facts as in the previous example, except that Fred transfers equipment worth $10,000 (adjusted basis of $12,000) and boot worth $15,000 (adjusted basis of $9,000). Fred's realized gain appears to be $4,000 ($25,000 amount realized – $21,000 adjusted basis). Since realization previously has served as a ceiling on recognition, it appears that the recognized gain is $4,000 (lower of realized gain of $4,000 or amount of appreciation on boot of $6,000). However, the recognized gain actually is $6,000 (full amount of the appreciation on the boot). In effect, Fred must calculate the like-kind and boot parts of the transaction separately. That is, the realized loss of $2,000 on the like-kind property is not recognized ($10,000 fair market value – $12,000 adjusted basis), and the $6,000 realized gain on the boot is recognized ($15,000 fair market value – $9,000 adjusted basis). ▼

BASIS AND HOLDING PERIOD OF PROPERTY RECEIVED

If an exchange does not qualify as nontaxable under § 1031, gain or loss is recognized, and the basis of property received in the exchange is the property's fair market value. If the exchange qualifies for nonrecognition, the basis of property received must be adjusted to reflect any postponed (deferred) gain or loss. The *basis* of *like-kind property* received in the exchange is the property's fair market value less postponed gain or plus postponed loss. If the exchange partially qualifies for nonrecognition (if recognition is associated with boot), the basis of like-kind property received in the exchange is the property's fair market value less postponed gain or plus postponed loss. The *basis* of any *boot* received is the boot's fair market value.

If there is a postponed loss, nonrecognition creates a situation in which the taxpayer has recovered *less* than the cost or other basis of the property exchanged in an amount equal to the unrecognized loss. If there is a postponed gain, the taxpayer has recovered *more* than the cost or other basis of the property exchanged in an amount equal to the unrecognized gain.

EXAMPLE 8

Jaime exchanges a building (used in his business) with an adjusted basis of $30,000 and fair market value of $38,000 for land with a fair market value of $38,000. The land is to be held as an investment. The exchange qualifies as like-kind (an exchange of business real property for investment real property). Thus, the basis of the land is $30,000 (the land's fair market value of $38,000 less the $8,000 postponed gain on the building). If the land is later sold for its fair market value of $38,000, the $8,000 postponed gain is recognized. ▼

EXAMPLE 9

Assume the same facts as in the previous example, except that the building has an adjusted basis of $48,000 and fair market value of only $38,000. The basis in the newly acquired land is $48,000 (fair market value of $38,000 plus the $10,000 postponed loss on the building). If the land is later sold for its fair market value of $38,000, the $10,000 postponed loss is recognized. ▼

The Code provides an alternative approach for determining the basis of like-kind property received:

> Adjusted basis of like-kind property surrendered
> + Adjusted basis of boot given
> + Gain recognized
> − Fair market value of boot received
> − Loss recognized
> = *Basis of like-kind property received*

This approach is logical in terms of the recovery of capital doctrine. That is, the unrecovered cost or other basis is increased by additional cost (boot given) or decreased by cost recovered (boot received). Any gain recognized is included in the basis of the new property. The taxpayer has been taxed on this amount and is now entitled to recover it tax-free. Any loss recognized is deducted from the basis of the new property. The taxpayer has received a tax benefit on that amount.

The **holding period** of the property surrendered in the exchange carries over and *tacks on* to the holding period of the like-kind property received.[6] The logic of this rule is derived from the basic concept of the new property as a continuation of the old investment. The boot received has a new holding period (from the date of exchange) rather than a carryover holding period.

Depreciation recapture potential carries over to the property received in a like-kind exchange.[7] See Chapter 17 for a discussion of this topic.

The following comprehensive example illustrates the like-kind exchange rules.

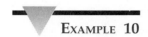

EXAMPLE 10

Vicki exchanged the following old machines for new machines in five independent like-kind exchanges:

Exchange	Adjusted Basis of Old Machine	Fair Market Value of New Machine	Adjusted Basis of Boot Given	Fair Market Value of Boot Received
1	$4,000	$9,000	$ –0–	$ –0–
2	4,000	9,000	3,000	–0–
3	4,000	9,000	6,000	–0–
4	4,000	9,000	–0–	3,000
5	4,000	3,500	–0–	300

Vicki's realized and recognized gains and losses and the basis of each of the like-kind properties received are as follows:

Exchange	Realized Gain (Loss)	Recognized Gain (Loss)	Old Adj. Basis	+	Boot Given	+	Gain Recognized	–	Boot Received	=	New Basis
1	$5,000	$ –0–	$ 4,000	+	$ –0–	+	$ –0–	–	$ –0–	=	$ 4,000*
2	2,000	–0–	4,000	+	3,000	+	–0–	–	–0–	=	7,000*
3	(1,000)	–(0)–	4,000	+	6,000	+	–0–	–	–0–	=	10,000**
4	8,000	3,000	4,000	+	–0–	+	3,000	–	3,000	=	4,000*
5	(200)	–(0)–	4,000	+	–0–	+	–0–	–	300	=	3,700**

*Basis may be determined in gain situations under the alternative method by subtracting the gain not recognized from the fair market value of the new property:
$9,000 – $5,000 = $4,000 for exchange 1.
$9,000 – $2,000 = $7,000 for exchange 2.
$9,000 – $5,000 = $4,000 for exchange 4.

**In loss situations, basis may be determined by adding the loss not recognized to the fair market value of the new property:
$9,000 + $1,000 = $10,000 for exchange 3.
$3,500 + $200 = $3,700 for exchange 5.

The basis of the boot received is the boot's fair market value.   ▼

---

[6] § 1223(1) and Reg. § 1.1223–1(a). For this carryover holding period rule to apply to like-kind exchanges after March 1, 1954, the like-kind property surrendered must have been either a capital asset or § 1231 property. See Chapters 16 and 17 for the discussion of capital assets and § 1231 property.
[7] Reg. §§ 1.1245–2(a)(4) and 1.1250–2(d)(1).

If the taxpayer either assumes a liability or takes property subject to a liability, the amount of the liability is treated as boot given. For the taxpayer whose liability is assumed or whose property is taken subject to the liability, the amount of the liability is treated as boot received. Example 11 illustrates the effect of such a liability. In addition, the example illustrates the tax consequences for both parties involved in the like-kind exchange.

EXAMPLE 11

Jane and Leo exchange real estate investments. Jane gives up property with an adjusted basis of $250,000 (fair market value $400,000) that is subject to a mortgage of $75,000 (assumed by Leo). In return for this property, Jane receives property with a fair market value of $300,000 (adjusted basis $200,000) and cash of $25,000.

- Jane's realized gain is $150,000. She gave up property with an adjusted basis of $250,000. Jane received $400,000 from the exchange ($300,000 fair market value of like-kind property plus $100,000 boot received). The boot received consists of the $25,000 cash received from Leo and Jane's mortgage of $75,000 that Leo assumes.
- Jane's recognized gain is $100,000. The realized gain of $150,000 is recognized to the extent of boot received.
- Jane's basis in the real estate received from Leo is $250,000. This basis can be computed by subtracting the postponed gain ($50,000) from the fair market value of the real estate received ($300,000). It can also be computed by adding the recognized gain ($100,000) to the adjusted basis of the real estate given up ($250,000) and subtracting the boot received ($100,000).
- Leo's realized gain is $100,000. Leo gave up property with an adjusted basis of $200,000 plus boot of $100,000 ($75,000 mortgage assumed + $25,000 cash) or a total of $300,000. Leo received $400,000 from the exchange (fair market value of like-kind property received).
- Leo has no recognized gain because he did not receive any boot. The entire realized gain of $100,000 is postponed.
- Leo's basis in the real estate received from Jane is $300,000. This basis can be computed by subtracting the postponed gain ($100,000) from the fair market value of the real estate received ($400,000). It can also be computed by adding the boot given ($75,000 mortgage assumed by Leo + $25,000 cash) to the adjusted basis of the real estate given up ($200,000).[8] ▼

INVOLUNTARY CONVERSIONS—§ 1033

GENERAL SCHEME

3   LEARNING OBJECTIVE
Explain the nonrecognition provisions available on the involuntary conversion of property.

Section 1033 provides that a taxpayer who suffers an involuntary conversion of property may postpone recognition of *gain* realized from the conversion. The objective of this provision is to provide relief to the taxpayer who has suffered hardship and does not have the wherewithal to pay the tax on any gain realized from the conversion. Postponement of realized gain is permitted to the extent that the taxpayer reinvests the amount realized from the conversion in replacement property. The rules for nonrecognition of gain are as follows:

- If the amount reinvested in replacement property *equals or exceeds* the amount realized, realized gain is *not recognized*.

---

[8]Example (2) of Reg. § 1.1031(d)—2 illustrates a special situation where both the buyer and the seller transfer liabilities that are assumed or property is acquired subject to a liability by the other party.

• If the amount reinvested in replacement property is *less than* the amount realized, realized gain *is recognized* to the extent of the deficiency.

If a *loss* occurs on an involuntary conversion, § 1033 does not modify the normal rules for loss recognition. That is, if realized loss otherwise would be recognized, § 1033 does not change the result.

INVOLUNTARY CONVERSION DEFINED

An **involuntary conversion** results from the destruction (complete or partial), theft, seizure, requisition or condemnation, or the sale or exchange under threat or imminence of requisition or condemnation of the taxpayer's property.[9] To prove the existence of a threat or imminence of condemnation, the taxpayer must obtain confirmation that there has been a decision to acquire the property for public use. In addition, the taxpayer must have reasonable grounds to believe the property will be taken.[10] The property does not have to be sold to the authority threatening to condemn it to qualify for § 1033 postponement. If the taxpayer satisfies the confirmation and reasonable grounds requirements, he or she can sell the property to another party.[11] Likewise, the sale of property to a condemning authority by a taxpayer who acquired the property from its former owner with the knowledge that the property was under threat of condemnation also qualifies as an involuntary conversion under § 1033.[12] A voluntary act, such as a taxpayer destroying his or her own property by arson, is not an involuntary conversion.[13]

ETHICAL CONSIDERATIONS

Purchasing Property in Expectation of Condemnation

The city of Richmond is going to condemn some buildings in a run-down section of the city to build a park. Steve's principal residence is one of the dilapidated buildings. His adjusted basis for the house and land is $60,000. The appraised value of the house and land is $52,000.

Steve is unaware of the future condemnation proceedings, but would like for his family to escape from the urban blight in which they are living. Therefore, when Ross, a realtor, indicates that he has a corporate client who would like to purchase Steve's property for $100,000, Steve is ecstatic and agrees to sell.

The purchasing corporation is owned by Ross and his wife. Ross is aware of the forthcoming condemnation proceedings. He considers himself a skilled negotiator and thinks he can obtain a 100 percent return on his investment. Once the corporation receives the condemnation proceeds, Ross intends to defer the recognition of the realized gain on the involuntary conversion through a timely acquisition of other rental property.

COMPUTING THE AMOUNT REALIZED

The amount realized from the condemnation of property usually includes only the amount received as compensation for the property.[14] Any amount received that is designated as severance damages by both the government and the taxpayer is not

---

[9] § 1033(a) and Reg. §§ 1.1033(a)–1(a) and –2(a).
[10] Rev.Rul. 63–221, 1963–2 C. B. 332, and *Joseph P. Balistrieri,* 38 TCM 526, T.C.Memo. 1979–115.
[11] Rev.Rul. 81–180, 1981–2 C.B. 161.

[12] Rev.Rul. 81–181, 1981–2 C.B. 162.
[13] Rev.Rul. 82–74, 1982–1 C.B. 110.
[14] *Pioneer Real Estate Co.,* 47 B.T.A. 886 (1942), *acq.* 1943 C.B. 18.

included in the amount realized. *Severance awards* usually occur when only a portion of the entire property is condemned (e.g., a strip of land is taken to build a highway). Severance damages are awarded because the value of the taxpayer's remaining property has declined as a result of the condemnation. Such damages reduce the basis of the property. However, if either of the following requirements is satisfied, the nonrecognition provision of § 1033 applies to the severance damages.

- Severance damages are used to restore the usability of the remaining property.
- The usefulness of the remaining property is destroyed by the condemnation, and the property is sold and replaced at a cost equal to or exceeding the sum of the condemnation award, severance damages, and sales proceeds.

EXAMPLE 12

The government condemns a portion of Ron's farmland to build part of an interstate highway. Because the highway denies his cattle access to a pond and some grazing land, Ron receives severance damages in addition to the condemnation proceeds for the land taken. Ron must reduce the basis of the property by the amount of the severance damages. If the amount of the severance damages received exceeds the adjusted basis, Ron recognizes gain. ▼

EXAMPLE 13

Assume the same facts as in the previous example, except that Ron used the proceeds from the condemnation and the severance damages to build another pond and to clear woodland for grazing. Therefore, all the proceeds are eligible for § 1033 treatment. Thus, there is no possibility of gain recognition as the result of the amount of the severance damages received exceeding the adjusted basis. ▼

REPLACEMENT PROPERTY

The requirements for replacement property generally are more restrictive than those for like-kind property under § 1031. The basic requirement is that the replacement property be similar or related in service or use to the involuntarily converted property.[15]

Different interpretations of the phrase *similar or related in service or use* apply if the involuntarily converted property is held by an *owner-user* rather than an *owner-investor* (e.g., lessor). A taxpayer who uses the property in his or her trade or business is subject to a more restrictive test in terms of acquiring replacement property. For an owner-user, the *functional use test* applies, and for an owner-investor, the *taxpayer use test* applies.

Taxpayer Use Test

The taxpayer use test for owner-investors provides the taxpayer with more flexibility in terms of what qualifies as replacement property than does the functional use test for owner-users. Essentially, the properties must be used by the taxpayer (the owner-investor) in similar endeavors. For example, rental property held by an owner-investor qualifies if replaced by other rental property, regardless of the type of rental property involved. The test is met when an investor replaces a manufacturing plant with a wholesale grocery warehouse if both properties are held for the production of rental income.[16] The replacement of a rental residence with a personal residence does not meet the test.[17]

---

[15] § 1033(a) and Reg. § 1.1033(a)–1.

[16] *Loco Realty Co. v. Comm.*, 62–2 USTC ¶9657, 10 AFTR2d 5359, 306 F.2d 207 (CA–8, 1962).

[17] Rev.Rul. 70–466, 1970–2 C.B. 165.

Functional Use Test

Under this test, the taxpayer's use of the replacement property and of the involuntarily converted property must be the same. Replacing a manufacturing plant with a wholesale grocery warehouse, whether rented or not, does not meet this test. As indicated above, the IRS applies the taxpayer use test to owner-investors. However, the functional use test still applies to owner-users (e.g., a manufacturer whose manufacturing plant is destroyed by fire is required to replace the plant with another facility of similar functional use). Replacing a rental residence with a personal residence does not meet this test.

Special Rules

Under one set of circumstances, the broader replacement rules for like-kind exchanges are substituted for the narrow replacement rules normally used for involuntary conversions. This beneficial provision applies if business real property or investment real property is condemned. Therefore, the taxpayer has substantially more flexibility in selecting replacement property. For example, improved real property can be replaced with unimproved real property.

The rules concerning the nature of replacement property are illustrated in Concept Summary 15–1.

TIME LIMITATION ON REPLACEMENT

The taxpayer normally has a two-year period after the close of the taxable year in which any gain is realized from the involuntary conversion to replace the property (*the latest date*).[18] This rule affords as much as three years from the date of

---

CONCEPT SUMMARY 15–1

Replacement Property Tests

Type of Property and User	Like-Kind Test	Taxpayer Use Test	Functional Use Test
Land used by a manufacturing company is condemned by a local government authority.	X		
Apartment and land held by an investor are sold due to the threat or imminence of condemnation.	X		
An investor's rented shopping mall is destroyed by fire; the mall may be replaced by other rental properties (e.g., an apartment building).		X	
A manufacturing plant is destroyed by fire; replacement property must consist of another manufacturing plant that is functionally the same as the property converted.			X
Personal residence of taxpayer is condemned by a local government authority; replacement property must consist of another personal residence.			X

---

[18] §§ 1033(a)(2)(B) and (g)(4) and Reg. § 1.1033(a)–2(c)(3).

realization of gain to replace the property if the realization of gain took place on the first day of the taxable year.[19] If the involuntary conversion involved the condemnation of real property used in a trade or business or held for investment, a three-year period is substituted for the normal two-year period. In this case, the taxpayer can actually have as much as four years from the date of realization of gain to replace the property.

EXAMPLE 14

Megan's warehouse is destroyed by fire on December 16, 1993. The adjusted basis is $325,000. Megan receives $400,000 from the insurance company on January 10, 1994. She is a calendar year taxpayer. The latest date for replacement is December 31, 1996 (the end of the taxable year in which realized gain occurred plus two years). The critical date is not the date the involuntary conversion occurred, but rather the date of gain realization. ▼

EXAMPLE 15

Assume the same facts as in the previous example, except Megan's warehouse is condemned. The latest date for replacement is December 31, 1997 (the end of the taxable year in which realized gain occurred plus three years). ▼

The *earliest date* for replacement typically is the date the involuntary conversion occurs. However, if the property is condemned, it is possible to replace the condemned property before this date. In this case, the earliest date is the date of the threat or imminence of requisition or condemnation of the property. The purpose of this provision is to enable the taxpayer to make an orderly replacement of the condemned property.

EXAMPLE 16

Assume the same facts as in Example 15. Megan can replace the warehouse before December 16, 1993 (the condemnation date). The earliest date for replacement is the date of the threat or imminence of requisition or condemnation of the warehouse. ▼

ETHICAL CONSIDERATIONS

Postponing Realized Gain from an Involuntary Conversion

Peggy, age 63 and in frail health, owns a furniture store in Petersburg. Due to competition from two large furniture retailers who opened stores in the Petersburg area during the past three years, Peggy's furniture store has been unprofitable.

Due to this lack of profitability as well as her advancing age, Peggy would like to retire. Unfortunately, she has been unable to locate a purchaser for her store. Her prayers seem to be answered when a tornado destroys her building and its contents. Fortunately, no one is injured or killed by the tornado.

Peggy anticipates that she can live on the insurance proceeds of $800,000 for the rest of her life. However, her realized gain on the involuntary conversion would produce a combined state and Federal tax liability of approximately $175,000. In order to forgo paying this amount associated with her 1994 income tax returns, Peggy elects postponement treatment under § 1033, indicating that she intends to replace the involuntarily converted property with similar property even though she does not intend to do so. Her justification, based on her participation in a 12-step program, is that she lives "one day at a time."

---

[19]The taxpayer can apply for an extension of this time period anytime before its expiration [Reg. § 1.1033(a)–2(c)(3)]. Also, the period for filing the application for extension can be extended if the taxpayer shows reasonable cause.

NONRECOGNITION OF GAIN

Nonrecognition of gain can be either mandatory or elective, depending upon whether the conversion is direct (into replacement property) or into money.

Direct Conversion

If the conversion is directly into replacement property rather than into money, nonrecognition of realized gain is *mandatory*. In this case, the basis of the replacement property is the same as the adjusted basis of the converted property. Direct conversion is rare in practice and usually involves condemnations. The following example illustrates the application of the rules for direct conversions.

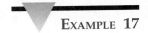

EXAMPLE 17

Lupe's property with an adjusted basis of $20,000 is condemned by the state. Lupe receives property with a fair market value of $50,000 as compensation for the property taken. Since the nonrecognition of realized gain is mandatory for direct conversions, Lupe's realized gain of $30,000 is not recognized, and the basis of the replacement property is $20,000 (adjusted basis of the condemned property). ▼

Conversion into Money

If the conversion is into money, "at the election of the taxpayer the gain shall be recognized only to the extent that the amount realized upon such conversion . . . exceeds the cost of such other property or such stock."[20] This is the usual case, and nonrecognition (postponement) is *elective*.

The basis of the replacement property is the property's cost less postponed (deferred) gain.[21] If the election to postpone gain is made, the holding period of the replacement property includes the holding period of the converted property.

Section 1033 applies *only to gains* and *not to losses*. Losses from involuntary conversions are recognized if the property is held for business or income-producing purposes. Personal casualty losses are recognized, but condemnation losses related to personal use assets (e.g., a personal residence) are neither recognized nor postponed.

Examples 18 and 19 illustrate the application of the involuntary conversion rules.

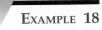

EXAMPLE 18

Walt's building (used in his trade or business), with an adjusted basis of $50,000, is destroyed by fire in 1994. Walt is a calendar year taxpayer. In 1994, he receives an insurance reimbursement of $100,000 for the loss. Walt invests $80,000 in a new building.

- Walt has until December 31, 1996, to make the new investment and qualify for the nonrecognition election.
- Walt's realized gain is $50,000 ($100,000 insurance proceeds received − $50,000 adjusted basis of old building).
- Assuming the replacement property qualifies as similar or related in service or use, Walt's recognized gain is $20,000. He reinvested $20,000 less than the insurance proceeds received ($100,000 proceeds − $80,000 reinvested). Therefore, his realized gain is recognized to that extent.
- Walt's basis in the new building is $50,000. This is the building's cost of $80,000 less the postponed gain of $30,000 (realized gain of $50,000 − recognized gain of $20,000).

---

[20] § 1033(a)(2)(A) and Reg. § 1.1033(a)–2(c)(1).   [21] § 1033(b).

- The computation of realization, recognition, and basis would apply even if Walt was a real estate dealer and the building destroyed by fire was part of his inventory. Unlike § 1031, § 1033 generally does not exclude inventory. ▼

EXAMPLE 19

Assume the same facts as in the previous example, except that Walt receives only $45,000 (instead of $100,000) of insurance proceeds. He has a realized and recognized loss of $5,000. The basis of the new building is the building's cost of $80,000. If the destroyed building was held for personal use, the recognized loss is subject to other limitations.[22] The loss of $5,000 is limited to the decline in fair market value of the property, and the amount of the loss is reduced first by $100 and then by 10% of adjusted gross income (refer to Chapter 7). ▼

INVOLUNTARY CONVERSION OF A PERSONAL RESIDENCE

The tax consequences of the involuntary conversion of a personal residence depend upon whether the conversion is a casualty or condemnation and whether a realized loss or gain results.

Loss Situations

If the conversion is a condemnation, the realized loss is not recognized. Loss from the condemnation of a personal use asset is never recognized. If the conversion is a casualty (a loss from fire, storm, etc.), the loss is recognized subject to the personal casualty loss limitations.

Gain Situations

If the conversion is a condemnation, the gain may be postponed under either § 1033 or § 1034. That is, the taxpayer may elect to treat the condemnation as a sale under the deferral of gain rules relating to the sale of a personal residence under § 1034 (presented subsequently). If the conversion is a casualty, the gain is postponed only under the involuntary conversion provisions.

REPORTING CONSIDERATIONS

Involuntary conversions from casualty and theft are reported first on Form 4684, Casualties and Thefts. Casualty and theft losses on personal use property for the individual taxpayer are carried from Form 4684 to Schedule A of Form 1040. For other casualty and theft items, the Form 4684 amounts are generally reported on Form 4797, Sales of Business Property, unless Form 4797 is not required. In the latter case, the amounts are reported directly on the tax return involved.

Except for personal use property, recognized gains and losses from involuntary conversions other than by casualty and theft are reported on Form 4797. As stated previously, if the property involved in the involuntary conversion (other than by casualty and theft) is personal use property, any realized loss is not recognized. Any realized gain is treated as gain on a voluntary sale.

4 LEARNING OBJECTIVE
Describe the provisions for postponing recognition of gain on the sale and replacement of a personal residence.

SALE OF A RESIDENCE—§ 1034

A realized loss from the sale of a **personal residence** is not recognized because the residence is personal use property. A realized gain is subject to taxation, however.

[22] § 165(c)(3) and Reg. § 1.165–7.

TAX IN THE NEWS

PRESIDENTIALLY DECLARED DISASTERS—THE BACK DOOR

The Revenue Reconciliation Act of 1993 has expanded involuntary conversion treatment to include principal residences damaged by presidentially declared disasters. A principal residence for this purpose includes either a residence owned by the taxpayer or a residence rented by the taxpayer (a rented residence will qualify with respect to the contents). The normal two-year replacement period for involuntary conversions is replaced with a four-year replacement period.

Section 1033(h) provides that exclusion treatment is available for insurance proceeds received for the residence contents which are unscheduled personal property.

The insurance proceeds received for the principal residence and scheduled personal property qualify for postponement treatment and are treated as received for the involuntary conversion of a single item of property. The reinvestment of the insurance proceeds in any property that is similar or related in service or use to the converted residence (or its contents) will be treated as the acquisition of property similar or related in service or use to that single item of property.

This provision was not included in either the House bill or the Senate bill. Rather, it was produced by the Joint Conference Committee. The effective date is retroactive to September 1, 1991. One of the supporters of this provision was Representative Stark of California. The retroactive effective date enables constituents from his East Bay District who were victims of fires in October 1991 to qualify.

SOURCE: Information from *Wall Street Journal,* September 3, 1993, p. A1; Earl C. Gottschalk, Jr., "Your Money Matters: Tax Aftermath of a Disaster Is a Complicated Ordeal," *Wall Street Journal,* September 28, 1993, pp. C1, C18; Elizabeth M. MacDonald, "Tax News: How a Disaster Can Now Turn into a Tax Break," *Money,* November 1993, p. 19.

The tax law includes two provisions under which all or part of the realized gain is either postponed or excluded from taxation. The first of these, § 1034, is discussed below. The second, § 121, is discussed later in the chapter.

Section 1034 provides for the *mandatory* nonrecognition of gain from the sale or exchange of a personal residence if the sales proceeds are reinvested in a replacement residence within a prescribed time period. Both the old and new residences must qualify as the taxpayer's principal residence. A houseboat or house trailer qualifies if it is used by the taxpayer as a principal residence.[23]

The reason for not recognizing gain when a residence is replaced by a new residence within the prescribed time period (discussed below) is that the new residence is viewed as a continuation of the investment. Also, if the proceeds from the sale are reinvested, the taxpayer does not have the wherewithal to pay tax on the realized gain. Beyond these fundamental concepts, Congress, in enacting § 1034, was concerned with the hardship of involuntary moves and the socially desirable objective of encouraging the mobility of labor.

REPLACEMENT PERIOD

For the nonrecognition treatment to apply, the old residence must be replaced by a new residence within a period *beginning two years before* the sale of the old

---

[23]Reg. § 1.1034–1(c)(3)(i).

residence and *ending two years after* the sale. This four-year period applies regardless of whether the new residence is purchased or constructed. The taxpayer must not only *acquire* the new residence during this period, but must *occupy* and use it as well. The occupancy requirement has been strictly construed by both the IRS and the courts, and even circumstances beyond a taxpayer's control do not excuse noncompliance.[24]

EXAMPLE 20

Gail sells her personal residence from which she realizes a gain of $50,000. She begins constructing a new residence immediately after the sale. However, unstable soil conditions and a trade union strike cause unforeseen delays. The new residence ultimately is completed and occupied by Gail 25 months after the sale of the old residence. Since the occupancy requirement has not been satisfied, § 1034 is inapplicable, and Gail must recognize a gain of $50,000 on the sale of the old residence. ▼

Taxpayers might be inclined to make liberal use of § 1034 as a means of speculating when the price of residential housing is rising. Without any time restriction on its use, § 1034 would permit deferral of gain on multiple sales of principal residences, each of which would result in an economic profit. The Code curbs this approach by precluding the application of § 1034 to any sales occurring within two years of its last use.

EXAMPLE 21

After Seth sells his principal residence (the first residence) in March 1993 for $150,000 (realized gain of $60,000), he buys and sells the following (all of which qualify as principal residences):

	Date of Purchase	**Date of Sale**	**Amount Involved**
Second residence	April 1993		$160,000
Second residence		May 1994	180,000
Third residence	June 1994		200,000

Because multiple sales have occurred within a period of two years, § 1034 does not apply to the sale of the second residence. Thus, the realized gain of $20,000 [$180,000 (selling price) − $160,000 (purchase price)] must be recognized. ▼

The two-year rule precluding multiple use of § 1034 could create a hardship where a taxpayer is transferred by his or her employer and has little choice in the matter. For this reason, § 1034 was amended to provide an exception to the two-year rule when the sale results from a change in the location of employment. To qualify for the exception, a taxpayer must meet the distance and length-of-employment requirements specified for the deduction of moving expenses under § 217.[25]

EXAMPLE 22

Assume the same facts as in the previous example, except that in February 1994, Seth's employer transfers him to a job in another state. Consequently, the sale of the second residence and the purchase of the third residence were due to the relocation of employment. If Seth satisfies the distance and length-of-employment requirements of § 217, no gain is recognized on the sale of the first and second residences. ▼

---

[24] *James A. Henry,* 44 TCM 844, T.C.Memo. 1982–469, and *William F. Peck,* 44 TCM 1030, T.C.Memo. 1982–506.

[25] Refer to Chapter 9 for the discussion of the rules governing the deduction for moving expenses.

The running of the time periods specified above (other than the two-year limit on multiple sales) is suspended during any time the taxpayer or spouse is on extended active duty (over 90 days or for an indefinite period) with the U.S. Armed Forces after the date the old residence is sold.[26] This suspension is limited to four years after the date the old residence is sold. A similar suspension is available to U.S. citizens who are employed outside the United States by nongovernmental employers (expatriates).[27]

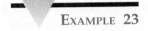

EXAMPLE 23   Iris, an employee of Blue Corporation, sold her principal residence in Baltimore on July 5, 1994, because she had been transferred to the Berlin office on a one-year assignment. Iris returns to the United States on July 1, 1995, after completing the assignment. The latest date for a qualifying replacement is July 1, 1997 (i.e., two years after the end of the suspension period). ▼

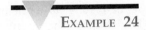

EXAMPLE 24   Assume the same facts as in the previous example, except that the assignment is for a three-year period. Therefore, Iris returns to the United States on July 1, 1997, after completing the assignment. Two years after the end of the suspension period is July 1, 1999. However, since the suspension period exception cannot result in extending the replacement time period beyond four years after the date the principal residence was sold, the latest date for a qualifying replacement is July 5, 1998. ▼

In one circumstance, the four-year limitation is extended for members of the U.S. Armed Forces. If they are stationed outside the United States or are required thereafter to reside in government quarters at a remote site, the four-year period is replaced with an eight-year period.[28]

PRINCIPAL RESIDENCE

Both the old and new residences must qualify as the taxpayer's principal residence. Whether property is the taxpayer's principal residence depends "... upon all the facts and circumstances in each case."[29]

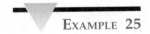

EXAMPLE 25   Mitch sells his principal residence and moves to Norfolk, Virginia, where he is employed. He decides to rent an apartment in Norfolk because of its proximity to his place of employment. He purchases a beach house in Virginia Beach that he occupies most weekends. Mitch does not intend to live in the beach house other than on weekends. The apartment in Norfolk is his principal place of residence. Therefore, the purchase of the beach house does not qualify as an appropriate replacement. ▼

If the old residence ceases to be the taxpayer's principal residence before its sale, the nonrecognition provision does not apply. For example, if the taxpayer abandons the old residence before its sale, the residence no longer qualifies as a principal residence.[30] If the old residence is converted to other than personal use (e.g., rental) before its sale, the nonrecognition provision does not apply. If the residence is only partially converted to business use, gain from the sale of the personal use portion still qualifies for nonrecognition. It is possible to convert part of a principal residence to business use and later to convert that part back to being part of the principal residence (e.g., a home office).[31]

---

[26] § 1034(h)(1).
[27] § 1034(k).
[28] § 1034(h)(2).
[29] Reg. § 1.1034–1(c)(3).

[30] *Richard T. Houlette,* 48 T.C. 350 (1967), and *Stolk v. Comm.,* 64–1 USTC ¶9228, 13 AFTR2d 535, 326 F.2d 760 (CA–2, 1964).
[31] Rev.Rul. 82–26, 1982–1 C.B. 114.

Temporarily renting out the old residence before sale does not necessarily terminate its status as the taxpayer's principal residence,[32] nor does temporarily renting out the new residence before it is occupied by the taxpayer. A related issue is whether a taxpayer who temporarily rents out the old residence while attempting to sell it is entitled to deduct expenses in excess of income relating to the rental. That is, is the old residence subject to the loss deduction rules for hobby loss activities? If it is, the deductions associated with the rental activity are limited to the rent income generated. The Tax Court concluded that since the property was considered to be the taxpayer's principal residence and as a result qualified for § 1034 postponement of gain, the property was subject to the hobby loss limitations. The Court of Appeals reversed the Tax Court and held that the hobby loss provisions did not apply.[33]

NONRECOGNITION OF GAIN REQUIREMENTS

Realized gain from the sale of the old residence is not recognized if the taxpayer reinvests an amount *at least equal* to the adjusted sales price of the old residence. Realized gain is recognized to the extent the taxpayer does not reinvest an amount at least equal to the adjusted sales price in a new residence. Therefore, the amount not reinvested is treated similarly to boot received in a like-kind exchange.

The **adjusted sales price** is the amount realized from the sale of the old residence less fixing-up expenses. The *amount realized* is the selling price less the selling expenses. *Selling expenses* include items such as the cost of advertising the property for sale, real estate broker commissions, legal fees in connection with the sale, and loan placement fees paid by the taxpayer as a condition of arranging financing for the buyer.

Fixing-up expenses are personal in nature and are incurred by the taxpayer to assist in the sale of the old residence. Fixing-up expenses include such items as ordinary repairs, painting, and wallpapering. To qualify as a fixing-up expense, the expense must (1) be incurred for work performed during the 90-day period ending on the date of the contract of sale, (2) be paid within 30 days after the date of the sale, and (3) not be a capital expenditure.

Although selling expenses are deductible in calculating the amount realized, fixing-up expenses are not. Therefore, fixing-up expenses do not have an impact on the calculation of realized gain or loss. However, since fixing-up expenses are deductible in calculating the adjusted sales price, they do have the potential for producing tax benefit in that they reduce the amount of the reinvestment required to qualify for nonrecognition treatment. Conversely, if a replacement residence is not acquired, the fixing-up expenses produce no tax benefit.

Reducing the amount of the required reinvestment by the amount of fixing-up expenses is another application of the wherewithal to pay concept. To the extent that the taxpayer has expended part of the funds received from the sale in preparing the old residence for sale, he or she does not have the funds available to reinvest in the new residence.

As previously mentioned, fixing-up expenses are not considered in determining realized gain. They are considered only in determining how much realized gain is to be postponed. In addition, fixing-up expenses have no direct effect on the basis of the new residence. Indirectly, though, through their effect on postponed gain, they can bring about a lesser basis for the new residence. The

---

[32] *Robert W. Aagaard*, 56 T.C. 191 (1971), *acq.* 1971–2 C.B. 1; *Robert G. Clapham*, 63 T.C. 505 (1975); Rev.Rul. 59–72, 1959–1 C.B. 203; and Rev.Rul. 78–146, 1978–1 C.B. 260.

[33] *Bolaris v. Comm.*, 85–2 USTC ¶9822, 56 AFTR2d 85–6472, 776 F.2d 1428 (CA–9, 1985).

▼ **FIGURE 15–1**
Sale-of-Residence Model

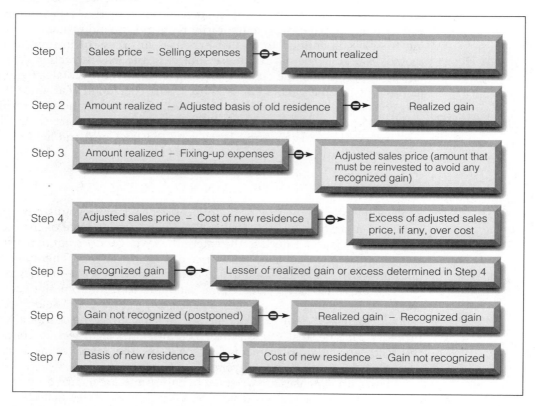

effects of fixing-up expenses on the computation of gain realized and recognized and on basis are illustrated in Figure 15–1 and in Example 26.

CAPITAL IMPROVEMENTS

Capital improvements are added to the adjusted basis of a personal residence. The adjusted basis is used in computing gain or loss on a subsequent sale or other disposition of the property. In calculating the cost of a replacement residence (for determining the nonrecognition of gain under § 1034), only capital improvements made during a certain time period are counted. The time period begins two years before the date of sale of the old residence and ends two years after that date (the time period during which the old residence can be replaced).[34]

If the taxpayer receives a residence by gift or inheritance, the residence will not qualify as a replacement residence. However, if the taxpayer makes substantial capital expenditures (e.g., reconstruction or additions) to the property within the replacement time period, these expenditures do qualify.[35]

BASIS AND HOLDING PERIOD OF THE NEW RESIDENCE

The *basis* of the new residence is the cost of the new residence less the realized gain not recognized (postponed gain). If there is any postponed gain, the *holding period* of the new residence includes the holding period of the old residence.

---

[34] *Charles M. Shaw,* 69 T.C. 1034 (1978); Reg. § 1.1034–1(c)(4)(ii); and Rev.Rul. 78–147, 1978–1 C.B. 261.

[35] Reg. §§ 1.1034–1(b)(7) and (9) and 1.1034–1(c)(4)(i).

Figure 15–1 summarizes the sale-of-residence concepts. Example 26 illustrates these concepts and the application of the nonrecognition provision.

EXAMPLE 26

Veneia, age 47, sells her personal residence (adjusted basis of $136,000) for $244,000. She receives only $229,400 after paying a brokerage fee of $14,600. Ten days before the sale, Veneia incurred and paid for qualified fixing-up expenses of $3,400. Two months later, Veneia acquires a new residence. Determine the gain, if any, she must recognize and the basis of the new residence under each of the following circumstances:

1. The new residence costs $230,000.
2. The new residence costs $210,000.
3. The new residence costs $110,000.

		1	2	3
Step 1:	Sales price	$ 244,000	$ 244,000	$ 244,000
	−Selling expenses	(14,600)	(14,600)	(14,600)
	=Amount realized	$ 229,400	$ 229,400	$ 229,400
Step 2:	Amount realized	$ 229,400	$ 229,400	$ 229,400
	−Adjusted basis	(136,000)	(136,000)	(136,000)
	=Realized gain	$ 93,400	$ 93,400	$ 93,400
Step 3:	Amount realized	$ 229,400	$ 229,400	$ 229,400
	−Fixing-up expenses	(3,400)	(3,400)	(3,400)
	=Adjusted sales price	$ 226,000	$ 226,000	$ 226,000
Step 4:	Adjusted sales price	$ 226,000	$ 226,000	$ 226,000
	−Cost of new residence	(230,000)	(210,000)	(110,000)
	=Excess of ASP over cost	$ −0−	$ 16,000	$ 116,000
Step 5:	Recognized gain (lesser of Step 2 or Step 4)	$ −0−	$ 16,000	$ 93,400
Step 6:	Realized gain	$ 93,400	$ 93,400	$ 93,400
	−Recognized gain	(−0−)	(16,000)	(93,400)
	=Postponed gain	$ 93,400	$ 77,400	$ −0−
Step 7:	Cost of new residence	$ 230,000	$ 210,000	$ 110,000
	−Postponed gain	(93,400)	(77,400)	(−0−)
	=Basis of new residence	$ 136,600	$ 132,600	$ 110,000

None of the realized gain of $93,400 is recognized in the first case because the actual reinvestment of $230,000 exceeds the required reinvestment of $226,000. In the second case, the recognized gain is $16,000 because the required reinvestment of $226,000 exceeds the actual reinvestment of $210,000 by this amount. In the third case, the required reinvestment of $226,000 exceeds the actual reinvestment of $110,000 by $116,000. Since this amount is greater than the realized gain of $93,400, the realized gain of $93,400 is recognized, and § 1034 deferral does not apply. ▼

REPORTING PROCEDURES

The taxpayer is required to report the details of the sale of the residence on the tax return for the taxable year in which gain is realized, even if all of the gain is postponed. If a new residence is acquired and occupied before filing, a statement should be attached to the return showing the purchase date, the cost, and date of occupancy. Form 2119, Sale or Exchange of Your Home, is used to show the details of the sale and replacement, and the taxpayer should retain a copy permanently as support for the basis of the new residence. If a replacement residence has not been purchased by the time the return is filed, the taxpayer should submit the details of the purchase on the return of the taxable year during which it occurs. If the old residence is not replaced within the prescribed time period, or if some recognized gain results, the taxpayer must file an amended return for the year in which the sale took place.

SALE OF A RESIDENCE—§ 121

5 **LEARNING OBJECTIVE**
Discuss the provisions for permanent exclusion of gain on the sale of a personal residence by taxpayers age 55 and older.

Under the **Section 121 exclusion,** taxpayers age 55 or older who sell or exchange their principal residence may *elect to exclude* up to $125,000 ($62,500 for married individuals filing separate returns) of realized gain from the sale or exchange.[36] The election can be made *only once.*[37] This provision differs from § 1034 where nonrecognition is mandatory and may occur many times during a taxpayer's lifetime. Section 121 also differs from § 1034 in that it does not require the taxpayer to purchase a new residence. The excluded gain is never recognized, whereas the realized gain not recognized under § 1034 is postponed by subtracting it from the cost of the new residence in calculating the adjusted basis.

This provision is the only case in the tax law where a realized gain from the disposition of property that is not recognized is excluded rather than merely postponed. The provision allows the taxpayer a permanent recovery of more than the cost or other basis of the residence tax-free.

Congress enacted § 121 simply to relieve older citizens of the large tax they might incur from the sale of a personal residence. The dollar and age limitations restrict the benefit of § 121 to taxpayers who presumably have a greater need for increased tax-free dollars.

EXCLUSION REQUIREMENTS

The taxpayer must be at least age 55 before the date of the sale and have *owned* and *used* the residence as a principal residence for at least *three years* during the *five-year* period ending on the date of sale. The ownership and use periods do not have to be the same period of time. Short temporary absences (e.g., vacations) count as periods of use. If the residence is owned jointly by husband and wife, only one of the spouses is required to meet these requirements if a joint return is filed for the taxable year in which the sale took place.

In determining whether the ownership and use period requirements are satisfied, transactions affecting prior residences may be relevant. If a former residence is involuntarily converted and any gain is postponed under § 1033, the holding period of the former residence is added to the holding period of the replacement residence for § 121 purposes. However, if the realized gain is postponed under § 1034 (sale-of-residence provision), the holding period of the former residence is not added to the holding period of the replacement residence for § 121 purposes. In this instance, the holding period of the replacement residence begins with the acquisition date of the replacement residence.

---

[36] §§ 121(a), (b), and (c). For married taxpayers, each spouse must consent.

[37] § 121(b)(2) and Reg. § 1.121–2(b). Only one election may be made by married individuals.

▼
EXAMPLE 27

Cole has lived in his residence since 1985. The residence is involuntarily converted in July 1994. He purchases a replacement residence in August 1994. When the replacement residence is subsequently sold, Cole includes the holding period of the involuntarily converted residence in determining whether he can satisfy the ownership and use requirements. ▼

▼
EXAMPLE 28

Assume the same facts as in the previous example, except that Cole's residence was not involuntarily converted. Instead, he sold it so that he could move into a larger house. When the replacement residence is subsequently sold, Cole is not permitted to include the holding period of the old residence in determining whether he can satisfy the ownership and use requirements. ▼

ETHICAL CONSIDERATIONS

A Couple's Approach to the § 121 Exclusion

Bob and Sandra, both age 67, live in Houston, Texas, where each owns a personal residence on which the realized gain from a sale would be $125,000. They plan to marry and move to Williamsburg, Virginia. Not wanting the burdens of home ownership, they intend to rent a house.

Bob and Sandra both satisfy the requirements for the § 121 exclusion. Because of the soft real estate market in Houston, they have been unsuccessful in selling their personal residences. Being aware that a married couple can qualify only once for the § 121 exclusion, they devise the following plan. Bob will sell his house to Sandra, and Sandra will sell her house to Bob for the fair market value. Each will elect § 121 exclusion treatment. They will then marry and move to Williamsburg. Upon the subsequent sale of the houses to external buyers, the recognized gain, if any, will be minimal, since the adjusted basis of each house will have stepped up to the fair market value on the prior sale to each other.

RELATIONSHIP TO OTHER PROVISIONS

The taxpayer can treat an involuntary conversion of a principal residence as a sale for purposes of § 121. Any gain not excluded under § 121 is then subject to postponement under § 1033 or § 1034 (condemnation only), assuming the requirements of those provisions are met.

Any gain from the sale of a residence not excluded under § 121 is subject to postponement under § 1034, assuming the requirements of that provision are met. Examples 29 and 30 illustrate this relationship.

MAKING AND REVOKING THE ELECTION

The election not to recognize gain under § 121 may be made or revoked at any time before the statute of limitations expires. Therefore, the taxpayer generally has until the *later* of (1) three years from the due date of the return for the year the gain is realized or (2) two years from the date the tax is paid to make or revoke the election. The election is made by attaching a signed statement (showing all the details of the sale) to the return for the taxable year in which the sale took place. Form 2119 is used for this purpose. The election is revoked by filing a signed statement (showing the taxpayer's name, Social Security number, and taxable year for which the election was made) indicating the revocation.[38]

COMPUTATION PROCEDURE

The following examples illustrate the application of both the § 121 and § 1034 provisions.

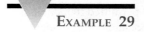

EXAMPLE 29

Keith sells his personal residence (adjusted basis of $32,000) for $205,000, of which he receives only $195,400 after paying the selling expenses. Ten days before the sale, he incurred and paid for qualified fixing-up expenses of $6,400. Keith is age 55 and elects the exclusion of gain under § 121. He does not acquire a replacement residence. ▼

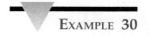

EXAMPLE 30

Assume the same facts as in the previous example, except that Keith acquires a new residence for $40,000 within the prescribed time period.

The solutions to Examples 29 and 30 are as follows:

	Example 29	Example 30
Amount realized ($205,000 – $9,600)	$ 195,400	$ 195,400
Adjusted basis	(32,000)	(32,000)
Realized gain	$ 163,400	$ 163,400
§ 121 exclusion	(125,000)	(125,000)
Realized gain after exclusion	$ 38,400	$ 38,400
Amount realized	$ 195,400	$ 195,400
Fixing-up expenses	(6,400)	(6,400)
Adjusted sales price	$ 189,000	$ 189,000
§ 121 exclusion	(125,000)	(125,000)
Adjusted sales price after exclusion	$ 64,000	$ 64,000
Cost of new residence	(–0–)	(40,000)
Excess of adjusted sales price after the exclusion over reinvestment	$ 64,000	$ 24,000
Recognized gain (lower of realized gain after exclusion or above excess)	$ 38,400	$ 24,000
Realized gain after exclusion	$ 38,400	$ 38,400
Recognized gain	(38,400)	(24,000)
Postponed gain	$ –0–	$ 14,400
Cost of new residence	$ –0–	$ 40,000
Postponed gain	(–0–)	(14,400)
Basis of new residence	$ –0–	$ 25,600

▼

Comparing the results of Examples 29 and 30 provides insight into the relationship between § 1034 and § 121. If Keith had not made the election to postpone gain under § 121 in Example 29, his recognized gain would have been $163,400 (the realized gain). Thus, the election resulted in the permanent exclusion of the $125,000 of realized gain by reducing the recognized gain to $38,400. Further

[38]Reg. §§ 1.121–4(b) and (c).

documentation of the permanent nature of the § 121 exclusion is provided in the calculation of the basis of the new residence in Example 30. The $40,000 cost of the residence is reduced only by the postponed gain of $14,400. That is, it is not reduced by the amount of the § 121 exclusion. To postpone all of the $38,400 realized gain after the exclusion, Keith would have needed to reinvest $64,000 (the adjusted sales price after the exclusion). Also, note that the Example 29 results demonstrate that the realized gain after the exclusion is the ceiling on recognition.

OTHER NONRECOGNITION PROVISIONS

The typical taxpayer experiences the sale of a residence or an involuntary conversion more frequently than the other types of nontaxable exchanges. Several additional nonrecognition provisions that are not as common are treated briefly in the remainder of this chapter.

EXCHANGE OF STOCK FOR PROPERTY—§ 1032

Under § 1032, a corporation does not recognize gain or loss on the receipt of money or other property in exchange for its stock (including treasury stock). In other words, a corporation does not recognize gain or loss when it deals in its own stock. This provision is consistent with the accounting treatment of such transactions.

CERTAIN EXCHANGES OF INSURANCE POLICIES—§ 1035

Under this provision, no gain or loss is recognized from the exchange of certain insurance contracts or policies. The rules relating to exchanges not solely in kind and the basis of the property acquired are the same as under § 1031. Exchanges qualifying for nonrecognition include the following:

- The exchange of life insurance contracts.
- The exchange of a life insurance contract for an endowment or annuity contract.
- The exchange of an endowment contract for another endowment contract that provides for regular payments beginning at a date not later than the date payments would have begun under the contract exchanged.
- The exchange of an endowment contract for an annuity contract.
- The exchange of annuity contracts.

EXCHANGE OF STOCK FOR STOCK OF THE SAME CORPORATION—§ 1036

A shareholder does not recognize gain or loss on the exchange of common stock solely for common stock in the same corporation or from the exchange of preferred stock for preferred stock in the same corporation. Exchanges between individual shareholders as well as between a shareholder and the corporation are included. The rules relating to exchanges not solely in kind and the basis of the property acquired are the same as under § 1031. For example, a nonrecognition exchange occurs when common stock with different rights, such as voting for nonvoting, is exchanged. A shareholder usually recognizes gain or loss from the exchange of common for preferred or preferred for common even though the stock exchanged is in the same corporation.

CERTAIN REACQUISITIONS OF REAL PROPERTY—§ 1038

Under this provision, no loss is recognized from the repossession of real property sold on an installment basis. Gain is recognized to a limited extent.

TRANSFERS OF PROPERTY BETWEEN SPOUSES OR INCIDENT TO DIVORCE—§ 1041

Section 1041 provides that transfers of property *between spouses or former spouses incident to divorce* are nontaxable transactions. Therefore, the basis to the recipient is a carryover basis. To be treated as incident to the divorce, the transfer must be related to the cessation of marriage or occur within one year after the date on which the marriage ceases.

Section 1041 also provides for nontaxable exchange treatment on property transfers *between spouses during marriage.* The basis to the recipient spouse is a carryover basis.

ROLLOVER OF PUBLICLY TRADED SECURITIES GAIN INTO SPECIALIZED SMALL BUSINESS INVESTMENT COMPANIES—§ 1044

The Revenue Reconciliation Act of 1993 provides a postponement opportunity associated with the sale of publicly traded securities. If the amount realized is reinvested in the common stock or partnership interest of a specialized small business investment company (SSBIC), the realized gain is not recognized. Any amount not reinvested will trigger the recognition of the realized gain on the sale to the extent of the deficiency. The taxpayer must reinvest the proceeds within 60 days of the date of sale in order to qualify. In calculating the basis of the SSBIC stock, the amount of the purchase price is reduced by the amount of the postponed gain.

Statutory ceilings are imposed on the amount of realized gain that can be postponed for any taxable year as follows:

- Individual taxpayer: Lesser of:
  - $50,000 ($25,000 for married filing separately).
  - $500,000 ($250,000 for married filing separately) reduced by the amount of such nonrecognized gain in prior taxable years.
- Corporate taxpayer: Lesser of:
  - $250,000.
  - $1,000,000 reduced by the amount of such nonrecognized gain in prior taxable years.

Investors ineligible for this postponement treatment include partnerships, S corporations, estates, and trusts.

Chapter 15 has covered certain situations in which realized gains or losses are not recognized (nontaxable exchanges). Chapters 16 and 17 are concerned with the *classification* of recognized gains and losses. That is, if a gain or loss is recognized, is it an ordinary or capital gain or loss? Chapter 16 discusses the tax consequences of capital gains and losses.

6 Learning Objective
Identify tax planning
opportunities related to the
nonrecognition provisions
discussed in the chapter.

LIKE-KIND EXCHANGES

Since application of the like-kind provisions is mandatory rather than elective, in certain instances it may be preferable to avoid qualifying for § 1031 nonrecognition. If the like-kind provisions do not apply, the end result may be the recognition of capital gain in exchange for a higher basis in the newly acquired asset. Also, the immediate recognition of gain may be preferable in certain situations. Examples where immediate recognition is beneficial include the following:

- Taxpayer has unused net operating loss carryovers.
- Taxpayer has unused general business credit carryovers.
- Taxpayer has suspended or current passive activity losses.
- Taxpayer expects his or her effective tax rate to increase in the future.

EXAMPLE 31

Alicia disposes of a machine (used in her business) with an adjusted basis of $3,000 for $4,000. She also acquires a new business machine for $9,000. If § 1031 applies, the $1,000 realized gain is not recognized, and the basis of the new machine is reduced by $1,000 (from $9,000 to $8,000). If § 1031 does not apply, a $1,000 gain is recognized and may receive favorable capital gain treatment to the extent that the gain is not recognized as ordinary income due to the depreciation recapture provisions (see Chapter 17). In addition, the basis for depreciation on the new machine is $9,000 rather than $8,000 since there is no unrecognized gain. ▼

The application of § 1031 nonrecognition treatment should also be avoided when the adjusted basis of the property being disposed of exceeds the fair market value.

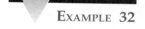

EXAMPLE 32

Assume the same facts as in the previous example, except the fair market value of the machine is $2,500. If § 1031 applies, the $500 realized loss is not recognized. To recognize the loss, Alicia should sell the old machine and purchase the new one. The purchase and sale transactions should be with different taxpayers. ▼

On the other hand, the like-kind exchange procedure can be utilized to control the amount of recognized gain.

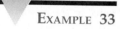

EXAMPLE 33

Rex has property with an adjusted basis of $40,000 and a fair market value of $100,000. Sandra wants to buy Rex's property, but Rex wants to limit the amount of recognized gain on the proposed transaction. Sandra acquires other like-kind property (from an outside party) for $80,000. She then exchanges this property and $20,000 cash for Rex's property. Rex has a realized gain of $60,000 ($100,000 amount realized − $40,000 adjusted basis). His recognized gain is only $20,000, the lower of the $20,000 boot received or the $60,000 realized gain. Rex's basis for the like-kind property is $40,000 ($40,000 adjusted basis + $20,000 gain recognized − $20,000 boot received). If Rex had sold the property to Sandra for its fair market value of $100,000, the result would have been a $60,000 recognized gain ($100,000 amount realized − $40,000 adjusted basis) to him. It is permissible for Rex to identify the like-kind property that he wants Sandra to purchase.[39] ▼

INVOLUNTARY CONVERSIONS

In certain cases, a taxpayer may prefer to recognize gain from an involuntary conversion. Keep in mind that § 1033, unlike § 1031 (dealing with like-kind exchanges), generally is an elective provision.

---

[39] *Franklin B. Biggs,* 69 T.C. 905 (1978); Rev.Rul. 57–244, 1957–1 C.B. 247; Rev.Rul. 73–476, 1973–2 C.B. 300; *Starker vs. U.S.,* 79–2 USTC ¶9541, 44 AFTR2d 79–5525, 602 F.2d 1341 (CA–9, 1979); and *Baird Publishing Co.,* 39 T.C. 608 (1962).

EXAMPLE 34

Ahmad has a $40,000 realized gain from the involuntary conversion of an office building. He reinvests the entire proceeds of $450,000 in a new office building. He does not elect to postpone gain under § 1033, however, because of an expiring net operating loss carryover that is offset against the gain. Therefore, none of the realized gain of $40,000 is postponed. By not electing § 1033 postponement, Ahmad's basis in the replacement property is the property's cost of $450,000 rather than $410,000 ($450,000 reduced by the $40,000 realized gain). ▼

SALE OF A PERSONAL RESIDENCE

Replacement Period Requirements

Several problems arise in avoiding the recognition of gain on the sale of a principal residence. Most of these problems can be resolved favorably through appropriate planning procedures. However, a few represent situations where the taxpayer has to accept the adverse tax consequences and possesses little, if any, planning flexibility. One pitfall concerns the failure to reinvest *all* of the proceeds from the sale of the residence in a new principal residence.

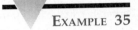

EXAMPLE 35

Rita sells her principal residence in January 1992 for $150,000 (adjusted basis of $40,000). Shortly thereafter, she purchases for $100,000 a 50-year-old house in a historical part of the community and uses it as her principal residence. Rita intends to significantly renovate the property over a period of time and make it more suitable to her living needs. In December 1994, she enters into a contract with a home improvement company to carry out the renovation at a cost of $60,000. It is clear that only $100,000 of the proceeds from the sale of the old residence has been reinvested in a new principal residence on a *timely* basis. Of the realized gain of $110,000, therefore, $50,000 ($150,000 adjusted sales price − $100,000 reinvested) must be recognized.[40] ▼

One problem that a taxpayer may not be in a position to do anything about is the acquisition of property *before* the beginning of the replacement period. Recall that the replacement period begins two years before the sale and ends two years after the sale.

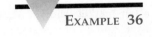

EXAMPLE 36

Tab's employer transfers him to a different city in July 1992, at which time Tab lists his house for sale with a realtor. Tab purchases a principal residence in the city to which he is transferred in September 1992. Because of market conditions, he is unable to sell his original residence until December 1994. Since the sale does not occur within two years of the purchase, the residence Tab bought in September 1992 is not a qualifying replacement residence. ▼

Principal Residence Requirement

Section 1034 will not apply unless the property involved is the taxpayer's principal residence. A potential hurdle arises in cases where the residence has been rented and therefore has not been occupied by the taxpayer for an extended period of time. Depending on the circumstances, the IRS may contend that the taxpayer has abandoned the property as his or her principal residence. The *key* to the abandonment issue is whether or not the taxpayer intended to reoccupy the property and use it as a principal residence upon returning to the locale. If the residence is, in fact, not reoccupied, the taxpayer should have a good reason to explain why it is not.

---

[40] It has been assumed that § 121 did not apply.

EXAMPLE 37

Lori's employer transfers her to another office out of the state on a three-year assignment. It is the understanding of the parties that the assignment is temporary, and upon its completion, Lori will return to the original job site. During her absence, she rents her principal residence and lives in an apartment at the new location. Lori has every intention of reoccupying her residence. However, when she returns from the temporary assignment, she finds that the residence no longer suits her needs. Specifically, the public school located nearby where she had planned to send her children has been closed. As a consequence, Lori sells the residence and replaces it with one more conveniently located to a public school. Under these circumstances, it would appear that Lori is in an excellent position to show that she has not abandoned the property as her principal residence. She can satisfactorily explain why she did not reoccupy the residence before its sale.[41] ▼

The principal residence requirement can cause difficulty when a taxpayer works in two places and maintains more than one household. In such cases, the principal residence will be the location where the taxpayer lives most of the time.[42]

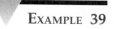

EXAMPLE 38

Hubert is a vice president of Green Corporation and in this capacity spends about an equal amount of time in the company's New York City and Miami offices. He owns a house in each location and expects to retire in about five years. At that time, he plans to sell his New York home and use some of the proceeds to make improvements on the Miami property. Both homes have appreciated in value since their acquisition, and Hubert expects the appreciation to continue. From a tax planning standpoint, Hubert should be looking toward the use of §§ 121 and 1034 to shelter some or all of the gain he will realize on the future sale of the New York City home.[43] To do this, he should arrange his affairs so as to spend more than six months each year at that location. Upon its sale, therefore, the New York home will be his principal residence. ▼

Section 121 Considerations

Older individuals who may be contemplating a move from their home to an apartment should consider the following possibilities for minimizing or deferring taxes:

- Wait until age 55 to sell the residence and elect under § 121 to exclude up to $125,000 of the realized gain.
- Sell the personal residence under an installment contract to spread the gain over several years.[44]
- Sell the personal residence and purchase a condominium instead of renting an apartment, thereby permitting further deferral of the unrecognized gain.

The use of § 121 should be carefully considered. Although the use avoids the immediate recognition of gain, the election expends the full $125,000 allowed.

EXAMPLE 39

In 1994 Kate, age 55, sells her personal residence for an amount that yields a realized gain of $5,000. Presuming Kate does not plan to reinvest the sales proceeds in a new principal residence (take advantage of the deferral possibility of § 1034), should she avoid the

---

[41] Rev.Rul. 78–146, 1978–1 C.B. 260. Compare *Rudolph M. Stucchi,* 35 TCM 1052, T.C.Memo. 1976–242.

[42] Rev.Rul. 77–298, 1977–2 C.B. 308.

[43] If Hubert qualifies, § 121 would allow the first $125,000 of gain to be excluded. Further gain might be avoided under § 1034 to the

extent the sales proceeds are applied toward improvements on the Miami home.

[44] § 453(a). See the discussion of the installment method in Chapter 18.

recognition of this gain by utilizing § 121? Electing § 121 means that Kate will waste $120,000 of her lifetime exclusion. ▼

In this connection, the use of § 121 by one spouse precludes the other spouse from later taking advantage of the exclusion.

▼
EXAMPLE 40

Assume the same facts as in the previous example, except that Kate was married to Wes at the time of the sale. Later, Kate and Wes are divorced and Wes marries Alice. If Kate has used the § 121 exclusion, it is unavailable to Wes and Alice even though either one of them may otherwise qualify. This result occurs because when Kate made the election for the 1994 sale, it was necessary for Wes to join with her in making the election even though the residence was owned separately by Kate. For Wes and Alice to be able to make the § 121 election, Wes and Kate must revoke their prior election. Another planning approach is for Alice to sell her residence before marrying Wes and to elect the exclusion on that sale. ▼

A taxpayer who is eligible to elect § 121 exclusion treatment may choose not to do so in order to remain eligible to elect it in the future. In arriving at this decision, consideration must be given to the probability that the taxpayer will satisfy the three-out-of-five-year ownership and use period requirements associated with a residence sale in the future. As previously mentioned, the holding period for the occupancy and use requirements does carry over for a § 1033 involuntary conversion but does not carry over for a § 1034 sale.

Taxpayers should maintain records of both the purchase and sale of personal residences since the sale of one residence results in an adjustment of the basis of the new residence if the deferral provisions of § 1034 apply. Form 2119 should be filed with the tax return and a copy retained as support for the basis of the new residence. Detailed cost records should be retained for an indefinite period.

KEY TERMS

Adjusted sales price,   15–19

Boot,   15–6

Fixing-up expenses,   15–19

Holding period,   15–8

Involuntary conversion,   15–10

Like-kind exchange,   15–3

Nontaxable exchange,   15–2

Personal residence,   15–15

Personalty,   15–4

Realty,   15–4

Section 121 exclusion,   15–22

▼
PROBLEM MATERIALS

DISCUSSION QUESTIONS

1. What is the justification for nontaxable exchange treatment?

2. Distinguish between a loss that is not recognized on a nontaxable exchange and a loss that is not recognized on the sale or exchange of a personal use asset.

3. Can the exchange of property held for productive use in a trade or business for investment property qualify for like-kind exchange treatment?

4. Can the exchange of personal use property for other personal use property qualify for like-kind exchange treatment?

5. Why would a taxpayer want to avoid like-kind exchange treatment?

X 6. Which of the following qualify as like-kind exchanges under § 1031?
   a. Improved for unimproved real estate.
   b. Vending machine (used in business) for inventory.
   c. Rental house for truck (used in business).
   d. Business equipment for securities.
   e. Warehouse for office building (both used for business).
   f. Personal residence for apartment building (held for investment).
   g. Rental house for land (both held for investment).
   h. Ten shares of stock in Blue Corporation for 10 shares of stock in Red Corporation.

7. Under what circumstances can the exchange of partnership interests qualify for like-kind exchange treatment?

8. If a taxpayer exchanges a personal use car for another car to be held for personal use, any realized loss is not recognized. However, if realized gain occurs, the realized gain is recognized. Why?

9. What is boot, and how does it affect the recognition of gain or loss on a like-kind exchange when received by the taxpayer? How is the recognition of gain or loss affected when boot is given?

10. Why does the receipt of boot in a like-kind exchange trigger the recognition of realized gain but not the recognition of realized loss?

11. The receipt of boot in a § 1031 exchange triggers the recognition of realized gain. The gain recognition will affect the basis of the property received by the taxpayer.
   a. Discuss the relationship between the realized gain and the boot received if the boot received is greater than the realized gain.
   b. Discuss the relationship between the realized gain and the boot received if the boot received is less than the realized gain.
   c. What effect does the recognition of gain have on the basis of the like-kind property received? Of the boot received?

12. In a like-kind exchange, the basis of the property received is the same as the adjusted basis of the property transferred. If boot is received, what effect does the boot have on the basis of the like-kind property received? If boot is given, what effect does the boot have on the basis of the like-kind property received?

13. In connection with like-kind exchanges, discuss each of the following:
   a. Realized gain.
   b. Realized loss.
   c. Recognized gain.
   d. Recognized loss.
   e. Postponed gain.
   f. Postponed loss.
   g. Basis of like-kind property received.
   h. Basis of boot received.

14. What is the holding period of like-kind property received in a like-kind exchange? For boot received? Why?

15. Mortgaged real estate may be received in a like-kind exchange. If the taxpayer assumes the mortgage, what effect does the mortgage have on the recognition of realized gain? On the basis of the real estate received?

X 16. What constitutes an involuntary conversion?

17. A taxpayer's appreciated property is involuntarily converted. She receives insurance proceeds equal to the fair market value of the property. What is the minimum amount the taxpayer must reinvest in qualifying property to defer recognition of realized gain?

18. What are the differences in the replacement requirement rules for involuntary conversions under the functional use test and the taxpayer use test?

19. Taxpayer's warehouse is destroyed by fire. What are the different tax options available to the taxpayer (a) if he has a realized gain and (b) if he has a realized loss?

20. What is the earliest date that a taxpayer can replace involuntarily converted property?

21. Discuss the tax options available to the taxpayer when the form of the transaction is (a) a direct involuntary conversion and (b) an indirect involuntary conversion.

22. When does the holding period begin in an involuntary conversion for which the similar property rule is applicable? The like-kind property rule?

23. Bob is notified by the city public housing authority on October 5, 1994, that his apartment building is going to be condemned as part of an urban renewal project. On October 12, 1994, Carol offers to buy the building from Bob. Bob sells the building to Carol on October 30, 1994. Condemnation occurs on February 1, 1995, and Carol receives the condemnation proceeds from the city. Assume both Bob and Carol are calendar year taxpayers.
    a. What is the earliest date that Bob can dispose of the building and qualify for § 1033 postponement treatment?
    b. Does the sale to Carol qualify as a § 1033 involuntary conversion?
    c. What is the latest date that Carol can acquire qualifying replacement property and qualify for postponement of the realized gain?
    d. What type of property will be qualifying replacement property?

24. Discuss the justification for nonrecognition of gain on the sale or exchange of a principal residence. Discuss the justification for disallowance of loss.

25. Jim sells his principal residence on September 18, 1994. Although he does not replace it until August 19, 1998, the replacement qualifies for postponement treatment under § 1034. Discuss how this replacement could satisfy the residence replacement period requirement.

26. What is a principal residence? Can a taxpayer have more than one principal residence at one point in time?

27. Peggy has owned and occupied a house as her principal residence for 10 years. She purchases a new residence in March 1994. She initially listed her old residence with a realtor in January 1994. Needing the cash flow, she rents the old residence to Joe for a six-month period beginning in March. She sells the old residence to Paul upon the expiration of the rental period in September. Does the sale of the old residence in September qualify as the sale of a principal residence?

28. Define each of the following associated with the sale of a residence:
    a. Amount realized.
    b. Adjusted sales price.
    c. Fixing-up expenses.

29. Explain how the following are determined on the sale or exchange of a residence:
    a. Realized gain.
    b. Recognized gain.
    c. Postponed gain.
    d. Basis of new residence.

30. Discuss the basis calculation formula as it applies to a new residence if:
    a. Realized gain is postponed.
    b. Realized loss is disallowed.
    c. Realized gain is recognized because the new residence is not acquired within the two-year time period from the sale of the old residence.

31. Can capital expenditures made to a house received by gift enable the taxpayer to qualify for postponement treatment under § 1034?

32. Why was § 121 enacted?

33. What does the § 121 exclusion cover? Is it elective? Does the old residence have to be replaced?

34. How many times can § 121 exclusion treatment be elected by a taxpayer? If the taxpayer is filing a joint return with his or her spouse, do both taxpayers have to meet the ownership and use requirements?

35. Can any other provision be applied to any remaining gain that is not excluded under § 121?

PROBLEMS

36. Kay owns undeveloped land with an adjusted basis of $55,000. She exchanges it for other undeveloped land worth $120,000.
    a. What are Kay's realized and recognized gain or loss?
    b. What is Kay's basis in the undeveloped land she receives?

37. Kareem owns an automobile that he uses exclusively in his business. The adjusted basis is $11,000, and the fair market value is $5,000. Kareem exchanges the car for a car that he will use exclusively in his business.
    a. What are Kareem's realized and recognized gain or loss?
    b. What is his basis in the car?
    c. What are the tax consequences to Kareem in (a) and (b) if he will use the car exclusively for personal purposes?

38. Bonnie owns a personal computer that she uses exclusively in her business. The adjusted basis is $5,000. Bonnie transfers the personal computer and cash of $4,000 to Don for a laser printer worth $10,000 that she will use in her business.
    a. Calculate Bonnie's recognized gain or loss on the exchange.
    b. Calculate Bonnie's basis for the printer.

39. Chee exchanges an automobile used exclusively in his business for a light-duty truck that will be used in his business. The adjusted basis for the automobile is $12,000, and the fair market value of the truck is $10,000.
    a. Calculate Chee's recognized gain or loss on the exchange.
    b. Calculate Chee's basis for the truck.

40. Susan owns a car that she uses exclusively for personal purposes. Its original cost was $15,000, and the fair market value is $7,000. She exchanges the car and $18,000 cash for a new car.
    a. Calculate Susan's realized and recognized gain or loss.
    b. Calculate Susan's basis for the new car.

41. Tom owns land and building with an adjusted basis of $125,000 and a fair market value of $275,000. Tom exchanges the land and building for land with a fair market value of $175,000 that he will use as a parking lot. In addition, he receives stock worth $100,000.
    a. What is Tom's realized gain or loss?
    b. His recognized gain or loss?
    c. The basis of the land and the stock received?

42. Olga owns a machine that she uses in her business. The adjusted basis is $60,000, and the fair market value is $90,000. She exchanges it for another machine worth $55,000. Olga also receives cash of $35,000.
    a. Calculate Olga's realized and recognized gain or loss on the exchange.
    b. Calculate Olga's basis for the new machine.

43. Ed owns investment land with an adjusted basis of $35,000. Polly has offered to purchase the land from Ed for $175,000 for use in a real estate development. The amount offered by Polly is $10,000 in excess of what Ed perceives as the fair market value of the land. Ed would like to dispose of the land to Polly but does not want to incur the tax liability that would result. He identifies an office building with a fair market value of $175,000 that he would like to acquire. Polly purchases the office building and then exchanges the office building for Ed's land.
    a. Calculate Ed's realized and recognized gain on the exchange and his basis for the office building.
    b. Calculate Polly's realized and recognized gain on the exchange and her basis in the land.

44. What is the basis of the new property in each of the following exchanges?
    a. Apartment building held for investment (adjusted basis $150,000) for office building to be held for investment (fair market value $200,000).
    b. Land and building used as a barber shop (adjusted basis $30,000) for land and building used as a grocery store (fair market value $350,000).
    c. Office building (adjusted basis $30,000) for bulldozer (fair market value $42,000), both held for business use.
    d. IBM common stock (adjusted basis $14,000) for Exxon common stock (fair market value $18,000).
    e. Rental house (adjusted basis $90,000) for mountain cabin to be held for personal use (fair market value $115,000).

45. Norm owns Machine A, which he uses in his business. The adjusted basis of Machine A is $12,000, and the fair market value is $15,000. Norm sells Machine A for $15,000 to Tim, who is a dealer. Norm then purchases Machine B, which would qualify as like-kind property, for $15,000 from Joan, who also is a dealer.
    a. What are Norm's realized and recognized gain on the sale of Machine A?
    b. What is Norm's basis for Machine B, which was acquired from Joan?
    c. What factors would motivate Norm to sell Machine A and purchase the replacement Machine B rather than exchange one machine for the other?
    d. Assume that the adjusted basis of Machine A is $15,000 and the fair market value of each machine is $12,000. Respond to (a) through (c).

46. Gus exchanges real estate held for investment plus stock for real estate to be held for investment. The stock transferred has an adjusted basis of $10,000 and a fair market value of $6,000. The real estate transferred has an adjusted basis of $15,000 and a fair market value of $22,000. The real estate acquired has a fair market value of $28,000.
    a. What is Gus's realized gain or loss?
    b. His recognized gain or loss?
    c. The basis of the newly acquired real estate?

47. Helen exchanges a machine (adjusted basis of $30,000 and fair market value of $55,000) and undeveloped land held for investment (adjusted basis of $100,000 and fair market value of $325,000) for land worth $320,000 to be used in her business. The undeveloped land has a mortgage of $60,000 that the other party to the exchange assumes.
    a. What is Helen's realized gain or loss?
    b. Her recognized gain or loss?
    c. The basis of the newly acquired real estate?

48. Determine the realized, recognized, and postponed gain or loss and the new basis for each of the following like-kind exchanges:

	Adjusted Basis of Old Asset	Boot Given	Fair Market Value of New Asset	Boot Received
a.	$ 7,000	$ –0–	$12,000	$4,000
b.	14,000	2,000	15,000	–0–
c.	3,000	7,000	8,000	500
d.	22,000	–0–	32,000	–0–
e.	10,000	–0–	11,000	1,000
f.	10,000	–0–	8,000	–0–

49. Shontelle owns an apartment house that has an adjusted basis of $900,000 but is subject to a mortgage of $300,000. She transfers the apartment house to Dave and receives from him $125,000 in cash and an office building with a fair market value of $800,000 at the time of the exchange. Dave assumes the $300,000 mortgage on the apartment house.
    a. What is Shontelle's realized gain or loss?
    b. Her recognized gain or loss?
    c. The basis of the newly acquired office building?

50. Carmen's office building, which has an adjusted basis of $200,000, is destroyed by a tornado. Since Carmen's business has excess office space, she decides not to replace the office building, but instead to contribute the proceeds to the working capital of her business.
    a. If the insurance proceeds are $225,000, what is Carmen's recognized gain or loss?
    b. If the insurance proceeds are $180,000, what is Carmen's recognized gain or loss?

51. For each of the following involuntary conversions, indicate whether the property acquired qualifies as replacement property:
    a. Frank owns a shopping mall that is destroyed by a tornado. The space in the mall was rented to various tenants. Frank uses the insurance proceeds to build a shopping mall in a neighboring community where no property has been damaged by tornadoes.
    b. Ivan owns a warehouse that he uses in his business. The warehouse is destroyed by fire. Due to economic conditions in the area, Ivan decides not to rebuild the warehouse. Instead, he uses the insurance proceeds to build a warehouse to be used in his business in another state.
    c. Ridge's personal residence is condemned as part of a local government project to widen the highway from two lanes to four lanes. He uses the condemnation proceeds to purchase another personal residence.

52. Do the following qualify for involuntary conversion treatment?
    a. Purchase of a sporting goods store as a replacement for a bookstore (used in a business) that was destroyed by fire.
    b. Sale of a home because a neighbor converted his residence into a nightclub.
    c. Purchase of an airplane to replace a shrimp boat (used in a business) that was wrecked by a hurricane.
    d. Taxpayer's residence destroyed by a tornado and replaced with another residence.
    e. Investor's purchase of an apartment building to replace a rental house. The rental house was destroyed by a flood.

53. The building that houses LaToya's designer clothing store is destroyed in a mud slide associated with a flood on June 27, 1994. LaToya had anticipated the flood and moved her inventory, furniture, and fixtures to a warehouse outside the floodplain on June 20, 1994. Her adjusted basis for the building is $150,000, and she receives insurance proceeds of $160,000 on July 15, 1994. LaToya intends to purchase another building for her store, but would like to have time to locate one in a safer location. Her taxable year ends on June 30.
    a. What are the earliest and latest dates that LaToya can make a qualified replacement?
    b. Assuming LaToya makes a qualified replacement costing $160,000, what are her realized gain, recognized gain, and basis for the replacement property?

54. Lynn's office building, which is used in her business, is destroyed by a hurricane in September 1994. The adjusted basis is $225,000. Lynn receives insurance proceeds of $350,000 in October 1994.
    a. Calculate Lynn's realized gain or loss, recognized gain or loss, and basis for the replacement property if she acquires an office building for $390,000 in October 1994.
    b. Calculate Lynn's realized gain or loss, recognized gain or loss, and basis for the replacement property if she acquires a warehouse for $330,000 in October 1994.
    c. Calculate Lynn's realized gain or loss and recognized gain or loss if she does not acquire replacement property.

55. Carlos's warehouse, which has an adjusted basis of $325,000 and a fair market value of $490,000, is condemned by an agency of the Federal government to make way for a highway interchange. The initial condemnation offer is $450,000. After substantial negotiations, the agency agrees to transfer to Carlos a surplus warehouse that he believes is worth $490,000.
    a. What are the recognized gain or loss and the basis of the replacement warehouse if Carlos's objective is to recognize as much gain as possible?
    b. What are the recognized gain or loss and the basis of the replacement warehouse if Carlos's objective is to minimize gain recognition?

56. What are the *maximum* postponed gain or loss and the basis for the replacement property for the following involuntary conversions?

	Property	Type of Conversion	Amount Realized	Adjusted Basis	Amount Reinvested
a.	Drugstore (business)	Condemned	$160,000	$120,000	$100,000
b.	Apartments (investment)	Casualty	100,000	120,000	200,000
c.	Grocery store (business)	Casualty	400,000	300,000	350,000
d.	Residence (personal)	Casualty	16,000	18,000	17,000
e.	Vacant lot (investment)	Condemned	240,000	160,000	240,000
f.	Residence (personal)	Casualty	20,000	18,000	19,000
g.	Residence (personal)	Condemned	18,000	20,000	26,000
h.	Apartments (investment)	Condemned	150,000	100,000	200,000

57. Rental property owned by Freda, a calendar year taxpayer, is destroyed by a tornado on January 1, 1994. Freda had originally paid $150,000 for the property, of which $125,000 was allocated to the building and $25,000 was allocated to the land. During the time Freda owned the property, MACRS deductions of $46,250 were taken. MACRS deductions of $57,500 would have been taken, except that Freda chose to forgo deductions of $11,250 one year when her tax return showed a net operating loss. Freda receives insurance proceeds of $60,000 in November 1994. As a result of continuing negotiations with the insurance company, Freda receives additional proceeds of $35,000 in August 1995.
    a. What is Freda's adjusted basis for the property?
    b. What is Freda's realized gain or loss on the involuntary conversion in 1994? In 1995?
    c. What is the latest date that Freda can replace the involuntarily converted property to qualify for § 1033 postponement?
    d. What is the latest date that Freda can replace the involuntarily converted property to qualify for § 1033 postponement if the form of the involuntary conversion is a condemnation?

58. Which of the following are selling expenses, fixing-up expenses, or neither?
    a. New swimming pool.
    b. Legal fees to clear title to residence.
    c. Painting exterior of residence.
    d. Repair of leaky plumbing.
    e. New roof.
    f. Advertising residence for sale.
    g. Painting living and dining rooms.
    h. Broker commissions.

59. Tina, age 42, has lived in her residence for three years. Her adjusted basis is $130,000. In February 1992, she decides to move to another neighborhood to reduce her commuting time and lists her residence for sale for $225,000. In May 1992, she moves to another residence that she has purchased for $240,000 at the beginning of the month. By April 1994, she has still not sold her old residence due to market conditions. She is becoming concerned that she will not satisfy the two-year replacement provision. Therefore, she is considering moving back into her old residence and selling her new residence. She anticipates no difficulty in selling the new residence for $250,000.
    a. Advise Tina regarding whether she should (1) sell her new residence and move back into her old residence or (2) stay in her new residence and continue to try to sell her old residence.
    b. If Tina moves back into her old residence, what is her adjusted basis for the old residence?

60. What are the realized, recognized, and postponed gain or loss, the new basis, and the adjusted sales price for each of the following? Assume that none of the taxpayers is 55 years of age or older.
   a. Susan sells her residence for $90,000. The adjusted basis was $55,000. The selling expenses were $5,000. The fixing-up expenses were $3,000. She did not reinvest in a new residence.
   b. Rocky sells his residence for $170,000. The adjusted basis was $120,000. The selling expenses were $4,000. The fixing-up expenses were $6,000. Rocky reinvested $160,000 in a new residence.
   c. Veneia sells her residence for $65,000. The adjusted basis was $35,000. The selling expenses were $1,000. The fixing-up expenses were $2,000. She reinvested $40,000.
   d. Barry sells his residence for $70,000. The adjusted basis was $65,000. The selling expenses were $6,000. He reinvested $80,000.
   e. Carl sells his residence for $100,000, and his mortgage is assumed by the buyer. The adjusted basis was $80,000; the mortgage, $50,000. The selling expenses were $4,000. The fixing-up expenses were $2,000. He reinvested $120,000.

61. Ted is a colonel in the U.S. Air Force who is stationed in Newport News, Virginia. He is being transferred to Turkey for a three-year tour of duty beginning on September 15, 1994. He sells his principal residence in Newport News on August 25, 1994, for $220,000. His adjusted basis is $120,000. The selling expenses are $12,000, and the fixing-up expenses are $3,000. He returns to the United States on September 15, 1997, and purchases a new residence for $210,000 in San Antonio, Texas, where he is now stationed.
   a. What is Ted's realized gain or loss?
   b. His recognized gain or loss?
   c. The basis of the residence?

62. On January 15, 1994, Kelly, a 48-year-old widow, buys a new residence for $180,000. On March 1, 1994, she sells for an adjusted sales price of $197,000 her old residence, which had an adjusted basis of $110,000. No fixing-up expenses are incurred. Between April 1 and June 30, 1994, she constructs an addition to her new house at a cost of $20,000.
   a. What is Kelly's realized gain or loss?
   b. Kelly's recognized gain or loss?
   c. Kelly's basis for the new residence?

63. Ned, age 47, sells his residence in Richmond on May 5, 1994, for $115,000. He incurs realtor's commissions of $6,900 and qualified fixing-up expenses of $2,000. His adjusted basis is $70,000. Ned sells the house because his employer assigns him to a temporary job in another state. Ned moves back to Richmond in December 1995. However, he has decided that he enjoys being relieved of the responsibilities of home ownership. Therefore, he rents an apartment and does not purchase another residence by May 5, 1996.
   a. What should Ned have reported on his 1994 return with respect to the sale of his residence?
   b. What should Ned do in 1996 when he has not replaced the residence within the required two-year period?

64. Pedro, age 57, is the sole owner of his principal residence. He has owned and occupied it for 10 years. Maria, his spouse, refuses to join him in making the § 121 election.
   a. Can Pedro elect the § 121 exclusion if he and Maria file a joint return? If so, what is the available amount of the exclusion?
   b. Can Pedro elect the § 121 exclusion if he files a separate return? If so, what is the available amount of the exclusion?
   c. If Maria joins Pedro in making the election, what is the available amount of the exclusion on a joint return? On a separate return?

65. Pat sold his residence, which he had owned and occupied for 20 years. The adjusted basis was $92,000, and the selling price was $275,000. The selling expenses were $16,000, and the fixing-up expenses were $5,000. He reinvested $90,000 in a new

residence. Pat is 57 years old. What are the realized, recognized, and postponed gain or loss, the new basis, and the adjusted sales price if his objective is to minimize the recognized gain?

66. Nell, Nina, and Nora, who are sisters, sell their principal residence in which they have lived for the past 20 years. The youngest of the sisters is age 58. The selling price is $555,000, selling expenses and legal fees are $15,000, and the adjusted basis is $60,000 (the fair market value of the residence when inherited from their parents 20 years ago). Since the sisters are going to live in rental housing, they do not plan to acquire another residence. Nell has contacted you on behalf of the three sisters regarding the tax consequences of the sale.
    a. Write a letter to Nell advising her of the tax consequences and how taxes can be minimized.
    b. Prepare a memo for the files.

67. Jeff and Jill are divorced on August 1, 1994. According to the terms of the divorce decree, Jeff's ownership interest in the house is to be transferred to Jill in exchange for the release from marital rights. Before the divorce, the house was jointly owned by Jeff and Jill. The adjusted basis and the fair market value at the date of the transfer are $150,000 and $200,000, respectively.
    a. Does the transfer of the house produce recognized gain to either Jeff or Jill?
    b. What is the basis of the house to Jill?
    c. If the same transfer was made by Jeff to Jill for $100,000 and was not associated with a divorce, would either Jeff or Jill have recognized gain?

68. Sam, age 63, owns a residence in which he has lived for 20 years. The residence is destroyed by fire on August 8, 1994. The adjusted basis is $90,000, and the fair market value is $300,000. Sam receives insurance proceeds of $300,000 for the residence. He is trying to decide whether to purchase a comparable house. He anticipates that he will retire in two years and will move to a warmer climate where he will rent in case he decides to live in different places.
    a. Advise Sam of the tax consequences of replacing versus not replacing the residence.
    b. Which do you recommend to him?

CUMULATIVE PROBLEMS

69. Tammy Walker, age 37, is a self-employed accountant. Tammy's Social Security number is 333–40–1111. Her address is 101 Glass Road, Richmond, VA 23236. Her income and expenses associated with her accounting practice for 1994 are as follows:

Revenues (cash receipts during 1994)	$186,000
Expenses	
Salaries	$ 83,000
Office supplies	1,100
Postage	500
Depreciation of equipment	25,000
Telephone	650
	$110,250

Since Tammy is a cash method taxpayer, she does not record her receivables as revenue until she receives cash payment. At the beginning of 1994, her accounts receivable were $17,000, and the balance had decreased to $8,000 by the end of the year. The balance on December 31, 1994, would have been $13,500, except that an account for $5,500 had become uncollectible in November.

Tammy used one room in her 10-room house as an office (400 square feet out of a total square footage of 4,000). She paid the following expenses related to the house during 1994:

Utilities	$4,000
Insurance	800
Property taxes	4,000
Repairs	1,400

Tammy had purchased the house on September 1, 1993, for $200,000. She sold her previous house on November 15, 1993, for $105,000. Her selling expenses had been $9,000, and qualified fixing-up expenses were $1,100. Tammy and her former husband, Lou, had purchased the house in 1991 for $80,000. Tammy had received Lou's 50% ownership interest as part of their divorce settlement in August 1992. Tammy had not used any part of the former residence as a home office.

Tammy has one child, Thomas, age 17. Thomas lives with his father during the summer and with Tammy for the rest of the year. Tammy can document that she spent $8,000 during 1994 for the child's support. The father normally provides about $2,000 per year, but this year he gave the child a new car for Christmas. The cost of the car was $18,000. The divorce decree is silent regarding the dependency exemption for the child.

Under the terms of the divorce decree, Tammy is to receive alimony of $800 per month. The payments will terminate at Tammy's death or if she should remarry.

Tammy provides part of the support of her mother, age 67. The total support for 1994 for her mother was as follows:

Social Security benefits	$4,800
From Tammy	1,900
From Bob, Tammy's brother	1,300
From Susan, Tammy's sister	2,000

Bob and Susan have both indicated their willingness to sign a multiple support waiver form if it will benefit Tammy.

Tammy's deductible itemized deductions during 1994, excluding any itemized deductions related to the house, were $11,000. She made estimated tax payments of $22,000.

Part 1—Tax Computation
Compute Tammy's lowest net tax payable or refund due for 1994. Suggested software (if available): *TurboTax* or *MacInTax* for tax return or WFT tax planning software.

Part 2—Tax Planning
Tammy and her former husband have been discussing the $800 alimony he pays her each month. Due to a health problem of his new wife, he does not feel that he can afford to continue to pay the $800 each month. He is in the 15% tax bracket. If Tammy will agree to decrease the amount by 25%, he will agree that the amount paid is not alimony for tax purposes. Assume that the other data used in calculating Tammy's taxable income for 1994 will apply for her 1995 tax return. Write a letter to Tammy that contains your advice on whether she should agree to her former husband's proposal. Also prepare a memo for the tax files. Suggested software (if available): WFT tax planning software.

70. Mary Gordon, age 41, is single and has no dependents. Mary's Social Security number is 999–00–1000. Mary resides at 9700 Linkmeadow, Sarasota, FL 33500. She is a self-employed operator of a sole proprietorship. During 1993, gross income from her business was $130,000, and business expenses were $75,000. In addition, she had the

following property transactions related to her business (not reflected in the preceding income and expense figures):

a.	Cash received on February 26, 1993, on trade of a parcel of land on the outskirts of town (held for two years as a site for a new warehouse) for a lot near Mary's store. Mary intends to build a new warehouse on the lot. The old parcel had a fair market value of $28,000 and adjusted basis of $25,000. The fair market value of the new lot was $21,000.	$ 7,000
b.	Condemnation award received on July 11, 1993, from the state for an acre of unimproved land (used for parking delivery vans) adjacent to the store (adjusted basis of the land was $12,000). The land had been purchased on October 3, 1988.	35,000
c.	Cost of an acre of unimproved land (purchased on September 18, 1993) across the street from the store (the land is to be used for parking delivery vans).	28,000

Mary's personal transactions for 1993 were as follows:

d.	Cash received on January 16, 1993, on exchange of 50 shares of Canary Corporation stock (adjusted basis of $20 a share, fair market value of $50 a share) for 50 shares of Tan Corporation stock (fair market value of $40 a share). Canary Corporation and Tan Corporation are not related, and Mary had held the Canary stock for two years.	500
e.	Amount realized on November 14, 1993, on the sale of a condominium Mary used as her personal residence. The condominium, which was built in 1975, was acquired in 1985 as a replacement for the house in which she formerly resided. She paid $65,000 for the condominium, and the amount realized for the house she sold was $80,000 (no fixing-up expenses, and adjusted basis was $50,000). Mary is moving into an apartment and does not intend to replace the condominium.	90,000
f.	Loss of amount Mary loaned to a friend in 1990 (the friend declared bankruptcy in 1993).	3,000
g.	Mary's interest income on personal savings accounts.	1,500
h.	Itemized deductions in 1993.	9,000
i.	Estimated Federal income tax payments.	31,000

Compute Mary's lowest net tax payable or refund due for 1993, assuming Mary makes any available elections that will reduce the tax. If you use tax forms for your computations, you will need Forms 1040, 2119, and 4797 and Schedules A, B, C, D, and SE. [Any gain recognized from item (a), (b), or (c) is § 1231 gain (discussed in Chapter 17), is reported on Form 4797 and Schedule D, and is to be treated as long-term capital gain.] Suggested software (if available): *TurboTax* or *MacInTax* for tax return or WFT tax planning software.

RESEARCH PROBLEMS

Research Problem 1.   Ralph and Agnes have lived in the city since their graduation from college which was over 20 years ago. They decide to move to the country. The adjusted basis of their residence is $85,000. The amount realized on the sale of the residence in July is $250,000. They purchase a farm in July, which has a residence, a barn, and 60 acres of land, for $300,000. Since the cost of the farm exceeds the amount realized on the sale of their residence, they believe that the realized gain on the sale is postponed under § 1034. Determine if their conclusion is correct.

Research Problem 2.   Matt owned 3,000 acres of timberland in Oregon. CZE Corporation offered to purchase the property for $4.5 million. Since the adjusted basis for the land was only $400,000, Matt did not want to have the large recognized gain that would result. CZE Corporation offered to purchase the land on the installment method and thereby spread the recognized gain over the period of the installment payments. Matt rejected the proposal and countered with the following proposal.

- Matt would transfer the land (fair market value of $4.5 million) to CZE Corporation in exchange for a five-year contract under which he would have the right to identify real property that CZE would purchase and transfer to him.

- At the end of the five-year period, the remainder of the $4.5 million that had not been so expended would be transferred to Matt in cash.

- During the five-year period, the amount of the $4.5 million not expended by the end of each year was to be increased by a growth factor of 12% per year.

a. Does the exchange qualify as a like-kind exchange under § 1031?
b. What is the appropriate treatment of the growth factor?

Partial list of research aids:
Starker v. U.S., 75–1 USTC ¶9443, 35 AFTR2d 75–1550 (D.Ct.Ore., 1975).

Research Problem 3.   Joyce owned property that had an adjusted basis of $125,000, of which $100,000 was allocated to the land and $25,000 to the building. The property was condemned by the state, and Joyce received a $275,000 condemnation award. She spent $400,000 for new property, of which $100,000 was allocable to the land and $300,000 to the building. What is the basis of the replacement property, and how is it allocated to the land and the building?

Partial list of research aids:
Reg. § 1.1033(c)–1(a).
Rev.Rul. 73–18, 1973–1 C.B. 368.

Research Problem 4.   You are the general manager of the San Diego Padres, Inc. In order for the Padres to become a serious contender for the pennant, you believe player changes are necessary. Discussions are in progress with the general manager of the Toronto Blue Jays. He has offered to trade Tony Fernandez (an all-star shortstop) and $5 million to the Padres in exchange for Joe Carter (an all-star outfielder) and Roberto Alomar (an all-star second baseman). You have countered by expressing an interest in receiving Fernandez and Fred McGriff (an all-star first baseman) rather than the cash. You believe that if you are going to give up the power provided by Carter, you need to get a power hitter in return (i.e., McGriff). In addition, you vaguely remember from your MBA days that a player trade with no cash involved will provide better tax results. Before you finalize a trade, you need to know the tax consequences. Obtain a written opinion from your CPA on the way you should structure the trade.

16

PROPERTY TRANSACTIONS: CAPITAL GAINS AND LOSSES

LEARNING OBJECTIVES

After completing Chapter 16, you should be able to:

1. Understand the rationale for separate reporting of capital gains and losses.

2. Distinguish capital assets from ordinary assets.

3. Understand the relevance of a sale or exchange to classification as a capital gain or loss and apply the special rules for the capital gain or loss treatment of the retirement of corporate obligations, options, patents, franchises, and lease cancellation payments.

4. Determine whether the holding period for a capital asset is long term or short term.

5. Describe the beneficial tax treatment for capital gains and the detrimental tax treatment for capital losses for both the noncorporate and corporate taxpayer.

6. Identify tax planning opportunities arising from the sale or exchange of capital assets.

General Considerations, 16–2

Rationale for Separate Reporting of Capital Gains and Losses, 16–2

General Scheme of Taxation, 16–3

Capital Assets, 16–3

Definition of a Capital Asset, 16–3

Effect of Judicial Action, 16–6

Statutory Expansions, 16–6

Sale or Exchange, 16–9

Worthless Securities, 16–9

Special Rule—Retirement of Corporate Obligations, 16–9

Options, 16–10

Patents, 16–12

Franchises, Trademarks, and Trade Names, 16–13

Lease Cancellation Payments, 16–15

Holding Period, 16–16

Review of Special Holding Period Rules, 16–17

Special Rules for Short Sales, 16–18

Tax Treatment of Capital Gains and Losses of Noncorporate Taxpayers, 16–20

Treatment of Capital Gains, 16–21

Treatment of Capital Losses, 16–23

Reporting Procedures, 16–24

Tax Treatment of Capital Gains and Losses of Corporate Taxpayers, 16–25

Tax Planning Considerations, 16–27

Importance of Capital Asset Status, 16–27

Planning for Capital Asset Status, 16–27

Effect of Capital Asset Status in Transactions Other Than Sales, 16–28

Stock Sales, 16–29

Maximizing Benefits, 16–29

Year-End Planning, 16–29

General ▼Considerations

RATIONALE FOR SEPARATE REPORTING OF CAPITAL GAINS AND LOSSES

1 Learning Objective
Understand the rationale for separate reporting of capital gains and losses.

Fourteen years ago, a taxpayer purchased 100 shares of IBM stock for $17 a share. This year the taxpayer sells the shares for $97 a share. Should the $80 per share gain receive any special tax treatment? The $80 gain has built up over 14 years, so it may not be fair to tax it the same as income that was all earned this year.

What if the stock had been purchased for $97 per share and sold for $17 a share? Should the loss be fully deductible? The tax law has an intricate approach to answering these investment activity–related questions.

As you study this chapter, keep in mind that how investment-related gains and losses are taxed can dramatically affect whether taxpayers make investments and which investments are made. Except for a brief discussion in Chapter 3, earlier chapters dwelt on how to determine the amount of gain or loss from a property disposition, but did not discuss the classification of gains and losses. This chapter will focus on that topic.

The tax law requires **capital gains** and **capital losses** to be separated from other types of gains and losses. There are two reasons for this treatment. First, long-term capital gains may be taxed at a lower rate than ordinary gains. An *alternative tax computation* is used to determine the tax when taxable income includes net long-term capital gain. Capital gains and losses must therefore be matched with one another to see if a net long-term capital gain exists. The alternative tax computation is discussed in the Tax Treatment of Capital Gains and Losses of Noncorporate Taxpayers portion of this chapter.

Why else does the Code require separate reporting of gains and losses and a determination of their tax character? The second reason is that a net capital loss is only deductible up to $3,000 per year. Excess loss over the annual limit carries over and may be deductible in a future tax year. Capital gains and losses must be matched with one another to see if a net capital loss exists.

For these reasons, capital gains and losses must be distinguished from other types of gains and losses. Most of this chapter and the next chapter describe the intricate rules for determining what type of gains and losses the taxpayer has.

As a result of the need to distinguish and separately match capital gains and losses, the individual tax forms include very extensive reporting requirements for capital gains and losses. This chapter explains the principles underlying the forms. The forms are illustrated with examples at the end of the chapter.

GENERAL SCHEME OF TAXATION

Recognized gains and losses must be properly classified. Proper classification depends upon three characteristics:

- The tax status of the property.
- The manner of the property's disposition.
- The holding period of the property.

The three possible tax statuses are capital asset, § 1231 asset, or ordinary asset. Property disposition may be by sale, exchange, casualty, theft, or condemnation. The two holding periods are one year or less (short term) and more than one year (long term).

The major focus of this chapter is capital gains and losses. Capital gains and losses usually result from the disposition of a capital asset. The most common disposition is a sale of the asset. Capital gains and losses can also result from the disposition of § 1231 assets, which is discussed in Chapter 17.

CAPITAL ASSETS

DEFINITION OF A CAPITAL ASSET

2 LEARNING OBJECTIVE
Distinguish capital assets from ordinary assets.

Personal use assets and investment assets are the most common capital assets owned by individual taxpayers. Personal use assets usually include items such as clothing, recreation equipment, a residence, and automobiles. Investment assets usually include corporate stocks and bonds, government bonds, and vacant land. Remember, however, that losses from the sale or exchange of personal use assets are not recognized. Therefore, the classification of such losses as capital losses can be ignored.

Due to the historical preferential treatment of capital gains, taxpayers have preferred that gains be capital gains rather than ordinary gains. As a result, a great many statutes, cases, and rulings have accumulated in the attempt to define what is and what is not a capital asset.

Capital assets are not directly defined in the Code. Instead, § 1221 defines what is *not* a capital asset. A **capital asset** is property held by the taxpayer (whether or not it is connected with the taxpayer's business) that is *not* any of the following:

- Inventory or property held primarily for sale to customers in the ordinary course of a business. The Supreme Court, in *Malat v. Riddell,* defined *primarily* as meaning *of first importance* or *principally.*[1]

---
[1] 66–1 USTC ¶9317, 17 AFTR2d 604, 86 S.Ct. 1030 (USSC, 1966).

TAX IN THE NEWS

GARAGE SALES AND TAXABLE GAINS

A recent income tax fraud trial involved a "professional garage sale person." The defendant bought items at a very low cost from garage sales in one part of a major city and then resold them at his own monthly "garage sale" in another part of the city. Although he made a very substantial profit, he did not report any income from the garage sales in his Federal income tax return. An IRS agent who lived near the defendant noticed the regular garage sales, chatted with the defendant about what was going on, and then launched a tax fraud investigation.

The taxpayer was convicted, fined, and sentenced to two years' probation. He, of course, had to file amended tax returns and pay back taxes plus interest and penalties. When he filed those amended tax returns, what type of gain should he have reported?

Normally, items sold at garage sales are personal use property. Such property is a capital asset because all personal use property is a capital asset. If the property is sold at a gain, the gain is a capital gain. If the property is sold at a loss, the loss is nondeductible because losses on personal use property are not deductible.

The court concluded that the defendant was in the garage sale business. Thus, the property sold at his sales was inventory and not a capital asset. Consequently, he had ordinary income rather than capital gain.

- Accounts and notes receivable acquired from the sale of inventory or acquired for services rendered in the ordinary course of business.
- Depreciable property or real estate used in a business.
- Certain copyrights; literary, musical, or artistic compositions; or letters, memoranda, or similar property held by (1) a taxpayer whose efforts created the property; (2) in the case of a letter, memorandum, or similar property, a taxpayer for whom it was produced; or (3) a taxpayer in whose hands the basis of the property is determined, for purposes of determining gain from a sale or exchange, in whole or in part by reference to the basis of such property in the hands of a taxpayer described in (1) or (2).
- U.S. government publications that are (1) received by a taxpayer from the U.S. government other than by purchase at the price at which they are offered for sale to the public or (2) held by a taxpayer whose basis, for purposes of determining gain from a sale or exchange, is determined by reference to a taxpayer described in (1).

The Code defines what is not a capital asset. From the preceding list, it is apparent that inventory, accounts and notes receivable, and most fixed assets of a business are not capital assets. The following discussion provides further detail on each part of the capital asset definition.

Inventory

What constitutes inventory is determined by the taxpayer's business.

EXAMPLE 1

Green Company buys and sells used cars. Its cars are inventory. Its gains from sale of the cars are ordinary income. ▼

EXAMPLE 2

Soong sells her personal use automobile at a $500 gain. The automobile is a personal use asset and, therefore, a capital asset. The gain is a capital gain. ▼

Accounts and Notes Receivable

Collection of an accrual basis account receivable usually does not result in a gain or loss because the amount collected equals the receivable's basis. The sale of an account or note receivable may generate a gain or loss, and the gain or loss is ordinary because the receivable is not a capital asset. The sale of an accrual basis receivable may result in a gain or loss because it will probably be sold for more or less than its basis. A cash basis account receivable has no basis. Sale of such a receivable will generate a gain. Collection of a cash basis receivable generates ordinary income rather than a gain. A gain usually requires a sale of the receivable. See the discussion of Sale or Exchange later in this chapter.

EXAMPLE 3

Oriole Company has accounts receivable of $100,000. Because it needs working capital, it sells the receivables for $83,000 to a financial institution. If Oriole is an accrual basis taxpayer, it has a $17,000 ordinary loss. Revenue of $100,000 would have been recorded and a $100,000 basis would have been established when the receivable was created. If Oriole is a cash basis taxpayer, it has $83,000 of ordinary income because it would not have recorded any revenue earlier; thus, the receivable has no tax basis. ▼

Business Fixed Assets

Depreciable personal property and real estate (both depreciable and nondepreciable) used by a business are not capital assets. Thus, *business fixed assets* are generally not capital assets. The Code has a very complex set of rules pertaining to such property. One of these rules is discussed under Real Property Subdivided for Sale in this chapter. Chapter 17 discusses the potential capital gain treatment under § 1231 for business fixed assets.

Copyrights and Creative Works

Generally, the person whose efforts led to the copyright or creative work has an ordinary asset, not a capital asset. *Creative works* include the works of authors, composers, and artists. Also, the person for whom a letter, memorandum, or other similar property was created has an ordinary asset. Finally, a person receiving a copyright, creative work, letter, memorandum, or similar property by gift from the creator or the person for whom the work was created has an ordinary asset.

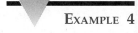

EXAMPLE 4

Wanda is a part-time music composer. A music publisher purchases one of her songs for $5,000. Wanda has a $5,000 ordinary gain from the sale of an ordinary asset. ▼

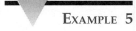

EXAMPLE 5

Ed received a letter from the President of the United States in 1962. In the current year, Ed sells the letter to a collector for $300. Ed has a $300 ordinary gain from the sale of an ordinary asset (because the letter was created for Ed). ▼

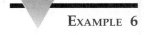

EXAMPLE 6

Isabella gives a song she composed to her son. The son sells the song to a music publisher for $5,000. The son has a $5,000 ordinary gain from the sale of an ordinary asset. If the son inherits the song from Isabella, his basis for the song is its fair market value at Isabella's death. The song is a capital asset because the son's basis is not related to Isabella's basis for the song. ▼

(Patents are subject to special statutory rules discussed later in the chapter.)

U.S. Government Publications

U.S. government publications received from the U.S. government (or its agencies) for a reduced price are not capital assets. This prevents a taxpayer from later donating the publications to charity and claiming a charitable contribution equal to the fair market value of the publications. A charitable contribution of a capital asset generally yields a deduction equal to the fair market value. A charitable contribution of an ordinary asset generally yields a deduction equal to less than the fair market value. If such property is received by gift from the original purchaser, the property is not a capital asset to the donee. (For a more comprehensive explanation of charitable contributions of property, refer to Chapter 10.)

EFFECT OF JUDICIAL ACTION

Court decisions play an important role in the definition of capital assets. Because the Code only lists categories of what are *not* capital assets, judicial interpretation is sometimes required to determine whether a specific item fits into one of those categories. The Supreme Court follows a literal interpretation of the categories. For instance, corporate stock is not mentioned in § 1221. Thus, corporate stock is *usually* a capital asset. However, what if corporate stock is purchased for resale to customers? Then it is *inventory* and not a capital asset because inventory is one of the categories in § 1221. (See the discussion of Dealers in Securities below.) A Supreme Court decision was required to distinguish between capital asset and non-capital asset status when a taxpayer who did not normally acquire stock for resale to customers acquired stock with the intention of resale.[2] The Court decided that since the stock was not acquired primarily for sale to customers (the taxpayer did not sell the stock to its regular customers), the stock was a capital asset.

Often the crux of the capital asset determination hinges on whether the asset is held for investment purposes (capital asset) or business purposes (ordinary asset). The taxpayer's *use* of the property often provides objective evidence.

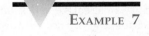

EXAMPLE 7

Ramon's business buys an expensive painting. If the painting is used to decorate Ramon's office and is not of investment quality, the painting is depreciable and, therefore, not a capital asset. If Ramon's business is buying and selling paintings, the painting is inventory and, therefore, an ordinary asset. If the painting is of investment quality and the business purchased it for investment, the painting is a capital asset, even though it serves a decorative purpose in Ramon's office. *Investment quality* generally means that the painting is expected to appreciate in value. ▼

Because of the uncertainty associated with capital asset status, Congress has enacted several Code Sections to clarify the definition. These statutory expansions of the capital asset definition are discussed in the following section.

STATUTORY EXPANSIONS

Congress has often expanded the § 1221 general definition of a capital asset.

---

[2] *Arkansas Best v. Comm.*, 88–1 USTC ¶9210, 61 AFTR2d 88–655, 108 S.Ct. 971 (USSC, 1988).

Dealers in Securities

As a general rule, securities (stocks, bonds, and other financial instruments) held by a dealer are considered to be inventory and are not, therefore, subject to capital gain or loss treatment. A *dealer in securities* is a merchant (e.g., a brokerage firm) that regularly engages in the purchase and resale of securities to customers. The dealer must identify any securities being held for investment. Generally, if a dealer clearly identifies certain securities as held for investment purposes by the close of business on the acquisition date, gain from the securities' sale will be capital gain. However, the gain will not be capital gain if the dealer ceases to hold the securities for investment prior to the sale. Losses are capital losses if at any time the securities have been clearly identified by the dealer as held for investment.[3]

EXAMPLE 8

Tracy is a securities dealer. She purchases 100 shares of Swan stock. If Tracy takes no further action, the stock is inventory and an ordinary asset. If she designates in her records that the stock is held for investment, the stock is a capital asset. Tracy must designate the investment purpose by the close of business on the acquisition date. If Tracy maintains her investment purpose and later sells the stock, the gain or loss is capital gain or loss. If Tracy redesignates the stock as held for resale (inventory) and then sells it, any gain is ordinary, but any loss is capital loss. Stock designated as held for investment and then sold at a loss always yields a capital loss. ▼

Real Property Subdivided for Sale

Substantial real property development activities may result in the owner being considered a dealer for tax purposes. Income from the sale of real estate property lots is treated as the sale of inventory (ordinary income) if the owner is considered to be a dealer. However, § 1237 allows real estate investors capital gain treatment if they engage in *limited* development activities. To be eligible for § 1237 treatment, the following requirements must be met:

- The taxpayer may not be a corporation.
- The taxpayer may not be a real estate dealer.
- No substantial improvements may be made to the lots sold. *Substantial* generally means more than a 10 percent increase in the value of a lot. Shopping centers and other commercial or residential buildings are considered substantial, while filling, draining, leveling, and clearing operations are not.
- The taxpayer must have held the lots sold for at least 5 years, except for inherited property. The substantial improvements test is less stringent if the property is held at least 10 years.

If the preceding requirements are met, all gain is capital gain until the tax year in which the *sixth* lot is sold. Sales of contiguous lots to a single buyer in the same transaction count as the sale of one lot. Beginning with the tax year the *sixth* lot is sold, some of the gain may be ordinary income. Five percent of the revenue from lot sales is potential ordinary income. That potential ordinary income is offset by any selling expenses from the lot sales. Practically, sales commissions often are at least 5 percent of the sales price, so none of the gain is treated as ordinary income.

---

[3]§§ 1236(a) and (b) and Reg. § 1.1236–1(a). Section 107(b)(1) of the Deficit Reduction Act of 1984 authorizes the Treasury to impose earlier identification deadlines than the close of the business day.

The Treasury could also provide by Regulations for a method of identification other than the taxpayer's records. At this writing, such Regulations have not been issued.

ETHICAL
CONSIDERATIONS

Capital Gain Treatment for Real Estate Developments

The difference between long-term capital gain and ordinary gain treatment of gains from subdivided real property can be very significant. The requirements of § 1237 are met only in very limited circumstances. In the rare case where § 1237 applies, the tax return preparer could easily overlook the § 1237 rules and erroneously report as ordinary gain what should be long-term capital gain.

The presence of such a narrow, but potentially crucial, exception to the general rule that inventory is not a capital asset makes the tax preparer's role demanding, frustrating, and useful. Only a knowledgeable tax preparer is likely to know about § 1237 and be able to apply it properly. The existence of the beneficial treatment of § 1237 imposes an additional ethical burden on a taxpayer who normally is a real estate developer to properly report the extent of the development activities so that inventory is not inappropriately classified as qualifying for § 1237 treatment.

Section 1237 does not apply to losses. A loss from the sale of subdivided real property is an ordinary loss unless the property qualifies as a capital asset under § 1221. The following example illustrates the application of § 1237.

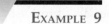

EXAMPLE 9

Ahmed owns a large tract of land and subdivides it for sale. Assume Ahmed meets all the requirements of § 1237 and during the tax year sells the first 10 lots to 10 different buyers for $10,000 each. Ahmed's basis in each lot sold is $3,000, and he incurs total selling expenses of $4,000 on the sales. Ahmed's gain is computed as follows:

Selling price (10 × $10,000)		$100,000	
Basis (10 × $3,000)		(30,000)	
Excess over basis		$ 70,000	
Five percent of selling price	$ 5,000		
Selling expenses	(4,000)		
Amount of ordinary income			$ 1,000
Five percent of selling price	$ 5,000		
Excess of expenses over 5% of selling price	–0–	(5,000)	
Capital gain			65,000
Total gain ($70,000 – $4,000 selling expenses)			$66,000

Lump-Sum Distributions

A *lump-sum distribution* is generally a distribution of an employee's entire qualified pension or profit sharing plan balance within one tax year. The distribution must result from the employee's (1) death, (2) reaching age 59½, or (3) separation from service with an employer. TRA of 1986 repealed a provision that allowed a portion of a lump-sum distribution to be treated as capital gain. However, partial capital gain treatment may still be available because transition rules allow certain taxpayers to continue using prior law. See Chapter 19 for a further discussion of lump-sum distributions.

Nonbusiness Bad Debts

A loan not made in the ordinary course of business is classified as a nonbusiness receivable. In the year the receivable becomes completely worthless, it is a *nonbusiness bad debt,* and the bad debt is treated as a short-term capital loss. Even if the receivable was outstanding for more than one year, the loss is still a short-term capital loss. Chapter 7 discusses nonbusiness bad debts more thoroughly.

SALE OR EXCHANGE

3   LEARNING OBJECTIVE
Understand the relevance of a sale or exchange to classification as a capital gain or loss and apply the special rules for the capital gain or loss treatment of the retirement of corporate obligations, options, patents, franchises, and lease cancellation payments.

Recognition of capital gain or loss usually requires a sale or exchange of a capital asset. The Code uses the term **sale or exchange,** but does not define it. Generally, a property sale involves the receipt of money by the seller and/or the assumption by the purchaser of the seller's liabilities. An exchange involves the transfer of property for other property. Thus, an involuntary conversion (casualty, theft, or condemnation) is not a sale or exchange. In several situations, the determination of whether a sale or exchange has taken place has been clarified by the enactment of Code Sections that specifically provide for sale or exchange treatment.

Recognized gains or losses from the cancellation, lapse, expiration, or any other termination of a right or obligation with respect to personal property (other than stock) that is or would be a capital asset in the hands of the taxpayer are capital gains or losses.[4] See the discussion under Options later in the chapter for more details.

WORTHLESS SECURITIES

Occasionally, securities such as stock and, especially, bonds may become worthless due to the insolvency of their issuer. If such a security is a capital asset, the loss is deemed to have occurred as the result of a sale or exchange on the *last day* of the tax year.[5] This last-day rule may have the effect of converting what otherwise would have been a short-term capital loss into a long-term capital loss. See Treatment of Capital Losses later in this chapter.

Section 1244 allows an ordinary deduction on disposition of stock at a loss. The stock must be that of a small business company, and the ordinary deduction is limited to $50,000 ($100,000 for married individuals filing jointly) per year. For a more detailed discussion, refer to Chapter 7.

SPECIAL RULE—RETIREMENT OF CORPORATE OBLIGATIONS

A debt obligation (e.g., a bond or note payable) may have a tax basis in excess of or less than its redemption value because it may have been acquired at a premium or discount. Consequently, the collection of the redemption value may result in a loss or gain. Generally, the collection of a debt obligation is *not* a sale or exchange. Therefore, any loss or gain cannot be a capital loss or gain because no sale or exchange has taken place. However, if the debt obligation was issued by a corporation or certain government agencies, the collection of the redemption value is treated as a sale or exchange.[6]

---

[4] § 1234A.
[5] § 165(g)(1).

[6] § 1271.

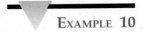

EXAMPLE 10

Fran acquires $1,000 of Osprey Corporation bonds for $980 in the open market. If the bonds are held to maturity, the $20 difference between Fran's collection of the $1,000 maturity value and her cost of $980 is treated as capital gain. If the obligation had been issued to Fran by an individual instead of by a corporation, her $20 gain would be ordinary, since she did not sell or exchange the debt. ▼

Original Issue Discount

The benefit of the sale or exchange exception that allows a capital gain from the collection of certain obligations is reduced when the obligation has original issue discount. **Original issue discount (OID)** arises when the issue price of a debt obligation is less than the maturity value of the obligation. OID must generally be amortized over the life of the debt obligation. The OID amortization increases the basis of the bond. Most new publicly traded bond issues do not carry OID since the stated interest rate is set to make the market price on issue the same as the bond's face amount. In addition, even if the issue price is less than the face amount, the difference is not considered to be OID if the difference is less than one-fourth of 1 percent of the redemption price at maturity multiplied by the number of years to maturity.[7]

In the case where OID does exist, it may or may not have to be amortized, depending upon the date the obligation was issued. When OID is amortized, the amount of gain upon collection, sale, or exchange of the obligation is correspondingly reduced. The obligations covered by the OID amortization rules and the method of amortization are presented in §§ 1272–1275. Similar rules for other obligations can be found in §§ 1276–1288.

EXAMPLE 11

Jane purchases $10,000 of newly issued White Corporation bonds for $6,000. The bonds have OID of $4,000. Jane must amortize the discount over the life of the bonds. The OID amortization *increases* Jane's interest income. (The bonds were selling at a discount because the market rate of interest was greater than the bonds' interest rate.) After Jane has amortized $1,800 of OID, she sells the bonds for $8,000. Jane has a capital gain of $200 [$8,000 − ($6,000 cost + $1,800 OID amortization)]. The OID amortization rules prevent Jane from converting ordinary interest income into capital gain. Without the OID amortization, Jane would have capital gain of $2,000 ($8,000 − $6,000 cost). ▼

OPTIONS

Frequently, a potential buyer of property wants some time to make the purchase decision, but wants to control the sale and/or the sale price in the meantime. **Options** are used to achieve these objectives. The potential purchaser (grantee) pays the property owner (grantor) for an option on the property. The grantee then becomes the option holder. The option usually sets a price at which the grantee can buy the property and expires after a specified period of time.

Sale of an Option

A grantee may sell or exchange the option rather than exercising it or letting it expire. Generally, the grantee's sale or exchange of the option results in capital gain or loss if the option property is (or would be) a capital asset to the grantee.[8]

---

[7] § 1273(a)(3).
[8] § 1234(a) and Reg. § 1.1234–1(a)(1). Stock options are discussed in Chapter 19.

▼

EXAMPLE 12

Rosa wants to buy some vacant land for investment purposes. She cannot afford the full purchase price. Instead, she convinces the landowner (grantor) to sell her the right to purchase the land for $100,000 anytime in the next two years. Rosa (grantee) pays $3,000 to obtain this option to buy the land. The option is a capital asset for Rosa because if she actually purchased the land, the land would be a capital asset. Three months after purchasing the option, Rosa sells it for $7,000. She has a $4,000 short-term capital gain on this sale since she held the option for one year or less. ▼

Failure to Exercise Options

If an option holder (grantee) fails to exercise the option, the lapse of the option is considered a sale or exchange on the option expiration date. Thus, the loss is a capital loss if the property subject to the option is (or would be) a capital asset in the hands of the grantee.

The grantor of an option on *stocks, securities, commodities, or commodity futures* receives short-term capital gain treatment upon the expiration of the option. Options on property other than stocks, securities, commodities, or commodity futures result in ordinary income to the grantor when the option expires. For example, an individual investor who owns certain stock (a capital asset) may sell a call option, entitling the buyer of the option to acquire the stock at a specified price higher than the value at the date the option is granted. The writer of the call receives a premium (e.g., 10 percent) for writing the option. If the price of the stock does not increase during the option period, the option will expire unexercised. Upon the expiration of the option, the grantor must recognize short-term capital gain. These provisions do not apply to options held for sale to customers (the inventory of a securities dealer).

Exercise of Options by Grantee

If the option is exercised, the amount paid for the option is added to the optioned property's selling price. This increases the gain (or reduces the loss) to the grantor resulting from the sale of the property. The grantor's gain or loss is capital or ordinary depending on the tax status of the property. The grantee adds the cost of the option to the basis of the property purchased.

▼

EXAMPLE 13

On September 1, 1988, Wes purchases 100 shares of Eagle Company stock for $5,000. On April 1, 1994, he writes a call option on the stock, giving the grantee the right to buy the stock for $6,000 during the following six-month period. Wes (the grantor) receives a call premium of $500 for writing the call.

- If the call is exercised by the grantee on August 1, 1994, Wes has $1,500 ($6,000 + $500 – $5,000) of long-term capital gain from the sale of the stock. The grantee has a $6,500 ($500 option premium + $6,000 purchase price) basis for the stock.
- Assume that Wes decides to sell his stock prior to exercise for $6,000 and enters into a closing transaction by purchasing a call on 100 shares of Eagle Company stock for $5,000. Since the Eagle stock is selling for $6,000, Wes must pay a call premium of $1,000. He recognizes a $500 short-term capital loss [$1,000 (call premium paid) – $500 (call premium received)] on the closing transaction. On the actual sale of the Eagle stock, Wes has a long-term capital gain of $1,000 [$6,000 (selling price) – $5,000 (cost)]. The grantee is not affected by Wes's closing transaction. The original option is still in existence, and the grantee's tax consequences will depend on what action the grantee takes—exercising the option, letting the option expire, or selling the option.
- Assume that the original option expired unexercised. Wes has a $500 short-term capital gain equal to the call premium received for writing the option. This gain is

not recognized until the option expires. The grantee has a loss from expiration of the option. The nature of the loss will depend upon whether the option was a capital asset or an ordinary asset. ▼

PATENTS

Transfer of a **patent** is treated as the sale or exchange of a long-term capital asset when all substantial rights to the patent (or an undivided interest that includes all such rights) are transferred by a holder.[9] The transferor/holder may receive payment in virtually any form. Lump-sum or periodic payments are most common. The amount of the payments also may be contingent on the transferee/purchaser's productivity, use, or disposition of the patent. If the transfer meets these requirements, any gain or loss is *automatically* a *long-term* capital gain or loss. Whether the asset was a capital asset for the transferor, whether a sale or exchange occurred, and how long the transferor held the patent are not relevant.

This special long-term capital gain or loss treatment for patents is intended to encourage technological progress. Ironically, authors, composers, and artists are not eligible for capital gain treatment when their creations are transferred. Books, songs, and artists' works may be copyrighted, but copyrights and the assets they represent are not capital assets. Thus, the disposition of those assets by their creators usually results in ordinary gain or loss. The following example illustrates the special treatment for patents.

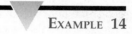

EXAMPLE 14

Mei-Yen, a druggist, invents a pill-counting machine, which she patents. In consideration of a lump-sum payment of $200,000 plus $10 per machine sold, Mei-Yen assigns the patent to Drug Products, Inc. Assuming Mei-Yen has transferred all substantial rights, the question of whether the transfer is a sale or exchange of a capital asset is not relevant. Mei-Yen automatically has a long-term capital gain from both the lump-sum payment and the $10 per machine royalty to the extent these proceeds exceed her basis for the patent. ▼

CONCEPT SUMMARY 16–1

Options

Event	Effect on Grantor	Effect on Grantee
Option is granted.	Receives value and has a contract obligation (a liability).	Pays value and has a contract right (an asset).
Option expires.	Has a short-term capital gain if the option property is stocks, securities, commodities, or commodity futures. Otherwise, gain is ordinary income.	Has a loss (capital loss if option property would have been a capital asset for the grantee).
Option is exercised.	Amount received for option increases proceeds from sale of the option property.	Amount paid for option becomes part of the basis of the option property purchased.
Option is sold or exchanged by grantee.	Result depends upon whether option later expires or is exercised (see above).	Could have gain or loss (capital gain or loss if option property would have been a capital asset for the grantee).

---

[9]§ 1235.

Substantial Rights

To receive favorable capital gain treatment, all *substantial rights* to the patent (or an undivided interest in it) must be transferred. All substantial rights to a patent means all rights (whether or not then held by the grantor) that are valuable at the time the patent rights (or an undivided interest in the patent) are transferred. All substantial rights have not been transferred when the transfer is limited geographically within the issuing country or when the transfer is for a period less than the remaining life of the patent. The circumstances of the entire transaction, rather than merely the language used in the transfer instrument, are to be considered in deciding whether all substantial rights have been transferred.[10]

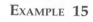

EXAMPLE 15

Assume Mei-Yen, the druggist in Example 14, only licensed Drug Products, Inc., to manufacture and sell the invention in Michigan. She retained the right to license the machine elsewhere in the United States. Mei-Yen has retained a substantial right and is not eligible for automatic long-term capital gain treatment. ▼

Holder Defined

The *holder* of a patent must be an *individual* and is usually the invention's creator. A holder may also be an individual who purchases the patent rights from the creator before the patented invention is reduced to practice. However, the creator's employer and certain parties related to the creator do not qualify as holders. Thus, in the common situation where an employer has all rights to an employee's inventions, the employer is not eligible for long-term capital gain treatment. More than likely, the employer will have an ordinary asset because the patent was developed as part of its business.

FRANCHISES, TRADEMARKS, AND TRADE NAMES

A mode of operation, a widely recognized brand name (trade name), and a widely known business symbol (trademark) are all valuable assets. These assets may be licensed (commonly known as franchising) by their owner for use by other

---

[10] Reg. § 1.1235–2(b)(1).

businesses. Many fast-food restaurants are franchises. The franchisee usually pays the owner (franchisor) an initial fee plus a contingent fee. The contingent fee is often based upon the franchisee's sales volume.

For Federal income tax purposes, a **franchise** is an agreement that gives the franchisee the right to distribute, sell, or provide goods, services, or facilities within a specified area.[11] A franchise transfer includes the grant of a franchise, transfers by one franchisee to another person, or the renewal of a franchise.

A franchise transfer is generally not a sale or exchange of a capital asset. Section 1253 provides that a transfer of a patent, trademark, or trade name is not a transfer of a capital asset when the transferor retains any significant power, right, or continuing interest in the property transferred.

Significant Power, Right, or Continuing Interest

Significant powers, rights, or continuing interests include control over assignment, quality of products and services, sale or advertising of other products or services, and the right to require that substantially all supplies and equipment be purchased from the transferor. Also included are the right to terminate the franchise at will and the right to substantial contingent payments. Most modern franchising operations involve some or all of these powers, rights, or continuing interests.

In the unusual case where no significant power, right, or continuing interest is retained by the transferor, a sale or exchange may occur, and capital gain or loss treatment may be available. For capital gain or loss treatment to be available, the asset transferred must qualify as a capital asset.

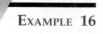

EXAMPLE 16

Orange, Inc., a franchisee, sells the franchise to a third party. Payments to Orange are not contingent, and all significant powers, rights, and continuing interests are transferred. The gain (payments – adjusted basis) on the sale is a capital gain to Orange. ▼

Noncontingent Payments

When the transferor retains a significant power, right, or continuing interest, the transferee's noncontingent payments to the transferor will be ordinary income to

---

[11] § 1253(b)(1).

the transferor. The franchisee capitalizes the payments and amortizes them over 15 years. The amortization is subject to recapture under § 1245.[12]

EXAMPLE 17

Grey Company signs a 10-year franchise agreement with DOH Donuts. Grey (the franchisee) makes payments of $3,000 per year for the first 8 years of the franchise agreement—a total of $24,000. Grey cannot deduct $3,000 per year as the payments are made. Instead, Grey may amortize the $24,000 total over 15 years. Thus, Grey may deduct $1,600 per year for each of the 15 years of the amortization period. The same result would occur if Grey made a $24,000 lump-sum payment at the beginning of the franchise period. Assuming DOH Donuts (the franchisor) retains significant powers, rights, or a continuing interest, it will have ordinary income when it receives the payments from Grey. ▼

Contingent Payments

Whether or not the tranferor retains a significant power, right, or continuing interest, contingent franchise payments are ordinary income for the franchisor and an ordinary deduction for the franchisee. For this purpose, a payment qualifies as a contingent payment only if the following requirements are met:

- The contingent amounts are part of a series of payments that are paid at least annually throughout the term of the transfer agreement.
- The payments are substantially equal in amount or are payable under a fixed formula.

EXAMPLE 18

TAK, a spicy chicken franchisor, transfers an eight-year franchise to Otis. TAK retains a significant power, right, or continuing interest. Otis, the franchisee, agrees to pay TAK 15% of sales. This contingent payment is ordinary income to TAK and a business deduction for Otis as the payments are made. ▼

Sports Franchises

Professional sports franchises (e.g., the Detroit Tigers) are not covered by § 1253.[13] However, § 1056 restricts the allocation of sports franchise acquisition costs to player contracts. Player contracts are usually one of the major assets acquired with a sports franchise. These contracts last only for the time stated in the contract. Therefore, owners of sports franchises would like to allocate franchise acquisition costs disproportionately to the contracts so that the acquisition costs will be amortizable over the contracts' lives. Section 1056 prevents this by generally limiting the amount that can be allocated to player contracts to no more than 50 percent of the franchise acquisition cost. In addition, the seller of the sports franchise has ordinary income under § 1245 for the portion of the gain allocable to the disposition of player contracts.[14]

LEASE CANCELLATION PAYMENTS

The tax treatment of payments received for canceling a lease depends on whether the recipient is the **lessor** or the **lessee** and whether the lease is a capital asset or not.

---

[12] See Chapter 17 for a discussion of the recapture provisions.
[13] § 1253(e).

[14] See Chapter 17 for a discussion of the recapture provisions.

Lessee Treatment

Lease cancellation payments received by a lessee are treated as an exchange.[15] Thus, these payments may be capital gains if the lease is a capital asset. Generally, a lessee's lease is a capital asset if the property (either personalty or realty) is used for the lessee's personal use (e.g., his or her residence). A lessee's lease is an ordinary asset if the property is used in the lessee's trade or business.[16]

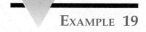

EXAMPLE 19

Mark owns an apartment building that he is going to convert into an office building. Vicki is one of the apartment tenants and receives $1,000 from Mark to cancel the lease. Vicki has a capital gain of $1,000 (which will be long term or short term depending upon how long she has held the lease). Mark has an ordinary deduction of $1,000. ▼

Lessor Treatment

Payments received by a lessor for a lease cancellation are always ordinary income because they are considered to be in lieu of rental payments.[17]

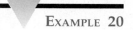

EXAMPLE 20

Floyd owns an apartment building near a university campus. Hui-Fen is one of the tenants. Hui-Fen is graduating early and offers Floyd $800 to cancel the apartment lease. Floyd accepts the offer. Floyd has ordinary income of $800. Hui-Fen has a nondeductible payment since the apartment was personal use property. ▼

HOLDING PERIOD

4   LEARNING OBJECTIVE
Determine whether the holding period for a capital asset is long term or short term.

Property must be held more than one year to qualify for long-term capital gain or loss treatment.[18] Property not held for the required long-term period will result in short-term capital gain or loss. To compute the **holding period,** start counting on the day after the property was acquired and include the day of disposition.

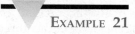

EXAMPLE 21

Marge purchases a capital asset on January 15, 1993, and sells it on January 16, 1994. Marge's holding period is more than one year. If Marge had sold the asset on January 15, 1994, the holding period would have been exactly one year, and the gain or loss would have been short term. ▼

To be held for more than one year, a capital asset acquired on the last day of any month must not be disposed of until on or after the first day of the thirteenth succeeding month.[19]

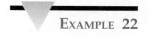

EXAMPLE 22

Leo purchases a capital asset on February 28, 1993. If Leo sells the asset on February 28, 1994, the holding period is one year, and Leo will have a short-term capital gain or loss. If Leo sells the asset on March 1, 1994, the holding period is more than one year, and he will have a long-term capital gain or loss. ▼

---

[15] § 1241 and Reg. § 1.1241–1(a).
[16] Reg. § 1.1221–1(b).
[17] *Hort v. Comm.,* 41–1 USTC ¶9354, 25 AFTR 1207, 61 S.Ct. 757 (USSC, 1941).

[18] § 1222.
[19] Rev.Rul. 66–7, 1966–1 C.B. 188.

REVIEW OF SPECIAL HOLDING PERIOD RULES

There are several special holding period rules.[20] The application of these rules depends on the type of asset and how it was acquired.

Nontaxable Exchanges

The holding period of property received in a like-kind exchange includes the holding period of the former asset if the property that has been exchanged is a capital asset or a § 1231 asset. In certain nontaxable transactions involving a substituted basis, the holding period of the former property is *tacked on* to the holding period of the newly acquired property.

EXAMPLE 23

Vern exchanges a business truck for another truck in a like-kind exchange. The holding period of the exchanged truck tacks on to the holding period of the new truck. ▼

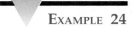
EXAMPLE 24

Alicia sells her personal residence and acquires a new residence. If the transaction qualifies for nonrecognition of gain on the sale of a residence, the holding period of the new residence includes the holding period of the former residence. ▼

Certain Nontaxable Transactions Involving a Carryover of Another Taxpayer's Basis

A former owner's holding period is tacked on to the present owner's holding period if the transaction is nontaxable and the former owner's basis carries over to the present owner.

EXAMPLE 25

Kareem acquires 100 shares of Robin Corporation stock for $1,000 on December 31, 1989. He transfers the shares by gift to Megan on December 31, 1993, when the stock is worth $2,000. Kareem's basis of $1,000 becomes the basis for determining gain or loss on a subsequent sale by Megan. Megan's holding period begins with the date the stock was acquired by Kareem. ▼

EXAMPLE 26

Assume the same facts as in Example 25, except that the fair market value of the shares is only $800 on the date of the gift. The holding period begins on the date of the gift if Megan sells the stock for a loss. The value of the shares at the date of the gift is used in the determination of basis. If she sells the shares for $500 on April 1, 1994, Megan has a $300 recognized capital loss, and the holding period is from December 31, 1993, to April 1, 1994 (thus, the loss is short term). ▼

Certain Disallowed Loss Transactions

Under several Code provisions, realized losses are disallowed. When a loss is disallowed, there is no carryover of holding period. Losses can be disallowed under § 267 (sale or exchange between related taxpayers) and § 262 (sale or exchange of personal use assets) as well as other Code Sections. Taxpayers who acquire property in a disallowed loss transaction will have a new holding period begin and will have a basis equal to the purchase price.

---

[20] § 1223.

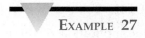

EXAMPLE 27

Janet sells her personal residence at a loss. She may not deduct the loss because it arises from the sale of personal use property. Janet purchases a replacement residence for more than the selling price of her former residence. Janet has a basis equal to the cost of the replacement residence, and her holding period begins when she acquires the replacement residence. ▼

Inherited Property

The holding period for inherited property is treated as long term no matter how long the property is actually held by the heir. The holding period of the decedent or the decedent's estate is not relevant for the heir's holding period.

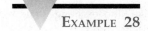

EXAMPLE 28

Shonda inherits Blue Company stock from her father. She receives the stock on April 1, 1994, and sells it on November 1, 1994. Even though the stock was not held more than one year, Shonda receives long-term capital gain or loss treatment on the sale. ▼

SPECIAL RULES FOR SHORT SALES

The holding period of property sold short is determined under special rules provided in § 1233. A **short sale** occurs when a taxpayer sells borrowed property and repays the lender with substantially identical property either held on the date of the sale or purchased after the sale. Short sales usually involve corporate stock. The seller's objective is to make a profit in anticipation of a decline in the stock's price. If the price declines, the seller in a short sale recognizes a profit equal to the difference between the sales price of the borrowed stock and the price paid for the replacement stock.

A *short sale against the box* occurs when the stock is borrowed from a broker by a seller who already owns the same stock. The *box* is the safe deposit box where stock owners routinely used to keep stock certificates. Although today stockbrokers generally keep stock certificates for their customers, the terminology short sale against the box is still used.

EXAMPLE 29

Chris does not own any shares of Brown Corporation. However, Chris sells 30 shares of Brown. The shares are borrowed from Chris's broker and must be replaced within 45 days. Chris has a short sale because he was short the shares he sold. He will *close* the short sale by purchasing Brown shares and delivering them to his broker. If the original 30 shares were sold for $10,000 and Chris later purchases 30 shares for $8,000, he will have a gain of $2,000. Chris's hunch that the price of Brown stock would decline was correct. Chris was able to profit from selling high and buying low. If Chris had to purchase Brown shares for $13,000 to close the short sale, he would have a loss of $3,000. In this case, Chris has sold low and bought high—not the result he wanted! Chris would be making a short sale against the box if he borrowed shares from his broker to sell and then closed the short sale by delivering other Brown shares he owned at the time he made the short sale. ▼

A short sale gain or loss is a capital gain or loss to the extent that the short sale property constitutes a capital asset of the taxpayer. The gain or loss is not recognized until the short sale is closed. Generally, the holding period of the short sale property is determined by how long the property used to close the short sale was held. However, if *substantially identical property* (e.g., other shares of the same stock) is held by the taxpayer, the short-term or long-term character of the short sale gain or loss may be affected:

- If substantially identical property has *not* been held for the long-term holding period on the short sale date, the short sale *gain or loss* is short term.

- If substantially identical property has *been* held for the long-term holding period on the short sale date, the short sale *gain* is long term if the substantially identical property is used to close the short sale and short term if it is not used to close the short sale.
- If substantially identical property has *been* held for the long-term holding period on the short sale date, the short sale *loss* is long term whether or not the substantially identical property is used to close the short sale.
- If substantially identical property is acquired *after* the short sale date and on or before the closing date, the short sale *gain or loss* is short term.

Concept Summary 16–2 summarizes the short sale rules.

The short sale rules are intended to prevent the conversion of short-term capital gains into long-term capital gains and long-term capital losses into short-term capital losses. The following examples illustrate the application of the short sale rules.

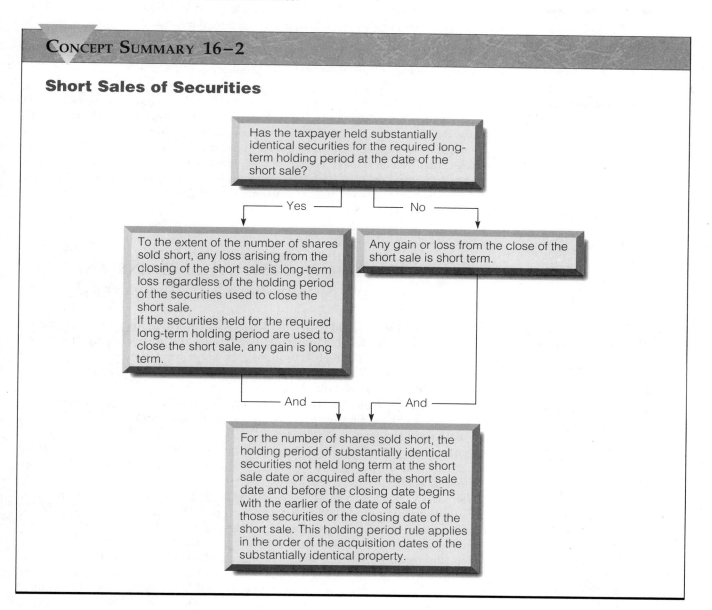

CONCEPT SUMMARY 16–2

Short Sales of Securities

Has the taxpayer held substantially identical securities for the required long-term holding period at the date of the short sale?

— Yes —

To the extent of the number of shares sold short, any loss arising from the closing of the short sale is long-term loss regardless of the holding period of the securities used to close the short sale.
If the securities held for the required long-term holding period are used to close the short sale, any gain is long term.

— No —

Any gain or loss from the close of the short sale is short term.

— And —   — And —

For the number of shares sold short, the holding period of substantially identical securities not held long term at the short sale date or acquired after the short sale date and before the closing date begins with the earlier of the date of sale of those securities or the closing date of the short sale. This holding period rule applies in the order of the acquisition dates of the substantially identical property.

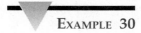

EXAMPLE 30

On January 4, 1994, Donald purchases five shares of Osprey Corporation common stock for $100. On April 14, 1994, he engages in a short sale of five shares of the same stock for $150. On August 15, Donald closes the short sale by repaying the borrowed stock with the five shares purchased on January 4. Donald has a $50 short-term capital gain from the short sale because he had not held substantially identical shares for the long-term holding period on the short sale date. ▼

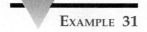

EXAMPLE 31

Assume the same facts as in the previous example, except that Donald closes the short sale on January 28, 1995, by repaying the borrowed stock with five shares purchased on January 27, 1995, for $200. The stock used to close the short sale was not the property purchased on January 4, 1994, but since Donald held short-term property at the April 14, 1994, short sale date, the gain or loss from closing the short sale is short term. Donald has a $50 short-term capital loss ($200 cost of stock purchased January 27, 1995, and a short sale selling price of $150). ▼

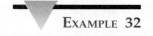

EXAMPLE 32

Assume the same facts as in Example 31. On January 31, 1995, Donald sells for $200 the stock purchased January 4, 1994. Donald's holding period for that stock begins January 28, 1995, because the holding period portion of the short sale rules applies to the substantially identical property in order of acquisition. Donald has a short-term capital gain of $100 ($100 cost of stock purchased January 4, 1994, and a selling price of $200). ▼

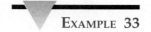

EXAMPLE 33

On January 4, 1994, Rita purchases five shares of Owl Corporation common stock for $100. She purchases five more shares of the same stock on April 14, 1994, for $200. On January 17, 1995, she sells short five shares of the same stock for $150. On September 30, 1995, she repays the borrowed stock with the five shares purchased on April 14, 1994, and sells the five shares purchased on January 4, 1994, for $200. Rita has a $50 long-term capital loss from the short sale because she held substantially identical shares for more than one year on the date of the short sale. Rita has a $100 long-term capital gain from the sale of the shares purchased on January 4, 1994. ▼

TAX TREATMENT OF CAPITAL GAINS AND LOSSES OF NONCORPORATE TAXPAYERS

5 ▼ **LEARNING OBJECTIVE**
Describe the beneficial tax treatment for capital gains and the detrimental tax treatment for capital losses for both the noncorporate and corporate taxpayer.

All taxpayers net their capital gains and losses. Short-term gains and losses (if any) are netted against one another, and long-term gains and losses (if any) are netted against one another. The results will be net short-term gain or loss and net long-term gain or loss. If these two net positions are of opposite sign (one is a gain and one is a loss), they are netted against one another.

Six possibilities exist for the result after all possible netting has been completed. Three of these final results are gains, and three are losses. One possible result is a net long-term capital gain (NLTCG). Net long-term capital gains of noncorporate taxpayers are subject to beneficial treatment. A second possibility is a net short-term capital gain (NSTCG). Third, the netting may result in both NLTCG and NSTCG.

The NLTCG portion of these net results is subject to a 28 percent maximum tax rate. Since the maximum individual tax rate on non-NLTCG (ordinary income and NSTCG) income is 39.6 percent, the 28 percent maximum tax rate on NLTCG may reduce the tax rate by as much as 11.6 percentage points. The alternative tax computation (discussed in the next section of this chapter) is used to get this tax saving.

The last three results of the capital gain and loss netting process are losses. Thus, a fourth possibility is a net long-term capital loss (NLTCL). A fifth result is a net short-term capital loss (NSTCL). Finally, a sixth possibility includes both an

NLTCL and an NSTCL. Neither NLTCLs nor NSTCLs are treated as ordinary losses. Treatment as an ordinary loss generally is preferable to capital loss treatment since ordinary losses are deductible in full while the deductibility of capital losses is subject to certain limitations. An individual taxpayer may deduct a maximum of $3,000 of net capital losses for a taxable year.[21]

TREATMENT OF CAPITAL GAINS

Computation of Net Capital Gain

As just discussed, the *first step* in the computation is to net all long-term capital gains and losses and all short-term capital gains and losses. The result is the taxpayer's net long-term capital gain (NLTCG) or loss (NLTCL) and net short-term capital gain (NSTCG) or loss (NSTCL).

▼ **EXAMPLE 34**

Some possible results of the first step in netting capital gains and losses are shown below. Assume that each case is independent (assume the taxpayer's only capital gains and losses are those shown in the given case).

Case	STCG	STCL	LTCG	LTCL	Result of Netting	Description of Result
A	$8,000	($5,000)			$3,000	NSTCG
B	2,000	(7,000)			(5,000)	NSTCL
C			$9,000	($1,000)	8,000	NLTCG
D			8,800	(9,800)	(1,000)	NLTCL

▼

The *second step* in netting capital gains and losses requires offsetting any positive and negative amounts that remain after the first netting step. This procedure is illustrated in the following examples.

▼ **EXAMPLE 35**

Assume that Sanjay had all the capital gains and losses specified in Cases B and C in Example 34:

Case C ($9,000 LTCG – $1,000 LTCL)	$ 8,000	NLTCG
Case B ($2,000 STCG – $7,000 STCL)	(5,000)	NSTCL
Excess of NLTCG over NSTCL	$ 3,000	

▼

The excess of NLTCG over NSTCL is defined as **net capital gain (NCG).** The result in Example 35 is a $3,000 NCG. There is an alternative tax computation when taxable income includes a NCG. The alternative tax computation taxes the NCG component of taxable income at a maximum tax rate of 28 percent. When taxable income including the NCG does not put the taxpayer into at least the 31 percent rate bracket, the alternative tax computation does not yield a tax benefit.

The NCG **alternative tax** is the summation of the following computations. It is illustrated in Example 36.

1. The tax computed using the regular rates on the greater of:
   a. Taxable income less the NCG, or
   b. The amount of taxable income taxed at a rate below 28 percent, plus
2. Twenty-eight percent of taxable income in excess of taxable income used in (1).

---

[21] § 1211(b).

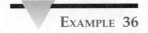

EXAMPLE 36

Tim, an unmarried taxpayer, has taxable income (TI) of $175,000. The TI includes NCG of $50,000. Tim's regular tax liability for 1994 is $52,639 [($22,750 × 15%) + 28%($55,100 − $22,750) + 31%($115,000 − $55,100) + 36%($175,000 − $115,000)]. His alternative tax on the NCG is calculated as follows:

1. Tax on greater of:
    a. TI less NCG ($175,000 − $50,000)
    b. TI taxed below 28% ($22,750), plus $34,639

2. 28% of TI exceeding TI used in (1)
    [28% × ($175,000 − $125,000)]   14,000

Alternative tax on TI including NCG $48,639

The NCG alternative tax saves Tim $4,000 ($52,639 − $48,639) in 1994. ▼

There is no special name for the excess of NSTCG over NLTCL, nor is there any special tax treatment. The nature of the gain is short term, and the gain is treated the same as ordinary gain and is included in the taxpayer's gross income.

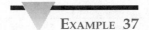

EXAMPLE 37

Assume that Nora had all the capital gains and losses specified in Cases A and D in Example 34:

Case A ($8,000 STCG − $5,000 STCL)	$ 3,000	NSTCG
Case D ($8,800 LTCG − $9,800 LTCL)	(1,000)	NLTCL
Excess of NSTCG over NLTCL	$ 2,000	

ETHICAL CONSIDERATIONS

Indexing Long-Term Capital Gains for Inflation

Tim, an economist, purchased a lot in a planned community for $100,000 in 1984. His intent at that time was to hold the land for investment. During the period from 1974 to 1984, golf course lots in the planned community had appreciated by 200 percent.

Each year Tim pays real property taxes of $1,000 to the county. In addition, he pays $1,200 annually to the homeowners' association for maintenance of the community, security, and garbage collection. He deducts the property taxes on his Federal income tax return and capitalizes the homeowners' association fee.

Tim sells the lot at the end of 1994 for $160,000. Inflation for the 10-year period has been 30 percent. Tim is aware that the Internal Revenue Code of 1986 includes a number of statutory indexing provisions. Although one is not specifically provided for capital asset transactions, Tim feels that the appropriate way for the sale of the land to be taxed is as follows:

Adjusted basis of land:	
Cost	$100,000
Homeowners' association fees ($1,200 × 10 years)	12,000
Inflation adjustment ($100,000 × 30%)	30,000
	$142,000
Amount realized	$160,000
Adjusted basis	(142,000)
Recognized gain	$ 18,000

Since Tim's marginal tax rate is 28 percent, his tax liability associated with the sales transaction is $5,040 ($18,000 × 28%).

TREATMENT OF CAPITAL LOSSES

Computation of Net Capital Loss

A **net capital loss (NCL)** results if capital losses exceed capital gains for the year. An NCL may be all long term, all short term, or part long and part short term.[22] The characterization of an NCL as long or short term is important in determining the capital loss deduction (discussed later in this chapter).

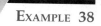

EXAMPLE 38
Three different individual taxpayers have the following capital gains and losses during the year:

Taxpayer	LTCG	LTCL	STCG	STCL	Result of Netting	Description of Result
Robert	$1,000	($2,800)	$1,000	($500)	($1,300)	NLTCL
Carlos	1,000	(500)	1,000	(2,800)	(1,300)	NSTCL
Troy	400	(1,200)	500	(1,200)	(1,500)	NLTCL ($800)
						NSTCL ($700)

Robert's NCL of $1,300 is all long term. Carlos's NCL of $1,300 is all short term. Troy's NCL is $1,500, $800 of which is long term and $700 of which is short term. ▼

Treatment of Net Capital Loss

An NCL is deductible from gross income to the extent of $3,000 per tax year.[23] Capital losses exceeding the loss deduction limits carry forward indefinitely. Thus, although there may or may not be beneficial treatment for capital gains, there is *unfavorable* treatment for capital losses in terms of the $3,000 annual limitation on deducting NCL against ordinary income. If the NCL includes both long-term and short-term capital loss, the short-term capital loss is counted first toward the $3,000 annual limitation.

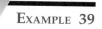

EXAMPLE 39
Burt has an NCL of $5,000, of which $2,000 is STCL and $3,000 is LTCL. Burt has a capital loss deduction of $3,000 ($2,000 of STCL and $1,000 of LTCL) with an LTCL carryforward of $2,000. ▼

Carryovers

Taxpayers are allowed to carry over unused capital losses indefinitely. The STCL and LTCL carried over retain their character as STCL or LTCL.

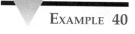

EXAMPLE 40
In 1993, Yoon incurred $1,000 of STCL and $11,000 of LTCL. In 1994, Yoon has a $400 LTCG.

- Yoon's NCL for 1993 is $12,000. Yoon deducts $3,000 ($1,000 STCL and $2,000 LTCL). He has $9,000 of LTCL carried forward to 1994.
- Yoon combines the $9,000 LTCL carryforward with the $400 LTCG for 1994. He has an $8,600 NLTCL for 1994. Yoon deducts $3,000 of LTCL in 1994 and carries forward $5,600 of LTCL to 1995. ▼

---

[22] Section 1222(10) defines a net capital loss as the net loss after the capital loss deduction. However, that definition confuses the discussion of net capital loss. Therefore, net capital loss is used here to mean the result after netting capital gains and losses and before

considering the capital loss deduction. The capital loss deduction is discussed under Treatment of Net Capital Loss in this chapter.
[23] § 1211(b)(1). Married persons filing separate returns are limited to a $1,500 deduction per taxable year.

When a taxpayer has both a capital loss deduction and negative taxable income, a special computation of the capital loss carryover is required.[24] Specifically, the capital loss carryover is the NCL minus the lesser of:

- The capital loss deduction claimed on the return.
- The negative taxable income increased by the capital loss deduction claimed on the return and the personal and dependency exemption deduction.

Without this provision, some of the tax benefit of the capital loss deduction would be wasted when the deduction drives taxable income below zero.

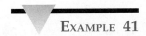

EXAMPLE 41

In 1994, Joanne has a $13,000 NCL (all long term), a $2,450 personal exemption deduction, and $4,000 negative taxable income. The negative taxable income includes a $3,000 capital loss deduction. The capital loss carryover to 1995 is $11,550 computed as follows:

- The $4,000 negative taxable income is treated as a negative number, but the capital loss deduction and personal exemption deduction are treated as positive numbers.
- $13,000 – the lesser of $3,000 (capital loss deduction) or $1,450 [– $4,000 (negative taxable income) + $3,000 (capital loss deduction) + $2,450 (personal exemption deduction)] = $13,000 – $1,450 = $11,550 carryover. ▼

REPORTING PROCEDURES

The following discusses only 1993 tax forms because the 1994 tax forms were not available at the time of this writing.

Capital gains and losses are reported on Schedule D of the 1993 Form 1040 (reproduced on page 16–26). Part I of Schedule D is used to report short-term capital gains and losses. Part II of Schedule D is used to report long-term capital gains and losses. Part III summarizes the results of Parts I and II. Part IV lists

---

CONCEPT SUMMARY 16–3

Noncorporate Taxpayer's Treatment of Net Capital Gain or Loss

Net Capital Gain Treatment Summarized

1. All long-term capital gain	28% alternative tax is available, but is not always beneficial.
2. All short-term capital gain	Taxable as ordinary income.
3. Part long-term and part short-term capital gain	Short-term capital gain portion taxable as ordinary income. 28% alternative tax is available for long-term capital gain portion, but is not always beneficial.

Net Capital Loss Treatment Summarized

4. All long-term capital loss	$1 of loss used to make $1 of deduction. Deduction is *for* AGI and limited to $3,000 per year. Portion of loss not used to make deduction carries forward indefinitely.
5. All short-term capital loss	$1 of loss used to make $1 of deduction. Deduction is *for* AGI and limited to $3,000 per year. Portion of loss not used to make deduction carries forward indefinitely.
6. Part long-term and part short-term capital loss	Short-term losses used first to make $3,000 deduction.

---

[24] § 1212(b).

additional short-term capital gains and losses. It is a continuation of Part I. Part V lists additional long-term capital gains and losses. It is a continuation of Part II. The Form 1040 instructions have a Schedule D tax worksheet that is used for the alternative tax computation for net long-term capital gains. Parts IV and V of Schedule D and the Schedule D tax worksheet are not reproduced here.

▼
EXAMPLE 42

During 1993, Erlyne Smith (Social Security number, 466–36–4596) had the following sales of capital assets (a 1993 example has been used, since a 1994 form was unavailable):

Description	Date Acquired	Date Sold	Selling Price	Cost Basis*
100 shares of Apple Corp. common stock	10/21/93	12/3/93	$11,000	$10,000
300 shares of Orange Corp. preferred stock	7/29/93	11/25/93	5,000	5,500
2,000 shares of Peach Corp. common stock	1/31/81	2/12/93	8,000	7,000
40 shares of Pear Corp. common stock	6/11/81	9/5/93	16,000	18,800

*Includes selling expenses (e.g., brokerage commissions).   ▼

Note that Erlyne's tax position is the same as that of Robert in Example 38. Thus, Erlyne has a NLTCL of $1,800 (Part II of Schedule D) and an NSTCG of $500 (Part I of Schedule D). These amounts are combined (see Part III of Schedule D) for a NLTCL of $1,300. All of the $1,300 is deductible *for* adjusted gross income as a capital loss deduction. There is no remaining capital loss to carry over to 1994. In completing a Schedule D for Erlyne Smith, it was assumed that she had no capital loss carryovers from prior years. Her total stock sales of $40,000 ($11,000 + $5,000 + $8,000 + $16,000) were reported to her by her broker on a Form 1099–B. ▼

Tax Treatment of Capital Gains and Losses of Corporate Taxpayers

The treatment of a corporation's net capital gain or loss differs from the rules for individuals. Briefly, the differences are as follows:

- There is a NCG alternative tax rate of 35 percent. However, since the maximum corporate tax rate is 35 percent, the alternative tax is not beneficial.
- Capital losses offset only capital gains. No deduction of capital losses is permitted against ordinary taxable income (whereas a $3,000 deduction is allowed to individuals).[25]
- There is a three-year carryback and a five-year carryover period for net capital losses.[26] Corporate carryovers and carrybacks are always treated as short term, regardless of their original nature.

▼
EXAMPLE 43

Sparrow Corporation has a $15,000 NLTCL for the current year and $57,000 of ordinary taxable income. Sparrow may not offset the $15,000 NLTCL against its ordinary income by

---

[25]§ 1211(a).   [26]§ 1212(a)(1).

SCHEDULE D (Form 1040)	Capital Gains and Losses	OMB No. 1545-0074
Department of the Treasury Internal Revenue Service	▶ Attach to Form 1040. ▶ See Instructions for Schedule D (Form 1040). ▶ Use lines 20 and 22 for more space to list transactions for lines 1 and 9.	19**93** Attachment Sequence No. **12**

Name(s) shown on Form 1040	Your social security number
Erlyne Smith	466 : 36 : 4596

Part I   Short-Term Capital Gains and Losses—Assets Held One Year or Less

(a) Description of property (Example: 100 sh. XYZ Co.)	(b) Date acquired (Mo., day, yr.)	(c) Date sold (Mo., day, yr.)	(d) Sales price (see page D-3)	(e) Cost or other basis (see page D-3)	(f) LOSS If (e) is more than (d), subtract (d) from (e)	(g) GAIN If (d) is more than (e), subtract (e) from (d)
1 100 shares Apple Corp. common	10/21/93	12/3/93	11,000	10,000		1,000
300 shares Orange Corp. preferred	7/29/93	11/25/93	5,000	5,500	500	

2 Enter your short-term totals, if any, from line 21	**2**				
3 **Total short-term sales price amounts.** Add column (d) of lines 1 and 2 . . .	**3**	16,000			
4 Short-term gain from Forms 2119 and 6252, and short-term gain or (loss) from Forms 4684, 6781, and 8824	**4**				
5 Net short-term gain or (loss) from partnerships, S corporations, and fiduciaries from Schedule(s) K-1	**5**				
6 Short-term capital loss carryover from 1992 Schedule D, line 38	**6**				
7 Add lines 1, 2, and 4 through 6, in columns (f) and (g)	**7**			(500)	1,000
8 **Net short-term capital gain or (loss).** Combine columns (f) and (g) of line 7	**8**				500

Part II   Long-Term Capital Gains and Losses—Assets Held More Than One Year

9 2,000 shares Peach Corp. common	1/31/81	2/12/93	8,000	7,000		1,000
40 shares Pear Corp. common	6/11/81	9/5/93	16,000	18,800	2,800	

10 Enter your long-term totals, if any, from line 23	**10**				
11 **Total long-term sales price amounts.** Add column (d) of lines 9 and 10 . . .	**11**	24,000			
12 Gain from Form 4797; long-term gain from Forms 2119, 2439, and 6252; and long-term gain or (loss) from Forms 4684, 6781, and 8824 . . .	**12**				
13 Net long-term gain or (loss) from partnerships, S corporations, and fiduciaries from Schedule(s) K-1	**13**				
14 Capital gain distributions	**14**				
15 Long-term capital loss carryover from 1992 Schedule D, line 45	**15**				
16 Add lines 9, 10, and 12 through 15, in columns (f) and (g)	**16**			(2,800)	1,000
17 **Net long-term capital gain or (loss).** Combine columns (f) and (g) of line 16	**17**				(1,800)

Part III   Summary of Parts I and II

18 Combine lines 8 and 17. If a loss, go to line 19. If a gain, enter the gain on Form 1040, line 13. **Note:** *If both lines 17 and 18 are gains, see the* **Schedule D Tax Worksheet** *on page D-4* . .	**18**	(1,300)
19 If line 18 is a (loss), enter here and as a (loss) on Form 1040, line 13, the **smaller** of these losses:		
a The (loss) on line 18; **or**		
b ($3,000) or, if married filing separately, ($1,500)	**19**	(1,300)
Note: *See the* **Capital Loss Carryover Worksheet** *on page D-4 if the loss on line 18 exceeds the loss on line 19 or if Form 1040, line 35, is a loss.*		

For Paperwork Reduction Act Notice, see Form 1040 instructions.   Cat. No. 11338H   Schedule D (Form 1040) 1993

taking a capital loss deduction. The $15,000 NLTCL becomes a $15,000 STCL for carryback and carryover purposes. This amount may be offset by capital gains in the three-year carryback period or, if not absorbed there, offset by capital gains in the five-year carryforward period. ▼

The rules applicable to corporations are discussed in greater detail in Chapter 20.

TAX PLANNING CONSIDERATIONS

IMPORTANCE OF CAPITAL ASSET STATUS

Why is capital asset status important when net long-term capital gain is subject to a maximum 28 percent tax rate? The 11.6 percent difference between the maximum 39.6 percent regular tax rate and the maximum 28 percent net long-term capital gain tax rate may generate significant tax savings for taxpayers in the highest regular tax bracket (and to a lesser extent for taxpayers in the 31 percent and 36 percent tax brackets) who can receive income in the form of long-term capital gains.

6 **LEARNING OBJECTIVE**
Identify tax planning opportunities arising from the sale or exchange of capital assets.

Capital asset status is also important because capital gains must be offset by capital losses. If a net capital loss results, the maximum deduction is $3,000 per year.

Consequently, capital gains and losses must be segregated from other types of gains and losses and must be reported separately on Schedule D of Form 1040.

PLANNING FOR CAPITAL ASSET STATUS

It is important to keep in mind that capital asset status often is a question of objective evidence. Thus, property that is not a capital asset to one party may qualify as a capital asset to another party.

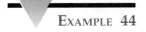

EXAMPLE 44

Diane, a real estate dealer, transfers by gift a tract of land to Jeff, her son. The land was recorded as part of Diane's inventory (it was held for resale) and was therefore not a capital asset to her. Jeff, however, treats the land as an investment. The land is a capital asset in Jeff's hands, and any later taxable disposition of the property by him will yield a capital gain or loss. ▼

ETHICAL CONSIDERATIONS

Assuring Capital Asset Status

The taxpayer is an antiques collector and is going to sell an antique purchased many years ago for a very large gain in 1994. The facts and circumstances indicate that the taxpayer might be classified as a dealer rather than an investor in antiques. The taxpayer will save $40,000 in taxes if the gain is treated as a long-term capital gain rather than as an ordinary gain.

The taxpayer is considering the following options as ways to assure the $40,000 tax savings:

• Give the antique to his daughter, who is an investment banker, to sell.
• Merely assume that he has held the antique as an investment.
• Exchange the antique in a like-kind exchange for another antique he wants.

If proper planning is carried out, even a dealer may obtain long-term capital gain treatment on the sale of the type of property normally held for resale.

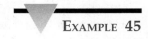

EXAMPLE 45

Jim, a real estate dealer, segregates tract A from the real estate he regularly holds for resale and designates the property as being held for investment purposes. The property is not advertised for sale and is disposed of several years later. The negotiations for the subsequent sale were initiated by the purchaser and not by Jim. Under these circumstances, it would appear that any gain or loss from the sale of tract A should be a capital gain or loss.[27] ▼

When a business is being sold, one of the major decisions usually concerns whether a portion of the sales price is goodwill. For the seller, goodwill generally represents the disposition of a capital asset. Goodwill has no basis and represents a residual portion of the selling price that cannot be allocated reasonably to the known assets. The amount of goodwill thus represents capital gain. The buyer purchasing goodwill has a capitalizable, 15-year amortizable asset—a disadvantageous situation.

Prior to the Revenue Reconciliation Act (RRA) of 1993, the buyer would prefer that the residual portion of the purchase price be allocated to a covenant not to compete (a promise that the seller will not compete against the buyer by conducting a business similar to the one that the buyer has purchased). Payments for a covenant not to compete are ordinary income to the seller, but were ordinary deductions for the buyer over the life of the covenant. However, RRA of 1993 now provides that a covenant is amortized over the same 15-year period as goodwill.

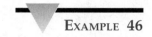

EXAMPLE 46

Marcia is buying Jack's dry cleaning proprietorship. An appraisal of the assets indicates that a reasonable purchase price would exceed the value of the known assets by $30,000. If the purchase contract does not specify the nature of the $30,000, the amount will be goodwill, and Jack will have a long-term capital gain of $30,000. Marcia will have a 15-year amortizable $30,000 asset. If Marcia is paying the extra $30,000 to prevent Jack from conducting another dry cleaning business in the area (a covenant not to compete), Jack will have $30,000 of ordinary income. Marcia will have a $30,000 deduction over the statutory 15-year amortization period rather than over the actual life of the covenant (e.g., 5 years). ▼

EFFECT OF CAPITAL ASSET STATUS IN TRANSACTIONS OTHER THAN SALES

The nature of an asset (capital or ordinary) is important in determining the tax consequences that result when a sale or exchange occurs. It may, however, be just as significant in circumstances other than a taxable sale or exchange. When a capital asset is disposed of, the result is not always a capital gain or loss. Rather, in general, the disposition must be a sale or exchange. Collection of a debt instrument having a basis less than the face value results in an ordinary gain rather than a capital gain even though the debt instrument is a capital asset. The collection is not a sale or exchange. Sale of the debt shortly before the due date for collection will not produce a capital gain.[28] If selling the debt in such circumstances could produce a capital gain but collecting could not, the narrow interpretation of what constitutes a capital gain or loss would be frustrated. Another illustration of the sale or exchange principle involves a donation of certain appreciated property to a qualified charity. Recall that in certain circumstances, the measure of the charitable contribution is fair market value when the property, if sold, would have yielded a long-term capital gain [refer to Chapter 10 and the discussion of § 170(e)].

---

[27] *Toledo, Peoria & Western Railroad Co.*, 35 TCM 1663, T.C.Memo. 1976–366.

[28] *Comm. v. Percy W. Phillips*, 60–1 USTC ¶9294, 5 AFTR2d 855, 275 F.2d 33 (CA–4, 1960).

EXAMPLE 47

Sharon wants to donate a tract of unimproved land (basis of $40,000 and fair market value of $200,000) held for the required long-term holding period to State University (a qualified charitable organization). However, Sharon currently is under audit by the IRS for capital gains she reported on certain real estate transactions during an earlier tax year. Although Sharon is not a licensed real estate broker, the IRS agent conducting the audit is contending that she has achieved dealer status by virtue of the number and frequency of the real estate transactions she has conducted. Under these circumstances, Sharon would be well-advised to postpone the donation to State University until her status is clarified. If she has achieved dealer status, the unimproved land may be inventory (refer to Example 45 for another possible result), and Sharon's charitable contribution deduction would be limited to $40,000. If not, and if the land is held as an investment, Sharon's deduction is $200,000 (the fair market value of the property). ▼

STOCK SALES

The following rules apply in determining the date of a stock sale:

- The date the sale is executed is the date of the sale. The execution date is the date the broker completes the transaction on the stock exchange.
- The settlement date is the date the cash or other property is paid to the seller of the stock. This date is *not* relevant in determining the date of sale.

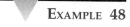

EXAMPLE 48

Lupe, a cash basis taxpayer, sells stock that results in a gain. The sale was executed on December 29, 1993. The settlement date is January 5, 1994. The date of sale is December 29, 1993 (the execution date). The holding period for the stock sold ends with the execution date. ▼

MAXIMIZING BENEFITS

Ordinary losses generally are preferable to capital losses because of the limitations imposed on the deductibility of net capital losses and the requirement that capital losses be used to offset capital gains. The taxpayer may be able to convert what would otherwise have been capital loss to ordinary loss. For example, business (but not nonbusiness) bad debts, losses from the sale or exchange of small business investment company stock, and losses from the sale or exchange of small business company stock all result in ordinary losses.[29]

Although capital losses can be carried over indefinitely, *indefinite* becomes definite when a taxpayer dies. Any loss carryovers not used by the taxpayer are permanently lost. That is, no tax benefit can be derived from the carryovers subsequent to death.[30] Therefore, the potential benefit of carrying over capital losses diminishes when dealing with older taxpayers.

It is usually beneficial to spread gains over more than one taxable year. In some cases, this can be accomplished through the installment sales method of accounting.

YEAR-END PLANNING

The following general rules can be applied for timing the recognition of capital gains and losses near the end of a taxable year:

- If the taxpayer already has recognized over $3,000 of capital loss, sell assets to generate capital gain equal to the excess of the capital loss over $3,000.

---

[29] §§ 166(d), 1242, and 1244. Refer to the discussion in Chapter 7.   [30] Rev.Rul. 74–175, 1974–1 C.B. 52.

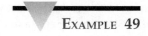

EXAMPLE 49

Kevin has already incurred a $6,000 LTCL. Kevin should generate $3,000 of capital gain. The gain will offset $3,000 of the loss. Thus, the remaining loss of $3,000 can be deducted against ordinary income. ▼

- If the taxpayer already has recognized capital gain, sell assets to generate capital loss equal to the capital gain. The gain will not be taxed, and the loss will be fully *deductible* against the gain.
- If the taxpayer's ordinary taxable income is already in the 28 percent bracket, it would make sense to recognize long-term capital gain rather than ordinary income where the taxpayer has a choice between the two. Such gain is taxed at the alternative rate of 28 percent whereas ordinary income may be taxed under the regular tax rates at 31 percent or more.

KEY TERMS

Alternative tax, 16–21	Lessee, 16–15	Original issue discount (OID), 16–10
Capital asset, 16–3	Lessor, 16–15	
Capital gains, 16–2	Net capital gain (NCG), 16–21	Patent, 16–12
Capital losses, 16–2		Sale or exchange, 16–9
Franchise, 16–14	Net capital loss (NCL), 16–23	
Holding period, 16–16	Options, 16–10	Short sale, 16–18

PROBLEM MATERIALS

DISCUSSION QUESTIONS

1. Why does the tax law require that capital gains and losses be separated from other types of gains and losses?

2. Proper classification of recognized gains and losses depends upon what three characteristics?

3. What are the most common capital assets owned by individual taxpayers?

✗ 4. Does the tax law define "capital asset"?

5. Todd owns the following assets. Which of them are capital assets?
   a. Ten shares of Standard Motors common stock.
   b. A copyright on a song Todd wrote.
   c. A U.S. government savings bond.
   d. A note Todd received when he loaned $100 to a friend.
   e. A very rare copy of "Your Federal Income Tax" (a U.S. government publication that Todd purchased many years ago from the U.S. Government Printing Office).
   f. Todd's personal use automobile.
   g. A letter Todd received from a former U.S. President. Todd received the letter because he had complained to the President about the President's foreign policy.

6. Why doesn't the collection of an accrual basis account receivable usually result in a gain or loss?

7. Does the creator of a copyrighted work generally have a capital asset?

8. Why do court decisions play an important role in the definition of capital assets?

9. In what circumstances may real estate held for resale receive capital gain treatment?

10. A loan made by a taxpayer is a nonbusiness receivable. If the loan is not paid because the debtor defaults, what are the tax consequences?

11. Recognition of capital gain or loss usually requires a sale or exchange of a capital asset. Define "sale" and "exchange."

12. A corporate bond is worthless due to a bankruptcy on May 10. At what date does the tax loss occur? (Assume the bond was held by an individual for investment purposes.)

13. Why does the Code require amortization of original issue discount? What is the effect of this amortization on the interest income of the taxpayer owning the bond? On the adjusted basis?

14. Mequoia, a real estate dealer, purchased for $25,000 a one-year option on 40 acres of farmland. If Mequoia is able to get the property rezoned for single-family residential development, she will exercise the option and purchase the land for $800,000. The rezoning effort is unsuccessful, and the option expires. How should the $25,000 be treated?

15. If a grantee of an option exercises the option, do the grantor's proceeds from the sale of the option property increase? Why?

16. When does the transfer of a patent result in long-term capital gain? Short-term capital gain? Ordinary income?

17. If an inventor's employer automatically has sole patent rights to the inventor's inventions, is the employer a holder of the patent?

18. What is a franchise? In practice, does the transfer of a franchise usually result in capital gain or loss treatment? Why or why not?

19. Under what circumstances is a contingent payment received by a franchise transferor from a transferee a capital gain?

20. When are lease cancellation payments received by a lessee capital in nature? When are lease cancellation payments received by a lessor capital in nature?

21. Taxpayer is the lessee and the lease is on the taxpayer's residence. Taxpayer makes a payment to the lessor to cancel the lease. Why is the payment nondeductible?

22. What does it mean when a capital asset has been held "short term"?

23. In determining the long-term holding period, how is the day of acquisition counted? The day of disposition?

24. Helen exchanges a computer used in her business for another computer that she will use in her business. The transaction qualifies as a like-kind exchange. Helen had held the computer given up in the exchange for four years. The computers are § 1231 assets. What is the holding period of the computer received in the exchange on the day of its acquisition?

25. Juan purchased corporate stock for $10,000 on April 10, 1993. On July 14, 1994, when the stock was worth $17,000, he gave it to his son, Miguel. When does Miguel's holding period for the stock begin?

26. John inherits stock on July 17, 1994. John's father had purchased the stock on April 10, 1993, for $12,000. The stock was worth $15,000 when the father died on December 20, 1993. The stock was worth $18,000 when John received it on July 17, 1994. When does John's holding period for the stock begin?

27. Define a short sale. Why does a seller enter into a short sale?

28. After all possible capital gain and loss netting is complete, what are the possibilities for outcomes that include a net long-term capital gain?

29. After all possible capital gain and loss netting is complete, what are the possibilities for outcomes that include a net long-term capital loss?

30. Which type of gain would a taxpayer prefer to recognize in 1994: long-term capital gain, short-term capital gain, or ordinary income?

31. Which type of loss would a taxpayer prefer to incur in 1994: long-term capital loss, short-term capital loss, or ordinary loss?

32. Differentiate between the capital loss carryover rules for unused capital losses of individuals and corporations.

PROBLEMS

33. Nancy had three property transactions during the year. She sold a vacation home used for personal purposes at a $21,000 gain. The home had been held for five years and had never been rented. Nancy also sold an antique clock for $3,500 that she had inherited from her grandmother. The clock was valued in Nancy's grandmother's estate at $5,000. Nancy owned the clock for only four months. Nancy sold these assets to finance her full-time occupation as a songwriter. Near the end of the year, Nancy sold one of the songs she had written two years earlier. She received cash of $38,000 and a royalty interest in revenues derived from the merchandising of the song. Nancy had no tax basis for the song. Nancy had no other income and $18,000 in deductible songwriting expenses. Assuming the year is 1994, what is Nancy's adjusted gross income?

34. Rashad is the owner of a sole proprietorship. The business is on the cash basis of accounting and has $40,000 of accounts receivable. Rashad is desperate for cash, so he sells the receivables to a collection agency for $23,000. How should Rashad treat this sale of the receivables? How would the answer differ if Rashad was on the accrual basis of accounting?

35. Lucy is a dealer in securities. She purchased $10,000 of stock several years ago. She designated it as held for investment by the end of the day she acquired it. Two years later, she decided that she no longer wanted to hold the stock for investment and, therefore, redesignated it as held for sale in the ordinary course of her business. During the current year, she sold the stock for $35,000.
    a. What are the amount and nature of her gain from disposition of the stock?
    b. Assume the stock was sold for $8,000. What are the amount and nature of the loss from disposition of the stock?

36. Abby sells real estate lots, but meets all the conditions of § 1237. In 1994, she sells six lots, one lot each to Betty, Carl, Donna, and Evelyn and two adjacent lots to Frank. The sales price of each lot is $20,000. Abby's basis is $15,000 for each lot. Sales expenses are $500 per lot.
    a. What is the realized and recognized gain?
    b. Explain the nature of the gain (ordinary income or capital gain).
    c. Would your answers change if the two lots sold to Frank were not adjacent? If so, how?

37. Sue has had a bad year with her investments. She lent a friend $3,700; the friend did not repay the loan when it was due, and then declared bankruptcy. The loan is totally uncollectible. Sue also was notified by her broker that the Willow corporate bonds she owned became worthless on October 13, 1994. She had purchased the bonds for $10,000 on October 10, 1993. What are the amount and nature of Sue's losses?

38. Fred purchases $100,000 of newly issued Gold Corporation bonds for $66,000. The bonds have original issue discount of $34,000. After Fred has held the bonds for two years and has amortized $14,000 of the original issue discount, he sells the bonds for $98,000. What is Fred's adjusted basis for the bonds when he sells them, and what are the amount and nature of the gain from the disposition of the bonds?

39. Tim paid $43,000 for a four-month option to acquire a song copyright. He tried to sign a major country and western star to record the song. Tim was not successful in signing the singer, and the option lapsed. Tim is not in the business of buying and recording

songs. Tim did not create the song on which he had an option. What are the amount and nature of Tim's loss?

40. Marta is looking for vacant land to buy. She would hold the land as an investment. For $1,000, she is granted an 11-month option on January 1, 1994, to buy 10 acres of vacant land for $25,000. The owner (who is holding the land for investment) paid $10,000 for the land several years ago.
    a. Does the landowner have gross income when $1,000 is received for granting the option?
    b. Does Marta have an asset when the option is granted?
    c. If the option lapses, does the landowner have a recognized gain? If so, what type of gain? Does Marta have a recognized loss? If so, what type of loss?
    d. If the option is exercised and an additional $25,000 is paid for the land, how much recognized gain does the seller have? What type of gain? What is Marta's tax basis for the property?

41. In each of the following independent situations, determine whether the sale at a gain of all substantial rights in a patent qualifies for capital gain treatment:
    a. The individual creator sells the patent to a manufacturing company. The creator is not an employee of the manufacturing company.
    b. A manufacturing company owns a patent developed by one of its employees. It has been using the patent in its manufacturing process. The company sells the patent along with the assets of the manufacturing process.
    c. An individual investor buys a patent that has not been reduced to practice from the individual creator. After holding it for three months, the investor sells it to a retail company.

42. Rocky purchases a 20-year franchise from Wearever Mufflers for $60,000. The $60,000 is payable at the rate of $12,000 per year for each of the first five years. Wearever retained significant powers and rights in the franchise agreement. How much may Rocky deduct in the first franchise year? How much and what type of income must Wearever report in the first franchise year?

43. Freys, Inc., sells a 12-year franchise to Reynaldo. The franchise contains many restrictions on how Reynaldo may operate his store. For instance, Reynaldo cannot use less than Grade 10 Idaho potatoes, must fry the potatoes at a constant 410 degrees, dress store personnel in Freys-approved uniforms, and have a Freys sign that meets detailed specifications on size, color, and construction. When the franchise contract is signed, Reynaldo makes a noncontingent $40,000 payment to Freys. During the same year, Reynaldo pays Freys $25,000—14% of Reynaldo's sales. How does Freys treat each of these payments? How does Reynaldo treat each of the payments?

44. Irene lives in an apartment near her college campus. Her lease runs out in July 1995, but her landlord could sell the building if he can convince all the tenants to cancel their leases and move out by the end of 1994. The landlord has offered Irene $1,000 to cancel her lease. Irene's lease began on August 1, 1994. What tax factors should Irene consider in deciding whether to take the landlord's offer?

45. Evelyn acquires 200 Copper Corporation common shares at $10 per share on October 13, 1987. On August 10, 1993, Evelyn gives the shares to her son, Bob. At the time of the gift, the shares are worth $40 each. On May 11, 1994, Bob sells the shares for $45 each. What is Bob's gain? Is it short or long term?

46. Dennis sells short 100 shares of ARC stock at $20 per share on January 15, 1994. He buys 200 shares of ARC stock on April 1, 1994, at $25 per share. On May 2, 1994, he closes the short sale by delivering 100 of the shares purchased on April 1.
    a. What are the amount and nature of Dennis's loss upon closing the short sale?
    b. When does the holding period for the remaining 100 shares begin?
    c. If Dennis sells (at $27 per share) the remaining 100 shares on January 20, 1995, what will be the nature of his gain or loss?

47. Elaine (single with no dependents) has the following transactions in 1994:

Adjusted gross income (exclusive of capital gains and losses)	$80,000
Long-term capital gain	12,000
Long-term capital loss	(5,000)
Short-term capital gain	1,000
Short-term capital loss	(1,900)

What is Elaine's net capital gain or loss?

48. In 1994, Betty (head of household with three dependents) had an $18,000 loss from the sale of a personal residence. She also purchased from an individual inventor for $8,000 (and resold in two months for $7,000) a patent on a rubber bonding process. The patent had not yet been reduced to practice. Betty purchased the patent as an investment. Additionally, she had the following capital gains and losses from stock transactions:

Long-term capital loss	($3,000)
Long-term capital loss carryover from 1993	(12,000)
Short-term capital gain	21,000
Short-term capital loss	(6,000)

What is Betty's net capital gain or loss?

49. In 1994, Wilbur (single with no dependents) engaged in various stock transactions. Wilbur purchased RST, Inc., common stock on January 10, for $8,000. The price began to plummet almost immediately. Wilbur sold the stock on March 31, 1994, for $3,000. Wilbur also had the following other stock transaction results: $500 STCG, $6,300 STCL, $700 LTCL, $43,500 LTCG. Wilbur has $210,000 of taxable income from sources other than those previously mentioned. The taxable income has already been adjusted the appropriate amount for the phase-out of the personal exemption deduction. What is Wilbur's net capital gain or loss? What is Wilbur's total tax liability?

50. In 1994, Venezia has a $4,800 net short-term capital loss and $8,030 of negative taxable income. She used the standard deduction and has one personal exemption. What is the amount of Venezia's capital loss carryover to 1995?

51. For 1994, Ahmad completes the following stock transactions:

	Date Acquired	Cost	Date Sold	Selling Price
1,000 shares ABC	1/6/94	$4,000	8/2/94	$8,000
200 shares DEF	7/1/82	8,800	9/18/94	9,400
3,500 shares GHI	5/2/94	7,000	11/2/94	8,900
5,000 shares JKL	8/5/94	9,700	12/15/94	5,000

What is Ahmad's includible gain or deductible loss resulting from these stock sales?

52. Consuela, a head of household with two dependents, has the following 1994 transactions:

Adjusted gross income (exclusive of capital gains and losses)	$125,250
Long-term capital loss	(5,000)
Long-term capital gain	20,000
Short-term capital loss carryover	(2,000)

a. What is Consuela's net capital gain or loss?
b. What is Consuela's taxable income assuming she does not itemize and has one personal exemption?
c. What is Consuela's tax on taxable income?

53. Purple Corporation has $16,800 of long-term capital loss for 1994 and $5,000 of other taxable income. What is its 1994 taxable income and the amount (if any) of its capital loss carryover?

CUMULATIVE PROBLEMS

54. Nikki Hassad is a graduate student at State University. She is single and has no dependents. During 1994, she had $25,500 wages from a full-time job she held until returning to school in August. Nikki received a $3,000 scholarship from State University and used all of the scholarship money to pay for tuition and fees. In June 1994, she won $35,000 with an instant lottery ticket and immediately invested in various stocks. The following table summarizes her stock transactions for 1994:

	Date Acquired	Cost	Date Sold	Selling Price
150 shares Clay	7/2/94	$5,000	12/11/94	$6,200
100 shares Gold	7/2/94	5,000	11/6/94	3,300
120 shares Iron	7/2/94	3,100	10/8/94	8,000
25 shares Sand	7/2/94	1,900		
100 shares Uranium	6/16/91	2,000	12/11/94	9,600

Nikki does not have many itemized deductions, so she will take the standard deduction. Her Social Security number is 393–86–4502, and she lives at 518 Marigold Lane, Okemos, MI 48864. She had $5,600 of Federal income tax withheld on her wages and $7,000 of Federal income tax withheld on her lottery winnings. She also made Federal estimated income tax payments of $3,500.

Compute Nikki's lowest legal tax liability for 1994. Suggested software (if available): *TurboTax* or *MacInTax* for tax return or WFT tax planning software.

Draft a brief letter to Nikki describing (1) how long she must hold the Sand stock for it to become "long term," (2) what the 1995 tax consequences would be if she sold that stock for a $4,000 long-term capital gain, and (3) what would happen if she was eligible for the alternative tax on long-term capital gains. Date the letter March 17, 1995.

55. Margaret Gill, age 33, has two dependents. She does not wish to have $3 go to the Presidential Election Campaign Fund. Margaret is an insurance adjuster. She resides at 2510 Grace Avenue, Richmond, VA 23100. Her Social Security number is 566–88–1000. The following information is for Margaret's 1993 tax year. She earned a $40,000 salary. Margaret received $35,000 of alimony and $40,000 of child support from her former husband. The children are Susan Gill (age 11, Social Security number 396–42–8909) and Jason Gill (age 9, Social Security number 396–43–9090). Both children lived with Margaret all year. On March 1, 1982, she purchased 500 shares of People's Power Company for $10,000. She sold those shares on October 14, 1993, for $8,500 after receiving nontaxable dividends totaling $2,600 (including $700 in 1993). She also received $300 in taxable dividends in 1993 from People's Power Company. On November 7, 1983, Margaret purchased 1,000 shares of Violet Corporation for $22,000. On February 12, 1993, she received an additional 100 shares in a nontaxable 10% stock dividend. On February 13, 1993, she sold those 100 shares for $2,500. During 1993, she paid $16,000 in deductible home mortgage interest, $7,000 in property taxes, $2,000 in state income taxes, $600 in sales tax, $2,300 in charitable contributions, and $1,500 in professional dues and subscriptions. Her employer withheld Federal income tax of $8,200. Compute Margaret's net tax payable or refund due for 1993. If you use tax forms for your computations, you will need Form 1040 and Schedules A, B, and D. Suggested software (if available): *TurboTax* or *MacInTax* for tax return or WFT tax planning software.

RESEARCH PROBLEMS

Research Problem 1. Warren and Betty Johnson own various plots of land in Eaton County, Michigan. They acquired the land at various times during the last 20 years. About every fourth year, the Johnsons subdivide one of the properties they own into lots. They then have water, sewer, natural gas, and electricity hookups put in on each lot and pave the new streets. The Johnsons have always treated their sales of such lots as sales of capital assets. Their previous tax returns were prepared by the accountant whose practice you recently purchased. Have the Johnsons used the proper tax treatment on their prior returns?

Partial list of research aids:
§§ 1221 and 1237 and *Jesse W. and Betty J. English,* 65 T.C.M. 2160, T.C.Memo, 1993–111.

Research Problem 2.   Clean Corporation runs a chain of dry cleaners. Borax is used heavily in Clean's dry cleaning process and has been in short supply several times in the past. Clean Corporation buys a controlling interest in Dig Corporation—a borax mining concern. Clean's sole reason for purchasing the Dig stock is to assure Clean of a continuous supply of borax if another shortage develops. Although borax must be refined before it is usable for dry cleaning purposes, a well-established commodities market exists for trading unrefined borax for refined borax. After owning the Dig stock for several years, Clean sells the stock at a loss because Dig is in difficult financial straits. Clean no longer needs to own Dig because Clean has obtained an alternative source of borax. What is the nature of Clean's loss on the disposition of the Dig Corporation stock? Write a letter to the taxpayer that contains your advice and prepare a memo for the tax files.

Research Problem 3.   Treasury bills are short-term debt obligations issued by the U.S. government. As a result of a very old IRS Revenue Ruling, Treasury bills are *not* capital assets. Treasury bill futures are speculative investments that, in effect, "bet" on the direction Treasury bill interest rates will take. Are Treasury bill futures capital assets?

Partial list of research aids:
Rev.Rul. 51, 1953–1 C.B. 497.
Don D. Dial, 58 TCM 1138, T.C.Memo. 1990–9.

C·H·A·P·T·E·R

17

PROPERTY TRANSACTIONS: SECTION 1231 AND RECAPTURE PROVISIONS

LEARNING OBJECTIVES

After completing Chapter 17, you should be able to:

1. Understand the rationale for and the nature and treatment of gains and losses from the disposition of business assets.

2. Distinguish §1231 assets from ordinary assets and capital assets and calculate the §1231 gain or loss.

3. Determine when §1245 recapture applies and how it is computed.

4. Determine when §1250 recapture applies and how it is computed.

5. Apply the special recapture provisions for related parties and IDC and be aware of the special recapture provision for corporations.

6. Describe and apply the reporting procedures for §§ 1231, 1245, and 1250.

7. Identify tax planning opportunities associated with §§ 1231, 1245, and 1250.

Section 1231 Assets, 17–3

Relationship to Capital Assets, 17–3

Justification for Favorable Tax Treatment, 17–4

Property Included, 17–5

Property Excluded, 17–5

Special Rules for Certain § 1231 Assets, 17–5

General Procedure for § 1231 Computation, 17–8

Section 1245 Recapture, 17–12

Section 1245 Property, 17–14

Observations on § 1245, 17–15

Section 1250 Recapture, 17–15

Computing Recapture on Nonresidential Real Property, 17–16

Computing Recapture on Residential Rental Housing, 17–18

Section 1250 Recapture Situations, 17–18

Considerations Common to §§ 1245 and 1250, 17–19

Exceptions, 17–19

Other Applications, 17–21

Special Recapture Provisions, 17–23

Special Recapture for Corporations, 17–23

Gain from Sale of Depreciable Property between Certain Related Parties, 17–23

Intangible Drilling Costs , 17–23

Reporting Procedures, 17–23

Tax Planning Considerations, 17–25

Timing of § 1231 Gain, 17–25

Timing of Recapture, 17–29

Postponing and Shifting Recapture, 17–29

Avoiding Recapture, 17–29

Businesses own many assets that are used in the business rather than held for resale. In financial accounting, such assets are known as "fixed assets." For example, a foundry's 30,000-pound stamping machine is a fixed asset. It is also a depreciable asset. The building housing the foundry is another fixed asset. This chapter largely deals with how to classify the gains and losses arising from the disposition of fixed assets. Chapter 8 discussed how to depreciate such assets. Chapter 15 discussed how to determine the adjusted basis and the amount of gain or loss from their disposition.

TAX IN THE NEWS

FIXED ASSETS FOR SALE

Small, sturdy building on corner lot. Large two-car garage. Two baths. Classic American styling. Close to main roads. Priced to sell. What is it? A gasoline station. Actually, 200 gasoline stations. Getty Petroleum sold them off. The gasoline stations were Getty's fixed assets. Both the buildings and the land were sold. Getty sold 125 of the 200 stations by listing them for sale and selling them to other oil companies. However, the other 75 stations were "slow movers," so Getty held the first-ever gas station auction. The bidders had to have at least a $5,000 certified check to bid. Getty used the auction to attract buyers who would "convert" the properties into beauty parlors, auto repair shops, and many other uses. Gas stations are very easy to convert because they are basically just a box.

SOURCE: Adapted from Mitchell Pacelle, "For Sale: Cheap Lots Near Main Roads; The Hitch: They Used to Be Gas Stations," *Wall Street Journal*, November 1, 1993, pp. B1, B5. Reprinted by permission of the *Wall Street Journal*, © 1993 Dow Jones & Company, Inc. All rights reserved worldwide.

A long-term capital gain was defined in Chapter 16 as the recognized gain from the sale or exchange of a capital asset held for the required long-term holding period.[1] This chapter is concerned with classification under § 1231, which applies to the sale or exchange of business properties and to certain involuntary conversions. The business properties are not capital assets because they are depreciable and/or are real property used in business or for the production of income. Section 1221(2) provides that such assets are not capital assets. Nonetheless, these business properties may be held for long periods of time and may be sold at a gain. Congress decided many years ago that such assets deserved *limited* capital gain–type treatment. Unfortunately, this limited capital gain–type treatment is very complex and difficult to understand.

Because the limited capital gain–type treatment sometimes gives too much tax advantage if assets are eligible for depreciation (or cost recovery), certain recapture rules may remove the capital gain treatment when depreciation is taken. Thus, this chapter also covers the recapture provisions that tax as ordinary income certain gains that might otherwise qualify for long-term capital gain treatment.

SECTION 1231 ASSETS

RELATIONSHIP TO CAPITAL ASSETS

1 **LEARNING OBJECTIVE**
Understand the rationale for and the nature and treatment of gains and losses from the disposition of business assets.

Depreciable property and real property used in business are not capital assets.[2] Thus, the recognized gains from the disposition of such property (principally machinery, equipment, buildings, and land) would appear to be ordinary income rather than capital gain. Due to § 1231, however, *net gain* from the disposition of such property is sometimes *treated* as *long-term capital gain.* A long-term holding period requirement must be met; the disposition must generally be from a sale, exchange, or involuntary conversion; and certain recapture provisions must be satisfied for this result to occur. Section 1231 may also apply to involuntary conversions of capital assets. Since an involuntary conversion is not a sale or exchange, such a disposition would not normally result in a capital gain.

If the disposition of depreciable property and real property used in business results in a *net loss,* § 1231 *treats* the *loss* as an *ordinary loss* rather than as a capital loss. Ordinary losses are fully deductible *for* adjusted gross income (AGI). Capital losses are offset by capital gains, and, if any loss remains, the loss is deductible to the extent of $3,000 per year for individuals and currently is not deductible at all by regular corporations. It seems, therefore, that § 1231 provides the *best* of both potential results: net gain may be treated as long-term capital gain, and net loss is treated as ordinary loss.

EXAMPLE 1

Roberto sells business land and building at a $5,000 gain and business equipment at a $3,000 loss. Both properties were held for the long-term holding period. Roberto's net gain is $2,000, and that net gain may (depending on various recapture rules discussed later in this chapter) be treated as a long-term capital gain under § 1231. ▼

---

[1] The long-term holding period is more than one year.
[2] § 1221(2).

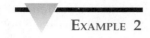

EXAMPLE 2

Samantha sells business equipment at a $10,000 loss and business land at a $2,000 gain. Both properties were held for the long-term holding period. Samantha's net loss is $8,000, and that net loss is an ordinary loss. ▼

The rules regarding § 1231 treatment do *not* apply to *all* business property. Important in this regard are the holding period requirements and the fact that the property must be either depreciable property or real estate used in business. Nor is § 1231 necessarily limited to business property. Transactions involving certain capital assets may fall into the § 1231 category. Thus, § 1231 singles out only some types of business property.

As discussed in Chapter 16, there is a beneficial tax rate for long-term capital gains. Section 1231 requires netting of **§ 1231 gains and losses.** If the result is a gain, it may be treated as a long-term capital gain. The net gain is added to the "real" long-term capital gains (if any) and netted with capital losses (if any). Thus, the net § 1231 gain may eventually be taxed at the alternative long-term capital gain rate or help avoid the unfavorable net capital loss result. The § 1231 gain and loss netting may result in a loss. In this case, the loss is an ordinary loss and is deductible *for* AGI. Finally, § 1231 assets are treated the same as capital assets for purposes of the appreciated property charitable contribution provisions (refer to Chapter 10).

JUSTIFICATION FOR FAVORABLE TAX TREATMENT

The favorable capital gain/ordinary loss treatment sanctioned by § 1231 can be explained by examining several historical developments. Before 1938, business property had been included in the definition of capital assets. Thus, if such property was sold for a loss (not an unlikely possibility during the depression years), a capital loss resulted. If, however, the property was depreciable and could be retained for its estimated useful life, much (if not all) of its costs could be recovered in the form of depreciation. Because the allowance for depreciation was fully deductible whereas capital losses were not, the tax law favored those who did not dispose of an asset. Congress recognized this inequity when it removed business property from the capital asset classification. During the period 1938–1942, therefore, all such gains and losses were ordinary gains and losses.

With the advent of World War II, two developments in particular forced Congress to reexamine the situation regarding business assets. First, the sale of business assets at a gain was discouraged because the gain would be ordinary income. Gains were common because the war effort had inflated prices. Second, taxpayers who did not want to sell their assets often were required to because the government acquired them through condemnation. Often, as a result of the condemnation awards, taxpayers who were forced to part with their property experienced large gains and were deprived of the benefits of future depreciation deductions. Of course, the condemnations constituted involuntary conversions, so taxpayers could defer the gain by timely reinvestment in property that was "similar or related in service or use." But where was such property to be found in view of wartime restrictions and other governmental condemnations? The end result did not seem equitable: a large ordinary gain due to government action and no possibility of deferral due to government restrictions.

In recognition of these conditions, in 1942, Congress eased the tax bite on the disposition of some business property by allowing preferential capital gain treatment. Thus, the present scheme of § 1231 and the dichotomy of capital gain/ordinary loss treatment evolved from a combination of economic considerations existing in 1938 and 1942.

PROPERTY INCLUDED

2 **LEARNING OBJECTIVE**
Distinguish § 1231 assets from ordinary assets and capital assets and calculate the § 1231 gain or loss.

Section 1231 property includes the following:

- Depreciable or real property used in business or for the production of income (principally machinery and equipment, buildings, and land).
- Timber, coal, or domestic iron ore to which § 631 applies.
- Livestock held for draft, breeding, dairy, or sporting purposes.
- Unharvested crops on land used in business.
- Certain nonpersonal use capital assets.

PROPERTY EXCLUDED

Section 1231 property does *not* include the following:

- Property not held for the long-term holding period. Since the benefit of § 1231 is long-term capital gain treatment, the holding period must correspond to the more-than-one-year holding period that applies to capital assets. Livestock must be held at least 12 months (24 months in some cases). Unharvested crops do not have to be held for the required long-term holding period, but the land must be held for the long-term holding period.
- Property where casualty losses exceed casualty gains for the taxable year. If a taxpayer has a net casualty loss, the individual casualty gains and losses are treated as ordinary gains and losses.
- Inventory and property held primarily for sale to customers.
- Copyrights; literary, musical, or artistic compositions, etc.; and certain U.S. government publications.
- Intangible assets such as accounts receivable and notes receivable.

SPECIAL RULES FOR CERTAIN § 1231 ASSETS

A rather diverse group of assets is included under § 1231. The following discussion summarizes the special rules for some of those assets.

Timber

A taxpayer can *elect* to treat the cutting of timber held for sale or for use in business as a sale or exchange.[3] If the taxpayer makes this election, the transaction qualifies under § 1231. The taxpayer must have owned the timber or a contract to cut it on the first day of the year and for the long-term holding period before the date the cutting takes place. The recognized § 1231 gain or loss is determined at the time the timber is cut and is equal to the difference between the timber's fair market value as of the first day of the taxable year and the adjusted basis for depletion. If a taxpayer sells the timber for more or less than the fair market value as of the first day of the taxable year in which it is cut, the difference is ordinary income or loss.

This provision was enacted to provide preferential treatment relative to the natural growth value of timber, which takes a relatively long time to mature. Congress believed this favorable treatment would encourage reforestation of timber lands. If a taxpayer disposes of timber held for the long-term holding period, either by sale or under a royalty contract (where the taxpayer retains an economic interest in the property), the disposal is treated as a sale of the timber. Therefore, any gain or loss qualifies under § 1231.

---

[3]§ 631(a) and Reg. § 1.631–1.

EXAMPLE 3

Several years ago, Tom purchased a tract of land with a substantial stand of trees on it. The land cost $40,000, and the timber cost $100,000. On the first day of 1994, the timber was appraised at $250,000. In August 1994, Tom cut the timber and sold it for $265,000. Tom elects to treat the cutting as a sale or exchange under § 1231. He has a $150,000 § 1231 gain ($250,000 − $100,000) and a $15,000 ordinary gain ($265,000 − $250,000).

What if the timber had been sold for $235,000? Tom would still have a $150,000 § 1231 gain, but would also have a $15,000 ordinary loss. The price for computation of § 1231 gain is the price at the beginning of the year. Any difference between that price and the sales price is ordinary gain or loss. Here, since the price declined by $15,000, Tom has an ordinary loss in that amount. ▼

Livestock

Cattle and horses must be held 24 months or more and other livestock must be held 12 months or more to qualify under § 1231.[4] The primary reason for enacting this provision was the considerable amount of litigation over the character of livestock (whether livestock was held primarily for sale to customers [ordinary income] or for use in a trade or business [§ 1231 property]). Poultry is not livestock for purposes of § 1231.

ETHICAL
CONSIDERATIONS

Determining How Long an Asset Has Been Held

George, a dairy farmer sells a milk cow for $12,000. Normally, George does not sell his cows, but he received an offer he could not refuse for this "super milker." George is not sure exactly when the cow was born, but he does know that it is the calf of another cow he owns. Consequently, he has a zero tax basis for the cow that was sold. George owns 500 cows.

When George's tax adviser points out that the cow must have been held 24 months to be eligible for § 1231 treatment, George gets very upset. The tax adviser knows that George's records are a mess. George thinks the cow was born "within the last 27 months." After the tax adviser explains the tax benefits of the sale qualifying for § 1231 treatment, George decides the cow was more than 24 months old.

Certain Nonpersonal Use Capital Assets

Nonpersonal use property disposed of by casualty or theft may receive § 1231 treatment. Nonpersonal use property includes capital assets held for the production of income, such as an investment painting or investment land. Nonpersonal use property also includes business property. The casualty or theft *long-term* gains and losses from nonpersonal use property are combined (see Concept Summary 17–1). If the result is a gain, the gains and losses are treated as § 1231 transactions. If the result is a loss, § 1231 does not apply. Instead, the gains are treated as ordinary (even though some of them may initially be capital gains), the business losses are deductible *for* AGI, and the other losses (even though some of them may initially be capital losses) are deductible *from* AGI as miscellaneous losses subject

---

[4] Note that the holding period is "12 months or more" and not "more than 12 months."

to the 2 percent of AGI limitation. Thus, a nonpersonal use capital asset that is disposed of by casualty or theft may or may not be a § 1231 asset, depending on the result of the netting process. For simplicity, the rest of this chapter will use the term *casualty* to mean casualty *or* theft.

Personal use property casualty gains and losses are not subject to the § 1231 rules. If the result of netting these gains and losses is a gain, the net gain is a capital gain. If the netting results in a loss, the net loss is a deduction *from* AGI to the extent it exceeds 10 percent of AGI.

Casualties, thefts, and condemnations are *involuntary conversions.* Notice that condemnation gains and losses are not included in the netting processes discussed above. Long-term *recognized* condemnation gains and losses from the disposition

---

Concept Summary 17–1

Section 1231 Netting Procedure

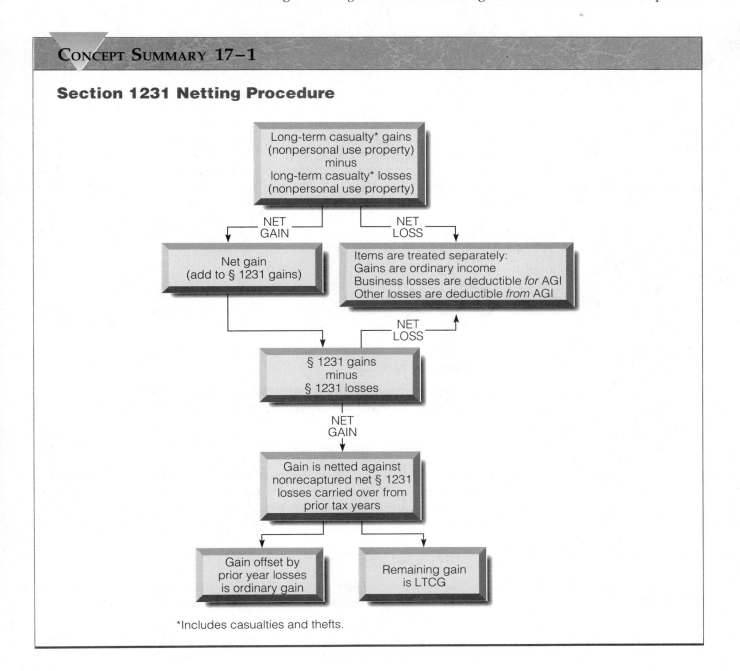

*Includes casualties and thefts.

of property held for business use and for the production of income are treated as § 1231 gains and losses. Involuntary conversion gains may be deferred if conversion proceeds are reinvested, but involuntary conversion losses are recognized (refer to Chapter 15) regardless of whether the conversion proceeds are reinvested.

This variation in treatment between casualty and condemnation gains and losses sheds considerable light on what § 1231 is all about. Section 1231 has no effect on whether or not realized gain or loss is recognized. Instead, it merely dictates how such gain or loss might be *classified* (ordinary or capital) under certain conditions.

Personal use property condemnation gains and losses are not subject to the § 1231 rules. The gains are capital gains, and the losses are nondeductible because they arise from the disposition of personal use property.

GENERAL PROCEDURE FOR § 1231 COMPUTATION

The tax treatment of § 1231 gains and losses depends on the results of a rather complex *netting* procedure. The steps in this netting procedure are as follows.

Step 1: Casualty Netting

Net all long-term gains and losses from casualties of nonpersonal use property. Casualty gains result when insurance proceeds exceed the adjusted basis of the property.

a. If the casualty gains exceed the casualty losses, add the excess to the other § 1231 gains for the taxable year.
b. If the casualty losses exceed the casualty gains, exclude all losses and gains from further § 1231 computation. If this is the case, all casualty gains are ordinary income. Business casualty losses are deductible *for* AGI. Other casualty losses are deductible *from* AGI.

Step 2: § 1231 Netting

After adding any net casualty gain from Step 1a to the other § 1231 gains and losses (including recognized nonpersonal use property condemnation gains and losses), net all § 1231 gains and losses.

a. If the gains exceed the losses, the net gain is offset by the nonrecaptured § 1231 losses (see below) from prior tax years. To the extent of this offset, the net § 1231 gain is classified as ordinary gain. Any remaining gain is long-term capital gain.

b. If the losses exceed the gains, all gains are ordinary income. Business losses are deductible *for* AGI. Other casualty losses are deductible *from* AGI.

Step 3: § 1231 Lookback

The net § 1231 gain from Step 2a is offset by the nonrecaptured net § 1231 losses for the five preceding taxable years. For 1994, the lookback years are 1989, 1990, 1991, 1992, and 1993. To the extent of the nonrecaptured net § 1231 loss, the current year net § 1231 gain is ordinary income. The *nonrecaptured* net § 1231 losses are those that have not already been used to offset net § 1231 gains. Only the net § 1231 gain exceeding this net § 1231 loss carryforward is given long-term capital gain treatment. Concept Summary 17–1 summarizes the § 1231 computational procedure. Examples 6 and 7 illustrate the **§ 1231 lookback** procedure.

Examples 4 through 7 illustrate the application of the § 1231 computation procedure.

EXAMPLE 4

During 1994, Ross had $125,000 of AGI before considering the following recognized gains and losses:

Capital Gains and Losses	
Long-term capital gain	$3,000
Long-term capital loss	(400)
Short-term capital gain	1,000
Short-term capital loss	(200)

Casualties	
Theft of diamond ring (owned four months)	$(800)*
Fire damage to personal residence (owned 10 years)	(400)*
Gain from insurance recovery on accidental destruction of business truck (owned two years)	200

§ 1231 Gains and Losses from Depreciable Business Assets Held Long Term	
Asset A	$ 300
Asset B	1,100
Asset C	(500)

Gains and Losses from Sale of Depreciable Business Assets Held Short Term	
Asset D	$ 200
Asset E	(300)

*As adjusted for the $100 floor on personal casualty losses.

Ross had no net § 1231 losses in tax years before 1994.

Disregarding the recapture of depreciation (discussed later in the chapter), Ross's gains and losses receive the following tax treatment:

- The diamond ring and the residence are personal use assets. Therefore, these casualties are not § 1231 transactions. The $800 (ring) plus $400 (residence) losses are potentially deductible *from* AGI. However, the total loss of $1,200 does not exceed 10% of AGI. Thus, only the business casualty remains. The $200 gain is added to the § 1231 gains.

- The gains from § 1231 transactions (Assets A, B, and C and the business casualty gain) exceed the losses by $1,100 ($1,600 − $500). This excess is a long-term capital gain and is added to Ross's other long-term capital gains.
- Ross's net long-term capital gain is $3,700 ($3,000 + $1,100 from § 1231 transactions − $400 long-term capital loss). Ross's net short-term capital gain is $800 ($1,000 − $200). The result is capital gain net income of $4,500. The $3,700 net long-term capital gain portion is eligible for the 28% alternative tax, and the $800 net short-term capital gain is subject to tax as ordinary income.[5]
- Ross treats the gain and loss from Assets D and E (depreciable business assets held for less than the long-term holding period) as ordinary gain and loss.

Results of the Gains and Losses on Ross's Tax Computation

NLTCG	$ 3,700
NSTCG	800
Ordinary gain from sale of Asset D	200
Ordinary loss from sale of Asset E	(300)
AGI from other sources	125,000
AGI	$129,400

- Ross will have personal casualty losses of $1,200 [$800 (diamond ring) + $400 (personal residence)]. A personal casualty loss is deductible only to the extent it exceeds 10% of AGI. Thus, none of the $1,200 is deductible ($129,400 × 10% = $12,940). ▼

EXAMPLE 5

Assume the same facts as in Example 4, except the loss from Asset C was $1,700 instead of $500.

- The treatment of the casualty losses is the same as in Example 4.
- The losses from § 1231 transactions now exceed the gains by $100 ($1,700 − $1,600). As a result, the gains from Assets A and B and the business casualty gain are ordinary income, and the loss from Asset C is a deduction *for* AGI (a business loss). The same result can be achieved by simply treating the $100 net loss as a deduction *for* AGI.
- Capital gain net income is $3,400 ($2,600 long-term + $800 short-term). The $2,600 net long-term capital gain portion is eligible for the 28% alternative tax, and the $800 net short-term capital gain is subject to tax as ordinary income.

Results of the Gains and Losses on Ross's Tax Computation

NLTCG	$ 2,600
NSTCG	800
Net ordinary loss on Assets A, B, and C and business casualty gain	(100)
Ordinary gain from sale of Asset D	200
Ordinary loss from sale of Asset E	(300)
AGI from other sources	125,000
AGI	$128,200

- None of the personal casualty losses will be deductible since $1,200 does not exceed 10% of $128,200. ▼

---

[5] Ross's taxable income (unless the itemized deductions and the personal exemption and dependency deductions are extremely large) will put him in at least the 31% tax bracket. Thus, the 28% alternative tax computation will yield a lower tax. See Example 36 in Chapter 16.

EXAMPLE 6

Assume the same facts as in Example 4, except that Ross has a $700 nonrecaptured net § 1231 loss from 1993.

- The treatment of the casualty losses is the same as in Example 4.
- The 1994 net § 1231 gain of $1,100 is treated as ordinary income to the extent of the 1993 nonrecaptured § 1231 loss of $700. The remaining $400 net § 1231 gain is a long-term capital gain and is added to Ross's other long-term capital gains.
- Ross's net long-term capital gain is $3,000 ($3,000 + $400 from § 1231 transactions – $400 long-term capital loss). Ross's net short-term capital gain is still $800 ($1,000 – $200). The result is capital gain net income of $3,800. The $3,000 net long-term capital gain portion is eligible for the 28% alternative tax, and the $800 net short-term capital gain is subject to tax as ordinary income.

Results of the Gains and Losses on Ross's Tax Computation

NLTCG	$ 3,000
NSTCG	800
Ordinary gain from recapture of § 1231 losses	700
Ordinary gain from sale of Asset D	200
Ordinary loss from sale of Asset E	(300)
AGI from other sources	125,000
AGI	$129,400

- None of the personal casualty losses will be deductible since $1,200 does not exceed 10% of $129,400. ▼

EXAMPLE 7

Assume the same facts as in Example 4, except that Ross had a net § 1231 loss of $2,700 in 1992 and a net § 1231 gain of $300 in 1993.

- The treatment of the casualty losses is the same as in Example 4.
- The 1992 net § 1231 loss of $2,700 will have carried over to 1993 and been offset against the 1993 net § 1231 gain of $300. Thus, the $300 gain will have been classified as ordinary income, and $2,400 of nonrecaptured 1992 net § 1231 loss will carry over to 1994. The 1994 net § 1231 gain of $1,100 will be offset against this loss, resulting in $1,100 of ordinary income. The nonrecaptured net § 1231 loss of $1,300 ($2,400 – $1,100) carries over to 1995.
- Capital gain net income is $3,400 ($2,600 net long-term capital gain + $800 net short-term capital gain). The $2,600 net long-term capital gain portion is eligible for the 28% alternative tax, and the $800 net short-term capital gain is subject to tax as ordinary income.

Results of the Gains and Losses on Ross's Tax Computation

NLTCG	$ 2,600
NSTCG	800
Ordinary gain from recapture of § 1231 losses	1,100
Ordinary gain from sale of Asset D	200
Ordinary loss from sale of Asset E	(300)
AGI from other sources	125,000
AGI	$129,400

- None of the personal casualty losses will be deductible since $1,200 does not exceed 10% of $129,400. ▼

SECTION 1245 RECAPTURE

3   LEARNING OBJECTIVE
Determine when § 1245 recapture applies and how it is computed.

Now that the basic rules of § 1231 have been introduced, it is time to add some complications. The Code contains two major *recapture* provisions—§§ 1245 and 1250. These provisions cause *gain* to be treated *initially* as ordinary gain. Thus, what may appear to be a § 1231 gain is ordinary gain instead. These recapture provisions may also cause a gain in a nonpersonal use casualty to be *initially* ordinary gain rather than casualty gain. Classifying gains (and losses) properly initially is important because improper initial classification may lead to incorrect mixing and matching of gains and losses. This section discusses the § 1245 recapture rules, and the next section discusses the § 1250 recapture rules.

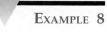

ETHICAL CONSIDERATIONS

Does Applying the Recapture Rules Make a Difference?

Due to their complexity, the § 1245 and § 1250 recapture rules require careful study to obtain a complete understanding. It is much easier just to assume that the sale of business fixed assets results in capital gain or loss. Certainly, most taxpayers expect that result. Quite often, taxable income is the same whether the recapture rules are properly applied or not. If ultimately there is *no difference* between taxable income with proper handling of recapture and taxable income without proper handling of recapture, is it not logical and practical for the tax return preparer simply to ignore the recapture rules?

Section 1245 prevents taxpayers from receiving the dual benefits of depreciation deductions that offset ordinary income plus § 1231 long-term capital gain treatment on the disposition of the depreciated property. Section 1245 applies primarily to non-real estate property such as machinery, trucks, and office furniture. Section 1245 requires recognized gain to be treated as ordinary income to the extent of depreciation taken on the property disposed of. Section 1245 does not apply if property is disposed of at a loss. Generally, the loss will be a § 1231 loss unless the form of the disposition is a casualty.

EXAMPLE 8

Alice purchased a $100,000 business machine and deducted $70,000 depreciation before selling it for $80,000. If it were not for § 1245, the $50,000 would be § 1231 gain ($80,000 amount realized – $30,000 adjusted basis). Section 1245 prevents this potentially favorable result by treating as ordinary income (not as § 1231 gain) any gain to the extent of depreciation taken. In this example, the entire $50,000 gain would be ordinary income. ▼

Section 1245 recapture provides, in general, that the portion of recognized gain from the sale or other disposition of § 1245 property that represents depreciation (including § 167 depreciation, § 168 cost recovery, § 179 immediate expensing, and § 197 amortization) is *recaptured* as ordinary income. Thus, in Example 8, $50,000 of the $70,000 depreciation taken is recaptured as ordinary income when the business machine is sold. Only $50,000 is recaptured rather than $70,000 because Alice is only required to recognize § 1245 recapture ordinary gain equal to the lower of the depreciation taken or the gain recognized. In Example 8, the recognized gain is lower than the depreciation taken.

TAX IN THE NEWS

RECAPTURING THE AMORTIZATION OF INTANGIBLE ASSETS

The Revenue Reconciliation Act of 1993 cleared up a major tax controversy—how to deduct the costs of intangible assets that have an uncertain life. The IRS had taken the position that such costs were capitalizable, but not amortizable. Section 197 now allows 15-year, straight-line amortization of intangible assets. Intangible assets include items like goodwill, going-concern value, customer lists, and similar items that are acquired when a business is purchased.

For instance, a national cable television company recently acquired a local cable television company by purchasing all of its assets. The most important asset acquired is the local company's subscribers. Those subscribers represent the future revenue stream.

The acquiring company must determine how much of the purchase price was paid for the "subscriber list." The amount paid is capitalized and then amortized over 15 years.

And now for the rest of the story! The amortization is subject to § 1245 recapture if the acquiring company later resells the local company's assets at a gain. Even though the subscriber list cannot be a § 1231 asset because it is intangible, the amortization is still subject to recapture by § 1245.

The method of depreciation (e.g., accelerated or straight-line) does not matter. All depreciation taken is potentially subject to recapture. Thus, § 1245 recapture is often referred to as *full recapture.* Any remaining gain after subtracting the amount recaptured as ordinary income will usually be § 1231 gain. The remaining gain would be casualty gain if it were disposed of in a casualty event. If the business machine in Example 8 had been disposed of by casualty and the $80,000 received had been an insurance recovery, Alice would still have a gain of $50,000, and the gain would still be recaptured by § 1245 as ordinary gain. The § 1245 recapture rules apply before there is any casualty gain. Since all the $50,000 gain is recaptured, no casualty gain arises from the casualty.

Although § 1245 applies primarily to non-real estate property, it does apply to certain real estate. Nonresidential real estate acquired after 1980 and before 1987 and for which accelerated depreciation (the statutory percentage method of the accelerated cost recovery system) is used is subject to the § 1245 recapture rules. Such property includes 15-year, 18-year, and 19-year nonresidential real estate.

The following examples illustrate the general application of § 1245.

EXAMPLE 9

On January 1, 1994, Gary sold for $13,000 a machine acquired several years ago for $12,000. He had taken $10,000 of depreciation on the machine.

- The recognized gain from the sale is $11,000. This is the amount realized of $13,000 less the adjusted basis of $2,000 ($12,000 cost – $10,000 depreciation taken).
- Depreciation taken is $10,000. Therefore, since § 1245 recapture gain is the lower of depreciation taken or gain recognized, $10,000 of the $11,000 recognized gain is ordinary income, and the remaining $1,000 gain is § 1231 gain.
- The § 1231 gain of $1,000 is also equal to the excess of the sales price over the original cost of the property ($13,000 – $12,000 = $1,000 § 1231 gain). ▼

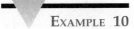

EXAMPLE 10

Assume the same facts as in the previous example, except the asset is sold for $9,000 instead of $13,000.

- The recognized gain from the sale is $7,000. This is the amount realized of $9,000 less the adjusted basis of $2,000.
- Depreciation taken is $10,000. Therefore, since the $10,000 depreciation taken exceeds the recognized gain of $7,000, the entire $7,000 recognized gain is ordinary income.
- The § 1231 gain is zero. There is no § 1231 gain because the selling price ($9,000) does not exceed the original purchase price ($12,000). ▼

EXAMPLE 11

Assume the same facts as in Example 9, except the asset is sold for $1,500 instead of $13,000.

- The recognized loss from the sale is $500. This is the amount realized of $1,500 less the adjusted basis of $2,000.
- Since there is a loss, there is no depreciation recapture. All of the loss is § 1231 loss. ▼

If § 1245 property is disposed of in a transaction other than a sale, exchange, or involuntary conversion, the maximum amount recaptured is the excess of the property's fair market value over its adjusted basis. See the discussion under Considerations Common to §§ 1245 and 1250 later in the chapter.

SECTION 1245 PROPERTY

Generally, **§ 1245 property** includes all depreciable personal property (e.g., machinery and equipment), including livestock. Buildings and their structural components generally are not § 1245 property. The following property is *also* subject to § 1245 treatment:

- Amortizable personal property such as goodwill, patents, copyrights, and leaseholds of § 1245 property. Professional baseball and football player contracts are § 1245 property.
- Amortization of reforestation expenditures and expensing of costs to remove architectural and transportation barriers to the handicapped and elderly.
- Section 179 immediate expensing of depreciable tangible personal property costs.
- Elevators and escalators acquired before January 1, 1987.
- Certain depreciable tangible real property (other than buildings and their structural components) employed as an integral part of certain activities such as manufacturing and production. For example, a natural gas storage tank where the gas is used in the manufacturing process is § 1245 property.
- Pollution control facilities, railroad grading and tunnel bores, on-the-job training, and child care facilities on which amortization is taken.
- Single-purpose agricultural and horticultural structures and petroleum storage facilities (e.g., a greenhouse or silo).
- As noted above, 15-year, 18-year, and 19-year nonresidential real estate for which accelerated cost recovery is used is subject to the § 1245 recapture rules, although it is technically not § 1245 property. Such property would have been placed in service after 1980 and before 1987.

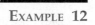

EXAMPLE 12

James acquired nonresidential real property on January 1, 1986, for $100,000. He used the statutory percentage method to compute the ACRS cost recovery. He sells the asset on

January 15, 1994, for $120,000. The amount and nature of James's gain are computed as follows:

Amount realized		$120,000
Adjusted basis		
Cost	$100,000	
Less cost recovery: 1986	(8,800)	
1987	(8,400)	
1988	(7,600)	
1989	(6,900)	
1990	(6,300)	
1991	(5,700)	
1992	(5,200)	
1993	(4,700)	
1994	(175)	
January 15, 1994, adjusted basis		(46,225)
Gain realized and recognized		$ 73,775

The gain of $73,775 is treated as ordinary income to the extent of *all* depreciation taken because the property is 19-year nonresidential real estate for which accelerated depreciation was used. Thus, James reports ordinary income of $53,775 ($8,800 + $8,400 + $7,600 + $6,900 + $6,300 + $5,700 + $5,200 + $4,700 + $175) and § 1231 gain of $20,000 ($73,775 − $53,775). ▼

OBSERVATIONS ON § 1245

- In most instances, the total depreciation taken will exceed the recognized gain. Therefore, the disposition of § 1245 property usually results in ordinary income rather than § 1231 gain. Thus, generally, no § 1231 gain will occur unless the § 1245 property is disposed of for more than its original cost. Refer to Examples 9 and 10.
- Recapture applies to the total amount of depreciation allowed or allowable regardless of the depreciation method used.
- Recapture applies regardless of the holding period of the property. Of course, the entire recognized gain would be ordinary income if the property were held for less than the long-term holding period because § 1231 would not apply.
- Section 1245 does not apply to losses, which receive § 1231 treatment.
- Gains from the disposition of § 1245 assets may also be treated as passive activity gains.

SECTION 1250 RECAPTURE

4   LEARNING OBJECTIVE
Determine when § 1250 recapture applies and how it is computed.

Generally, **§ 1250 property** is depreciable real property (principally buildings and their structural components) that is not subject to § 1245.[6] Intangible real property, such as leaseholds of § 1250 property, is also included.

---

[6] As previously discussed, in one limited circumstance, § 1245 does apply to nonresidential real estate. If the nonresidential real estate was placed in service after 1980 and before 1987 and accelerated depreciation was used, the § 1245 recapture rules rather than the § 1250 recapture rules apply.

Section 1250 recapture is substantially less punitive than § 1245 recapture since only the amount of additional depreciation is subject to recapture. To have additional depreciation, accelerated depreciation must have been taken on the asset. Straight-line depreciation (except for property held one year or less) is not recaptured. Since real property placed in service after 1986 can only be depreciated using the straight-line method, there will be *no § 1250 depreciation recapture* on such property.

Section 1250 was enacted in 1964 for depreciable real property and has been revised many times. The provision prevents taxpayers from receiving the benefits of both *accelerated* depreciation (or cost recovery) deductions and subsequent long-term capital gain treatment upon the disposition of real property. If straight-line depreciation is taken on the property, § 1250 does not apply. Nor does § 1250 apply if the real property is sold at a loss. The loss will generally be a § 1231 loss unless the property is disposed of by casualty.

Section 1250 as originally enacted required recapture of a percentage of the additional depreciation deducted by the taxpayer. **Additional depreciation** is the excess of accelerated depreciation actually deducted over depreciation that would have been deductible if the straight-line method had been used. Since only the additional depreciation is subject to recapture, § 1250 recapture is often referred to as *partial recapture*.

Post-1969 additional depreciation on nonresidential real property is subject to 100 percent recapture (see Example 13). Post-1969 additional depreciation on residential property may be subject to less than 100 percent recapture (see Example 14).

If § 1250 property is disposed of in a transaction other than a sale, exchange, or involuntary conversion, the maximum amount recaptured is the excess of the property's fair market value over the adjusted basis. For example, if a corporation distributes property to its shareholders as a dividend, the property will have been disposed of at a gain if the fair market value is greater than the adjusted basis. The maximum amount of § 1250 recapture will be the amount of the gain.

The following discussion describes the computational steps prescribed in § 1250 and reflected on Form 4797 (Sales of Business Property).

COMPUTING RECAPTURE ON NONRESIDENTIAL REAL PROPERTY

For § 1250 property other than residential rental property, the potential recapture is equal to the amount of additional depreciation taken since December 31, 1969. This nonresidential real property includes buildings such as offices, warehouses, factories, and stores. (The definition of and rules for residential rental housing are discussed later in the chapter.) The lower of the potential § 1250 recapture amount or the recognized gain is ordinary income. The following general rules apply:

- Post-1969 additional depreciation is depreciation taken in excess of straight-line after December 31, 1969.
- If the property is held for one year or less (usually not the case), all depreciation taken, even under the straight-line method, is additional depreciation.
- Special rules apply to dispositions of substantially improved § 1250 property. These rules are rather technical, and the reader should consult the examples in the Regulations for illustrations of their application.[7]

---

[7] § 1250(f) and Reg. § 1.1250–5.

The following procedure is used to compute recapture on nonresidential real property under § 1250:

- Determine the recognized gain from the sale or other disposition of the property.
- Determine post-1969 additional depreciation.
- The lower of the recognized gain or the post-1969 additional depreciation is ordinary income.
- If any recognized gain remains (total recognized gain less recapture), it is § 1231 gain. However, it would be casualty gain if the disposition was by casualty.

The following example shows the application of the § 1250 computational procedure.

EXAMPLE 13   On January 3, 1980, Larry acquired a new building at a cost of $200,000 for use in his business. The building had an estimated useful life of 50 years and no estimated salvage value. Depreciation has been taken under the 150% declining-balance method through December 31, 1993. Pertinent information with respect to depreciation taken follows:

Year	Undepreciated Balance (Beginning of the Year)	Current Depreciation Provision	Straight-Line Depreciation	Additional Depreciation
1980	$200,000	$ 6,000	$ 4,000	$ 2,000
1981	194,000	5,820	4,000	1,820
1982	188,180	5,645	4,000	1,645
1983	182,535	5,476	4,000	1,476
1984	177,059	5,312	4,000	1,312
1985	171,747	5,152	4,000	1,152
1986	166,595	4,998	4,000	998
1987	161,597	4,848	4,000	848
1988	156,749	4,702	4,000	702
1989	152,047	4,561	4,000	561
1990	147,486	4,425	4,000	425
1991	143,061	4,292	4,000	292
1992	138,769	4,163	4,000	163
1993	134,606	4,038	4,000	38
Total 1980–1993		$69,432	$56,000	$13,432

On January 2, 1994, Larry sold the building for $180,000. Compute the amount of his § 1250 ordinary income and § 1231 gain.

- Larry's recognized gain from the sale is $49,432. This is the difference between the $180,000 amount realized and the $130,568 adjusted basis ($200,000 cost − $69,432 depreciation taken).
- Post-1969 additional depreciation is $13,432.
- The amount of post-1969 ordinary income is $13,432. Since the post-1969 additional depreciation of $13,432 is less than the recognized gain of $49,432, the entire gain is not recaptured.
- The remaining $36,000 ($49,432 − $13,432) gain is § 1231 gain.   ▼

COMPUTING RECAPTURE ON RESIDENTIAL RENTAL HOUSING

Section 1250 recapture applies to the sale or other disposition of residential rental housing. Property qualifies as *residential rental housing* only if at least 80 percent of gross rent income is rent income from dwelling units.[8] The rules are the same as for other § 1250 property, except that only the post-1975 additional depreciation may be recaptured. The post-1969 through 1975 recapture percentage is 100 percent less one percentage point for each full month the property is held over 100 months.[9] Therefore, the additional depreciation for periods after 1975 is initially applied against the recognized gain, and such amounts may be recaptured in full as ordinary income. If any of the recognized gain is not absorbed by the recapture rules pertaining to the post-1975 period, the remaining gain is § 1231 gain.

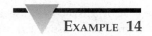

EXAMPLE 14

Assume the same facts as in the previous example, except the building is residential rental housing.

- Post-1975 ordinary income is $13,432 (post-1975 additional depreciation of $13,432).
- The remaining $36,000 ($49,432 – $13,432) gain is § 1231 gain. ▼

Under § 1250, when straight-line depreciation is used, there is no § 1250 recapture potential unless the property is disposed of in the first year of use. Before 1987, accelerated depreciation on real estate generally was available. For real property placed in service after 1986, however, only straight-line depreciation is allowed. Therefore, the § 1250 recapture rules do not apply to such property unless the property is disposed of in the first year of use.

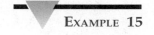

EXAMPLE 15

Sanjay acquires a residential rental building on January 1, 1993, for $300,000. He receives an offer of $450,000 for the building in 1994 and sells it on December 23, 1994.

- Sanjay takes $20,909 [($300,000 × .03485) + ($300,000 × .03636 × 11.5/12) = $20,909] of total depreciation for 1993 and 1994, and the adjusted basis of the property is $279,091 ($300,000 – $20,909).
- Sanjay's recognized gain is $170,909 ($450,000 – $279,091).
- All of the gain is § 1231 gain. ▼

SECTION 1250 RECAPTURE SITUATIONS

The § 1250 recapture rules apply to the following property for which accelerated depreciation was used:

- Residential real estate acquired before 1987.
- Nonresidential real estate acquired before 1981.
- Real property used predominantly outside the United States.
- Certain government-financed or low-income housing described in § 1250(a)(1)(B).

---

[8] § 168(e)(2)(A) and Reg. § 1.167(j)–3(b)(1)(i). Note that there may be residential, nonrental housing (e.g., a bunkhouse on a cattle ranch). Such property is commonly regarded as "nonresidential real estate." The rules for such property were discussed in the previous section.

[9] §§ 1250(a)(1) and (2) and Reg. § 1.1250–1(d)(1)(i)(c). Since the post-1969 through 1975 recapture percentage is 100% less one percentage point for each full month the property is held over 100 months, this approach now yields a zero percentage no matter when the property was acquired in the 1969–1975 period. For instance, if a building was acquired on January 3, 1975, and sold on January 3, 1994, it would have been held 228 months. The recapture percentage is zero because 100% – (228% – 100%) is less than zero.

CONCEPT SUMMARY 17–2

Comparison of § 1245 and § 1250 Depreciation Recapture

	§ 1245	§ 1250
Property affected	All depreciable personal property, but also nonresidential real property acquired after December 31, 1980, and before January 1, 1987, for which accelerated cost recovery was used. Also includes miscellaneous items such as § 179 expense and § 197 amortization of patents and copyrights.	Residential real property acquired after December 31, 1980, and before January 1, 1987, on which accelerated cost recovery was taken. Nonresidential real property acquired after December 31, 1969, and before January 1, 1976, on which accelerated depreciation was taken. Residential real and nonresidential real property acquired after December 31, 1975, and before January 1, 1981, on which accelerated depreciation was taken.
Depreciation recaptured	Potentially all depreciation taken. If the selling price is greater than or equal to the original cost, all depreciation is recaptured. If the selling price is between the adjusted basis and the original cost, only some depreciation is recaptured.	Additional depreciation (the excess of accelerated cost recovery over straight-line cost recovery or the excess of accelerated depreciation over straight-line depreciation).
Limit on recapture	Lower of depreciation taken or gain recognized.	Lower of additional depreciation or gain recognized.
Treatment of gain exceeding recapture gain	Usually § 1231 gain.	Usually § 1231 gain.
Treatment of loss	No depreciation recapture; loss is usually § 1231 loss.	No depreciation recapture; loss is usually § 1231 loss.

Concept Summary 17–2 compares and contrasts the § 1245 and § 1250 depreciation recapture rules.

CONSIDERATIONS COMMON TO
§§ 1245 AND 1250

EXCEPTIONS

Recapture under §§ 1245 and 1250 does not apply to the following transactions.

Gifts

The recapture potential carries over to the donee.[10]

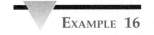

EXAMPLE 16

Wade gives his daughter, Helen, § 1245 property with an adjusted basis of $1,000. The amount of recapture potential is $700. Helen uses the property in her business and claims

---

[10]§§ 1245(b)(1) and 1250(d)(1) and Reg. §§ 1.1245–4(a)(1) and 1.1250–3(a)(1).

further depreciation of $100 before selling it for $1,900. Helen's recognized gain is $1,000 ($1,900 amount realized − $900 adjusted basis), of which $800 is recaptured as ordinary income ($100 depreciation taken by Helen + $700 recapture potential carried over from Wade). The remaining gain of $200 is § 1231 gain. Even if Helen used the property for personal purposes, the $700 recapture potential would still be carried over. ▼

Death

Although not a very attractive tax planning approach, death eliminates all recapture potential.[11] In other words, any recapture potential does not carry over from a decedent to an estate or heir.

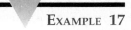
EXAMPLE 17

Assume the same facts as in Example 16, except Helen receives the property as a result of Wade's death. The $700 recapture potential from Wade is extinguished. Helen has a basis for the property equal to the property's fair market value (assume $1,700) at Wade's death. She will have a $300 gain when the property is sold because the selling price ($1,900) exceeds the property's adjusted basis ($1,700 original basis to Helen − $100 depreciation) by $300. Because of § 1245, $100 is ordinary income. The remaining gain of $200 is § 1231 gain. ▼

Charitable Transfers

The recapture potential reduces the amount of the charitable contribution deduction under § 170.[12]

EXAMPLE 18

Kanisha donates to her church § 1245 property with a fair market value of $10,000 and an adjusted basis of $7,000. Assume that the amount of recapture potential is $2,000 (the amount of recapture that would occur if the property were sold). Her charitable contribution deduction (subject to the limitations discussed in Chapter 10) is $8,000 ($10,000 fair market value − $2,000 recapture potential). ▼

Certain Nontaxable Transactions

These are transactions in which the transferor's adjusted basis of property carries over to the transferee.[13] The recapture potential also carries over to the transferee.[14] Included in this category are transfers of property pursuant to the following:

- Nontaxable incorporations under § 351.
- Certain liquidations of subsidiary companies under § 332.
- Nontaxable contributions to a partnership under § 721.
- Nontaxable reorganizations.

Gain may be recognized in these transactions if boot is received. If gain is recognized, it is treated as ordinary income to the extent of the recapture potential or recognized gain, whichever is lower.[15]

---

[11] §§ 1245(b)(2) and 1250(d)(2).

[12] § 170(e)(1)(A) and Reg. § 1.170A−4(b)(1). In certain circumstances, § 1231 gain also reduces the amount of the charitable contribution. See § 170(e)(1)(B).

[13] §§ 1245(b)(3) and 1250(d)(3) and Reg. §§ 1.1245−4(c) and 1.1250−3(c).

[14] Reg. §§ 1.1245−2(a)(4) and −2(c)(2) and 1.1250−2(d)(1) and (3) and −3(c)(3).

[15] §§ 1245(b)(3) and 1250(d)(3) and Reg. §§ 1.1245−4(c) and 1.1250−3(c). Some of these special corporate problems are discussed in Chapter 20. Partnership contributions are also discussed in Chapter 20.

Like-Kind Exchanges (§ 1031) and Involuntary Conversions (§ 1033)

Realized gain will be recognized to the extent of boot received under § 1031. Realized gain also will be recognized to the extent the proceeds from an involuntary conversion are not reinvested in similar property under § 1033. Such recognized gain is subject to recapture as ordinary income under §§ 1245 and 1250. The remaining recapture potential, if any, carries over to the property received in the exchange.

EXAMPLE 19

Anita exchanges § 1245 property with an adjusted basis of $300 for § 1245 property with a fair market value of $6,000. The exchange qualifies as a like-kind exchange under § 1031. Anita also receives $1,000 cash (boot). Her realized gain is $6,700 ($7,000 amount realized − $300 adjusted basis of property). Assuming the recapture potential is $7,500, Anita recognizes § 1245 gain of $1,000 because she received boot of $1,000. The remaining recapture potential of $6,500 carries over to the like-kind property received. ▼

OTHER APPLICATIONS

Sections 1245 and 1250 apply notwithstanding any other provisions in the Code.[16] That is, the recapture rules under these Sections *override* all other Sections. Special applications include installment sales and property dividends.

Installment Sales

Recapture gain is recognized in the year of the sale regardless of whether gain is otherwise recognized under the installment method.[17] All gain is ordinary income until the recapture potential is fully absorbed. Nonrecapture (§ 1231) gain is recognized under the installment method as cash is received.

EXAMPLE 20

Seth sells § 1245 property for $20,000, to be paid in 10 annual installments of $2,000 each plus interest at 10%. Seth realizes a $6,000 gain from the sale, of which $4,000 is attributable to depreciation taken. If Seth uses the installment method, he recognizes the entire $4,000 of recapture gain as ordinary income in the year of the sale. The $2,000 of nonrecapture (§ 1231) gain will be recognized at the rate of $200 per year for 10 years. ▼

Gain is also recognized on installment sales in the year of sale in an amount equal to the § 179 (immediate expensing) deductions taken with respect to the property sold.

Property Dividends

A corporation generally recognizes gain if it distributes appreciated property as a dividend. Recapture under §§ 1245 and 1250 applies to the extent of the lower of the recapture potential or the excess of the property's fair market value over the adjusted basis.[18]

---

[16] §§ 1245(d) and 1250(i).

[17] § 453(i). The installment method of reporting gains on the sale of property is discussed in Chapter 18.

[18] § 311(b) and Reg. §§ 1.1245–1(c) and −6(b) and 1.1250–1(a)(4), −1(b)(4), and −1(c)(2).

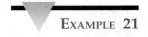

EXAMPLE 21   Emerald Corporation distributes § 1245 property as a dividend to its shareholders. The amount of the recapture potential is $300, and the excess of the property's fair market value over the adjusted basis is $800. Emerald recognizes $300 of ordinary income and $500 of § 1231 gain. ▼

Concept Summary 17–3 integrates the depreciation recapture rules with the § 1231 netting process. It is an expanded version of Concept Summary 17–1.

CONCEPT SUMMARY   17–3

Depreciation Recapture and § 1231 Netting Procedure

*Includes casualties and thefts.

SPECIAL RECAPTURE PROVISIONS

SPECIAL RECAPTURE FOR CORPORATIONS

5 **LEARNING OBJECTIVE**
Apply the special recapture provisions for related parties and IDC and be aware of the special recapture provision for corporations.

Corporations (other than S corporations) selling depreciable real estate may have ordinary income in addition to that required by § 1250.[19] See the discussion of this topic in Chapter 20.

GAIN FROM SALE OF DEPRECIABLE PROPERTY BETWEEN CERTAIN RELATED PARTIES

When the sale or exchange of property, which in the hands of the *transferee* is depreciable property (principally machinery, equipment, and buildings, but not land), is between certain related parties, any gain recognized is ordinary income.[20] This provision applies to both direct and indirect sales or exchanges. A **related party** is defined as an individual and his or her controlled corporation or partnership or a taxpayer and any trust in which the taxpayer (or the taxpayer's spouse) is a beneficiary.

EXAMPLE 22

Isabella sells a personal use automobile (therefore nondepreciable) to her controlled corporation. The automobile, which was purchased two years ago, originally cost $5,000 and is sold for $7,000. The automobile is to be used in the corporation's business. If the related-party provision did not exist, Isabella would realize a $2,000 long-term capital gain. The income tax consequences would be favorable because Isabella's controlled corporation is entitled to depreciate the automobile based upon the purchase price of $7,000. Under the related-party provision, Isabella's $2,000 gain is ordinary income. ▼

INTANGIBLE DRILLING COSTS

Taxpayers may elect to either *expense or capitalize* intangible drilling and development costs for oil, gas, or geothermal properties.[21] **Intangible drilling and development costs (IDC)** include operator (one who holds a working or operating interest in any tract or parcel of land) expenditures for wages, fuel, repairs, hauling, and supplies. These expenditures must be incident to and necessary for the drilling of wells and preparation of wells for production. In most instances, taxpayers elect to expense IDC to maximize tax deductions during drilling.

Intangible drilling and development costs are subject to § 1254 recapture when the property is disposed of. The gain on the disposition of the property is subject to recapture as ordinary income.

REPORTING PROCEDURES

6 **LEARNING OBJECTIVE**
Describe and apply the reporting procedures for §§ 1231, 1245, and 1250.

Noncapital gains and losses are reported on Form 4797, Sales of Business Property. Before filling out Form 4797, however, Form 4684, Casualties and Thefts, must be completed to determine whether or not any casualties will enter into the § 1231 computation procedure. Recall that gains from casualties may be recaptured by

---

[19] § 291(a)(1).
[20] § 1239.

[21] § 263(c).

§ 1245 or § 1250. These gains will not appear on Form 4684. Only long-term nonrecaptured nonpersonal use property casualty gains are netted against long-term nonpersonal use property casualty losses to determine whether there is a net gain to transfer to Part I of Form 4797.

Because the 1994 tax forms were unavailable at this writing, 1993 tax forms are used in the remainder of the discussion.

Form 4797 is divided into four parts, summarized as follows:

Part	Function
I	To report regular § 1231 gains and losses (including recognized gains and losses from certain involuntary conversions [condemnations]).
II	To report ordinary gains and losses.
III	To determine the portion of the gain that is subject to recapture (e.g., §§ 1245 and 1250 gain).
IV	Computation of recapture amounts under §§ 179 and 280F when business use of depreciable property drops to 50% or less.

Generally, the best approach to completing Form 4797 is to start with Part III. Once the recapture amount has been determined, it is transferred to Part II. The balance of any gain remaining after the recapture has been accounted for is transferred from Part III to Part I. Also transferred to Part I is any net gain from certain casualties and thefts as reported on Form 4684 (refer to above and Chapter 15). If the netting process in Part I results in a gain, it is reduced by the nonrecaptured net § 1231 losses from prior years (line 9 of Part I). Any remaining gain is shifted to Schedule D, Capital Gains and Losses, of Form 1040. If the netting process in Part I of Form 4797 results in a loss, it goes to Part II to be treated as an ordinary loss.

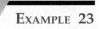 **EXAMPLE 23**

For 1993, Troy Williams (Social Security number 467–85–3036) had the following recognized gains and losses (a 1993 example has been used since 1994 forms were unavailable):

Sale of Depreciable Business Assets Held Long Term	
Asset A (Note 1)	$36,500
Asset B (Note 2)	23,538
Asset C (Note 3)	(880)

Sale of Depreciable Business Assets Held Short Term	
Asset D (Note 4)	$ (600)

Capital Assets	
Long-term gain (Note 5)	$ 3,000
Short-term loss (Note 6)	(200)

Note 1. Asset A was acquired on June 23, 1990, for $50,000. It was five-year MACRS property, and four years' cost recovery allowances totaled $38,480. The property was sold for $48,020 on August 31, 1993.

Note 2.   Asset B was purchased on May 10, 1986, for $37,000. It was 19-year ACRS property. Using the statutory percentage method, cost recovery totaled $17,538. The property was sold for $43,000 on January 10, 1993. The building was residential rental property, and straight-line cost recovery for the period of ownership would have totaled $13,061.

Note 3.   Asset C was purchased on December 9, 1990, for $16,000. It was five-year MACRS property, and four years' cost recovery totaled $12,314. The property was sold for $2,806 on December 30, 1993.

Note 4.   Asset D was purchased for $7,000 on July 27, 1993. It was five-year MACRS property but proved unsuitable to Troy's business. Troy sold it for $6,400 on November 3, 1993.

Note 5.   The LTCG resulted from the sale of 100 shares of Orange Corporation stock purchased for $10,000 on April 5, 1986. The shares were sold on October 21, 1993, for $13,223. Expenses of sale were $223.

Note 6.   The STCL resulted from the sale of 50 shares of Blue Corporation stock purchased for $350 on March 14, 1993. The shares were sold for $170 on August 20, 1993. Expenses of sale were $20.

The sale of assets A and B at a gain results in the recapture of cost recovery deductions. That recapture is shown in Part III of Form 4797. Some of the gain from the sale of asset B exceeds the recapture amount and is carried from line 34 to Part I, line 6, of Form 4797. On line 2, the loss from asset C appears. Part I is where the § 1231 netting process takes place. Assume Troy Williams has no nonrecaptured net § 1231 losses from prior years. The net gain on line 8 is transferred to Schedule D, line 12. In Part II of Form 4797, the ordinary gains are accumulated. On line 14, the recapture from line 33 (Part III) is shown. On line 11, the loss from asset D is shown. The net gain on line 20 is ordinary income and is transferred to Form 1040, line 15.

Schedule D, Part I, line 1, reports the short-term capital loss from the Blue Corporation stock. Part II of Schedule D has the net § 1231 gain transferred from Form 4797 on line 12 and the Orange Corporation gain on line 9. The net capital gain is determined on line 18, Part III. The capital gain is then carried to line 13 of Form 1040.

Form 4797 and Schedule D (Parts I–III) for Troy Williams are reproduced on the following pages. ▼

The 1993 tax forms solution for Example 23 appear on the following pages.

TAX PLANNING CONSIDERATIONS

7   **LEARNING OBJECTIVE**
Identify tax planning opportunities associated with §§ 1231, 1245, and 1250.

TIMING OF § 1231 GAIN

Although §§ 1245 and 1250 recapture much of the gain from the disposition of business property, sometimes § 1231 gain is still substantial. For instance, land held as a business asset will generate either § 1231 gain or § 1231 loss. If the taxpayer already has a capital loss for the year, the sale of land at a gain should be postponed so that the net § 1231 gain is not netted against the capital loss. The capital loss deduction will therefore be maximized for the current tax year, and the capital loss carryforward (if any) may be offset against the gain when the land is sold. If the taxpayer already has a § 1231 loss, § 1231 gains might be postponed to maximize the ordinary loss deduction this year. However, the carryforward of nonrecaptured § 1231 losses will make the § 1231 gain next year an ordinary gain.

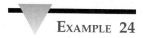

EXAMPLE 24

Mark has a $2,000 net STCL for 1994. He could sell business land for a $3,000 § 1231 gain. He will have no other capital gains and losses or § 1231 gains and losses in 1994 or 1995. He has no nonrecaptured § 1231 losses from prior years. Mark is in the 28% tax bracket in 1994 and 1995. If he sells the land in 1994, he will have a $1,000 net LTCG ($3,000 § 1231 gain − $2,000

| Form **4797** | | **Sales of Business Property** (Also Involuntary Conversions and Recapture Amounts Under Sections 179 and 280F(b)(2)) ▶ Attach to your tax return.   ▶ See separate instructions. | | OMB No. 1545-0184 **1993** Attachment Sequence No. **27** |

Department of the Treasury Internal Revenue Service

| Name(s) shown on return Troy Williams | Identifying number 467-85-3036 |

1   Enter here the gross proceeds from the sale or exchange of real estate reported to you for 1993 on Form(s) 1099-S (or a substitute statement) that you will be including on line 2, 11, or 22 . . . . | 1 |

Part I **Sales or Exchanges of Property Used in a Trade or Business and Involuntary Conversions From Other Than Casualty or Theft—Property Held More Than 1 Year**

(a) Description of property	(b) Date acquired (mo., day, yr.)	(c) Date sold (mo., day, yr.)	(d) Gross sales price	(e) Depreciation allowed or allowable since acquisition	(f) Cost or other basis, plus improvements and expense of sale	(g) LOSS ((f) minus the sum of (d) and (e))	(h) GAIN ((d) plus (e) minus (f))
2							
Asset C	12/9/90	12/30/90	2,806	12,314	16,000	880	

3   Gain, if any, from Form 4684, line 39 . . . . | **3** |
4   Section 1231 gain from installment sales from Form 6252, line 26 or 37 . . . . | **4** |
5   Section 1231 gain or (loss) from like-kind exchanges from Form 8824 . . . . | **5** |
6   Gain, if any, from line 34, from other than casualty or theft . . . . | **6** | 19,061 |
7   Add lines 2 through 6 in columns (g) and (h) . . . . | **7** (880) | 19,061 |
8   Combine columns (g) and (h) of line 7. Enter gain or (loss) here, and on the appropriate line as follows: | **8** | 18,181 |

Partnerships—Enter the gain or (loss) on Form 1065, Schedule K, line 6. Skip lines 9, 10, 12, and 13 below.

S corporations—Report the gain or (loss) following the instructions for Form 1120S, Schedule K, lines 5 and 6. Skip lines 9, 10, 12, and 13 below, unless line 8 is a gain and the S corporation is subject to the capital gains tax.

All others—If line 8 is zero or a loss, enter the amount on line 12 below and skip lines 9 and 10. If line 8 is a gain and you did not have any prior year section 1231 losses, or they were recaptured in an earlier year, enter the gain as a long-term capital gain on Schedule D and skip lines 9, 10, and 13 below.

9   Nonrecaptured net section 1231 losses from prior years (see instructions) . . . . | **9** |
10   Subtract line 9 from line 8. If zero or less, enter -0-. Also enter on the appropriate line as follows (see instructions): | **10** |

S corporations—Enter this amount (if more than zero) on Schedule D (Form 1120S), line 13, and skip lines 12 and 13 below.

All others—If line 10 is zero, enter the amount from line 8 on line 13 below. If line 10 is more than zero, enter the amount from line 9 on line 13 below, and enter the amount from line 10 as a long-term capital gain on Schedule D.

Part II **Ordinary Gains and Losses**

11   Ordinary gains and losses not included on lines 12 through 18 (include property held 1 year or less):

(a)	(b)	(c)	(d)	(e)	(f)	(g)	(h)
Asset D	7/27/93	11/3/93	6,400	0	7,000	600	

12   Loss, if any, from line 8 . . . . | **12** |
13   Gain, if any, from line 8, or amount from line 9 if applicable . . . . | **13** |
14   Gain, if any, from line 33 . . . . | **14** | 40,977 |
15   Net gain or (loss) from Form 4684, lines 31 and 38a . . . . | **15** |
16   Ordinary gain from installment sales from Form 6252, line 25 or 36 . . . . | **16** |
17   Ordinary gain or (loss) from like-kind exchanges from Form 8824 . . . . . | **17** |
18   Recapture of section 179 expense deduction for partners and S corporation shareholders from property dispositions by partnerships and S corporations (see instructions) . . . . . | **18** |
19   Add lines 11 through 18 in columns (g) and (h) . . . . | **19** (600) | 40,977 |
20   Combine columns (g) and (h) of line 19. Enter gain or (loss) here, and on the appropriate line as follows: . . . | **20** | 40,377 |
a   For all except individual returns: Enter the gain or (loss) from line 20 on the return being filed.
b   For individual returns:
  (1)   If the loss on line 12 includes a loss from Form 4684, line 35, column (b)(ii), enter that part of the loss here and on line 20 of Schedule A (Form 1040). Identify as from "Form 4797, line 20b(1)." See instructions . . . . | **20b(1)** | 0 |
  (2)   Redetermine the gain or (loss) on line 20, excluding the loss, if any, on line 20b(1). Enter here and on Form 1040, line 15 . . | **20b(2)** | 40,377 |

For Paperwork Reduction Act Notice, see page 1 of separate instructions.   Cat. No. 13086I   Form **4797** (1993)

Form 4797 (1993)

Page **2**

| **Part III** | Gain From Disposition of Property Under Sections 1245, 1250, 1252, 1254, and 1255 |

21	(a) Description of section 1245, 1250, 1252, 1254, or 1255 property:	(b) Date acquired (mo., day, yr.)	(c) Date sold (mo., day, yr.)
A	Asset A	6/23/90	8/31/93
B	Asset B	5/10/86	1/10/93
C			
D			

	Relate lines 21A through 21D to these columns	▶		Property A	Property B	Property C	Property D
22	Gross sales price (**Note:** See line 1 before completing.)	22		48,020	43,000		
23	Cost or other basis plus expense of sale	23		50,000	37,000		
24	Depreciation (or depletion) allowed or allowable	24		38,480	17,538		
25	Adjusted basis. Subtract line 24 from line 23	25		11,520	19,462		
26	Total gain. Subtract line 25 from line 22	26		36,500	23,538		
27	**If section 1245 property:**						
a	Depreciation allowed or allowable from line 24	27a		38,480			
b	Enter the **smaller** of line 26 or 27a	27b		36,500			
28	**If section 1250 property:** If straight line depreciation was used, enter -0- on line 28g, except for a corporation subject to section 291.				4,477		
a	Additional depreciation after 1975 (see instructions)	28a					
b	Applicable percentage multiplied by the **smaller** of line 26 or line 28a (see instructions)	28b			4,477		
c	Subtract line 28a from line 26. If residential rental property or line 26 is not more than line 28a, skip lines 28d and 28e	28c			19,061		
d	Additional depreciation after 1969 and before 1976	28d			0		
e	Enter the **smaller** of line 28c or 28d	28e			0		
f	Section 291 amount (corporations only)	28f			0		
g	Add lines 28b, 28e, and 28f	28g			4,477		
29	**If section 1252 property:** Skip this section if you did not dispose of farmland or if this form is being completed for a partnership.						
a	Soil, water, and land clearing expenses	29a					
b	Line 29a multiplied by applicable percentage (see instructions)	29b					
c	Enter the **smaller** of line 26 or 29b	29c					
30	**If section 1254 property:**						
a	Intangible drilling and development costs, expenditures for development of mines and other natural deposits, and mining exploration costs (see instructions)	30a					
b	Enter the **smaller** of line 26 or 30a	30b					
31	**If section 1255 property:**						
a	Applicable percentage of payments excluded from income under section 126 (see instructions)	31a					
b	Enter the **smaller** of line 26 or 31a	31b					

Summary of Part III Gains. Complete property columns A through D, through line 31b before going to line 32.

32	Total gains for all properties. Add columns A through D, line 26	32	60,038
33	Add columns A through D, lines 27b, 28g, 29c, 30b, and 31b. Enter here and on line 14	33	40,977
34	Subtract line 33 from line 32. Enter the portion from casualty or theft on Form 4684, line 33. Enter the portion from other than casualty or theft on Form 4797, line 6	34	19,061

| **Part IV** | Recapture Amounts Under Sections 179 and 280F(b)(2) When Business Use Drops to 50% or Less |

See instructions for Part IV.

			(a) Section 179	(b) Section 280F(b)(2)
35	Section 179 expense deduction or depreciation allowable in prior years	35		
36	Recomputed depreciation (see instructions)	36		
37	Recapture amount. Subtract line 36 from line 35. See instructions for where to report	37		

SCHEDULE D
(Form 1040)

Department of the Treasury
Internal Revenue Service

Capital Gains and Losses

▶ Attach to Form 1040.   ▶ See Instructions for Schedule D (Form 1040).
▶ Use lines 20 and 22 for more space to list transactions for lines 1 and 9.

OMB No. 1545-0074

1993

Attachment
Sequence No. **12**

Name(s) shown on Form 1040   Troy Williams

Your social security number
467 : 85 : 3036

| Part I | Short-Term Capital Gains and Losses—Assets Held One Year or Less |

(a) Description of property (Example: 100 sh. XYZ Co.)	(b) Date acquired (Mo., day, yr.)	(c) Date sold (Mo., day, yr.)	(d) Sales price (see page D-3)	(e) Cost or other basis (see page D-3)	(f) LOSS If (e) is more than (d), subtract (d) from (e)	(g) GAIN If (d) is more than (e), subtract (e) from (d)
1 Blue Corp. (50 shares)	3/14/93	8/20/93	170	370	200	

2 Enter your short-term totals, if any, from line 21 . . . . **2**

3 **Total short-term sales price amounts.** Add column (d) of lines 1 and 2 . . . **3**   170

4 Short-term gain from Forms 2119 and 6252, and short-term gain or (loss) from Forms 4684, 6781, and 8824 . . . . **4**

5 Net short-term gain or (loss) from partnerships, S corporations, and fiduciaries from Schedule(s) K-1 . . . . **5**

6 Short-term capital loss carryover from 1992 Schedule D, line 38 . . . . **6**

7 Add lines 1, 2, and 4 through 6, in columns (f) and (g) . . . . **7** (200   )

8 **Net short-term capital gain or (loss).** Combine columns (f) and (g) of line 7 . . . . . . **8**   (200)

| Part II | Long-Term Capital Gains and Losses—Assets Held More Than One Year |

9 Orange Corp. (100 shares)	4/5/86	10/21/93	13,223	10,223		3,000

10 Enter your long-term totals, if any, from line 23 . . . . **10**

11 **Total long-term sales price amounts.** Add column (d) of lines 9 and 10 . . . **11**   13,223

12 Gain from Form 4797; long-term gain from Forms 2119, 2439, and 6252; and long-term gain or (loss) from Forms 4684, 6781, and 8824 . . . **12**   18,181

13 Net long-term gain or (loss) from partnerships, S corporations, and fiduciaries from Schedule(s) K-1 . . . . **13**

14 Capital gain distributions **14**

15 Long-term capital loss carryover from 1992 Schedule D, line 45 . . . . **15**

16 Add lines 9, 10, and 12 through 15, in columns (f) and (g) **16** (21,181

17 **Net long-term capital gain or (loss).** Combine columns (f) and (g) of line 16 . . . . **17**   21,181

| Part III | Summary of Parts I and II |

18 Combine lines 8 and 17. If a loss, go to line 19. If a gain, enter the gain on Form 1040, line 13.
    Note: If both lines 17 and 18 are gains, see the **Schedule D Tax Worksheet** on page D-4 . . **18**   20,981

19 If line 18 is a (loss), enter here and as a (loss) on Form 1040, line 13, the **smaller** of these losses:
   a The (loss) on line 18; **or**
   b ($3,000) or, if married filing separately, ($1,500) . . . . **19** (   )
    Note: See the **Capital Loss Carryover Worksheet** on page D-4 if the loss on line 18 exceeds the loss on line 19 **or** if Form 1040, line 35, is a loss.

For Paperwork Reduction Act Notice, see Form 1040 instructions.   Cat. No. 11338H   Schedule D (Form 1040) 1993

STCL) and will pay a tax of $280 ($1,000 × 28%). If Mark sells the land in 1995, he will have a 1994 tax savings of $560 ($2,000 capital loss deduction × 28% tax rate on ordinary income). In 1995, he will pay tax of $840 ($3,000 gain × 28%). By postponing the sale for a year, Mark will have the use of $840 ($560 + $280). ▼

EXAMPLE 25

Beth has a $15,000 § 1231 loss in 1994. She could sell business equipment for a $20,000 § 1231 gain and a $12,000 § 1245 gain. Beth is in the 28% tax bracket in 1994 and 1995. She has no nonrecaptured § 1231 losses from prior years. If she sells the equipment in 1994, she will have a $5,000 net § 1231 gain and $12,000 of ordinary gain. Her tax would be $4,760 [($5,000 § 1231 gain × 28%) + ($12,000 ordinary gain × 28%)].

If Beth postpones the equipment sale until 1995, she would have a 1994 ordinary loss of $15,000 and tax savings of $4,200 ($15,000 × 28%). In 1995, she would have $5,000 of § 1231 gain (the 1994 § 1231 loss carries over and recaptures $15,000 of the 1995 § 1231 gain as ordinary income) and $27,000 of ordinary gain. Her tax would be $8,960 [($5,000 § 1231 gain × 28%) + ($27,000 ordinary gain × 28%)]. By postponing the equipment sale, Beth has the use of $8,960 ($4,200 + $4,760). ▼

TIMING OF RECAPTURE

Since recapture is usually not triggered until the property is sold or disposed of, it may be possible to plan for recapture in low-bracket or loss years. If a taxpayer has net operating loss carryovers that are about to expire, the recognition of ordinary income from recapture may be advisable to absorb the loss carryovers.

EXAMPLE 26

Ahmad has a $15,000 net operating loss carryover that will expire this year. He owns a machine that he plans to sell in the early part of next year. The expected gain of $17,000 from the sale of the machine will be recaptured as ordinary income under § 1245. Ahmad sells the machine before the end of this year and offsets $15,000 of the ordinary income against the net operating loss carryover. ▼

POSTPONING AND SHIFTING RECAPTURE

It is also possible to postpone recapture or to shift the burden of recapture to others. For example, recapture is avoided upon the disposition of a § 1231 asset if the taxpayer replaces the property by entering into a like-kind exchange. In this instance, recapture potential is merely carried over to the newly acquired property (refer to Example 19).

Recapture can be shifted to others through the gratuitous transfer of § 1245 or § 1250 property to family members. A subsequent sale of such property by the donee will trigger recapture to the donee rather than the donor (refer to Example 16). This procedure would be advisable only if the donee is in a lower income tax bracket than the donor.

AVOIDING RECAPTURE

The immediate expensing election (§ 179) is subject to § 1245 recapture. If the election is not made, the § 1245 recapture potential will accumulate more slowly (refer to Chapter 8). Since using the immediate expense deduction complicates depreciation and book accounting for the affected asset, not taking the deduction may make sense even though the time value of money might indicate it should be taken.

KEY TERMS

Additional depreciation, 17–16

Intangible drilling and development costs (IDC), 17–23

Nonpersonal use property, 17–6

Related party, 17–23

Section 1231 gains and losses, 17–4

Section 1231 lookback, 17–9

Section 1231 property, 17–5

Section 1245 property, 17–14

Section 1245 recapture, 17–12

Section 1250 property, 17–15

Section 1250 recapture, 17–16

PROBLEM
MATERIALS

DISCUSSION QUESTIONS

1. What types of transactions involving capital assets are included under § 1231? Why wouldn't they qualify for long-term capital gain treatment without § 1231?

2. Does § 1231 treatment apply to all business property?

3. The disposition of depreciable business property results in a net loss. How is the net loss treated for tax purposes?

4. What two developments near the start of World War II caused Congress to reexamine the tax treatment of business assets?

5. Name two types of assets that are neither § 1231 assets nor capital assets.

6. Does § 1231 property include depreciable business property held for the short-term holding period?

7. Is it possible to recognize both a gain and a loss on the sale of timber in one taxable year? How?

8. How long must a farmer who raises rabbits hold the rabbits before they become § 1231 assets?

9. Nonpersonal use property held long term is disposed of by casualty, but the insurance proceeds result in a gain. This is the only nonpersonal use property casualty during the year. How is the gain treated?

10. Do casualty gains from disposition of personal use assets receive § 1231 treatment?

11. Are recognized long-term business asset condemnation gains treated as § 1231 gains? (Ignore the possibility of depreciation recapture.)

12. How are personal use property condemnation gains and losses treated?

13. List the three steps in the § 1231 netting procedure.

14. How does the *lookback rule* change the character of a current-year net § 1231 gain?

15. Fully depreciated business equipment purchased for $75,000 was stolen from Max. It was not recovered, and the insurance reimbursement was $10,000. Is this $10,000 gain subject to depreciation recapture? Why?

16. Several years ago, business equipment was purchased for $3,000, and the entire purchase was immediately deducted under § 179. Is the § 179 expense subject to recapture under § 1245?

17. If a farmer buys a pig and uses MACRS, are the cost recovery deductions subject to § 1245 recapture if the pig is sold at a gain?

18. What is "additional depreciation"?

19. Differentiate between the types of property covered by §§ 1245 and 1250.

20. If depreciable real property is sold at a loss after being held long term, does § 1250 apply?

21. Why does § 1250 generally not apply to real estate acquired after 1986?

22. What is the definition of residential rental housing?

23. Do any of the recapture provisions apply to real property that is owned by a U.S. taxpayer, but used in Italy?

24. Death eliminates all recapture potential. Do you agree? Why or why not?

25. Does recapture apply when § 1245 property is donated to charity?

26. What provisions of the Internal Revenue Code do the §§ 1245 and 1250 recapture rules override?

27. May an installment sale trigger § 1245 recapture even though no gain would otherwise be currently recognizable?

28. What happens to depreciation recapture potential under either § 1245 or § 1250 when a corporate taxpayer distributes depreciable equipment as a property dividend? Assume the equipment would have been sold at a gain if it were sold rather than distributed.

29. May corporations transferring real estate have depreciation recapture in addition to § 1250 recapture?

30. In general, how does the related-party ordinary income provision differ from §§ 1245 and 1250?

31. Are intangible drilling and development costs subject to recapture?

32. What three tax forms may be required to properly report the gains and losses discussed in Chapter 17?

33. Where in the tax forms is the §§ 1245 and 1250 depreciation recapture shown?

34. On what tax form and where on that form does the § 1231 netting process to determine whether there is a net § 1231 gain or loss take place?

PROBLEMS

35. Sue-Jen purchased a contract to cut timber on a 100-acre tract of land in South Dakota in March 1992 for $20,000. On January 1, 1993, the timber had a fair market value of $50,000. Because of careless cutting in November 1993, when the fair market value was $55,000, the wood was sold on January 30, 1994, for $49,000.
    a. What gain (loss) was realized in 1992, 1993, and 1994? What gain (loss) was recognized in 1992, 1993, and 1994?
    b. What was the nature of the gains (losses) in (a)? What assumption must be made?
    c. Does the answer change if the timber was sold in December 1993? Why?
    d. If the timber was worth only $18,000 on January 1, 1993, was cut in November when worth $21,000, and was sold in December for $19,000, how would the answers to (a) and (b) change?

36. Bob owns a farming sole proprietorship. During the year, Bob sold a milk cow that he had owned for 13 months and a workhorse that he had owned for 56 months. The cow had an adjusted basis of $800 and was sold for $550. The horse had an adjusted basis of $350 and was sold for $1,000. Bob also has a $200 long-term capital loss from the sale of corporate stock. He has $55,000 of other AGI (not associated with the items above) for the year. He has no net § 1231 losses from previous years. What is the nature of the gains or losses from the disposition of the farm animals, and what is Bob's AGI for the year?

37. Vicki has the following net § 1231 results for each of the years shown. What would be the nature of the net gains in 1993 and 1994?

Tax Year	Net § 1231 Loss	Net § 1231 Gain
1989	$ 5,000	
1990	17,000	
1991	35,000	
1992		$10,000
1993		30,000
1994		25,000

38. Troy, who owns and operates a farm business, had the following transactions during 1994:

   • Damage from the wreck of a business machine held more than one year due to a hurricane ($15,000 loss).

   • Sale of a mechanical rake bought on April 1 and sold on September 1 ($600 loss).

   • Sale of farmland with unharvested crops, held four years ($12,000 gain).

   • Recovery on theft of a family brooch owned for 10 years ($10,000 gain).

   • Fire in silo on December 6, purchased May 8 ($1,000 loss).

   • Sale of grist mill owned 11 years ($3,000 loss).

   • Sale of 15 shares of ABC Corporation stock held four months ($1,800 gain).

   a. How is each transaction treated?
   b. What is Troy's 1994 AGI?

39. Rose Company owns two lathes. Lathe A was purchased several years ago for $15,000, has a $10,000 adjusted basis, and was sold in 1994 for $11,000. Lathe B was purchased several years ago for $8,000, has a $6,000 adjusted basis, and was sold in 1994 for $2,000. What are the amount and nature of the recognized gain or loss from the disposition of each asset?

40. Tan Corporation sold machines A and B during the current year. The machines had been purchased for $180,000 and $240,000, respectively. The machines were purchased eight years ago and were depreciated to zero. Machine A was sold for $40,000, and machine B for $260,000. What amount of gain is recognized by Tan, and what is the nature of the gain?

41. On March 1, 1990, Cardinal Company buys and places in service a new seven-year machine for $25,000. On April 1, 1994, Cardinal sells the machine for $3,000. Cost recovery deductions to date have been $17,841.
   a. What is Cardinal's realized and recognized loss?
   b. What is the nature of the loss?
   c. How much would Cardinal have to sell the machine for to avoid any gain or loss from the disposition? Is the machine still a § 1231 asset when there is no gain or loss on its disposition?

42. Green Manufacturing purchases a $3,000,000 propane storage tank and places it on a permanent framework outside its plant. The propane is drawn from the tank through a hose and valve system into the burners underneath Green's chemical vats. After $1,800,000 of cost recovery has been taken on the tank, it is sold for $2,300,000. What are the nature and amount of Green's gain or loss from the disposition of the tank?

43. On June 1, 1991, Sparrow Enterprises (not a corporation) acquired a retail store for $400,000. The store was 31.5-year real property, and the straight-line cost recovery method was used. The store was sold on June 21, 1994, for $370,000. Cost recovery taken totaled $38,000. What are the amount and nature of Sparrow's gain or loss from disposition of the store?

44. On January 1, 1984, Esteban acquired a $600,000 residential building for use in his rental activity. He took $450,000 of cost recovery on the building before disposing of it for

$800,000 on January 1, 1994. For the period Esteban held the building, straight-line cost recovery would have been $400,000. What are the amount and nature of Esteban's gain from the disposition of the property?

45. Dave is the sole proprietor of a trampoline shop. During 1994, the following transactions occurred:

- Unimproved land adjacent to the store was condemned by the city on February 1. The condemnation proceeds were $25,000. The land, acquired in 1982, had an allocable basis of $15,000. Dave has additional parking across the street and plans to use the condemnation proceeds to build his inventory.

- A truck used to deliver trampolines was sold on January 2 for $3,500. The truck was purchased on January 2, 1990, for $6,000. On the date of sale, the adjusted basis was $2,509.

- Dave sold an antique rowing machine at an auction. Net proceeds were $3,900. The rowing machine was purchased as used equipment 17 years ago for $5,200 and is fully depreciated.

- Dave sold an apartment building for $200,000 on September 1. The rental property was purchased on September 1, 1991, for $150,000 and was being depreciated over a 27.5-year life using the straight-line method. At the date of sale, the adjusted basis was $124,783.

- Dave's personal yacht was stolen September 5. The yacht had been purchased in August at a cost of $25,000. The fair market value immediately preceding the theft was $20,000. Dave was insured for 50% of the original cost, and he received $12,500 on December 1.

- Dave sold a Buick on May 1 for $9,600. The vehicle had been used exclusively for personal purposes. It was purchased on September 1, 1989, for $10,800.

- An adding machine used by Dave's bookkeeper was sold on June 1. Net proceeds of the sale were $135. The machine was purchased on June 2, 1990, for $350. It was being depreciated over a five-year life employing the straight-line method. The adjusted basis on the date of sale was $95.

- Dave's trampoline stretching machine (owned two years) was stolen on May 5, but the business's insurance company will not pay any of the machine's value because Dave failed to pay the insurance premium. The machine had a fair market value of $8,000 and an adjusted basis of $6,000 at the time of theft.

- Dave had AGI of $4,000 from sources other than those described above.

   a. For each transaction, what are the amount and nature of recognized gain or loss?
   b. What is Dave's 1994 AGI?

46. On January 1, 1986, Cora Hassant acquired depreciable real property for $100,000. She used accelerated depreciation to compute the asset's cost recovery. The asset was sold for $89,000 on January 3, 1994, when its adjusted basis was $46,225. Straight-line cost recovery for the period of time the asset was held would have been $44,300.
   a. What are the amount and nature of the gain if the real property was residential?
   b. What are the amount and nature of the gain if the real property was nonresidential?
   c. Cora is curious about how the recapture rules differ for residential rental real estate acquired in 1986 and for residential rental real estate acquired in 1987 and thereafter. Write a letter to Cora explaining the differences. Her address is 2345 Westridge Street #23, Homer, MT 67342.

47. On February 10, 1994, Amy sold land A ($55,000 cost; $45,000 sales price), land B ($35,000 cost; $75,000 sales price), and building B ($40,000 cost; $45,000 sales price). Land A was vacant land that Amy had purchased for investment in 1986. Land B had building B on it, and both assets had been purchased in January 1993. The building was used in Amy's business, and $1,375 of cost recovery had been taken on it. Amy has $14,000 nonrecaptured § 1231 losses from prior years. What are the amount and nature of each gain or loss, and what is Amy's AGI for 1994?

48. LaShona donates to her church § 1245 property with a $13,000 fair market value and a $10,000 adjusted basis. There would be $2,000 depreciation recapture if the property had been sold. What is LaShona's charitable contribution deduction? (Ignore the charitable contribution deduction limitations discussed in Chapter 10.)

49. Paul owned a § 1245 asset with an adjusted basis of $5,000. He had deducted cost recovery of $6,000 ($5,000 adjusted basis + $6,000 cost recovery = $11,000 original cost). On May 1, 1992, when the fair market value was $22,500, Paul made a gift of the asset to his daughter, Caroline. She used the asset in her business for two years (deducting an additional $2,000 of cost recovery). On November 7, 1994, Caroline sold the asset for $36,000.
    a. What is Caroline's basis for the asset on November 7, 1994?
    b. What are the amount and character of Caroline's recognized gain?
    c. How would your answers in (a) and (b) differ if Caroline had received the asset as a result of Paul's death?

50. Burt transferred forklifts used in his factory with recapture potential of $6,500 to a dealer in exchange for new forklifts worth $8,000 and $1,500 of marketable securities. The transaction qualified as a § 1031 like-kind exchange. Burt had an adjusted basis of $6,000 in the equipment.
    a. What is Burt's realized and recognized gain or loss?
    b. What is the nature of the recognized gain or loss?
    c. How would your answer to (a) or (b) change if no marketable securities were involved?

51. Cathy sells § 1245 property for $35,000, to be paid in 10 annual installments of $3,500 each plus interest at 8%. Cathy realizes a $12,000 gain from the sale, of which $12,000 is attributable to depreciation taken. Cathy would like to use the installment method to recognize the gain on the sale. May she do so?

52. Magenta Corporation owns business machinery that cost $45,000 and has a $32,000 adjusted basis. Magenta does not need the machine anymore, but its only shareholder, Jerry, would like to use it for his personal use. The machine has a $37,000 fair market value. How much gain (if any) and what kind of gain will Magenta recognize if it distributes the machine to Jerry as a property dividend?

53. Orange Corporation sells depreciable equipment for $59,000 to its sole shareholder, Jane. Orange had a $45,000 adjusted basis for the equipment and had originally paid $85,000 for it. Jane will use the equipment in her sole proprietorship business. The $59,000 sale price is the property's fair market value at the time of the sale. What are the consequences of this sale for Orange? For Jane?

54. Refer to the sample Form 4797 and Form 1040 Schedule D in the text. Form 4797, Part I, line 2h shows $43,000. Part I, line 9 shows $11,000. What amount should appear on Schedule D, line 12?

55. Refer to the sample Form 4797 and Form 1040 Schedule D in the text. Form 4797, Part III, line 32 shows $43,000. Part III, line 33 shows $11,000. What amount should appear on Part II, line 14?

56. Refer to the sample 1993 Form 4797 and Form 1040 Schedule D in the text. Ernest has the following items on these forms:

Item	Form 4797		Schedule D
Property A (§ 1245 property)	Line 24	$86,000	
	Line 26	96,000	
Property B (§ 1250 property)	Line 26	34,000	
	Line 28a	32,000	
Property C			Line 9 ($3,000)

Ernest has no nonrecaptured § 1231 losses from prior years. What is Ernest's entry on line 12 of Schedule D?

CUMULATIVE PROBLEMS

57. Glen and Diane Okumura are married, file a joint return, and live at 39 Kaloa Street, Honolulu, Hawaii 56790. Glen's Social Security number is 777–88–2000 and Diane's is 888–77–1000. The Okumuras have two dependent children, Amy (age 15) and John (age 9). Glen works for the Hawaii Public Works Department, and Diane owns a retail dress shop. The Okumuras had the following transactions during 1994:
   a. Glen earned $57,000 in wages and had Federal income tax withholding of $14,000.
   b. Diane had net income of $98,000 from the dress shop and made Federal income tax estimated payments of $104,000.
   c. The Okumuras sold a small apartment building for $465,000 on November 15, 1994. The building was acquired in October 1988 for $300,000, cost recovery was $86,820.
   d. Diane sold a delivery truck used in her business. The truck cost $35,000, $21,700 of cost recovery had been taken, and it was sold for $18,000.
   e. The Okumuras received $13,000 in dividends on various domestic corporation stock that they own.
   f. The Okumuras sold stock for a $15,000 long-term capital gain and other stock at a $6,000 short-term capital loss.
   g. The Okumuras had the following itemized deductions: $1,000 unreimbursed medical expenses; $10,500 personal use property taxes; $7,000 qualified residence interest; $3,000 consumer interest; $1,500 of Glen's unreimbursed employee business expenses; $535 of investment-related expenses; and $6,300 of state income taxes paid.

Compute the Okumuras' 1994 net tax payable or refund due. (Ignore self-employment tax.) Suggested software (if available): *TurboTax* or *MacInTax* for tax return or WFT tax planning software.

58. Linda Franklin is an attorney. She is single and lives at 1619 Merry Lane, Cantone, TN 16703. Her Social Security number is 345–67–8900. Linda receives a salary of $45,000. During 1993, she had the following property transactions:
   a. Sales of stock held for investment:

Stock	Selling Price	Basis	Date Sold	Date Acquired
Acme Corporation	$2,000	$ 1,400	6/30/1993	12/31/1992
Bareham Corporation	8,000	10,500	12/31/1993	7/15/1993
Cronin, Inc.	9,400	5,400	7/26/1993	5/2/1983
Davis Corporation	1,800	2,900	10/18/1993	10/17/1984

   b. Complete destruction of a personal use travel trailer in a wreck on August 1 (adjusted basis, $6,500; fair market value, $5,000; reimbursement for loss by insurance company, $3,000). Linda had bought the trailer on June 12, 1987.
   c. Sale of photocopying machine used in business for $2,800 on November 6. Linda had acquired the machine on April 29, 1991, for $4,000 and had taken $2,163 of cost recovery on it.
   d. Sale of typewriter used in business on January 15 for $500. The typewriter was acquired on May 8, 1991, at a cost of $1,000; cost recovery of $395 had been deducted.
   e. Cash dividends of $5,000 (all from Bareham stock).

Compute Linda Franklin's AGI from these transactions. If you use tax forms in your computations, you will need Forms 1040, 4684, and 4797 and Schedule D. Suggested software (if available): *TurboTax* or *MacInTax* for tax return or WFT tax planning software.

RESEARCH PROBLEMS

Research Problem 1.   Sidney owns a professional football franchise. He has received an offer of $80 million for the franchise, all the football equipment, the rights to concession receipts, the rights to a stadium lease, and the rights to all the player contracts he owns. Most of the players have been with the team for quite a long time and have contracts that were signed several years ago. The contracts have been substantially depreciated. Sidney is concerned about potential § 1245 recapture when the contracts are sold. He has heard about "previously unrecaptured depreciation with respect to initial contracts" and would like to know more about it. Find a definition for that phrase and write an explanation of it.

Partial list of research aids:
§ 1245(a)(4).

Research Problem 2.   On May 10, 1986, Dave purchased a $160,000 building (but not the land) that was 60 feet wide, 80 feet deep, and two stories high. The front 60 feet of the 80-foot first-floor depth was rented as a retail store. The remaining 20 feet of the first floor and all of the second floor were rented for residential use. The retail portion of the property rented for $25 per square foot per year, and the residential portion of the property rented for $15 per square foot per year. The building was fully occupied throughout the time Dave owned it. Dave used the ACRS statutory percentages and sold the building for $140,000 on December 31, 1994. Dave is unsure whether all the depreciation is subject to recapture by § 1245, some of it is subject to recapture by § 1250, or none of it is subject to recapture.

Does § 1245 or § 1250 recapture apply in this situation? Write a letter to Dave that contains your advice and prepare a memo for the tax files.

Research Problem 3.   Amata is both a real estate developer and the owner and manager of rental real estate. Amata is retiring and is going to sell both the land he is holding for future development and the rental properties he owns. Straight-line depreciation was used to depreciate the rental real estate. The rental properties will be sold at a substantial loss, and the development property will be sold at a substantial gain. What is the nature of these gains and losses?

Partial list of research aids:
§§ 1221 and 1231.
Tollis v. Comm., 65 T.C.M. 1951, T.C.Memo 1993–63.

Research Problem 4.   During 1994, Honest John's Auto Sales, a dealer in new and used cars, sold some new cars, some used cars, some company cars (used in the business to run errands, etc.), and some demonstrators. Since Honest John's is a dealer, can any of these sales be considered sales of § 1231 assets?

Partial list of research aids:
§ 1231(b).
Latimer-Looney Chevrolet, Inc., 19 T.C. 120 (1952), *acq.*

VI

ACCOUNTING PERIODS, ACCOUNTING METHODS, AND DEFERRED COMPENSATION

Part VI provides a more comprehensive examination of the accounting periods and accounting methods that were introduced in Part II. A discussion of special accounting methods is also included. Part VI concludes with an analysis of the tax consequences of deferred compensation transactions.

Chapter 18

Accounting Periods and Methods

Chapter 19

Deferred Compensation

ACCOUNTING PERIODS AND METHODS

LEARNING OBJECTIVES

After completing Chapter 18, you should be able to:

1. Understand the relevance of the accounting period concept, the different types of accounting periods, and the limitations on their use.

2. Apply the cash method, accrual method, and hybrid method of accounting.

3. Utilize the procedure for changing accounting methods.

4. Determine when the installment method of accounting can be utilized and apply the related calculation techniques.

5. Understand the alternative methods of accounting for long-term contracts (the completed contract method and the percentage of completion method) including the limitations on the use of the completed contract method.

6. Understand when accounting for inventories must occur, recognize the types of costs that must be included in inventories, and apply the LIFO method.

7. Identify tax planning opportunities related to accounting periods and accounting methods.

Accounting Periods, 18–3

In General, 18–3

Making the Election, 18–7

Changes in the Accounting Period, 18–7

Taxable Periods of Less Than One Year, 18–8

Mitigation of the Annual Accounting Period Concept, 18–9

Accounting Methods, 18–10

Permissible Methods, 18–10

Cash Receipts and Disbursements Method—Cash Basis, 18–11

Accrual Method, 18–12

Hybrid Method, 18–15

Change of Method, 18–15

Special Accounting Methods, 18–19

Installment Method, 18–19

Disposition of Installment Obligations, 18–25

Interest on Deferred Taxes, 18–25

Electing Out of the Installment Method, 18–26

Long-Term Contracts, 18–26

Inventories, 18–31

Determining Inventory Cost, 18–32

The LIFO Election, 18–36

Tax Planning Considerations, 18–37

Taxable Year, 18–37

Cash Method of Accounting, 18–37

Installment Method, 18–37

LIFO, 18–38

Tax practitioners must deal with the issue of *when* particular items of income and expense are recognized as well as the basic issue of *whether* the items are includible in taxable income. Earlier chapters discussed the types of income subject to tax (gross income and exclusions) and allowable deductions (the *whether* issue).[1] This chapter focuses on the related issue of the periods in which income and deductions are reported (the *when* issue). Generally, a taxpayer's income and deductions must be assigned to particular 12-month periods—calendar years or fiscal years.

Income and deductions are placed within particular years through the use of tax accounting methods. The basic accounting methods are the cash method,

---

TAX IN THE NEWS

ACCELERATION OF INCOME

Hillary Rodham Clinton had the opportunity to receive compensation income in 1992 or 1993. She chose to accelerate the income into 1992. This appears to be at variance with the normal tax planning mode of deferring the reporting of income and accelerating the reporting of deductions.

One possible explanation for reporting the income in 1992 rather than in 1993 is that the family's taxable income was expected to be greater in 1993 than in 1992. However, while the President earns substantially more as President of the United States than as the Governor of Arkansas, the First Lady earns substantially less than she did as a partner in an Arkansas law firm.

Another possible explanation is the expectation that the Revenue Reconciliation Act of 1993 with its retroactive increase in tax rates would be passed by Congress. In any event, the First Lady followed sound tax advice in accelerating the income into 1992.

SOURCE: Information from several sources, among them "Hillary Rodham Laffer?" *Wall Street Journal*, April 22, 1993, p. A14.

---

[1] See Chapters 4, 5, and 6.

accrual method, and hybrid method. Other special purpose methods are available for specific circumstances or types of transactions such as the installment method and the methods used for long-term construction contracts.

Over the long run, the accounting period used by a taxpayer will not affect the aggregate amount of reported taxable income. However, taxable income for any particular year may vary significantly due to the use of a particular reporting period. Also, through the choice of accounting methods or accounting periods, it is possible to postpone the recognition of taxable income and to enjoy the benefits from deferring the related tax. This chapter discusses the taxpayer's alternatives for accounting periods and accounting methods.

ACCOUNTING PERIODS

IN GENERAL

1 LEARNING OBJECTIVE
Understand the relevance of the accounting period concept, the different types of accounting periods, and the limitations on their use.

A taxpayer who keeps adequate books and records may be permitted to elect a **fiscal year,** a 12-month period ending on the *last day* of a month other than December, for the **accounting period.** Otherwise, a *calendar year* must be used.[2] Frequently, corporations can satisfy the record-keeping requirements and elect to use a fiscal year.[3] Often the fiscal year conforms to a natural business year (e.g., a summer resort's fiscal year may end on September 30, after the close of the season). Individuals seldom use a fiscal year because they do not maintain the necessary books and records and because complications can arise as a result of changes in the tax law (e.g., often the transition rules and effective dates differ for fiscal year taxpayers).

Generally, a taxable year may not exceed 12 calendar months. However, if certain requirements are met, a taxpayer may elect to use an annual period that varies from 52 to 53 weeks.[4] In that case, the year-end must be on the same day of the week (e.g., the Tuesday falling closest to October 31 or the last Tuesday in October). The day of the week selected for ending the year will depend upon business considerations. For example, a retail business that is not open on Sundays may end its tax year on a Sunday so that it can take an inventory without interrupting business operations.

EXAMPLE 1

Wade is in the business of selling farm supplies. His natural business year terminates at the end of October with the completion of harvesting. At the end of the fiscal year, Wade must take an inventory, which is most easily accomplished on a Tuesday. Therefore, Wade could adopt a 52–53 week tax year ending on the Tuesday closest to October 31. If Wade selects this method, the year-end date may fall in the following month if that Tuesday is closer to October 31. The tax year ending in 1994 will contain 52 weeks beginning on Wednesday, November 3, 1993, and ending on Tuesday, November 1, 1994. The tax year ending in 1995 will have 52 weeks beginning on Wednesday, November 2, 1994, and ending on Tuesday, October 31, 1995. ▼

Partnerships and S Corporations

When a partner's tax year and the partnership's tax year differ, the partner will enjoy a deferral of income. This results because the partner reports his or her share

---

[2] § 441(c) and Reg. § 1.441–1(b)(1)(ii).
[3] Reg. § 1.441–1(e)(2).

[4] § 441(f).

of the partnership's income and deductions for the partnership's tax year ending within or with the partner's tax year.[5] For example, if the tax year of the partnership ends on January 31, a calendar year partner will not report partnership profits for the first 11 months of the partnership tax year until the following year. Therefore, partnerships are subject to special tax year requirements.

In general, the partnership tax year must be the same as the tax year of the majority interest partners. The **majority interest partners** are the partners who own a greater than 50 percent interest in the partnership capital and profits. If the majority owners do not have the same tax year, the partnership must adopt the same tax year as its principal partners. A **principal partner** is a partner with a 5 percent or more interest in the partnership capital or profits.[6]

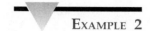

EXAMPLE 2

The RST Partnership is owned equally by Rose Corporation, Silver Corporation, and Tom. The partners have the following tax years.

	Partner's Tax Year Ending
Rose	June 30
Silver	June 30
Tom	December 31

The partnership's tax year must end on June 30. If Silver Corporation's as well as Tom's year ended on December 31, the partnership would be required to adopt a calendar year. ▼

If the principal partners do not all have the same tax year and no majority of partners have the same tax year, the partnership must use a year that results in the *least aggregate deferral* of income.[7] Under the **least aggregate deferral method,** the different tax years of the principal partners are tested to determine which produces the least aggregate deferral. This is calculated by first multiplying the combined percentages of the principal partners with the same tax year by the months of deferral for the test year. Once this is done for each set of principal partners with the same tax year, the resulting products are summed to produce the aggregate deferral. After calculating the aggregate deferral for each of the test years, the test year with the smallest summation (the least aggregate deferral) is the tax year for the partnership.

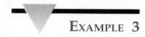

EXAMPLE 3

The DE Partnership is owned equally by Diane and Emily. Diane's fiscal year ends on March 31, and Emily's fiscal year ends on August 31. The partnership must use the partner's fiscal year that will result in the least aggregate deferral of income. Therefore, the fiscal years ending March 31 and August 31 must both be tested.

	Test for Fiscal Year Ending March 31			
Partner	**Year Ends**	**Profit %**	**Months of Deferral**	**Product**
Diane	3–31	50	0	0
Emily	8–31	50	5	2.5
Aggregate deferral months				2.5

---

[5] Reg. § 1.706–1(a).
[6] §§ 706(b)(1)(B) and 706(b)(3).

[7] Temp.Reg. § 1.706–1T(a)(2).

Thus, with a year ending March 31, Emily would be able to defer her half of the income for five months. That is, Emily's share of the partnership income for the fiscal year ending March 31, 1995, would not be included in her income until August 31, 1995.

Partner	Year Ends	Profit %	Months of Deferral	Product
Diane	3–31	50	7	3.5
Emily	8–31	50	0	0
Aggregate deferral months				3.5

Test for Fiscal Year Ending August 31

Thus, with a year ending August 31, Diane would be able to defer her half of the income for seven months. That is, Diane's share of the partnership income for the fiscal year ending August 31, 1995, would not be included in her income until March 31, 1996.

The year ending March 31 must be used because it results in the least aggregate deferral of income. ▼

Generally, S corporations must adopt a calendar year.[8] However, partnerships and S corporations may *elect* an otherwise *impermissible year* under any of the following conditions:

- A business purpose for the year can be demonstrated.[9]
- The partnership's or S corporation's year results in a deferral of not more than three months' income, and the entity agrees to make required tax payments.[10]
- The entity retains the same year as was used for the fiscal year ending in 1987, provided the entity agrees to make required tax payments.

Business Purpose

The only business purpose for a fiscal year that the IRS has acknowledged is the need to conform the tax year to the natural business year of a business.[11] Generally, only seasonal businesses have a natural business year. For example, the natural business year for a department store may end on January 31, after Christmas returns have been processed and clearance sales have been completed.

Required Tax Payments

Under this system, tax payments are due from the partnership or S corporation by April 15 of each tax year.[12] The amount due is computed by applying the highest individual tax rate plus 1 percent to an estimate of the deferral period income. The deferral period runs from the close of the fiscal year to the end of the calendar year. Estimated income for this period is based on the average monthly earnings for the previous fiscal year. The amount due is reduced by the amount of required tax payments for the previous year.[13]

---

[8] §§ 1378(a) and (b).
[9] §§ 706(b)(1)(C) and 1378(b)(2).
[10] § 444.
[11] Rev.Rul. 87–57, 1987–2 C.B. 117.

[12] §§ 444(c) and 7519. No payment is required if the calculated amount is $500 or less.
[13] § 7519(b).

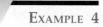

EXAMPLE 4

Brown, Inc., an S corporation, elected a fiscal year ending September 30. Bob is the only shareholder. For the fiscal year ending September 30, 1994, Brown earned $100,000. The required tax payment for the previous year was $5,000. The corporation must pay $5,150 by April 15, 1995, calculated as follows:

$$(\$100,000 \times 3/12 \times 40.6\%^*) - \$5,000 = \$5,150$$

*Maximum § 1 rate of 39.6% + 1%.   ▼

Personal Service Corporations

A **personal service corporation (PSC)** is a corporation whose shareholder-employees provide personal services (e.g., medical, dental, legal, accounting, engineering, actuarial, consulting, or performing arts). Generally, a PSC must use a calendar year.[14] However, a PSC can *elect* a fiscal year under any of the following conditions:

- A business purpose for the year can be demonstrated.
- The PSC year results in a deferral of not more than three months' income, the corporation pays the shareholder-employee's salary during the portion of the calendar year after the close of the fiscal year, and the salary for that period is at least proportionate to the shareholder-employee's salary received for the fiscal year.[15]
- The PSC retains the same year it used for the fiscal year ending in 1987, provided it satisfies the latter two requirements in the preceding option.

EXAMPLE 5

Nancy's corporation paid Nancy a salary of $120,000 during its fiscal year ending September 30, 1994. The corporation cannot satisfy the business purpose test for a fiscal year. The corporation can continue to use its fiscal year without any negative tax effects, provided Nancy receives at least $30,000 (3 months/12 months × $120,000) as salary during the period October 1 through December 31, 1994. ▼

If the salary test is not satisfied, the PSC can retain the fiscal year, but the corporation's deduction for salary for the fiscal year is limited to the following:

A + A(F/N)

Where A = Amount paid after the close of the fiscal year

       F = Number of months in fiscal year minus number of months from the end of the fiscal year to the end of the ongoing calendar year

       N = Number of months from the end of the fiscal year to the end of the ongoing calendar year

EXAMPLE 6

Assume the corporation in the previous example paid Nancy $10,000 of salary during the period October 1 through December 31, 1994. The deduction for Nancy's salary for the corporation's fiscal year ending September 30, 1995, is thus limited to $40,000 calculated as follows:

$$\$10,000 + \left[\$10,000\left(\frac{12-3}{3}\right)\right] = \$10,000 + \$30,000 = \$40,000$$

    ▼

---

[14] § 441(i).
[15] §§ 444 and 280H.

MAKING THE ELECTION

A taxpayer elects to use a calendar or fiscal year by the timely filing of his or her initial tax return. For all subsequent years, the taxpayer must use this same period unless approval for change is obtained from the IRS.[16]

CHANGES IN THE ACCOUNTING PERIOD

A taxpayer must obtain consent from the IRS before changing the tax year.[17] This power to approve or not to approve a change is significant in that it permits the IRS to issue authoritative administrative guidelines that must be met by taxpayers who wish to change their accounting period. An application for permission to change tax years must be made on Form 1128, Application for Change in Accounting Period. The application must be filed on or before the fifteenth day of the second calendar month following the close of the short period that results from the change in accounting period.[18]

▼
EXAMPLE 7

Beginning in 1994, Gold Corporation, a calendar year taxpayer, would like to switch to a fiscal year ending March 31. The corporation must file Form 1128 by May 15, 1994. ▼

IRS Requirements

The IRS will not grant permission for the change unless the taxpayer can establish a substantial business purpose for the request. One substantial business purpose is to change to a tax year that coincides with the *natural business year* (the completion of an annual business cycle). The IRS applies an objective gross receipts test to determine if the entity has a natural business year. At least 25 percent of the entity's gross receipts for the 12-month period must be realized in the final 2 months of the 12-month period for three consecutive years.[19]

▼
EXAMPLE 8

A Virginia Beach motel had gross receipts as follows:

	1992	**1993**	**1994**
July–August receipts	$ 300,000	$250,000	$ 325,000
September 1–August 31 receipts	1,000,000	900,000	1,250,000
Receipts for 2 months divided by receipts for 12 months	30.0%	27.8%	26.0%

Since it satisfies the natural business year test, the motel will be allowed to use a fiscal year ending August 31. ▼

---

[16] Reg. §§ 1.441–1(b)(3) and 1.441–1(b)(4).
[17] § 442. Under certain conditions, corporations are allowed to change tax years without obtaining IRS approval. See Reg. § 1.442–1(c)(1).
[18] Reg. § 1.442–1(b)(1). In Example 7, the first period after the change in accounting period (January 1, 1994, through March 31,

1994) is less than a 12-month period and is referred to as a *short period.*
[19] Rev.Proc. 87–32, 1987–1 C.B. 131, and Rev.Rul. 87–57, 1987–2 C.B. 117.

The IRS usually establishes certain conditions that the taxpayer must accept if the approval for change is to be granted. In particular, if the taxpayer has a net operating loss for the short period, the IRS may require that the loss be carried forward and allocated equally over the 6 following years.[20] As you may recall (refer to Chapter 7), net operating losses are ordinarily carried back for 3 years and forward for 15 years.

EXAMPLE 9

Parrot Corporation changed from a calendar year to a fiscal year ending September 30. The short-period return for the nine months ending September 30, 1994, reflected a $60,000 net operating loss. The corporation had taxable income for 1991, 1992, and 1993. As a condition for granting approval, the IRS requires Parrot to allocate the $60,000 loss over the next six years, rather than carrying the loss back to the three preceding years (the usual order for applying a net operating loss). Thus, Parrot Corporation will reduce its taxable income by $10,000 each year ending September 30, 1995, through September 30, 2000. ▼

TAXABLE PERIODS OF LESS THAN ONE YEAR

A **short taxable year** (or **short period**) is a period of less than 12 calendar months. A taxpayer may have a short year for (1) the first income tax return, (2) the final income tax return, or (3) a change in the tax year. If the short period results from a change in the taxpayer's annual accounting period, the taxable income for the period must be annualized. Due to the progressive tax rate structure, taxpayers could reap benefits from a short-period return if some adjustments were not required. Thus, the taxpayer is required to do the following:

1. Annualize the short-period income.

$$\text{Annualized income} = \text{Short-period income} \times \frac{12}{\text{Number of months in the short period}}$$

2. Compute the tax on the annualized income.
3. Convert the tax on the annualized income to a short-period tax.

$$\text{Short-period tax} = \text{Tax on annualized income} \times \frac{\text{Number of months in the short period}}{12}$$

EXAMPLE 10

Gray Corporation obtained permission to change from a calendar year to a fiscal year ending September 30, beginning in 1994. For the short period January 1 through September 30, 1994, the corporation's taxable income was $48,000. The relevant tax rates and the resultant short-period tax are as follows:

Amount of Taxable Income	Tax Calculation
$1–$50,000	15% of taxable income
$50,001–$75,000	$7,500 plus 25% of taxable income in excess of $50,000
Annualized income ($48,000 × ¹²⁄₉) = 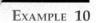 $64,000	

Amount of Taxable Income	Tax Calculation
Tax on annualized income	
$7,500 + .25 ($64,000 − $50,000) =	
$7,500 + $3,500 = $11,000	
Short-period tax = ($11,000 × 9/12) = $8,250	
Annualizing the income increased the tax by $1,050:	
Tax with annualizing	$8,250
Tax without annualizing (.15 × $48,000)	7,200
	$1,050

▼

Rather than annualize the short-period income, the taxpayer can elect to calculate the tax for a 12-month period beginning on the first day of the short period and (2) convert the tax in (1) to a short-period tax as follows:[21]

$$\frac{\text{Taxable income for short period}}{\text{Taxable income for the 12-month period}} \times \frac{\text{Tax on the 12 months of}}{\text{income}}$$

EXAMPLE 11

Assume Gray Corporation's taxable income for the calendar year 1994 was $60,000. The tax on the full 12 months of income would have been $10,000 [$7,500 + .25($60,000 − $50,000)]. The short-period tax would be $8,000 ($48,000/$60,000 × $10,000). Thus, if the corporation utilized this option, the tax for the short period would be $8,000 (rather than $8,250, as calculated in Example 10). ▼

For individuals, annualizing requires some special adjustments:[22]

- Deductions must be itemized for the short period (the standard deduction is not allowed).
- Personal and dependency exemptions must be prorated.

Fortunately, individuals rarely change tax years.

MITIGATION OF THE ANNUAL ACCOUNTING PERIOD CONCEPT

Several provisions in the Code are designed to give the taxpayer relief from the seemingly harsh results that may be produced by the combined effects of an arbitrary accounting period and a progressive rate structure. For example, under the net operating loss carryback and carryover rules, a loss in one year can be carried back and offset against taxable income for the preceding 3 years. Unused net operating losses are then carried over for 15 years.[23] In addition, the Code provides special relief provisions for casualty losses pursuant to a disaster and for the reporting of insurance proceeds from destruction of crops.[24]

Restoration of Amounts Received under a Claim of Right

The court-made **claim of right doctrine** applies when the taxpayer receives property as income and treats it as his or her own but a dispute arises over the taxpayer's rights to the income.[25] According to the doctrine, the taxpayer must include the amount as income in the year of receipt. The rationale for the doctrine

---

[21] § 443(b)(1).
[22] § 443(b)(2) and Reg. § 1.443–1(a)(2).
[23] § 172. Refer to Chapter 7.

[24] §§ 165(i) and 451(d). Refer to Chapter 7.
[25] *North American Consolidated Oil Co. v. Burnet*, 3 USTC ¶943, 11 AFTR 16, 52 S.Ct. 613 (USSC, 1932).

is that the Federal government cannot await the resolution of all disputes before exacting a tax. As a corollary to the doctrine, if the taxpayer is later required to repay the funds, generally a deduction is allowed in the year of repayment.[26]

▼
EXAMPLE 12

In 1994, Pedro received a $5,000 bonus computed as a percentage of profits. In 1995, Pedro's employer determined that the 1994 profits had been incorrectly computed, and Pedro had to refund the $5,000 in 1995. Pedro was required to include the $5,000 in his 1994 income, but he can claim a $5,000 deduction in 1995. ▼

In Example 12 the transactions were a wash; that is, the income and deduction were the same ($5,000). Suppose, however, Pedro was in the 36 percent tax bracket in 1994 but in the 15 percent bracket in 1995. Without some relief provision, the mistake would be costly to Pedro. He paid $1,800 tax in 1994 (.36 × $5,000), but the deduction reduced his tax liability in 1995 by only $750 (.15 × $5,000). The Code does provide the needed relief in such cases. Under § 1341, when income that has been taxed under the claim of right doctrine must later be repaid, in effect, the taxpayer gets to apply to the deduction the tax rate of the year that will produce the greatest tax benefit. Thus, in Example 12, the repayment in 1995 would reduce Pedro's 1995 tax liability by the greater 1994 rate (.36) applied to the $5,000. However, relief is provided only in cases where the tax is significantly different; that is, when the deduction for the amount previously included in income exceeds $3,000.

▼ ACCOUNTING METHODS

PERMISSIBLE METHODS

2   LEARNING OBJECTIVE
Apply the cash method, accrual method, and hybrid method of accounting.

Section 446 requires the taxpayer to compute taxable income using the method of accounting regularly employed in keeping his or her books, provided the method clearly reflects income. The Code recognizes the following as generally permissible **accounting methods:**

- The cash receipts and disbursements method.
- The accrual method.
- A hybrid method (a combination of cash and accrual).

The Regulations refer to these alternatives as *overall methods* and add that the term *method of accounting* includes not only the overall method of accounting of the taxpayer but also the accounting treatment of any item.[27]

Generally, any of the three methods of accounting may be used if the method is consistently employed and clearly reflects income. However, the taxpayer is required to use the accrual method for sales and costs of goods sold if inventories are an income-producing factor to the business.[28] Other situations in which the accrual method is required are discussed later. Special methods are also permitted for installment sales, long-term construction contracts, and farmers.

A taxpayer who has more than one trade or business may use a different method of accounting for each trade or business activity.[29] Furthermore, a different method of accounting may be used to determine income from a trade or business than is used to compute nonbusiness items of income and deductions.[30]

---

[26] *U.S. v. Lewis*, 51–1 USTC ¶9211, 40 AFTR 258, 71 S.Ct. 522 (USSC, 1951).
[27] Reg. § 1.446–1(a)(1).

[28] Reg. § 1.446–1(a)(4)(i).
[29] § 446(d).
[30] Reg. § 1.446–1(c)(1)(iv)(b).

EXAMPLE 13

Linda operates a grocery store and owns stock and bonds. The sales and cost of goods sold from the grocery store must be computed by the accrual method because inventories are material. However, Linda can report her dividends and interest under the cash method. ▼

The Code grants the IRS broad powers to determine whether the taxpayer's accounting method *clearly reflects income*. Thus, if the method employed does not clearly reflect income, the IRS has the power to prescribe the method to be used by the taxpayer.[31]

CASH RECEIPTS AND DISBURSEMENTS METHOD— CASH BASIS

Most individuals and many businesses use the cash basis to report income and deductions. The popularity of this method can largely be attributed to its simplicity and flexibility.

Under the **cash method,** income is not recognized until the taxpayer actually receives, or constructively receives, cash or its equivalent. Cash is constructively received if it is available to the taxpayer.[32] Deductions are generally permitted in the year of payment. Thus, year-end accounts receivable, accounts payable, and accrued income and deductions are not included in the determination of taxable income.

In many cases, a taxpayer using the cash method can choose the year in which a deduction is claimed simply by postponing or accelerating the payment of expenses. For fixed assets, however, the cash basis taxpayer claims deductions through depreciation or amortization, the same as an accrual basis taxpayer does. In addition, prepaid expenses must be capitalized and amortized if the life of the asset extends substantially beyond the end of the tax year.[33] Most courts have applied the one-year rule to determine whether capitalization and amortization are required. According to this rule, capitalization is required only if the asset has a life that extends beyond the tax year following the year of payment.[34]

Restrictions on Use of the Cash Method

Using the cash method to measure income from a merchandising or manufacturing operation would often yield a distorted picture of the results of operations. Income for the period would largely be a function of when payments were made for goods or materials. Thus, the Regulations prohibit the use of the cash method (and require the accrual method) to measure sales and cost of goods sold if inventories are material to the business.[35]

The prohibition on the use of the cash method if inventories are material and the rules regarding prepaid expenses (discussed above) are intended to assure that annual income is clearly reflected. However, certain taxpayers may not use the cash method of accounting for Federal income tax purposes regardless of whether inventories are material. The accrual basis must be used to report the income earned by (1) a corporation (other than an S corporation), (2) a partnership with a

---

[31] § 446(b).
[32] Reg. § 1.451–1(a). Refer to Chapter 4 for a discussion of constructive receipt.

[33] Reg. § 1.461–1(a)(1).
[34] *Zaninovich v. Comm.,* 80–1 USTC ¶9342, 45 AFTR2d 80–1442, 616 F.2d 429 (CA–9, 1980), *rev'g* 69 T.C. 605 (1978). Refer to Chapter 6 for further discussion of the one-year rule.
[35] Reg. § 1.446–1(a)(4)(i).

corporate partner, and (3) a tax shelter.[36] This accrual basis requirement has three exceptions:[37]

- A farming business.
- A qualified personal service corporation (e.g., a corporation performing services in health, law, engineering, architecture, accounting, actuarial science, performing arts, or consulting).
- An entity that is not a tax shelter whose average annual gross receipts for the most recent three-year period are $5 million or less.

Farming

Although inventories are material to farming operations, the IRS long ago created an exception to the general rule that allows farmers to use the cash method of accounting.[38] The purpose of the exception is to relieve the small farmer from the bookkeeping burden of accrual accounting. However, tax shelter promoters recognized, for example, that by deducting the costs of a crop in one tax year and harvesting the crop in a later year, income could be deferred from tax. Thus, §§ 447 and 464 were enacted to prevent certain farming corporations and limited partnerships (farming syndicates) from using the cash method.[39]

Farmers who are allowed to use the cash method of accounting must nevertheless capitalize their costs of raising trees when the preproduction period is greater than two years.[40] Thus, a cash basis apple farmer must capitalize the cost of raising trees until the trees produce in merchantable quantities. Cash basis farmers can elect not to capitalize these costs, but if the election is made, the alternative depreciation system (refer to Chapter 8) must be used for all farming property.

Generally, the cost of purchasing an animal must be capitalized. However, the cash basis farmer's cost of raising the animal can be expensed.[41]

ACCRUAL METHOD

All Events Test for Income

Under the **accrual method,** an item is generally included in gross income for the year in which it is earned, regardless of when the income is collected. An item of income is earned when (1) all the events have occurred to fix the taxpayer's right to receive the income and (2) the amount of income (the amount the taxpayer has a right to receive) can be determined with reasonable accuracy.[42]

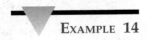

EXAMPLE 14

Andre, a calendar year taxpayer who uses the accrual basis of accounting, was to receive a bonus equal to 6% of Blue Corporation's net income for its fiscal year ending each June 30. For the fiscal year ending June 30, 1994, Blue Corporation had net income of $240,000, and for the six months ending December 31, 1994, the corporation's net income was $150,000. Andre will report $14,400 (.06 × $240,000) for 1994 because his rights to the amount became fixed when Blue Corporation's year closed. However, Andre would not accrue income based on the corporation's profits for the last six months of 1994 since his right to the income does not accrue until the close of the corporation's tax year. ▼

---

[36] § 448(a). For this purpose, the hybrid method of accounting is considered the same as the cash method.
[37] § 448(b).
[38] Reg. § 1.471–6(a).
[39] Section 447(c) contains counter-exceptions that allow certain closely held corporations to use the cash method. See also § 464(c).

[40] § 263A(d).
[41] Reg. § 1.162–12(a).
[42] Reg. § 1.451–1(a). Refer to Chapter 4 for further discussion of the accrual basis.

In a situation where the accrual basis taxpayer's right to income is being contested and the income has not yet been collected, generally no income is recognized until the dispute has been settled.[43] Before the settlement, "all of the events have not occurred that fix the right to receive the income."

All Events and Economic Performance Tests for Deductions

An **all events test** applies to accrual basis deductions. A deduction cannot be claimed until (1) all the events have occurred to create the taxpayer's liability and (2) the amount of the liability can be determined with reasonable accuracy.[44] Once these requirements are satisfied, the deduction will be permitted only if economic performance has occurred.[45]

The **economic performance test** addresses situations in which the taxpayer has either of the following obligations:

1. To pay for services or property to be provided in the future.
2. To provide services or property (other than money) in the future.

When services or property are to be provided to the taxpayer in the future (situation 1), economic performance occurs when the property or services are actually provided by the other party.

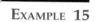

EXAMPLE 15

An accrual basis calendar year taxpayer, JAB, Inc., promoted a boxing match held in the company's arena on December 31, 1994. CLN, Inc., had contracted to clean the arena for $5,000, but did not actually perform the work until January 1, 1995. JAB, Inc., did not pay the $5,000 until 1996. Although financial accounting would require JAB, Inc., to accrue the $5,000 cleaning expense in 1994 to match the revenues from the fight, the economic performance test was not satisfied until 1995, when CLN, Inc., performed the service. Thus, JAB, Inc., must deduct the expense in 1995. ▼

If the taxpayer is obligated to provide property or services (situation 2), economic performance occurs (and thus the deduction is allowed) in the year the taxpayer provides the property or services.

EXAMPLE 16

Copper Corporation, an accrual basis taxpayer, is in the strip mining business. According to the contract with the landowner, the company must reclaim the land. The estimated cost of reclaiming land mined in 1994 was $500,000, but the land was not actually reclaimed until 1996. The all events test was satisfied in 1994. The obligation existed, and the amount of the liability could be determined with reasonable accuracy. However, the economic performance test was not satisfied until 1996. Therefore, the deduction is not allowed until 1996.[46] ▼

The economic performance test is waived, and thus year-end accruals can be deducted, if all the following conditions (*recurring item exception*) are met:

* The obligation exists and the amount of the liability can be reasonably estimated.
* Economic performance occurs within a reasonable period (but not later than 8½ months after the close of the taxable year).
* The item is recurring in nature and is treated consistently by the taxpayer.
* Either the accrued item is not material, or accruing it results in a better matching of revenues and expenses.

[43] *Burnet v. Sanford & Brooks Co.*, 2 USTC ¶636, 9 AFTR 603, 51 S.Ct. 150 (USSC, 1931).
[44] § 461(h)(4).
[45] § 461(h).
[46] See § 468 for an elective method for reporting reclamation costs.

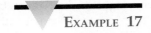

EXAMPLE 17

Green Corporation often sells goods that are on hand but cannot be shipped for another week. Thus, the sales account usually includes revenues for some items that have not been shipped at year-end. Green Corporation is obligated to pay shipping costs. Although the company's obligation for shipping costs can be determined with reasonable accuracy, economic performance is not satisfied until Green (or its agent) actually delivers the goods. However, accruing shipping costs on sold items will better match expenses with revenues for the period. Therefore, the company should be allowed to accrue the shipping costs on items sold but not shipped at year-end. ▼

The economic performance test as set forth in the Code does not address all possible accrued expenses. That is, in some cases, the taxpayer incurs cost even though no property or services were received. In these instances, according to Regulations, economic performance generally is not satisfied until the liability is paid. The following liabilities are cases in which payment is generally the only means of satisfying economic performance:[47]

1. Workers' compensation.
2. Torts.
3. Breach of contract.
4. Violation of law.
5. Rebates and refunds.
6. Awards, prizes, and jackpots.
7. Insurance, warranty, and service contracts.[48]
8. Taxes.

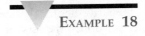

EXAMPLE 18

Yellow Corporation sold defective merchandise that injured a customer. Yellow admitted liability in 1994, but did not pay the claim until January 1995. The customer's tort claim cannot be deducted until it is paid. ▼

However, items (5) through (8) above are eligible for the aforementioned recurring item exception.

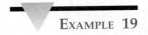

EXAMPLE 19

Pelican Corporation filed its 1994 state income tax return in March 1995. At the time the return was filed, Pelican was required to pay an additional $5,000. The state taxes are eligible for the recurring item exception. Thus, the $5,000 of state income taxes can be deducted on the corporation's 1994 Federal tax return. The deduction is allowed because all the events had occurred to fix the liability as of the end of 1994, the payment was made within 8 ½ months after the end of the tax year, the item is recurring in nature, and allowing the deduction in 1994 produces a good matching of revenues and expenses. ▼

Reserves

Generally, the all events and economic performance tests will prevent the use of reserves (e.g., for product warranty expense) frequently used in financial accounting to match expenses with revenues. However, small banks are allowed to use a bad debt reserve.[49] Furthermore, an accrual basis taxpayer in a service business is permitted to not accrue revenue that appears uncollectible based on experience. In effect, this approach indirectly allows a reserve.[50]

---

[47] Reg. §§ 1.461–4(g)(2)–(6) and 1.461–5(c).
[48] This item applies to contracts the taxpayer enters into for his or her own protection, rather than the taxpayer's liability as insurer, warrantor, or service provider.

[49] § 585.
[50] § 448(d)(5).

HYBRID METHOD

A **hybrid method** of accounting involves the use of more than one method. For example, a taxpayer who uses the accrual basis to report sales and cost of goods sold but uses the cash basis to report other items of income and expense is employing a hybrid method. The Code permits the use of a hybrid method provided the taxpayer's income is clearly reflected.[51] A taxpayer who uses the accrual method for business expenses must also use the accrual method for business income (a cash method may not be used for income items if the taxpayer's expenses are accounted for under the accrual method).

It may be preferable for a business that is required to report sales and cost of goods sold on the accrual method to report other items of income and expense under the cash method. The cash method permits greater flexibility in the timing of income and expense recognition.

CHANGE OF METHOD

3 LEARNING OBJECTIVE
Utilize the procedure for changing accounting methods.

The taxpayer, in effect, makes an election to use a particular accounting method when an initial tax return is filed using that method. If a subsequent change in method is desired, the taxpayer must obtain the permission of the IRS. The request for change is made on Form 3115, Application for Change in Accounting Method. Generally, the form must be filed within the first 180 days of the taxable year of the desired change.[52]

As previously mentioned, the term *accounting method* encompasses not only the overall accounting method used by the taxpayer (the cash or accrual method) but also the treatment of any material item of income or deduction.[53] Thus, a change in the method of deducting property taxes from a cash basis to an accrual basis that results in a deduction for taxes in a different year constitutes a change in

---

[51] § 446(c).
[52] Reg. § 1.446–1(e)(3). The deadline may be extended to within the first nine months of the year of the change if the taxpayer can show good cause for the delay in filing the request.

[53] Reg. § 1.446–1(a)(1).

TAX IN THE NEWS

AUTOMOBILE DEALERS SANDWICHED BETWEEN TWO TAX ACCOUNTING RULES

Automobile dealers sell extended warranty contracts that cover periods as long as five years. Under the prepaid income rules, the automobile dealers are required to report all of the income from the warranty contract in the year of receipt. The dealer generally purchases an insurance contract to cover the warranty for the customer. With the insurance contract, the customer can have the warranty services performed at any dealer, and the insurance company will pay the expense. The dealer is generally out of the picture once the insurance contract is purchased. However, because the insurance protection extends over more than one tax year, the dealer is required to amortize the cost of the policy over the insured period. Thus, the prepaid income rules accelerate the recognition of income while the rules for capitalization and amortization defer the deductions.

SOURCE: Some of the information is from "IRS Rules on Extended Warranties," *Deloitte & Touche Review*, September 21, 1992, p. 6.

an accounting method. Another example of accounting method change is a change involving the method or basis used in the valuation of inventories. However, a change in treatment resulting from a change in underlying facts does not constitute a change in the taxpayer's method of accounting.[54] For example, a change in employment contracts so that an employee accrues one day of vacation pay for each month of service rather than 12 days of vacation pay for a full year of service is a change in the underlying facts and is therefore not an accounting method change.

Correction of an Error

A change in accounting method should be distinguished from the *correction of an error.* The taxpayer can correct an error (by filing amended returns) without permission, and the IRS can simply adjust the taxpayer's liability if an error is discovered on audit of the return. Some examples of errors are incorrect postings, errors in the calculation of tax liability or tax credits, deductions of business expense items that are actually personal, and omissions of income and deductions.[55] Unless the taxpayer or the IRS corrects the error within the statute of limitations, the taxpayer's total lifetime taxable income will be overstated or understated by the amount of the error.

Change from an Incorrect Method

An *incorrect accounting method* is the consistent (year-after-year) use of an incorrect rule to report an item of income or expense. The incorrect accounting method generally will not affect the taxpayer's total lifetime income (unlike the error). That is, an incorrect method has a self-balancing mechanism. For example, deducting freight on inventory in the year the goods are purchased, rather than when the inventory is sold, is an incorrect accounting method. The total cost of goods sold over the life of the business is not affected, but the year-to-year income is incorrect.[56]

---

[54] Reg. § 1.446–1(e)(2)(ii)
[55] Reg. § 1.446–1(e)(2)(ii)(b).

[56] But see *Korn Industries v. U.S.*, 76–1 USTC ¶9354, 37 AFTR2d 76–1228, 532 F.2d 1352 (Ct.Cls., 1976).

If a taxpayer is employing an incorrect method of accounting, permission must be obtained from the IRS to change to a correct method. An incorrect method is not treated as a mechanical error that can be corrected by merely filing an amended tax return.

The tax return preparer as well as the taxpayer will be subject to penalties if the tax return is prepared using an incorrect method of accounting and permission for a change to a correct method has not been requested.[57]

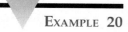

ETHICAL CONSIDERATIONS

A Change in Accounting Method

Tom, a CPA, recently obtained a new client, the Egret Engineering Corporation (annual gross receipts of $2 million). The company's previous accountant had filed all returns by the accrual method of accounting, the same method that was used to prepare financial statements submitted when the company applied for a loan in its first year of operation. Tom recognizes that under the accrual method of accounting the company is paying tax on its accounts receivable, whereas under the cash method of accounting the income could be deferred until the cash is collected. In many cases, it takes the company three months to collect a receivable. Tom also recognizes that the IRS will not allow the corporation to change to the cash method.

Therefore, Tom is considering the following plan: A new corporation would be formed. Each shareholder in Egret would own the same percentage of stock in the new corporation. The key element of the plan is that the new corporation would elect the cash method of accounting. Egret would complete its contracts in progress, collect its receivables, and gradually be liquidated. Meanwhile all new business would be channeled into the new corporation.

Net Adjustments Due to Change in Accounting Method

In the year of a change in accounting method, some items of income and expense may have to be adjusted to prevent the change from distorting taxable income.

EXAMPLE 20

In 1994, White Corporation, with consent from the IRS, switched from the cash to the accrual basis for reporting sales and cost of goods sold. The corporation's accrual basis gross profit for the year was computed as follows:

Sales		$100,000
Beginning inventory	$ 15,000	
Purchases	60,000	
Less: Ending inventory	(10,000)	
Cost of goods sold		(65,000)
Gross profit		$ 35,000

At the end of the previous year, White Corporation had accounts receivable of $25,000 and accounts payable for merchandise of $34,000. The accounts receivable from the previous year in the amount of $25,000 were never included in gross income since White was on the

---

[57] § 446(f). See *West's Federal Taxation: Corporations, Partnerships, Estates, and Trusts,* Chapter 16.

cash basis and did not recognize the uncollected receivables. In the current year, the $25,000 was not included in the accrual basis sales since the sales were made in a prior year. Therefore, a $25,000 adjustment to income is required to prevent the receivables from being omitted from income.

The corollary of the failure to recognize a prior year's receivables is the failure to recognize a prior year's accounts payable. The beginning of the year's accounts payable was not included in the current or prior year's purchases. Thus, a deduction for the $34,000 was not taken in either year and is therefore included as an adjustment to income for the period of change.

An adjustment is also required to reflect the $15,000 beginning inventory that White deducted (due to the use of a cash method of accounting) in the previous year. In this instance, the cost of goods sold during the year of change was increased by the beginning inventory and resulted in a double deduction.

The net adjustment due to the change in accounting method is computed as follows:

Beginning inventory (deducted in prior and current year)	$ 15,000
Beginning accounts receivable (omitted from income)	25,000
Beginning accounts payable (omitted from deductions)	(34,000)
Net increase in taxable income	$ 6,000

Disposition of the Net Adjustment

Generally, if the IRS *requires* the taxpayer to change an accounting method, the net adjustment is added to or subtracted from the income for the year of the change. In cases of positive (an increase in income) adjustments in excess of $3,000, the taxpayer is allowed to calculate the tax by spreading the adjustment over one or more previous years.[58]

To encourage taxpayers to *voluntarily* change from incorrect methods and to facilitate changes from one correct method to another, the IRS generally allows the taxpayer to spread the adjustment into future years. Assuming the taxpayer files a timely request for change (Form 3115), the allocation periods in Concept Summary 18–1 generally apply.[59]

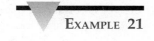

EXAMPLE 21   White Corporation in Example 20 voluntarily changed from an incorrect method (the cash basis was incorrect because inventories were material to the business) to a correct method. The company must add $2,000 (⅓ × $6,000 positive adjustment) to its 1994, 1995, and 1996 income. ▼

CONCEPT SUMMARY 18–1

Adjustment Periods

Change	Type of Adjustment	Allocation Period
Incorrect to correct method	Positive	Three years—year of change and the two succeeding years
Incorrect to correct method	Negative	Year of change
Correct to correct	Positive	Six years—year of change and the five succeeding years
Correct to correct	Negative	Six years—year of change and the five succeeding years

---

[58] § 481(b).   [59] Rev.Proc. 92–20, 1992–1 C.B. 301.

Special Accounting Methods

Generally, accrual basis taxpayers recognize income when goods are sold and shipped to the customer. Cash basis taxpayers generally recognize income from a sale on the collection of cash from the customer. The tax law provides special accounting methods for certain installment sales and long-term contracts. These special methods were enacted, in part, to assure that the tax will be due when the taxpayer is best able to pay the tax.

INSTALLMENT METHOD

4 **LEARNING OBJECTIVE**
Determine when the installment method of accounting can be utilized and apply the related calculation techniques.

Under the general rule for computing the gain or loss from the sale of property, the taxpayer recognizes the entire amount of gain or loss upon the sale or other disposition of the property.

EXAMPLE 22

Mark sells property to Fran for $10,000 cash plus Fran's note (fair market value and face amount of $90,000). Mark's basis for the property was $15,000. Gain or loss is computed under either the cash or accrual basis as follows:

Amount realized	
Cash down payment	$ 10,000
Note receivable	90,000
	$100,000
Basis in the property	(15,000)
Realized gain	$ 85,000

In Example 22, the general rule for recognizing gain or loss requires Mark to pay a substantial amount of tax on the gain in the year of sale even though he received only $10,000 cash. Congress enacted the installment sales provisions to prevent this sort of hardship by allowing the taxpayer to spread the gain from installment sales over the collection period. The installment method is a very important planning tool because of the tax deferral possibilities.

Eligibility and Calculations

The **installment method** applies to *gains* (but not losses) from the sale of property where the seller will receive at least one payment *after* the year of sale. For many years, practically all gains from the sale of property were eligible for the installment method. However, in recent years, the Code has been amended to *deny* the use of the installment method for the following:[60]

- Gains on property held for sale in the ordinary course of business.
- Depreciation recapture under § 1245 or § 1250.
- Gains on stocks or securities traded on an established market.

As an exception to the first item, the installment method may be used to report gains from sales of the following:[61]

- Time-share units (e.g., the right to use real property for two weeks each year).
- Residential lots (if the seller is not to make any improvements).
- Any property used or produced in the trade or business of farming.

---

[60] §§ 453(b), (i), and (l).

[61] § 453(l)(2).

The Nonelective Aspect

Regardless of the taxpayer's method of accounting, as a general rule, eligible sales *must* be reported by the installment method.[62] A special election is required to report the gain by any other method of accounting (see the discussion in a subsequent section of this chapter).

Computing the Gain for the Period

The gain reported on each sale is computed by the following formula:

$$\frac{\text{Total gain}}{\text{Contract price}} \times \text{Payments received} = \text{Recognized gain}$$

The taxpayer must compute each variable as follows:

1. *Total gain* is the selling price reduced by selling expenses and the adjusted basis of the property. The selling price is the total consideration received by the seller, including notes receivable from the buyer and the seller's liabilities assumed by the buyer.
2. *Contract price* is the selling price less the seller's liabilities that are assumed by the buyer. Generally, the contract price is the amount, other than interest, the seller will receive from the purchaser.
3. *Payments received* are the collections on the contract price received in the tax year. This generally is equal to the cash received less the interest income collected for the period. If the buyer pays any of the seller's expenses, the seller regards the amount paid as a payment received.

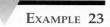

EXAMPLE 23

The seller is not a dealer, and the facts are as follows:

Sales price		
Cash down payment	$ 1,000	
Seller's mortgage assumed	3,000	
Notes payable to the seller	13,000	$ 17,000
Selling expenses		(500)
Seller's basis		(10,000)
Total gain		$ 6,500

The contract price is $14,000 ($17,000 – $3,000). Assuming the $1,000 is the only payment in the year of sale, the recognized gain in that year is computed as follows:

$$\frac{\$6,500 \text{ (total gain)}}{\$14,000 \text{ (contract price)}} \times \$1,000 = \$464 \quad \begin{matrix} \text{(gain recognized} \\ \text{in year of sale)} \end{matrix} \quad \blacktriangledown$$

If the sum of the seller's basis and selling expenses is less than the liabilities assumed by the buyer, the difference must be added to the contract price and to the payments (treated as *deemed payments*) received in the year of sale.[63] This adjustment to the contract price is required so that the ratio of total gain to contract price will not be greater than one. The adjustment also accelerates the reporting of income from the deemed payments.

---

[62] § 453(a).
[63] Temp.Reg. § 15a.453–1(b)(2)(iii).

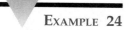

EXAMPLE 24

Assume the same facts as in Example 23, except that the seller's basis in the property is only $2,000. The total gain, therefore, is $14,500 [$17,000 − ($2,000 + $500)]. Payments in the year of sale are $1,500 and are calculated as follows:

Down payment	$1,000
Excess of mortgage assumed over seller's basis and expenses ($3,000 − $2,000 − $500)	500
	$1,500

The contract price is $14,500 [$17,000 (selling price) − $3,000 (seller's mortgage assumed) + $500 (excess of mortgage assumed over seller's basis and selling expenses)]. The gain recognized in the year of sale is computed as follows:

$$\frac{\$14,500 \text{ (total gain)}}{\$14,500 \text{ (contract price)}} \times \$1,500 = \$1,500$$

In subsequent years, all amounts the seller collects on the note principal ($13,000) will be recognized gain ($13,000 × 100%). ▼

As previously discussed, gains attributable to ordinary income recapture under §§ 1245 and 1250 are *ineligible* for installment reporting. Therefore, the § 1245 or § 1250 gain realized must be recognized in the year of sale, and the installment sale gain is the remaining gain.

EXAMPLE 25

Olaf sold an apartment building for $50,000 cash and a $75,000 note due in two years. Olaf's basis in the property was $25,000, and he recaptured $40,000 ordinary income under § 1250.

Olaf's realized gain is $100,000 ($125,000 − $25,000), and the $40,000 recapture must be recognized in the year of sale. Of the $60,000 remaining § 1231 gain, $24,000 must be recognized in the year of sale:

$$\frac{\S 1231 \text{ gain}}{\text{Contract price}} \times \text{Payments received} = \frac{\$125,000 - \$25,000 - \$40,000}{\$125,000} \times \$50,000$$

$$= \frac{\$60,000}{\$125,000} \times \$50,000 = \$24,000$$

The remaining realized gain of $36,000 ($60,000 − $24,000) will be recognized as the $75,000 note is collected. ▼

Imputed Interest

Sections 483 and 1274 provide that if a deferred payment contract for the sale of property with a selling price greater than $3,000 does not contain a reasonable interest rate, a reasonable rate is imputed. The imputing of interest effectively restates the selling price of the property to equal the sum of the payments at the date of the sale and the discounted present value of the future payments. The difference between the present value of a future payment and the payment's face amount is taxed as interest income, as discussed in the following paragraphs. Thus, the **imputed interest** rules prevent sellers of capital assets from increasing the selling price to reflect the equivalent of unstated interest on deferred payments and thereby converting ordinary (interest) income into long-term capital gains. In addition, the imputed interest rules are important because they affect the timing of income recognition.

Generally, if the contract does not charge at least the Federal rate, interest will be imputed at the Federal rate. The Federal rate is the interest rate the Federal government pays on new borrowing and is published monthly by the IRS.[64]

As a general rule, the buyer and seller must account for interest on the accrual basis with semiannual compounding.[65] Requiring the use of the accrual basis assures that the seller's interest income and the buyer's interest expense are reported in the same tax year. Under pre-1984 law, the cash basis seller did not report interest income until it was actually collected, but an accrual basis buyer could deduct the interest as it accrued. The following example illustrates the calculation and amortization of imputed interest.

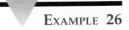

EXAMPLE 26

Peggy, a cash basis taxpayer, sold land on January 1, 1994, for $100,000 cash and $3 million due on December 31, 1995, with 5% interest payable December 31, 1994, and December 31, 1995. At the time of the sale, the Federal rate was 8% (compounded semiannually). Because Peggy did not charge at least the Federal rate, interest will be imputed at 8% (compounded semiannually).

Date	Payment	Present Value (at 8%) on 1/1/1994	Imputed Interest
12/31/1994	$ 150,000	$ 138,750	$ 11,250
12/31/1995	3,150,000	2,693,250	456,750
	$3,300,000	$2,832,000	$468,000

Thus, the selling price will be restated to $2,932,000 ($100,000 + $2,832,000) rather than $3,100,000 ($100,000 + $3,000,000), and Peggy will recognize interest income in accordance with the following amortization schedule:

	Beginning Balance	Interest Income (at 8%)*	Received	Ending Balance
1994	$2,832,000	$231,091	$ 150,000	$2,913,091
1995	2,913,091	236,909	3,150,000	–0–

*Compounded semiannually.

Congress has created several exceptions regarding the rate at which interest is imputed and the method of accounting for the interest income and expense. The general rules and exceptions are summarized in Concept Summary 18–2.

Related-Party Sales of Nondepreciable Property

If the Code did not contain special rules, a taxpayer could make an installment sale of property to a related party (e.g., a family member) who would obtain a basis in the property equal to the purchase price (the fair market value of the property). Then, the purchasing family member could immediately sell the property to an unrelated party for cash with no recognized gain or loss (the amount realized

---

[64]§ 1274(d)(1). There are three Federal rates: short-term (not over three years), mid-term (over three years but not over nine years), and long-term (over nine years).

[65]§§ 1274(a), 1273(a), and 1272(a).

would equal the basis). The related-party purchaser would not pay the installment note to the selling family member until a later year or years. The net result would be that the family has the cash, but no taxable gain is recognized until the intrafamily transfer of the cash (the purchasing family member makes payments on the installment note).

Under special rules designed to combat the scheme described above, the proceeds from the subsequent sale (the second sale) by the purchasing family member are treated as though they were used to pay the installment note due the selling family member (the first sale). As a result, the recognition of gain from the original sale between the related parties is accelerated.[66]

CONCEPT SUMMARY 18–2

Interest on Installment Sales

	Imputed Interest Rate
General rule	Federal rate
Exceptions:	
• Principal amount not over $2.8 million.[1]	Lesser of Federal rate or 9%
• Sale of land (with a calendar year ceiling of $500,000) between family members (the seller's spouse, brothers, sisters, ancestors, or lineal descendants).[2]	Lesser of Federal rate or 6%

	Method of Accounting for Interest	
	Seller's Interest Income	**Buyer's Interest Expense**
General rule[3]	Accrual	Accrual
Exceptions:		
• Total payments under the contract are $250,000 or less.[4]	Taxpayer's overall method	Taxpayer's overall method
• Sale of a farm (sales price of $1 million or less).[5]	Taxpayer's overall method	Taxpayer's overall method
• Sale of a principal residence.[6]	Taxpayer's overall method	Taxpayer's overall method
• Sale for a note with a principal amount of not over $2 million, the seller is on the cash basis, the property sold is not inventory, and the buyer agrees to report expense by the cash method.[7]	Cash	Cash

1. § 1274A. This amount is adjusted annually for inflation. For 1993, the amount is $3,332,400.
2. §§ 1274(c)(3)(F) and 483(e).
3. §§ 1274(a) and 1272(a)(3).
4. §§ 1274(c)(3)(C) and 483.
5. §§ 1274(c)(3)(A) and 483.
6. §§ 1274(c)(3)(B) and 483.
7. § 1274A(c). This amount is adjusted annually for inflation. For 1993, the amount is $2,380,300.

---

[66]§ 453(e).

However, even with these special rules, Congress did not eliminate the benefits of all related-party installment sales.

- Related parties include the first seller's brothers, sisters, ancestors, lineal descendants, controlled corporations, and partnerships, trusts, and estates in which the seller has an interest.[67]
- There is no acceleration if the second disposition occurs more than two years after the first sale.[68]

Thus, if the taxpayer can sell the property to an unrelated party (not a related party) or patient family member, the intrafamily installment sale is still a powerful tax planning tool. Other exceptions also can be applied in some circumstances.[69]

ETHICAL
CONSIDERATIONS

A Related-Party Installment Sale Has Unexpected Results

Amos has been in the farming business for over 40 years. Since he is nearing retirement age—although he will never retire—he would like to slow down. He decides to sell 300 acres of his land to his 26-year-old son, Chuck, for $465,000 so Chuck can go into the farming business. Amos's basis for the land is $50,000. Since Chuck does not have much equity and Amos would like to keep the financing of the land in the family, the sales contract calls for a $15,000 down payment and annual payments of $30,000 for 15 years plus interest at 8 percent. Amos anticipates Chuck's profit from the farm will be adequate to cover these payments and provide Chuck with a decent living.

Chuck makes the payment for the first year. Unfortunately, he then gets involved with some young people from a nearby city and develops a drug problem. To finance his drug dependency, 14 months after acquiring the farm, he sells it for $500,000 cash to a real estate developer who intends to build 1,000 tract houses on the land.

When Amos learns of this, he is furious. He disowns Chuck and vows never to speak to him again.

Now Amos's CPA tells him that he has another problem. The sale of the land by Chuck should be treated as if Chuck had paid Amos the remaining balance on the installment sale. The CPA explains to Amos that this result occurs because his original sale to Chuck was a related-party transaction. Amos finds this ridiculous and says he no longer has a son.

Related-Party Sales of Depreciable Property

The installment method cannot be used to report a gain on the sale of depreciable property to a controlled entity. The purpose of this rule is to prevent the seller from deferring gain (until collections are received) while the related purchaser is enjoying a stepped-up basis for depreciation purposes.[70]

The prohibition on the use of the installment method applies to sales between the taxpayer and a partnership or corporation in which the taxpayer holds a

---

[67] § 453(f)(1), cross-referencing §§ 267(b) and 318(a). Although spouses are related parties, the exemption of gain between spouses (§ 1041) makes the second-disposition rules inapplicable when the first sale was between spouses.

[68] § 453(e)(2). But see § 453(e)(2)(B) for extensions of the two-year period.

[69] See §§ 453(e)(6) and (7).

[70] § 453(g).

more-than-50 percent interest. Constructive ownership rules are used in applying the ownership test (e.g., the taxpayer is considered to own stock owned by a spouse and certain other family members).[71] However, if the taxpayer can establish that tax avoidance was not a principal purpose of the transaction, the installment method can be used to report the gain.

EXAMPLE 27

Ali purchased an apartment building from his controlled corporation, Emerald Corporation. Ali was short of cash at the time of the purchase (December 1994), but was to collect a large cash payment in January 1995. The agreement required Ali to pay the entire arm's length price in January 1995. Ali had good business reasons for acquiring the building. Emerald Corporation should be able to convince the IRS that tax avoidance was not a principal purpose for the installment sale because the tax benefits are not overwhelming. The corporation will report all of the gain in the year following the year of sale, and the building must be expensed over 27.5 years (the cost recovery period). ▼

DISPOSITION OF INSTALLMENT OBLIGATIONS

Generally, a taxpayer must recognize the deferred profit from an installment sale when the obligation is transferred to another party or otherwise relinquished. The rationale for accelerating the gain is that the deferral should continue for no longer than the taxpayer owns the installment obligation.[72]

The gift or cancellation of an installment note will be treated as a taxable disposition by the donor. The amount realized from the cancellation is the face amount of the note if the parties (obligor and obligee) are related to each other.[73]

EXAMPLE 28

Liz cancels a note issued by Tina (Liz's daughter) that arose in connection with the sale of property. At the time of the cancellation, the note had a basis to Liz of $10,000, a face amount of $25,000, and a fair market value of $20,000. Presuming the initial sale by Liz qualified as an installment sale, the cancellation would result in gain of $15,000 ($25,000 − $10,000) to Liz. ▼

Certain exceptions to the recognition of gain provisions are provided for transfers of installment obligations pursuant to tax-free incorporations under § 351, contributions of capital to a partnership, certain corporate liquidations, transfers due to the taxpayer's death, and transfers between spouses or incident to divorce.[74] In such instances, the deferred profit is merely shifted to the transferee, who is responsible for the payment of tax on the subsequent collections of the installment obligations.

INTEREST ON DEFERRED TAXES

With the installment method, the seller earns interest on the receivable. The receivable includes the deferred gain. Thus, one could argue that the seller is earning interest on the deferred taxes. Some commentators reason that the government is, in effect, making interest-free loans to taxpayers who report gains by the installment method. Following the argument that the amount of the deferred taxes is a loan, the taxpayer is required to pay interest on the deferred taxes in some situations.[75]

---

[71] §§ 1239(b) and (c).
[72] § 453B(a).
[73] § 453B(f)(2).

[74] §§ 453B(c), (d), and (g). See Chapter 20 for a discussion of some of these subjects.
[75] § 453A.

The taxpayer is required to pay interest on the deferred taxes only if both of the following requirements are met:

- The installment obligation arises from the sale of property (other than farming property) for more than $150,000.
- Such installment obligations outstanding at the close of the tax year exceed $5 million.

Interest on the deferred taxes is payable only for the portion of the taxes that relates to the installment obligations in *excess* of $5 million. The interest is calculated using the underpayment rate in § 6621.

ELECTING OUT OF THE INSTALLMENT METHOD

A taxpayer can *elect not to use* the installment method. The election is made by reporting on a timely filed return the gain computed by the taxpayer's usual method of accounting (cash or accrual).[76] However, the Regulations provide that the amount realized by a cash basis taxpayer cannot be less than the value of the property sold. This rule differs from the usual cash basis accounting rules (discussed earlier),[77] which measure the amount realized in terms of the fair market value of the property received. The net effect of the Regulations is to allow the cash basis taxpayer to report his or her gain as an accrual basis taxpayer. The election is frequently applied to year-end sales by taxpayers who expect to be in a higher tax bracket in the following year.

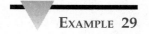

EXAMPLE 29

On December 31, 1994, Jaime sold land to Veneia for $20,000 (fair market value). The cash was to be paid on January 4, 1995. Jaime is a cash basis taxpayer, and his basis in the land is $8,000. Jaime has a large casualty loss and very little other income in 1994. Thus, his marginal tax rate in 1994 is 15%. He expects his rate to increase to 36% in 1995.

The transaction constitutes an installment sale because a payment will be received in a tax year after the tax year of disposition. Veneia's promise to pay Jaime is an installment obligation, and under the Regulations, the value of the installment obligation is equal to the value of the property sold ($20,000). If Jaime elects out of the installment method, he would shift $12,000 of gain ($20,000 − $8,000) from the expected 36% rate in 1995 to the 15% rate in 1994. The expected tax savings of $2,520 [(.36 − .15) × ($12,000)] may exceed the benefit of the tax deferral available with the installment method. ▼

Revocation of the Election

Permission of the IRS is required to revoke an election not to use the installment method.[78] The stickiness of the election is an added peril.

5 **LEARNING OBJECTIVE**
Understand the alternative methods of accounting for long-term contracts (the completed contract method and the percentage of completion method) including the limitations on the use of the completed contract method.

LONG-TERM CONTRACTS

A **long-term contract** is a building, installation, construction, or manufacturing contract that is entered into but not completed within the same tax year. However, a *manufacturing* contract is long term *only* if the contract is to manufacture (1) a unique item not normally carried in finished goods inventory or (2) items that normally require more than 12 calendar months to complete.[79] An item is *unique* if

---

[76] § 453(d) and Temp.Reg. § 15a.453–1(d). See also Rev.Rul. 82–227, 1982–2 C.B. 89.
[77] Refer to Chapter 4, Example 5.

[78] § 453(d)(3) and Temp.Reg. § 15a.453–1(d)(4).
[79] § 460(f) and Reg. § 1.451–3(b).

it is designed to meet the customer's particular needs and is not suitable for use by others. A contract to perform services (e.g., auditing or legal services) is not considered a contract for this purpose and thus cannot qualify as a long-term contract.

▼
EXAMPLE 30

Rocky, a calendar year taxpayer, entered into two contracts during the year. One contract was to construct a building foundation. Work was to begin in October 1993 and was to be completed by June 1994. The contract is long term because it will not be entered into and completed in the same tax year. The fact that the contract requires less than 12 calendar months to complete is not relevant because the contract is not for manufacturing. The second contract was for architectural services to be performed over two years. These services will not qualify for long-term contract treatment because the taxpayer will not build, install, construct, or manufacture a product. ▼

Generally, the taxpayer must accumulate all of the direct and indirect costs incurred under a contract. This means the production costs must be accumulated and allocated to individual contracts. Furthermore, mixed services costs, costs that benefit contracts as well as the general administrative operations of the business, must be allocated to production. Concept Summary 18–3 lists the types of costs that must be accumulated and allocated to contracts. The taxpayer must develop reasonable bases for cost allocations.[80]

▼
EXAMPLE 31

Falcon, Inc., uses detailed cost accumulation records to assign labor and materials to its contracts in progress. The total cost of fringe benefits is allocated to a contract on the following basis:

$$\frac{\text{Labor on the contract}}{\text{Total salaries and labor}} \times \text{Total cost of fringe benefits}$$

Similarly, storage and handling costs for materials are allocated to contracts on the following basis:

$$\frac{\text{Contract materials}}{\text{Materials purchases}} \times \text{Storage and handling costs}$$

The cost of the personnel operations, a mixed services cost, is allocated between production and general administration based on the number of employees in each function. The personnel cost allocated to production is allocated to individual contracts on the basis of the formula used to allocate fringe benefits. ▼

The accumulated costs are deducted when the revenue from the contract is recognized. Generally, two methods of accounting are used in varying circumstances to determine when the revenue from a contract is recognized:[81]

- The completed contract method.
- The percentage of completion method.

The completed contract method may be used for (1) home construction contracts (contracts in which at least 80 percent of the estimated costs are for dwelling units in buildings with four or fewer units) and (2) certain other real

---

[80] Reg. §§ 1.263A–1T(b)(3)(iii)(A)(1) and 1.451–3(d)(9).
[81] § 460.

CONCEPT SUMMARY 18–3

Contract Costs, Mixed Services Costs, and Current Expense Items for Contracts

	Contracts Eligible for the Completed Contract Method	Other Contracts
Contract costs:		
Direct materials (a part of the finished product).	Capital	Capital
Indirect materials (consumed in production but not in the finished product, e.g., grease and oil for equipment).	Capital	Capital
Storage, handling, and insurance on materials.	Expense	Capital
Direct labor (worked on the product).	Capital	Capital
Indirect labor (worked in the production process but not directly on the product, e.g., a construction supervisor).	Capital	Capital
Fringe benefits for direct and indirect labor (e.g., vacation, sick pay, unemployment, and other insurance).	Capital	Capital
Pension costs for direct and indirect labor:		
• Current cost.	Expense	Capital
• Past service costs.	Expense	Capital
Depreciation on production facilities:		
• For financial statements.	Capital	Capital
• Tax depreciation in excess of financial statements.	Expense	Capital
Depreciation on idle facilities.	Expense	Expense
Property taxes, insurance, rent, and maintenance on production facilities.	Capital	Capital
Bidding expenses—successful.	Expense	Capital
Bidding expenses—unsuccessful.	Expense	Expense
Interest to finance real estate construction.	Capital	Capital
Interest to finance personal property:		
• Production period of one year or less.	Expense	Expense
• Production period exceeds one year and costs exceed $1 million.	Capital	Capital
• Production period exceeds two years.	Capital	Capital
Mixed services costs:		
• Personnel operations.	Expense	Allocate
• Data processing.	Expense	Allocate
• Purchasing.	Expense	Allocate
Selling, general, and administrative expenses (including an allocated share of mixed services)	Expense	Expense
Losses	Expense	Expense

estate construction contracts. Other real estate contracts can qualify for the completed contract method if the following requirements are satisfied:

- The contract is expected to be completed within the two-year period beginning on the commencement date of the contract.
- The contract is performed by a taxpayer whose average annual gross receipts for the three taxable years preceding the taxable year in which the contract is entered into do not exceed $10 million.

All other contractors must use the percentage of completion method.

Completed Contract Method

Under the **completed contract method,** no revenue from the contract is recognized until the contract is completed and accepted. However, a taxpayer may not delay completion of a contract for the principal purpose of deferring tax.[82]

In some instances, the original contract price may be disputed, or the buyer may want additional work to be done on a long-term contract. If the disputed amount is substantial (it is not possible to determine whether a profit or loss will ultimately be realized on the contract), the Regulations provide that no amount of income or loss is recognized until the dispute is resolved. In all other cases, the profit or loss (reduced by the amount in dispute) is recognized in the current period on completion of the contract. However, additional work may need to be performed with respect to the disputed contract. In this case, the difference between the amount in dispute and the actual cost of the additional work will be recognized in the year the work is completed rather than in the year in which the dispute is resolved.[83]

EXAMPLE 32

Ted, a calendar year taxpayer utilizing the completed contract method of accounting, constructed a building for Khalid under a long-term contract. The gross contract price was $500,000. Ted finished construction in 1994 at a cost of $475,000. When Khalid examined the building, he insisted that the building be repainted or the contract price be reduced. The estimated cost of repainting is $10,000. Since under the terms of the contract, Ted is assured of a profit of at least $15,000 ($500,000 – $475,000 – $10,000) even if the dispute is ultimately resolved in Khalid's favor, Ted must include $490,000 ($500,000 – $10,000) in gross income and is allowed deductions of $475,000 for 1994.

In 1995, Ted and Khalid resolve the dispute, and Ted repaints certain portions of the building at a cost of $6,000. Ted must include $10,000 in 1995 gross income and may deduct the $6,000 expense in that year. ▼

EXAMPLE 33

Assume the same facts as in the previous example, except the estimated cost of repainting the building is $50,000. Since the resolution of the dispute completely in Khalid's favor would mean a net loss on the contract for Ted ($500,000 – $475,000 – $50,000 = $25,000 loss), Ted does not recognize any income or loss until the year the dispute is resolved. ▼

Frequently, a contractor receives payment at various stages of completion. For example, when the contract is 50 percent complete, the contractor may receive 50 percent of the contract price less a retainage. The taxation of these payments is generally governed by Regulation § 1.451–5 "advance payments for goods and long-term contracts" (discussed in Chapter 4). Generally, contractors are permitted to defer the advance payments until the payments are recognized as income under the taxpayer's method of accounting.

---

[82] Reg. § 1.451–3(b)(2).

[83] Reg. § 1.451–3(d)(2)(ii)–(vii), Example (2).

Percentage of Completion Method

The percentage of completion method must be used to account for long-term contracts unless the taxpayer qualifies for one of the two exceptions that permit the completed contract method to be used (home construction contracts and certain other real estate construction contracts).[84] Under the **percentage of completion method,** a portion of the gross contract price is included in income during each period as the work progresses. The revenue accrued each period is computed as follows:[85]

$$\frac{C}{T} \times P$$

Where C = Contract costs incurred during the period

T = Estimated total cost of the contract

P = Contract price

All of the costs allocated to the contract during the period are deductible from the accrued revenue.[86] Because T in this formula is an estimate that frequently differs from total actual costs, which are not known until the contract has been completed, the profit on a contract for a particular period may be overstated or understated.

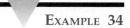

EXAMPLE 34

Tan, Inc., entered into a contract that was to take two years to complete, with an estimated cost of $2,250,000. The contract price was $3,000,000. Costs of the contract for 1994, the first year, totaled $1,350,000. The gross profit reported by the percentage of completion method for 1994 was $450,000 [($1,350,000/$2,250,000 × $3,000,000) − $1,350,000]. The contract was completed at the end of 1995 at a total cost of $2,700,000. In retrospect, 1994 profit should have been $150,000 [($1,350,000/$2,700,000 × $3,000,000) − $1,350,000]. Thus, taxes were overpaid for 1994. ▼

A *de minimis* rule enables the contractor to delay the recognition of income for a particular contract under the percentage of completion method. If less than 10 percent of the estimated contract costs have been incurred by the end of the taxable year, the taxpayer can elect to defer the recognition of income and the related costs until the taxable year in which cumulative contract costs are at least 10 percent of the estimated contract costs.[87]

Lookback Provisions

In the year a contract is completed, a *lookback* provision requires the recalculation of annual profits reported on the contract under the percentage of completion method. Interest is paid to the taxpayer if taxes were overpaid, and interest is payable by the taxpayer if there was an underpayment.[88]

EXAMPLE 35

Assume Tan, Inc., in Example 34, was in the 35% tax bracket in both years and the relevant interest rate was 10%. For 1994, the company paid excess taxes of $105,000 [($450,000 − $150,000) × .35]. When the contract is completed at the end of 1995, Tan, Inc., should receive interest of $10,500 for one year on the tax overpayment ($105,000 × .10). ▼

---

[84] Certain residential construction contracts that do not qualify for the completed contract method may nevertheless use that method to account for 30% of the profit from the contract, with the remaining 70% reported by the percentage of completion method.

[85] § 460(b)(1)(A).

[86] Reg. § 1.451–3(c)(3).

[87] § 460(b)(5).

[88] § 460(b)(2).

INVENTORIES

6 **LEARNING OBJECTIVE**
Understand when accounting for inventories must occur, recognize the types of costs that must be included in inventories, and apply the LIFO method.

Generally, tax accounting and financial accounting for inventories are much the same:

- The use of inventories is necessary to clearly reflect the income of any business engaged in the production and sale or purchase and sale of goods.[89]
- The inventories should include all finished goods, goods in process, and raw materials and supplies that will become part of the product (including containers).
- Inventory rules must give effect to the *best* accounting practice of a particular trade or business, and the taxpayer's method should be consistently followed from year to year.
- All items included in inventory should be valued at either (1) cost or (2) the lower of cost or market value.

The following are *not* acceptable methods or practices in valuing inventories:

- A deduction for a reserve for anticipated price changes.
- The use of a constant price or nominal value for a so-called normal quantity of materials or goods in stock (e.g., the base stock method).
- The inclusion in inventory of stock in transit to which title is not vested in the taxpayer.
- The direct costing approach (excluding fixed indirect production costs from inventory).
- The prime costing approach (excluding all indirect production costs from inventory).

The reason for the similarities between tax and financial accounting for inventories is that § 471 sets forth what appears to be a two-prong test. Under this provision "inventories shall be taken . . . on such basis . . . as conforming as nearly as may be to the *best accounting practice* in the trade or business and as most *clearly reflecting the income.*" The best accounting practice is synonymous with generally accepted accounting principles (hereafter referred to as GAAP). However, the IRS determines whether an inventory method clearly reflects income.

In *Thor Power Tool Co. v. Comm.*, there was a conflict between the two tests.[90] The taxpayer's method of valuing obsolete parts was in conformity with GAAP. The IRS, however, successfully argued that the clear reflection of income test was not satisfied because the taxpayer's procedures for valuing its inventories were contrary to the Regulations. Under the taxpayer's method, inventories for parts in excess of estimated future sales were written off (expensed), although the parts were kept on hand and their asking prices were not reduced. [Under Regulation § 1.471–4(b), inventories cannot be written down unless the selling prices also are reduced.] The taxpayer contended that conformity to GAAP creates a presumption that the method clearly reflects income. The Supreme Court disagreed, concluding that the clear reflection of income test was *paramount.* Moreover, it is the opinion of the IRS that controls in determining whether the method of inventory clearly reflects income. Thus, the best accounting practice test was

---

[89] § 471(a) and Reg. §§ 1.471–1 and –2.
[90] 79–1 USTC ¶9139, 43 AFTR2d 79–362, 99 S.Ct. 773 (USSC, 1979).

rendered practically meaningless. It follows that the taxpayer's method of inventory must strictly conform to the Regulations regardless of what GAAP may require.

DETERMINING INVENTORY COST

For merchandise purchased, cost is the invoice price less trade discounts plus freight and other handling charges.[91] Cash discounts approximating a fair interest rate can be deducted or capitalized at the taxpayer's option, providing the method used is consistently applied.

Uniform Capitalization

In 1986, Congress added § 263A, which significantly affects the inventory rules, to the Code. Section 263A provides that for inventory and property produced by the taxpayer, "... (A) the direct cost of such property, and (B) such property's share of those indirect costs (including taxes) part or all of which are allocable to such property" must be capitalized. The Committee Reports observe that Congress is attempting to achieve a set of capitalization rules that will apply to all types of businesses: contractors, manufacturers, farmers, wholesalers, and retailers.[92] Congress has labeled the system the **uniform capitalization rules,** and practitioners refer to the rules as a *super-full absorption costing system.*

To value inventory under the uniform capitalization rules, a *producer* must apply the following steps:

- Classify all costs into three categories: (1) production, (2) general administrative expense, and (3) mixed services.
- Allocate mixed services costs to production and general administrative expenses.[93]
- Allocate the production costs between the cost of goods sold and the ending inventory.

Concept Summary 18–3 (see the "Other Contracts" column) lists typical items that are included in the three classes of costs. The mixed services costs should be allocated to production on a rational basis. For example, the costs of operating the personnel department may be allocated between production and general administration based on the number of applications processed or the number of employees. In lieu of allocating each mixed services cost, the taxpayer can elect a *simplified method* whereby the total of all mixed services costs is allocated to production as follows:[94]

$$\text{MSP} = \frac{\text{TP}}{\text{TC}} \times \text{TMS}$$

Where MSP = Mixed services costs allocated to production

TP = Total production costs, other than interest and mixed services

TC = Total costs, other than interest, state, local or foreign income taxes, and mixed services costs

TMS = Total mixed services costs

[91] Reg. § 1.471–3(b).

[92] H. Rep. 99–841, 99th Cong., 2nd Sess., 1986, pp. 302–309. See also Reg. § 1.263A–1(a).

[93] Producers with mixed services costs of less than $200,000 for the year are not required to allocate mixed services costs if the simplified method is used to allocate their production costs. Reg. § 1.263A–1(b)(12).

[94] Reg. § 1.263A–1(h)(5).

The usual cost accounting techniques (e.g., average cost per equivalent unit) can be used to allocate the costs between the cost of goods sold and the ending inventory.

Alternatively, the producer can elect to allocate mixed services costs to production on the basis of labor charges only (production labor as a percentage of total labor costs).

The costs included in the inventory of *wholesalers and retailers* are comparable to those of the producer. However, many of these costs are captured in the price these taxpayers pay for the goods. The following additional costs must be capitalized by these taxpayers:

- All storage costs for wholesalers.
- Offsite storage costs for retailers.
- Purchasing costs (e.g., buyers' wages or salaries).
- Handling, processing, assembly, and repackaging.
- The portion of mixed services costs allocable to these functions.

Mixed services costs must be allocated to offsite storage, purchasing, and packaging on the basis of direct labor costs of these departments as a percentage of total payroll. Thus, the storage, purchasing, and packaging costs allocated to ending inventory include some mixed services costs.

The uniform capitalization rules may result in some costs being capitalized for tax purposes but not for financial accounting purposes. For example, a wholesaler's or a manufacturer's storage costs are generally expensed for financial reporting purposes, but are capitalized for tax purposes. Also, the taxpayer may capitalize straight-line depreciation of production equipment for financial accounting purposes, but the total tax depreciation must be capitalized under uniform capitalization.

Lower of Cost or Market

Except for those taxpayers who use the LIFO method, inventories may be valued at the **lower of cost or market (replacement cost).**[95] Taxpayers using LIFO must value inventory at cost. However, the write-down of damaged or shopworn merchandise and goods that are otherwise unsalable at normal prices is not considered to be an application of the lower of cost or market method. Such items should be valued at bona fide selling price less direct cost of disposal.[96]

In the case of excess inventories (as in *Thor Power Tool Co.*, discussed above), the goods can be written down only to the taxpayer's offering price. If the offering price on the goods is not reduced, the goods must be valued at cost.

▼
EXAMPLE 36

The Cardinal Publishing Company invested $50,000 in printing 10,000 copies of a book. Although only 7,000 copies were sold in the first 3 years and none in the next 5 years, management is convinced that the book will become a classic in 20 years. Cardinal leaves the price the same as it was when the book was first distributed ($15 per copy). The remaining 3,000 books must be valued at cost ($15,000). Note that the tax law provides an incentive for the taxpayer to destroy or abandon its excess inventory and obtain an immediate deduction rather than wait for the event of future sales. ▼

In applying the lower of cost or market method, *each* item included in the inventory must be valued at the lower of its cost or market value.[97]

---

[95] Reg. § 1.472–4
[96] Reg. § 1.471–2(c).

[97] Reg. § 1.471–4(c).

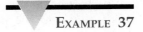

EXAMPLE 37

The taxpayer's ending inventory is valued as follows:

Item	Cost	Market	Lower of Cost or Market
A	$5,000	$ 4,000	$4,000
B	3,000	2,000	2,000
C	1,500	6,000	1,500
	$9,500	$12,000	$7,500

Under the lower of cost or market method, the taxpayer's inventory would be valued at $7,500 rather than $9,500. ▼

Determining Cost—Specific Identification, FIFO, and LIFO

In some cases, it is feasible to determine the cost of the particular item sold. For example, an automobile dealer can easily determine the specific cost of each automobile that has been sold. However, in most businesses it is necessary to resort to a flow of goods assumption such as *first in, first out* (FIFO), *last in, first out* (LIFO), or an *average cost* method. A taxpayer may use any of these methods, provided the method selected is consistently applied from year to year.

During a period of rising prices, LIFO will generally produce a lower ending inventory valuation and will result in a greater cost of goods sold than would be obtained under the FIFO method. The following example illustrates how LIFO and FIFO affect the computation of the cost of goods sold.

EXAMPLE 38

On January 1, 1994, the taxpayer opened a retail store to sell refrigerators. At least 10 refrigerators must be carried in inventory to satisfy customer demands. The initial investment in the 10 refrigerators is $5,000. During the year, 10 refrigerators were sold at $750 each and were replaced at a cost of $6,000 ($600 each). Gross profit under the LIFO and FIFO methods is computed as follows:

		FIFO		LIFO
Sales (10 × $750)		$ 7,500		$ 7,500
Beginning inventory	$ 5,000		$ 5,000	
Purchases	6,000		6,000	
	$11,000		$11,000	
Ending inventory				
10 × $600	(6,000)			
10 × $500			(5,000)	
Cost of goods sold		(5,000)		(6,000)
Gross profit		$ 2,500		$ 1,500

▼

Dollar-Value LIFO

In the previous example, the taxpayer was buying and selling a single product, a particular model of a refrigerator. The taxpayer employed the specific goods LIFO technique. Under the specific goods approach, if the identical items are not on hand at the end of the period, the LIFO inventory is depleted, and all of the deferred profit must be recaptured. Thus, taxpayers who frequently change the items carried in inventory would realize little benefit from LIFO. However, the dollar-value LIFO technique avoids the LIFO depletion problem associated with the specific goods technique.

Under **dollar-value LIFO,** each inventory item is assigned to a pool. A *pool* is a collection of similar items and is treated as a separate inventory. Determining whether items are similar involves considerable judgment. In general, however, the taxpayer would prefer broad pools so that when a particular item is sold out, it can be replaced by increases in other items in the same pool. Generally, all products manufactured at a particular plant can be treated as a pool.[98] A department store may have a separate pool for each department. An automobile dealer may have separate pools for new cars, lightweight trucks, heavy-duty trucks, and car and truck parts.

At the end of the period, the ending inventory must be valued at the current year prices and then at the LIFO base period (the year LIFO was adopted). The ratio of the ending inventory at current prices to the ending inventory at base period prices is the *LIFO index.* If the total current inventory at base period prices is greater than the base period inventory at base period prices, a LIFO layer must be added. The LIFO index is applied to the LIFO layer to convert it to current prices.

EXAMPLE 39

Black Company adopted LIFO effective January 1, 1994. The base LIFO inventory (from December 31, 1993) was $1,000,000. On December 31, 1994, the inventory was $1,320,000 at end-of-1994 prices and $1,200,000 at end-of-1993 (the base period) prices. Thus, Black added a 1994 layer of $200,000 ($1,200,000 − $1,000,000) at base period prices. The layer must be converted to 1994 prices as follows:

$$\text{LIFO index} = \$1,320,000/\$1,200,000 = 1.10$$

$$\text{1994 layer} \times \text{LIFO index} = \$200,000 \times 1.10 = \$220,000$$

Therefore, the 1994 ending inventory is $1,000,000 + $220,000 = $1,220,000.

The inventory on December 31, 1995, is $1,325,000 using 1995 prices and $1,250,000 using base period prices. Thus, the LIFO index for 1995 is $1,325,000/$1,250,000 = 1.06. The LIFO inventory is $1,273,000 as computed below:

BLACK COMPANY
LIFO Inventory
December 31, 1995

	Base Period Cost	LIFO Index	LIFO Layers
Base inventory	$1,000,000	1.00	$1,000,000
1994 layer	200,000	1.10	220,000
1995 layer	50,000	1.06	53,000
	$1,250,000		$1,273,000

ETHICAL CONSIDERATIONS

Protecting the LIFO Reserve

The Swan Company has been using the LIFO inventory method for the past 20 years and has accumulated a substantial LIFO reserve. During the current year, the company's employees went on strike. By early December, all of the inventories had

[98] See, generally, Reg. § 1.472–8.

been depleted. Sugar is the major raw material used in the company's product. The company is considering the following plan to avoid depletion of the LIFO reserve. In late December, the company will purchase a large quantity of sugar. Also, in December, the company will enter into a contract to sell the sugar to a broker. The sugar purchased will not actually be delivered to Swan. Instead, the seller will hold the sugar until early January and then deliver it directly to the broker.

THE LIFO ELECTION

A taxpayer may adopt LIFO by merely using the method in the tax return for the year of the change and by attaching Form 970 (Application to Use LIFO Inventory Method) to the tax return. Thus, a taxpayer does not have to request approval for changes within the first 180 days of the tax year. Once the election is made, it cannot be revoked. However, a prospective change from LIFO to any other inventory method can be made if the consent of the IRS is obtained.[99]

The beginning inventory valuation for the first year LIFO is used is computed by the costing method employed in the preceding year. Thus, the beginning LIFO inventory is generally the same as the closing inventory for the preceding year. However, since lower of cost or market cannot be used in conjunction with LIFO, previous write-downs to market for items included in the beginning inventory must be restored to income. The amount the inventories are written up is an adjustment due to a change in accounting method.[100] However, the usual rules for disposition of the adjustments under Revenue Procedure 92–20 are not applicable.[101] The taxpayer is allowed to spread the adjustment ratably over the year of the change and the two succeeding years.

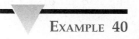

EXAMPLE 40

In 1993, Chee used the lower of cost or market FIFO inventory method. The FIFO cost of his ending inventory was $30,000, and the market value of the inventory was $24,000. Therefore, the ending inventory for 1993 was $24,000. Chee switched to LIFO in 1994 and was required to write up the beginning inventory to $30,000. Chee must add $2,000 ($6,000 ÷ 3) to his income for each of the years 1994, 1995, and 1996. ▼

Congress added this provision to the Code to overrule the previous IRS policy of requiring the taxpayer to include the entire adjustment in income for the year preceding the change to LIFO.[102]

Once the LIFO election is made for tax purposes, the taxpayer's financial reports to owners and creditors must also be prepared on the basis of LIFO.[103] The *conformity* of financial reports to tax reporting is specifically required by the Code and is strictly enforced by the IRS. However, the Regulations permit the taxpayer to make a footnote disclosure of the net income computed by another method of inventory valuation (e.g., FIFO).[104]

[99] Reg. §§ 1.472–3(a) and 1.472–5 and Rev.Proc. 84–74, 1984–2 C.B. 736 at 742.

[100] Reg. § 1.472–2(c). In Rev.Rul. 76–282, 1976–2 C.B. 137, the IRS required the restoration of write-downs for damaged and shopworn goods when the taxpayer switched to LIFO.

[101] I.R.B. No. 12, 10.

[102] § 472(d), overruling the IRS position cited in Footnote 100.

[103] § 472(c).

[104] Reg. § 1.472–2(e).

**TAX PLANNING
CONSIDERATIONS**

7 | **LEARNING OBJECTIVE**

Identify tax planning
opportunities related to
accounting periods and
accounting methods.

TAXABLE YEAR

Under the general rules for tax years, partnerships and S corporations frequently will be required to use a calendar year. However, if the partnership or S corporation can demonstrate a business purpose for a fiscal year, the IRS will allow the entity to use the requested year. The advantage to a fiscal year is that the calendar year partners and S corporation shareholders may be able to defer from tax the income earned from the close of the fiscal year until the end of the calendar year. Tax advisers for these entities should apply the IRS's gross receipts test described in Revenue Procedure 87–32 to determine if permission for the fiscal year will be granted.

CASH METHOD OF ACCOUNTING

The cash method of accounting gives the taxpayer considerable control over the recognition of expenses and some control over the recognition of income. This method can be used by proprietorships, partnerships, and small corporations (gross receipts of $5 million or less) that provide services (inventories are not material to the service business). Farmers (except certain farming corporations) can also use the cash method.

INSTALLMENT METHOD

Unlike the accrual and cash methods, the installment method results in an interest-free loan (of deferred taxes) from the government. Thus, the installment method is a powerful tax planning tool and should be considered when a sale of eligible property is being planned. Note, however, that the provision that requires interest to be paid on the deferred taxes on certain installment obligations reduces this benefit.

Related Parties

Intrafamily installment sales can still be a useful family tax planning tool. If the related party holds the property more than two years, a subsequent sale will not accelerate the gain from the first disposition. Patience and forethought are rewarded.

   The 6 percent limitation on imputed interest on sales of land between family members enables the seller to convert ordinary income into capital gain or make what is, in effect, a nontaxable gift. If the selling price is raised to adjust for the low interest rate charges on an installment sale, the seller has more capital gain but less ordinary income than would be realized from a sale to an unrelated party. If the selling price is not raised and the specified interest of 6 percent is charged, the seller enables the relative to have the use of the property without having to pay for its full market value. As an additional benefit, the bargain sale is not a taxable gift.

Disposition of Installment Obligations

A disposition of an installment obligation is also a serious matter. Gifts of the obligations will accelerate income to the seller. The list of taxable and nontaxable dispositions of installment obligations should not be trusted to memory. In each instance where transfers of installment obligations are contemplated, the practitioner should conduct research to be sure he or she knows the consequences.

LIFO

During periods of inflation, LIFO results in the deferral of tax. The only major disadvantage to LIFO is the financial-tax conformity requirement. However, this disadvantage can be overcome through footnote disclosure of earnings as computed under FIFO.

KEY TERMS

Accounting methods, 18-10

Accounting period, 18-3

Accrual method, 18-12

All events test, 18-13

Cash method, 18-11

Claim of right doctrine, 18-9

Completed contract method, 18-29

Dollar-value LIFO, 18-35

Economic performance test, 18-13

Fiscal year, 18-3

Hybrid method, 18-15

Imputed interest, 18-21

Installment method, 18-19

Least aggregate deferral method, 18-4

Long-term contract, 18-26

Lower of cost or market (replacement cost), 18-33

Majority interest partners, 18-4

Percentage of completion method, 18-30

Personal service corporation (PSC), 18-6

Principal partner, 18-4

Short taxable year (short period), 18-8

Uniform capitalization rules, 18-32

PROBLEM MATERIALS

DISCUSSION QUESTIONS

1. Megan recently began conducting an office supply business as a corporation. Vito began conducting his law practice through a corporation. Neither corporation has made an S election. What tax year alternatives are available to Megan's business that are not available to Vito's business?

2. Why would a C corporation want to use a tax year other than a calendar year?

3. Debra is a practicing accountant. Over 90% of her work is done for individuals and S corporations. In the tax season just ended, Debra found that she could not continue to provide high-quality services for so many calendar year clients. Therefore, she plans to propose to some of her S corporation clients that the corporation change to a fiscal year ending September 30. What problems will Debra encounter in getting her clients to agree to a change in tax year?

4. How does a partnership establish a business purpose for a tax year that differs from its partners' tax years?

5. Dan, a calendar year taxpayer, recently became a licensed orthopedic surgeon. He has incorporated his practice. Dan's brother suggested that the corporation's tax year

should end on September 30 and thus avoid the end-of-the-calendar-year rush. What complications could result from the corporation filing its return on the basis of a fiscal year ending September 30?

6. In which of the following situations must a taxpayer annualize income?
   a. The first tax year.
   b. The year an individual marries.
   c. The final return.
   d. A year of a change in the tax year.

7. Jack is a cash basis taxpayer. In 1993, when Jack was in the 31% marginal tax bracket, he received $25,000 for services provided for Jane. In 1994, Jack discovered that he had overcharged Jane by $4,000 in 1993. Therefore, he immediately refunded Jane the $4,000. As a result of some unusually large expenses in 1994, Jack's taxable income for the year was only $5,000. What special tax treatment is afforded the $4,000 payment?

8. Quinn is the sole shareholder of an accrual basis S corporation, Red, Inc. If Quinn forms another S corporation, Purple, Inc., does the fact that Red uses the accrual method mean that Purple is required to use the accrual method?

9. Why would a business generally prefer to use the cash method of accounting?

10. Rita buys and sells produce. Her annual gross receipts are less than $5 million. Approximately 30% of her sales are on account. Rita sells all of her inventory each day. Thus, she has no beginning or ending inventory each year. Is Rita required to use the accrual method of accounting?

11. Earl, a certified public accountant, recently obtained a new client. The client is a retail grocery store that has used the cash method to report its income since it began doing business. Will Earl incur any liability if he prepares the tax return in accordance with the cash method and does not advise the client of the necessity of seeking the IRS's permission to change to the accrual method?

12. In December 1994, a cash basis taxpayer paid January through June 1995 management fees in connection with his rental properties. The fees were $4,000 per month. Compute the 1994 expense under the following assumptions:
    a. The fees were paid by an individual who derived substantially all of his income from the properties.
    b. The fees were paid by a tax-shelter partnership.

13. Osprey Corporation, an accrual basis taxpayer, had taxable income for 1994. However, Osprey's accountant was ill, and the taxable income for 1994 was not computed until July 1995. The state income tax return for 1994 was filed in August 1995, and $3,000 in state income taxes were paid at that time. Can the 1994 state income taxes be deducted in calculating the corporation's 1994 Federal taxable income?

14. Compare the cash basis and accrual basis of accounting as applied to the following:
    a. Fixed assets.
    b. Prepaid rent income.
    c. Prepaid interest expense.
    d. A note received for services performed if the market value and face amount of the note differ.

15. When are reserves for estimated expenses allowed for tax purposes? What is the role of the matching concept in tax accounting?

16. What difference does it make whether the taxpayer or the IRS initiates the change in accounting method?

17. Generally, what is the deadline for a taxpayer filing a request for a change from an incorrect accounting method?

18. Generally, what incentives are provided to encourage a taxpayer to change voluntarily from an incorrect method of accounting?

19. Which of the following require the permission of the IRS?
    a. A change from the cash to the accrual basis for deducting property tax expenses.
    b. The correction of a prior year's return when the double-declining balance method was incorrectly used to compute the amortization of a patent.
    c. A change from direct costing to the full absorption method of valuing inventories.
    d. A change from the FIFO to the LIFO inventory method.
    e. A change from cost to the lower of cost or market method of valuing inventories.
    f. A write-down of damaged merchandise to net realizable value when the taxpayer has consistently used cost to value the inventories.
    g. The use of the lower of cost or market method in conjunction with the LIFO inventory method.
    h. A change from the LIFO to the FIFO inventory method.

20. What difference does it make whether the taxpayer is deemed to have used an incorrect accounting method versus having committed an error?

21. Irene has made Sara an offer on the purchase of a capital asset. Irene will pay (1) $200,000 cash or (2) $50,000 cash and a 9% installment note for $150,000 guaranteed by City Bank of New York. If Sara sells for $200,000 cash, she will invest the after-tax proceeds in certificates of deposit yielding 9% interest. Sara's cost of the asset is $25,000. Why would Sara prefer the installment sale?

22. Which of the following are eligible for installment reporting? Assume some payments are received after the year of sale and the sales are for gains.
    a. Fully depreciated equipment sold for $50,000. The original cost of the equipment was $75,000.
    b. Sale of a tractor by a farm equipment dealer.
    c. Sale of stock in a family-controlled corporation.
    d. Sale of residential lots.

23. Juan, a cash basis taxpayer, sold land in December 1994. At the time of the sale, Juan received $10,000 cash and a note for $90,000 due in 90 days. Juan expects to be in a much higher tax bracket in 1995. Should Juan report the sale in 1994 or 1995?

24. How does the buyer's assumption of the seller's liabilities in an installment sale affect the following?
    a. Selling price.
    b. Contract price.
    c. Buyer's payments in the year of sale.

25. On June 1, 1992, Father sold land to Son for $100,000. Father reported the gain by the installment method, with the gain to be spread over five years. In May 1994, Son received an offer of $150,000 for the land, to be paid over three years. What would be the tax consequences of Son's sale?

26. In 1993, Bhaskar sold a building to his 100% controlled corporation. The entire purchase price is to be paid in 1994. When should Bhaskar report the gain on the sale of the building?

27. What is the tax effect of a gift of an installment obligation?

28. Who can use the completed contract method to report income?

29. What is the purpose of the lookback rules applicable to long-term contracts reported by the percentage of completion method?

30. What are the implications of underestimating the costs of a contract whose income is reported by the percentage of completion method?

31. What is *market* for purposes of applying the lower of cost or market inventory method?

32. Contrast the procedures for changing to the LIFO inventory method with the general requirements for making a change in an accounting method.

33. Discuss the problems that could result from footnote disclosures of net income computed by the FIFO method when the taxpayer uses the LIFO method to report its taxable income.

PROBLEMS

34. Red, White, and Blue are unrelated corporations engaged in real estate development. The three corporations formed a joint venture (treated as a partnership) to develop a tract of land. Assuming the venture does not have a natural business year, what tax year must the joint venture adopt under the following circumstances?

		Tax Year Ending	Interest in Joint Venture
a.	Red	Sept. 30	60%
	White	June 30	20%
	Blue	March 31	20%
b.	Red	Sept. 30	30%
	White	June 30	40%
	Blue	January 31	30%

35. The Cardinal Wholesale Company is an S corporation that began business on March 1, 1994. Robert, a calendar year taxpayer, owns 100% of the Cardinal stock. He has $400,000 taxable income from other sources each year. Robert will work approximately 30 hours a week for the corporation. Cardinal sells swimming pool supplies, and its natural business year ends in September. Approximately 80% of Cardinal's gross receipts occur in June through September.
    a. What tax year should Cardinal elect, assuming that Robert anticipates the company will produce a net profit for all years?
    b. What tax year should Cardinal elect, assuming it will lose $10,000 a month for the first 12 months and an average of $5,000 a month for the next 12 months? In the third year, the corporation will earn taxable income.

36. Zack conducted his professional practice through Zack, Inc. The corporation uses a fiscal year ending September 30 even though the business purpose test for a fiscal year cannot be satisfied. For the year ending September 30, 1994, the corporation paid Zack a salary of $150,000, and during the period January through September 1994, the corporation paid him a salary of $120,000.
    a. How much salary should Zack receive during the period October 1 through December 31, 1994?
    b. Assume Zack received only $30,000 salary during the period October 1 through December 31, 1994. What would be the consequences to Zack, Inc.?

37. Owl Corporation is in the business of sales and home deliveries of fuel oil and currently uses a calendar year for reporting its taxable income. However, Owl's natural business year ends May 31. For the short period, January 1, 1994, through May 31, 1994, the corporation earned $31,500. Assume the corporate tax rates are as follows: 15% on taxable income of $50,000 or less, 25% on taxable income over $50,000 but not over $75,000, and 34% on taxable income over $75,000.
    a. What must Owl Corporation do to change its taxable year?
    b. Compute Owl Corporation's tax for the short period.

38. Jim, a cash basis taxpayer, owned a building that he leased to Edith. In 1994, Edith prepaid the 1995 rent. During 1995, the building was destroyed by fire. Under the lease agreement, Jim was required to refund $6,000 to Edith. Also, in June 1994, Jim paid the insurance premium on the property for the next 12 months. After the building was destroyed in 1995, Jim got a $600 refund on the insurance premium. He was in the 31% marginal tax bracket in 1994 and in the 15% marginal tax bracket in 1995. What are the effects of the refunds on Jim's 1995 tax liability?

39. Compute the taxpayer's income or deductions for 1994 using (1) the cash basis and (2) the accrual basis for each of the following:
    a. In 1994, the taxpayer purchased new equipment for $100,000. The taxpayer paid $25,000 in cash and gave a $75,000 interest-bearing note for the balance. The

equipment has a MACRS life of five years, the mid-year convention applies, and the § 179 election was not made.

b. In December 1994, the taxpayer collected $10,000 for January rents. In January 1995, the taxpayer collected $2,000 for December 1994 rents.

c. In December 1994, the taxpayer paid office equipment insurance premiums for January–June 1995 of $30,000.

40. Which of the following businesses must use the accrual method of accounting?
   a. A corporation with annual gross receipts of $12 million from equipment rentals.
   b. A partnership (not a tax shelter) engaged in farming and with annual gross receipts of $8 million.
   c. A corporation that acts as an insurance agent, with annual gross receipts of $1 million.
   d. A manufacturer with annual gross receipts of $600,000.
   e. A retailer with annual gross receipts of $250,000.

41. Pink Company calculated its accrual basis income for its first year of operations. Net income before tax was $30,000. For tax purposes, the company would like to elect the method that will minimize its taxable income for the year. Compute Pink's minimum taxable income, given the following information at the end of the first year:

Inventory	$19,000
Accounts receivable	25,000
Office supplies	1,800
Prepaid insurance (6 months)	1,200
Accounts payable (merchandise)	5,000

42. Ron receives appliances from the manufacturer on consignment and collects a 5% commission on any sales made during the year. Ron is an accrual basis taxpayer and made total sales of $750,000 during the year. However, the manufacturer is usually a few weeks behind in recording Ron's sales and at the end of the year recorded only $600,000 in sales. Ron argues that he should report income for the year of only $30,000 (5% × $600,000), since that was all he had a right to receive for the year. Ron had no right to the commissions on the other $150,000 sales until the manufacturer reported them in the following year. What is Ron's correct taxable income for the year? Explain.

43. Determine when Helen, an accrual basis taxpayer, should record the expenses in each of the following cases:
   a. A customer returned defective merchandise to Helen in December 1994. The customer claimed the goods did not meet specifications and threatened to sue Helen for breach of contract. Helen admitted liability in 1994, but did not pay the damages until January 1995.
   b. A customer slipped and fell on the business premises in 1994. Helen admitted liability, and a settlement was reached late in the year. Under the terms of the settlement, Helen was to pay the customer's medical expenses. By the end of 1994, the total medical expenses associated with the injury were determined. However, some of the expenses were for doctor visits that were to be spread over an 18-month period, and payments would not be made until the time of the visits.
   c. In March 1995, Helen filed her 1994 state income tax return and paid the balance due on 1994 state income taxes.

44. In 1994, the taxpayer was required to switch from the cash to the accrual basis of accounting for sales and cost of goods sold. Taxable income for 1994 computed under the cash basis was $40,000. Relevant account balances were as follows:

	Beginning of the Year	End of the Year
Accounts receivable	$24,000	$30,000
Accounts payable	9,000	8,000
Inventory	7,000	4,000

Compute the following:

a. The adjustment due to the change in accounting method.

b. The accrual basis taxable income for 1994.

45. Crow Finance Company experiences bad debts of about 5% of its outstanding loans. At the end of the year, the company had outstanding receivables of $18 million. This balance included $3 million of accrued interest receivable. Crow's loan loss reserve for the year was computed as follows:

Balance, January 1, 1994	$750,000
Accounts written off as uncollectible	
Loans made in 1994	(10,000)
Loans made in prior years	(35,000)
Collections on loans previously written off	9,000
Adjustment to required balance	186,000
Balance, December 31, 1994	$900,000

a. Determine the effects of the above on Crow's taxable income for 1994.

b. Assume that Crow has used the reserve method to compute its taxable income for the 10 years the company has been in existence. In 1994, you begin preparing Crow's tax return. What should be done with regard to the reserve?

46. In 1994, the taxpayer changed from the cash to the accrual basis of accounting for sales, cost of goods sold, and accrued expenses. Taxable income for 1994 computed under the cash method was $45,000. Relevant account balances are as follows:

	Beginning of the Year	**End of the Year**
Accounts receivable	$ 5,000	$11,000
Accounts payable	–0–	–0–
Accrued expenses	2,000	3,000
Inventory	10,000	16,000

a. Compute the accrual basis taxable income for 1994 and the adjustment due to the change in accounting method.

b. Assuming the change was voluntary, how will the adjustment due to the change be treated?

47. Floyd, a cash basis taxpayer, has agreed to sell land to Beige, Inc., a well-established and highly profitable company. Beige is willing to (1) pay $100,000 cash or (2) pay $25,000 cash and the balance ($75,000) plus interest at 10% (the Federal rate) in two years. Floyd is in the 35% marginal tax bracket (combined Federal and state) for all years and believes he can reinvest the sales proceeds and earn a 14% before-tax rate of return.

a. Should Floyd accept the deferred payments option if his basis in the land is $10,000?

b. Do you think your results would change if Floyd's basis in the land is $90,000?

48. Kay, who is not a dealer, sold an apartment house to Polly during the current year (1994). The closing statement for the sale is as follows:

Total selling price		$100,000
Add: Polly's share of property taxes (6 months) paid by Kay		2,500
Less: Kay's 11% mortgage assumed by Polly	$55,000	
Polly's refundable binder ("earnest money") paid in 1993	1,000	
Polly's 11% installment note given to Kay	30,000	
Kay's real estate commissions and attorney's fees	7,500	(93,500)
Cash paid to Kay at closing		$ 9,000
Cash due from Polly = $9,000 + $7,500 expenses		$ 16,500

During 1994, Kay collected $4,000 in principal on the installment note and $2,000 interest. Kay's basis in the property was $70,000 [$85,000 – $15,000 (depreciation)], and there was $9,000 in potential depreciation recapture under § 1250. The Federal rate is 9%.

a. Compute the following:
   1. Total gain.
   2. Contract price.
   3. Payments received in the year of sale.
   4. Recognized gain in the year of sale and the character of such gain.

(*Hint:* Think carefully about the manner in which the property taxes are handled before you begin your computations.)

b. Same as (a)(2) and (3), except Kay's basis in the property was $45,000.

49. On June 30, 1994, Kelly sold property for $250,000 cash on the date of sale and a $750,000 note due on September 30, 1995. No interest was stated in the contract. The present value of the note (using 13.2%, which was the Federal rate) was $640,000. Kelly's basis in the property was $400,000, and $40,000 of the gain was depreciation recapture under § 1245. Expenses of the sale totaled $10,000, and Kelly was not a dealer in the property sold.
   a. Compute Kelly's gain to be reported in 1994.
   b. Compute Kelly's interest income for 1995.

50. On July 1, 1993, a cash basis taxpayer sold land for $800,000 due on the date of the sale and $6 million principal and $741,600 interest (6%) due on June 30, 1995. The seller's basis in the land was $1 million. The Federal short-term rate was 8%, compounded semiannually.
   a. Compute the seller's interest income and gain in 1993, 1994, and 1995.
   b. Same as (a), except that the amount due in two years was $2 million principal and $508,800 interest and the purchaser will use the cash method to account for interest.

51. Maria made an installment sale of land and a building to Ned. There was no ordinary income recapture on the building. At the time of the sale, the Federal rate was 8%, and the market rate on similar contracts was 10%. Under the contract, Ned would make payments as follows:

Cash at closing, July 1, 1994	$ 50,000
Interest at 9%, due June 30, 1995*	27,607
Interest at 9%, due June 30, 1996*	27,607
Principal due June 30, 1996	300,000

*Interest is compounded semiannually.

   a. Will interest be imputed on the contract?
   b. Assuming Maria is a cash basis taxpayer, what is her interest income for 1994 under the contract?
   c. Assuming Ned is an accrual basis taxpayer, what is his interest expense for 1994 under the contract?

52. On December 30, 1994, Father sold land to Son for $10,000 cash and a 7% installment note with a face amount of $190,000. In 1995, after paying $30,000 on the principal of the note, Son sold the land. In 1996, Son paid Father $25,000 on the note principal. Father's basis in the land was $50,000. Assuming Son sold the land for $250,000, compute Father's taxable gain in 1995.

53. George sold land to an unrelated party in 1993. His basis in the land was $40,000, and the selling price was $100,000—$25,000 payable at closing and $25,000 (plus 10% interest) due January 1, 1994, 1995, and 1996. What would be the tax consequences of the following? [Treat each part independently and assume (1) George did not elect out

of the installment method and (2) the installment obligations have values equal to their face amounts.]

a. In 1994, George gave to his daughter the right to collect all future payments on the installment obligations.

b. In 1994, after collecting the payment due on January 1, George transferred the installment obligation to his 100% controlled corporation in exchange for additional shares of stock.

c. On December 31, 1994, George received the payment due on January 1, 1995. On December 15, 1995, George died, and the remaining installment obligation was transferred to George's estate. The estate collected the amount due on January 1, 1996.

54. The Dove Construction Company reports its income by the completed contract method. At the end of 1994, the company completed a contract to construct a building at a total cost of $980,000. The contract price was $1,200,000. However, the customer refused to accept the work and would not pay anything on the contract because he claimed the roof did not meet specifications. Dove's engineers estimated it would cost $140,000 to bring the roof up to the customer's standards. In 1995, the dispute was settled in the customer's favor; the roof was improved at a cost of $170,000, and the customer accepted the building and paid the $1,200,000.

a. What would be the effects of the above on Dove's taxable income for 1994 and 1995?

b. Same as (a), except Dove had $1,100,000 accumulated cost under the contract at the end of 1994.

55. Rust Company is a real estate construction company with average annual gross receipts of $3 million. Rust uses the completed contract method, and the contracts require 18 months to complete. Which of the following costs would be allocated to construction in progress by Rust?

a. The payroll taxes on direct labor.

b. The current services pension costs for employees whose wages are included in direct labor.

c. Accelerated depreciation on equipment used on contracts.

d. Sales tax on materials assigned to contracts.

e. The past service costs for employees whose wages are included in direct labor.

f. Bidding expenses for contracts awarded.

56. Indicate the accounting method that should be used to compute the income from the following contracts:

a. A contract to build six jet aircraft.

b. A contract to build a new home. The contractor's average annual gross receipts are $15 million.

c. A contract to manufacture 3,000 pairs of boots for a large retail chain. The manufacturer has several contracts to produce the same boot for other retailers.

d. A contract to pave a parking lot. The contractor's average annual gross receipts are $2 million.

57. Ostrich Company makes gasoline storage tanks. Everything produced is under contract (that is, the company does not produce until it gets a contract for a product). Ostrich makes three basic models. However, the tanks must be adapted to each individual customer's location and needs (e.g., the location of the valves, the quality of the materials and insulation). Discuss the following issues relative to Ostrich's operations:

a. An examining IRS agent contends that each of the company's contracts is to produce a "unique product." What difference does it make whether the product is unique rather than a "shelf item"?

b. Producing one of the tanks takes over one year from start to completion, and the total cost is in excess of $1 million. What costs must be capitalized for this contract that are not subject to capitalization for a contract with a shorter duration and lower cost?

    c. What must Ostrich do with the costs of bidding on contracts?

    d. Ostrich frequently makes several cost estimates for a contract, using various estimates of materials costs. These costs fluctuate almost daily. Assuming Ostrich must use the percentage of completion method to report the income from the contract, what will be the consequence if the company uses the highest estimate of a contract's cost and the actual cost is closer to the lowest estimated cost?

58. Swallow Company is a large real estate construction company that reports its income by the percentage of completion method. In 1995, the company completed a contract at a total cost of $1,960,000. The contract price was $2,400,000. At the end of 1994, the year the contract was begun, Swallow estimated the total cost of the contract would be $2,100,000, and total accumulated costs on the contract at the end of 1994 were $1,400,000. The relevant tax rate is 34%, and the relevant Federal interest rate is 7%. Assume that all returns were filed and taxes were paid on March 15 following the close of the calendar tax year.

    a. Compute the gross profit on the contract for 1994 and 1995.

    b. Compute the lookback interest due with the 1995 return.

59. How would interest provisions in the tax law impact upon the following events?

    a. The taxpayer reports income by the percentage of completion method. In 1995, the taxpayer completed a real estate construction contract that yielded a total profit of $750,000. One-half of the costs of the contract were incurred in 1994, and the taxpayer reported $400,000 as percentage of completion profit that year. The disproportionate profit reported in 1994 was due to an overestimation of the total profit on the contract.

    b. The contractor in (a) received progress payments from the customer, but generally the total cost accumulated on the contract was $100,000 greater than the progress payments. The contractor financed the balance of the cost with a bank loan. The customer financed the payments made with a construction loan.

    c. The contractor in (a) completed the contract at the end of 1995. At that time, the customer owed the contractor $100,000. Also, in 1995, the customer went bankrupt, and the contractor was unable to collect the $100,000.

60. Determine whether the following costs must be added to inventory:

    a. The taxpayer bottles wine as part of his wholesale business and must incur $150,000 in warehousing to store the wine for six months before the wine is offered for sale. The taxpayer owns the warehouse.

    b. Interest allocable to the wine in storage [in (a)] is $30,000.

    c. A real estate developer incurred $50,000 interest during construction.

    d. A chain of retail stores operates a warehouse. The total cost of operating the warehouse (e.g., depreciation, wages) for the year was $2 million, of which $500,000 is attributable to (allocated on the basis of costs) storing goods still on hand at year-end.

61. Flamingo Company produces small machinery. The company also produces parts used to repair the machinery. The parts may be sold for several years after the company has discontinued the product. Flamingo has on hand parts with an original cost of $600,000. The total offering price on these goods is $960,000. However, the company expects to sell only 80% of the parts on hand. The excess parts are kept in case the estimates are incorrect.

    a. Can Flamingo deduct the excess inventory under the lower of cost or market rule?

    b. Assume that Flamingo deducted the cost of the excess parts on hand. While the parts were still on hand, the company elected LIFO. What are the implications of the change in inventory method?

62. Lavender Manufacturing Company began business in the current year. The company uses the simplified method to allocate mixed services costs to production. The company's costs and expenses for the year were as follows:

Direct labor	$1,250,000
Direct materials	2,000,000
Factory supervision	200,000
Personnel department	100,000
Computer operations	50,000
General administration	150,000
Marketing	100,000
Interest	25,000
	$3,875,000

a. Determine Lavender's total production costs for the year.

b. What suggestions can you offer regarding the allocation of the company's mixed services costs?

63. In 1994, Gail changed from the use of the lower of cost or market FIFO method to the LIFO method. The ending inventory for 1993 was computed as follows:

Item	FIFO Cost	Replacement Cost	Lower of Cost or Market
A	$10,000	$18,000	$10,000
B	25,000	20,000	20,000
			$30,000

a. What is the correct beginning inventory in 1994 under the LIFO method?

b. What immediate tax consequences (if any) would result from the switch to LIFO?

64. Amber Company has used the dollar-value LIFO technique for the past three years. The company has only one inventory pool. Its beginning inventory for the current year was computed as follows:

	Base Period Cost	LIFO Index	LIFO Layer
Base inventory	$1,250,000	1.0	$1,250,000
Year 1 layer	450,000	1.1	495,000
Year 2 layer	100,000	.90	90,000
	$1,800,000		$1,835,000

The ending inventory is $1,955,000 at current period prices and $1,700,000 at base period prices. Determine the company's LIFO inventory value as of the end of the current year.

65. Your client, Bob Young, is negotiating a sale of investment real estate for $12 million. Bob believes that the buyer would pay cash of $8 million and a note for $4 million, or $3 million cash and a note for $9 million. The notes will pay interest at slightly above the market rate. Bob realizes that the second option involves more risks of collection, but he is willing to accept that risk if the tax benefits of the installment sale are substantial. Write a letter to Bob advising him of the tax consequences of choosing the lower down payment and larger note option, assuming he has no other installment receivables.

RESEARCH PROBLEMS

Research Problem 1.   Amber Company is a wholesaler with a fiscal year ending October 31, after it has shipped all of its Christmas goods. Management at Amber is considering changing its terms of sale for some of its goods so that the goods are on consignment until November 30, and title does not pass to the retailer until that date. Under present terms, title to the goods passes at the time of shipment. Management would like to know the tax consequences of the change in terms.

Partial list of research aids:
Hallmark Cards, Inc. & Subsidiaries, 90 T.C. 26 (1988).

Research Problem 2.   Violet Company discovered certain equipment used in its repair operations had been accounted for as inventory rather than as fixed assets. This incorrect treatment applied to all years in which the equipment had been used, and all of those years are open under the statute of limitations. Violet filed amended returns for all years affected by the incorrect treatment to obtain a refund of overpayments of taxes for the years affected. The IRS refused to accept the amended returns. The IRS reasoned that Violet was actually changing accounting methods and this can only be accomplished through a request for change in methods. In addition, the IRS concluded that an adjustment due to a voluntary change in accounting method must be taken into income for the year of the change. Is the IRS correct? Write a letter to Violet Company that contains your advice and prepare a memo for the tax files.

Research Problem 3.   Your client is an automobile dealer, selling a full range of new automobiles manufactured by a domestic company and also a line of foreign-made automobiles. Prices of new cars have steadily increased over the past several years, and you believe your client could defer profits by electing LIFO. Where can you find specific guidance for establishing pools and techniques for pricing the dollar-value LIFO inventory for an automobile dealer?

Research Problem 4.   You recently contracted to perform tax services for a new funeral home. In preparing the initial tax return, you must decide whether the funeral home can use the cash method of accounting. When discussing this issue with the manager, the manager points out that the company is actually a service business and that the only materials involved are caskets, which average only 15% of the price of a funeral. Is the funeral home required to use the accrual method of accounting?

Research Problem 5.   State law requires Clear Cola Company to sell its beverages in returnable bottles. Customers pay a deposit for the bottles, and Clear is required to refund the deposit to anyone who returns the bottles. Grocery stores collect the deposits and pay the customers for returned bottles and then are reimbursed by Clear. The company unsuccessfully argued that the collections of the deposits should not be treated as income. Subsequently, the company argued that if income must be recognized from the receipt of a deposit, a deduction should be allowed for the estimated amounts that must be paid to the customers. Clear estimates that 80% of all bottles are returned. Can Clear accrue a deduction for the estimated cost of bottles that will be returned and thus accurately match revenue and expenses?

19

DEFERRED COMPENSATION

LEARNING OBJECTIVES

After completing Chapter 19, you should be able to:

1. Distinguish between qualified (defined contribution and defined benefit) and nonqualified compensation arrangements.

2. Identify the qualification requirements for qualified plans.

3. Discuss the tax consequences of qualified plans.

4. Calculate the limitations on contributions to and benefits from qualified plans.

5. Understand the qualified plan (Keogh plan) available to a self-employed person.

6. Describe the benefits of an Individual Retirement Account (IRA).

7. Understand the rationale for nonqualified deferred compensation plans and the related tax treatment.

8. Explain the value of restricted property plans.

9. Differentiate the tax treatment of qualified and nonqualified stock options.

OUTLINE

Qualified Pension, Profit Sharing, and Stock Bonus Plans, 19–3

Types of Plans, 19–4

Qualification Requirements, 19–7

Tax Consequences to the Employee and Employer, 19–12

Limitations on Contributions to and Benefits from Qualified Plans, 19–16

Top-Heavy Plans, 19–18

Cash or Deferred Arrangement Plans, 19–19

Retirement Plans for Self-Employed Individuals, 19–20

Coverage Requirements, 19–21

Contribution Limitations, 19–21

Individual Retirement Accounts (IRAs), 19–22

General Rules, 19–22

Penalty Taxes for Excess Contributions, 19–25

Taxation of Benefits, 19–25

Nonqualified Deferred Compensation Plans, 19–27

Underlying Rationale for Tax Treatment, 19–27

Tax Treatment to the Employer and Employee, 19–28

Restricted Property Plans, 19–31

General Provisions, 19–31

Substantial Risk of Forfeiture, 19–32

Special Election Available, 19–32

Employer Deductions, 19–33

Stock Options, 19–34

In General, 19–34

Incentive Stock Options, 19–34

Nonqualified Stock Options, 19–36

Tax Planning Considerations, 19–37

Deferred Compensation, 19–37

Qualified Plans, 19–38

Self-Employed Retirement Plans, 19–38

Individual Retirement Accounts, 19–38

Comparison of § 401(k) Plan with IRA, 19–39

Nonqualified Deferred Compensation (NQDC) Plans, 19–40

Stock Options, 19–40

Flexible Benefit Plans, 19–41

This chapter discusses the various types of deferred compensation arrangements available to employees and self-employed individuals. With **deferred compensation,** an employee receives compensation for services after the period when the services were performed. The tax law encourages employers to offer deferred compensation plans to their employees to supplement the Federal Social Security retirement system. Contributions to qualified pension, profit sharing, or stock bonus plans offer three major advantages:

- Contributions are immediately deductible by the employer.
- Employees are not taxed until these funds are made available to them.
- Income earned by the plan trust, which has received the contributions, is not subject to tax until made available to the employees.

A variety of deferred compensation arrangements are being offered to employees, including the following:

- Qualified profit sharing plans.
- Qualified pension plans.
- Employee stock ownership plans.
- Cash or deferred arrangement plans.
- Tax-deferred annuities.
- Incentive stock option plans.
- Nonqualified deferred compensation plans.
- Restricted property plans.
- Cafeteria benefit plans.

With the new higher 39.6 percent individual tax bracket, taxpayers may lower their tax bill by participating in more deferred compensation arrangements. Further, the new $1 million per year compensation deduction limitation on the top five executives of publicly traded companies may cause these executives to shift compensation payments into both qualified and nonqualified deferred compensation arrangements.

In addition to the various types of deferred compensation, employees may receive other valuable fringe benefits. Examples of such benefits include group term life insurance, medical reimbursement plans, company-supplied automobiles, education expense reimbursement plans, and group legal services.[1]

The Code, in certain circumstances, prohibits a deduction for certain types of fringe benefits such as a golden parachute payment. Refer to the subsequent discussion under Nonqualified Deferred Compensation Plans.

1   LEARNING OBJECTIVE
Distinguish between qualified (defined contribution and defined benefit) and nonqualified compensation arrangements.

QUALIFIED PENSION, PROFIT SHARING, AND STOCK BONUS PLANS

The Federal government has encouraged private pension and profit sharing plans to keep retired people from becoming dependent on the government. Therefore, the Federal tax law provides substantial tax benefits for plans that meet certain

---

TAX IN THE NEWS

DIG IT OUT

Indeed, employee benefit plans are the most valuable source of tax breaks and savings opportunities most people have, providing all of their medical coverage, life insurance, and retirement savings (apart from Social Security). "For most employees, the tax savings in benefit plans exceed the deductions they're taking on their income tax returns," says Lance Tane, a partner with Kwasha Lipton, a benefits consulting firm in Fort Lee, New Jersey. "Not making the right choices with your benefits is like not cashing a couple of your paychecks."

But a lot of employees don't make the right choices because they don't take time to find out what they've got and how to make the best use of their options. "Benefit programs today are a lot like VCRs," says Mr. Tane. "They've been engineered with a lot of value-added features, but most users don't get the benefits because they don't take time to read the manual."

Michael Hayes, an actuary with Hewitt Associates, a benefits consulting firm in Lincolnshire, Illinois, agrees. "It may feel like doing your income taxes," he says, "but it's worth the time."

Paying attention to your benefit plan is more crucial than ever these days because cost-conscious employers are making benefits harder to obtain. Increasingly, they are shifting the costs to employees and to taxpayers.

Another good reason for employees to get in the driver's seat when it comes to their benefit plans is that they can't always count on their employer to tell them what's best for them. Overworked human resource staffs are already struggling to juggle all the changes taking place and may not have the time or expertise to explain all the options in a program. "At many companies, employee benefits are like buried treasure: The company may give you a map, but you have to dig to get it," says Mr. Tane.

SOURCE: Reprinted from Ellen E. Schultz, "How to Get the Most Out of Your Benefit Plan," *Wall Street Journal,* July 9, 1993, p. C1. Reprinted by permission of the *Wall Street Journal,* © 1993 Dow Jones & Company, Inc. All rights reserved worldwide.

---

[1] Refer to the discussions in Chapters 4 and 5.

requirements. The major requirement for qualification is that a plan not discriminate in favor of highly compensated employees.

TYPES OF PLANS

There are three types of qualified plans: pension, profit sharing, and stock bonus plans.

Pension Plans

A **pension plan** is a deferred compensation arrangement that provides for systematic payments of definitely determinable retirement benefits to employees who meet the requirements set forth in the plan. Benefits are generally measured by and based on such factors as years of service and employee compensation. Employer contributions under a qualified pension plan must *not* depend on profits. In addition, they must be sufficient to provide definitely determinable benefits on some actuarial basis (except for a defined contribution pension plan).

There are basically two types of qualified pension plans: defined benefit plans and defined contribution plans.

A **defined benefit plan** includes a formula that defines the benefits employees are to receive.[2] Under such a plan, an employer must make annual contributions based upon actuarial computations that will be sufficient to pay the vested retirement benefits. If a plan document permits, employees may make contributions to the pension fund. Separate accounts are not maintained for each participant. A defined benefit plan provides some sense of security for employees since the benefits may be expressed in fixed dollar amounts.

Under a **defined contribution pension plan** (or money purchase plan), a separate account must be maintained for each participant. Benefits are based solely on (1) the amount contributed and (2) income from the fund that accrues to the participant's account.[3] In essence, the plan defines the amount the employer is required to contribute (e.g., a flat dollar amount, an amount based on a special formula, or an amount equal to a certain percentage of compensation). Consequently, actuarial calculations are not required to determine the employer's annual contribution. Upon retirement, an employee's pension depends on the value of his or her account. Although it is not mandatory, a plan may require or permit employee contributions to the pension fund.

EXAMPLE 1

The qualified pension plan of Rose Company calls for both the employer and employee to contribute annually to the pension trust an amount equal to 5% of the employee's compensation. Since the employer's rate of contribution is fixed, this pension plan is a defined contribution plan. If the plan called for contributions sufficient to provide retirement benefits equal to 30% of the employee's average salary for the last five years, it would be a defined benefit plan. ▼

Concept Summary 19–1 compares and contrasts a defined benefit plan and a defined contribution plan.

---

[2]§ 414(j).   [3]§ 414(i).

ETHICAL
CONSIDERATIONS

Underfunded Pension Plans

The rate of return that a business projects on the investments in its pension plan can cause underfunding. For example, General Motors assumed an 11 percent rate of return in order to reduce the amount of money set aside for retirees in its retirement plan. Since the plan only earned 6.4 percent because of low interest rates, the gap between what GM promised and the amount set aside was $14 billion in 1992. The shortfall may be $19 billion in 1993.

Representative J. J. Pickle indicates that "the ability of companies to manipulate their assumptions allows them to avoid properly funding pension plans, which, in some cases, are already significantly underfunded."

Of course, the problem of underfunding is even worse with state and municipal employees' pension trusts. Callan Associates believe that public pension funds are setting

---

CONCEPT SUMMARY 19–1

Defined Benefit Plan and Defined Contribution Plan Compared

Defined Benefit Plan	Defined Contribution Plan
Includes a pension plan.	Includes profit sharing, stock bonus, money purchase, target benefit, qualified cash or deferred compensation, and employee stock ownership plans.
Determinable benefits based upon years of service and average compensation. Benefits calculated by a formula.	An account for each participant. Ultimate benefits depend upon contributions and investment performance.
Maximum annual *benefits* payable may not exceed the smaller of (1) $118,800 (in 1994)* or (2) 100% of the participant's average earnings in the three highest years of employment.	Maximum annual *contribution* to an account may not exceed the smaller of (1) $30,000** or (2) 25% of the participant's compensation (15% for a profit sharing plan).
Forfeitures must reduce subsequent funding costs and cannot increase the benefits any participant can receive under the plan.	Forfeitures may be allocated to the accounts of remaining participants.
Subject to minimum funding requirement in order to avoid penalties.	Exempt from funding requirements.
Greater administrative and actuarial costs and greater reporting requirements.	Costs and reporting requirements less burdensome.
Subject to plan termination insurance.	Not subject to plan termination insurance.
More favorable to employees who are older when plan is adopted since it is possible to fund higher benefits over a shorter period.	More favorable to younger employees since, over a longer period, higher benefits may result.

*This amount is indexed annually.
**The $30,000 amount becomes subject to indexing when the dollar limitation for a defined benefit plan exceeds $120,000.

aside only about 89 percent of the funds needed to provide workers with pension benefits.

How can a company with an underfunded plan justify increasing income for shareholders by reducing pension contributions for employees?

Profit Sharing Plans

A **profit sharing plan** is a deferred compensation arrangement established and maintained by an employer to provide for employee participation in the company's profits. Contributions are paid from the employer's current or accumulated profits to a trustee and are commingled in a single trust fund. Thus, an employer does not have to have a profit for the current year to make a contribution (the contribution can be from accumulated profits).

In a profit sharing plan, separate accounts are maintained for each participant. The plan must provide a definite, predetermined formula for allocating the contributions (made to the trustee) among the participants. Likewise, it must include a definite, predetermined formula for distributing the accumulated funds after a fixed number of years, on the attainment of a stated age, or on the occurrence of certain events such as illness, layoff, or retirement. A company is not required to contribute a definite, predetermined amount to the plan, although substantial and recurring contributions must be made to meet the permanency requirement. Forfeitures arising under this plan do not have to be used to reduce the employer's contribution. Instead, forfeitures may be used to increase the individual accounts of the remaining participants as long as these increases do not result in prohibited discrimination.[4] Since a profit sharing plan does not necessarily emphasize retirement income, benefits to employees may normally be distributed through lump-sum payouts.

Stock Bonus Plans

A **stock bonus plan** is another form of deferred compensation. In this case, an employer establishes and maintains the plan in order to contribute shares of its stock. The contributions need not be dependent on the employer's profits. A stock bonus plan is subject to the same requirements as a profit sharing plan for purposes of allocating and distributing the stock among the employees.[5] Any benefits of the plan are distributable in the form of stock of the employer company, except that distributable fractional shares may be paid in cash.

Employee Stock Ownership Plans

An **employee stock ownership plan (ESOP)** is a stock bonus trust that qualifies as a tax-exempt employee trust under § 401(a). Technically, an ESOP is a defined contribution plan that is either a qualified stock bonus plan or a stock bonus and a money purchase plan, each of which is qualified under § 401(a). An ESOP must invest primarily in qualifying employer securities.[6]

Since the corporation can contribute stock rather than cash, there is no cash-flow drain. If stock is contributed, no cash outlay is required, and the

---

[4] Reg. §§ 1.401–1(b) and 1.401–4(a)(1)(iii).
[5] Reg. § 1.401–1(b)(1)(iii).
[6] § 4975(e)(7).

corporation receives a tax deduction equal to the fair market value of the stock. Under § 1032, the employer-corporation does not recognize a gain or loss on the contributed stock. The corporation may deduct dividends paid in cash (or dividends used to repay certain ESOP loans) on shares held by an ESOP. The tax savings accruing under the plan may have a favorable impact on the company's working capital. An ESOP also provides flexibility, since contributions may vary from year to year and, in fact, may be omitted in any one year.[7]

A company can fund the ESOP by acquiring outstanding shares of stock from its shareholders, who receive capital gain treatment upon the sale of their stock. Owners of small closely held corporations may elect nonrecognition treatment for any gain realized on the sale of securities to an ESOP where qualified replacement property [defined in § 1042(c)(4)] is purchased during a 15-month period. This 15-month period begins 3 months before the date of the sale and ends 12 months after that date.[8] Nonrecognition treatment is permitted only if the seller has held the securities for at least three years prior to the sale to the ESOP.

Employees are not subject to tax until they receive a distribution of stock or cash from the trust. Distributions to employees may be made entirely in cash or partly in cash and partly in employer securities. A participant must have the right to demand the entire distribution in the form of employer securities.[9]

EXAMPLE 2

Gray Company establishes an ESOP for its employees and contributes unissued stock to the ESOP trust. The company receives a deduction for the contribution, and there is no cash-flow drain. The employees are not subject to tax until a subsequent stock or cash distribution from the trust. ▼

EXAMPLE 3

The ESOP of Gray Company borrows $100,000 from City Bank in January 1994. The loan is secured by the stock interest and is guaranteed by the company. The ESOP buys stock for the trust from a shareholder of Gray Company for $100,000. The shareholder has owned the stock for four years. The shares are then allocated among the employees' retirement accounts. The shareholder obtains capital gain treatment on the sale or can elect nonrecognition treatment if qualified replacement securities are purchased during a 15-month period. Gray Company makes deductible contributions to the ESOP, which, in turn, pays off the loan. ▼

QUALIFICATION REQUIREMENTS

2 LEARNING OBJECTIVE
Identify the qualification requirements for qualified plans.

A number of qualification requirements must be satisfied in order for a plan to receive favorable tax treatment. To be *qualified*, a plan must meet the following requirements:

- Exclusive benefit requirement.
- Nondiscrimination requirements.
- Participation and coverage requirements.
- Vesting requirements.
- Distribution requirements.

These qualification rules are highly technical and numerous. Thus, an employer should submit a retirement plan to the IRS for a determination letter regarding the qualified status of the plan and trust. A favorable determination

---

[7] Reg. § 1.401–1(b)(2).
[8] Refer to the discussion in Chapter 15.

[9] § 409(h)(1).

letter may be expected within 6 to 12 months, indicating that the plan meets the qualification requirements and that the trust is tax-exempt. However, the continued qualification of the plan depends upon its actual operations. Therefore, the operations of the plan should be reviewed periodically.

Exclusive Benefit Requirement

A pension, profit sharing, or stock bonus trust must be created by an employer for the exclusive benefit of employees or their beneficiaries. Under a prudent person concept, the IRS specifies four investment conditions for meeting the *exclusive benefit* requirement:[10]

- The cost of the investment must not exceed the fair market value at the time of purchase.
- A fair return commensurate with prevailing rates must be provided.
- Sufficient liquidity must be maintained to permit distributions in accordance with the terms of the qualified plan.
- The safeguards and diversity that a prudent investor would adhere to must be present.

Nondiscrimination Requirements

The contributions and benefits under a plan must *not discriminate* in favor of highly compensated employees. A plan is not considered discriminatory merely because the contributions and benefits on behalf of the employees are uniformly related to their compensation.[11] For example, a pension plan that provides for the allocation of employer contributions based upon a flat 3 percent of each employee's compensation would not be discriminatory even though highly paid employees receive greater benefits.

Qualified plans may be *integrated* with Social Security (employer FICA contributions for covered employees may be taken into account) to avoid giving lower-level employees proportionately greater benefits or contributions. Integrated plans may not reduce a participant's benefits or contributions to less than one-half of what they would have been without integration.

Participation and Coverage Requirements

A qualified plan must provide, at a minimum, that all employees in the covered group who are 21 years of age are eligible to participate after completing one year of service. A year of service is generally defined as the completion of 1,000 hours of service within a measuring period of 12 consecutive months. As an alternative, where the plan provides that 100 percent of an employee's accrued benefits will be vested upon entering the plan, the employee's participation may be postponed until the later of age 21 or two years from the date of employment.[12] Once the age and service requirements are met, an employee must begin participating no later than the *earlier* of the following:

- The first day of the first plan year beginning after the date upon which the requirements were satisfied.
- Six months after the date on which the requirements were satisfied.[13]

---

[10] § 401(a); Rev.Rul. 65–178, 1965–2 C.B. 94, and Rev.Rul. 73–380, 1973–2 C.B. 124.

[11] §§ 401(a)(4) and (5).

[12] §§ 410(a)(1)(A) and (B).

[13] § 410(a)(4).

EXAMPLE 4

Coffee Corporation has a calendar year retirement plan covering its employees. The corporation adopts the most restrictive eligibility rules permitted. Wilma, age 21, is hired on January 31, 1993, and meets the service requirement over the next 12 months (completes at least 1,000 hours by January 31, 1994). Wilma must be included in this plan no later than July 31, 1994, because the 6-month limitation would be applicable. If the company had adopted the two-year participation rule, Wilma must be included in the plan no later than July 31, 1995. ▼

Since a qualified plan must be primarily for the benefit of employees and be nondiscriminatory, the plan has to cover a reasonable percentage of the company employees. A plan will be qualified only if it satisfies one of the following tests:[14]

- The plan benefits at least 70 percent of all non-highly compensated employees (the *percentage test*).
- The plan benefits a percentage of non-highly compensated employees equal to at least 70 percent of the percentage of highly compensated employees benefiting under the plan (the *ratio test*).
- The plan meets the *average benefits test*.

If a company has no highly compensated employees, the retirement plan will automatically satisfy the coverage rules.

To satisfy the *average benefits test*, the plan must benefit any employees who qualify under a classification set up by the employer and found by the Secretary of the Treasury not to be discriminatory in favor of highly compensated employees (the *classification test*). In addition, the average benefit percentage for non-highly compensated employees must be at least 70 percent of the average benefit percentage for highly compensated employees. The *average benefit percentage* means, with respect to any group of employees, the average of the benefit percentages calculated separately for each employee in the group. The term *benefit percentage* means the employer-provided contributions (including forfeitures) or benefits of an employee under all qualified plans of the employer, expressed as a percentage of that employee's compensation.

An employee is a **highly compensated employee** if, at any time during the year or the preceding year, the employee satisfies *any* of the following:[15]

- Was a 5 percent owner of the company.
- Received more than $99,000 (in 1994) in annual compensation from the employer.
- Received more than $66,000 (in 1994) in annual compensation from the employer *and* was a member of the top-paid group of the employer.
- Was an officer of the company and received compensation greater than 150 percent of the maximum statutory dollar amount of the annual addition to a defined contribution plan ($30,000 × 150% = $45,000).

An employee who is among the top 20 percent of the employees on the basis of compensation paid during the year is a member of the top-paid group. The $66,000 and $99,000 amounts are indexed annually.[16]

An additional *minimum participation* test must also be met. A plan must cover at least 40 percent of all employees or, if fewer, at least 50 employees on one representative day of the plan year. In determining all employees, nonresident

---

[14]§ 410(b).
[15]§§ 401(a)(4) and 414(q).

[16]The indexed amounts for 1994 are provided.

aliens, certain union members, and employees not fulfilling the minimum age or years-of-service requirement of the plan may be excluded.[17]

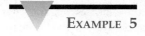

EXAMPLE 5   Rust Corporation's retirement plan meets the 70% test (the percentage test) because 70% of all non-highly compensated employees are benefited. The company has 100 employees, but only 38 of these employees are covered by the plan. Therefore, this retirement plan does not meet the minimum participation requirement. ▼

Vesting Requirements

An employee's right to accrued benefits derived from his or her own contributions must be nonforfeitable from the date of contribution. The accrued benefits derived from employer contributions must be nonforfeitable in accordance with one of two alternative minimum vesting schedules. The purpose of the **vesting requirements** is to protect an employee who has worked a reasonable period of time for an employer from losing employer contributions because of being fired or changing jobs.

A plan will not be a qualified plan unless a participant's employer-provided benefits vest at least as rapidly as under one of *two alternative minimum vesting schedules.* To satisfy the *first alternative,* a participant must have a nonforfeitable right to 100 percent of his or her accrued benefits derived from employer contributions upon completion of five years of service (five-year or cliff vesting). The *second alternative* is satisfied if a participant has a nonforfeitable right at least equal to a percentage of the accrued benefits derived from employer contributions as depicted in Table 19–1 (graded vesting). Of the two alternatives, cliff vesting minimizes administration expenses for a company and provides more vesting for a long-term employee. Neither vesting schedule applies to top-heavy plans.

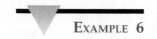

EXAMPLE 6   Mitch has six years of service completed as of February 2, 1994, his employment anniversary date. If his defined benefit plan has a five-year (cliff) vesting schedule, 100% of Mitch's accrued benefits are vested. If, however, the plan uses the graded vesting rule, Mitch's nonforfeitable percentage is 80%. ▼

Distribution Requirements

Uniform *minimum distribution rules* exist for all qualified defined benefit and defined contribution plans, Individual Retirement Accounts (IRAs) and annuities, unfunded deferred compensation plans of state and local governments and tax-exempt employers, and tax-sheltered custodial accounts and annuities. Distributions must begin no later than April 1 of the calendar year following the

▼ **TABLE 19–1**
Three-to-Seven-Year Vesting

Years of Service	Nonforfeitable Percentage
3	20%
4	40%
5	60%
6	80%
7 or more	100%

[17] §§ 401(a)(26) and 410(b)(3) and (4).

calendar year in which the participant attains age 70½. This commencement date is not affected by the actual date of retirement or termination.[18]

Once age 70½ is reached, minimum annual distributions must be made over the life of the participant or the lives of the participant and a designated individual beneficiary. The amount of the required minimum distribution for a particular year is determined by dividing the account balance as of December 31 of the prior year by the applicable life expectancy. The life expectancy of the owner and his or her beneficiary is based upon the expected return multiples in the Regulations, using ages attained within the calendar year the participant reaches age 70½.[19]

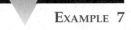

EXAMPLE 7

Beth reaches age 70½ in 1994, and she will also be age 71 in 1994. Her retirement account (an IRA) has a balance of $120,000 on December 31, 1993. Beth must withdraw $7,843 for the 1994 calendar year, assuming her multiple is 15.3 ($120,000 ÷ 15.3). This distribution need not be made until April 1, 1995, but a second distribution must be made by December 31, 1995. ▼

Failure to make a minimum required distribution to a particular participant results in a 50 percent nondeductible excise tax on the excess in any taxable year of the amount that should have been distributed over the amount that actually was distributed. The tax is imposed on the individual required to take the distribution (the payee).[20] The Secretary of the Treasury is authorized to waive the tax for a given taxpayer year if the taxpayer is able to establish that the shortfall is due to reasonable error and that reasonable steps are being taken to remedy the shortfall.

If a taxpayer receives an *early distribution* from a qualified retirement plan, a 10 percent additional tax is levied on the full amount of any distribution includible in gross income.[21] For this purpose, the term qualified retirement plan includes a qualified defined benefit plan or defined contribution plan, a tax-sheltered annuity or custodial account, or an IRA. Certain distributions, however, are *not* treated as early distributions:

- Made on or after the date the employee attains age 59½.
- Made to a beneficiary (or the estate of an employee) on or after the death of the employee.
- Attributable to the employee's being disabled.
- Made as part of a scheduled series of substantially equal periodic payments (made not less frequently than annually) for the life of the participant (or the joint lives of the participant and the participant's beneficiary).
- Made to an employee after separation from service because of early retirement under the plan after attaining age 55. This exception to early distribution treatment does not apply to an IRA.
- Used to pay medical expenses to the extent that the expenses are deductible under § 213 (determined regardless of whether or not the taxpayer itemizes deductions). This exception to early distribution treatment does not apply to an IRA.

A 15 percent excise tax is imposed on excess distributions from qualified plans.[22] The tax is levied on the individual with respect to whom the excess distribution is made and is reduced by the amount of the tax imposed on early

[18] § 401(a)(9).
[19] Reg. § 1.72–9. Refer to Chapter 4.
[20] § 4974(a).

[21] § 72(t). See Ltr.Rul. 8837071.
[22] § 4981A.

distributions (to the extent attributable to the excess distribution). An *excess distribution* is the aggregate amount of the retirement distributions during the taxable year for an individual to the extent that amount exceeds the greater of $150,000 or $112,500 (1994 indexed amount is $148,500). Thus, for 1994 the annual limitation is $150,000. Once the indexed $112,500 amount exceeds the $150,000, the indexed amount will become the annual limit. The following distributions are *not* subject to this limitation:

- Any retirement distribution made after the death of the individual.
- Any retirement distribution payable to an alternate payee in conformance with a qualified domestic relations order.
- Any retirement distribution attributable to the employee's investment in the contract (after-tax contributions).
- Any retirement distribution not included in gross income by reason of a rollover contribution.

If the taxpayer elects lump-sum distribution treatment, the $150,000 limit is applied separately to the lump-sum distribution and is increased to five times the generally applicable limit with respect to that distribution (to $750,000).

EXAMPLE 8

Emily, age 65, has accumulated $960,000 in a defined contribution plan, $105,000 of which represents her own after-tax contributions. Receiving a lump-sum distribution would result in an excise tax of $15,750.

Account balance	$ 960,000
Less after-tax contributions	(105,000)
Less lump-sum limitation	(750,000)
Amount subject to tax	$ 105,000
15% excise tax	× .15
Excise tax due	$ 15,750

If Emily receives the distribution in the form of an annuity over her expected lifetime of 20 years, her yearly distributions of $48,000 *plus* related interest would probably be less than the $150,000 annual distribution limit. ▼

A grandfather provision exists with respect to accrued benefits as of August 1, 1986.[23]

TAX CONSEQUENCES TO THE EMPLOYEE AND EMPLOYER

In General

3   LEARNING OBJECTIVE
Discuss the tax consequences
of qualified plans.

Although employer contributions to qualified plans are generally deductible immediately (subject to contribution and deductibility rules), these amounts are not subject to taxation until distributed to employees.[24] If benefits are paid with respect to an employee (to a creditor of the employee, a child of the employee, etc.), the benefits paid are treated as if paid to the employee. When benefits are distributed to employees, or paid with respect to an employee, the employer does not receive another deduction.

---

[23] § 4981A(c)(5).

[24] § 402(a)(1).

The tax benefit to the employee amounts to a substantial tax deferral and may be viewed as an interest-free loan from the government to the trust fund. Another advantage of a qualified plan is that any income earned by the trust is not taxable to the trust.[25] Employees, in effect, are taxed on such earnings when they receive the retirement benefits.

The taxation of amounts received by employees in periodic or installment payments is generally subject to the annuity rules in § 72 (refer to Chapter 4). Employee contributions have previously been subject to tax and are therefore included in the employee's *investment in the contract.* Two other alternative options are available for benefit distributions. A taxpayer may roll over the benefits into an IRA or another qualified employer retirement plan.[26] A taxpayer also may receive the distribution in a lump-sum payment.

Lump-Sum Distributions from Qualified Plans

The annuity rules do not apply to a **lump-sum distribution.** All such payments are taxed in one year. Since lump-sum payments have been accumulated over a number of years, bunching retirement benefits into one taxable year may impose a high tax burden because of progressive rates. To overcome this bunching effect, for many years the tax law has provided favorable treatment for certain lump-sum distributions. Major changes were made in the lump-sum distribution rules by TRA of 1986. Transitional provisions allow a participant who reached age 50 before January 1, 1986 (born before 1936) to elect the pre-1987 rules on a limited basis.

Under the pre-1987 rules, the taxable amount is allocated between a capital gain portion and an ordinary income portion (which may be subject to a special 10-year averaging treatment).[27] That portion attributable to the employee's service before 1974 qualifies for capital gain treatment. That portion attributable to the employee's service after 1973 is included as ordinary income when received and may be taxed under the 10-year averaging provision. An employee must be a plan participant for at least five years to take advantage of the 10-year averaging option. It is possible to defer tax on some or all of the distribution, provided that the employee elects to roll over the distribution by transferring the proceeds to an IRA or another qualified employer retirement plan.[28]

An employee may *elect* to treat all of the distribution as ordinary income subject to the 10-year forward averaging provision.[29] In some instances, ordinary income treatment is preferable to long-term capital gain treatment because of the favorable averaging technique.

Special preferential averaging treatment of qualified lump-sum distributions can be used only once during a recipient's lifetime. In the case of a small lump-sum distribution, a recipient may prefer to pay ordinary income tax on the amount and save the averaging election for a larger lump-sum distribution in the future.

To determine the tax on a lump-sum distribution, it is necessary to compute the taxable portion of the distribution by subtracting employee contributions and the net unrealized appreciation in the value of any distributed securities of the

---

[25] § 501(a).
[26] Refer to the subsequent discussion in this chapter under Individual Retirement Accounts (IRAs).

[27] § 402(e)(1)(C) of the IRC of 1954.
[28] § 402(a)(5).
[29] § 402(e)(4)(L).

employer corporation.[30] The taxable amount is then reduced by a minimum distribution allowance to arrive at the amount that is eligible for the 10-year income averaging provisions.[31] The following portion of the lump-sum distribution is treated as a long-term capital gain:

$$\text{Taxable amount} \times \frac{\text{Years of service before 1974}}{\text{Total years of service}}$$
(computed without being reduced by the minimum distribution allowance)

The applicable capital gain rate is 20 percent.

After 1986, subject to the transition rule for recipients born before 1936 mentioned earlier, the 10-year forward averaging rule for lump-sum distributions is replaced by a 5-year forward averaging rule.[32] Only one lump-sum distribution received after age 59½ is eligible for the averaging treatment. Furthermore, capital gain treatment for lump-sum distributions (associated with participation before 1974) is repealed.

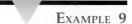

EXAMPLE 9   Esteban, age 65 and married, retires at the end of 1994 and receives a lump-sum distribution of $100,000 from his company's profit sharing plan. This plan includes $5,000 of his own contributions and $10,000 of unrealized appreciation on his employer's common stock. Esteban was a participant in the plan for 25 years. Since Esteban attained age 50 before January 1, 1986, he is eligible to elect the pre-1987 10-year forward averaging technique (using 1986 rates and the **zero bracket amount**). Refer to the computation model in Concept Summary 19–2.

CONCEPT SUMMARY 19–2

Model for Lump-Sum Distribution Computation

1. Start with the total lump-sum distribution and deduct any employee contributions and unrealized appreciation in employer securities.
2. Divide the result into the capital gain portion and the ordinary income portion.*
3. Multiply the capital gain portion by the capital gain rate of 20%.
4. Reduce the ordinary income portion by the minimum distribution allowance.
5. Divide the ordinary income portion into 5 or 10 equal portions, whichever is appropriate.
6. Compute the tax on the result in step 5 using the 1986 or current rate schedules (whichever is appropriate) for single taxpayers.
7. Multiply the resulting tax by 5 or 10, whichever is appropriate.
8. Add the results in steps 3 and 7.

*In certain circumstances, none of the taxable amount of the distribution will be eligible for capital gain treatment. In other circumstances, the taxpayer may choose to treat none of the taxable amount as capital gain even though part could qualify.

---

[30] Section 402(e)(4)(J) provides that before any distribution a taxpayer may elect not to have this subtraction associated with employer securities apply.

[31] Section 402(e)(1)(D) defines the *minimum distribution allowance* as the smaller of $10,000 or one-half of the total taxable amount of the lump-sum distribution, reduced by 20% of the amount, if any, by which such total taxable amount exceeds $20,000. Thus, for lump-sum distributions of $70,000 or more, there will be no minimum distribution allowance.

[32] § 402(e)(1).

Taxable portion of the lump-sum distribution		$85,000
Less: Minimum distribution allowance (½ of the taxable amount up to $20,000)	$ 10,000	
Less: 20% of the taxable amount in excess of $20,000: 20% × ($85,000 – $20,000)	(13,000)	
Minimum distribution allowance		–0–
Taxable amount		$85,000
Computation of tax under 10-year averaging: Long-term capital gain portion:		
$85,000 × $\frac{\text{4 (service before 1974)}}{\text{25 (total service years)}}$ = $13,600 × .20 =		$ 2,720
Ordinary income portion: 10 times the tax on $9,620 [33] [¹⁄₁₀ ($85,000 – $13,600) + $2,480]		9,729
Tax on lump-sum distribution		$12,449

Thus, Esteban's capital gain on the distribution is $13,600 and is subject to a 20% capital gain rate. Here Esteban may wish to elect to treat the entire distribution as ordinary income using the 10-year forward averaging approach rather than taxing the capital gain portion at the 20% capital gain rate. The tax liability of $11,905 would be less than the previously calculated tax liability of $12,449. The capital gain on the unrealized appreciation in the employer's common stock is not taxable until Esteban sells the stock. In essence, the cost basis of the securities to the trust becomes the tax basis to the employee.[34] If Esteban keeps the securities until he dies, there may be some income tax savings on this gain to the extent his estate or heirs obtain a step-up in basis. ▼

If Esteban (in Example 9) uses the 5-year forward averaging provision instead, the following results are produced:

Taxable amount	$85,000	
Computation of tax under 5-year averaging: Long-term capital gain portion:		
$85,000 × $\frac{\text{4 (service before 1974)}}{\text{25 (total service years)}}$ = $13,600 × .20 =		$ 2,720
Ordinary income portion: 5 times the tax on $14,280[35] ⅕ ($85,000 – $13,600)		10,710
Tax on lump-sum distribution		$13,430

Thus, Esteban's capital gain on the distribution is $13,600 (the same as in the 10-year averaging calculation). The capital gain is subject to a 20 percent capital gain rate.[36] Once again the taxpayer may wish to elect to treat the entire distribution as ordinary income using the 5-year forward averaging approach rather than taxing the capital gain portion at the 20 percent capital gain rate. The tax liability of $12,750 would be less than the previously calculated tax liability of

[33] In making this tax computation, it is necessary to use the 1986 Tax Rate Schedule for single taxpayers and to add $2,480 (the zero bracket amount) to the taxable income. Thus, the tax was computed on $9,620, which is $7,140 (¹⁄₁₀ of $71,400) plus $2,480. Note that the tax rates provided in the instructions for Form 4972 (Tax on Lump-Sum Distributions) have already been adjusted for the zero bracket amount (i.e., it is not necessary to add the zero bracket amount in making the calculation).

[34] § 402(e)(4)(J).

[35] In making this tax computation, it is necessary to use the 1994 Tax Rate Schedule for single taxpayers.

[36] Note that since Esteban qualifies under the transition rules (attained age 50 before January 1, 1986), he is eligible to elect capital gain treatment in conjunction with 5-year forward averaging.

$13,430. Since the ordinary income tax under 10-year forward averaging is less than the ordinary income tax under 5-year forward averaging, it appears that Esteban's best alternative is to use the 10-year forward averaging provision and treat the capital gain as ordinary income.

LIMITATIONS ON CONTRIBUTIONS TO AND BENEFITS FROM QUALIFIED PLANS

In General

4 **LEARNING OBJECTIVE**
Calculate the limitations on contributions to and benefits from qualified plans.

The limitations on contributions to and benefits from qualified plans appearing in § 415 must be written into a qualified plan. The plan terminates if these limits are exceeded. Section 404 sets the limits on deductibility applicable to the employer. The limit on the amount deductible under § 404 may have an impact on the amount the employer is willing to contribute. In fact, under § 404(j), a defined benefit plan or defined contribution plan is not allowed a deduction for the amount that exceeds the § 415 limitations.

Defined Contribution Plans

Under a *defined contribution plan* (money purchase pension, profit sharing, or stock bonus plan), the annual addition to an employee's account cannot exceed the smaller of $30,000 or 25 percent of the employee's compensation.[37] The $30,000 amount is to be indexed once the statutory ceiling for defined benefit plans (discussed next) reaches $120,000.

Defined Benefit Plans

Under a *defined benefit plan,* the annual benefit payable to an employee is limited to the smaller of $118,800 (in 1994)[38] or 100 percent of the employee's average compensation for the highest three years of employment. This benefit limit is subject to a $10,000 *de minimis* floor. The $118,800 limitation is reduced actuarially if the benefits begin before the Social Security normal retirement age (currently age 65). The $118,800 amount is increased actuarially if the benefits begin after the Social Security normal retirement age. The dollar limit on annual benefits ($118,800) is reduced by one-tenth for each year of *participation* under 10 years by the employee. Furthermore, the 100 percent of compensation limitation and the $10,000 *de minimis* floor are reduced proportionately for a participant who has less than 10 years of *service* with the employer.[39]

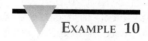

EXAMPLE 10

Adam's average compensation for the highest three years of employment is $87,000. Although the § 415(b)(1) limitation does not limit the deduction, the defined benefit plan would not qualify if the plan provides for benefits in excess of the smaller of (1) $87,000 or (2) $118,800 for Adam in 1994 (assuming retirement age of 65). ▼

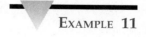

EXAMPLE 11

Peggy has participated for four years in a defined benefit plan and has six years of service with her employer. Her average compensation for the three highest years is $50,000. Her four years of participation reduce her dollar limitation to $47,520 ($118,800 × ⁴⁄₁₀). Her six years of service reduce her 100% of compensation limitation to 60%. Therefore, her limit on annual benefits is $30,000 ($50,000 × 60%). ▼

---

[37]§ 415(c).
[38]This amount is indexed annually.

[39]§ 415(b).

For collectively bargained plans with at least 100 participants, the annual dollar limitation is the greater of $68,212 or one-half of the $118,800 monetary limit.

The amount of compensation that may be taken into account under any plan is limited to $150,000 (in 1994).[40] Thus, the benefits highly compensated individuals receive may be smaller as a percentage of their pay than those received by non-highly compensated employees.

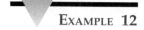

EXAMPLE 12

Swan Corporation has a defined contribution plan with a 10% contribution formula. An employee earning less than $150,000 in 1994 would not be affected by this includible compensation limitation. However, an employee earning $300,000 in 1994 would have only 5% of compensation allocated to his or her account because of the $150,000 limit on includible compensation. ▼

Two methods can be used to determine the maximum deduction a corporation is permitted for contributions to pension plans. First, an aggregate cost method allows an actuarially determined deduction based on a level amount, or a level percentage, of compensation over the remaining future service of covered participants. Second, the employer is permitted to deduct the so-called normal cost plus no more than 10 percent of the past service costs.

The employer's contribution is deductible in the tax year such amounts are paid to the pension trust. However, both cash and accrual basis employers may defer the payment of contributions with respect to any tax year until the date fixed for filing the taxpayer's Federal income tax return for that year (including extensions).[41] In effect, the corporation is allowed a deduction to the extent it is compelled to make such contributions to satisfy the funding requirement. If an amount in excess of the allowable amount is contributed in any tax year, the excess may be carried forward and deducted in succeeding tax years (to the extent the carryover plus the succeeding year's contribution does not exceed the deductible limitation for that year).[42]

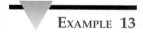

EXAMPLE 13

During 1994, Green Corporation contributes $17,500 to its qualified pension plan. Normal cost for this year is $7,200, and the amount necessary to pay retirement benefits on behalf of employee services before 1994 is $82,000 (past service costs). The corporation's maximum deduction would be $15,400. This amount consists of the $7,200 normal cost plus 10% ($8,200) of the past service costs. The corporation would have a $2,100 [$17,500 (contribution) – $15,400 (deduction)] contribution carryover. ▼

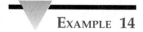

EXAMPLE 14

Assume in the previous example that Green Corporation has normal cost in 1995 of $7,200 and contributes $10,000 to the pension trust. The corporation's maximum deduction would be $15,400. Green Corporation may deduct $12,100, composed of this year's contribution ($10,000) plus the $2,100 contribution carryover. ▼

A 10 percent excise tax is imposed on nondeductible contributions. The tax is levied on the employer making the contribution. The tax applies to nondeductible contributions for the current year and any nondeductible contributions for the preceding year that have not been eliminated by the end of the current year (as a carryover or by being returned to the employer in the current year).[43]

---

[40] §§ 401(a)(17) and 404(l). This amount is to be indexed annually.
[41] §§ 404(a)(1) and (6).

[42] § 404(a)(1)(D).
[43] § 4972.

Profit Sharing and Stock Bonus Plan Limitations

The maximum deduction permitted to an employer each year for contributions to profit sharing and stock bonus plans is 15 percent of the compensation paid or accrued with respect to plan participants. Any nondeductible excess, a so-called contribution carryover, may be carried forward indefinitely and deducted in subsequent years. The maximum deduction in any succeeding year is 15 percent of all compensation paid or accrued during that taxable year. An employer can circumvent the 15 percent limitation by establishing a money purchase pension plan as a supplement to the profit sharing or stock bonus plan. When there are two or more plans, a maximum deduction of 25 percent of the compensation paid is allowable.[44]

TOP-HEAVY PLANS

A special set of rules is imposed upon so-called top-heavy plans to discourage retirement plans from conferring disproportionate benefits upon key employees. Top-heaviness is determined on an annual basis.

In general, a **top-heavy plan** allocates more than 60 percent of the cumulative benefits to key employees; a plan may also be part of a top-heavy plan. *Key employees* are defined as follows:

- Officers. However, for purposes of this definition, only the smaller of (1) 50 officers or (2) three employees or 10 percent of all employees (whichever is greater) may be considered officers.
- The 10 employees owning the largest interest in the employer (using the constructive ownership rules of § 318).
- A greater-than-5 percent owner of the employer.
- A greater-than-1 percent owner of the employer with annual compensation in excess of $150,000.[45]

An employee need fall within only one of these categories to be classified as a key employee. However, a key employee does not include officers paid $45,000 or less a year. In addition, for purposes of the 10-employees provision, a key employee does not include an employee whose annual compensation from the employer is $30,000 or less. Employees receiving no compensation for five years are disregarded in testing for top-heavy status.

A top-heavy plan must provide for greater portability for participants who are non-key employees. An employee's right to the accrued benefits derived from employer contributions must become nonforfeitable under either of two vesting schedules. Under the first schedule, an employee who has at least three years of service with the employer must have a nonforfeitable right to 100 percent of his or her accrued benefits derived from employer contributions. Under the second schedule, a six-year graded vesting schedule must be met (see Table 19–2).[46]

To prevent an employer from avoiding the top-heavy rules by establishing a one-person corporate shell, § 269A allows the IRS to allocate any income or deductions between a personal service corporation and its employee-owner. An employee-owner is any employee who owns more than 10 percent of the outstanding stock of the personal service corporation on any day during the tax year.

---

[44] §§ 404(a)(3)(A) and (a)(7).
[45] § 416(i)(1).

[46] § 416(b).

▼ **TABLE 19–2**
Top-Heavy Graded Vesting

Years of Service	Vested Percentage
2	20%
3	40%
4	60%
5	80%
6 or more	100%

CASH OR DEFERRED ARRANGEMENT PLANS

A *cash or deferred arrangement plan,* hereafter referred to as a **§ 401(k) plan,** allows participants to elect either to receive up to $9,240 (in 1994)[47] in cash (taxed currently) or to have a contribution made on their behalf to a profit sharing or stock bonus plan. The plan may also be in the form of a salary reduction agreement between an eligible participant and an employer under which a contribution will be made only if the participant elects to reduce his or her compensation or to forgo an increase in compensation.

Any pretax amount elected by the employee as a plan contribution is not includible in gross income and is 100 percent vested. Any employer contributions are tax deferred, as are earnings on contributions in the plan.

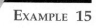

EXAMPLE 15

Sam participates in a § 401(k) plan of his employer. The plan permits the participants to choose between a full salary or a reduced salary where the reduction becomes a before-tax contribution to a retirement plan. Sam elects to contribute 10% of his annual compensation of $30,000 to the plan. Income taxes are paid on only $27,000. No income taxes are paid on the $3,000—or on any earnings—until it is distributed from the plan to Sam. The main benefit of a § 401(k) plan is that Sam can shift a portion of his income to a later taxable year. ▼

The maximum employee annual elective contribution to a § 401(k) plan is $9,240 (in 1994), but that amount is reduced dollar for dollar by other salary-reduction contributions to tax-sheltered annuities and simplified employee pension plans. Elective contributions in excess of the maximum limitation are taxable in the year of deferral. These amounts may be distributed from the plan tax-free before April 15 of the following year. Excess amounts not timely distributed will be taxable in the year of distribution, even though they were included in income in the year of deferral.

A 10 percent excise tax is imposed on the employer for excess contributions not withdrawn from the plan within 2½ months after the close of the plan year. The plan will lose its qualified status if these excess contributions (and any related income) are not withdrawn by the end of the plan year following the plan year in which the excess contributions were made.[48]

EXAMPLE 16

Carmen, an employee of a manufacturing corporation, defers $11,240 in a § 401(k) plan in 1994. The $2,000 excess deferral, along with the appropriate earnings, must be returned to Carmen by April 15, 1995. This $2,000 excess amount plus related income is taxable to her

---

[47] This amount is indexed annually.

[48] § 4979(a).

CHOICES IN 401(K) PLANS?

Until this past April, employees of Duke Power, the Charlotte, North Carolina, utility, had two ways to save for retirement. Participants in the company's § 401(k) savings plan could direct a portion of each paycheck into either Duke Power stock or U.S. savings bonds. The plan didn't offer much in the way of diversification, but it was easy to figure out. Of 18,000 employees, 17,000 signed up.

Today, the choices call for a lot more thought. Besides company stock, Duke Power offers five mutual funds: a money market fund, a Ginnie Mae fund, a balanced fund that invests 60 percent in stocks and 40 percent in bonds, an index fund that tracks the Standard and Poor's index of 500 large-company stocks, and a global fund that invests in stocks all over the world. Instead of being limited to quarterly switches, employees can move their money around any time by calling a toll-free phone number. But all the new freedom to customize portfolios seems to have frozen most Duke employees in their tracks. Two and a half months after the new plan's launch, only 400 employees with § 401(k)s are using it. The other 16,600 so far are standing pat—with 95 percent of their savings in company stock.

The shift at Duke Power is a sign of change to come for the 16 million U.S. workers who invest in § 401(k)s. New Labor Department rules effective next January have companies scrambling to give § 401(k) plan participants more and better choices. The rules protect companies from being held liable if employees' investments disappoint them—a distinct possibility when the only offerings are company stock, a money market account, and maybe a guaranteed investment contract (GIC), an insurance product similar to a bank certificate of deposit. To qualify for the shield, though, companies must include at least three diversified options—mutual funds, for example.

SOURCE: Reprinted with permission from "A Revolution in Retirement Planning," *U.S. News and World Report*, June 14, 1993, p. 86. Copyright 1993 U.S. News & World Report, Inc.

in 1994 and will be taxed again upon distribution (if made after April 15, 1995). There will be a 10% tax on Carmen's employer on any excess contributions not returned within 2½ months after the close of the plan year. ▼

Complicated antidiscrimination provisions apply to § 401(k) plans.

RETIREMENT PLANS FOR SELF-EMPLOYED INDIVIDUALS

5   **LEARNING OBJECTIVE**
Understand the qualified plan (Keogh plan) available to a self-employed person.

Self-employed individuals (e.g., partners and sole proprietors) and their employees are eligible to receive qualified retirement benefits under what are known as **H.R. 10 (Keogh) plans.** Because of contribution limitations and other restrictions, self-employed plans previously were less attractive than corporate plans. Contributions and benefits of a self-employed person now are subject to the general corporate provisions. Basically, self-employed persons are now on a parity with corporate employees. Consequently, Keogh plans can now provide a self-employed person with an adequate retirement base.

A variety of funding vehicles can be used for Keogh investments, such as mutual funds, annuities, real estate shares, certificates of deposit, debt instruments, commodities, securities, and personal properties. Investment in most collectibles is not allowed in a self-directed plan. When an individual decides to make all investment decisions, a self-directed retirement plan is established. Otherwise the individual may prefer to invest the funds with a financial institution such as a broker, a bank, or a savings and loan institution.

COVERAGE REQUIREMENTS

Generally, the corporate coverage rules apply to Keogh plans. Thus, the percentage, ratio, and average benefits tests previously discussed also apply to self-employed plans. In addition, the more restrictive top-heavy plan rules apply to Keogh plans.[49] An individual covered under a qualified corporate plan as an employee may also establish a Keogh plan for earnings from self-employment.

CONTRIBUTION LIMITATIONS

A self-employed individual may annually contribute the smaller of $30,000 or 25 percent of earned income to a *defined contribution* Keogh plan.[50] However, if the defined contribution plan is a profit sharing plan, a 15 percent deduction limit applies. Under a *defined benefit* Keogh plan, the annual benefit payable to an employee is limited to the smaller of $118,800 (in 1994) or 100 percent of the employee's average compensation for the three highest years of employment.[51] An employee includes a self-employed person. More restrictive rules apply to a top-heavy plan.

Earned income refers to net earnings from self-employment as defined in § 1402(a).[52] Net earnings from self-employment means the gross income derived by an individual from any trade or business carried on by that individual, less appropriate deductions, plus the distributive share of income or loss from a partnership.[53] Earned income is reduced by contributions to a Keogh plan on the individual's behalf.[54]

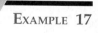

EXAMPLE 17

Pat, a partner, has earned income in 1994 (before any Keogh contribution) of $130,000. The maximum contribution to a defined contribution plan is $26,000, calculated from the following formula: $130,000 - .25X = X$, where X is earned income reduced by Pat's Keogh contribution. Solving this equation, $X = \$104,000$; thus, the contribution limit is $.25 \times \$104,000 = \$26,000$. To achieve the maximum contribution of $30,000, Pat would have to earn at least $150,000. In essence, a self-employed individual can contribute 20% of *gross* earned income. (Pat could contribute only 13.043% of self-employment gross earned income if this were a profit sharing plan.) ▼

Many Keogh plans will be considered top-heavy plans (refer to the previous discussion). For nondiscrimination purposes, the 25 percent limitation on the employee contribution is computed on the first $150,000 (in 1994) of earned income.

---

[49] § 401(d).
[50] § 415(c)(1).
[51] § 415(b)(1). This amount is indexed annually.

[52] § 401(c)(2).
[53] § 1402(a).
[54] § 401(c)(2)(A)(v).

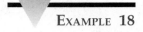

EXAMPLE 18

Terry, a self-employed accountant, has a money purchase plan with a contribution rate of 15% of compensation. Terry's earned income before the retirement contribution is $250,000. Terry's contribution would be limited to $19,565 ($150,000 − .15X = X), since X = $130,435 and .15 × $130,435 = $19,565. ▼

Although a Keogh plan must be established before the end of the year in question, contributions may be made up to the normal filing date for that year.

INDIVIDUAL RETIREMENT ACCOUNTS (IRAS)

GENERAL RULES

6   LEARNING OBJECTIVE
Describe the benefits of an Individual Retirement Account (IRA).

Employees not covered by another qualified plan can establish their own tax-deductible **IRAs.** The contribution ceiling is the smaller of $2,000 (or $2,250 for spousal IRAs) or 100 percent of compensation.[55] If the taxpayer or spouse is an active participant in another qualified plan, the IRA deduction limitation is phased out *proportionately* between certain adjusted gross income (AGI) ranges, as shown in Table 19–3.[56]

AGI is calculated taking into account any § 469 passive losses and § 86 taxable Social Security benefits and ignoring any § 911 foreign income exclusion, § 135 savings bonds interest exclusion, and the IRA deduction. There is a $200 floor on the IRA deduction limitation for individuals whose AGI is not above the phase-out range.

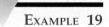

EXAMPLE 19

In 1994, Mr. and Mrs. Smith had compensation income of $27,000 and $20,000, respectively. Their AGI for 1994 was $47,000. Mr. Smith was an active participant in his employer's qualified retirement plan. Mr. and Mrs. Smith may *each* contribute $600 to an IRA. The deductible amount for each is reduced from $2,000 by $1,400 because of the phase-out mechanism:

$$\frac{\$7,000}{\$10,000} \times \$2,000 = \$1,400 \text{ reduction}$$ ▼

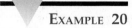

EXAMPLE 20

An unmarried individual is an active participant in his employer's qualified retirement plan. With AGI of $34,500, he would normally have an IRA deduction limit of $100 {$2,000 − [($34,500 − $25,000)/$10,000 × $2,000]}. However, because of the special floor provision, a $200 IRA deduction is allowable. ▼

To the extent that an individual is ineligible to make a deductible contribution to an IRA, *nondeductible contributions* can be made to separate accounts.[57] The

▼ **TABLE 19–3**
Phase-Out of IRA
Deduction

AGI Filing Status	Phase-Out Begins	Phase-Out Ends
Single and head of household	$25,000	$35,000
Married, filing joint return	40,000	50,000
Married, filing separate return	−0−	10,000

---

[55] §§ 219(b)(1) and (c)(2).
[56] § 219(g). However, a special rule in § 219(g)(4) allows a married person filing a separate return to avoid the phase-out rules even though the spouse is an active participant. The individual must live apart from the spouse at all times during the taxable year and must not be an active participant in another qualified plan.
[57] § 408(o).

nondeductible contribution will be subject to the same dollar limits for deductible contributions of $2,000 of earned income ($2,250 for a spousal IRA). Income in the account accumulates tax-free until distributed. Only the account earnings will be taxed (account basis equals the contributions made by the taxpayer) upon distribution. A taxpayer may elect to treat deductible IRA contributions as nondeductible. If an individual has no taxable income for the year after taking into account other deductions, the election would be beneficial. The election is made on the individual's tax return for the taxable year to which the designation relates.

Simplified Employee Pension Plans

An employer may contribute to an IRA covering an employee an amount equal to the lesser of $30,000 or 15 percent of the employee's earned income.[58] In such a plan, the corporation must make contributions for *each* employee who has reached age 21, has performed service for the employer during the calendar year and at least three of the five preceding calendar years, and has received at least $396 (in 1994) in compensation from the employer for the year.[59] Known as **simplified employee pension (SEP) plans,** these plans are subject to many of the same restrictions applicable to qualified plans (e.g., age and period-of-service requirements, top-heavy rules, and nondiscrimination limitations). Concept Summary 19–3 compares a SEP with a Keogh plan.

Employees who participate in salary-reduction SEPs may elect to have contributions made to the SEP or to receive contributions in cash.[60] If an employee

---

CONCEPT SUMMARY 19–3

Keogh Plan and SEP Compared

	Keogh	SEP
Form	Trust.*	IRA.
Establishment	By end of year.	By extension due date of employer.
Type of plan	Qualified.	Qualified.
Contributions to plan	By extension due date.	By extension due date of employer.
Vesting rules	Qualified plan rules.	100% immediately.
Participants' rules	Flexible.	Stricter.
Lump-sum distributions and averaging	Yes, favorable 5-year or 10-year forward averaging.	No, ordinary income.
$5,000 death benefit exclusion	Yes.	No.
Deduction limitation	Varies.*	Smaller of $30,000 or 15% of earned income.
Self as trustee	Yes.	No.

*For a defined contribution pension plan, the limit is the smaller of $30,000 or 20% of self-employment income. A defined contribution profit sharing plan has a 13.043% deduction limit. A defined benefit Keogh plan's limit is the smaller of $118,800 (in 1994) or 100% of the employee's average compensation for the highest three years of employment.

---

[58] § 408(j).
[59] § 408(k)(2). This amount is indexed annually.

[60] § 408(k)(6).

elects to have contributions made on his or her behalf to the SEP, the contribution is not treated as having been distributed or made available to the employee (i.e., no constructive receipt). The election to have amounts contributed to a SEP or received in cash is available only if at least 50 percent of the employees eligible to participate elect to have amounts contributed to the SEP. This exception to the constructive receipt principle is available only in a taxable year in which the employer maintaining the SEP has 25 or fewer employees eligible to participate at all times during the preceding year. In addition, the deferral percentage for each highly compensated employee cannot exceed 125 percent of the average deferral percentage for all other eligible employees.

The amounts contributed to a SEP by an employer on behalf of an employee and the elective deferrals under a SEP are excludible from gross income. Elective deferrals under a SEP are subject to a statutory ceiling of $9,240 (in 1994). Only $150,000 (in 1994) in compensation may be taken into account in making the SEP computation. An employer is permitted to elect to use its taxable year rather than the calendar year for purposes of determining contributions to a SEP.[61]

Spousal IRA

If both spouses work, each can individually establish an IRA. When only one spouse is employed, an IRA can be established for the nonemployed spouse if the employed spouse is eligible to establish an IRA. The maximum deduction for the individual and spouse is the lesser of 100 percent of the compensation income of the working spouse or $2,250. One spouse is permitted to elect to be treated, for this purpose, as having no earned income, thus allowing the contributing spouse to make the additional $250 contribution to an IRA. The contribution may be allocated to either spouse in any amount up to $2,000, and a joint return must be filed. The spousal IRA deduction is also proportionately reduced for active participants whose AGI exceeds the above target ranges.

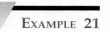

EXAMPLE 21

Tony, who is married, is eligible to establish an IRA. He received $30,000 in compensation in 1994. Tony can contribute a total of $2,250 to a spousal IRA, to be divided in any manner between the two spouses, except that no more than $2,000 can be allocated to either spouse. ▼

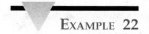

EXAMPLE 22

Assume the same facts as in the previous example, except that Tony's wife has earned income of $100. Absent the election to treat the wife's earned income as zero, the maximum IRA contribution is $2,100 ($2,000 for Tony and $100 for Tony's wife). With the election, $2,250 can be contributed under the spousal IRA provision. ▼

Alimony is considered to be earned income for purposes of IRA contributions. Thus, a person whose only income is alimony can contribute to an IRA.[62]

Timing of Contributions

Contributions (both deductible and nondeductible) can be made to an IRA anytime before the due date of the individual's tax return.[63] For example, an individual can establish and contribute to an IRA through April 15, 1995 (the return due date), and deduct this amount on his or her tax return for 1994. IRA

---

[61] § 404(h)(1)(A). The $9,240 and $150,000 amounts are indexed annually.

[62] § 219(f)(1).
[63] § 219(f)(3).

contributions that are made during a tax return extension period do not satisfy the requirement of being made by the return due date. An employer can make contributions up until the time of the due date for filing the return (including extensions) and treat those amounts as a deduction for the prior year.[64] As noted earlier, a similar rule applies to Keogh plans. However, the Keogh plan must be established before the end of the tax year. Contributions to the Keogh plan may then be made anytime before the due date of the individual's tax return.

PENALTY TAXES FOR EXCESS CONTRIBUTIONS

A cumulative, nondeductible 6 percent excise penalty tax is imposed on the smaller of (1) any excess contributions or (2) the market value of the plan assets determined as of the close of the tax year. *Excess contributions* are any contributions that exceed the maximum limitation and contributions that are made during or after the tax year in which the individual reaches age 70½.[65] A taxpayer is not allowed a deduction for excess contributions. If the excess is corrected by contributing less than the deductible amount for a later year, a deduction then is allowable in the later year as a *makeup* deduction.

An excess contribution is taxable annually until returned to the taxpayer or reduced by the underutilization of the maximum contribution limitation in a subsequent year. The 6 percent penalty tax can be avoided if the excess amounts are returned.[66]

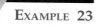

EXAMPLE 23

Nancy, age 55, establishes an IRA in 1994 and contributes $2,300 in cash to the plan. She has earned income of $22,000. Nancy is allowed a $2,000 deduction *for* AGI for 1994. Assuming the market value of the plan assets is at least $300, there is a nondeductible 6% excise penalty tax of $18 ($300 × 6%). The $300 may be subject to an additional penalty tax in future years if it is not returned to Nancy or reduced by underutilization of the $2,000 maximum contribution limitation. ▼

TAXATION OF BENEFITS

A participant has a zero basis in the *deductible* contributions to an IRA because such contributions are not taxed currently.[67] Once retirement payments are received, they are ordinary income and are not subject to the 5-year or 10-year averaging allowed for lump-sum distributions. Payments made to a participant from deductible IRAs before age 59½ are subject to a nondeductible 10 percent penalty tax on such actual, or constructive, payments.[68]

All IRAs of an individual are treated as one contract, and all distributions during a taxable year are treated as one distribution. If an individual who previously has made both deductible and nondeductible IRA contributions makes a withdrawal from an IRA during a taxable year, the excludible amount must be calculated. The amount excludible from gross income for the taxable year is calculated by multiplying the amount withdrawn by a percentage. The percentage is calculated by dividing the individual's aggregate nondeductible IRA contributions by the aggregate balance of all his or her IRAs (including rollover IRAs and SEPs).[69]

[64] § 404(h)(1)(B).
[65] §§ 4973(a)(1) and (b).
[66] §§ 408(d)(4) and 4973(b)(2).
[67] § 408(d)(1).

[68] § 72(t). There are limited exceptions to the penalty on early distributions.
[69] § 408(d)(2).

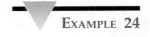

EXAMPLE 24

Carl, age 59, has a $12,000 deductible IRA and a $2,000 nondeductible IRA (without any earnings). Carl withdraws $1,000 from the nondeductible IRA in 1994. The excludible portion is $143 ($2,000/$14,000 × $1,000), and the includible portion is $857 ($12,000/ $14,000 × $1,000). Carl must pay a 10% penalty tax on a prorated portion considered withdrawn from the deductible IRA and earnings in either type of IRA. Thus, the 10% penalty tax is $85.70 (10% × $857). ▼

Rollovers

An IRA may be the recipient of a rollover from another qualified plan, including another IRA. Such a distribution from a qualified plan is not included in gross income if it is transferred within 60 days of receipt to an IRA or another qualified plan. For a series of distributions that constitute a lump-sum distribution, the 60-day period does not begin until the last distribution. Amounts received from IRAs may be rolled over tax-free only once in a 12-month period. If a person has more than one IRA, the one-year waiting period applies separately to each IRA.[70]

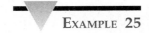

EXAMPLE 25

Nonemployer stock worth $60,000 is distributed to an employee from a qualified retirement plan. Hubert, the employee, sells the stock within 60 days for $60,000 and transfers one-half of the proceeds to an IRA. Hubert will have $30,000 of ordinary income, which is not eligible for 5-year or 10-year forward averaging or for the capital gain treatment for pre-1974 contributions. One-half of the distribution, or $30,000, does escape taxation because of the rollover. ▼

A tax-free rollover for distributions from qualified plans is an alternative to the taxable 5-year or 10-year forward averaging techniques. Any rollover amount in an IRA may later be rolled over into another qualified plan if the IRA consists of only the amounts from the original plan. The amount of nondeductible employee contributions included in a distribution may not be rolled over, but that amount is tax-free because the contributions were made with after-tax dollars. Partial rollovers are allowed, but the maximum amount that may be rolled over may not exceed the portion of the distribution that is otherwise includible in gross income. Rollovers are not available for minimum distributions once age 70½ is reached.

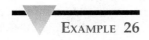

EXAMPLE 26

Jane withdraws $1,500 from her IRA on May 2, 1994, but she redeposits it in the same IRA on June 28, 1994. Although this was a partial rollover and Jane may have used the funds for a limited time, this is a tax-free rollover.[71] ▼

A rollover is different from a direct transfer of funds from a qualified plan to an IRA or another qualified plan by a trustee or issuer. A direct transfer is not subject to the one-year waiting period and the withholding rules.[72] Further, in many states, IRA amounts are subject to claims of creditors, which is not the case for employer plans.

An employer must withhold 20 percent of any lump-sum distributions unless the transfer is a direct transfer to an IRA or another qualified plan. This provision is effective for distributions after December 31, 1992.[73]

---

[70] § 408(d)(3)(B) and Prop.Reg. 1.408–4(b)(4).
[71] Ltr.Rul. 9010007.

[72] Temp.Reg. 35.3405–1.
[73] § 3405(c).

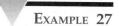

EXAMPLE 27

Kay receives a distribution from a qualified retirement plan. The amount of the distribution would have been $20,000, but Kay receives only $16,000 ($20,000 – $4,000) as a result of the 20% withholding provision. After several weeks, Kay decides to contribute $20,000 (the gross amount of the distribution) to her IRA. Since she received only $16,000, she will need to contribute $4,000 from another source in order to make a $20,000 contribution. Kay will be able to claim a refund for the $4,000 that was withheld when she files her tax return for the year. ▼

Distributions to an IRA are generally not eligible for 5- or 10-year averaging or capital gain treatment. An exception applies in the case of a conduit IRA, where the sole assets of a plan are rolled over into an IRA, and the assets are then rolled into a qualified plan. With a conduit IRA, the lump-sum distribution from the original plan is still eligible for the special tax treatments.

NONQUALIFIED DEFERRED COMPENSATION PLANS

UNDERLYING RATIONALE FOR TAX TREATMENT

7   LEARNING OBJECTIVE
Understand the rationale for nonqualified deferred compensation plans and the related tax treatment.

Nonqualified deferred compensation (NQDC) plans provide a flexible way for executives, particularly those in the 36 or 39.6 percent tax brackets, to defer income taxes on income payments until a possible lower tax bracket year. Where the deferred compensation is credited with annual earnings until payment, the entire deferred compensation, not the after-tax amount, is generating investment income. Also, most deferred compensation plans do not have to meet the discrimination, funding, coverage, and other requirements of qualified plans. In addition to these advantages for the employee, the employer may not have a current cash outflow.

The doctrine of constructive receipt is an important concept relating to the taxability of nonqualified deferred compensation.[74] In essence, if a taxpayer irrevocably earns income but may elect to receive it now or at a later date, the income is constructively received and is immediately taxed. Income is not constructively received, however, if the taxpayer's control over the amounts earned is subject to substantial limitations or restrictions.

Another important concept is the economic benefit theory. Although a taxpayer does not have a present right to income, the income will be taxable if a right in the form of a negotiable promissory note exists. Notes and other evidences of indebtedness received in payment for services constitute income to the extent of their fair market value at the time of the transfer.[75]

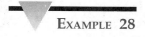

EXAMPLE 28

Eagle Corporation and Bill, a cash basis employee, enter into an employment agreement that provides an annual salary of $120,000 to Bill. Of this amount, $100,000 is to be paid in current monthly installments, and $20,000 is to be paid in 10 annual installments beginning at Bill's retirement or death. Although Eagle Corporation maintains a separate account for Bill, that account is not funded (Bill is merely an unsecured creditor of the corporation). The $20,000 is not considered constructively received and is deferred. Compensation of $100,000 is currently taxable to Bill and deductible to Eagle. The other $20,000 will be taxable and deductible when paid in future years. ▼

---

[74] § 451(a) and Reg. § 1.451–2.   [75] Reg. § 1.61–2(d)(4).

TAX TREATMENT TO THE EMPLOYER AND EMPLOYEE

The tax treatment of an NQDC plan depends on whether it is *funded* or *unfunded* and whether it is *forfeitable* or *nonforfeitable*. In an unfunded NQDC plan, the employee relies upon the company's mere promise to make the compensation payment in the future. An unfunded, unsecured promise to pay, not represented by a negotiable note, effectively defers the recognition of income. Thus, the employee is taxed later when the compensation is actually paid or made available.[76] Similarly, the employer is allowed a deduction when the employee recognizes income.[77]

The employer can set up an escrow account to accumulate deferred payments on behalf of the employee. These funds may be invested by the escrow agent for the benefit of the employee.[78] By avoiding income recognition until the benefits from the escrow custodial account are received, the employee postpones the tax. An escrow arrangement can be appropriate for a professional athlete or entertainer whose income is earned in a few peak years.

▼

EXAMPLE 29

Ted, a professional athlete, is to receive a bonus for signing an employment contract. An NQDC plan is established to defer the income beyond Ted's peak income years. His employer transfers the bonus to an escrow agent who invests the funds in securities, etc., which may act as a hedge against inflation. The bonus is deferred for 10 years and becomes payable gradually in years 11 through 15. The bonus is taxable to Ted and deductible by his employer when Ted receives the payments in years 11 through 15. ▼

It is also possible to provide for NQDC through an internally funded revocable trust or through an externally funded nonexempt trust.[79] The detailed requirements for such arrangements are beyond the scope of this text. Generally, however, funded NQDC plans must be forfeitable to keep the compensation payments from being taxable immediately. In most instances, employees prefer to have some assurance that they will ultimately receive benefits from the NQDC (that the plan provides for nonforfeitable benefits). In such instances, the plan will have to be unfunded to prevent immediate taxation to the employee. Note that most funded NQDC plans are subject to many of the provisions that apply to qualified plans.

When to Use an NQDC Arrangement

As a general rule, NQDC plans are more appropriate for executives in a financially secure company. Because of the need for currently disposable income, such plans are usually not appropriate for young employees.

An NQDC plan can reduce an employee's overall tax payments by deferring the taxation of income to later years (possibly when the employee is in a lower tax bracket). In effect, these plans may produce a form of income averaging. Further, NQDC plans may discriminate in favor of shareholders, officers, specific highly compensated key employees, or a single individual.

Certain disadvantages should be noted. Nonqualified plans are usually required to be unfunded, which means that an employee is not assured that funds

---

[76] Rev.Rul. 60–31, 1960–1 C.B. 174; Reg. § 1.451–2(a); *U.S. v. Basye,* 73–1 USTC ¶9250, 31 AFTR2d 73–802, 93 S.Ct. 1080 (USSC, 1973).
[77] §§ 404(a) and (d).

[78] Rev.Rul. 55–525, 1955–2 C.B. 543.
[79] Rev.Rul. 67–289, 1967–2 C.B. 163; Reg. § 1.83–1(a).

ultimately will be available to pay the benefits. Also, the employer's tax deduction is postponed until the employee is taxed on those payments.

Golden Parachute Arrangements

Certain excessive severance payments to employees may be penalized. The Code denies a deduction to an employer who makes a payment of cash or property to an employee or independent contractor that satisfies both of the following conditions:

- The payment is contingent on a change of ownership of a corporation through a stock or asset acquisition.
- The aggregate present value of the payment equals or exceeds three times the employee's (or independent contractor's) average annual compensation.[80]

The law recognizes that a corporation may provide monetary benefits to key employees if those employees lose their jobs as a result of a change in ownership of the corporation. These payments may be unreasonable or not really for services rendered. The Code refers to such payments as **golden parachute payments,** a term that, in essence, means *excess severance pay.* The disallowed amount is the excess of the payment over a statutory base amount (a five-year average of compensation if the taxpayer was an employee for the entire five-year period). Further, a 20 percent excise tax is imposed on the recipient on the receipt of these parachute payments, to be withheld at the time of payment.[81]

EXAMPLE 30

Irene, an executive, receives a golden parachute payment of $380,000 from her employer. Her average annual compensation for the most recent five tax years is $120,000. The corporation will be denied a deduction for $260,000 ($380,000 payment − $120,000 base amount). Irene's excise tax is $52,000 ($260,000 × 20%). ▼

Golden parachute payments do not include payments to or from qualified pension, profit sharing, stock bonus, annuity, or simplified employee pension plans. Also excluded is the amount of the payment that, in fact, represents reasonable compensation for personal services actually rendered or to be rendered. S corporations are not subject to the golden parachute rules. Generally, corporations that do not have stock that is readily tradable on an established securities market or elsewhere are also exempt. Such excluded payments are not taken into account when determining whether the threshold (the aggregate present value calculation) is exceeded.

Publicly Held Companies' Compensation Limitation

For purposes of both the regular income tax and the alternative minimum tax, the deductible compensation for the top five executives of publicly traded companies is limited to $1 million for each executive. A company is publicly held if the corporation has common stock listed on a national securities exchange.[82]

This new deduction limitation applies when the compensation deduction would otherwise be taken. For example, in the case of a nonqualified stock option (NSO), which is discussed later in this chapter, the deduction is normally taken in

---

[80] § 280G.
[81] § 4999.

[82] § 162(m).

TAX IN THE NEWS

GOLDEN HANDCUFFS

Infuriated by talent raids staged by departing executives, many big companies are erecting elaborate new antidefection defenses.

The motive is self-preservation: Job-hopping executives can wreak considerable havoc by recruiting trusted lieutenants. "It can be terrible to lose one executive. But when several leave, a company can be devastated," says Joseph Bachelder, a New York lawyer and executive-pay specialist.

To prevent that, a number of companies "are taking out their golden handcuffs and anything else they can to chain top performers to the wall," notes David B. Radden, a senior vice president with recruiters Paul R. Ray & Company.

At Compaq Computer Corporation, for example, executives forfeit special pension plans if they try to recruit talent when they leave. American Express Company has established employment agreements for many executives that include noncompete and nonsolicitation agreements. And Paine-Webber Group, Inc.'s money-management unit, Mitchell Hutchins Institutional Investors, Inc., recently gave stars more money to sign employment agreements, which tie them to the company for at least 18 months.

SOURCE: Reprinted from Julie A. Lopez, "Firms Use Contracts and Cash to Prevent Talent Raids by Departing Executives," *Wall Street Journal*, July 9, 1993, p. B1. Reprinted by permission of the *Wall Street Journal*, © 1993 Dow Jones & Company, Inc. All rights reserved worldwide.

the year the NSO is exercised, even though the option was granted with respect to services performed in a prior year.

Certain types of compensation are *not* subject to this new deduction limit and are not taken into account in determining whether other compensation exceeds $1 million:

- Compensation payable on a commission basis.
- Compensation payable solely on account of the attainment of one or more performance goals when certain requirements involving the approval of outside directors and shareholders are met.
- Payments to a tax-qualified retirement plan (including salary reduction contributions).
- Amounts that are excludible from an executive's gross income (such as employer-provided health benefits and miscellaneous fringe benefits).

The most important exception is performance-based compensation. Compensation qualifies for this exception only if the following conditions are satisfied:

- The compensation is paid solely on account of the attainment of one or more performance goals.
- The performance goals are established by a compensation committee consisting solely of two or more outside directors.
- The material terms under which the compensation is to be paid (including the performance goals) are disclosed to and approved by the shareholders in a separate vote prior to payment.
- Prior to payment, the compensation committee certifies that the performance goals and any other material terms were in fact satisfied.

Compensation (other than stock options or other stock appreciation rights) is not treated as paid solely on account of the attainment of one or more performance goals unless the compensation is paid to the particular executive under a preestablished objective performance formula or standard that precludes discretion. In essence, a third party with knowledge of the relevant performance results could calculate the amount to be paid to the particular executive. A performance goal is broadly defined and includes, for example, any objective performance standard that is applied to the individual executive, a business unit (e.g., a division or a line of business), or the corporation as a whole. Performance standards could include increases in stock price, market share, sales, or earnings per share.

ETHICAL CONSIDERATIONS

Limiting Compensation for Executives But Not for Other Highly Paid Employees

The top five executives of publicly traded corporations have a $1 million limit on deductible compensation. During 1992, the average compensation for two hundred of the highest-paid chief financial officers was $458,636. However, many of these CFOs had salaries ranging as high as $3 million. During 1991, Leon Hirsch at U.S. Surgical was paid $118 million, Anthony O'Reilly at H. J. Heinz was paid $75 million, and Martin Wygod at Medco Containment received $33.7 million.

The average salary for a player in the American League or National League on the opening day of the 1993 baseball season was $1.12 million. Ken Hrbek of the Minnesota Twins is paid $3 million per season. Kansas City's George Brett gets $2.5 million. Oakland's Ruben Sierra has a $28 million, five-year contract, as does his teammate Mark McGwire. Kansas City pitcher David Cone has a three-year $18 million deal, and Detroit's Cecil Fielder has a $36 million, five-year deal. In football, the Dallas Cowboys' Emmitt Smith and the Buffalo Bills' Thurman Thomas each have four-year contracts worth approximately $13.5 million.

Similarly, many television and movie performers are receiving huge salaries (e.g., David Letterman). Yet these entertainers and professional sports players are not subject to the $1 million compensation cap. Some question the fairness of a policy which subjects business executives to a compensation limitation while allowing entertainers and sports stars to be exempt.

RESTRICTED PROPERTY PLANS

GENERAL PROVISIONS

8 LEARNING OBJECTIVE
Explain the value of restricted property plans.

A **restricted property plan** is an arrangement whereby an employer transfers property (e.g., stock of the employer-corporation) to a provider of services at no cost or at a bargain price. The purpose of a restricted stock plan is to retain the services of key employees who might otherwise leave. The employer hopes that such compensation arrangements will encourage company growth and attainment of performance objectives. Section 83 was enacted in 1969 to provide rules for the taxation of incentive compensation arrangements, which previously were governed by judicial and administrative interpretations. Although the following discussion refers to an employee as the provider of the services, the services need not be performed by an employee (§ 83 also applies to independent contractors).

As a general rule, if an employee performs services and receives property (e.g., stock), the fair market value of that property in excess of any amount paid by the employee is includible in his or her gross income. The time for inclusion is the earlier of (1) the time the property is no longer subject to a substantial risk of forfeiture or (2) the time the property is transferable by the employee. The fair market value of the property is determined without regard to any restriction, except a restriction that by its terms will never lapse.[83] Since the amount of the compensation is determined at the date that the restrictions lapse or when the property is transferable, the opportunity to generate capital gain treatment on the property is denied during a period when the ordinary income element is being deferred.

EXAMPLE 31

On October 1, 1990, Blue Corporation sold 100 shares of its stock to Ahmad, an employee, for $10 per share. At the time of the sale, the fair market value of the stock was $100 per share. Under the terms of the sale, each share of stock was nontransferable and subject to a substantial risk of forfeiture (which was not to lapse until October 1, 1994). Evidence of these restrictions was stamped on the face of the stock certificates. On October 1, 1994, the fair market value of the stock was $250 per share. Since the stock was nontransferable and was subject to a substantial risk of forfeiture, Ahmad did not include any compensation in gross income during 1990 (assuming no special election was made). Instead, Ahmad was required to include $24,000 of compensation in gross income [100 shares × ($250 less $10 per share)] during 1994. If for some reason the substantial risk of forfeiture had occurred (e.g., the plan required Ahmad to surrender the stock to the corporation if he voluntarily terminated his employment with the company before October 1, 1994) and Ahmad never received the stock certificates, he would have been allowed a capital loss of $1,000 (the extent of his investment). ▼

SUBSTANTIAL RISK OF FORFEITURE

A **substantial risk of forfeiture** exists if a person's rights to full enjoyment of property are conditioned upon the future performance, or the refraining from the performance, of substantial services by that individual.[84] For example, if an employee must return the property (receiving only his or her original cost, if any) should there be a failure to complete a substantial period of service (for any reason), the property is subject to a substantial risk of forfeiture. Another such situation exists when an employer can compel an employee to return the property due to a breach of a substantial covenant not to compete. Any substantial risk of forfeiture should be stated on the face of the stock certificates. Assuming that a substantial risk of forfeiture does not exist, the property received is valued at its fair market value, ignoring any restrictions, except for one instance dealing with closely held stock.

SPECIAL ELECTION AVAILABLE

An employee may elect within 30 days after the receipt of restricted property to recognize immediately as ordinary income the fair market value in excess of the amount paid for the property. Any appreciation in the value of the property after receipt is classified as capital gain instead of ordinary income. No deduction is allowed to the employee for taxes paid on the original amount included in income if the property is subsequently forfeited.[85] The employee is permitted to take a

---

[83] § 83(a)(1); *Miriam Sakol,* 67 T.C. 986 (1977); *T. M. Horwith,* 71 T.C. 932 (1979).

[84] § 83(c); Regulation § 1.83–3(c)(2) includes several examples of restricted property arrangements.
[85] § 83(b).

capital loss for any amounts that were actually paid for the property. Furthermore, in such a case, the employer must repay taxes saved by any compensation deduction taken in the earlier year.[86]

Any increase in value between the time the property is received and the time it becomes either nonforfeitable or transferable is taxed as ordinary income if the employee does not make a special election. However, if the employee elects to be taxed immediately on the difference between the cost and fair market value on the date of issue, any future appreciation is treated as capital gain. In determining whether the gain is long term or short term, the holding period starts when the employee is taxed on the ordinary income.[87]

EXAMPLE 32

On July 1, 1984, Sparrow Company sold 100 shares of its preferred stock, worth $15 per share, to Diane (an employee) for $5 per share. The sale was subject to Diane's agreement to resell the preferred shares to the company for $5 per share if she terminated her employment during the following 10 years. Assume that the stock had a value of $25 per share on July 1, 1994, and Diane sold the stock for $30 per share on October 10, 1994. Diane made the special election to include the original spread (between the value in 1984 of $15 and the amount paid of $5) in income for 1984. Diane was required to recognize $1,000 of compensation income in 1984 ($15 − $5 = $10 ×100 shares), at which time her holding period in her stock began. Diane's tax basis in the stock was $1,500 ($1,000 + $500). When the preferred stock was sold in 1994, Diane recognized a $1,500 long-term capital gain ($30 × 100 shares − $1,500). ▼

EXAMPLE 33

Assume the same facts as in Example 32, except that Diane sells the stock in 1995 (rather than 1994). She would not recognize any gain in 1994 when the substantial risk of forfeiture lapses. Instead, Diane would recognize the $1,500 long-term capital gain in 1995. ▼

This special provision is usually not elected since it results in an immediate recognition of income and adverse tax consequences result from a subsequent forfeiture. However, the special election may be attractive in the following situations:

- The bargain element is relatively small.
- Substantial appreciation is expected in the future.
- A high probability exists that the restrictions will be met.

EMPLOYER DEDUCTIONS

At the time the employee is required to include the compensation in income, the employer is allowed a tax deduction for the same amount. The employer must withhold on this amount in accordance with § 3402. In the no-election situation, the deduction is limited to the fair market value of the restricted property (without regard to the restrictions) at the time the restrictions lapse, reduced by the amount originally paid for the property by the employee.[88] When the employee elects to be taxed immediately, the corporate deduction also is accelerated and deductible in like amount. In cases of deferred income recognition, the employer can receive a very sizable deduction if the property has appreciated.

EXAMPLE 34

On March 14, 1992, Gold Corporation sold to Harry, an employee, 10 shares of Gold common stock for $100 per share. Both the corporation and Harry were calendar year

---

[86] Reg. §§ 1.83–6(c) and 2(a).
[87] § 1223(6).

[88] Reg. § 1.83–6(a).

taxpayers. The common stock was subject to a substantial risk of forfeiture and was nontransferable; both conditions were to lapse on March 14, 1994. At the time of the sale, the fair market value of the common stock (without considering the restrictions) was $1,000 per share. On March 14, 1994, when the fair market value of the stock was $2,000 per share, the restrictions lapsed. Harry did not make a special election. In 1994, Harry realized ordinary income of $19,000 (10 shares at $2,000 per share less the $100 per share he had paid). Likewise, Gold Corporation was allowed a $19,000 compensation deduction in 1994. ▼

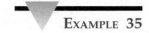
EXAMPLE 35

In the previous example, assume that Harry had made the special election. Since he was taxed on $9,000 in 1992, the corporation was allowed to deduct a like amount in 1992. No deduction would be available in 1994. ▼

STOCK OPTIONS

IN GENERAL

9 **LEARNING OBJECTIVE**
Differentiate the tax treatment of qualified and nonqualified stock options.

Various equity types of stock option programs are available for an employee's compensation package. Some authorities believe that some form of *equity kicker* is needed to attract new management, convert key officers into *partners* by giving them a share of the business, and retain the services of executives who might otherwise leave. Encouraging the managers of a business to have a proprietary interest in its successful operation should provide executives with a key motive to expand the company and improve its profits. In addition, under certain conditions, stock options may fall outside the $1 million cap on the salaries of the top five executives of publicly traded companies.

A **stock option** gives an individual the right to purchase a stated number of shares of stock from a corporation at a certain price within a specified period of time. The optionee must be under no obligation to purchase the stock, and the option may be revocable by the corporation. The option must be in writing, and its terms must be clearly expressed.[89]

INCENTIVE STOCK OPTIONS

An equity type of stock option called an *incentive stock options (ISO)* is available for options granted after 1975 and exercised after 1980.[90] An ISO arrangement receives much the same tax treatment previously accorded to restricted and qualified stock option plans. There are no tax consequences when the option is granted, but the *spread* (the excess of the fair market value of the share at the date of exercise over the option price)[91] is a tax preference item for purposes of the alternative minimum tax. The determination of fair market value is made without regard to any lapse restrictions (a restriction that will expire after a period of time). After the option is exercised and when the stock is sold, any gain from the sale is taxed as a long-term capital gain if certain holding period requirements are met. To qualify as a long-term capital gain, the employee must not dispose of the stock within two years after the option is granted or within one year after acquiring the stock.[92] If

---

[89] Reg. §§ 1.421–1(a)(1) and –7(a)(1).
[90] Qualified stock options were available under § 422 (prior to repeal by the Revenue Reconciliation Act of 1990) for certain qualified options granted before May 21, 1976. These qualified

stock options had many of the statutory requirements of ISOs, but ISOs have a more favorable tax treatment.
[91] §§ 422(a), 421(a)(1), and 57(a)(3).
[92] § 422(a)(1).

the employee meets the holding period requirements, none of these transactions generate any business deduction for the employer.[93]

Since some beneficial treatment for long-term capital gains for the individual was restored beginning in 1991 and tax rates were increased in 1993, ISOs have regained some of their tax appeal on the gain side. In addition, an employee who has capital losses would prefer capital gain treatment.

EXAMPLE 36

Wren Corporation granted an ISO for 100 shares of its stock to Rocky, an employee, on March 18, 1991. The option price was $100, and the fair market value was $100 on the date of the grant. Rocky exercised the option on April 1, 1993, when the market value of the stock was $200 per share. He sells the stock on April 6, 1994, for $300 per share. Rocky did not recognize any ordinary income on the date of the grant or the exercise date since the option qualified as an ISO. Wren received no compensation deduction. Rocky has a $10,000 tax preference item on the exercise date. He has a long-term capital gain of $20,000 [($300 − $100) × 100] upon the sale of the stock in 1994, since the one-year and two-year holding periods and other requirements have been met. ▼

As a further requirement for ISO treatment, the option holder must be an employee of the issuing corporation from the date the option is granted until 3 months (12 months if disabled) before the date of exercise. Exceptions are made for parent and subsidiary situations, corporate reorganizations, and liquidations. The holding period and the employee-status rules just described (the one-year, two-year, and three-month requirements) are waived in the case of the death of an employee. Also, in certain situations involving an insolvent employee, the holding period rules are modified.[94]

EXAMPLE 37

Assume the same facts as in the previous example, except that Rocky was not employed by Wren Corporation for six months before the date he exercised the options. Rocky must recognize ordinary income to the extent of the spread, assuming there was no substantial risk of forfeiture. Thus, Rocky recognizes $10,000 [($200 − $100) × 100] of ordinary income on the exercise date, since he was not an employee of Wren Corporation at all times during the period beginning on the grant date and ending three months before the exercise date. Wren is allowed a deduction at the same time that Rocky reports the ordinary income. ▼

If the holding period requirements are not satisfied but all other conditions are met, the tax is still deferred to the point of the sale. However, the difference between the option price and the value of the stock at the date the option was exercised will be treated as ordinary income. The difference between the amount realized for the stock and the value of the stock at the date of exercise will be short-term or long-term capital gain, depending on the holding period of the stock itself. The employer will be allowed a deduction equal to the amount recognized by the employee as ordinary income.

EXAMPLE 38

Assume the same facts as in Example 36, except that Rocky sells the stock on March 22, 1994, for $290 per share. Since Rocky did not hold the stock itself for at least one year, $10,000 of the gain is treated as ordinary income in 1994, and Wren Corporation is allowed a $10,000 compensation deduction in 1994. The remaining $9,000 is a short-term capital gain ($29,000 − $20,000). ▼

---

[93] § 421(a)(2).

[94] §§ 422(a)(2) and (c)(3).

Qualification Requirements for Incentive Stock Option Plans

An **incentive stock option** is an option to purchase stock of a corporation granted to an individual for any reason connected with his or her employment.[95] The option is granted by the employer-corporation or by a parent or subsidiary corporation of the employer-corporation. An employee can use company stock to pay for the stock when exercising an option without disqualifying the ISO plan.

For an option to qualify as an ISO, the terms of the option itself must meet the following conditions:

- The option must be granted under a plan specifying the number of shares of stock to be issued and the employees or class of employees eligible to receive the options. The plan must be approved by the shareholders of the corporation within 12 months before or after the plan is adopted.
- The option must be granted within 10 years of the date the plan is adopted or of the date the plan is approved by the shareholders, whichever date is earlier.
- The option must by its terms be exercisable only within 10 years of the date it is granted.
- The option price must equal or exceed the fair market value of the stock at the time the option is granted. This requirement is deemed satisfied if there has been a good faith attempt to value the stock accurately, even if the option price is less than the stock value.
- The option by its terms must be nontransferable other than at death and must be exercisable during the employee's lifetime only by the employee.
- The employee must not, immediately before the option is granted, own stock representing more than 10 percent of the voting power or value of all classes of stock in the employer-corporation or its parent or subsidiary. (Here, the attribution rules of § 267 are applied in modified form.) However, the stock ownership limitation will be waived if the option price is at least 110 percent of the fair market value (at the time the option is granted) of the stock subject to the option and the option by its terms is not exercisable more than five years from the date it is granted.[96]

An overall limitation is imposed on the amount of ISOs that can be exercised in one year. This limit is set at $100,000 per year (based on the value of the stock determined at the time the option is granted) per employee.

NONQUALIFIED STOCK OPTIONS

A **nonqualified stock option (NQSO)** does not satisfy the statutory requirements for ISOs. In addition, a stock option that otherwise would qualify as an ISO will be treated as an NQSO if the terms of the stock option provide that it is not an ISO. If the NQSO has a readily ascertainable fair market value (e.g., the option is traded on an established exchange), the value of the option must be included in the employee's income at the date of grant. Thereafter, capital gain or loss is recognized only upon the disposal of the optioned stock. The employee's basis is the amount paid for the stock plus any amount reported as ordinary income. The employer obtains a corresponding tax deduction at the same time and to the extent that ordinary income is recognized by the employee.[97]

---

[95] § 422(b).
[96] § 422(c)(5).

[97] Reg. §§ 1.421–6(c), (d), (e), and (f); Reg. § 1.83–7.

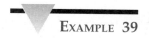

EXAMPLE 39

On February 1, 1993, Janet was granted an NQSO to purchase 100 shares of stock from her employer at $10 per share. On this date, the option was selling for $2 on an established exchange. Janet exercised the option on March 30, 1994, when the stock was worth $20 per share. On June 5, 1994, Janet sold the optioned stock for $22 per share.

- Janet must report ordinary income of $200 ($2 × 100 shares) on the date of grant (February 1, 1993), since the option has a readily ascertainable fair market value.
- Upon the sale of the stock (June 5, 1994), Janet must report a long-term capital gain of $1,000 [($22 − $12) × 100 shares].
- At the date of grant (February 1, 1993), the employer will receive a tax deduction of $200, the amount of income reported by Janet. ▼

If an NQSO does not have a readily ascertainable fair market value, an employee does not recognize income at the grant date. However, as a general rule, ordinary income must be reported in the year of exercise (the difference between the fair market value of the stock at the exercise date and the option price).[98] The amount paid by the employee for the stock plus the amount reported as ordinary income becomes the basis. Any appreciation above that basis is taxed as a long-term capital gain upon disposition (assuming the stock is held for the required long-term holding period after exercise). The corporation receives a corresponding tax deduction at the same time and to the extent that ordinary income is recognized by the employee.

EXAMPLE 40

On February 3, 1992, Maria was granted an NQSO for 100 shares of common stock at $10 per share. On the date of the grant, there was no readily ascertainable fair market value for the option. Maria exercised the options on January 3, 1993, when the stock was selling for $15 per share. She sold one-half of the shares on April 15, 1993, and the other half on September 17, 1994. The sale price on both dates was $21 per share. Maria would not recognize any income on the grant date (February 3, 1992) but would recognize $500 ($1,500 − $1,000) of ordinary income on the exercise date (January 3, 1993). She would recognize a short-term capital gain of $300 on the sale of the first half in 1993 and a $300 long-term capital gain on the sale of the second batch of stock in 1994 [½ ($2,100 − $1,500)]. ▼

The major *advantages* of NQSOs can be summarized as follows:

- A tax deduction is available to the corporation without a cash outlay.
- The employee receives capital gain treatment on any appreciation in the stock starting either at the exercise date or at the date of grant if the option has a readily ascertainable fair market value.
- Options can be issued at more flexible terms than under ISO plans (e.g., longer exercise period and discount on exercise price).

A major *disadvantage* is that the employee must recognize ordinary income on the exercise of the option or at the date of grant if the option has a readily ascertainable market value, without receiving cash to pay the tax.

TAX PLANNING CONSIDERATIONS

DEFERRED COMPENSATION

With the new higher 39.6 percent individual tax rate, taxpayers may try to lower their tax burden by participating in more deferred compensation arrangements. The new $1 million annual limit on the compensation deduction for the top five

---

[98] Reg. § 1.83–7(a); Reg. § 1.421–6(d).

executives of publicly traded companies may cause a shift into § 401(k) plans, qualified retirement plans, and especially nonqualified deferred compensation arrangements. However, the amount of compensation that can be taken into consideration for purposes of calculating contributions or benefits under a qualified pension or profit sharing plan has been reduced to $150,000.

The tightening of the antidiscrimination rules may increase the costs to the employer of providing deferred compensation. Restrictions upon the deductibility of interest expense make it more costly for an employee to borrow money as part of a compensation program. Payment of compensation in cash in 1994 still may be beneficial, however, especially if individual tax rates continue to increase in future years.

QUALIFIED PLANS

Qualified plans provide maximum tax benefits for employers, since the employer receives an immediate tax deduction for contributions to such plans and the income that is earned on the contributions is not taxable to the employer. The employer contributions and the trust earnings are not taxed to the employees until those funds are made available to them.

Qualified plans are most appropriate where it is desirable to provide benefits for a cross section of employees. In some closely held corporations, the primary objective is to provide benefits for the officer-shareholder group and other highly paid personnel. The nondiscrimination requirements that must be met in a qualified plan may prevent such companies from attaining these objectives. Thus, a nonqualified arrangement may be needed as a supplement to, or used in lieu of, the qualified plan.

SELF-EMPLOYED RETIREMENT PLANS

A Keogh or IRA participant may make a deductible contribution for a tax year up to the time prescribed for filing the individual's tax return. A Keogh plan must have been established by the end of the tax year (December 31) to obtain a current deduction for the contribution made in the subsequent year. An individual can establish an IRA after the end of the tax year and still receive a current deduction for the contribution made in the subsequent year. However, since the deductibility of contributions to IRAs has been restricted for many middle-income and upper-income taxpayers, Keogh plans are likely to become more important.

INDIVIDUAL RETIREMENT ACCOUNTS

Fewer taxpayers are now allowed to make deductible contributions to IRAs. A working taxpayer not covered by another qualified plan may still deduct IRA contributions up to the smaller of $2,000 or 100 percent of earned income. If both spouses work, each may individually establish an IRA. Where only one spouse has earned income, an IRA may be established for the nonworking spouse. A total of $2,250 may then be contributed to the two IRAs. If the nonworking spouse has a small amount of income (e.g., jury duty), an election may be made to ignore such income for spousal IRA purposes.

A married couple may put $4,000 into an IRA when one spouse works for the other spouse. This requires paying the *employee spouse* $2,000 in salary and having him or her make an independent contribution to an IRA. This extra $2,000, is subject to FICA, however.

A single working taxpayer covered by another retirement plan may deduct a $2,000 IRA contribution only if AGI is less than $25,000 a year. For married couples filing jointly, the ceiling is $40,000. The IRA deduction is reduced proportionately as AGI increases within a $10,000 phase-out range above the $25,000 and $40,000 ceilings.

IRA and Keogh participants can self-direct their investments into a wide variety of assets. The participant self-directs the investments into various assets even though the assets are under the control of a trustee or custodian. The acquisition of collectibles (e.g., art, gems, metals) by an IRA or self-directed Keogh or corporate plan is treated as a distribution (taxed). For an IRA or Keogh participant under age 59½, there is also a 10 percent premature distribution penalty. However, state-issued coins and gold and silver eagle coins issued by the United States may be placed in IRAs.

COMPARISON OF § 401(k) PLAN WITH IRA

Most employees will find a § 401(k) plan more attractive than an IRA. Probably the biggest limitation of an IRA is the $2,000 maximum shelter. Under § 401(k), employees are permitted to shelter compensation up to $9,240 (in 1994).[99] The restrictions on deducting contributions to IRAs for many middle-income and upper-income taxpayers may cause many employees to utilize § 401(k) plans more frequently.

Another difference between § 401(k) plans and IRAs is the manner in which the money is treated. Money placed in an IRA may be tax deductible, whereas dollars placed in a § 401(k) plan are considered to be deferred compensation. Thus, a § 401(k) reduction may reduce profit sharing payments, group life insurance, and Social Security benefits. Concept Summary 19–4 compares a § 401(k) plan with an IRA.

CONCEPT SUMMARY 19–4

Section 401(k) Plan and IRA Compared

	§ 401(k) Plan	IRA
Deduction limitation	Smaller of $9,240 (in 1994) or approximately 25% of total earnings. Limited by antidiscrimination requirements of § 401(k)(3).	$2,000 or 100% of compensation.
Distributions	Early withdrawal possible if for early retirement (55 or over) or to pay medical expenses.	10% penalty for early withdrawals.
Effect on gross earnings	Gross salary reduction, which may reduce profit sharing contributions, Social Security benefits, and group life insurance.	No effect.
Employer involvement	Must keep records; monitor for compliance with antidiscrimination test.	Minimal.
Lump-sum distributions	Favorable 5-year or 10-year forward averaging.	Ordinary income.
Timing of contribution	Within 30 days of plan year-end or due date of employer's return.*	Grace period up to due date of tax return.
Loans from plan	Yes.	No.

*Elective contributions must be made to the plan no later than 30 days after the end of the plan year, and nonelective contributions no later than the due date of the tax return (including extensions).

---

[99] This amount is indexed annually.

NONQUALIFIED DEFERRED COMPENSATION (NQDC) PLANS

Nonqualified deferred compensation arrangements such as restricted property plans can be useful to attract executive talent or to provide substantial retirement benefits for executives. A restricted property plan may be used to retain a key employee of a closely held company when management continuity problems are anticipated. Without such employees, the untimely death or disability of one of the owners might cause a disruption of the business with an attendant loss in value for his or her heirs. Such plans may discriminate in favor of officers and other highly paid employees. The employer, however, does not receive a tax deduction until the employee is required to include the deferred compensation in income (upon the lapse of the restrictions).

The principal advantage of NQDC plans is that the employee can defer the recognition of income to future periods when his or her income tax bracket may be lower (e.g., during retirement years). The time value benefits from the deferral of income should also be considered. However, with the trend toward increasing rates, an executive with a deferred compensation arrangement entered into in a prior year may wish to accelerate the income into 1994 since individual tax rates in future years may be even higher.

The principal disadvantage of NQDC plans could be the bunching effect that takes place on the expiration of the period of deferral. In some cases, planning can alleviate this result.

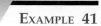

EXAMPLE 41

During 1994, Kelly, an executive, enters into an agreement to postpone a portion of her payment for current services until retirement. The deferred amount is not segregated from the company's general assets and is subject to normal business risk. The entire payment, not the after-tax amount, is invested in securities and variable annuity contracts. Kelly is not taxed on the payment in 1994, and the company receives no deduction in 1994. If Kelly receives the deferred payment in a lump sum when she retires, the tax rates may be higher and more progressive than in 1994. Thus, Kelly may wish to arrange for a number of payments to be made to her or a designated beneficiary over a number of years. ▼

STOCK OPTIONS

Rather than paying compensation in the form of corporate stock, an alternative approach is to issue options to purchase stock at a specific price to an employee. Stock option plans are used more frequently by publicly traded companies than by closely held companies. This difference is due to the problems of determining the value of the stock of a company that is not publicly held.

Nonqualified stock options (NQSOs) are more flexible and less restrictive than incentive stock options (ISOs). For example, the holding period for an NQSO is not as long as that for an ISO. Further, the option price of an NQSO may be less than the fair market value of the stock at the time the option is granted. An NQSO creates an employer deduction that lowers the cost of the NQSO to the employer. The employer may pass along this tax savings to the employee in the form of a cash payment. Both the employer and the employee may be better off by combining NQSOs with additional cash payments rather than using ISOs. See Concept Summary 19–5.

CONCEPT SUMMARY 19-5

Incentive Stock Options and Nonqualified Stock Options Compared

	ISO	NQSO
Granted at any price	No	Yes
May have any duration	No	Yes
Governing Code Section	§ 422	§ 83
Spread subject to alternative minimum tax	Yes	No
Deduction to employer for spread	No	Yes
Type of gain/loss on disposal	Capital	Capital
Statutory amount ($100,000) limitation	Yes	No

FLEXIBLE BENEFIT PLANS

Employees may be permitted to choose from a package of employer-provided fringe benefits.[100] In these so-called **cafeteria benefit plans,** some of the benefits chosen by an employee may be taxable, and some may be statutory nontaxable benefits (e.g., health and accident insurance and group term life insurance).

Employer contributions made to a flexible plan are included in an employee's gross income only to the extent that the employee actually elects the taxable benefits. Certain nondiscrimination standards with respect to coverage, eligibility for participation, contributions, and benefits must be met. Thus, such a plan must cover a fair cross section of employees. Also, a flexible plan cannot include an election to defer compensation, and a key employee is not exempt from taxation on the taxable benefits made available where more than 25 percent of the statutory nontaxable benefits are provided to key employees.

KEY TERMS

Cafeteria benefit plan, 19–41

Deferred compensation,   19–2

Defined benefit plan, 19–4

Defined contribution pension plan,   19–4

Employee stock ownership plan (ESOP),   19–6

Golden parachute payments,   19–29

Highly compensated employee,   19–9

H.R. 10 (Keogh) plan, 19–20

Incentive stock option (ISO),   19–36

Individual Retirement Account (IRA),   19–22

---

[100] § 125.

Lump-sum distribution, 19–13

Nonqualified deferred compensation (NQDC) plan, 19–27

Nonqualified stock option (NQSO), 19–36

Pension plan, 19–4

Profit sharing plan, 19–6

Restricted property plan, 19–31

Section 401(k) plan, 19–19

Simplified employee pension (SEP) plan, 19–23

Stock bonus plan, 19–6

Stock option, 19–34

Substantial risk of forfeiture, 19–32

Top-heavy plan, 19–18

Vesting requirements, 19–10

Zero bracket amount, 19–14

PROBLEM MATERIALS

DISCUSSION QUESTIONS

1. Compare and contrast defined contribution and defined benefit pension plans.

2. Compare and contrast qualified pension and profit sharing plans.

3. Determine whether each of the following independent statements best applies to a defined contribution plan (DCP), defined benefit plan (DBP), both (B), or neither (N):
   a. Includes an employee stock ownership plan (ESOP).
   b. Forfeitures can be allocated to the remaining participants' accounts.
   c. Requires greater reporting requirements and more actuarial and administrative costs.
   d. Forfeitures can revert to the employer.
   e. More favorable to employees who are older at the time the plan is adopted.
   f. Employee forfeitures can be used to reduce future contributions by the employer.
   g. May exclude employees who begin employment within five years of normal retirement age.
   h. Annual addition to each employee's account may not exceed the smaller of $30,000 or 25% of the employee's salary.
   i. The final benefit to a participant depends upon investment performance.
   j. To avoid penalties, the amount of annual contributions must meet minimum funding requirements.

4. Indicate whether the following statements apply to a pension plan (P), a profit sharing plan (PS), both (B), or neither (N):
   a. Forfeited amounts can be used to reduce future contributions by the employer.
   b. Allocation of forfeitures may discriminate in favor of the prohibited group (highly compensated employees).
   c. Forfeitures can revert to the employer.
   d. Forfeitures can increase plan benefits by allocating the forfeitures to participants.
   e. An annual benefit of $60,000 could be payable on behalf of a participant.
   f. More favorable to employees who are older at the time the qualified plan is adopted.

5. When will the $30,000 maximum annual contribution to a defined contribution plan be indexed?

6. What are the tax and financial advantages accruing to a company that adopts an employee stock ownership plan (ESOP) for employees?

7. List the qualification requirements that must be satisfied in order for a qualified plan to receive favorable tax treatment.

8. Is it possible to provide greater vested benefits for highly paid employees and still meet the nondiscrimination requirements under a qualified pension plan? Explain.

9. Once the age and service requirements are met, when must an employee begin participating in a qualified plan?

10. What is vesting, and how will vesting requirements help employees who do not remain with one employer during their working years?

11. What are the minimum coverage requirements for qualified pension or profit sharing plans?

12. Discuss the tax consequences to employee, employer, and the trust of a qualified pension or profit sharing plan.

13. What three alternative options are available for distributions of benefits from a qualified retirement plan?

14. How are lump-sum distributions from qualified plans taxed to the recipients (capital gain or ordinary income)? Is income averaging available to an employee who receives a lump-sum distribution?

15. Which of the following would be considered a tax benefit or advantage of a qualified retirement plan?
    a. Certain lump-sum distributions may be subject to capital gain treatment.
    b. Employer contributions are currently deductible.
    c. Employee contributions are currently deductible.
    d. The qualified trust is tax-exempt as to all income (other than unrelated business income).
    e. In a lump-sum distribution, any capital gain tax on the portion attributable to any unrealized appreciation in the stock of the employer at the time of distribution is deferred until the time the employee disposes of the stock in a taxable transaction.
    f. Election may be made to allow a lump-sum distribution to be subject to a 5-year or 10-year forward averaging technique.

16. What ceiling limitations have been placed on employer contributions (relative to individual employees) to defined contribution and defined benefit plans?

17. Define the term *key employee* for purposes of a top-heavy plan.

18. What is a top-heavy plan?

19. Determine the 1994 indexed amounts for the following items:
    a. Maximum annual contribution to a defined contribution plan.
    b. Maximum annual benefits payable by a defined benefit plan.
    c. The $150,000 or $112,500 amounts for calculating the 15% excise tax imposed on excess distributions.
    d. The maximum amount of the annual contribution to a cash or deferred arrangement plan.

20. Discuss the differences between a Keogh plan and an Individual Retirement Account (IRA).

21. What tax-free alternative is available for the 5-year or 10-year forward averaging techniques for lump-sum distributions?

22. For which of the following situations is a nonqualified deferred compensation plan taxable under the constructive receipt doctrine?
    a. The contract is funded, and there is no substantial risk of forfeiture.
    b. Same as (a), except the employee must work for three years.
    c. An agreement to defer payment is entered into after compensation is earned.
    d. The agreement is entered into before services are rendered.
    e. In (a), the contract is not funded.

23. What is the major disadvantage of a nonqualified deferred compensation plan?

24. What is a golden parachute arrangement?

25. Explain the difference in the tax treatment of an employer and employee with respect to the general rule (no election) and the special election under § 83(b) when dealing with a restricted property plan. Explain the risk aspect of this tax provision.

26. What is a substantial risk of forfeiture? Why is it necessary to impose this restriction on the transfer of restricted property?

27. Determine which of the following conditions would cause options to fall *outside* the qualification requirements for incentive stock options:
    a. The employee disposes of his stock within 15 months from the date of the granting of the options.
    b. The employee is allowed to exercise the options up to 12 years from the date the options are granted.
    c. The employee is transferred to the parent of the corporation six months before he exercises the options.
    d. The option price is 112% of the fair market value of the stock on the grant date, and the shareholder owns 15% of the stock.
    e. The option may be exercised by the employee's spouse in the event of the employee's death.

28. Would a 30-year-old corporate executive in the 39.6% tax bracket prefer an extra $20,000 bonus or the option to purchase $20,000 worth of securities for $8,000 from the employer under a nonqualified stock option plan in 1994?

x 29. Compare and contrast an IRA and a § 401(k) plan. p. 19-39

30. Explain what is meant by a cafeteria benefit plan.

31. Indicate whether each of the following items is considered a nonqualified compensation plan (N), a qualified compensation plan (Q), or both (B):
    a. Individual Retirement Account.
    b. Incentive stock option.
    c. Group term life insurance.
    d. Cafeteria plan.
    e. Pension plan.
    f. Employee stock ownership plan.
    g. Nonqualified stock option.
    h. Keogh plan.
    i. Simplified employee pension plan.

PROBLEMS

32. Red Corporation has a total of 1,000 employees, of whom 700 are non-highly compensated. The retirement plan covers 300 non-highly compensated employees and 200 highly compensated employees. Does this plan satisfy the minimum coverage test for 1994?

33. Cardinal Corporation's pension plan benefits 620 of its 1,000 highly compensated employees during 1994. How many of its 620 non-highly compensated employees must benefit to meet the ratio test for the minimum coverage requirement?

34. A retirement plan covers 72% of the non-highly compensated individuals. The plan benefits 49 of the 131 employees. Determine if the participation requirement is met for 1994.

35. An employee of Robin, Inc., has completed five years of employment and is 50% vested in her retirement plan. Does this plan meet the minimum vesting standards required for 1994?

36. Tyronne, age 46, is the sole remaining participant of a money purchase pension plan. The plan is terminated, and a $150,000 taxable distribution is made to Tyronne. Calculate the amount of any early distribution penalty tax.

37. In 1994, Cheryl receives a $170,000 distribution from her qualified retirement plan. If this amount is not a lump-sum distribution, calculate the amount of any excess distribution penalty tax. Cheryl made no after-tax contributions to the plan.

38. George received a distribution from a qualified plan that was entitled to capital gain treatment under § 402(a)(2). The 100 shares of the employer company stock received

have a tax basis of $20 per share and a fair market value of $85 per share. George sold this stock five months after the distribution for $110 per share. Calculate the amount and character of any gain to George.

39. When Leif retires in 1994, he receives a lump-sum distribution of $50,000 from a noncontributory qualified pension plan. His active period of participation was from January 1, 1971, through December 31, 1978. Assume that Leif attained age 50 before January 1, 1986. If Leif files a joint return with his wife in 1994 and elects to use the 10-year forward averaging provision, calculate (a) his separate tax on this distribution and (b) the capital gain portion.

40. Veneia receives a $150,000 lump-sum distribution in 1994 from a contributory pension plan, which includes employer common stock with net unrealized appreciation of $20,000. Veneia contributed $20,000 to the qualified plan while she was an active participant from February 10, 1973, to February 10, 1978. Assume that Veneia attained age 50 before January 1, 1986.
    a. Calculate the total taxable amount.
    b. Calculate the separate tax assuming Veneia elects to use the 5-year or 10-year forward averaging provision.
    c. Calculate the capital gain portion. (Treat part of a calendar month as one month.)

41. Wade has been an active participant in a defined benefit plan for 17 years. During his last 5 years of employment, Wade earned $20,000, $30,000, $45,000, $50,000, and $60,000, respectively (representing his highest income years).
    a. Calculate Wade's maximum allowable benefits from this qualified plan (assume there are fewer than 100 participants) in 1994.
    b. Assume that Wade's average compensation for his three high years is $132,000. Calculate Wade's maximum allowable benefits.

42. The compensation paid by Orange Corporation to the plan participants of a profit sharing plan in 1994 was $33,300. During 1994, Orange Corporation contributed $10,000 to the plan.
    a. Calculate Orange Corporation's deductible amount for 1994.
    b. Calculate the amount of the contribution carryover from 1994.

43. Determine the maximum contributions to a qualified plan in the following independent situations:
    a. Andre is covered by a money purchase pension plan and has an annual salary of $140,000 in 1994.
    b. Nan is a participant in a profit sharing plan and has an annual salary of $110,000 in 1994.
    c. Pete is a participant in a money purchase pension plan and has an annual salary of $220,000 in 1994. The plan has a 10% contribution formula.

44. Determine the maximum annual benefits payable to an employee from a defined benefit plan in the following independent situations:
    a. Quincy, age 65, has been a participant for 12 years, and his highest average compensation for 3 years is $85,000.
    b. Wendy, age 66, has been a participant for 8 years (11 years of service), and her highest average compensation for 3 years is $86,000.
    c. Paul, age 67, has been a participant for 11 years in a collectively bargained plan with 238 participants. His highest average compensation for 3 years is $70,300.

45. During 1994, Keith is a key employee of a top-heavy pension plan. His salary is $275,000. Calculate Keith's maximum contribution to such a defined benefit plan.

46. Heron Company's defined benefit plan allocates $200,000 of the $300,000 of cumulative benefits to key employees. Determine the consequences of this allocation.

47. Nora has 5 years of service completed as of March 2, 1994, her employment anniversary date. Her plan uses the graded vesting rule.
    a. How much is Nora's nonforfeitable percentage if the plan is not top-heavy?

b. Assume the plan is top-heavy in 1994. How much is Nora's nonforfeitable percentage?

c. Assume the plan is top-heavy in 1994 and the company uses cliff vesting. How much is Nora's nonforfeitable percentage?

48. Miguel, a single individual, participates in a § 401(k) plan of his employer. The plan permits participants to choose between a full salary or a reduced salary where the reduction becomes a before-tax contribution to a retirement plan. Miguel elects to contribute 10% of his annual compensation of $82,000 to the plan. On what amount of his salary are income taxes paid in 1994?

49. Susan earns $220,000 of self-employment net income in 1994 in a sole proprietorship.
    a. Calculate the maximum amount that Susan can deduct for contributions to a defined contribution Keogh plan.
    b. Suppose Susan contributes more than the allowable amount to the Keogh plan. What are the consequences to her?
    c. Can Susan retire and begin receiving Keogh payments at age 55?

50. Larry, a married individual filing a joint return, is a member of a Keogh pension plan. For 1994, his AGI is $42,000, and Larry would like to contribute as much as is allowed to an IRA. Calculate the amount that Larry can contribute and the amount he can deduct.

51. Answer the following independent questions with respect to IRA contributions:
    a. During 1994, Juan earns a salary of $25,000 and is not an active participant in any other qualified plan. His wife has no earned income. What is the maximum total deductible contribution to their IRAs? Juan wishes to contribute as much as possible to his own IRA.
    b. Abby has earned income during 1994 of $23,000, and her husband has earned income of $1,900. They are not active participants in any other qualified plan. What is the maximum contribution to their IRAs?
    c. Leo's employer makes a contribution of $3,500 to Leo's simplified employee pension plan. If Leo's earned income is $27,000 and AGI is $24,000 during 1994, what amount, if any, can he also contribute to an IRA?

52. Egret Company pays bonuses to its key executives each year. The specific employees to receive bonuses and the amount of bonus for each recipient are determined on December 1 of each year. Each employee eligible for a bonus may decide on or before November 15 of each year to postpone the receipt of the bonus until retirement or death. An employee electing to postpone receipt of a bonus is allowed to designate, at any time before retirement, the time and manner of the postretirement payments and to designate the persons to receive any amount payable after death. Since most employees elect to defer their bonuses, separate accounts are not maintained for each employee. Under this program, Jack elects to receive his $60,000 bonus in cash, and Ellen elects to defer the receipt of her $65,000 bonus until 1999. When would these bonuses be taxed to these two executives and be deductible by Egret Company?

53. Lori is a disqualifying individual, as defined under § 280G, who receives a possible golden parachute payment of $520,000 from her employer. Her base amount (average annual compensation for the most recent five tax years) is $200,000.
    a. Calculate the amount deductible by Lori's employer and any excise tax payable by Lori.
    b. Assume that Lori's base amount is $110,000 and she receives $310,000. Calculate the employer's deduction and Lori's excise tax.

54. James, an executive, receives a $600,000 payment under a golden parachute agreement entered into on January 14, 1994. James's base amount from Silver Corporation is $140,000.
    a. What amount is not deductible to Silver Corporation under § 280G?
    b. What total tax must James pay, assuming a 39.6% tax rate?
    c. Answer (a) and (b) assuming the payment is $400,000.

55. On February 20, 1994, Tim (an executive of Hawk Corporation) purchased 100 shares of Hawk stock (selling at $20 a share) for $10. A condition of the transaction was that Tim

must resell the stock to Hawk at cost if he voluntarily leaves the company within five years of receiving the stock (assume this represents a substantial risk of forfeiture).

a. Assuming that no special election is made under § 83(b), what amount, if any, is taxable to Tim in 1994?

b. Five years later when the stock is selling for $40 a share, Tim is still employed by Hawk. What amount of ordinary income, if any, is taxable to Tim?

c. What amount, if any, is deductible by Hawk as compensation expense five years later?

d. Should Tim make the § 83(b) special election in 1994? What amount would be taxable in 1994 if he makes the special election?

e. In (d), what amount would be deductible by Hawk five years later?

f. Under (d), assume Tim sold all the stock six years later for $65 per share. How much capital gain is included in his gross income?

g. In (d), what loss is available to Tim if he voluntarily resigns in 1998 before the five-year period and does not sell the stock back to the corporation?

h. In (g), in the year Tim resigns, what amount, if any, would be taxable to Hawk Corporation?

56. On July 2, 1990, Black Corporation sold 1,000 of its common shares (worth $14 per share) to Earl, an employee, for $5 per share. The sale was subject to Earl's agreement to resell the shares to the corporation for $5 per share if his employment is terminated within the following four years. The shares had a value of $24 per share on July 2, 1994. Earl sold the shares for $31 per share on September 16, 1994. No special election under § 83(b) is made.

a. What amount, if any, will be taxed to Earl on July 2, 1990?

b. On July 2, 1994?

c. On September 16, 1994?

d. What deduction, if any, will Black Corporation obtain?

e. Assume the same facts but that Earl makes the election under § 83(b). What amount, if any, will be taxed to Earl on July 2, 1990?

f. Will the assumption made in (e) have any effect on any deduction Black Corporation will receive? Explain.

57. Rosa exercises incentive stock options for 100 shares of Copper Corporation stock on May 21, 1994, at the option price of $100 per share when the fair market value is $120 per share. She sells the 100 shares of common stock three and one-half years later for $140.

a. Calculate the total long-term capital gain on this sale.

b. Assume Rosa holds the stock seven months and sells the shares for $140 per share. Calculate any ordinary income on the sale.

c. In (b), what amount can Copper Corporation deduct?

d. Suppose Rosa holds the stock for two years and sells the shares for $115 per share. Calculate any capital gain on this transaction.

e. In (a), assume the options are nonqualified options with a nonascertainable fair market value on the date of the grant. Calculate total long-term capital gain, if any, in the year of sale.

f. In (e), assume that each option has an ascertainable fair market value of $10 on the date of the grant and no substantial risk of forfeiture exists. Calculate total long-term capital gain, if any, on the date of the sale.

58. On November 19, 1992, Rex is granted a nonqualified stock option to purchase 100 shares of Tan Company (on that date the stock is selling for $8 per share and the option price is $9 per share). Rex exercises the option on August 21, 1993, when the stock is selling for $10 per share. Five months later, Rex sells the shares for $11.50 per share.

a. What amount is taxable to Rex in 1992?

b. What amount is taxable to Rex in 1993?

c. What amount and type of gain are taxable to Rex in 1994?

d. What amount, if any, is deductible by Tan Company in 1993?

e. What amount, if any, is recognized in 1994 if the stock is sold for $9.50 per share?

RESEARCH PROBLEMS

Research Problem 1.   Mr. Sanjay Baker and his sister owned and operated a mail-order business in corporate form. The corporation used the homes of Mr. Baker and his sister for corporate mail-order activities (assembling, storing inventory, etc.). The corporation paid Mr. Baker and the sister rent for the use of the homes. The payments were deducted as rent and reported by the two parties on their tax returns. The IRS disallowed most of the deduction, contending that the rent was excessive. Is the excessive rent deductible as compensation? Write a letter to Mr. Baker that contains your advice and prepare a memo for the tax files.

Partial list of research aids:
Multnomah Operating Co., 57–2 USTC ¶9979, 52 AFTR 672, 248 F.2d 661 (CA–9, 1957).

Research Problem 2.   Kareem had been a participant in the pension plan of Post, Inc., since 1974. In 1992, he terminated employment with Post, Inc., and became an employee of Daily, Inc. In 1973, the IRS issued a letter that the pension plan was qualified under § 401(a) and that the pension trust was therefore exempt from tax under § 501(a). In 1994, the Commissioner examined the pension plan and determined that the plan discriminated among salaried employees. The Commissioner revoked the plan's qualified status and the trust's exempt status retroactively to January 1, 1992. When Kareem changed jobs in 1992, he rolled over his distribution from the pension plan to an IRA under § 402(a)(5). Discuss Kareem's tax situation.

Research Problem 3.   Frank and Polly were married, but Frank died on February 25, 1994. During 1994, Frank earned $5,226 in wages, but Polly had no earned income. Neither had contributed any money to an IRA during 1994. What amount, if any, can be contributed to Frank's IRA and/or Polly's spousal IRA?

Research Problem 4.   Determine the validity of the use of a rabbi trust for a nonqualified deferred compensation plan. How does a secular trust differ from a rabbi trust?

Research Problem 5.   What is a phantom stock plan? Outline the tax treatment. Could a phantom stock payment be considered performance-based compensation for purposes of the $1 million deduction limitation on executive pay?

CORPORATIONS AND PARTNERSHIPS

The primary orientation of this text is toward basic tax concepts and the individual taxpayer. Although many of these tax concepts also apply to corporations and partnerships, numerous tax concepts apply specifically to corporations or partnerships. An overview of these provisions is presented in Part VII. Comprehensive coverage of these topics appears in *West's Federal Taxation: Corporations, Partnerships, Estates, and Trusts.*

Chapter 20
Corporations and Partnerships

20

CORPORATIONS AND PARTNERSHIPS

LEARNING OBJECTIVES

After completing Chapter 20, you should be able to:

1. Identify those entities that are treated as corporations for Federal income tax purposes.

2. Contrast the income tax treatment of individuals with that applicable to corporations.

3. Recognize and calculate the tax deductions available only to corporations.

4. Understand the tax rules governing the formation of corporations.

5. Understand the tax rules governing the operation of corporations.

6. Understand the tax rules governing the liquidation of corporations.

7. Appreciate the utility and effect of the Subchapter S election.

8. Understand the tax consequences of forming and operating a partnership.

9. Evaluate the advantages and disadvantages of the various forms for conducting a business.

OUTLINE

What Is a Corporation?, 20–3

Compliance with State Law, 20–3

The Association Approach, 20–4

Limited Liability Companies, 20–4

Income Tax Considerations, 20–5

General Tax Consequences of Different Forms of Business Entities, 20–5

Individuals and Corporations Compared—An Overview, 20–5

Specific Provisions Compared, 20–6

Deductions Available Only to Corporations, 20–10

Determination of Corporate Tax Liability, 20–13

Corporate Filing Requirements, 20–14

Reconciliation of Corporate Taxable Income and Accounting Income, 20–14

Forming the Corporation, 20–17

Capital Contributions, 20–17

Transfers to Controlled Corporations, 20–18

Operating the Corporation, 20–19

Dividend Distributions, 20–19

Stock Redemptions, 20–22

Liquidating the Corporation, 20–22

General Rule of § 331, 20–22

Exception to the General Rule, 20–23

Basis Determination—§§ 334 and 338, 20–23

Effect of the Liquidation on the Corporation, 20–23

The S Election, 20–24

Justification for the Election, 20–24

Operational Rules, 20–26

Partnerships, 20–30

Nature of Partnership Taxation, 20–30

Partnership Formation, 20–30

Partnership Operation, 20–32

Tax Planning Considerations, 20–35

Corporate versus Noncorporate Forms of Business Organization, 20–35

Regular Corporation versus S Status, 20–35

Use of an Entity to Reduce the Family Income Tax Burden, 20–36

Until now this text has concentrated on the Federal income taxation of individual taxpayers. However, even the most basic business decisions require some awareness of the tax implications of other business forms.

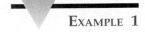

EXAMPLE 1

Gina and Tom are contemplating entering into a new business venture that will require additional capital investment by other parties. As the venture will involve financial risk, both Gina and Tom are concerned about personal liability. Further, they would prefer to avoid any income taxes at the entity level. Both Gina and Tom would like to take advantage of any losses the venture may generate during its formative period. ▼

In choosing the form for the venture, Gina and Tom will have to consider using a corporation. The corporate form limits a shareholder's liability to the amount invested in the stock. Regular corporations, however, are subject to the corporate income tax. Furthermore, losses incurred by corporations do not pass through to the shareholders. Perhaps the ideal solution would be to use the corporate form and elect to be taxed as an S corporation. The election would avoid the corporate income tax and permit the pass-through of losses while providing limited liability for the shareholders.

Although the resolution of the problem posed by Example 1 seems simple enough, it did not consider the possible use of a partnership. More important, the decision required *some* knowledge of corporations and the S corporation election. This chapter is intended to provide such knowledge by briefly reviewing the tax consequences of the various forms of business organization.

What Is a Corporation?

COMPLIANCE WITH STATE LAW

1   **LEARNING OBJECTIVE**
Identify those entities that are treated as corporations for Federal income tax purposes.

A company must comply with the specific requirements for corporate status under state law. For example, it is necessary to draft and file articles of incorporation with the state regulatory agency, be granted a charter, and issue stock to shareholders.

Compliance with state law, although important, is not the only requirement that must be met to qualify for corporate *tax* status. For example, a corporation qualifying under state law may be disregarded as a taxable entity if it is a mere sham lacking in economic substance. The key consideration is the degree of business activity conducted at the corporate level.

EXAMPLE 2   Gene and Mike are joint owners of a tract of unimproved real estate that they wish to protect from future creditors. Gene and Mike form Falcon Corporation, to which they transfer the land in return for all of the corporation's stock. The corporation merely holds title to the land and conducts no other activities. In all respects, Falcon Corporation meets the legal requirements of a corporation under applicable state law. Nevertheless, Falcon might not be recognized as a separate entity for corporate tax purposes under these facts.[1] ▼

EXAMPLE 3   Assume the same facts as in Example 2. In addition to holding title to the land, Falcon Corporation leases the property, collects rents, and pays the property taxes. Falcon probably would be treated as a corporation for Federal income tax purposes because of the scope of its activities. ▼

In some instances, the IRS has attempted to disregard (or collapse) a corporation in order to make the income taxable directly to the shareholders.[2] In other cases, the IRS has asserted that the corporation is a separate taxable entity so as to assess tax at the corporate level and to tax corporate distributions to shareholders as dividend income (double taxation).[3]

ETHICAL CONSIDERATIONS

Filing Status: Corporation versus Individual

Vernon owns an apartment project that he recently inherited from his mother. The property is located out of state, and its existence is unknown to Vernon's wife, Helen. Vernon and Helen are not getting along with each other, and a divorce appears imminent. To protect the apartment project from any property settlement incident to a divorce, Vernon transfers it to a newly formed corporation. Before any tax forms have been filed for the corporation, a major fire completely destroys the apartments. Since the property was not insured, a large casualty loss develops.

---

[1] See *Paymer v. Comm.*, 45–2 USTC ¶9353, 33 AFTR 1536, 150 F.2d 334 (CA–2, 1945).

[2] *Floyd Patterson*, 25 TCM 1230, T.C. Memo. 1966–239, *aff'd.* in 68–2 USTC ¶9471, 22 AFTR2d 5810 (CA–2, 1968).

[3] *Raffety Farms Inc. v. U.S.*, 75–1 USTC ¶9271, 35 AFTR2d 75–811, 511 F.2d 1234 (CA–8, 1975).

Vernon decides to claim the casualty loss on the separate individual income tax return he files. He plans to disregard the corporation because it was only created to hide assets from a spiteful spouse. As a result, he neither will file tax returns for the corporation nor notify the IRS that it ever was formed.

THE ASSOCIATION APPROACH

An organization not qualifying as a regular corporation under state law may nevertheless be taxed as a corporation under the association approach. The designation given to an entity under the state law is not controlling. For example, a partnership of physicians has been treated as an association even though state law prohibited the practice of medicine in the corporate form. The partnership thus was subject to the Federal income tax rules applicable to corporations.[4] Another sensitive area involves limited partnerships where the only general partner is a corporation. Unless certain prescribed guidelines are carefully followed, the IRS will treat the partnership as an association.[5]

Whether or not an entity will be considered an **association** for Federal income tax purposes depends upon the number of corporate characteristics it possesses. According to court decisions and the Regulations, corporate characteristics include the following:[6]

1. Associates.
2. An objective to carry on a business and divide the gains therefrom.
3. Continuity of life.
4. Centralized management.
5. Limited liability.
6. Free transferability of interests.

The Regulations state that an unincorporated organization shall not be classified as an association unless it possesses *more* corporate than noncorporate characteristics. In making this determination, the characteristics common to both corporate and noncorporate business organizations are to be disregarded. Both corporations and partnerships generally have associates (shareholders and partners) and an objective to carry on a business and divide the gains. Therefore, only if a partnership has at least three of attributes 3 through 6 will it be treated as an association (taxable as a corporation).

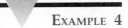

EXAMPLE 4

The Green Partnership agreement provides for the following: the partnership terminates with the withdrawal of a partner; all of the partners have authority to participate in the management of the partnership; all of the partners are individually liable for the debts of the partnership; and a partner may not freely transfer his or her interest in the partnership to another. None of corporate attributes 3 through 6 are present. Since the majority requirement of the Regulations is not satisfied, Green is not taxable as an association. ▼

LIMITED LIABILITY COMPANIES

At the beginning of 1994, 36 states had adopted statutes allowing **limited liability companies.** These organizations have the corporate feature of limited liability, so the owners have no personal liability for the debts of the business. This type of

---

[4] *U.S. v. Kintner,* 54–2 USTC ¶9626, 46 AFTR 995, 216 F.2d 418 (CA–5, 1954).

[5] Rev.Proc. 89–12, 1989–1 C.B. 798.
[6] Reg. § 301.7701–2(a).

organization is becoming increasingly popular for professional groups. In most cases, the owners want the organization to be treated as a partnership for Federal income tax purposes, so as to avoid the double tax resulting from operating as a corporation. Often, centralized management is present, but the other key corporate characteristics (i.e., continuity of life and free transferability of interests) are absent.[7]

INCOME TAX CONSIDERATIONS

GENERAL TAX CONSEQUENCES OF DIFFERENT FORMS OF BUSINESS ENTITIES

2   **LEARNING OBJECTIVE**
Contrast the income tax treatment of individuals with that applicable to corporations.

Business operations may be conducted as a sole proprietorship, as a partnership, or in corporate form.

- Sole proprietorships are not separate taxable entities. The owner of the business reports all business transactions on his or her individual income tax return.
- Partnerships are not subject to the income tax. Under the *conduit* concept, the various tax attributes of the partnership's operations flow through to the individual partners to be reported on their personal income tax returns.
- The regular corporate form of doing business carries with it the imposition of the corporate income tax. The corporation is recognized as a separate taxpaying entity. Income is taxed to the corporation as earned and taxed again to the shareholders as dividends when distributed.
- A regular corporation may elect to be taxed as an S corporation. This special treatment is similar (although not identical) to the partnership rules. Income tax is generally avoided at the corporate level, and shareholders are taxed currently on the taxable income of the S corporation.

INDIVIDUALS AND CORPORATIONS COMPARED— AN OVERVIEW

Similarities between Corporate and Individual Tax Rules

The gross income of a corporation is determined in much the same manner as for individuals. Both individuals and corporations are entitled to exclusions from gross income, such as interest on municipal bonds. Gains and losses from property transactions are also treated similarly. For example, whether a gain or loss is capital or ordinary depends on the nature and use of the asset rather than the type of taxpayer. Upon the sale or other taxable disposition of depreciable personalty, the recapture rules of § 1245 make no distinction between corporate and noncorporate taxpayers. In the case of the recapture of depreciation on real property (§ 1250), however, corporate taxpayers experience more severe tax consequences. As illustrated later, corporations must recognize as additional ordinary income 20 percent of the excess of the amount that would be recaptured under § 1245 over the amount recaptured under § 1250.

The business deductions of corporations parallel those available to individuals. Corporate deductions are allowed for all ordinary and necessary expenses

---

[7]See Chapter 13 of *West's Federal Taxation: Corporations, Partnerships, Estates, and Trusts.*

paid or incurred in carrying on a trade or business. Corporations may also deduct interest, certain taxes, losses, bad debts, depreciation, cost recovery, charitable contributions subject to corporate limitation rules, net operating losses, research and experimental expenditures, and other less common deductions.

Many of the tax credits available to individuals, such as the foreign tax credit, can be claimed by corporations. Not available to corporations are certain credits that are personal in nature. Examples of credits not available to corporations include the credit for child and dependent care expenses, the credit for the elderly or disabled, and the earned income credit.

Corporations usually have the same choices of accounting periods as do individuals. Like an individual, a corporation may choose a calendar year or a fiscal year for reporting purposes. Corporations do enjoy greater flexibility in the election of a tax year. For example, corporations usually can have different tax years from those of their shareholders. Also, a newly formed corporation generally has a free choice of any approved accounting period without having to obtain the consent of the IRS. As noted in Chapter 18, however, personal service corporations are subject to severe restrictions on the use of a fiscal year.

The use of the cash method of accounting is denied to large corporations (those with average annual gross receipts in excess of $5 million). Smaller corporations as well as qualified personal service corporations and other corporations engaged in the trade or business of farming have a choice between the cash or accrual method of accounting for tax purposes. Both individuals and corporations that maintain inventory for sale to customers are required to use the accrual method of accounting for determining sales and cost of goods sold.

Dissimilarities

Both noncorporate and corporate taxpayers are subject to progressive income tax rates. For individuals, the rates are 15, 28, 31, 36, and 39.6 percent. For corporations, the rates are 15, 25, 34, and 35 percent. Corporate taxpayers lose the benefits of the lower brackets (using a phase-out approach) once taxable income reaches a certain level. Noncorporate taxpayers, however, continue to enjoy the benefits of the lower brackets even though they have reached the higher taxable income levels.

Both corporate and noncorporate taxpayers are subject to the alternative minimum tax (AMT). For AMT purposes, many adjustments and tax preference items are the same for both, but other adjustments and tax preferences apply only to corporations or only to individuals. Corporate tax rates are discussed later in the chapter. The AMT is discussed at length in Chapter 12. See also the coverage in *West's Federal Taxation: Corporations, Partnerships, Estates, and Trusts.*

All allowable corporate deductions are treated as business expenses. The determination of adjusted gross income, so essential for individuals, has no relevance to corporations. Corporations need not be concerned with classifying deductions into *deduction for* and *deduction from* categories.[8]

SPECIFIC PROVISIONS COMPARED

Corporate and individual tax rules also differ in the following areas:

- Capital gains and losses.
- Recapture of depreciation.

---

[8] The standard deduction, itemized deductions, and personal and dependency exemptions are not available to corporations.

- Charitable contributions.
- Net operating losses.
- Special deductions for corporations.

Capital Gains and Losses

Both corporate and noncorporate taxpayers are required to aggregate gains and losses from the taxable sale or exchange of capital assets. (Refer to Chapter 16 for a description of the netting process that takes place after the aggregation has been completed.) For net long-term capital gains, individual taxpayers enjoy an advantage (the alternative tax). In no event will the gains be taxed at a rate in excess of 28 percent. In the case of corporations, all capital gains are treated as ordinary income. Therefore, the net long-term capital gains of a corporation could be taxed at a rate of 35 percent (the highest rate applicable to corporations).

Significant differences exist in the treatment of capital losses for income tax purposes. Individuals, for example, can annually deduct up to $3,000 of net capital losses against ordinary income. Corporations are not permitted to use net capital losses to offset ordinary income. Net capital losses can be used only to offset past or future capital gains.[9] Unlike individuals, corporations are not allowed an unlimited carryover period for capital losses. Instead, they may carry back excess capital losses to the three preceding years, applying them initially to the earliest year. If not exhausted by the carryback, remaining unused capital losses may be carried over for a period of five years from the year of the loss.[10]

When carried back or over, *both* short-term capital losses and long-term capital losses are treated as short-term capital losses by corporate taxpayers. For noncorporate taxpayers, a capital loss does not lose its identity. Thus, long-term capital losses of noncorporate taxpayers are carried forward as long-term capital losses, and short-term capital losses are carried forward as short-term capital losses.

EXAMPLE 5   Hawk Corporation, a calendar year taxpayer, incurs a long-term net capital loss of $5,000 for 1994. None of the capital loss may be deducted in 1994. Hawk may, however, carry the loss back to years 1991, 1992, and 1993 (in this order) and offset any capital gains recognized in these years. If the carryback does not exhaust the loss, the loss may be carried over to 1995, 1996, 1997, 1998, and 1999 (in this order). Such capital loss carrybacks or carryovers are treated as short-term capital losses. ▼

Recapture of Depreciation

Corporations selling depreciable real estate may have ordinary income in addition to that required by § 1250. Under § 291, the additional ordinary income element is 20 percent of the excess of the § 1245 recapture potential over the § 1250 recapture. As a result, the § 1231 gain is correspondingly decreased by the additional recapture.

EXAMPLE 6   Condor Corporation purchases residential real property on January 3, 1984, for $300,000. Accelerated cost recovery is taken in the amount of $226,250 before the property is sold on January 5, 1994, for $250,000. Straight-line cost recovery would have been $201,667 (using a 15-year recovery period under ACRS).

---

[9] §§ 1211(a) and (b).   [10] § 1212(a).

First, determine realized gain:

Sales price		$250,000
Less adjusted basis:		
Cost of property	$ 300,000	
Less cost recovery	(226,250)	(73,750)
Realized gain		$176,250

Second, determine § 1245 recapture potential. This is the lesser of $176,250 (realized gain) or $226,250 (cost recovery claimed), or $176,250. Third, determine § 1250 recapture amount:

Cost recovery taken	$ 226,250
Less straight-line cost recovery	(201,667)
§ 1250 ordinary income	$ 24,583

Fourth, because the taxpayer is a corporation, determine the additional § 291 amount:

§ 1245 recapture potential	$176,250
Less § 1250 recapture amount	(24,583)
Excess § 1245 recapture potential	$151,667
Apply § 291 percentage	× 20%
Additional ordinary income under § 291	$ 30,333

Condor Corporation's realized and recognized gain of $176,250 is accounted for as follows:

Ordinary income under § 1250	$ 24,583
Ordinary income under § 291	30,333
§ 1231 gain	121,334
Total recognized gain	$176,250

▼

Charitable Contributions

Generally, a charitable contribution deduction is allowed only for the tax year in which the payment is made. However, an important exception is made for accrual basis corporations. The deduction may be claimed in the tax year *preceding* payment if the following conditions are satisfied:

* The contribution is authorized by the board of directors by the end of that tax year *and*
* The contribution is paid on or before the fifteenth day of the third month of the next tax year.[11]

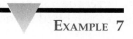

EXAMPLE 7

On December 28, 1994, the board of directors of Dove Corporation, a calendar year, accrual basis taxpayer, authorizes a $5,000 donation to a qualified charity. The donation is paid on March 14, 1995. Dove Corporation may claim the $5,000 donation as a deduction for 1994. As an alternative, Dove may claim the deduction in 1995 (the year of payment). ▼

Like individuals, corporations are not permitted an unlimited charitable contribution deduction. In any one year, a corporate taxpayer is limited to 10 percent of taxable income. For this purpose, taxable income is computed without regard to the charitable contribution deduction, any net operating loss carryback

[11]§ 170(a)(2).

or capital loss carryback, or the dividends received deduction.[12] Any contributions in excess of the 10 percent limitation are carried over to the five succeeding tax years. Any carryover must be added to subsequent contributions and is subject to the 10 percent limitation. In applying the limitation, the most recent contributions must be deducted first.[13]

EXAMPLE 8

During 1994, Eagle Corporation (a calendar year taxpayer) had the following income and expenses:

Income from operations	$140,000
Expenses from operations	110,000
Dividends received	10,000
Charitable contributions made in 1994	5,000

For the purposes of the 10% limitation only, Eagle Corporation's taxable income is $40,000 ($140,000 − $110,000 + $10,000). Consequently, the allowable charitable contribution deduction for 1994 is $4,000 (10% × $40,000). The $1,000 unused portion of the contribution is carried over to 1995, 1996, 1997, 1998, and 1999 (in that order) until exhausted. ▼

EXAMPLE 9

Assume the same facts as in Example 8. In 1995, Eagle Corporation has taxable income (after adjustments) of $50,000 and makes a charitable contribution of $4,800. The maximum deduction allowed for 1995 is $5,000 (10% × $50,000). The first $4,800 of the allowed deduction must be allocated to the 1995 contributions, and the $200 excess is carried over from 1994. The remaining $800 of the 1994 contribution is carried over to 1996, etc. ▼

As noted in Chapter 10, the deduction for charitable contributions of ordinary income property is limited to the lesser of the fair market value or the adjusted basis of the property. A special rule permits a corporation to contribute inventory (ordinary income property) to certain charitable organizations and receive a deduction equal to the adjusted basis plus one-half of the difference between the fair market value and the adjusted basis of the property.[14] In no event, however, may the deduction exceed twice the adjusted basis of the property. To qualify for this exception, the inventory must be used by the charity in its exempt purpose for the care of *children*, the *ill*, or the *needy*.

EXAMPLE 10

In the current year, Robin Company (a retail clothier) donates sweaters and overcoats to Sheltering Arms (a qualified charity caring for the homeless). The clothing is inventory and has a basis of $10,000 and a fair market value of $14,000. If Robin is a corporation, the charitable contribution that results is $12,000 [$10,000 (basis) + $2,000 (50% of the appreciation of $4,000)]. In contrast, if Robin is not a corporation, the charitable contribution is limited to $10,000 (basis). ▼

Net Operating Losses

The computation of a net operating loss (NOL) for individuals was discussed in Chapter 7. Corporations are not subject to the complex adjustments required for individuals (e.g., a corporation has no adjustments for nonbusiness deductions or capital gains and losses). Corporations are subject to fewer adjustments than individuals are because a corporation's loss more clearly approximates a true

[12] § 170(b)(2).
[13] § 170(d)(2).

[14] § 170(e)(3).

economic loss. Artificial deductions (e.g., personal and dependency exemptions) that merely generate paper losses are not permitted for corporations.

In computing the NOL of a corporation, the dividends received deduction (discussed below) can be claimed in determining the amount of the loss.[15] Corporate NOLs may be carried back 3 years and forward 15 years (or taxpayers may elect to forgo the carryback period) to offset taxable income for those years.

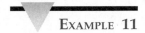

EXAMPLE 11

In 1994, Wren Corporation has gross income of $200,000 and deductions of $300,000, excluding the dividends received deduction. Wren received taxable dividends of $100,000 from Exxon stock. Wren has an NOL of $170,000, computed as follows:

Gross income (including Exxon dividends)		$200,000
Less: Business deductions	$300,000	
Dividends received deduction (70% × $100,000)	70,000	370,000
Taxable income (loss)		($170,000) ▼

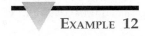

EXAMPLE 12

Assume the same facts as in Example 11 and that Wren Corporation had taxable income of $40,000 in 1991. The NOL of $170,000 is carried back to 1991 (unless Wren elects not to carry back the loss to that year). The carryover to 1992 is $130,000, computed as follows:

Taxable income for 1991	$ 40,000
Less: NOL carryback from 1994	170,000
Carryover of unabsorbed 1994 loss	($130,000) ▼

In Example 12, the carryback to 1991 might have been ill-advised if Wren Corporation had little, if any, taxable income in 1992 and 1993 and if it anticipated large amounts of taxable income in the immediate future. In that case, the *election to forgo* the carryback might generate greater tax savings. In this regard, three points should be considered. First, the time value of the tax refund that is lost by not using the carryback procedure must be considered. Second, the election to forgo an NOL carryback is irrevocable. Thus, it cannot be changed later if the future high profits do not materialize. Third, future increases or decreases in corporate income tax rates that can reasonably be anticipated should be considered.

DEDUCTIONS AVAILABLE ONLY TO CORPORATIONS

Dividends Received Deduction

3   LEARNING OBJECTIVE
Recognize and calculate the tax deductions available only to corporations.

The purpose of the **dividends received deduction** is to prevent triple taxation. Without the deduction, income paid to a corporation in the form of a dividend would be subject to taxation for a second time (once to the distributing corporation) with no corresponding deduction to the distributing corporation. A third level of tax would be assessed on the shareholders when the recipient corporation distributed the income to its shareholders. Since the dividends received deduction may be less than 100 percent, the law provides only partial relief.

The amount of the dividends received deduction depends upon the percentage of ownership the recipient corporate shareholder holds in the corporation making the dividend distribution.[16] For dividends received or accrued, the *deduction percentage* is summarized as follows:

---

[15]§ 172(d).   [16]§ 243(a).

Percentage of Ownership by Corporate Shareholder	Deduction Percentage
Less than 20%	70%
20% or more (but less than 80%)	80%
80% or more	100%

The dividends received deduction may be limited to a percentage of the taxable income of a corporation computed without regard to the NOL deduction, the dividends received deduction, or any capital loss carryback to the current tax year. The percentage of taxable income limitation corresponds to the deduction percentage. Thus, if a corporate shareholder owns less than 20 percent of the stock in the distributing corporation, the dividends received deduction is limited to 70 percent of taxable income (as previously defined). However, this limitation does not apply if the corporation has an NOL for the current taxable year.[17]

In working with these myriad rules, the following steps need to be taken:

1. Multiply the dividends received by the deduction percentage.
2. Multiply the taxable income (as previously defined) by the deduction percentage.
3. The deduction is limited to the lesser of Step 1 or Step 2, unless subtracting the amount derived from Step 1 from taxable income (as previously defined) generates a negative number. If so, the amount derived in Step 1 should be used.

TAX IN THE NEWS

THERE MAY BE NO FREE PARKING

Many factors influence the choice of legal form for a business entity. Frequently cited as a benefit for the corporate form is limited liability. In addition, as a result of the Revenue Reconciliation Act of 1993, the maximum corporate tax rate (35 percent) is now lower than the maximum individual tax rate (39.6 percent).

A new factor has now arrived on the scene—free parking. The Energy Policy Act of 1992 makes what previously was free parking subject to taxation. An exclusion still is provided to the extent the value of the free parking does not exceed $155 per month.

However, the exclusion treatment does not apply to many accountants, lawyers, and consultants. The reason is that many professionals operate in the partnership form. For free parking to be excludible, the taxpayer receiving it must be an employee. For this purpose, a partner does not qualify as an employee.

The apparent solution is to change the business form to a corporation. One firm that has decided to do so, partially based on the free parking exclusion, is the Washington law firm McDermott, Will, & Emery. According to Mary Hevener, a fringe benefit specialist with the firm, it was the free parking that pushed them to incorporate: "It was the last straw."

SOURCE: Information from Paulette Thomas, "New Tax Means All Free Parking Won't Be Free," *Wall Street Journal*, January 10, 1994, pp. B1, B5.

---

[17] § 246(b).

EXAMPLE 13

Crane, Osprey, and Gull Corporations, three unrelated calendar year corporations, have the following transactions for 1994:

	Crane Corporation	Osprey Corporation	Gull Corporation
Gross income from operations	$ 400,000	$ 320,000	$ 260,000
Expenses from operations	(340,000)	(340,000)	(340,000)
Dividends received from domestic corporations (less than 20% ownership)	200,000	200,000	200,000
Taxable income before the dividends received deduction	$ 260,000	$ 180,000	$ 120,000

In determining the dividends received deduction, use the step procedure just described:

	Crane Corporation	Osprey Corporation	Gull Corporation
Step 1: (70% × $200,000)	$140,000	$140,000	$140,000
Step 2:			
70% × $260,000 (taxable income)	$182,000		
70% × $180,000 (taxable income)		$126,000	
70% × $120,000 (taxable income)			$ 84,000
Step 3:			
Lesser of Step 1 or Step 2	$140,000	$126,000	
Generates an NOL			$140,000

Osprey Corporation is subject to the 70 percent of taxable income limitation. It does not qualify for the loss rule treatment, since subtracting $140,000 (Step 1) from $180,000 does not yield a loss. Gull Corporation qualifies for the loss rule treatment because subtracting $140,000 (Step 1) from $120,000 does yield a loss. In summary, each corporation has the following dividends received deduction for 1994: $140,000 for Crane, $126,000 for Osprey, and $140,000 for Gull. If a corporation already has an NOL before any dividends received deduction is claimed, the full dividends received deduction (as calculated in Step 1) is allowed.

Deduction of Organizational Expenditures

Under § 248, a corporation may elect to amortize organizational expenses over a period of 60 months or more. If the election is not made on a timely basis, the expenditures cannot be deducted until the corporation ceases to conduct business and liquidates. The election is made in a statement attached to the corporation's return for its first taxable year.

Organizational expenditures include the following:

- Legal services incident to organization (e.g., drafting the corporate charter, by-laws, minutes of organizational meetings, terms of original stock certificates).
- Necessary accounting services.

- Expenses of temporary directors and of organizational meetings of directors and shareholders.
- Fees paid to the state of incorporation.

Expenditures that do not qualify include those connected with issuing or selling shares of stock or other securities (e.g., commissions, professional fees, and printing costs) or with the transfer of assets to a corporation. These expenditures are generally added to the capital account and are not subject to amortization.

DETERMINATION OF CORPORATE TAX LIABILITY

Income Tax Rates

The Revenue Reconciliation Act of 1993 revised the corporate rate schedule for tax years beginning after 1992. The rates *were not changed for taxable income of $10 million or less.* For corporations with taxable income in excess of $10 million, a new rate of 35 percent applies to the excess. As additional tax at the rate of 3 percent (not to exceed $100,000) is imposed on taxable income in excess of $15 million.[18] In effect, the rate brackets on corporations are as follows:

Taxable Income	Tax Rate
Not over $50,000	15%
Over $50,000 but not over $75,000	25%
Over $75,000 but not over $100,000	34%
Over $100,000 but not over $335,000	39%*
Over $335,000 but not over $10,000,000	34%
Over $10,000,000 but not over $15,000,000	35%
Over $15,000,000 but not over $18,333,333	38%**
Over $18,333,333	35%

*Five percent of this rate represents a phase-out of the benefits of the lower tax rates on the first $75,000 of taxable income.
**Three percent of this rate represents a phase-out of the benefits of the lower tax rate (34% rather than 35%) on the first $10 million of taxable income.

EXAMPLE 14

A calendar year corporation has taxable income of $90,000 for 1994. The income tax liability will be $18,850 determined as follows: $7,500 (15% × $50,000) + $6,250 (25% × $25,000) + $5,100 (34% × $15,000).

If the corporate taxable income were $17,000,000, the corporate tax liability would be $5,910,000.

34% × $10,000,000	=	$3,400,000
35% × 5,000,000	=	1,750,000
38% × 2,000,000	=	760,000
		$5,910,000

Qualified personal service corporations are taxed at a flat 35 percent rate on all taxable income. They do not enjoy the tax savings of the lower brackets. For this purpose, a *qualified* **personal service corporation** is one that is substantially

---

[18] § 11(b). Corporations with a fiscal year that includes some of 1992 may have to make a weighted-average computation. § 15.

employee owned and engages in one of the following activities: health, law, engineering, architecture, accounting, actuarial science, performing arts, or consulting.

Alternative Minimum Tax

Corporations are subject to an alternative minimum tax (AMT) that is structured in the same manner as that applicable to individuals. The AMT for corporations, as for individuals, defines a more expansive tax base than for the regular tax. Like individuals, corporations are required to apply a minimum tax rate to the expanded base and pay the difference between the tentative AMT liability and the regular tax. Many of the adjustments and tax preference items necessary to arrive at alternative minimum taxable income (AMTI) are the same for individuals and corporations. Although the objective of the AMT is the same for individuals and for corporations, the rate and exemptions are different. Computation of the AMT is discussed in Chapter 12.[19]

CORPORATE FILING REQUIREMENTS

A corporation must file a return whether it has taxable income or not.[20] A corporation that was not in existence throughout an entire annual accounting period is required to file a return for the fraction of the year during which it was in existence. In addition, the corporation must file a return even though it has ceased to do business if it has valuable claims for which it will bring suit. It is relieved of filing returns once it ceases business and dissolves.

The corporate return is filed on Form 1120 unless the corporation is a small corporation entitled to file the shorter Form 1120–A. Among the *several* requirements for filing Form 1120–A are gross receipts (or sales) of less than $500,000 and total assets of less than $500,000. Corporations making the S corporation election (discussed later in the chapter) file on Form 1120S.

The return must be filed on or before the fifteenth day of the third month following the close of the corporation's tax year. Corporations can receive an automatic extension of six months for filing the corporate return by filing Form 7004 by the due date of the return. However, the IRS may terminate an extension by mailing a 10-day notice to the taxpayer corporation.[21]

A corporation must make payments of estimated tax unless its tax liability can reasonably be expected to be less than $500.[22] For 1994, the payments must equal 100 percent of the corporation's final tax. These payments may be made in four installments due on or before the fifteenth day of the fourth, sixth, ninth, and twelfth months of the corporate taxable year. The full amount of the unpaid tax is due on the date of the return. Failure to make the required estimated tax prepayments will result in a nondeductible penalty being imposed on the corporation. The penalty can be avoided, however, if any of various exceptions apply.[23]

RECONCILIATION OF CORPORATE TAXABLE INCOME AND ACCOUNTING INCOME

Taxable income and accounting net income are seldom the same amount. For example, a difference may arise if the corporation uses accelerated depreciation for tax purposes and straight-line depreciation for accounting purposes.

---

[19] See also the coverage in *West's Federal Taxation: Corporations, Partnerships, Estates, and Trusts.*
[20] § 6012(a)(2).

[21] § 6081.
[22] § 6655(f).
[23] See § 6655 for the penalty involved and the various exceptions.

Many items of income for accounting purposes, such as proceeds from a life insurance policy on the death of a corporate officer and interest on municipal bonds, may not be includible in calculating taxable income. Some expense items for accounting purposes, such as expenses to produce tax-exempt income, estimated warranty reserves, a net capital loss, and Federal income taxes, are not deductible for tax purposes.

Schedule M–1 on the last page of Form 1120 is used to reconcile accounting net income (net income after Federal income taxes) with taxable income (as computed on the corporate tax return before the deduction for a net operating loss and the dividends received deduction). In the left-hand column of Schedule M–1, net income per books is added to the following: the Federal income tax liability for the year, the excess of capital losses over capital gains (which cannot be deducted in the current year), income for tax purposes that is not income in the current year for accounting purposes, and expenses recorded on the books that are not deductible on the tax return. In the right-hand column, income recorded on the books that is not currently taxable or is tax-exempt and deductions for tax purposes that are not expenses for accounting purposes are totaled and subtracted from the left-hand column total to arrive at taxable income (before the net operating loss or dividends received deductions).

EXAMPLE 15

During 1994, Crow Corporation had the following transactions:

Net income per books (after tax)	$92,400
Taxable income	50,000
Federal income tax liability (15% × $50,000)	7,500
Interest income from tax-exempt bonds	5,000
Interest paid on loan, the proceeds of which were used to purchase the tax-exempt bonds	500
Life insurance proceeds received as a result of the death of a key employee	50,000
Premiums paid on key employee life insurance policy	2,600
Excess of capital losses over capital gains	2,000

For book and tax purposes, Crow determines depreciation under the straight-line method. Crow's Schedule M–1 for the current year follows.

Schedule M-1	**Reconciliation of Income (Loss) per Books With Income per Return** (See instructions.)		
1 Net income (loss) per books	92,400	**7** Income recorded on books this year not included on this return (itemize):	
2 Federal income tax	7,500	Tax-exempt interest $ 5,000 Life	
3 Excess of capital losses over capital gains .	2,000	insurance proceeds on key	
4 Income subject to tax not recorded on books this year (itemize): _____		employee $50,000	55,000
_____		**8** Deductions on this return not charged against book income this year (itemize):	
5 Expenses recorded on books this year not deducted on this return (itemize):		**a** Depreciation . . . . $ _____	
a Depreciation . . . . $ _____		**b** Contributions carryover $ _____	
b Contributions carryover $ _____		_____	
c Travel and entertainment $ Int. on tax-exempt bonds $500, Prem. on key employee ins. $2,600	3,100	_____	
6 Add lines 1 through 5	105,000	**9** Add lines 7 and 8	55,000
		10 Income (line 28, page 1)—line 6 less line 9	50,000

Schedule M–2 reconciles unappropriated retained earnings at the beginning of the year with unappropriated retained earnings at year-end. Beginning balance plus net income per books, as entered on line 1 of Schedule M–1, less dividend distributions during the year equals ending retained earnings. Other sources of increases or decreases in retained earnings are also listed on Schedule M–2.

Summary of Income Tax Consequences

	Individuals	Corporations
Computation of gross income	§ 61.	§ 61.
Computation of taxable income	§§ 62, 63(b) through (h).	§ 63(a). Concept of AGI has no relevance.
Deductions	Trade or business (§ 162); nonbusiness (§ 212); some personal and employee expenses (generally deductible as itemized deductions).	Trade or business (§ 162).
Charitable contributions	Limited in any tax year to 50% of AGI; 30% for long-term capital gain property unless election is made to reduce fair market value of gift; 20% for long-term capital gain property contributed to private nonoperating foundations.	Limited in any tax year to 10% of taxable income computed without regard to the charitable contribution deduction, net operating loss or capital loss carryback, and dividends received deduction.
	Time of deduction—year in which payment is made.	Time of deduction—year in which payment is made unless accrual basis taxpayer. Accrual basis corporation may take deduction in year preceding payment if contribution was authorized by board of directors by end of that year and contribution is paid by fifteenth day of third month of following year.
Casualty losses	$100 floor on nonbusiness casualty and theft losses; nonbusiness casualty and theft losses deductible only to extent losses exceed 10% of AGI.	Deductible in full.
Depreciation recapture for § 1250 property	Recaptured to extent accelerated depreciation exceeds straight-line.	20% of excess of amount that would be recaptured under § 1245 over amount recaptured under § 1250 is additional ordinary income under § 291.
Net operating loss	Adjusted for nonbusiness deductions over nonbusiness income and for personal and dependency exemptions.	Generally no adjustments.
Dividend exclusion or deduction	None.	Generally 70% of dividends received.
Long-term capital gains	Taxed at a rate no higher than 28%.	Taxed using regular corporate rates.
Capital losses	Only $3,000 of capital loss can offset ordinary income; loss is carried forward indefinitely to offset capital gains or ordinary income up to $3,000; carryovers remain long term or short term (as the case may be).	Can offset only capital gains; carried back three years and forward five years; carrybacks and carryovers are treated as short-term losses.
Passive activity losses	Generally deductible only against income from passive activities.	For regular corporations, no limitation on deductibility. Personal service corporations and certain closely held corporations, however, are subject to same limitations as imposed on individuals. A closely held corporation is one where 5 or fewer individuals own more than 50% of the stock either directly or indirectly.

	Individuals	Corporations
Alternative minimum tax	Applied at a graduated rate schedule of 26% and 28% to AMT base (taxable income as modified by certain adjustments plus preference items minus exemption amount); exemption allowed depending on filing status (e.g., $45,000 for married filing jointly); exemption phase-out begins when AMTI reaches a certain amount (e.g., $150,000 for married filing jointly).	Applied at a 20% rate to AMT base (taxable income as modified by certain adjustments plus preference items minus exemption amount); $40,000 exemption allowed but phase-out begins once AMTI reaches $150,000; adjustments and tax preference items similar to those applicable to individuals but also include 75% of adjusted current earnings (ACE) over AMTI.
Tax rates	Progressive with five rates (15%, 28%, 31%, 36%, and 39.6%).	Progressive with four rates (15%, 25%, 34%, and 35%); lower brackets phased out at higher levels.

EXAMPLE 16

Assume the same facts as in Example 15. Crow Corporation's beginning balance in unappropriated retained earnings is $125,000, and Crow distributed a cash dividend of $30,000 to its shareholders during the year. Based on these further assumptions, Crow has the following Schedule M–2 for the current year.

Schedule M-2	Analysis of Unappropriated Retained Earnings per Books (Line 25, Schedule L)				
1	Balance at beginning of year	125,000	5 Distributions: a Cash		30,000
2	Net income (loss) per books	92,400	b Stock		
3	Other increases (itemize):		c Property		
			6 Other decreases (itemize):		
4	Add lines 1, 2, and 3	217,400	7 Add lines 5 and 6		30,000
			8 Balance at end of year (line 4 less line 7)		187,400

FORMING THE CORPORATION

CAPITAL CONTRIBUTIONS

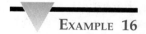

4 **LEARNING OBJECTIVE**
Understand the tax rules governing the formation of corporations.

The receipt of money or property in exchange for capital stock produces neither recognized gain nor loss to the recipient corporation.[24] Gross income of a corporation does not include shareholders' contributions of money or property to the capital of the corporation.[25] Contributions by nonshareholders are also excluded from the gross income of a corporation.[26] The basis of the property (capital transfers by nonshareholders) to the corporation is zero.

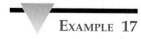

EXAMPLE 17

A city donates land worth $200,000 to Cardinal Corporation as an inducement for it to locate in the city. The receipt of the land does not represent gross income. The land's basis to the corporation is zero. ▼

Thin Capitalization

The advantages of capitalizing a corporation with debt may be substantial. Interest on debt is deductible by the corporation, while dividend payments are not.

---

[24] § 1032.
[25] § 118.

[26] *Edwards v. Cuba Railroad Co.,* 1 USTC ¶139, 5 AFTR 5398, 45 S.Ct. 614 (USSC, 1925).

Further, the shareholders are not taxed on loan repayments unless the payments exceed basis. If a company is capitalized solely with common stock, subsequent repayments of such capital contributions are likely to be treated as dividends to the shareholders.

In certain instances, the IRS will contend that debt is really an equity interest (**thin capitalization**) and will deny the shareholders the tax advantages of debt financing. If the debt instrument has too many features of stock, it may be treated as a form of stock, and principal and interest payments are treated as dividends.[27]

The form of the instrument will not assure debt treatment, but failure to observe certain formalities in creating the debt may lead to an assumption that the purported debt is a form of stock. The debt should be in proper legal form, bear a legitimate rate of interest, have a definite maturity date, and be repaid on a timely basis. Payments should not be contingent upon earnings. Further, the debt should not be subordinated to other liabilities, and proportionate holdings of stock and debt should be avoided or minimized.

TRANSFERS TO CONTROLLED CORPORATIONS

Without special provisions in the Code, a transfer of property to a corporation in exchange for its stock would be a sale or exchange of property and would constitute a taxable transaction to the transferor shareholder. Section 351 provides for the nonrecognition of gain or loss upon such transfers of property if the transferors are in control of the corporation immediately after the transfer. Gain or loss is merely postponed in a manner similar to a like-kind exchange.[28] The following requirements must be met to qualify under § 351:

- The transferors must be in control of the corporation immediately after the exchange. *Control* is defined as ownership of at least 80 percent of the total combined voting power of all classes of stock entitled to vote and at least 80 percent of the total number of shares of all other classes of stock.[29]
- Realized gain (but not loss) is recognized to the extent that the transferors receive property other than stock. Such nonqualifying property is commonly referred to as boot.

If the requirements of § 351 are satisfied and no boot is involved, nonrecognition of gain or loss is *mandatory.*

Basis Considerations and Computation of Gain

The nonrecognition of gain or loss is accompanied by a carryover of basis. The basis of stock received in a § 351 transfer is determined as follows:

- Start with the adjusted basis of the property transferred by the shareholder.
- Add any gain recognized by the shareholder as a result of the transfer.
- Subtract the fair market value of any boot received by the shareholder from the corporation.[30]

The basis of properties received by the corporation is the basis in the hands of the transferor increased by the amount of any gain recognized to the transferor shareholder.[31]

---

[27] Section 385 lists several factors that might be used to determine whether a debtor-creditor relationship or a shareholder-corporation relationship exists.

[28] Refer to the discussion in Chapter 15.

[29] § 368(c).

[30] § 358(a).

[31] § 362(a).

EXAMPLE 18

Ann and Lori form Bluejay Corporation. Ann transfers property with an adjusted basis of $30,000 and a fair market value of $60,000 for 50% of the stock. Lori transfers property with an adjusted basis of $40,000 and a fair market value of $60,000 for the remaining 50% of the stock. The realized gain ($30,000 for Ann and $20,000 for Lori) is not recognized on the transfer because the transfer qualifies under § 351. The basis of the stock to Ann is $30,000, and the basis of the stock to Lori is $40,000. Bluejay Corporation has a basis of $30,000 in the property transferred by Ann and a basis of $40,000 in the property transferred by Lori. ▼

EXAMPLE 19

Mike and John form Condor Corporation with the following investments: Mike transfers property (adjusted basis of $30,000 and fair market value of $70,000), and John transfers cash of $60,000. Each receives 50 shares of the Condor stock, but Mike also receives $10,000 in cash. Assume each share of the Condor stock is worth $1,200. Mike's realized gain is $40,000, determined as follows:

Value of the Condor stock received [50 (shares) × $1,200 (value per share)]	$ 60,000
Cash received	10,000
Amount realized	$ 70,000
Less basis of property transferred	(30,000)
Realized gain	$ 40,000

Mike's recognized gain is $10,000, the lesser of the realized gain ($40,000) or the fair market value of the boot received ($10,000). Mike's basis in the Condor stock is $30,000, computed as follows:

Basis in the property transferred	$ 30,000
Plus recognized gain	10,000
	$ 40,000
Less boot received	(10,000)
Basis to Mike of the Condor stock	$ 30,000

Condor Corporation's basis in the property transferred by Mike is $40,000 [$30,000 (basis of the property to Mike) + $10,000 (gain recognized by Mike)]. John neither realizes nor recognizes gain or loss and will have a basis in the Condor stock of $60,000. ▼

Shareholders who receive noncash boot have a basis in the property equal to the fair market value. The receipt of stock for the performance of *services* always results in ordinary income to the transferor shareholder. An example might be an attorney who does not charge a fee for incorporating a business but instead receives the value equivalent in stock of the newly formed corporation.

OPERATING THE CORPORATION

DIVIDEND DISTRIBUTIONS

5 LEARNING OBJECTIVE
Understand the tax rules governing the operation of corporations.

Corporate distributions of cash or property to shareholders are treated as ordinary dividend income to the extent the corporation has accumulated *or* current earnings and profits (E & P).[32] In determining the source of the distribution, a dividend is deemed to have been made initially from current E & P.

---

[32] § 316.

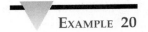

EXAMPLE 20   As of January 1, 1994, Teal Corporation has a deficit in accumulated E & P of $30,000. For tax year 1994, it has current E & P of $10,000. In 1994, the corporation distributes $5,000 to its shareholders. The $5,000 distribution is treated as a taxable dividend, since it is deemed to have been made from current E & P. This is the case even though Teal still has a deficit in its accumulated E & P at the end of 1994. ▼

If a corporate distribution is not covered by E & P (either current or past), it is treated as a return of capital (refer to the discussion of the recovery of capital doctrine in Chapter 4). This treatment allows the shareholder to apply the amount of the distribution against the basis of the stock investment and therefore represents a nontaxable return of capital. Any amount received in excess of the stock basis is classified as a capital gain (if the stock is a capital asset in the hands of the shareholder).

EXAMPLE 21   When Mallard Corporation has no E & P (either current or accumulated), it distributes cash of $30,000 to its sole shareholder, Helen. The basis of Helen's stock investment is $20,000. Based on these facts, the $30,000 distribution Helen receives is accounted for as follows:

Return of capital (nontaxable)	$20,000
Capital gain	10,000
Total amount of distribution	$30,000

After the distribution, Helen has a basis of zero in her stock investment. ▼

Concept of Earnings and Profits

The term **earnings and profits** is not defined in the Code, although § 312 does include certain transactions that affect E & P. Although E & P and the accounting concept of retained earnings have certain similarities, they differ in numerous respects. For example, although a nontaxable stock dividend is treated as a capitalization of retained earnings for accounting purposes, it does not decrease E & P for tax purposes. Taxable dividends do reduce E & P but cannot yield a deficit. Referring to Example 21, after the distribution, Mallard Corporation's E & P remains zero rather than being a negative amount.

Generally, *current E & P* for a taxable year is taxable income plus or minus certain adjustments (e.g., an addition is made for tax-exempt income). Federal income taxes are subtracted from taxable income in arriving at current E & P. *Accumulated E & P* is the sum of the corporation's past current E & P. A detailed discussion of the concept of E & P is beyond the scope of this chapter.

Property Dividends

A distribution of property to a shareholder is measured by the fair market value of the property on the date of distribution. The shareholder's basis in the property received is also the fair market value.[33]

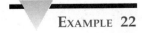

EXAMPLE 22   Drake Corporation has E & P of $60,000. It distributes land with a fair market value of $50,000 (adjusted basis of $30,000) to its sole shareholder, Art. Art has a taxable dividend of $50,000 and a basis in the land of $50,000. ▼

---

[33] § 301.

A corporation that distributes appreciated property to its shareholders as a dividend must recognize the amount of the appreciation as gain.

EXAMPLE 23

Assume the same facts as in Example 22. Drake Corporation must recognize a gain of $20,000 on the distribution it made to Art. ▼

However, if the property distributed has a basis in excess of its fair market value, the distributing corporation cannot recognize any loss.

Constructive Dividends

Many taxpayers mistakenly assume that dividend consequences do not take place unless the distribution carries the formalities of a dividend (declaration date, record date, payment date). They further assume that dividends must be paid out to all shareholders on a pro rata basis. This may not be the case when closely held corporations are involved. Here, the key to dividend treatment depends upon whether the shareholders derive a benefit from the corporation that cannot be otherwise classified (e.g., reasonable salary). The following are examples of **constructive dividends**:

- Salaries paid to shareholder-employees that are not reasonable (refer to Example 6 in Chapter 6).
- Interest on debt owed by the corporation to shareholders that is reclassified as equity because the corporation is thinly capitalized (refer to the earlier discussion in this chapter).
- Excessive rent paid by a corporation for the use of shareholder property. Whether the rent is excessive is to be tested by use of the arm's length standard (refer to Example 24 in Chapter 1).
- Advances to shareholders that are not bona fide loans.
- Interest-free (or below-market) loans to shareholders. In this situation, the dividend component is the difference between the interest provided for, if any, and that calculated using the market rate.
- Shareholder use of corporate property for less than an arm's length rate.
- Absorption by the corporation of a shareholder's personal expenses.
- Bargain purchase of corporate property by shareholders.

Like regular dividends, constructive dividends must be covered by E & P to carry dividend income consequences to the shareholders. As noted above, however, constructive dividends need not be available to all shareholders on a pro rata basis.

Although dividends reduce the E & P of a corporation, they are not deductible for income tax purposes. In this regard, certain constructive dividends could have subtle tax consequences for all parties concerned.

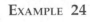

EXAMPLE 24

Grouse Corporation makes a loan to one of its shareholders, Hal. No interest is provided for, but application of the market rate would produce $20,000 of interest for the term of the loan. Presuming the loan is bona fide, the following results occur:

- Hal has dividend income of $20,000.
- Grouse Corporation has interest income of $20,000.
- Hal might obtain an interest deduction of $20,000.

Not only does Grouse Corporation have to recognize income of $20,000, but it also obtains no income tax deduction for the $20,000 constructive dividend. ▼

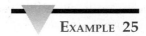

EXAMPLE 25

Assume the same facts as in Example 24, except that the loan to Hal was not bona fide. In this event, the full amount of the loan is regarded as a dividend to Hal. Therefore, the interest element is not a factor, since no bona fide loan ever existed. ▼

STOCK REDEMPTIONS

If a corporation redeems a shareholder's stock (a **stock redemption**), one of two possible outcomes occurs:

- The redemption may qualify as a sale or exchange under § 302 or § 303. In that case, capital gain or loss treatment usually applies to the qualifying shareholders.
- The redemption will be treated as a dividend under § 301, provided the distributing corporation has E & P.

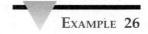

EXAMPLE 26

Reba owns 300 shares of Snipe Corporation stock as an investment. The shares have a basis to Reba of $100 each, for a total of $30,000. When the fair market value of a share is $200, Snipe redeems 200 of Reba's shares. If the redemption qualifies for sale or exchange treatment, the result is a capital gain to Reba of $20,000 [$40,000 (redemption price) – $20,000 (basis in 200 shares)]. Reba's basis in the remaining 100 shares is $10,000 [$30,000 (basis in the original shares) – $20,000 (basis in the shares redeemed)]. ▼

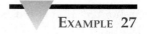

EXAMPLE 27

Assume the same facts as in Example 26, except that the redemption does not qualify for sale or exchange treatment. Presuming adequate E & P, the redemption results in $40,000 dividend income. Reba's basis in the remaining 100 shares now becomes $30,000, or $300 per share. ▼

A stock redemption qualifies as a sale or exchange if it meets any of the safe harbors of § 302 or § 303.

LIQUIDATING THE CORPORATION

6   LEARNING OBJECTIVE
Understand the tax rules governing the liquidation of corporations.

Unlike dividend distributions or stock redemptions, where the distributing corporation continues its operations, **liquidating distributions** occur during the termination of the business. All debts are paid, and any remaining corporate assets are distributed pro rata to the shareholders in exchange for their stock. Once these distributions are completed, the corporation undergoing liquidation will cease to be a separate tax entity.

GENERAL RULE OF § 331

Under the general rule, the shareholders recognize gain or loss in a corporate liquidation. The amount of recognized gain or loss is measured by the difference between the fair market value of the assets received from the corporation and the adjusted basis of the stock surrendered. The shareholders recognize capital gain or loss if the stock is a capital asset.[34]

---

[34] If the stock is held as an investment, which is usually the case, gain or loss will be capital. Stock owned by a broker probably will be inventory and therefore will not constitute a capital asset. Thus, the gain or loss on this type of stock is ordinary and not capital.

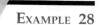

EXAMPLE 28

Pursuant to a complete liquidation, Starling Corporation distributes $100,000 in cash to Edna, one of its shareholders. If Edna's basis in the stock surrendered is $40,000, she must recognize a gain of $60,000. If Edna held the stock as an investment, the $60,000 gain will be capital gain—either short term or long term (depending on the holding period). ▼

EXCEPTION TO THE GENERAL RULE

Section 332 is an exception to the general rule that the shareholder recognizes gain or loss on a corporate liquidation. If a parent corporation liquidates a subsidiary corporation in which it owns at least 80 percent of the voting power and value of the stock, no gain or loss is recognized by the parent company. The subsidiary must distribute all of its property in complete liquidation of all of its stock within the taxable year or within three years from the close of the tax year in which the first distribution occurred.

BASIS DETERMINATION—§§ 334 AND 338

General Rule

Where gain or loss is recognized upon the complete liquidation of a corporation, the basis of the property received by the shareholders is the property's fair market value.[35]

Subsidiary Liquidation Basis Rules

The general rule is that the property received by the parent corporation in a complete liquidation of its subsidiary under § 332 has the same basis it had in the hands of the subsidiary (a carryover basis).[36] The parent's basis in the stock of the liquidated subsidiary disappears.

EXAMPLE 29

Swallow, the parent corporation, has a basis of $20,000 in the stock of Shrike Corporation, a subsidiary in which it owns 85% of all classes of stock. Swallow purchased the stock of Shrike Corporation 10 years ago. In the current year, Swallow liquidates Shrike Corporation and receives assets worth $50,000 with a tax basis to Shrike of $40,000. Swallow Corporation would have a basis of $40,000 in the assets, with a potential gain upon sale of $10,000. Swallow's original $20,000 basis in the Shrike stock disappears. ▼

An exception to the carryover of basis rule is provided in § 338. Under this exception, the parent company may elect to receive a basis for the assets equal to the adjusted basis of the stock of the subsidiary. In effect, the initial acquisition of the subsidiary is treated as if the parent company had acquired the assets (rather than the stock) of the subsidiary.

EFFECT OF THE LIQUIDATION ON THE CORPORATION

Having examined what happens to the shareholder upon the liquidation of a corporation, what happens at the corporate level? Here, § 336 applies to dictate the tax consequences to the corporation being liquidated.

Under § 336, the distributing corporation recognizes gain or loss upon complete liquidation. In this regard, it does not matter whether the corporation

---

[35] § 334(a).

[36] § 334(b)(1).

distributes the property in-kind (*as is*) to the shareholders or first sells the property and then distributes the proceeds.

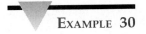

EXAMPLE 30

Pursuant to a complete liquidation, Grackle Corporation distributes the following assets to its shareholders: undeveloped land held as an investment (basis of $150,000 and fair market value of $140,000) and marketable securities (basis of $160,000 and fair market value of $200,000). Since Grackle is treated as if it had sold the property, a gain of $40,000 results from the securities, and a loss of $10,000 results from the land. ▼

ETHICAL CONSIDERATIONS

Necessity for Filing a Corporate Tax Return

For many years, Hanna has owned and operated several apartment buildings. In 1990 and upon the advice of her attorney, Hanna transferred the apartment buildings to a newly formed corporation. Her main reason for incorporating the business was to achieve limited liability.

Every year since 1990, Hanna has prepared and filed a Form 1120 for the corporation. No corporate income tax has been paid since, after the deduction of various expenses (including Hanna's salary), the corporation has zero taxable income.

In 1994, Hanna decides that filing Form 1120 is a waste of time. Instead, she will report all of the financial activities of the apartment business on her own individual Form 1040.

The deductibility of losses may be restricted by the related-party rules (refer to Chapter 6) if certain conditions exist (e.g., the distributions are not pro rata).[37]

A wholly owned subsidiary corporation does not recognize gain or loss when the parent corporation uses the carryover basis option of § 334(b)(1). The reason for the special treatment is that the subsidiary's basis (and all other tax attributes) in the assets carries over to the parent corporation.

THE S ELECTION

JUSTIFICATION FOR THE ELECTION

7   LEARNING OBJECTIVE
Appreciate the utility and effect of the Subchapter S election.

Numerous nontax reasons exist for operating a business in the corporate form (e.g., limited liability). Consequently, the existence of income tax disadvantages (e.g., double taxation of corporate income and shareholder dividends) should not deter business people from using the corporate form. To prevent tax considerations from interfering with the exercise of sound business judgment, Congress enacted Subchapter S of the Code.

To qualify for S status, the corporation must be a **small business corporation**.[38] This includes any corporation that has the following characteristics:

- Is a domestic corporation.
- Is not a member of an affiliated group.
- Has no more than 35 shareholders.

---

[37] § 336(d).   [38] § 1361(b).

- Has as its shareholders only individuals, estates, and certain trusts.
- Does not have a nonresident alien as a shareholder.
- Has only one class of stock outstanding.

These characteristics must continue to exist if an electing S corporation is to maintain S status.

Making the Election

The election is made by filing Form 2553, and *all* shareholders must consent. Special rules apply to husbands and wives where stock is jointly held and to minors.

To be effective for the current year, the election must be filed anytime during the preceding taxable year or on or before the fifteenth day of the third month of the current year.[39]

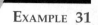

EXAMPLE 31

Heron, a calendar year taxpayer, is a regular corporation that wishes to elect S status for 1994. If the election is filed anytime from January 1, 1993, through March 15, 1994, it will be effective for 1994. ▼

Loss of the Election

The S election may be terminated *voluntarily* (a majority of the shareholders file to revoke the election) or *involuntarily*. An involuntary termination may occur in *any* of the following ways:

- The corporation ceases to qualify as a small business corporation (e.g., the number of shareholders exceeds 35, or a partnership becomes a shareholder).
- The corporation has passive investment income (e.g., interest, dividends) in excess of 25 percent of gross receipts for a period of three consecutive years. This possibility applies only if the corporation was previously a regular corporation and has earnings and profits from that period.

If the holders of a *majority* of the shares consent to a voluntary revocation of S status, the election to revoke must be made on or before the fifteenth day of the third month of the tax year to be effective for that year.

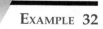

EXAMPLE 32

The shareholders of Stork Corporation, a calendar year S corporation, elect to revoke the election on January 4, 1994. Assuming the election is duly executed and timely filed, Stork will become a regular corporation for calendar year 1994. If the election to revoke is not made until June 1994, Stork will not become a regular corporation until calendar year 1995. ▼

Suppose the shareholders in Example 32 file the election to revoke on January 4, 1994, but do not want the revocation to take place until 1995. If the election so specifies, Stork Corporation will cease to have S status as of January 1, 1995.

In the case where S status is lost because of a disqualifying act (involuntarily), the loss of the election takes effect as of the date on which the event occurs.

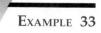

EXAMPLE 33

Crow Corporation has been a calendar year S corporation for several years. On August 13, 1994, one of its shareholders sells her stock to Kite Corporation. Since Crow Corporation no longer satisfies the definition of a small business corporation (it has another corporation as

---

[39] § 1362.

PROPOSED S CORPORATION LEGISLATION

Senators David Pryor (Democrat-Arkansas) and John Danforth (Republican-Missouri) have introduced tax legislation that better reflects the practicalities of operating a small business in the 1990s. According to Sam Starr, a Coopers & Lybrand tax partner who specializes in S corporation taxation, the legislation would make it easier for S corporations to obtain financing and would provide more flexibility in terms of corporate structure and the ability to grow. Currently, 1.6 million small businesses are operating as S corporations.

The legislation would remove some of the artificial restrictions that hinder S corporations, provide more options for structuring business transactions, and put S corporations on a more even playing field with partnerships and C corporations. Among the proposed changes are the following:

1. Increase the number of permitted shareholders from 35 to 50.
2. Treat all the members of a family as a single shareholder.
3. Expand the types of trusts that are eligible shareholders.
4. Allow new types of shareholders, thereby increasing sources of financing. These would include tax-exempt organizations, pension plans and employee stock option plans, and nonresident aliens.
5. Permit "plain vanilla" preferred stock to be issued.
6. Permit venture capitalists to hold convertible debentures that would be "safe-harbored" from classification as a second class of stock.
7. Allow S corporations to own 80 percent or more of another corporation's stock.
8. Permit S corporation elections even if certain administrative mistakes occur.
9. Treat S corporation shareholders the same as C corporation shareholders for purposes of tax-favored fringe benefits.

SOURCE: Adapted by permission of Coopers & Lybrand from "Legislation Improves Outlook for S Corporations," *Washington Perspective*, December 1993, p. 1.

a shareholder), the election has been involuntarily terminated. For calendar year 1994, therefore, Crow will be an S corporation through August 12 and a regular corporation from August 13 through December 31, 1994. ▼

In the event the election is lost through a violation of the passive investment income limitation, the loss of S status starts at the beginning of the next tax year.

Barring certain exceptions, the loss of the election places the corporation in a five-year holding period before S status can be reelected.

OPERATIONAL RULES

The S corporation is primarily a tax-reporting rather than a taxpaying entity. In this respect, the entity is taxed much like a partnership.[40] Under the conduit

---

[40] This is not to imply that an S corporation is always free from the income tax. For example, a tax may be imposed on certain built-in gains or certain excessive passive investment income.

concept, the taxable income and losses of an S corporation flow through to the shareholders who report them on their personal income tax returns.

To ascertain the annual tax consequences to each shareholder, it is necessary to carry out two steps at the S corporation level. First, all corporate transactions that will flow through to the shareholders on an *as is* basis under the conduit approach must be set aside. Second, what remains is aggregated as the taxable income of the S corporation and is allocated to each shareholder on a per-share and per-day of stock ownership basis.[41]

Separately Stated Items

The following are some of the items that do not lose their identity as they pass through the S corporation and are therefore picked up by each shareholder on an *as is* basis:

- Tax-exempt income.
- Long-term and short-term capital gains and losses.
- Section 1231 gains and losses.
- Charitable contributions.
- Foreign tax credits.
- Depletion.
- Nonbusiness income or loss under § 212.
- Intangible drilling costs.
- Investment interest, income, and expenses covered under § 163(d).
- Certain portfolio income.
- Passive activity gains, losses, and credits under § 469.
- AMT adjustments and tax preference items.

These items are separately stated because each may lead to a different tax result when combined with a particular shareholder's other transactions.

EXAMPLE 34

Arnold and Jean are equal shareholders in Lark Corporation (an S corporation). For calendar year 1994, each must account for one-half of a corporate short-term capital gain of $6,000. Arnold has no other capital asset transactions, and Jean has a short-term capital loss of $3,000 from the sale of stock in IBM Corporation. In terms of overall effect, the difference between the two taxpayers is significant. Although both must report the short-term capital gain pass-through, Jean will neutralize its inclusion in gross income by offsetting it with the $3,000 short-term capital loss from the sale of the IBM stock. To Arnold, the short-term capital gain pass-through results in additional ordinary income of $3,000. ▼

Taxable Income

After the separately stated items have been removed, the balance represents the taxable income of the S corporation. In arriving at taxable income, the dividends received deduction and the net operating loss deduction are not allowed. An S corporation does come under the regular corporate rules, however, for purposes of amortization of organizational expenditures.

Once taxable income has been determined, it passes through to each shareholder as of the last day of the S corporation's tax year.

---

[41] § 1366.

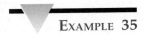

EXAMPLE 35

Harrier Corporation, a calendar year S corporation, had the following transactions during the current year:

Sales		$ 40,000
Cost of goods sold		(23,000)
Other income		
*Tax-exempt interest	$ 300	
*Long-term capital gain	500	800
Other expenses		
*Charitable contributions	$ 400	
Advertising expense	1,500	
Other operating expenses	2,000	
*Short-term capital loss	150	(4,050)
Net income per books		$ 13,750

When the items that are to be separately stated (those preceded by an asterisk [*]) and shown *as is* by each shareholder are withdrawn, Harrier has the following taxable income:

Sales		$ 40,000
Cost of goods sold		(23,000)
Other expenses		
Advertising expense	$1,500	
Other operating expenses	2,000	(3,500)
Taxable income		$ 13,500

▼

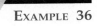

EXAMPLE 36

If Oscar owned 10% of the stock in Harrier Corporation (refer to Example 35) during all of the current year, he must account for the following:

Separately stated items	
Tax-exempt interest	$ 30
Long-term capital gain	50
Charitable contributions	40
Short-term capital loss	15
Taxable income (10% of $13,500)	1,350

Some of the separately stated items need not be reported on Oscar's individual income tax return (e.g., the tax-exempt interest). Others must be reported but may not lead to tax consequences. Oscar picks up his share of Harrier's taxable income ($1,350) as ordinary income. ▼

Treatment of Losses

As previously noted, separately stated loss items (e.g., capital losses, § 1231 losses) flow through to the shareholders on an *as is* basis. Their treatment by a shareholder depends on the shareholder's individual income tax position. If the S corporation's taxable income determination results in an operating loss, it also passes through to the shareholders. As is the case with separately stated items, the amount of the loss each shareholder receives depends on the stock ownership during the year.

EXAMPLE 37

In 1994, Oriole Corporation (a calendar year S corporation) incurred an operating loss of $36,500. During 1994, Jason's ownership in Oriole was as follows: 20% for 200 days and 30% for 165 days. Jason's share of the loss is determined as follows:

[$36,500 × (200/365)] × 20% = $4,000
[$36,500 × (165/365)] × 30% = 4,950
Total loss $8,950

Presuming the basis limitation does not come into play (see the following discussion), Jason deducts $8,950 in arriving at adjusted gross income. ▼

Basis Determination

A shareholder's *basis* in the stock of an S corporation, like that of a regular corporation, is the original investment plus additional capital contributions less return of capital distributions. At this point, however, the symmetry disappears. Generally, basis is increased by the pass-through of income items (including those separately stated) and decreased by the loss items (including those separately stated).[42]

EXAMPLE 38

In 1994, Warbler Corporation is formed with an investment of $100,000, of which Janice contributed $20,000 for a 20% stock interest. A timely S election is made, and for 1994, Warbler earns taxable income of $15,000. Janice's basis in her stock investment now becomes $23,000 [$20,000 (original capital contribution) + $3,000 (the 20% share of the corporation's taxable income assigned to Janice)]. ▼

Distributions by an S corporation reduce the basis of a shareholder's stock investment. However, if the amount of the distribution exceeds basis, the excess normally receives capital gain treatment.

As previously noted, operating losses of an S corporation pass through to the shareholders and reduce the basis in their stock investment. Because the basis of the stock cannot fall below zero, an excess loss is then applied against the basis of any loans the shareholder may have made to the corporation.

EXAMPLE 39

Flamingo Corporation, a calendar year S corporation, has an operating loss of $60,000 for 1994. Norman, a 50% shareholder, has an adjusted basis of $25,000 in his stock investment and has made loans to the corporation of $5,000. Based on these facts, Norman may take full advantage of the $30,000 loss (50% of $60,000) on his 1994 individual income tax return. Norman's basis in the stock and the loans must be reduced accordingly, and both will be zero after the pass-through. ▼

In the event the basis limitation precludes an operating loss from being absorbed, the loss can be carried forward and deducted when and if it is covered by basis.

EXAMPLE 40

Assume the same facts as in Example 39, except that Norman had not made any loans to Flamingo Corporation. Further assume that Flamingo has taxable income of $15,000 in

---

[42] § 1367.

the following year (1995). Norman's tax situation for 1994 and 1995 is summarized as follows:

Ordinary loss for 1994	$25,000
Restoration of stock basis in 1995 (50% of $15,000)	7,500
Income to be reported in 1995	7,500
Loss allowed for 1995 ($30,000 – $25,000)	5,000
Basis in stock account after 1995 ($7,500 – $5,000)	2,500

Thus, Norman's unabsorbed loss of $5,000 from 1994 carries over to 1995 and is applied against the $7,500 of ordinary income for that year. ▼

PARTNERSHIPS

NATURE OF PARTNERSHIP TAXATION

8   LEARNING OBJECTIVE
Understand the tax consequences of forming and operating a partnership.

Unlike corporations, partnerships are not considered separate taxable entities. Each member of a partnership is subject to income tax on his or her distributive share of the partnership's income, even if an actual distribution is not made. The tax return (Form 1065) required of a partnership serves only to provide information necessary in determining the character and amount of each partner's distributive share of the partnership's income and expense. Because a partnership acts as a conduit, items that pass through to the partners do not lose their identity. For example, tax-exempt income earned by a partnership is picked up by the partners as tax-exempt income. In this regard, partnerships function in much the same fashion as S corporations, which also serve as conduits.

A partnership is considered a separate taxable entity for purposes of making various elections and selecting its taxable year, method of depreciation, and accounting method. A partnership is also treated as a separate legal entity under civil law with the right to own property in its own name and to transact business free from the personal debts of its partners.

PARTNERSHIP FORMATION

Recognition of Gain or Loss

The general rule is that no gain or loss is recognized by a partnership or any of its partners on the contribution of property in exchange for a capital interest in the partnership.[43] The general rule also applies to all subsequent contributions of property.

There are certain exceptions to the nonrecognition of gain or loss rule including the following:

- If a partner transfers property to the partnership and receives money or other consideration as a result, the transaction will be treated as a sale or exchange rather than as a contribution of capital.
- If a partnership interest is received in exchange for services rendered or to be rendered by the partner to the partnership, the fair market value of the transferred capital interest is regarded as compensation for services ren-

---

[43] § 721.

dered. In such cases, the recipient of the capital interest must recognize the amount as ordinary income in the year actually or constructively received.

- If property that is subject to a liability in excess of its basis is contributed to a partnership, the contributing partner may recognize gain.

Basis of a Partnership Interest

The contributing *partner's basis* in the partnership interest received is the sum of money contributed plus the adjusted basis of any other property transferred to the partnership.[44]

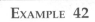

EXAMPLE 41

In return for the contribution of property (with a basis of $50,000 and a fair market value of $80,000) and cash of $10,000 to the Brown Partnership, Marcia receives a 10% capital interest worth $90,000. Although Marcia has a realized gain of $30,000 ($90,000 – $60,000) on the transfer, none of the gain is recognized. The basis of her interest in the Brown Partnership is $60,000 [$50,000 (basis of property contributed) + $10,000 (cash contribution)]. ▼

A partner's basis in the partnership interest is determined without regard to any amount reflected on the partnership's books as capital, equity, or a similar account.

EXAMPLE 42

Marge and Clyde form the equal Blue Partnership with a cash contribution of $30,000 from Marge and a property contribution (adjusted basis of $18,000 and fair market value of $30,000) from Clyde. Although the books of the Blue Partnership may reflect a credit of $30,000 to each partner's capital account, only Marge has a tax basis of $30,000 in her partnership interest. Clyde's tax basis in his partnership interest is $18,000, the amount of his tax basis in the property contributed to the partnership. ▼

After its initial determination, the basis of a partnership interest is subject to continuous fluctuations. A partner's basis is increased by additional contributions and the sum of his or her current and prior years' distributive share of the following:

- Taxable income of the partnership, including capital gains.
- Tax-exempt income of the partnership.
- The excess of the deductions for depletion over the basis of the partnership's property subject to depletion.[45]

Similarly, the basis of a partner's interest is decreased, but not below zero, by distributions of partnership property and by the sum of the current and prior years' distributive share of the following:

- Partnership losses, including capital losses.
- Partnership expenditures that are not deductible in computing taxable income or loss and that are not capital expenditures.

Changes in the liabilities (including trade accounts payable, bank loans, etc.) of a partnership also affect the basis of a partnership interest. A partner's basis is increased by his or her assumption of partnership liabilities and by his or her pro rata share of liabilities incurred by the partnership. Likewise, the partner's basis is decreased by the amount of any personal liabilities assumed by the partnership and by the pro rata share of any decreases in the liabilities of the partnership.

[44] § 722.

[45] § 705(a).

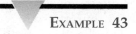

EXAMPLE 43

Tony, Martha, and Carolyn form the Orange Partnership with the following contributions: cash of $50,000 from Tony for a 50% interest in capital and profits, cash of $25,000 from Martha for a 25% interest, and property valued at $33,000 from Carolyn for a 25% interest. The property contributed by Carolyn has an adjusted basis of $15,000 and is subject to a mortgage of $8,000, which is assumed by the partnership. Carolyn's basis in her interest in the Orange Partnership is $9,000, determined as follows:

Adjusted basis of Carolyn's contributed property	$15,000
Less portion of mortgage assumed by Tony and Martha and treated as a distribution of money to Carolyn (75% of $8,000)	(6,000)
Basis of Carolyn's interest in Orange Partnership	$ 9,000

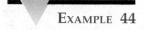

EXAMPLE 44

Assuming the same facts as in Example 43, Tony and Martha have a basis in their partnership interests of $54,000 and $27,000, respectively.

	Tony	Martha
Cash contribution	$50,000	$25,000
Plus portion of mortgage assumed and treated as an additional cash contribution:		
(50% of $8,000)	4,000	
(25% of $8,000)		2,000
Basis of interest in Orange Partnership	$54,000	$27,000

Partnership's Basis in Contributed Property

The *basis of property* contributed to a partnership by a partner is the adjusted basis of the property to the contributing partner at the time of the contribution.[46] Additionally, the holding period of the property for the partnership includes the period during which the property was held by the contributing partner. This is logical, since the partnership's basis in the property is the same basis the property had in the hands of the partner.[47]

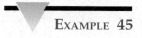

EXAMPLE 45

In 1994, Roger contributed equipment with an adjusted basis of $10,000 and fair market value of $30,000 to the Red Partnership in exchange for a one-third interest in the partnership. No gain or loss is recognized by Roger. The basis in the equipment is $10,000 to the Red Partnership. If Roger had acquired the equipment in 1986, the holding period for the Red Partnership would include the period from 1986 through 1994. ▼

PARTNERSHIP OPERATION

Measuring and Reporting Partnership Income

Although a partnership is not subject to Federal income taxation, it is required to determine its taxable income and file an income tax return for information purposes.[48] The tax return, Form 1065, is due on the fifteenth day of the fourth month following the close of the taxable year of the partnership.

---

[46] § 723.
[47] § 1223(2).

[48] § 6031.

In measuring and reporting partnership income, certain transactions must be segregated and reported separately on the partnership return. Items such as charitable contributions, capital gains and losses, and foreign taxes are excluded from partnership taxable income and are allocated separately to the partners.[49] These items must be segregated and allocated separately because they affect the computation of various exclusions, deductions, and credits at the individual partner level. For example, one of the partners may have made personal charitable contributions in excess of the ceiling limitations on his or her individual tax return. Therefore, partnership charitable contributions are excluded from partnership taxable income and are reported separately on the partnership return.

A second step in the measurement and reporting process is the computation of the partnership's ordinary income or loss. The taxable income of a partnership is computed in the same manner as the taxable income of an individual taxpayer. However, a partnership is not allowed the following deductions:[50]

- The deduction for personal and dependency exemptions.
- The deduction for taxes paid to foreign countries or possessions of the United States.
- The deduction for charitable contributions.
- The deduction for net operating losses.
- The additional itemized deductions allowed individuals in §§ 211 through 219.

The partnership's ordinary income or loss and each of the items requiring separate treatment are reported in the partnership's information return and allocated to the partners in accordance with their distributive shares.

Limitation on Partner's Share of Losses

A partner's deduction of the distributive share of partnership losses (including capital losses) could be limited. The limitation is the adjusted basis of the partnership interest at the end of the partnership year in which the losses were incurred.

The limitation for partnership loss deductions is similar to that applicable to losses of S corporations. Like S corporation losses, partnership losses may be carried forward by the partner and utilized against future increases in the basis of the partnership interest. Such increases might result from additional capital contributions to the partnership, from additional partnership liabilities, or from future partnership income.

EXAMPLE 46

Florence and Donald do business as the Green Partnership, sharing profits and losses equally. All parties use the calendar year for tax purposes. As of January 1, 1994, Florence's basis in her partnership interest is $25,000. The partnership sustained an operating loss of $80,000 in 1994 and earned a profit of $70,000 in 1995. For the calendar year 1994, Florence may claim only $25,000 of her $40,000 distributive share of the partnership loss (one-half of the $80,000 loss). As a result, the basis in her partnership interest is reduced to zero as of January 1, 1995, and she must carry forward the remaining $15,000 of partnership losses. ▼

EXAMPLE 47

Assuming the same facts as in Example 46, what are the income tax consequences for Florence in 1995? Since the partnership earned a profit of $70,000 for the calendar year 1995,

---

[49] § 702(a).
[50] § 703(a).

Florence reports income from the partnership of $20,000 ($35,000 distributive share of income for 1995 less the $15,000 loss not allowed for 1994). The adjusted basis of her partnership interest now becomes $20,000. ▼

Transactions between Partner and Partnership

A partner engaging in a transaction with the partnership is generally regarded as a nonpartner or outsider. However, the Code includes certain exceptions to prevent unwarranted tax avoidance. For instance, losses from the sale or exchange of property are disallowed if they arise in either of the following cases:

- Between a partnership and a person whose direct or indirect interest in the capital or profits of the partnership is more than 50 percent.
- Between two partnerships in which the same persons own more than a 50 percent interest in the capital or profits.[51]

If one of the purchasers later sells the property, any gain realized will be recognized only to the extent that it exceeds the loss previously disallowed.

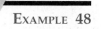

EXAMPLE 48

Pat owns a 60% interest in the capital and profits of the Rose Partnership. In the current year, Pat sells property with an adjusted basis of $50,000 to the partnership for its fair market value of $35,000. The $15,000 loss is not deductible since Pat's ownership interest is more than 50%. If the Rose Partnership later sells the property for $40,000, none of the $5,000 (sale price of $40,000 less adjusted basis to partnership of $35,000) gain will be recognized since it is offset by $5,000 of the previously disallowed loss of $15,000. The unused loss of $10,000, however, is of no tax benefit either to the partnership or to Pat. ▼

Payments made by a partnership to one of its partners for services rendered or for the use of capital, to the extent they are determined without regard to the income of the partnership, are treated by the partnership in the same manner as payments made to a person who is not a partner. Referred to as **guaranteed payments,** these are generally deductible by the partnership as a business expense.[52] The payments must be reported as ordinary income by the receiving partner. Their deductibility distinguishes guaranteed payments from a partner's distributive share of income that is not deductible by the partnership.

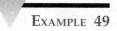

EXAMPLE 49

Under the terms of the Silver Partnership agreement, Kim is entitled to a fixed annual salary of $18,000 without regard to the income of the partnership. He is also to share in the profits and losses of the partnership as a one-third partner. After deducting the guaranteed payment, the partnership has $36,000 of ordinary income. Kim must include $30,000 as ordinary income on his income tax return for his tax year with or within which the partnership tax year ends ($18,000 guaranteed payment + his one-third distributive share of partnership income of $12,000). ▼

Other Partnership Considerations

Complex tax provisions involving liquidating and nonliquidating distributions and the sale of a partnership interest are beyond the scope of this text and are discussed in depth in *West's Federal Taxation: Corporations, Partnerships, Estates, and Trusts.*

---

[51] § 707(b)(1).   [52] § 707(c).

**TAX PLANNING
CONSIDERATIONS**

9   LEARNING OBJECTIVE
Evaluate the advantages and
disadvantages of the various
forms for conducting a
business.

CORPORATE VERSUS NONCORPORATE FORMS OF BUSINESS ORGANIZATION

The decision to use the corporate form in conducting a trade or business must be weighed carefully. Besides the nontax aspects of the corporate form (limited liability, continuity of life, free transferability of interest, centralized management), tax ramifications play an important role in any such decision. Close attention should be paid to the following:

1. The corporate form means the imposition of the corporate income tax. Corporate-source income will be taxed twice—once as earned by the corporation and again when distributed to the shareholders. Since dividends are not deductible, a strong incentive exists in a closely held corporation to structure corporate distributions in a deductible form. The shareholders may bail out profits in the form of salaries, interest, or rents. These procedures lead to a multitude of problems, one of which, the reclassification of debt as equity, has been discussed. The problems of unreasonable salaries and rents were discussed in Chapter 6.

2. The applicable income tax rates also affect the choice of the form for doing business. Unfortunately, because of the wide range of possibilities involved (15 to 39.6 percent for individuals and 15 to 35 percent for corporations), this factor must be considered on a case-by-case basis. For example, the corporate form is very appealing if the anticipated taxable income falls within the 25 percent bracket while the shareholder's individual bracket is 39.6 percent. Here, the time value of the taxes saved (by not distributing dividends and postponing the effect of the double tax) could make operating a business in the corporate form advantageous.

3. Corporate-source income loses its identity as it passes through the corporation to the shareholders. Thus, items possessing preferential tax treatment (e.g., interest on municipal bonds) are not taxed as such to the shareholders.

4. As noted earlier, it may be difficult for shareholders to recover some or all of their investment in the corporation without an ordinary income result. Recall that most corporate distributions are treated as dividends to the extent of the corporation's earnings and profits. Structuring the capital of the corporation to include debt is a partial solution to this problem. Thus, the shareholder-creditor could recoup part of his or her investment through the tax-free payment of principal. Too much debt, however, may lead to the debt being reclassified as equity.

5. Corporate losses cannot be passed through to the shareholders.

6. The liquidation of a corporation may generate tax consequences to both the corporation and its shareholders.

7. The corporate form provides the shareholders with the opportunity to be treated as employees for tax purposes if they render services to the corporation. This status makes a number of attractive tax-sheltered fringe benefits available (e.g., group term life insurance). These benefits are not available to partners and sole proprietors.

REGULAR CORPORATION VERSUS S STATUS

Due to the pass-through concept, the use of S status generally avoids the income tax at the corporate level, bringing the individual income tax into play. As noted in item 2 in the previous section, the differential between the rates applicable to noncorporate and corporate taxpayers makes this a factor to be considered. The S election enables a business to operate in the corporate form, avoid the corporate income tax, and depending on taxable income, possibly take advantage of the lower rates usually applicable to individuals. Also, losses incurred at the corporate level pass through to the shareholders, who will utilize them on their individual returns (compare with item 5).

Electing S status can present several problems. First, the election is available only to small business corporations. Consequently, many corporations will not qualify for the election. Second, S corporations are subject to the rules governing regular corporations unless otherwise specified in the Code. For example, if an S corporation carries out a stock redemption or is liquidated, the rules covering regular corporations apply. Third, some states do not recognize S status for purposes of state and local taxation. Therefore, an S corporation might be subject to a state franchise tax (refer to Chapter 1) or a state or local income tax.

USE OF AN ENTITY TO REDUCE THE FAMILY INCOME TAX BURDEN

One objective of tax planning is to keep the income from a business within the family unit but to disperse the income in such a manner as to minimize the overall tax burden. To the extent feasible, therefore, income should be shifted from higher-bracket to lower-bracket family members.

Unfortunately, the income from property (a business) cannot be shifted to another without also transferring an interest in the property. If, for example, a father wants to assign income from his sole proprietorship to his children, he must form a partnership or incorporate the business.[53] In either case, the transfer of the interest may be subject to the Federal gift tax. But any potential gift tax can be eliminated or controlled through judicious use of the annual exclusion, the election to split gifts (for married donors), and the unified tax credit (refer to the discussion of the Federal gift tax in Chapter 1).

Consequently, the first problem to be resolved becomes which form of business organization will best fit the objective of income shifting. For the partnership form, one major obstacle arises. The family partnership rules of § 704(e) preclude the assignment of income to a family member unless capital is a material income-producing factor. If not, the family member must contribute substantial or vital services. Ordinarily, capital is not a material income-producing factor if the income of the business consists principally of compensation for personal services performed by members or employees of the partnership. Conversely, capital is a material income-producing factor if the operation of the business entails a substantial investment in physical assets (e.g., inventory, plant, machinery, or equipment).

Income shifting through the use of a partnership, therefore, may be ineffectual if a personal service business is involved. In fact, it could be hopeless if the assignees are minors. The use of the corporate form usually involves no such impediment. Regardless of the nature of the business, a gift of stock carries with it the attributes of ownership. Thus, dividends paid on stock are taxed to the owner of the stock.

But what if the corporate form is utilized and the S election is made? A new hurdle arises under the Code. Section 1366(e) authorizes the IRS to make adjustments in situations where shareholders are not being adequately compensated for the value of their services or capital provided to an S corporation in a family setting.

---

[53] Income shifting will not work, however, if the minor is under 14 years of age. In such cases, net unearned income (refer to the discussion in Chapter 3) of the child is taxed at the parents' tax rate. § 1(g).

EXAMPLE 50

The stock of an S corporation is held equally by Roy and his three minor children (ages 14, 15, and 16). Without help from his children, Roy runs the business for which he pays himself an annual salary of $20,000. If $50,000 is a reasonable amount for the value of these services, the IRS may allocate $30,000 of the corporation's taxable income from the children to Roy. ▼

Thus, an S corporation suffers from the same vulnerability that exists with family partnerships.

A further factor that favors the corporate form (either a regular or an S corporation) as a device for income splitting is the ease with which it can be carried out. Presuming the entity already exists, the transfer of stock merely requires an entry in the corporation's stock ledger account. In contrast, a gift of a partnership interest probably requires an amendment to the articles of copartnership. If minors are to be the assignees (donees), a state's Uniform Gifts to Minors Act provides a useful and flexible means of holding a stock interest until the assignees become adults.[54] In the case of a partnership interest, however, a guardianship may have to be set up to achieve the same flexibility. In summary, the transfer of stock is more convenient and, since it usually avoids legal problems, can be less expensive.

Regardless of the form of organization used for the business, income shifting will not take place unless the transfer is complete.[55] If the donor continues to exercise control over the interest transferred and does not recognize and protect the ownership rights of the donee, the IRS may argue that the transfer is ineffective for tax purposes. In that case, the income from the transferred interest continues to be taxed to the donor.

KEY TERMS

Association, 20–4

Constructive dividends, 20–21

Dividends received deduction, 20–10

Earnings and profits, 20–20

Guaranteed payments, 20–34

Limited liability companies, 20–4

Liquidating distribution, 20–22

Organizational expenditures, 20–12

Personal service corporation, 20–13

Small business corporation, 20–24

Stock redemption, 20–22

Thin capitalization (corporation), 20–18

PROBLEM
MATERIALS

DISCUSSION QUESTIONS

1. What is the role of state law in determining whether or not an entity will be classified as a corporation for Federal income tax purposes?

2. Under what circumstances might the disregard of the corporate entity produce a favorable result for the IRS?

---

[54] The Uniform Gifts to Minors Act is explained in Chapter 4.

[55] *Ginsberg v. Comm.*, 74–2 USTC ¶9660, 34 AFTR2d 74–5760, 502 F.2d 965 (CA–6, 1974), and *Michael F. Beirne*, 61 T.C. 268 (1973).

3. When will an entity be classified as a corporation under the association approach?

4. Why are limited liability companies advantageous?

5. When contrasted with the partnership, the corporate form of doing business results in another layer of Federal income tax. Explain.

6. Are the net long-term capital gains of individual taxpayers taxed in the same manner as those of corporate taxpayers? Explain.

7. Contrast the corporate tax rules for deducting net capital losses with the rules for individuals. Are the corporate capital loss rules *more or less* favorable than the capital loss provisions for individuals? Why?

8. Do corporations have to recapture more depreciation than noncorporate taxpayers? Explain.

9. What requirements must be met to properly accrue a charitable contribution that is paid in the year following the year of the deduction?

10. How are corporate charitable contributions treated when they exceed the maximum limitations?

11. Is it possible for a corporation to donate inventory to a charitable organization and claim some of the appreciation as a deduction? Explain.

12. Why would a corporation elect not to carry back an NOL to a particular year?

13. What is the rationale for the dividends received deduction for corporate shareholders?

14. The amount of the dividends received deduction may depend on the percentage of ownership held by the corporate shareholder. Explain.

15. Distinguish between expenditures that qualify as organizational expenditures and those that do not qualify.

16. Under what circumstances may a corporation file a Form 1120–A (rather than Form 1120)?

17. What purpose does the Schedule M–1 reconciliation of Form 1120 serve for the taxpayer? For the IRS?

18. What does Schedule M–2 of Form 1120 accomplish?

19. To encourage a corporation to open a manufacturing facility in the community, a city donates land to the corporation. Does the donation generate income to the corporation? What basis will the corporation have in the land?

20. Why is it usually advantageous to capitalize a corporation by using debt? Is it possible that the debt will be reclassified as equity? Why?

21. If § 351 applies, no realized gain or loss is ever recognized. Comment on the validity of this statement.

22. When a corporation receives property in a nontaxable exchange under § 351, what is its income tax basis in the property?

23. Does it matter to a corporation whether a shareholder-transferor has recognized gain on a § 351 transfer? Why or why not?

24. In return for the performance of legal services, Imelda receives stock in newly formed Swallow Corporation. What is Imelda's income tax situation for this stock?

25. How do the following transactions affect the earnings and profits of a corporation?
    a. A nontaxable stock dividend issued to the shareholders.
    b. Receipt of interest on municipal bonds.
    c. Federal corporate income tax liability.

26. When is a distribution by a corporation to its shareholders treated by the shareholders as a return of capital? When can a shareholder have a capital gain on a distribution received from a corporation?

27. A corporation distributes a property dividend to its shareholders.
    a. Is any gain or loss recognized by the distributing corporation?
    b. What basis will the shareholders have in the property?

28. Angelo, the sole shareholder of Bunting Corporation, sells property to the corporation for $10,000 more than its fair market value. Discuss the tax ramifications of this transaction.

29. What difference does it make whether a corporation's redemption of its stock qualifies as a sale or exchange?

30. What is the usual tax effect to a shareholder when the corporation liquidates?

31. On March 19, 1994, the holders of 80% of the shares of Falcon Corporation, a calendar year taxpayer, elect to terminate S status. For what year will Falcon first become a regular corporation?

32. What are some examples of separately stated items that pass through "as is" to an S corporation's shareholders? Why is this procedure required?

33. If an S corporation incurs an operating loss, how is the loss apportioned to the shareholders?

34. Compare the nonrecognition of gain or loss on contributions to a partnership with the similar provision found in corporate formation (§ 351). What are the major differences and similarities?

35. Under what circumstances does the receipt of a partnership interest result in the recognition of ordinary income? What is the effect of this on the partnership and the other partners?

36. How is a contributing partner's basis in a partnership interest determined?

37. What transactions or events will cause a partner's basis in his or her partnership interest to fluctuate continuously?

38. Describe the two-step approach used in determining partnership income. Why is the computation necessary?

39. To what extent can a partner deduct his or her distributive share of partnership losses? What happens to any unused losses?

40. What are guaranteed payments? When might such payments be used?

PROBLEMS

41. Canary Corporation has net short-term capital gains of $10,000 and net long-term capital losses of $90,000 during 1994. Taxable income from other sources is $400,000. Prior years' transactions included the following:

1990	Net short-term capital gains	$40,000
1991	Net long-term capital gains	20,000
1992	Net short-term capital gains	30,000
1993	Net long-term capital gains	20,000

    a. How are the capital gains and losses treated on the 1994 tax return?
    b. Compute the capital loss carryback to the carryback years.
    c. Compute the amount of capital loss carryover, if any, and designate the years to which the loss may be carried.

42. Starling Corporation acquired residential rental property on January 3, 1986, for $100,000. The property was depreciated using the accelerated method and a 19-year recovery period under ACRS. Depreciation in the amount of $53,775 was claimed. Straight-line depreciation for the period would have been $42,321. Starling sold the property on January 1, 1994, for $110,000. What is the gain on the sale, and how is it taxed?

43. Assume the property in Problem 42 was a commercial building and Starling Corporation used the straight-line method of depreciation with a 19-year recovery period under ACRS. What would be the gain on the sale, and how would it be taxed?

44. During 1994, Bluebird Corporation, a calendar year taxpayer, had the following income and expenses:

Income from operations	$450,000
Expenses from operations	330,000
Dividends from domestic corporations	30,000
NOL carryover from 1993	9,000

On May 1, 1994, Bluebird made a contribution to a qualified charitable organization of $21,000 in cash (not included in any of the items listed above).
   a. Determine Bluebird's deduction for charitable contributions for 1994.
   b. What happens to any portion of the contribution not deductible in 1994?

45. Lark Company is a wholesale grocery business. During 1994, it donated canned and dried food (held as inventory) to the local Salvation Army. The basis of the food is $15,000, and it has a fair market value of $18,000. Based on the following assumptions, what amount qualifies as a charitable contribution?
   a. Lark Company is a sole proprietorship.
   b. Lark Company is a regular corporation.

46. During 1994, Raven Corporation had net income from operations of $300,000. In addition, Raven received dividends in the following amounts: $20,000 from Flicker Corporation and $30,000 from Blackbird Corporation. Raven owns 14% of the stock of Flicker and 40% of the stock of Blackbird. Determine Raven Corporation's dividends received deduction for 1994.

47. In each of the following independent situations, determine the dividends received deduction. Assume that none of the corporate shareholders owns 20% or more of the stock in the corporation paying the dividends.

	Thrush Corporation	Wren Corporation	Warbler Corporation
Income from operations	$ 700,000	$ 800,000	$ 700,000
Expenses of operations	(600,000)	(900,000)	(740,000)
Qualifying dividends	100,000	200,000	200,000

48. In each of the following independent situations, determine the corporation's income tax liability. Assume that all corporations use a calendar year for tax purposes, and that the tax year involved is 1994.

	Taxable Income
Cardinal Corporation	$ 40,000
Sparrow Corporation	110,000
Robin Corporation	400,000
Nighthawk Corporation	11,000,000
Jay Corporation (a qualified personal service corporation)	100,000

49. Using the following legend, classify each statement accordingly:

Legend
I = Applies to the income taxation of individuals.
C = Applies to the income taxation of regular corporations.
B = Applies to the income taxation of both individuals and regular corporations.
N = Applies to the income taxation of neither individuals nor regular corporations.

a. Net capital losses cannot be carried back.
b. Net capital losses can be carried over indefinitely.
c. Net capital losses cannot offset other income.
d. Net long-term capital gains cannot be taxed at a rate in excess of 28%.
e. An accrual basis taxpayer cannot deduct charitable contributions until the year of payment.
f. A dividends received deduction may be available.
g. The application of § 1250 (the recapture of depreciation claimed on certain real property) may yield more ordinary income.
h. The concept of adjusted gross income (AGI) has no relevance.
i. Percentage limitations may restrict the amount of charitable deductions that can be claimed in any one tax year.
j. Casualty losses are deductible in full.
k. Tax rates are progressive.
l. More adjustments are necessary to arrive at an NOL deduction.

50. Ellen and Dick form Crane Corporation with the following investments: Ellen transfers cash of $300,000, and Dick transfers land worth $320,000. The land has an adjusted basis to Dick of $290,000. Each of the transferors receives 50% of the stock of Crane Corporation. In addition to stock, Dick receives $20,000 cash from Crane. All of Crane's stock has a fair market value of $600,000.
a. Do the transfers qualify under § 351?
b. What is Dick's realized gain (or loss)? Recognized gain (or loss)?
c. What is Dick's basis in the Crane stock?
d. What is Crane Corporation's basis in the land?

51. Zina and Walter form Flamingo Corporation with the following investments: Zina transfers cash of $200,000 while Walter transfers land worth $230,000 (adjusted basis of $250,000). In return, each receives 50% of Flamingo's stock. In addition to stock, Walter receives $30,000 cash from Flamingo. All of Flamingo's stock has a fair market value of $400,000.
a. What is Walter's realized gain (or loss)? Recognized gain (or loss)?
b. What is Walter's basis in the Flamingo stock?
c. What is Flamingo Corporation's basis in the land?

52. Francene, the sole shareholder of Swift Corporation, has a basis of $10,000 in her stock investment. At a time when Swift Corporation has E & P of $8,000, it distributes cash of $20,000 to Francene. What are the tax consequences to Francene of the $20,000 distribution?

53. The stock of Pintail Corporation is held equally by Rick and by Tern Corporation. At a time when Pintail Corporation has E & P of $300,000, it distributes the following property dividends to Rick and to Tern Corporation:

	Asset Distributed	Adjusted Basis to Pintail Corporation	Fair Market Value
To Rick	Land (parcel A)	$ 40,000	$110,000
To Tern Corporation	Land (parcel B)	130,000	110,000

a. What are the income tax consequences to Rick?

b. What are the income tax consequences to Tern Corporation?

c. What are the income tax consequences to Pintail Corporation?

54. At a time when Longspur Corporation has ample earnings and profits, it redeems 500 of Cynthia's 1,500 shares for their fair market value of $500,000 ($1,000 for each share). All of Cynthia's shares were acquired 10 years ago as an investment and have an adjusted basis of $150,000 ($100 for each share).

a. Describe the tax effect of the redemption if it qualifies for sale or exchange treatment.

b. Describe the tax effect of the redemption if it does not qualify for sale or exchange treatment.

55. In the current year, Shearwater Corporation is liquidated under the general rules of § 331. The company distributes its only asset (land with a fair market value of $100,000 and adjusted basis of $20,000) to Oscar, who holds all of the Shearwater stock as an investment. Oscar's basis in the Shearwater stock is $60,000. Shearwater Corporation has E & P of $10,000.

a. What are the amount and character of the gain or loss recognized by Oscar upon receiving the land in exchange for the stock?

b. What is Oscar's basis in the land?

c. Is there any tax effect to Shearwater Corporation? Explain.

56. Ten years ago, Albatross Corporation purchased all of the stock of Kingbird Corporation for $100,000. In the current year, Kingbird has a basis in its assets of $300,000 and a fair market value of $400,000. Albatross liquidates Kingbird Corporation and receives all of its assets. The exception to the carryover basis rule does not apply.

a. Does Albatross Corporation recognize any gain as a result of the liquidation?

b. What is Albatross Corporation's basis for the assets it receives from Kingbird Corporation?

57. During 1994, Canary Corporation (a calendar year, accrual basis S corporation) had the following transactions:

Sales	$500,000
Cost of goods sold	300,000
Long-term capital gain	4,000
Short-term capital loss	3,000
Charitable contributions	6,000
Salaries and wages	20,000
Interest on municipal bonds	2,000
Advertising expense	5,000
Cash dividends on Texaco stock	7,000

a. Determine Canary Corporation's separately stated items for 1994.

b. Determine Canary Corporation's taxable income for 1994.

58. Julius owns all of the stock of Mockingbird Corporation, a calendar year S corporation. For calendar year 1994, Mockingbird anticipates an operating loss of $20,000 and could, if deemed worthwhile, sell a stock investment that would generate a $3,000 long-term capital loss. Julius has an adjusted basis of $5,000 in the Mockingbird stock. He anticipates no capital asset transactions and expects to be in the 36% tax bracket in 1994.

a. Can you recommend a course of action that can save Julius taxes for 1994?

b. Write a letter to Julius explaining your recommendations.

59. In 1994, Heron Corporation (a calendar year S corporation) had an NOL of $73,000. Otto, a calendar year individual, held stock in Heron Corporation as follows: 40% for 200 days and 60% for 165 days. Based on these facts, what is Otto's loss pass-through for 1994?

60. Sam, Bob, and Clara form the Beige Partnership on January 1, 1994. In exchange for a 30% capital interest, Sam transfers property (basis of $14,000, fair market value of $25,000) subject to a liability of $10,000. The liability is assumed by the partnership. Bob transfers property (basis of $24,000, fair market value of $15,000) for a 30% capital interest, and Clara transfers cash of $20,000 for the remaining 40% capital interest.
    a. How much gain must Sam recognize on the transfer?
    b. What is Sam's basis in his partnership interest?
    c. How much loss may Bob recognize on the transfer?
    d. What is Bob's basis in his partnership interest?
    e. What is Clara's basis in her partnership interest?
    f. What basis will the Beige Partnership have in the property transferred by Sam? The property transferred by Bob?
    g. What would be the tax consequences to Sam if the basis of the property he contributed is only $9,000?

61. As of January 1, 1993, Victor had a basis of $26,000 in his 25% capital interest in the Gray Partnership. He and the partnership use the calendar year for tax purposes. The partnership incurred an operating loss of $120,000 for 1993 and a profit of $80,000 for 1994.
    a. How much, if any, loss may Victor recognize for 1993?
    b. How much income must Victor recognize for 1994?
    c. What basis will Victor have in his partnership interest as of January 1, 1994?
    d. What basis will Victor have in his partnership interest as of January 1, 1995?
    e. What year-end tax planning would you suggest to ensure that a partner could deduct all of his or her share of any partnership losses?

62. Sarah owns a 51% interest in the capital and profits of the Rose Partnership. In 1993, Sarah sells property (adjusted basis of $120,000) to the partnership for the property's fair market value of $109,000. In 1994, Rose Partnership sells the same property to an outsider for $112,000.
    a. What are Sarah's tax consequences on the 1993 sale?
    b. What are Rose Partnership's tax consequences on the 1994 sale?

RESEARCH PROBLEMS

Research Problem 1. Roland and Peter are brothers and equal shareholders in Condor Corporation, a calendar year taxpayer. In 1994, as employees, they incurred certain travel and entertainment expenditures on behalf of Condor Corporation. Because Condor was in a precarious financial condition, Roland and Peter decided not to seek reimbursement for these expenditures. Instead, on his own individual return (Form 1040), each brother deducted what he had spent. Upon audit of the returns filed by Roland and Peter for 1994, the IRS disallowed these expenditures. Do you agree? Why or why not?

Partial list of research aids:
Roy L. Harding, 29 TCM 789, T.C.Memo. 1970–179.

Research Problem 2. Leonora incorporates her retail clothing business. She transfers all her business assets (total basis of $100,000 and fair market value of $95,000) along with business liabilities of $10,000 and a personal note in the amount of $15,000 to the corporation for 100% of its stock. The note is for money borrowed from the bank six months before incorporation to finance improvements on her home. What are the tax consequences of the transfer?

Research Problem 3. On March 1, Marie and Jennifer, the two shareholders of Pelican Corporation, held a meeting at their business office. They decided to terminate the S election prospectively, as of July 1 of the current year. They were expecting a large amount of income in the last half of the tax year. Jennifer prepared the necessary statement of revocation, obtained Marie's signature, signed the statement herself, and planned to mail it to the IRS the next day.

Jennifer had a heart attack during the night and was confined to the hospital for 20 days. She failed to mail the revocation until March 21.

In August, Marie learned of the slipup and became worried. On August 31, she gave a share of Pelican stock to her Canadian cousin who lives in Ontario. She did not inform the IRS of the transfer.

Does Pelican Corporation still have S corporation status? Explain.

 Research Problem 4. Ms. Bland and a number of her friends want to diversify their investment portfolios. With this in mind, they form a partnership to which they transfer appreciated securities. Each transferor receives an interest in the new partnership proportionate to the value of the securities transferred. Will the creation of the partnership be tax-free? Why or why not?

a. Prepare a letter to Ms. Bland giving your advice.

b. Prepare a memo for your firm's client files.

APPENDIX A
Tax Rate Schedules and Tables

1993   Income Tax Rate Schedules   A–2

1993   Tax Tables   A–3

1994   Income Tax Rate Schedules   A–9

1993 Tax Rate Schedules

Single—Schedule X

If taxable income is: Over—	But not over—	The tax is:	of the amount over—
$0	$ 22,100	................15%	$0
22,100	53,500	3,315.00 + 28%	22,100
53,000	115,000	12,107.00 + 31%	53,500
115,000	250,000	31,172.00 + 36%	115,000
250,000	....	79,772.00 + 39.6%	250,000

Head of household—Schedule Z

If taxable income is: Over—	But not over—	The tax is:	of the amount over—
$0	$ 29,600	................15%	$0
29,600	76,400	$4,440.00 + 28%	29,600
76,400	127,500	17,544.00 + 31%	76,400
127,500	250,000	33,385.00 + 36%	127,500
250,000	....	77,485.00 + 39.6%	250,000

Married filing jointly or Qualifying widow(er)—Schedule Y-1

If taxable income is: Over—	But not over—	The tax is:	of the amount over—
$0	$ 36,900	................15%	$0
36,900	89,150	$5,535.00 + 28%	36,900
89,150	140,000	20,165.00 + 31%	89,150
140,000	250,000	35,928.50 + 36%	140,000
250,000	....	75,528.50 + 39.6%	250,000

Married filing separately—Schedule Y-2

If taxable income is: Over—	But not over—	The tax is:	of the amount over—
$0	$ 18,450	................15%	$0
18,450	44,575	$2,767.50 + 28%	18,450
44,575	70,000	10,082.50 + 31%	44,575
70,000	125,000	17,964.25 + 38%	70,000
125,000	....	37,764.25 + 39.6%	125,000

1993 Tax Table

Use if your taxable income is less than $100,000. If $100,000 or more, use the Tax Rate Schedules.

Example. Mr. and Mrs. Brown are filing a joint return. Their taxable income on line 37 of Form 1040 is $25,300. First, they find the $25,300–25,350 income line. Next, they find the column for married filing jointly and read down the column. The amount shown where the income line and filing status column meet is $3,799. This is the tax amount they must enter on line 38 of their Form 1040.

Sample Table

At least	But less than	Single	Married filing jointly *	Married filing separately	Head of a household
			Your tax is—		
25,200	25,250	4,190	3,784	4,665	3,784
25,250	25,300	4,204	3,791	4,679	3,791
25,300	25,350	4,218	(3,799)	4,693	3,799
25,350	25,400	4,232	3,806	4,707	3,806

If line 37 (taxable income) is— At least	But less than	Single	Married filing jointly *	Married filing separately	Head of a house-hold
			Your tax is—		
0	5	0	0	0	0
5	15	2	2	2	2
15	25	3	3	3	3
25	50	6	6	6	6
50	75	9	9	9	9
75	100	13	13	13	13
100	125	17	17	17	17
125	150	21	21	21	21
150	175	24	24	24	24
175	200	28	28	28	28
200	225	32	32	32	32
225	250	36	36	36	36
250	275	39	39	39	39
275	300	43	43	43	43
300	325	47	47	47	47
325	350	51	51	51	51
350	375	54	54	54	54
375	400	58	58	58	58
400	425	62	62	62	62
425	450	66	66	66	66
450	475	69	69	69	69
475	500	73	73	73	73
500	525	77	77	77	77
525	550	81	81	81	81
550	575	84	84	84	84
575	600	88	88	88	88
600	625	92	92	92	92
625	650	96	96	96	96
650	675	99	99	99	99
675	700	103	103	103	103
700	725	107	107	107	107
725	750	111	111	111	111
750	775	114	114	114	114
775	800	118	118	118	118
800	825	122	122	122	122
825	850	126	126	126	126
850	875	129	129	129	129
875	900	133	133	133	133
900	925	137	137	137	137
925	950	141	141	141	141
950	975	144	144	144	144
975	1,000	148	148	148	148

1,000

At least	But less than	Single	Married filing jointly *	Married filing separately	Head of a house-hold
1,000	1,025	152	152	152	152
1,025	1,050	156	156	156	156
1,050	1,075	159	159	159	159
1,075	1,100	163	163	163	163
1,100	1,125	167	167	167	167
1,125	1,150	171	171	171	171
1,150	1,175	174	174	174	174
1,175	1,200	178	178	178	178
1,200	1,225	182	182	182	182
1,225	1,250	186	186	186	186
1,250	1,275	189	189	189	189
1,275	1,300	193	193	193	193

If line 37 (taxable income) is— At least	But less than	Single	Married filing jointly *	Married filing separately	Head of a house-hold
			Your tax is—		
1,300	1,325	197	197	197	197
1,325	1,350	201	201	201	201
1,350	1,375	204	204	204	204
1,375	1,400	208	208	208	208
1,400	1,425	212	212	212	212
1,425	1,450	216	216	216	216
1,450	1,475	219	219	219	219
1,475	1,500	223	223	223	223
1,500	1,525	227	227	227	227
1,525	1,550	231	231	231	231
1,550	1,575	234	234	234	234
1,575	1,600	238	238	238	238
1,600	1,625	242	242	242	242
1,625	1,650	246	246	246	246
1,650	1,675	249	249	249	249
1,675	1,700	253	253	253	253
1,700	1,725	257	257	257	257
1,725	1,750	261	261	261	261
1,750	1,775	264	264	264	264
1,775	1,800	268	268	268	268
1,800	1,825	272	272	272	272
1,825	1,850	276	276	276	276
1,850	1,875	279	279	279	279
1,875	1,900	283	283	283	283
1,900	1,925	287	287	287	287
1,925	1,950	291	291	291	291
1,950	1,975	294	294	294	294
1,975	2,000	298	298	298	298

2,000

At least	But less than	Single	Married filing jointly *	Married filing separately	Head of a house-hold
2,000	2,025	302	302	302	302
2,025	2,050	306	306	306	306
2,050	2,075	309	309	309	309
2,075	2,100	313	313	313	313
2,100	2,125	317	317	317	317
2,125	2,150	321	321	321	321
2,150	2,175	324	324	324	324
2,175	2,200	328	328	328	328
2,200	2,225	332	332	332	332
2,225	2,250	336	336	336	336
2,250	2,275	339	339	339	339
2,275	2,300	343	343	343	343
2,300	2,325	347	347	347	347
2,325	2,350	351	351	351	351
2,350	2,375	354	354	354	354
2,375	2,400	358	358	358	358
2,400	2,425	362	362	362	362
2,425	2,450	366	366	366	366
2,450	2,475	369	369	369	369
2,475	2,500	373	373	373	373
2,500	2,525	377	377	377	377
2,525	2,550	381	381	381	381
2,550	2,575	384	384	384	384
2,575	2,600	388	388	388	388
2,600	2,625	392	392	392	392
2,625	2,650	396	396	396	396
2,650	2,675	399	399	399	399
2,675	2,700	403	403	403	403

If line 37 (taxable income) is— At least	But less than	Single	Married filing jointly *	Married filing separately	Head of a house-hold
			Your tax is—		
2,700	2,725	407	407	407	407
2,725	2,750	411	411	411	411
2,750	2,775	414	414	414	414
2,775	2,800	418	418	418	418
2,800	2,825	422	422	422	422
2,825	2,850	426	426	426	426
2,850	2,875	429	429	429	429
2,875	2,900	433	433	433	433
2,900	2,925	437	437	437	437
2,925	2,950	441	441	441	441
2,950	2,975	444	444	444	444
2,975	3,000	448	448	448	448

3,000

At least	But less than	Single	Married filing jointly *	Married filing separately	Head of a house-hold
3,000	3,050	454	454	454	454
3,050	3,100	461	461	461	461
3,100	3,150	469	469	469	469
3,150	3,200	476	476	476	476
3,200	3,250	484	484	484	484
3,250	3,300	491	491	491	491
3,300	3,350	499	499	499	499
3,350	3,400	506	506	506	506
3,400	3,450	514	514	514	514
3,450	3,500	521	521	521	521
3,500	3,550	529	529	529	529
3,550	3,600	536	536	536	536
3,600	3,650	544	544	544	544
3,650	3,700	551	551	551	551
3,700	3,750	559	559	559	559
3,750	3,800	566	566	566	566
3,800	3,850	574	574	574	574
3,850	3,900	581	581	581	581
3,900	3,950	589	589	589	589
3,950	4,000	596	596	596	596

4,000

At least	But less than	Single	Married filing jointly *	Married filing separately	Head of a house-hold
4,000	4,050	604	604	604	604
4,050	4,100	611	611	611	611
4,100	4,150	619	619	619	619
4,150	4,200	626	626	626	626
4,200	4,250	634	634	634	634
4,250	4,300	641	641	641	641
4,300	4,350	649	649	649	649
4,350	4,400	656	656	656	656
4,400	4,450	664	664	664	664
4,450	4,500	671	671	671	671
4,500	4,550	679	679	679	679
4,550	4,600	686	686	686	686
4,600	4,650	694	694	694	694
4,650	4,700	701	701	701	701
4,700	4,750	709	709	709	709
4,750	4,800	716	716	716	716
4,800	4,850	724	724	724	724
4,850	4,900	731	731	731	731
4,900	4,950	739	739	739	739
4,950	5,000	746	746	746	746

Continued on next page

* This column must also be used by a qualifying widow(er).

1993 Tax Table—Continued

* This column must also be used by a qualifying widow(er).

5,000

At least	But less than	Single	Married filing jointly *	Married filing separately	Head of a household
5,000	5,050	754	754	754	754
5,050	5,100	761	761	761	761
5,100	5,150	769	769	769	769
5,150	5,200	776	776	776	776
5,200	5,250	784	784	784	784
5,250	5,300	791	791	791	791
5,300	5,350	799	799	799	799
5,350	5,400	806	806	806	806
5,400	5,450	814	814	814	814
5,450	5,500	821	821	821	821
5,500	5,550	829	829	829	829
5,550	5,600	836	836	836	836
5,600	5,650	844	844	844	844
5,650	5,700	851	851	851	851
5,700	5,750	859	859	859	859
5,750	5,800	866	866	866	866
5,800	5,850	874	874	874	874
5,850	5,900	881	881	881	881
5,900	5,950	889	889	889	889
5,950	6,000	896	896	896	896

6,000

At least	But less than	Single	Married filing jointly *	Married filing separately	Head of a household
6,000	6,050	904	904	904	904
6,050	6,100	911	911	911	911
6,100	6,150	919	919	919	919
6,150	6,200	926	926	926	926
6,200	6,250	934	934	934	934
6,250	6,300	941	941	941	941
6,300	6,350	949	949	949	949
6,350	6,400	956	956	956	956
6,400	6,450	964	964	964	964
6,450	6,500	971	971	971	971
6,500	6,550	979	979	979	979
6,550	6,600	986	986	986	986
6,600	6,650	994	994	994	994
6,650	6,700	1,001	1,001	1,001	1,001
6,700	6,750	1,009	1,009	1,009	1,009
6,750	6,800	1,016	1,016	1,016	1,016
6,800	6,850	1,024	1,024	1,024	1,024
6,850	6,900	1,031	1,031	1,031	1,031
6,900	6,950	1,039	1,039	1,039	1,039
6,950	7,000	1,046	1,046	1,046	1,046

7,000

At least	But less than	Single	Married filing jointly *	Married filing separately	Head of a household
7,000	7,050	1,054	1,054	1,054	1,054
7,050	7,100	1,061	1,061	1,061	1,061
7,100	7,150	1,069	1,069	1,069	1,069
7,150	7,200	1,076	1,076	1,076	1,076
7,200	7,250	1,084	1,084	1,084	1,084
7,250	7,300	1,091	1,091	1,091	1,091
7,300	7,350	1,099	1,099	1,099	1,099
7,350	7,400	1,106	1,106	1,106	1,106
7,400	7,450	1,114	1,114	1,114	1,114
7,450	7,500	1,121	1,121	1,121	1,121
7,500	7,550	1,129	1,129	1,129	1,129
7,550	7,600	1,136	1,136	1,136	1,136
7,600	7,650	1,144	1,144	1,144	1,144
7,650	7,700	1,151	1,151	1,151	1,151
7,700	7,750	1,159	1,159	1,159	1,159
7,750	7,800	1,166	1,166	1,166	1,166
7,800	7,850	1,174	1,174	1,174	1,174
7,850	7,900	1,181	1,181	1,181	1,181
7,900	7,950	1,189	1,189	1,189	1,189
7,950	8,000	1,196	1,196	1,196	1,196

8,000

At least	But less than	Single	Married filing jointly *	Married filing separately	Head of a household
8,000	8,050	1,204	1,204	1,204	1,204
8,050	8,100	1,211	1,211	1,211	1,211
8,100	8,150	1,219	1,219	1,219	1,219
8,150	8,200	1,226	1,226	1,226	1,226
8,200	8,250	1,234	1,234	1,234	1,234
8,250	8,300	1,241	1,241	1,241	1,241
8,300	8,350	1,249	1,249	1,249	1,249
8,350	8,400	1,256	1,256	1,256	1,256
8,400	8,450	1,264	1,264	1,264	1,264
8,450	8,500	1,271	1,271	1,271	1,271
8,500	8,550	1,279	1,279	1,279	1,279
8,550	8,600	1,286	1,286	1,286	1,286
8,600	8,650	1,294	1,294	1,294	1,294
8,650	8,700	1,301	1,301	1,301	1,301
8,700	8,750	1,309	1,309	1,309	1,309
8,750	8,800	1,316	1,316	1,316	1,316
8,800	8,850	1,324	1,324	1,324	1,324
8,850	8,900	1,331	1,331	1,331	1,331
8,900	8,950	1,339	1,339	1,339	1,339
8,950	9,000	1,346	1,346	1,346	1,346

9,000

At least	But less than	Single	Married filing jointly *	Married filing separately	Head of a household
9,000	9,050	1,354	1,354	1,354	1,354
9,050	9,100	1,361	1,361	1,361	1,361
9,100	9,150	1,369	1,369	1,369	1,369
9,150	9,200	1,376	1,376	1,376	1,376
9,200	9,250	1,384	1,384	1,384	1,384
9,250	9,300	1,391	1,391	1,391	1,391
9,300	9,350	1,399	1,399	1,399	1,399
9,350	9,400	1,406	1,406	1,406	1,406
9,400	9,450	1,414	1,414	1,414	1,414
9,450	9,500	1,421	1,421	1,421	1,421
9,500	9,550	1,429	1,429	1,429	1,429
9,550	9,600	1,436	1,436	1,436	1,436
9,600	9,650	1,444	1,444	1,444	1,444
9,650	9,700	1,451	1,451	1,451	1,451
9,700	9,750	1,459	1,459	1,459	1,459
9,750	9,800	1,466	1,466	1,466	1,466
9,800	9,850	1,474	1,474	1,474	1,474
9,850	9,900	1,481	1,481	1,481	1,481
9,900	9,950	1,489	1,489	1,489	1,489
9,950	10,000	1,496	1,496	1,496	1,496

10,000

At least	But less than	Single	Married filing jointly *	Married filing separately	Head of a household
10,000	10,050	1,504	1,504	1,504	1,504
10,050	10,100	1,511	1,511	1,511	1,511
10,100	10,150	1,519	1,519	1,519	1,519
10,150	10,200	1,526	1,526	1,526	1,526
10,200	10,250	1,534	1,534	1,534	1,534
10,250	10,300	1,541	1,541	1,541	1,541
10,300	10,350	1,549	1,549	1,549	1,549
10,350	10,400	1,556	1,556	1,556	1,556
10,400	10,450	1,564	1,564	1,564	1,564
10,450	10,500	1,571	1,571	1,571	1,571
10,500	10,550	1,579	1,579	1,579	1,579
10,550	10,600	1,586	1,586	1,586	1,586
10,600	10,650	1,594	1,594	1,594	1,594
10,650	10,700	1,601	1,601	1,601	1,601
10,700	10,750	1,609	1,609	1,609	1,609
10,750	10,800	1,616	1,616	1,616	1,616
10,800	10,850	1,624	1,624	1,624	1,624
10,850	10,900	1,631	1,631	1,631	1,631
10,900	10,950	1,639	1,639	1,639	1,639
10,950	11,000	1,646	1,646	1,646	1,646

11,000

At least	But less than	Single	Married filing jointly *	Married filing separately	Head of a household
11,000	11,050	1,654	1,654	1,654	1,654
11,050	11,100	1,661	1,661	1,661	1,661
11,100	11,150	1,669	1,669	1,669	1,669
11,150	11,200	1,676	1,676	1,676	1,676
11,200	11,250	1,684	1,684	1,684	1,684
11,250	11,300	1,691	1,691	1,691	1,691
11,300	11,350	1,699	1,699	1,699	1,699
11,350	11,400	1,706	1,706	1,706	1,706
11,400	11,450	1,714	1,714	1,714	1,714
11,450	11,500	1,721	1,721	1,721	1,721
11,500	11,550	1,729	1,729	1,729	1,729
11,550	11,600	1,736	1,736	1,736	1,736
11,600	11,650	1,744	1,744	1,744	1,744
11,650	11,700	1,751	1,751	1,751	1,751
11,700	11,750	1,759	1,759	1,759	1,759
11,750	11,800	1,766	1,766	1,766	1,766
11,800	11,850	1,774	1,774	1,774	1,774
11,850	11,900	1,781	1,781	1,781	1,781
11,900	11,950	1,789	1,789	1,789	1,789
11,950	12,000	1,796	1,796	1,796	1,796

12,000

At least	But less than	Single	Married filing jointly *	Married filing separately	Head of a household
12,000	12,050	1,804	1,804	1,804	1,804
12,050	12,100	1,811	1,811	1,811	1,811
12,100	12,150	1,819	1,819	1,819	1,819
12,150	12,200	1,826	1,826	1,826	1,826
12,200	12,250	1,834	1,834	1,834	1,834
12,250	12,300	1,841	1,841	1,841	1,841
12,300	12,350	1,849	1,849	1,849	1,849
12,350	12,400	1,856	1,856	1,856	1,856
12,400	12,450	1,864	1,864	1,864	1,864
12,450	12,500	1,871	1,871	1,871	1,871
12,500	12,550	1,879	1,879	1,879	1,879
12,550	12,600	1,886	1,886	1,886	1,886
12,600	12,650	1,894	1,894	1,894	1,894
12,650	12,700	1,901	1,901	1,901	1,901
12,700	12,750	1,909	1,909	1,909	1,909
12,750	12,800	1,916	1,916	1,916	1,916
12,800	12,850	1,924	1,924	1,924	1,924
12,850	12,900	1,931	1,931	1,931	1,931
12,900	12,950	1,939	1,939	1,939	1,939
12,950	13,000	1,946	1,946	1,946	1,946

13,000

At least	But less than	Single	Married filing jointly *	Married filing separately	Head of a household
13,000	13,050	1,954	1,954	1,954	1,954
13,050	13,100	1,961	1,961	1,961	1,961
13,100	13,150	1,969	1,969	1,969	1,969
13,150	13,200	1,976	1,976	1,976	1,976
13,200	13,250	1,984	1,984	1,984	1,984
13,250	13,300	1,991	1,991	1,991	1,991
13,300	13,350	1,999	1,999	1,999	1,999
13,350	13,400	2,006	2,006	2,006	2,006
13,400	13,450	2,014	2,014	2,014	2,014
13,450	13,500	2,021	2,021	2,021	2,021
13,500	13,550	2,029	2,029	2,029	2,029
13,550	13,600	2,036	2,036	2,036	2,036
13,600	13,650	2,044	2,044	2,044	2,044
13,650	13,700	2,051	2,051	2,051	2,051
13,700	13,750	2,059	2,059	2,059	2,059
13,750	13,800	2,066	2,066	2,066	2,066
13,800	13,850	2,074	2,074	2,074	2,074
13,850	13,900	2,081	2,081	2,081	2,081
13,900	13,950	2,089	2,089	2,089	2,089
13,950	14,000	2,096	2,096	2,096	2,096

Continued on next page

1993 Tax Table—*Continued*

14,000

At least	But less than	Single	Married filing jointly *	Married filing separately	Head of a household
14,000	14,050	2,104	2,104	2,104	2,104
14,050	14,100	2,111	2,111	2,111	2,111
14,100	14,150	2,119	2,119	2,119	2,119
14,150	14,200	2,126	2,126	2,126	2,126
14,200	14,250	2,134	2,134	2,134	2,134
14,250	14,300	2,141	2,141	2,141	2,141
14,300	14,350	2,149	2,149	2,149	2,149
14,350	14,400	2,156	2,156	2,156	2,156
14,400	14,450	2,164	2,164	2,164	2,164
14,450	14,500	2,171	2,171	2,171	2,171
14,500	14,550	2,179	2,179	2,179	2,179
14,550	14,600	2,186	2,186	2,186	2,186
14,600	14,650	2,194	2,194	2,194	2,194
14,650	14,700	2,201	2,201	2,201	2,201
14,700	14,750	2,209	2,209	2,209	2,209
14,750	14,800	2,216	2,216	2,216	2,216
14,800	14,850	2,224	2,224	2,224	2,224
14,850	14,900	2,231	2,231	2,231	2,231
14,900	14,950	2,239	2,239	2,239	2,239
14,950	15,000	2,246	2,246	2,246	2,246

15,000

At least	But less than	Single	Married filing jointly *	Married filing separately	Head of a household
15,000	15,050	2,254	2,254	2,254	2,254
15,050	15,100	2,261	2,261	2,261	2,261
15,100	15,150	2,269	2,269	2,269	2,269
15,150	15,200	2,276	2,276	2,276	2,276
15,200	15,250	2,284	2,284	2,284	2,284
15,250	15,300	2,291	2,291	2,291	2,291
15,300	15,350	2,299	2,299	2,299	2,299
15,350	15,400	2,306	2,306	2,306	2,306
15,400	15,450	2,314	2,314	2,314	2,314
15,450	15,500	2,321	2,321	2,321	2,321
15,500	15,550	2,329	2,329	2,329	2,329
15,550	15,600	2,336	2,336	2,336	2,336
15,600	15,650	2,344	2,344	2,344	2,344
15,650	15,700	2,351	2,351	2,351	2,351
15,700	15,750	2,359	2,359	2,359	2,359
15,750	15,800	2,366	2,366	2,366	2,366
15,800	15,850	2,374	2,374	2,374	2,374
15,850	15,900	2,381	2,381	2,381	2,381
15,900	15,950	2,389	2,389	2,389	2,389
15,950	16,000	2,396	2,396	2,396	2,396

16,000

At least	But less than	Single	Married filing jointly *	Married filing separately	Head of a household
16,000	16,050	2,404	2,404	2,404	2,404
16,050	16,100	2,411	2,411	2,411	2,411
16,100	16,150	2,419	2,419	2,419	2,419
16,150	16,200	2,426	2,426	2,426	2,426
16,200	16,250	2,434	2,434	2,434	2,434
16,250	16,300	2,441	2,441	2,441	2,441
16,300	16,350	2,449	2,449	2,449	2,449
16,350	16,400	2,456	2,456	2,456	2,456
16,400	16,450	2,464	2,464	2,464	2,464
16,450	16,500	2,471	2,471	2,471	2,471
16,500	16,550	2,479	2,479	2,479	2,479
16,550	16,600	2,486	2,486	2,486	2,486
16,600	16,650	2,494	2,494	2,494	2,494
16,650	16,700	2,501	2,501	2,501	2,501
16,700	16,750	2,509	2,509	2,509	2,509
16,750	16,800	2,516	2,516	2,516	2,516
16,800	16,850	2,524	2,524	2,524	2,524
16,850	16,900	2,531	2,531	2,531	2,531
16,900	16,950	2,539	2,539	2,539	2,539
16,950	17,000	2,546	2,546	2,546	2,546

17,000

At least	But less than	Single	Married filing jointly *	Married filing separately	Head of a household
17,000	17,050	2,554	2,554	2,554	2,554
17,050	17,100	2,561	2,561	2,561	2,561
17,100	17,150	2,569	2,569	2,569	2,569
17,150	17,200	2,576	2,576	2,576	2,576
17,200	17,250	2,584	2,584	2,584	2,584
17,250	17,300	2,591	2,591	2,591	2,591
17,300	17,350	2,599	2,599	2,599	2,599
17,350	17,400	2,606	2,606	2,606	2,606
17,400	17,450	2,614	2,614	2,614	2,614
17,450	17,500	2,621	2,621	2,621	2,621
17,500	17,550	2,629	2,629	2,629	2,629
17,550	17,600	2,636	2,636	2,636	2,636
17,600	17,650	2,644	2,644	2,644	2,644
17,650	17,700	2,651	2,651	2,651	2,651
17,700	17,750	2,659	2,659	2,659	2,659
17,750	17,800	2,666	2,666	2,666	2,666
17,800	17,850	2,674	2,674	2,674	2,674
17,850	17,900	2,681	2,681	2,681	2,681
17,900	17,950	2,689	2,689	2,689	2,689
17,950	18,000	2,696	2,696	2,696	2,696

18,000

At least	But less than	Single	Married filing jointly *	Married filing separately	Head of a household
18,000	18,050	2,704	2,704	2,704	2,704
18,050	18,100	2,711	2,711	2,711	2,711
18,100	18,150	2,719	2,719	2,719	2,719
18,150	18,200	2,726	2,726	2,726	2,726
18,200	18,250	2,734	2,734	2,734	2,734
18,250	18,300	2,741	2,741	2,741	2,741
18,300	18,350	2,749	2,749	2,749	2,749
18,350	18,400	2,756	2,756	2,756	2,756
18,400	18,450	2,764	2,764	2,764	2,764
18,450	18,500	2,771	2,771	2,775	2,771
18,500	18,550	2,779	2,779	2,789	2,779
18,550	18,600	2,786	2,786	2,803	2,786
18,600	18,650	2,794	2,794	2,817	2,794
18,650	18,700	2,801	2,801	2,831	2,801
18,700	18,750	2,809	2,809	2,845	2,809
18,750	18,800	2,816	2,816	2,859	2,816
18,800	18,850	2,824	2,824	2,873	2,824
18,850	18,900	2,831	2,831	2,887	2,831
18,900	18,950	2,839	2,839	2,901	2,839
18,950	19,000	2,846	2,846	2,915	2,846

19,000

At least	But less than	Single	Married filing jointly *	Married filing separately	Head of a household
19,000	19,050	2,854	2,854	2,929	2,854
19,050	19,100	2,861	2,861	2,943	2,861
19,100	19,150	2,869	2,869	2,957	2,869
19,150	19,200	2,876	2,876	2,971	2,876
19,200	19,250	2,884	2,884	2,985	2,884
19,250	19,300	2,891	2,891	2,999	2,891
19,300	19,350	2,899	2,899	3,013	2,899
19,350	19,400	2,906	2,906	3,027	2,906
19,400	19,450	2,914	2,914	3,041	2,914
19,450	19,500	2,921	2,921	3,055	2,921
19,500	19,550	2,929	2,929	3,069	2,929
19,550	19,600	2,936	2,936	3,083	2,936
19,600	19,650	2,944	2,944	3,097	2,944
19,650	19,700	2,951	2,951	3,111	2,951
19,700	19,750	2,959	2,959	3,125	2,959
19,750	19,800	2,966	2,966	3,139	2,966
19,800	19,850	2,974	2,974	3,153	2,974
19,850	19,900	2,981	2,981	3,167	2,981
19,900	19,950	2,989	2,989	3,181	2,989
19,950	20,000	2,996	2,996	3,195	2,996

20,000

At least	But less than	Single	Married filing jointly *	Married filing separately	Head of a household
20,000	20,050	3,004	3,004	3,209	3,004
20,050	20,100	3,011	3,011	3,223	3,011
20,100	20,150	3,019	3,019	3,237	3,019
20,150	20,200	3,026	3,026	3,251	3,026
20,200	20,250	3,034	3,034	3,265	3,034
20,250	20,300	3,041	3,041	3,279	3,041
20,300	20,350	3,049	3,049	3,293	3,049
20,350	20,400	3,056	3,056	3,307	3,056
20,400	20,450	3,064	3,064	3,321	3,064
20,450	20,500	3,071	3,071	3,335	3,071
20,500	20,550	3,079	3,079	3,349	3,079
20,550	20,600	3,086	3,086	3,363	3,086
20,600	20,650	3,094	3,094	3,377	3,094
20,650	20,700	3,101	3,101	3,391	3,101
20,700	20,750	3,109	3,109	3,405	3,109
20,750	20,800	3,116	3,116	3,419	3,116
20,800	20,850	3,124	3,124	3,433	3,124
20,850	20,900	3,131	3,131	3,447	3,131
20,900	20,950	3,139	3,139	3,461	3,139
20,950	21,000	3,146	3,146	3,475	3,146

21,000

At least	But less than	Single	Married filing jointly *	Married filing separately	Head of a household
21,000	21,050	3,154	3,154	3,489	3,154
21,050	21,100	3,161	3,161	3,503	3,161
21,100	21,150	3,169	3,169	3,517	3,169
21,150	21,200	3,176	3,176	3,531	3,176
21,200	21,250	3,184	3,184	3,545	3,184
21,250	21,300	3,191	3,191	3,559	3,191
21,300	21,350	3,199	3,199	3,573	3,199
21,350	21,400	3,206	3,206	3,587	3,206
21,400	21,450	3,214	3,214	3,601	3,214
21,450	21,500	3,221	3,221	3,615	3,221
21,500	21,550	3,229	3,229	3,629	3,229
21,550	21,600	3,236	3,236	3,643	3,236
21,600	21,650	3,244	3,244	3,657	3,244
21,650	21,700	3,251	3,251	3,671	3,251
21,700	21,750	3,259	3,259	3,685	3,259
21,750	21,800	3,266	3,266	3,699	3,266
21,800	21,850	3,274	3,274	3,713	3,274
21,850	21,900	3,281	3,281	3,727	3,281
21,900	21,950	3,289	3,289	3,741	3,289
21,950	22,000	3,296	3,296	3,755	3,296

22,000

At least	But less than	Single	Married filing jointly *	Married filing separately	Head of a household
22,000	22,050	3,304	3,304	3,769	3,304
22,050	22,100	3,311	3,311	3,783	3,311
22,100	22,150	3,322	3,319	3,797	3,319
22,150	22,200	3,336	3,326	3,811	3,326
22,200	22,250	3,350	3,334	3,825	3,334
22,250	22,300	3,364	3,341	3,839	3,341
22,300	22,350	3,378	3,349	3,853	3,349
22,350	22,400	3,392	3,356	3,867	3,356
22,400	22,450	3,406	3,364	3,881	3,364
22,450	22,500	3,420	3,371	3,895	3,371
22,500	22,550	3,434	3,379	3,909	3,379
22,550	22,600	3,448	3,386	3,923	3,386
22,600	22,650	3,462	3,394	3,937	3,394
22,650	22,700	3,476	3,401	3,951	3,401
22,700	22,750	3,490	3,409	3,965	3,409
22,750	22,800	3,504	3,416	3,979	3,416
22,800	22,850	3,518	3,424	3,993	3,424
22,850	22,900	3,532	3,431	4,007	3,431
22,900	22,950	3,546	3,439	4,021	3,439
22,950	23,000	3,560	3,446	4,035	3,446

* This column must also be used by a qualifying widow(er).

Continued on next page

1993 Tax Table—*Continued*

If line 37 (taxable income) is—		And you are—				If line 37 (taxable income) is—		And you are—				If line 37 (taxable income) is—		And you are—			
At least	But less than	Single	Married filing jointly *	Married filing separately	Head of a household	At least	But less than	Single	Married filing jointly *	Married filing separately	Head of a household	At least	But less than	Single	Married filing jointly *	Married filing separately	Head of a household
		Your tax is—						Your tax is—						Your tax is—			
23,000						**26,000**						**29,000**					
23,000	23,050	3,574	3,454	4,049	3,454	26,000	26,050	4,414	3,904	4,889	3,904	29,000	29,050	5,254	4,354	5,729	4,354
23,050	23,100	3,588	3,461	4,063	3,461	26,050	26,100	4,428	3,911	4,903	3,911	29,050	29,100	5,268	4,361	5,743	4,361
23,100	23,150	3,602	3,469	4,077	3,469	26,100	26,150	4,442	3,919	4,917	3,919	29,100	29,150	5,282	4,369	5,757	4,369
23,150	23,200	3,616	3,476	4,091	3,476	26,150	26,200	4,456	3,926	4,931	3,926	29,150	29,200	5,296	4,376	5,771	4,376
23,200	23,250	3,630	3,484	4,105	3,484	26,200	26,250	4,470	3,934	4,945	3,934	29,200	29,250	5,310	4,384	5,785	4,384
23,250	23,300	3,644	3,491	4,119	3,491	26,250	26,300	4,484	3,941	4,959	3,941	29,250	29,300	5,324	4,391	5,799	4,391
23,300	23,350	3,658	3,499	4,133	3,499	26,300	26,350	4,498	3,949	4,973	3,949	29,300	29,350	5,338	4,399	5,813	4,399
23,350	23,400	3,672	3,506	4,147	3,506	26,350	26,400	4,512	3,956	4,987	3,956	29,350	29,400	5,352	4,406	5,827	4,406
23,400	23,450	3,686	3,514	4,161	3,514	26,400	26,450	4,526	3,964	5,001	3,964	29,400	29,450	5,366	4,414	5,841	4,414
23,450	23,500	3,700	3,521	4,175	3,521	26,450	26,500	4,540	3,971	5,015	3,971	29,450	29,500	5,380	4,421	5,855	4,421
23,500	23,550	3,714	3,529	4,189	3,529	26,500	26,550	4,554	3,979	5,029	3,979	29,500	29,550	5,394	4,429	5,869	4,429
23,550	23,600	3,728	3,536	4,203	3,536	26,550	26,600	4,568	3,986	5,043	3,986	29,550	29,600	5,408	4,436	5,883	4,436
23,600	23,650	3,742	3,544	4,217	3,544	26,600	26,650	4,582	3,994	5,057	3,994	29,600	29,650	5,422	4,444	5,897	4,447
23,650	23,700	3,756	3,551	4,231	3,551	26,650	26,700	4,596	4,001	5,071	4,001	29,650	29,700	5,436	4,451	5,911	4,461
23,700	23,750	3,770	3,559	4,245	3,559	26,700	26,750	4,610	4,009	5,085	4,009	29,700	29,750	5,450	4,459	5,925	4,475
23,750	23,800	3,784	3,566	4,259	3,566	26,750	26,800	4,624	4,016	5,099	4,016	29,750	29,800	5,464	4,466	5,939	4,489
23,800	23,850	3,798	3,574	4,273	3,574	26,800	26,850	4,638	4,024	5,113	4,024	29,800	29,850	5,478	4,474	5,953	4,503
23,850	23,900	3,812	3,581	4,287	3,581	26,850	26,900	4,652	4,031	5,127	4,031	29,850	29,900	5,492	4,481	5,967	4,517
23,900	23,950	3,826	3,589	4,301	3,589	26,900	26,950	4,666	4,039	5,141	4,039	29,900	29,950	5,506	4,489	5,981	4,531
23,950	24,000	3,840	3,596	4,315	3,596	26,950	27,000	4,680	4,046	5,155	4,046	29,950	30,000	5,520	4,496	5,995	4,545
24,000						**27,000**						**30,000**					
24,000	24,050	3,854	3,604	4,329	3,604	27,000	27,050	4,694	4,054	5,169	4,054	30,000	30,050	5,534	4,504	6,009	4,559
24,050	24,100	3,868	3,611	4,343	3,611	27,050	27,100	4,708	4,061	5,183	4,061	30,050	30,100	5,548	4,511	6,023	4,573
24,100	24,150	3,882	3,619	4,357	3,619	27,100	27,150	4,722	4,069	5,197	4,069	30,100	30,150	5,562	4,519	6,037	4,587
24,150	24,200	3,896	3,626	4,371	3,626	27,150	27,200	4,736	4,076	5,211	4,076	30,150	30,200	5,576	4,526	6,051	4,601
24,200	24,250	3,910	3,634	4,385	3,634	27,200	27,250	4,750	4,084	5,225	4,084	30,200	30,250	5,590	4,534	6,065	4,615
24,250	24,300	3,924	3,641	4,399	3,641	27,250	27,300	4,764	4,091	5,239	4,091	30,250	30,300	5,604	4,541	6,079	4,629
24,300	24,350	3,938	3,649	4,413	3,649	27,300	27,350	4,778	4,099	5,253	4,099	30,300	30,350	5,618	4,549	6,093	4,643
24,350	24,400	3,952	3,656	4,427	3,656	27,350	27,400	4,792	4,106	5,267	4,106	30,350	30,400	5,632	4,556	6,107	4,657
24,400	24,450	3,966	3,664	4,441	3,664	27,400	27,450	4,806	4,114	5,281	4,114	30,400	30,450	5,646	4,564	6,121	4,671
24,450	24,500	3,980	3,671	4,455	3,671	27,450	27,500	4,820	4,121	5,295	4,121	30,450	30,500	5,660	4,571	6,135	4,685
24,500	24,550	3,994	3,679	4,469	3,679	27,500	27,550	4,834	4,129	5,309	4,129	30,500	30,550	5,674	4,579	6,149	4,699
24,550	24,600	4,008	3,686	4,483	3,686	27,550	27,600	4,848	4,136	5,323	4,136	30,550	30,600	5,688	4,586	6,163	4,713
24,600	24,650	4,022	3,694	4,497	3,694	27,600	27,650	4,862	4,144	5,337	4,144	30,600	30,650	5,702	4,594	6,177	4,727
24,650	24,700	4,036	3,701	4,511	3,701	27,650	27,700	4,876	4,151	5,351	4,151	30,650	30,700	5,716	4,601	6,191	4,741
24,700	24,750	4,050	3,709	4,525	3,709	27,700	27,750	4,890	4,159	5,365	4,159	30,700	30,750	5,730	4,609	6,205	4,755
24,750	24,800	4,064	3,716	4,539	3,716	27,750	27,800	4,904	4,166	5,379	4,166	30,750	30,800	5,744	4,616	6,219	4,769
24,800	24,850	4,078	3,724	4,553	3,724	27,800	27,850	4,918	4,174	5,393	4,174	30,800	30,850	5,758	4,624	6,233	4,783
24,850	24,900	4,092	3,731	4,567	3,731	27,850	27,900	4,932	4,181	5,407	4,181	30,850	30,900	5,772	4,631	6,247	4,797
24,900	24,950	4,106	3,739	4,581	3,739	27,900	27,950	4,946	4,189	5,421	4,189	30,900	30,950	5,786	4,639	6,261	4,811
24,950	25,000	4,120	3,746	4,595	3,746	27,950	28,000	4,960	4,196	5,435	4,196	30,950	31,000	5,800	4,646	6,275	4,825
25,000						**28,000**						**31,000**					
25,000	25,050	4,134	3,754	4,609	3,754	28,000	28,050	4,974	4,204	5,449	4,204	31,000	31,050	5,814	4,654	6,289	4,839
25,050	25,100	4,148	3,761	4,623	3,761	28,050	28,100	4,988	4,211	5,463	4,211	31,050	31,100	5,828	4,661	6,303	4,853
25,100	25,150	4,162	3,769	4,637	3,769	28,100	28,150	5,002	4,219	5,477	4,219	31,100	31,150	5,842	4,669	6,317	4,867
25,150	25,200	4,176	3,776	4,651	3,776	28,150	28,200	5,016	4,226	5,491	4,226	31,150	31,200	5,856	4,676	6,331	4,881
25,200	25,250	4,190	3,784	4,665	3,784	28,200	28,250	5,030	4,234	5,505	4,234	31,200	31,250	5,870	4,684	6,345	4,895
25,250	25,300	4,204	3,791	4,679	3,791	28,250	28,300	5,044	4,241	5,519	4,241	31,250	31,300	5,884	4,691	6,359	4,909
25,300	25,350	4,218	3,799	4,693	3,799	28,300	28,350	5,058	4,249	5,533	4,249	31,300	31,350	5,898	4,699	6,373	4,923
25,350	25,400	4,232	3,806	4,707	3,806	28,350	28,400	5,072	4,256	5,547	4,256	31,350	31,400	5,912	4,706	6,387	4,937
25,400	25,450	4,246	3,814	4,721	3,814	28,400	28,450	5,086	4,264	5,561	4,264	31,400	31,450	5,926	4,714	6,401	4,951
25,450	25,500	4,260	3,821	4,735	3,821	28,450	28,500	5,100	4,271	5,575	4,271	31,450	31,500	5,940	4,721	6,415	4,965
25,500	25,550	4,274	3,829	4,749	3,829	28,500	28,550	5,114	4,279	5,589	4,279	31,500	31,550	5,954	4,729	6,429	4,979
25,550	25,600	4,288	3,836	4,763	3,836	28,550	28,600	5,128	4,286	5,603	4,286	31,550	31,600	5,968	4,736	6,443	4,993
25,600	25,650	4,302	3,844	4,777	3,844	28,600	28,650	5,142	4,294	5,617	4,294	31,600	31,650	5,982	4,744	6,457	5,007
25,650	25,700	4,316	3,851	4,791	3,851	28,650	28,700	5,156	4,301	5,631	4,301	31,650	31,700	5,996	4,751	6,471	5,021
25,700	25,750	4,330	3,859	4,805	3,859	28,700	28,750	5,170	4,309	5,645	4,309	31,700	31,750	6,010	4,759	6,485	5,035
25,750	25,800	4,344	3,866	4,819	3,866	28,750	28,800	5,184	4,316	5,659	4,316	31,750	31,800	6,024	4,766	6,499	5,049
25,800	25,850	4,358	3,874	4,833	3,874	28,800	28,850	5,198	4,324	5,673	4,324	31,800	31,850	6,038	4,774	6,513	5,063
25,850	25,900	4,372	3,881	4,847	3,881	28,850	28,900	5,212	4,331	5,687	4,331	31,850	31,900	6,052	4,781	6,527	5,077
25,900	25,950	4,386	3,889	4,861	3,889	28,900	28,950	5,226	4,339	5,701	4,339	31,900	31,950	6,066	4,789	6,541	5,091
25,950	26,000	4,400	3,896	4,875	3,896	28,950	29,000	5,240	4,346	5,715	4,346	31,950	32,000	6,080	4,796	6,555	5,105

* This column must also be used by a qualifying widow(er).

Continued on next page

1993 Tax Table—*Continued*

32,000

At least	But less than	Single	Married filing jointly *	Married filing separately	Head of a household
32,000	32,050	6,094	4,804	6,569	5,119
32,050	32,100	6,108	4,811	6,583	5,133
32,100	32,150	6,122	4,819	6,597	5,147
32,150	32,200	6,136	4,826	6,611	5,161
32,200	32,250	6,150	4,834	6,625	5,175
32,250	32,300	6,164	4,841	6,639	5,189
32,300	32,350	6,178	4,849	6,653	5,203
32,350	32,400	6,192	4,856	6,667	5,217
32,400	32,450	6,206	4,864	6,681	5,231
32,450	32,500	6,220	4,871	6,695	5,245
32,500	32,550	6,234	4,879	6,709	5,259
32,550	32,600	6,248	4,886	6,723	5,273
32,600	32,650	6,262	4,894	6,737	5,287
32,650	32,700	6,276	4,901	6,751	5,301
32,700	32,750	6,290	4,909	6,765	5,315
32,750	32,800	6,304	4,916	6,779	5,329
32,800	32,850	6,318	4,924	6,793	5,343
32,850	32,900	6,332	4,931	6,807	5,357
32,900	32,950	6,346	4,939	6,821	5,371
32,950	33,000	6,360	4,946	6,835	5,385

33,000

At least	But less than	Single	Married filing jointly *	Married filing separately	Head of a household
33,000	33,050	6,374	4,954	6,849	5,399
33,050	33,100	6,388	4,961	6,863	5,413
33,100	33,150	6,402	4,969	6,877	5,427
33,150	33,200	6,416	4,976	6,891	5,441
33,200	33,250	6,430	4,984	6,905	5,455
33,250	33,300	6,444	4,991	6,919	5,469
33,300	33,350	6,458	4,999	6,933	5,483
33,350	33,400	6,472	5,006	6,947	5,497
33,400	33,450	6,486	5,014	6,961	5,511
33,450	33,500	6,500	5,021	6,975	5,525
33,500	33,550	6,514	5,029	6,989	5,539
33,550	33,600	6,528	5,036	7,003	5,553
33,600	33,650	6,542	5,044	7,017	5,567
33,650	33,700	6,556	5,051	7,031	5,581
33,700	33,750	6,570	5,059	7,045	5,595
33,750	33,800	6,584	5,066	7,059	5,609
33,800	33,850	6,598	5,074	7,073	5,623
33,850	33,900	6,612	5,081	7,087	5,637
33,900	33,950	6,626	5,089	7,101	5,651
33,950	34,000	6,640	5,096	7,115	5,665

34,000

At least	But less than	Single	Married filing jointly *	Married filing separately	Head of a household
34,000	34,050	6,654	5,104	7,129	5,679
34,050	34,100	6,668	5,111	7,143	5,693
34,100	34,150	6,682	5,119	7,157	5,707
34,150	34,200	6,696	5,126	7,171	5,721
34,200	34,250	6,710	5,134	7,185	5,735
34,250	34,300	6,724	5,141	7,199	5,749
34,300	34,350	6,738	5,149	7,213	5,763
34,350	34,400	6,752	5,156	7,227	5,777
34,400	34,450	6,766	5,164	7,241	5,791
34,450	34,500	6,780	5,171	7,255	5,805
34,500	34,550	6,794	5,179	7,269	5,819
34,550	34,600	6,808	5,186	7,283	5,833
34,600	34,650	6,822	5,194	7,297	5,847
34,650	34,700	6,836	5,201	7,311	5,861
34,700	34,750	6,850	5,209	7,325	5,875
34,750	34,800	6,864	5,216	7,339	5,889
34,800	34,850	6,878	5,224	7,353	5,903
34,850	34,900	6,892	5,231	7,367	5,917
34,900	34,950	6,906	5,239	7,381	5,931
34,950	35,000	6,920	5,246	7,395	5,945

35,000

At least	But less than	Single	Married filing jointly *	Married filing separately	Head of a household
35,000	35,050	6,934	5,254	7,409	5,959
35,050	35,100	6,948	5,261	7,423	5,973
35,100	35,150	6,962	5,269	7,437	5,987
35,150	35,200	6,976	5,276	7,451	6,001
35,200	35,250	6,990	5,284	7,465	6,015
35,250	35,300	7,004	5,291	7,479	6,029
35,300	35,350	7,018	5,299	7,493	6,043
35,350	35,400	7,032	5,306	7,507	6,057
35,400	35,450	7,046	5,314	7,521	6,071
35,450	35,500	7,060	5,321	7,535	6,085
35,500	35,550	7,074	5,329	7,549	6,099
35,550	35,600	7,088	5,336	7,563	6,113
35,600	35,650	7,102	5,344	7,577	6,127
35,650	35,700	7,116	5,351	7,591	6,141
35,700	35,750	7,130	5,359	7,605	6,155
35,750	35,800	7,144	5,366	7,619	6,169
35,800	35,850	7,158	5,374	7,633	6,183
35,850	35,900	7,172	5,381	7,647	6,197
35,900	35,950	7,186	5,389	7,661	6,211
35,950	36,000	7,200	5,396	7,675	6,225

36,000

At least	But less than	Single	Married filing jointly *	Married filing separately	Head of a household
36,000	36,050	7,214	5,404	7,689	6,239
36,050	36,100	7,228	5,411	7,703	6,253
36,100	36,150	7,242	5,419	7,717	6,267
36,150	36,200	7,256	5,426	7,731	6,281
36,200	36,250	7,270	5,434	7,745	6,295
36,250	36,300	7,284	5,441	7,759	6,309
36,300	36,350	7,298	5,449	7,773	6,323
36,350	36,400	7,312	5,456	7,787	6,337
36,400	36,450	7,326	5,464	7,801	6,351
36,450	36,500	7,340	5,471	7,815	6,365
36,500	36,550	7,354	5,479	7,829	6,379
36,550	36,600	7,368	5,486	7,843	6,393
36,600	36,650	7,382	5,494	7,857	6,407
36,650	36,700	7,396	5,501	7,871	6,421
36,700	36,750	7,410	5,509	7,885	6,435
36,750	36,800	7,424	5,516	7,899	6,449
36,800	36,850	7,438	5,524	7,913	6,463
36,850	36,900	7,452	5,531	7,927	6,477
36,900	36,950	7,466	5,542	7,941	6,491
36,950	37,000	7,480	5,556	7,955	6,505

37,000

At least	But less than	Single	Married filing jointly *	Married filing separately	Head of a household
37,000	37,050	7,494	5,570	7,969	6,519
37,050	37,100	7,508	5,584	7,983	6,533
37,100	37,150	7,522	5,598	7,997	6,547
37,150	37,200	7,536	5,612	8,011	6,561
37,200	37,250	7,550	5,626	8,025	6,575
37,250	37,300	7,564	5,640	8,039	6,589
37,300	37,350	7,578	5,654	8,053	6,603
37,350	37,400	7,592	5,668	8,067	6,617
37,400	37,450	7,606	5,682	8,081	6,631
37,450	37,500	7,620	5,696	8,095	6,645
37,500	37,550	7,634	5,710	8,109	6,659
37,550	37,600	7,648	5,724	8,123	6,673
37,600	37,650	7,662	5,738	8,137	6,687
37,650	37,700	7,676	5,752	8,151	6,701
37,700	37,750	7,690	5,766	8,165	6,715
37,750	37,800	7,704	5,780	8,179	6,729
37,800	37,850	7,718	5,794	8,193	6,743
37,850	37,900	7,732	5,808	8,207	6,757
37,900	37,950	7,746	5,822	8,221	6,771
37,950	38,000	7,760	5,836	8,235	6,785

38,000

At least	But less than	Single	Married filing jointly *	Married filing separately	Head of a household
38,000	38,050	7,774	5,850	8,249	6,799
38,050	38,100	7,788	5,864	8,263	6,813
38,100	38,150	7,802	5,878	8,277	6,827
38,150	38,200	7,816	5,892	8,291	6,841
38,200	38,250	7,830	5,906	8,305	6,855
38,250	38,300	7,844	5,920	8,319	6,869
38,300	38,350	7,858	5,934	8,333	6,883
38,350	38,400	7,872	5,948	8,347	6,897
38,400	38,450	7,886	5,962	8,361	6,911
38,450	38,500	7,900	5,976	8,375	6,925
38,500	38,550	7,914	5,990	8,389	6,939
38,550	38,600	7,928	6,004	8,403	6,953
38,600	38,650	7,942	6,018	8,417	6,967
38,650	38,700	7,956	6,032	8,431	6,981
38,700	38,750	7,970	6,046	8,445	6,995
38,750	38,800	7,984	6,060	8,459	7,009
38,800	38,850	7,998	6,074	8,473	7,023
38,850	38,900	8,012	6,088	8,487	7,037
38,900	38,950	8,026	6,102	8,501	7,051
38,950	39,000	8,040	6,116	8,515	7,065

39,000

At least	But less than	Single	Married filing jointly *	Married filing separately	Head of a household
39,000	39,050	8,054	6,130	8,529	7,079
39,050	39,100	8,068	6,144	8,543	7,093
39,100	39,150	8,082	6,158	8,557	7,107
39,150	39,200	8,096	6,172	8,571	7,121
39,200	39,250	8,110	6,186	8,585	7,135
39,250	39,300	8,124	6,200	8,599	7,149
39,300	39,350	8,138	6,214	8,613	7,163
39,350	39,400	8,152	6,228	8,627	7,177
39,400	39,450	8,166	6,242	8,641	7,191
39,450	39,500	8,180	6,256	8,655	7,205
39,500	39,550	8,194	6,270	8,669	7,219
39,550	39,600	8,208	6,284	8,683	7,233
39,600	39,650	8,222	6,298	8,697	7,247
39,650	39,700	8,236	6,312	8,711	7,261
39,700	39,750	8,250	6,326	8,725	7,275
39,750	39,800	8,264	6,340	8,739	7,289
39,800	39,850	8,278	6,354	8,753	7,303
39,850	39,900	8,292	6,368	8,767	7,317
39,900	39,950	8,306	6,382	8,781	7,331
39,950	40,000	8,320	6,396	8,795	7,345

40,000

At least	But less than	Single	Married filing jointly *	Married filing separately	Head of a household
40,000	40,050	8,334	6,410	8,809	7,359
40,050	40,100	8,348	6,424	8,823	7,373
40,100	40,150	8,362	6,438	8,837	7,387
40,150	40,200	8,376	6,452	8,851	7,401
40,200	40,250	8,390	6,466	8,865	7,415
40,250	40,300	8,404	6,480	8,879	7,429
40,300	40,350	8,418	6,494	8,893	7,443
40,350	40,400	8,432	6,508	8,907	7,457
40,400	40,450	8,446	6,522	8,921	7,471
40,450	40,500	8,460	6,536	8,935	7,485
40,500	40,550	8,474	6,550	8,949	7,499
40,550	40,600	8,488	6,564	8,963	7,513
40,600	40,650	8,502	6,578	8,977	7,527
40,650	40,700	8,516	6,592	8,991	7,541
40,700	40,750	8,530	6,606	9,005	7,555
40,750	40,800	8,544	6,620	9,019	7,569
40,800	40,850	8,558	6,634	9,033	7,583
40,850	40,900	8,572	6,648	9,047	7,597
40,900	40,950	8,586	6,662	9,061	7,611
40,950	41,000	8,600	6,676	9,075	7,625

* This column must also be used by a qualifying widow(er).

Continued on next page

1993 Tax Table—Continued

41,000

At least	But less than	Single	Married filing jointly*	Married filing separately	Head of a household
41,000	41,050	8,614	6,690	9,089	7,639
41,050	41,100	8,628	6,704	9,103	7,653
41,100	41,150	8,642	6,718	9,117	7,667
41,150	41,200	8,656	6,732	9,131	7,681
41,200	41,250	8,670	6,746	9,145	7,695
41,250	41,300	8,684	6,760	9,159	7,709
41,300	41,350	8,698	6,774	9,173	7,723
41,350	41,400	8,712	6,788	9,187	7,737
41,400	41,450	8,726	6,802	9,201	7,751
41,450	41,500	8,740	6,816	9,215	7,765
41,500	41,550	8,754	6,830	9,229	7,779
41,550	41,600	8,768	6,844	9,243	7,793
41,600	41,650	8,782	6,858	9,257	7,807
41,650	41,700	8,796	6,872	9,271	7,821
41,700	41,750	8,810	6,886	9,285	7,835
41,750	41,800	8,824	6,900	9,299	7,849
41,800	41,850	8,838	6,914	9,313	7,863
41,850	41,900	8,852	6,928	9,327	7,877
41,900	41,950	8,866	6,942	9,341	7,891
41,950	42,000	8,880	6,956	9,355	7,905

42,000

At least	But less than	Single	Married filing jointly*	Married filing separately	Head of a household
42,000	42,050	8,894	6,970	9,369	7,919
42,050	42,100	8,908	6,984	9,383	7,933
42,100	42,150	8,922	6,998	9,397	7,947
42,150	42,200	8,936	7,012	9,411	7,961
42,200	42,250	8,950	7,026	9,425	7,975
42,250	42,300	8,964	7,040	9,439	7,989
42,300	42,350	8,978	7,054	9,453	8,003
42,350	42,400	8,992	7,068	9,467	8,017
42,400	42,450	9,006	7,082	9,481	8,031
42,450	42,500	9,020	7,096	9,495	8,045
42,500	42,550	9,034	7,110	9,509	8,059
42,550	42,600	9,048	7,124	9,523	8,073
42,600	42,650	9,062	7,138	9,537	8,087
42,650	42,700	9,076	7,152	9,551	8,101
42,700	42,750	9,090	7,166	9,565	8,115
42,750	42,800	9,104	7,180	9,579	8,129
42,800	42,850	9,118	7,194	9,593	8,143
42,850	42,900	9,132	7,208	9,607	8,157
42,900	42,950	9,146	7,222	9,621	8,171
42,950	43,000	9,160	7,236	9,635	8,185

43,000

At least	But less than	Single	Married filing jointly*	Married filing separately	Head of a household
43,000	43,050	9,174	7,250	9,649	8,199
43,050	43,100	9,188	7,264	9,663	8,213
43,100	43,150	9,202	7,278	9,677	8,227
43,150	43,200	9,216	7,292	9,691	8,241
43,200	43,250	9,230	7,306	9,705	8,255
43,250	43,300	9,244	7,320	9,719	8,269
43,300	43,350	9,258	7,334	9,733	8,283
43,350	43,400	9,272	7,348	9,747	8,297
43,400	43,450	9,286	7,362	9,761	8,311
43,450	43,500	9,300	7,376	9,775	8,325
43,500	43,550	9,314	7,390	9,789	8,339
43,550	43,600	9,328	7,404	9,803	8,353
43,600	43,650	9,342	7,418	9,817	8,367
43,650	43,700	9,356	7,432	9,831	8,381
43,700	43,750	9,370	7,446	9,845	8,395
43,750	43,800	9,384	7,460	9,859	8,409
43,800	43,850	9,398	7,474	9,873	8,423
43,850	43,900	9,412	7,488	9,887	8,437
43,900	43,950	9,426	7,502	9,901	8,451
43,950	44,000	9,440	7,516	9,915	8,465

44,000

At least	But less than	Single	Married filing jointly*	Married filing separately	Head of a household
44,000	44,050	9,454	7,530	9,929	8,479
44,050	44,100	9,468	7,544	9,943	8,493
44,100	44,150	9,482	7,558	9,957	8,507
44,150	44,200	9,496	7,572	9,971	8,521
44,200	44,250	9,510	7,586	9,985	8,535
44,250	44,300	9,524	7,600	9,999	8,549
44,300	44,350	9,538	7,614	10,013	8,563
44,350	44,400	9,552	7,628	10,027	8,577
44,400	44,450	9,566	7,642	10,041	8,591
44,450	44,500	9,580	7,656	10,055	8,605
44,500	44,550	9,594	7,670	10,069	8,619
44,550	44,600	9,608	7,684	10,083	8,633
44,600	44,650	9,622	7,698	10,098	8,647
44,650	44,700	9,636	7,712	10,114	8,661
44,700	44,750	9,650	7,726	10,129	8,675
44,750	44,800	9,664	7,740	10,145	8,689
44,800	44,850	9,678	7,754	10,160	8,703
44,850	44,900	9,692	7,768	10,176	8,717
44,900	44,950	9,706	7,782	10,191	8,731
44,950	45,000	9,720	7,796	10,207	8,745

45,000

At least	But less than	Single	Married filing jointly*	Married filing separately	Head of a household
45,000	45,050	9,734	7,810	10,222	8,759
45,050	45,100	9,748	7,824	10,238	8,773
45,100	45,150	9,762	7,838	10,253	8,787
45,150	45,200	9,776	7,852	10,269	8,801
45,200	45,250	9,790	7,866	10,284	8,815
45,250	45,300	9,804	7,880	10,300	8,829
45,300	45,350	9,818	7,894	10,315	8,843
45,350	45,400	9,832	7,908	10,331	8,857
45,400	45,450	9,846	7,922	10,346	8,871
45,450	45,500	9,860	7,936	10,362	8,885
45,500	45,550	9,874	7,950	10,377	8,899
45,550	45,600	9,888	7,964	10,393	8,913
45,600	45,650	9,902	7,978	10,408	8,927
45,650	45,700	9,916	7,992	10,424	8,941
45,700	45,750	9,930	8,006	10,439	8,955
45,750	45,800	9,944	8,020	10,455	8,969
45,800	45,850	9,958	8,034	10,470	8,983
45,850	45,900	9,972	8,048	10,486	8,997
45,900	45,950	9,986	8,062	10,501	9,011
45,950	46,000	10,000	8,076	10,517	9,025

46,000

At least	But less than	Single	Married filing jointly*	Married filing separately	Head of a household
46,000	46,050	10,014	8,090	10,532	9,039
46,050	46,100	10,028	8,104	10,548	9,053
46,100	46,150	10,042	8,118	10,563	9,067
46,150	46,200	10,056	8,132	10,579	9,081
46,200	46,250	10,070	8,146	10,594	9,095
46,250	46,300	10,084	8,160	10,610	9,109
46,300	46,350	10,098	8,174	10,625	9,123
46,350	46,400	10,112	8,188	10,641	9,137
46,400	46,450	10,126	8,202	10,656	9,151
46,450	46,500	10,140	8,216	10,672	9,165
46,500	46,550	10,154	8,230	10,687	9,179
46,550	46,600	10,168	8,244	10,703	9,193
46,600	46,650	10,182	8,258	10,718	9,207
46,650	46,700	10,196	8,272	10,734	9,221
46,700	46,750	10,210	8,286	10,749	9,235
46,750	46,800	10,224	8,300	10,765	9,249
46,800	46,850	10,238	8,314	10,780	9,263
46,850	46,900	10,252	8,328	10,796	9,277
46,900	46,950	10,266	8,342	10,811	9,291
46,950	47,000	10,280	8,356	10,827	9,305

47,000

At least	But less than	Single	Married filing jointly*	Married filing separately	Head of a household
47,000	47,050	10,294	8,370	10,842	9,319
47,050	47,100	10,308	8,384	10,858	9,333
47,100	47,150	10,322	8,398	10,873	9,347
47,150	47,200	10,336	8,412	10,889	9,361
47,200	47,250	10,350	8,426	10,904	9,375
47,250	47,300	10,364	8,440	10,920	9,389
47,300	47,350	10,378	8,454	10,935	9,403
47,350	47,400	10,392	8,468	10,951	9,417
47,400	47,450	10,406	8,482	10,966	9,431
47,450	47,500	10,420	8,496	10,982	9,445
47,500	47,550	10,434	8,510	10,997	9,459
47,550	47,600	10,448	8,524	11,013	9,473
47,600	47,650	10,462	8,538	11,028	9,487
47,650	47,700	10,476	8,552	11,044	9,501
47,700	47,750	10,490	8,566	11,059	9,515
47,750	47,800	10,504	8,580	11,075	9,529
47,800	47,850	10,518	8,594	11,090	9,543
47,850	47,900	10,532	8,608	11,106	9,557
47,900	47,950	10,546	8,622	11,121	9,571
47,950	48,000	10,560	8,636	11,137	9,585

48,000

At least	But less than	Single	Married filing jointly*	Married filing separately	Head of a household
48,000	48,050	10,574	8,650	11,152	9,599
48,050	48,100	10,588	8,664	11,168	9,613
48,100	48,150	10,602	8,678	11,183	9,627
48,150	48,200	10,616	8,692	11,199	9,641
48,200	48,250	10,630	8,706	11,214	9,655
48,250	48,300	10,644	8,720	11,230	9,669
48,300	48,350	10,658	8,734	11,245	9,683
48,350	48,400	10,672	8,748	11,261	9,697
48,400	48,450	10,686	8,762	11,276	9,711
48,450	48,500	10,700	8,776	11,292	9,725
48,500	48,550	10,714	8,790	11,307	9,739
48,550	48,600	10,728	8,804	11,323	9,753
48,600	48,650	10,742	8,818	11,338	9,767
48,650	48,700	10,756	8,832	11,354	9,781
48,700	48,750	10,770	8,846	11,369	9,795
48,750	48,800	10,784	8,860	11,385	9,809
48,800	48,850	10,798	8,874	11,400	9,823
48,850	48,900	10,812	8,888	11,416	9,837
48,900	48,950	10,826	8,902	11,431	9,851
48,950	49,000	10,840	8,916	11,447	9,865

49,000

At least	But less than	Single	Married filing jointly*	Married filing separately	Head of a household
49,000	49,050	10,854	8,930	11,462	9,879
49,050	49,100	10,868	8,944	11,478	9,893
49,100	49,150	10,882	8,958	11,493	9,907
49,150	49,200	10,896	8,972	11,509	9,921
49,200	49,250	10,910	8,986	11,524	9,935
49,250	49,300	10,924	9,000	11,540	9,949
49,300	49,350	10,938	9,014	11,555	9,963
49,350	49,400	10,952	9,028	11,571	9,977
49,400	49,450	10,966	9,042	11,586	9,991
49,450	49,500	10,980	9,056	11,602	10,005
49,500	49,550	10,994	9,070	11,617	10,019
49,550	49,600	11,008	9,084	11,633	10,033
49,600	49,650	11,022	9,098	11,648	10,047
49,650	49,700	11,036	9,112	11,664	10,061
49,700	49,750	11,050	9,126	11,679	10,075
49,750	49,800	11,064	9,140	11,695	10,089
49,800	49,850	11,078	9,154	11,710	10,103
49,850	49,900	11,092	9,168	11,726	10,117
49,900	49,950	11,106	9,182	11,741	10,131
49,950	50,000	11,120	9,196	11,757	10,145

* This column must also be used by a qualifying widow(er).

Continued on next page

1994 Tax Rate Schedules

Single—Schedule X

If taxable income is: Over—	But not over—	The tax is:	of the amount over—
$0	$22,750	........15%	$0
22,750	55,100	$3,412.50 + 28%	22,750
55,100	115,000	12,470.50 + 31%	55,100
115,000	250,000	31,039.50 + 36%	115,000
250,000	....	79,639.50 + 39.6%	250,000

Head of household—Schedule Z

If taxable income is: Over—	But not over—	The tax is:	of the amount over—
$0	$30,500	........15%	$0
30,500	78,700	$4,575.00 + 28%	30,500
78,700	127,500	18,071.00 + 31%	78,700
127,500	250,000	33,199.00 + 36%	127,500
250,000	....	77,299.00 + 39.6%	250,000

Married filing jointly or Qualifying widow(er)—Schedule Y-1

If taxable income is: Over—	But not over—	The tax is:	of the amount over—
$0	$38,000	........15%	$0
38,000	91,850	$5,700.00 + 28%	38,000
91,850	140,000	20,778.00 + 31%	91,850
140,000	250,000	35,704.50 + 36%	140,000
250,000	....	75,304.50 + 39.6%	250,000

Married filing separately—Schedule Y-2

If taxable income is: Over—	But not over—	The tax is:	of the amount over—
$0	$19,000	........15%	$0
19,000	45,925	$2,850.00 + 28%	19,000
45,925	70,000	10,389.00 + 31%	45,925
70,000	125,000	17,852.25 + 36%	70,000
125,000	....	37,652.25 + 39.6%	125,000

APPENDIX B
Tax Forms

Form 1040EZ	Income Tax Return for Single Filers With No Dependents	B–3
Form 1040A	U.S. Individual Income Tax Return (Short Form)	B–5
Schedule 1	Interest and Dividend Income	B–7
Form 1040	U.S. Individual Income Tax Return	B–8
Schedules A & B	Itemized Deductions; Interest and Dividend Income	B–10
Schedule C	Profit or Loss Business	B–12
Schedule D	Capital Gains and Losses and Reconciliation of Forms 1099–B	B–14
Schedule E	Supplemental Income and Loss	B–16
Schedule EIC	Earned Income Credit	B–18
Schedule R	Credit for the Elderly or the Disabled	B–20
Schedule SE	Self-Employment Tax	B–22
Form 1040-ES	Estimated Tax for Individuals	B–24
Form 2106	Employee Business Expenses	B–30
Form 2119	Sale of Your Home	B–32
Form 2120	Multiple Support Declaration	B–33
Form 2210	Underpayment of Estimated Tax by Individuals and Fiduciaries	B–34
Form 2441	Child and Dependent Care Expenses	B–36

Form 3800	General Business Credit	**B–38**
Form 3903	Moving Expenses	**B–39**
Form 4255	Recapture of Investment Credit	**B–40**
Form 4562	Depreciation and Amortization	**B–42**
Form 4684	Casualties and Thefts	**B–44**
Form 4797	Sales of Business Property	**B–46**
Form 4868	Application for Automatic Extension of Time to File U.S. Individual Income Tax Return	**B–48**
Form 4952	Investment Interest Expense Deduction	**B–49**
Form 4972	Tax on Lump-Sum Distributions	**B–51**
Form 6251	Alternative Minimum Tax—Individuals	**B–53**
Form 6252	Installment Sale Income	**B–54**
Form 8283	Noncash Charitable Contributions	**B–55**
Form 8332	Release of Claim to Exemption for Child of Divorced or Separated Parents	**B–57**
Form 8582	Passive Activity Loss Limitations	**B–58**
Form 8606	Nondeductible IRA Contributions, IRA Basis, and Nontaxable IRA Distributions	**B–59**
Form 8615	Tax for Children Under Age 14 Who Have Investment Income of More Than $1,100	**B–61**
Form 8829	Expenses for Business Use of Your Home	**B–63**

Department of the Treasury—Internal Revenue Service

Form
1040EZ

Income Tax Return for Single and Joint Filers With No Dependents 1993

OMB No. 1545-0675

Use the IRS label
(See page 10.)
Otherwise, please print.

L A B E L
H E R E

Print your name (first, initial, last)

If a joint return, print spouse's name (first, initial, last)

Home address (number and street). If you have a P.O. box, see page 11.　Apt. no.

City, town or post office, state and ZIP code. If you have a foreign address, see page 11.

Your social security number

Spouse's social security number

See instructions on back and in Form 1040EZ booklet.

Presidential Election Campaign
(See page 11.)

Note: *Checking "Yes" will not change your tax or reduce your refund.*
Do you want $3 to go to this fund?　▶
If a joint return, does your spouse want $3 to go to this fund?　▶

Yes　No

Dollars　Cents

Filing status

1 ☐ Single ☐ Married filing joint return (even if only one had income)

Report your income

Attach Copy B of Form(s) W-2 here. Attach any tax payment on top of Form(s) W-2.

Note: *You must check Yes or No.*

2　Total wages, salaries, and tips. This should be shown in box 1 of your W-2 form(s). Attach your W-2 form(s).　2

3　Taxable interest income of $400 or less. If the total is over $400, you cannot use Form 1040EZ.　3

4　Add lines 2 and 3. This is your **adjusted gross income.**　4

5　Can your parents (or someone else) claim you on their return?
☐ **Yes.** Do worksheet on back; enter amount from line G here.
☐ **No.** If **single,** enter 6,050.00. If **married,** enter 10,900.00. For an explanation of these amounts, see back of form.　5

6　Subtract line 5 from line 4. If line 5 is larger than line 4, enter 0. This is your **taxable income.**　6

Figure your tax

7　Enter your Federal income tax withheld from box 2 of your W-2 form(s).　7

8　**Tax.** Look at line 6 above. Use the amount on **line 6** to find your tax in the tax table on pages 24–28 of the booklet. Then, enter the tax from the table on this line.　8

Refund or amount you owe

9　If line 7 is larger than line 8, subtract line 8 from line 7. This is your **refund.**　9

10　If line 8 is larger than line 7, subtract line 7 from line 8. This is the **amount you owe.** For details on how to pay, including what to write on your payment, see page 16.　10

Sign your return

Keep a copy of this form for your records.

I have read this return. Under penalties of perjury, I declare that to the best of my knowledge and belief, the return is true, correct, and accurately lists all amounts and sources of income I received during the tax year.

Your signature

Spouse's signature if joint return

Date　Your occupation　Date　Spouse's occupation

For IRS Use Only — Please do not write in boxes below.

For Privacy Act and Paperwork Reduction Act Notice, see page 4.　Cat. No. 11329W　Form 1040EZ (1993)

1993   Instructions for Form 1040EZ

Use this form if	• Your filing status is single or married filing jointly. • You (and your spouse if married) were under 65 on January 1, 1994, and not blind at the end of 1993. • You do not claim any dependents. • Your taxable income (line 6) is less than $50,000. • You had **only** wages, salaries, tips, and taxable scholarship or fellowship grants, and your taxable interest income was $400 or less. **But** if you earned tips, including allocated tips, that are not included in box 5 and box 7 of your W-2, you may not be able to use Form 1040EZ. See page 13. • You did not receive any advance earned income credit payments. **Caution:** *If married and either you or your spouse had total wages of over $57,600, you may not be able to use this form. See page 6.* If you are not sure about your filing status, see page 12. If you have questions about dependents, call Tele-Tax (see page 22) and listen to topic 354. If you **can't use this form,** call Tele-Tax (see page 22) and listen to topic 352.

Filling in your return	Because this form is read by a machine, please print your numbers inside the boxes like this: $9\ 8\ 7\ 6\ 5\ 4\ 3\ 2\ 1\ 0$ Do not type your numbers. Do not use dollar signs. Most people can fill in the form by following the instructions on the front. But you will have to use the booklet if you received a scholarship or fellowship grant or tax-exempt interest income, such as on municipal bonds. Also, use the booklet if you received a Form 1099-INT showing income tax withheld (backup withholding). **Remember,** you must report all wages, salaries, and tips even if you don't get a W-2 form from your employer. You must also report all your taxable interest income, including interest from banks, savings and loans, credit unions, etc., even if you don't get a Form 1099-INT. If you paid someone to prepare your return, see page 17.

Worksheet for dependents who checked "Yes" on line 5	Use this worksheet to figure the amount to enter on line 5 if someone can claim you (or your spouse if married) as a dependent, even if that person chooses not to do so. To find out if someone can claim you as a dependent, call Tele-Tax (see page 22) and listen to topic 354.
	
	A. Enter the amount from line 2 on the front. **A.** _____
	B. Minimum standard deduction. **B.** _____600.00
	C. Enter the LARGER of line A or line B here. **C.** _____
	D. Maximum standard deduction. If single, enter 3,700.00; if married, enter 6,200.00. **D.** _____
	E. Enter the SMALLER of line C or line D here. This is your standard deduction. **E.** _____
	F. Exemption amount.
	   • If single, enter 0.
	   • If married and both you and your spouse can be claimed as dependents, enter 0.
	   • If married and only one of you can be claimed as a dependent, enter 2,350.00. **F.** _____
	G. Add lines E and F. Enter the total here and on line 5 on the front. **G.** _____
	
	If you checked "No" on line 5 because no one can claim you (or your spouse if married) as a dependent, enter on line 5 the amount shown below that applies to you.
	
	• Single, enter 6,050.00. This is the total of your standard deduction (3,700.00) and personal exemption (2,350.00).
	• Married, enter 10,900.00. This is the total of your standard deduction (6,200.00), exemption for yourself (2,350.00), and exemption for your spouse (2,350.00).

Avoid mistakes	Please see page 17 of the Form 1040EZ booklet for a list of common mistakes to avoid that will help you make sure your form is filled in correctly.

Mailing your return	Mail your return by **April 15, 1994.** Use the envelope that came with your booklet. If you don't have that envelope, see page 29 for the address to use.

Form

1040A

Department of the Treasury—Internal Revenue Service

U.S. Individual Income Tax Return   **1993**

IRS Use Only—Do not write or staple in this space.

Label

(See page 15.)

Use the IRS label.
Otherwise, please print or type.

L
A
B
E
L

H
E
R
E

Your first name and initial	Last name

If a joint return, spouse's first name and initial	Last name

Home address (number and street). If you have a P.O. box, see page 16.	Apt. no.

City, town or post office, state, and ZIP code. If you have a foreign address, see page 16.

OMB No. 1545-0085

Your social security number

Spouse's social security number

For Privacy Act and Paperwork Reduction Act Notice, see page 4.

Presidential Election Campaign Fund (See page 16.)
Do you want $3 to go to this fund? . . . .
If a joint return, does your spouse want $3 to go to this fund?

Yes	No

Note: *Checking "Yes" will not change your tax or reduce your refund.*

Check the box for your filing status

(See page 16.)

Check only one box.

1 ☐ Single
2 ☐ Married filing joint return (even if only one had income)
3 ☐ Married filing separate return. Enter spouse's social security number above and full name here. ▶ _____
4 ☐ Head of household (with qualifying person). (See page 17.) If the qualifying person is a child but not your dependent, enter this child's name here. ▶ _____
5 ☐ Qualifying widow(er) with dependent child (year spouse died ▶ 19___). (See page 18.)

Figure your exemptions

(See page 19.)

If more than seven dependents, see page 22.

6a ☐ **Yourself.** If your parent (or someone else) can claim you as a dependent on his or her tax return, **do not** check box 6a. But be sure to check the box on line 18b on page 2.

b ☐ **Spouse**

c **Dependents:**

(1) Name (first, initial, and last name)	(2) Check if under age 1	(3) If age 1 or older, dependent's social security number	(4) Dependent's relationship to you	(5) No. of months lived in your home in 1993
_____				
_____				
_____				
_____				
_____				
_____				
_____				

No. of boxes checked on 6a and 6b ____

No. of your children on 6c who:
• lived with you ____
• didn't live with you due to divorce or separation (see page 22) ____

Dependents on 6c not entered above ____

d If your child didn't live with you but is claimed as your dependent under a pre-1985 agreement, check here . . . . ▶ ☐

e Total number of exemptions claimed.

Add numbers entered on lines above ☐

Figure your total income

Attach Copy B of your Forms W-2 and 1099-R here.

If you didn't get a W-2, see page 24.

If you are attaching a check or money order, put it on top of any Forms W-2 or 1099-R.

7 Wages, salaries, tips, etc. This should be shown in box 1 of your W-2 form(s). Attach Form(s) W-2.   **7**

8a **Taxable** interest income (see page 25). If over $400, also complete and attach Schedule 1, Part I.   **8a**

b **Tax-exempt** interest. DO NOT include on line 8a.   **8b**

9 Dividends. If over $400, also complete and attach Schedule 1, Part II.   **9**

10a Total IRA distributions.   **10a**   **10b** Taxable amount (see page 26).   **10b**

11a Total pensions and annuities.   **11a**   **11b** Taxable amount (see page 26).   **11b**

12 Unemployment compensation (see page 30).   **12**

13a Social security benefits.   **13a**   **13b** Taxable amount (see page 30).   **13b**

14 Add lines 7 through 13b (far right column). This is your **total income.** ▶ **14**

Figure your adjusted gross income

15a Your IRA deduction (see page 32).   **15a**

b Spouse's IRA deduction (see page 32).   **15b**

c Add lines 15a and 15b. These are your **total adjustments.**   **15c**

16 Subtract line 15c from line 14. This is your **adjusted gross income.** If less than $23,050 and a child lived with you, see page 63 to find out if you can claim the "Earned income credit" on line 28c. ▶ **16**

Cat. No. 11327A

1993 Form 1040A page 1

1993 Form 1040A page 2

Name(s) shown on page 1	Your social security number

Figure your standard deduction, exemption amount, and taxable income

17   Enter the amount from line 16.   **17**

18a   Check if: ☐ **You** were 65 or older   ☐ Blind   **Enter number of boxes checked** ▶ **18a** ☐
     ☐ **Spouse** was 65 or older   ☐ Blind

  b   If your parent (or someone else) can claim you as a dependent, check here . . . . ▶ **18b** ☐

  c   If you are married filing separately and your spouse files Form 1040 and itemizes deductions, see page 36 and check here ▶ **18c** ☐

19   Enter the **standard deduction** shown below for your filing status. **But if you checked any box on line 18a or b,** go to page 36 to find your standard deduction. **If you checked box 18c,** enter -0-.
- Single—$3,700   ● Head of household—$5,450
- Married filing jointly or Qualifying widow(er)—$6,200
- Married filing separately—$3,100   **19**

20   Subtract line 19 from line 17. If line 19 is more than line 17, enter -0-.   **20**

21   Multiply $2,350 by the total number of exemptions claimed on line 6e.   **21**

22   Subtract line 21 from line 20. If line 21 is more than line 20, enter -0-. This is your **taxable income.** ▶ **22**

Figure your tax, credits, and payments

If you want the IRS to figure your tax, see the instructions for line 22 on page 37.

23   Find the tax on the amount on line 22. Check if from: ☐ Tax Table (pages 50–55) or   ☐ Form 8615 (see page 38).   **23**

24a   Credit for child and dependent care expenses. Complete and attach Schedule 2.   **24a**

  b   Credit for the elderly or the disabled. Complete and attach Schedule 3.   **24b**

  c   Add lines 24a and 24b. These are your **total credits.**   **24c**

25   Subtract line 24c from line 23. If line 24c is more than line 23, enter -0-.   **25**

26   Advance earned income credit payments from Form W-2.   **26**

27   Add lines 25 and 26. This is your **total tax.** ▶ **27**

28a   Total Federal income tax withheld. If any tax is from Form(s) 1099, check here. ▶ ☐   **28a**

  b   1993 estimated tax payments and amount applied from 1992 return.   **28b**

  c   **Earned income credit.** Complete and attach Schedule EIC.   **28c**

  d   Add lines 28a, 28b, and 28c. These are your **total payments.** ▶ **28d**

Figure your refund or amount you owe

29   If line 28d is more than line 27, subtract line 27 from line 28d. This is the amount you **overpaid.**   **29**

30   Amount of line 29 you want **refunded to you.**   **30**

31   Amount of line 29 you want **applied to your 1994 estimated tax.**   **31**

32   If line 27 is more than line 28d, subtract line 28d from line 27. This is the **amount you owe.** For details on how to pay, including what to write on your payment, see page 42.   **32**

33   Estimated tax penalty (see page 43). Also, include on line 32.   **33**

Sign your return

Keep a copy of this return for your records.

Under penalties of perjury, I declare that I have examined this return and accompanying schedules and statements, and to the best of my knowledge and belief, they are true, correct, and accurately list all amounts and sources of income I received during the tax year. Declaration of preparer (other than the taxpayer) is based on all information of which the preparer has any knowledge.

▶ Your signature	Date	Your occupation
▶ Spouse's signature. If joint return, BOTH must sign.	Date	Spouse's occupation

Paid preparer's use only

Preparer's signature ▶	Date	Check if self-employed ☐	Preparer's social security no.
Firm's name (or yours if self-employed) and address ▶		E.I. No.	
		ZIP code	

1993 Form 1040A page 2

Schedule 1
(Form 1040A)

Department of the Treasury—Internal Revenue Service

**Interest and Dividend Income
for Form 1040A Filers**

1993

OMB No. 1545-0085

Name(s) shown on Form 1040A

Your social security number

Part I

**Interest
income**

(See pages 25
and 56.)

Note: *If you received a Form 1099–INT, Form 1099–OID, or substitute statement from a brokerage firm, enter the firm's name and the total interest shown on that form.*

1 List name of payer. If any interest is from a seller-financed mortgage and the buyer used the property as a personal residence, see page 56 and list this interest first. Also, show that buyer's social security number and address.

	Amount
1	

2 Add the amounts on line 1. | 2 | |

3 Excludable interest on series EE U.S. savings bonds issued after 1989 from Form 8815, line 14. You MUST attach Form 8815 to Form 1040A. | 3 | |

4 Subtract line 3 from line 2. Enter the result here and on Form 1040A, line 8a. | 4 | |

Part II

**Dividend
income**

(See pages 25
and 57.)

Note: *If you received a Form 1099–DIV or substitute statement from a brokerage firm, enter the firm's name and the total dividends shown on that form.*

5 List name of payer

	Amount
5	

6 Add the amounts on line 5. Enter the total here and on Form 1040A, line 9. | 6 | |

For Paperwork Reduction Act Notice, see Form 1040A instructions. Cat. No. 12075R **1993 Schedule 1 (Form 1040A) page 1**

Form **1040**

Department of the Treasury—Internal Revenue Service

U.S. Individual Income Tax Return 19**93**

IRS Use Only—Do not write or staple in this space.

For the year Jan. 1–Dec. 31, 1993, or other tax year beginning _____ , 1993, ending _____ , 19___ | OMB No. 1545-0074

Label

(See instructions on page 12.)

Use the IRS label. Otherwise, please print or type.

L A B E L   H E R E

Your first name and initial _____ Last name _____

If a joint return, spouse's first name and initial _____ Last name _____

Home address (number and street). If you have a P.O. box, see page 12. _____ Apt. no. _____

City, town or post office, state, and ZIP code. If you have a foreign address, see page 12. _____

Your social security number _____

Spouse's social security number _____

For Privacy Act and Paperwork Reduction Act Notice, see page 4.

Presidential Election Campaign
(See page 12.)

Do you want $3 to go to this fund? . . . .

If a joint return, does your spouse want $3 to go to this fund? . . . .

Yes | No

Note: *Checking "Yes" will not change your tax or reduce your refund.*

Filing Status

(See page 12.)

Check only one box.

1 ☐ Single

2 ☐ Married filing joint return (even if only one had income)

3 ☐ Married filing separate return. Enter spouse's social security no. above and full name here. ▶ _____

4 ☐ Head of household (with qualifying person). (See page 13.) If the qualifying person is a child but not your dependent, enter this child's name here. ▶ _____

5 ☐ Qualifying widow(er) with dependent child (year spouse died ▶ 19___). (See page 13.)

Exemptions

(See page 13.)

6a ☐ **Yourself.** If your parent (or someone else) can claim you as a dependent on his or her tax return, **do not** check box 6a. But be sure to check the box on line 33b on page 2.

b ☐ **Spouse** . . . .

c **Dependents:**

If more than six dependents, see page 14.

(1) Name (first, initial, and last name)	(2) Check if under age 1	(3) If age 1 or older, dependent's social security number	(4) Dependent's relationship to you	(5) No. of months lived in your home in 1993

No. of boxes checked on 6a and 6b _____

No. of your children on 6c who:
- **lived with you** _____
- **didn't live with you due to divorce or separation (see page 15)** _____

Dependents on 6c not entered above _____

d If your child didn't live with you but is claimed as your dependent under a pre-1985 agreement, check here ▶ ☐

e Total number of exemptions claimed . . . .

Add numbers entered on lines above ▶ ☐

Income

Attach Copy B of your Forms W-2, W-2G, and 1099-R here.

If you did not get a W-2, see page 10.

If you are attaching a check or money order, put it on top of any Forms W-2, W-2G, or 1099-R.

7 Wages, salaries, tips, etc. Attach Form(s) W-2 . . . . . . | 7

8a Taxable interest income (see page 16). Attach Schedule B if over $400 . . . . | 8a

b Tax-exempt interest (see page 17). DON'T include on line 8a | 8b |

9 Dividend income. Attach Schedule B if over $400 . . . . | 9

10 Taxable refunds, credits, or offsets of state and local income taxes (see page 17) . . | 10

11 Alimony received . . . . | 11

12 Business income or (loss). Attach Schedule C or C-EZ . . . . . . | 12

13 Capital gain or (loss). Attach Schedule D . . . . | 13

14 Capital gain distributions not reported on line 13 (see page 17) . . . | 14

15 Other gains or (losses). Attach Form 4797 . . . . | 15

16a Total IRA distributions . | 16a | b Taxable amount (see page 18) | 16b

17a Total pensions and annuities | 17a | b Taxable amount (see page 18) | 17b

18 Rental real estate, royalties, partnerships, S corporations, trusts, etc. Attach Schedule E | 18

19 Farm income or (loss). Attach Schedule F . . . . | 19

20 Unemployment compensation (see page 19) . . . . | 20

21a Social security benefits | 21a | b Taxable amount (see page 19) | 21b

22 Other income. List type and amount—see page 20 _____ | 22

23 Add the amounts in the far right column for lines 7 through 22. This is your **total income** ▶ | 23

Adjustments to Income

(See page 20.)

24a Your IRA deduction (see page 20) . . . . | 24a |

b Spouse's IRA deduction (see page 20) . . . . . . | 24b |

25 One-half of self-employment tax (see page 21) . . . | 25 |

26 Self-employed health insurance deduction (see page 22) | 26 |

27 Keogh retirement plan and self-employed SEP deduction | 27 |

28 Penalty on early withdrawal of savings . . . . . | 28 |

29 Alimony paid. Recipient's SSN ▶ _____ | 29 |

30 Add lines 24a through 29. These are your **total adjustments** . . . . ▶ | 30

Adjusted Gross Income

31 Subtract line 30 from line 23. This is your **adjusted gross income.** *If this amount is less than $23,050 and a child lived with you, see page EIC-1 to find out if you can claim the "Earned Income Credit" on line 56* . . . . ▶ | 31

Cat. No. 11320B

Form **1040** (1993)

Form 1040 (1993)

Page **2**

Tax Computation

(See page 23.)

32 Amount from line 31 (adjusted gross income) . . . . | 32 |

33a Check if: ☐ **You** were 65 or older, ☐ Blind; ☐ **Spouse** was 65 or older, ☐ Blind.
Add the number of boxes checked above and enter the total here . . . . ▶ **33a** | |

b If your parent (or someone else) can claim you as a dependent, check here . ▶ **33b** ☐

c If you are married filing separately and your spouse itemizes deductions or you are a dual-status alien, see page 24 and check here . . . . ▶ **33c** ☐

34 Enter the larger of your:
Itemized deductions from Schedule A, line 26, **OR**
Standard deduction shown below for your filing status. **But if you checked any box on line 33a or b,** go to page 24 to find your standard deduction. If you checked **box 33c,** your standard deduction is zero.
- Single—$3,700   • Head of household—$5,450
- Married filing jointly or Qualifying widow(er)—$6,200
- Married filing separately—$3,100
| 34 |

If you want the IRS to figure your tax, see page 24.

35 Subtract line 34 from line 32 . . . . | 35 |

36 If line 32 is $81,350 or less, multiply $2,350 by the total number of exemptions claimed on line 6e. If line 32 is over $81,350, see the worksheet on page 25 for the amount to enter . | 36 |

37 **Taxable income.** Subtract line 36 from line 35. If line 36 is more than line 35, enter -0- . | 37 |

38 Tax. Check if from **a** ☐ Tax Table, **b** ☐ Tax Rate Schedules, **c** ☐ Schedule D Tax Worksheet, or **d** ☐ Form 8615 (see page 25). Amount from Form(s) 8814 ▶ **e** _____ | 38 |

39 Additional taxes (see page 25). Check if from **a** ☐ Form 4970 **b** ☐ Form 4972 . . . | 39 |

40 Add lines 38 and 39 . . . . ▶ | 40 |

Credits

(See page 25.)

41 Credit for child and dependent care expenses. Attach Form 2441 | 41 |

42 Credit for the elderly or the disabled. Attach Schedule R . . | 42 |

43 Foreign tax credit. Attach Form 1116 . . . . | 43 |

44 Other credits (see page 26). Check if from **a** ☐ Form 3800 **b** ☐ Form 8396 **c** ☐ Form 8801 **d** ☐ Form (specify)_____ | 44 |

45 Add lines 41 through 44 . . . . | 45 |

46 Subtract line 45 from line 40. If line 45 is more than line 40, enter -0- . . . . . . ▶ | 46 |

Other Taxes

47 Self-employment tax. Attach Schedule SE. Also, see line 25 . . . . | 47 |

48 Alternative minimum tax. Attach Form 6251 . . . . | 48 |

49 Recapture taxes (see page 26). Check if from **a** ☐ Form 4255 **b** ☐ Form 8611 **c** ☐ Form 8828 | 49 |

50 Social security and Medicare tax on tip income not reported to employer. Attach Form 4137 | 50 |

51 Tax on qualified retirement plans, including IRAs. If required, attach Form 5329 . . . | 51 |

52 Advance earned income credit payments from Form W-2 . . . . | 52 |

53 Add lines 46 through 52. This is your **total tax** . . . . ▶ | 53 |

Payments

Attach Forms W-2, W-2G, and 1099-R on the front.

54 Federal income tax withheld. If any is from Form(s) 1099, check ▶ ☐ | 54 |

55 1993 estimated tax payments and amount applied from 1992 return . | 55 |

56 **Earned income credit.** Attach Schedule EIC . . . . . | 56 |

57 Amount paid with Form 4868 (extension request) . . . . | 57 |

58a Excess social security, Medicare, and RRTA tax withheld (see page 28) . | 58a |

b Deferral of additional 1993 taxes. Attach Form 8841 . . . . | 58b |

59 Other payments (see page 28). Check if from **a** ☐ Form 2439 **b** ☐ Form 4136 . . . . | 59 |

60 Add lines 54 through 59. These are your **total payments** . . . . ▶ | 60 |

Refund or Amount You Owe

61 If line 60 is more than line 53, subtract line 53 from line 60. This is the amount you **OVERPAID**. ▶ | 61 |

62 Amount of line 61 you want **REFUNDED TO YOU**. . . . . ▶ | 62 |

63 Amount of line 61 you want **APPLIED TO YOUR 1994 ESTIMATED TAX** ▶ | 63 |

64 If line 53 is more than line 60, subtract line 60 from line 53. This is the **AMOUNT YOU OWE**. For details on how to pay, including what to write on your payment, see page 29 . . . | 64 |

65 Estimated tax penalty (see page 29). Also include on line 64 | 65 |

Sign Here

Keep a copy of this return for your records.

Under penalties of perjury, I declare that I have examined this return and accompanying schedules and statements, and to the best of my knowledge and belief, they are true, correct, and complete. Declaration of preparer (other than taxpayer) is based on all information of which preparer has any knowledge.

▶ Your signature | Date | Your occupation

▶ Spouse's signature. If a joint return, BOTH must sign. | Date | Spouse's occupation

Paid Preparer's Use Only

Preparer's signature ▶ | Date | Check if self-employed ☐ | Preparer's social security no.

Firm's name (or yours if self-employed) and address ▶ | E.I. No. | ZIP code

SCHEDULES A&B	Schedule A—Itemized Deductions	OMB No. 1545-0074

(Form 1040)

(Schedule B is on back)

1993

Department of the Treasury
Internal Revenue Service

▶ **Attach to Form 1040.** ▶ **See Instructions for Schedules A and B (Form 1040).**

Attachment
Sequence No. **07**

Name(s) shown on Form 1040 | Your social security number

Medical and Dental Expenses

Caution: *Do not include expenses reimbursed or paid by others.*

1 Medical and dental expenses (see page A-1) . . . . | **1**
2 Enter amount from Form 1040, line 32 . | **2**
3 Multiply line 2 above by 7.5% (.075) . . . . | **3**
4 Subtract line 3 from line 1. If zero or less, enter -0- . . . . ▶ | **4**

Taxes You Paid

(See page A-1.)

5 State and local income taxes . . . . | **5**
6 Real estate taxes (see page A-2) . . . . | **6**
7 Other taxes. List—include personal property taxes ▶ | **7**
....
8 Add lines 5 through 7 . . . . ▶ | **8**

Interest You Paid

(See page A-2.)

9a Home mortgage interest and points reported to you on Form 1098 | **9a**
b Home mortgage interest not reported to you on Form 1098. If paid to the person from whom you bought the home, see page A-3 and show that person's name, identifying no., and address ▶
....
....

Note: Personal interest is not deductible.

.... | **9b**
10 Points not reported to you on Form 1098. See page A-3 for special rules . . . . | **10**
11 Investment interest. If required, attach Form 4952. (See page A-3.) . . . . | **11**
12 Add lines 9a through 11 . . . . ▶ | **12**

Gifts to Charity

(See page A-3.)

Caution: *If you made a charitable contribution and received a benefit in return, see page A-3.*

13 Contributions by cash or check . . . . | **13**
14 Other than by cash or check. If over $500, you **MUST** attach Form 8283 . . . . | **14**
15 Carryover from prior year . . . . | **15**
16 Add lines 13 through 15 . . . . ▶ | **16**

Casualty and Theft Losses

17 Casualty or theft loss(es). Attach Form 4684. (See page A-4.) . . . . ▶ | **17**

Moving Expenses

18 Moving expenses. Attach Form 3903 or 3903-F. (See page A-4.) . . . . . . ▶ | **18**

Job Expenses and Most Other Miscellaneous Deductions

(See page A-5 for expenses to deduct here.)

19 Unreimbursed employee expenses—job travel, union dues, job education, etc. If required, you **MUST** attach Form 2106. (See page A-4.) ▶ ----------------------
.... | **19**
20 Other expenses—investment, tax preparation, safe deposit box, etc. List type and amount ▶ --------------
.... | **20**
21 Add lines 19 and 20 . . . . | **21**
22 Enter amount from Form 1040, line 32 . | **22**
23 Multiply line 22 above by 2% (.02) . . . . | **23**
24 Subtract line 23 from line 21. If zero or less, enter -0- . . . . ▶ | **24**

Other Miscellaneous Deductions

25 Other—from list on page A-5. List type and amount ▶ ----------------------------
.... ▶ | **25**

Total Itemized Deductions

26 Is the amount on Form 1040, line 32, more than $108,450 (more than $54,225 if married filing separately)?
● **NO.** Your deduction is not limited. Add lines 4, 8, 12, 16, 17, 18, 24, and 25 and enter the total here. Also enter on Form 1040, line 34, the **larger** of this amount or your standard deduction.
● **YES.** Your deduction may be limited. See page A-5 for the amount to enter. ▶ | **26**

For Paperwork Reduction Act Notice, see Form 1040 instructions.   Cat. No. 11330X   **Schedule A (Form 1040) 1993**

Schedules A&B (Form 1040) 1993   OMB No. 1545-0074   Page **2**

Name(s) shown on Form 1040. Do not enter name and social security number if shown on other side.

Your social security number

Schedule B—Interest and Dividend Income
Attachment Sequence No. **08**

Part I Interest Income

(See pages 16 and B-1.)

Note: If you received a Form 1099-INT, Form 1099-OID, or substitute statement from a brokerage firm, list the firm's name as the payer and enter the total interest shown on that form.

Note: If you had over $400 in taxable interest income, you must also complete Part III.

Interest Income	Amount
1 List name of payer. If any interest is from a seller-financed mortgage and the buyer used the property as a personal residence, see page B-1 and list this interest first. Also show that buyer's social security number and address ▶	**1**
2 Add the amounts on line 1	**2**
3 Excludable interest on series EE U.S. savings bonds issued after 1989 from Form 8815, line 14. You MUST attach Form 8815 to Form 1040	**3**
4 Subtract line 3 from line 2. Enter the result here and on Form 1040, line 8a ▶	**4**

Part II Dividend Income

(See pages 17 and B-1.)

Note: If you received a Form 1099-DIV or substitute statement from a brokerage firm, list the firm's name as the payer and enter the total dividends shown on that form.

Note: If you had over $400 in gross dividends and/or other distributions on stock, you must also complete Part III.

Dividend Income	Amount
5 List name of payer. Include gross dividends and/or other distributions on stock here. Any capital gain distributions and nontaxable distributions will be deducted on lines 7 and 8 ▶	**5**
6 Add the amounts on line 5	**6**
7 Capital gain distributions. Enter here and on Schedule D* .	**7**	
8 Nontaxable distributions. (See the inst. for Form 1040, line 9.)	**8**	
9 Add lines 7 and 8	**9**
10 Subtract line 9 from line 6. Enter the result here and on Form 1040, line 9 . ▶	**10**

*If you received capital gain distributions but do not need Schedule D to report any other gains or losses, see the instructions for Form 1040, lines 13 and 14.

Part III Foreign Accounts and Trusts

(See page B-2.)

If you had over $400 of interest or dividends OR had a foreign account or were a grantor of, or a transferor to, a foreign trust, you must complete this part. | Yes | No |

11a At any time during 1993, did you have an interest in or a signature or other authority over a financial account in a foreign country, such as a bank account, securities account, or other financial account? See page B-2 for exceptions and filing requirements for Form TD F 90-22.1 . . . .

b If "Yes," enter the name of the foreign country ▶

12 Were you the grantor of, or transferor to, a foreign trust that existed during 1993, whether or not you have any beneficial interest in it? If "Yes," you may have to file Form 3520, 3520-A, or 926 .

For Paperwork Reduction Act Notice, see Form 1040 instructions.   **Schedule B (Form 1040) 1993**

SCHEDULE C (Form 1040)	Profit or Loss From Business	OMB No. 1545-0074

SCHEDULE C (Form 1040)

Department of the Treasury
Internal Revenue Service

Profit or Loss From Business
(Sole Proprietorship)
▶ Partnerships, joint ventures, etc., must file Form 1065.
▶ Attach to Form 1040 or Form 1041. ▶ See Instructions for Schedule C (Form 1040).

OMB No. 1545-0074

1993

Attachment
Sequence No. **09**

Name of proprietor

Social security number (SSN)

A Principal business or profession, including product or service (see page C-1)

B Enter principal business code (see page C-6) ▶

C Business name. If no separate business name, leave blank.

D Employer ID number (EIN), if any

E Business address (including suite or room no.) ▶ ....
City, town or post office, state, and ZIP code

F Accounting method: **(1)** ☐ Cash **(2)** ☐ Accrual **(3)** ☐ Other (specify) ▶ ....

G Method(s) used to value closing inventory: **(1)** ☐ Cost **(2)** ☐ Lower of cost or market **(3)** ☐ Other (attach explanation) **(4)** ☐ Does not apply (if checked, skip line H)

	Yes	No

H Was there any change in determining quantities, costs, or valuations between opening and closing inventory? If "Yes," attach explanation . . . .

I Did you "materially participate" in the operation of this business during 1993? If "No," see page C-2 for limit on losses. . . .

J If you started or acquired this business during 1993, check here . . . . ▶ ☐

Part I   Income

1	Gross receipts or sales. **Caution:** *If this income was reported to you on Form W-2 and the "Statutory employee" box on that form was checked, see page C-2 and check here* . . . . ▶ ☐	1
2	Returns and allowances	2
3	Subtract line 2 from line 1	3
4	Cost of goods sold (from line 40 on page 2)	4
5	**Gross profit.** Subtract line 4 from line 3	5
6	Other income, including Federal and state gasoline or fuel tax credit or refund (see page C-2) . . .	6
7	**Gross income.** Add lines 5 and 6 . . . . ▶	7

Part II   Expenses. Caution: *Do not enter expenses for business use of your home on lines 8–27. Instead, see line 30.*

8	Advertising	8	19 Pension and profit-sharing plans	19	
9	Bad debts from sales or services (see page C-3) .	9	20 Rent or lease (see page C-4):		
			a Vehicles, machinery, and equipment .	20a	
10	Car and truck expenses (see page C-3)	10	b Other business property . .	20b	
11	Commissions and fees. . .	11	21 Repairs and maintenance . .	21	
12	Depletion.	12	22 Supplies (not included in Part III) .	22	
13	Depreciation and section 179 expense deduction (not included in Part III) (see page C-3) . .	13	23 Taxes and licenses	23	
			24 Travel, meals, and entertainment:		
14	Employee benefit programs (other than on line 19) . . .	14	a Travel	24a	
15	Insurance (other than health) .	15	b Meals and entertainment .		
16	Interest:		c Enter 20% of line 24b subject to limitations (see page C-4) .		
a	Mortgage (paid to banks, etc.) .	16a			
b	Other	16b	d Subtract line 24c from line 24b	24d	
17	Legal and professional services	17	25 Utilities	25	
			26 Wages (less jobs credit) . .	26	
18	Office expense	18	27 Other expenses (from line 46 on page 2)	27	

28	**Total expenses** before expenses for business use of home. Add lines 8 through 27 in columns. . ▶	28
29	Tentative profit (loss). Subtract line 28 from line 7	29
30	Expenses for business use of your home. Attach **Form 8829**	30
31	**Net profit or (loss).** Subtract line 30 from line 29.	
	• If a profit, enter on **Form 1040, line 12,** and ALSO on **Schedule SE, line 2** (statutory employees, see page C-5). Fiduciaries, enter on Form 1041, line 3.	31
	• If a loss, you MUST go on to line 32.	
32	If you have a loss, check the box that describes your investment in this activity (see page C-5).	
	• If you checked 32a, enter the loss on **Form 1040, line 12,** and ALSO on **Schedule SE, line 2** (statutory employees, see page C-5). Fiduciaries, enter on Form 1041, line 3.	32a ☐ All investment is at risk.
	• If you checked 32b, you MUST attach **Form 6198.**	32b ☐ Some investment is not at risk.

For Paperwork Reduction Act Notice, see Form 1040 instructions.   Cat. No. 11334P   Schedule C (Form 1040) 1993

Schedule C (Form 1040) 1993   Page **2**

Part III	**Cost of Goods Sold** (see page C-5)			
33	Inventory at beginning of year. If different from last year's closing inventory, attach explanation . .	33		
34	Purchases less cost of items withdrawn for personal use	34		
35	Cost of labor. Do not include salary paid to yourself	35		
36	Materials and supplies	36		
37	Other costs	37		
38	Add lines 33 through 37	38		
39	Inventory at end of year	39		
40	**Cost of goods sold.** Subtract line 39 from line 38. Enter the result here and on page 1, line 4 . .	40		

Part IV	**Information on Your Vehicle.** Complete this part **ONLY** if you are claiming car or truck expenses on line 10 and are not required to file Form 4562 for this business.

41   When did you place your vehicle in service for business purposes? (month, day, year) ▶ ..../........../........ .

42   Of the total number of miles you drove your vehicle during 1993, enter the number of miles you used your vehicle for:

a   Business .... b   Commuting c   Other ....

43   Do you (or your spouse) have another vehicle available for personal use? . . . . ☐ Yes   ☐ No

44   Was your vehicle available for use during off-duty hours? . . . . ☐ Yes   ☐ No

45a   Do you have evidence to support your deduction? . . . . ☐ Yes   ☐ No
  b   If "Yes," is the evidence written? . . . . ☐ Yes   ☐ No

Part V	**Other Expenses.** List below business expenses not included on lines 8–26 or line 30.

....		
....		
....		
....		
....		
....		
....		
....		
....		
46 **Total other expenses.** Enter here and on page 1, line 27	46	

✪ *Printed on recycled paper*

SCHEDULE D
(Form 1040)

Department of the Treasury
Internal Revenue Service

Capital Gains and Losses

▶ Attach to Form 1040.   ▶ See Instructions for Schedule D (Form 1040).

▶ Use lines 20 and 22 for more space to list transactions for lines 1 and 9.

OMB No. 1545-0074

1993

Attachment
Sequence No. **12**

Name(s) shown on Form 1040

Your social security number

Part I   Short-Term Capital Gains and Losses—Assets Held One Year or Less

(a) Description of property (Example: 100 sh. XYZ Co.)	(b) Date acquired (Mo., day, yr.)	(c) Date sold (Mo., day, yr.)	(d) Sales price (see page D-3)	(e) Cost or other basis (see page D-3)	(f) LOSS If (e) is more than (d), subtract (d) from (e)	(g) GAIN If (d) is more than (e), subtract (e) from (d)
1						

2	Enter your short-term totals, if any, from line 21	**2**		
3	**Total short-term sales price amounts.** Add column (d) of lines 1 and 2 . . .	**3**		
4	Short-term gain from Forms 2119 and 6252, and short-term gain or (loss) from Forms 4684, 6781, and 8824	**4**	
5	Net short-term gain or (loss) from partnerships, S corporations, and fiduciaries from Schedule(s) K-1	**5**	
6	Short-term capital loss carryover from 1992 Schedule D, line 38	**6**	
7	Add lines 1, 2, and 4 through 6, in columns (f) and (g)	**7** (	)
8	**Net short-term capital gain or (loss).** Combine columns (f) and (g) of line 7	**8**

Part II   Long-Term Capital Gains and Losses—Assets Held More Than One Year

9						

10	Enter your long-term totals, if any, from line 23	**10**		
11	**Total long-term sales price amounts.** Add column (d) of lines 9 and 10 . . .	**11**		
12	Gain from Form 4797; long-term gain from Forms 2119, 2439, and 6252; and long-term gain or (loss) from Forms 4684, 6781, and 8824	**12**	
13	Net long-term gain or (loss) from partnerships, S corporations, and fiduciaries from Schedule(s) K-1	**13**	
14	Capital gain distributions	**14**	
15	Long-term capital loss carryover from 1992 Schedule D, line 45	**15**	
16	Add lines 9, 10, and 12 through 15, in columns (f) and (g)	**16** (	)
17	**Net long-term capital gain or (loss).** Combine columns (f) and (g) of line 16	**17**

Part III   Summary of Parts I and II

18	Combine lines 8 and 17. If a loss, go to line 19. If a gain, enter the gain on Form 1040, line 13. **Note:** *If both lines 17 and 18 are gains, see the Schedule D Tax Worksheet on page D-4* . .	**18**
19	If line 18 is a (loss), enter here and as a (loss) on Form 1040, line 13, the **smaller** of these losses:	
a	The (loss) on line 18; **or**	
b	($3,000) or, if married filing separately, ($1,500)	**19** ( )
	Note: *See the Capital Loss Carryover Worksheet on page D-4 if the loss on line 18 exceeds the loss on line 19 or if Form 1040, line 35, is a loss.*	

For Paperwork Reduction Act Notice, see Form 1040 instructions.   Cat. No. 11338H   Schedule D (Form 1040) 1993

Schedule D (Form 1040) 1993 — Attachment Sequence No. **12** — Page **2**

Name(s) shown on Form 1040. Do not enter name and social security number if shown on other side. | Your social security number

Part IV   Short-Term Capital Gains and Losses—Assets Held One Year or Less *(Continuation of Part I)*

(a) Description of property (Example: 100 sh. XYZ Co.)	(b) Date acquired (Mo., day, yr.)	(c) Date sold (Mo., day, yr.)	(d) Sales price (see page D-3)	(e) Cost or other basis (see page D-3)	(f) LOSS If (e) is more than (d), subtract (d) from (e)	(g) GAIN If (d) is more than (e), subtract (e) from (d)
20						

21 Short-term totals. Add columns (d), (f), and (g) of line 20. Enter here and on line 2   .   **21**

Part V   Long-Term Capital Gains and Losses—Assets Held More Than One Year *(Continuation of Part II)*

22						

23 Long-term totals. Add columns (d), (f), and (g) of line 22. Enter here and on line 10   .   **23**

SCHEDULE E (Form 1040)	Supplemental Income and Loss	OMB No. 1545-0074

SCHEDULE E
(Form 1040)

Department of the Treasury
Internal Revenue Service

Supplemental Income and Loss

(From rental real estate, royalties, partnerships,
S corporations, estates, trusts, REMICs, etc.)

► **Attach to Form 1040 or Form 1041.**   ► **See Instructions for Schedule E (Form 1040).**

OMB No. 1545-0074

19 93

Attachment
Sequence No. **13**

Name(s) shown on return | Your social security number

Part I **Income or Loss From Rental Real Estate and Royalties** Note: *Report income and expenses from your business of renting personal property on* **Schedule C** *or* **C-EZ** *(see page E-1). Report farm rental income or loss from* **Form 4835** *on page 2, line 39.*

1 Show the kind and location of each **rental real estate property:**

A ....

B ....

C ....

2 For each rental real estate property listed on line 1, did you or your family use it for personal purposes for more than the greater of 14 days or 10% of the total days rented at fair rental value during the tax year? (See page E-1.)

	Yes	No
A		
B		
C		

Income:

		Properties			Totals
		A	B	C	(Add columns A, B, and C.)
3 Rents received	3				3
4 Royalties received	4				4

Expenses:

5 Advertising	5				
6 Auto and travel (see page E-2)	6				
7 Cleaning and maintenance	7				
8 Commissions	8				
9 Insurance	9				
10 Legal and other professional fees	10				
11 Management fees	11				
12 Mortgage interest paid to banks, etc. (see page E-2)	12				12
13 Other interest	13				
14 Repairs	14				
15 Supplies	15				
16 Taxes	16				
17 Utilities	17				
18 Other (list) ►	18				
19 Add lines 5 through 18	19				19
20 Depreciation expense or depletion (see page E-2)	20				20
21 Total expenses. Add lines 19 and 20	21				
22 Income or (loss) from rental real estate or royalty properties. Subtract line 21 from line 3 (rents) or line 4 (royalties). If the result is a (loss), see page E-2 to find out if you must file **Form 6198**	22				
23 Deductible rental real estate loss. **Caution:** *Your rental real estate loss on line 22 may be limited. See page E-3 to find out if you must file* **Form 8582**	23	( )	( )	( )	

24 **Income.** Add positive amounts shown on line 22. **Do not** include any losses .... | 24 |

25 **Losses.** Add royalty losses from line 22 and rental real estate losses from line 23. Enter the total losses here .... | 25 | ( ) |

26 Total rental real estate and royalty income or (loss). Combine lines 24 and 25. Enter the result here. If Parts II, III, IV, and line 39 on page 2 do not apply to you, also enter this amount on Form 1040, line 18. Otherwise, include this amount in the total on line 40 on page 2 .... | 26 |

For Paperwork Reduction Act Notice, see Form 1040 instructions.   Cat. No. 11344L   **Schedule E (Form 1040) 1993**

Schedule E (Form 1040) 1993   Attachment Sequence No. **13**   Page **2**

Name(s) shown on return. Do not enter name and social security number if shown on other side.	Your social security number

Note: *If you report amounts from farming or fishing on Schedule E, you must enter your gross income from those activities on line 41 below.*

Part II   Income or Loss From Partnerships and S Corporations

If you report a loss from an at-risk activity, you MUST check either column **(e)** or **(f)** of line 27 to describe your investment in the activity. See page E-4. If you check column **(f)**, you must attach **Form 6198**.

27	(a) Name	(b) Enter P for partnership; S for S corporation	(c) Check if foreign partnership	(d) Employer identification number	Investment At Risk? (e) All is at risk	(f) Some is not at risk
A						
B						
C						
D						
E						

	Passive Income and Loss		Nonpassive Income and Loss		
	(g) Passive loss allowed (attach **Form 8582** if required)	(h) Passive income from **Schedule K-1**	(i) Nonpassive loss from **Schedule K-1**	(j) Section 179 expense deduction from **Form 4562**	(k) Nonpassive income from **Schedule K-1**
A					
B					
C					
D					
E					

28a	Totals					
b	Totals					

29	Add columns (h) and (k) of line 28a	29	
30	Add columns (g), (i), and (j) of line 28b	30	( )
31	Total partnership and S corporation income or (loss). Combine lines 29 and 30. Enter the result here and include in the total on line 40 below	31	

Part III   Income or Loss From Estates and Trusts

32	(a) Name	(b) Employer identification number
A		
B		
C		

	Passive Income and Loss		Nonpassive Income and Loss	
	(c) Passive deduction or loss allowed (attach **Form 8582** if required)	(d) Passive income from **Schedule K-1**	(e) Deduction or loss from **Schedule K-1**	(f) Other income from **Schedule K-1**
A				
B				
C				

33a	Totals			
b	Totals			

34	Add columns (d) and (f) of line 33a	34	
35	Add columns (c) and (e) of line 33b	35	( )
36	Total estate and trust income or (loss). Combine lines 34 and 35. Enter the result here and include in the total on line 40 below	36	

Part IV   Income or Loss From Real Estate Mortgage Investment Conduits (REMICs)—Residual Holder

37	(a) Name	(b) Employer identification number	(c) Excess inclusion from Schedules Q, line 2c (see page E-4)	(d) Taxable income (net loss) from Schedules Q, line 1b	(e) Income from Schedules Q, line 3b

38	Combine columns (d) and (e) only. Enter the result here and include in the total on line 40 below	38	

Part V   Summary

39	Net farm rental income or (loss) from **Form 4835**. Also, complete line 41 below	39	
40	TOTAL income or (loss). Combine lines 26, 31, 36, 38, and 39. Enter the result here and on Form 1040, line 18 . . . . ▶	40	
41	**Reconciliation of Farming and Fishing Income:** Enter your **gross** farming and fishing income reported in Parts II and III and on line 39 (see page E-4) 41		

SCHEDULE EIC (Form 1040A or 1040) Department of the Treasury Internal Revenue Service	**Earned Income Credit** ▶ Attach to Form 1040A or 1040. ▶ See Instructions for Schedule EIC.	OMB No. 1545-0074 **1993** Attachment Sequence No. **43**
Name(s) shown on return		**Your social security number**

Want the IRS to figure the credit for you? Just fill in this page. We'll do the rest.

General Information

To take this credit ▶
- You **must** have worked and earned **less** than $23,050, **and**
- Your adjusted gross income (Form 1040A, line 16, or Form 1040, line 31) **must** be **less** than $23,050, **and**
- Your filing status can be any status **except** married filing a separate return, **and**
- You **must** have at least one qualifying child (see boxes below), **and**
- You **cannot** be a qualifying child yourself.

A **qualifying child** is a child who: ▶

is your:		**was (at the end of 1993):**		**who:**
son daughter adopted child grandchild stepchild or foster child	**A N D**	under age 19 or under age 24 and a full-time student or any age and permanently and totally disabled	**A N D**	lived with you in the U.S. for more than half of 1993* (or all of 1993 if a foster child*)

*If the child didn't live with you for the required time (for example, was born in 1993), see the **Exception** on page 64 (1040A) or page EIC-2 (1040).

Do you have at least one qualifying child?	**No** ▶	You **cannot** take the credit. Enter "NO" next to line 28c of Form 1040A (or line 56 of Form 1040).
	Yes ▶	Go to line 1. But if the child was married or is also a qualifying child of another person (other than your spouse if filing a joint return), first see page 64 (1040A) or page EIC-2 (1040).

Information About Your Qualifying Child or Children

If more than two qualifying children, see page 65 (1040A) or page EIC-2 (1040). **1(a)** Child's name (first, initial, and last name)	**(b)** Child's year of birth	For a child born **before 1975**, check if child was—		**(e)** If child was born **before 1993**, enter the child's social security number	**(f)** Child's relationship to you (for example, son, grandchild, etc.)	**(g)** Number of months child lived with you in the U.S. in 1993
		(c) a student **under age 24** at end of 1993	**(d)** disabled (see booklet)			
	19			: :		
	19			: :		

Caution: *If a child you listed above was born in 1993 **and** you chose to claim the credit or exclusion for child care expenses for this child on **Schedule 2** (Form 1040A) or **Form 2441** (Form 1040), check here* . . . . ▶ ☐

Do you want the IRS to figure the credit for you?	**Yes** ▶	Fill in lines 2 and 3; **and** enter the amount from Form 1040A, line 16, or Form 1040, line 31, here. ▶ $
	No ▶	Go to page 2 on the back now.

Other Information

2	Enter any **nontaxable earned income** (see page 65 (1040A) or page EIC-2 (1040)) such as military housing and subsistence or contributions to a 401(k) plan. Also, list type and amount here. ▶ _____	**2**	
3	Enter the total amount you paid in 1993 for health insurance that covered at least one qualifying child. See instructions	**3**	

If you want the IRS to figure the credit for you:	**S T O P** ▶	**Attach this schedule to your return.** • If filing Form **1040A**, print "EIC" on the line next to line 28c. • If filing Form **1040**, print "EIC" on the dotted line next to line 56.

For Paperwork Reduction Act Notice, see Form 1040A or 1040 instructions.   Cat. No. 13339M   **Schedule EIC (Form 1040A or 1040) 1993**

Schedule EIC (Form 1040A or 1040) 1993

Figure Your Basic Credit

4 Enter the amount from line 7 of Form 1040A or Form 1040. If you received a taxable scholarship or fellowship grant, see instructions **4**

5 Enter any **nontaxable earned income** (see page 65 (1040A) or page EIC-2 (1040)) such as military housing and subsistence or contributions to a 401(k) plan. Also, list type and amount here. ▶ --
-- **5**

6 **Form 1040 Filers Only:** If you were self-employed **or** used Sch. C or C-EZ as a statutory employee, enter the amount from the worksheet on page EIC-3 . . . . **6**

7 **Earned income.** Add lines 4, 5, and 6. If $23,050 or more, you **cannot** take the credit. Enter "NO" next to line 28c of Form 1040A (or line 56 of Form 1040) . . . . ▶ **7**

8 Use **line 7** above to find your credit in **TABLE A** on pages **69 and 70** (1040A) or pages **EIC-4 and 5** (1040). Enter here **8**

9 **Adjusted gross income.** Enter the amount from Form 1040A, line 16, or Form 1040, line 31 ▶ **9**

10 **Is line 9 $12,200 or more?**

   YES. Use **line 9** to find your credit in **TABLE A** on pages **69 and 70** (1040A) or pages **EIC-4 and 5** (1040). Enter here **10**
   NO. Go to line 11.

11 **Basic credit:**
   • If you answered "YES" to line 10, enter the **smaller** of line 8 or line 10.
   • If you answered "NO" to line 10, enter the amount from line 8. } **11**

   Next: To take the health insurance credit, fill in lines 12–16. To take the extra credit for a child born in 1993, fill in lines 17–19. Otherwise, go to line 20 now.

Figure Your Health Insurance Credit

12 Use **line 7** above to find your credit in **TABLE B** on page **71** (1040A) or page **EIC-6** (1040). Enter here **12**

13 **Is line 9 above $12,200 or more?**

   YES. Use **line 9** to find your credit in **TABLE B** on page **71** (1040A) or page **EIC-6** (1040). Enter here. **13**
   NO. Go to line 14.

14 • If you answered "YES" to line 13, enter the **smaller** of line 12 or line 13.
   • If you answered "NO" to line 13, enter the amount from line 12. } **14**

15 Enter the total amount you paid in 1993 for health insurance that covered at least one qualifying child. See instructions **15**

16 **Health insurance credit.** Enter the **smaller** of line 14 or line 15 . . . . **16**

Figure Your Extra Credit for Child Born in 1993

   Take this credit **only** if you did not take the credit or exclusion for child care expenses on **Schedule 2** or **Form 2441** for the same child.

   TIP: You can take **both** the basic credit and the extra credit for your child born in 1993.

17 Use **line 7** above to find your credit in **TABLE C** on page **72** (1040A) or page **EIC-7** (1040). Enter here **17**

18 **Is line 9 above $12,200 or more?**

   YES. Use **line 9** to find your credit in **TABLE C** on page **72** (1040A) or page **EIC-7** (1040). Enter here **18**
   NO. Go to line 19.

19 **Extra credit for child born in 1993:**
   • If you answered "YES" to line 18, enter the **smaller** of line 17 or line 18.
   • If you answered "NO" to line 18, enter the amount from line 17. } **19**

Figure Your Total Earned Income Credit

20 Add lines 11, 16, and 19. Enter the total here and on Form 1040A, line 28c (or on Form 1040, line 56). This is your **total earned income credit** . . . . ▶ **20**

   TIP: Do you want the earned income credit added to your take-home pay in 1994? To see if you qualify, get **Form W-5** from your employer or by calling the IRS at 1-800-829-3676.

Schedule R
(Form 1040)

Department of the Treasury
Internal Revenue Service

Credit for the Elderly or the Disabled

▶ Attach to Form 1040.   ▶ See separate instructions for Schedule R.

OMB No. 1545-0074

1993

Attachment
Sequence No. **16**

Name(s) shown on Form 1040 | Your social security number

You may be able to use Schedule R to reduce your tax if by the end of 1993:

- You were age 65 or older, **OR** ● You were under age 65, you retired on **permanent and total** disability, and you received taxable disability income.

But you must also meet other tests. See the separate instructions for Schedule R.
Note: *In most cases, the IRS can figure the credit for you. See page 25 of the Form 1040 instructions.*

Part I   Check the Box for Your Filing Status and Age

If your filing status is:	And by the end of 1993:	Check only one box:
Single, Head of household, or Qualifying widow(er) with dependent child	**1** You were 65 or older **1**	☐
	2 You were under 65 and you retired on permanent and total disability . . . **2**	☐
	3 Both spouses were 65 or older **3**	☐
	4 Both spouses were under 65, but only one spouse retired on permanent and total disability **4**	☐
Married filing a joint return	**5** Both spouses were under 65, and both retired on permanent and total disability **5**	☐
	6 One spouse was 65 or older, and the other spouse was under 65 and retired on permanent and total disability **6**	☐
	7 One spouse was 65 or older, and the other spouse was under 65 and **NOT** retired on permanent and total disability **7**	☐
Married filing a separate return	**8** You were 65 or older and you lived apart from your spouse for all of 1993 . . **8**	☐
	9 You were under 65, you retired on permanent and total disability, and you lived apart from your spouse for all of 1993 . . . . **9**	☐

If you checked box 1, 3, 7, or 8, skip Part II and complete Part III on the back. All others, complete Parts II and III.

Part II   Statement of Permanent and Total Disability (Complete **only** if you checked box 2, 4, 5, 6, or 9 above.)

IF: 1 You filed a physician's statement for this disability for 1983 or an earlier year, or you filed a statement for tax years after 1983 and your physician signed line B on the statement, **AND**

2 Due to your continued disabled condition, you were unable to engage in any substantial gainful activity in 1993, check this box . . . . ▶ ☐

- If you checked this box, you do not have to file another statement for 1993.
- If you **did not** check this box, have your physician complete the following statement.

Physician's Statement (See instructions at bottom of page 2.)

I certify that _____
                              Name of disabled person

was permanently and totally disabled on January 1, 1976, or January 1, 1977, **OR** was permanently and totally disabled on the date he or she retired. If retired after December 31, 1976, enter the date retired. ▶ _____
Physician: Sign your name on **either** line A or B below.

A The disability has lasted or can be expected to last continuously for at least a year . . . . _____
                                                      Physician's signature   Date

B There is no reasonable probability that the disabled condition will ever improve . . . . _____
                                                      Physician's signature   Date

Physician's name | Physician's address

For Paperwork Reduction Act Notice, see Form 1040 instructions.   Cat. No. 11359K   Schedule R (Form 1040) 1993

Schedule R (Form 1040) 1993

Page **2**

Part III — Figure Your Credit

10 If you checked (in Part I): **Enter:**

Box 1, 2, 4, or 7 . . . . $5,000

Box 3, 5, or 6 . . . . $7,500   **10**

Box 8 or 9 . . . . $3,750

Caution: *If you checked box 2, 4, 5, 6, or 9 in Part I, you* **MUST** *complete line 11 below. All others, skip line 11 and enter the amount from line 10 on line 12.*

11 If you checked:

- Box 6 in Part I, add $5,000 to the taxable disability income of the spouse who was under age 65. Enter the total.
- Box 2, 4, or 9 in Part I, enter your taxable disability income.   **11**
- Box 5 in Part I, add your taxable disability income to your spouse's taxable disability income. Enter the total.

TIP: For more details on what to include on line 11, see the instructions.

12
- If you completed line 11, look at lines 10 and 11. Enter the **smaller** of the two amounts.   **12**
- All others, enter the amount from line 10.

13 Enter the following pensions, annuities, or disability income that you (and your spouse if filing a joint return) received in 1993:

a Nontaxable part of social security benefits, and

Nontaxable part of railroad retirement benefits treated as social security. See instructions.   **13a**

b Nontaxable veterans' pensions, and

Any other pension, annuity, or disability benefit that is excluded from income under any other provision of law. See instructions.   **13b**

c Add lines 13a and 13b. (Even though these income items are not taxable, they **must** be included here to figure your credit.) If you did not receive any of the types of nontaxable income listed on line 13a or 13b, enter -0- on line 13c **13c**

14 Enter the amount from Form 1040, line 32   **14**

15 If you checked (in Part I): **Enter:**

Box 1 or 2 . . . . $7,500

Box 3, 4, 5, 6, or 7 . . . . $10,000   **15**

Box 8 or 9 . . . . . . $5,000

16 Subtract line 15 from line 14. If line 15 is more than line 14, enter -0- **16**

17 Divide line 16 above by 2 . . . .   **17**

18 Add lines 13c and 17 . . . .   **18**

19 Subtract line 18 from line 12. If line 18 is more than line 12, stop here; you **cannot** take the credit. Otherwise, go to line 21 . . . .   **19**

20 Decimal amount used to figure the credit . . . .   **20**   × .15

21 Multiply line 19 above by the decimal amount (.15) on line 20. Enter the result here and on Form 1040, line 42. **Caution:** *If you file Schedule C, C-EZ, D, E, or F (Form 1040), your credit may be limited. See the instructions for line 21 for the amount of credit you can claim* **21**

Instructions for Physician's Statement

Taxpayer

If you retired after December 31, 1976, enter the date you retired in the space provided in Part II.

Physician

A person is permanently and totally disabled if **both** of the following apply:

1. He or she cannot engage in any substantial gainful activity because of a physical or mental condition, and

2. A physician determines that the disability has lasted or can be expected to last continuously for at least a year or can lead to death.

SCHEDULE SE **(Form 1040)** Department of the Treasury Internal Revenue Service	**Self-Employment Tax** ▶ See Instructions for Schedule SE (Form 1040). ▶ Attach to Form 1040.	OMB No. 1545-0074 19**93** Attachment Sequence No. **17**

Name of person with **self-employment** income (as shown on Form 1040)	Social security number of person with **self-employment** income ▶

Who Must File Schedule SE

You must file Schedule SE if:

● Your wages (and tips) subject to social security AND Medicare tax (or railroad retirement tax) were less than $135,000; **AND**

● Your net earnings from self-employment from other than church employee income (line 4 of Short Schedule SE or line 4c of Long Schedule SE) were $400 or more; **OR**

● You had church employee income of $108.28 or more. Income from services you performed as a minister or a member of a religious order **is not** church employee income. See page SE-1.

Note: *Even if you have a loss or a small amount of income from self-employment, it may be to your benefit to file Schedule SE and use either "optional method" in Part II of Long Schedule SE. See page SE-3.*

Exception. If your only self-employment income was from earnings as a minister, member of a religious order, or Christian Science practitioner, **AND** you filed Form 4361 and received IRS approval not to be taxed on those earnings, **DO NOT** file Schedule SE. Instead, write "Exempt–Form 4361" on Form 1040, line 47.

May I Use Short Schedule SE or MUST I Use Long Schedule SE?

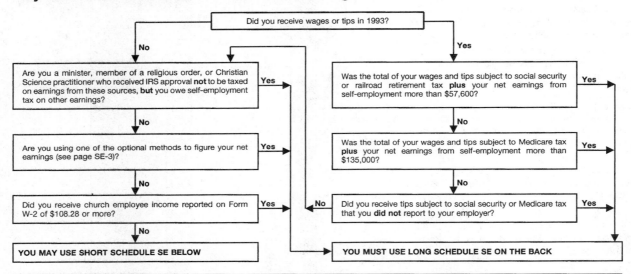

Section A—Short Schedule SE. Caution: *Read above to see if you can use Short Schedule SE.*

1	Net farm profit or (loss) from Schedule F, line 36, and farm partnerships, Schedule K-1 (Form 1065), line 15a	**1**
2	Net profit or (loss) from Schedule C, line 31; Schedule C-EZ, line 3; and Schedule K-1 (Form 1065), line 15a (other than farming). Ministers and members of religious orders see page SE-1 for amounts to report on this line. See page SE-2 for other income to report	**2**
3	Combine lines 1 and 2	**3**
4	**Net earnings from self-employment.** Multiply line 3 by 92.35% (.9235). If less than $400, **do not** file this schedule; you do not owe self-employment tax . . . . ▶	**4**
5	**Self-employment tax.** If the amount on line 4 is: ● $57,600 or less, multiply line 4 by 15.3% (.153) and enter the result. ● More than $57,600 but less than $135,000, multiply the amount in excess of $57,600 by 2.9% (.029). Then, add $8,812.80 to the result and enter the total. ● $135,000 or more, enter $11,057.40. Also enter on **Form 1040, line 47. (Important:** You are allowed a deduction for **one-half** of this amount. Multiply line 5 by 50% (.5) and enter the result on **Form 1040, line 25.)**	**5**

For Paperwork Reduction Act Notice, see Form 1040 instructions.   Cat. No. 11358Z   Schedule SE (Form 1040) 1993

Schedule SE (Form 1040) 1993   Attachment Sequence No. **17**   Page **2**

Name of person with **self-employment** income (as shown on Form 1040)	Social security number of person with **self-employment** income ▶	

Section B—Long Schedule SE

Part I   Self-Employment Tax

Note: *If your only income subject to self-employment tax is church employee income, skip lines 1 through 4b. Enter -0- on line 4c and go to line 5a. Income from services you performed as a minister or a member of a religious order **is not** church employee income. See page SE-1.*

A   If you are a minister, member of a religious order, or Christian Science practitioner **AND** you filed Form 4361, but you had $400 or more of **other** net earnings from self-employment, check here and continue with Part I . . . . . ▶ ☐

1	Net farm profit or (loss) from Schedule F, line 36, and farm partnerships, Schedule K-1 (Form 1065), line 15a. **Note:** *Skip this line if you use the farm optional method. See page SE-3* . .	**1**	
2	Net profit or (loss) from Schedule C, line 31; Schedule C-EZ, line 3; and Schedule K-1 (Form 1065), line 15a (other than farming). Ministers and members of religious orders see page SE-1 for amounts to report on this line. See page SE-2 for other income to report. **Note:** *Skip this line if you use the nonfarm optional method. See page SE-3*	**2**	
3	Combine lines 1 and 2	**3**	
4a	If line 3 is more than zero, multiply line 3 by 92.35% (.9235). Otherwise, enter amount from line 3	**4a**	
b	If you elected one or both of the optional methods, enter the total of lines 17 and 19 here . .	**4b**	
c	Combine lines 4a and 4b. If less than $400, **do not** file this schedule; you do not owe self-employment tax. **Exception.** If less than $400 and you had church employee income, enter -0- and continue . ▶	**4c**	
5a	Enter your church employee income from Form W-2. **Caution:** *See page SE-1 for definition of church employee income* . . **5a**		**5b**	
b	Multiply line 5a by 92.35% (.9235). If less than $100, enter -0-	**5b**	
6	**Net earnings from self-employment.** Add lines 4c and 5b	**6**	
7	Maximum amount of combined wages and self-employment earnings subject to social security tax or the 6.2% portion of the 7.65% railroad retirement (tier 1) tax for 1993	**7**	57,600 00
8a	Total social security wages and tips (from Form(s) W-2) and railroad retirement (tier 1) compensation **8a**			
b	Unreported tips subject to social security tax (from Form 4137, line 9) **8b**			
c	Add lines 8a and 8b	**8c**	
9	Subtract line 8c from line 7. If zero or less, enter -0- here and on line 10 and go to line 12a ▶	**9**	
10	Multiply the **smaller** of line 6 or line 9 by 12.4% (.124)	**10**	
11	Maximum amount of combined wages and self-employment earnings subject to Medicare tax or the 1.45% portion of the 7.65% railroad retirement (tier 1) tax for 1993	**11**	135,000 00
12a	Total Medicare wages and tips (from Form(s) W-2) and railroad retirement (tier 1) compensation **12a**			
b	Unreported tips subject to Medicare tax (from Form 4137, line 14) . **12b**			
c	Add lines 12a and 12b	**12c**	
13	Subtract line 12c from line 11. If zero or less, enter -0- here and on line 14 and go to line 15 .	**13**	
14	Multiply the **smaller** of line 6 or line 13 by 2.9% (.029)	**14**	
15	**Self-employment tax.** Add lines 10 and 14. Enter here and on **Form 1040, line 47. (Important:** You are allowed a deduction for **one-half** of this amount. Multiply line 15 by 50% (.5) and enter the result on **Form 1040, line 25.)**	**15**	

Part II   Optional Methods To Figure Net Earnings (See page SE-3.)

Farm Optional Method. You may use this method **only** if **(a)** Your gross farm income[1] was not more than $2,400 **or (b)** Your gross farm income[1] was more than $2,400 and your net farm profits[2] were less than $1,733.

16	Maximum income for optional methods	**16**	1,600 00
17	Enter the **smaller** of: two-thirds (⅔) of gross farm income[1] (not less than zero) **or** $1,600. Also, include this amount on line 4b above	**17**	

Nonfarm Optional Method. You may use this method **only** if **(a)** Your net nonfarm profits[3] were less than $1,733 and also less than 72.189% of your gross nonfarm income,[4] **and (b)** You had net earnings from self-employment of at least $400 in 2 of the prior 3 years. **Caution:** *You may use this method no more than five times.*

18	Subtract line 17 from line 16	**18**	
19	Enter the **smaller** of: two-thirds (⅔) of gross nonfarm income[4] (not less than zero) **or** the amount on line 18. Also, include this amount on line 4b above	**19**	

[1]From Schedule F, line 11, and Schedule K-1 (Form 1065), line 15b.   [3]From Schedule C, line 31; Schedule C-EZ, line 3; and Schedule K-1 (Form 1065), line 15a.
[2]From Schedule F, line 36, and Schedule K-1 (Form 1065), line 15a.   [4]From Schedule C, line 7; Schedule C-EZ, line 1; and Schedule K-1 (Form 1065), line 15c.

Form **1040-ES**	**Estimated Tax for Individuals**	OMB No. 1545-0087

Department of the Treasury
Internal Revenue Service

This package is primarily for first-time filers of estimated tax.

1994

Paperwork Reduction Act Notice

We ask for the information on the payment vouchers to carry out the Internal Revenue laws of the United States. You are required to give us the information. We need it to ensure that you are complying with these laws and to allow us to figure and collect the right amount of tax.

The time needed to complete the worksheets and prepare and file the payment vouchers will vary depending on individual circumstances. The estimated average time is: **Recordkeeping, 1 hr., 19 min.; Learning about the law, 19 min.; Preparing the worksheets and payment vouchers, 49 min.; Copying, assembling, and sending the payment voucher to the IRS, 10 min.** If you have comments concerning the accuracy of these time estimates or suggestions for making this package easier, we would be happy to hear from you. You can write to both the **Internal Revenue Service,** Attention: Reports Clearance Officer, PC:FP, Washington, DC 20224; and the **Office of Management and Budget,** Paperwork Reduction Project (1545-0087), Washington, DC 20503. **DO NOT** send the payment vouchers to either of these offices. Instead, see **Where To File Your Payment Voucher** on page 5.

Purpose of This Package

Use this package to figure and pay your estimated tax. Estimated tax is the method used to pay tax on income that is not subject to withholding; for example, earnings from self-employment, interest, dividends, rents, alimony, unemployment compensation, etc.

This package is primarily for first-time filers who are or may be subject to paying estimated tax. This package can also be used if you did not receive or have lost your preprinted 1040-ES package. The estimated tax worksheet on page 3 will help you figure the correct amount to pay. The vouchers in this package are for crediting your estimated tax payments to your account correctly. Use the **Record of Estimated Tax Payments** on page 5 to keep track of the payments you have made and the number and amount of your remaining payments.

After we receive your first payment voucher from this package, we will mail you a preprinted 1040-ES package with your name, address, and social security number on each payment voucher. Use the preprinted vouchers to make your **remaining** estimated tax payments for the year. This will speed processing, reduce processing costs, and reduce the chance of errors.

Do not use the vouchers in this package to notify the IRS of a **change of address.** If you have a new address, get **Form 8822,** Change of Address, by calling 1-800-TAX-FORM (1-800-829-3676). Send the completed form to the Internal Revenue Service Center where you filed your last tax return. The Service Center will update your record and send you new preprinted payment vouchers.

Note: *Continue to use your old preprinted payment vouchers to make payments of estimated tax until you receive the new package of preprinted payment vouchers.*

Who Must Make Estimated Tax Payments

In most cases, you must make estimated tax payments if you expect to owe, after subtracting your withholding and credits, at least $500 in tax for 1994, and you expect your withholding and credits to be less than the **smaller** of:

1. 90% of the tax shown on your 1994 tax return, or
2. 100% of the tax shown on your 1993 tax return (110% of that amount if you are not a farmer or a fisherman and the adjusted gross income shown on that return is more than $150,000 or, if married filing separately for 1994, more than $75,000).

However, if you did not file a 1993 tax return or that return did not cover all 12 months, item 2 above does not apply.

Exception. You do not have to pay estimated tax if you were a U.S. citizen or resident alien for all of 1993 and you had no tax liability for the full 12-month 1993 tax year.

The estimated tax rules apply to:
- U.S. citizens and residents,
- Residents of Puerto Rico, the Virgin Islands, Guam, the Commonwealth of the Northern Mariana Islands, and American Samoa, and
- Nonresident aliens (use Form 1040-ES (NR)).

If you also receive salaries and wages, you can avoid having to make estimated tax payments by asking your employer to take more tax out of your earnings. To do this, file a new **Form W-4,** Employee's Withholding Allowance Certificate, with your employer.

Caution: You may not make joint estimated tax payments if you or your spouse is a nonresident alien, you are separated under a decree of divorce or separate maintenance, or you and your spouse have different tax years.

Additional Information You May Need

Most of the information you will need can be found in:
   Pub. 505, Tax Withholding and Estimated Tax.
Other available information:
   Pub. 553, Highlights of 1993 Tax Changes, and
   Instructions for the 1993 Form 1040 or 1040A.
For forms and publications, call 1-800-TAX-FORM (1-800-829-3676). For assistance, call 1-800-829-1040.

Tax Law Changes Effective for 1994

Use your 1993 tax return as a guide in figuring your 1994 estimated tax, but be sure to consider the changes noted in this section. For more information on most of the following provisions and other changes that may affect your 1994 estimated tax, see Pub. 553.

Figuring Estimated Tax. The rules for figuring estimated tax based on your prior year's tax have changed. See **Who Must Make Estimated Tax Payments** on this page.

Expiration of Self-Employed Health Insurance Deduction. At the time this package went to print, the self-employed health insurance deduction was scheduled to expire December 31, 1993.

Self-Employment Tax. Beginning in 1994, the limit on the amount of self-employment income subject to the 2.9% Medicare tax has been repealed. The entire amount of your net self-employment earnings of at least $400, including amounts over $135,000, is now subject to the Medicare tax.

Business Meals and Entertainment. Beginning in 1994, the deductible portion of business meal costs and entertainment expenses has been reduced from 80% to 50%.

Club Dues. No deduction is allowed for amounts paid or incurred after 1993 for membership dues in any club organized for business, pleasure, recreation, or other social purpose. This includes business, social, athletic, luncheon, sporting, airline, and hotel clubs.

Travel Expenses. No deduction is allowed for travel expenses paid or incurred after 1993 for a spouse, dependent, or other individual accompanying you on business travel, unless that spouse, dependent, or other individual is your employee and the travel is for a bona fide business purpose and would otherwise be deductible by that person.

Taxable Social Security Benefits. If your 1994 income, including one-half of your social security or equivalent railroad retirement benefits, is more than $34,000 if you are single (more than $44,000 if you are married filing jointly), more of your benefits may be taxable. For some people, up to 85% will be taxable. For details, including rules for married persons filing separately and a worksheet to figure your taxable benefits, see Pub. 553.

Earned Income Credit. The maximum earned income, income limitation, and credit amounts have been increased. But the health insurance credit and the extra credit for a child born

Cat. No. 11340T

(Continued on page 2)

during the year are no longer allowed. Also, new rules allow certain individuals without qualifying children to take the credit.

Charitable Contributions. Generally, no deduction is allowed for any charitable contribution of $250 or more made after 1993, unless you obtain a written acknowledgement from the charitable organization.

Moving Expenses. For expenses incurred after 1993, the deduction for expenses of moving to a new home in connection with beginning work at a new location is allowed only if your new principal workplace is at least 50 miles farther from your former home than was your former principal workplace. In addition, deductible moving expenses are limited to the costs of moving your household goods and personal effects from your former home to your new home and transportation and lodging expenses en route from your former home to your new home. Meals, pre-move househunting expenses, temporary quarters expenses, and qualified real estate expenses are no longer deductible. Also, deductible moving expenses incurred after 1993 and reimbursed by your employer are no longer included in your gross income. Unreimbursed moving expenses that are deductible are claimed as an adjustment to income (i.e., you no longer need to itemize deductions to deduct these expenses).

Rental Real Estate Losses and Credits of Real Estate Professionals. For tax years beginning after 1993, certain individuals who materially participate in real property trades or businesses, and who perform more than one-half of their personal services and more than 750 hours of services during the year in those trades or businesses, are not subject to the passive activity limitations on losses and credits from rental real estate activities in which they materially participate. A real property trade or business means any real property development, redevelopment, construction, reconstruction, acquisition, conversion, rental, operation, management, leasing, or brokerage trade or business. Services performed as an employee are not treated as performed in a real property trade or business, unless the employee owns more than 5% of the stock (or more than 5% of the capital or profits interest) in the employer.

Standard Deduction for 1994. If you do not itemize your deductions, you may take the 1994 standard deduction listed below:

Filing Status	Standard Deduction
Married filing jointly or Qualifying widow(er)	$6,350
Head of household	$5,600
Single	$3,800
Married filing separately	$3,175

Caution: If you can be claimed as a dependent on another person's 1994 return, your standard deduction is the greater of $600 or your earned income, up to the standard deduction amount.

An additional amount is added to the standard deduction if:

1. You are an unmarried individual (single or head of household) and are:

65 or older or blind	$950
65 or older and blind	$1,900

2. You are a married individual (filing jointly or separately) or a qualifying widow(er) and are:

65 or older or blind	$750
65 or older and blind	$1,500
Both spouses 65 or older	$1,500 *
Both spouses 65 or older and blind	$3,000 *

* If married filing separately, these amounts apply only if you can claim an exemption for your spouse.

To Figure Your Estimated Tax Use

- The **1994 Estimated Tax Worksheet** on page 3.
- The instructions on page 4 for the worksheet on page 3.
- The **1994 Tax Rate Schedules** below.
- Your 1993 tax return and instructions as a guide to figuring your income, deductions, and credits (but be sure to consider the tax law changes noted earlier).

If you receive your income unevenly throughout the year (e.g., you operate your business on a seasonal basis), you may be able to lower or eliminate the amount of your required estimated tax payment for one or more periods by using the annualized income installment method. See Pub. 505 for details.

To amend or correct your estimated tax, see **Amending Estimated Tax Payments** on page 4.

1994 Tax Rate Schedules

Caution: *Do not use these Tax Rate Schedules to figure your 1993 taxes. Use only to figure your 1994 estimated taxes.*

Single—Schedule X

If line 5 is: Over—	But not over—	The tax is:	of the amount over—
$0	$22,750	. . . . 15%	$0
22,750	55,100	$3,412.50 + 28%	22,750
55,100	115,000	12,470.50 + 31%	55,100
115,000	250,000	31,039.50 + 36%	115,000
250,000	. . . .	79,639.50 + 39.6%	250,000

Head of household—Schedule Z

If line 5 is: Over—	But not over—	The tax is:	of the amount over—
$0	$30,500	. . . . 15%	$0
30,500	78,700	$4,575.00 + 28%	30,500
78,700	127,500	18,071.00 + 31%	78,700
127,500	250,000	33,199.00 + 36%	127,500
250,000	. . . .	77,299.00 + 39.6%	250,000

Married filing jointly or Qualifying widow(er)—Schedule Y-1

If line 5 is: Over—	But not over—	The tax is:	of the amount over—
$0	$38,000	. . . . 15%	$0
38,000	91,850	$5,700.00 + 28%	38,000
91,850	140,000	20,778.00 + 31%	91,850
140,000	250,000	35,704.50 + 36%	140,000
250,000	. . . .	75,304.50 + 39.6%	250,000

Married filing separately—Schedule Y-2

If line 5 is: Over—	But not over—	The tax is:	of the amount over—
$0	$19,000	. . . . 15%	$0
19,000	45,925	$2,850.00 + 28%	19,000
45,925	70,000	10,389.00 + 31%	45,925
70,000	125,000	17,852.25 + 36%	70,000
125,000	. . . .	37,652.25 + 39.6%	125,000

1994 Estimated Tax Worksheet (keep for your records)

1	Enter amount of adjusted gross income you expect in 1994 (see instructions)	**1**
2	• If you plan to itemize deductions, enter the estimated total of your itemized deductions. **Caution:** If line 1 above is over $111,800 ($55,900 if married filing separately), your deduction may be reduced. See Pub. 505 for details. • If you do not plan to itemize deductions, see **Standard Deduction for 1994** on page 2, and enter your standard deduction here.	**2**
3	Subtract line 2 from line 1	**3**
4	Exemptions. Multiply $2,450 by the number of personal exemptions. If you can be claimed as a dependent on another person's 1994 return, your personal exemption is not allowed. **Caution:** If line 1 above is over $167,700 ($139,750 if head of household; $111,800 if single; $83,850 if married filing separately), get Pub. 505 to figure the amount to enter	**4**
5	Subtract line 4 from line 3	**5**
6	**Tax.** Figure your tax on the amount on line 5 by using the 1994 Tax Rate Schedules on page 2. DO NOT use the Tax Table or the Tax Rate Schedules in the 1993 Form 1040 or Form 1040A instructions. **Caution:** If you have a net capital gain and line 5 is over $91,850 ($78,700 if head of household; $55,100 if single; $45,925 if married filing separately), get Pub. 505 to figure the tax	**6**
7	Additional taxes (see instructions)	**7**
8	Add lines 6 and 7	**8**
9	Credits (see instructions). Do not include any income tax withholding on this line	**9**
10	Subtract line 9 from line 8. Enter the result, but not less than zero	**10**
11	Self-employment tax. Estimate of 1994 net earnings from self-employment $_____; if **$60,600 or less,** multiply the amount by 15.3%; if **more than $60,600,** multiply the amount in excess of $60,600 by 2.9%. Add $9,271.80 to the result and enter the total. **Caution:** If you also have wages subject to social security tax, get Pub. 505 to figure the amount to enter. . . .	**11**
12	Other taxes (see instructions)	**12**
13a	Add lines 10 through 12	**13a**
b	Earned income credit and credit from **Form 4136**	**13b**
c	Subtract line 13b from line 13a. Enter the result, but not less than zero. **THIS IS YOUR TOTAL 1994 ESTIMATED TAX** . . . . ▶	**13c**

		14a	14b	
14a	Multiply line 13c by 90% (66⅔% for farmers and fishermen) . . .	**14a**		
b	Enter 100% of the tax shown on your 1993 tax return (110% of that amount if you are not a farmer or a fisherman and the adjusted gross income shown on that return is more than $150,000 or, if married filing separately for 1994, more than $75,000)		**14b**	

c	Enter the **smaller** of line 14a or 14b. **THIS IS YOUR REQUIRED ANNUAL PAYMENT TO AVOID A PENALTY** . . . . ▶	**14c**
	Caution: Generally, if you do not prepay (through income tax withholding and estimated tax payments) at least the amount on line 14c, you may owe a penalty for not paying enough estimated tax. To avoid a penalty, make sure your estimate on line 13c is as accurate as possible. Even if you pay the required annual payment, you may still owe tax when you file your return. If you prefer, you may pay the amount shown on line 13c. For more details, get Pub. 505.	
15	Income tax withheld and estimated to be withheld during 1994 (including income tax withholding on pensions, annuities, certain deferred income, etc.)	**15**
16	Subtract line 15 from line 14c. (**Note:** *If zero or less, or line 13c minus line 15 is less than $500, stop here. You are not required to make estimated tax payments.*)	**16**
17	If the first payment you are required to make is due April 15, 1994, enter ¼ of line 16 (minus any 1993 overpayment that you are applying to this installment) here and on your payment voucher(s)	**17**

Instructions for Worksheet on Page 3

Line 1—If you are self-employed, be sure to take into account the deduction for one-half of your self-employment tax. For details on figuring your adjusted gross income, see **Expected Adjusted Gross Income** in Pub. 505.

Line 7—Additional Taxes. Enter the additional taxes from **Form 4970**, Tax on Accumulation Distribution of Trusts, or **Form 4972**, Tax on Lump-Sum Distributions.

Line 9—Credits. See Pub. 553 and the 1993 Form 1040, lines 41 through 45, or Form 1040A, lines 24a and 24b, and the related instructions.

Line 11—Self-Employment Tax. If you and your spouse make joint estimated tax payments and you both have self-employment income, figure the self-employment tax for each of you separately. Enter the total on line 11. When figuring your estimate of 1994 net earnings from self-employment, be sure to use only 92.35% of your total net profit from self-employment.

Line 12—Other Taxes. Enter any other taxes, such as tax on early distributions from a qualified retirement plan (including your IRA), annuity, or modified endowment contract (entered into after June 20, 1988); and alternative minimum tax. Do not include any deferral of additional 1993 taxes or recapture of a Federal mortgage subsidy. Also, do not include social security and Medicare tax on tip income not reported to your employer or uncollected employee social security and Medicare or RRTA tax on tips or group-term life insurance.

Payment Due Dates

You may pay all of your estimated tax by April 15, 1994, or in four equal amounts by the dates shown below:

1st payment	April 15, 1994
2nd payment	June 15, 1994
3rd payment	Sept. 15, 1994
4th payment	Jan. 17, 1995*

*You do not have to make the payment due January 17, 1995, if you file your 1994 Form 1040 or 1040A by January 31, 1995, **AND** pay the entire balance due with your return.

Note: *Payments are due by the dates indicated whether or not you are outside the United States and Puerto Rico.*

If, after March 31, 1994, you have a large change in income, deductions, additional taxes, or credits that requires you to start making estimated tax payments, you should figure the amount of your estimated tax payments by using the annualized income installment method, as explained in Pub. 505. Although your payment due dates will be the same as shown above, the payment amounts will vary based on your income, deductions, additional taxes, and credits for the months ending before each payment due date. As a result, this method may allow you to skip or lower the amount due for one or more payments. If you use the annualized income installment method, be sure to file **Form 2210**, Underpayment of Estimated Tax by Individuals and Fiduciaries, with your 1994 tax return, even if no penalty is owed.

Farmers and Fishermen. If at least two-thirds of your gross income for 1993 or 1994 is from farming or fishing, you may do one of the following:

● Pay all of your estimated tax by January 17, 1995, or

● File your 1994 Form 1040 by March 1, 1995, and pay the total tax due. In this case, 1994 estimated payments are not required.

Fiscal Year Filers. You are on a fiscal year if your 12-month tax period ends on any day except December 31. Due dates for fiscal year filers are the 15th day of the 4th, 6th, and 9th months for your current fiscal year and the 1st month of the following fiscal year. If any payment date falls on a Saturday, Sunday, or legal holiday, use the next working day.

Amending Estimated Tax Payments

To change or amend your estimated payments, refigure your total estimated payments due (line 16 of the worksheet on page 3). Then use the worksheets under **Amended estimated tax** in Pub. 505 to figure the payment due for each remaining payment period. If an estimated tax payment for a previous period is less than one-fourth of your amended estimated tax, you may owe a penalty when you file your return.

When a Penalty Is Applied

In some cases, you may owe a penalty when you file your return. The penalty is imposed on each underpayment for the number of days it remains unpaid. A penalty may be applied if you did not pay enough estimated tax or you did not make the payments on time or in the required amount. A penalty may apply even if you have an overpayment on your tax return.

The penalty may be waived under certain conditions. See Pub. 505 for details.

How To Complete and Use the Payment Voucher

There is a separate voucher for each due date. Please be sure you use the voucher with the correct due date shown in the upper right corner. Complete and send in the voucher **only** if you are making a payment. To complete your voucher:

● Type or print your name, address, and social security number in the space provided on the voucher. If filing a joint voucher, also enter your spouse's name and social security number.

● Enter on the payment line of the voucher only the amount you are sending in. When making payments of estimated tax, be sure to take into account any 1993 overpayment that you choose to credit against your 1994 tax, but do not include the overpayment amount on this line.

● Enclose your payment, making the check or money order payable to: "Internal Revenue Service" (not "IRS").

● Write your social security number and "1994 Form 1040-ES" on your check or money order.

● Do not staple or attach your payment to the voucher.

● Mail your payment voucher to the address shown on page 5 for the place where you live.

● Fill in the **Record of Estimated Tax Payments** on page 5 for your files.

If you changed your name and made estimated tax payments using your old name, attach a statement to the front of your 1994 Form 1040 or 1040A. List all of the estimated tax payments you and your spouse made for 1994, the address where you made the payments, and the name(s) and social security number(s) under which you made the payments.

Record of Estimated Tax Payments (see page 4 for correct payment due dates)

Payment number	(a) Date	(b) Amount paid	(c) 1993 overpayment credit applied	(d) Total amount paid and credited (add (b) and (c))
1				
2				
3				
4				
Total . . . . ▶				

Where To File Your Payment Voucher

Mail your payment voucher to the Internal Revenue Service at the address shown below for the place where you live. **Do not** mail your tax return to this address. Also, do not mail your estimated tax payments to the address shown in the Form 1040 or 1040A instructions.

Note: *For proper delivery of your estimated tax payment, you must include the P.O. box number, if any, in the address.*

If you live in: ▼	Use this address: ▼
New Jersey, New York (New York City and counties of Nassau, Rockland, Suffolk, and Westchester)	P.O. Box 162 Newark, NJ 07101-0162
New York (all other counties), Connecticut, Maine, Massachusetts, New Hampshire, Rhode Island, Vermont	P.O. Box 371999 Pittsburgh, PA 15250-7999
Delaware, District of Columbia, Maryland, Pennsylvania, Virginia	P.O. Box 839 Newark, NJ 07101-0839
Florida, Georgia, South Carolina	P.O. Box 105900 Atlanta, GA 30348-5900
Indiana, Kentucky, Michigan, Ohio, West Virginia	P.O. Box 7422 Chicago, IL 60680-7422
Alabama, Arkansas, Louisiana, Mississippi, North Carolina, Tennessee	P.O. Box 1219 Charlotte, NC 28201-1219

Illinois, Iowa, Minnesota, Missouri, Wisconsin	P.O. Box 970006 St. Louis, MO 63197-0006
Kansas, New Mexico, Oklahoma, Texas	P.O. Box 970001 St. Louis, MO 63197-0001
Alaska, Arizona, California (counties of Alpine, Amador, Butte, Calaveras, Colusa, Contra Costa, Del Norte, El Dorado, Glenn, Humboldt, Lake, Lassen, Marin, Mendocino, Modoc, Napa, Nevada, Placer, Plumas, Sacramento, San Joaquin, Shasta, Sierra, Siskiyou, Solano, Sonoma, Sutter, Tehama, Trinity, Yolo, and Yuba), Colorado, Idaho, Montana, Nebraska, Nevada, North Dakota, Oregon, South Dakota, Utah, Washington, Wyoming	P.O. Box 510000 San Francisco, CA 94151-5100
California (all other counties), Hawaii	P.O. Box 54030 Los Angeles, CA 90054-0030
American Samoa	P.O. Box 839 Newark, NJ 07101-0839
The Commonwealth of the Northern Mariana Islands	P.O. Box 839 Newark, NJ 07101-0839
Puerto Rico (or if excluding income under section 933)	P.O. Box 839 Newark, NJ 07101-0839

Guam: Nonpermanent residents	P.O. Box 839 Newark, NJ 07101-0839
Permanent residents*	Department of Revenue and Taxation Government of Guam 378 Chalan San Antonio Tamuning, GU 96911

* You must prepare separate vouchers for estimated income tax and self-employment tax payments. Send the income tax vouchers to the Guam address and the self-employment tax vouchers to the address for Guam nonpermanent residents shown above.

Virgin Islands: Nonpermanent residents	P.O. Box 839 Newark, NJ 07101-0839
Permanent residents*	V.I. Bureau of Internal Revenue Lockhart Gardens No. 1-A Charlotte Amalie St. Thomas, VI 00802

* You must prepare separate vouchers for estimated income tax and self-employment tax payments. Send the income tax vouchers to the V.I. address and the self-employment tax vouchers to the address for V.I. nonpermanent residents shown above.

All A.P.O. and F.P.O. addresses	P.O. Box 839 Newark, NJ 07101-0839
Foreign country: U.S. citizens and those filing Form 2555, Form 2555-EZ, or Form 4563	P.O. Box 839 Newark, NJ 07101-0839

Tear off here

Form **1040-ES** Department of the Treasury Internal Revenue Service	**1994** Payment Voucher **4**		OMB No. 1545-0087

		Calendar year—Due Jan. 17, 1995

File only if you are making a payment of estimated tax. Return this voucher with check or money order payable to the **"Internal Revenue Service."** Please write your social security number and "1994 Form 1040-ES" on your check or money order. Please do not send cash. Enclose, but do not staple or attach, your payment with this voucher.

Amount of payment	Please type or print	Your first name and initial	Your last name	Your social security number
		If joint payment, complete for spouse		
		Spouse's first name and initial	Spouse's last name	Spouse's social security number
$		Address (number, street, and apt. no.)		
		City, state, and ZIP code		

For Paperwork Reduction Act Notice, see instructions on page 1.   **Page 5**

Form **1040-ES**
Department of the Treasury
Internal Revenue Service

1994 Payment **3**
Voucher

OMB No. 1545-0087

File only if you are making a payment of estimated tax. Return this voucher with check or money order payable to the "**Internal Revenue Service.**" Please write your social security number and "1994 Form 1040-ES" on your check or money order. Please do not send cash. Enclose, but do not staple or attach, your payment with this voucher.

Calendar year—Due Sept. 15, 1994

Amount of payment	Please type or print	Your first name and initial	Your last name	Your social security number
		If joint payment, complete for spouse		
		Spouse's first name and initial	Spouse's last name	Spouse's social security number
$ ---------------------		Address (number, street, and apt. no.)		
		City, state, and ZIP code		

For Paperwork Reduction Act Notice, see instructions on page 1.

.... **Tear off here** ....

Form **1040-ES**
Department of the Treasury
Internal Revenue Service

1994 Payment **2**
Voucher

OMB No. 1545-0087

File only if you are making a payment of estimated tax. Return this voucher with check or money order payable to the "**Internal Revenue Service.**" Please write your social security number and "1994 Form 1040-ES" on your check or money order. Please do not send cash. Enclose, but do not staple or attach, your payment with this voucher.

Calendar year—Due June 15, 1994

Amount of payment	Please type or print	Your first name and initial	Your last name	Your social security number
		If joint payment, complete for spouse		
		Spouse's first name and initial	Spouse's last name	Spouse's social security number
$ ---------------------		Address (number, street, and apt. no.)		
		City, state, and ZIP code		

For Paperwork Reduction Act Notice, see instructions on page 1.

.... **Tear off here** ....

Form **1040-ES**
Department of the Treasury
Internal Revenue Service

1994 Payment **1**
Voucher

OMB No. 1545-0087

File only if you are making a payment of estimated tax. Return this voucher with check or money order payable to the "**Internal Revenue Service.**" Please write your social security number and "1994 Form 1040-ES" on your check or money order. Please do not send cash. Enclose, but do not staple or attach, your payment with this voucher.

Calendar year—Due April 15, 1994

Amount of payment	Please type or print	Your first name and initial	Your last name	Your social security number
		If joint payment, complete for spouse		
		Spouse's first name and initial	Spouse's last name	Spouse's social security number
$ ---------------------		Address (number, street, and apt. no.)		
		City, state, and ZIP code		

For Paperwork Reduction Act Notice, see instructions on page 1.

Page 7

Form **2106**

Department of the Treasury
Internal Revenue Service

Employee Business Expenses

▶ See separate instructions.

▶ Attach to Form 1040.

OMB No. 1545-0139

1993

Attachment
Sequence No. **54**

Your name	Social security number	Occupation in which expenses were incurred

Part I   **Employee Business Expenses and Reimbursements**

STEP 1   Enter Your Expenses

		Column A Other Than Meals and Entertainment		Column B Meals and Entertainment	
1	Vehicle expense from line 22 or line 29	1		//////	
2	Parking fees, tolls, and transportation, including train, bus, etc., that **did not** involve overnight travel	2		//////	
3	Travel expense while away from home overnight, including lodging, airplane, car rental, etc. **Do not** include meals and entertainment	3		//////	
4	Business expenses not included on lines 1 through 3. **Do not** include meals and entertainment	4		//////	
5	Meals and entertainment expenses (see instructions)	5	//////		
6	**Total expenses.** In Column A, add lines 1 through 4 and enter the result. In Column B, enter the amount from line 5	6		//////	

Note: *If you were not reimbursed for any expenses in Step 1, skip line 7 and enter the amount from line 6 on line 8.*

STEP 2   Enter Amounts Your Employer Gave You for Expenses Listed in STEP 1

7	Enter amounts your employer gave you that were **not** reported to you in box 1 of Form W-2. Include any amount reported under code "L" in box 13 of your Form W-2 (see instructions) . . .	7		//////	

STEP 3   Figure Expenses To Deduct on Schedule A (Form 1040)

8	Subtract line 7 from line 6	8		//////	
	Note: *If **both columns** of line 8 are zero, **stop here.** If Column A is less than zero, report the amount as income on Form 1040, line 7, and enter -0- on line 10, Column A.*		//////	//////	
9	Enter 20% (.20) of line 8, Column B	9	//////		
10	In Column A, enter the amount from line 8. In Column B, subtract line 9 from line 8	10		//////	
11	Add the amounts on line 10 of both columns and enter the total here. **Also, enter the total on Schedule A (Form 1040), line 19.** (Qualified performing artists and individuals with disabilities, see the instructions for special rules on where to enter the total.) . . . . ▶	11			

For Paperwork Reduction Act Notice, see instructions.   Cat. No. 11700N   Form **2106** (1993)

Form 2106 (1993)

Page **2**

Part II — Vehicle Expenses (See instructions to find out which sections to complete.)

Section A.—General Information

			(a) Vehicle 1	(b) Vehicle 2
12	Enter the date vehicle was placed in service	12	/ /	/ /
13	Total miles vehicle was driven during 1993	13	miles	miles
14	Business miles included on line 13	14	miles	miles
15	Percent of business use. Divide line 14 by line 13	15	%	%
16	Average daily round trip commuting distance	16	miles	miles
17	Commuting miles included on line 13	17	miles	miles
18	Other personal miles. Add lines 14 and 17 and subtract the total from line 13	18	miles	miles

19 Do you (or your spouse) have another vehicle available for personal purposes? ☐ Yes ☐ No

20 If your employer provided you with a vehicle, is personal use during off duty hours permitted? ☐ Yes ☐ No ☐ Not applicable

21a Do you have evidence to support your deduction? ☐ Yes ☐ No

21b If "Yes," is the evidence written? ☐ Yes ☐ No

Section B.—Standard Mileage Rate (Use this section only if you own the vehicle.)

22	Multiply line 14 by 28¢ (.28). Enter the result here and on line 1. (Rural mail carriers, see instructions.)	22	

Section C.—Actual Expenses

			(a) Vehicle 1		(b) Vehicle 2	
23	Gasoline, oil, repairs, vehicle insurance, etc.	23				
24a	Vehicle rentals	24a				
b	Inclusion amount (see instructions)	24b				
c	Subtract line 24b from line 24a	24c				
25	Value of employer-provided vehicle (applies only if 100% of annual lease value was included on Form W-2—see instructions)	25				
26	Add lines 23, 24c, and 25	26				
27	Multiply line 26 by the percentage on line 15	27				
28	Depreciation. Enter amount from line 38 below	28				
29	Add lines 27 and 28. Enter total here and on line 1	29				

Section D.—Depreciation of Vehicles (Use this section only if you own the vehicle.)

			(a) Vehicle 1		(b) Vehicle 2	
30	Enter cost or other basis (see instructions)	30				
31	Enter amount of section 179 deduction (see instructions)	31				
32	Multiply line 30 by line 15 (see instructions if you elected the section 179 deduction)	32				
33	Enter depreciation method and percentage (see instructions)	33				
34	Multiply line 32 by the percentage on line 33 (see instructions)	34				
35	Add lines 31 and 34	35				
36	Enter the limitation amount from the table in the line 36 instructions	36				
37	Multiply line 36 by the percentage on line 15	37				
38	Enter the **smaller** of line 35 or line 37. Also, enter this amount on line 28 above	38				

Form **2119**	**Sale of Your Home**	OMB No. 1545-0072
Department of the Treasury Internal Revenue Service	▶ Attach to Form 1040 for year of sale. ▶ See separate instructions. ▶ Please print or type.	19**93** Attachment Sequence No. **20**

Your first name and initial. If a joint return, also give spouse's name and initial.   Last name   **Your social security number**

Fill in Your Address Only If You Are Filing This Form by Itself and Not With Your Tax Return	Present address (no., street, and apt. no., rural route, or P.O. box no. if mail is not delivered to street address)	**Spouse's social security number**
	City, town or post office, state, and ZIP code	

Part I   General Information

1   Date your former main home was sold (month, day, year) . . . . ▶   **1**   /   /
2   Have you bought or built a new main home? . . . . ☐ Yes ☐ No
3   Is or was any part of either main home rented out or used for business? If "Yes," see instructions . . ☐ Yes ☐ No

Part II   Gain on Sale—Do not include amounts you deduct as moving expenses.

4   Selling price of home. Do not include personal property items you sold with your home . .   **4**
5   Expense of sale (see instructions) **5**
6   Amount realized. Subtract line 5 from line 4 . . . .   **6**
7   Adjusted basis of home sold (see instructions) **7**
8   **Gain on sale.** Subtract line 7 from line 6 . . . .   **8**

Is line 8 more than zero?	— Yes ——▶	If line 2 is "Yes," you **must** go to Part III or Part IV, whichever applies. If line 2 is "No," go to line 9.
	— No ——▶	**Stop** and attach this form to your return.

9   If you haven't replaced your home, do you plan to do so within the **replacement period** (see instructions)? ☐ Yes ☐ No
    • If line 9 is "Yes," stop here, attach this form to your return, and see **Additional Filing Requirements** in the instructions.
    • If line 9 is "No," you **must** go to Part III or Part IV, whichever applies.

Part III   One-Time Exclusion of Gain for People Age 55 or Older—By completing this part, you are electing to take the one-time exclusion (see instructions). If you are not electing to take the exclusion, go to Part IV now.

10   Who was age 55 or older on the date of sale? . . . . ☐ You ☐ Your spouse ☐ Both of you
11   Did the person who was age 55 or older own and use the property as his or her main home for a total of at least 3 years (except for short absences) of the 5-year period before the sale? If "No," go to Part IV now . . ☐ Yes ☐ No
12   At the time of sale, who owned the home? . . . . ☐ You ☐ Your spouse ☐ Both of you
13   Social security number of spouse at the time of sale if you had a different spouse from the one above. If you were not married at the time of sale, enter "None" . . . . ▶   **13**
14   **Exclusion.** Enter the **smaller** of line 8 or $125,000 ($62,500 if married filing separate return). Then, go to line 15 . . . .   **14**

Part IV   Adjusted Sales Price, Taxable Gain, and Adjusted Basis of New Home

15   If line 14 is blank, enter the amount from line 8. Otherwise, subtract line 14 from line 8 . .   **15**
    • If line 15 is zero, stop and attach this form to your return.
    • If line 15 is more than zero and line 2 is "Yes," go to line 16 now.
    • If you are reporting this sale on the installment method, stop and see the instructions.
    • All others, stop and **enter the amount from line 15 on Schedule D, col. (g), line 4 or line 12.**
16   Fixing-up expenses (see instructions for time limits) **16**
17   If line 14 is blank, enter amount from line 16. Otherwise, add lines 14 and 16 . . . . .   **17**
18   **Adjusted sales price.** Subtract line 17 from line 6 . . . .   **18**
19a   Date you moved into new home ▶ [/ /]   **b** Cost of new home (see instructions)   **19b**
20   Subtract line 19b from line 18. If zero or less, enter -0- **20**
21   **Taxable gain.** Enter the **smaller** of line 15 or line 20 . . . .   **21**
    • If line 21 is zero, go to line 22 and attach this form to your return.
    • If you are reporting this sale on the installment method, see the line 15 instructions and go to line 22.
    • All others, **enter the amount from line 21 on Schedule D, col. (g), line 4 or line 12,** and go to line 22.
22   Postponed gain. Subtract line 21 from line 15 . . . .   **22**
23   **Adjusted basis of new home.** Subtract line 22 from line 19b **23**

Sign Here Only If You Are Filing This Form by Itself and Not With Your Tax Return   Under penalties of perjury, I declare that I have examined this form, including attachments, and to the best of my knowledge and belief, it is true, correct, and complete.

Your signature   Date   Spouse's signature   Date

▶ _____   ▶ _____   _____
    If a joint return, both must sign.

For Paperwork Reduction Act Notice, see separate instructions.   Cat. No. 11710J   Form **2119** (1993)

♲ *Printed on recycled paper*

Form 2120
(Rev. January 1994)

Department of the Treasury
Internal Revenue Service

Multiple Support Declaration

▶ **Attach to Form 1040 or Form 1040A of Person Claiming the Dependent.**

OMB No. 1545-0071
Expires 1-31-97

Attachment
Sequence No. **50**

Name of person claiming the dependent

Social security number

During the calendar year 19 ...., I paid over 10% of the support of

----
Name of person

I could have claimed this person as a dependent except that I did not pay over 50% of his or her support. I understand that this person named above is being claimed as a dependent on the income tax return of

----
Name

Address

I agree not to claim this person as a dependent on my Federal income tax return for any tax year that began in this calendar year.

Your signature

Your social security number

-----------------   ---
Date   Address (number, street, apt. no.)

City, state, and ZIP code

Instructions

Paperwork Reduction Act Notice

We ask for the information on this form to carry out the Internal Revenue laws of the United States. You are required to give us the information. We need it to ensure that you are complying with these laws and to allow us to figure and collect the right amount of tax.

The time needed to complete and file this form will vary depending on individual circumstances. The estimated average time is: **Recordkeeping,** 7 minutes; **Learning about the law or the form,** 2 minutes; **Preparing the form,** 7 minutes; and **Copying, assembling, and sending the form to the IRS,** 10 minutes.

If you have comments concerning the accuracy of these time estimates or suggestions for making this form more simple, we would be happy to hear from you. You can write to both the IRS and the Office of Management and Budget at the addresses listed in the instructions of the tax return with which this form is filed.

Purpose of Form

When two or more individuals together pay over 50% of another person's support, Form 2120 or a similar statement is used to allow one of them to claim the person as a dependent for tax purposes.

The similar statement must contain the same information that is required by this form.

Who Can Claim the Dependent

To claim someone as a dependent, you must pay over 50% of that person's living expenses (support).

If no one meets this support test, but two or more of you together provide over 50% of a person's support, then one of you can claim that person as a dependent.

To claim the dependent, you must meet **all three** of the following requirements:

1. You paid over 10% of the support, and

2. All others who paid over 10% agree not to claim the person as a dependent, and

3. The other four dependency tests are met. See **Dependents** in the Form 1040 or Form 1040A instructions.

All contributors who provided over 10% support must choose which one of them will claim the dependent. If you will be claiming the dependent, see **How To File** below.

If you are a 10% contributor but **will not** be claiming the dependent, complete and sign a Form 2120 or similar statement. Give it to the person claiming the dependent.

How To File

If you are claiming the dependent, you must attach to your tax return a Form 2120 or similar statement that is completed and signed by each of the 10% contributors who are not claiming the dependent for the tax year. Be sure your name and social security number are at the top of each Form 2120 or similar statement.

Additional Information

See **Pub. 501,** Exemptions, Standard Deduction, and Filing Information, for more information.

Form 2210

Department of the Treasury
Internal Revenue Service

Underpayment of
Estimated Tax by Individuals and Fiduciaries
▶ See separate instructions.
▶ Attach to Form 1040, Form 1040A, Form 1040NR, or Form 1041.

OMB No. 1545-0140

19 93

Attachment
Sequence No. **06**

Name(s) shown on tax return | Identifying number

Note: *In most cases, you **do not** need to file Form 2210. The IRS will figure any penalty you owe and send you a bill. File Form 2210 **only** if one or more boxes in Part I apply to you. If you do not need to file Form 2210, you still may use it to figure your penalty. Enter the amount from line 20 or line 32 on the penalty line of your return, but do not attach Form 2210.*

Part I | **Reasons For Filing**—If 1a, b, c, or d below applies to you, you may be able to lower or eliminate your penalty. But you MUST check the boxes that apply and file Form 2210 with your tax return. If 1e or f below applies to you, check that box and file Form 2210 with your tax return.

1 Check whichever boxes apply (if none apply, see the **Note** above):

a ☐ You request a **waiver.** In certain circumstances, the IRS will waive all or part of the penalty. See the instructions for **Waiver of Penalty.**

b ☐ You use the **annualized income installment method.** If your income varied during the year, this method may reduce the amount of one or more required installments. See the **Instructions for Schedule B.**

c ☐ You had Federal income tax withheld from wages and you treat it as paid for estimated tax purposes when it was **actually** withheld instead of in equal amounts on the payment due dates. See the instructions for line 22.

d ☐ (1) You made estimated tax payments for 1990, 1991, or 1992 (or were charged an estimated tax penalty for any of those years), **AND**
   (2) Your adjusted gross income (AGI) is more than $75,000 (more than $37,500 if married filing separately), **AND**
   (3) Your 1993 **modified** AGI exceeds your 1992 AGI by more than $40,000 (more than $20,000 if married filing separately), **AND**
   (4) Your 2nd, 3rd, or 4th required installment (column (b), (c), or (d) of line 21) is based on **either** your 1992 tax **or** 90% of your 1993 **modified** tax.

   See the **Instructions for Schedule A** for more information.

e ☐ Conditions (1), (2), and (4) (but not condition (3)) in box 1d apply to you, and your 1993 AGI exceeds your 1992 AGI by more than $40,000 (more than $20,000 if married filing separately). If you check this box, you must also attach a computation of your 1993 modified AGI.

f ☐ One or more of your required installments (line 21) are based on your 1992 tax and you filed or are filing a joint return for either 1992 or 1993 but not for both years.

Part II | **All Filers Must Complete This Part**

2	Enter your 1993 tax after credits (see instructions)	2	
3	Other taxes (see instructions)	3	
4	Add lines 2 and 3	4	
5	Earned income credit	5	
6	Credit for Federal tax paid on fuels	6	
7	Add lines 5 and 6	7	
8	Current year tax. Subtract line 7 from line 4	8	
9	Multiply line 8 by 90% (.90)	9	
10	Withholding taxes. **Do not** include any estimated tax payments on this line (see instructions) .	10	
11	Subtract line 10 from line 8. If less than $500, **stop** here; **do not** complete or file this form. You do not owe the penalty	11	
12	Tax shown on your prior year (1992) return. **(Caution:** *See instructions.*)	12	
13	Enter the **smaller** of line 9 or line 12 (see instructions)	13	

Part III | **Short Method (Caution:** *Read the instructions to see if you can use the short method. If you checked box **1b, c,** or **d** in Part I, skip this part and go to Part IV.)*

14	Enter the amount, if any, from line 10 above	14	
15	Enter the total amount, if any, of estimated tax payments you made	15	
16	Add lines 14 and 15	16	
17	**Total underpayment for year.** Subtract line 16 from line 13. If zero or less, stop here; you do not owe the penalty. Do not file Form 2210 unless you checked box 1e or f above	17	
18	Multiply line 17 by .04655	18	
19	• If the amount on line 17 was paid **on or after** 4/15/94, enter -0-. • If the amount on line 17 was paid **before** 4/15/94, make the following computation to find the amount to enter on line 19. Amount on line 17 ✕ Number of days paid before 4/15/94 ✕ .00019	19	
20	**PENALTY.** Subtract line 19 from line 18. Enter the result here and on Form 1040, line 65; Form 1040A, line 33; Form 1040NR, line 66; or Form 1041, line 26 . . . . ▶	20	

For Paperwork Reduction Act Notice, see page 1 of separate instructions. | Cat. No. 11744P | Form **2210** (1993)

Form 2210 (1993) Page **2**

Part IV **Regular Method** (See the instructions if you are filing Form 1040NR.)

Section A—Figure Your Underpayment		Payment Due Dates			
		(a) 4/15/93	(b) 6/15/93	(c) 9/15/93	(d) 1/15/94
21 Required installments. If box 1b applies, enter the amounts from Schedule B, line 26. If you must use Schedule A to figure your penalty (and box 1b does not apply), enter the amounts from Schedule A, line 5, 8, or 19, whichever applies. All others, enter ¼ of line 13, Form 2210, in each column	21				
22 Estimated tax paid and tax withheld (see instructions). For column (a) only, also enter the amount from line 22 on line 26. If line 22 is equal to or more than line 21 for all payment periods, stop here; you do not owe the penalty. Do not file Form 2210 unless you checked a box in Part I . . . . *Complete lines 23 through 29 of one column before going to the next column.*	22				
23 Enter amount, if any, from line 29 of previous column	23	///////			
24 Add lines 22 and 23	24	///////			
25 Add amounts on lines 27 and 28 of the previous column	25	///////			
26 Subtract line 25 from line 24. If zero or less, enter -0-. For column (a) only, enter the amount from line 22 .	26				
27 If the amount on line 26 is zero, subtract line 24 from line 25. Otherwise, enter -0-	27	///////			///////
28 Underpayment. If line 21 is equal to or more than line 26, subtract line 26 from line 21. Then go to line 23 of next column. Otherwise, go to line 29 . . ▶	28				
29 Overpayment. If line 26 is more than line 21, subtract line 21 from line 26. Then go to line 23 of next column	29				

Section B—Figure the Penalty (Complete lines 30 and 31 of one column before going to the next column.)

		4/15/93	6/15/93	9/15/93	1/15/94
30 Number of days FROM the date shown above line 30 TO the date the amount on line 28 was paid **or** 4/15/94, whichever is earlier	30	Days:	Days:	Days:	Days:
31 $\dfrac{\text{Underpayment on line 28 (see instructions)}}{} \times \dfrac{\text{Number of days on line 30}}{365} \times .07$ ▶	31	$	$	$	$

32 **PENALTY.** Add the amounts in each column of line 31. Enter the total here and on Form 1040, line 65; Form 1040A, line 33; Form 1040NR, line 66; or Form 1041, line 26 . . . . ▶ | 32 | $

Form **2441**

Department of the Treasury
Internal Revenue Service

Child and Dependent Care Expenses

▶ Attach to Form 1040.

▶ See separate instructions.

OMB No. 1545-0068

1993

Attachment
Sequence No. **21**

Name(s) shown on Form 1040

Your social security number

You need to understand the following terms to complete this form: **Dependent Care Benefits, Earned Income, Qualified Expenses,** and **Qualifying Person(s).** See **Important Terms** on page 1 of the Form 2441 instructions. Also, if you had a child born in 1993 and line 32 of Form 1040 is less than $23,050, see **A Change To Note** on page 2 of the instructions.

Part I **Persons or Organizations Who Provided the Care**—You **must** complete this part.
(If you need more space, use the bottom of page 2.)

1	(a) Care provider's name	(b) Address (number, street, apt. no., city, state, and ZIP code)	(c) Identifying number (SSN or EIN)	(d) Amount paid (see instructions)

2	Add the amounts in column (d) of line 1	**2**
3	Enter the number of **qualifying persons** cared for in 1993 . . . . ▶	

Did you receive **dependent care benefits?**	**NO** ──────▶	Complete only Part II below.
	YES ──────▶	Complete Part III on the back now.

Part II **Credit for Child and Dependent Care Expenses**

4	Enter the amount of **qualified expenses** you incurred and paid in 1993. DO NOT enter more than $2,400 for one qualifying person or $4,800 for two or more persons. If you completed Part III, enter the amount from line 25	**4**
5	Enter YOUR **earned income**	**5**
6	If married filing a joint return, enter YOUR SPOUSE'S earned income (if student or disabled, see instructions); **all others,** enter the amount from line 5	**6**
7	Enter the **smallest** of line 4, 5, or 6	**7**
8	Enter the amount from Form 1040, line 32	**8**
9	Enter on line 9 the decimal amount shown below that applies to the amount on line 8	

If line 8 is—		Decimal amount is	If line 8 is—		Decimal amount is
Over	But not over		Over	But not over	
$0	10,000	.30	$20,000	22,000	.24
10,000	12,000	.29	22,000	24,000	.23
12,000	14,000	.28	24,000	26,000	.22
14,000	16,000	.27	26,000	28,000	.21
16,000	18,000	.26	28,000	No limit	.20
18,000	20,000	.25			

9 ✕ .

10	Multiply **line 7** by the decimal amount on line 9. Enter the result. Then, see the instructions for the amount of credit to enter on Form 1040, line 41	**10**

Caution: *If you paid $50 or more in a calendar quarter to a person who worked in your home, you must file an employment tax return. Get* **Form 942** *for details.*

For Paperwork Reduction Act Notice, see separate instructions.   Cat. No. 11862M   Form **2441** (1993)

Part III Dependent Care Benefits—Complete this part **only** if you received these benefits.

11 Enter the total amount of **dependent care benefits** you received for 1993. This amount should be shown in box 10 of your W-2 form(s). DO NOT include amounts that were reported to you as wages in box 1 of Form(s) W-2 . . . . **11**

12 Enter the amount forfeited, if any. See the instructions **12**

13 Subtract line 12 from line 11 . . . . **13**

14 Enter the total amount of **qualified expenses** incurred in 1993 for the care of the qualifying person(s) **14**

15 Enter the **smaller** of line 13 or 14 . . . . **15**

16 Enter YOUR **earned income** **16**

17 If married filing a joint return, enter YOUR SPOUSE'S earned income (if student or disabled, see the line 6 instructions); if married filing a separate return, see the instructions for the amount to enter; **all others,** enter the amount from line 16 . . **17**

18 Enter the **smallest** of line 15, 16, or 17 . . . . **18**

19 **Excluded benefits.** Enter here the **smaller** of the following:

- The amount from line 18, or
- $5,000 ($2,500 if married filing a separate return **and** you were required to enter your spouse's earned income on line 17). **19**

20 **Taxable benefits.** Subtract line 19 from line 13. Also, include this amount on Form 1040, line 7. On the dotted line next to line 7, write "DCB" **20**

To claim the child and dependent care credit, complete
lines 21–25 below, and lines 4–10 on the front of this form.

21 Enter the amount of qualified expenses you incurred and paid in 1993. DO NOT include on this line any excluded benefits shown on line 19 . . . . **21**

22 Enter $2,400 ($4,800 if two or more qualifying persons) . . . **22**

23 Enter the amount from line 19 . . . . **23**

24 Subtract line 23 from line 22. If zero or less, **STOP**. You cannot take the credit. **Exception.** If you paid 1992 expenses in 1993, see the line 10 instructions **24**

25 Enter the **smaller** of line 21 or 24 here **and** on line 4 on the front of this form **25**

Form **3800**

Department of the Treasury
Internal Revenue Service

General Business Credit

▶ **Attach to your tax return.**

▶ **See separate instructions.**

OMB No. 1545–0895

1993

Attachment
Sequence No. **22**

Name(s) as shown on return

Identifying number

Part I   Tentative Credit

1a	Current year investment credit (Form 3468, Part I)	**1a**		
b	Current year jobs credit (Form 5884, Part I)	**1b**		
c	Current year credit for alcohol used as fuel (Form 6478)	**1c**		
d	Current year credit for increasing research activities (Form 6765, Part III)	**1d**		
e	Current year low-income housing credit (Form 8586, Part I)	**1e**		
f	Current year enhanced oil recovery credit (Form 8830, Part I)	**1f**		
g	Current year disabled access credit (Form 8826, Part I)	**1g**		
h	Current year renewable electricity production credit (Form 8835, Part I)	**1h**		
i	Other current year credit(s). Check if from ☐ Form 8845 ☐ Form 8846 ☐ Form 8847	**1i**		
j	**Current year general business credit.** Add lines 1a through 1i	**1j**		
2	Passive activity credits included on lines 1a through 1i (see instructions).	**2**		
3	Subtract line 2 from line 1j	**3**		
4	Passive activity credits allowed for 1993 (see instructions)	**4**		
5	Carryforward of general business, WIN, or ESOP credit to 1993 (see instructions for the schedule to attach)	**5**		
6	Carryback of general business credit to 1993 (see instructions)	**6**		
7	**Tentative general business credit.** Add lines 3 through 6	**7**		

Part II   General Business Credit Limitation Based on Amount of Tax

8a	Individuals. Enter amount from Form 1040, line 40		⎫		
b	Corporations. Enter amount from Form 1120, Schedule J, line 3 (or Form 1120-A, Part I, line 1)		⎬ **8**		
c	Other filers. Enter regular tax before credits from your return		⎭		
9	Credits that reduce regular tax before the general business credit—				
a	Credit for child and dependent care expenses (Form 2441, line 10)	**9a**			
b	Credit for the elderly or the disabled (Schedule R (Form 1040), line 21)	**9b**			
c	Mortgage interest credit (Form 8396, line 11)	**9c**			
d	Foreign tax credit (Form 1116, line 32, or Form 1118, Sch. B, line 12)	**9d**			
e	Possessions tax credit (Form 5735, line 14)	**9e**			
f	Orphan drug credit (Form 6765, line 10)	**9f**			
g	Credit for fuel from a nonconventional source	**9g**			
h	Qualified electric vehicle credit (Form 8834, line 17)	**9h**			
i	Add lines 9a through 9h		**9i**		
10	Net regular tax. Subtract line 9i from line 8		**10**		
11	Tentative minimum tax (see instructions):				
a	Individuals. Enter amount from Form 6251, line 26		⎫		
b	Corporations. Enter amount from Form 4626, line 14		⎬ **11**		
c	Estates and trusts. Enter amount from Form 1041, Schedule H, line 37		⎭		
12	Net income tax:				
a	Individuals. Add line 10 above and line 28 of Form 6251		⎫		
b	Corporations. Add line 10 above and line 16 of Form 4626		⎬ **12**		
c	Estates and trusts. Add line 10 above and line 39 of Form 1041, Schedule H		⎭		
13	If line 10 is more than $25,000, enter 25% (.25) of the excess (see instructions)		**13**		
14	Subtract line 11 or line 13, whichever is greater, from line 12. If less than zero, enter -0- . .		**14**		
15	**General business credit allowed for current year.** Enter the **smaller** of line 7 or line 14. Also enter this amount on Form 1040, line 44; Form 1120, Schedule J, line 4e; Form 1120-A, Part I, line 2a; or on the appropriate line of your return. (Individuals, estates, and trusts, see instructions if the credit for increasing research activities is claimed. C corporations, see instructions for Schedule A if any regular investment credit carryforward is claimed. See the instructions if the corporation has undergone a post-1986 "ownership change.")		**15**		

For Paperwork Reduction Act Notice, see page 2 of this form.   Cat. No. 12392F   Form **3800** (1993)

Form **3903**	**Moving Expenses**	OMB No. 1545-0062

Form **3903**

Department of the Treasury
Internal Revenue Service

Moving Expenses

▶ **Attach to Form 1040.**

▶ **See separate instructions.**

OMB No. 1545-0062

19**93**

Attachment
Sequence No. **62**

Name(s) shown on Form 1040 | Your social security number

Caution: *If you are a member of the armed forces, see the instructions before completing this form.*

1	Enter the number of miles from your **old home** to your **new workplace**	1	
2	Enter the number of miles from your **old home** to your **old workplace**	2	
3	Subtract line 2 from line 1. Enter the result but not less than zero. ▶	3	

If line 3 is 35 or more miles, complete the rest of this form. Also, see **Time Test** in the instructions. If line 3 is less than 35 miles, you may not deduct your moving expenses.

Part I Moving Expenses

Note: *Any payments your employer made for any part of your move (including the value of any services furnished in kind) should be included on your W-2 form. Report that amount on **Form 1040, line 7.** See **Reimbursements** in the instructions.*

Section A—Transportation of Household Goods

| 4 | Transportation and storage for household goods and personal effects | 4 | |

Section B—Expenses of Moving From Old To New Home

5	Travel and lodging **not** including meals	5	
6	Total meals	6	
7	Multiply line 6 by 80% (.80)	7	
8	Add lines 5 and 7	8	

Section C—Pre-move Househunting Expenses and Temporary Quarters
(for any 30 days in a row after getting your job)

9	Pre-move travel and lodging **not** including meals	9	
10	Temporary quarters expenses **not** including meals	10	
11	Total meal expenses for both pre-move househunting and temporary quarters	11	
12	Multiply line 11 by 80% (.80)	12	
13	Add lines 9, 10, and 12	13	

Section D—Qualified Real Estate Expenses

| 14 | Expenses of (check one) **a** ☐ selling or exchanging your old home, or
b ☐ if renting, settling an unexpired lease. | 14 | |
| 15 | Expenses of (check one) **a** ☐ buying your new home, or
b ☐ if renting, getting a new lease. | 15 | |

Part II Dollar Limits and Moving Expense Deduction

Note: *If you and your spouse moved to separate homes, see the instructions.*

16	Enter the **smaller** of: • The amount on line 13, or • $1,500 ($750 if married filing a separate return and at the end of 1993 you lived with your spouse who also started work in 1993).	16	
17	Add lines 14, 15, and 16	17	
18	Enter the **smaller** of: • The amount on line 17, or • $3,000 ($1,500 if married filing a separate return and at the end of 1993 you lived with your spouse who also started work in 1993).	18	
19	Add lines 4, 8, and 18. Enter the total here and on Schedule A, line 18. This is your **moving expense deduction** ▶	19	

For Paperwork Reduction Act Notice, see separate instructions.   Cat. No. 12490K   Form **3903** (1993)

🔁 *Printed on recycled paper*

Form **4255** (Rev. April 1991) Department of the Treasury Internal Revenue Service	**Recapture of Investment Credit** (Including Energy Investment Credit) ▶ Attach to your income tax return.	OMB No. 1545-0166 Expires 4-30-94 Attachment Sequence No. **65**

Name(s) as shown on return	Taxpayer Identifying number

Properties	Kind of property—State whether recovery or nonrecovery (see the Instructions for Form 3468 for definitions). If energy property, show type. Also indicate if rehabilitation expenditure property.
A	
B	
C	
D	

Original Investment Credit

Computation Steps: (see Specific Instructions)	Properties A	B	C	D
1 Original rate of credit.				
2 Date property was placed in service				
3 Cost or other basis				
4 Original estimated useful life or class of property.				
5 Applicable percentage				
6 Original qualified investment (Multiply line 3 by the percentage on line 5.)				
7 Original credit (Multiply line 6 by the percentage on line 1.)				
8 Date property ceased to be qualified investment credit property				
9 Number of full years between the date on line 2 and the date on line 8				

Computation of Recapture Tax

10 Recapture percentage (from instructions)				
11 Tentative recapture tax (Multiply line 7 by the percentage on line 10.)				

12 Add line 11, columns A through D

13 Enter tax from property ceasing to be at risk, or for which there was an increase in nonqualified nonrecourse financing (attach separate computation).

14 Total—Add lines 12 and 13

15 Portion of original credit (line 7) not used to offset tax in any year, plus any carryback and carryforward of credits you can now apply to the original credit year because you have freed up tax liability in the amount of the tax recaptured (Do not enter more than line 14—see instructions)

16 Total increase in tax—Subtract line 15 from line 14. Enter here and on the appropriate line of your tax return

General Instructions

(Section references are to the Internal Revenue Code before amendment by the Revenue Reconciliation Act of 1990 (the Act), unless otherwise noted.)

Paperwork Reduction Act Notice.—We ask for the information on this form to carry out the Internal Revenue laws of the United States. You are required to give us the information. We need it to ensure that you are complying with these laws and to allow us to figure and collect the right amount of tax.

The time needed to complete and file this form will vary depending on individual circumstances. The estimated average time is:

Recordkeeping . . . . . 7 hr., 53 min.

Learning about the law or the form . . . . . 2 hr., 23 min.

Preparing and sending the form to IRS . . . . . 2 hr., 37 min.

If you have comments concerning the accuracy of these time estimates or suggestions for making this form more simple, we would be happy to hear from you. You can write to both the IRS and the Office of Management and Budget at the addresses listed in the instructions of the tax return with which this form is filed.

Purpose of Form.—Use Form 4255 to figure the increase in tax for the recapture of investment credit for regular and energy property.

You must refigure the credit if you took it in an earlier year, but disposed of the property before the end of the recapture period or the useful life you used to figure the original credit. You must also refigure the credit if you returned leased property (on which you had taken a credit) to the lessor before the end of the recapture period or useful life.

You must refigure the credit if you changed the use of property so that it no longer qualifies as regular or energy investment credit property. For example, you must refigure the credit if you change the use of property from business use to personal use, or if there is any decrease in the percentage of business use of investment credit property. See sections 50(a)(2) (as

amended by the Act), 47(a)(3), 47(a)(5)(C), and 49(e)(2) for information on recapture for progress expenditure property. Also see the instructions for line 13 regarding recapture if property ceases to be at risk, or if there is an increase in nonqualified, nonrecourse financing related to certain at-risk property placed in service after July 18, 1984.

If certain "listed property" (i.e., automobiles, certain other vehicles, computers, and property used for entertainment, recreation, or amusement) placed in service after June 18, 1984, ceases to be used more than 50% for business, you may have to recapture investment credit taken on the property. See section 280F for details.

An election to be treated as an S corporation does not automatically trigger recapture of investment credit taken before the election was effective. However, the S corporation is liable for any recapture of investment credit taken before the election.

If property on which you took both regular and energy investment credit ceases to be energy credit property, but still qualifies as regular investment credit property, you need only refigure the energy investment credit. However, if you took both credits, and you dispose of the property, or the property ceases to be both energy and regular investment credit property, you must refigure both credits.

If you are an S corporation, a partnership, or an estate or trust that allocated any or all of the investment credit to your shareholders, partners, or beneficiaries, you must give them the information they need to refigure the credit. See Regulations sections 1.47-4, 1.47-5 and 1.47-6.

Partners, shareholders and beneficiaries.—If your Schedule K-1 shows that you must recapture investment credit taken in an earlier year, you will need your retained copy of the original Form 3468 to complete lines 1 through 9 of this Form 4255.

Special Rules.—If you took a credit on the following kinds of property, see the sections listed below before you complete Form 4255:

Property	Section
Motion picture films and video tapes	.47(a)(8)
Ships	.46(g)(4)
Commuter highway vehicles	.47(a)(4)

If you took any nonconventional source fuel credit, see section 29(b)(4).

If, before the end of the recapture period, you dispose of recovery property placed in service after 1982 (or the business use percentage decreases), increase the basis of this property by 50% of the recapture amount unless you originally made the section 48(q)(4) election to take a reduced credit instead of reducing the basis of the property.

Note: *The Act changed these rules for property eligible for the rehabilitation credit under section 47, as amended by the Act. Increase the basis of this property by 100% of the recapture amount instead of 50%. For details, see sections 50(c)(2) and 50(c)(3), as amended by the Act.*

Specific Instructions

Note: *Do not figure the recapture tax on lines 1 through 12 for property ceasing to be at risk, or if there is an increase in nonqualified, nonrecourse financing related to certain at-risk property placed in service after July 18, 1984. Figure the recapture tax for these properties on separate schedules and enter the recapture tax on line 13. Include any unused credit for these properties on line 15.*

Lines A through D.—Describe the property for which you must refigure the credit.

Complete lines 1 through 11 for each property on which you are refiguring the credit. Use a separate column for each item. If you must recapture both the energy investment credit and the regular investment credit for the same item, use a separate column for each credit. If you need more columns, use additional Forms 4255, or other schedules with all the information shown on Form 4255. Enter the total from the separate sheets on line 12.

Line 1.—Enter the rate you used to figure the original credit from the tables below:

Regular Investment Property

Qualifying property acquired or constructed and placed in service 10%

If at the time the credit was taken the regular 10% credit above was subject to all or part of the 35% reduction under section 49(c), reduce the 10% accordingly.

For example, if a 10% regular credit was used in calendar year 1987 when it was reduced by 17.5% under section 49(c), enter 8.25% on line 1 (10% minus 17.5% of 10%). If parts of the credit were used in different tax

years (for example, part in 1986 when the full 10% was allowed, part in 1987 when the 10% credit was reduced under 49(c) by a portion of 35%, and part in 1988 when the credit was reduced by 35%), use a weighted average based on the portion of the credit used in each year.

Be sure to include any ESOP credit, or other credits listed under the special rules above.

See section 46(b)(4) for the rates for qualified rehabilitation expenditures made after 1981.

Energy Investment Property

See the table in section 46(b)(2)(A) for a listing of the energy percentages. For property eligible under section 48(a), as amended by the Act, the percentage is 10%.

Reforestation Credit Property

The reforestation percentage is 10% for property eligible under section 48(b), as amended by the Act.

Line 2.—For both recovery and nonrecovery property, enter the first day of the first month, and the year, that the property was available for service.

Line 3.—Enter the cost or other basis that you used to figure the original credit.

Line 4.—Enter the estimated useful life that you used to figure the original credit for nonrecovery property. Enter the class of property for recovery property.

Line 5.—Enter the applicable percentage that you used to figure the original qualified investment from the tables below:

Nonrecovery Property

Original estimated useful life	Applicable percentage
3 or more but less than 5 years	33⅓%
5 or more but less than 7 years	66⅔%
7 or more years	100%

Recovery Property

Class of property	Applicable percentage
Other	100%

Section 48(q) Election Recovery Property

(Placed in service after 12/31/82 and before 1/1/86)

Class of property	Applicable percentage
Other	80%

Generally, the applicable percentage will be 100% for property eligible for the investment credit under section 46, as amended by the Act.

Line 8.—Generally, this will be the date you disposed of the property. See Regulations section 1.47-1(c) for more information.

Line 9.—Do not enter partial years. If the property was held less than 12 months, enter zero.

Line 10.—Enter the recapture percentage from the following tables:

Nonrecovery Property

If number of full years on line 9 of Form 4255 is:	3 or more but less than 5 years is:	5 or more but less than 7 years is:	7 or more years is:
0	100	100	100
1	100	100	100
2	100	100	100
3	0	50	66.6
4	0	50	66.6
5	0	0	33.3
6	0	0	33.3

Recovery Property

If number of full years on line 9 of Form 4255 is:	The recapture percentage for: Other than 3-year property is:
0	100
1	80
2	60
3	40
4	20

For property eligible for the investment credit under section 46, as amended by the Act, the recapture percentage is the same as the recapture percentage in the above table for Recovery Property.

Decrease in Business Use.—If you take investment credit for property and the percentage of business use in a later year falls below the percentage for the year placed in service, you are treated as having disposed of part of the property and may have to recapture part of the investment credit.

Line 12.—If you have used more than one Form 4255, or separate sheets to list additional items on which you figured an increase in tax, write on the dotted line "Tax from attached, $ . . . ." Include the amount in the total for line 12.

Line 13.—For certain taxpayers, the basis or cost of property placed in service after February 18, 1981, is limited to the amount the taxpayer is at risk for the property at year-end. For property placed in service after July 18, 1984, the basis or cost must be reduced by the amount of any "nonqualified, nonrecourse financing" related to the property at year-end. If property ceases to be at risk in a later year, or if there is an increase in nonqualified, nonrecourse financing, recapture may be required. See section 49(b), as amended by the Act, for details. Attach a separate computation schedule to figure the recapture tax and enter the total tax on line 13.

Line 15.—If you did not use all the credit you originally figured, either in the year you figured it or in a carryback or carryforward year, you do not have to recapture the amount of the credit you did not use. In refiguring the credit for the original credit year, be sure to take into account any carryforwards from previous years, plus any carrybacks arising within the 3 taxable years after the original credit year that are now allowed because the recapture and recomputation of the original credit made available some additional tax liability in that year. See Regulations section 1.47-1(d) and Revenue Ruling 72-221 for more information.

Note: *You must also take into account any applicable 35% reduction in credit under section 49(c)(2) when computing the amount to enter on line 15.*

Figure the unused portion on a separate sheet and enter it on this line. Do not enter more than the recapture tax on line 14.

Reminder: Be sure to adjust your current unused credit to reflect any unused portion of the original credit that was entered on line 15 of this form.

Form **4562**	**Depreciation and Amortization**	OMB No. 1545-0172
Department of the Treasury Internal Revenue Service	**(Including Information on Listed Property)** ► **See separate instructions.** ► **Attach this form to your return.**	**1993** Attachment Sequence No. **67**

Name(s) shown on return	Identifying number

Business or activity to which this form relates

Part I **Election To Expense Certain Tangible Property (Section 179)** (Note: *If you have any "Listed Property," complete Part V before you complete Part I.*)

1	Maximum dollar limitation (If an enterprise zone business, see instructions.)	**1**	$17,500
2	Total cost of section 179 property placed in service during the tax year (see instructions) . .	**2**	
3	Threshold cost of section 179 property before reduction in limitation	**3**	$200,000
4	Reduction in limitation. Subtract line 3 from line 2, but do not enter less than -0-	**4**	
5	Dollar limitation for tax year. Subtract line 4 from line 1, but do not enter less than -0-. (If married filing separately, see instructions.)	**5**	

(a) Description of property	(b) Cost	(c) Elected cost	
6			

7	Listed property. Enter amount from line 26.	**7**	
8	Total elected cost of section 179 property. Add amounts in column (c), lines 6 and 7 . . .	**8**	
9	Tentative deduction. Enter the smaller of line 5 or line 8	**9**	
10	Carryover of disallowed deduction from 1992 (see instructions)	**10**	
11	Taxable income limitation. Enter the smaller of taxable income or line 5 (see instructions) . .	**11**	
12	Section 179 expense deduction. Add lines 9 and 10, but do not enter more than line 11 . .	**12**	
13	Carryover of disallowed deduction to 1994. Add lines 9 and 10, less line 12 ►	**13**	

Note: *Do not use Part II or Part III below for listed property (automobiles, certain other vehicles, cellular telephones, certain computers, or property used for entertainment, recreation, or amusement). Instead, use Part V for listed property.*

Part II **MACRS Depreciation For Assets Placed in Service ONLY During Your 1993 Tax Year (Do Not Include Listed Property)**

(a) Classification of property	(b) Month and year placed in service	(c) Basis for depreciation (business/investment use only—see instructions)	(d) Recovery period	(e) Convention	(f) Method	(g) Depreciation deduction
14 General Depreciation System (GDS) (see instructions):						
a 3-year property						
b 5-year property						
c 7-year property						
d 10-year property						
e 15-year property						
f 20-year property						
g Residential rental property			27.5 yrs.	MM	S/L	
			27.5 yrs.	MM	S/L	
h Nonresidential real property				MM	S/L	
				MM	S/L	
15 Alternative Depreciation System (ADS) (see instructions):						
a Class life					S/L	
b 12-year			12 yrs.		S/L	
c 40-year			40 yrs.	MM	S/L	

Part III **Other Depreciation (Do Not Include Listed Property)**

16	GDS and ADS deductions for assets placed in service in tax years beginning before 1993 (see instructions)	**16**	
17	Property subject to section 168(f)(1) election (see instructions)	**17**	
18	ACRS and other depreciation (see instructions)	**18**	

Part IV **Summary**

19	Listed property. Enter amount from line 25.	**19**	
20	**Total.** Add deductions on line 12, lines 14 and 15 in column (g), and lines 16 through 19. Enter here and on the appropriate lines of your return. (Partnerships and S corporations—see instructions)	**20**	
21	For assets shown above and placed in service during the current year, enter the portion of the basis attributable to section 263A costs (see instructions)	**21**	

For Paperwork Reduction Act Notice, see page 1 of the separate instructions.   Cat. No. 12906N   Form **4562** (1993)

Form 4562 (1993)

Page **2**

Part V — Listed Property—Automobiles, Certain Other Vehicles, Cellular Telephones, Certain Computers, and Property Used for Entertainment, Recreation, or Amusement

For any vehicle for which you are using the standard mileage rate or deducting lease expense, complete only 22a, 22b, columns (a) through (c) of Section A, all of Section B, and Section C if applicable.

Section A—Depreciation and Other Information (Caution: See instructions for limitations for automobiles.)

22a Do you have evidence to support the business/investment use claimed? ☐ **Yes** ☐ **No**   **22b** If "Yes," is the evidence written? ☐ **Yes** ☐ **No**

(a) Type of property (list vehicles first)	(b) Date placed in service	(c) Business/ investment use percentage	(d) Cost or other basis	(e) Basis for depreciation (business/investment use only)	(f) Recovery period	(g) Method/ Convention	(h) Depreciation deduction	(i) Elected section 179 cost
23 Property used more than 50% in a qualified business use (see instructions):								
		%						
		%						
		%						
24 Property used 50% or less in a qualified business use (see instructions):								
		%			S/L –			
		%			S/L –			
		%			S/L –			

25 Add amounts in column (h). Enter the total here and on line 19, page 1 . . . . . | **25** |

26 Add amounts in column (i). Enter the total here and on line 7, page 1 . . . . | **26** |

Section B—Information Regarding Use of Vehicles—If you deduct expenses for vehicles:

● *Always complete this section for vehicles used by a sole proprietor, partner, or other "more than 5% owner," or related person.*
● *If you provided vehicles to your employees, first answer the questions in Section C to see if you meet an exception to completing this section for those vehicles.*

	(a) Vehicle 1		(b) Vehicle 2		(c) Vehicle 3		(d) Vehicle 4		(e) Vehicle 5		(f) Vehicle 6	
27 Total business/investment miles driven during the year (DO NOT include commuting miles)												
28 Total commuting miles driven during the year												
29 Total other personal (noncommuting) miles driven												
30 Total miles driven during the year. Add lines 27 through 29												
	Yes	No	Yes	No	Yes	No	Yes	No	Yes	No	Yes	No
31 Was the vehicle available for personal use during off-duty hours?												
32 Was the vehicle used primarily by a more than 5% owner or related person?												
33 Is another vehicle available for personal use?												

Section C—Questions for Employers Who Provide Vehicles for Use by Their Employees

Answer these questions to determine if you meet an exception to completing Section B. **Note:** *Section B must always be completed for vehicles used by sole proprietors, partners, or other more than 5% owners or related persons.*

	Yes	No
34 Do you maintain a written policy statement that prohibits all personal use of vehicles, including commuting, by your employees?		
35 Do you maintain a written policy statement that prohibits personal use of vehicles, except commuting, by your employees? (See instructions for vehicles used by corporate officers, directors, or 1% or more owners.)		
36 Do you treat all use of vehicles by employees as personal use?		
37 Do you provide more than five vehicles to your employees and retain the information received from your employees concerning the use of the vehicles?		
38 Do you meet the requirements concerning qualified automobile demonstration use (see instructions)? . .		

Note: *If your answer to 34, 35, 36, 37, or 38 is "Yes," you need not complete Section B for the covered vehicles.*

Part VI — Amortization

(a) Description of costs	(b) Date amortization begins	(c) Amortizable amount	(d) Code section	(e) Amortization period or percentage	(f) Amortization for this year
39 Amortization of costs that begins during your 1993 tax year:					

40 Amortization of costs that began before 1993 . . . . | **40** |

41 **Total.** Enter here and on "Other Deductions" or "Other Expenses" line of your return . . . | **41** |

Form **4684**

Department of the Treasury
Internal Revenue Service

Casualties and Thefts

▶ See separate instructions.
▶ Attach to your tax return.
▶ Use a separate Form 4684 for each different casualty or theft.

OMB No. 1545-0177

1993

Attachment
Sequence No. **26**

Name(s) shown on tax return | Identifying number

SECTION A—Personal Use Property (Use this section to report casualties and thefts of property **not** used in a trade or business or for income-producing purposes.)

1 Description of properties (show type, location, and date acquired for each):

Property **A** ....

Property **B** ....

Property **C** ....

Property **D** ....

Properties (Use a separate column for each property lost or damaged from one casualty or theft.)

		A	B	C	D
2	Cost or other basis of each property				
3	Insurance or other reimbursement (whether or not you filed a claim). See instructions				
	Note: *If line 2 is **more than** line 3, skip line 4.*				
4	Gain from casualty or theft. If line 3 is **more than** line 2, enter the difference here and skip lines 5 through 9 for that column. See instructions if line 3 includes insurance or other reimbursement you did not claim, or you received payment for your loss in a later tax year				
5	Fair market value **before** casualty or theft				
6	Fair market value **after** casualty or theft				
7	Subtract line 6 from line 5				
8	Enter the **smaller** of line 2 or line 7				
9	Subtract line 3 from line 8. If zero or less, enter -0-				

10	Casualty or theft loss. Add the amounts on line 9. Enter the total	**10**	
11	Enter the amount from line 10 or $100, whichever is **smaller**	**11**	
12	Subtract line 11 from line 10	**12**	
	Caution: *Use only one Form 4684 for lines 13 through 18.*		
13	Add the amounts on line 12 of all Forms 4684	**13**	
14	Combine the amounts from line 4 of all Forms 4684	**14**	
15	• If line 14 is **more than** line 13, enter the difference here and on Schedule D. Do not complete the rest of this section (see instructions). • If line 14 is **less than** line 13, enter -0- here and continue with the form. • If line 14 is **equal to** line 13, enter -0- here. Do not complete the rest of this section.	**15**	
16	If line 14 is **less than** line 13, enter the difference	**16**	
17	Enter 10% of your adjusted gross income (Form 1040, line 32). Estates and trusts, see instructions	**17**	
18	Subtract line 17 from line 16. If zero or less, enter -0-. Also enter result on Schedule A (Form 1040), line 17. Estates and trusts, enter on the "Other deductions" line of your tax return	**18**	

For Paperwork Reduction Act Notice, see page 1 of separate instructions.   Cat. No. 12997O   Form **4684** (1993)

Form 4684 (1993)   Attachment Sequence No. **26**   Page **2**

Name(s) shown on tax return. Do not enter name and identifying number if shown on other side.	Identifying number

SECTION B—Business and Income-Producing Property (Use this section to report casualties and thefts of property used in a trade or business or for income-producing purposes.)

Part I **Casualty or Theft Gain or Loss** (Use a separate Part I for each casualty or theft.)

19 Description of properties (show type, location, and date acquired for each):

Property **A** ....

Property **B** ....

Property **C** ....

Property **D** ....

Properties (Use a separate column for each property lost or damaged from one casualty or theft.)

		A	B	C	D
20	Cost or adjusted basis of each property				
21	Insurance or other reimbursement (whether or not you filed a claim). See the instructions for line 3. **Note:** If line 20 is **more than** line 21, skip line 22.				
22	Gain from casualty or theft. If line 21 is **more than** line 20, enter the difference here and on line 29 or line 34, column (c), except as provided in the instructions for line 33. Also, skip lines 23 through 27 for that column. See the instructions for line 4 if line 21 includes insurance or other reimbursement you did not claim, or you received payment for your loss in a later tax year				
23	Fair market value **before** casualty or theft				
24	Fair market value **after** casualty or theft				
25	Subtract line 24 from line 23				
26	Enter the **smaller** of line 20 or line 25				
	Note: If the property was totally destroyed by casualty or lost from theft, enter on line 26 the amount from line 20.				
27	Subtract line 21 from line 26. If zero or less, enter -0-				
28	Casualty or theft loss. Add the amounts on line 27. Enter the total here and on line 29 **or** line 34 (see instructions).			28	

Part II **Summary of Gains and Losses** (from separate Parts I)

(a) Identify casualty or theft	(b) Losses from casualties or thefts		(c) Gains from casualties or thefts includible in income
	(i) Trade, business, rental or royalty property	(ii) Income-producing property	

Casualty or Theft of Property Held One Year or Less

29	_____	( )	( )	
		( )	( )	
30	Totals. Add the amounts on line 29	( )	( )	

31 Combine line 30, columns (b)(i) and (c). Enter the net gain or (loss) here and on Form 4797, line 15. If Form 4797 is not otherwise required, see instructions ... | 31 |

32 Enter the amount from line 30, column (b)(ii) here and on Schedule A (Form 1040), line 20. Partnerships, S corporations, estates and trusts, see instructions ... | 32 |

Casualty or Theft of Property Held More Than One Year

33 Casualty or theft gains from Form 4797, line 34 ... | 33 |

| 34 | _____ | ( ) | ( ) | |

35 Total losses. Add amounts on line 34, columns (b)(i) and (b)(ii) ... | 35 ( ) ( ) |

36 Total gains. Add lines 33 and 34, column (c) ... | 36 |

37 Add amounts on line 35, columns (b)(i) and (b)(ii) ... | 37 |

38 If the loss on line 37 is **more than** the gain on line 36:

a Combine line 35, column (b)(i) and line 36, and enter the net gain or (loss) here. Partnerships and S corporations see the note below. All others enter this amount on Form 4797, line 15. If Form 4797 is not otherwise required, see instructions ... | 38a |

b Enter the amount from line 35, column (b)(ii) here. Partnerships and S corporations see the note below. Individuals enter this amount on Schedule A (Form 1040), line 20. Estates and trusts, enter on the "Other deductions" line of your tax return | 38b |

39 If the loss on line 37 is **equal to** or **less than** the gain on line 36, combine these lines and enter here. Partnerships, see the note below. All others, enter this amount on Form 4797, line 3 | 39 |

Note: Partnerships, enter the amount from line 38a, 38b, or line 39 on Form 1065, Schedule K, line 7. S corporations, enter the amount from line 38a or 38b on Form 1120S, Schedule K, line 6.

Form **4797**

Department of the Treasury
Internal Revenue Service

Sales of Business Property

(Also Involuntary Conversions and Recapture Amounts
Under Sections 179 and 280F(b)(2))

▶ Attach to your tax return.   ▶ See separate instructions.

OMB No. 1545-0184

19**93**

Attachment
Sequence No. **27**

Name(s) shown on return

Identifying number

| 1 | Enter here the gross proceeds from the sale or exchange of real estate reported to you for 1993 on Form(s) 1099-S (or a substitute statement) that you will be including on line 2, 11, or 22 . . . . | 1 | |

Part I **Sales or Exchanges of Property Used in a Trade or Business and Involuntary Conversions From Other Than Casualty or Theft—Property Held More Than 1 Year**

(a) Description of property	(b) Date acquired (mo., day, yr.)	(c) Date sold (mo., day, yr.)	(d) Gross sales price	(e) Depreciation allowed or allowable since acquisition	(f) Cost or other basis, plus improvements and expense of sale	(g) LOSS ((f) minus the sum of (d) and (e))	(h) GAIN ((d) plus (e) minus (f))
2							

3	Gain, if any, from Form 4684, line 39	3	
4	Section 1231 gain from installment sales from Form 6252, line 26 or 37	4	
5	Section 1231 gain or (loss) from like-kind exchanges from Form 8824	5	
6	Gain, if any, from line 34, from other than casualty or theft	6	
7	Add lines 2 through 6 in columns (g) and (h)	7 ( )	
8	Combine columns (g) and (h) of line 7. Enter gain or (loss) here, and on the appropriate line as follows:	8	

Partnerships—Enter the gain or (loss) on Form 1065, Schedule K, line 6. Skip lines 9, 10, 12, and 13 below.

S corporations—Report the gain or (loss) following the instructions for Form 1120S, Schedule K, lines 5 and 6. Skip lines 9, 10, 12, and 13 below, unless line 8 is a gain and the S corporation is subject to the capital gains tax.

All others—If line 8 is zero or a loss, enter the amount on line 12 below and skip lines 9 and 10. If line 8 is a gain and you did not have any prior year section 1231 losses, or they were recaptured in an earlier year, enter the gain as a long-term capital gain on Schedule D and skip lines 9, 10, and 13 below.

| 9 | Nonrecaptured net section 1231 losses from prior years (see instructions) . . . . | 9 | |
| 10 | Subtract line 9 from line 8. If zero or less, enter -0-. Also enter on the appropriate line as follows (see instructions): | 10 | |

S corporations—Enter this amount (if more than zero) on Schedule D (Form 1120S), line 13, and skip lines 12 and 13 below.

All others—If line 10 is zero, enter the amount from line 8 on line 13 below. If line 10 is more than zero, enter the amount from line 9 on line 13 below, and enter the amount from line 10 as a long-term capital gain on Schedule D.

Part II **Ordinary Gains and Losses**

| 11 | Ordinary gains and losses not included on lines 12 through 18 (include property held 1 year or less): |

12	Loss, if any, from line 8	12	
13	Gain, if any, from line 8, or amount from line 9 if applicable	13	
14	Gain, if any, from line 33	14	
15	Net gain or (loss) from Form 4684, lines 31 and 38a	15	
16	Ordinary gain from installment sales from Form 6252, line 25 or 36	16	
17	Ordinary gain or (loss) from like-kind exchanges from Form 8824	17	
18	Recapture of section 179 expense deduction for partners and S corporation shareholders from property dispositions by partnerships and S corporations (see instructions)	18	
19	Add lines 11 through 18 in columns (g) and (h)	19 ( )	
20	Combine columns (g) and (h) of line 19. Enter gain or (loss) here, and on the appropriate line as follows: . . .	20	
a	For all except individual returns: Enter the gain or (loss) from line 20 on the return being filed.		
b	For individual returns:		
	(1) If the loss on line 12 includes a loss from Form 4684, line 35, column (b)(ii), enter that part of the loss here and on line 20 of Schedule A (Form 1040). Identify as from "Form 4797, line 20b(1)." See instructions	20b(1)	
	(2) Redetermine the gain or (loss) on line 20, excluding the loss, if any, on line 20b(1). Enter here and on Form 1040, line 15 .	20b(2)	

For Paperwork Reduction Act Notice, see page 1 of separate instructions.   Cat. No. 13086I   Form **4797** (1993)

Part III Gain From Disposition of Property Under Sections 1245, 1250, 1252, 1254, and 1255

21	(a) Description of section 1245, 1250, 1252, 1254, or 1255 property:	(b) Date acquired (mo., day, yr.)	(c) Date sold (mo., day, yr.)
A			
B			
C			
D			

	Relate lines 21A through 21D to these columns ▶		Property A	Property B	Property C	Property D
22	Gross sales price (**Note:** See line 1 before completing.)	22				
23	Cost or other basis plus expense of sale	23				
24	Depreciation (or depletion) allowed or allowable	24				
25	Adjusted basis. Subtract line 24 from line 23	25				
26	Total gain. Subtract line 25 from line 22	26				
27	**If section 1245 property:**					
a	Depreciation allowed or allowable from line 24	27a				
b	Enter the **smaller** of line 26 or 27a	27b				
28	**If section 1250 property:** If straight line depreciation was used, enter -0- on line 28g, except for a corporation subject to section 291.					
a	Additional depreciation after 1975 (see instructions)	28a				
b	Applicable percentage multiplied by the **smaller** of line 26 or line 28a (see instructions)	28b				
c	Subtract line 28a from line 26. If residential rental property or line 26 is not more than line 28a, skip lines 28d and 28e	28c				
d	Additional depreciation after 1969 and before 1976	28d				
e	Enter the **smaller** of line 28c or 28d	28e				
f	Section 291 amount (corporations only)	28f				
g	Add lines 28b, 28e, and 28f	28g				
29	**If section 1252 property:** Skip this section if you did not dispose of farmland or if this form is being completed for a partnership.					
a	Soil, water, and land clearing expenses	29a				
b	Line 29a multiplied by applicable percentage (see instructions)	29b				
c	Enter the **smaller** of line 26 or 29b	29c				
30	**If section 1254 property:**					
a	Intangible drilling and development costs, expenditures for development of mines and other natural deposits, and mining exploration costs (see instructions)	30a				
b	Enter the **smaller** of line 26 or 30a	30b				
31	**If section 1255 property:**					
a	Applicable percentage of payments excluded from income under section 126 (see instructions)	31a				
b	Enter the **smaller** of line 26 or 31a	31b				

Summary of Part III Gains. Complete property columns A through D, through line 31b before going to line 32.

32	Total gains for all properties. Add columns A through D, line 26	32	
33	Add columns A through D, lines 27b, 28g, 29c, 30b, and 31b. Enter here and on line 14	33	
34	Subtract line 33 from line 32. Enter the portion from casualty or theft on Form 4684, line 33. Enter the portion from other than casualty or theft on Form 4797, line 6	34	

Part IV Recapture Amounts Under Sections 179 and 280F(b)(2) When Business Use Drops to 50% or Less
See instructions for Part IV.

			(a) Section 179	(b) Section 280F(b)(2)
35	Section 179 expense deduction or depreciation allowable in prior years	35		
36	Recomputed depreciation (see instructions)	36		
37	Recapture amount. Subtract line 36 from line 35. See instructions for where to report	37		

Form **4868**

Department of the Treasury
Internal Revenue Service

Application for Automatic Extension of Time To File U.S. Individual Income Tax Return

▶ This is not an extension of time to pay your tax.
▶ See separate instructions.

OMB No. 1545-0188

1993

	Your first name and initial	Last name	Your social security number
Please Type or Print	If a joint return, spouse's first name and initial	Last name	Spouse's social security number
	Home address (number, street, and apt. no. or rural route). If you have a P.O. box, see the instructions.		
	City, town or post office, state, and ZIP code		

I request an automatic 4-month extension of time to August 15, 1994, to file Form 1040EZ, Form 1040A, or Form 1040 for the calendar year 1993 or to _____, 19____, for the fiscal tax year ending _____, 19____.

Part I   **Individual Income Tax**—You must complete this part.

1 **Total tax liability for 1993.** This is the amount you expect to enter on Form 1040EZ, line 8; Form 1040A, line 27; or Form 1040, line 53. If you expect this amount to be zero, enter -0-.   **1**

   *Caution: You **MUST** enter an amount on line 1 or your extension will be denied. You can estimate this amount, but be as exact as you can with the information you have. If we later find that your estimate was not reasonable, the extension will be null and void.*

2 **Total payments for 1993.** This is the amount you expect to enter on Form 1040EZ, line 7; Form 1040A, line 28d; or Form 1040, line 60   **2**

3 **BALANCE DUE.** Subtract line 2 from line 1. If line 2 is more than line 1, enter -0-. For details on how to pay, including what to write on your payment, see the instructions   ▶   **3**

Part II   **Gift or Generation-Skipping Transfer (GST) Tax**—Complete this part if you expect to owe either tax.

Caution: Do not include income tax on lines 5a and 5b. See the instructions.

4 If you or your spouse plan to file a gift tax return (Form 709 or 709-A) for 1993, generally due by April 15, 1994, see the instructions and check here   . . .   Yourself ▶ ☐   Spouse ▶ ☐

5a Enter the amount of gift or GST tax **you** are paying with this form **5a**

  b Enter the amount of gift or GST tax **your spouse** is paying with this form **5b**

Signature and Verification

Under penalties of perjury, I declare that I have examined this form, including accompanying schedules and statements, and to the best of my knowledge and belief, it is true, correct, and complete; and, if prepared by someone other than the taxpayer, that I am authorized to prepare this form.

▶ _____ | Date _____ | ▶ _____ | Date _____
Your signature | | Spouse's signature, if filing jointly |

▶ _____ | | Date _____
Preparer's signature (other than taxpayer) | |

If you want correspondence regarding this extension to be sent to you at an address other than that shown above or to an agent acting for you, please enter the name of the agent and/or the address where it should be sent.

	Name
Please Type or Print	Number and street (include suite, room, or apt. no.) or P.O. box number if mail is not delivered to street address
	City, town or post office, state, and ZIP code

For Paperwork Reduction Act Notice, see separate instructions.   Cat. No. 13141W   Form **4868** (1993)

Form **4952**

Department of the Treasury
Internal Revenue Service

Investment Interest Expense Deduction

▶ Attach to your tax return.

OMB No. 1545-0191

1993

Attachment
Sequence No. **12A**

Name(s) shown on return

Identifying number

Part I	**Total Investment Interest Expense**		
1	Investment interest expense paid or accrued in 1993. See instructions	1	
2	Disallowed investment interest expense from 1992 Form 4952, line 5	2	
3	**Total investment interest expense.** Add lines 1 and 2	3	

Part II	**Net Investment Income**		
4a	Gross income from property held for investment (excluding any net gain from the disposition of property held for investment)	4a	
b	Net gain from the disposition of property held for investment . . . 4b		
c	Net capital gain from the disposition of property held for investment 4c		
d	Subtract line 4c from line 4b. If zero or less, enter -0-	4d	
e	Enter all or part of the amount on line 4c that you elect to include in investment income. Do not enter more than the amount on line 4b. See instructions . . . . ▶	4e	
f	Investment income. Add lines 4a, 4d, and 4e. See instructions	4f	
5	Investment expenses. See instructions	5	
6	**Net investment income.** Subtract line 5 from line 4f. If zero or less, enter -0-	6	

Part III	**Investment Interest Expense Deduction**		
7	Disallowed investment interest expense to be carried forward to 1994. Subtract line 6 from line 3. If zero or less, enter -0-	7	
8	**Investment interest expense deduction.** Enter the smaller of line 3 or 6. See instructions . .	8	

Paperwork Reduction Act Notice

We ask for the information on this form to carry out the Internal Revenue laws of the United States. You are required to give us the information. We need it to ensure that you are complying with these laws and to allow us to figure and collect the right amount of tax.

The time needed to complete and file this form will vary depending on individual circumstances. The estimated average time is:

Recordkeeping . . . . . . 13 min.
Learning about the
law or the form . . . . . 15 min.
Preparing the form . . . . 21 min.
Copying, assembling, and
sending the form to the IRS . . 10 min.

If you have comments concerning the accuracy of these time estimates or suggestions for making this form more simple, we would be happy to hear from you. You can write to both the IRS and the Office of Management and Budget at the addresses listed in the instructions for the tax return with which this form is filed.

General Instructions

Section references are to the Internal Revenue Code unless otherwise noted.

A Change To Note

Beginning in 1993, for purposes of computing your investment interest expense deduction, net capital gain from the disposition of property held for investment is excluded from investment income. However, you may elect to include in your investment income all or

part of the net capital gain from the disposition of property held for investment if you also reduce the amount of net capital gain eligible for the 28% maximum capital gains rate by the same amount. See the instructions for line 4e on page 2.

Purpose of Form

Interest expense paid by an individual, estate, or a trust on a loan that is allocable to property held for investment may not be fully deductible in the current year. Form 4952 is used to figure the amount of investment interest expense deductible for the current year and the amount, if any, to carry forward to future years.

For more details, get **Pub. 550**, Investment Income and Expenses.

Cat. No. 13177Y

Form **4952** (1993)

Who Must File

If you are an individual, estate, or a trust, and you claim a deduction for investment interest expense, you must complete and attach Form 4952 to your tax return, unless **all** of the following apply:

● Your only investment income was from interest or dividends,

● You have no other deductible expenses connected with the production of interest or dividends,

● Your investment interest expense is not more than your investment income, and

● You have no carryovers of investment interest expense from 1992.

Allocation of Interest Expense Under Temporary Regulations Section 1.163-8T

If you paid or accrued interest on a loan and you used the proceeds of the loan for more than one purpose, you may have to allocate the interest paid. This is necessary because of the different rules that apply to investment interest, personal interest, trade or business interest, home mortgage interest, and passive activity interest. See Pub. 550.

Specific Instructions
Part I—Total Investment Interest Expense
Line 1

Enter the investment interest paid or accrued during the tax year, regardless of when the indebtedness was incurred. Investment interest is interest paid or accrued on a loan (or part of a loan) that is allocable to property held for investment (as defined below).

Be sure to include investment interest expense reported to you on Schedule K-1 from a partnership or an S corporation. Include amortization of bond premium on taxable bonds purchased after October 22, 1986, but before January 1, 1988, unless you elected to offset amortizable bond premium against the interest payments on the bond. A taxable bond is a bond on which the interest is includible in gross income.

Investment interest expense does not include the following:

● Home mortgage interest.

● Interest expense that is properly allocable to a passive activity. A passive activity is any business activity in which you **do not** materially participate and any rental activity regardless of participation. See the separate instructions for **Form 8582,** Passive Activity Loss Limitations, for the material participation tests and the definition of "rental activity."

● Any interest expense that is capitalized, such as construction interest subject to section 263A.

● Interest expense related to tax-exempt interest income under section 265.

Property held for investment.—Property held for investment includes property that produces income (unless derived in the ordinary course of a trade or business) from interest, dividends, annuities, or royalties; and gains from the disposition of property that produces those types of income or is held for investment. However, it does not include an interest in a passive activity.

Property held for investment also includes an interest in an activity of conducting a trade or business in which you did not materially participate and that is not a passive activity. For example, a working interest in an oil or gas property that is not a passive activity is property held for investment if you did not materially participate in the activity.

Part II—Net Investment Income
Line 4a

Gross income from property held for investment to be entered on line 4a includes income (unless derived in the ordinary course of a trade or business) from:

● Interest,

● Dividends (except Alaska Permanent Fund dividends),

● Annuities, and

● Royalties.

If you are filing **Form 8814,** Parents' Election To Report Child's Interest and Dividends, part or all of your child's income may be included on line 4a. See Form 8814 for details.

Also, include on line 4a net income from the following passive activities:

● Rental of substantially nondepreciable property,

● Equity-financed lending activities, and

● Acquisition of certain interests in a pass-through entity licensing intangible property.

See Regulations section 1.469-2(f)(10) for details.

Net passive income from a passive activity of a publicly traded partnership (as defined in section 469(k)(2)) is also included in investment income. See Notice 88-75, 1988-2 C.B. 386, for details.

Include investment income reported to you on Schedule K-1 from a partnership or an S corporation. Also include net investment income from an estate or a trust.

Do not include on line 4a any net gain from the disposition of property held for investment. Instead, enter this amount on line 4b.

Line 4b

Net gain from the disposition of property held for investment is the excess, if any, of total gains over total losses from the disposition of property held for investment. When figuring this amount, be sure to include capital gain distributions from mutual funds.

Line 4c

Net capital gain from the disposition of property held for investment is the excess, if any, of net long-term capital gain over net short-term capital loss from the disposition of property held for investment. When figuring this amount, be sure to include capital gain distributions from mutual funds.

Line 4e

Enter all or part of the amount on line 4c, but not more than the amount on line 4b, that you choose to include in investment income. If you make an entry on line 4e and you are using the **Schedule D Tax Worksheet** on page D-4 of the Form 1040 instructions (or Part VI of Schedule D (Form 1041)), you must also reduce the amount of net capital gain eligible for the 28% maximum capital gains

rate by the amount on this line. Therefore, you should consider the effect on your tax using the maximum capital gains rate before making an entry on this line.

Line 5

Investment expenses are your allowed deductions, other than interest expense, directly connected with the production of investment income. For example, depreciation or depletion allowed on assets that produce investment income is an investment expense.

Be sure to include investment expenses reported to you on Schedule K-1 from a partnership or an S corporation.

Investment expenses do not include any deductions taken into account in determining your income or loss from a passive activity.

If you have investment expenses that are included as a miscellaneous itemized deduction on Schedule A (Form 1040), line 20, you may not have to use all of the amount for purposes of Form 4952, line 5. The 2% adjusted gross income limitation on Schedule A may reduce the amount.

To figure the amount to use, compare the amount of the investment expenses included on Schedule A, line 20, with the total miscellaneous expenses on Schedule A, line 24. The smaller of the investment expenses included on line 20 or the total on line 24 is the amount to use to figure the investment expenses from Schedule A for line 5.

Example. Assume Schedule A, line 20, includes investment expenses of $3,000, and line 24 is $1,300 after the 2% adjusted gross income limitation. Investment expenses from Schedule A of $1,300 are used to figure the amount of investment expenses for line 5. If investment expenses of $800 were included on line 20 and line 24 was $1,300, investment expenses from Schedule A of $800 would be used.

Part III—Investment Interest Expense Deduction
Line 8

This is the amount you may deduct as investment interest expense.

Individuals.—Enter the amount from line 8 on Schedule A (Form 1040), line 11, even if all or part of it is attributable to a partnership or an S corporation. However, if any portion of this amount is attributable to royalties, enter that part of the interest expense on Schedule E (Form 1040).

Estates and trusts.—Enter the amount from line 8 on Form 1041, line 10.

Form 6198.—If any portion of the deductible investment interest expense is attributable to an activity for which you are not at risk, you must also use **Form 6198,** At-Risk Limitations, to figure your deductible investment interest expense. Enter the portion attributable to the at-risk activity on Form 6198, line 4. Reduce Form 4952, line 8, by the amount entered on Form 6198. See Form 6198 and its instructions for more details, especially the instructions for line 4 of that form.

Alternative minimum tax.—Deductible interest expense is an adjustment for alternative minimum tax purposes. Get Form 6251, Alternative Minimum Tax—Individuals, or Form 1041, Schedule H, for estates and trusts.

 Printed on recycled paper

Form **4972**

Department of the Treasury
Internal Revenue Service

Tax on Lump-Sum Distributions
(Use This Form Only for Lump-Sum Distributions From
Qualified Retirement Plans)

► **Attach to Form 1040 or Form 1041.** ► **See separate instructions.**

OMB No. 1545-0193

1993

Attachment
Sequence No. **28**

Name of recipient of distribution

Identifying number

Part I	Complete this part to see if you qualify to use Form 4972.		Yes	No
1	Did you roll over any part of the distribution? If "Yes," do not complete the rest of this form	**1**		
2	Was the retirement plan participant born before 1936? If "No," do not complete the rest of this form . .	**2**		
3	Was this a lump-sum distribution from a qualified pension, profit-sharing, or stock bonus plan? (See **Distributions That Qualify for the 20% Capital Gain Election or for 5- or 10-Year Averaging** in the instructions.) If "No," do not complete the rest of this form	**3**		
4	Was the participant in the plan for at least 5 years before the year of the distribution?	**4**		
5	Was this distribution paid to you as a beneficiary of a plan participant who died?	**5**		
	If you answered "No" to both questions 4 **and** 5, do not complete the rest of this form.			
6	Was the plan participant:			
a	An employee who received the distribution because he or she quit, retired, was laid off, or was fired? . .	**6a**		
b	Self-employed or an owner-employee who became permanently and totally disabled before the distribution?	**6b**		
c	Age 59½ or older at the time of the distribution?	**6c**		
	If you answered "No" to question 5 and **all** parts of question 6, do not complete the rest of this form.			
7	Did you use Form 4972 in a prior year for any distribution received after 1986 for the same plan participant, including yourself, for whom the 1993 distribution was made? If "Yes," do not complete the rest of this form	**7**		

If you qualify to use this form, you may choose to use Part II, Part III, or Part IV; **or** Part II and Part III; **or** Part II and Part IV.

Part II	Complete this part to choose the 20% capital gain election. (See instructions.)		
8	Capital gain part from box 3 of Form 1099-R. (See instructions.)	**8**	
9	Multiply line 8 by 20% (.20) and enter here. If you do not choose to use Part III or Part IV, also enter the amount on Form 1040, line 39, or Form 1041, Schedule G, line 1b.	**9**	

Part III	Complete this part to choose the 5-year averaging method. (See instructions.)		
10	Ordinary income from Form 1099-R, box 2a minus box 3. If you did not complete Part II, enter the taxable amount from box 2a of Form 1099-R. (See instructions.)	**10**	
11	Death benefit exclusion. (See instructions.)	**11**	
12	Total taxable amount—Subtract line 11 from line 10	**12**	
13	Current actuarial value of annuity, if applicable (from Form 1099-R, box 8)	**13**	
14	Adjusted total taxable amount—Add lines 12 and 13. If this amount is $70,000 or more, skip lines 15 through 18, and enter this amount on line 19	**14**	
15	Multiply line 14 by 50% (.50), but **do not** enter more than $10,000 . **15**		
16	Subtract $20,000 from line 14. If line 14 is $20,000 or less, enter -0- **16**		
17	Multiply line 16 by 20% (.20) **17**		
18	Minimum distribution allowance—Subtract line 17 from line 15	**18**	
19	Subtract line 18 from line 14	**19**	
20	Federal estate tax attributable to lump-sum distribution. Do not deduct on Form 1040 or Form 1041 the amount attributable to the ordinary income entered on line 10. (See instructions.) . .	**20**	
21	Subtract line 20 from line 19	**21**	
22	Multiply line 21 by 20% (.20)	**22**	
23	Tax on amount on line 22. See the Tax Rate Schedule for the 5-Year Method in the instructions	**23**	
24	Multiply line 23 by five (5). If line 13 is blank, skip lines 25 through 30, and enter this amount on line 31	**24**	
25	Divide line 13 by line 14 and enter the result as a decimal. (See instructions.)	**25**	× .
26	Multiply line 18 by the decimal amount on line 25	**26**	
27	Subtract line 26 from line 13	**27**	
28	Multiply line 27 by 20% (.20)	**28**	
29	Tax on amount on line 28. See the Tax Rate Schedule for the 5-Year Method in the instructions	**29**	
30	Multiply line 29 by five (5)	**30**	
31	Subtract line 30 from line 24. (Multiple recipients, see instructions.)	**31**	
32	Tax on lump-sum distribution—Add Part II, line 9, and Part III, line 31. Enter on Form 1040, line 39, or Form 1041, Schedule G, line 1b . . . . ►	**32**	

For Paperwork Reduction Act Notice, see separate instructions.

Cat. No. 13187U

Form **4972** (1993)

Form 4972 (1993)   Page **2**

Part IV	**Complete this part to choose the 10-year averaging method.** (See instructions.)			
33	Ordinary income part from Form 1099-R, box 2a minus box 3. If you did not complete Part II, enter the taxable amount from box 2a of Form 1099-R. (See instructions.)	33		
34	Death benefit exclusion. (See instructions.)	34		
35	Total taxable amount—Subtract line 34 from line 33	35		
36	Current actuarial value of annuity, if applicable (from Form 1099-R, box 8)	36		
37	Adjusted total taxable amount—Add lines 35 and 36. If this amount is $70,000 or more, skip lines 38 through 41, and enter this amount on line 42	37		
38	Multiply line 37 by 50% (.50), but **do not** enter more than $10,000 .	38			
39	Subtract $20,000 from line 37. If line 37 is $20,000 or less, enter -0-	39			
40	Multiply line 39 by 20% (.20)	40			
41	Minimum distribution allowance—Subtract line 40 from line 38	41		
42	Subtract line 41 from line 37	42		
43	Federal estate tax attributable to lump-sum distribution. Do not deduct on Form 1040 or Form 1041 the amount attributable to the ordinary income entered on line 33. (See instructions.) . .	43		
44	Subtract line 43 from line 42	44		
45	Multiply line 44 by 10% (.10)	45		
46	Tax on amount on line 45. See the Tax Rate Schedule for the 10-Year Method in the instructions	46		
47	Multiply line 46 by ten (10). If line 36 is blank, skip lines 48 through 53, and enter this amount on line 54	47		
48	Divide line 36 by line 37 and enter the result as a decimal. (See instructions.)	48	× .	
49	Multiply line 41 by the decimal amount on line 48	49		
50	Subtract line 49 from line 36	50		
51	Multiply line 50 by 10% (.10)	51		
52	Tax on amount on line 51. See the Tax Rate Schedule for the 10-Year Method in the instructions	52		
53	Multiply line 52 by ten (10)	53		
54	Subtract line 53 from line 47. (Multiple recipients, see instructions.)	54		
55	Tax on lump-sum distribution—Add Part II, line 9, and Part IV, line 54. Enter on Form 1040, line 39, or Form 1041, Schedule G, line 1b . . . . ▶	55		

Printed on recycled paper

Form **6251**

Department of the Treasury
Internal Revenue Service

Alternative Minimum Tax—Individuals

▶ See separate instructions.

▶ Attach to Form 1040 or Form 1040NR.

OMB No. 1545-0227

1993

Attachment
Sequence No. **32**

Name(s) shown on Form 1040

Your social security number

Part I Adjustments and Preferences

1	If you itemized deductions on Schedule A (Form 1040), go to line 2. If you did not itemize deductions, enter your standard deduction from Form 1040, line 34, and skip to line 6 . .	**1**	
2	Medical and dental expenses. See instructions	**2**	
3	Taxes. Enter the amount from Schedule A, line 8	**3**	
4	Certain interest on a home mortgage not used to buy, build, or improve your home . . .	**4**	
5	Miscellaneous itemized deductions. Enter the amount from Schedule A, line 24	**5**	
6	Refund of taxes. Enter any tax refund from Form 1040, line 10 or 22	**6**	( )
7	Investment interest. Enter difference between regular tax and AMT deduction	**7**	
8	Post-1986 depreciation. Enter difference between regular tax and AMT depreciation . . .	**8**	
9	Adjusted gain or loss. Enter difference between AMT and regular tax gain or loss	**9**	
10	Incentive stock options. Enter excess of AMT income over regular tax income	**10**	
11	Passive activities. Enter difference between AMT and regular tax income or loss	**11**	
12	Beneficiaries of estates and trusts. Enter the amount from Schedule K-1 (Form 1041), line 8	**12**	
13	Tax-exempt interest from private activity bonds issued after 8/7/86	**13**	
14	Other. Enter the amount, if any, for each item and enter the total on line 14.		

a Charitable contributions .		**g** Long-term contracts . .	
b Circulation expenditures .		**h** Loss limitations . . .	
c Depletion		**i** Mining costs	
d Depreciation (pre-1987) .		**j** Pollution control facilities .	
e Installment sales . . .		**k** Research and experimental	
f Intangible drilling costs .		**l** Tax shelter farm activities .	
		m Related adjustments . .	**14**

15	**Total Adjustments and Preferences.** Combine lines 1 through 14 . . . . ▶	**15**	

Part II Alternative Minimum Taxable Income

16	Enter the amount from **Form 1040, line 35.** If less than zero, enter as a (loss) . . . . ▶	**16**	
17	Net operating loss deduction, if any, from Form 1040, line 22. Enter as a positive amount .	**17**	
18	If Form 1040, line 32, is over $108,450 (over $54,225 if married filing separately), enter your itemized deductions limitation, if any, from line 9 of the worksheet for Schedule A, line 26	**18**	( )
19	Combine lines 15 through 18 . . . . ▶	**19**	
20	Alternative tax net operating loss deduction. See instructions	**20**	
21	**Alternative Minimum Taxable Income.** Subtract line 20 from line 19. (If married filing separately and line 21 is more than $165,000, see instructions.) . . . . ▶	**21**	

Part III Exemption Amount and Alternative Minimum Tax

22 **Exemption Amount.** (If this form is for a child under age 14, see instructions.)

If your filing status is:	And line 21 is not over:	Enter on line 22:	
Single or head of household	$112,500	$33,750	
Married filing jointly or qualifying widow(er)	150,000	45,000	**22**
Married filing separately	75,000	22,500	

If line 21 is **over** the amount shown above for your filing status, see instructions.

23	Subtract line 22 from line 21. If zero or less, enter -0- here and on lines 26 and 28 . ▶	**23**	
24	If line 23 is $175,000 or less ($87,500 or less if married filing separately), multiply line 23 by 26% (.26). Otherwise, see instructions	**24**	
25	Alternative minimum tax foreign tax credit. See instructions	**25**	
26	Tentative minimum tax. Subtract line 25 from line 24 . . . . ▶	**26**	
27	Enter your tax from Form 1040, line 38 (plus any amount from Form 4970 included on Form 1040, line 39), minus any foreign tax credit from Form 1040, line 43	**27**	
28	**Alternative Minimum Tax.** (If this form is for a child under age 14, see instructions.) Subtract line 27 from line 26. If zero or less, enter -0-. Enter here and on Form 1040, line 48 . . ▶	**28**	

For Paperwork Reduction Act Notice, see separate instructions.   Cat. No. 13600G   Form **6251** (1993)

Form **6252**

Department of the Treasury
Internal Revenue Service

Installment Sale Income

▶ See separate instructions.   ▶ Attach to your tax return.
▶ Use a separate form for each sale or other disposition of property on the installment method.

OMB No. 1545-0228

19**93**

Attachment
Sequence No. **79**

Name(s) shown on return	Identifying number

1   Description of property ▶ ....

2a   Date acquired (month, day, and year) ▶ |___/___/___| **b** Date sold (month, day, and year) ▶ |___/___/___|

3   Was the property sold to a related party after May 14, 1980? See instructions . . . . ☐ Yes ☐ No

4   If the answer to question 3 is "Yes," was the property a marketable security? If "Yes," complete Part III. If "No," complete Part III for the year of sale and for 2 years after the year of sale. . . . . ☐ Yes ☐ No

Part I   Gross Profit and Contract Price. Complete this part for the year of sale only.

5	Selling price including mortgages and other debts. Do not include interest whether stated or unstated	**5**	
6	Mortgages and other debts the buyer assumed or took the property subject to, but not new mortgages the buyer got from a bank or other source .	**6**	
7	Subtract line 6 from line 5	**7**	
8	Cost or other basis of property sold	**8**	
9	Depreciation allowed or allowable	**9**	
10	Adjusted basis. Subtract line 9 from line 8	**10**	
11	Commissions and other expenses of sale.	**11**	
12	Income recapture from Form 4797, Part III. See instructions . .	**12**	
13	Add lines 10, 11, and 12	**13**	
14	Subtract line 13 from line 5. If zero or less, **stop here.** Do not complete the rest of this form .	**14**	
15	If the property described on line 1 above was your main home, enter the total of lines 14 and 22 from Form 2119. Otherwise, enter -0-.	**15**	
16	**Gross profit.** Subtract line 15 from line 14	**16**	
17	Subtract line 13 from line 6. If zero or less, enter -0- . .	**17**	
18	**Contract price.** Add line 7 and line 17	**18**	

Part II   Installment Sale Income. Complete this part for the year of sale and any year you receive a payment or have certain debts you must treat as a payment on installment obligations.

19	Gross profit percentage. Divide line 16 by line 18. For years after the year of sale, see instructions	**19**	
20	**For year of sale only**—Enter amount from line 17 above; otherwise, enter -0-	**20**	
21	Payments received during year. See instructions. Do not include interest whether stated or unstated	**21**	
22	Add lines 20 and 21.	**22**	
23	Payments received in prior years. See instructions. Do not include interest whether stated or unstated.	**23**	
24	**Installment sale income.** Multiply line 22 by line 19	**24**	
25	Part of line 24 that is ordinary income under recapture rules. See instructions	**25**	
26	Subtract line 25 from line 24. Enter here and on Schedule D or Form 4797. See instructions .	**26**	

Part III   Related Party Installment Sale Income. Do not complete if you received the final payment this tax year.

27   Name, address, and taxpayer identifying number of related party ....

....

28   Did the related party, during this tax year, resell or dispose of the property ("second disposition")? . . . ☐ Yes ☐ No

29   **If the answer to question 28 is "Yes," complete lines 30 through 37 below unless one of the following conditions is met. Check only the box that applies.**

   a ☐ The second disposition was more than 2 years after the first disposition (other than dispositions of marketable securities). If this box is checked, enter the date of disposition (month, day, year) ▶ |___/___/___|

   b ☐ The first disposition was a sale or exchange of stock to the issuing corporation.

   c ☐ The second disposition was an involuntary conversion where the threat of conversion occurred after the first disposition.

   d ☐ The second disposition occurred after the death of the original seller or buyer.

   e ☐ It can be established to the satisfaction of the Internal Revenue Service that tax avoidance was not a principal purpose for either of the dispositions. If this box is checked, attach an explanation. See instructions.

30	Selling price of property sold by related party	**30**	
31	Enter contract price from line 18 for year of first sale	**31**	
32	Enter the **smaller** of line 30 or line 31	**32**	
33	Total payments received by the end of your 1993 tax year. Add lines 22 and 23	**33**	
34	Subtract line 33 from line 32. If zero or less, enter -0-	**34**	
35	Multiply line 34 by the gross profit percentage on line 19 for year of first sale	**35**	
36	Part of line 35 that is ordinary income under recapture rules. See instructions	**36**	
37	Subtract line 36 from line 35. Enter here and on Schedule D or Form 4797. See instructions .	**37**	

For Paperwork Reduction Act Notice, see separate instructions.   Cat. No. 13601R   Form **6252** (1993)

✿ *Printed on recycled paper*

Form **8283**
(Rev. November 1992)

Department of the Treasury
Internal Revenue Service

Noncash Charitable Contributions

▶ Attach to your tax return if the total deduction claimed
for all property contributed exceeds $500.

▶ See separate instructions.

OMB No. 1545-0908
Expires 11-30-95

Attachment
Sequence No. **55**

Name(s) shown on your income tax return

Identifying number

Note: *Figure the amount of your contribution deduction before completing this form. See your tax return instructions.*

Section A—Include in this section **only** items (or groups of similar items) for which you claimed a deduction of $5,000 or less per item or group, and certain publicly traded securities (see instructions).

Part I Information on Donated Property—If you need more space, attach a statement.

1	(a) Name and address of the donee organization	(b) Description of donated property
A		
B		
C		
D		
E		

Note: *If the amount you claimed as a deduction for an item is $500 or less, you do not have to complete columns (d), (e), and (f).*

	(c) Date of the contribution	(d) Date acquired by donor (mo., yr.)	(e) How acquired by donor	(f) Donor's cost or adjusted basis	(g) Fair market value	(h) Method used to determine the fair market value
A						
B						
C						
D						
E						

Part II Other Information—If you gave less than an entire interest in property listed in Part I, complete lines 2a–2e. If restrictions were attached to a contribution listed in Part I, complete lines 3a–3c.

2 If less than the entire interest in the property is contributed during the year, complete the following:

a Enter letter from Part I that identifies the property _____. If Part II applies to more than one property, attach a separate statement.

b Total amount claimed as a deduction for the property listed in Part I: **(1)** For this tax year _____
(2) For any prior tax years _____.

c Name and address of each organization to which any such contribution was made in a prior year (complete only if different than the donee organization above).

Name of charitable organization (donee)

Address (number, street, and room or suite no.)

City or town, state, and ZIP code

d For tangible property, enter the place where the property is located or kept _____

e Name of any person, other than the donee organization, having actual possession of the property _____

3 If conditions were attached to any contribution listed in Part I, answer the following questions and attach the required statement (see instructions):

		Yes	No
a	Is there a restriction, either temporary or permanent, on the donee's right to use or dispose of the donated property?		
b	Did you give to anyone (other than the donee organization or another organization participating with the donee organization in cooperative fundraising) the right to the income from the donated property or to the possession of the property, including the right to vote donated securities, to acquire the property by purchase or otherwise, or to designate the person having such income, possession, or right to acquire?		
c	Is there a restriction limiting the donated property for a particular use?		

For Paperwork Reduction Act Notice, see separate instructions.   Cat. No. 62299J   Form **8283** (Rev. 11-92)

Form 8283 (Rev. 11-92)   Page **2**

Name(s) shown on your income tax return	Identifying number

Section B—Appraisal Summary—Include in this section only items (or groups of similar items) for which you claimed a deduction of more than $5,000 per item or group. Report contributions of certain publicly traded securities only in Section A.

If you donated art, you may have to attach the complete appraisal. See the **Note** in Part I below.

Part I   **Information on Donated Property**—To be completed by the taxpayer and/or appraiser.

4   Check type of property:

☐ Art* (contribution of $20,000 or more)   ☐ Real Estate   ☐ Gems/Jewelry   ☐ Stamp Collections
☐ Art* (contribution of less than $20,000)   ☐ Coin Collections ☐ Books   ☐ Other

*Art includes paintings, sculptures, watercolors, prints, drawings, ceramics, antique furniture, decorative arts, textiles, carpets, silver, rare manuscripts, historical memorabilia, and other similar objects.

Note: *If your total art contribution deduction was $20,000 or more, you must attach a complete copy of the signed appraisal. See instructions.*

5	(a) Description of donated property (if you need more space, attach a separate statement)	(b) If tangible property was donated, give a brief summary of the overall physical condition at the time of the gift	(c) Appraised fair market value
A			
B			
C			
D			

	(d) Date acquired by donor (mo., yr.)	(e) How acquired by donor	(f) Donor's cost or adjusted basis	(g) For bargain sales, enter amount received	See instructions	
					(h) Amount claimed as a deduction	(i) Average trading price of securities
A						
B						
C						
D						

Part II   **Taxpayer (Donor) Statement**—List each item included in Part I above that is separately identified in the appraisal as having a value of $500 or less. See instructions.

I declare that the following item(s) included in Part I above has to the best of my knowledge and belief an appraised value of not more than $500 (per item). Enter identifying letter from Part I and describe the specific item: _____

Signature of taxpayer (donor) ▶   Date ▶

Part III   **Certification of Appraiser**

I declare that I am not the donor, the donee, a party to the transaction in which the donor acquired the property, employed by, married to, or related to any of the foregoing persons, or an appraiser regularly used by any of the foregoing persons and who does not perform a majority of appraisals during the taxable year for other persons.

Also, I declare that I hold myself out to the public as an appraiser or perform appraisals on a regular basis; and that because of my qualifications as described in the appraisal, I am qualified to make appraisals of the type of property being valued. I certify that the appraisal fees were not based upon a percentage of the appraised property value. Furthermore, I understand that a false or fraudulent overstatement of the property value as described in the qualified appraisal or this appraisal summary may subject me to the civil penalty under section 6701(a) (aiding and abetting the understatement of tax liability). I affirm that I have not been barred from presenting evidence or testimony by the Director of Practice.

Sign Here

Signature ▶	Title ▶	Date of appraisal ▶
Business address (including room or suite no.)		Identifying number
City or town, state, and ZIP code		

Part IV   **Donee Acknowledgment**—To be completed by the charitable organization.

This charitable organization acknowledges that it is a qualified organization under section 170(c) and that it received the donated property as described in Section B, Part I, above on _____
                                                                                                (Date)

Furthermore, this organization affirms that in the event it sells, exchanges, or otherwise disposes of the property (or any portion thereof) within 2 years after the date of receipt, it will file an information return (**Form 8282,** Donee Information Return) with the IRS and furnish the donor a copy of that return. This acknowledgment does not represent concurrence in the claimed fair market value.

Name of charitable organization (donee)	Employer identification number
Address (number, street, and room or suite no.)	City or town, state, and ZIP code
Authorized signature	Title	Date

Form **8332**
(Rev. March 1993)

Department of the Treasury
Internal Revenue Service

Release of Claim to Exemption for Child of Divorced or Separated Parents

ATTACH to noncustodial parent's return each year exemption claimed.

OMB No. 1545-0915
Expires 3-31-96

Attachment
Sequence No. **51**

Name(s) of parent claiming exemption

Social security number

Part I Release of Claim to Exemption for Current Year

I agree not to claim an exemption for_____
Name(s) of child (or children)

for the tax year 19_____ .

_____
Signature of parent releasing claim to exemption

Social security number

Date

If you choose not to claim an exemption for this child (or children) for future tax years, complete Part II.

Part II Release of Claim to Exemption for Future Years *(If completed, see Noncustodial Parent below.)*

I agree not to claim an exemption for_____
Name(s) of child (or children)

for the tax year(s)_____ .
(Specify. See instructions.)

_____
Signature of parent releasing claim to exemption

Social security number

Date

General Instructions

Paperwork Reduction Act Notice.—We ask for the information on this form to carry out the Internal Revenue laws of the United States. You are required to give us the information. We need it to ensure that you are complying with these laws and to allow us to figure and collect the right amount of tax.

The time needed to complete and file this form will vary depending on individual circumstances. The estimated average time is: **Recordkeeping, 7 min.; Learning about the law or the form, 5 min.; Preparing the form, 7 min.; and Copying, assembling, and sending the form to the IRS, 14 min.**

If you have comments concerning the accuracy of these time estimates or suggestions for making this form more simple, we would be happy to hear from you. You can write to both the IRS and the Office of Management and Budget at the addresses listed in the instructions for the return with which this form is filed.

Purpose of Form.—If you are a **custodial parent,** you may use this form to release your claim to your child's exemption. To do so, complete this form and give it to the **noncustodial parent** who will claim the child's exemption. Then, the noncustodial parent must attach this form or a similar statement to his or her tax return each year the exemption is claimed.

You are the **custodial parent** if you had custody of the child for most of the year. You are the **noncustodial parent** if you had custody for a shorter period of time or did not have custody at all.

Instead of using this form, you (the custodial parent) may use a similar statement as long as it contains the same information required by this form.

Children of Divorced or Separated Parents.—Special rules apply to determine if the support test is met for children of parents who are divorced or legally separated under a decree of divorce or separate maintenance or separated under a written separation agreement. The rules also apply to children of parents who did not live together at any time during the last 6 months of the year, even if they do not have a separation agreement.

The general rule is that the custodial parent is treated as having provided over half of the child's support if:

1. The child received over half of his or her total support for the year from both of the parents, **AND**

2. The child was in the custody of one or both of his or her parents for more than half of the year.

Note: *Public assistance payments, such as Aid to Families with Dependent Children, are not support provided by the parents.*

If both **1** and **2** above apply, and the other four dependency tests in the instructions for Form 1040 or Form 1040A are also met, the custodial parent can claim the child's exemption.

Exception. The general rule does not apply if **any** of the following applies:

• The custodial parent agrees not to claim the child's exemption by signing this form or similar statement. The noncustodial parent **must** attach this form or similar statement to his or her tax return for the tax year. See **Custodial Parent** later.

• The child is treated as having received over half of his or her total support from a person under a multiple support agreement **(Form 2120, Multiple Support Declaration).**

• A pre-1985 divorce decree or written separation agreement states that the noncustodial parent can claim the child as a dependent. But the noncustodial parent must provide at least $600 for the child's support during the year. The noncustodial parent must also check the box on line 6d of Form 1040 or Form 1040A. This rule does not apply if the decree or agreement was changed after 1984 to say that the noncustodial parent cannot claim the child as a dependent.

Additional Information.—For more details, get **Pub. 504,** Divorced or Separated Individuals.

Specific Instructions

Custodial Parent.—You may agree to release your claim to the child's exemption for the current tax year or for future years, or both.

• Complete **Part I** if you agree to release your claim to the child's exemption for the current tax year.

• Complete **Part II** if you agree to release your claim to the child's exemption for any or all future years. If you do, write the specific future year(s) or "all future years" in the space provided in Part II.

Noncustodial Parent.—Attach Form 8332 or a similar statement to your tax return for the tax year in which you claim the child's exemption. You may claim the exemption **only** if the other four dependency tests in the Form 1040 or Form 1040A instructions are met.

Note: *If the custodial parent completed Part II, you **must** attach a copy of this form to your tax return for each future year in which you claim the exemption.*

Form **8582**

Department of the Treasury
Internal Revenue Service

Passive Activity Loss Limitations

▶ See separate instructions.
▶ Attach to Form 1040 or Form 1041.

OMB No. 1545-1008

19**93**

Attachment
Sequence No. **88**

Name(s) shown on return

Identifying number

Part I   **1993 Passive Activity Loss**

Caution: *See the instructions for Worksheets 1 and 2 on page 7 before completing Part I.*

Rental Real Estate Activities With Active Participation (For the definition of active participation see **Active Participation in a Rental Real Estate Activity** on page 3 of the instructions.)

1a Activities with net income (from Worksheet 1, column (a)) . . .	**1a**	
b Activities with net loss (from Worksheet 1, column (b))	**1b** ( )	
c Prior year unallowed losses (from Worksheet 1, column (c)) . .	**1c** ( )	
d Combine lines 1a, 1b, and 1c		**1d**

All Other Passive Activities

2a Activities with net income (from Worksheet 2, column (a)) . . .	**2a**	
b Activities with net loss (from Worksheet 2, column (b))	**2b** ( )	
c Prior year unallowed losses (from Worksheet 2, column (c)) . .	**2c** ( )	
d Combine lines 2a, 2b, and 2c		**2d**

3 Combine lines 1d and 2d. If the result is net income or zero, see the instructions for line 3. If this line and line 1d are losses, go to line 4. Otherwise, enter -0- on line 9 and go to line 10 .   **3**

Part II   **Special Allowance for Rental Real Estate With Active Participation**

Note: *Enter all numbers in Part II as positive amounts. (See instructions on page 7 for examples.)*

4 Enter the **smaller** of the loss on line 1d or the loss on line 3	**4**	
5 Enter $150,000. If married filing separately, see the instructions .	**5**	
6 Enter modified adjusted gross income, but not less than zero (see instructions)	**6**	
	Note: *If line 6 is equal to or greater than line 5, skip lines 7 and 8, enter -0- on line 9, and then go to line 10. Otherwise, go to line 7.*	
7 Subtract line 6 from line 5	**7**	
8 Multiply line 7 by 50% (.5). **Do not** enter more than $25,000. If married filing separately, see instructions		**8**
9 Enter the **smaller** of line 4 or line 8		**9**

Part III   **Total Losses Allowed**

10 Add the income, if any, on lines 1a and 2a and enter the total **10**

11 **Total losses allowed from all passive activities for 1993.** Add lines 9 and 10. See the instructions to find out how to report the losses on your tax return **11**

For Paperwork Reduction Act Notice, see separate instructions.   Cat. No. 63704F   Form **8582** (1993)

Form **8606**

Department of the Treasury
Internal Revenue Service

Nondeductible IRAs
(Contributions, Distributions, and Basis)
▶ Please see What Records Must I Keep? below.
▶ Attach to Form 1040, Form 1040A, or Form 1040NR.

OMB No. 1545-1007

1993

Attachment
Sequence No. **47**

Name. If married, file a separate Form 8606 for each spouse. See instructions.

Your social security number

Fill in Your Address Only If You Are Filing This Form by Itself and Not With Your Tax Return ▷

Home address (number and street, or P.O. box if mail is not delivered to your home)

Apt. no.

City, town or post office, state, and ZIP code

Contributions, Nontaxable Distributions, and Basis

1	Enter your IRA contributions for 1993 that you choose to be nondeductible. Include those made during 1/1/94–4/15/94 that were for 1993. See instructions	1	
2	Enter your total IRA basis for 1992 and earlier years. See instructions	2	
3	Add lines 1 and 2	3	

Did you receive any IRA distributions (withdrawals) in 1993?
— No → Enter the amount from line 3 on line 12. Then, **stop** and read **When and Where To File** on page 2.
— Yes → Go to line 4.

4	Enter only those contributions included on line 1 that were made during 1/1/94–4/15/94. This amount will be the same as line 1 if all of your nondeductible contributions for 1993 were made in 1994 by 4/15/94. See instructions	4	
5	Subtract line 4 from line 3	5	
6	Enter the total value of **ALL** your IRAs as of 12/31/93 plus any outstanding rollovers. See instructions	6	
7	Enter the total IRA distributions received during 1993. Do not include amounts rolled over before 1/1/94. See instructions	7	
8	Add lines 6 and 7	8	
9	Divide line 5 by line 8 and enter the result as a decimal (to at least two places). Do not enter more than "1.00"	9	× .
10	Multiply line 7 by line 9. This is the amount of your **nontaxable distributions for 1993**	10	
11	Subtract line 10 from line 5. This is the **basis in your IRA(s) as of 12/31/93**	11	
12	Add lines 4 and 11. This is your **total IRA basis for 1993 and earlier years**	12	

Taxable Distributions for 1993

13	Subtract line 10 from line 7. Enter the result here and on Form 1040, line 16b; Form 1040A, line 10b; or Form 1040NR, line 17b, whichever applies	13	

Sign Here Only If You Are Filing This Form by Itself and Not With Your Tax Return

Under penalties of perjury, I declare that I have examined this form, including accompanying attachments, and to the best of my knowledge and belief, it is true, correct, and complete.

▶ Your signature

▶ Date

General Instructions

Paperwork Reduction Act Notice.—We ask for the information on this form to carry out the Internal Revenue laws of the United States. You are required to give us the information. We need it to ensure that you are complying with these laws and to allow us to figure and collect the right amount of tax.

The time needed to complete and file this form will vary depending on individual circumstances. The estimated average time is: **Recordkeeping, 26 min.; Learning about the law or the form, 7 min.; Preparing the form, 22 min.; and Copying, assembling, and sending the form to the IRS, 20 min.**

If you have comments concerning the accuracy of these time estimates or suggestions for making this form more simple, we would be happy to hear from

you. You can write to both the IRS and the Office of Management and Budget at the addresses listed in the Instructions for Form 1040, Form 1040A, or Form 1040NR.

Purpose of Form

Use Form 8606 to report your IRA contributions that you choose to be nondeductible. For example, if you cannot deduct all of your contributions because of the income limits for IRAs, you may want to make nondeductible contributions.

Also use Form 8606 to figure the basis in your IRA(s) and the taxable part of any distibutions you received in 1993 if you have ever made nondeductible contributions.

Your **basis** is the total of all your nondeductible IRA contributions minus the total of all nontaxable IRA distributions received. It is to your advantage to keep

track of your basis because it is used to figure the nontaxable part of future distributions.

Note: To figure your deductible IRA contributions, use the Instructions for Form 1040 or Form 1040A, whichever applies.

Who Must File

You must file Form 8606 for 1993 if:
- You made nondeductible contributions to your IRA for 1993, **or**
- You received IRA distributions in 1993 **and** you have ever made nondeductible contributions to any of your IRAs.

What Records Must I Keep?

To verify the nontaxable part of distributions from your IRA, keep a copy of this form together with copies of the following forms and records until all distributions are made from your IRA(s):

Cat.No. 63966F

Form **8606** (1993)

- Page 1 of Forms 1040 (or Forms 1040A or Forms 1040NR) filed for each year you make a nondeductible contribution.
- Forms 5498 or similar statements received each year showing contributions you made.
- Forms 5498 or similar statements you received showing the value of your IRA(s) for each year you received a distribution.
- Forms 1099-R and W-2P received for each year you received a distribution.

When and Where To File

Attach Form 8606 to your 1993 Form 1040, Form 1040A, or Form 1040NR.

If you are required to file Form 8606 but do not have to file an income tax return because you do not meet the requirements for filing a return, you still **must** file Form 8606 with the Internal Revenue Service at the same time and place you would be required to file Form 1040, Form 1040A, or Form 1040NR.

Penalty for Not Filing

If you are required to file Form 8606 but do not do so, you will have to pay a $50 penalty for each failure to file this form unless you can show reasonable cause.

Penalty for Overstatement

If you overstate your nondeductible contributions for any tax year, you must pay a $100 penalty for each overstatement unless it was due to reasonable cause.

Additional Information

For more details on nondeductible contributions, IRA basis, and distributions, get **Pub. 590**, Individual Retirement Arrangements (IRAs).

Amending Form 8606

After you file your return, you may change a nondeductible contribution made on a prior year's return to a deductible contribution or vice versa. To do this, complete a new Form 8606 showing the revised information and attach it to **Form 1040X**, Amended U.S. Individual Income Tax Return. Send both of these forms to the Internal Revenue Service Center shown in the Form 1040X instructions for your area.

Specific Instructions

Section references are to the Internal Revenue Code.

Note: *If you received an IRA distribution in 1993 and you also made IRA contributions for 1993 that may not be fully deductible because of the income limits, you need to make a special computation before completing this form. For details, including how to complete Form 8606, see Tax Treatment of Distributions in Chapter 6 of Pub. 590.*

Name and Social Security Number

If you file a joint return on Form 1040 or Form 1040A, enter the name and social security number of the spouse whose IRA information is shown.

Line 1

If you used IRA Worksheet 2 in the Form 1040 or Form 1040A instructions, include the following on line 1 of Form 8606:

- The amount shown on line 10 of IRA Worksheet 2 (Form 1040) or line 8 of IRA Worksheet 2 (Form 1040A) that you choose to make nondeductible.
- The part, if any, of the amount shown on line 9 of IRA Worksheet 2 (Form 1040) or line 7 of IRA Worksheet 2 (Form 1040A) that you choose to make nondeductible. You cannot take a deduction for the part included on line 1.

Note: *Enter any nondeductible contributions for your **nonworking spouse** from the appropriate lines of IRA Worksheet 2 on line 1 of your spouse's separate Form 8606.*

If none of your contributions are deductible, you may choose to make up to $2,000 (but not more than your earned income) of your contributions nondeductible. Enter on line 1 of Form 8606 your contributions that you choose to make nondeductible.

If contributions were also made to your nonworking spouse's IRA, you may choose to make nondeductible contributions up to $2,250 (but not more than your earned income). Enter on line 1 of your Form 8606 the total nondeductible contributions you are making to your IRA. Enter the balance on line 1 of your nonworking spouse's Form 8606. Do not enter more than $2,000 on either your or your spouse's Form 8606. Also, the total of the two amounts cannot be more than $2,250.

If you used IRA Worksheet 1 in the Form 1040 or Form 1040A instructions but choose not to deduct the full amount shown on line 3 of that worksheet, subtract the amount you are deducting from the amount on line 3. Enter the result on line 1 of your Form 8606.

If contributions were made to your nonworking spouse's IRA but you choose not to deduct the full amount shown on line 8 of IRA Worksheet 1, subtract the amount you are deducting for your nonworking spouse from the amount on line 8. Enter the result on line 1 of your nonworking spouse's Form 8606.

Line 2

If this is the first year you are required to file Form 8606, enter zero. If you filed a Form 8606 for any year **after 1988,** enter the amount from line 14 of the **last** Form 8606 you filed. Otherwise, enter the total of the amounts from lines 7 and 16 of your **1988** Form 8606. Or, if you didn't file a 1988 Form 8606, enter the total of the amounts from lines 4 and 13 of your **1987** Form 8606.

Line 4

If you made contributions in 1993 and 1994 that are for 1993, you may choose to apply the contributions made in 1993 first to nondeductible contributions and then to deductible contributions, or vice versa. But the amount on line 1 minus the amount on line 4 cannot be more than the IRA contributions you actually made in 1993.

Example. You made contributions of $1,000 in 1993, and $1,000 in 1994. $1,500 of your contributions are deductible and $500 are nondeductible. You choose $500 of your contribution in 1993 to be nondeductible. In this case, the $500 would be entered on line 1, but not on line 4, and would become part of your basis for 1993.

Line 5

Although the 1993 IRA contributions you made during 1/1/94–4/15/94 (line 4) can be treated as nondeductible for purposes of line 1, they are not included in your basis for purposes of figuring the nontaxable part of any distributions you received in 1993. This is why you subtract line 4 from line 3.

Line 6

Enter the total value of **ALL** your IRAs as of 12/31/93 **plus** any outstanding rollovers. You should receive a statement by 1/31/94 for each IRA account showing the value on 12/31/93. A **rollover** is a tax-free distribution from one IRA that is contributed to another IRA. The rollover must be completed within 60 days of receiving the distribution from the first IRA. An **outstanding rollover** is any amount distributed to you from one IRA within 60 days of the end of 1993 (between Nov. 2 and Dec. 31) that you did not roll over to another IRA by 12/31/93, but that you roll over to another IRA in 1994 within the normal 60-day rollover period.

Line 7

Do not include on line 7:

- Distributions received in 1993 and rolled over to another IRA by 12/31/93,
- Outstanding rollovers included on line 6,
- Contributions under section 408(d)(4) returned to you on or before the due date of the return, or
- Excess contributions under section 408(d)(5) returned to you after the due date of the return.

Line 11

This is the total of your nondeductible IRA contributions made in 1993 and earlier years minus the total of any nontaxable IRA distributions received in those years.

Line 12

This is the total of your IRA basis as of 12/31/93 and any nondeductible IRA contributions for 1993 that you made in 1994 by 4/15/94.

This amount will be used on Form 8606 in future years if you make nondeductible IRA contributions or receive distributions.

Form **8615**	**Tax for Children Under Age 14**	OMB No. 1545-0998

Tax for Children Under Age 14
Who Have Investment Income of More Than $1,200
► See instructions below and on back.
► Attach ONLY to the child's Form 1040, Form 1040A, or Form 1040NR.

1993

Department of the Treasury
Internal Revenue Service

Attachment
Sequence No. **33**

Child's name shown on return

Child's social security number

A Parent's name (first, initial, and last). **Caution:** See instructions on back before completing.

B Parent's social security number

C Parent's filing status (check one):
☐ Single ☐ Married filing jointly ☐ Married filing separately ☐ Head of household ☐ Qualifying widow(er)

Step 1 **Figure child's net investment income**

1 Enter child's investment income, such as taxable interest and dividend income. See instructions. If this amount is $1,200 or less, **stop here;** do not file this form **1**

2 If the child DID NOT itemize deductions on Schedule A (Form 1040 or Form 1040NR), enter $1,200. If the child ITEMIZED deductions, see instructions **2**

3 Subtract line 2 from line 1. If the result is zero or less, **stop here;** do not complete the rest of this form but ATTACH it to the child's return **3**

4 Enter child's **taxable** income from Form 1040, line 37; Form 1040A, line 22; or Form 1040NR, line 36 **4**

5 Enter the **smaller** of line 3 or line 4 here . . . . ► **5**

Step 2 **Figure tentative tax based on the tax rate of the parent listed on line A**

6 Enter parent's **taxable** income from Form 1040, line 37; Form 1040A, line 22; Form 1040EZ, line 6; or Form 1040NR, line 36. If the parent transferred property to a trust, see instructions . . **6**

7 Enter the total net investment income, if any, from Forms 8615, line 5, of ALL OTHER children of the parent identified above. **Do not** include the amount from line 5 above **7**

8 Add lines 5, 6, and 7 . . . . **8**

9 Tax on line 8 based on the **parent's** filing status. See instructions. If from Schedule D Tax Worksheet, enter amount from line 4 of that worksheet here ► _____ **9**

10 Enter parent's tax from Form 1040, line 38; Form 1040A, line 23; Form 1040EZ, line 8; or Form 1040NR, line 37. If from Schedule D Tax Worksheet, enter amount from line 4 of that worksheet here ► _____ **10**

11 Subtract line 10 from line 9. If line 7 is blank, enter on line 13 the amount from line 11; skip lines 12a and 12b **11**

12a Add lines 5 and 7 . . . . **12a** | |

b Divide line 5 by line 12a. Enter the result as a decimal (rounded to two places) . . . . . . **12b** × .

13 Multiply line 11 by line 12b . . . . ► **13**

Step 3 **Figure child's tax—If lines 4 and 5 above are the same, go to line 16 now.**

14 Subtract line 5 from line 4 . . . . **14** | |

15 Tax on line 14 based on the **child's** filing status. See instructions. If from Schedule D Tax Worksheet, enter amount from line 4 of that worksheet here ► _____ **15**

16 Add lines 13 and 15 . . . . **16**

17 Tax on line 4 based on the **child's** filing status. See instructions. If from Schedule D Tax Worksheet, check here . . . . ► ☐ **17**

18 Enter the **larger** of line 16 or line 17 here and on Form 1040, line 38; Form 1040A, line 23; or Form 1040NR, line 37. Be sure to check the box for "Form 8615" even if line 17 is more than line 16 . ► **18**

General Instructions

A Change To Note.—If line 8 of Form 8615 is over $70,000 (over $140,000 if the parent's filing status is married filing jointly or qualifying widow(er)), the election to defer additional 1993 taxes may apply to the child. Get **Form 8841,** Deferral of Additional 1993 Taxes, for details. If the election is made, Form 1040A **cannot** be filed for the child.

Purpose of Form.—For children under age 14, investment income over $1,200 is taxed at the parent's rate if the parent's rate is higher than the child's rate. If the child's investment income is more than $1,200, use this form to figure the child's tax.

Investment Income.—As used on this form, "investment income" includes all taxable income other than earned income as defined on page 2. It includes income such as taxable interest, dividends, capital gains, rents, royalties, etc. It also includes pension and annuity income and income (other than earned income) received as the beneficiary of a trust.

Who Must File.—Generally, Form 8615 must be filed for any child who was under age 14 on January 1, 1994, had more than $1,200 of investment income, and is required to file a tax return. If neither parent was alive on December 31, 1993, do not use Form 8615.

Instead, figure the child's tax in the normal manner.

Note: *The parent may be able to elect to report the child's interest and dividends on his or her return. If the parent makes this election, the child will not have to file a return or Form 8615. For more details, see the instructions for Form 1040 or Form 1040A, or get **Form 8814,** Parents' Election To Report Child's Interest and Dividends.*

Additional Information.—For more details, get **Pub. 929,** Tax Rules for Children and Dependents.

Incomplete Information for Parent.—If the parent's taxable income or filing status or the net investment income of

For Paperwork Reduction Act Notice, see back of form.   Cat. No. 64113U   Form **8615** (1993)

the parent's other children is not known by the due date of the child's return, reasonable estimates may be used. Write "Estimated" on the appropriate line(s) of Form 8615. For more details, see Pub. 929.

Amended Return.—If after the child's return is filed, the parent's taxable income is changed or the net investment income of any of the parent's other children is changed, the child's tax must be refigured using the adjusted amounts. If the child's tax is changed as a result of the adjustment(s), file **Form 1040X,** Amended U.S. Individual Income Tax Return, to correct the child's tax.

Alternative Minimum Tax.—A child whose tax is figured on Form 8615 may owe the alternative minimum tax. For details, get **Form 6251,** Alternative Minimum Tax—Individuals, and its instructions.

Line Instructions

Section references are to the Internal Revenue Code.

Lines A and B.—If the child's parents were married to each other and filed a joint return, enter the name and social security number (SSN) of the parent who is listed first on the joint return. For example, if the father's name is listed first on the return and his SSN is entered in the block labeled "Your social security number," enter his name on line A and his SSN on line B.

If the parents were married but filed separate returns, enter the name and SSN of the parent who had the **higher** taxable income. If you do not know which parent had the higher taxable income, see Pub. 929.

If the parents were unmarried, treated as unmarried for Federal income tax purposes, or separated either by a divorce or separate maintenance decree, enter the name and SSN of the parent who had custody of the child for most of the year (the custodial parent).

Exception. If the custodial parent remarried and filed a joint return with his or her new spouse, enter the name and SSN of the person listed first on the joint return, even if that person is not the child's parent. If the custodial parent and his or her new spouse filed separate returns, enter the name and SSN of the person with the **higher** taxable income, even if that person is not the child's parent.

Note: *If the parents were unmarried but lived together during the year with the child, enter the name and SSN of the parent who had the **higher** taxable income.*

Line 1.—If the child had no earned income (defined later), enter the child's adjusted gross income from Form 1040, line 32; Form 1040A, line 17; or Form 1040NR, line 32.

If the child had earned income, use the following worksheet to figure the amount to enter on line 1. But if the child files **Form 2555,** Foreign Earned Income, or **Form 2555-EZ,** Foreign Earned Income Exclusion, has a net loss from self-employment, or claims a net operating loss deduction, **do not** use the worksheet below. Instead, use the worksheet in Pub. 929 to figure the amount to enter on line 1.

Worksheet (keep a copy for your records)

1. Enter the amount from the child's Form 1040, line 23; Form 1040A, line 14; or Form 1040NR, line 24, whichever applies . . . _____

2. Enter the child's **earned income** (defined below) plus any deduction the child claims on Form 1040, line 28, or Form 1040NR, line 28, whichever applies _____

3. Subtract line 2 from line 1. Enter the result here and on Form 8615, line 1 . . _____

Earned income includes wages, tips, and other payments received for personal services performed. Generally, earned income is the total of the amounts reported on Form 1040, lines 7, 12, and 19; Form 1040A, line 7; or Form 1040NR, lines 8, 13, and 20.

Line 2.—If the child itemized deductions, enter on line 2 the **greater** of:
- $600 plus the portion of the amount on Schedule A (Form 1040), line 26, or Schedule A (Form 1040NR), line 17, that is directly connected with the production of the investment income on Form 8615, line 1; **OR**
- $1,200.

Line 6.—If the parent's taxable income is less than zero, enter zero on line 6. If the parent filed a joint return, enter the taxable income shown on that return even if the parent's spouse is not the child's parent. If the parent transferred property to a trust which sold or exchanged the property during the year at a gain, include any gain that was taxed to the trust under section 644 in the amount entered on line 6. Enter "Section 644" and the amount to the right of the line 6 entry. Also, see the instructions for line 10.

Line 9.—Figure the tax using the Tax Table, Tax Rate Schedules, or the Schedule D Tax Worksheet, whichever applies. If any net capital gain is included on lines 5, 6, and/or 7, the tax on the amount on line 8 may be less if the Schedule D Tax Worksheet can be used to figure the tax. See Pub. 929 for details on how to figure the net capital gain included on line 8 and how to complete the worksheet. The Schedule D Tax Worksheet should be used to figure the tax if:

the parent's filing status is:	AND	the amount on Form 8615, line 8, is over:
• Single		$53,500
• Married filing jointly or Qualifying widow(er)		$89,150
• Married filing separately		$44,575
• Head of household		$76,400

If the Schedule D Tax Worksheet is used to figure the tax, enter on Form 8615, line 9, the amount from line 13 of that worksheet. Also, enter the amount from line 4 of that worksheet in the space next to line 9 of Form 8615.

Line 10.—If the parent filed a joint return, enter the tax shown on that return even if the parent's spouse is not the child's parent. If the parent filed Form 8814, enter "Form 8814" and the total tax from line 8 of Form(s) 8814 in the space next to line 10 of Form 8615.

If line 6 includes any gain taxed to a trust under section 644, add the tax imposed under section 644(a)(2)(A) to the tax shown on the parent's return. Enter the total on line 10 instead of the tax from the parent's return. Also, enter "Section 644" next to line 10.

Line 15.—Figure the tax using the Tax Table, Tax Rate Schedule X, or the Schedule D Tax Worksheet, whichever applies. If line 14 is more than $53,500 and includes any net capital gain, the tax may be less if the Schedule D Tax Worksheet is used to figure the tax. See Pub. 929 for details on how to figure the net capital gain included on line 14 and how to complete the worksheet.

Line 17.—Figure the tax as if these rules did not apply. For example, if the child files Schedule D and can use the Schedule D Tax Worksheet to figure his or her tax, complete that worksheet.

Paperwork Reduction Act Notice.—We ask for the information on this form to carry out the Internal Revenue laws of the United States. You are required to give us the information. We need it to ensure that you are complying with these laws and to allow us to figure and collect the right amount of tax.

The time needed to complete and file this form will vary depending on individual circumstances. The estimated average time is: **Recordkeeping,** 13 min.; **Learning about the law or the form,** 12 min.; **Preparing the form,** 45 min.; and **Copying, assembling, and sending the form to the IRS,** 17 min.

If you have comments concerning the accuracy of these time estimates or suggestions for making this form more simple, we would be happy to hear from you. You can write to both the IRS and the Office of Management and Budget at the addresses listed in the instructions of the tax return with which this form is filed.

 Printed on recycled paper

Form 8829

Department of the Treasury
Internal Revenue Service

Expenses for Business Use of Your Home

▶ File only with Schedule C (Form 1040). Use a separate Form 8829 for each home you used for business during the year.

▶ See separate instructions.

OMB No. 1545-1266

1993

Attachment Sequence No. **66**

Name(s) of proprietor(s)   Your social security number

Part I — Part of Your Home Used for Business

1	Area used regularly and exclusively for business, regularly for day care, or for inventory storage. See instructions	1	
2	Total area of home	2	
3	Divide line 1 by line 2. Enter the result as a percentage	3	%

- For day-care facilities not used exclusively for business, also complete lines 4–6.
- All others, skip lines 4–6 and enter the amount from line 3 on line 7.

4	Multiply days used for day care during year by hours used per day	4	hr.
5	Total hours available for use during the year (365 days × 24 hours). See instructions	5	8,760 hr.
6	Divide line 4 by line 5. Enter the result as a decimal amount	6	.
7	Business percentage. For day-care facilities not used exclusively for business, multiply line 6 by line 3 (enter the result as a percentage). All others, enter the amount from line 3 ▶	7	%

Part II — Figure Your Allowable Deduction

8 Enter the amount from Schedule C, line 29, **plus** any net gain or (loss) derived from the business use of your home and shown on Schedule D or Form 4797. If more than one place of business, see instructions — **8**

See instructions for columns **(a)** and **(b)** before completing lines 9–20.

			(a) Direct expenses	(b) Indirect expenses	
9	Casualty losses. See instructions	9			
10	Deductible mortgage interest. See instructions	10			
11	Real estate taxes. See instructions	11			
12	Add lines 9, 10, and 11	12			
13	Multiply line 12, column (b) by line 7		13		
14	Add line 12, column (a) and line 13				14
15	Subtract line 14 from line 8. If zero or less, enter -0-				15
16	Excess mortgage interest. See instructions	16			
17	Insurance	17			
18	Repairs and maintenance	18			
19	Utilities	19			
20	Other expenses. See instructions	20			
21	Add lines 16 through 20	21			
22	Multiply line 21, column (b) by line 7		22		
23	Carryover of operating expenses from 1992 Form 8829, line 41		23		
24	Add line 21 in column (a), line 22, and line 23				24
25	Allowable operating expenses. Enter the **smaller** of line 15 or line 24				25
26	Limit on excess casualty losses and depreciation. Subtract line 25 from line 15				26
27	Excess casualty losses. See instructions	27			
28	Depreciation of your home from Part III below	28			
29	Carryover of excess casualty losses and depreciation from 1992 Form 8829, line 42	29			
30	Add lines 27 through 29				30
31	Allowable excess casualty losses and depreciation. Enter the **smaller** of line 26 or line 30				31
32	Add lines 14, 25, and 31				32
33	Casualty loss portion, if any, from lines 14 and 31. Carry amount to **Form 4684**, Section B				33
34	Allowable expenses for business use of your home. Subtract line 33 from line 32. Enter here and on Schedule C, line 30. If your home was used for more than one business, see instructions ▶				34

Part III — Depreciation of Your Home

35	Enter the **smaller** of your home's adjusted basis or its fair market value. See instructions	35	
36	Value of land included on line 35	36	
37	Basis of building. Subtract line 36 from line 35	37	
38	Business basis of building. Multiply line 37 by line 7	38	
39	Depreciation percentage. See instructions	39	%
40	Depreciation allowable. Multiply line 38 by line 39. Enter here and on line 28 above. See instructions	40	

Part IV — Carryover of Unallowed Expenses to 1994

41	Operating expenses. Subtract line 25 from line 24. If less than zero, enter -0-	41	
42	Excess casualty losses and depreciation. Subtract line 31 from line 30. If less than zero, enter -0-	42	

For Paperwork Reduction Act Notice, see page 1 of separate instructions.   Cat. No. 13232M   Form **8829** (1993)

APPENDIX C
Glossary of Tax Terms

The words and phrases in this glossary have been defined to reflect their conventional use in the field of taxation. The definitions may therefore be incomplete for other purposes.

A

Accelerated cost recovery system (ACRS). A method in which the cost of tangible property is recovered over a prescribed period of time. Enacted by the Economic Recovery Tax Act (ERTA) of 1981 and substantially modified by the Tax Reform Act (TRA) of 1986 (the modified system is referred to as MACRS), the approach disregards salvage value, imposes a period of cost recovery that depends upon the classification of the asset into one of various recovery periods, and prescribes the applicable percentage of cost that can be deducted each year. § 168.

Accelerated depreciation. Various methods of depreciation that yield larger deductions in the earlier years of the life of an asset than the straight-line method. Examples include the double declining-balance and the sum-of-the-years' digits methods of depreciation. § 167.

Accident and health benefits. Employee fringe benefits provided by employers through the payment of health and accident insurance premiums or the establishment of employer-funded medical reimbursement plans. Employers generally are entitled to a deduction for such payments, whereas employees generally exclude the fringe benefits from gross income. §§ 105 and 106.

Accountable plan. An accountable plan is a type of expense reimbursement plan that requires an employee to render an adequate accounting to the employer and return any excess reimbursement or allowance. If the expense qualifies, it will be treated a deduction *for* AGI.

Accounting income. The accountant's concept of income is generally based upon the realization principle. Financial accounting income may differ from taxable income (e.g., accelerated depreciation might be used for Federal income tax and straight-line depreciation for financial accounting purposes). Differences are included in a reconciliation of taxable and accounting income on Schedule M–1 of Form 1120 for corporations. Seventy-five percent of the excess of adjusted current earnings over alternative minimum taxable income is an adjustment for alternative minimum tax purposes for a corporation. See *alternative minimum tax* and *economic income.*

Accounting method. The method under which income and expenses are determined for tax purposes. Major accounting methods are the cash basis and the accrual basis. Special methods are available for the reporting of gain on installment sales, recognition of income on construction projects (the completed contract and percentage of completion methods), and the valuation of inventories (last-in, first-out and first-in, first-out). §§ 446–474. See also *accrual method, cash method, completed contract method, percentage of completion method,* etc.

Accounting period. The period of time, usually a year, used by a taxpayer for the determination of tax liability. Unless a fiscal year is chosen, taxpayers must determine and pay their income tax liability by using the calendar year (January 1 through December 31) as the period of measurement. An example of a fiscal year is July 1 through June 30. A change in accounting period (e.g., from a calendar year to a fiscal year) generally requires the consent of the IRS. A new taxpayer, such as a newly formed corporation or an estate created upon the death of an individual taxpayer, is free to select either a calendar or a fiscal year without the consent of the IRS. Limitations exist on the accounting period that may be selected by a partnership, an S corporation, and a personal service corporation. §§ 441–444.

Accrual basis. See *accrual method.*

Accrual method. A method of accounting that reflects expenses incurred and income earned for any one tax year. In contrast to the cash basis of accounting, expenses do not have to be paid to be deductible nor does income have to be received to be taxable. Unearned income (e.g., prepaid interest and rent) generally is taxed in the year of receipt regardless of the method of accounting used by the taxpayer. § 446(c)(2). See also *accounting method, cash method,* and *unearned income.*

Accumulated earnings tax. A special tax imposed on corporations that accumulate (rather than distribute) their earnings beyond the reasonable needs of the business. The tax is imposed on accumulated taxable income and is imposed in addition to the corporate income tax. §§ 531–537.

ACE adjustment. See *adjusted current earnings (ACE) adjustment* and *business untaxed reported profits*.

Acquiescence. In agreement with the result reached. The IRS follows a policy of either acquiescing (*A, Acq.*) or nonacquiescing (*NA, Non-Acq.*) in the results reached in the Regular decisions of the U.S. Tax Court.

ACRS. See *accelerated cost recovery system*.

Active income. Active income includes wages, salary, commissions, bonuses, profits from a trade or business in which the taxpayer is a material participant, gain on the sale or other disposition of assets used in an active trade or business, income from intangible property if the taxpayer's personal efforts significantly contributed to the creation of the property, and income from a qualified low-income housing project that is not subject to the passive loss limitations under transitional rules. The passive loss rules require classification of income and losses into three categories with active income being one of them.

Active participation. A term that is relevant for both the at-risk rules and the passive activity loss rules associated with rental real estate activities. For the at-risk rules, the following factors indicate active participation: (1) making decisions involving the operation or management of the activity, (2) performing services for the activity, and (3) hiring and discharging employees. For the passive activity loss rules, the taxpayer must participate in the making of management decisions in a significant and bona fide sense.

Additional depreciation. The excess of the amount of depreciation actually deducted over the amount that would have been deducted had the straight-line method been used. § 1250(b). See also *Section 1250 recapture*.

Adjusted basis. The cost or other basis of property reduced by depreciation (cost recovery) allowed or allowable and increased by capital improvements. See also *basis* and *realized gain or loss*.

Adjusted current earnings (ACE) adjustment. An adjustment in computing corporate alternative minimum taxable income (AMTI), computed at 75 percent of the excess of adjusted current earnings and profits computations over AMTI. ACE computations reflect longer and slower cost recovery deductions and other restrictions on the timing of certain recognition events. Exempt interest, life insurance proceeds, and other receipts that are included in earnings and profits but not in taxable income also increase the ACE adjustment. See also *alternative minimum tax, business untaxed reported profits, and earnings and profits*.

Adjusted gross income (AGI). A determination peculiar to individual taxpayers. Generally, it represents gross income less business expenses, expenses attributable to the production of rent or royalty income, the allowed capital loss deduction, and certain personal expenses (deductions *for* AGI). § 62. See also *gross income*.

Adjusted sales price. The amount realized from the sale of a residence reduced by the fixing-up expenses is the adjusted sales price. An amount equal to the adjusted sales price must be reinvested in a replacement residence to defer the recognition of the realized gain on the sale of a residence. See also *amount realized, fixing-up expenses*, and *realized gain*.

Ad valorem tax. A tax imposed on the value of property. The most familiar ad valorem tax is that imposed by states, counties, and cities on real estate. Ad valorem taxes can, however, be imposed upon personal property (e.g., a motor vehicle tax based on the value of an automobile). §§ 164(a)(1) and (2).

Advance payments. In general, prepayments for services or goods are includible in gross income upon receipt of the advance payments (for both accrual and cash basis taxpayers). However, Rev.Proc. 71–21 (1971–2 C.B. 549) provides guidelines for the deferral of tax on certain advance payments providing specific conditions are met.

AFTR. Published by Research Institute of America (formerly by Prentice-Hall), *American Federal Tax Reports* contains all of the Federal tax decisions issued by the U.S. District Courts, U.S. Court of Federal Claims, U.S. Courts of Appeals, and U.S. Supreme Court.

AFTR2d. The second series of the *American Federal Tax Reports*.

Alimony and separate maintenance payments. Alimony and separate maintenance payments are includible in the gross income of the recipient and are deductible by the payor. The payments must be made in discharge of a legal obligation arising from a marital or family relationship. Child support and voluntary payments are not treated as alimony. Alimony is deductible *for* AGI. §§ 62(10), 71, and 215. See also *child support payments*.

Alimony recapture. The amount of alimony that previously has been included in the gross income of the recipient and deducted by the payor that now is deducted by the recipient and included in the gross income of the payor as the result of front-loading. § 71(f).

All events test. For accrual method taxpayers, income is earned when (1) all the events have occurred that fix the right to receive the income and (2) the amount can be determined with reasonable accuracy. Accrual of income cannot be postponed simply because a portion of the income may have to be returned in a subsequent period. The all events test also is utilized to determine when expenses can be deducted by an accrual basis taxpayer. The application of the test could cause a variation between the treatment of an item for accounting and for tax purposes. For example, a reserve for warranty expense may be properly accruable under generally accepted accounting principles but not be deductible under the Federal income tax law. Because of the application of the all events test, the deduction becomes available in the year the warranty obligation becomes fixed and the amount is determinable with reasonable certainty. See also *economic performance test*. Reg. §§ 1.446–1(c)(1)(ii) and 1.461–1(a)(2).

Alternate valuation date. Property passing from a person by reason of death may be valued for death tax purposes as of the date of death or the alternate valuation date. The alternate valuation date is six months from the date of death or the date the property is disposed of by the estate, whichever comes first. To use the alternate valuation date, the executor or administrator of the estate must make an affirmative election. The election of the alternate valuation date is not available unless it decreases both the amount of the gross estate *and* the estate tax liability. §§ 1014(a) and 2032.

Alternative depreciation system. A cost recovery system that produces a smaller deduction than would be calculated under ACRS or MACRS. The alternative system must be used in certain instances and can be elected in other instances. § 168(g). See also *cost recovery allowance.*

Alternative minimum tax (AMT). The alternative minimum tax is imposed only to the extent it exceeds the regular income tax (in effect, the tax liability is the greater of the tax liability calculated using the AMT rules and that calculated using the regular income tax rules). The AMT rates (26 and 28 percent for the individual taxpayer and 20 percent for the corporate taxpayer) are applied to the AMT base. The AMT base is calculated by modifying taxable income for the following: (1) add tax preferences, (2) add certain adjustments, (3) deduct certain adjustments, and (4) deduct the exemption amount. §§ 55–59. See also *adjusted current earnings (ACE) adjustment* and *business untaxed reported profits.*

Alternative tax. An option that is allowed in computing the tax on net capital gain. The rate is 35 percent of net capital gain for corporations and 28 percent for noncorporate taxpayers. For 1988 through 1990, the alternative tax did not produce a beneficial result. For 1991 and thereafter, the alternative tax can produce beneficial results for the noncorporate taxpayer because the regular tax rates can be as high as 39.6 percent. §§ 1(h) and 1201. See also *net capital gain.*

Amortization. The allocation (and charge to expense) of the cost or other basis of an intangible asset over a statutory period of 15 years. Examples of amortizable intangibles include patents, copyrights, covenants not to compete, acquired goodwill, and leasehold interests. See also *estimated useful life* and *goodwill.*

Amount realized. The amount received by a taxpayer on the sale or other disposition of property. The amount realized is the sum of the cash and the fair market value of any property or services received, plus any related debt assumed by the buyer. Determining the amount realized is the starting point for arriving at realized gain or loss. The amount realized is defined in § 1001(b) and the related Regulations. See also *realized gain or loss* and *recognized gain or loss.*

Annuity. A fixed sum payable to a person at specified intervals for a specific period of time or for life. Payments represent a partial return of capital and a return (interest) on the capital investment. Therefore, an exclusion ratio must be used to compute the amount of nontaxable income. The exclusion ratio is used until the annuitant has recovered his or her investment in the annuity contract. Thereafter, all of the annuity payments received are included in gross income. If the annuitant dies before his or her investment is recovered, a deduction is allowed. § 72. See also *qualified pension or profit sharing plan.*

Appellate court. For Federal tax purposes, appellate courts include the Courts of Appeals and the Supreme Court. If the party losing in the trial (or lower) court is dissatisfied with the result, the dispute may be carried to the appropriate appellate court. See also *Court of Appeals* and *trial court.*

Arm's length transaction. The standard under which unrelated parties would determine an exchange price for a transaction. Suppose, for example, Cardinal Corporation sells property to its sole shareholder for $10,000. In testing whether the $10,000 is an "arm's length" price, one would ascertain the price that would have been negotiated between the corporation and an unrelated party in a bargained exchange.

Asset Depreciation Range system. A system of estimated useful lives for categories of tangible assets prescribed by the IRS. The system provides a range for each category that extends from 20 percent above to 20 percent below the guideline class lives prescribed by the IRS.

Assignment of income. A procedure whereby a taxpayer attempts to avoid the recognition of income by assigning the property that generates the income to another. Such a procedure will not avoid the recognition of income by the taxpayer making the assignment if it can be said that the income was earned at the point of the transfer. In this case, usually referred to as an anticipatory assignment of income, the income will be taxed to the person who earns it.

Association. An organization treated as a corporation for Federal tax purposes even though it may not qualify as such under applicable state law. An entity designated as a trust or a partnership, for example, may be classified as an association if it clearly possesses corporate attributes. Corporate attributes include centralized management, continuity of life, free transferability of interests, and limited liability. § 7701(a)(3).

At-risk limitation. Under the at-risk rules, a taxpayer's deductible losses from an activity for any taxable year are limited to the amount the taxpayer has at risk at the end of the taxable year. The initial amount considered at-risk is generally the sum of the amount of cash and the adjusted basis of property contributed to the activity and amounts borrowed for use in the activity for which the taxpayer is personally liable or has pledged as security property not used in the activity.

Attribution. Under certain circumstances, the tax law applies attribution rules to assign to one taxpayer the ownership interest of another taxpayer. If, for example, the stock of Gold Corporation is held 60 percent by Marsha and 40 percent by Sid, Marsha may be deemed to own 100 percent of Gold Corporation if she and Sid are mother and son. In that case, the stock owned by Sid is attributed to Marsha. See, for example, §§ 267 and 318.

Audit.   Inspection and verification of a taxpayer's return or other transactions possessing tax consequences. See also *correspondence audit*, *field audit*, and *office audit*.

Automatic mileage method.   See *automobile expenses*.

Automobile expenses.   Automobile expenses are generally deductible only to the extent the automobile is used in business or for the production of income. Personal commuting expenses are not deductible. The taxpayer may deduct actual expenses (including depreciation and insurance) or the standard (automatic) mileage rate may be used (27.5 cents per mile for 1991, 28 cents per mile for 1992, 28 cents per mile for 1993, and 29 cents per mile for 1994) during any one year. Automobile expenses incurred for medical purposes or in connection with job-related moving expenses are deductible to the extent of actual out-of-pocket expenses or at the rate of 9 cents per mile (12 cents for charitable activities). See also *transportation expenses*.

B

Bad debts.   A deduction is permitted if a business account receivable subsequently becomes partially or completely worthless, providing the income arising from the debt previously was included in income. Available methods are the specific charge-off method and the reserve method. However, except for certain financial institutions, TRA of 1986 repealed the use of the reserve method for 1987 and thereafter. If the reserve method is used, partially or totally worthless accounts are charged to the reserve. A nonbusiness bad debt deduction is allowed as a short-term capital loss if the loan did not arise in connection with the creditor's trade or business activities. Loans between related parties (family members) generally are classified as nonbusiness. § 166. See also *nonbusiness bad debts*.

Basis.   The acquisition cost assigned to an asset for income tax purposes. For assets acquired by purchase, the basis is the cost (§ 1012). Special rules govern the basis of property received by virtue of another's death (§ 1014) or by gift (§ 1015), the basis of stock received on a transfer of property to a controlled corporation (§ 358), the basis of the property transferred to the corporation (§ 362), and the basis of property received upon the liquidation of a corporation (§§ 334 and 338). See also *adjusted basis*.

Book value.   The net amount of an asset after reduction by a related reserve. The book value of accounts receivable, for example, is the face amount of the receivables less the reserve for bad debts. The book value of a building is the cost less the accumulated depreciation.

Boot.   Cash or property of a type not included in the definition of a nontaxable exchange. The receipt of boot will cause an otherwise nontaxable transfer to become taxable to the extent of the lesser of the fair market value of such boot or the realized gain on the transfer. Examples of nontaxable exchanges that could be partially or completely taxable due to the receipt of boot include transfers to controlled corporations [§ 351(b)] and like-kind exchanges [§ 1031(b)]. See also *realized gain or loss* and *recognized gain or loss*.

Bribes and illegal payments.   Section 162 denies a deduction for bribes or kickbacks, fines and penalties paid to a government official or employee for violation of law, and two-thirds of the treble damage payments made to claimants for violation of the antitrust law. Denial of a deduction for bribes and illegal payments is based upon the judicially established principle that allowing such payments would be contrary to public policy.

B.T.A.   The Board of Tax Appeals was a trial court that considered Federal tax matters. This court is now the U.S. Tax Court.

Burden of proof.   The requirement in a lawsuit to show the weight of evidence and thereby gain a favorable decision. Except in cases of tax fraud, the burden of proof in a tax case generally will be on the taxpayer.

Business bad debt.   A debt created or acquired in connection with a trade or business of the taxpayer, or a debt the loss from the worthlessness of which is incurred in the taxpayer's trade or business. A business bad debt is deducted as an ordinary deduction.

Business energy tax credit.   See *energy tax credit—business property*.

Business expenses.   See *trade or business expenses*.

Business gifts.   Business gifts are deductible only to the extent that each gift does not exceed $25 per person per year. Exceptions are made for gifts costing $4 or less and for certain employee awards. § 274(b).

Business untaxed reported profits.   Such profits are a positive adjustment for purposes of the corporate alternative minimum tax. For taxable years beginning after 1989, the amount is 75 percent of the excess of adjusted current earnings over the alternative minimum taxable income (AMTI). This adjustment was replaced in 1990 with the ACE adjustment. §§ 56(c)(1) and (g). See also *adjusted current earnings (ACE) adjustment* and *alternative minimum tax*.

C

Cafeteria benefit plan.   An employee benefit plan under which an employee is allowed to select from among a variety of employer-provided fringe benefits. Some of the benefits may be taxable and some may be statutory nontaxable benefits (e.g., health and accident insurance and group term life insurance). The employee is taxed only on the taxable benefits selected. A cafeteria benefit plan is also referred to as a flexible benefit plan.

Canons of taxation.   Criteria used in the selection of a tax base that were originally discussed by Adam Smith in *The*

Wealth of Nations. Canons of taxation include equality, convenience, certainty, and economy.

Capital asset. Broadly speaking, all assets are capital except those specifically excluded by the Code. Major categories of noncapital assets include property held for resale in the normal course of business (inventory), trade accounts and notes receivable, and depreciable property and real estate used in a trade or business (§ 1231 assets). § 1221. See also *capital gain* and *capital loss.*

Capital contributions. Various means by which a shareholder makes additional funds available to the corporation (placed at the risk of the business) without the receipt of additional stock. Such contributions are added to the basis of the shareholder's existing stock investment and do not generate income to the corporation. § 118.

Capital expenditure. An expenditure that should be added to the basis of the property improved. For income tax purposes, this generally precludes a full deduction for the expenditure in the year paid or incurred. Any capital recovery in the form of a tax deduction must come in the form of depreciation. § 263.

Capital gain. The gain from the sale or exchange of a capital asset. See also *capital asset* and *net capital gain.*

Capital gain net income. If the total capital gains for the tax year exceed the total capital losses, the result is capital gain net income. Note that the term does not distinguish between the long-term and short-term gains. § 1222(9). See also *net capital gain.*

Capital gain or loss holding period. The period of time that a capital asset is held by the taxpayer. To qualify for long-term treatment, the asset must be held for more than one year. See also *holding period.*

Capital loss. The loss from the sale or exchange of a capital asset. See also *capital asset.*

Cash basis. See *accounting method* and *cash method.*

Cash equivalent doctrine. Generally, a cash basis taxpayer does not report income until cash is constructively or actually received. Under the cash equivalent doctrine, cash basis taxpayers are required to report income if they receive the equivalent of cash (e.g., property is received) in a taxable transaction.

Cash method. See *cash receipts method.*

Cash receipts method. A method of accounting under which the taxpayer generally reports income when cash is collected and reports expenses when cash payments are made. However, for fixed assets, the cash basis taxpayer claims deductions through depreciation or amortization in the same manner as an accrual basis taxpayer. Prepaid expenses must be capitalized and amortized if the life of the asset extends "substantially beyond" the end of the tax year. See also *constructive receipt.*

Casualty loss. A casualty is defined as "the complete or partial destruction of property resulting from an identifiable event of a sudden, unexpected or unusual nature" (e.g., floods, storms, fires, auto accidents). Individuals may deduct a casualty loss only if the loss is incurred in a trade or business or in a transaction entered into for profit or arises from fire, storm, shipwreck, or other casualty or from theft. Individuals usually deduct personal casualty losses as itemized deductions subject to a $100 nondeductible amount and to an annual floor equal to 10 percent of adjusted gross income that applies after the $100 per casualty floor has been applied. Special rules are provided for the netting of certain casualty gains and losses. See also *disaster loss* and *Section 1231 gains and losses.*

C corporation. A corporation that has not elected conduit treatment under § 1361. See also *S corporation status.*

Cert. den. By denying the Writ of Certiorari, the U.S. Supreme Court refuses to accept an appeal from a U.S. Court of Appeals. The denial of certiorari does not, however, mean that the U.S. Supreme Court agrees with the result reached by the lower court.

Certiorari. Appeal from a U.S. Court of Appeals to the U.S. Supreme Court is by Writ of Certiorari. The Supreme Court does not have to accept the appeal and usually does not (*cert. den.*) unless there is a conflict among the lower courts that needs to be resolved or a constitutional issue is involved.

Change in accounting method. A change in the taxpayer's method of accounting (e.g., from FIFO to LIFO) generally requires prior approval from the IRS. Generally, a request must be filed within 180 days after the beginning of the taxable year of the desired change. In some instances, the permission for change will not be granted unless the taxpayer agrees to certain adjustments prescribed by the IRS.

Change in accounting period. A taxpayer must obtain the consent of the IRS before changing his or her tax year. Income for the short period created by the change must be annualized.

Charitable contributions. Contributions are deductible (subject to various restrictions and ceiling limitations) if made to qualified nonprofit charitable organizations. A cash basis taxpayer is entitled to a deduction solely in the year of payment. Accrual basis corporations may accrue contributions at year-end if payment is properly authorized before the end of the year and payment is made within two and one-half months after the end of the year. § 170.

Child and dependent care credit. A tax credit ranging from 20 percent to 30 percent of employment-related expenses (child and dependent care expenses) for amounts of up to $4,800 is available to individuals who are employed (or deemed to be employed) and maintain a household for a dependent child under age 13, disabled spouse, or disabled dependent. § 21.

Child support payments. Payments for child support do not constitute alimony and are therefore not includible in gross income by the recipient or deductible as alimony by the payor. Generally, none of the amounts paid are regarded as child support unless the divorce decree or separation agreement specifically calls for child support payments. However, if the amount of the payment to the former spouse would be reduced upon the happening of a contingency related to a child (e.g., the child attains age 21 or dies), the amount of the future reduction in the payment will be deemed child support for post-1984 agreements and decrees. § 71(c). See also *alimony payments.*

Circuit Court of Appeals.   See *Court of Appeals.*

Claim of right doctrine.   A judicially imposed doctrine applicable to both cash and accrual basis taxpayers that holds that an amount is includible in income upon actual or constructive receipt if the taxpayer has an unrestricted claim to the payment. For the tax treatment of amounts repaid when previously included in income under the claim of right doctrine, see § 1341.

Claims Court.   One of three Federal trial courts that consider Federal tax controversy. Now known as the U.S. Court of Federal Claims, appeal from this court (formerly to the U.S. Supreme Court) now goes to the Court of Appeals for the Federal Circuit. See also *trial court.*

Clear reflection of income.   The IRS has the authority to redetermine a taxpayer's income using a method that clearly reflects income if the taxpayer's method does not do so. § 446(b). In addition, the IRS may apportion or allocate income among various related businesses if income is not "clearly reflected." § 482.

Closely held corporation.   A corporation where the stock ownership is not widely dispersed. Instead, a few shareholders are in control of corporate policy and are in a position to benefit personally from that policy.

Community property.   Louisiana, Texas, New Mexico, Arizona, California, Washington, Idaho, Nevada, and Wisconsin have community property systems. The rest of the states are classified as common law jurisdictions. The difference between common law and community property systems centers around the property rights possessed by married persons. In a common law system, each spouse owns whatever he or she earns. Under a community property system, one-half of the earnings of each spouse is considered owned by the other spouse. Assume, for example, Alice and Jeff are husband and wife and their only income is the $50,000 annual salary Jeff receives. If they live in New York (a common law state), the $50,000 salary belongs to Jeff. If, however, they live in Texas (a community property state), the $50,000 salary is divided equally, in terms of ownership, between Jeff and Alice. See also *separate property.*

Compensatory damages.   Damages received or paid by the taxpayer can be classified as compensatory damages or as punitive damages. Compensatory damages are those paid to compensate one for harm caused by another. Compensatory damages are excludible from the recipient's gross income. See *punitive damages.*

Completed contract method.   A method of reporting gain or loss on certain long-term contracts. Under this method of accounting, gross income and expenses are recognized in the tax year in which the contract is completed. Reg. § 1.451–3. Limitations exist on a taxpayer's ability to use the completed contract method. § 460. See also *percentage of completion method* and *long-term contracts.*

Component depreciation.   The process of dividing an asset (e.g., a building) into separate components or parts for the purpose of calculating depreciation. The advantage of dividing an asset into components is to use shorter depreciation lives for selected components under § 167. Generally, the same cost recovery period must be used for all the components of an asset under § 168.

Condemnation.   The taking of property by a public authority. The property is condemned as the result of legal action, and the owner is compensated by the public authority. The power to condemn property is known as the right of eminent domain.

Conduit concept.   An approach assumed by the tax law in the treatment of certain entities and their owners. Specific tax characteristics pass through the entity without losing their identity. For example, items of income and expense, capital gains and losses, tax credits, etc., realized by a partnership pass through the partnership (a conduit) and are subject to taxation at the partner level. Also, in an S corporation, certain items pass through and are reported on the returns of the shareholders.

Constructive ownership.   See *attribution.*

Constructive receipt.   If income is unqualifiedly available, it will be subject to the income tax even though it is not physically in the taxpayer's possession. An example is accrued interest on a savings account. Under the constructive receipt of income concept, the interest will be taxed to a depositor in the year it is available rather than the year actually withdrawn. The fact that the depositor uses the cash basis of accounting for tax purposes is irrelevant. See Reg. § 1.451–2.

Consumer interest.   Interest expense of the taxpayer of a personal nature (not trade or business interest, investment interest, qualified residence interest, or passive activity interest). TRA of 1986 provided that no deduction is permitted for consumer interest. However, the provision was not fully effective until 1991. § 163(h). See also *qualified residence interest.*

Contributions to the capital of a corporation.   See *capital contributions.*

Convention expenses.   Travel expenses incurred in attending a convention are deductible if the meetings are related to a taxpayer's trade or business or job-related activities. If, however, the convention trip is primarily for pleasure, no deduction is permitted for transportation expenses. Likewise, if the expenses are for attending a convention related to the production of income (§ 212), no deduction is permitted. Specific limitations are provided for foreign convention expenses. See § 274(n) for the limitations on the deductions for meals. § 274(h).

Correspondence audit. An audit conducted by the IRS by mail. Typically, the IRS writes to the taxpayer requesting the verification of a particular deduction, exemption, or credit. The completion of a special form or the remittance of copies of records or other support is all that is requested of the taxpayer. To be distinguished from a *field audit* or an *office audit*.

Cost depletion. Depletion that is calculated based on the adjusted basis of the asset. The adjusted basis is divided by the expected recoverable units to determine the depletion per unit. The depletion per unit is multiplied by the units sold during the tax year to calculate cost depletion. See also *percentage depletion*.

Cost recovery allowance. The portion of the cost of an asset written off under ACRS (or MACRS), which replaced the depreciation system as a method for writing off the cost of an asset for most assets placed in service after 1980 (after 1986 for MACRS). § 168. See also *alternative depreciation system*.

Cost recovery period. A period specified in the Code for writing off the cost of an asset under ACRS or MACRS.

Court of Appeals. Any of 13 Federal courts that consider tax matters appealed from the U.S. Tax Court, U.S. Court of Federal Claims, or a U.S. District Court. Appeal from a U.S. Court of Appeals is to the U.S. Supreme Court by Writ of Certiorari. See also *appellate court*.

Court of Federal Claims. See *Claims Court*.

Court of original jurisdiction. The Federal courts are divided into courts of original jurisdiction and appellate courts. The dispute between the taxpayer and the IRS is first considered by a court of original jurisdiction (i.e., a trial court). The four Federal courts of original jurisdiction are the U.S. Tax Court, U.S. District Court, the Court of Federal Claims, and the Small Claims Division of the U.S. Tax Court. See *Court of Appeals*.

Credit for child and dependent care. See *child and dependent care credit*.

D

Death benefit. A payment made by an employer to the beneficiary or beneficiaries of a deceased employee on account of the death of the employee. Under certain conditions, the first $5,000 of the payment is exempt from the income tax. § 101(b)(1).

Death tax. See *estate tax*.

Declaration of estimated tax. A procedure whereby individuals and corporations are required to make quarterly installment payments of estimated tax. Individuals are required to make the declaration and file quarterly payments of the estimated tax if certain requirements are met. In 1994, a declaration is not required for an individual whose estimated tax is reasonably expected to be less than $500.

Deductions for adjusted gross income. See *adjusted gross income*.

Deductions from adjusted gross income. See *itemized deductions*.

Deferred compensation. Compensation that will be taxed when received or upon the removal of certain restrictions on receipt and not when earned. Contributions by an employer to a qualified pension or profit sharing plan on behalf of an employee are an example. The contributions will not be taxed to the employee until the funds are made available or distributed to the employee (e.g., upon retirement). See also *qualified pension or profit sharing plan*.

Deficiency. Additional tax liability owed by a taxpayer and assessed by the IRS. See also *statutory notice of deficiency*.

Defined benefit plan. Qualified plans can be dichotomized into defined benefit plans and defined contribution plans. Under a defined benefit plan, a formula defines the benefits employees are to receive. The formula usually includes years of service, employee compensation, and some stated percentage. The employer must make annual contributions based on actuarial computations that will be sufficient to pay the vested retirement benefits. See also *defined contribution plan* and *pension plan*.

Defined contribution plan. Qualified plans can be dichotomized into defined benefit plans and defined contribution plans. Under a defined contribution plan, a separate account is maintained for each covered employee. The employee's benefits under the plan are based solely on (1) the amount contributed and (2) income from the fund that accrues to the employee's account. The plan defines the amount the employer is required to contribute (e.g., a flat dollar amount, an amount based on a special formula, or an amount equal to a certain percentage of compensation). See also *defined benefit plan* and *pension plan*.

De minimis fringe. Benefits provided to employees that are too insignificant to warrant the time and effort required to account for the benefits received by each employee and the value of those benefits. Such amounts are excludible from the employee's gross income. § 132.

Dependency deduction. See *personal and dependency exemptions*.

Depletion. The process by which the cost or other basis of a natural resource (e.g., an oil or gas interest) is recovered upon extraction and sale of the resource. The two ways to determine the depletion allowance are the cost and percentage (or statutory) methods. Under the cost method, each unit of production sold is assigned a portion of the cost or other basis of the interest. This is determined by dividing the cost or other basis by the total units expected to be recovered. Under the percentage (or statutory) method, the tax law provides a special percentage factor for different types of minerals and other natural resources. This percentage is multiplied by the gross income from the interest to arrive at the depletion allowance. §§ 613 and 613A.

Depreciation. The deduction of the cost or other basis of a tangible asset over the asset's estimated useful life. § 167. For intangible assets, see *amortization*. For natural resources, see *depletion*. Also see *estimated useful life*. The depreciation system was replaced by ACRS for most assets placed in service after 1980 (by MACRS for most assets placed in service after 1986) but still applies for assets placed in service before 1981. See also *recapture of depreciation*.

Determination letter. Upon the request of a taxpayer, a District Director will comment on the tax status of a completed transaction. Determination letters are most frequently used to clarify employee versus self-employed status, to determine whether a pension or profit sharing plan qualifies under the Code, and to determine the tax-exempt status of certain nonprofit organizations.

Direct charge-off method. See *specific charge-off method*.

Disabled access credit. A tax credit whose purpose is to encourage small businesses to make their businesses more accessible to disabled individuals. The credit is equal to 50 percent of the eligible expenditures that exceed $250 but do not exceed $10,250. Thus, the maximum amount for the credit is $5,000. The adjusted basis for depreciation is reduced by the amount of the credit. § 44. See also *general business credit*.

Disaster area loss. A casualty sustained in an area designated as a disaster area by the President of the United States. In such an event, the disaster loss may be treated as having occurred in the taxable year immediately preceding the year in which the disaster actually occurred. Thus, immediate tax benefits are provided to victims of a disaster. § 165(i). See also *casualty loss*.

Dissent. To disagree with the majority. If, for example, Judge Brown disagrees with the result reached by Judges Charles and Davis (all of whom are members of the same court), Judge Brown could issue a dissenting opinion.

District Court. A Federal District Court is a trial court for purposes of litigating (among others) Federal tax matters. It is the only trial court where a jury trial can be obtained. See also *trial court*.

Dividends received deduction. A deduction allowed a shareholder that is a corporation for dividends received from a domestic corporation. The percentage applied in calculating the dividends received deduction varies according to the percentage of stock ownership. If the stock ownership percentage is less than 20 percent, the percentage is 70 percent of the dividends received. If the stock ownership percentage is at least 20 percent but less than 80 percent, the percentage is 80 percent. If the stock ownership percentage is at least 80 percent, the percentage is 100 percent. §§ 243–246A.

Dollar value lifo. An inventory technique that focuses on the dollars invested in the inventory rather than the particular items on hand each period. Each inventory item is assigned to a pool. A pool is a collection of similar items and is treated as a separate inventory. At the end of the period, each pool is valued in terms of prices at the time LIFO was adopted (base period prices), whether or not the particular items were actually on hand in the year LIFO was adopted, to compare with current prices to determine if there has been an increase or decrease in inventories.

E

Earned income. Income from personal services as distinguished from income generated by property. See §§ 32 and 911 and the related Regulations.

Earned income credit. A refundable tax credit whose purpose is to provide assistance to certain low-income individuals. To receive the most beneficial treatment, the taxpayer must have qualifying children. However, it is possible to qualify for the credit without having a child. To calculate the credit for a taxpayer with one or more children for 1994, a statutory rate of 26.3 percent is multiplied by the earned income (subject to a statutory maximum of $7,750 with one qualifying child or $8,425 with two or more qualifying children). Once the earned income exceeds $11,000, the credit is phased out using a 15.98 percent rate for one qualifying child and a 17.68 percent rate for two or more qualifying children. For the qualifying taxpayer without children, the credit is calculated on a maximum earned income of $4,000 applying a 7.65 percent rate with the phaseout beginning at $5,000 applying the same rate. § 32.

Earnings and profits. A tax concept peculiar to corporate taxpayers that measures economic capacity to make a distribution to shareholders that is not a return of capital. Such a distribution will result in dividend income to the shareholders to the extent of the corporation's current and accumulated earnings and profits.

Economic income. The change in the taxpayer's net worth, as measured in terms of market values, plus the value of the assets the taxpayer consumed during the year. Because of the impracticality of this income model, it is not used for tax purposes. See also *accounting income*.

Economic performance test. One of the requirements that must be satisfied in order for an accrual basis taxpayer to deduct an expense. The accrual basis taxpayer first must satisfy the all events test. That test is not deemed satisfied until economic performance occurs. This occurs, when property or services are provided to the taxpayer, or in the case in which the taxpayer is required to provide property or services, whenever the property or services are actually provided by the taxpayer. See also *all events test*.

Education expenses. Employees may deduct education expenses if such items are incurred either (1) to maintain or improve existing job-related skills or (2) to meet the express requirements of the employer or the requirements imposed by law to retain employment status. The expenses are not deductible if the education is required to meet the minimum educational standards for the taxpayer's job or if the education qualifies the individual for a new trade or business. Reg. § 1.162–5.

Educational savings bonds.   United States Series EE bonds whose proceeds are used for qualified higher educational expenses for the taxpayer, the taxpayer's spouse, or a dependent. The interest may be excluded from gross income, provided the taxpayer's adjusted gross income does not exceed certain amounts. § 135.

Employee expenses.   The deductions *for* adjusted gross income include reimbursed expenses and certain expenses of performing artists. All other employee expenses are deductible *from* adjusted gross income. § 62. See also *trade or business expenses*.

Employee stock ownership plan (ESOP).   A type of defined contribution plan that qualifies as a tax-exempt employee trust. The ESOP must invest primarily in qualifying employer securities. A major benefit of an ESOP to the employer corporation is that it can contribute stock rather than cash, and receive a tax deduction equal to the fair market value of the stock.

Employment taxes.   Employment taxes are those taxes that an employer must pay on account of its employees. Employment taxes include FICA (Federal Insurance Contributions Act) and FUTA (Federal Unemployment Tax Act) taxes. Employment taxes are paid to the IRS in addition to income tax withholdings at specified intervals. Such taxes can be levied on the employees, the employer, or both. See also *FICA tax* and *FUTA tax*.

Energy tax credit—business property.   A 10 percent tax credit is available to businesses that invest in certain energy property. The purpose of the credit is to create incentives for conservation and to penalize the increased use of oil and gas. The business energy tax credit applies to equipment with an estimated useful life of at least three years that uses fuel or feedstock other than oil or natural gas (e.g., solar, geothermal). §§ 46(2) and 48(a). See also *estimated useful life* and *investment tax credit*.

Entertainment expenses.   These expenses are deductible only if they are directly related to or associated with a trade or business. Various restrictions and documentation requirements have been imposed upon the deductibility of entertainment expenses to prevent abuses by taxpayers. See, for example, the provision contained in § 274(n) that disallows 50 percent of entertainment expenses. § 274.

Estate tax.   A tax imposed on the right to transfer property by reason of death. Thus, an estate tax is levied on the decedent's estate and not on the heir receiving the property. §§ 2001 and 2002. See also *inheritance* tax.

Estimated tax.   The amount of tax (including alternative minimum tax and self-employment tax) an individual expects to owe for the year after subtracting tax credits and income tax withheld. The estimated tax must be paid in installments at designated intervals (e.g. for the individual taxpayer, by April 15, June 15, September 15, and January 15 of the following year).

Estimated useful life.   The period over which an asset will be used by a particular taxpayer. Although the period cannot be longer than the estimated physical life of an asset, it could be shorter if the taxpayer does not intend to keep the asset until it wears out. Assets such as goodwill do not have an estimated useful life. The estimated useful life of an asset is essential to measuring the annual tax deduction for depreciation and amortization. An asset subject to ACRS or MACRS is written off over a specified cost recovery period rather than over its estimated useful life. In addition, most intangibles are now amortized over a 15-year statutory period.

Excise tax.   A tax on the manufacture, sale, or use of goods or on the carrying on of an occupation or activity. Also a tax on the transfer of property. Thus, the Federal estate and gift taxes are, theoretically, excise taxes.

Extraordinary personal services.   These are services provided by individuals where the customers' use of the property is incidental to their receipt of the services. For example, a patient's use of a hospital bed is incidental to his or her use of medical services. This is one of the six exceptions to determine whether an activity is a passive rental activity.

F

Fair market value.   The amount at which property would change hands between a willing buyer and a willing seller, neither being under any compulsion to buy or sell and both having reasonable knowledge of the relevant facts. Reg. § 20.2031–1(b).

F.2d.   An abbreviation for the Second Series of the *Federal Reporter*, the official series where decisions of the U.S. Claims Court (before October 1982) and the U.S. Courts of Appeals are published.

F.Supp.   The abbreviation for the *Federal Supplement*, the official series where the reported decisions of the U.S. District Courts are published.

Federal district court.   See *district court*.

FICA tax.   An abbreviation which stands for Federal Insurance Contributions Act, commonly referred to as the Social Security tax. The FICA tax is comprised of the Social Security tax (old age, survivors, and disability insurance) and the Medicare tax (hospital insurance) and is imposed on both employers and employees. See also *employment taxes*.

Field audit.   An audit by the IRS conducted on the business premises of the taxpayer or in the office of the tax practitioner representing the taxpayer. To be distinguished from a *correspondence audit* or an *office audit*.

Finalized regulation. See *regulations.*

First-in, first-out (FIFO). An accounting method for determining the cost of inventories. Under this method, the inventory on hand is deemed to be the sum of the cost of the most recently acquired units. See also *last-in, first-out (LIFO).*

Fixing-up expense. An expense that is incurred to assist in the sale of a residence and is deductible in calculating the adjusted sales price. Fixing-up expenses include such items as ordinary repairs, painting, and wallpapering. To qualify, the expense must (1) be incurred on work performed during the 90-day period ending on the date of the contract of sale, (2) be paid within 30 days after the date of the sale, and (3) not be a capital expenditure. § 1034. See also *adjusted sales price.*

Foreign earned income exclusion. The foreign earned income exclusion is a relief provision that applies to U.S. citizens working in a foreign country. To qualify for the exclusion, the taxpayer must be either a bona fide resident of the foreign country or present in the country for 330 days during any 12 consecutive months. The exclusion is limited to $70,000. § 911.

Foreign tax credit or deduction. Both individual taxpayers and corporations may claim a foreign tax credit on income earned and subject to tax in a foreign country or U.S. possession. As an alternative to the credit, a deduction may be taken for the foreign taxes paid. §§ 27, 164, and 901–905.

Franchise. An agreement that gives the transferee the right to distribute, sell, or provide goods, services, or facilities within a specified area. The cost of obtaining a franchise may be amortized over a statutory period of 15 years. In general, the franchisor's gain on the sale of franchise rights is an ordinary gain because the franchisor retains a significant power, right, or continuing interest in the subject of the franchise. §§ 197 and 1253.

Franchise tax. A tax levied on the right to do business in a state as a corporation. Although income considerations may come into play, the tax usually is based on the capitalization of the corporation.

Fringe benefits. Compensation or other benefits received by an employee that are not in the form of cash. Some fringe benefits (e.g., accident and health plans, group term life insurance) may be excluded from the employee's gross income and therefore are not subject to the Federal income tax.

Fruit and the tree metaphor. The courts have held that an individual who earns income from property or services cannot assign that income to another. For example, a father cannot assign his earnings from commissions to his child and escape income tax on those amounts.

FUTA tax. An employment tax levied on employers. Jointly administered by the Federal and state governments, the tax provides funding for unemployment benefits. FUTA applies at a rate of 6.2 percent in 1994 on the first $7,000 of covered wages paid during the year for each employee. The Federal government allows a credit for FUTA paid (or allowed under a merit rating system) to the state. The credit cannot exceed 5.4 percent of the covered wages. See also *unemployment taxes.*

G

General business credit. The summation of various non-refundable business credits, including the investment tax credit, jobs credit, research activities credit, low-income housing credit, and disabled access credit. The amount of general business credit that can be used to reduce the tax liability is limited to the taxpayer's net income tax reduced by the greater of (1) the tentative minimum tax or (2) 25 percent of the net regular tax liability that exceeds $25,000. Unused general business credits can be carried back 3 years and forward 15 years. § 38.

Gift. A transfer of property for less than adequate consideration. Gifts usually occur in a personal setting (such as between members of the same family). Gifts are excluded from the income tax but may be subject to the *gift tax.*

Gift tax. A tax imposed on the transfer of property by gift. The tax is imposed upon the donor of a gift and is based upon the fair market value of the property on the date of the gift. §§ 2501–2524.

Golden parachute payments. A severance payment to employees that meets the following requirements: (1) the payment is contingent on a change of ownership of a corporation through a stock or asset acquisition and (2) the aggregate present value of the payment equals or exceeds three times the employee's average annual compensation. To the extent the severance payment meets these conditions, a deduction is disallowed to the employer for the excess of the payment over a statutory base amount (a five-year average of compensation if the taxpayer was an employee for the entire five-year period). In addition, a 20 percent excise tax is imposed on the employee who receives the excess severance pay. §§ 280G and 4999.

Goodwill. The ability of a business to generate income in excess of a normal rate on assets due to superior managerial skills, market position, new product technology, etc. In the purchase of a business, goodwill represents the difference between the purchase price and the fair market value of the net assets acquired. Goodwill is an intangible asset that possesses an indefinite life. However, since acquired goodwill is a § 197 intangible asset, it is amortized over a 15-year statutory period. Self-created goodwill cannot be amortized. Reg. § 1.167(a)–3. See also *amortization.*

Government bonds issued at a discount. Certain U.S. government bonds (Series E and EE) are issued at a discount and do not pay interest during the life of the bonds. Instead, the bonds are redeemable at increasing fixed amounts. Thus, the difference between the purchase price and the amount received upon redemption represents interest income to the holder. A cash basis taxpayer may defer recognition of gross income until the bonds are redeemed. For Series EE savings bonds issued after 1989, the interest otherwise taxable at redemption can be excluded if the bonds are qualified educational savings bonds. As an alternative to deferring recognition of gross income until the bonds are redeemed, the taxpayer may elect to include in gross income on an annual basis the annual increase in the value of the bonds. § 454.

Gross income.   Income subject to the Federal income tax. Gross income does not include income for which the Code permits exclusion treatment (e.g., interest on municipal bonds). For a manufacturing or merchandising business, gross income means gross profit (gross sales or gross receipts less cost of goods sold). § 61 and Reg. § 1.61–3(a).

Group term life insurance.   Life insurance coverage permitted by an employer for a group of employees. Such insurance is renewable on a year-to-year basis and does not accumulate in value (i.e., no cash surrender value is built up). The premiums paid by the employer on the insurance are not taxed to an employee on coverage of up to $50,000 per person. § 79 and Reg. § 1.79–1(a).

H

Half-year convention.   The half-year convention is a cost recovery convention that assumes all property is placed in service at mid-year and thus provides for a half-year's cost recovery for that year.

Head of household.   An unmarried individual who maintains a household for another and satisfies certain conditions set forth in § 2(b). Such status enables the taxpayer to use a set of income tax rates [see § 1(b)] that are lower than those applicable to other unmarried individuals [§ 1(c)] but higher than those applicable to surviving spouses and married persons filing a joint return [§ 1(a)]. See also *tax rate schedules*.

Highly compensated employee.   The employee group is generally divided into two categories for fringe benefit (including pension and profit sharing plans) purposes. These are (1) highly compensated employees and (2) non-highly compensated employees. For most fringe benefits, if the fringe benefit plan discriminates in favor of highly compensated employees, it will not be a qualified plan with respect, at a minimum, to the highly compensated employees.

Hobby loss.   A nondeductible loss arising from a personal hobby as contrasted with an activity engaged in for profit. Generally, the law provides a rebuttable presumption that an activity is engaged in for profit if profits are earned during any three or more years during a five-year period. § 183. See also *vacation home*.

Holding period.   The period of time property has been held for income tax purposes. The holding period is crucial in determining whether gain or loss from the sale or exchange of a capital asset is long term or short term. § 1223. See also *capital gain or loss holding period*.

Home office expenses.   See *office-in-the-home expenses*.

H.R. 10 plan.   See *self-employment retirement plan*.

Hybrid method.   A combination of the accrual and cash methods of accounting. That is, the taxpayer may account for some items of income on the accrual method (e.g., sales and cost of goods sold) and other items (e.g., interest income) on the cash method.

I

Imputed interest.   For certain long-term sales of property, the IRS can convert some of the gain from the sale into interest income if the contract does not provide for a minimum rate of interest to be paid by the purchaser. The application of this procedure has the effect of forcing the seller to recognize less long-term capital gain and more ordinary income (interest income). §§ 483 and 1274 and the Regulations thereunder. In addition, interest income and interest expense are imputed (deemed to exist) on interest-free or below-market rate loans between certain related parties. § 7872. See also *interest-free loans*.

Incentive stock option.   A type of stock option which receives favorable tax treatment. If various qualification requirements can be satisfied, there are no recognition tax consequences when the stock option is granted. However, the spread (the excess of the fair market value at the date of exercise over the option price) is a tax preference item for purposes of the alternative minimum tax. The gain on disposition of the stock resulting from the exercise of the stock option will be classified as long-term capital gain if certain holding period requirements are met (the employee must not dispose of the stock within two years after the option is granted or within one year after acquiring the stock). § 422. See *nonqualified stock option (NQSO)*.

Income.   For tax purposes, an increase in wealth that has been realized.

Independent contractor.   A self-employed person as distinguished from one who is employed as an employee.

Individual retirement account (IRA).   Individuals with earned income who are not active participants in qualified retirement plans are permitted to set aside up to 100 percent of their salary per year (generally not to exceed $2,000 or $2,250 for a spousal IRA) for a retirement account. The amount set aside can be deducted by the taxpayer and will be subject to income tax only upon withdrawal. Specific requirements are established for the withdrawal of such funds, and penalties are provided for failure to comply. If the employee is an active participant in a qualified retirement plan, the IRA deduction is phased out once adjusted gross income exceeds certain amounts. Even if the IRA deduction has been completely phased out, the taxpayer can still make a nondeductible contribution. § 219. See also *simplified employee pensions*.

Inheritance tax. An excise tax levied on the heir based on the value of property received from a decedent. See also *estate tax.*

Installment method. A method of accounting enabling a taxpayer to spread the recognition of gain on the sale of property over the payout period. Under this procedure, the seller computes the gross profit percentage from the sale (the gain divided by the contract price) and applies it to each payment received to arrive at the gain to be recognized. §§ 453 and 453A.

Intangible drilling and development costs. Taxpayers may elect to expense or capitalize (subject to amortization) intangible drilling and development costs. However, ordinary income recapture provisions apply to oil and gas properties on a sale or other disposition if the expense method is elected. §§ 263(c) and 1254(a).

Interest-free loans. Bona fide loans that carry no interest (or a below-market rate). If made in a nonbusiness setting, the imputed interest element is treated as a gift from the lender to the borrower. If made by a corporation to a shareholder, a constructive dividend could result. In either event, the lender may recognize interest income and the borrower may be able to deduct interest expense. § 7872.

Interpretive regulation. A Regulation issued by the Treasury Department which purports to explain the meaning of a particular Code Section. An interpretive Regulation is given less deference than a legislative Regulation. See also *legislative regulation* and *procedural regulation.* § 7805.

Investigation of a new business. Expenditures by taxpayers who are not engaged in a trade or business incurred in the evaluation of prospective business activities (acquiring an existing business or entering into a new trade or business). If the expenditures are general, it is the position of the IRS that no deduction is permitted even if the investigation is abandoned because the taxpayer is not engaged in a trade or business. The courts, however, have permitted a loss deduction providing the expenditures were specific.

Investment indebtedness. If funds are borrowed by noncorporate taxpayers for the purpose of purchasing or continuing to hold investment property, some portion of the interest expense deduction may be disallowed. The interest deduction is generally limited to net investment income. Amounts that are disallowed may be carried forward and treated as investment interest of the succeeding year. § 163(d).

Investment tax credit. A tax credit that usually was equal to 10 percent (unless a reduced credit was elected) of the qualified investment in tangible personalty used in a trade or business. If the tangible personalty had a recovery period of five years or more, the full cost of the property qualified for the credit. Only 60 percent of cost qualified for property with a recovery period of three years. However, the regular investment tax credit was repealed by TRA of 1986 for property placed in service after December 31, 1985. §§ 46–48. See also *general business credit, recapture of investment tax credit,* and *Section 38 property.*

Involuntary conversion. The loss or destruction of property through theft, casualty, or condemnation. Any gain realized on an involuntary conversion can, at the taxpayer's election, be postponed (deferred) for Federal income tax purposes if the owner reinvests the proceeds within a prescribed period of time in property that is similar or related in service or use. § 1033. See also *nontaxable exchange.*

IRA. See *individual retirement account.*

Itemized deductions. Certain personal expenditures allowed by the Code as deductions *from* adjusted gross income. Examples include certain medical expenses, interest on home mortgages, and charitable contributions. Itemized deductions are reported on Schedule A of Form 1040. Certain miscellaneous itemized deductions are reduced by 2 percent of the taxpayer's adjusted gross income. In addition, a taxpayer whose adjusted gross income exceeds $100,000 ($50,000 for married filing separately) must reduce the itemized deductions by 3 percent of the excess of adjusted gross income over $100,000. For 1994, the indexed amount for the $100,000 is $111,800, and the indexed amount for the $50,000 is $55,900. Medical, casualty and theft, and investment interest deductions are not subject to the 3 percent reduction. The 3 percent reduction may not reduce itemized deductions that are subject to the reduction to below 20 percent of their initial amount. §§ 63(d), 67, and 68.

J

Jobs credit. Employers are allowed a tax credit equal to 40 percent of the first $6,000 of wages (per eligible employee) for the first year of employment. Eligible employees include certain hard-to-employ individuals (e.g., youths from low-income families, handicapped persons). The employer's deduction for wages is reduced by the amount of the credit taken. For qualified summer youth employees, the 40 percent rate is applied to the first $3,000 of qualified wages. §§ 51 and 52.

K

Keogh plan. See *self-employment retirement plan.*

L

Last-in, first-out (LIFO). An accounting method for valuing inventories for tax purposes. Under this method, it is assumed that the inventory on hand is valued at the cost of the earliest acquired units. § 472 and the related Regulations. See also *first-in, first-out (FIFO).*

Least aggregate deferral method. An algorithm set forth in the Regulations to determine the tax year for a partnership with partners whose tax years differ. The tax year is selected which produces the least aggregate deferral of income.

Legislative regulation. Some Code Sections give the Secretary of the Treasury or his delegate the authority to prescribe Regulations to carry out the details of administration or to otherwise complete the operating rules. Regulations issued pursuant to this type of authority truly possess the force and effect of law. In effect, Congress is almost delegating its legislative powers to the Treasury Department. See also *interpretive regulation* and *procedural regulation.*

Lessee. One who rents property from another. In the case of real estate, the lessee is also known as the tenant.

Lessor. One who rents property to another. In the case of real estate, the lessor is also known as the landlord.

Letter rulings. Issued upon a taxpayer's request, by the National Office of the IRS, they describe how the IRS will treat a proposed transaction for tax purposes. They apply only to the taxpayer who asks for and obtains the ruling, but post-1984 rulings may be substantial authority for purposes of avoiding the accuracy-related penalties. The IRS limits the issuance of letter rulings to restricted, preannounced areas of taxation.

Life insurance proceeds. Generally, life insurance proceeds paid to a beneficiary upon the death of the insured are exempt from Federal income tax. An exception is provided when a life insurance contract has been transferred for valuable consideration to another individual who assumes ownership rights. In that case, the proceeds are income to the assignee to the extent that the proceeds exceed the amount paid for the policy plus any subsequent premiums paid. Insurance proceeds may be subject to the Federal estate tax if the decedent retained any incidents of ownership in the policy before death or if the proceeds are payable to the decedent's estate. §§ 101 and 2042.

Like-kind exchange. An exchange of property held for productive use in a trade or business or for investment (except inventory, stocks and bonds, and partnership interests) for other investment or trade or business property. Unless non-like-kind property is received (boot), the exchange will be nontaxable. § 1031. See also *boot* and *nontaxable exchange.*

Limited expensing. See *Section 179 expensing.*

Liquidation of a corporation. In a complete or partial liquidation of a corporation, amounts received by the shareholders in exchange for their stock are usually treated as a sale or exchange of the stock resulting in capital gain or loss treatment. § 331. Special rules apply to the liquidation of a subsidiary under § 332. Generally, a liquidation is a taxable event to the corporation. § 336. Special rules apply to a parent corporation that is liquidating a subsidiary. § 337.

Listed property. The term listed property includes (1) any passenger automobile, (2) any other property used as a means of transportation, (3) any property of a type generally used for purposes of entertainment, recreation, or amusement, (4) any computer or peripheral equipment (with an exception for exclusive business use), (5) any cellular telephone (or other similar telecommunications equipment), and (6) any other property of a type specified in Regulations. If listed property is predominantly used for business, the taxpayer is allowed to use the statutory percentage method of cost recovery. Otherwise, the straight-line cost recovery method must be used.

Long-term contract. A building, installation, construction, or manufacturing contract that is entered into but not completed within the same tax year. A manufacturing contract is a long-term contract only if the contract is to manufacture (1) a unique item not normally carried in finished goods inventory or (2) items that normally require more than 12 calendar months to complete. The two available methods to account for long-term contracts are the percentage of completion method and the completed contract method. The completed contract method can be used only in limited circumstances. § 460. See also *completed contract method* and *percentage of completion method.*

Lower of cost or market. An elective inventory method, whereby the taxpayer may value inventories at the lower of the taxpayer's actual cost, or the current replacement cost of the goods. This method cannot be used in conjunction with the LIFO inventory method.

Low-income housing. Low-income housing is rental housing that is a dwelling unit for low- or moderate-income individuals or families. Beneficial tax treatment is in the form of the *low-income housing credit.* § 42. See also *accelerated cost recovery system.*

Low-income housing credit. Beneficial treatment to owners of low-income housing is provided in the form of a tax credit. The calculated credit is claimed in the year the building is placed in service and in the following nine years. § 42. See also *general business credit.*

Lump-sum distribution. Payment of the entire amount due at one time rather than in installments. Such distributions often occur from qualified pension or profit sharing plans upon the retirement or death of a covered employee. The recipient of a lump-sum distribution may recognize both long-term capital gain and ordinary income upon the receipt of the distribution. The ordinary income portion may be subject to a special five-year or ten-year income averaging provision. § 402(e).

M

MACRS. See *accelerated cost recovery system (ACRS).*

Majority interest partners. Partners who have more than a 50 percent interest in partnership profits and capital, counting only those partners who have the same taxable year, are referred to as majority interest partners. The term is of significance in determining the appropriate taxable year of a partnership. § 706(b). See also *accounting period* and *principal partner.*

Marital deduction. A deduction allowed upon the transfer of property from one spouse to another. The deduction is allowed under the Federal gift tax for lifetime (inter vivos) transfers or under the Federal estate tax for death (testamentary) transfers. §§ 2056 and 2523.

Material participation. If an individual taxpayer materially participates in a nonrental trade or business activity, any loss from that activity is treated as an active loss that can be offset against active income. Material participation is achieved by meeting any one of seven tests provided in the Regulations.

Medical expenses. Medical expenses of an individual, spouse, and dependents are allowed as an itemized deduction to the extent that such amounts (less insurance reimbursements) exceed 7.5 percent of adjusted gross income. § 213.

Mid-month convention. The mid-month convention is a cost recovery convention that assumes property is placed in service in the middle of the month that it is actually placed in service.

Mid-quarter convention. The mid-quarter convention is a cost recovery convention that assumes property placed in service during the year is placed in service at the middle of the quarter in which it is actually placed in service. The mid-quarter convention applies if more than 40% of the value of property (other than eligible real estate) is placed in service during the last quarter of the year.

Mitigation of the annual accounting period concept. Various tax provisions that provide relief from the effect of the finality of the annual accounting period concept. For example, the *net operating loss* provisions provide relief to a taxpayer whose business profits and losses for different taxable years fluctuate. See also *accounting period.*

Moving expenses. A deduction *for* AGI is permitted to employees and self-employed individuals provided certain tests are met. The taxpayer's new job must be at least 50 miles farther from the old residence than the old residence was from the former place of work. In addition, an employee must be employed on a full-time basis at the new location for 39 weeks in the 12-month period following the move. Deductible moving expenses include the cost of moving the household and personal effects, transportation, and lodging expenses during the move. The cost of meals during the move are not deductible. Qualified moving expenses that are paid (or reimbursed) by the employer can be excluded from the employee's gross income. In this case, the related deduction is not permitted. §§ 62(a)(15), 132(a)(6), and 217.

N

Necessary. Appropriate and helpful in furthering the taxpayer's business or income-producing activity. §§ 162(a) and 212. See also *ordinary.*

Net capital gain. The excess of the net long-term capital gain for the tax year over the net short-term capital loss. The net capital gain of an individual taxpayer is eligible for the alternative tax. § 1222(11). See also *alternative tax.*

Net capital loss. The excess of the losses from sales or exchanges of capital assets over the gains from sales or exchanges of such assets. Up to $3,000 per year of the net capital loss may be deductible by noncorporate taxpayers against ordinary income. The excess net capital loss carries over to future tax years. For corporate taxpayers, the net capital loss cannot be offset against ordinary income, but it can be carried back 3 years and forward 5 years to offset net capital gains. §§ 1211, 1212, and 1221(10).

Net operating loss. To mitigate the effect of the annual accounting period concept, § 172 allows taxpayers to use an excess loss of one year as a deduction for certain past or future years. In this regard, a carryback period of 3 years and a carryforward period of 15 years are allowed. See also *mitigation of the annual accounting period concept.*

Net worth method. An approach used by the IRS to reconstruct the income of a taxpayer who fails to maintain adequate records. Under this approach, the gross income for the year is the increase in net worth of the taxpayer (assets in excess of liabilities) with appropriate adjustment for nontaxable receipts and nondeductible expenditures. The net worth method often is used when tax fraud is suspected.

Ninety-day letter. See *statutory notice of deficiency.*

No-additional-cost-services. Services that the employer may provide the employee at no additional cost to the employer. Generally, the benefit is the ability to utilize employer's excess capacity (vacant seats on an airliner). Such amounts are excludible from the recipient's gross income. § 132.

Nonaccountable plan. An expense reimbursement plan that does not have an accountability feature. The result is that employee expenses must be claimed as deductions *from* AGI. An exception is moving expenses which are deductions *for* AGI. See also *accountable plan.*

Nonacquiescence. Announcement of disagreement by the IRS on the result reached by the U.S. Tax Court in a Regular Decision. Sometimes abbreviated *non-acq.* or *NA.* See also *acquiescence.*

Nonbusiness bad debts. A bad debt loss not incurred in connection with a creditor's trade or business. The loss is deductible as a short-term capital loss and will be allowed only in the year the debt becomes entirely worthless. In addition to family loans, many investor losses fall into the classification of nonbusiness bad debts. § 166(d). See also *bad debts.*

Nonqualified deferred compensation plans. Compensation arrangements that are frequently offered to executives. Such plans may include stock options, restricted stock, etc. Often, an executive may defer the recognition of taxable income. The employer, however, does not receive a tax deduction until the employee is required to include the compensation in income. See also *restricted property.*

Nonqualified stock option (NQSO). A type of stock option that does not satisfy the statutory requirements of an incentive stock option. If the NQSO has a readily ascertainable fair market value (e.g., the option is traded on an established exchange), the value of the option must be included in the employee's gross income at the date of the grant. Otherwise, the employee does not recognize income at the grant date. Instead, ordinary income is recognized in the year of exercise of the option. See also *incentive stock options*.

Nonrecourse debt. An obligation on which the endorser is not personally liable. An example of a nonrecourse debt is a mortgage on real estate acquired by a partnership without the assumption of any liability on the mortgage by the partnership or any of the partners. The acquired property generally is pledged as collateral for the loan.

Nonrefundable credit. A nonrefundable credit is a credit that is not paid if it exceeds the taxpayer's tax liability. Some nonrefundable credits qualify for carryback and carryover treatment. See also *refundable credit*.

Nontaxable exchange. A transaction in which realized gains or losses are not recognized. The recognition of gain or loss is postponed (deferred) until the property received in the nontaxable exchange is subsequently disposed of in a taxable transaction. Examples are § 1031 like-kind exchanges, § 1033 involuntary conversions, and § 1034 sale of a residence. See also *involuntary conversion* and *like-kind exchange*.

O

Occupational tax. A tax imposed on various trades or businesses. A license fee that enables a taxpayer to engage in a particular occupation.

Office audit. An audit by the IRS of a taxpayer's return that is conducted in the agent's office. To be distinguished from a *correspondence audit* or a *field audit*.

Office-in-the-home expenses. Employment and business-related expenses attributable to the use of a residence (e.g., den or office) are allowed only if the portion of the residence is exclusively used on a regular basis as a principal place of business of the taxpayer or as a place of business that is used by patients, clients, or customers. If the expenses are incurred by an employee, the use must be for the convenience of the employer as opposed to being merely appropriate and helpful. § 280A.

Open transaction. A judicially imposed doctrine that allows the taxpayer to defer all gain until he or she has collected an amount equal to the adjusted basis of assets transferred pursuant to an exchange transaction. This doctrine has been applied where the property received in an exchange has no ascertainable fair market value due to the existence of contingencies. The method is permitted only in very limited circumstances. See also *recovery of capital doctrine*.

Options. The sale or exchange of an option to buy or sell property results in capital gain or loss if the property is a capital asset. Generally, the closing of an option transaction results in short-term capital gain or loss to the writer of the call and the purchaser of the call option. § 1234.

Ordinary. Common and accepted in the general industry or type of activity in which the taxpayer is engaged. It comprises one of the tests for the deductibility of expenses incurred or paid in connection with a trade or business; for the production or collection of income; for the management, conservation, or maintenance of property held for the production of income; or in connection with the determination, collection, or refund of any tax. §§ 162(a) and 212. See also *necessary*.

Organizational expenses. A corporation may elect to amortize organizational expenses over a period of 60 months or more. Certain expenses of organizing a company do not qualify for amortization (e.g., expenditures connected with issuing or selling stock or other securities). § 248.

Original issue discount. The difference between the issue price of a debt obligation (e.g., a corporate bond) and the maturity value of the obligation when the issue price is *less than* the maturity value. OID represents interest and must be amortized over the life of the debt obligation using the effective interest method. The difference is not considered to be original issue discount for tax purposes when it is less than one-fourth of 1 percent of the redemption price at maturity multiplied by the number of years to maturity. §§ 1272 and 1273(a)(3).

Outside salesperson. An outside salesperson solicits business away from the employer's place of business on a full-time basis. The employment-related expenses of an outside salesperson are itemized deductions unless reimbursed by the employer. If reimbursed, such expenses are deductible *for* AGI.

P

Partnerships. A partnership is treated as a conduit and is not subject to taxation. Various items of partnership income, expenses, gains, and losses flow through to the individual partners and are reported on the partners' personal income tax returns.

Passive activity. A trade or business activity in which the taxpayer does not materially participate is subject to limitations on the deduction of losses and credits. Rental activities (subject to an exception) and limited partnership interests are inherently passive. However, relief from passive activity limitation treatment is provided for certain rental real estate if the taxpayer actively participates in the activity. The annual ceiling on the relief is $25,000. § 469. See also *portfolio income*.

Passive investment income. As defined in § 1362(d)(3)(D), passive investment income means gross receipts from royalties, certain rents, dividends, interest, annuities, and gains from the sale or exchange of stock and securities. Revocation of the S corporation election may occur in certain cases when the S corporation has passive investment income in excess of 25 percent of gross receipts for a period of three consecutive years.

Passive loss. Any loss from (1) activities in which the taxpayer does not materially participate, (2) rental activities (subject to an exception), or (3) tax shelter activities. Net passive losses cannot be used to offset income from nonpassive sources. Rather, they are suspended until the taxpayer either generates net passive income (and a deduction of the losses is allowed) or disposes of the underlying property (at which time the loss deductions are allowed in full). Landlords who actively participate in the rental activities can deduct up to $25,000 of passive losses annually. However, this amount is phased out when the landlord's AGI exceeds $100,000. See also *portfolio income.*

Patent. A patent is an intangible asset that may be amortized over a statutory 15-year period as a § 197 intangible. The sale of a patent usually results in favorable long-term capital gain treatment. §§ 197 and 1235.

Pension plan. A type of deferred compensation arrangement that provides for systematic payments of definitely determinable retirement benefits to employees who meet the requirements set forth in the plan. See also *defined benefit plan* and *defined contribution plan.*

Percentage depletion. Percentage depletion is depletion based on a statutory percentage applied to the gross income from the property. The taxpayer deducts the greater of cost depletion or percentage depletion. § 613. See also *cost depletion.*

Percentage of completion method. A method of reporting gain or loss on certain long-term contracts. Under this method of accounting, the gross contract price is included in income as the contract is being completed. § 460 and Reg. § 1.451–3. See also *completed contract method and long-term contracts.*

Personal and dependency exemptions. The tax law provides an exemption for each individual taxpayer and an additional exemption for the taxpayer's spouse if a joint return is filed. An individual may also claim a dependency exemption for each dependent, provided certain tests are met. The amount of the personal and dependency exemptions is $2,350 in 1993 and $2,450 in 1994. The amount is indexed for inflation. The exemption is subject to phase-out once adjusted gross income exceeds certain statutory threshold amounts. § 151.

Personal casualty gain. The recognized gain from any involuntary conversion of personal use property arising from fire, storm, shipwreck, or other casualty, or from theft. See also *personal casualty loss.*

Personal casualty loss. The recognized loss from any involuntary conversion of personal use property arising from fire, storm, shipwreck, or other casualty, or from theft. See also *personal casualty gain.*

Personal expenses. Expenses of an individual for personal reasons that are not deductible unless specifically provided for under the tax law. § 262.

Personal property. Generally, all property other than real estate. It is sometimes referred to as personalty when real estate is termed realty. Personal property also can refer to property that is not used in a taxpayer's trade or business or held for the production or collection of income. When used in this sense, personal property can include both realty (e.g., a personal residence) and personalty (e.g., personal effects such as clothing and furniture).

Personal residence. The sale of a personal residence generally results in the recognition of capital gain (but not loss). However, the gain may be deferred if the adjusted sales price of the old residence is reinvested in the purchase of a new residence within certain prescribed time periods. Also, taxpayers age 55 or older may exclude $125,000 of the gain from tax, provided certain requirements are met. §§ 1034 and 121.

Personal services corporation (PSC). A corporation the principal activity of which is the performance of personal services (e.g., health, law, engineering, architecture, accounting, actuarial science, performing arts, or consulting) and such services are substantially performed by the employee-owners.

Personalty. All property other than realty (real estate). Personalty usually is categorized as tangible or intangible property. Tangible personalty includes such assets as machinery and equipment, automobiles and trucks, and office equipment. Intangible personalty includes stocks and bonds, goodwill, patents, trademarks, and copyrights.

Points. Loan origination fees that may be deductible as interest by a buyer of property. A seller of property who pays points is required to reduce the selling price and therefore does not receive an interest deduction. See *prepaid interest* for the timing of the interest deduction.

Pollution control facilities. A certified pollution control facility, the cost of which may be amortized over a 60-month period if the taxpayer elects. § 169.

Portfolio income. The term is relevant in applying the limitation on passive activity losses and credits. Although normally considered passive in nature, for this purpose portfolio income is treated as nonpassive. Therefore, net passive losses and credits cannot be offset against portfolio income. Examples of portfolio income are interest, dividends, annuities, and certain royalties. § 469. See also *passive activity.*

Precedents. A previously decided court decision which is recognized as authority for the disposition of future decisions.

Prepaid expenses. Cash basis as well as accrual basis taxpayers usually are required to capitalize prepayments for rent, insurance, etc., that cover more than one year. Deductions are taken during the period the benefits are received.

Prepaid interest. In effect, the Code places cash basis taxpayers on an accrual basis for purposes of recognizing a deduction for prepaid interest. Thus, interest paid in advance is deductible as an interest expense only as it accrues. The one exception to this rule involves the interest element when a cash basis taxpayer pays points to obtain financing for the purchase of a principal residence (or to make improvements thereto) if the payment of points is an established business practice in the area in which the indebtedness is incurred and the amount involved is not excessive. § 461(g). See also *points.*

Principal partner. A partner with a 5 percent or greater interest in partnership capital or profits. § 706(b)(3). See also *majority interest partners.*

Prizes and awards. The fair market value of a prize or award generally is includible in gross income. However, exclusion is permitted if the prize or award is made in recognition of religious, charitable, scientific, educational, artistic, literary, or civic achievement, and the recipient transfers the award to a qualified governmental unit or a nonprofit organization. In that case, the recipient must be selected without any action on his or her part to enter a contest or proceeding, and the recipient must not be required to render substantial future services as a condition of receiving the prize or award. § 74.

Procedural regulation. A Regulation issued by the Treasury Department that is a housekeeping-type instruction indicating information that taxpayers should provide the IRS as well as information about the internal management and conduct of the IRS itself. See also *interpretive regulation* and *legislative regulation.*

Profit-sharing plan. A deferred compensation plan established and maintained by an employer to provide for employee participation in the company's profits. Contributions are paid from the employer's current or accumulated profits to a trustee. Separate accounts are maintained for each participant employee. The plan must provide a definite, predetermined formula for allocating the contributions among the participants. It also must include a definite, predetermined formula for distributing the accumulated funds after a fixed number of years, on the attainment of a stated age, or on the occurrence of certain events such as illness, layoff, or retirement.

Proposed Regulation. A Regulation issued by the Treasury Department in proposed, rather than final, form. The interval between the proposal of a Regulation and its finalization permits taxpayers and other interested parties to comment on the propriety of the proposal. See also *finalized regulation* and *regulations.*

Public policy limitation. See *bribes and illegal payments.*

Punitive damages. Damages received or paid by the taxpayer can be classified as compensatory damages or as punitive damages. Punitive damages are those awarded to punish the defendant for gross negligence or the intentional infliction of harm. Such damages are includible in gross income unless the claim arises out of physical injury or physical sickness. See also *compensatory damages.*

Q

Qualified employee discounts. Discounts offered employees on merchandise or services that the employer ordinarily sells or provides to customers. The discounts must be generally available to all employees. In the case of property, the discount cannot exceed the employer's gross profit (the sales price cannot be less than the employer's cost). In the case of services, the discounts cannot exceed 20% of the normal sales price. § 132.

Qualified pension or profit sharing plan. An employer-sponsored plan that meets the requirements of § 401. If these requirements are met, none of the employer's contributions to the plan will be taxed to the employee until distributed to him or her (§ 402). The employer will be allowed a deduction in the year the contributions are made (§ 404). See also *annuity* and *deferred compensation.*

Qualified real property business indebtedness. Indebtedness which was incurred or assumed by the taxpayer in connection with real property used in a trade or business and is secured by such real property. The taxpayer must not be a C corporation. For qualified real property business indebtedness, the taxpayer may elect to exclude some or all of the income realized from cancellation of debt on qualified real property. If the election is made, the basis of the property must be reduced by the amount excluded. The amount excluded cannot be greater than the excess of the principal amount of the outstanding debt over the fair market value (net of any other debt outstanding on the property) of the property securing the debt.

Qualified residence interest. A term relevant in determining the amount of interest expense the individual taxpayer may deduct as an itemized deduction for what otherwise would be disallowed as a component of personal interest (consumer interest). Qualified residence interest consists of interest paid on qualified residences (principal residence and one other residence) of the taxpayer. Debt that qualifies as qualified residence interest is limited to $1 million of debt to acquire, construct, or substantially improve qualified residences (acquisition indebtedness) plus $100,000 of other debt secured by qualified residences (home equity indebtedness). The home equity indebtedness may not exceed the fair market value of a qualified residence reduced by the acquisition indebtedness for that residence. § 163(h)(3). See also *consumer interest.*

Qualified transportation fringe. Transportation benefits provided by the employer to the employee. Such benefits include (1) transportation in a commuter highway vehicle between the employee's residence and the place of employment, (2) a transit pass, and (3) qualified parking. Qualified transportation fringes are excludible from the employee's gross income to the extent categories (1) and (2) above do not exceed $60 per month and category (3) does not exceed $155 per month. § 132.

Qualified tuition reduction plan. A type of fringe benefit plan which is available to employees of nonprofit educational institutions. Such employees (and the spouse and dependent children) are allowed to exclude a tuition waiver pursuant to a qualified tuition reduction plan from gross income. The exclusion applies to undergraduate tuition. In limited circumstances, the exclusion also applies to the graduate tuition of teaching and research assistants.

R

RAR. A revenue agent's report, which reflects any adjustments made by the agent as a result of an audit of the taxpayer. The RAR is mailed to the taxpayer along with the 30-day letter, which outlines the appellate procedures available to the taxpayer.

Realized gain or loss. The difference between the amount realized upon the sale or other disposition of property and the adjusted basis of the property. § 1001. See also *adjusted basis* and *recognized gain or loss.*

Realty. All real estate, including land and buildings. Permanent improvements to a building (fixtures) become realty if their removal would cause significant damage to the property. An example of a fixture is the installation of a central air conditioning or heating system to a building. Thus, personalty can become realty through the fixture reclassification.

Reasonable needs of the business. See *accumulated earnings tax.*

Recapture. To recover the tax benefit of a deduction or a credit previously taken.

Recapture of depreciation. Upon the disposition of depreciable property used in a trade or business, gain or loss is determined measured by the difference between the consideration received (the amount realized) and the adjusted basis of the property. Before the enactment of the recapture of depreciation provisions of the Code, any such gain recognized could be § 1231 gain and usually qualified for long-term capital gain treatment. The recapture provisions of the Code (e.g., §§ 1245 and 1250) may operate to convert some or all of the previous § 1231 gain into ordinary income. The justification for recapture of depreciation is that it prevents a taxpayer from deducting depreciation at ordinary income rates and having the related gain on disposition taxed at capital gain rates. The recapture of depreciation rules do not apply when the property is disposed of at a loss. See also *residential rental property, Section 1231 gains and losses, Section 1245 recapture,* and *Section 1250 recapture.*

Recapture of investment tax credit. When investment tax credit property is disposed of or ceases to be used in the trade or business of the taxpayer, some or all of the investment tax credit claimed on the property may be recaptured as additional tax liability. The amount of the recapture is the difference between the amount of the credit originally claimed and what should have been claimed in light of the length of time the property was actually held or used for qualifying purposes. § 50. See also *investment tax credit.*

Recapture potential. Reference is to property that, if disposed of in a taxable transaction, would result in the recapture of depreciation (§§ 1245 or 1250) and/or of the investment tax credit (§ 50).

Recognized gain or loss. The portion of realized gain or loss that is considered in computing taxable income. See also *realized gain or loss.*

Recovery of capital doctrine. When a taxable sale or exchange occurs, the seller may be permitted to recover his or her investment (or other adjusted basis) in the property before gain or loss is recognized. See also *open transaction.*

Refundable credit. A refundable credit is a credit that is paid to the taxpayer even if the amount of the credit (or credits) exceeds the taxpayer's tax liability. See also *nonrefundable credit.*

Regulations. Treasury Department Regulations represent the position of the IRS as to how the Internal Revenue Code is to be interpreted. Their purpose is to provide taxpayers and IRS personnel with rules of general and specific application to the various provisions of the tax law. Regulations are published in the *Federal Register* and in all tax services. See also *interpretive regulation, legislative regulation, procedural regulation,* and *proposed regulation.*

Rehabilitation expenditures credit. A credit that is based on expenditures incurred to rehabilitate industrial and commercial buildings and certified historic structures. The credit, an extension of the regular investment tax credit, is intended to discourage businesses from moving from older, economically distressed areas to newer locations and to encourage the preservation of historic structures. § 47. See *rehabilitation expenditures credit recapture.*

Rehabilitation expenditures credit recapture. When property that qualifies for the rehabilitation expenditures credit is disposed of or ceases to be used in the trade or business of the taxpayer, some or all of the tax credit claimed on the property may be recaptured as additional tax liability. The amount of the recapture is the difference between the amount of the credit claimed originally and what should have been claimed in light of the length of time the property was actually held or used for qualifying purposes. § 50. See *rehabilitation expenditures credit.*

Related-party transactions. The tax law places restrictions upon the recognition of gains and losses between related parties because of the potential for abuse. For example, restrictions are placed on the deduction of losses from the sale or exchange of property between related parties. A related party includes a corporation controlled by the taxpayer. § 267.

Rental activity. Any activity where payments are received principally for the use of tangible property is a rental activity. Temporary Regulations provide that in certain circumstances activities involving rentals of real and personal property are not to be treated as rental activities. There are six exceptions listed in the Temporary Regulations.

Research activities credit. A tax credit whose purpose is to encourage research and development. It consists of two components: the incremental research activities credit and the basic research credit. The incremental research activities credit is equal to 20 percent of the excess of qualified research expenditures over the base amount. The basic research credit is equal to 20 percent of the excess of basic research payments over the base amount. § 41. See also *general business credit*.

Research and experimentation expenditures. The Code provides three alternatives for the tax treatment of research and experimentation expenditures. They may be expensed in the year paid or incurred, deferred subject to amortization, or capitalized. If the taxpayer does not elect to expense such costs or to defer them subject to amortization (over 60 months), the expenditures must be capitalized. § 174. Two types of research activities credits are available: the basic research credit and the incremental research activities credit. The rate for each type is 20 percent. § 41.

Reserve for bad debts. A method of accounting whereby an allowance is permitted for estimated uncollectible accounts. Actual write-offs are charged to the reserve, and recoveries of amounts previously written off are credited to the reserve. The Code permits only certain financial institutions to use the reserve method. § 166. See also *specific charge-off method*.

Reserve method. See *reserve for bad debts*.

Reserves for estimated expenses. Except in the limited case for bad debts, reserves for estimated expenses (e.g., warranty service costs) are not permitted for tax purposes even though such reserves are appropriate for financial accounting purposes. See also *all events test*.

Residential rental property. Buildings for which at least 80 percent of the gross rents are from dwelling units (e.g., an apartment building). This type of building is distinguished from nonresidential (commercial or industrial) buildings in applying the recapture of depreciation provisions. The term also is relevant in distinguishing between buildings that are eligible for a 27.5-year life versus a 39-year (or 31.5-year) life for MACRS purposes. Generally, residential buildings receive preferential treatment. §§ 168(e)(2) and 1250. See also *recapture of depreciation*.

Restricted property. An arrangement whereby an employer transfers property (usually stock) to an employee at a bargain price (for less than the fair market value). If the transfer is accompanied by a substantial risk of forfeiture and the property is not transferable, no compensation results to the employee until the restrictions disappear. An example of a substantial risk of forfeiture would be a requirement that the employee return the property if his or her employment is terminated within a specified period of time. § 83. See also *nonqualified deferred compensation plans* and *substantial risk of forfeiture*.

Retirement of corporate obligations. The retirement of corporate and certain government obligations is considered to be a sale or exchange. Gain or loss, upon the retirement of a corporate obligation, therefore, is treated as capital gain or loss rather than as ordinary income or loss. §§ 1271–1275.

Return of capital doctrine. See *recovery of capital doctrine*.

Revenue neutrality. A description that characterizes tax legislation when it neither increases nor decreases the revenue result. Thus, any tax revenue losses are offset by tax revenue gains.

Revenue Procedure. A matter of procedural importance to both taxpayers and the IRS concerning the administration of the tax law is issued by the National Office of the IRS as a Revenue Procedure (abbreviated Rev.Proc.). A Revenue Procedure is first published in an *Internal Revenue Bulletin* (I.R.B.) and later transferred to the appropriate *Cumulative Bulletin* (C.B.). Both the *Internal Revenue Bulletin* and the *Cumulative Bulletin* are published by the U.S. Government Printing Office.

Revenue Ruling. A Revenue Ruling (abbreviated Rev.Rul.) is issued by the National Office of the IRS to express an official interpretation of the tax law as applied to specific transactions. It is more limited in application than a Regulation. A Revenue Ruling is first published in an *Internal Revenue Bulletin* (I.R.B.) and later transferred to the appropriate *Cumulative Bulletin* (C.B.). Both the *Internal Revenue Bulletin* and the *Cumulative Bulletin* are published by the U.S. Government Printing Office.

S

Sale or exchange. A requirement for the recognition of capital gain or loss. Generally, the seller of property must receive money or relief from debt in order to have sold the property. An exchange involves the transfer of property for other property. Thus, *collection* of a debt is neither a sale nor an exchange. The term *sale or exchange* is not defined by the Code.

Sales tax. A transaction tax imposed upon the sale of goods. It usually is based on a specified percentage of the value of the property sold. A sales tax is to be distinguished from an excise tax, since a sales tax applies to a broad variety of commodities.

Salvage value. The estimated amount a taxpayer will receive upon the disposition of an asset used in the taxpayer's trade or business. Salvage value is relevant in calculating depreciation under § 167, but is not relevant in calculating cost recovery under § 168.

Scholarships. Scholarships are generally excluded from the gross income of the recipient unless the payments are a disguised form of compensation for services rendered. However, the Code imposes restrictions on the exclusion. The recipient must be a degree candidate. The excluded amount is limited to amounts used for tuition, fees, books, supplies, and equipment required for courses of instruction. Amounts received for room and board are not eligible for the exclusion. § 117.

S corporation status. An elective provision permitting certain small business corporations (§ 1361) and their shareholders to elect (§ 1362) to be treated for income tax purposes in accordance with the operating rules of §§ 1363–1379. Of major significance are the facts that S status avoids the corporate income tax and corporate losses can be claimed by the shareholders. See also *C corporation*.

Section 38 property. Property that qualified for the investment tax credit. Generally, this included all tangible property (other than real estate) used in a trade or business. § 48 prior to repeal by the Revenue Reconciliation Act of 1990. See also *investment tax credit*.

Section 121 exclusion. An exclusion of $125,000 of realized gain available to taxpayers who are age 55 or over associated with the sale of their principal residence. The taxpayer must have owned and occupied the residence for at least three years during the five-year period ending on the date of sale. The exclusion treatment is elective and the election can be made only once. If married, both spouses must consent to the election. § 121.

Section 179 expensing. The ability to deduct a capital expenditure in the year an asset is placed in service rather than over the asset's useful life or cost recovery period. The annual ceiling on the deduction is $17,500. However, the deduction is reduced dollar for dollar when § 179 property placed in service during the taxable year exceeds $200,000. In addition, the amount expensed under § 179 cannot exceed the aggregate amount of taxable income derived from the conduct of any trade or business by the taxpayer.

Section 401(k) plan. A cash or deferred arrangement plan which allows participants to elect to receive up to $9,240 in 1994 in cash (taxed currently) or to have a contribution made on their behalf to a profit sharing or stock bonus plan (excludible from gross income). The plan may also be in the form of a salary reduction agreement between the participant and the employer.

Section 1231 assets. Depreciable assets and real estate used in a trade or business and held for the required long-term holding period. Under certain circumstances, the classification also includes timber, coal, domestic iron ore, livestock (held for draft, breeding, dairy, or sporting purposes), and unharvested crops. § 1231(b).

Section 1231 gains and losses. If the net result of the combined gains and losses from the taxable dispositions of § 1231 assets plus the net gain from the involuntary conversion of nonpersonal use assets is a gain, the gains and losses from § 1231 assets are treated as long-term capital gains and losses. In arriving at § 1231 gains, however, the depreciation recapture provisions (e.g., §§ 1245 and 1250) are first applied to produce ordinary income. If the net result of the combination is a loss, the gains and losses from § 1231 assets are treated as ordinary gains and losses. § 1231(a). See also *recapture of depreciation*.

Section 1244 stock. Stock issued under § 1244 by qualifying small business corporations. If § 1244 stock is disposed of at a loss or becomes worthless, the shareholders may claim an ordinary loss rather than the usual capital loss. The annual ceiling on the ordinary loss treatment is $50,000 ($100,000 for married individuals filing jointly). See also *worthless securities*.

Section 1245 property. Property that is subject to the recapture of depreciation under § 1245. For a definition of § 1245 property, see § 1245(a)(3). See also *Section 1245 recapture*.

Section 1245 recapture. Upon a taxable disposition of § 1245 property, all depreciation claimed on the property after 1961 will be recaptured as ordinary income (but not to exceed the recognized gain from the disposition). See also *recapture of depreciation*.

Section 1250 property. Real estate that is subject to the recapture of depreciation under § 1250. For a definition of § 1250 property, see § 1250(c). See also *Section 1250 recapture*.

Section 1250 recapture. Upon a taxable disposition of § 1250 property, some or all of the additional depreciation claimed on the property may be recaptured as ordinary income. Various recapture rules apply depending upon the type of property (residential or nonresidential real estate) and the date acquired. Generally, the additional depreciation is recaptured in full to the extent of the gain recognized. See also *additional depreciation* and *recapture of depreciation*.

Self-employment retirement plan. A designation for retirement plans available to self-employed taxpayers. Also referred to as H.R. 10 and Keogh plans. Under such plans, a taxpayer may deduct each year up to either 20 percent of net earnings from self-employment or $30,000, whichever is less. If the plan is a profit sharing plan, the percentage is 13.043 percent.

Self-employment tax. In 1994, a tax of 12.4 percent is levied on individuals with net earnings from self-employment (up to $60,600) to provide Social Security benefits (i.e., the old age, survivors, and disability insurance portion) for such individuals. In addition, in 1994, a tax of 2.9 percent is levied on individuals with net earnings from self-employment (with no statutory ceiling) to provide Medicare benefits (i.e., the hospital insurance portion) for such individuals. If a self-employed individual also receives wages from an employer that are subject to FICA, the self-employment tax will be reduced if total income subject to Social Security is more than $60,600. A partial deduction is allowed in calculating the self-employment tax. Individuals with net earnings of $400 or more from self-employment are subject to this tax.

Separate property. In a community property jurisdiction, separate property is the property that belongs entirely to one of the spouses. Generally, it is property acquired before marriage or acquired after marriage by gift or inheritance. See also *community property*.

Severance tax. A tax imposed upon the extraction of natural resources.

Short sales. A short sale occurs when a taxpayer sells borrowed property (usually stock) and repays the lender with substantially identical property either held on the date of the short sale or purchased after the sale. No gain or loss is recognized until the short sale is closed, and such gain or loss is generally short term. § 1233.

Short taxable year (short period). A tax year that is less than 12 months. A short taxable year may occur in the initial reporting period, the final tax year, or when the taxpayer changes tax years.

Significant participation activity. There are seven tests to determine whether an individual has achieved material participation in an activity, one of which is based on more than 500 hours of participation in significant participation activities. A significant participation activity is one in which the individual's participation exceeds 100 hours during the year.

Simplified employee pensions. An employer may make contributions to an employee's IRA in amounts not exceeding the lesser of 15 percent of compensation or $30,000 per individual. These employer-sponsored simplified employee pensions are permitted only if the contributions are nondiscriminatory and are made on behalf of all employees who have attained age 21 and have worked for the employer during at least three of the five preceding calendar years. § 219(b). See also *individual retirement account.*

Small business corporation. A corporation that satisfies the definition of § 1361(b), § 1244(c)(3), or both. Satisfaction of § 1361(b) permits an S corporation election, and satisfaction of § 1244 enables the shareholders of the corporation to claim an ordinary loss. See also *S corporation status* and *Section 1244 stock.*

Small business stock. See *small business corporation.*

Small claims division. A subsidiary division of the U.S. Tax Court. The jurisdiction of the Small Claims division is limited to small claims (i.e., claims of $10,000 or less). The proceedings of the Small Claims Division are informal and there is no appeal of the findings.

Specific charge-off method. A method of accounting for bad debts in which a deduction is permitted only when an account becomes partially or completely worthless. See also *reserve for bad debts.*

Standard deduction. The individual taxpayer can either itemize deductions or take the standard deduction. The amount of the standard deduction depends on the taxpayer's filing status (single, head of household, married filing jointly, surviving spouse, or married filing separately). For 1994, the amount of the standard deduction ranges from $3,175 to $6,350. Additional standard deductions of either $750 (for married taxpayers) or $950 (for single taxpayers) are available if the taxpayer is either blind or age 65 or over. Limitations exist on the amount of the standard deduction of a taxpayer who is another taxpayer's dependent. Beginning in 1989, the standard deduction amounts are adjusted for inflation each year. § 63(c). See also *zero bracket amount.*

Statute of limitations. Provisions of the law that specify the maximum period of time in which action may be taken on a past event. Code §§ 6501–6504 contain the limitation periods applicable to the IRS for additional assessments, and §§ 6511–6515 relate to refund claims by taxpayers.

Statutory notice of deficiency. Commonly referred to as the 90-day letter, this notice is sent to a taxpayer upon request, upon the expiration of the 30-day letter, or upon exhaustion by the taxpayer of his or her administrative remedies before the IRS. The notice gives the taxpayer 90 days in which to file a petition with the U.S. Tax Court. If a petition is not filed, the IRS will issue a demand for payment of the assessed deficiency. §§ 6211–6216. See also *thirty-day letter.*

Stock bonus plan. A type of deferred compensation plan in which the employer establishes and maintains the plan and contributes employer stock to the plan for the benefit of employees. The contributions need not be dependent on the employer's profits. Any benefits of the plan are distributable in the form of employer stock, except that distributable fractional shares may be paid in cash.

Stock option. The right to purchase a stated number of shares of stock from a corporation at a certain price within a specified period of time.

Stock redemptions. The redemption of the stock of a shareholder by the issuing corporation will be treated as a sale or exchange of the stock if the redemption is not a dividend. §§ 301 and 302.

Substantial risk of forfeiture. A term that is relevant associated with a restricted property plan. Generally, an employee who receives property (e.g., stock of the employer-corporation) from the employee at a bargain price or at no cost must include the bargain element in gross income. However, the employee does not have to do so if there is a substantial risk of forfeiture. A substantial risk of forfeiture exists if a person's rights to full enjoyment of property are conditioned upon the future performance, or the refraining from the performance, of substantial services by the individual. § 83. See also *restricted property.*

Super-full absorption costing rules. See *uniform capitalization rules.*

T

Targeted jobs tax credit. See *jobs credit.*

Taxable year. The annual period over which income is measured for income tax purposes. Most individuals use a calendar year, but many businesses use a fiscal year based on the natural business year.

Tax avoidance. The minimization of one's tax liability by taking advantage of legally available tax planning opportunities. Tax avoidance can be contrasted with tax evasion, which entails the reduction of tax liability by illegal means.

Tax benefit rule. A rule that limits the recognition of income from the recovery of an expense or loss properly deducted in a prior tax year to the amount of the deduction that generated a tax benefit. § 111.

Tax Court. The U.S. Tax Court is one of three trial courts of original jurisdiction that decide litigation involving Federal income, estate, or gift taxes. It is the only trial court where the taxpayer need not first pay the deficiency assessed by the IRS. The Tax Court will not have jurisdiction over a case unless the statutory notice of deficiency (90-day letter) has been issued by the IRS and the taxpayer files the petition for hearing within the time prescribed.

Tax credit. A tax credit is an amount that directly reduces a taxpayer's tax liability. The tax benefit received from a tax credit is not dependent on the taxpayer's marginal tax rate, whereas the benefit of a tax deduction is dependent on the taxpayer's tax bracket.

Tax credit for elderly or disabled. An elderly (age 65 and over) or disabled taxpayer may receive a tax credit amounting to 15 percent of $5,000 ($7,500 for qualified married individuals filing jointly). This amount is reduced by Social Security benefits, excluded pension benefits, and one-half of the taxpayer's adjusted gross income in excess of $7,500 ($10,000 for married taxpayers filing jointly). § 22.

Tax-free exchange. Transfers of property specifically exempted from Federal income tax consequences. Examples are a transfer of property to a controlled corporation under § 351(a) and a like-kind exchange under § 1031(a). The recognition of gain or loss is postponed, rather than being permanently excluded, through the assignment of a carryover basis to the replacement property.

Tax home. Since travel expenses of an employee are deductible only if the taxpayer is away from home, the deductibility of such expenses rests upon the definition of tax home. The IRS position is that tax home is the business location, post, or station of the taxpayer. If an employee is temporarily reassigned to a new post for a period of one year or less, the taxpayer's home should be his or her personal residence and the travel expenses should be deductible. If the assignment is for more than two years, the IRS position is that it is indefinite or permanent and the taxpayer is therefore not in travel status. If the assignment is for between one and two years, the IRS position is that the location of the tax home will be determined on the basis of the facts and circumstances. The courts are in conflict regarding what constitutes a person's home for tax purposes. For such costs paid or incurred after December 31, 1992, the Energy Policy Act of 1992 provides that the taxpayer shall not be treated as temporarily away from home if the employment period exceeds one year. Thus, in this situation, the tax home will be the place of employment. See also *travel expenses.*

Tax preference items. Those items set forth in § 57 that may result in the imposition of the alternative minimum tax. See also *alternative minimum tax.*

Tax rate schedules. Rate schedules appearing in Appendix A that are used by upper-income taxpayers and those not permitted to use the tax table. Separate rate schedules are provided for married individuals filing jointly, head of household, single taxpayers, estates and trusts, and married individuals filing separate returns. § 1.

Tax research. The method used to determine the best available solution to a situation that possesses tax consequences. Both tax and nontax factors are considered.

Tax shelters. The typical tax shelter generated large losses in the early years of the activity. Investors would offset these losses against other types of income and, therefore, avoid paying income taxes on this income. These tax shelter investments could then be sold after a few years and produce capital gain income which is taxed at a lower rate than ordinary income. The passive loss rules and the at-risk rules now limit tax shelter deductions.

Tax table. A tax table appearing in Appendix A that is provided for taxpayers with less than $100,000 of taxable income. Separate columns are provided for single taxpayers, married taxpayers filing jointly, head of household, and married taxpayers filing separately. § 3.

Technical advice memoranda (TAM). TAMs are issued by the National Office of the IRS in response to questions raised by IRS field personnel during audits. They deal with completed rather than proposed transactions and are often requested for questions related to exempt organizations and employee plans.

Temporary regulation. A Regulation issued by the Treasury Department in temporary form. When speed is critical, the Treasury Department issues temporary Regulations which take effect immediately. These Regulations have the same authoritative value as final Regulations and may be cited as precedent for three years. Temporary Regulations are also issued as proposed Regulations. See also *proposed regulation* and *finalized regulation.*

Theft loss. A loss from larceny, embezzlement, and robbery. It does not include misplacement of items. See also *casualty loss.*

Thin corporation. When debt owed by a corporation to its shareholders is large relative to its capital structure (stock and shareholder equity), the IRS may contend that the corporation is thinly capitalized. In effect, this means that some or all of the debt will be reclassified as equity. The immediate result is to disallow any interest deduction to the corporation on the reclassified debt. To the extent of the corporation's earnings and profits, interest payments and loan repayments on the reclassified debt are treated as dividends to the shareholders. § 385.

Thirty-day letter. A letter that accompanies a revenue agent's report (RAR) issued as a result of an IRS audit of a taxpayer (or the rejection of a taxpayer's claim for refund). The letter outlines the taxpayer's appeal procedure before the IRS. If the taxpayer does not request any such procedures within the 30-day period, the IRS will issue a *statutory notice of deficiency* (the 90-day letter).

Timber. Special rules apply to the recognition of gain from the sale of timber. A taxpayer may elect to treat the cutting of timber that is held for sale or use in a trade or business as a sale or exchange. If the holding period requirements are met, the gain is recognized as § 1231 gain and may therefore receive long-term capital gain treatment. § 631.

Top-heavy plan. A type of retirement plan which primarily benefits key employees. Such plans allocate more than 60 percent of the cumulative benefits to key employees. Special rules are imposed to discourage retirement plans from conferring disproportionate benefits on key employees.

Trade or business expenses. Deductions *for* AGI that are attributable to a taxpayer's business or profession. Some employee expenses may also be treated as trade or business expenses. See also *employee expenses.*

Transportation expenses. Transportation expenses for an employee include only the cost of transportation (taxi fares, automobile expenses, etc.) in the course of employment when the employee is not away from home in travel status. Commuting expenses are not deductible. See also *automobile expenses.*

Travel expenses. Travel expenses include meals (subject to a 50 percent disallowance) and lodging and transportation expenses while away from home in the pursuit of a trade or business (including that of an employee). See also *tax home.*

Trial court. The court of original jurisdiction; the first court to consider litigation. In Federal tax controversies, trial courts include U.S. District Courts, the U.S. Tax Court, and the U.S. Court of Federal Claims. See also *appellate court.*

U

Unearned (prepaid) income. For tax purposes, prepaid income (e.g., rent) is taxable in the year of receipt. In certain cases involving advance payments for goods and services, income may be deferred. See Rev.Proc. 71–21 (1971–2 C.B. 549) and Reg. § 1.451–5. See also *accrual method.*

Uniform capitalization rules. The Regulations under section 263A which provide a set of rules that all taxpayers (regardless of the particular industry) can use to determine the items of cost (and means of allocating those costs) that must be capitalized with respect to the production of tangible property.

Unreasonable compensation. Under § 162(a)(1), a deduction is allowed for "reasonable" salaries or other compensation for personal services actually rendered. To the extent compensation is excessive ("unreasonable"), no deduction will be allowed. The problem of unreasonable compensation usually is limited to closely held corporations where the mo-

tivation is to pay out profits in some form deductible to the corporation. Deductible compensation, therefore, becomes an attractive substitute for nondeductible dividends when the shareholders are also employees of the corporation.

U.S. Court of Federal Claims. See *Claims Court.*

Use tax. A use tax is an ad valorem tax, usually at the same rate as the sales tax, on the use or consumption of tangible personalty. The purpose of a use tax is to prevent the avoidance of a sales tax.

U.S. Supreme Court. The highest appellate court or the court of last resort in the Federal court system and in most states. The constitutionality of a tax law of a small number of tax decisions of the U.S. Courts of Appeal are reviewed by the U.S. Supreme Court under its certiorari procedure.

U.S. Tax Court. See *Tax Court.*

USTC. Published by Commerce Clearing House, *U.S. Tax Cases* contain all of the Federal tax decisions issued by the U.S. District Courts, U.S. Court of Federal Claims, U.S. Courts of Appeals, and the U.S. Supreme Court.

V

Vacation home. The Code places restrictions upon taxpayers who rent their residences or vacation homes for part of the tax year. The restrictions may result in a scaling down of expense deductions for the taxpayers. § 280A. See also *hobby loss.*

Value added tax (VAT). A national sales tax that taxes the increment in value as goods move through the production process. A VAT is much used in other countries, but has not yet been incorporated as part of the U.S. Federal tax structure.

Vesting requirements. In order to be a qualified deferred compensation arrangement, a vesting requirement must be satisfied. Under this provision, an employee's right to accrued plan benefits derived from employer contributions must be nonforfeitable in accordance with one of two vesting timeperiod schedules.

W

Wash sale. A loss from the sale of stock or securities that is disallowed because the taxpayer has within 30 days before or after the sale acquired stock or securities that are substantially identical to those sold. § 1091.

Wherewithal to pay. This concept recognizes the inequity of taxing a transaction when the taxpayer lacks the means with which to pay the tax. Under it, there is a correlation between the imposition of the tax and the ability to pay the tax. It is particularly suited to situations in which the taxpayer's economic position has not changed significantly as a result of the transaction.

Withholding allowances. The number of withholding allowances serves as the basis for determining the amount of income taxes withheld from an employee's salary or wages. The more withholding allowances claimed, the less income tax withheld by an employer. An employee may claim withholding allowances for personal exemptions for self and spouse (unless claimed as a dependent of another person), dependency exemptions, and special withholding allowances.

Working condition fringe.   A type of fringe benefit received by the employee that is excludible from the employee's gross income. It consists of property or services provided (paid or reimbursed) by the employer for which the employee could take a tax deduction if the employee had paid for them. § 132.

Worthless securities.   A loss (usually capital) is allowed for a security that becomes worthless during the year. The loss is deemed to have occurred on the last day of the year. Special rules apply to securities of affiliated companies and small business stock. § 165. See also *Section 1244 stock.*

Writ of certiorari.   See *certiorari.*

Z

Zero bracket amount.   A deduction that was generally available to all individual taxpayers in arriving at taxable income. It represented the equivalent of the standard deduction for taxable years before 1987. The taxpayer did not take a deduction for the zero bracket amount because it was built into the tax tables and tax rate schedules. Because the amount was built-in, if the taxpayer itemized deductions, only the excess itemized deductions (amount of the itemized deductions in excess of the zero bracket amount) were deductible. TRA of 1986 repealed the zero bracket amount and replaced it with the standard deduction for 1987 and thereafter. The zero bracket amount for 1986 is presently used in the 10-year forward averaging calculation for lump-sum distributions. § 63(c). See also *standard deduction.*

APPENDIX D-1
Table of Code Sections Cited

[See Title 26 U.S.C.A.]

I.R.C. Sec.	This Work Page
1	2–7, 18–6
1(a)	3–23
1(g)	3–18, 20–36
1.162–21(b)	6–44
1–5	2–6
2	2–7, 2–9
2(a)	2–6, 3–24
2(a)(1)(A)	2–6, 2–7
2(b)	3–25, 3–41
2(b)(1)(A)(i)	3–25
2(b)(1)(B)	3–25
5	2–6
11	2–6
11(b)	20–13
11–12	2–6
12(d)	2–7
15	20–13
21	13–21, 13–24
21(c)	13–23
22	13–19, 13–24
27	13–20, 13–25
31	13–24
32	13–17, 13–24
38	13–25
38(c)	13–5
39(a)(1)	13–6
41	7–18, 13–11, 13–25, 13–49
41(b)(3)(A)	13–12
41(d)	13–12
41(e)	13–14
42	13–15, 13–25
44	13–16, 13–25
46	13–25
47	13–8
48(q)	8–6
50(c)	13–8
51	13–10, 13–25
55(c)	12–21
56	12–27
56(a)(2)	12–10

I.R.C. Sec.	This Work Page
56(b)(2)(A)(i)	12–6
56(g)(6)	12–26
57	12–27
57(a)(3)	19–34
58	12–27
59(e)(2)(A)	12–8
59(e)(2)(D)	12–11
59(e)(2)(E)	12–11
61	4–2, 20–16
61(a)	3–3
61(a)(3)	14–6
61(a)(12)	5–30
62	2–16, 3–4, 6–3
62(a)(1)	6–31, 7–15, 9–3
62(a)(1) or (3)	6–31
62(a)(1) or (4)	6–31
62(a)(2)	9–22
62(a)(2)(A)	6–31
62(a)(2)(B)	6–31
62(a)(4)	6–4, 6–31, 7–15
62(a)(10)	7–35
62(a)(15)	6–31, 9–13
62(b)	9–22
63(a)	2–41, 20–16
63(b)–(h)	20–16
63(c)(1)	3–6
63(c)(5)	3–9
63(c)(6)	3–9
63(d)	6–4
66	2–35, 4–18
67	5–21, 6–31, 9–25
67(b)(3)	7–15
68	10–27
71	4–19
71–90	4–19
71(b)(1)	4–20
71(c)(2)	4–23
71(f)	4–21
71(f)(5)(A)	4–22
71(f)(5)(C)	4–22

I.R.C. Sec.	This Work Page
72	19–13
72(b)	4–29
72(c)(3)	4–28
72(q)	4–28
72(t)	19–11, 19–25
73	4–14
74	4–30
74(b)	4–31
74(c)	4–31, 5–4
79	4–31, 5–4
79(d)	4–33, 5–24
83	19–31, 19–41
83(a)	4–10
83(a)(1)	19–32
83(b)	19–32, 19–43, 19–47
83(c)	19–32
85	4–33
86	4–33, 5–4, 19–22
101	5–4, 14–29
101–150	5–2
101(a)	5–5
101(a)(1)	14–29
101(b)	5–4, 5–7
102	5–3, 5–4
102(a)	14–11
102(c)	5–5
103	5–4, 6–29
103(a)	5–26
103(b)	5–27
104	5–4
104(a)	5–12
104(a)(1)	5–12
104(a)(2)	5–11
104(a)(3)	5–13
105	5–4, 5–14
105(a)	5–13
105(b)	5–13
105(c)	5–14
105(h)	5–14, 5–24
106	5–4, 5–13
107	5–4, 5–16, 13–48
107(1)	13–49
107(b)(1)	16–7
108	5–4, 5–30
108(a)	5–31
108(b)	5–31
108(c)	5–31
108(e)	5–31
108(e)(5)	5–31
108(e)(6)	5–31
108(f)	5–31
108(g)	5–31
109	5–3, 5–4, 14–23
111	5–4, 5–29

I.R.C. Sec.	This Work Page
111(a)	5–29
112	5–4
117	4–30, 5–4, 9–15
117(a)	2–31, 5–8
117(b)	5–9
117(d)	5–10
118	20–17
119	5–4, 5–14, 5–20
119(a)	5–14
119(d)	5–16
121	5–4, 14–8, 15–2, 15–3, 15–16, 15–22, 15–23, 15–24, 15–25, 15–28, 15–29, 15–30, 15–32, 15–33, 15–37
121(a)	15–22
121(b)	15–22
121(b)(2)	15–22
121(c)	15–22
123	5–4
125	5–4, 5–17, 19–41
127	5–4, 5–17, 9–15
127(b)(2)	5–24
129	5–4, 5–17
131	5–4
132	5–4, 5–19
132(a)(6)	9–13
132(c)	5–20
132(d)	5–21
132(f)	5–22
132(g)	9–13
132(j)(1)	5–22, 5–24
132(j)(3)	5–21
132(j)(4)	5–17
134	5–4, 5–17
135	5–4, 5–28, 19–22
151(c)(1)	2–31, 3–14
151(c)(1)(B)	2–23, 2–31
151(c)(2)	2–29, 2–31, 3–14
151(d)	2–23
151(d)(2)	2–29, 2–31
152(a)	2–31, 3–13, 3–25
152(b)(2)	3–13
152(b)(5)	2–43, 3–13
152(c)	3–12
152(d)	2–23, 3–41
152(e)	3–13
162	6–3, 6–5, 6–12, 6–31, 20–16
162(a)	6–4, 6–31, 6–44, 9–3, 9–8
162(a)(1)	6–6
162(a)(2)	6–31
162(c)	6–11
162(c)(1)	6–5
162(c)(2)	9–36
162(e)	6–14
162(f)	6–11, 6–44

I.R.C. Sec.	This Work Page
162(g)	6–11
162(m)	19–29
163(a)	6–31, 10–11
163(d)	10–11, 20–27
163(h)(3)	10–13, 10–40
164	10–8, 10–9, 13–21
164(a)(1)	6–31
164(a)(2)	6–31
164(a)(3)	6–31
164(f)	13–37
165	6–7
165(a)	14–6
165(c)	7–9
165(c)(1)	6–31
165(c)(3)	6–31, 7–13, 15–15
165(g)	7–7
165(g)(1)	16–9
165(h)	7–12, 7–16
165(h)(4)(E)	7–13
165(i)	7–14, 18–9
165(k)	7–12
165(l)	7–6
166	6–31
166(a)	7–3
166(d)	16–29
167	8–3, 14–23, 17–12
168	8–3, 14–23, 17–12
168(b)	8–7, 8–11
168(b)(5)	8–14
168(c)	8–11
168(d)(3)	8–8
168(d)(4)(A)	8–8
168(e)	8–7, 8–11
168(e)(2)(A)	17–18
168(e)(3)	8–21
168(f)	8–4
168(g)	8–21
168(g)(3)(B)	8–21
169	12–20
170	6–31, 10–16, 17–20
170(a)(2)	20–8
170(b)(2)	20–9
170(c)	10–16, 10–18
170(d)(2)	20–9
170(e)	16–28
170(e)(1)(A)	10–41, 17–20
170(e)(1)(B)	17–20
170(e)(3)	20–9
170(f)(8)	10–19
170(i)	10–17
170(j)	10–17
170(l)	10–17
171(c)	14–6
172	7–20, 18–9

I.R.C. Sec.	This Work Page
172(d)	7–21, 20–10
173(a)	12–5
174	7–17, 13–14
174(b)(2)	7–18
179	8–1, 8–14, 8–15, 8–17, 8–22, 8–29, 8–43, 8–44, 8–45, 8–46, 8–47, 8–48, 9–7, 9–27, 12–7, 13–48, 14–23, 17–12, 17–14, 17–19, 17–21, 17–24, 17–29, 17–30, 18–42
179(b)	8–14
179(d)	8–14
183	2–17, 6–18, 6–32, 6–35
183(b)(2)	6–17
183(d)	6–18
195	6–16
195(a)	2–41
197	6–26, 8–23, 8–44, 17–12, 17–13, 17–19
197(a)	8–23
211	2–6
211–219	20–33
212	3–6, 6–3, 6–4, 6–5, 6–6, 6–29, 6–31, 9–21, 9–25, 10–24, 20–16, 20–27
212(1)	2–6
212(3)	10–5
213	6–31, 19–11
213(a)	6–25
213(c)	10–7
213(d)(1)(A)	10–3
213(d)(2)	10–5
215	4–19, 7–35
217	15–17
217(a)	9–12
217(b)	9–13
217(c)(2)	9–35
219	6–4
219(b)(1)	19–22
219(c)(2)	19–22
219(f)(1)	19–24
219(f)(3)	19–24
219(g)	19–22
219(g)(4)	19–22
241	2–6
243(a)	20–10
246(b)	20–11
248	20–12
262	6–25, 6–31, 10–2, 10–24, 16–17
263A	18–32
263A(d)	18–12
263(a)(1)	6–25
263(c)	17–23
265	6–29, 6–44
265(a)(2)	10–15
267	6–27, 14–17, 14–18, 14–25, 14–26, 16–17, 19–36
267(a)(1)	6–27, 14–6
267(b)	15–4, 18–24
267(d)	14–17, 14–18

I.R.C. Sec.	This Work Page
269A	19–18
269A(b)(2)	11–5
274	8–20
274(a)(1)(A)	9–17
274(a)(3)	9–18
274(b)(1)	9–19
274(c)	9–10
274(d)	8–21, 9–23
274(e)(2)	9–16
274(e)(4)	9–17, 9–35
274(e)(9)	9–16
274(h)(1)	9–8
274(i)	8–21
274(j)	4–31
274(k)	9–17
274(k)(1)(B)	9–18
274(l)	9–19
274(m)(2)	9–9
274(m)(3)	9–9
274(n)	9–16
274(n)(2)	9–16
276	6–13
280A	6–19
280A–280H	2–6
280A(c)(1)	9–20, 9–36
280A(d)	6–20, 6–23
280A(g)	6–20
280C(c)	13–14
280E	6–13
280F	8–16, 17–24
280F(a)(2)	8–17
280F(b)(2)	8–18
280F(b)(3)	8–18
280F(b)(4)	8–16
280F(d)(1)	8–17
280F(d)(4)	8–16
280F(d)(5)	8–17
280G	19–29, 19–46
280H	18–6
291	20–7, 20–8, 20–16
291(a)(1)	17–23
301	20–20, 20–22
301(c)	5–27
302	20–22
303	20–22
305(a)	5–27, 14–10
305(b)	5–27
307(a)	14–10
307(b)	14–11
311(b)	17–21
312	20–20
316	20–19
316(a)	5–27
318	19–18
318(a)	18–24
331	20–2, 20–22, 20–42

I.R.C. Sec.	This Work Page
332	17–20, 20–23
334	20–2, 20–23
334(a)	20–23
334(b)(1)	20–23, 20–24
336	20–23
336(d)	20–24
338	20–2, 20–23
341(e)	2–25
351	17–20, 18–25, 20–18, 20–19, 20–38, 20–39, 20–41
358(a)	20–18
362(a)	20–18
368(c)	20–18
385	20–18
401(a)	19–6, 19–8, 19–48
401(a)(4)	19–8, 19–9
401(a)(5)	19–8
401(a)(9)	19–11
401(a)(17)	19–17
401(a)(26)	19–10
401(c)(2)	19–21
401(c)(2)(A)(v)	19–21
401(d)	19–21
401(k)	19–2, 19–19, 19–20, 19–38, 19–39, 19–42, 19–44, 19–46
401(k)(3)	19–39
402(a)(1)	19–12
402(a)(2)	19–44
402(a)(5)	19–13, 19–48
402(e)(1)	19–14
402(e)(1)(C)	19–13
402(e)(1)(D)	19–14
402(e)(4)(J)	19–14, 19–15
402(e)(4)(L)	19–13
404	19–16
404(a)(1)(6)	19–17
404(a)(1)(D)	19–17
404(a)(3)(A)	19–18
404(a)(7)	19–18
404(a)(d)	19–28
404(h)(1)(A)	19–24
404(h)(1)(B)	19–25
404(j)	19–16
404(l)	19–17
408(d)(1)	19–25
408(d)(2)	19–25
408(d)(3)(B)	19–26
408(d)(4)	19–25
408(j)	19–23
408(k)(2)	19–23
408(k)(6)	19–23
408(o)	19–22
409(h)(1)	19–7
410(a)(1)(A)	19–8
410(a)(1)(B)	19–8

I.R.C. Sec.	This Work Page
410(a)(4)	19–8
410(b)	19–9
410(b)(3)	19–10
410(b)(4)	19–10
414(i)	19–4
414(j)	19–4
414(q)	19–9
415	19–16
415(b)	19–16
415(b)(1)	19–16, 19–21
415(c)	19–16
415(c)(1)	19–21
416(b)	19–18
416(i)(1)	19–18
421	4–22
421(a)	12–12
421(a)(1)	19–34
421(a)(2)	19–35
422	19–34, 19–41
422(a)	19–34
422(a)(1)	19–34
422(a)(2)	19–35
422(b)	19–36
422(c)(3)	19–35
422(c)(5)	19–36
422(e)	4–23
441(a)	4–7
441(c)	18–3
441(d)	4–7
441(f)	18–3
441(i)	18–6
442	18–7
443(b)(1)	18–9
443(b)(2)	18–9
444	18–5, 18–6
444(c)	18–5
446	18–10
446(a)	6–7
446(b)	4–7, 4–12, 6–7, 18–11
446(c)	18–15
446(d)	18–10
446(e)	4–7, 6–7
446(f)	18–17
447	18–12
447(c)	18–12
448	6–9
448(a)	18–12
448(b)	18–12
448(d)	11–5
448(d)(5)	18–14
451(a)	19–27
451(d)	18–9
453	2–33
453A	4–7, 18–25
453(a)	4–7, 15–29, 18–20
453(b)	4–7

I.R.C. Sec.	This Work Page
453B(a)	18–25
453B(c)	18–25
453B(d)	18–25
453B(f)(2)	18–25
453B(g)	18–25
453(b),(i),(l)	18–19
453(d)	18–26
453(d)(3)	18–26
453(e)	18–23
453(e)(2)	18–24
453(e)(2)(B)	18–24
453(e)(6)	18–24
453(e)(7)	18–24
453(f)(1)	18–24
453(g)	18–24
453(i)	17–21
453(l)	18–19
453(l)(2)	18–19
454(a)	4–11
460	18–27
460(b)(1)(A)	18–30
460(b)(2)	18–30
460(b)(5)	18–30
460(f)	18–26
461(g)(1)	10–16
461(g)(2)	10–14, 10–40
461(h)	18–13
461(h)(1)	6–9
461(h)(2)(A)	6–9
461(h)(2)(B)	6–9
461(h)(3)(A)	6–10
461(h)(4)	18–13
464	18–12
464(c)	18–12
465(b)(1)	11–3
465(e)	11–4
468	18–13
469	11–6, 11–11, 11–13, 11–18, 19–22, 20–27
469(a)	11–4
469(b)	11–22
469(c)(2)	11–13
469(d)(2)	11–22
469(f)	11–26
469(g)(2)	11–26
469(g)(3)	11–26
469(i)	11–23
469(i)(6)	11–23
469(j)(2)	11–5
469(j)(5)	11–24
469(j)(6)	11–26
469(j)(8)	11–13
471	18–31
471(a)	18–31
472(c)	12–26, 18–36
472(d)	18–36

I.R.C. Sec.	This Work Page
481(b)	18–18
483	18–21, 18–23
483(e)	18–23
501	10–18
501(a)	19–13, 19–48
585	18–14
611(a)	8–26
612	8–25
613	8–28
613A	8–26
613(a)	8–26
617(a)	12–10
631	17–5
631(a)	17–5
652(a)	4–17
662(a)	4–17
702(a)	20–33
703(a)	20–33
704(e)	20–36
705(a)	20–31
706(a)	4–16
706(b)(1)(B)	18–4
706(b)(1)(C)	18–5
706(b)(3)	18–4
707	14–17
707(b)(1)	20–34
707(c)	20–34
721	11–27, 17–20, 20–30
722	20–31
723	20–32
901–908	13–20
904	13–21
911	5–4, 5–29, 19–22
911(a)	5–25
911(c)	5–25
911(d)	5–25
912(1)(C)	6–44
1001(a)	14–3
1001(b)	14–3
1001(c)	14–6
1011	14–13
1011(a)	14–4
1012	14–8
1014	11–26
1014(a)	14–14
1014(b)(6)	14–16
1014(e)	14–16
1015(a)	14–11
1015(d)(6)	14–12
1016(a)	14–4
1016(a)(2)	14–5
1016(a)(4)	14–5
1016(a)(5)	14–5
1017	5–30
1031	11–27, 14–8, 15–2, 15–3, 15–4, 15–5, 15–6, 15–7, 15–11, 15–15, 15–25, 15–27, 15–31, 15–41, 17–21, 17–34
1031(a)	15–3
1032	15–2, 15–25, 19–7, 20–17
1033	14–8, 15–2, 15–9, 15–10, 15–11, 15–13, 15–14, 15–15, 15–22, 15–23, 15–27, 15–28, 15–30, 15–32, 15–36, 17–21
1033(a)	15–10, 15–11
1033(a)(2)(A)	15–14
1033(a)(2)(B)	15–12
1033(b)	15–14
1033(g)(4)	15–12
1033(h)	15–16
1034	10–13, 14–8, 14–20, 15–2, 15–15, 15–16, 15–17, 15–19, 15–20, 15–21, 15–22, 15–23, 15–24, 15–28, 15–29, 15–30, 15–32
1034(h)(1)	15–18
1034(h)(2)	15–18
1034(k)	15–18
1035	15–2, 15–25
1036	15–2, 15–25
1038	15–2, 15–26
1041	4–20, 14–17, 15–2, 15–26, 18–24
1042(c)(4)	19–7
1044	15–26
1056	16–15
1060	14–9
1091	14–19
1091(a)	14–19
1091(b)	14–19
1091(d)	14–19
1211(a)	16–25, 20–7
1211(b)	16–21
1211(b)(1)	16–23
1212(a)	20–7
1212(a)(1)	16–25
1212(b)	16–24
1221	3–27, 16–3, 16–6, 16–8, 16–36
1221(1)	2–6
1221(2)	17–3
1221(3)	10–41
1222	16–16
1222(10)	16–23
1223	16–17
1223(1)	15–8
1223(2)	14–13, 14–18, 20–32
1223(4)	14–19
1223(5)	14–10, 14–11
1223(6)	19–33
1223(11)	14–17
1231	6–26, 10–21, 14–9, 15–8, 15–40, 16–3, 16–5, 16–17, 16–31, 17–1, 17–2, 17–3, 17–4, 17–5, 17–6, 17–7, 17–8, 17–9, 17–10, 17–11, 17–12, 17–13, 17–14, 17–15, 17–16, 17–17, 17–18, 17–19, 17–20, 17–21, 17–22, 17–23, 17–24, 17–25, 17–29, 17–30, 17–31, 17–32, 17–33, 17–35, 17–36, 18–21, 20–7, 20–8, 20–27, 20–28
1231(b)	17–36
1232A(a)	14–5

I.R.C. Sec.	This Work Page
1232A(c)(5)	14–5
1232(a)(2)(A)	14–5
1233	16–18
1233(a)	2–34
1233(b)(2)	2–34
1234A	16–9
1234(a)	16–10
1235	16–12
1236(a)	16–7
1236(b)	16–7
1237	16–7, 16–8, 16–32, 16–36
1239	17–23
1239(b)	18–25
1239(c)	18–25
1241	16–16
1242	16–29
1244	7–1, 7–8, 7–9, 7–26, 7–27, 7–28, 7–29, 7–32, 16–9, 16–29
1245	7–1, 8–5, 16–15, 17–2, 17–12, 17–13, 17–14, 17–15, 17–16, 17–19, 17–20, 17–21, 17–22, 17–23, 17–24, 17–25, 17–29, 17–30, 17–31, 17–34, 17–36, 18–19, 18–21, 18–44, 20–5, 20–7, 20–8, 20–16
1245(a)(4)	17–36
1245(b)(1)	17–19
1245(b)(2)	17–20
1245(b)(3)	17–20
1245(d)	17–21
1250	17–1, 17–2, 17–12, 17–14, 17–15, 17–16, 17–17, 17–18, 17–19, 17–21, 17–23, 17–24, 17–25, 17–29, 17–30, 17–31, 17–34, 17–36, 18–19, 18–21, 18–44, 20–5, 20–7, 20–8, 20–16, 20–41
1250(a)(1)(B)	17–18
1250(a)(1)	17–18
1250(a)(2)	17–18
1250(d)(1)	17–19
1250(d)(2)	17–20
1250(d)(3)	17–20
1250(f)	17–16
1250(i)	17–21
1253	16–14, 16–15
1253(b)(1)	16–14
1253(e)	16–15
1254	17–23
1271	16–9
1272–1275	16–10
1272(a)	18–22
1272(a)(2)	4–11
1272(a)(3)	4–11, 18–23
1273(a)	4–11, 18–22
1273(a)(3)	16–10
1274	18–21, 18–23
1274A	18–23
1274A(c)	18–23
1274(a)	18–22
1274(c)(3)(A)	18–23
1274(c)(3)(B)	18–23

I.R.C. Sec.	This Work Page
1274(c)(3)(C)	18–23
1274(c)(3)(F)	18–23
1274(d)(1)	18–22
1276–1288	16–10
1341	18–10
1361(a)	4–17
1361(b)	20–24
1361–1379	2–6
1362	20–25
1366	4–17, 20–27
1366(e)	20–36
1367	20–29
1378(a)	18–5
1378(b)	18–5
1378(b)(2)	18–5
1402(a)	19–21
1402(a)(8)	13–49
1402(a)(12)	13–37
1843(c)(2)	4–22
2032(a)(1)	14–14
2032(c)	14–14
2040(a)	14–17
3401	13–29
3402	3–17, 13–29, 19–33
3403	13–26
3406(a)	13–34
4942	10–21
4972	19–17
4973(a)(1)	19–25
4973(b)	19–25
4973(b)(2)	19–25
4974(a)	19–11
4975(e)(7)	19–6
4979(a)	19–19
4981A	19–11
4981A(c)(5)	19–12
4999	19–29
6012(a)(1)	3–21
6012(a)(2)	20–14
6017	13–36
6031	20–32
6072(a)	3–22
6081	20–14
6110	2–11
6110(j)(3)	2–12, 12–6
6202	3–17
6621	18–26
6654	13–26
6654(b)(2)	13–35
6654(b)(3)	13–36
6654(c)(1)	13–35
6655	20–14
6655(f)	20–14
6656	13–26
6659	10–41
6661	2–29

I.R.C. Sec.	This Work Page	I.R.C. Sec.	This Work Page
6662	2–28	7805(e)	2–9
6662(b)(3)	10–41	7852(d)	2–8
6662(c)	2–27	7872(a)(1)	4–24
7482(a)(c)	2–17	7872(b)(2)	4–24
7519	18–5	7872(c)	4–25
7519(b)	18–5	7872(c)(2)	4–26
7701(a)(2)	2–41	7872(c)(3)	4–27
7805	2–8	7872(d)	4–26
7805(a)	2–9	7872(f)(2)	4–24

APPENDIX D-2
Table of Regulations Cited

Temporary Treasury Regulations

Temp.Reg. Sec.	This Work Page
1.1(i)–1T	2–9
1.79–3T	4–31
1.263A–1(a)	18–32
1.263A–1(h)(5)	18–32
1.263A–1T(b)(3)(iii)(A)(1)	18–27
1.469–1T(e)(3)(ii)	11–13
1.469–1T(e)(3)(iv)	11–14
1.469–1T(e)(3)(vi)(B) – (E)	11–14
1.469–2T(a)(2)	11–19
1.469–2T(c)(2)	11–19
1.469–2T(c)(2)(i) – (iii)	11–25
1.469–2T(c)(3)	11–19
1.469–2T(c)(4)	11–19
1.469–2T(c)(7)	11–19
1.469–2T(d)	11–20
1.469–5T(b)(2)	11–11
1.469–5T(e)(3)(ii)	11–13
1.469–5T(f)(3)	11–13
1.469–5T(j)	11–10
1.706–1T(a)(2)	18–4
15a.453–1(b)(2)(iii)	18–20
15a.453–1(d)	18–26
15a.453–1(d)(4)	18–26
35.3405–1	19–26
3405(c)	19–26

Proposed Treasury Regulations

Prop.Reg. Sec.	This Work Page
1.2	2–9
1.117–6(a)(3)(i)	5–8
1.117–6(b)(2)	5–9
1.117–6(d)	5–10
1.117–6(h)	5–9
1.280A–3(c)	6–20
1.280A–3(d)(4)	6–22
1.408–4(b)(4)	19–26
1.461–4(g)(2)–(6)	18–14

Proposed Treasury Regulations

Prop.Reg. Sec.	This Work Page
1.461–5(c)	18–14
1.469–4	11–16
1.469–4(c)(2)	11–16
1.469–4(c)(3)	11–17
1.469–4(d)	11–17
1.469–4(h)	11–17
1.482–2	2–42
1.7872–2(b)(1)(i)	4–26

Treasury Regulations

Reg. Sec.	This Work Page
1.2	2–9
1.61–1(a)	4–6
1.61–2 T(j)	5–24
1.61–2(d)(2)(i)	14–8
1.61–2(d)(4)	19–27
1.61–3(a)	6–13
1.61–6(a)	14–6, 14–9
1.61–9(c)	4–16
1.61–12	4–6
1.67–1T(a)(1)(iv)	6–18
1.72–7(c)(1)	5–7
1.72–9	4–28, 19–11
1.79–3(d)(2)	4–31
1.83–1(a)	19–28
1.83–2(a)	19–33
1.83–3(c)(2)	19–32
1.83–6(a)	19–33
1.83–6(c)	19–33
1.83–7	19–36
1.83–7(a)	19–37
1.101–7T	5–7
1.106–1	5–13
1.107–1	5–16
1.117–2(a)	5–8
1.119–1(c)(1)	5–15
1.119–1(f)	5–15

Treasury Regulations

Reg. Sec.	This Work Page
1.121–2(b)	15–22
1.121–4(b)(c)	15–24
1.132–1(b)	5–20
1.132–2	5–19
1.151–3(a)	2–41, 3–14
1.151–3(b)	2–29, 2–31, 3–14
1.151–3(c)	3–14
1.152–1(c)	2–23, 2–31, 3–11
1.162–12(a)	18–12
1.162–17(b)(4)	9–23
1.162–2(b)(1)	9–10
1.162–5(b)(2)(iii)	9–14
1.162–5(b)(2)	9–14
1.162–5(b)(3)	9–14
1.162–5(b)(3)(ii)	9–15
1.162–8	6–6
1.164–4(a)	10–9
1.165–1(a)	14–6
1.165–1(d)(2)	7–10
1.165–1(d)(2)(i)	7–11
1.165–7	15–15
1.165–7(a)(2)(ii)	7–13
1.165–8(a)(2)	7–10
1.165–8(d)	7–10
1.165–9(b)(2)	14–20
1.166	7–3
1.166–1(e)	7–3
1.166–5(d)	7–5
1.167(g)–1	14–13, 14–20
1.167(j)–3(b)(1)(i)	17–18
1.170A–1(e)	10–41
1.170A–4(b)(1)	17–20
1.170A–4(b)(3)(ii)(b)	10–22
1.172–3(a)	7–21
1.174–2(a)(1)	7–18
1.179–1(e)	8–16
1.183–1(b)(1)	6–18
1.183–2(b)(1)–(9)	6–17, 6–33
1.212–1(d)	6–6
1.212–1(f)	9–14
1.212–1(g)	6–4
1.213–1(e)(1)(v)	10–3
1.263A–1(b)(12)	18–32
1.263(a)–1(b)	6–25
1.267(d)–1(a)	14–17
1.267(d)–1(c)(3)	14–18
1.274–4	9–10
1.274–5T(c)(3)	9–23
1.280F–6T(e)	8–17
1.280F–7T(a)	8–19
1.301–1(j)	14–8
1.307–1(a)	14–10
1.401–1(b)	19–6

Treasury Regulations

Reg. Sec.	This Work Page
1.401–1(b)(1)(iii)	19–6
1.401–1(b)(2)	19–7
1.401–4(a)(1)(iii)	19–6
1.421–1(a)(1)–7(a)(1)	19–34
1.421–6(c)	19–36
1.421–6(d)	19–36, 19–37
1.421–6(e)	19–36
1.421–6(f)	19–36
1.441–1(b)(1)(ii)	18–3
1.441–1(b)(3)	18–7
1.441–1(b)(4)	18–7
1.441–1(e)(2)	18–3
1.442–1(b)(1)	18–7
1.442–1(c)(1)	18–7
1.443–1(a)(2)	18–9
1.446–1(a)(1)	18–10, 18–15
1.446–1(a)(2)	6–7
1.446–1(a)(3)	4–8
1.446–1(a)(4)(i)	18–10, 18–11
1.446–1(c)(1)(iv)(b)	18–10
1.446–1(c)(1)(i)	4–8
1.446–1(c)(2)(i)	4–7
1.446–1(e)(2)(ii)	18–16
1.446–1(e)(2)(ii)(b)	18–16
1.446–1(e)(3)	18–15
1.451–1(a)	4–8, 18–11, 18–12
1.451–2	19–27
1.451–2(a)	4–9, 19–28
1.451–2(b)	4–10
1.451–3	4–7
1.451–3(b)	18–26
1.451–3(b)(2)	18–29
1.451–3(c)(3)	18–30
1.451–3(d)(2)(ii)–(vii)	18–29
1.451–3(d)(9)	18–27
1.451–5	4–37, 18–29
1.451–5(b)	4–13
1.451–5(c)	4–13
1.461–1(a)	6–9
1.461–1(a)(1)	18–11
1.461–1(a)(2)	6–10
1.471–1–2	18–31
1.471–2(c)	18–33
1.471–3(b)	18–32
1.471–4(b)	18–31
1.471–4(c)	18–33
1.471–6(a)	18–12
1.472–2(c)	18–36
1.472–2(e)	18–36
1.472–3(a)	18–36
1.472–4	18–33
1.472–5	18–36
1.472–8	18–35

Treasury Regulations

Reg. Sec.	This Work Page
1.611–1(b)	8–24
1.631–1	17–5
1.641(a)–0(c)	2–16
1.706–1(a)	18–4
1.706–1(a)(1)	4–16
1.871–2(b)	5–25
1.1001–1(a)	14–3
1.1001–1(b)	14–3
1.1001–1(b)(2)	14–4
1.1001–1(c)(1)	14–3
1.1001–2(a)	5–30
1.1002–1(a)	14–6
1.1002–1(c)	15–2
1.1011–1	14–4, 14–13
1.1012–1(a)	14–8
1.1012–1(b)	14–4
1.1012–1(c)(1)	14–9
1.1015–1(a)(1)	14–11
1.1015–1(a)(3)	14–11
1.1016–1	14–4
1.1016–3(a)(1)(i)	14–5
1.1016–5(a)	14–5
1.1016–5(b)	14–5
1.1016–6(a)	14–5
1.1031(a)–1(a)	15–3
1.1031(a)–1(b)	15–4
1.1031(a)–2(j)–1	15–4
1.1031(a)–3(g)(2)	2–41
1.1031(d)–2	15–9
1.1033(a)–1	15–11
1.1033(a)–1(a)–2(a)	15–10
1.1033(a)–2(c)(1)	15–14
1.1033(a)–2(c)(3)	15–12, 15–13
1.1033(c)–1(a)	15–41
1.1034–1(b)(7)(9)	15–20
1.1034–1(c)(3)	15–18
1.1034–1(c)(3)(i)	15–16

Treasury Regulations

Reg. Sec.	This Work Page
1.1034–1(c)(4)(i)	15–20
1.1034–1(c)(4)(ii)	15–20
1.1091–1(a)	14–19
1.1091–1(a)(f)	14–19
1.1091–1(c)	14–19
1.1091–2(a)	14–19
1.1221–1(b)	16–16
1.1223–1(a)	15–8
1.1223–1(b)	14–13
1.1223–1(d)	14–19
1.1223–1(e)	14–10, 14–11
1.1223–1(f)	14–11
1.1234–1(a)(1)	16–10
1.1235–2(b)(1)	16–13
1.1236–1(a)	16–7
1.1241–1(a)	16–16
1.1245–1(c)–6(b)	17–21
1.1245–2(a)(4)	15–8
1.1245–2(a)(4)–2(c)(2)	17–20
1.1245–4(a)(1)	17–19
1.1245–4(c)	17–20
1.1250–1(a)(4) –1(b)(4)–1(c)(2)	17–21
1.1250–1(d)(1)(i)(c)	17–18
1.1250–2(d)(1)	15–8
1.1250–2(d)(1)(3)–3(c)(3)	17–20
1.1250–3(a)(1)	17–19
1.1250–3(c)	17–20
1.1250–5	17–16
1.1502–75(c)(2)(i)	2–41
1.6013–1(a)(1)	3–30
1.6081–4	3–22
1.6661–3(b)(2)	2–28
31.3401(c)–(1)(b)	9–3
301.6114–1	2–8
301.6712–1	2–8
301.7701–2(a)	20–4

APPENDIX D-3
Table of Revenue Procedures and Revenue Rulings Cited

Revenue Procedure

Rev.Proc.	This Work Page
71–21	4–13, 4–14, 4–36
83–35	8–5
83–78	2–42
84–74	18–36
85–16	18–8
87–1	2–27
87–32	18–7, 18–37
87–56	2–36, 8–7, 8–22, 8–48, 12–10
87–57	8–36, 8–42, 15–5
89–12	20–4
92–20	18–18, 18–36
92–71	6–28
93–51	10–5
93–151	9–6
94–3	2–11

Revenue Rulings

Rev.Rul.	This Work Page
51	16–36
54–567	2–29
55–261	10–4
55–273	4–51
55–525	19–28
56–60	14–14
56–406	14–19
57–244	15–27
57–344	3–11
57–345	10–8
57–418	6–16
58–419	3–11
59–72	15–19
59–86	14–13
60–31	19–28
61	4–5
61–119	15–6
61–186	3–41
62–102	5–7

Revenue Rulings

Rev.Rul.	This Work Page
63–221	15–10
63–232	7–10
64–221	3–41
65–34	2–29
65–178	19–8
65–235	2–36
66–7	16–16
67–289	19–28
67–297	10–14
68–212	10–4
68–579	5–43
68–662	6–12
69–185	2–42
69–292	9–14
70–466	15–11
70–622	10–8
71–190	10–11
71–425	5–4
72–312	4–15
72–545	6–25
72–592	7–9
73–18	15–41
73–380	19–8
73–476	15–27
74–78	9–14
74–175	16–29
75–14	6–18
75–168	9–7
75–380	9–5
75–448	5–9
76–111	14–37
76–282	18–36
77–37	2–41
77–298	15–29
78–39	6–8
78–146	15–19
78–146	15–29
78–147	15–20
78–340	10–4
79–379	4–16

Revenue Rulings

Rev.Rul.	This Work Page
80	5–15
80–52	4–10
80–335	6–8
81–180	15–10
81–181	15–10
82–26	15–18
82–74	15–10
82–196	5–13
82–202	5–30
82–208	10–11
82–227	18–26

Rev.Rul.	This Work Page
83–3	6–44
84–108	5–12
85–97	5–11
85–135	2–41
85–143	5–11
87–22	10–14
87–57	18–5
87–106	10–5
90–23	9–5
92–62	2–10
94–1	13–15

APPENDIX E
Citator Example

ILLUSTRATION OF THE USE OF THE CITATOR[1]

BACKGROUND

The *Federal Tax Citator* is a separate multivolume service with monthly supplements. Cases reported by the *Citator* are divided into the various issues involved. Since the researcher may be interested in only one or two issues, only those cases involving the particular issue need to be checked.

The *Federal Tax Citator* includes the following volumes, each of which covers a particular period of time:

- Volume 1 (1863–1941)
- Volume 2 (1942–1948)
- Volume 3 (1948–1954)
- Volume 1, Second Series (1954–1977)
- Volume 2, Second Series (1978–1989)
- Cumulative supplement (1990–1993)
- Monthly cumulative supplements (paperback)

Through the use of symbols, the *Citator* indicates whether a decision has been followed, explained, criticized, questioned, or overruled by a later court decision. These symbols are reproduced in Figure E–1.

EXAMPLE

Determine the background and validity of *Adda v. Comm.*, 37 AFTR 654, 171 F.2d 457 (CA–4, 1948).

SOLUTION

Turning directly to the case itself (reproduced as Figure E–2), note the two issues involved (issues 1 and 2). For purposes of emphasis, these issues have been bracketed and identified by a marginal notation in the figure. The reason for the division of the issues becomes apparent when the case is traced through the *Citator*.

---

[1] Features in the *Federal Tax Citator* that do not appear in the CCH *Citator* include the following: (1) distinguishes between the various issues in the case, (2) lists all court decisions that cite the court decision being researched, (3) indicates the relationship (e.g., explained, criticized, followed, or overruled) between the court decision being researched and subsequent decisions, and (4) pinpoints the exact page on which one court decision is cited by another court decision. Prior to the acquisition of Prentice-Hall Information Services, the *Federal Tax Citator* was published by Prentice-Hall. The *Federal Tax Citator* is now published by Research Institute of America.

▼ **FIGURE E–1**

Citator Symbols*

COURT DECISIONS

Judicial History of the Case

a	affirmed (by decision of a higher court)
d	dismissed (appeal to a higher court dismissed)
m	modified (decision modified by a higher court, or on rehearing)
r	reversed (by a decision of a higher court)
s	same case (e.g., on rehearing)
rc	related case (companion cases and other cases arising out of the same subject matter are so designated)
x	certiorari denied (by the Supreme Court of the United States)
(C or G)	The Commissioner or Solicitor General has made the appeal
(T)	Taxpayer has made the appeal
(A)	Tax Court's decision acquiesced in by Commissioner
(NA)	Tax Court's decision nonacquiesced in by Commissioner
sa	same case affirmed (by the cited case)
sd	same case dismissed (by the cited case)
sm	same case modified (by the cited case)
sr	same case reversed (by the cited case)
sx	same case—certiorari denied

Syllabus of the Cited Case

iv	four (on all fours with the cited case)
f	followed (the cited case followed)
e	explained (comment generally favorable, but not to a degree that indicates the cited case is followed)
k	reconciled (the cited case reconciled)
n	dissenting opinion (cited in a dissenting opinion)
g	distinguished (the cited case distinguished either in law or on the facts)
l	limited (the cited case limited to its facts. Used when an appellate court so limits a prior decision, or a lower court states that in its opinion the cited case should be so limited)
c	criticized (adverse comment on the cited case)
q	questioned (the cited case not only criticized, but its correctness questioned)
o	overruled

*Reproduced from the *Federal Tax 2nd Citator* with the permission of the publisher, Research Institute of America, Englewood Cliffs, NJ 07632.

Refer to Volume 3 of the First Series (covering the period from October 7, 1948, through July 29, 1954) of the *Federal Tax Citator*. The case reference is located on page 5505, which is reproduced in Figure E–3.

Correlating the symbols in Figure E–1 with the shaded portion of Figure E–3 reveals the following information about *Adda v. Comm.*:

- Application for certiorari (appeal to the U.S. Supreme Court) filed by the taxpayer (T) on March 1, 1949.
- Certiorari was denied (x) by the U.S. Supreme Court on April 18, 1949.

▼ **FIGURE E–2**

ADDA v. COMMISSIONER OF INTERNAL REVENUE   457
Cite as 171 F.2d 457

ADDA v. COMMISSIONER OF INTERNAL REVENUE.

No. 5796.

United States Court of Appeals
Fourth Circuit.

Dec. 3, 1948.

ISSUE 1

1. **Internal revenue** ⬅792

Where nonresident alien's brother residing in United States traded for alien's benefit on commodity exchanges in United States at authorization of alien, who vested full discretion in brother with regard thereto, and many transactions were effected through different brokers, several accounts were maintained, and substantial gains and losses realized, transactions constituted a "trade or business," profits of which were "capital gains" taxable as income to the alien. 26 U.S.C.A. § 211(b).

See Words and Phrases, Permanent Edition, for other judicial constructions and definitions of "Capital Gains" and "Trade or Business".

ISSUE 2

2. **Internal revenue** ⬅792

The exemption of a nonresident alien's commodity transactions in the United States provided for by the Internal Revenue Code does not apply where alien has agent in United States using his own discretion in effecting transactions for alien's account. 26 U.S.C.A. § 211(b).

———◆———

On Petition to Review the Decision of The Tax Court of the United States.

Petition by Fernand C. A. Adda to review a decision of the Tax Court redetermining a deficiency in income tax imposed by the Commissioner of Internal Revenue.

Decision affirmed.

Rollin Browne and Mitchell B. Carroll, both of New York City, for petitioner.

Irving I. Axelrad, Sp. Asst. to Atty. Gen. (Theron Lamar Caudle, Asst. Atty. Gen., and Ellis N. Slack and A. F. Prescott, Sp. Assts. to Atty. Gen., on the brief), for respondent.

Before PARKER, Chief Judge, and SOPER and DOBIE, Circuit Judges.

PER CURIAM.

[1, 2] This is a petition by a non-resident alien to review a decision of the Tax Court. Petitioner is a national of Egypt, who in the year 1941 was residing in France. He had a brother who at that time was residing in the United States and who traded for petitioner's benefit on commodity exchanges in the United States in cotton, wool, grains, silk, hides and copper. This·trading was authorized by petitioner who vested full discretion in his brother with regard thereto, and it resulted in profits in the sum of $193,857.14. The Tax Court said: "While the number of transactions or the total amount of money involved in them has not been stated, it is apparent that many transactions were effected through different brokers, several accounts were maintained, and gains and losses in substantial amounts were realized. This evidence shows that the trading was extensive enough to amount to a trade or business, and the petitioner does not contend, nor has he shown, that the transactions were so infrequent or inconsequential as not to amount to a trade or business." We agree with the Tax Court that, for reasons adequately set forth in its opinion, this income was subject to taxation, and that the exemption of a non-resident alien's commodity transactions in the United States, provided by section 211(b) of the Internal Revenue Code, 26 U.S.C.A. § 211(b), does not apply to a case where the alien has an agent in the United States using his own discretion in effecting the transactions for the alien's account. As said by the Tax Court, "Through such transactions the alien is engaging in trade or business within the United States, and the profits on these transactions are capital gains taxable to him." Nothing need be added to the reasoning of the Tax Court in this connection, and the decision will be affirmed on its opinion.

Affirmed.

- The trial court decision is reported in 10 T.C. 273 and was affirmed on appeal (sa) to the Fourth Court of Appeals.
- During the time frame of Volume 3 of the *Citator* (October 7, 1948, through July 29, 1954), one decision (*Milner Hotels, Inc.*) has agreed "on all fours with the cited case" (iv). One decision (*Comm. v. Nubar*) has limited the cited case to its facts (l) and two decisions (*The Scottish American Investment Co., Ltd.* and *Zareh Nubar*) have distinguished the cited case on issue number one (g-1).

▼ **FIGURE E–3**

» Adamson — Adler «   5505

ADAMSON, JAMES H. & MARION C. v
U. S., — F Supp —, 36 AFTR 1529, 1946
P.-H. ¶ 72,418 (DC Calif) (See Adamson
v U. S.)
ADAMSON, R. R., MRS. — BTA —, 1934 (P.-
H.) BTA Memo. Dec. ¶ 34,370
ADAMSON v U. S., 26 AFTR 1188 (DC Calif,
Sept 8, 1939)
 iv—Coggan, Linus C., 1939 (P.-H.) BTA
  Memo. Dec. page 39—806
ADAMSON; U. S. v, 161 F(2d) 942, 35 AFTR
1404 (CCA 9)
 1—Lazier v U. S., 170 F(2d) 524, 37 AFTR
  545, 1948 P.-H. page 73,174 (CCA 8)
 1—Grace Bros., Inc. v Comm., 173 F(2d)
  178, 37 AFTR 1014, 1949 P.-H. page 72,433
  (CCA 9)
 1—Briggs; Hofferbert v, 178 F(2d) 744, 38
  AFTR 1219, 1950 P.-H. page 72,267 (CCA
  4)
 1—Rogers v Comm., 180 F(2d) 722, 39 AFTR
  115, 1950 P.-H. page 72,531 (CCA 3)
 1—Lamar v Granger, 99 F Supp 41, 40
  AFTR 270, 1951 P.-H. page 72,945 (DC Pa)
 1—Herbert v Riddell, 103 F Supp 383, 41
  AFTR 975, 1952 P.-H. page 72,383 (DC
  Calif)
 1—Hudson, Galvin, 20 TC 737, 20-1953
  P.-H. TC 418
ADAMSON v U. S., — F Supp —, 36 AFTR
1529, 1946 P.-H. ¶ 72,418 (DC Calif, Jan
28, 1946)
ADAMS-ROTH BAKING CO., 8 BTA 458
 1—Gunderson Bros. Engineering Corp., 16
  TC 129, 16-1951 P.-H. TC 72
ADAMSTON FLAT GLASS CO. v COMM.,
162 F(2d) 875, 35 AFTR 1579 (CCA 6)
 4—Forrest Hotel Corp. v. Fly, 112 F Supp
  789, 43 AFTR 1080, 1953 P.-H. page 72,856
  (DC Miss)
ADDA v COMM., 171 F(2d) 457, 37 AFTR 654,
1948 P.-H. ¶ 72,655 (CCA 4, Dec 3, 1948)
Cert. filed, March 1, 1949 (T)
No cert. (G) 1949 P-H ¶ 71,050
 x—Adda v Comm., 336 US 952, 69 S Ct 883,
  93 L Ed 1107, April 18, 1949 (T)
 sa—Adda, Fernand C. A., 10 TC 273 (No.
  33), ¶ 10.33 P.-H. TC 1948
 iv—Milner Hotels, Inc., N. Y., 173 F(2d)
  567, 37 AFTR 1170, 1949 P.-H. page 72,528
  (CCA 6)
 1—Nubar; Comm. v, 185 F(2d) 588, 39 AFTR
  1315, 1950 P.-H. page 73,423 (CCA 4)
 g-1—Scottish Amer. Invest. Co., Ltd.,
  The, 12 TC 59, 12-1949 P.-H. TC 32
 g-1—Nubar, Zareh, 13 TC 579, 13-1949
  P.-H. TC 318
ADDA, FERNAND C. A., 10 TC 273 (No.
33), ¶ 10.33 P.-H. TC 1948 (A) 1948-2 CB 1
 a—Adda v Comm., 171 F(2d) 457, 37 AFTR
  654, 1948 P.-H. ¶ 72,655 (CCA 4)
 1—Nubar; Comm. v, 185 F(2d) 588, 39 AFTR
  1315, 1950 P.-H. page 73,423 (CCA 4)
 g-1—Scottish Amer. Invest. Co., Ltd.,
  The, 12 TC 59, 12-1949 P.-H. TC 32
 g-1—Nubar, Zareh, 13 TC 579, 13-1949
  P.-H. TC 318
ADDA, FERNAND C. A., 10 TC 1291 (No.
168), ¶ 10.168 P.-H. TC 1948 (A) 1953-1
CB 3, 1953 P.-H. ¶ 76,453 (NA) 1948-2
CB 5, 1948 P.-H. ¶ 76,434 withdrawn
 1—Scottish Amer. Invest. Co., Ltd., The,
  12 TC 59, 12-1949 P.-H. TC 32
ADDA INC., 9 TC 199 (A) 1949-1 CB 1, 1949
P.-H. ¶ 76,260 (NA) 1947-2 CB 6 withdrawn
 a—Adda, Inc.; Comm. v, 171 F(2d) 367, 37
  AFTR 641, 1948 P.-H. ¶ 72,654 (CCA 2)
 a—Adda, Inc.; Comm. v, 171 F(2d) 367, 37
  AFTR 641, 1949 P.-H. ¶ 72,303 (CCA 2)
 e-1—G.C.M. 26069, 1949-2 CB 38, 1949 P.-H.
  page 76,226
 3—Koshland, Execx.; U. S. v, 208 F(2d)
  640, — AFTR —, 1953 P.-H. page 73,597
  (CCA 9)
 4—Kent, Otis Beall, 1954 (P. H.) TC
  Memo. Dec. page 54—47

ADDA, INC.; COMM. v, 171 F(2d) 367, 37
AFTR 641, 1948 P.-H. ¶ 72,654 (CCA 2, Dec
6, 1948)
 sa—Adda, Inc., 9 TC 199
 s—Adda, Inc.; Comm. v, 171 F(2d) 367, 37
  AFTR 641, 1949 P.-H. ¶ 72,303 (CCA 2) reh.
  den.
 e-1—G.C.M. 26069, 1949-2 CB 39, 1949 P.-H.
  page 76,227
 e-2—G.C.M. 26069, 1949-2 CB 39, 1949 P.-H.
  page 76,227
ADDA, INC.; COMM. v, 171 F(2d) 367, 37
AFTR 641, 1949 P.-H. ¶ 72,303 (CCA 2, Dec
6, 1948) reh. den.
 sa—Adda, Inc., 9 TC 199
 s—Adda, Inc.; Comm. v, 171 F(2d) 367, 37
  AFTR 641, 1948 P.-H. ¶ 72,654 (CCA 2)
ADDISON-CHEVROLET SALES, INC. v
CHAMBERLAIN, L. A. & NAT. BANK
OF WASH., THE, — F Supp —, — AFTR
—, 1954 P.-H. ¶ 72,550 (DC DC) (See
Campbell v Chamberlain)
ADDISON v COMM., 177 F(2d) 521, 38 AFTR
821, 1949 P.-H. ¶ 72,637 (CCA 8, Nov 3,
1949)
 sa—Addison, Irene D., — TC —, 1948
  (P.-H.) TC Memo. Dec. ¶ 48,177
 1—Roberts, Supt. v U. S., 115 Ct Cl 439,
  87 F Supp 937, 38 AFTR 1314, 1950 P.-H.
  page 72,292
 1—Cold Metal Process Co., The, 17 TC
  934, 17-1951 P.-H. TC 512
 1—Berger, Samuel & Lillian, 1954 (P.-H.)
  TC Memo. Dec. page 54—232
 2—Urquhart, George Gordon & Mary F.,
  20 TC 948, 20-1953 P.-H. TC 536
ADDISON, IRENE D., — TC —, 1948 (P.-
H.) TC Memo. Dec. ¶ 48,177
App (T) Jan 14, 1949 (CCA 8)
 a—Addison v Comm., 177 F(2d) 521, 38
  AFTR 821, 1949 P.-H. ¶ 72,637 (CCA 8)
 1—Urquhart, George Gordon & Mary F.,
  20 TC 948, 20-1953 P.-H. TC 536
ADDITON, HARRY L. & ANNIE S., 3
TC 427
 1—Lum, Ralph E., 12 TC 379, 12-1949 P.-H.
  TC 204
 1—Christie, John A. & Elizabeth H., —
  TC —, 1949 (P.-H.) TC Memo. Dec.
  page 49—795
ADDRESSOGRAPH - MULTIGRAPH
CORP., 1945 (P.-H.) TC Memo. Dec.
¶ 45,058
 f-10—Rev. Rul. 54-71, 1954 P.-H. page
  76.453
ADDRESSOGRAPH-MULTIGRAPH CORP.
v U. S., 112 Ct Cl 201, 78 F Supp 111, 37
AFTR 53, 1948 P.-H. ¶ 72,504 (June 1, 1948)
No cert (G) 1949 P.-H. ¶ 71,041
 1—New Oakmont Corp., The v U. S., 114
  Ct Cl 686, 86 F Supp 901, 38 AFTR 924, 1949
  P.-H. page 73,181
ADELAIDE PARK LAND, 25 BTA 211
 g—Amer. Security & Fidelity Corp., — BTA
  —, 1940 (P.-H.) BTA Memo. Dec. page
  40—571
ADELPHI PAINT & COLOR WORKS,
INC., 18 BTA 436
 1—Neracher, William A., — BTA —, 1939
  (P.-H.) BTA Memo. Dec. page 39—69
 1—Lyman-Hawkins Lumber Co., — BTA —,
  1939 (P.-H.) BTA Memo. Dec. page 39—350
ADEMAN v U. S., 174 F(2d) 283, 37 AFTR
1406 (CCA 9, April 25, 1949)
ADICONIS, NOELLA L. (PATNAUDE),
1953 (P.-H.) TC Memo. Dec. ¶ 53,305
ADJUSTMENT BUREAU OF ST. LOUIS
ASSN., OF CREDIT MEN, 21 BTA 232
 1—Cook County Loss Adjustment Bureau,
  — BTA —, 1940 (P.-H.) BTA Memo. Dec.
  page 40—331
ADKINS, CHARLES I., — BTA —, 1933
 (P.-H.) BTA Memo. Dec. ¶ 33,457
ADLER v COMM., 77 F(2d) 733, 16 AFTR 162
(CCA 5)
 g-2—McEuen v Comm., 196 F(2d) 130, 41
  AFTR 1172, 1952 P.-H. page 72,604 (CCA 5)

Copyright 1955 by Prentice Hall, Inc.—Federal Tax Citator

Reference to Volume 1 of the *Citator* Second Series (covering the period from 1954 through 1977) shows the *Adda v. Comm.* case on page 25, which is reproduced in Figure E–4.

Correlating the symbols in Figure E–1 with the shaded portion of Figure E–4 reveals the following additional information about *Adda v. Comm.*:

- The case was cited without comment in two rulings and two cases: *Rev.Rul. 56–145, Rev.Rul. 56–392, Balanovski,* and *Liang.*
- It was followed in *Asthmanefrin Co.* (f-1).
- It was distinguished in *de Vegvar* and *Purvis* (g-1).
- It was reconciled in *deKrause* (k-1).

Reference to the "Court Decisions" section of Volume 2, Second Series of the *Citator* (covering the period from 1978 through 1989) shows that *Adda v. Comm.* was cited in *Judith C. Connelly* and *Robert E. Cleveland,* with each case limited to its facts (l). This page (22) is reproduced in Figure E–5.

The *Citator* includes a cumulative supplement (i.e., 1990–1993), and a cumulative monthly supplement is published each month. Be sure to refer to these supplements, or very recent citations might be overlooked. No citations appear in the supplements for *Adda v. Comm.*

Except as otherwise noted, it appears that *Adda v. Comm.* has withstood the test of time.

▼ **FIGURE E–4**

ADASKAVICH—ADELSON
25

ADASKAVICH, STEPHEN A. v U.S., 39 AFTR2d 77-517, 422 F Supp 276 (DC Mont) (See Wiegand. Charles J., Jr v U.S.)

AD. AURIEMA, INC., 1943 P-H TC Memo ¶ 43,422
  e-1—Miller v U.S., 13 AFTR2d 1515, 166 Ct Cl 257, 331 F2d 859

ADAY v SUPERIOR CT. OF ALAMEDA COUNTY, 8 AFTR2d 5367, 13 Cal Reptr 415, 362 P2d 47 (Calif, 5-11-61)

ADCO SERVICE, INC., ASSIGNEE v CYBERMATICS, INC., 36 AFTR2d 75-6342 (NJ) (See Adco Service. Inc., Assignee v Graphic Color Plate)

ADCO SERVICE, INC., ASSIGNEE v GRAPHIC COLOR PLATE, 36 AFTR2d 75-6342 (NJ, Supr Ct, 11-10-75)

ADCO SERVICE, INC., ASSIGNEE v GRAPHIC COLOR PLATE, INC., 36 AFTR2d 75-6342 (NJ) (See Adco Service. Inc., Assignee v Graphic Color Plate)

ADDA v COMM., 171 F2d 457, 37 AFTR 654 (USCA 4)
  —Rev. Rul. 56-145, 1956-1 CB 613
  1—Balanovski. U.S. v. 236 F2d 304, 49 AFTR 2013 (USCA 2)
  1—Liang. Chang Hsiao. 23 TC 1045, 23-1955 P-H TC 624
  f-1—Asthmanefrin Co., Inc., 25 TC 1141, 25-1956 P-H TC 639
  g-1—de Vegvar, Edward A. Neuman. 28 TC 1061. 28-1957 P-H TC 599
  g-1—Purvis, Ralph E. & Patricia Lee. 1974 P-H TC Memo 74-669
  k-1—deKrause. Piedad Alvarado. 1974 P-H TC Memo 74-1291
  1—Rev. Rul. 56-392. 1956-2 CB 971

ADDA, FERNAND C.A., 10 TC 273, ¶ 10,133 P-H TC 1948
  1—Balanovski. U.S. v. 236 F2d 303, 49 AFTR 2012 (USCA 2)
  1—Liang. Chang Hsiao. 23 TC 1045, 23-1955 P-H TC 624
  g-1—de Vegvar, Edward A. Neuman. 28 TC 1061. 28-1957 P-H TC 599
  g-1—Purvis, Ralph E. & Patricia Lee. 1974 P-H TC Memo 74-669
  k-1—deKrause. Piedad Alvarado. 1974 P-H TC Memo 74-1291

ADDA, INC., 9 TC 199
  Pardee. Marvin L., Est. of, 49 TC 152, 49 P-H TC 107 [See 9 TC 206-208]
  f-1—Asthmanefrin Co., Inc., 25 TC 1141, 25-1956 P-H TC 639
  1—Keil Properties, Inc. (Dela), 24 TC 1117, 24-1955 P-H TC 615
  1—Saffan, Samuel. 1957 P-H TC Memo 57—701
  1—Rev. Rul. 56-145, 1956-1 CB 613
  1—Rev. Rul. 56-392, 1956-2 CB 971
  4— Midler Court Realty, Inc., 61 TC 597, 61 P-H TC 368

ADDA, INC.; COMM. v, 171 F2d 367, 37 AFTR 641 (USCA 2)
  1—Pardee. Marvin L., Est. of, 49 TC 152, 49 P-H TC 107
  1—Saffan, Samuel. 1957 P-H TC Memo 57-701
  2—Midler Court Realty, Inc., 61 TC 597, 61 P-H TC 368

ADDELSTON, ALBERT A. & SARAH M., 1965 P-H TC Memo ¶ 65,215

ADDISON v COMM., 177 F2d 521, 38 AFTR 821 (USCA 8)
  g-1—Industrial Aggregate Co v U.S., 6 AFTR2d 5963. 284 F2d 645 (USCA 8)
  1—Sturgeon v McMahon, 155 F Supp 630, 52 AFTR 789 (DC NY)
  1—Gilmore v U.S., 16 AFTR2d 5211, 5213, 245 F Supp 384, 386 (DC Calif)
  1—Waldheim & Co., Inc., 25 TC 599, 25-1955 P-H TC 332
  g-1—Galewitz, Samuel & Marian, 50 TC 113, 50 P-H TC 79
  1 —Buder, G. A., Est. of, 1963 P-H TC Memo 63-345
  e-1—Rhodes, Lynn E. & Martha E., 1963 P-H TC Memo 63-1374
  2—Shipp v Comm., 217 F2d 402. 46 AFTR 1170 (USCA 9)

ADDISON—Contd.
  g-2—Industrial Aggregate Co v U.S., 6 AFTR2d 5964, 284 F2d 645 (USCA 8)
  e-2—Buder, Est. of v Comm., 13 AFTR2d 1238, 330 F2d 443 (USCA 8)
  2—Iowa Southern Utilities Co. v Comm., 14 AFTR2d 5063, 333 F2d 385 (USCA 8)
  2—Kelly, Daniel, S.W., 23 TC 687, 23-1955 P-H TC 422
  f-2—Morgan, Joseph P., Est. of, 37 TC 36, 37, 37-1961 P-H TC 26, 27
  n-2—Woodward, Fred W. & Elsie M., 49 TC 385, 49 P-H TC 270

ADDISON, IRENE D., 1948 P-H TC Memo ¶ 48,177
  1—Waldheim & Co., Inc., 25 TC 599, 25-1955 P-H TC 332
  f-1—Morgan, Joseph P., Est. of, 37 TC 36, 37, 37-1961 P-H TC 26, 27
  1—Buder, G. A., Est. of, 1963 P-H TC Memo 63-345
  e-1—Rhodes. Lynn E. & Martha E., 1963 P-H TC Memo 63-1374

ADDISON, JOHN MILTON, BKPT; U.S. v, 20 AFTR2d 5630, 384 F2d 748 (USCA 5) (See Rochelle Jr., Trtee; U.S. v)

ADDRESSOGRAPH - MULTIGRAPH CORP., 1945 P-H TC Memo ¶ 45,058
  Conn. L. & P. Co., The v U.S., 9 AFTR2d 679, 156 Ct Cl 312, 314, 299 F2d 264
  Copperhead Coal Co., Inc., 1958 P-H TC Memo 58-33
  1—Seas Shipping Co., Inc. v Comm., 19 AFTR2d 596, 371 F2d 529 (USCA 2)
  e-1—Hitchcock, E. R., Co., The v U.S., 35 AFTR2d 75-1207, 514 F2d 487 (USCA 2)
  f-2—Vulcan Materials Co. v U.S., 25 AFTR2d 70-446, 308 F Supp 57 (DC Ala)
  f-3—Marlo Coil Co. v U.S., 1969 P-H 58,133 (Ct Cl Comr Rep)
  4—United Gas Improvement Co v Comm., 240 F2d 318, 50 AFTR 1354 (USCA 3)
  10—St. Louis Co. (Del) (in Dissolution) v U.S., 237 F2d 156, 50 AFTR 257 (USCA 3)

ADDRESSOGRAPH - MULTIGRAPH CORP. v U.S., 112 Ct Cl 201, 78 F Supp 111, 37 AFTR 53
  f-1—St. Joseph Lead Co v U.S., 9 AFTR2d 712, 299 F2d 350 (USCA 2)
  e-1—Central & South West Corp v U.S., 1968 P-H 58,175 (Ct Cl Comr Rep)
  1—Smale & Robinson, Inc. v U.S., 123 F Supp 469, 46 AFTR 375 (DC Calif)
  1—St. Joseph Lead Co. v U.S., 7 AFTR2d 401, 190 F Supp 640 (DC NY)
  1—Eisenstadt Mfg. Co., 28 TC 230, 28-1957 P-H TC 132
  f-2—St. Joseph Lead Co. v U.S., 9 AFTR2d 712, 299 F2d 350 (USCA 2)
  f-3—Consol, Coppermines Corp. v U.S., 8 AFTR2d 5873, 155 Ct Cl 736, 296 F2d 745

ADELAIDE PARK LAND, 25 BTA 211
  g—Custom Component Switches, Inc v U.S., 19 AFTR2d 560 (DC Calif) [See 25 BTA 215]
  O'Connor, John C., 1957 P-H TC Memo 57-190

ADELBERG, MARVIN & HELEN, 1971 P-H TC Memo ¶ 71,015

ADELMAN v U.S., 27 AFTR2d 71-1464, 440 F2d 991 (USCA 9, 5-3-71)
  sa—Adelman v U.S., 24 AFTR2d 69-5769, 304 F Supp 599 (DC Calif)

ADELMAN v U.S., 24 AFTR2d 69-5769, 304 F Supp 599 (DC Calif, 9-30-69)
  a—Adelman v U.S., 27 AFTR2d 71-1464, 440 F2d 991 (USCA 9)

ADELSON, SAMUEL; U.S. v, 52 AFTR 1798 (DC RI) (See Sullivan Co., Inc.: U.S. v)

ADELSON v U.S., 15 AFTR2d 246, 342 F2d 332 (USCA 9, 1-13-65)
  sa—Adelson v U.S., 12 AFTR2d 5010, 221 F Supp 31 (DC Calif)
  g-1—Greenlee, L. C. & Gladys M., 1966 P-H TC Memo 66-985
  f-1—Cochran, Carol J., 1973 P-H TC Memo 73-459
  f-1—Marchionni. Siro L., 1976 P-H TC Memo 76-1321
  f-2—Krist, Edwin F. v Comm., 32 AFTR2d 73-5663, 483 F2d 1351 (USCA 2)
  f-2—Fugate v U.S., 18 AFTR2d 5607, 259 F Supp 401 (DC Tex) [See 15 AFTR2d 249, 342 F2d 335]

▼ **FIGURE E–5**

22	ADAMSON—ADELSON

ADAMSON, LEE A., 1981 PH TC Memo ¶ 81,285 (See Petty, R. M. & Allene A.)

ADAMSON, RAY P., 1981 PH TC Memo ¶ 81,285 (See Petty, R. M. & Allene A.)

ADAMSON, ROY & CATHERINE, 1986 PH TC Memo ¶ 86,489
 f-1—Dew, James Edward, 91 TC 626, 91 PH TC 310
 e-1—Telfeyan, Louis & Lynn, 1988 PH TC Memo 88-2146
 e-1—Bullock, Kenneth & Gail, 1988 PH TC Memo 88-2706

ADAMSON, SANDRA L., 1981 PH TC Memo ¶ 81,285 (See Petty, R. M. & Allene A.)

ADAMSON; U.S. v, 161 F2d 942, 35 AFTR 1404 (USCA 9)
 e-1—Inco Electroenergy Corp., 1987 PH TC Memo 87-2295

ADAMUCCI, RICHARD, 1987 PH TC Memo ¶ 87,378 (See Batastini, Paul J. & Amelia)

ADCOCK, HOMER & DOROTHY, 1982 PH TC Memo ¶ 82,206
 e-1—Kauffman, Wilma G., 1982 PH TC Memo 82-2193
 e-1—Scallen, Stephen B. & Chacke Y., 1987 PH TC Memo 87-2134

ADDA v COMM., 171 F2d 457, 37 AFTR 654 (USCA 4)
 1—Connelly, Judith C., 1982 PH TC Memo 82-2866
 1—Cleveland, Robert E., 1983 PH TC Memo 83-1223

ADDA, FERNAND C.A., 10 TC 273, ¶ 10.133 PH TC 1948
 1—Connelly, Judith C., 1982 PH TC Memo 82-2866
 1—Cleveland, Robert E., 1983 PH TC Memo 83-1223

ADDA, INC., 9 TC 199
 e—Hodges, Irene McLaughlin & Thomas Lyman, 1985 PH TC Memo 85-2062 [See 9 TC 210-211]
 1—Security Bancorp, Inc v U.S., 48 AFTR2d 81-5514 (DC Mich)
 4—Watson Land Co., 1983 PH TC Memo 83-744

ADDA, INC.; COMM. v, 171 F2d 367, 37 AFTR 641 (USCA 2)
 Security Bancorp, Inc v U.S., 48 AFTR2d 81-5514 (DC Mich)
 Watson Land Co., 1983 PH TC Memo 83-744
 e—Hodges, Irene McLaughlin & Thomas Lyman, 1985 PH TC Memo 85-2062

ADDEO, ARTHUR J., Jr. & MARY, 1984 PH TC Memo ¶ 84,493
 e-1—Brown, Stewart L., 1986 PH TC Memo 86-1153

ADDINGTON, DOUGLAS F., 1986 PH TC Memo ¶ 86,358 (See Hoak, Roderick C. & Cornelia)

ADDINGTON, WILLIAM H. & DONNA L., 1980 PH TC Memo ¶ 80,046
 a—Court Order, 10-20-81, 663 F2d 104 (USCA 5)
 d—1981 PH 61,000 (USCA 10)

ADDISON, ALBERT I., 1979 PH TC Memo ¶ 79,317
 e-1—Ridenour, Harry P., Jr. v U.S., 52 AFTR2d 83-5589, 3 Cl Ct 134
 e-1—Reinhardt, Jules & Marilyn D., 85 TC 526, 85 PH TC 299

ADDISON INTERNAT., INC., 90 TC 1207, ¶ 90.78 PH TC
 a—Addison Internat., Inc. v Comm., 64 AFTR2d 89-5747, 887 F2d 660 (USCA 6)
 rc—Rocky Mountain Associates Internat., Inc., 90 TC 1241, 1242, 90 PH TC 637, 638
 g-1—Butka, David J. & Sabine I., 91 TC 130, 91 PH TC 66

ADDISON INTERNAT., INC. v COMM., 64 AFTR2d 89-5747, 887 F2d 660 (USCA 6, 10-10-89)
 sa—Addison Internat., Inc., 90 TC 1207, ¶ 90.78 PH TC

ADDRESSOGRAPH-MULTIGRAPH CORP., 1945 PH TC Memo ¶ 45,058
 1—Buffalo Wire Works Co., Inc., 74 TC 938, 74 PH TC 509
 g-1—Maier Brewing Co., 1987 PH TC Memo 87-1978

ADEE, ALLEN R., TRUST NO. 1 v U.S., 52 AFTR2d 83-6437 (DC Kan, 7-19-83)

ADEE, DONALD P., TRUSTEE v U.S., 52 AFTR2d 83-6437 (DC Kan) (See Adee, Allen R., Trust No. 1 v U.S.)

ADEE, JACK R., TRUSTEE v U.S., 52 AFTR2d 83-6437 (DC Kan) (See Adee, Allen R., Trust No. 1 v U.S.)

ADELBERG, MARVIN & HELEN M., 1985 PH TC Memo ¶ 85,597
 a—Court Order, 1-21-87, 811 F2d 1507 (USCA 9)
 e-1—Chao, Wen Y. & Ching J., 92 TC 1144, 92 PH TC 577
 e-1—Nicklo, Joseph J., 1988 PH TC Memo 88-1199

ADELEKE, JOEL & CATHERINE A., 1980 PH TC Memo ¶ 80,479
 e-1—Pike-Biegunski, Maciej Jan & Denise Nadine, 1984 PH TC Memo 84-1123

ADELMAN v U.S., 27 AFTR2d 71-1464, 440 F2d 991 (USCA 9)
 e-1—Barbados #7 Ltd., 92 TC 813, 92 PH TC 409

ADELMAN v U.S., 24 AFTR2d 69-5769, 304 F Supp 599 (DC Calif)
 e-2—Barbados #7 Ltd., 92 TC 813, 92 PH TC 409

ADELSON, SHELDON G. v U.S., 54 AFTR2d 84-5428, 737 F2d 1569 (USCA Fed, 6-28-84)
 remg—Adelson, Sheldon G. v U.S., 52 AFTR2d 83-5211 (Cl Ct)
 s—Adelson, Sheldon G. v U.S., 51 AFTR2d 83-574 (Cl Ct) 535 F Supp 1082
 s—Adelson, Sheldon G. v U.S., 54 AFTR2d 84-5959, 6 Cl Ct 102
 rc—Adelson, Sheldon G. v U.S., 57 AFTR2d 86-736, 782 F2d 1010 (USCA Fed)
 rc—Adelson, Sheldon G. v U.S., 59 AFTR2d 87-993, 12 Cl Ct 231
 e-1—Larson, Roger Roy, In re, 62 AFTR2d 88-5801, 862 F2d 117 (USCA 7)
 e-1—Raab, George S. v I.R.S., 57 AFTR2d 86-715, 86-716 (DC Pa)

ADELSON, SHELDON G. v U.S., 57 AFTR2d 86-736, 782 F2d 1010 (USCA Fed, 1-29-86)
 remg—Adelson, Sheldon G. v U.S., 54 AFTR2d 84-5959, 6 Cl Ct 102
 rc—Adelson, Sheldon G. v U.S., 54 AFTR2d 84-5428, 737 F2d 1569 (USCA Fed)
 rc—Adelson, Sheldon G. v U.S., 52 AFTR2d 83-5211, 2 Cl Ct 591
 rc—Adelson, Sheldon G. v U.S., 51 AFTR2d 83-574, 1 Cl Ct 61, 553 F Supp 1082
 rc—Adelson, Sheldon G. v U.S., 59 AFTR2d 87-993, 12 Cl Ct 231

ADELSON, SHELDON G. v U.S., 51 AFTR2d 83-574, 1 Cl Ct 61, 553 F Supp 1082 (12-27-82)
 s—Adelson, Sheldon G. v U.S., 54 AFTR2d 84-5428, 737 F2d 1569 (USCA Fed)
 s—Adelson, Sheldon G. v U.S., 52 AFTR2d 83-5211, 2 Cl Ct 591
 rc—Adelson, Sheldon G. v U.S., 57 AFTR2d 86-736, 782 F2d 1010 (USCA Fed)
 rc—Adelson, Sheldon G. v U.S., 54 AFTR2d 84-5959, 6 Cl Ct 102
 rc—Adelson, Sheldon G. v U.S., 59 AFTR2d 87-993, 12 Cl Ct 231
 e-1—Mann, Guy L. Est. of, 53 AFTR2d 84-1304, 731 F2d 273 (USCA 5)

ADELSON, SHELDON G. v U.S., 52 AFTR2d 83-5211, 2 Cl Ct 591 (6-14-83)
 remd—Adelson, Sheldon G. v U.S., 54 AFTR2d 84-5428, 737 F2d 1569 (USCA Fed)
 s—Adelson, Sheldon G. v U.S., 51 AFTR2d 83-574 (Cl Ct) 553 F Supp 1082
 rc—Adelson, Sheldon G. v U.S., 57 AFTR2d 86-736, 782 F2d 1010 (USCA Fed)
 rc—Adelson, Sheldon G. v U.S., 54 AFTR2d 84-5959, 6 Cl Ct 102
 rc—Adelson, Sheldon G. v U.S., 59 AFTR2d 87-993, 12 Cl Ct 231

ADELSON, SHELDON G. v U.S., 54 AFTR2d 84-5959, 6 Cl Ct 102 (9-12-84)
 remd—Adelson, Sheldon G. v U.S., 57 AFTR2d 86-736, 782 F2d 1010 (USCA Fed)
 s—Adelson, Sheldon G. v U.S., 54 AFTR2d 84-5428, 737 F2d 1569 (USCA Fed)
 rc—Adelson, Sheldon G. v U.S., 51 AFTR2d 83-574, 1 Cl Ct 61, 553 F Supp 1082
 rc—Adelson, Sheldon G. v U.S., 52 AFTR2d 83-5211, 2 Cl Ct 591
 rc—Adelson, Sheldon G. v U.S., 59 AFTR2d 87-993, 12 Cl Ct 231

Reproduced from the *Federal Tax 2nd Citator* with the permission of the publisher, Research Institute of America, Englewood Cliffs, NJ 07632.

APPENDIX F
Comprehensive Tax Return Problems

PROBLEM 1

1. Arnold J. and Pat W. Alford, ages 46 and 44, are married and file a joint income tax return. Arnold is a specialist in horticulture and is employed by the Mid-West Seed Corporation as director of their research activities. Pat is a school teacher and is employed by St. Alban's Middle School, a private institution owned and operated by a religious group. Salary and tax withholdings for 1993 were:

	Salary	Federal	State
Arnold	$68,000	$4,780	$2,580
Pat	31,000	3,010	1,250

2. The Alfords have always lived and worked in Des Moines, IA. They reside at 312 Drake Avenue, Des Moines, IA 50312. Living with them are their three children, Nancy (age 14), Martin (age 16), and Irene (age 21). Also living with the Alfords is Arnold's widower father, Paul (age 71). Irene is a full-time student at Drake University. During the year, she earned $3,000 from a part-time job. Paul received $9,000 in Social Security benefits, which he deposited in his savings account. The Alfords contributed more than 50 percent of the support of their children and of Paul.

3. The Alfords contribute 25 percent of the support of Pat's aunt, Martha Bates, who lives with Pat's sister. The remainder of Martha's support is received from Pat's sister and two brothers, 25 percent each. Pat's sister and brothers have signed a multiple support agreement allowing Pat to claim the dependency exemption for Martha. As noted below, the Alfords have provided their share of support by paying Martha's medical expenses.

4. Relevant Social Security numbers are:

Arnold	478–12–6024
Pat	477–19–1022
Nancy	479–22–6018
Martin	479–29–5025
Irene	479–31–4129
Paul	481–15–6113
Martha	480–42–1266

5. Because Paul is confined to a wheelchair due to a stroke he suffered several years ago, the Alfords spent $8,300 during the year adding impairment-related improvements to their personal residence (e.g., wheelchair ramps, widening of hallway, bathtub railings). A friend who is in the real estate business estimates that these changes increased the value of the residence by $3,000.

6. During 1993, the Alfords had flood damage to their personal residence. They purchased this house on June 15, 1972, and paid $65,000 for it. A professional appraisal, for which the Alfords paid $400, reflects that the value of the residence decreased by $15,000 ($110,000 before and $95,000 after) due to the flood. The Alford's homeowner's insurance policy does not cover flood damage.

7. On June 1, 1989, and as a favor to a former college roommate, Arnold lent $5,000 to Lyle Petit. Lyle signed a note, maturity date of June 1, 1993, with annual interest of 10 percent. Arnold has never recovered any of the loan or received any interest. Lyle was declared bankrupt in April of 1993 and is currently under investigation for mail fraud.

8. Pat has a Bachelor of Education degree which she received many years ago. Recently, the directors at St. Alban's School resolved that all of its teachers must earn a Master of Education degree in order to continue in their present jobs. The teachers were allowed ten years in which to satisfy this new requirement. During the summer of 1993, Pat enrolled at a local university and took several graduate courses in education. Pat lived at home and commuted to her classes. Her expenses were as follows:

Books and tuition	$1,600
Tranportation	
Bus fares	65
Personal auto mileage (150 miles)	?
Meals while on campus (between classes)	82
Parking charges	31

When Pat did not take the bus, usually on rainy days, she drove the family auto (use the automatic mileage method—28 cents for 1993). When Pat drove, she had to pay for on-campus parking.

9. During 1993, the Alfords sold the following stocks:

Robin Corporation (400 shares common)	July 5	$32,000
Canary Corporation (300 shares preferred)	August 10	15,000

The Robin Corporation stock had been received from Pat's mother as a gift on January 2, 1993, when it had a fair market value of $31,000. Her mother had purchased the stock on June 1, 1992, for $30,500. No gift tax was due or paid on the mother's gift.

The Canary Corporation stock was inherited by Arnold from his mother. The mother died on December 10, 1992, and her estate was settled on March 3, 1993 (the day Arnold received the stock). The stock was worth $14,500 on December 10, 1992, and $14,700 on March 3, 1993. Arnold has found a broker's statement that shows his mother purchased the stock on September 9, 1992, for $14,100 (including brokerage fee).

10. Besides any other items mentioned elsewhere, the Alfords had the following receipts for 1993:

Interest on CD (Iowa State Bank)		$1,800
Interest on city of Des Moines general purpose bonds		1,500
Dividends		
Robin Corporation stock	$1,200	
Canary Corporation stock	900	2,100
Riverboat casino winnings		3,300
Garage sale after flood of damaged household goods (reasonable cost estimate of items sold is $6,000)		800

11. As to medical expenses, the Alfords had the following during 1993:

Hospital and doctor bills for Martha	$4,100
Arnold's contribution toward the cost of his employer's medical insurance premiums	2,400
Insurance recovery for 1992 expenses under employment medical policy	920
Orthodontia expenses for children	3,400
Prescription drugs	1,300
Doctor bills for family	1,150
Tonsillectomy for Nancy (surgeon and hospital)	1,600
Wheelchair and hearing aid for Paul	2,050

The $920 insurance recovery for the year 1992 was for medical expenses the Alfords deducted on their 1992 Federal income tax return.

The Alfords have not yet submitted any claims to the insurance company for their 1993 medical expenses. They estimate that, after the required deductible, the reimbursed amount will be $1,400.

12. Other expenditures for 1993 are summarized below:

Interest on home mortgage	$5,200
Property taxes on home	3,750
Payment of church pledge ($300 was for the 1992 remaining balance)	2,700
Additional state income tax due for 1992	210
School supplies Pat uses for her classes (not provided by St. Alban's School)	205
Professional dues (Arnold and Pat)	305
Professional journals (Arnold and Pat)	280
Lab coats (used by Arnold at work)	310
Laundry of lab coats	85
Safety goggles and shoes (used by Arnold at work)	160
Riverboat casino losses (supported by adequate records)	3,600

13. The Alfords do not wish to designate a contribution to the Presidential Election Campaign Fund. If they have overpaid, any refund is to be applied toward the 1994 Federal income tax liability.

Requirements

You are to prepare a joint Federal income tax return for the Alfords for 1993.

PROBLEM 2

1. Keith L. Darger, age 40, is divorced and lives alone at 409 Maple Lane, Cincinnati, OH 45211. He provides more than half of the cost of maintaining a household for Nancy Darger, who lives in an apartment nearby. Nancy, age 66, is Keith's widowed mother and qualifies as his dependent.

2. Keith and Rita were married eighteen years ago and were divorced in 1990. Rita was awarded custody of their only child, David, now twelve years old. Under the divorce decree, Keith must pay Rita $500 each month until David reaches age 21 or dies

(whichever occurs first). Upon the occurrence of either event, the monthly payment becomes $200. Since Keith and Rita have been alternating claiming David as a dependent, Rita did not complete and send to Keith a Form 8332 for 1993. Keith sent Rita the required $6,000 ($500 × 12 months) for 1993. Furthermore, he sent Rita an additional $900 for dental work she had done on her teeth. He also paid an optometrist/optician $350 for David's eye exams and prescription glasses.

3. Keith is a licensed hair stylist and beautician and operates his own salon under the business name of "Keith's Coiffures." Although it varies as to number, Keith's business consists of four to six stations operated by himself and other licensed beauticians. The beauticians who work in the salon are treated as independent contractors. In this regard, each has his or her own telephone line. They maintain their own appointment books, have their own customers, and collect and keep the fees charged. For the use of the work stations and various facilities (e.g., hair dryers, shampoo sinks, waiting area), each pays Keith a monthly rental. Keith does not control their work hours, although most choose to follow Keith's own work schedule.

4. Keith's Coiffures is well-known for its selection and quality of men's hairpieces (i.e., toupees) and women's wigs. The business also sells a considerable quantity of beauty products (e.g., conditioners, shampoos, curling irons). Some of these items are sold to other beauticians but most are sold to regular patrons and walk-in customers.

5. Keith's Coiffures is located at 4369 Glover Street, Cincinnati, OH 45211. The employer identification number is 31–0009521; the professional activity code for beauticians is 8110.

6. The building in which the business is located is rented under a long-term lease for $1,050 each month. Keith pays his own utilities. Before Keith moved in, the landlord customized the facilities so as to be suited for its intended use. The only employee Keith has is a shampoo person, who also performs light janitorial services. Keith hires an outside service to do the heavier janitorial duties. Likewise, a local accounting group is on retainer to keep the financial records and prepare the tax returns for the business.

7. Keith's Coiffures had the following receipts for 1993:

Sales of cosmetics	$18,000
Sales of hairpieces, wigs	25,000
Fees received from patrons by Keith (including tips received)	35,700
Rent charged other beauticians	21,800

The amounts shown for the retail sales of cosmetics, hairpieces, and wigs, include state sales tax.

8. Keith's Coiffures has the following expenses for 1993:

Purchases of cosmetics	$10,000
Purchases of hairpieces, wigs	12,000
Operating supplies (shampoo, permanent wave solution, color, etc.)	4,700
Rent for building	12,600
Utilities and telephone	5,210
Payroll expense	4,800
Payroll taxes (FICA, FUTA, state unemployment)	430
Sales taxes remitted to state	2,100
Health insurance coverage for employee	950
City of Cincinnati occupation permit for 1993	350
State beautician license fee	400
Liability insurance premiums (coverage is for calendar years 1993–1995)	6,000

Casualty insurance on business furnishings and equipment for 1993	1,200
Janitorial services	2,400
Accounting services ($400 was for preparation of personal tax return)	4,000
Waiting room furniture	2,700
Magazine subscriptions for waiting room	175
Advertising	800
Fine paid to city of Cincinnati	210

9. Keith decided to completely renovate the furnishings in his waiting room. Consequently, he spent $2,700 for chairs, sofa, lamps, coffee table, etc., all placed in service on April 20, 1993. The old furnishings were given to patrons or thrown away. The old furniture was completely depreciated and had a zero tax basis. Keith has always followed a policy of claiming as much depreciation as soon as possible. All of his other business assets (e.g., hair driers, work-station chairs) have been fully depreciated by 1993.

10. The fine paid to the city was assessed by the Sanitation Department. Keith had failed, in accordance with a city ordinance, to separate the trash of the business into recyclable and nonrecyclable bins.

11. In late 1992, a transient customer visiting the city had purchased a hairpiece from the business for $180. The customer's check was not deposited until early 1993 and ultimately proved fraudulent. The sale was reported on Keith's 1992 tax return. Keith has no doubt that he will never collect the $180 due him.

12. Keith maintains an inventory as to the merchandise he sells. The business inventories (based on the lower of cost or market) are as follows:

	12/31/92	12/31/93
Hairpieces and wigs	$3,000	$2,800
Cosmetics	2,010	2,200

13. In 1993, Keith was audited by both the city and the state as to his 1992 income tax returns. As a result of the audit, he had to pay the city an additional $120 but he received a refund from the state of $180.

14. Except for the inventory and purchases accounts, Keith operates the business on a cash method. Customers pay for services as rendered. Sales income is recorded when the merchandise is sold. Keith does not extend credit but does accept payment by charge card and check (see item 11 above).

15. Keith's medical expenses for 1993, and not mentioned elsewhere, included the following:

Gall bladder operation (includes hospital and surgeon's charges) for Nancy	$2,400
Annual physical for Keith	700
Dentist charges for Keith (includes crown, bridges, fillings, etc.)	6,200
Hernia operation (includes hospital and surgeon's charges)	3,200
Prescription medicines	900
Medical insurance premiums	2,900

In March of 1993, Keith purchased a medical insurance policy. The policy does not cover anyone but Keith and his one employee (see item 6 above). The premium for the employee coverage is stated separately at item 8. Also, the policy does not apply to dental bills. Keith filed a claim with the insurance company in late December. He received a check in January of 1994 which, after the appropriate deductible, was for $3,020.

16. Keith's other expenses are listed below:

Property taxes on residence	$4,800
Interest on home mortgage	6,000
Annual dues for membership in the American Association of Beauticians	150
Professional journals	320

17. Keith has always itemized his deductions because even without substantial medical expenses, his deductions from adjusted gross income have exceeded the standard deductions by more than $5,000.

18. Keith had no stock transactions in 1993 but he does have a $4,000 long-term capital loss carryover from 1992.

19. Keith's other income for 1993 is summarized below:

Interest income from a savings account at Enterprise Bank	$6,000
Cash dividend from AT&T	4,000

20. Keith made estimated tax payments for 1993 as follows:

City income tax	$ 600
Ohio income tax	2,400
Federal income and self-employment taxes (paid $1,400 quarterly)	5,600

21. Relevant social security numbers are—

Keith Darger	268–01–5869
Nancy Darger	301–42–2657
Rita Darger	300–52–7981
David Darger	302–64–1826

Requirements

You are to prepare Keith's Federal income tax return for 1993. Keith does not desire that $3 be directed to the Presidential Election Campaign fund. If he has overpaid his 1993 taxes, he wants to have the amount applied to his 1994 estimated tax.

APPENDIX G
Table of Cases Cited

A

Aagaard, Robert W., 15–19
Allen, Mary Francis, 7–10
American Automobile Association v. U.S., 4–12
Anderson, Comm. v., 5–15
Anton, M. G., 4–16
Appeal of (see name of party)
Arcade Realty Co., 10–15
Arkansas Best Corp. v. Comm., 16–6
Armantrout, Richard T., 5–9
Armstrong v. Phinney, 5–15
Artnell Co. v. Comm., 4–13
Augustus v. Comm., 2–26

B

Baird Publishing Co., 15–27
Baist, George A., 9–28
Balistrieri, Joseph P., 15–10
Barbados #6 Ltd., 2–43
Bassett, Robert S., 10–7
Basye, U.S. v., 19–28
Baxter v. Comm., 4–9
Bedell v. Comm., 4–8
Beime, Michael F., 20–37
Bhalla, C.P., 5–8
Biggs, Franklin B., 15–27
Bingler v. Johnson, 5–8
Boise Cascade Corp. v. U.S., 4–13
Bolaris v. Comm., 15–19
Bolton v. Comm., 6–21
Bonaire Development Co. v. Comm., 6–9
Briggs v. U.S., 5–15
Brown v. Comm., 7–35
Brown v. Helvering, 4–8
Bruun, Helvering v., 5–3
Burke, U.S. v., 5–11
Burnet v. Sanford & Brooks Co., 4–9, 18–13

C

Carr, Jack D., 2–20
Carter, Estate of v. Comm., 5–7
Caruth Corp. v. U.S., 4–16

Church, Wade E., 5–11
Clapham, Robert G., 15–19
Cohen, Theodore H., 4–10
Comm. v. _____ (see opposing party)
Consolidated-Hammer Dry Plate & Film Co. v. Comm., 4–13
Continental Trust Co., 10–15
Cooper, Howard Sherman, 9–14
Correll, U.S. v., 9–7
Cowden v. Comm., 4–10
Crane v. Comm., 14–5, 14–39
Crowther, Charles, 2–42

D

Daly, Estate of, 5–3
Davidson, Collin J., 9–14
Davis, U.S. v., 4–20, 14–6
Delman, Estate of, 5–30
Delp, F. S., 10–4
Deputy v. du Pont, 6–5
Doak, Comm. v., 5–15
Donruss, U.S. v., 2–21
Doyle v. Mitchell Bros. Co., 4–6
Dreicer v. Comm. v., 2–17
Duberstein, Comm. v., 2–17, 5–3, 10–17
Dunn & McCarthy v. Comm., 6–5
Durden, Ray, 2–42
Dyer, J. Raymond, 6–6

E

Ebben, Leo G., 14–39
Edwards v. Cuba R. Co., 20–17
Eisner v. Macomber, 4–5, 5–27
Estate of (see name of party)

F

Farm Service Cooperative, 2–42
Faulconer v. Comm., 6–33
Fausner v. Comm., 9–5
Fay v. Helvering, 7–10
Finkbohner v. U.S., 2–20
Fischer, L. M., 4–10

Flint v. Stone Tracy Co., 1–5
Frank, Morton, 6–16
F.W. Woolworth Co., 2–9

G

Galt v. Comm., 4–15
Ginsberg v. Comm., 20–37
Glenshaw Glass v. Comm., 5–12
Golconda Mining Corp., 2–42
Goldberg, Harry H., 6–25
Golsen, Jack E., 2–16
Goode v. Comm., 7–35
Groetzinger v. Comm., 7–2
Guenther, Kenneth W., 9–28

H

Hallmark Cards Inc. & Subsidiaries v. Comm., 18–48
Harding, Roy L., 20–43
Hawkins, C.A., 5–11
Heininger, Comm. v., 6–6
Helvering v. _____ (see opposing party)
Henry, James A., 15–17
Hilliard v. U.S., 3–41
Hillsboro Nat. Bank v. Comm., 6–9
Horst, Helvering v., 4–15
Hort v. Comm., 16–16
Horwith, T.M., 19–32
Houlette, Richard T., 15–18

I

Industrial Valley Bank & Trust Co., 2–27
Indianapolis Power & Light Co., Comm. v., 4–13

J

Jackson, John J., 2–42
Jacobson, Comm. v., 5–31
James v. U.S., 4–3

K

Kahler, C. F., 4–8
Keller v. Comm., 6–9
Kennedy, Jr. v. Comm., 6–6
Kieselbach v. Comm., 5–26
Kintner, U.S. v., 20–4
Kirby Lumber Co., U.S. v., 4–6, 5–30
Kluger Associates, Inc., 14–11
Korn Industries, Inc. v. U.S., 18–16
Kowalski, Comm. v., 5–15

L

Landfield Finance Co. v. U.S., 5–5
Lang, Grace E., 2–42
Lazisky, Albert A., 2–42

Lennard, Milton S., 2–41
Lesslie, Thomas E., 10–30
Lester v. Comm., 4–23
Lewis, U.S. v., 18–10
Lincoln Electric Co., Comm. v., 6–6
Lindeman, J.B., 5–15
Loco Realty Co. v. Comm., 15–11
Longue Vue Foundation, 2–42
Lucas v. Earl, 4–14
Lucas v. North Texas Lumber Co., 4–8
Lynch v. Turrish, 14–5

M

Maid of the Mist Corporation and Affiliated Corporations, 2–42
Malat v. Riddell, 16–3
Mantell, John, 4–12
Marshman, Comm. v., 14–6
McCrary, Ronald W., 10–41
McWilliams v. Comm., 6–27, 14–21
Merchants' Loan & Trust Co. v. Smietanka, 4–3
Merians v. Sidney, 2–42
Miller, Harris M., 2–9
Miller, J.O., 8–48
Mitnick, Moses (Also Known as Eddie Lewis), 9–8
Moran, Comm. v., 5–15
Mulherin, Brian C., 9–28
Multnomah Operating Co., 19–48

N

National Muffler Dealers Ass'n, Inc. v. U.S., 2–27
Neuhoff, Ann R., 2–27
New Colonial Ice Co. v. Helvering, 6–2
Newman, Comm. v., 2–33
Nico, Severino R., 2–28
North American Oil Consolidated v. Burnet, 4–9, 18–9

O

Old Colony R. Co. v. Comm., 10–11
O'Malley v. Ames, 14–6
Ostheimer v. U.S., 4–51

P

Page v. Rhode Island Hospital Trust Co., 6–8
Papineau, G.A., 5–15
Patterson, Floyd, 20–3
Pauli, Karl, 2–19
Paymer v. Comm., 20–3
Peacock, Cassius L., III, 3–13
Peck, William F., 15–17
Pfeifer, Donald R., 10–4
Phillips, Comm. v., 16–28
Pioneer Real Estate Co., 15–10
Pollock v. Farmers' Loan & Trust Co., 1–5, 5–26
Pulvers v. Comm., 7–10

R

Raffety Farms Inc. v. U.S., 20–3
Recchie v. U.S., 2–20

Riach v. Frank, 10–4
Roberts, William M., 10–40
Robertson v. U.S., 5–3
Robinson v. U.S., 5–15
Roemer v. Comm., 5–11, 5–12
Rogers, U.S. v., 7–10
Rollert Residuary Trust, 2–42
Rose, Erie H., 10–9
Rosenberg v. Comm., 7–10
Roszkos, Louis E., 2–42
Rowan Companies, Inc. v. U.S., 5–14
Rubnitz, Alan A., 10–29
Rutkin v. U.S., 4–5

S

Sakol, Miriam, 19–32
Sargent v. Comm., 4–14
Schlude v. Comm., 4–12
Schwartz, Henry W., 2–41
Shaw, Charles M., 15–20
Sherman, Stephen G., 9–28
Shopmaker v. U.S., 7–10
Simons-Eastern Co. v. U.S., 2–20, 2–24
Simpson v. U.S., 2–42, 5–7
Snow v. Comm., 7–18
Soliman, Comm. v., 9–20
Solomon, Stephen L., 7–10
South Carolina v. Baker, 5–26
Stark, Nelda C., 2–27
Starker v. U.S., 15–27, 15–41
Stolk v. Comm., 15–18
Strauss, Julia A., 4–8
Stucchi, Rudolph M., 15–29
Sullivan, Comm. v., 6–12

T

Tank Truck Rentals, Inc. v. Comm., 6–10
Tauferner v. U.S., 9–4

Tellier, Comm. v., 6–12
Thor Power Tool Co. v. Comm., 4–5, 18–31
Toledo, Peoria & Western Railroad Company, 16–28
Tomerlin Trust, James O., 2–9
Tougher v. Comm., 5–15
Tufts v. Comm., 2–42, 14–6
Tyler, W. David, 9–23

U

United States v. _____ (see opposing party)
United States Trust Co. of New York v. Anderson, 5–26
Untermann, John T., 2–43

V

Venstra & DeHavaan Coal Co., 4–13
Vogel Fertilizer Co., U.S. v., 2–27

W

Ward, Dwight A., 6–16
Washington, Alexander, 4–20
Welch v. Helvering, 6–5
Whitaker, William T., 9–23
Wilkerson, Donald L., 10–29
Wisconsin Cheeseman, Inc. v. U.S., 6–29
Withers, LaVar M., 10–30
Woods Investment Co., 2–41

Y

York v. Comm., 6–15

Z

Zaninovich v. Comm., 6–9, 18–11
Zarin v. Comm., 4–2

APPENDIX H
Depreciation

INTRODUCTION

Cost recovery, amortization, and depletion are presented in Chapter 8. For most fixed assets (e.g., machinery, equipment, furniture, fixtures, buildings) placed in service after December 31, 1980, the Economic Recovery Tax Act of 1981 (ERTA) has replaced the depreciation system with the cost recovery system.[1] The general relationship between the depreciation system and the cost recovery system is summarized in Exhibit H–1.

Despite ERTA, a discussion of § 167 depreciation is still relevant for two reasons. First, assets that were placed in service prior to 1981 are still in use. Second, certain assets placed in service after 1980 are not eligible to use the cost recovery system and therefore must be depreciated. They include property placed in service after 1980 whose life is not based on years (e.g., units-of-production method).

DEPRECIATION

Section 167 permits a depreciation deduction in the form of a reasonable allowance for the exhaustion, wear and tear, and obsolescence of business property and property held for the production of income (e.g., rental property held by an investor).[2] Obsolescence refers to normal technological change due to reasonably foreseeable economic conditions. If rapid or abnormal obsolescence occurs, a taxpayer may change to a shorter estimated useful life if there is a "clear and convincing basis for the redetermination." Depreciation deductions are *not* permitted for personal use property.

▼ **EXHIBIT H–1**
Depreciation and Cost Recovery: Relevant Time Periods

System	Date Property Is Placed in Service
§ 167 depreciation	Before January 1, 1981, and *certain* property placed in service after December 31, 1980.
Original accelerated cost recovery system (ACRS)	After December 31, 1980, and before January 1, 1987.
Modified accelerated cost recovery system (MACRS)	After December 31, 1986.

---

[1] Depreciation is covered in § 167 and cost recovery (ACRS and MACRS) is covered in § 168.

[2] § 167(a) and Reg. § 1.167(a)–1.

The taxpayer must adopt a reasonable and consistent plan for depreciating the cost or other basis of assets over the estimated useful life of the property (e.g., the taxpayer cannot arbitrarily defer or accelerate the amount of depreciation from one year to another). The basis of the depreciable property must be reduced by the depreciation allowed and by not less than the allowable amount.[3] The *allowed* depreciation is the depreciation actually taken, whereas the *allowable* depreciation is the amount that could have been taken under the applicable depreciation method. If the taxpayer does not claim any depreciation on property during a particular year, the basis of the property still must be reduced by the amount of depreciation that should have been deducted (the allowable depreciation).

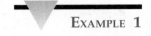

EXAMPLE 1

On January 1, Ted paid $7,500 for a truck to be used in his business. He chose a five-year estimated useful life, no salvage value, and straight-line depreciation. Thus, the allowable depreciation deduction was $1,500 per year. However, depreciation actually taken (allowed) was as follows:

Year 1	$1,500
Year 2	–0–
Year 3	–0–
Year 4	1,500
Year 5	1,500

The adjusted basis of the truck must be reduced by the amount of allowable depreciation of $7,500 ($1,500 × 5 years) even though Ted claimed only $4,500 depreciation during the five-year period. Therefore, if Ted sold the truck at the end of Year 5 for $1,000, he would recognize a $1,000 gain, since the adjusted basis of the truck is zero. ▼

QUALIFYING PROPERTY AND BASIS FOR DEPRECIATION

The use rather than the character of property determines whether a depreciation deduction is permitted. Property must be used in a trade or business or held for the production of income to qualify as depreciable.

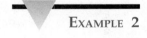

EXAMPLE 2

Carol is a self-employed CPA who maintains her office in a room in her home. The room, which is used exclusively for her business, comprises 20% of the square footage of her house. Carol is permitted a depreciation deduction only for the business use part of the house. No depreciation deduction is permitted for the 80% of the square footage of her house that is used as her residence. ▼

The basis for depreciation generally is the adjusted cost basis used to determine gain if the property is sold or otherwise disposed of.[4] However, if personal use assets are converted to business or income-producing use, the basis for depreciation *and* for loss is the *lower* of the adjusted basis or fair market value at the time of the conversion of the property.[5] As a result of this lower of basis rule, losses that occurred while the property was personal use property will not be recognized for tax purposes through the depreciation of the property.

---

[3] § 1016(a)(2) and Reg. § 1.167(a)–10(a).
[4] § 167(c).

[5] Reg. § 1.167(g)–1.

EXAMPLE 3   Hans acquires a personal residence for $30,000. Four years later, when the fair market value is only $25,000, he converts the property to rental use. The basis for depreciation is $25,000, since the fair market value is less than the adjusted basis. The $5,000 decline in value is deemed to be personal (since it occurred while the property was held for personal use) and therefore nondeductible. ▼

The Regulations provide that tangible property is depreciable only to the extent that the property is subject to wear and tear, decay or decline from natural causes, exhaustion, and obsolescence.[6] Thus, land and inventory are not depreciable, but land improvements are depreciable (e.g., paved surfaces, fences, landscaping).

OTHER DEPRECIATION CONSIDERATIONS

In determining the amount of the depreciation deduction, the following additional considerations need to be addressed:

- The salvage value of the asset.
- The choice of depreciation methods.
- The useful life of the asset.

For property subject to depreciation under § 167, taxpayers generally must take into account the **salvage value** (assuming there is a salvage value) of an asset in calculating depreciation. An asset cannot be depreciated below its salvage value. However, the Code permits a taxpayer to disregard salvage value for amounts up to 10 percent of the basis in the property. This provision applies to tangible personal property (other than livestock) with an estimated useful life of three years or more.[7]

EXAMPLE 4   Green Company acquired a machine for $10,000 in 1980 with an estimated salvage value of $3,000 after 15 years. The company may disregard salvage value to the extent of $1,000 and compute the machine's depreciation based upon a cost of $10,000 less $2,000 salvage value. The adjusted basis may be reduced to $2,000 (depreciation of $8,000 may be taken) even though the actual salvage value is $3,000. ▼

This provision was incorporated into the law to reduce the number of IRS-taxpayer disputes over the amount of the salvage value that should be used.

Another consideration is the *choice of depreciation methods* from among the several allowed. The following alternative depreciation methods are permitted for property placed into service before January 1, 1981, and for the aforementioned property placed in service after December 31, 1980, for which cost recovery is not permitted:

- The straight-line (SL) method (cost basis less salvage value ÷ estimated useful life).
- The declining-balance method (DB) using a rate not to exceed twice the straight-line rate. Common methods include 200 percent DB (double-declining balance), 150 percent DB, and 125 percent DB. Salvage value is not taken into account under any of the declining-balance methods. However, no further depreciation can be claimed once net book value (cost minus depreciation) and salvage value are the same.
- The sum-of-the-years' digits method (SYD).

---

[6] Reg. § 1.167(a)–2.   [7] Reg. §§ 1.167(a)–1(c) and (f)–1.

• Any other consistent method that does not result in greater total depreciation being claimed during the first two-thirds of the useful life than would have been allowable under the double-declining balance method. Permissible methods include machine hours and the units-of-production method.

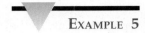
EXAMPLE 5

On January 1, 1980, Diego acquired a new machine to be used in his business. The asset cost $10,000 with an estimated salvage value of $2,000 and a four-year estimated useful life.[8] The following amounts of depreciation could be deducted, depending on the method of depreciation used:

	1980	1981	1982	1983
1. Straight-line:				
$10,000 cost less ($2,000 salvage value reduced by 10% of cost) ÷ 4 years	$2,250	$2,250	$2,250	$2,250
2. Double-declining balance:				
a. $10,000 × 50% (twice the straight-line rate)	5,000			
b. ($10,000 − $5,000) × 50%		2,500		
c. ($10,000 − $5,000 − $2,500) × 50%			1,250	
d. ($10,000 − $5,000 − $2,500 − $1,250) × 50%				250[9]
3. Sum-of-the-years' digits:* $10,000 cost less ($2,000 salvage value reduced by 10% of cost) or $9,000				
a. $9,000 × 4/10	3,600			
b. $9,000 × 3/10		2,700		
c. $9,000 × 2/10			1,800	
d. $9,000 × 1/10				900

*The formula for the sum-of-the-years' digits (SYD) method is

$$\text{Cost} - \text{Salvage value} \times \frac{\text{Remaining life at the beginning of the year}}{\text{Sum-of-the-years' digits of the estimated life}}$$

In this example, the denominator for SYD is 1 + 2 + 3 + 4, or 10. The numerator is 4 for Year 1 (the number of years left at the beginning of Year 1), 3 for Year 2, etc. The denominator can be calculated by the following formula:

$$S = \frac{Y(Y + 1)}{2} \text{ where } Y = \text{estimated useful life}$$

$$S = \frac{4(4 + 1)}{2} = 10$$

▼

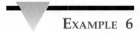
EXAMPLE 6

Using the depreciation calculations in Example 5, the depreciation reserve (accumulated depreciation) and net book value at the end of 1983 are as follows:

---

[8] A four-year life is used to illustrate the different depreciation methods. Note that an asset placed in service in 1980 must have a useful life of at least 15 years in order for depreciation to be deducted in 1994.

[9] Total depreciation taken cannot exceed cost minus estimated salvage value ($1,000 in this example).

	Cost	–	Depreciation	=	Net Book Value*
Straight-line	$10,000		$9,000		$1,000
Double-declining balance	10,000		9,000		1,000
Sum-of-the-years' digits	10,000		9,000		1,000

*Note that an asset may not be depreciated below its salvage value even when a declining-balance method is used. ▼

In 1969, Congress placed certain restrictions on the use of accelerated methods for new and used realty that are subject to the depreciation rules under § 167. These restrictions were imposed to reduce the opportunities for using real estate investments as tax shelters. The use of accelerated depreciation frequently resulted in the recognition of ordinary tax losses on economically profitable real estate ventures.

The following methods were permitted for residential and nonresidential real property:

	Nonresidential Real Property (Commercial and Industrial Buildings, Etc.)	Residential Real Property (Apartment Buildings, Etc.)
New property acquired after July 24, 1969, and generally before January 1, 1981	150% DB, SL	200% DB, SYD, 150% DB, or SL
Used property acquired after July 24, 1969, and generally before January 1, 1981	SL	125% DB (if estimated useful life is 20 years or greater) or SL

Congress chose to permit accelerated methods (200 percent declining-balance and sum-of-the-years' digits) for new residential rental property. Presumably, the desire to stimulate construction of new housing units justified the need for such accelerated methods.

Restrictions on the use of accelerated methods were not imposed on new tangible personalty (e.g., machinery, equipment, and automobiles). However, the 200 percent declining-balance and sum-of-the-years' digits methods were not permitted for used tangible personal property. The depreciation methods permitted for *used* tangible personal property were as follows:

	Useful Life of Three Years or More	Useful Life of Less Than Three Years
Used tangible personal property acquired after July 24, 1969, and generally before January 1, 1981	150% DB, SL	SL

Since the acquisition of used property does not result in any net addition to gross private investment in our economy, Congress chose not to provide as rapid accelerated depreciation for used property.

The determination of a *useful life* for a depreciable asset often led to disagreement between taxpayers and the IRS. One source of information was the company's previous experience and policy with respect to asset maintenance and utilization. Another source was the guideline lives issued by the IRS.[10] In 1971, the IRS guideline life system was modified and liberalized by the enactment of the **Asset Depreciation Range (ADR) system.**[11]

KEY TERMS

Asset Depreciation Range (ADR) system, H–6

Salvage value,   H–3

---

[10] Rev.Proc. 72–10, 1972–1 C.B. 721, superseded by Rev.Proc. 83–35, 1983–1 C.B. 745.

[11] Reg. § 1.167(a)–11.

INDEX

Abandoned spouse rules, **3**:26
Accelerated cost recovery system
  (ACRS), **8**:2, **8**:4–5
  business and personal use of
    automobiles and other listed
    property, **8**:16–21
  eligible property, **8**:5
  personalty: recovery periods and
    methods, **8**:5–7
  realty: recovery periods and methods,
    8:10–11
  straight-line election, **8**:13–14
  tables for, **8**:35, **8**:37–39, **8**:41
  tax planning for, **8**:29–33
ACCESS, **2**:34
Accident and health insurance benefits,
  plan paid for by employee, **5**:12–13
  plan paid for by employer, **5**:13–14
Accountable plans for employee
  expenses, **9**:23–24
Accounting income, **4**:4–5
Accounting methods, **4**:7, **18**:10–11
  accrual method, **4**:8–9, **18**:12–14
  cash receipts method, **4**:7–8,
    18:11–12
  change of method, **18**:15–18
  completed contract method, **12**:12
  hybrid method, **4**:9, **18**:15
  importance of in accounting for
    deductions and losses, **6**:7–8
  installment method, **18**:19–26
  long-term contracts, **18**:26–32
Accounting periods, **18**:3
  business purpose, **18**:5
  changes in accounting period, **18**:7–8
  making the election, **18**:7
  mitigation of annual accounting
    period concept, **18**:9–10
  partnerships and S corporations,
    18:3–5
  personal service corporations, **18**:6
  required tax payments, **18**:5–6
  taxable periods of less than one year,
    18:8–9
Accounts and notes receivable, **16**:5
Accrual method of accounting, **4**:8–9
  deducting expenses under, **6**:9–10
  deferral of advance payments for
    goods, **4**:13

deferral of advance payments for
  services, **4**:13–14
prepaid income, **4**:12–13
Acquiescence, of IRS in Tax Court
  decisions, **2**:19
Acquisition indebtedness, **10**:13
Actions on Decisions (AODs), **2**:12
Ad valorem taxes, **1**:6
  on personalty, **1**:8
  on realty, **1**:6–8
  use taxes, **1**:10
Adjusted basis, **14**:4
Adjusted current earnings (ACE)
  adjustment, **12**:25–27
Adjusted gross income (AGI), **1**:14,
  3:4–6
  deductions for, **3**:4, **6**:2, **6**:3–4
  deductions from, **6**:2–3. *See also*
    Itemized deductions
  modified adjusted gross income
    (MAGI), **4**:33–34
Adjusted sales price of personal
  residence, **15**:19
Administrative sources of tax law, **2**:8
  Actions on Decisions (AODs), **2**:12
  determination letters, **2**:11
  General Counsel Memoranda
    (GCMs), **2**:12
  letter rulings, **2**:9, **2**:10–11
  Revenue Rulings, and Revenue
    Procedures, **2**:9–10
  Technical Advice Memoranda
    (TAMs), **2**:11–12
  Treasury Decisions (TDs), **2**:11
  Treasury Department Regulations,
    2:8–9
Age test, for earned income credit, **13**:18
Agent, income received by, **4**:16
Alimony recapture, **4**:20–23
Alimony and separate maintenance
  payments, **4**:19–20
  child support, **4**:23
  front-loading, **4**:20–23
  post-1984 agreements and decrees,
    4:20
  tax planning and, **4**:38
All events test,
  for deductions, **18**:13–14
  for income, **18**:12–13

Allocable parental tax, **3**:19
Alternate valuation amount, **14**:14
Alternative depreciation system (ADS),
  8:21–22, **8**:42–43, **12**:8–9
Alternative minimum tax (AMT),
  corporate, **12**:24–25, **20**:14
  adjustments, **12**:25
    applicable only to corporations,
      12:25–27
    applicable to individuals and
      corporations, **12**:25
  exemption, **12**:28
  tax preferences, **12**:27–28
individual, **12**:2–3
  adjustments, **12**:3, **12**:4–5
    adjusted gain or loss, **12**:13–14
    alternative tax net operating loss
      deduction, **12**:14–15
    circulation expenses, **12**:8
    depreciation of post-1986
      personal property, **12**:9–10
    depreciation of post-1986 real
      property, **12**:8–9
    direction of adjustments, **12**:8
    expenditures requiring 10-year
      write-off, **12**:10–11
    incentive stock options, **12**:12–13
    itemized deductions, **12**:15–18
    other adjustments, **12**:18
    passive activity losses, **12**:11–12
    pollution control facilities, **12**:10
    use of completed contract
      method of accounting, **12**:12
  alternative tax adjusted gross
    income (ATAGI), **12**:5–8
  computation of, **12**:22–23
  exemption amount, **12**:21–22
  preferences, **12**:3, **12**:5
    amortization of certified pollution
      control facilities, **12**:20–21
    depreciation, **12**:19–20
    intangible drilling costs, **12**:19
    interest on private activity bonds,
      12:19
    percentage depletion, **12**:18–19
  rate schedule, **12**:22
  regular tax liability, **12**:22
  table for, **8**:42
  tax planning for, **12**:28–29

Alternative minimum taxable income (AMTI), **12**:2–5, **12**:21

Alternative tax adjusted gross income (ATAGI), **12**:5–6

Alternative tax net operating loss deduction (ATNOLD), **12**:14–15

American Federal Tax Reports (AFTR), **2**:20

Amortizable Section 197 intangibles, **8**:23

Amortization, **8**:3, **8**:22–24
   tax planning for, **8**:33

Amount realized, from sale or other disposition of property, **14**:3–4

Annual accounting period concept, mitigation of, **1**:28–29, **18**:9–10

Annuities, income from, **4**:27–30

Appellate Courts, **2**:15–18

Assets,
   business versus personal use of, **1**:8
   classification of, **1**:8
   expensing of under Section 179, **8**:14–16
   Section 1231 assets, **17**:3–11

Assignment of income, **4**:14

Associations, **20**:4

At-risk limits, **11**:3–4

Audit process, **1**:19
   selection of returns, **1**:19
   settlement procedures, **1**:20–21
   types of audits, **1**:20

Automatic mileage method of computing auto expense, **9**:6–7

Automobile expenses,
   commuting expenses as, **9**:4–7
   computation of, **9**:6–7

Automobiles,
   leased, **8**:19–21
   as listed property, **8**:16–19

Awards, income from, **4**:30–31

Backup withholding, **13**:34

Bad debts, **7**:3, **7**:7
   business versus nonbusiness, **7**:4–5
   loans between related parties, **7**:5–6
   loss of deposits in insolvent financial institutions, **7**:6
   specific charge-off method, **7**:3–4

Bankruptcy, IRS and, **2**:15

Basic research payments, **13**:14–15

Basis,
   adjusted, of property, **14**:4
   cost basis of property, **14**:8–11
   determination of in S corporation, **20**:29–30
   effect of Section 179 expensing on, **8**:15–16
   gift basis of property, **14**:11–14
   of like-kind property, **15**:7–8
   of new personal residence, **15**:20–21
   partner's in partnership, **20**:31, **20**:32
   of property acquired from decedent, **14**:14–17

stepped-down, **14**:14
stepped-up, **14**:14
summary of adjustments to, **14**:22–24

Benefit received rule, **10**:17

Boot, in like-kind exchange, **15**:6–7

Bracket creep, **1**:29–30

Business bad debt, **7**:4–5

Business energy credits, **13**:10

Business expenses and losses,
   business versus nonbusiness losses, **6**:7
   as deductions for AGI, **6**:4–6
   ordinary and necessary requirement for, **6**:5–6
   reasonableness requirement, **6**:6

Business fixed assets, **16**:5

Business gifts, **9**:19–20

Business meals, deductibility of, **9**:17–18

Cafeteria plans, **5**:17–18

Calendar year, **4**:6

Capital assets,
   definition of, **3**:27–28, **16**:3–4
      accounts and notes receivable, **16**:5
      business fixed assets, **16**:5
      copyrights and creative works, **16**:5
      inventory, **16**:4–5
      U.S. government publications, **16**:6
   effect of judicial action, **16**:6
   holding period, **16**:16
      review of special holding period rules, **16**:7
         certain disallowed loss transactions, **16**:17–18
         certain nontaxable transactions involving carryover of another taxpayer's basis, **16**:17
         inherited property, **16**:18
         nontaxable exchanges, **16**:17
         special rules for short sales, **16**:18–20
   nonpersonal use, **17**:6–8
   relationship to Section 1231 assets, **17**:3–4
   sale or exchange, **16**:9
      franchises, trademarks, and trade names, **16**:13–15
      lease cancellation payments, **16**:15
      options, **16**:10–12
      patents, **16**:12–13
      special rule—retirement of corporate obligations, **16**:9–10
      worthless securities, **16**:9
   statutory expansions, **16**:6
      dealers in securities, **16**:7
      lump sum distributions, **16**:8
      nonbusiness bad debts, **16**:9
      real property subdivided for sale, **16**:7–8
   tax planning for, **16**:25–30

Capital contributions, **20**:17–18

Capital expenditures,
   disallowance of deductions for, **6**:25–26
   for medical purposes, **10**:4–5
   tax planning for, **6**:33

Capital gain property, **10**:21–22

Capital gains,
   computation of, **3**:28
   reporting, **16**:2–3
   tax treatment of, for corporate taxpayers, **16**:25–27, **20**:7
   tax treatment of, for noncorporate taxpayers, **16**:20–22, **26**:24–25

Capital losses, **3**:28–29
   corporate, **3**:29
   limitation on, **3**:28–29
   reporting, **16**:2–3
   tax treatment of, for corporate taxpayers, **16**:25–27, **20**:7
   tax treatment of, for noncorporate taxpayers, **16**:20, **16**:23–25

Cash receipts method of accounting, **4**:7–8, **18**:11
   amounts received under an obligation to repay, **4**:12
   constructive receipt, **4**:9–10
   deducting expenses under, **6**:8–9
   farming and, **18**:12
   original issue discount, **4**:11
   restrictions on use of, **18**:11–12
   Series E and Series EE bonds, **4**:11–12
   tax deferral and, **4**:36
   tax planning for, **18**:37

Casualty losses, **7**:9, **7**:25, **7**:26
   personal casualty gains and losses, **7**:16–17

Charitable contributions, **10**:16
   by corporations, **20**:8–9
   criteria for a gift, **10**:16–17
      benefit received rule, **10**:17
      contribution of services, **10**:17
      nondeductible items, **10**:18
   limitation on deduction of, **10**:20–21
      capital gain property, **10**:21–22
      contribution carryovers, **10**:24
      fifty percent ceiling, **10**:22–23
      ordinary income property, **10**:21
      thirty percent ceiling, **10**:23
      twenty percent ceiling, **10**:24
   qualified organizations, **10**:18
   recapture potential and, **17**:20
   record-keeping and valuation requirements, **10**:19–20
   tax planning for, **10**:30–31
   time of deduction, **10**:18–19

Child and dependent care expenses, tax credit for, **13**:21–22, **13**:24
   calculation of credit, **13**:23
   dependent care assistance program, **13**:23
   earned income ceiling, **13**:22
   eligibility, **13**:22
   eligible employment-related expenses, **13**:22

reporting requirements, **13**:23
tax planning for, **13**:39–41
Child support, **4**:23
Children,
tax planning for income of, **3**:30
taxation of unearned income of, **3**:18–20
Circuit Court of Appeals, **2**:15
Circulation expenditures, **12**:8
Citizenship or residency test for dependency exemption, **3**:14
Claim of right doctrine, **18**:9–10
Clear business purpose test, for deducting business meals, **9**:18
Closely held corporations, passive loss rules and, **11**:5–6
Club dues, deductibility of, **9**:18
Common law states, survivor's share of property in, **14**:16–17
Community property states, income in, **4**:17–18
spouses living apart, **4**:18–19
survivor's share of property in, **14**:16
tax planning in, **4**:38
Commuting expenses, **9**:4–5
Compensation-related loans, **4**:27
Compensatory damages, **5**:10–11
Completed contract method of accounting, **18**:29
use of for AMT purposes, **12**:12
Congress, intent of in enacting tax legislation, **2**:4
Constructive dividends, **20**:21–22
Constructive ownership, **6**:28
Constructive receipt, **4**:9–10
Controlled corporations, transfers to, **20**:18–19
Conventions, travel to, **9**:8–9
Copyrights and creative works, **16**:5
Corporate income tax, **1**:3
Corporate obligations, retirement of, **16**:9–10
Corporation-shareholder loans, **4**:27
Corporations, **20**:3–4. *See also* S corporations
association approach, **20**:4
filing requirements, **20**:14
formation of, **20**:17
capital contributions, **20**:17–18
transfers to controlled corporations, **20**:18–19
income tax considerations, **20**:5
capital gains and losses, **20**:7
charitable contributions, **20**:8–9
deduction of organizational expenditures, **20**:12–13
dividends received deduction, **20**:10–12
individuals and corporations compared, **20**:5–7, **20**:16–17
net operating losses, **20**:9–10
recapture of depreciation, **20**:7–8
tax consequences, **20**:5

limited liability companies, **20**:4–5
liquidation, **20**:22–24
operations, **20**:19
dividend distribution, **20**:19–22
stock distributions, **20**:22
reconciliation of corporate taxable income and accounting income, **20**:14–15, **20**:17
special recapture for, **17**:23
tax liability, **20**:13
alternative minimum tax, **20**:14
income tax rates, **20**:13–14
tax planning for, **20**:35–37
Correspondence audit, **1**:20
Cost basis of property, **14**:8–11
Cost depletion, **8**:25–26
Court of original jurisdiction, **2**:12
appeals of decisions in, **2**:15–18
Cumulative Bulletin, **2**:10, **2**:19
Current Tax Payment Act, **1**:4

Daily Tax Reports, **2**:11
De minimis fringes, **5**:21
De minimis fringe benefit rule, **9**:16
Death benefits for employees, **5**:7–8
Death, elimination of recapture potential by, **17**:20
Death taxes, **1**:11
Federal estate tax, **1**:11–12
state death taxes, **1**:12
Deathbed gifts, **14**:15–16
Deductions, **3**:5. *See also* Itemized deductions; Standard deduction
for adjusted gross income, **6**:3–4, **7**:2
all events test for, **18**:13–14
business versus nonbusiness losses, **6**:7
classification of, **6**:2–3, **6**:31
disallowance possibilities, **6**:10
excessive executive compensation, **6**:14–15
expenditures incurred for taxpayer's benefit or taxpayer's obligation, **6**:23–25
expenses and interest relating to tax-exempt income, **6**:29–30
hobby losses, **6**:16–19
investigation of a business, **6**:15–16
political contributions and lobbying activities, **6**:13–14
public policy limitation, **6**:10
expenses relating to an illegal business, **6**:12–13
justification for denying deductions, **6**:10–12
legal expenses incurred in defense of civil or criminal penalties, **6**:12
rental of vacation homes, **6**:19–23
substantiation requirements, **6**:28
transactions between related parties, **6**:26–28

economic performance test for, **18**:13–14
from adjusted gross income, **6**:2–3, **7**:2
production of income expenses, **6**:4–6
reporting procedures, **6**:7
tax planning for, **6**:30
timing of expense recognition, **6**:7–8
accrual method requirements, **6**:9–10
cash method requirements, **6**:8–9
trade or business expenses, **6**:4–6
ordinary and necessary requirement, **6**:5–6
reasonableness requirement, **6**:6
Deemed substantiation, of employee expenses, **9**:23–24
Deferred compensation, **19**:2–3
Individual Retirement Accounts, **19**:22–27
nonqualified deferred compensation plans, **19**:27–31
qualified pension, profit sharing, and stock bonus plans, **19**:3–20
restricted property plans, **19**:31–34
retirement plans for self-employed individuals, **19**:20–22, **19**:23
stock options, **19**:34–37
tax planning for, **19**:37–41
Defined benefit pension plan, **19**:4, **19**:5, **19**:16–18
Defined contribution pension plan, **19**:4–5, **19**:16
Dependency exemptions, **3**:11
citizenship or residency test, **3**:14
gross income test, **3**:14
joint return test, **3**:14
phase-out of, **3**:14–15
relationship or member-of-the-household test, **3**:13
support test, **3**:11–13
tax planning for, **3**:30–32
Dependents,
special limitations on standard deduction and personal exemption of, **3**:10
tax filing rules for, **3**:21–22
Depletion, **8**:3, **8**:24–25
intangible drilling and development costs, **8**:24–25
methods of, **8**:25
cost depletion, **8**:25–26
effect of intangible drilling costs on, **8**:27–28
percentage depletion, **8**:26–27
special recapture for, **17**:23
tax planning for, **8**:33
Depreciation, **8**:2, **8**:3
alternative depreciation system (ADS), **8**:21–22
AMT and, **12**:19–20
basis for on depreciable gift property, **14**:13–14
recapture of for corporations, **20**:7–8

Determination letters, **2**:11
Disabled access credit, **13**:16–17
Disallowed loss transactions, holding period for, **16**:17–18
Disaster area losses, **7**:11–12, **7**:26
Discharge of indebtedness, income from, **5**:30–31
Dividend received deduction, **20**:10–12
Dividends,
   constructive, **20**:21–22
   distribution of, **20**:19–22
   excluded from gross income, **5**:27
   as income, **4**:15–16
   property, **20**:20–21
Divorce. *See* Alimony and separate maintenance payments
Dollar-value LIFO, **18**:34–35
Domestic travel, deduction of expenses for, **9**:9–10
Domestic workers, withholding for, **13**:34
Dual basis property, **14**:11–12

Earned income credit, **13**:17–18
   advance payment, **13**:19
   earned income credit table, **13**:18
   eligibility requirements, **13**:18–19
Earnings and profits (E & P), **20**:20
Economic considerations and tax law, **1**:24–26
Economic income, **4**:3–4
Economic performance test, **6**:9, **18**:13–14
Economic Recovery Tax Act of 1981 (ERTA), **8**:2
Education, travel as, **9**:9
Education expenses, **9**:13–14
   classification of specific items, **9**:15
   maintaining or improving existing skills, **9**:14–15
   other provisions, **9**:15
   requirements imposed by law or by employer for retention of employment, **9**:14
   tax planning for, **9**:28
Educational savings bonds, income from excluded from gross income, **5**:28–29
Elderly or disabled taxpayers, tax credit for, **13**:19–20
Eligible access expenditures, **13**:16–17
Employee death benefits, **5**:7–8
Employee status,
   employee expenses, **9**:4, **9**:27
      classification of, **9**:22
         accountable plans, **9**:23–24
         nonaccountable plans, **9**:24
         reporting procedures, **9**:24–25
      education expenses, **9**:13–15
      entertainment expenses, **9**:16–20
      miscellaneous employee expenses, **9**:21–22
      moving expenses, **9**:11–13

office in the home, **9**:20–21
   transportation expenses, **9**:4–7
   travel expenses, **9**:7–11
   unreimbursed, **9**:25–26
   tax planning for, **9**:27–28
   versus self-employment, **9**:2–4
Employee stock ownership plans (ESOP), **19**:6–7
Employees of educational institutions, exclusion of value of campus housing, **5**:16
Employment taxes, **1**:16, **13**:26
   coverage requirements, **13**:26–28
   Federal Insurance Contributions Act (FICA) taxes, **1**:16–17, **13**:26, **13**:28–29
   Federal Unemployment Tax Act (FUTA) taxes, **1**:17
Energy Policy Act of 1992, **5**:21–22
Entertainment expenses, **9**:16
   classification of, **9**:17
   dollar limitations, **9**:16–17
   restriction upon deductibility of, **9**:17
      business gifts, **9**:19–20
      business meals, **9**:17–18
      club dues, **9**:18
      tickets purchased for entertainment, **9**:19
   tax planning for, **9**:28
Equity considerations and tax law, **1**:27–30
Estate tax, **1**:11–12
Estimated tax, for individuals, **13**:35
Excessive executive compensation, deductibility of, **6**:14–15
   tax planning for, **6**:32
Excise taxes, **1**:3
   Federal, **1**:9
   state, **1**:9
Exemptions, **3**:8. *See also* Dependency exemptions; Personal exemptions
   phase-out of, **3**:14–15
Expensing of assets, **8**:14–16
Extraordinary personal services, **11**:14

Fair market value of property, **14**:4
Family tax planning, **13**:40–41
Farming, accounting method for, **18**:12
Federal customs duties, **1**:17–18
Federal District Court, **2**:12
Federal estate tax, **1**:11–12
Federal excise taxes, **1**:9
Federal gift tax, **1**:12–13
Federal income tax. *See* Income tax
Federal Insurance Contributions Act. *See* FICA
Federal Register, **2**:9
Federal Second Series, **2**:20
Federal Supplement Series, **2**:20
Federal Tax Articles, **2**:24
Federal Tax Coordinator 2d, **2**:24

Federal Unemployment Tax Act. *See* FUTA
FICA (Federal Insurance Contributions Act) taxes, **1**:16–17
Field audit, **1**:20
FIFO (first in, first out), **18**:34
Fiscal year, **4**:6–7
Fixing-up expenses of personal residence, **15**:19
Foreign earned income, excluded from gross income, **5**:24–26
Foreign Sales Corporations, **1**:25–26
Foreign tax credit, **13**:20–21
   tax planning for, **13**:39
Foreign travel, deduction of expenses for, **9**:10–11
Franchise tax, **1**:18
Franchises, **16**:13–14
   contingent payments, **16**:15
   noncontingent payments, **16**:14–15
   significant power, right, or continuing interest, **16**:14
   sports franchises, **16**:15
Fringe benefits, **5**:17
   exclusion of from gross income, **5**:17
   cafeteria plans, **5**:17–18
   general classes of excluded benefits, **5**:18–19, **5**:23
   de minimis fringes, **5**:21, **5**:23–24
   no-additional-cost services, **5**:19–20
   nondiscrimination provisions, **5**:22–24
   qualified employee discounts, **5**:20
   qualified transportation fringe, **5**:21–22
   working condition fringes, **5**:21
   tax planning for, **5**:31–32
   taxable, **5**:24
Front-loading, of property settlements, **4**:20–23
Fruit and tree metaphor, **4**:14
Functional use test, in involuntary conversion, **15**:11
FUTA (Federal Unemployment Tax Act) taxes, **1**:17

Gain,
   adjusted, for AMT, **12**:13–14
   nonrecognition of, **14**:6–7
      in involuntary conversion, **15**:14–15
   recognition of, **14**:6
   under Section 1231, **17**:4, **17**:7
General business tax credit, **13**:5–6
General Counsel Memoranda (GCMs), **2**:12
Gift basis of property, **14**:11–14
Gift loans, **4**:26–27
Gift taxes, **1**:12
   adjustments to property basis and, **1**:12–13

Federal gift tax, **1**:12–13
state gift taxes, **1**:13–15
Gifts,
excluded from gross income, **5**:3, **5**:5
recapture potential of, **17**:19–20
Golden parachute arrangements, **19**:29
Golsen decision, **2**:16–17
Goodwill, special allocation rule and, **14**:9–10
Gross income, **3**:3–5. *See also* Adjusted gross income (AGI); Income
alimony and separate maintenance payments, **4**:19–23
annuities, **4**:27–30
child support, **4**:23
definition, **4**:3
economic and accounting concepts, **4**:3–5
exclusions from, **5**:2, **5**:4
cafeteria plans, **5**:17–18
compensation for injuries and sickness, **5**:10–13
de minimis fringes, **5**:21, **5**:23–24
dividends, **5**:27
educational savings bonds, **5**:28–29
employee death benefits, **5**:7–8
employer-sponsored accident and health plans, **5**:13–14
foreign earned income, **5**:24–26
gifts and inheritances, **5**:3, **5**:5
income from discharge of indebtedness, **5**:30–31
interest on certain state and local government obligations, **5**:26–27
life insurance proceeds, **5**:5–7
meals and lodging, **5**:14–17
no-additional-cost services, **5**:19–20
nondiscrimination provisions, **5**:22–24
qualified employee discounts, **5**:20
qualified transportation fringe, **5**:21–22
scholarships, **5**:8–10
statutory authority, **5**:2–3
working condition fringes, **5**:21
form of receipt, **4**:6
group term life insurance, **4**:31–32
imputed interest, **4**:23–27
prizes and awards, **4**:30–31
recovery of capital doctrine and, **4**:6
Social Security benefits, **4**:32–35
tax benefit rule, **5**:29
unemployment compensation, **4**:32
year of inclusion, **4**:6–14
Gross income test,
for dependency exemption, **3**:14
tax planning for, **3**:31
Group term life insurance, income from, **4**:31–32

Half-year convention, **8**:6
Heads of household, tax rates for, **3**:25

Hobby losses, **6**:16–17
general rules, **6**:17
presumptive rule of Sec. 183, **6**:18–19
tax planning for, **6**:32–33
Holding period,
of capital assets, **16**:16–20
of like-kind property, **15**:8–9
of new residence, **15**:20–21
for property acquired by gift, **14**:13
Home equity loans, **10**:13–14
Home office expenses, **9**:20–21
House of Representatives, **2**:3–5
House Ways and Means Committee, **2**:3–5
Housing interest, AMT and, **12**:16–17
H.R. 10 (Keogh) plans, **19**:20–22, **19**:23
Hybrid method of accounting, **4**:9, **18**:15

Illegal business, deductibility of expenses incurred in, **6**:12–13
Imputed interest,
on below-market loans, **4**:23–27
in installment method of accounting, **18**:21–22, **18**:24
Incentive stock option, **19**:34–36
Incentive stock options (ISOs), **12**:12–13
Income, **3**:3, **4**:3. *See also* Adjusted gross income (AGI)
accounting and tax concepts of, **4**:5–6
all events test for, **18**:12–13
assignment of, **4**:14
in community property states, **4**:17–18
exclusion of, **3**:3, **3**:4
from discharge of indebtedness, **5**:30–31
gross, **3**:3–5
portfolio, **11**:18
prepaid, **4**:12–13
sources of, **4**:14
partnerships, S corporations, trusts, and estates, **4**:16–17
personal services, **4**:14
property, **4**:15–16
received by an agent, **4**:16
tax exempt, deductibility of expenses and interest relating to, **6**:29–30
unearned, **3**:18
Income tax, **1**:14
amount of withholding, **13**:29–33
Federal income taxes, **1**:14
history of, **1**:2–4
local income taxes, **1**:15
as source of revenue for Federal government, **1**:3–4
state income taxes, **1**:14–15
Individual Retirement Accounts (IRAs), **1**:26, **19**:22–23
deductibility of contributions to, **9**:22
simplified employee pension plans, **19**:23–24
spousal IRA, **19**:24
tax planning for, **19**:38–39

timing of contributions, **19**:24–25
penalty taxes for excess contributions, **19**:25
taxation of benefits, **19**:25–27
Inflation, tax law and, **1**:29–30
Inheritance tax, **1**:11
Inherited property, holding period for, **16**:18
Injuries and sickness, compensation for, **5**:10–13
Installment method of accounting, **18**:19
computing gain, **18**:20–21
disposition of installment obligations, **18**:25
electing out of, **18**:26
eligibility and calculations, **18**:19
imputed interest, **18**:21–22, **18**:24
interest on deferred taxes, **18**:25–26
nonelective aspect of, **18**:20
related-party sales of depreciable party, **18**:24–25
related-party sales of nondepreciable property, **18**:22–24
tax planning for, **18**:37–38
Installment sales, recapture potential of, **17**:21
Insurance,
accident and health benefits provided by employee-paid plans, **5**:12–13
accident and health benefits provided by employer-sponsored plans, **5**:13–14
medical insurance premiums, **10**:6
Insurance policies, certain exchanges of (Section 1035), **15**:25
Intangible drilling and development costs (IDC), **8**:24–25
AMT and, **12**:19
effect of on depletion, **8**:27–28
special recapture for, **17**:23
Inter vivos gifts, **5**:3
Interest,
AMT and, **12**:16–18
on certain state and local government obligations excluded from gross income, **5**:26–27
classification of interest expense, **10**:16
deductibility of, **10**:11
interest paid for services, **10**:14
interest paid to related parties, **10**:15
investment interest, **10**:11–13
prepayment penalty, **10**:14–15
qualified residence interest, **10**:13–14
tax-exempt securities, **10**:15
as income, **4**:15
restrictions on deductibility and timing considerations, **10**:15
prepaid interest, **10**:16
taxpayer's obligation, **10**:15
time of deduction, **10**:15
tax planning for deduction of, **10**:29

Interest and penalties, **1**:22–23
Internal Revenue Bulletin, **2**:19
Internal Revenue Bulletin (I.R.B.), **2**:10,
  2:11
Internal Revenue Code, origin of, **2**:2–3
Internal Revenue Code (IRC),
  of 1939, **1**:3, **2**:3
  of 1954, **1**:3, **2**:3
  of 1986, **1**:3, **2**:3
  arrangement of, **2**:6
  citing, **2**:6–7
  interpreting, **2**:25–26
Internal Revenue Service (IRS), **1**:18–19
  acquiescence or nonacquiescence of in
    Tax Court decisions, **2**:19
  influence of on tax laws, **1**:31–32
Interpretive Regulations, **2**:27
Inventories, **18**:31–32
  determining inventory cost, **18**:32
    dollar-value LIFO, **18**:34–35
    lower of cost or market, **18**:33–34
    specific identification, FIFO, and
      LIFO, **18**:34
    uniform capitalization, **18**:32–33
  LIFO election, **18**:36
Inventory, **16**:4–5
Investigation expenses for new or
  expanded business, deductibility of,
  6:15–16
Investment earnings, arising from
  reinvestment of life insurance
  proceeds, **5**:6–7
Investment income, **10**:12
  tax planning for, **5**:32–33
Investment interest,
  AMT and, **12**:17–18
  deductibility of, **10**:11–13
Investment tax credit (ITC), **13**:7
  computation of qualified investment
    and amount of credit, **13**:7
  qualifying property, **13**:7
  reduction of basis for, **8**:6–7
  reduction of, **13**:8
Involuntary conversions (Section 1033),
  15:9–10
  computing amount realized, **15**:10–11
  involuntary conversion of personal
    residence, **15**:15
  nonrecognition of gain, **15**:14–15
  recapture potential of, **17**:21
  replacement property, **15**:11–12
  reporting considerations, **15**:15
  time limitation on replacement,
    15:12–13
Itemized deductions, **3**:6, **3**:7, **10**:24–25.
  See also Deductions
  AMT and, **12**:15–18
  charitable contributions, **10**:16–24
  comprehensive example of Schedule
    A, **10**:25–26
  interest, **10**:11–16
  limitations on, **9**:25–26
  medical expenses, **10**:2–8
  miscellaneous, **10**:24–25

overall limitation on certain itemized
  deductions, **10**:27
tax planning for, **10**:28–31
taxes, **10**:8–11

Jobs credit, **13**:10
  computation of for qualified summer
    youth employees, **13**:11
  computation of regular credit,
    13:10–11
Joint Conference Committee, **2**:3–5
Joint return test,
  for dependency exemption, **3**:14
  tax planning for, **3**:30–31
Judicial sources of tax law, **2**:12–13
  appellate courts, **2**:15–18
  assessing validity of, **2**:28–29
  judicial citations, **2**:18
    U.S. District Court, Court of Federal
      Claims, Courts of Appeals,
      2:20–21
    U.S. Supreme Court, **2**:21
    U.S. Tax Court, **2**:18–20
  trial courts, **2**:13–15

Keogh (H.R. 10) plans, **1**:26, **19**:20–22,
  19:23, **19**:38–39
Kiddie tax, **3**:18

Lease cancellation payments, **16**:15–16
Least aggregate deferral method of
  accounting, **18**:4
Legal expenses, deductibility of, **6**:12
Legislative Regulations, **2**:27
Letter Ruling Review, **2**:11
Letter rulings, **2**:9, **2**:10–11
LEXIS, **2**:34
Life insurance, tax planning for, **5**:31
Life insurance proceeds, excluded from
  gross income, **5**:5–7
LIFO (last in, first out), **18**:34, **18**:36
  tax planning for, **18**:38
Like-kind exchanges (Section 1031), **15**:3
  basis and holding period of property
    received, **15**:7–9
  boot, **15**:6–7
  exchange requirement, **15**:5–6
  like-kind property, **15**:4–5
  recapture potential of, **17**:21
Limited liability companies, **20**:4–5
Limited partners, passive loss rules for,
  11:13
Listed property, **8**:16–21
Loans,
  imputed interest on below-market,
    4:23–27
  tax treatment of, **4**:12
Lobbying expenditures, deductibility of,
  6:13–14
Long-term capital gains (LTCG), **3**:28

Long-term capital losses (LTCL), **3**:28
Long-term contracts, **18**:26–29
  completed contract method, **18**:29
  lookback provisions, **18**:30
  percentage of completion method,
    18:30
Lookback provisions, **18**:30
  Section 1231, **17**:9–11
Losses. *See also* Capital losses; Net
  operating losses; Passive activity
  losses
  adjusted, for AMT, **12**:13–14
  business versus nonbusiness, **6**:7
  of individuals, **7**:9, **7**:17
    casualty losses, **7**:9
    events that are not casualties, **7**:10
    measuring amount of loss, **7**:12–15
    personal casualty gains and losses,
      7:16–17
    statutory framework for deducting,
      7:15
    theft losses, **7**:10–11
    when to deduct casualty losses,
      7:11
      disaster area losses, **7**:11–12
  in S corporation, **20**:28–29
  under Section 1231, **17**:4, **17**:7
Low-income housing credit, **13**:15–16
Lower of cost or market (replacement
  cost), **18**:33–34
Lump-sum distributions, **16**:8
  from qualified pension plans,
    19:13–16

Marginal tax rate, tax planning and,
  3:29
Marriage penalty, **3**:24
Mass tax, **1**:4
Meals and lodging furnished for
  convenience of employer, **5**:14–16
Medical expenses, **10**:2–3
  AMT and, **12**:16
  capital expenditures for medical
    purposes, **10**:4–5
  defined, **10**:3–4
  medical expenses incurred for spouse
    and dependents, **10**:6–7
  medical insurance premiums, **10**:6
  reimbursements, **10**:7–8
  tax planning for, **3**:32, **10**:28–29
  transportation and lodging expenses
    for medical treatment, **10**:5–6
  year of deduction, **10**:7
Medical reimbursement plans, **5**:14
Member-of-the-household test for
  dependency exemption, **3**:13
Mid-quarter convention, **8**:8–10
Military personnel, exclusion of value
  of housing from gross income, **5**:17
Ministers of the gospel, exclusion of
  value of housing from gross income,
  5:16

Modified accelerated cost recovery system (MACRS), **8**:2
business and personal use of automobiles and other listed property, **8**:16–21
classification of property, **8**:7–10
residential real estate cost recovery, **8**:11–12
straight-line election, **8**:13–14, **8**:15
tables for, **8**:36, **8**:40–41
tax planning for, **8**:29–33
Modified adjusted gross income (MAGI), **4**:33–34, **5**:29
Moving expenses, **9**:11–12
distance test, **9**:12
tax planning for, **9**:27–28
time test, **9**:12
treatment of, **9**:13
Multiple support agreement, **3**:12
Multiple taxation, **1**:28

Net capital gain alternative tax, **16**:21–22
Net capital loss (NCL), **16**:23–24
Net investment income, **10**:12
Net long-term capital gain (NLTCG), **3**:28
Net long-term capital gains (NLTCG), **16**:20–22
Net long-term capital loss (NLTCL), **3**:28, **16**:20
Net operating losses (NOL), **7**:19–20
alternative tax net operating loss deduction (ATNOLD), **12**:14–15
carryback and carryover periods, **7**:20–21
computation of, **7**:21–23, **7**:24–25
computing for corporation, **20**:9–10
recomputation of tax liability for year to which NOL is carried, **7**:23–24
tax planning for, **7**:26–27
Net short-term capital gain (NSTCG), **3**:28
Net short-term capital gains (NSTCG), **16**:20–22
Net short-term capital loss (NSTCL), **3**:28
Net short-term capital losses (NSTCL), **16**:20
Net unearned income, **3**:18–19
No-additional-cost services as fringe benefits, **5**:19–20
Nonaccountable plan for reimbursing employee business expenses, **9**:24
Nonacquiescence, of IRS in Tax Court decisions, **2**:19
Nonbusiness bad debts, **7**:4, **7**:5, **16**:9
Nondiscrimination provisions for employee fringe benefits, **5**:22, **5**:24
Nonpersonal use property, **17**:6–8
Nonqualified deferred compensation plans, **19**:27
tax planning for, **19**:40–41

tax treatment to the employer and employee, **19**:28
golden parachute, **19**:29
publicly-held companies' compensation limitation, **19**:29–31
when to use, **19**:28–29
Nonqualified stock option (NSO), **19**:29–31
Nonrefundable tax credits, **13**:4–5
Nontaxable exchanges, **15**:2–3
certain reacquisitions of real property (Section 1038), **15**:26
exchange of stock for property (Section 1032), **15**:25
exchange of stock for stock of same corporation (Section 1036),**15**:25–26
holding period rules for, **16**:17
involuntary conversions (Section 1033), **15**:9–15
like-kind exchanges (Section 1031), **15**:3–9
of passive activities, **11**:27
rollover of publicly traded securities gain into specialized small business investment companies (Section 1044), **15**:26
sale of personal residence (Section 121), **15**:22–25
sale of personal residence (Section 1034), **15**:15–22
transfers of property between spouses or incident to a divorce (Section 1041), **15**:26
Nontaxable stock rights, **14**:10–11
Nursing home expenses, **10**:3

Occupational taxes, **1**:18
Office audit, **1**:20
Optional straight-line method of cost recovery, **8**:6
Options, **16**:10
exercise of, **16**:11–12
failure to exercise, **16**:11
sale of, **16**:10–11
Ordinary income property, **10**:21
Ordinary and necessary requirement, for trade and business expenses, **6**:5–6
Organizational expenses, deduction of, **20**:12–13
Original issue discount (OID), **4**:11, **16**:10

Partnerships, **20**:30
accounting periods in, **18**:3–5
formation of, **20**:30–32
income in, **4**:16–17
operations, **20**:32–34
Passive activity losses, AMT and, **12**:11–12

classification of income and losses, **11**:18–19
deductions not treated as passive, **11**:20
disposition of passive interests, **11**:25–26
at death, **11**:26
by gift, **11**:26
installment sale, **11**:26
nontaxable exchange, **11**:27
passive activity changes to active, **11**:26–27
identification of passive activity, **11**:16–17
grouping rental activities, **11**:17
regrouping of activities, **11**:17–18
income not treated as passive, **11**:19
material participation, **11**:7–8
facts and circumstances test, **11**:10–11
limited partners, **11**:13
participation defined, **11**:12–13
in a real property trade or business, **11**:11–12
tests based on current participation, **11**:8–9
tests based on prior participation, **11**:10
passive activities defined, **11**:6–7
passive credits, **11**:22–23
real estate rental activities, **11**:23–24
rental activities, **11**:13–15
suspended losses, **11**:20–21, **11**:20–22
tax planning for, **11**:28–29
taxpayers subject to, **11**:4
closely held corporations, **11**:5–6
personal service corporations, **11**:5
transition rules for passive losses (1987–1990), **11**:27–28
Passive credits, **11**:22–23
Patents, **16**:12–13
Penalties and interest, **1**:22–23
Pension plans, **19**:4–6
Per diem allowance, **9**:23–24
Percentage of completion method of accounting, **18**:30
Percentage depletion, **8**:26–27
AMT and, **12**:18–19
Personal casualty gains and losses, **7**:16–17
Personal exemptions, **3**:10
phase-out of, **3**:14–15
Personal expenditures, deductibility of. *See* Itemized deductions
disallowance of, **6**:25
Personal injury, tax treatment of damages received for, **5**:11
Personal property, depreciation of post-1986 personal property for AMT, **12**:9–10
Personal residence, capital improvements to, **15**:20

involuntary conversion of, **15**:15
sale of
Section 121, **15**:22
computation procedures, **15**:24–25
exclusion requirements, **15**:22–23
making and revoking the election, **15**:23–24
relationship to other provisions, **15**:23
tax planning for, **15**:29–30
Section 1034, **15**:15–16
basis and holding period of new residence, **15**:20–21
capital improvements, **15**:20
nonrecognition of gain requirement, **15**:19–20
principal residence requirement, **15**:18–19
replacement period, **15**:16–18
reporting procedures, **15**:21–22
tax planning for, **15**:28–29
Personal service corporations (PSCs), **11**:5, **18**:6, **20**:13–14
Personal use assets, sale, exchange, or condemnation of, **14**:6–7
Personalty, **8**:4
ACRS treatment of, **8**:5–7
ad valorem taxes on, **1**:8
as like-kind property, **15**:4
MACRS treatment of, **8**:7–10
tangible, **10**:22
Political contributions, deductibility of, **6**:13
Pollock v. Farmers' Loan and Trust Co., **1**:3
Pollution control facilities, amortization of cost of, **12**:10, **12**:20–21
Portfolio income, **11**:18
Precedents, **2**:16
Prepaid income, **4**:12–13
tax deferral and, **4**:36–37
Prepaid interest, **10**:16
Prepayment penalty, **10**:14–15
Primary residence, **6**:23
conversion to rental property, **6**:23
Primary valuation amount, **14**:14
Private activity bonds, interest on and AMT, **12**:19
Private Letter Rulings, **2**:11
Prizes, income from, **4**:30–31
Procedural Regulations, **2**:27
Profit sharing plans, **19**:6
Property, **3**:26–27
acquired from a decedent, **14**:14–15
deathbed gifts, **14**:15–16
holding period, **14**:17
survivor's share of property, **14**:16–17
bargain purchase of, **14**:8–9
basis adjustments summarized, **14**:22–24
capital asset defined, **3**:27–28
capital gain property, **10**:21–22
capital gains computation, **3**:28

capital loss limitation, **3**:28–29
capital losses computation, **3**:28
classification of under ACRS, **8**:5–6
classification of under MACRS, **8**:7–10
conversion of from personal to business or income-producing use, **14**:19–21
cost basis of, **14**:8–9
allocation problems, **14**:9–11
identification problems, **14**:9
cost identification and documentation considerations, **14**:25
disallowed losses, **14**:17
related taxpayers, **14**:17–18
wash sales, **14**:19
dual-basis, **14**:11–12
gift basis of, **14**:11
adjustment for gift tax, **14**:12–13
basis for depreciation, **14**:13–14
holding period, **14**:13
rules if no gift tax is paid, **14**:11–12
income from, **4**:15
dividends, **4**:15–16
interest, **4**:15
in like-kind exchanges, **15**:4–9
listed, **8**:16–21
nonpersonal use, **17**:6–8
nonrecognized gain or loss, **14**:6
sale, exchange, or condemnation of personal use assets, **14**:6–7
ordinary income property, **10**:21
realized gain or loss on, **14**:2–3
adjusted basis, **14**:4, **14**:21–22
amount realized, **14**:3–4, **14**:21
capital additions, **14**:4–5
capital recoveries, **14**:5–6
sale or other disposition, **14**:3
recognized gain or loss, **14**:6
recovery of capital doctrine, **14**:7–8
replacement property tests, **15**:12
Section 1231 property, **17**:5
Section 1245 property, **17**:14–15
Section 1250 property, **17**:15–19
tax planning for
disallowed losses, **14**:26–27
gifts and bequests, **14**:25–26
transfers of between spouses or incident to divorce (Section 1041), **15**:26
Property dividends, **20**:20–21
recapture potential of, **17**:21–22
Property taxes, **1**:6, **10**:9
ad valorem taxes on personalty, **1**:8
ad valorem taxes on realty, **1**:6–8
Public Law 99–121, **8**:11
Punitive damages, tax treatment of, **5**:12

Qualified employee discounts, **5**:20
Qualified financial institution, **7**:6
Qualified higher education expenses, **5**:28

Qualified individuals (who can elect to deduct losses on deposits in qualified financial institutions), **7**:6
Qualified pension, profit sharing, and stock bonus plans, **19**:3–4
cash or deferred arrangement plans, **19**:19–20
limitations on contributions to and benefits from, **19**:16
defined benefit plans, **19**:16–18
defined contribution plans, **19**:16
qualification requirements, **19**:7–8
distribution requirements, **19**:10–12
exclusive benefit requirement, **19**:8
nondiscrimination requirements, **19**:8
participation and coverage requirements, **19**:8–10
vesting requirements, **19**:10
tax consequences to employee and employer, **19**:12–13
lump-sum distributions, **19**:13–16
top-heavy plans, **19**:18–19
types of plans, **19**:4
employee stock ownership plans, **19**:6–7
pension plans, **19**:4–6
profit sharing plans, **19**:6
stock bonus plans, **19**:6
Qualified real property business indebtedness, **5**:30–31
Qualified rental period, **6**:23
Qualified residence interest, **10**:13–14
Qualified transportation fringe, **5**:21–22
Qualified tuition reduction plans, **5**:9–10
Qualifying child, **13**:18

Real estate rental activities, passive loss rules for, **11**:23–24
Real property,
certain reacquisitions of (Section 1038), **15**:26
depreciation of post-1986 real property for AMT, **12**:8–9
nonresidential real property, computing recapture on, **17**:16–17
residential rental housing, computing recapture on, **17**:18
subdivided for sale, asset status of, **16**:7–8
Real property trade or business, passive loss rules for, **11**:11–12
Realty, **8**:4
ad valorem taxes on, **1**:6–8
as like-kind property, **15**:4
recovery periods and methods under ACRS, **8**:10–11
Reasonableness requirement, for trade and business expenses, **6**:6

Recapture,
  computing for nonresidential real
    property, **17**:16−17
  computing for residential rental
    housing, **17**:18
  exceptions to Sections 1245 and 1250,
    17:19
    certain nontaxable transactions,
      17:20
    charitable transfers, **17**:20
    death, **17**:20
    gifts, **17**:19−20
    installment sales, **17**:21
    like-kind exchanges (Section 1031)
      and involuntary conversions
      (Section 1033), **17**:21
    property dividends, **17**:21−22
  gain from sale of depreciable property
    between certain related parties,
    17:23
  intangible drilling costs and
    depletion, **17**:23
  reporting procedures, **17**:23−25
  Section 1245 recapture, **17**:12−15,
    17:19
  Section 1250 recapture, **17**:15−19
  special recapture for corporations,
    17:23
  tax planning for, **17**:29
Recovery of capital doctrine, **4**:6,
  14:7−8
Refund, computation of, **3**:17−18
Refundable tax credits, **13**:4−5
Refunds, statute of limitations on,
  1:21−22
Rehabilitation expenditures tax credit,
  13:8−9
  recapture of tax credit, **13**:9−10
Related parties,
  disallowed losses between,
    14:17−18
  exchange of like-kind property
    between, **15**:4
  interest paid to, **10**:15
  loans between, **7**:5−6, **7**:25−26
  sale of depreciable property and,
    18:24−25
  sale of nondepreciable property and,
    18:22−24
  transactions between, **6**:26−27
    losses, **6**:27
    relationship and constructive
      ownership, **6**:27−28
    unpaid interest and expenses,
      6:27
Relationship test,
  for dependency exemption, **3**:13
  for earned income credit, **13**:18
Rental activities,
  grouping of, **11**:17
  passive loss rules for, **11**:13−15,
    11:23−24
Replacement cost (lower of cost or
  market), **18**:33−34

Research activities credit, **7**:18, **13**:11
  basic, **13**:14−15
  incremental, **13**:11−14
Research and experimental
  expenditures, **7**:17−18
  deferral and amortization method,
    7:18−19
  expense method, **7**:18
Reserve method for computing
  deductions for bad debts, **7**:3
Reserves, **18**:14
Reserves for estimated expenses, **6**:10
Residency test, for earned income credit,
  13:18
Residential rental housing, computing
  recapture on, **17**:18
Residential rental real estate, MACRS
  treatment of, **8**:11−12
Restricted property plans, **19**:31−32
  employer deductions, **19**:33−34
  special election available, **19**:32−33
  substantial risk of forfeiture, **19**:32
Revenue Act of 1913, **1**:3
Revenue Act of 1916, **1**:11
Revenue Act of 1948, **1**:31
Revenue Agent's Report (RAR), **1**:20
Revenue needs and tax law, **1**:24
Revenue neutrality, **1**:24
Revenue Procedures, **2**:9, **2**:10
Revenue Reconciliation Act of 1989, **5**:12
Revenue Reconciliation Act of 1993,
  8:12, **15**:26, **20**:13
Revenue Reconciliation Act (RRA) of
  1990, **2**:3
Revenue Reconciliation Act (RRA) of
  1993, **1**:24, **1**:25, **1**:30, **6**:14, **6**:15, **6**:33
Revenue Rulings, **2**:9−10
  assessing validity of, **2**:27−28
Right of offset, **14**:17

S corporations, **20**:24−26
  accounting periods in, **18**:3−5
  operational rules, **20**:26−27
    basis determination, **20**:29−30
    separately stated items, **20**:27
    taxable income, **20**:27−28
    treatment of losses, **20**:28−29
  tax planning for, **20**:35−37
Sales taxes, **1**:10−11
Scholarships, **5**:8−9
  disguised compensation, **5**:9
  qualified tuition reduction plans,
    5:9−10
  timing issues, **5**:9
Section 179 expensing of assets, **8**:14−16
Section 401(k) plans, **19**:19−20, **19**:39
Section 1231 assets, **17**:3
  general procedure for Section 1231
    computation, **17**:8−11
  justification for favorable tax
    treatment, **17**:4
  netting procedure, **17**:7, **17**:8−11

  property included and excluded, **17**:5
  relationship to capital assets, **17**:3−4
  special rules for, **17**:5
    certain nonpersonal use capital
      assets, **17**:6−8
    livestock, **17**:6
    timber, **17**:5−6
  tax planning for, **17**:25, **17**:29
Section 1231 gains and losses, **17**:4, **17**:7
Section 1244 stock. *See* Small business
  stock
Securities,
  as inventory for dealers, **16**:7
  worthless, **16**:9
Self-employed persons, **13**:34−35
  deduction of expenses, **9**:3
  estimated tax for, **13**:35
  penalty on underpayments,
    13:35−36
  retirement plans for (H.R. 10 or
    Keogh plans), **19**:20−22, **19**:23
  self-employment tax, **13**:36−39
  tax planning for, **9**:26−27
Self-employment, versus employee
  status, **9**:2−4
Self-employment tax, **13**:36−39
Senate, **2**:3−5
Senate Finance Committee, **2**:3−5
Series E and Series EE bonds, **4**:11−12
  income from excluded from gross
    income, **5**:28−29
  tax planning for, **5**:33
Severance taxes, **1**:11
Short sales, special rules for, **16**:18−20
Short taxable year, **18**:8−9
Short-term capital gains (STCG), **3**:28
Short-term capital losses (STCL), **3**:28
Significant participation activity, **11**:9
Simplified employee pension (SEP)
  plans, **19**:23024
Sixteenth Amendment, **1**:3, **5**:26
Small business corporations, **20**:24−25
  income in, **4**:17
Small business stock, deducting losses
  on, **7**:8−9
Small Claims Division of U.S. Tax
  Court, **2**:12−15
Smith, Adam, **1**:4−5
Social considerations and tax law,
  1:26−27
Social Security benefits, as income,
  4:32−35
Specific charge-off method of
  accounting for bad debts, **7**:3−4
Sports franchises, **16**:15
Spousal IRA, **19**:24
Standard deduction, **3**:6−8
  individuals not eligible for, **3**:9
Stare decisis, doctrine of, **2**:12
State death taxes, **1**:12
State excise tax, **1**:9
State gift taxes, **1**:13−14
State and local income taxes, **1**:14−15,
  10:10−11

Statute of limitations, **1**:21
  assessment by the IRS, **1**:21
  limitation on refunds, **1**:21–22
Statutory percentage method of cost
  recovery, **8**:6
Statutory sources of tax law, **2**:2
  effect of tax treaties, **2**:7
  legislative process, **2**:3–5
  origin of Internal Revenue Code,
    2:2–3
Stepped-down basis, **14**:14
Stepped-up basis, **14**:14
Stock,
  exchange of for property (Section
    1032), **15**:25
  exchange of for stock of same
    corporation (Section 1036), **15**:25–26
Stock bonus plans, **19**:6
Stock dividends, excluded from gross
  income, **5**:27
Stock options, **19**:34
  incentive stock options, **19**:34–36
  nonqualified stock options, **19**:36–37
  tax planning for, **19**:40–41
Stock redemptions, **20**:22
Stock sales, tax planning for, **16**:29
Substantial risk of forfeiture, **19**:32
Support test,
  for dependency exemption, **3**:11–13
  tax planning for, **3**:31
Supreme Court Register (S.Ct.), **2**:21
Surviving spouse, **3**:24–25
Suspended losses, **11**:20–21

Tangible personalty, **10**:22
Tax administration, **1**:18
  the audit process, **1**:19–21
  interest and penalties, **1**:22–23
  Internal Revenue Service, **1**:18–19
  statute of limitations, **1**:21–22
  tax practice, **1**:23–24
Tax avoidance, **2**:32–33
  below-market loans and, **4**:25–26
Tax base, **1**:5
Tax benefit rule, **5**:29, **10**:7–8
Tax credits, **13**:2–3, **13**:24–25
  business energy credits, **13**:10
  child and dependent care expenses,
    13:21–24
  disabled access credit, **13**:16–17
  earned income credit, **13**:17–19
  for elderly or disabled taxpayers,
    13:19–20
  foreign tax credit, **13**:20–21
  general business credit, **13**:5–7
  investment tax credit, **13**:7–8
  jobs credit, **13**:10–11
  low-income housing credit, **13**:15–16
  refundable versus Nonrefundable
    credits, **13**:4–5
  rehabilitation expenditures, **13**:8–10
  research activities credit, **13**:11–14
  tax policy considerations, **13**:3–4

Tax deferral, **4**:35
  cash basis accounting and, **4**:36
  prepaid income, **4**:36–37
  selection of investments, **4**:35–36
Tax determination, **3**:15
  computation of net taxes payable or
    refund due, **3**:17–18
  tax rate schedule method, **3**:16–17
  tax table method, **3**:15–16
  unearned income of children under 14
    taxed at parents' rate, **3**:18–20
Tax evasion, **2**:32–33
Tax filing, **3**:20, **3**:20–21
  filing status, **3**:23
    abandoned spouse rules, **3**:26
    rates for heads of household, **3**:25
    rates for married individuals,
      3:23–25
    rates for single taxpayers, **3**:23
  requirements for dependents, **3**:21–22
  selecting proper form, **3**:22
  when and where to file, **3**:22–23
Tax formula, **3**:2–3
  application of, **3**:8
  components of, **3**:3
    adjusted gross income, **3**:5–6
    deductions for adjusted gross
      income, **3**:5
    exclusions, **3**:3, **3**:4
    exemptions, **3**:8
    gross income, **3**:3–5
    itemized deductions, **3**:6, **3**:7
    standard deduction, **3**:6–8
  individuals not eligible for standard
    deduction, **3**:9
  special limitations for individuals
    who can be claimed as dependents,
    3:10
Tax home, determination of, **9**:8
Tax law, **1**:24. *See also* Tax research
  economic considerations, **1**:24–26
  equity considerations, **1**:27–30
  influence of the courts on, **1**:33
  influence of the Internal Revenue
    Service on, **1**:31–32
  judicial concepts relating to, **1**:33–34
  political considerations, **1**:30–31
  primary sources of, **2**:28
  revenue needs, **1**:24
  secondary sources of, **2**:28–29
  social considerations, **1**:26–27
  sources of, **2**:1
    administrative sources, **2**:8–12
    judicial sources, **2**:12–20
    statutory sources, **2**:2–7
  state and local government influence
    on, **1**:31
Tax Notes, **2**:11
Tax payment procedures, **13**:26, **13**:27
  amount of FICA taxes, **13**:28–29
  amount of income tax withholding,
    13:29–33
  backup withholding, **13**:34
  coverage requirements, **13**:26–28

  employment taxes, **13**:26, **13**:27
  procedures applicable to
    self-employed persons, **13**:34–35
    estimated tax for individuals, **13**:15
    penalty on underpayments,
      13:35–36
    self-employment tax, **13**:36–39
  reporting and payment procedures,
    13:33–34
  withholding on other amounts, **13**:34
Tax periodicals, **2**:24–25
Tax planning, **2**:32
  alimony, **4**:38
  alternative minimum tax (AMT),
    12:28–29
  amortization, **8**:33
  basis adjustments, **14**:24–25
  capital assets, **15**:25–30
  capital expenditures, **6**:33
  cash method of accounting, **18**:37
  charitable contributions, **10**:30–31
  community property, **4**:38
  computer-assisted tax research,
    2:34–35
  corporate versus noncorporate forms
    of business organization, **20**:35
  cost recovery, **8**:29–33
  credit for child and dependent care
    expenses, **13**:39–41
  dependency exemptions, **3**:30–32
  depletion, **8**:34
  disallowed losses, **14**:26–27
  documentation of related-taxpayer
    loans, casualty losses, and theft
    losses, **7**:25–26
  education expenses, **9**:28
  employee benefits, **5**:31–32
  entertainment expenses, **9**:28
  excessive executive compensation,
    6:32
  family income tax reduction by use of
    entity, **20**:36–37
  family tax planning, **13**:40–41
  follow-up procedures, **2**:33
  foreign tax credit, **13**:39
  gifts and bequests, **14**:25–26
  hobby losses, **6**:32–33
  home ownership, **4**:35
  income of minor children, **3**:30
  installment method of accounting,
    18:37–38
  interest deduction, **10**:29
  investment income, **5**:32–33
  involuntary conversions, **15**:27–28
  itemized deductions, **10**:28
  life insurance, **5**:31
  LIFO, **18**:38
  like-kind exchanges, **15**:27
  medical deductions, **10**:28–29
  medical expenses, **3**:32
  moving expenses, **9**:27–28
  nontax considerations, **2**:32
  nontaxable economic benefits, **4**:35
  passive losses, **11**:28–29

practical application, **2**:33–34
recapture, **17**:29
regular corporation versus S status, **20**:35–36
sale of personal residence (Sections 1034 and 121), **15**:28–30
Section 1231 gain, **17**:25, **17**:29
self-employed individuals, **9**:26–27
shifting deductions between employer and employee, **9**:27
shifting income to relatives, **4**:37–38
tax avoidance and tax evasion, **2**:32–33
tax deferral, **4**:35–37
tax rate differentials, **3**:29–30
taxable year, **18**:37
time value of tax deductions, **6**:30
transportation and travel expenses, **9**:27
unreasonable compensation, **6**:30, **6**:32
wash sales, **14**:27
withholding arrangements, **13**:41
Tax practice, **1**:23
ethical guidelines, **1**:23
statutory penalties, **1**:23–24
Tax preferences, **12**:3, **12**:5
Tax Rate Schedules, **3**:16–17
Tax rates, **1**:5
abandoned spouse rules, **3**:26
for heads of household, **3**:25
for married individuals, **3**:23–25
for single taxpayers, **3**:23
Tax Reform Act (TRA) of 1986, **1**:24, **1**:25, **1**:30, **2**:3, **3**:18
Tax research, **2**:22–23
arriving at a solution or at alternative solutions, **2**:29
assessing validity of tax law sources, **2**:25–29
communicating, **2**:29–31
computer-assisted, **2**:34–35
identifying the problem, **2**:23
locating appropriate tax law sources, **2**:23–24
tax periodicals, **2**:24–25
working with tax services, **2**:24
refining the problem, **2**:23
Tax services, **2**:23–24
Tax shelters, **11**:2–3
Tax structure, **1**:5
criteria used in selection of, **1**:4–5
incidence of taxation, **1**:5–6
tax base, **1**:5
tax rates, **1**:5
Tax Table, **3**:15–16
Tax treaties, **2**:8
Tax-exempt income, deductibility of expenses and interest relating to, **6**:29–30
Taxable year, **4**:6–7
short, **18**:8–9
tax planning for, **18**:37

Taxation, incidence of, **1**:5–6
Taxes,
death taxes, **1**:11–12
deductibility of, **10**:8–9
employment taxes, **1**:16–17
Federal custom duties, **1**:17–18
gift taxes, **1**:12–14
income taxes, **1**:14–16
property taxes, **1**:6–8
property taxes, assessments, and apportionment of taxes, **10**:9–10
state and local income taxes, **10**:10–11
transaction taxes, **1**:8–11
value added taxes (VAT), **1**:18
Taxpayer use test, in involuntary conversion, **15**:11
Taxpayer's benefit or obligation, expenses incurred for, **6**:23–25
TAXRIA, **2**:34
Technical Advice Memoranda (TAMs), **2**:12
Technical Advice Memorandum 9320003, **12**:5, **12**:6
Technical and Miscellaneous Revenue Act of 1988, **2**:3, **2**:8
Tentative minimum tax, **13**:5
Theft losses, **7**:10–11, **7**:25–26
Thin capitalization problem, **20**:17–18
Tickets purchased for entertainment, deductibility of, **9**:19
Top-heavy retirement plans, **19**:18–19
Trademarks and trade names, **16**:13–14
contingent payments, **16**:15
noncontingent payments, **16**:14–15
significant power, right, or continuing interest, **16**:14
Transaction taxes, **1**:8–9
Federal excise taxes, **1**:9
general sales taxes, **1**:10
severance taxes, **1**:11
state excise taxes, **1**:9
Transportation expenses, **9**:4
computation of auto expenses, **9**:6–7
for medical treatment, **10**:5–6
qualified expenditures, **9**:4–6
tax planning for, **9**:27
Travel expenses, **9**:7
away-from-home requirement, **9**:7–8
combined business and pleasure travel, **9**:9–11
restrictions on travel expenses, **9**:8–9
tax planning for, **9**:27
Treasury Decisions, **2**:9, **2**:11
Treasury Department Regulations, **2**:8–9
assessing validity of, **2**:26–27
finalized, **2**:9
interpretive, **2**:27
legislative, **2**:27
procedural, **2**:27
proposed, **2**:9
temporary, **2**:9

Trial courts, **2**:13–15
Tuition expenses, **10**:4

Underpayment of tax, penalty on, **13**:35–36
Unearned income, **3**:18–19
Unemployment compensation, as income, **4**:32
Unified transfer tax schedule, **1**:13
Uniform capitalization rules, **18**:32–33
Uniform Gifts to Minors Act, **4**:37
United States Supreme Court Reports (U.S.), **2**:21
Unreasonable compensation, tax planning for, **6**:30, **6**:32
Unreimbursed employee expenses, **9**:25–26
tax planning for, **9**:28
U.S. Court of Federal Claims, **2**:12–15
judicial citations in, **2**:20–21
U.S. District Court, **2**:12–15
judicial citations in, **2**:20–21
U.S. government publications, as assets, **16**:6
U.S. Supreme Court, **2**:16
appeals to, **2**:17
judicial citations in, **2**:21
U.S. Tax Cases (USTC), **2**:20
U.S. Tax Court, **2**:12–15
citations in, **2**:18–20
U.S. Tax Reporter, **2**:24
Use tax, **1**:10

Vacation homes,
conversion to rental property, **6**:23
personal/rental use, **6**:21–23
primarily personal use, **6**:19–20
primarily rental use, **6**:20–21
rental of, **6**:19, **6**:24
Value added taxes (VAT), **1**:18

Wash sales, **14**:19, **14**:27
WESTLAW, **2**:34
Wherewithal to pay concept, **1**:28
Withholding,
backup, **13**:34
for domestic workers, **13**:34
for FICA and FUTA, **13**:26, **13**:27, **13**:28–29
of income tax, **13**:29–33
reporting and payment procedures, **13**:33–34
tax planning for, **13**:41
Withholding allowances, **13**:30
Workers's compensation, tax treatment of, **5**:12
Working condition fringes, **5**:21
Worthless securities, **7**:7–8, **16**:9
small business stock, **7**:8–9
Writ of Certiorari, **2**:17